Financial Accounting

FOURTH EDITION

J. DAVID SPICELAND
University of Memphis

WAYNE THOMAS
University of Oklahoma

DON HERRMANN
Oklahoma State University

Dedicated to

David's wife Charlene, daughters Denise and Jessica, and three sons Michael David, Michael, and David

Wayne's wife Julee, daughter Olivia, and three sons Jake, Eli, and Luke

Don's wife Mary, daughter Rachel, and three sons David, Nathan, and Micah

FINANCIAL ACCOUNTING, FOURTH EDITION

Published by McGraw-Hill Education, 2 Penn Plaza, New York, NY 10121. Copyright © 2016 by McGraw-Hill Education. All rights reserved. Printed in the United States of America. Previous editions © 2014, 2011, and 2009. No part of this publication may be reproduced or distributed in any form or by any means, or stored in a database or retrieval system, without the prior written consent of McGraw-Hill Education, including, but not limited to, in any network or other electronic storage or transmission, or broadcast for distance learning.

Some ancillaries, including electronic and print components, may not be available to customers outside the United States.

This book is printed on acid-free paper.

3 4 5 6 7 8 9 LWI 21 20 19 18 17

ISBN 978-1-259-30795-9
MHID 1-259-30795-6

Senior Vice President, Products & Markets:
  Kurt L. Strand
Vice President, General Manager, Products & Markets:
  Marty Lange
Vice President, Content Design & Delivery: *Kimberly Meriwether David*
Managing Director: *Tim Vertovec*
Senior Brand Manager: *Natalie King*
Director, Product Development: *Rose Koos*
Product Developer: *Danielle Andries*
Marketing Manager: *Kyle Burdette*
Digital Product Developer: *Kevin Moran*

Director, Content Design & Delivery: *Linda Avenarius*
Program Manager: *Daryl Horrocks*
Lead Content Project Manager: *Pat Frederickson*
Content Project Manager: *Angela Norris*
Buyer: *Laura M. Fuller*
Senior Designer: *Srdjan Savanovic*
Content Licensing Specialists: *Carrie Burger* and *Lori Slattery*
Cover Image: ©*Paul Zizka, Getty Images*
Compositor: *SPi Global*
Printer: *LSC Communications*

All credits appearing on page or at the end of the book are considered to be an extension of the copyright page.

Library of Congress Cataloging-in-Publication Data

Spiceland, J. David, 1949- author.
    Financial accounting / J. David Spiceland, Wayne Thomas,
Don Herrmann.—Fourth edition.
    pages cm
    ISBN 978-1-259-30795-9 (alk. paper)
    1. Accounting. I. Thomas, Wayne, 1969- author. II. Herrmann, Don author. III. Title.
    HF5636.S77 2016
    657—dc23

                                                                2015028700

The Internet addresses listed in the text were accurate at the time of publication. The inclusion of a website does not indicate an endorsement by the authors or McGraw-Hill Education, and McGraw-Hill Education does not guarantee the accuracy of the information presented at these sites.

mheducation.com/highered

About the Authors

DAVID SPICELAND

David Spiceland is professor of accounting at the University of Memphis, where he teaches intermediate accounting and other financial accounting courses at the undergraduate and master's levels. He received his BS degree in finance from the University of Tennessee, his MBA from Southern Illinois University, and his PhD in accounting from the University of Arkansas.

Professor Spiceland's primary research interests are in earnings management and educational research. He has published articles in a variety of journals including *The Accounting Review, Accounting and Business Research, Journal of Financial Research,* and *Journal of Accounting Education.* David has received university and college awards and recognition for his teaching, research, and technological innovations in the classroom. David is lead author of McGraw-Hill's best-selling *Intermediate Accounting* text.

David is the Memphis Tigers' No. 1 basketball fan. He enjoys playing basketball, is a former all-state linebacker, and an avid fisherman. Cooking is a passion for David, who served as sous chef for Paula Deen at a Mid-South Fair cooking demonstration.

WAYNE THOMAS

Wayne Thomas is the John T. Steed Chair in Accounting at the University of Oklahoma, where he teaches introductory financial accounting to nearly 600 students per year. He received his bachelor's degree in accounting from Southwestern Oklahoma State University, and his master's and PhD in accounting from Oklahoma State University.

Professor Thomas's primary research interests are in markets-based accounting research, financial disclosures, financial statement analysis, and international accounting issues. He previously served as an editor of *The Accounting Review* and has published articles in a variety of journals including *The Accounting Review, Journal of Accounting and Economics, Journal of Accounting Research, Review of Accounting Studies,* and *Contemporary Accounting Research.* He has won several research awards, including the American Accounting Association's Competitive Manuscript Award. Professor Thomas has won teaching awards at the university, college, and departmental levels, and has received the Outstanding Educator Award from the Oklahoma Society of CPAs. Wayne is a co-author on McGraw-Hill's best-selling *Intermediate Accounting,* with David Spiceland.

Wayne enjoys playing sports (basketball, tennis, golf, and ping pong), solving crossword puzzles, and coaching little league sports. He has participated in several adventure races, like you'll read about in the Great Adventures continuing problem at the end of each chapter.

DON HERRMANN

Don Herrmann is the Deloitte Professor of Accounting at Oklahoma State University, where he teaches financial accounting and intermediate accounting, and is director of the doctoral program. He received his bachelor's degree in business from John Brown University, his master's degree in accounting from Kansas State University, and his PhD in accounting from Oklahoma State University.

Professor Herrmann's research interests are in earnings forecasts, segment reporting, financial statement analysis, and international accounting issues. He is past president of the American Accounting Association International Section and has served on the editorial and review board of the top research journal in the field of accounting, *The Accounting Review.* He has published articles in a variety of journals including *The Accounting Review, Journal of Accounting Research, Accounting Horizons, Journal of Business, Finance, and Accounting,* and the *Journal of Accounting and Public Policy.* Don Herrmann and Wayne Thomas often work together, having co-authored over 15 research articles. Professor Herrmann has received teaching awards at the department, college, and university levels, including Professor of the Year in the University Greek System.

Don, like his co-authors, is a big sports fan. He played tennis on scholarship in college and enjoys playing soccer, basketball, running, biking, and swimming. He also coaches soccer, basketball, and little league baseball in his hometown.

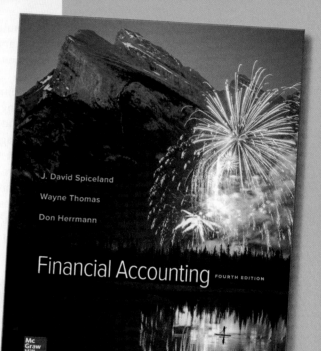

Don't you love those moments in your course when students are fully engaged? When the "Aha!" revelations are bursting like fireworks? David Spiceland, Wayne Thomas, and Don Herrmann have developed a unique set of materials based directly on their collective years in the classroom. They've brought together best practices like highlighting Common Mistakes, offering frequent Let's Review exercises, integrating the course with a running Continuing Problem, demonstrating the relevance of the course with real-world companies and decision analysis, and communicating it all in a student-friendly conversational writing style. After the proven success of the first three editions of *Financial Accounting*, we are confident that the fourth edition will not only motivate, engage, and challenge students—it will illuminate the financial accounting course like never before.

Spiceland's Accounting Series

To allow *Financial Accounting* to be part of a complete learning system, authors David Spiceland and Wayne Thomas have teamed up with Jim Sepe and Mark Nelson to offer *Intermediate Accounting*. Now in its eighth edition, *Intermediate Accounting* uses the same approach that makes *Financial Accounting* a success—conversational writing style with a real-world focus, decision maker's perspective, innovative pedagogy, and author-prepared assignments and supplements. The Spiceland Accounting Series is fully integrated with McGraw-Hill's Connect, an educational platform that seamlessly joins Spiceland's superior content with enhanced digital tools to deliver precisely what a student needs, when and how they need it.

EDUCATION IS CHANGING . . .

At McGraw-Hill, the Spiceland: *Financial Accounting* authors recognize that teaching is **part art and part science** and have been mastering the art and science of teaching in their own classrooms for years. Based on this experience and their interactions with thousands of faculty members, students, and business owners who have shared their insight, this approach has been crafted, refined, and continues to evolve to embody successful teaching and learning strategies. While the importance of financial accounting to successful business management remains constant, the ways in which students learn and are motivated continue to evolve. In today's fast-paced technology age, students are engaged when they believe topics are relevant. The authors' targeted insight into the student experience is crafted through research in addition to the information our technology can share. Through the intuitive SmartBook technology, the authors are able to analyze data that shows where students are struggling and refine their pedagogy to provide additional focus in these areas. *It is through understanding the science of what works and the art in how the teaching methodologies are executed, that* Spiceland: **Financial Accounting** *continues to build on its successful approach in this edition.*

McGraw Hill Education

We can drive results by understanding how the mind works.

Making the science of learning work for you. Simply.

Because learning changes everything.™

SO ARE WE.

CREATING FUTURE BUSINESS LEADERS

From the first edition of *Financial Accounting,* the authors have been talking with standard setters, auditors, and business leaders across the country to ensure their materials are consistent with what's being practiced in the business world. For example, in the fourth edition, we now cover installment notes early in the chapter on long-term liabilities based on feedback that loans with monthly principle and interest payments are very common in the business world. Coverage of installment notes is also practical for students who may be considering a car loan or a home loan in the not so distant future.

The authors believe that the foundation students get in the first financial accounting course is paramount to their business success. In keeping with the feedback from business leaders and instructors, the authors have focused their approach on four key areas:

- **Building Student Interest**
- **Helping Students Become Better Problem Solvers**
- **Fostering Decision-Making and Analysis Skills**
- **Using Technology to Enhance Learning**

By honing in on these key areas, the result is a better-prepared student who has a greater potential to take a leadership role when he or she graduates and enters the business world.

Building Student Interest

The first step in student engagement is real-world relevance. The authors of *Financial Accounting* do this by making the course relevant to students by exposing them to interesting, real-world examples that are applicable to their lives and future careers, and by crafting their narrative and its supporting features in an approachable and straightforward style.

Helping Students Become Better Problem Solvers

Helping students understand each piece of the accounting cycle and then how it is interconnected is central to the financial accounting course. The authors have taken care to carefully organize and streamline the materials with features like in-chapter **Let's Review** problems for students to check their understanding and prepare them to successfully complete the assigned End-of-Chapter material. The **Common Mistakes** feature is a student favorite, as it helps them avoid mistakes commonly made in the homework. **General Ledger Problems** further review the accounting cycle and allow students to see the big picture of how information flows through the financial statements.

Fostering Decision-Making and Analysis Skills

Decision-making and analysis skills are key ingredients in creating future business leaders. In building a strong foundation in problem-solving, students are better equipped to expand their understanding into how financial information affects businesses. Students are given opportunities to explore real business decision-making practices in each chapter—**Decision Maker's Perspectives** and **Decision Points**—and employ decision making in their homework assignments using materials like the **Great Adventures** continuing case and the Analysis portion of most **General Ledger Problems.**

Using Technology to Enhance Learning

Many of today's students are visual learners and technology driven. Spiceland: *Financial Accounting* reinforces students' conceptual understanding with elements like SmartBook and with video-based instruction using **Interactive Illustrations** and **Interactive Presentations.** The end-of-chapter exercises are supplemented with video-driven **Guided Examples.** Connect brings this all together to facilitate an interactive and personalized learning environment.

NEW IN THE FOURTH EDITION

We have received an incredible amount of feedback from over 600 reviewers and focus group participants. The list of changes and improvements on the next few pages is testament to the many hours that reviewers spent thinking about and analyzing our earlier editions, helping us to make *Financial Accounting* the **best book of its kind.**

Overall Updates in the Fourth Edition

- **Updated content to reflect latest FASB pronouncements** including terminology related to the upcoming changes in Revenue Recognition and Inventory.
- **Usage data** from SmartBook and Connect were used in developing changes to the 4th Edition.
- **Revised illustrations** in the new edition to continue to offer clear and visual learning tools for students.
- **Feature stories, real-world examples, and ratio analyses** were updated to include the most recent year of company data available.
- **Added content and new illustrations in Chapters 1–3** to build students' understanding of the framework of financial accounting and the accounting cycle activities during the year versus the end of the year.
- **Revised Chapter 9 on long-term liabilities** to first discuss installment notes (like car loans or home loans), leases, and an overview of bonds for instructors that prefer less detailed coverage of bonds. A detailed coverage of bonds is also provided later in the chapter for instructors that prefer a more in-depth coverage of bonds payable.
- **Revised Chapter 12 to eliminate the discussion of extraordinary items** in accordance with a recent FASB standard.
- **Fifteen New General Ledger Problems** have been added to the current offering, including some Great Adventures questions in this format. General Ledger Problems that were previously in Connect only, are also now available in the text.
- **Additional Accounting Cycle Problems** were added to Chapter 3

and to the later topical Chapters 5–10. Students can see how more advanced transactions related to receivables, inventory, depreciable assets, current and long-term liabilities, and equities work through an entire accounting cycle.
- **New Excel Simulations** covering financial accounting topics are now available in Connect. These questions allow students to practice their Excel skills within their Connect assignments using relevant accounting functions and activities. Assistance is provided on Excel basics so that instructors don't have to teach students Excel, and activities are auto-graded and provide feedback to students.
- **Over 400 new test bank questions** were added, including both multiple choice and computational questions.
- **Instructional PowerPoint slides** now include Concept Checks to help test students' comprehension during the lecture.

CHAPTER 1

- Added discussion of the distinction between expenses and dividends.
- Revised **Illustration 1–4** to make relationship among measurement categories more evident.
- Revised discussion to explain the basic format of the income statement in **Illustration 1–5.**
- Revised discussion throughout to be consistent with the new revenue recognition standard (ASU 2014-09).
- Provided a reference to the role of the PCAOB when discussing the auditor's report.
- Updated **AP1–2, AP1–3,** and **AP1–4** for American Eagle and The Buckle's most recent financial information.

CHAPTER 2

- Redesigned **Illustration 2–1** to make the six-step process of measuring external transactions more apparent.
- Emphasized in a Key Point the distinction between steps (2) and (3) of the measurement process in **Illustrations 2–1.**

- Revised **Illustration 2-3** to make clear the components of the expanded accounting equation.
- Separated the discussion of transactions (6) and (7) and discussed new revenue recognition principle in both (ASU 2014-09).
- Added discussion of difference between recording an expense versus an asset at the end of transaction (9) in **Part A.**
- Revised **Illustration 2–5** to improve clarity of effects of debits and credits on the accounting equation.
- Revised **Illustration 2–6** to make clear the effects of debits and credits on the expanded accounting equation.
- Moved up coverage of the chart of accounts to **Learning Objective 2–4.**
- Revised **Illustration 2–10** to show basic format of a general ledger account.
- For transactions (1) and (2), demonstrated posting to the general ledger accounts.
- Changed the account title from Unearned Revenue to Deferred Revenue, consistent with ASU 2014-09.
- Moved the Let's Review to follow **LO2–5** and demonstrated posting to the Cash account.
- Updated **AP2–2, AP2–3,** and **AP2–4** for American Eagle and The Buckle's most recent financial information.

CHAPTER 3

- Revised the definition of the Revenue Recognition Principle to be consistent with the new revenue recognition standard (ASU 2014-09).
- Revised entire discussion in **Part A** to continue the example of Eagle Golf Academy from **Chapters 1** and **2.**
- Discussed the revenue recognition principle in relation to transactions (6), (7), and (8) of Eagle Golf Academy.
- Discussed expense recognition in relation to transactions (4), (5), and (9) of Eagle Golf Academy.
- Added new **Illustrations 3–1** and **3–2** to highlight differences between accrual-basis accounting and cash-basis accounting for Eagle Golf Academy.
- Added new **Illustration 3–4** to explain four types of adjusting entries.

- Eliminated mini-financial statements under each of the eight adjusting entries in **Part B**.
- Changed company to Federal Express in **Illustrations 3–6** and to Netflix in **Illustration 3–7**.
- Added adjusting entry for interest receivable to demonstrate the flip side of the adjusting entry for interest payable.
- Revised **Illustration 3–10** to show adjusted trial balance.
- Added new Decision Maker's Perspective for the classified balance sheet.
- Added new General Ledger/Accounting Cycle review **Exercise 3–21**.
- Added **Problems 3–9A** and **3–9B** to require completion of the full accounting cycle.
- Updated **AP3–2**, **AP3–3**, and **AP3–4** for American Eagle and The Buckle's most recent financial information.

CHAPTER 4

- Added **Illustration 4–1** to graphically depict the Fraud Triangle.
- Added **Illustration 4–7** to graphically depict the components of the balance of cash.
- Revised discussion of deposits outstanding and checks outstanding.
- Added illustration to help identify deposits outstanding in a bank reconciliation.
- Added illustration to help identify checks outstanding in a bank reconciliation.
- Added bullet-point discussion of items involved in reconciling the company's balance of cash (Step 2).
- Added **Illustration 4–11** to summarize items included in the bank reconciliation.
- Changed **Learning Objective 4–6** to reflect the broader concept of accounting for employee purchases (in addition to petty cash).
- Added discussion of internal controls over employee purchases in **Learning Objective 4–6**.
- Separated section on Statement of Cash Flows to a new **Part C**, and included brief discussion of the reporting of restricted cash in the balance sheet.

- Revised the Analysis section to include comparison of Regal Entertainment to Cinemark Holdings.
- Revised **Review Questions 25** and **26**, **Brief Exercise 4–13**, and **Exercises 4–12** and **4–13** for employee purchases.
- Revised **Review Questions 29** and **30**, **Brief Exercise 4–18**, and **Exercise 4–20** for cash analysis.
- Updated **AP4–2**, **AP4–3**, and **AP4–4** for American Eagle and The Buckle's most recent financial information.

CHAPTER 5

- In Part A, added discussion of the new revenue recognition rules (ASU No. 2014-09) related to sales discounts, sales returns, and sales allowances.
- Added new **Illustration 5–3** to demonstrate accounting for contra revenue transactions.
- Added discussion of **Illustration 5–6** explaining why accounts in the "Not Yet Due" column have a percentage uncollectible.
- Added discussion of role of subsidiary ledgers and control accounts to expand on **Illustrations 5–6** and **5–7**.
- Provided additional discussion of the use of two entries to record cash collection on accounts previously written off.
- Revised **Illustration 5–12** to make timing difference between Allowance Method and Direct Write-off Method more apparent.
- Revised analysis of Tenet Healthcare versus Lifepoint Hospitals to show impact of cash collections on profitability.
- Added new **Brief Exercises 5–12** and **5–13** for the direct write-off method and **Brief Exercise 5–19** for matching terms.
- Added new General Ledger/Accounting Cycle review **Exercise 5–21**.
- Updated **AP5–2**, **AP5–3**, and **AP5–4** for American Eagle and The Buckle's most recent financial information.

CHAPTER 6

- Revised **Illustration 6–1** to better demonstrate inventory differences between a manufacturing company versus a merchandising company.

- Revised **Illustration 6–4** to include actual titles in Best Buy's multiple-step income statement.
- Revised discussion of Best Buy's multiple-step income statement based on new illustration.
- Updated discussion of inventory to lower of cost and "net realizable value" (instead of "market"), based on the FASB's recent simplification project. Companies using LIFO or the retail inventory method are excluded from the change.
- Revised **Illustration 6–19** to better illustrate the concept of lower of cost and net realizable value.
- Updated inventory analysis section to include comparison of Best Buy and Tiffany's.
- Added new General Ledger/Accounting Cycle review **Exercise 6–21**.
- Updated **AP6–2**, **AP6–3**, and **AP6–4** for American Eagle and The Buckle's most recent financial information.

CHAPTER 7

- Updated the WorldCom feature story.
- Updated the Balance Sheet for Darden Restaurants(**Illustration 7–1**).
- Revised the **Illustration 7–5** on the world's top 10 brands.
- Expanded the discussion on the use of an Accumulated Depreciation account rather than simply crediting the asset account.
- Explained that most companies have separate Accumulated Depreciation accounts for each separate asset or asset class.
- Added an equation to calculate the depreciation rate under the double-declining-balance method.
- Added color borders to the depreciation schedules in the text to better identify the depreciation method used in the schedule.
- Briefly expanded the discussion on intangible assets.
- Added a new list describing that (1) companies purchase intangible assets and (2) companies create intangible assets internally.
- Clarified the calculation and recording of goodwill and revised the text example.

- Revised the discussion on intangible assets subject to amortization to better explain the use of service life and residual value in computing amortization for intangible assets.
- Added a footnote referring to the standard on nonmonetary transactions *(FASB ASC 846)*.
- Expanded the analysis section to compare return on assets for Walmart vs. Costco (Target could no longer be used as they reported a loss in the most recent year).
- Revised and simplified the discussion on asset impairments.
- Added a new General Ledger/Accounting Cycle review **Exercise 7–21.**
- Changed **Problems 7–9A** and **7–9B** to allow instructors to assign algo versions of these analysis problems in Connect.
- Updated **AP7–2, AP7–3,** and **AP7–4** for American Eagle and The Buckle's most recent financial information.

CHAPTER 8
- Updated the feature story.
- Updated the partial balance sheet for Southwest Airlines (**Illustration 8–2**).
- Added a summary reconciling gross monthly pay to net monthly pay.
- Removed footnote about temporary payroll tax holiday in 2011 and 2012.
- Updated FICA base salary amount to $118,500 in 2015 in the text and EOC.
- Updated the section on unearned revenues to instead use the term deferred revenues consistent with the terminology used in the new revenue recognition standard.
- Added a new Common Mistake that some students think "Deferred Revenue" is a revenue account.
- Simplified the recording of Sales Tax Payable by removing the alternative method.

- Updated **Illustration 8–6,** Southwest Airlines disclosure of the current portion of long-term debt and long-term debt.
- Revised the example for recording the estimated warranty liability and actual warranty work.
- Updated the liquidity analysis comparing United Airlines and American Airlines.
- Added **Illustration 8–10** to summarize the effects of changes in current assets and current liabilities on the liquidity ratios.
- Added a new General Ledger/Accounting Cycle review **Exercise 8–16.**
- Changed **Problems 8–9A** and **8–9B** to allow instructors to assign algo versions of these analysis problems in Connect.
- Updated **AP8–2, AP8–3,** and **AP8–4** for American Eagle and The Buckle's most recent financial information.

CHAPTER 9
- Redesigned the chapter to provide instructors greater flexibility in the coverage of long-term liabilities. Instructors that prefer an overview of long-term liabilities including installment notes, leases, and bonds can just cover **Part A.** Instructors that prefer a detailed coverage of bonds can also cover **Part B** (Pricing a Bond) and/or **Part C** (Recording Bonds Payable).
- Moved the discussion of installment notes and leases early in the chapter.
- Revised the discussion of the amortization schedule for an installment note.
- Moved the Decision Maker's Perspective describing why some companies lease rather than buy to the beginning of the section on leases.
- Updated the footnote disclosure of minimum lease payments for Six Flags, Inc.

- Added clarification next to the **Part B** heading to indicate that **Part B** is designed as a stand-alone section and can be omitted without loss of understanding of the remaining topics in the chapter.
- Revised **Illustration 9-12** (differences among stated rate, market rate, and bond issue price) for greater clarity.
- Updated the comparison of Coca-Cola vs. PepsiCo in the analysis section.
- Revised the discussion of the times interest earned ratio.
- Changed the order of the end of chapter material to match the redesign of the chapter text.
- Added a new General Ledger/Accounting Cycle review **Exercise 9-19.**
- Changed **Problems 9-7A** and **9-7B** to allow instructors to assign algo versions of these analysis problems in Connect.
- Updated **AP9-2, AP9-3,** and **AP9-4** for American Eagle and The Buckle's most recent financial information.

CHAPTER 10
- Revised the feature story.
- Updated **Illustration 10–1** for American Eagle.
- Added a reference to Ali Baba, the largest technology IPO ever.
- Simplified the equations below **Illustration 10–6** relating to authorized and issued shares.
- Added an equation to help students better identify retained earnings.
- Added **Illustration 10–13** to help students understand how net income, net losses, and dividends impact the balance in retained earnings over time.
- Added a new decision point on retained earnings.
- Added a new common mistake related to students incorrectly paying dividends on treasury stock.

- Revised the discussion on the stock-holders' equity section for American Eagle in **LO10–7**.
- Moved the decision maker's perspective entitled "Why Doesn't Stockhold-ers' Equity Equal the Market Value of Equity?" from the analysis section to Part C on reporting stockholders' equity.
- Revised the equity analysis sec-tion to compare Ralph Lauren with Abercrombie.
- Added the dividend yield as a new ratio in the equity analysis section and updated all EOC material.
- Added new General Ledger/Account-ing Cycle review **Exercise 10–17**.
- Changed **Problems 10–7A** and **10–7B** to allow instructors to assign algo versions of these analysis problems in Connect.
- Updated **AP10–2, AP10–3,** and **AP10–4** for American Eagle and The Buckle's most recent financial information.

CHAPTER 11
- Updated the feature story.
- Added a definition of cash inflows and cash outflows at the beginning of **part A.**
- Reformatted **Illustration 11–2** to make it easier for students to read and use as a guide for homework.
- Updated **Illustration 11–7** to better show the basic format for the state-ment of cash flows.
- Deleted the two summary journal entries in the chapter to provide more concise explanations of items reconcil-ing net income to operating cash flows.
- Moved **Illustration 11-8** to the begin-ning of the operating section providing

a helpful summary of increases and decreases in adjusting net income to operating cash flows.
- Added an additional box to bet-ter demonstrate how an increase in accounts receivable causes sales rev-enue to be higher than cash inflows.
- Added a Let's Review following the operating activities section.
- Added a new introduction to the investing activities section to give students an overall sense of investing activities before going into more detail.
- Added a new introduction to the financing activities section to give students an overall sense of financing activities before going into more detail.
- Revised the cash flow analysis to com-pare Apple vs. Google. (Dell is now a private firm with data no longer pub-licly available.)
- Revised the introduction to the direct method to emphasize that the only dif-ference between the indirect and direct methods is in the operating section.
- Changed **Problems 11–4A** and **11–4B** to allow instructors to assign algo ver-sions of these analysis problems in Connect.
- Updated **AP11–2, AP11–3,** and **AP11–4** for American Eagle and The Buckle's most recent financial information.

CHAPTER 12
- Revised the feature story to list some of the top professional athletes sponsored by Under Armour.
- Updated all data and discussion for the vertical and horizontal analysis of Under Armour and Nike.

- Updated all the risk ratios and discus-sion in comparing Under Armour with Nike.
- Updated the list of companies held by Berkshire Hathaway to include com-pany names that students can better recognize.
- Updated all the profitability ratios and discussion in comparing Under Armour and Nike.
- Revised the discussion and definition of discontinued operations based on the FASBs new guidelines.
- Added a new example of discontinued operations for Nike related to the Sale of Cole Hann (footwear, handbags, and accessories).
- Eliminated the discussion of extraor-dinary items based on the FASB's new guidelines.
- Revised the IFRS box titled "Do International Standards Influence the FASB?"
- Updated **Illustration 12–26** to account for the FASB's new guidelines elimi-nating the reporting of extraordinary items.
- In discussing "other revenues and expenses", deleted the example of Marie Callendar's and replaced it with an example for Nike.
- Added a summary to the final section that accounting is not just black and white. There are many gray areas in accounting requiring management judgment.
- Updated all EOC material to eliminate the recording of extraordi-nary items.
- Added a new internet research project using yahoo finance (**AP12–6**).

BUILDING STUDENT INTEREST

With a wide variety of students enrolled in the financial accounting course, getting them interested in the content and making it enjoyable to learn can be challenging. Spiceland: *Financial Accounting* achieves this by using relevant examples and context that relate well to students, making the content both approachable and easy to digest.

Part of the unique art in how the authors of Spiceland: *Financial Accounting* approach the material is through their signature **Conversational Writing Style.** The authors took special care to write chapters that foster a friendly dialogue between the text and each individual student. The tone of the presentation is intentionally conversational—creating the impression of *speaking with* **the student,** as opposed to *speaking at* the student. This conversational writing style has been a proven success with Spiceland's *Intermediate Accounting* (now in its eighth edition), and that same approach has led to the success of Spiceland: *Financial Accounting.*

> **This text has a logical layout and incorporates tools** to keep the student's attention. It makes the student think about the impact on the financials based upon the different principles and estimates selected.
>
> — Victor Stanton, *University of California–Berkeley*

Layered in with the conversational tone, the authors' infusion of relevant examples from real companies that flow throughout each chapter's content, provide a compelling reason for students to take interest in the material.

> The text is very detailed, but **not overly technical.** It is written at a level and in a way that is highly user friendly.
>
> —PeterWoodlock, *Youngstown State University*

Real-World Focus Students are able to retain more information when they see how concepts are applied in the real world. Each chapter begins with a **Feature Story** that involves real companies and offers business insights related to the material in the chapter. As the chapter's topics are being presented, reference back to the companies in the Feature Story and other related companies are introduced to help keep the subject feeling real. The authors understand that students are engaged best when the discussion involves real companies that students find interesting and whose products or services are familiar, such as **Apple, American Eagle Outfitters, Best Buy, Six Flags, Regal Entertainment,** and **Google.** In **Chapter 12,** full financial statement analysis is provided for **Nike** versus **Under Armour.**

This focus is also carried into areas of the end-of-chapter material, where students can demonstrate their analysis and understanding of real-world situations.

> Most importantly, it **offers opportunities for students to have insights into accounting careers** via Career Corners.
>
> —Chuo-Hsuan Lee, *SUNY–Plattsburgh*

To help students be forward-thinking about their careers, discussions are included to bring the business world front and center. The **Career Corner** boxes highlight the relevance of accounting by showing how a particular topic in the chapter relates to a business career. This feature is intended to increase the relevance of the material for both accounting *majors* and *nonmajors.*

HELPING STUDENTS BECOME BETTER PROBLEM SOLVERS

> This text is very well written and offers a set of end-of-chapter problems that **progressively challenges students** and directs them to **build problem-solving skills.** —Gregg S. Woodruff, *Western Illinois University*

In becoming a good problem-solver, it's crucial that students have the right tools and guidance to help them along the way—especially when learning the accounting cycle. The **accounting cycle chapters** clearly distinguish activities During the Period (Chapter 2) from End of the Period (Chapter 3). Chapters 4-10 cover specific topics in **balance sheet order**. Throughout the chapters, several features keep students on the right track as they learn the accounting process.

Let's Review sections within each chapter test students' comprehension of key concepts. These short review exercises, with solutions, are intended to reinforce understanding of specific chapter material and allow students to apply concepts and procedures learned in the chapter prior to attempting their homework assignment. Each Let's Review exercise also contains **Suggested Homework**, which enables instructors to easily assign corresponding homework. For the fourth edition, 22 Let's Review sections are "interactive" and provide students **video-based instruction** on how to solve the exercise and model that approach for related homework.

> Easy to read, love the Key Points and Common Mistakes—**these sound like me talking to my students** and are exactly the points I make in class! Really!
>
> —Christa Morgan, *Georgia Perimeter College*

Key Points provide quick synopses of the critical pieces of information presented throughout each chapter. Key Points within each chapter's Learning Objectives are also summarized at the end of each chapter, providing students with a convenient study guide.

> Very easy to read!!! I like the Key Points and Common Mistakes segments in each chapter. These features would really help my students as they read the text and study for exams. I also like the **simplicity of each chapter.**
>
> — David Juriga, *St. Louis Community College*

Common Mistakes made by financial accounting students are highlighted throughout each of the chapters. With greater awareness of the pitfalls the average student will find in a first accounting class, students can avoid making the same mistakes and gain a deeper understanding of the chapter material.

COMMON MISTAKE

Dividends represent the payment of cash but are not considered an expense in running the business. Students sometimes mistakenly include the amount of dividends as an expense in the income statement, rather than as a distribution of net income in the statement of stockholders' equity.

> The "Flip Side" and "Common Mistakes" sections are outstanding and are **likely to be among the favorite parts of the content** for students.
>
> — Christian Wurst, *Temple University*

The **Flip Side** feature demonstrates how various transactions are viewed by each side. Including the "flip side" of a transaction—in context—enhances the student's understanding of both the initial and the related transaction. Selected homework materials also include the Flip Side transactions, to reinforce student understanding.

FOSTERING DECISION-MAKING & ANALYSIS SKILLS

In today's environment, business graduates are being asked more than ever to be equipped in analyzing data and making decisions. To address this need, each chapter includes **Decision Maker's Perspective** sections, which offer insights into how the information discussed in the chapters affects decisions made by investors, creditors, managers, and others. Each chapter also contains **Decision Points** highlighting specific decisions in the chapter that can be made using financial accounting information.

Decision Maker's Perspective

Investors Understand One-Time Gains

Investors typically take a close look at the components of a company's profits. For example, **Ford Motor Company** announced that it had earned a net income for the fourth quarter (the final three months of the year) of $13.6 billion. Analysts had expected Ford to earn only $1.7 to $2.0 billion for that period. The day that Ford announced this earnings news, its stock price *fell* about 4.5%.

Why would Ford's stock price fall on a day when the company reported these seemingly high profits? A closer inspection of Ford's income statement shows that it included a one-time gain of $12.4 billion for the fourth quarter. After subtracting this one-time gain, Ford actually earned only about $1.2 billion from normal operations, easily missing analysts' expectations. This disappointing earnings performance is the reason the company's stock price fell.

Analysis sections are offered at the end of topical chapters (4–11). These sections analyze the ratios of two real companies related to that chapter's theme. Students are able to see how companies' different business strategies affect their financial ratios. The **Financial Statement Analysis** chapter (12) allows students to take a deep dive into these concepts by analyzing the financial statements of Nike and Under Armour.

General Ledger Problems have students demonstrate their understanding of Ratio Analysis based on a list of transactions and subsequent financial statements. In addition, multiple other opportunities are available for students to practice decision-making and analysis skills in Connect and in the text itself.

The **Additional Perspectives** section of each chapter offers cases and activities designed to allow students to apply the knowledge and skills they've learned to real, realistic, or provocative situations. Students are placed in the role of decision maker, presented with a set of information, and asked to draw conclusions that test their understanding of the issues discussed in the chapters. Each chapter offers an engaging mix of activities and opportunities to perform real-world financial accounting analysis, conduct internet research, understand earnings management, address ethical dilemma, and practice written communication.

The **Great Adventures Continuing Problem** progresses from chapter to chapter, encompassing the accounting issues of each new chapter as the story unfolds. This problem allows students to see how each chapter's topics can be integrated into the operations of a single company. This problem is also available in McGraw-Hill Connect.

Financial Analysis: American Eagle Outfitters, Inc. & The Buckle, Inc. ask students to gather information from the annual report of American Eagle, located in Appendix A and Buckle, in Appendix B. **Comparative Analysis**—In addition to separately analyzing the financial information of American Eagle and Buckle, students are asked to compare financial information between the two companies.

Connect and Spiceland's *Financial Accounting* are tightly integrated to continue honing students' conceptual understanding, problem-solving, decision-making & analysis skills.

McGraw Hill Education **connect®**

All end-of-chapter items in the textbook that can be built into Connect have been included with feedback and explanations and many with **Guided Examples** to help students work through their homework in an effective manner.

Additional algorithms and a greatly expanded test bank have been added as well, allowing students more practice and you more opportunities for students to demonstrate their understanding.

Extensive End-Of-Chapter Questions are available in the text and Connect:
- Brief Exercises
- Exercises (A & B set)
- Problems (A & B set)
- Great Adventures Continuing Problem
- Comprehensive Problems spanning multiple chapters

Available within Connect, **SmartBook** makes study time as productive and efficient as possible. It identifies and closes knowledge gaps through a continually adapting reading experience that provides personalized learning resources at the precise moment of need. This ensures that every minute spent with SmartBook is returned to the student as the most value-added minute possible. The result? More confidence, better grades, and greater success

Connect Insight offers instructors and students with a highly visual analytics dashboard designed to provide valuable insights into what is occurring in the course. For instructors, Insight identifies areas in which groups of students are struggling and succeeding in their section(s). The analytics dashboard then allows instructors to view individual strengths and weaknesses, which can provide the blueprint for student success in the course. For students, Insight identifies individual strengths and weaknesses, as well as providing prescriptive advice on actions the student can take to shore up knowledge gaps. Connect Insight is a key differentiator in McGraw-Hill's technology offer!

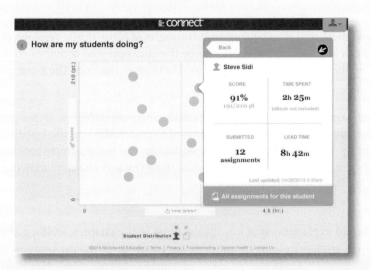

TWO NEW CONNECT PROBLEM TYPES:

General Ledger Problems

Expanded general ledger problems provide a much-improved student experience when working with accounting cycle questions with improved navigation and less scrolling. Students can audit their mistakes by easily linking back to their original entries and are able to see how the numbers flow through the various financial statements. Many General Ledger Problems include an analysis tab that allows students to demonstrate their critical thinking skills and a deeper understanding of accounting concepts.

Excel Simulations

New Simulated Excel questions, assignable within Connect, allow students to practice their Excel skills—such as basic formulas and formatting—within the content of financial accounting. These questions feature animated, narrated Help and Show Me tutorials (when enabled), as well as automatic feedback and grading for both students and professors.

ADDITIONAL VIDEO-BASED INSTRUCTION:

Guided Examples

Guided Examples provide narrated, animated, and step-by-step walkthroughs of algorithmic versions of assigned exercises in Connect, allowing the student to identify, review, or reinforce the concepts and activities covered in class. Guided Examples provide immediate feedback and focus on the areas where students need the most guidance.

Interactive Presentations

The Interactive Presentations provide engaging narratives of all chapter learning objectives in an assignable, interactive online format. They follow the structure of the text and are organized to match the specific learning objectives within each chapter of *Financial Accounting*. While the interactive presentations are not meant to replace the textbook, they provide additional explanation and enhancement of material from the text chapter, allowing students to learn, study, and practice with instant feedback at their own pace.

Interactive Illustrations

Interactive Illustrations provide video-based explanations of key illustrations in the chapter, walking students step-by-step through the illustration, to deepen students' understanding of the concepts or the calculations shown.

Required=Results

McGraw-Hill Connect®
Learn Without Limits

Connect is a teaching and learning platform that is proven to deliver better results for students and instructors.

Connect empowers students by continually adapting to deliver precisely what they need, when they need it, and how they need it, so your class time is more engaging and effective.

Course outcomes improve with Connect.

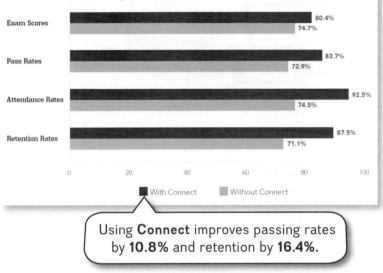

	With Connect	Without Connect
Exam Scores	80.4%	74.7%
Pass Rates	83.7%	72.9%
Attendance Rates	92.5%	74.5%
Retention Rates	87.5%	71.1%

Using **Connect** improves passing rates by **10.8%** and retention by **16.4%**.

88% of instructors who use **Connect** require it; instructor satisfaction **increases** by 38% when **Connect** is required.

Analytics

Connect Insight®

Connect Insight is Connect's new one-of-a-kind visual analytics dashboard—now available for both instructors and students—that provides at-a-glance information regarding student performance, which is immediately actionable. By presenting assignment, assessment, and topical performance results together with a time metric that is easily visible for aggregate or individual results, Connect Insight gives the user the ability to take a just-in-time approach to teaching and learning, which was never before available. Connect Insight presents data that empowers students and helps instructors improve class performance in a way that is efficient and effective.

Connect helps students achieve better grades

		A	B	C	D	F
With Connect		36%	29.5%	22%	4.3%	
Without Connect		22.2%	22.3%	25.6%	9.8%	

Based on McGraw-Hill Education Connect Effectiveness Study 2013

Students can view their results for any **Connect** course.

Adaptive

THE FIRST AND ONLY **ADAPTIVE READING EXPERIENCE** DESIGNED TO TRANSFORM THE WAY STUDENTS READ

> More students earn **A's** and **B's** when they use McGraw-Hill Education **Adaptive** products.

SmartBook®

Proven to help students improve grades and study more efficiently, SmartBook contains the same content within the print book, but actively tailors that content to the needs of the individual. SmartBook's adaptive technology provides precise, personalized instruction on what the student should do next, guiding the student to master and remember key concepts, targeting gaps in knowledge and offering customized feedback, and driving the student toward comprehension and retention of the subject matter. Available on smartphones and tablets, SmartBook puts learning at the student's fingertips—anywhere, anytime.

> Over **4 billion questions** have been answered, making McGraw-Hill Education products more intelligent, reliable, and precise.

STUDENTS WANT Mc Graw Hill Education **SMARTBOOK®**

95% of students reported **SmartBook** to be a more effective way of reading material

100% of students want to use the Practice Quiz feature available within **SmartBook** to help them study

100% of students reported having reliable access to off-campus wifi

90% of students say they would purchase **SmartBook** over print alone

95% reported that **SmartBook** would impact their study skills in a positive way

Mc Graw Hill Education

*Findings based on a 2015 focus group survey at Pellissippi State Community College administered by McGraw-Hill Education

The version of *Financial Accounting* you are reading would not be the same book without the valuable suggestions, keen insights, and constructive criticisms of the list of reviewers below. Each professor listed here contributed in substantive ways to the organization of chapters, coverage of topics, and selective use of pedagogy. We are grateful to them for taking the time to read each chapter and offer their insights.

Joe Abrokwa, *University of West Georgia*
Dawn Addington, *Central New Mexico Community College, Main*
Janice Ammons, *Quinnipiac University*
Bill Bailey, *Weber State University*
Lisa Banks, *Mott Community College*
Cindy Bolt, *The Citadel*
John Borke, *University of Wisconsin Platteville*
Bruce Bradford, *Fairfield University*
Phil Brown, *Harding University*
Sandra Byrd, *Missouri State University*
Ed Bysiek, *Saint Bonaventure University*
Julia Camp, *Providence College*
Mark Camma, *Atlantic Cape Community College*
Kam Chan, *Pace University*
Lawrence Chui, *University of St. Thomas*
Raymond Clark, *California State University, East Bay*
Jackie Conrecode, *Florida Gulf Coast University*
Amy Cooper, *University of Alaska, Fairbanks*
Cathy DeHart, *Gonzaga University*
Mingcherng Deng, *Baruch College*
Harry DeWolf, *Mount Hood Community College*
Patricia Dorris Crenny, *Villanova University*
Yun Fan, *University of Houston–Houston*
Cory Frad, *Muscatine Community College*
Jackie Franklin, *Spokane Falls Community College*
Christopher Ferro, *College of DuPage*
Joshua Filzen, *University of Nevada, Reno*
Lisa Gillespie, *Loyola University Chicago*
Penny Hahn, *KCTCS Henderson Community College*
Marcye Hampton, *University of Central Florida-Orlando*
Candy Heino, *Anoka Ramsey Community College*
Kenneth Horowitz, *Mercer County Community College*
Maggie Houston, *Wright State University – Dayton*
Laura Ilcisin, *University of Nebraska at Omaha*
Shelley Kane, *Wake Technical Community College*
Gokhan Karahan, *University of Alaska Anchorage*
Elizabeth Kidd, *Gannon University, Erie*
Marie Kelly, *Stephen F. Austin State University*
Stephen Kolenda, *Hartwick College*
Tal Kroll, *Ozarks Technical Community College*
Steven LaFave, *Augsburg College*
Judy Lincoln, *San Diego Mesa College*
Jason Lee, *SUNY Plattsburgh*
James Lukawitz, *University of Memphis*
Mabel Machin, *Valencia College Osceola*
Josephine Mathias, *Mercer County Community College*
Lynn Mazzola, *Nassau Community College*
Brenda McVey, *Green River Community College–Auburn*

Mary Ann Merryman, *Saint Mary's College*
Earl Mitchell, *Santa Ana College*
Edna Mitchell, *Polk State College – Winter Haven*
Liz Moliski, *Concordia University–TX*
Jody Murphy, *Colby Sawyer College*
Anthony Newton, *Highland Community College*
Jennifer Oliver, *Quinebaug Valley Community College*
Wendy Potratz, *University of Wisconsin Oshkosh*
Jared Plummer, *North Carolina State University Raleigh*
Jean Riley-Schultz, *University of Nebraska Lincoln*
Shawn Roberson, *King College*
Rebecca Rosner, *Hofstra University*
Anwar Salimi, *California State Polytechnic University, Pomona*
Larry Sallee, *Winona State University*
Monica Salomon, *University of West Florida*
Richard Sarkisian, *Camden County College*
Gary Schader, *Kean University*
Richard Schroeder, *University North Carolina, Charlotte*
Randall Serrett, *University of Houston Downtown*
Amber Sheeler, *North Carolina Wesleyan College*
Gregory Sinclair, *San Francisco State University*
Phil Smilanick, *Truckee Meadows Community College*
Judy Smith, *Parkland College*
Nancy Snow, *University of Toledo*
Bill Stinde, *Glendale Community College*
Edith Strickland, *Tallahassee Community College*
Dennis Stovall, *Colorado State University*
Gracelyn Stuart-Tuggle, *Palm Beach State College, South*
James Sugden, *Orange Coast College*
Denise Teixeira, *Chemeketa Community College*
Peter Theuri, *Northern Kentucky University*
Robin Thomas, *North Carolina State University Raleigh*
Lana Tuss, *Chemeketa Community College*
Lisa Victoravich, *University of Denver*
Cindy Vance, *Shepherd University*
Stacy R. Wade, *Western Kentucky University*
Jan Workman, *East Carolina University*

SECOND EDITION REVIEWERS

Dawn Addington, *Central New Mexico Community College*
Peter Aghimien, *Indiana University–South Bend*
Nasrollah Ahadiat, *California State Polytechnical University–Pomona*
James J. Aitken, *Central Michigan University*
Charles Aldridge, *Western Kentucky University*
Dave Alldredge, *Salt Lake Community College*
Fouad Alnajjar, *Baker College*
Janice Ammons, *Quinnipiac University*

Mark Anderson, *University of Texas at Dallas*
Steven Ault, *Montana State Unviersity–Bozeman*
Craig Bain, *Northern Arizona University*
Kashi Balachandran, *New York University*
Patricia C. Bancroft, *Bridgewater State College*
Randall P. Bandura, *Frostburg State University*
Lisa Banks, *Mott Community College*
Joyce Barden, *DeVry University*
Michael Barendse, *Grossmont College*
Carroll Barnes, *Milwaukee Area Technical College*
Cheryl Bartlett, *Central New Mexico Community College*
Ellen Bartley, *Saint Joseph's College–Suffolk*
Glenellyn Barty, *Northern Kentucky University*
Ira W. Bates, *Florida A&M University*
Mohammad S. Bazaz, *Oakland University*
Stephen Benner, *Eastern Illinois University*
Amy Bentley, *Tallahassee Community College*
Larry Bergin, *Winona State University*
Mark Bezik, *Concordia University*
Brenda Bindschatel, *Green River Community College–Auburn*
Cynthia Birk, *University of Nevada–Reno*
Eddy Birrer, *Gonzaga University*
Sandra Bitenc, *University of Texas at Arlington*
Claude Black, *Seattle Central Community College*
Janell Blazovich, *University of Saint Thomas*
David Bojarsky, *California State University–Long Beach*
Charlie Bokemeier, *Michigan State University*
Jack Borke, *University of Wisconsin–Platteville*
Lisa N. Bostick, *The University of Tampa*
Amy Bourne, *Oregon State University*
Benoit Boyer, *Sacred Heart University*
Thomas Brady, *University of Dayton*
Jerold K. Braun, *Daytona State College*
Molly Brown, *James Madison University*
Linnae Bryant, *Chicago State University*
R. Eugene Bryson, *University of Alabama–Huntsville*
Georgia Buckles, *Manchester Community College*
Charles I. Bunn, *Wake Tech Community College*
Esther Bunn, *Stephen F. Austin State University*
Jacqueline Burke, *Hofstra University*
Sandra Byrd, *Missouri State University*
Edward J. Bysiek, *Saint Bonaventure University*
Scott Cairns, *Shippensburg University of PA*
Ernest Carraway, *North Carolina State University*
Pat Carter, *Green River Community College–Auburn*
Bruce Cassel, *Dutchess Community College*
Gayle Chaky, *Dutchess Community College*
Valrie Chambers, *Texas A&M University*
Kam C. Chan, *Pace University*
Mike Chatham, *Radford University*

Betty Chavis, *California State University–Fullerton*
Al Chen, *North Carolina State University–Raleigh*
Xiaoyan Cheng, *University of Nebraska at Omaha*
Alan Cherry, *Loyola Marymount University*
Bea Chiang, *The College of New Jersey*
Carolyn Christesen, *Westchester Community College*
Cal Christian, *East Carolina University*
Tony Cioffi, *Lorain County Community College*
Jay Cohen, *Oakton Community College*
Leslie Cohen, *University of Arizona*
Taleah Collum, *Jacksonville State University*
Norman Colter, *University of New Mexico–Albuquerque*
Elizabeth Conner, *University of Colorado–Denver*
Jackie Conrecode, *Florida Gulf Coast University*
Debora Constable, *Georgia Perimeter College*
Pat Cook, *Manchester Community College*
Betty Cossitt, *University of Nevada–Reno*
Meg Costello Lambert, *Oakland Community College*
Samantha Cox, *Wake Tech Community College*
Leonard Cronin, *Rochester Community & Technical College*
Jim Crowther, *Kirkwood Community College*
Jill Cunningham, *Santa Fe College*
Wagih Dafashy, *George Mason University*
Karl Dahlberg, *Rutgers University*
Dori Danko, *Grand Valley State University*
Kreag Danvers, *Clarion University of PA*
Alan Davis, *Community College of Philadelphia*
Harold Davis, *Southeastern Louisiana University*
Mark DeFond, *University of Southern California*
Guenther DerManelian, *Johnson & Wales University*
Patricia Derrick, *Salisbury University*
Mike Deschamps, *Miracosta College*
Rosemond Desir, *Colorado State University*
Carlton Donchess, *Bridgewater State College*
Alex Dontoh, *New York University*
Jamie Doran, *Muhlenberg College*
John Draut, *Saint Xavier University*
Lisa Dutchik, *Kirkwood Community College*
Carol Dutton, *South Florida Community College*
Tammy Duxbury, *Bryant University*
Cynthia Eakin, *University of the Pacific*
Jeff Edwards, *Portland Community College–Sylvania*
Susan Eldridge, *University of Nebraska–Omaha*
Ryan Enlow, *University of Nevada–Las Vegas*
Sheri Erickson, *Minnesota State University–Moorhead*
Harlan Etheridge, *University of Louisiana–Lafayette*
Robert Everett, *Lewis & Clark Community College*
Alan Falcon, *Loyola Marymount University*
Darius Fatemi, *Northern Kentucky University*
Andrew Felo, *Penn State University*
Janice Fergusson, *University of South Carolina*
Kathleen Fitzpatrick, *University of Toledo–Scott Park*
Linda Flaming, *Monmouth University*
Amy Ford, *Western Illinois University*
John Fortner, *Daytona State College–Daytona Beach*

Brenda Fowler, *Alamance Community College*
Martha Lou Fowler, *Missouri Western State University*
Tom Fuhrmann, *Missouri Western State University*
Harlan Fuller, *Illinois State University*
Ed Furticella, *Purdue University*
Mohamed Gaber, *SUNY Plattsburgh*
John Gardner, *University of Wisconsin–La Crosse*
Roger Gee, *San Diego Mesa College*
Daniel Gibbons, *Waubonsee Community College*
Michael Gilkey, *Palomar College*
Lisa Gillespie, *Loyola University*
Marc Giullian, *Montana State University–Bozeman*
Ruth Goran, *Northeastern Illinois University*
Sherry Gordon, *Palomar College*
M. David Gorton, *Eastern Washington University–Spokane*
Jill Goslinga, *University of Florida–Gainesville*
Janet Grange, *Chicago State University*
Tony Greig, *Purdue University*
Andrew Griffith, *Iona College–New Rochelle*
Sanjay Gupta, *Valdosta State University*
Geoffrey Gurka, *Mesa State College*
Jeffry Haber, *Iona College*
Abo-El-Yazeed Habib, *Minnesota State University–Mankato*
Ronald Halsac, *Community College of Allegheny County*
Heidi Hansel, *Kirkwood Community College*
Thomas Bowe Hansen, *University of New Hampshire*
Sheldon Hanson, *Chippewa Valley Technical College*
Coby Harmon, *University of California–Santa Barbara*
Randall Hartman, *Lock Haven University of Pennsylvania*
Syd Hasan, *George Mason University*
Erskine Hawkins, *Georgia Perimeter College*
Laurie Hays, *Western Michigan University*
Daniel He, *Monmouth University*
Haihong He, *California State University–Los Angeles*
Kevin Hee, *San Diego State University*
Sheri Henson, *Western Kentucky University*
Joshua Herbold, *University of Montana*
Joyce Hicks, *Saint Mary's College*
Margaret Hicks, *Howard University*
Dan Hinchliffe, *University of North Carolina–Asheville*
Frank Hodge, *University of Washington*
Anthony Holder, *Case Western Reserve University*
Mary Hollars, *Vincennes University*
Cynthia Hollenbach, *University of Denver*
Linda Holmes, *University of Wisconsin–Whitewater*
Sharon Hoover-Dice, *Clinton Community College*
Steven Hornik, *University of Central Florida*
Kathy Hsiao Yu Hsu, *University of Louisiana–Lafayette*
Marsha Huber, *Otterbein College*
Robert Huddleston, *Dixie State College*

Peggy Ann Hughes, *Montclair State University*
Laura Ilcisin, *University of Nebraska at Omaha*
Paula Irwin, *Muhlenberg College*
Steve Jablonsky, *Colorado State University*
Cynthia Jackson, *Northeastern University*
Norma Jacobs, *Austin Community College*
Marianne James, *California State University–Los Angeles*
Todd Jensen, *Sierra College*
Cathy Jeppson, *California State University–Northridge*
Raymond Johnson, *Guilford College*
Shondra Johnson, *Bradley University*
Rita Jones, *Columbus State University*
Sandra F. Jordan, *Florida State College*
Mark Judd, *University of San Diego*
David Juriga, *Saint Louis Community College–Forest Park*
Robert Kachur, *Richard Stockton College of New Jersey*
Elliot Kamlet, *Binghamton University*
Shelley Kane, *Wake Tech Community College*
Kathryn Kapka, *University of Texas–Tyler*
Loisanne Kattelman, *Weber State University*
Ann Kelley, *Providence College*
Rebecca A. Kerr, *University of South Carolina*
Stephen Kerr, *Bradley University*
Lara Kessler, *Grand Valley State University*
Tim Kizirian, *California State University–Chico*
Janice Klimek, *University of Central Missouri*
Christine Kloezeman, *Glendale Community College*
John Koeplin, *University of San Francisco*
Stephen A. Kolenda, *Hartwick College*
Emil Koren, *Saint Leo University*
Dennis Kovach, *Community College of Allegheny County*
Sudha Krishnan, *California State University–Long Beach*
Tal Kroll, *Ozarks Technical Community College*
Joan Lacher, *Nassau Community College*
Steven J. LaFave, *Augsburg College*
Bradley Lail, *North Carolina State University–Raleigh*
Sheldon Langsam, *Western Michigan University*
Cathy Larson, *Middlesex Community College*
Douglas A. Larson, *Salem State College*
Laurie Larson-Gardner, *Valencia Community College*
Doug Laufer, *Metropolitan State College of Denver*
Michael D. Lawrence, *Portland Community College*
Suzanne Lay, *Mesa State College*
Chuo-Hsuan Lee, *SUNY Plattsburgh*
Deborah Lee, *Northeastern State University*
Christy Lefevers-Land, *Catawba Valley Community College*
Pamela Legner, *College of DuPage*
Stacy LeJeune, *Nicholls State University*
Elliott Levy, *Bentley College*
Xu Li, *University of Texas at Dallas*
Beixin Lin, *Montclair State University*

Joseph Lipari, *Montclair State University*
Jane Livingstone, *Western Carolina University*
William Lloyd, *Lock Haven University of Pennsylvania*
Joseph Lupino, *Saint Mary's College of California*
Anna Lusher, *Slippery Rock University of PA*
Kirk Lynch, *Sandhills Community College*
Nancy Lynch, *West Virginia University*
Mostafa Maksy, *Northeastern Illinois University*
Sal Marino, *Westchester Community College*
Diane Marker, *University of Toledo–Scott Park*
Angie Martin, *Tarrant County College*
James Martin, *Washburn University*
Peter Martino, *Johnson & Wales University*
Christian Mastilak, *Xavier University*
Josephine Mathias, *Mercer County Community College*
Betsy Mayes, *University of North Carolina–Asheville*
Lynn Mazzola, *Nassau Community College*
Maureen McBeth, *College of DuPage*
Florence McGovern, *Bergen Community College*
Brian L. McGuire, *University of Southern Indiana*
Allison McLeod, *University of North Texas*
Chris McNamara, *Finger Lakes Community College*
Sara Melendy, *Gonzaga University*
Terri Meta, *Seminole Community College*
Kathleen M. Metcalf, *Muscatine Community College*
Jean Meyer, *Loyola University*
Pam Meyer, *University of Louisiana–Lafayette*
James Miller, *Gannon University*
Julie Miller, *Chippewa Valley Technical College*
Claudette Milligan, *Trident Technical College*
Tim Mills, *Eastern Illinois University*
Richard Minot, *University of California–Irvine*
Susan Minton, *Prairie View A&M University*
Laurel Bond Mitchell, *University of Redlands*
Laura Mizaur, *Creighton University*
Richard A. Moellenberndt, *Washburn University*
Kathy Moffeit, *West Georgia University*
J. Lowell Mooney, *Georgia Southern University*
Tommy Moores, *University of Nevada–Las Vegas*
Arabian Morgan, *Orange Coast College*
Michelle Moshier, *University at Albany*
Gerald Motl, *Xavier University*
Matthew Muller, *Adirondack Community College*
Lisa Murawa, *Mott Community College*
Volkan Muslu, *University of Texas at Dallas*
Al Nagy, *John Carroll University*
Lisa Nash, *Vincennes University*
Sia Nassiripour, *William Paterson University*
Presha Neidermeyer, *West Virginia University*
Micki Nickla, *Ivy Tech Community College of Indiana*
Tracie Nobles, *Austin Community College*
Kelly Noe, *Stephen F. Austin State University*
Hossein Noorian, *Wentworth Institute of Technology*
Rosemary Nurre, *College of San Mateo*

Barbara Nyden, *Missouri State University–West Plains*
Dan O'Brien, *North Central Technical College*
Ron O'Brien, *Fayetteville Tech Community College*
Kanalis Ockree, *Washburn University*
Karen Osterheld, *Bentley College*
Robert A. Pacheco, *Massasoit Community College*
Don Pagach, *North Carolina State University–Raleigh*
Janet Papiernik, *Indiana University/Purdue University–Ft Wayne*
Glenn Pate, *Palm Beach Community College*
Rukshad Patel, *College of DuPage*
Keith F. Patterson, *Brigham Young University*
Mary B. Pearson, *Southern Utah University*
Nori Pearson, *Washington State University*
Reed Peoples, *Austin Community College–Northridge*
Richard J. Pettit, *Mountain View College*
Jan Pitera, *Broome Community College*
John Plouffe, *California State University–Los Angeles*
Linda Poulson, *Elon University*
Matthew Probst, *Ivy Tech Community College of Indiana*
John Purisky, *Salem State University*
William Quilliam, *Florida Southern College*
Atul Rai, *Wichita State University*
Richard Rand, *Tennessee Tech University*
David Randolph, *Xavier University*
July Ratley, *Shasta College*
Donald J. Raux, *Siena College*
Aaron Reeves, *Saint Louis Community College–Forest Park*
Patrick Reihing, *Nassau Community College*
Raymond Reisig, *Pace University*
Gayle Richardson, *Bakersfield College*
Laura Rickett, *Kent State University*
Jean Riley-Schultz, *University of Nebraska–Lincoln*
Jennifer Robinson, *Trident Technical College*
Sharon Robinson, *Frostburg State University*
Joanne Rockness, *University of North Carolina–Wilmington*
Leroy Rogero, *University of Dayton*
Carol Rogers, *Central New Mexico Community College*
Miles Romney, *University of San Diego*
Richard Roscher, *University of North Carolina–Wilmington*
Mark Ross, *Western Kentucky University*
John A. Rude, *Bloomsburg University of PA*
Robert Russ, *Northern Kentucky University*
Huldah A. Ryan, *Iona College*
Anwar Salimi, *California State Poly University–Pomona*
Angela Sandberg, *Jacksonville State University*
Amy Santos, *State College of Florida*

Noema Santos, *Manatee Community College–Bradenton*
Lynn Saubert, *Radford University*
Mary Scarborough, *Tyler Junior College*
Gary Schader, *Kean University*
Linda Schain, *Hofstra University*
Megan Schaupp, *West Virginia University*
Arnold Schneider, *Georgia Institute of Technology*
Michael Scott, *Glendale Community College*
Tony Scott, *Norwalk Community College*
Ali Sedaghat, *Loyola University Maryland*
Steve Sefcik, *University of Washington*
Joann Segovia, *Minnesota State University–Moorhead*
Ann E. Selk, *University of Wisconsin–Green Bay*
Michael Serif, *Dowling College*
Randall Serrett, *University of Houston–Downtown*
Suzanne Sevalstad, *University of Nevada*
Kathy Sevigny, *Bridgewater State College*
Sheila Shain, *Santa Ana College*
Geeta Shankar, *University of Dayton*
Robbie Sheffy, *Tarrant County College*
Deanna M. Shively, *Saint Mary's College*
Lori Simonsen, *University of Nebraska at Omaha*
Margie Sinclair-Parish, *Lewis & Clark Community College*
Mike Skaff, *College of the Sequoias*
Mike Slaubaugh, *Indiana University/Purdue University–Ft Wayne*
Nathan Slavin, *Hofstra University*
Erik Slayter, *California Polytechnic University*
G. Phillip Smilanick, *Truckee Meadows Community College*
Becky L. Smith, *York College of PA*
Gene Smith, *Eastern New Mexico University*
Gerald A. Smith, *University of Northern Iowa*
Peggy Smith, *Baker College–Flint*
Sondra Smith, *West Georgia University*
Warren Smock, *Ivy Tech Community College of Indiana*
Kenneth Snow, *Florida State College*
Dale Spencer, *New Mexico State University–Las Cruces*
Mary Speth, *Sandhills Community College*
Barbara Squires, *Corning Community College*
Victor Stanton, *University of California, Berkeley*
Diane Stark, *Phoenix College*
Jenny Staskey, *Northern Arizona University*
Maureen Stefanini, *Worcester State College*
Dean A. Steria, *SUNY Plattsburgh*
Charles Stivason, *Marshall University*
Ron Stone, *California State University–Northridge*
Dennis Stovall, *Grand Valley State University*
Arlene Strawn, *Tallahassee Community College*
Edith Strickland, *Tallahassee Community College*
Ron Strittmater, *North Hennepin Community College*

MORE THANKS . . .

Gloria Stuart, *Georgia Southern University*
Diane Sturek, *IUPUI–Indianapolis*
Alan Styles, *California State University–San Marcos*
John Surdick, *Xavier University*
Jan Sweeney, *Bernard M. Baruch College*
Paulette Tandy, *University of Nevada–Las Vegas*
Linda Tarrago, *Hillsborough Community College*
Karen Teitel, *College of the Holy Cross*
Sue Terzian, *Wright State University–Dayton*
Peter Theuri, *Northern Kentucky University*
Michael F. Thomas, *Humboldt State University*
Robin Thomas, *North Carolina State University–Raleigh*
Amanda Thompson, *Marshall University*
Dorothy Thompson, *North Central Texas College*
Lisa Thornton Buehler, *Truckee Meadows Community College*
Paula Tigerman, *Black Hawk College*
Theresa Tiggeman, *University of the Incarnate Word*
Melanie Torborg, *Minnesota School of Business*
Yvette Travis, *Bishop State Community College*
Mario Tripaldi, *Hudson County Community College*
Jinhee Trone, *Santa Ana College*
Nancy Uddin, *Monmouth University*
Karen Varnell, *Tarleton State University*
Stacy R. Wade, *Western Kentucky University*
Elisabeth Peltier Wagner, *Bernard M. Baruch College*
Mary Jeanne Walsh, *La Salle University*
Stephen Walsh, *Clark College*
Li Wang, *University of Akron*
Larry Watkins, *Northern Arizona University*
Olga Dupuis Watts, *McNeese State University*
Andrea Weickgenannt, *Northern Kentucky University*
Patti Weiss, *John Carroll University*
Mary Ann Welden, *Wayne State University*
Kristin Wentzel, *La Salle University*
Cathy West, *University of Massachusetts–Amherst*
Cheryl Westen, *Western Illinois University*
Sally Whitney, *Colorado State University*
Jane Wiese, *Valencia Community College East*
Gayle Williams, *Sacramento City College*
Gideon Wray, *Pennsylvania College of Technology*
Allen Wright, *Hillsborough Community College*
Christine Wright, *Seminole State College–Sanford*
Lorraine Wright, *North Carolina State University–Raleigh*
Christian Wurst, *Temple University*
Kathryn Yarbrough, *Appalachian State University*
Gregory C. Yost, *University of West Florida*
Thomas M. Young, *Lone Star College*
Marjorie Yuschak, *Sacred Heart University*
Tom Zeller, *Loyola University–Chicago*
Emmanuel Zur, *Bernard M. Baruch College*
Robert Zwicker, *Pace University*

FIRST EDITION REVIEWERS

James J. Aitken, *Central Michigan University*
Christie P. Anderson, *Whitworth University*
Marjorie Ashton, *Truckee Meadows Community College*
Steven Ault, *Montana State University–Bozeman*
Tim Baker, *California State University–Fresno*
Joyce Barden, *DeVry University–Phoenix*
Deborah F. Beard, *Southeast Missouri State University*
Judy Benish, *Fox Valley Tech College*
Joseph Berlinski, *Prairie State College*
Eddy Birrer, *Gonzaga University*
Jack Borke, *University of Wisconsin–Platteville*
Lisa N. Bostick, *The University of Tampa*
Bruce Bradford, *Fairfield University*
Thomas Brady, *University of Dayton*
Linda Bressler, *University of Houston–Downtown*
Madeline Brogan, *North Harris College*
Carol Brown, *Oregon State University*
Helen Brubeck, *San Jose State University*
R. Eugene Bryson, *University of Alabama–Huntsville*
Charles I. Bunn, *Wake Tech Community College*
Ron Burrows, *University of Dayton*
Thane Butt, *Champlain College*
Sandra Byrd, *Missouri State University*
Kay C. Carnes, *Gonzaga University*
Bea Bih-Horng Chiang, *The College of New Jersey*
Cal Christian, *East Carolina University*
John Coulter, *Western New England College*
Sue Cullers, *Tarleton State University*
Kreag Danvers, *Clarion University of PA*
Peggy Dejong, *Kirkwood Community College*
Laura Delaune, *Louisiana State University–Baton Rouge*
Shannon Donovan, *Bridgewater State College*
Allan Drebin, *Northwestern University*
Ahmed Ebrahim, *State University of NY–New Paltz*
Thomas Finnegan, *University of Illinois–Champaign*
Linda Flaming, *Monmouth University*
Martha Lou Fowler, *Missouri Western State University*
Tom Fuhrmann, *Missouri Western State University*
Mohamed Gaber, *State University of New York–Plattsburgh*
Rena Galloway, *State Fair Community College*
Margaret Garnsey, *Siena College*
David L. Gilbertson, *Western Washington University*
Lisa Gillespie, *Loyola University–Chicago*
Ruth Goran, *Northeastern Illinois University*
Jeffry Haber, *Iona College–New Rochelle*
Heidi Hansel, *Kirkwood Community College*
Sheldon Hanson, *Chippewa Valley Tech College*
Al Hartgraves, *Emory University*
Bob Hartman, *University of Iowa–Iowa City*

K.D. Hatheway-Dial, *University of Idaho*
John Hathorn, *Metro State College of Denver*
Byron K. Henry, *Howard University*
Joshua Herbold, *University of Montana*
Margaret Hicks, *Howard University*
Mary Hollars, *Vincennes University*
Sharon Hoover-Dice, *Clinton Community College*
Steven Hornik, *University of Central Florida*
Marsha Huber, *Otterbein College*
David Hurtt, *Baylor University*
Laura Ilcisin, *University of Nebraska–Omaha*
Paula Irwin, *Muhlenberg College*
Marianne James, *California State University–Los Angeles*
Raymond Johnson, *Guilford College*
Melissa Jordan, *College of DuPage*
David Juriga, *St. Louis Community College–Forest Park*
Dennis L. Kovach, *Community College of Allegheny County*
Steven J. LaFave, *Augsburg College*
Phillip D. Landers, *Pennsylvania College of Technology*
Douglas A. Larson, *Salem State College*
Laurie Larson-Gardner, *Valencia Community College East*
Daniel Law, *Gonzaga University*
Suzanne Lay, *Mesa State College*
Christy Lefevers-Land, *Catawba Valley Community College*
Joseph Lipari, *Montclair State University*
Chao-Shin Liu, *University of Notre Dame*
Mostafa Maksy, *Northeastern Illinois University*
S. A. Marino, *SUNY/Westchester Community College*
Dawn Massey, *Fairfield University*
Joyce Matthews, *Central New Mexico Community College*
Mark McCarthy, *East Carolina University*
Robert W. McGee, *Barry University*
Chris McNamara, *Finger Lakes Community College*
Kathleen M. Metcalf, *Muscatine Community College*
Herbert L. Meyer, *Scott Community College–Davenport*
Jean Meyer, *Loyola University*
Pam Meyer, *University of Louisiana–Lafayette*
Laurel Bond Mitchell, *University of Redlands*
Richard A. Moellenberndt, *Washburn University*
Dennis P. Moore, *Worcester State College*
Tommy Moores, *University of Nevada–Las Vegas*
Ron O'Brien, *Fayetteville Tech Community College*
George Pate, *Robeson Community College*
Keith Patterson, *Brigham Young University–Idaho*
Susanna Pendergast, *Western Illinois University*
Jan Pitera, *Broome Community College*
John Plouffe, *California State University–Los Angeles*

AND MORE THANKS . . .

Alan Ransom, *Cypress College*
Laura Rickett, *Kent State University*
John A. Rude, *Bloomsburg University of PA*
Amy Santos, *Manatee Community College–Bradenton*
Dick Schroeder, *University of North Carolina–Charlotte*
Ann E. Selk, *University of Wisconsin–Green Bay*
Seleshi Sisaye, *Duquesne University*
Rodney Smith, *California State University–Long Beach*

Nancy L. Snow, *University of Toledo*
Victor Stanton, *University of California–Berkeley*
Gracelyn Stuart, *Palm Beach Community College*
John J. Surdick, *Xavier University*
G. A. Swanson, *Tennessee Tech University*
Aida Sy, *University of Bridgeport*
Christine Tan, *Baruch College*
Steve Teeter, *Utah Valley State College*
Peter Theuri, *Northern Kentucky University*
Ada Till, *Prairie View A&M University*
Michael Tyler, *Barry University*

Joan Van Hise, *Fairfield University*
Marcia R. Veit, *University of Central Florida*
Stacy R. Wade, *Western Kentucky University*
Susan Wessels, *Meredith College*
Peter Woodlock, *Youngstown State University*
Gregg S. Woodruff, *Western Illinois University*
Christian Wurst, *Temple University–Philadelphia*
Thomas M. Young, *Lone Star College–Tomball*
Benny Zachry, *Nicholls State University*
Lin Zheng, *Georgia College and State University*
Robert Zwicker, *Pace University*

We also would like to acknowledge the many talented people who contributed to the creation of this fourth edition and thank them for their valuable contributions. Ilene Leopold Persoff of Long Island University/LIU Post did a wonderful job accuracy checking our manuscript. Mark McCarthy of East Carolina University contributed a helpful accuracy check of the page proofs; we thank him for his speedy and insightful comments. Jack Terry contributed the Excel templates that accompany the end-of-chapter material. We also appreciate the willingness of The Buckle, Inc., and American Eagle Outfitters, Inc., to allow us to use their companies' annual reports.

We appreciate the excellent *Connect* accuracy checking work completed by Beth Woods, Teressa Farough, and Mark McCarthy of East Carolina University, Bill Padley of Madison Area Technical College and all of the staff at ANSR Source. Janice Fergusson at the University of South Carolina did an excellent job accuracy checking our Testbank.

We also appreciate the expert attention given to this project by the staff at McGraw-Hill Education, especially Tim Vertovec, Managing Director; Natalie King, Senior Brand Manager; Kyle Burdette, Marketing Manager; Danielle Andries, Product Developer; Patricia Plumb, Director of Digital Content; Kevin Moran, Digital Product Developer; Pat Frederickson, Lead Content Project Manager; Angela Norris, Content Project Manager; Srdjan Savanovic, Senior Designer; and Laura Fuller, Buyer. Thanks, too, to Sarah Wood and Christina Sanders of Agate Publishing, for so ably stepping in to complete work on the supplements.

SUPPLEMENTS WITH THE SAME VOICE

Last but not least, we thank the authors of *Financial Accounting*, who write all of the major **supplements**, including the Solutions Manual, Instructor's Manual, all end-of-chapter material, additional online Exercises, and the Test Bank. The test bank includes over 3,000 questions, including more than 1,900 multiple-choice questions and more than 1,125 other types of questions and problems. The authors actively engage in the development of ALL technology-related supplements, such as SmartBook, end-of-chapter Questions, including our new General Ledger Problems, Interactive Illustrations, Let's Review Problems, Auto-Graded Excel Simulations and PowerPoints.

Contents in Brief

Contents

CHAPTER
11 Statement of Cash Flows 504

Apple Inc.: Cash Flows at the Core 505

CHAPTER
12 Financial Statement Analysis 560

Under Armour: Making the Competition Sweat 561

Contents Image Credits: Chapter 1 © AP Images/Cliff Owen; Chapter 2 © AP Images/ Reed Saxon; Chapter 3 © AP Images/Emile Wamsteker; Chapter 4 © Altrendo Images/ Getty Images; Chapter 5 © Comstock Images/SuperStock, RF; Chapter 6 © Susan Van Etten/PhotoEdit; Chapter 7 © AP Images/Louis Lanzano; Chapter 8 © Aaron M. Sprecher/Bloomberg/Getty Images; Chapter 9 © Thinkstock/Getty Images, RF; Chapter 10 © Bloomberg/Getty Images; Chapter 11 © AP Images/Rex Features; Chapter 12 © Tim Casey.

Fireworks Images Credits: © Comstock/PunchStock, RF and © Comstock Images/ Jupiterimages, RF.

CHAPTER 1

A Framework for Financial Accounting

Learning Objectives

AFTER STUDYING THIS CHAPTER, YOU SHOULD BE ABLE TO:

- **LO1–1** Describe the two primary functions of financial accounting.
- **LO1–2** Understand the business activities that financial accounting measures.
- **LO1–3** Determine how financial accounting information is communicated through financial statements.
- **LO1–4** Describe the role that financial accounting plays in the decision-making process.
- **LO1–5** Explain the term generally accepted accounting principles (GAAP) and describe the role of GAAP in financial accounting.
- **LO1–6** Identify career opportunities in accounting.

Appendix

- **LO1–7** Explain the nature of the conceptual framework used to develop generally accepted accounting principles.

BERKSHIRE HATHAWAY: SPEAKING THE LANGUAGE OF BUSINESS

"You have to understand accounting and you have to understand the nuances of accounting. It's the language of business and it's an imperfect language, but unless you are willing to put in the effort to learn accounting—how to read and interpret financial statements—you really shouldn't select stocks yourself." —Warren Buffett

Warren Buffett is the chairman and CEO of **Berkshire Hathaway**, a holding company that invests billions of dollars in other companies. In 1965, Warren Buffet acquired control of Berkshire Hathaway, and the company's stock has returned an amazing 1,826,163% over the 50-year period from 1965–2014. That means anyone investing $1,000 in Berkshire Hathaway's stock in 1965 would have watched their investment grow to nearly $20,000,000 by the end of 2014. By 2014, Buffett's personal net worth had grown to $72 billion, making him one of the richest people in the world according to *Forbes* magazine.

Feature Story

Some of Buffett's more famous investments have included companies such as Coca-Cola, Dairy Queen, American Express, Gillette, GEICO, and Heinz. How did he decide which stocks to purchase? Over ten thousand company stocks are available in the United States and thousands more on stock exchanges around the world. How did he separate the successful companies from the unsuccessful ones?

Buffett explains that the key to identifying good stocks is to look for companies having a durable competitive advantage. In other words, look for companies that are expected to produce *profits* for a long time because they have achieved a sustainable advantage over their rivals. How do you do this? There are, of course, many factors to consider, but Buffett explains that the primary source of this information comes from analyzing companies' financial accounting information—the subject of this book.

As you read through the chapters, you'll begin to understand the purpose of financial accounting to measure the business transactions of a company and then to communicate those measurements to investors, like Warren Buffett, in formal accounting reports called *financial statements*. It is from these financial statements that investors base their decisions on buying and selling a company's stock.

© AP Images/Cliff Owen

ACCOUNTING AS A MEASUREMENT/ COMMUNICATION PROCESS

Welcome to accounting. A common misconception about this course is that it is a math class, much like college algebra, calculus, or business statistics. You will soon see that this is *not* a math class. Don't say to yourself, "I'm not good at math so I probably won't be good at accounting." Though it's true that we use numbers heavily throughout each chapter, accounting is far more than adding, subtracting, and solving for unknown variables. So, what exactly is accounting? We'll take a close look at this next.

Defining Accounting

■ **LO1–1**
Describe the two primary functions of financial accounting.

Accounting is "the language of business." More precisely, accounting is a system of maintaining records of a company's operations and communicating that information to decision makers. Perhaps the earliest use of such systematic recordkeeping dates back thousands of years to ancient Mesopotamia (present-day Iraq), where records were kept of delivered agricultural products. Using accounting to maintain a record of multiple transactions allowed for better exchange among individuals and aided in the development of more complex societies.[1] In this class, you'll learn how to read, interpret, and communicate using the language of business.

Millions of people every day must make informed decisions about companies. Illustration 1–1 identifies some of those people and examples of decisions they make about the companies.

ILLUSTRATION 1–1

Decisions People Make About Companies

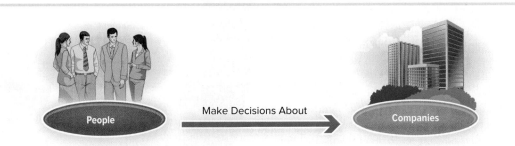

1. **Investors** decide whether to invest in stock.
2. **Creditors** decide whether to lend money.
3. **Customers** decide whether to purchase products.
4. **Suppliers** decide the customer's ability to pay for supplies.
5. **Managers** decide production and expansion.
6. **Employees** decide employment opportunities.
7. **Competitors** decide market share and profitability.
8. **Regulators** decide on social welfare.
9. **Tax authorities** decide on taxation policies.
10. **Local communities** decide on environmental issues.

To make the decisions outlined in Illustration 1–1, these people need information. This is where accounting plays a key role. As Illustration 1–2 shows, accountants **measure the activities of the company and communicate those measurements to others.**

Accounting information that is provided for *internal* users (managers) is referred to as **managerial accounting;** that provided to *external* users is referred to as **financial accounting.** In this book, we focus on financial accounting. Formally defined, the two functions of financial accounting are to measure business activities of a company and then to communicate those measurements to *external* parties for decision-making purposes.

As you study the business activities discussed in this book, it is important for you to keep in mind this "framework" for financial accounting. For each activity, ask yourself:

1. How is the business activity being measured?
2. How is the business activity being communicated?

---

[1]S. Basu and G. Waymire. 2006. Recordkeeping and Human Evolution. *Accounting Horizons* 20 (3): 201–229.

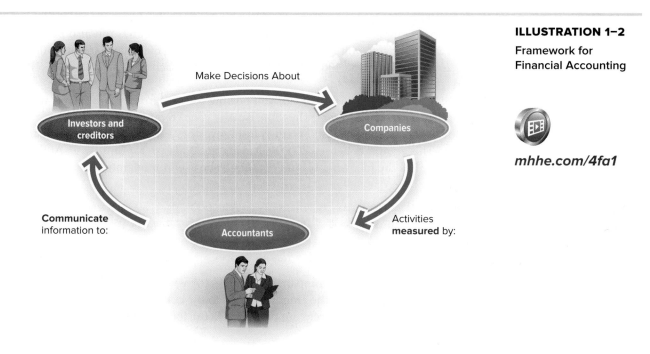

ILLUSTRATION 1–2
Framework for
Financial Accounting

mhhe.com/4fa1

These are the two functions of financial accounting. You'll better understand *why* this process exists by thinking about *how* the measurements being communicated help people make better decisions.

For example, **investors** want to make good decisions related to buying and selling their shares of the company's stock: Will the company's stock increase or decrease in value? The value of a stock is directly tied to the company's ability to make a profit, so what activities reflect the company's profitability? How should those activities be measured, and how should they be communicated in formal accounting reports?

As another example, **creditors** make decisions related to lending money to the company: Will the company be able to repay its debt and interest when they come due? How can debt activity be measured and how can it be communicated so that creditors better understand the ability of the company to have sufficient cash to repay debt and interest in the short term and the long term?

KEY POINT

The functions of financial accounting are to measure business activities of a company and to communicate information about those activities to investors and creditors and other outside users for decision-making purposes.

User's Guide For
learning objectives
throughout this book,
you will see boxed
sections, like this one,
titled *Key Point*. These
boxed items will highlight
the central focus of the
learning objectives.

Measuring Business Activities

■ **LO1–2**
Understand the business
activities that financial
accounting measures.

Let's first look at the typical activities of a start-up business. We'll do this with a simple example. Suppose you want to start a golf academy. The purpose of the academy is to provide lessons to develop junior players for top university programs and perhaps even one day to play on the PGA Tour. Let's look at some initial activities of your new company, which you've decided to name **Eagle Golf Academy.**

Let's assume you need about $35,000 to get the business up and going. You don't have that amount of money to start the business, so you begin by looking for investors. With their money, **investors** buy ownership in the company and have the right to share in the company's profits. Each share of ownership is typically referred to as a share of common stock. For your company, let's say you sell 1,000 shares of common stock for $25 each, receiving cash of $25,000 from investors. The 1,000 shares include 300 sold to your grandparents for $7,500, giving them 30% (= 300/1,000) ownership in the company. You also purchase 100 shares for $2,500, giving you 10% ownership. The remaining 600 shares include 300 to your parents, 200 to a friend, and 100 to your high school golf coach. You now have $25,000 from investors.

To raise the remaining cash needed, you borrow $10,000 from a local bank, which you agree to repay within three years. Thus, the bank is your **creditor.**

Now, with the $35,000 of cash obtained from investors and creditors, the company buys equipment. This equipment costs $24,000, leaving $11,000 cash for future use. At this point, your company has the following resources that can be used for operations.

Cash	$11,000	} Resources
Equipment	24,000	
	$35,000	

Who has the claims to the company's resources? Answer: The investors and creditors. Creditors have claims equal to the amount loaned to the company, $10,000. In other words, $10,000 of the company's resources are promised to the local bank. Investors have claims to all remaining resources, $25,000.

Creditors (local bank)	$10,000	} Claims to Resources
Investors (common stock)	25,000	
	$35,000	

Notice that you are both the manager and an investor. You manage the resources of the company on behalf of the owners (stockholders, in this case), while you are also an investor helping to align your interests with the other investors in the company. This is common in many start-up businesses. Mark Cuban, the owner of the Dallas Mavericks and a tech savvy entrepreneur, refers to a manager that also owns shares in the company as having "skin in the game." Companies that issue shares of stock often form as corporations.

Formally defined, a corporation is a company that is legally separate from its owners. The advantage of being legally separate is that the stockholders have limited liability. **Limited liability** prevents stockholders from being held personally responsible for the financial obligations of the corporation. Stockholders of Eagle Golf Academy can lose their investment of $25,000 if the company fails, but they cannot lose any of their personal assets (such as homes, cars, computers, and furniture).

Other common business forms include sole proprietorships and partnerships. A sole proprietorship is a business owned by one person; a partnership is a business owned by two or more persons. If you had decided to start Eagle Golf Academy without outside investors, you could have formed a sole proprietorship, or you and a friend could have formed a partnership. However, because you did not have the necessary resources to start the business, being a sole proprietorship (or even one member of a partnership) was not a viable option. Thus, a disadvantage of selecting the sole proprietorship or partnership form of business is that owners must have sufficient personal funds to finance the business in addition to the ability to borrow money. Another disadvantage of being a sole proprietorship or partnership is that neither offers limited liability. Owners (and partners) are held personally responsible for the activities of the business.

Sole proprietorships and partnerships do offer the advantage of lower taxes compared to corporations. Sole proprietorships and partnerships are taxed at the owner's personal income tax rate, which is typically lower than the corporate income tax rate. In addition, a corporation's income is taxed twice (known as *double taxation*): (1) the company first pays corporate income taxes on income it earns and (2) stockholders then pay personal income taxes when the company distributes that income as dividends to them.

Because most of the largest companies in the United States are corporations, in this book we will focus primarily on accounting from a corporation's perspective. Focusing on corporations also highlights the importance of financial accounting—to measure and communicate activities of a company for investors (stockholders) and creditors (lenders, such as a local bank). (A more detailed discussion of the advantages and disadvantages of a corporation is provided in Chapter 10.)

We'll continue the example of Eagle Golf Academy in more detail in a moment. For now, we can see that the company has engaged in financing and investing activities, and it will soon begin operating activities.

- *Financing activities* include transactions the company has with investors and creditors, such as issuing stock ($25,000) and borrowing money from a local bank ($10,000).
- *Investing activities* include transactions involving the purchase and sale of resources that are expected to benefit the company for several years, such as the purchase of equipment for $24,000. With the necessary resources in place, the company is ready to begin operations.
- *Operating activities* will include transactions that relate to the primary operations of the company, such as providing products and services to customers and the associated costs of doing so, like rent, salaries, utilities, taxes, and advertising.

Assets, Liabilities, and Stockholders' Equity. What information would Eagle's investors and creditors be interested in knowing to determine whether their investment in the company was a good decision? **Ultimately, investors and creditors want to know about the company's resources and their claims to those resources.** Accounting uses some conventional names to describe such resources and claims.

The resources of a company are referred to as assets. At this point, Eagle Golf Academy has two assets—cash and equipment. Of course, there are many other possible resources that a company can have, such as supplies, inventory for sale to customers, buildings, and land. You'll learn about these and many other assets throughout this book.

As discussed earlier, two parties have claims to the resources of the company—investors and creditors. Amounts owed to creditors are liabilities. Eagle Golf Academy has a liability of $10,000 to the local bank. Other examples of liabilities would be amounts owed to suppliers, employees, utility companies, and the government (in the form of taxes). Liabilities are claims that must be paid by a specified date.

Investors, or owners, have claims to any resources of the company not owed to creditors. In the case of Eagle Golf Academy, this amount is $25,000. We refer to owners' claims to resources as stockholders' equity, because stockholders are the owners.

The relationship among the three measurement categories is called the accounting equation, which is depicted in Illustration 1–3. It shows that a company's assets equal its liabilities plus stockholders' equity. Alternatively, a company's resources equal creditors' and owners' claims to those resources.

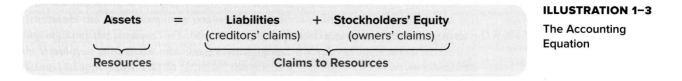

Assets	=	Liabilities (creditors' claims)	+	Stockholders' Equity (owners' claims)
Resources		Claims to Resources		

ILLUSTRATION 1–3

The Accounting Equation

As with any equation, we can move the components around. To isolate stockholders' equity, for example, we can subtract liabilities from both sides of the equal sign.

Assets (resources)	−	Liabilities (creditors' claims)	=	Stockholders' Equity (owners' claims)

Eagle has assets of $35,000 and liabilities of $10,000. How much equity do stockholders have? They have $35,000 − $10,000, or $25,000.

The accounting equation illustrates a fundamental model of business valuation. The value of a company to its owners equals total resources of the company minus amounts owed to creditors. Creditors expect to receive only resources equal to the amount owed them. Stockholders, on the other hand, can claim all resources in excess of the amount owed to creditors.

Revenues, Expenses, and Dividends.   Of course, all owners hope their claims to the company's resources increase over time. This increase occurs when the company makes a profit. Stockholders claim all resources in excess of amounts owed to creditors; thus, profits of the company are claimed solely by stockholders.

We calculate a company's profits by comparing its revenues and expenses. Revenues are the amounts recorded when the company sells products or provides services to customers. For example, when you or one of your employees provides golf training to a customer, the company records revenue. However, as you've probably heard, "It takes money to make money." To operate the academy, you'll encounter many costs. For example, you'll have costs related to salaries, rent, supplies, and utilities. We record these amounts as expenses. Expenses are the costs of providing products and services.

We measure the difference between revenues and expenses as net income. All businesses want revenues to be greater than expenses, producing a positive net income and adding to stockholders' equity in the business. However, if expenses exceed revenues, as happens from time to time, the difference between them is a negative amount—a **net loss.**

You'll notice the use of the term *net* to describe a company's profitability. In business, the term *net* is used often to describe the difference between two amounts. Here, we measure revenues *net* of (or minus) expenses, to calculate the net income or net loss. If we assume that by the end of the first month of operations Eagle Golf Academy has total revenues of $7,200 and total expenses of $6,000, then we would say that the company has *net income* of $1,200 for the month. This amount of profit increases stockholders' claims to resources but has no effect on creditors' claims.

When a business has positive net income, it may either distribute those profits back to its stockholders or retain those profits to pay for future operations. Suppose you decide that because Eagle Golf Academy has net income of $1,200, a cash payment of $200 should be returned to stockholders at the end of the month. These cash payments to stockholders are called dividends.

The other $1,000 of net income adds to stockholders' equity of the company. Thus, when Eagle has net income of $1,200, stockholders receive a total benefit of $1,200, equal to $200 of dividends received plus $1,000 increase in stockholders' equity in the company they own.

Dividends are not an expense.   Recall earlier we defined expenses as the costs necessary to run the business to produce revenues. Dividends, on the other hand, are not costs related to providing products and services to *customers;* dividends are cash returned to the *owners* of the company—the stockholders.

Common Terms Other common names for net income include *earnings* or *profit.*

Let's Review

User's Guide Let's Review exercises test your comprehension of key concepts covered in the chapter text.

Suggested Homework:
BE1–4;
E1–2, E1–3;
P1–2A&B

Match the term with the appropriate definition.

1. _____ Assets
2. _____ Liabilities
3. _____ Stockholders' Equity
4. _____ Dividends
5. _____ Revenues
6. _____ Expenses

A. Costs of selling products or services.
B. Sales of products or services to customers.
C. Amounts owed.
D. Distributions to stockholders.
E. Owners' claims to resources.
F. Resources of a company.

Solution:

1. F; 2. C; 3. E; 4. D; 5. B; 6. A

In summary, the measurement role of accounting is to create a record of the activities of a company. To make this possible, a company must maintain an accurate record of its assets, liabilities, stockholders' equity, revenues, expenses, and dividends. Be sure you understand the meaning of these items. We will refer to them throughout this book. Illustration 1–4 summarizes the business activities and the categories that measure them.

ILLUSTRATION 1–4
Business Activities and Their Measurement

Activities Related to:	Measurement Category	Relationship
• Resources of the company • Amounts owed • Stockholders' investment	• Assets • Liabilities • Stockholders' equity	**Accounting Equation** **(A = L + SE)**
• Distributions to stockholders	• Dividends	
• Sales of products or services • Costs of providing sales	• Revenues • Expenses	**Net Income** **(R − E = NI)**

KEY POINT

The measurement role of accounting is to create a record of the activities of a company. To make this possible, a company must maintain an accurate record of its assets, liabilities, stockholders' equity, revenues, expenses, and dividends.

As you learn to measure business activities, you will often find it helpful to consider both sides of the transaction: When someone pays cash, someone else receives cash; when someone borrows money, another lends money. Likewise, an expense for one company can be a revenue for another company; one company's asset can be another company's liability. Throughout this book, you will find discussions of the "flip side" of certain transactions, indicated by the icon you see here. In addition, certain homework problems, also marked by the icon, will ask you specifically to address the "flip side" in your computations. (See Exercise 1–2 for the first such example.)

Flip Side

Communicating through Financial Statements

We've discussed that different business activities produce assets, liabilities, stockholders' equity, dividends, revenues, and expenses, and that the first important role of financial accounting is to *measure* the relevant transactions of a company. Its second vital role is to *communicate* these business activities to those outside the company. The primary means of communicating business activities is through financial statements. Financial statements are periodic reports published by the company for the purpose of providing information to external users. There are four primary financial statements:

■ **LO1–3**
Determine how financial accounting information is communicated through financial statements.

1. Income statement
2. Statement of stockholders' equity
3. Balance sheet
4. Statement of cash flows

These financial statements give investors and creditors the key information they need when making decisions about a company: Should I buy the company's stock? Should I lend money to the company? Is management efficiently operating the company? **Without these financial statements, it would be difficult for those outside the company to see what's going on inside.**

Let's go through a simple set of financial statements to see what they look like. We'll continue with our example of Eagle Golf Academy. Actual companies' financial statements often report items you haven't yet encountered. However, because actual companies' financial information will be useful in helping you understand certain accounting topics, we'll sample them often throughout this book.

INCOME STATEMENT

The income statement is a financial statement that reports the company's revenues and expenses over an interval of time. It shows whether the company was able to generate enough revenue to cover the expenses of running the business. If revenues exceed expenses, then the company reports *net income:*

Revenues − Expenses = Net Income

If expenses exceed revenues, then the company reports a *net loss.*

On December 1, Eagle Golf Academy begins operations by offering lessons to junior golfers. For the first month of operations, Eagle Golf Academy reports its income statement as shown in Illustration 1–5.

Common Terms Other common names for the income statement include *statement of operations, statement of income, and profit and loss statement.*

ILLUSTRATION 1–5

Income Statement for Eagle Golf Academy

EAGLE GOLF ACADEMY Income Statement For the month ended December 31	
Revenues	
Service revenue	**$7,200**
Expenses	
Rent expense	500
Supplies expense	1,000
Salaries expense	3,100
Utilities expense	900
Interest expense	100
Other expenses	400
Total expenses	6,000
Net income	**$1,200**

Here are some specifics about Eagle's income statement:

- **Heading**—The heading includes the company's name, the title of the financial statement, and the time period covered by the financial statement.
- **Sections**—The two sections in the income statement are revenues and expenses, discussed earlier. The difference between them is net income.
- **Accounts**—Within each section are accounts and their balances. An account maintains a record of the business activities related to a particular item over a period of time. For example, the Service Revenue account balance is the summation of all service revenue activities during the period.
- **Underlines**—In a financial statement, a single underline generally represents a subtotal (in this case, total expenses), while a double underline indicates a final total (in this case, revenues minus expenses, or net income).

Now let's analyze what the numbers in the income statement represent. We can determine from the income statement that for the month of December Eagle Golf Academy provided services to customers for $7,200. This means that Eagle provides golf training and bills customers for a total of $7,200 for the month of December. Total expenses associated with generating those revenues, including rent, supplies, salaries, utilities, interest, and other expenses, are $6,000 for the month of December. These are typical costs that we might expect of any company. The income statement shows that revenues *exceed* expenses ($7,200 is greater than $6,000), and thus the academy is able to report net income of $1,200.

The fact that Eagle reports a positive net income is, in some sense, a signal of the company's success. The company is able to charge its customers a price higher than the costs of running the business. Do you assume most companies sell their products and services for a profit? It's not as easy as you might think. In recent years, companies such as **American Airlines, Sony, Alcoa, Sprint, Toys "R" Us, Blackberry, Office Depot**, and thousands of others have reported net losses.

KEY POINT

The income statement compares revenues and expenses for the current period to assess the company's ability to earn a profit from running its operations.

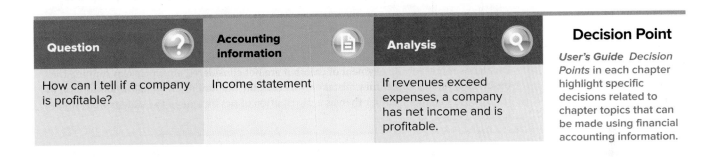

Question	Accounting information	Analysis
How can I tell if a company is profitable?	Income statement	If revenues exceed expenses, a company has net income and is profitable.

Decision Point

User's Guide Decision Points in each chapter highlight specific decisions related to chapter topics that can be made using financial accounting information.

STATEMENT OF STOCKHOLDERS' EQUITY

The statement of stockholders' equity is a financial statement that summarizes the changes in stockholders' equity over an interval of time. The reporting period coincides with the time period covered by the income statement.

Stockholders' equity has two primary components—common stock and retained earnings. Recall that common stock represents amounts invested by stockholders (the owners of the corporation) when they purchase shares of stock. Common stock is an *external* source of stockholders' equity.

Retained earnings, on the other hand, is an *internal* source of stockholders' equity. Retained earnings represents the cumulative amount of net income, earned over the life of the company, that has been kept (retained) in the business rather than distributed to stockholders as dividends (not retained). Since all profits of the company are owned by stockholders, any net income in excess of dividends paid to stockholders represents additional stockholders' equity. Thus, both common stock and retained earnings make up total stockholders' equity:

$$\text{Stockholders' Equity} = \text{Common Stock} + \text{Retained Earnings}$$

Illustration 1–6 shows the statement of stockholders' equity for Eagle Golf Academy. When Eagle begins operations on December 1, the balances of common stock and retained earnings are **$0**. This would be true of any company beginning operations. Now, let's see what happens to the two components of stockholders' equity in the month of December.

The first column shows that Eagle issues 1,000 shares of common stock for $25 per share, so the balance of common stock increases by **$25,000**. The second column shows that the balance of retained earnings increases by the amount of net income less any dividends paid to stockholders. For the month of December, net income was $1,200, and dividends paid to stockholders was $200, so retained earnings increased by $1,000 (= $1,200 − $200). **The balance of retained earnings equals the amount of "earnings retained" (not paid out in the form of dividends) over the life of the company.** The third column shows that the two components—common stock and retained earnings—add to equal total stockholders' equity.

ILLUSTRATION 1–6

Statement of
Stockholders' Equity for
Eagle Golf Academy

Beginning balances
are zero only because
this is the first month
of operations for Eagle.
Normally, beginning
balances for Common
Stock and Retained
Earnings equal ending
balances from the
previous period.

Note that the $1,200
in blue comes from the
income statement in
Illustration 1–5.

Accounting convention
uses parentheses to
signify an amount to
be subtracted (such
as dividends here) or
negative amounts (such
as a net loss in the
income statement).

User's Guide
Throughout each
chapter, you will see
sections titled *Common
Mistake.* Information in
these boxes will help you
avoid common mistakes
on exams, quizzes, and
homework.

EAGLE GOLF ACADEMY
Statement of Stockholders' Equity
For the month ended December 31

	Common Stock	Retained Earnings	Total Stockholders' Equity
Beginning balance (Dec. 1)	$ -0-	$ -0-	$ -0-
Issuance of common stock	25,000		25,000
Add: **Net income for the period**		1,200	1,200
Less: Dividends		(200)	(200)
Ending balance (Dec. 31)	$25,000	$ 1,000	$26,000

 **COMMON MISTAKE**

Dividends represent the payment of cash but are not considered an expense in running the business. Students sometimes mistakenly include the amount of dividends as an expense in the income statement, rather than as a distribution of net income in the statement of stockholders' equity.

By adding common stock of $25,000 and the retained earnings of $1,000, we calculate the balance of total stockholders' equity at December 31 to be **$26,000**. The company creates value *externally* through investment by owners (common stock), and *internally* by generating and retaining profits (retained earnings).

KEY POINT

The statement of stockholders' equity reports information related to changes in common stock and retained earnings each period. The change in retained earnings equals net income less dividends for the period.

Decision Point

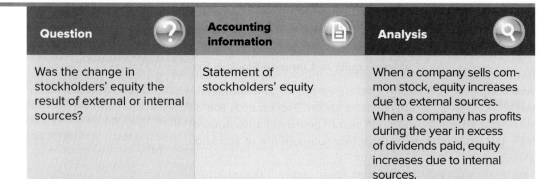

Question	Accounting information	Analysis
Was the change in stockholders' equity the result of external or internal sources?	Statement of stockholders' equity	When a company sells common stock, equity increases due to external sources. When a company has profits during the year in excess of dividends paid, equity increases due to internal sources.

BALANCE SHEET

The balance sheet is a financial statement that presents the financial position of the company on a particular date. The financial position of a company is summarized by the accounting equation (see Illustration 1–3):

$$\text{Assets} = \text{Liabilities} + \text{Stockholders' Equity}$$

As discussed earlier, this equation provides a fundamental model of business valuation. Assets are the resources of the company, and liabilities are amounts owed to creditors. Stockholders have equity in the company to the extent that assets exceed liabilities. Creditors also need to understand the balance sheet; it's the company's assets that will be used to pay liabilities (the amounts due creditors) as they become due.

Illustration 1–7 shows the balance sheet of Eagle Golf Academy. The first thing to notice is the time period included in the heading. Recall that the income statement and statement of stockholders' equity both show activity over an *interval of time.* The balance sheet, in contrast, reports assets, liabilities, and stockholders' equity at a *point in time.* For example, Eagle's income statement shows revenue and expense activity occurring *from* December 1 *to* December 31; its balance sheet shows assets, liabilities, and stockholders' equity of the company *on* December 31.

The income statement is like a video (shows events over time), whereas a balance sheet is like a photograph (shows events at a point in time).

ILLUSTRATION 1–7

Balance Sheet for Eagle Golf Academy

Common Terms Another name for the balance sheet is the *statement of financial position.*

EAGLE GOLF ACADEMY
Balance Sheet
December 31

Assets		Liabilities	
Cash	$ 6,900	Accounts payable	$ 2,300
Accounts receivable	2,700	Salaries payable	300
Supplies	1,300	Utilities payable	900
Equipment, net	23,600	Interest payable	100
Other assets	5,500	Notes payable	10,000
		Other liabilities	400
		Total liabilities	14,000
		Stockholders' Equity	
		Common stock	25,000
		Retained earnings	1,000
		Total stockholders' equity	**26,000**
Total assets	**$40,000**	Total liabilities and stockholders' equity	**$40,000**

We show the stockholders' equity items in purple here, to indicate they came from the statement of stockholders' equity (Illustration 1–6).

Let's take a look at Eagle's assets—the resources of the company. Eagle has assets that are familiar to most companies. *Cash* is a resource because it can be used to make purchases. *Accounts receivable* represent money the company expects to "receive" in the future from customers to whom it has already provided products or services. While accounts receivable are not cash now, the right to receive cash in the future is a benefit, and thus receivables are a resource of the company. *Supplies* include resources used to run the golf academy, such as paper, cleaning supplies, and golf balls. *Equipment* is a resource that can be used to provide services to customers. There are many other assets a business can have, and we will discuss those in other chapters. **For now, understand that assets are the resources of the company that are expected to provide benefits to the company in the future.** Total assets of Eagle Golf Academy on December 31 equal $40,000.

Total liabilities on December 31 equal $14,000. These include amounts owed to regular vendors (accounts payable), as well as amounts owed for other items such as employee salaries, utilities, interest, and bank borrowing (notes payable). **Many liabilities are referred to as "payables," to signify amounts the company will "pay" in the future.**

The difference between assets and liabilities of **$26,000** represents stockholders' equity. Total stockholders' equity includes the amount of common stock plus the amount of retained earnings from the statement of stockholders' equity. Notice that the amounts listed in the balance sheet show that the accounting equation balances:

Total assets must equal total liabilities and stockholders' equity.

Assets	=	Liabilities	+	Stockholders' Equity
(resources)		(creditors' claims)		(owners' claims)
$40,000	**=**	**$14,000**	**+**	**$26,000**

 KEY POINT

The balance sheet demonstrates that the company's resources (assets) equal creditors' claims (liabilities) plus owners' claims (stockholders' equity) to those resources on a particular date.

Decision Point

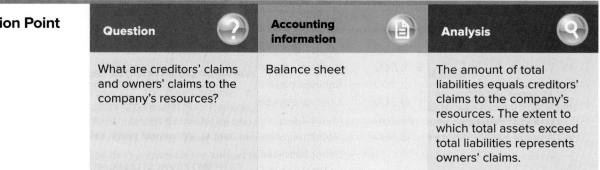

Question	Accounting information	Analysis
What are creditors' claims and owners' claims to the company's resources?	Balance sheet	The amount of total liabilities equals creditors' claims to the company's resources. The extent to which total assets exceed total liabilities represents owners' claims.

STATEMENT OF CASH FLOWS

The statement of cash flows is a financial statement that measures activities involving cash receipts and cash payments over an interval of time. We can classify all cash transactions into three categories that correspond to the three fundamental business activities—operating, investing, and financing:

- **Operating cash flows** include cash receipts and cash payments for transactions involving revenue and expense activities during the period. In other words, operating activities include the cash effects of the same activities that are reported in the income statement to calculate net income.
- **Investing cash flows** generally include cash transactions for the purchase and sale of investments and long-term assets. Long-term assets are resources owned by a company that are thought to provide benefits for more than one year.
- **Financing cash flows** include cash transactions with lenders, such as borrowing money and repaying debt, and with stockholders, such as issuing stock and paying dividends.

Illustration 1–8 provides the statement of cash flows for Eagle Golf Academy. Notice that the three sections in the statement of cash flows show the types of inflows and outflows of cash during the period. Inflows are shown as positive amounts; outflows are shown in parentheses to indicate negative cash flows. The final line in each section shows, in the right-most column, the difference between inflows and outflows as *net cash flow* for that type of activity.

 KEY POINT

The statement of cash flows reports cash transactions from operating, investing, and financing activities for the period.

ILLUSTRATION 1–8
Statement of Cash Flows for Eagle Golf Academy

EAGLE GOLF ACADEMY
Statement of Cash Flows
For the month ended December 31

Cash Flows from Operating Activities

Cash inflows:		
From customers	$ 4,900	
Cash outflows:		
For salaries	(2,800)	
For rent	(6,000)	
Net cash flows from operating activities		$ (3,900)

Cash Flows from Investing Activities

Purchase equipment	(24,000)	
Net cash flows from investing activities		(24,000)

Cash Flows from Financing Activities

Issue common stock	25,000	
Borrow from bank	10,000	
Pay dividends	(200)	
Net cash flows from financing activities		34,800
Net increase in cash		6,900
Cash at the beginning of the period		-0-
Cash at the end of the period		$ 6,900

Remember, amounts in parentheses indicate outflows of cash.

Decision Maker's Perspective

The statement of cash flows can be an important source of information to investors and creditors. For example, investors use the relationship between net income (revenues minus expenses) and operating cash flows (cash flows from revenue and expense activities) to forecast a company's future profitability. Creditors compare operating cash flows and investing cash flows to assess a company's ability to repay debt. Financing activities provide information to investors and creditors about the mix of external financing of the company.

User's Guide Decision Maker's Perspective sections discuss the usefulness of accounting information to decision makers such as investors, creditors, and company managers.

The total of the net cash flows from operating, investing, and financing activities equals the *net change in cash* during the period:

$$\text{Change in cash} = \text{Operating cash flows} + \text{Investing cash flows} + \text{Financing cash flows}$$

For Eagle, that net change in cash for December was an increase of $6,900. That amount equals the sum of its operating cash flows of −$3,900, investing cash flows of −$24,000, and financing cash flows of $34,800. We next add the beginning balance of cash. Because this is the first month of operations for Eagle, cash at the beginning of the period is zero. The ending balance of cash is the same as that reported in the balance sheet in Illustration 1–7. This reconciliation of the beginning and ending cash balances emphasizes that the statement of cash flows explains *why* the cash reported in the balance sheet changed from one period to the next.

THE LINKS AMONG FINANCIAL STATEMENTS

The four financial statements are linked, because events that are reported in one financial statement often affect amounts reported in another. Many times, a single business transaction, such as receiving cash from a customer when providing services, will affect more than

© Photodisc/Getty Images, RF

one of the financial statements. Providing services to a customer, for example, results in revenues recorded in the income statement, which are used to calculate net income. Net income, in turn, is reported in the calculation of retained earnings in the statement of stockholders' equity. Then, the ending balance of retained earnings is reported in the balance sheet. **Thus, any transaction that affects the income statement ultimately affects the balance sheet through the balance of retained earnings.** The cash received from customers will be reported as part of the ending cash balance in the balance sheet and as part of operating cash flows in the statement of cash flows.

Illustration 1–9 shows the links among the financial statements of Eagle Golf Academy in Illustrations 1–5, 1–6, 1–7, and 1–8. Link (1) shows that net income from the income statement is reported in the statement of stockholders' equity as part of the calculation of retained earnings. Link (2) shows that after we calculate the balance of retained earnings, the amount of total stockholders' equity can be reported in the balance sheet. Finally, link (3) demonstrates that the balance of cash in the balance sheet equals the amount of cash reported in the statement of cash flows.

ILLUSTRATION 1–9

Links among Financial Statements

[1] Notice that the amount of net income in the income statement reappears in the statement of stockholders' equity.

[2] Notice that the ending balance in the statement of stockholders' equity reappears in the balance sheet.

[3] Notice that the amount of cash in the balance sheet reappears as the ending cash balance in the statement of cash flows.

EAGLE GOLF ACADEMY
Income Statement

Revenues	$7,200
Expenses	6,000
Net income	$1,200

EAGLE GOLF ACADEMY
Statement of Stockholders' Equity

	Common Stock	Retained Earnings	Total Stockholders' Equity
Beginning balance (Dec. 1)	$ -0-	$ -0-	$ -0-
Issuances	25,000		25,000
Add: Net income		1,200	1,200
Less: Dividends		(200)	(200)
Ending balance (Dec. 31)	$25,000	$1,000	$26,000

EAGLE GOLF ACADEMY
Balance Sheet

Cash	$ 6,900	Liabilities	$14,000
Other assets	33,100	Stockholders' equity	26,000
		Total liabilities and	
Total assets	$40,000	stockholders' equity	$40,000

EAGLE GOLF ACADEMY
Statement of Cash Flows

Cash flows from operating activities	$ (3,900)
Cash flows from investing activities	(24,000)
Cash flows from financing activities	34,800
Net increase in cash	6,900
Cash at the beginning of the year	-0-
Cash at the end of the year	$ 6,900

Test your understanding of what you've read so far. The Computer Shop repairs laptops, desktops, and mainframe computers. On December 31, 2018, the company reports the following year-end amounts:

Let's Review

Assets:	Cash	$10,000	Revenues:	Service	$65,000
	Supplies	8,000			
	Equipment, net	26,000			
			Expenses:	Rent	6,000
Liabilities:	Accounts payable	4,000		Supplies	14,000
	Notes payable	10,000		Salaries	40,000

mhhe.com/4fa3

Additional information:

a. The balance of retained earnings at the beginning of the year is $7,000.

b. The company pays dividends of $1,000 on December 31, 2018.

c. Common stock is $15,000 at the beginning of the year, and additional shares are issued for $4,000 during 2018.

Required:

Prepare the (1) income statement, (2) statement of stockholders' equity, and (3) balance sheet.

Solution:

Suggested Homework:
BE1–7, BE1–8;
E1–6, E1–7, E1–8;
P1–3A&B, P1–5A&B

1. Income statement:

THE COMPUTER SHOP
Income Statement
Year ended Dec. 31, 2018

Revenues:	
Service revenue	$65,000
Expenses:	
Rent expense	6,000
Supplies expense	14,000
Salaries expense	40,000
Net income	$ 5,000

2. Statement of stockholders' equity:

THE COMPUTER SHOP
Statement of Stockholders' Equity
Year ended Dec. 31, 2018

	Common Stock	Retained Earnings	Total Stockholders' Equity
Beginning balance (Jan. 1)	$15,000	$ 7,000	$22,000
Issuance of common stock	4,000		4,000
Add: Net income		5,000	5,000
Less: Dividends		(1,000)	(1,000)
Ending balance (Dec. 31)	$19,000	$11,000	$30,000

3. Balance sheet:

THE COMPUTER SHOP
Balance Sheet
December 31, 2018

Assets		Liabilities	
Cash	$10,000	Accounts payable	$ 4,000
Supplies	8,000	Notes payable	10,000
Equipment	26,000	**Stockholders' Equity**	
		Common stock	19,000
		Retained earnings	11,000
		Total liabilities and stockholders' equity	
Total assets	$44,000		$44,000

KEY POINT

All transactions that affect revenues or expenses reported in the income statement ultimately affect the balance sheet through the balance in retained earnings.

OTHER INFORMATION REPORTED TO OUTSIDERS

The financial statements are a key component of a company's *annual report,* the term most often used to describe the formal document detailing a company's activities and financial performance. As the name suggests, annual reports are provided by companies each year. Two other important components of the annual report are: (1) management's discussion and analysis and (2) note disclosures to the financial statements.

The **management discussion and analysis** (MD&A) section typically includes management's views on significant events, trends, and uncertainties pertaining to the company's operations and resources. **Note disclosures** offer additional information either to explain the information presented in the financial statements or to provide information not included in the financial statements. For example, companies are required to report total revenues in the income statement, but they also often report revenues itemized by geographic region in a note disclosure. We'll discuss these items throughout this book. For now, if you'd like to see an abbreviated version of an actual company's annual report with financial statements, see Appendix A (**American Eagle Outfitters**) or Appendix B (**Buckle**) near the end of this book.

Making Decisions with Accounting Information

■ LO1–4

Describe the role that financial accounting plays in the decision-making process.

To this point, you've had a simple, first look at how companies measure and communicate financial information to external users. Subsequent chapters will provide an even more detailed view of this measurement/communication process. However, before proceeding, it's important to first consider why we are studying financial accounting. Does it matter? In other words, does the use of financial accounting information result in better business decisions?

One of the rewarding things about studying financial accounting is that it does matter! The concepts in this course have an impact on everyday business decisions as well as wide-ranging economic consequences. We'll see an example of this next and then more examples throughout the rest of this book.

Most prospering economies in the world today are structured around free markets. In free markets, firms are allowed to compete and customers are free to choose from a variety of products and services. From which company do you prefer to buy a laptop computer—**Dell**, **Hewlett-Packard**, or **Apple**? Competition among these companies helps determine the prices they charge customers and the amounts they spend on computer components, salaries, manufacturing and distribution facilities, warranties, research and development, and other business-related activities. Can these companies offer you the laptop computer you want for a price above their costs? If they can, they'll earn a profit and stay in business. If they cannot, they'll eventually go out of business. Because companies know they are directly competing with each other, they work harder and more efficiently to please you, the customer.

Successful companies use their resources efficiently to sell products and services for a profit. When a company is able to make a profit, investors and creditors are willing to transfer their resources to it, and the company will expand its profitable operations even further.

Unsuccessful companies either offer lower-quality products and services or do not efficiently keep their costs low. In either case, they are not profitable. When a company is unprofitable, investors will neither invest in nor lend to the firm. Without these sources of financing, eventually the company will fail. Clearly, you don't want to invest in an unsuccessful company and then watch your investment shrink as the company loses your money.

But how do investors and creditors know the successful companies from the unsuccessful companies? Here's where financial accounting enters the picture. Investors and creditors rely heavily on financial accounting information in making investment and lending decisions.

As Illustration 1–10 demonstrates, investors and creditors have cash they are willing to invest. How do they decide which investment option provides the better opportunity? Most often, they analyze companies' financial accounting information in making their decision. In fact, **financial accounting information is essential to making good business decisions.**

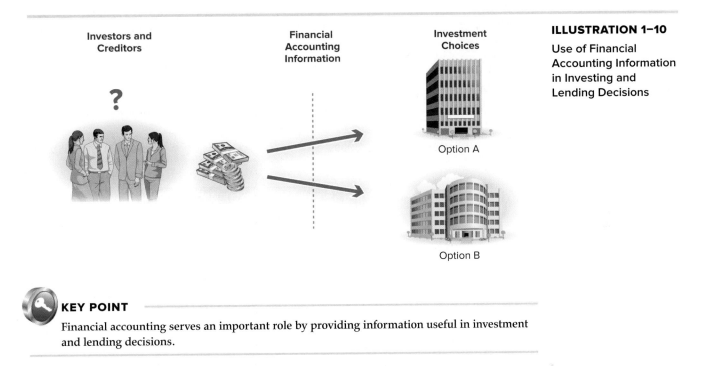

Investors and Creditors	Financial Accounting Information	Investment Choices

Option A

Option B

ILLUSTRATION 1–10

Use of Financial Accounting Information in Investing and Lending Decisions

KEY POINT

Financial accounting serves an important role by providing information useful in investment and lending decisions.

To demonstrate the importance of financial accounting information to investment decisions, we can look at the relationship between changes in stock prices and changes in net income over 20 years. As an investor, you will make money from an increase in the stock price of a company in which you invest (you can sell the stock for more than you bought it). So as an investor, you are looking for companies whose stock price is likely to increase. Is there a way to find such companies? Interestingly, there is: **No other single piece of company information better explains companies' stock price performance than does financial accounting net income,** the bottom line in the income statement.

What if you were able to accurately predict the direction of companies' changes in net income over the next year—that is, whether it would increase or decrease—and then you invested $1,000 in companies that were going to have an *increase*? In contrast, what if instead you invested in companies that would have a *decrease* in net income? Illustration 1–11 shows what would happen to your $1,000 investment over 20 years for each scenario.

You can see that if you had invested $1,000 in companies with an increase in net income, your investment would have increased to $18,183 over the 20-year period. (The amount would have been much higher without the extraordinary events surrounding the financial crisis in 2008.) If instead you had invested $1,000 in companies with a decrease in net income, your $1,000 investment would have shrunk to $139 over this same period. This dramatic difference in the value of the investment demonstrates the importance of financial accounting information to investors. This book will provide you a thorough understanding of how net income is calculated and presented in financial statements. As you can see from the charts above, if you are able to predict the change in financial accounting's measure of profitability—net income—then you can predict the change in stock prices as well.

ILLUSTRATION 1–11

Relationship between Changes in Stock Prices and Changes in Net Income over a 20-Year Period

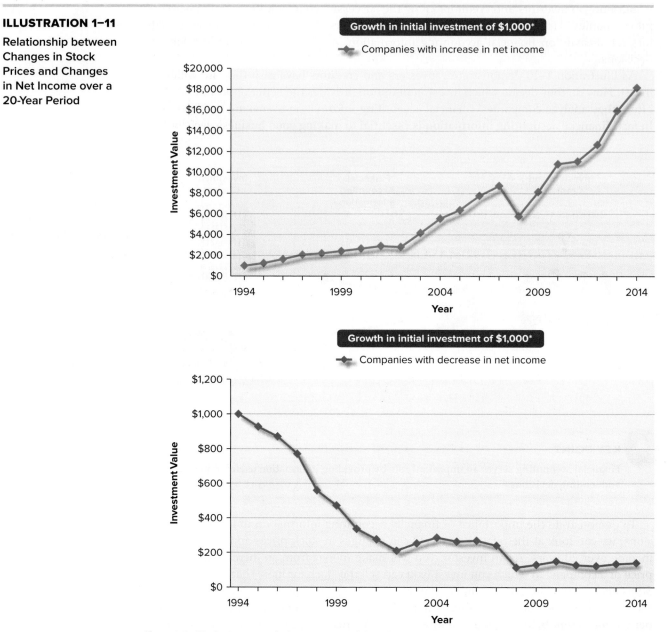

*Amounts in this chart represent the investment growth based on the median stock return of each group each year. Companies included in this analysis are all U.S. companies with listed stocks, which averages about 6,000 companies per year.

Investors and creditors also use information reported in the balance sheet. Consider a company's total liabilities, often referred to as *total debt*. Expanding debt levels limit management's ability to respond quickly and effectively to business situations. The "overhanging" debt, which involves legal obligation of repayment, restricts management's ability to engage in new profit-generating activities. Increased debt levels also increase interest payment burdens on the company. Failure to pay interest or to repay debt can result in creditors forcing the company to declare bankruptcy and go out of business. Understandably, then, investors and creditors keep a close eye on the company's debt level and its ability to repay.

 KEY POINT

No single piece of company information better explains companies' stock price performance than does financial accounting net income. A company's debt level is an important indicator of management's ability to respond to business situations and the possibility of bankruptcy.

FINANCIAL ACCOUNTING INFORMATION

Recall that accounting serves two main functions: It (1) measures business activities and (2) communicates those measurements to investors and creditors so they can make decisions. Although this process might seem straightforward, some issues have been heavily debated, and the answers have changed over time. How do we measure assets? When do we record revenues? What do we classify as an expense? How should we present financial statements? Next, we'll take a look at factors that shape the measurement and communication processes of financial accounting.

Financial Accounting Standards

Because financial accounting information is so vital to investors and creditors, formal standards have been established. The rules of financial accounting are called Generally Accepted Accounting Principles, often abbreviated as GAAP (pronounced *gap*). The fact that all companies use these same rules is critical to financial statement users. It helps investors to accurately *compare* financial information among companies when they are making decisions about where to invest or lend their resources.

■ **LO1–5**
Explain the term generally accepted accounting principles (GAAP) and describe the role of GAAP in financial accounting.

STANDARD SETTING TODAY

Financial accounting and reporting standards in the United States are established primarily by the Financial Accounting Standards Board (FASB) (pronounced either by the letters themselves or as *faz-be*). The FASB is an independent, private-sector body with full-time voting members and a very large support staff. Members include representatives from the accounting profession, large corporations, financial analysts, accounting educators, and government agencies.

Not all countries follow the same accounting and reporting standards. For example, accounting practices differ between the United States, the United Kingdom, and Japan. In recent years, the accounting profession has undertaken a project whose goal is to eliminate differences in accounting standards around the world. The standard-setting body responsible for this convergence effort is the International Accounting Standards Board (IASB), as detailed in the following box.

For information about the activities of the Financial Accounting Standards Board, see its website, ***www.fasb.org***.

For information about the activities of the International Accounting Standards Board, see its website, ***www.iasb.org***.

INTERNATIONAL FINANCIAL REPORTING STANDARDS (IFRS)

WHAT IS THE IASB?

The global counterpart to the FASB is the International Accounting Standards Board (IASB). In many ways, this organization functions like the FASB. The IASB's objectives are (1) to develop a single set of high-quality, understandable global accounting standards, (2) to promote the use of those standards, and (3) to bring about the convergence of national accounting standards and international accounting standards around the world. In 2002, the FASB and IASB signed the Norwalk Agreement, formalizing their commitment to convergence of U.S. and international accounting standards. The standards being developed and promoted by the IASB are called International Financial Reporting Standards (IFRS). The FASB and IASB have made several efforts to converge U.S. GAAP and IFRS, although important differences remain. (*For more discussion, see Appendix E.*)

User's Guide Discussion on *International Financial Reporting Standards* (IFRS) are included throughout the book to emphasize the growing importance of international accounting standards throughout the world. Appendix E at the back of the book provides a detailed discussion of differences between IFRS and U.S. GAAP.

More than 120 countries have chosen to forgo their own country-specific standards and either require or allow International Financial Reporting Standards as their national standards. That movement, coupled with the convergence of U.S. GAAP and IFRS, caused many to predict that both sets of rules, or perhaps only IFRS, would be acceptable for financial reporting in the United States. Currently, however, that seems unlikely.

 KEY POINT

> The rules of financial accounting are called generally accepted accounting principles (GAAP). The Financial Accounting Standards Board (FASB) is an independent, private body that has primary responsibility for the establishment of GAAP in the United States.

STANDARD SETTING IN THE PAST CENTURY

Pressures on the accounting profession to establish uniform accounting standards began to surface after the stock market crash of 1929. The Dow Jones Industrial Average, a major stock market index in the United States, fell 40% over the period September 3 to October 29 that year. The Dow bottomed out in July 1932, after losing 89% of its value.

Many blamed financial accounting for the stock market crash and the ensuing Great Depression of the 1930s. At the time of the crash, accounting practices and reporting procedures were not well established, providing the opportunity for companies to engage in inaccurate financial reporting to enhance their reported performance. This led to many stocks being valued too highly. As investors began to recognize this, their confidence in the stock market fell. They panicked and sold stocks in a frenzy. The Dow did not reach precrash levels again until 1954.

The 1933 Securities Act and the Securities Exchange Act of 1934 were designed to restore investor confidence in financial accounting. The 1933 act sets forth accounting and disclosure requirements for initial offerings of securities (stocks and bonds). The 1934 act created a government agency, the **Securities and Exchange Commission (SEC).** The 1934 act gives the SEC the power to require companies that publicly trade their stock to prepare periodic financial statements for distribution to investors and creditors.

While Congress has given the SEC both the power and the responsibility for setting accounting and reporting standards for publicly traded companies, the SEC has delegated the primary responsibility for setting accounting standards to the private sector, currently the FASB. Note that the SEC delegated only the responsibility, not the authority, to set these standards. The power still lies with the SEC. If the SEC does not agree with a particular standard issued by the FASB, it can force a change in the standard. In fact, it has done so in the past.

THE IMPORTANCE OF AUDITORS

For many businesses, there is a natural separation between those who run the business (managers) and those who own the business or finance operations (investors and creditors). This separation creates the need to ensure honest financial reporting. While it is the responsibility of management to apply GAAP when communicating with investors and creditors through financial statements, sometimes those in charge of preparing financial statements do not always follow the rules. Instead, some purposely provide misleading financial accounting information, commonly referred to as "cooking the books." The phrase implies that the accounting records ("books") have been presented in an altered form ("cooked"). Managers may cook the books for several reasons, such as to hide the poor operating performance of the company or to increase their personal wealth at stockholders' expense.

To help ensure that management has in fact appropriately applied GAAP, the SEC requires independent outside verification of the financial statements of publicly traded companies. Such independent examination is done by auditors, who are *not* employees of the company, but who are hired by the company as an independent party to express a professional opinion of the extent to which financial statements are prepared in compliance with GAAP and are free of material misstatement. If auditors find mistakes or fraudulent

Common Terms The auditor's report is also commonly referred to as the *auditor's opinion.*

reporting behavior, they require the company to correct all significant information before issuing financial statements. **Auditors play a major role in investors' and creditors' decisions by adding credibility to a company's financial statements.**

Illustration 1–12 presents an excerpt from the auditor's report for **Dick's Sporting Goods, Inc.** The auditor's report indicates that the financial statements for the period mentioned have been prepared in conformity with GAAP.

ILLUSTRATION 1–12

Excerpts from the Independent Auditor's Report of Dick's Sporting Goods, Inc.

DICK'S SPORTING GOODS, INC.
Report of Independent Auditors

To the Board of Directors and Stockholders of
Dick's Sporting Goods, Inc.
Pittsburgh, Pennsylvania

We have audited the accompanying consolidated balance sheets of Dick's Sporting Goods, Inc. and subsidiaries (the "Company") as of January 31, 2015, and February 1, 2014, and the related consolidated statements of income, comprehensive income, changes in stockholders' equity, and cash flows for each of the three years in the period ended January 31, 2015. These financial statements are the responsibility of the Company's management. Our responsibility is to express an opinion on these financial statements based on our audits.

In our opinion, such consolidated financial statements present fairly, in all material respects, the financial position of Dick's Sporting Goods, Inc. and subsidiaries as of January 31, 2015, and February 1, 2014, and the results of their operations and their cash flows for each of the three years in the period ended January 31, 2015, in conformity with accounting principles generally accepted in the United States of America.

To further enhance the credibility of financial reporting, Congress established in 2002 the **Public Company Accounting Oversight Board (PCAOB).** The role of the PCAOB is to ensure that auditors follow a strict set of guidelines when conducting their audits of public companies' financial statements. The PCAOB is a government entity that, simply stated, "audits the auditors."

OBJECTIVES OF FINANCIAL ACCOUNTING

After measuring business activities and communicating those measurements to investors and creditors, what do financial accountants hope to have achieved? What benefit will their services have brought to users of financial statements? The FASB has explicitly stated the specific objectives of financial accounting. These objectives are presented in Illustration 1–13.

ILLUSTRATION 1–13

Objectives of Financial Accounting

Financial accounting should provide information that:

1. Is useful to investors and creditors in making decisions.
2. Helps to predict cash flows.
3. Tells about economic resources, claims to resources, and changes in resources and claims.

The first objective is specific to investors and creditors. In addition to those users, though, financial accounting information is likely to have general usefulness to other groups of external users, who are interested in essentially the same financial aspects of a business as are investors and creditors. Some of these other groups were discussed in Illustration 1–1.

The second objective refers to the specific cash flow information needs of investors and creditors. The third objective emphasizes the need for information about economic resources (assets) and claims to those resources (liabilities and stockholders' equity) and their changes over time.

 KEY POINT

> The primary objective of financial accounting is to provide useful information to investors and creditors in making decisions.

Underlying these three key objectives is a conceptual framework that is the foundation upon which financial accounting is built. We discuss the FASB's conceptual framework in detail in the appendix to this chapter.

An Ethical Foundation

Like all structures, accounting requires a strong foundation. For accounting, part of that foundation is the ethical behavior of those who practice its rules. You have probably encountered the topic of ethics in other business courses. Ethics refers to a code or moral system that provides criteria for evaluating right and wrong behavior. Investors, creditors, government, and the general public rely on general ethical behavior among those who record and report the financial activities of businesses. A lack of public trust in financial reporting can undermine business and the economy. Indeed, the dramatic collapse of **Enron** in 2001 and the dismantling of the international public accounting firm of **Arthur Andersen** in 2002 severely shook investors' confidence in the stock market. Some questioned the credibility of corporate America as well as the accounting profession itself.

Public outrage over accounting scandals at high-profile companies increased the pressure on lawmakers to pass measures that would restore credibility and investor confidence in the financial reporting process. These pressures resulted in the issuance of what is commonly referred to as the Sarbanes-Oxley Act (SOX), named for the two congressmen who sponsored the bill. The Sarbanes-Oxley Act provides for the regulation of auditors and the types of services they furnish to clients, increases accountability of corporate executives, addresses conflicts of interest for securities analysts, and provides for stiff criminal penalties for violators. These increased requirements have dramatically increased the need for good accounting and, at the same time, highlighted the value of accounting information to investors and creditors. We discuss the specific provisions of SOX in more detail in Chapter 4.

Important as such legislation is in supporting the ethical foundation of accounting, it is equally important that accountants themselves have their own personal standards for ethical conduct. You cannot, though, just go out and suddenly obtain ethics when you need them. ("I'd like a pound of ethics, please.") Rather, accountants need to *develop* their ability to identify ethical situations and know the difference between right and wrong in the context of the accounting topics you will learn in this course. One of the keys to ethical decision making is having an appreciation for how your actions affect others.

When you face ethical dilemmas in your professional life (and indeed in your personal life), you can apply the following simple framework as you think through what to do:

1. Identify the ethical situation and the people who will be affected (the stakeholders).
2. Specify the options for alternative courses of action.
3. Understand the impact of each option on the stakeholders.
4. Make a decision.

Throughout the book, we will discuss some ethical decisions relating to accounting and will make clear their financial impact. These discussions will give you opportunities to practice some ethical decision-making in a classroom setting.

ETHICAL DILEMMA

© BananaStock/PunchStock, RF

You have been the manager of a local restaurant for the past five years. Because of increased competition, you notice you're getting fewer customers. Despite all your attempts to attract new customers and cut costs, the restaurant's profitability continues to decline. The restaurant owner tells you that if this year's profit is lower than last year's, you'll lose your job.

When preparing financial statements at the end of the year, you notice that this year's profit *is* lower. You know that by purposely understating certain expenses, you can falsely report higher profits to the owner for this year. That will allow you to keep your job for at least one more year and look for a new job in the meantime.

What should you do? What if you really believe the lower profitability is caused by factors outside your control? Would this make the false reporting acceptable?

User's Guide
Throughout the book, you will see boxed discussions of *Ethical Dilemmas.* These dilemmas are designed to raise your awareness of accounting issues that have ethical ramifications.

CAREERS IN ACCOUNTING

PART C

Whether you plan to major in accounting or not, this section is important for you. Accounting majors need to realize the many different options available upon graduation. Those who do not plan to major in accounting need a solid understanding of the many different business decisions involving accounting information.

After completing the first course in accounting, you will have some idea whether you enjoy accounting and might like to major in it. You will also find out through exams, quizzes, and homework whether you have the aptitude to be good at it. Realize, however, that besides being good at the technical side of accounting, you will need interpersonal skills such as working well in teams, making presentations to clients, and leading co-workers in complex projects. If you do major in accounting, the job prospects are numerous.

Demand for Accounting

One of the greatest benefits of an accounting degree is the wide variety of job opportunities it opens to you. With an accounting degree you can apply for almost any position available to finance majors. However, it doesn't work the other way: Finance majors often lack the accounting background necessary to apply for accounting positions.

For the past several years, accounting has ranked as one of the top majors on university campuses. Because of their importance in our society, accountants are in high demand. And because of this high demand, accounting salaries are on the rise. Starting salaries are among the highest of all majors across the university.

Career Options in Accounting

The first big decision a student makes as an accounting major is the choice between a career in public accounting and a career in private accounting.

■ **LO1–6**
Identify career opportunities in accounting.

PUBLIC ACCOUNTING

Public accounting firms are professional service firms that traditionally have focused on three areas: auditing, tax preparation/planning, and business consulting. We already have discussed the role of *auditors* in attesting to the conformity of companies' financial statements with GAAP. *Tax preparation/planning* is an increasingly important activity in the United States, as the complexity of tax laws related to personal and corporate taxes continues

# CAREER CORNER

Over 20,000 employees join public accounting firms in entry-level jobs each year, and thousands more go into other areas of accounting. While financial accountants learn how to measure business transactions and prepare financial reports, they also learn a great deal about the business itself. Because of this widespread business knowledge, accountants often play a key role on the management team. In fact, it should come as no surprise to learn that most chief financial officers (CFOs) started their careers as accountants.

Accounting, because of its dynamic and professional nature, offers an attractive career option. You can learn more about a career in accounting by visiting the website of the American Institute of Certified Public Accountants (*www.aicpa.org*). There, you can look under the *Career* link to find current information about job opportunities, salaries, work life for women, how to write a resume, how to interview, and other general career advice. For salary and other job-related information, consult the website of the U.S. Bureau of Labor Statistics (*www.bls.gov*). There are a wide variety of jobs in accounting and therefore a wide variety of starting salaries, typically ranging from $50,000 to $70,000. The demand for accounting positions is expected to grow 13% per year for the next 10 years.

© Digital Vision/Punchstock, RF

to increase. *Business consulting* is perhaps the most lucrative activity of accountants. Managers who want to better understand their companies' financial strengths and weaknesses often turn to public accountants for guidance. Who knows the business activities better than the one measuring and communicating them?

If you choose a career in public accounting, the next big decision is whether to work for one of the "Big 4" public accounting firms (**Deloitte**, **Ernst & Young**, **Pricewaterhouse-Coopers**, and **KPMG**) or one of the thousands of medium or smaller-sized firms. The Big 4 firms are huge, each having annual revenues in the billions. They audit almost all the Fortune 500 companies in the United States and most of the largest companies around the world, and they hire thousands of accounting majors each year. The thousands of smaller international, regional, and local accounting firms also hire thousands of accounting majors right out of college.

Most public accountants become *Certified Public Accountants (CPAs)*. You become a CPA by passing the four parts of the CPA exam and meeting minimum work experience requirements (in some states). Most states require that you have 150 semester hours (225 quarter hours) of college credit to take the exam. Becoming a CPA can provide a big boost in salary and long-term job opportunities.

User's Guide
Throughout the book, you will see sections titled *Career Corner.* These sections highlight a link between a particular topic and a business career, and thus are intended for both accounting majors and nonmajors.

PRIVATE ACCOUNTING

A career in **private accounting** means providing accounting services to the company that employs you. Every major company in the world needs employees with training and experience in financial accounting, management accounting, taxation, internal auditing, and accounting information systems. Whereas working as a public accountant provides the advantage of experience working with a number of different clients, private accountants sometimes earn higher starting salaries. In fact, many accounting students begin their careers in public accounting, gaining experience across a wide array of companies and industries, and then eventually switch over to one of their favorite clients as private accountants. Other students take positions directly in private accounting right out of college.

Because of their special training and valuable knowledge base, both public and private accountants are expanding their roles to include the following: financial planning, information technology development, financial analysis, forensic accounting, information risk management, investment banking, environmental accounting, tax law, FBI work, management consulting, and much, much more. Illustration 1–14 outlines just a few of the many career options in public and private accounting. In addition, there are career opportunities in government accounting and education.

KEY POINT

Because of the high demand for accounting graduates, wide range of job opportunities, and increasing salaries, this is a great time to obtain a degree in accounting.

ILLUSTRATION 1–14
Some of the Career Options in Accounting

	Public Accounting (Big 4 and Non-Big 4)	Private Accounting
Who are the clients?	Corporations Governments Nonprofit organizations Individuals	Your particular employer
What are the traditional career opportunities?	Auditors Tax preparers/planners Business consultants	Financial accountants Managerial accountants Internal auditors Tax preparers Payroll managers
What other career opportunities are available?	Financial planners Information technology developers Financial analysts Forensic accountants Information risk managers Investment bankers Environmental accountants Financial advisors Tax lawyers	Information managers Management advisors Tax planners Acquisition specialists FBI agents Sports agents

CONCEPTUAL FRAMEWORK

APPENDIX

The FASB establishes financial accounting standards based on a **conceptual framework,** which you can think of as the "theory" of accounting. In much the same way that our nation's Constitution provides the underlying principles that guide the "correctness" of all laws, the FASB's conceptual framework prescribes the correctness of financial accounting rules. Having a conceptual framework provides standard setters with a benchmark for creating a consistent set of financial reporting rules now and in the future. It also provides others with a *written* framework so that everyone understands the underlying concepts that accountants are to consider in preparing and interpreting financial accounting information.

■ **LO1–7**
Explain the nature of the conceptual framework used to develop generally accepted accounting principles.

 KEY POINT

The conceptual framework provides an underlying foundation for the development of accounting standards and interpretation of accounting information.

In the chapter, we discussed the three objectives of financial accounting as outlined in the FASB's conceptual framework. Financial accounting should provide information that:

1. Is useful to investors and creditors in making decisions.
2. Helps to predict cash flows.
3. Tells about economic resources, claims to resources, and changes in resources and claims.

To satisfy these stated objectives, financial reporting of accounting information should possess certain characteristics to be useful. What are the desired characteristics? Illustration 1–15 provides a graphical depiction of the qualitative characteristics of useful financial information.

Notice that at the top of the figure is decision usefulness—the ability of the information to be useful in decision making. Accounting information should help investors, lenders, and other creditors make important decisions about providing funds to a company.

ILLUSTRATION 1–15   Qualitative Characteristics of Useful Financial Information

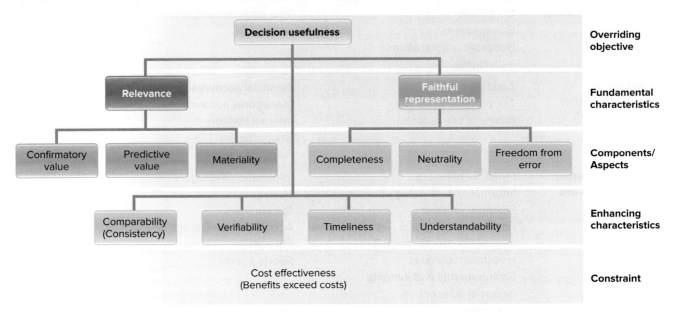

FUNDAMENTAL QUALITATIVE CHARACTERISTICS

The two fundamental decision-specific qualitative characteristics that make accounting information useful are *relevance* and *faithful representation.* Both are critical. No matter how representative, if information is not relevant to the decision at hand, it is useless. Conversely, relevant information is of little value if it does not faithfully represent the underlying activity.

Relevance.   To have relevance, accounting information should possess *confirmatory value* and/or *predictive value.* Generally, useful information will possess both of these components. For example, the ability of **Nike** to report a positive net income confirms that its management is effectively and efficiently using the company's resources to sell quality products. In this case, net income has *confirmatory value.* At the same time, reporting a positive and growing net income for several consecutive years should provide information that has *predictive value* for the company's future cash-generating ability.

Materiality reflects the impact of financial accounting information on investors' and creditors' decisions. Unless an item is material in amount or nature—that is, sufficient in amount or nature to affect a decision—it need not be reported in accordance with GAAP. Based on the concept of materiality, Nike probably does not record all its assets as assets. Most companies record assets such as wastebaskets and staplers as *expenses,* even though these items will benefit the company for a long period. Recording a $6 wastebasket as a current expense instead of a long-term asset for a multibillion-dollar company like Nike has no impact on investors' decisions. Thus, materiality is an aspect of the relevance characteristic with regard to values users deem significant in their decision-making process.

Faithful representation.   To be a faithful representation of business activities, accounting information should be complete, neutral, and free from error. *Completeness* means including all information necessary for faithful representation of the business activity the firm is reporting. For example, when Nike reports inventory in its balance sheet, investors understand it to represent *all* items (and only those items) that are intended for sale to customers in the ordinary course of business. If the amount reported for inventory includes only some of the items to be sold, then it lacks completeness. Adequate note disclosure is another important component of completeness. Nike must disclose in the notes to the financial statements the method it used to calculate inventory reported on its balance sheet. (We discuss alternative inventory methods in Chapter 6.)

Neutrality means to be unbiased, and this characteristic is highly related to the establishment of accounting standards. Because of the topic and the nature of the business, sometimes a new accounting standard may affect one group of companies over others. In such cases, the FASB must convince the financial community that this was a *consequence* of the standard, and not an *objective* used to set the standard. For example, the FASB requires that all research and development (R&D) costs be reported as an expense in the income statement, reducing the current year's net income. The FASB's objective in adopting this approach was not to weaken the financial appearance of those companies in R&D-intensive industries, such as telecommunications, pharmaceuticals, and software, even though that may have been an effect.

Freedom from error indicates that reported amounts reflect the best available information. As you'll come to find out in this course, some amounts reported in the financial statements are based on estimates, and the accuracy of those estimates is subject to uncertainty. Because of this, financial statements are not expected to be completely free of error, but they are expected to reflect management's unbiased judgments and due diligence in reflecting appropriate accounting principles.

 KEY POINT

To be useful for decision making, accounting information should have relevance and faithful representation.

ENHANCING QUALITATIVE CHARACTERISTICS

Four enhancing qualitative characteristics are comparability, verifiability, timeliness, and understandability. Comparability refers to the ability of users to see similarities and differences between two different business activities. For example, how does **Nike**'s net income compare with net income for other sports apparel companies such as **Under Armour**? Comparability also refers to the ability of users to see similarities and differences in the same company over time. How does Nike's net income this year compare to last year's? Closely related to the notion of comparability is consistency. Consistency refers to the use of similar accounting procedures either over time for the same company, or across companies at the same point in time. Comparability of financial information is the overriding goal, while consistency of accounting procedures is a means of achieving that goal.

Verifiability implies a consensus among different measurers. For instance, different graders will arrive at the same exam score for multiple-choice tests, but they are more likely to differ in scoring essay exams. Multiple-choice tests are highly verifiable. The same idea holds in the business world. For example, the price Nike pays to purchase a trademark of another company is usually verifiable because there is an exchange of cash at a certain point in time. In contrast, the value of a patent for a new product or design that Nike develops internally over an extended period is more subjective and less verifiable.

Firms must also disclose information related to net income that is *timely*. Timeliness refers to information being available to users early enough to allow them to use it in the decision process. Large companies like Nike are required to report information related to net income within 40 days after the end of the quarter and within 60 days after the end of the year.

Understandability means that users must be able to understand the information within the context of the decision they are making. This is a user-specific quality because users will differ in their ability to comprehend any set of information.

COST CONSTRAINT

Sometimes, certain information involves more time and effort than the information is worth. For example, if a friend asks what you did today, she probably wants to know the general outline of your day, but does not want to hear a recital of every move you made. Similarly, there may be a cost constraint (limit) to reporting financial information.

The cost constraint suggests that financial accounting information is provided only when the benefits of doing so exceed the costs. For example, knowing the profit margin earned by Nike in each country provides decision-useful information to investors and creditors. However, this information is also helpful to the company's current and potential competitors such as Under Armour as it makes its own expansion plans. The competitive costs of providing this information may outweigh the benefits.

UNDERLYING ASSUMPTIONS

For the qualitative characteristics described above to be applied to accounting information, four basic assumptions must be made to support the existence of GAAP. As pictured in Illustration 1–16, they are (1) the economic entity assumption, (2) the monetary unit assumption, (3) the periodicity assumption, and (4) the going concern assumption.

ILLUSTRATION 1–16

Assumptions That Underlie GAAP

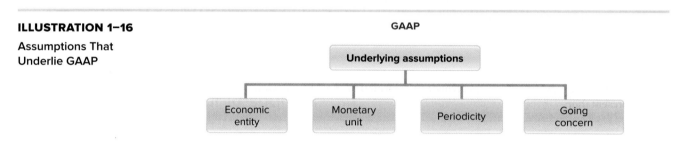

Economic Entity Assumption. The economic entity assumption states that we can identify all economic events with a particular economic entity. In other words, only business transactions involving Nike should be reported as part of Nike's financial accounting information. Another key aspect of this assumption is the distinction between the economic activities of owners and those of the company. For example, Nike co-founder and chairman Phil Knight's personal residence is not an asset of Nike, Inc.

Monetary Unit Assumption. Information would be difficult to use if, for example, we listed assets as "three machines, two trucks, and a building." According to the monetary unit assumption, in order to *measure* financial statement elements, we need a unit or scale of measurement. The dollar in the United States is the most appropriate common denominator to express information about financial statement elements and changes in those elements. In Europe, the common denominator is the euro. Nike has operations throughout the world, so it must translate all its financial information to U.S. dollars under the monetary unit assumption.

Periodicity Assumption. The periodicity assumption relates to the qualitative characteristic of *timeliness*. External users need *periodic* information to make decisions. The periodicity assumption divides the economic life of an enterprise (presumed to be indefinite) into artificial time periods for periodic financial reporting. Corporations like Nike, whose securities are publicly traded, are required to provide financial information to the SEC on a quarterly *and* an annual basis. Quarterly reports are more timely, while annual reports allow the full application of GAAP.

Going Concern Assumption. The going concern assumption states that in the absence of information to the contrary, a business entity will continue to operate indefinitely. This assumption is critical to many broad and specific accounting principles. It provides justification for measuring many assets based on their original costs (a practice known as the *historical cost principle*). If we knew an enterprise was going to cease operations in the near future, we would measure assets and liabilities not at their original costs but at their current liquidation values.

In addition to the four basic assumptions that underlie GAAP are four principles (historical cost, full disclosure, realization, and matching) that guide the application of GAAP. We will explain each of these in an appropriate context in later chapters.

 KEY POINTS BY LEARNING OBJECTIVE

LO1–1   Describe the two primary functions of financial accounting.

The functions of financial accounting are to measure business activities of a company and to communicate information about those activities to investors and creditors and other outside users for decision-making purposes.

LO1–2   Understand the business activities that financial accounting measures.

The measurement role of accounting is to create a record of the activities of a company. To make this possible, a company must maintain an accurate record of its assets, liabilities, stockholders' equity, revenues, expenses, and dividends.

LO1–3   Determine how financial accounting information is communicated through financial statements.

The income statement compares revenues and expenses for the current period to assess the company's ability to earn a profit from running its operations.

The statement of stockholders' equity reports information related to changes in common stock and retained earnings each period. The change in retained earnings equals net income less dividends for the period.

The balance sheet demonstrates that the company's resources (assets) equal creditors' claims (liabilities) plus owners' claims (stockholders' equity) to those resources on a particular date.

The statement of cash flows reports cash transactions from operating, investing, and financing activities for the period.

All transactions that affect revenues or expenses reported in the income statement ultimately affect the balance sheet through the balance in retained earnings.

LO1–4   Describe the role that financial accounting plays in the decision-making process.

Financial accounting serves an important role by providing information useful in investment and lending decisions.

No single piece of company information better explains companies' stock price performance than does financial accounting net income. A company's debt level is an important indicator of management's ability to respond to business situations and the possibility of bankruptcy.

LO1–5   Explain the term generally accepted accounting principles (GAAP) and describe the role of GAAP in financial accounting.

The rules of financial accounting are called generally accepted accounting principles (GAAP). The Financial Accounting Standards Board (FASB) is an independent, private body that has primary responsibility for the establishment of GAAP in the United States.

The primary objective of financial accounting is to provide useful information to investors and creditors in making decisions.

LO1–6   Identify career opportunities in accounting.

Because of the high demand for accounting graduates, the wide range of job opportunities, and increasing salaries, this is a great time to obtain a degree in accounting.

Appendix

LO1–7   Explain the nature of the conceptual framework used to develop generally accepted accounting principles.

The conceptual framework provides an underlying foundation for the development of accounting standards and interpretation of accounting information.

To be useful for decision making, accounting information should have relevance and faithful representation.

GLOSSARY

Accounting: A system of maintaining records of a company's operations and communicating that information to decision makers. **p. 4**

Accounting equation: Equation that shows a company's resources (assets) equal creditors' and owners' claims to those resources (liabilities and stockholders' equity). **p. 7**

Assets: Resources of a company. **p. 7**

Auditors: Trained individuals hired by a company as an independent party to express a professional opinion of the conformity of that company's financial statements with GAAP. **p. 22**

Balance sheet: A financial statement that presents the financial position of the company on a particular date. **p. 12**

Comparability: The ability of users to see similarities and differences between two different business activities. **p. 29**

Consistency: The use of similar accounting procedures either over time for the same company, or across companies at the same point in time. **p. 29**

Corporation: An entity that is legally separate from its owners. **p. 6**

Cost constraint: Financial accounting information is provided only when the benefits of doing so exceed the costs. **p. 30**

Decision usefulness: The ability of the information to be useful in decision making. **p. 27**

Dividends: Cash payments to stockholders. **p. 8**

Economic entity assumption: All economic events with a particular economic entity can be identified. **p. 30**

Ethics: A code or moral system that provides criteria for evaluating right and wrong behavior. **p. 24**

Expenses: Costs of providing products and services. **p. 8**

Faithful representation: Accounting information that is complete, neutral, and free from error. **p. 28**

Financial accounting: Measurement of business activities of a company and communication of those measurements to external parties for decision-making purposes. **p. 4**

Financial Accounting Standards Board (FASB): An independent, private body that has primary responsibility for the establishment of GAAP in the United States. **p. 21**

Financial statements: Periodic reports published by the company for the purpose of providing information to external users. **p. 9**

Generally accepted accounting principles (GAAP): The rules of financial accounting. **p. 21**

Going concern assumption: In the absence of information to the contrary, a business entity will continue to operate indefinitely. **p. 30**

Income statement: A financial statement that reports the company's revenues and expenses over an interval of time. **p. 10**

International Accounting Standards Board (IASB): An international accounting standard-setting body responsible for the convergence of accounting standards worldwide. **p. 21**

International Financial Reporting Standards (IFRS): The standards being developed and promoted by the International Accounting Standards Board. **p. 21**

Liabilities: Amounts owed to creditors. **p. 7**

Monetary unit assumption: A unit or scale of measurement can be used to measure financial statement elements. **p. 30**

Net income: Difference between revenues and expenses. **p. 8**

Partnership: Business owned by two or more persons. **p. 6**

Periodicity assumption: The economic life of an enterprise (presumed to be indefinite) can be divided into artificial time periods for financial reporting. **p. 30**

Relevance: Accounting information that possesses confirmatory value and/or predictive value, and that is material. **p. 28**

Retained earnings: Cumulative amount of net income earned over the life of the company that has been kept (retained) in the business rather than distributed to stockholders as dividends (not retained). **p. 11**

Revenues: Amounts recorded when the company sells products or services to customers. **p. 8**

Sarbanes-Oxley Act (SOX): Formally titled the Public Company Accounting Reform and Investor Protection Act of 2002, this act provides regulation of auditors and the types of services they furnish to clients, increases accountability of corporate executives, addresses conflicts of interest for securities analysts, and provides for stiff criminal penalties for violators. **p. 24**

Sole proprietorship: A business owned by one person. **p. 6**

Statement of cash flows: A financial statement that measures activities involving cash receipts and cash payments over an interval of time. **p. 14**

Statement of stockholders' equity: A financial statement that summarizes the changes in stockholders' equity over an interval of time. **p. 11**

Stockholders' equity: Stockholders', or owners', claims to resources, which equal the difference between total assets and total liabilities. **p. 7**

Timeliness: Information being available to users early enough to allow them to use it in the decision process. **p. 29**

Understandability: Users must understand the information within the context of the decision they are making. **p. 29**

Verifiability: A consensus among different measurers. **p. 29**

SELF-STUDY QUESTIONS

1. Based on the introductory section of this chapter, which course is most like financial accounting? **(LO1–1)**
   a. College algebra.
   b. Foreign language.
   c. Molecular biology.
   d. Physical education.

2. Financial accounting serves which primary function(s)? **(LO1–2)**
   a. Measures business activities.
   b. Communicates business activities to interested parties.
   c. Makes business decisions on behalf of interested parties.
   d. Both a. and b. are functions of financial accounting.

3. Resources of a company are referred to as: **(LO1–2)**
   a. Liabilities.
   b. Stockholders' equity.
   c. Dividends.
   d. Assets.

4. Sales of products or services are referred to as: **(LO1–2)**
   a. Assets.
   b. Revenues.
   c. Liabilities.
   d. Expenses.

5. Which financial statement conveys a company's ability to generate profits in the current period? **(LO1–3)**
   a. Income statement.
   b. Statement of cash flows.
   c. Balance sheet.
   d. Statement of stockholders' equity.

6. Which financial statement shows that a company's resources equal claims to those resources? **(LO1–3)**
   a. Income statement.
   b. Statement of stockholders' equity.
   c. Balance sheet.
   d. Statement of cash flows.

7. Why does financial accounting have a positive impact on our society? **(LO1–4)**
   a. It entails a detailed transaction record necessary for filing taxes with the Internal Revenue Service (IRS).
   b. It allows investors and creditors to redirect their resources to successful companies and away from unsuccessful companies.
   c. It prevents competitors from being able to steal the company's customers.
   d. It provides a system of useful internal reports for management decision making.

8. The body of rules and procedures that guide the measurement and communication of financial accounting information is known as: **(LO1–5)**
   a. Standards of Professional Compliance (SPC).
   b. Code of Ethical Decisions (COED).
   c. Rules of Financial Reporting (RFP).
   d. Generally Accepted Accounting Principles (GAAP).

9. What is a benefit to a career in accounting? **(LO1–6)**
   a. High salaries.
   b. Wide range of job opportunities.
   c. High demand for accounting graduates.
   d. All of the above.

10. What are the two fundamental qualitative characteristics identified by the Financial Accounting Standards Board's (FASB) conceptual framework? **(LO1–7)**
    a. Relevance and faithful representation.
    b. Materiality and efficiency.
    c. Comparability and consistency.
    d. Costs and benefits.

Note: For answers, see the last page of the chapter.

For additional study materials, including 10 more multiple-choice Self-Study Questions, visit Connect.

REVIEW QUESTIONS

1. Explain what it means to say that an accounting class is not the same as a math class. ■ **LO1–1**

2. Identify some of the people interested in making decisions about a company. ■ **LO1–1**

3. What is the basic difference between financial accounting and managerial accounting? ■ **LO1–1**

4. What are the two primary functions of financial accounting? ■ **LO1–1**

5. What are the three basic business activities that financial accounting seeks to measure and communicate to external parties? Define each. ■ **LO1–2**

■ **LO1–2**   6. What are a few of the typical financing activities for a company like **United Parcel Service, Inc. (UPS)**, the world's largest package delivery company and a leading global provider of specialized transportation and logistics services?

■ **LO1–2**   7. What are a few of the typical investing activities for a company like **Trump Entertainment Resorts, Inc.**, a leading gaming company that owns and operates casinos, resorts, and hotels?

■ **LO1–2**   8. What are a few of the typical operating activities for a company like **Oracle Corporation**, one of the world's leading suppliers of software for information management?

■ **LO1–2**   9. What are the three major legal forms of business organizations? Which one is chosen by most of the largest companies in the United States?

■ **LO1–2**   10. Provide the basic definition for each of the account types: assets, liabilities, stockholders' equity, dividends, revenues, and expenses.

■ **LO1–2**   11. What are the major advantages and disadvantages of each of the legal forms of business organizations?

■ **LO1–3**   12. What are the four primary financial statements? What basic information is shown on each?

■ **LO1–3**   13. What does it mean to say that the income statement, statement of stockholders' equity, and statement of cash flows measure activity over an *interval of time*, but the balance sheet measures activity at a *point in time?*

■ **LO1–3**   14. Give some examples of the basic revenues and expenses for a company like **The Walt Disney Company**.

■ **LO1–3**   15. What is the accounting equation? Which financial statement reports the accounting equation?

■ **LO1–3**   16. Give some examples of the basic assets and liabilities of a company like **Walmart**.

■ **LO1–3**   17. "The retained earnings account is a link between the income statement and the balance sheet." Explain what this means.

■ **LO1–3**   18. What are the three types of cash flows reported in the statement of cash flows? Give an example of each type of activity for a company like **Oakley, Inc.**, a designer, manufacturer, and distributor of high-performance eyewear, footwear, watches, and athletic equipment.

■ **LO1–3**   19. In addition to financial statements, what are some other ways to disclose financial information to external users?

■ **LO1–4**   20. How does financial accounting have an impact on society?

■ **LO1–5**   21. What is meant by GAAP? Why should companies follow GAAP in reporting to external users?

■ **LO1–5**   22. Which body is primarily responsible for the establishment of GAAP in the United States? What body serves this function on an international basis?

■ **LO1–5**   23. In general terms, explain the terms U.S. GAAP and IFRS.

■ **LO1–5**   24. What was the primary reason for the establishment of the 1933 Securities Act and the 1934 Securities Exchange Act? What power does the Securities and Exchange Commission (SEC) have?

■ **LO1–5**   25. What is the role of the auditor in the financial reporting process?

■ **LO1–5**   26. What are the three primary objectives of financial reporting?

■ **LO1–6**   27. What are some of the benefits to obtaining a degree in accounting? What is the difference between a career in public accounting and private accounting? What are some of the traditional careers of accounting graduates? What new areas are accountants expanding into?

■ **LO1–7**   28. Discuss the terms *relevance* and *faithful representation* as they relate to financial accounting information.

29. What are the three components/aspects of relevance? What are the three components/aspects of faithful representation?

■ **LO1–7**

30. What is meant by the term *cost effectiveness* in financial reporting?

■ **LO1–7**

31. Define the four basic assumptions underlying GAAP.

■ **LO1–7**

BRIEF EXERCISES

BE1–1 Indicate whether the definition provided is true or false.

Define accounting (LO1–1)

(True/False) Accounting can be defined as:

1. _____ The language of business.
2. _____ A measurement/communication process.
3. _____ A mathematics course.

BE1–2 Match each business activity with its description.

Identify the different types of business activities (LO1–2)

Business Activities	Descriptions
1. _____ Financing	a. Transactions related to revenues and expenses.
2. _____ Investing	b. Transactions with lenders and owners.
3. _____ Operating	c. Transactions involving the purchase and sale of productive assets.

BE1–3 Match each form of business organization with its description.

Identify the different forms of business organizations (LO1–2)

Business Organizations	Descriptions
1. _____ Sole proprietorship	a. Business owned by two or more persons.
2. _____ Partnership	b. Entity legally separate from its owners.
3. _____ Corporation	c. Business owned by a single person.

BE1–4 Match each account type with its description.

Recognize the different account classifications (LO1–2)

Account Classifications	Descriptions
1. _____ Assets	a. Sales of products or services.
2. _____ Liabilities	b. Owners' claims to resources.
3. _____ Stockholders' equity	c. Distributions to stockholders.
4. _____ Dividends	d. Costs of selling products or services.
5. _____ Revenues	e. Resources of a company.
6. _____ Expenses	f. Amounts owed.

BE1–5 For each transaction, indicate whether each account would be classified in the balance sheet as (a) an asset, (b) a liability, or (c) stockholders' equity; in the income statement as (d) a revenue or (e) an expense; or in the statement of stockholders' equity as (f) a dividend.

Assign account classifications (LO1–2)

Account Classifications	Accounts	Related Transactions
1. _____	Rent expense	Cost of rent.
2. _____	Interest revenue	Interest earned on savings account.
3. _____	Dividends	Cash payments to stockholders.
4. _____	Land	Land used for operations.
5. _____	Accounts payable	Amounts owed to suppliers.

BE1–6 For each transaction, indicate whether each account would be classified in the balance sheet as (a) an asset, (b) a liability, or (c) stockholders' equity; in the income statement as (d) a revenue or (e) an expense; or in the statement of stockholders' equity as (f) a dividend.

Assign account classifications (LO1–2)

Account Classifications	Account	Related Transactions
1. _____	Utilities payable	Amounts owed for utilities.
2. _____	Cash	Cash available for use.
3. _____	Salaries expense	Cost of salaries.
4. _____	Common stock	Shares of ownership sold to investors.
5. _____	Service revenue	Sale of services to customers.

Describe each financial statement (LO1–3)

BE1–7 Match each financial statement with its description.

Financial Statements	Related Transactions
1. _____ Income statement	a. Change in owners' claims to resources.
2. _____ Statement of stockholders' equity	b. Profitability of the company.
3. _____ Balance sheet	c. Change in cash as a result of operating, investing, and financing activities.
4. _____ Statement of cash flows	d. Resources equal creditors' and owners' claims to those resources.

Determine the location of items in financial statements (LO1–3)

BE1–8 Determine on which financial statement you find the following items.

Financial Statements	Items
1. _____ Income statement	a. The change in retained earnings due to net income and dividends.
2. _____ Statement of stockholders' equity	b. Amount of cash received from borrowing money from a local bank.
3. _____ Balance sheet	c. Revenue from sales to customers during the year.
4. _____ Statement of cash flows	d. Total amounts owed to workers at the end of the year.

Identify different groups engaged in providing high-quality financial reporting (LO1–5)

BE1–9 Each of these parties plays a role in the quality of financial reporting. Match each group with its function.

Groups	Functions
1. _____ Financial Accounting Standards Board	a. Group that has been given power by Congress to enforce the proper application of financial reporting rules for companies whose securities are publicly traded.
2. _____ International Accounting Standards Board	b. Independent, private-sector group that is primarily responsible for setting financial reporting standards in the United States.
3. _____ Securities and Exchange Commission	c. Independent intermediaries that help to ensure that management appropriately applies financial reporting rules in preparing the company's financial statements.
4. _____ Auditors	d. Body that is attempting to develop a single set of high-quality, understandable global accounting standards.

Identify the objectives of financial accounting (LO1–5)

BE1–10 Indicate which of the following are objectives of financial accounting.

(Yes/No)	Objectives
1. _____	Provide information that is useful to investors and creditors.
2. _____	Guarantee that businesses will not go bankrupt.
3. _____	Provide information about resources and claims to resources.
4. _____	Prevent competitors from offering lower-priced products.
5. _____	Provide information to help users in predicting future cash flows.
6. _____	Maximize tax revenue to the federal government.

BE1–11 Below are possible career opportunities for those earning a degree in accounting. Indicate whether the statement related to each career is true or false.

Identify careers for accounting majors (LO1–6)

(True/False)   Someone earning a degree in accounting could pursue the following career:

1. _____ Auditor
2. _____ Tax preparer
3. _____ Business consultant
4. _____ Financial planner
5. _____ Forensic investigator
6. _____ Tax planner
7. _____ Financial analyst
8. _____ Information technology developer
9. _____ Investment banker
10. _____ Tax lawyer
11. _____ FBI agent
12. _____ Information risk manager

BE1–12 Match each of the components of relevance with its definition.

Identify the components/aspects of relevance (LO1–7)

Relevance	Definitions
1. _____ Confirmatory value	a. Information is useful in helping to forecast future outcomes.
2. _____ Predictive value	b. Information provides feedback on past activities.
3. _____ Materiality	c. The nature or amount of an item has the ability to affect decisions.

BE1–13 Match each of the components of faithful representation with its definition.

Identify the components/ aspects of faithful representation (LO1–7)

Faithful Representation	Definition
1. _____ Freedom from error	a. All information necessary to describe an item is reported.
2. _____ Neutrality	b. Information that does not bias the decision maker.
3. _____ Completeness	c. Reported amounts reflect the best available information.

EXERCISES

McGraw Hill Education **connect**

E1–1 The following provides a list of transactions and a list of business activities.

Identify the different types of business activities (LO1–2)

Transactions	Business Activities
1. _____ Borrow from the bank.	a. Financing
2. _____ Provide services to customers.	b. Investing
3. _____ Issue common stock to investors.	c. Operating
4. _____ Purchase land.	
5. _____ Pay rent for the current period.	
6. _____ Pay dividends to stockholders.	
7. _____ Purchase building.	

Required:

Match the transaction with the business activity by indicating the letter that corresponds to the appropriate business activity.

E1–2 Falcon Incorporated has the following transactions with Wildcat Corporation.

Identify account classifications and business activities (LO1–2)

Flip Side of E1–3

Transactions	Falcon's Related Account
1. Falcon purchases common stock of Wildcat.	Investment
2. Falcon borrows from Wildcat by signing a note.	Notes payable
3. Wildcat pays dividends to Falcon.	Dividend revenue
4. Falcon provides services to Wildcat.	Service revenue
5. Falcon pays interest to Wildcat on borrowing.	Interest expense

Required:

1. For each transaction, indicate whether Falcon would classify each account in the balance sheet as (a) an asset, (b) a liability, or (c) stockholders' equity; in the income statement as (d) a revenue or (e) an expense; or in the statement of stockholders' equity as (f) a dividend.
2. Classify the type of activity as financing, investing, or operating.

Identify account classifications and business activities (LO1–2)

E1–3 The transactions in this problem are identical to those in E1–2, but now with a focus on Wildcat.

Flip Side of E1–2

Transactions	Wildcat's Related Account
1. Falcon purchases common stock of Wildcat.	Common stock
2. Falcon borrows from Wildcat by signing a note.	Notes receivable
3. Wildcat pays dividends to Falcon.	Dividend
4. Falcon provides services to Wildcat.	Service fee expense
5. Falcon pays interest to Wildcat on borrowing.	Interest revenue

Required:

1. For each transaction, indicate whether Wildcat would classify each account in the balance sheet as (a) an asset, (b) a liability, or (c) stockholders' equity; in the income statement as (d) a revenue or (e) an expense; or in the statement of stockholders' equity as (f) a dividend.
2. Classify the type of activity as financing, investing, or operating.

Calculate net income and stockholders' equity (LO1–2)

E1–4 Eagle Corp. operates magnetic resonance imaging (MRI) clinics throughout the Northeast. At the end of the current period, the company reports the following amounts: Assets = $50,000; Liabilities = $27,000; Dividends = $3,000; Revenues = $14,000; Expenses = $9,000.

Required:

1. Calculate net income.
2. Calculate stockholders' equity at the end of the period.

Calculate net loss and stockholders' equity (LO1–2)

E1–5 Cougar's Accounting Services provides low-cost tax advice and preparation to those with financial need. At the end of the current period, the company reports the following amounts: Assets = $19,000; Liabilities = $15,000; Revenues = $28,000; Expenses = $33,000.

Required:

1. Calculate net loss.
2. Calculate stockholders' equity at the end of the period.

Prepare an income statement (LO1–3)

E1–6 Below are the account balances for Cowboy Law Firm at the end of December.

Accounts	Balances
Cash	$ 5,400
Salaries expense	2,200
Accounts payable	3,400
Retained earnings	3,900
Utilities expense	1,200
Supplies	13,800
Service revenue	9,300
Common stock	6,000

Required:

Use only the appropriate accounts to prepare an income statement.

Prepare a statement of stockholders' equity (LO1–3)

E1–7 At the beginning of the year (January 1), Buffalo Drilling has $11,000 of common stock outstanding and retained earnings of $8,200. During the year, Buffalo reports net income of $8,500 and pays dividends of $3,200. In addition, Buffalo issues additional common stock for $8,000.

Required:

Prepare the statement of stockholders' equity at the end of the year (December 31).

E1–8 Wolfpack Construction has the following account balances at the end of the year.

Prepare a balance sheet (LO1–3)

Accounts	Balances
Equipment	$26,000
Accounts payable	3,000
Salaries expense	33,000
Common stock	11,000
Land	18,000
Notes payable	20,000
Service revenue	39,000
Cash	6,000
Retained earnings	?

Required:

Use only the appropriate accounts to prepare a balance sheet.

E1–9 Tiger Trade has the following cash transactions for the period.

Prepare a statement of cash flows (LO1–3)

Accounts	Amounts
Cash received from sale of products to customers	$ 40,000
Cash received from the bank for long-term loan	45,000
Cash paid to purchase factory equipment	(50,000)
Cash paid to merchandise suppliers	(12,000)
Cash received from the sale of an unused warehouse	13,000
Cash paid to workers	(24,000)
Cash paid for advertisement	(4,000)
Cash received for sale of services to customers	30,000
Cash paid for dividends to stockholders	(6,000)

Required:

1. Calculate the ending balance of cash, assuming the balance of cash at the beginning of the period is $5,000.
2. Prepare a statement of cash flows.

E1–10 On December 31, Fighting Okra Cooking Services reports the following revenues and expenses.

Link the income statement to the statement of stockholders' equity (LO1–3)

Service revenue	$75,000	Rent expense	$10,600
Postage expense	1,500	Salaries expense	24,000
Legal fees expense	2,400	Supplies expense	14,500

In addition, the balance of common stock at the beginning of the year was $200,000, and the balance of retained earnings was $32,000. During the year, the company issued additional shares of common stock for $25,000 and paid dividends of $10,000.

Required:

1. Prepare an income statement.
2. Prepare a statement of stockholders' equity.

E1–11 At the beginning of 2018, Artichoke Academy reported a balance in common stock of $150,000 and a balance in retained earnings of $50,000. During the year, the company issued additional shares of stock for $40,000, earned net income of $30,000, and paid dividends of $10,000. In addition, the company reported balances for the following assets and liabilities on December 31.

Link the statement of stockholders' equity to the balance sheet (LO1–3)

Assets		Liabilities	
Cash	$ 52,600	Accounts payable	$ 9,100
Supplies	13,400	Utilities payable	2,400
Prepaid rent	24,000	Salaries payable	3,500
Land	200,000	Notes payable	15,000

Required:
1. Prepare a statement of stockholders' equity.
2. Prepare a balance sheet.

Link the balance sheet to the statement of cash flows (LO1–3)

E1–12 Squirrel Tree Services reports the following amounts on December 31.

Assets		Liabilities and Stockholders' Equity	
Cash	$ 7,700	Accounts payable	$ 9,700
Supplies	1,800	Salaries payable	3,500
Prepaid insurance	3,500	Notes payable	20,000
Building	72,000	Common stock	40,000
		Retained earnings	11,800

In addition, the company reported the following cash flows.

Cash Inflows		Cash Outflows	
Customers	$60,000	Employee salaries	$22,000
Borrow from the bank (note)	20,000	Supplies	4,000
Sale of investments	10,000	Dividends	6,500
		Purchase building	62,000

Required:
1. Prepare a balance sheet.
2. Prepare a statement of cash flows.

Compute missing amounts from financial statements (LO1–3)

E1–13 Each of the following independent situations represents amounts shown on the four basic financial statements.

1. Revenues = $27,000; Expenses = $18,000; Net income = _____.
2. Increase in stockholders' equity = $17,000; Issuance of common stock = $11,000; Net income = $12,000; Dividends = _____.
3. Assets = $24,000; Stockholders' equity = $15,000; Liabilities = _____.
4. Total change in cash = $26,000; Net operating cash flows = $34,000; Net investing cash flows = ($17,000); Net financing cash flows = _____.

Required:
Fill in the missing blanks using your knowledge of amounts that appear on the financial statements.

Calculate the balance of retained earnings (LO1–3)

E1–14 During its first five years of operations, Red Raider Consulting reports net income and pays dividends as follows.

Year	Net Income	Dividends	Retained Earnings
1	$1,700	$ 600	_____
2	2,200	600	_____
3	3,100	1,500	_____
4	4,200	1,500	_____
5	5,400	1,500	_____

Required:

Calculate the balance of retained earnings at the end of each year. Note that retained earnings will always equal $0 at the beginning of year 1.

E1–15 Below are approximate amounts related to retained earnings reported by five companies in previous years.

1. **Coca-Cola** reports an increase in retained earnings of $3.2 billion and net income of $6.9 billion. What is the amount of dividends?
2. **PepsiCo** reports an increase in retained earnings of $3.4 billion and dividends of $2.6 billion. What is the amount of net income?
3. **Google** reports an increase in retained earnings of $1.6 billion and net income of $1.6 billion. What is the amount of dividends?
4. **Sirius Satellite Radio** reports beginning retained earnings of −$1.6 billion, net loss of $1.0 billion, and $0 dividends. What is the amount of ending retained earnings?
5. **Abercrombie & Fitch** reports ending retained earnings of $1.56 billion, net income of $0.43 billion, and dividends of $0.06 billion. What is the amount of beginning retained earnings?

Calculate amounts related to the balance of retained earnings **(LO1–3)**

Required:

Calculate the answer to each.

E1–16 Below are approximate amounts related to balance sheet information reported by five companies in previous years.

1. **ExxonMobil** reports total assets of $228 billion and total liabilities of $107 billion. What is the amount of stockholders' equity?
2. **Citigroup** reports total liabilities of $1,500 billion and stockholders' equity of $110 billion. What is the amount of total assets?
3. **Amazon.com** reports total assets of $4.7 billion and total stockholders' equity of $0.3 billion. What is the amount of total liabilities?
4. **Nike** reports an increase in assets of $1.2 billion and an increase in liabilities of $0.3 billion. What is the amount of the change in stockholders' equity?
5. **Kellogg** reports a decrease in liabilities of $0.34 billion and an increase in stockholders' equity of $0.02 billion. What is the amount of the change in total assets?

Use the accounting equation to calculate amounts related to the balance sheet **(LO1–3)**

Required:

Calculate the answer to each.

E1–17 Below are approximate amounts related to cash flow information reported by five companies in previous years.

1. **Kraft Foods** reports operating cash flows of $3.6 billion, investing cash flows of $0.6 billion, and financing cash flows of −$4.2 billion. What is the amount of the change in total cash?
2. **Sara Lee** reports operating cash flows of $1.4 billion, investing cash flows of −$0.3 billion, and financing cash flows of −$1.4 billion. If the beginning cash amount is $0.7 billion, what is the ending cash amount?
3. **Performance Food Group** reports operating cash flows of $0.07 billion, investing cash flows of $0.63 billion, and a change in total cash of $0.04 billion. What is the amount of cash flows from financing activities?
4. **Smithfield Foods** reports operating cash flows of $0.60 billion, financing cash flows of $0.42 billion, and a change in total cash of $0.02 billion. What is the amount of cash flows from investing activities?
5. **Tyson Foods** reports investing cash flows of −$1.42 billion, financing cash flows of $1.03 billion, and a change in total cash of $0.02 billion. What is the amount of cash flows from operating activities?

Calculate missing amounts related to the statement of cash flows **(LO1–3)**

Required:

Calculate the answer to each.

E1–18 Below are concepts associated with the role of the auditor in financial reporting.

Understand the role of the auditor **(LO1–5)**

Concept	Description
1. ____ Securities and Exchange Commission	a. Phrase meaning to present the accounting records in an altered format.
2. ____ Need for auditing	b. Auditors are not employees of the company they audit.
3. ____ Cooking the books	c. Responsible for applying generally accepted accounting principles (GAAP).
4. ____ Management	d. Regulatory body that requires audits of all publicly traded companies.
5. ____ Auditor	e. Separation of management from those who own the business or finance operations.
6. ____ Independent	f. Party that reports on whether a company's financial statements are in accordance with GAAP.
7. ____ Opinion	g. View expressed by an auditor as to the accuracy of a company's financial statements.

Required:

Match each concept with its description.

Identify the purpose of qualitative characteristics (LO1–7)

E1–19 The qualitative characteristics outlined in the FASB's conceptual framework include:

Fundamental Characteristics		Enhancing Characteristics
Relevance	**Faithful Representation**	g. Comparability
a. Confirmatory value	d. Completeness	h. Verifiability
b. Predictive value	e. Neutrality	i. Timeliness
c. Materiality	f. Freedom from error	j. Understandability

Consider the following independent situations.
1. In deciding whether to invest in **Southwest Airlines** or **American Airlines**, investors evaluate the companies' income statements. _____
2. To provide the most reliable information about future sales, **Walmart**'s management uses an appropriate process to estimate the decline in inventory value each year. _____
3. In deciding whether to loan money, **Wells Fargo** uses balance sheet information to forecast the probability of bankruptcy. _____
4. **IBM** is required to issue public financial statements within 60 days of its year-end. _____
5. Employees of **Starbucks** can use the company's financial statements to analyze the efficiency with which management has conducted operations over the past year. _____
6. When first requiring firms to prepare a statement of cash flows, the FASB's intent was not to discourage or promote investment in the automobile industry. _____
7. When **Harley-Davidson** reports revenue for the year, the amount includes sales not only in the United States but also those outside the United States. _____
8. The amount of total assets reported by **General Mills** can be substantiated by its auditors. _____
9. The **Cheesecake Factory** prepares its balance sheet in a clear format using basic accounting terminology to allow users to easily comprehend the company's assets, liabilities, and stockholders' equity. _____
10. **Target** prepays $600 to rent a post office box for the next six months and decides to record the entire payment to Rent expense (instead of Prepaid rent) in the current month. _____

Required:

Determine which qualitative characteristic best applies to each situation. Note: Each of the 10 characteristics is used once and only once.

E1–20 Below are the four underlying assumptions of generally accepted accounting principles.

Identify business assumptions underlying GAAP **(LO1–7)**

Assumptions	Descriptions
1. _____ Economic entity	a. A common denominator is needed to measure all business activities.
2. _____ Going concern	b. Economic events can be identified with a particular economic body.
3. _____ Periodicity	c. In the absence of information to the contrary, it is anticipated that a business entity will continue to operate indefinitely.
4. _____ Monetary unit	d. The economic life of a company can be divided into artificial time intervals for financial reporting.

Required:

Match each business assumption with its description.

PROBLEMS: SET A

P1–1A Below are typical transactions for **Hewlett-Packard**.

Classify business activities **(LO1–2)**

Type of Business Activity	Transactions
1. _____	Pay amount owed to the bank for previous borrowing.
2. _____	Pay utility costs.
3. _____	Purchase equipment to be used in operations.
4. _____	Provide services to customers.
5. _____	Purchase office supplies.
6. _____	Purchase a building.
7. _____	Pay workers' salaries.
8. _____	Pay for research and development costs.
9. _____	Pay taxes to the IRS.
10. _____	Sell common stock to investors.

Required:

Indicate whether each transaction is classified as a financing, investing, or operating activity.

P1–2A Account classifications include assets, liabilities, stockholders' equity, dividends, revenues, and expenses.

Assign account classifications **(LO1–2)**

Account Classifications	Accounts	Related Transactions
1. _____	Common stock	Sale of common stock to investors.
2. _____	Equipment	Equipment used for operations.
3. _____	Salaries payable	Amounts owed to employees.
4. _____	Service revenue	Sales of services to customers.
5. _____	Utilities expense	Cost of utilities.
6. _____	Supplies	Purchase of office supplies.
7. _____	Research and development expense	Cost of research and development.
8. _____	Land	Property used for operations.
9. _____	Income tax payable	Amounts owed to the IRS for taxes.
10. _____	Interest payable	Amount of interest owed on borrowing.

Prepare financial statements (LO1–3)

User's Guide Problems marked with this icon can be solved using Microsoft Excel templates.

Required:

For each transaction, indicate whether the related account would be classified in the balance sheet as (a) an asset, (b) a liability, or (c) stockholders' equity; in the income statement as (d) a revenue or (e) an expense; or in the statement of stockholders' equity as (f) a dividend.

P1–3A Longhorn Corporation provides low-cost food delivery services to senior citizens. At the end of the year, the company reports the following amounts:

Cash	$ 1,200	Service revenue	$67,700
Equipment	29,000	Cost of goods sold	53,400
Accounts payable	4,400	(food expense)	
Delivery expense	2,600	Buildings	40,000
Salaries expense	5,500	Supplies	3,400
		Salaries payable	800

In addition, the company had common stock of $40,000 at the beginning of the year and issued an additional $4,000 during the year. The company also had retained earnings of $18,200 at the beginning of the year.

Required:

Prepare the income statement, statement of stockholders' equity, and balance sheet for Longhorn Corporation.

Understand the format of financial statements and the links among them (LO1–3)

P1–4A Below are incomplete financial statements for Bulldog, Inc.

BULLDOG, INC.
Income Statement

Revenues	$39,000
Expenses:	
Salaries	(a)
Advertising	6,000
Utilities	4,000
Net income	(b)

BULLDOG, INC.
Statement of Stockholders' Equity

	Common Stock	Retained Earnings	Total S. Equity
Beginning balance	$10,000	$7,000	$17,000
Issuances	1,100		1,100
Add: Net income		(c)	(c)
Less: Dividends		(3,000)	(3,000)
Ending balance	$11,100	$10,000	$21,100

BULLDOG, INC.
Balance Sheet

Assets		Liabilities	
Cash	$ 4,000	Accounts payable	(d)
Accounts receivable	3,000	**Stockholders' Equity**	
Supplies	9,000	Common stock	(e)
Equipment	10,000	Retained earnings	(f)
		Total liabilities and	
Total assets	$26,000	stockholders' equity	(g)

Required:

Calculate the missing amounts.

Prepare financial statements (LO1–3)

P1–5A Cornhusker Company provides the following information at the end of 2018.

Cash remaining	$ 4,800
Rent expense for the year	7,000
Land that has been purchased	21,000
Retained earnings	12,400
Utility expense for the year	4,900
Accounts receivable from customers	7,200
Service revenue earned during the year	37,000
Salary expense for the year	13,300
Accounts payable to suppliers	2,200
Dividends paid to shareholders during the year	3,200
Common stock that has been issued prior to 2018	16,000
Salaries owed at the end of the year	2,400
Insurance expense for the year	3,500

Required:
Prepare the income statement, statement of stockholders' equity, and balance sheet for Cornhusker Company on December 31, 2018. No common stock is issued during 2018, and the balance of retained earnings at the beginning of 2018 equals $7,300.

P1–6A The four underlying assumptions of generally accepted accounting principles are economic entity, monetary unit, periodicity, and going concern. Consider the four independent situations below.

Identify underlying assumptions of GAAP (LO1–7)

1. Jumbo's is a local restaurant. Due to a bad shipment of potatoes, several of the company's customers become ill, and the company receives considerable bad publicity. Revenues are way down, several of its bills are past due, and the company is making plans to close the restaurant at the end of the month. The company continues to report its assets in the balance sheet at historical (original) cost.
2. Gorloks Tax Services is owned and operated by Sam Martin. The company has the usual business assets: land, building, cash, equipment, and supplies. In addition, Sam decides to buy a boat for him and his family to enjoy on the weekends. Sam includes the boat as an asset on the balance sheet of Gorloks Tax Services.
3. Claim Jumpers International, a U.S.-based company, has operations in the United States and in Europe. For the current year, the company purchased two trucks in the United States for $10,000 and three trucks in Europe for €20,000 (euros). Because of the differences in currencies, the company reported "Five Trucks" with no corresponding amount in the balance sheet.
4. Cobbers Etc. sells specialty music equipment ranging from African bongo drums to grand pianos. Because of the fluctuating nature of the business, management decides to publish financial statements only when a substantial amount of activity has taken place. Its last set of financial statements covered a period of 14 months, and the set of financial statements before that covered a period of 18 months.

Required:
For each situation, indicate which of the underlying assumptions of GAAP is violated.

P1–7A Listed below are nine terms and definitions associated with the FASB's conceptual framework.

Understand the components of the FASB's conceptual framework (LO1–7)

Terms	Definitions
1. _____ Completeness	a. Requires the consideration of the costs and value of information.
2. _____ Comparability	
3. _____ Neutrality	b. Ability to make comparisons between firms.
4. _____ Understandability	c. Comprehending the meaning of accounting information.
5. _____ Cost effectiveness	
6. _____ Verifiability	d. Including all information necessary to report the business activity.
	e. The business will last indefinitely unless there is evidence otherwise.

Terms	Definitions
7. _____ Decision usefulness	f. Recording transactions only for the company.
8. _____ Economic entity assumption	g. Implies consensus among different measures.
9. _____ Going concern assumption	h. Accounting should be useful in making decisions.
	i. Accounting information should not favor a particular group.

Required:

Pair each term with its related definition.

PROBLEMS: SET B

connect

Classify accounts (LO1–2)

P1–1B Below are typical transactions for **Caterpillar Inc.**

Type of Business Activity	Transactions
1. _____	Pay for advertising.
2. _____	Pay dividends to stockholders.
3. _____	Collect cash from customer for previous sale.
4. _____	Purchase a building to be used for operations.
5. _____	Purchase equipment.
6. _____	Sell land.
7. _____	Receive a loan from the bank by signing a note.
8. _____	Pay suppliers for purchase of supplies.
9. _____	Provide services to customers.
10. _____	Invest in securities of another company.

Required:

Indicate whether each transaction is classified as a financing, investing, or operating activity.

Assign business transactions to account classifications (LO1–2)

P1–2B Account classifications include assets, liabilities, stockholders' equity, dividends, revenues, and expenses.

Account Classifications	Accounts	Related Transactions
1. _____	Cash	Receive cash from customers.
2. _____	Service revenue	Provide services to customers.
3. _____	Supplies	Purchase supplies.
4. _____	Buildings	Purchase factory for operations.
5. _____	Advertising expense	Pay for cost of advertising.
6. _____	Equipment	Purchase equipment for operations.
7. _____	Interest expense	Pay for cost of interest.
8. _____	Accounts payable	Purchase supplies on credit.
9. _____	Dividends	Distribute cash to stockholders.
10. _____	Notes payable	Borrow from the bank.

Required:

For each transaction, indicate whether the related account would be classified in the balance sheet as (a) an asset, (b) a liability, or (c) stockholders' equity; in the income statement as (d) a revenue or (e) an expense; or in the statement of stockholders' equity as (f) a dividend.

Prepare financial statements (LO1–3)

P1–3B Gator Investments provides financial services related to investment selections, retirement planning, and general insurance needs. For the current year, the company reports the following amounts:

Advertising expense	$ 33,500	Service revenue	$127,600
Buildings	150,000	Interest expense	3,500
Salaries expense	65,100	Utilities expense	15,500
Accounts payable	6,400	Equipment	27,000
Cash	5,500	Notes payable	30,000

In addition, the company had common stock of $100,000 at the beginning of the year and issued an additional $11,000 during the year. The company also had retained earnings of $30,300 at the beginning of the year and paid dividends of $5,200.

Required:
Prepare the income statement, statement of stockholders' equity, and balance sheet for Gator Investments.

P1–4B Below are incomplete financial statements for Cyclone, Inc.

Understand the format of financial statements and the link among them (LO1–3)

CYCLONE, INC.
Income Statement

Revenues	(a)
Expenses:	
Salaries	$13,000
Rent	7,000
Advertising	5,000
Net income	(b)

CYCLONE, INC.
Statement of Stockholders' Equity

	Common Stock	Retained Earnings	Total S. Equity
Beginning balance	$14,000	$7,000	$21,000
Issuances of stock	(c)		(c)
Add: Net income		5,000	5,000
Less: Dividends		(d)	(d)
Ending balance	$17,000	$8,000	$25,000

CYCLONE, INC.
Balance Sheet

Assets		Liabilities	
Cash	$ 1,100	Accounts payable	$4,000
Supplies	(e)	**Stockholders' Equity**	
Land	6,000	Common stock	(g)
Building	16,000	Retained earnings	(h)
		Total liabilities and	
Total assets	(f)	stockholders' equity	(i)

Required:
Calculate the missing amounts.

P1–5B Tar Heel Corporation provides the following information at the end of 2018.

Prepare financial statements (LO1–3)

Salaries payable to workers at the end of the year	$ 3,300
Advertising expense for the year	10,400
Building that has been purchased	80,000
Supplies at the end of the year	4,600
Retained earnings	40,000
Utility expense for the year	6,000
Note payable to the bank	25,000
Service revenue earned during the year	69,400
Salary expense for the year	26,700
Accounts payable to suppliers	7,700
Dividends paid to shareholders during the year	(?)
Common stock that has been issued, including $6,000 that was issued this year	27,000
Cash remaining	5,200
Interest expense for the year	2,100
Accounts receivable from customers	13,200

Required:

Prepare the income statement, statement of stockholders' equity, and balance sheet for Tar Heel Corporation on December 31, 2018. The balance of retained earnings at the beginning of the year equals $26,800.

Identify underlying
assumptions of GAAP
(LO1–7)

P1–6B The four underlying assumptions of generally accepted accounting principles are economic entity, monetary unit, periodicity, and going concern. Consider the following four independent situations.

1. Mound Builders Groceries has over 1,000 grocery stores throughout the Northwest. Approximately 200,000 customers visit its stores each day. Because of the continual nature of grocery sales, the company does not publish an income statement. The company feels that it has an indefinite life and a periodic report would mislead investors.
2. Trolls Shipping provides delivery of packages between the United States and Japan. During the current year, the company delivered 3,000 packages for its U.S. customers totaling $25,000 in revenue. For its Japanese customers, the company delivered 1,000 packages totaling ¥1,000,000 (yen). The company's income statement indicates that total revenue equals 4,000 packages delivered with no corresponding amount in the income statement.
3. Slugs Typewriter has provided some of the finest typewriters in town for the past 50 years. Because of the advance of electronic word processors and computers, customer demand has dwindled over the years to almost nothing in the current year and the company can no longer pay its debts. For the most recent year, the company reports its assets in the balance sheet at historical (original) cost.
4. Blue Hose Carpet specializes in the installation of carpet and wood flooring. The company has the usual business expenses: salaries, supplies, utilities, advertising, and taxes. John Brewer, the company's owner, took his wife and two daughters to Disney World. John reported the airfare and hotel expenses in the income statement of Blue Hose Carpet.

Required:

For each situation, indicate which of the underlying assumptions of GAAP is violated.

Understand the
components of the FASB's
conceptual framework
(LO1–7)

P1–7B Listed below are several terms and definitions associated with the FASB's conceptual framework.

Terms	Definitions
1. _____ Predictive value	a. Decreases in equity resulting from transfers to owners.
2. _____ Relevance	b. Business transactions are measured using a common denominator.
3. _____ Timeliness	c. The indefinite life of a company can be broken into definite periods.
4. _____ Dividends	d. Information helps in understanding prior activities.
5. _____ Confirmatory value	e. Agreement between a measure and the phenomenon it represents.
6. _____ Faithful representation	f. Information arrives prior to the decision.
7. _____ Materiality	g. Information is related to the decision at hand.
8. _____ Monetary unit assumption	h. Information is useful in predicting the future.
9. _____ Periodicity assumption	i. Concerns the relative size of an item and its effect on decisions.

Required:

Pair each term with its related definition.

ADDITIONAL PERSPECTIVES

Great Adventures

**Continuing
Problem**

(The Great Adventures problem continues in each chapter.)

AP1–1 Tony Matheson plans to graduate from college in May 2018 after spending four years earning a degree in sports and recreation management. Since beginning T-ball at age five, he's been actively involved in sports and enjoys the outdoors. Each summer growing up, he and his father would spend two weeks at a father/son outdoor camp. These fond memories are part of the reason he chose his major. He wants to remain involved in these outdoor activities and provide others with the same adventures he was able to share with his dad. He decides to start an outdoor adventure company. However, he's not sure he has the business background necessary to do this.

This is where Suzie Ramos can help. Suzie also plans to graduate in May 2018 with a major in business. Suzie and Tony first met their sophomore year and have been friends ever since as they share a strong interest in sports and outdoor activities.

They decide to name their company Great Adventures. They will provide clinics for a variety of outdoor activities such as kayaking, mountain biking, rock climbing, wilderness survival techniques, orienteering, backpacking, and other adventure sports.

Required:

1. What are the three primary forms of business organizations Tony and Suzie might choose for Great Adventures? Explain the advantages and disadvantages of each. Which form do you recommend for Great Adventures?
2. Discuss some of the typical financing, investing, and operating activities that a company like Great Adventures is likely to have.
3. What specific account names for assets, liabilities, stockholders' equity, revenues, and expenses would the company likely use to record its business transactions?
4. To report company performance, Suzie plans to prepare the four primary financial statements. Explain the type of information provided by each statement.

American Eagle Outfitters, Inc.

Financial Analysis

AP1–2 Financial information for **American Eagle** is presented in **Appendix A** at the end of the book.

Required:

1. Determine the amounts American Eagle reports for total assets, total liabilities, and total stockholders' equity in the balance sheet for the most recent year. Verify that the basic accounting equation balances.
2. American Eagle refers to its income statement using another name. What is it?
3. Determine the amounts American Eagle reports for net sales and net income in its income statement for the most recent year.
4. For investing activities, what are the largest inflows and largest outflows for the most recent year reported in the statement of cash flows? For financing activities, what are the largest inflows and largest outflows?
5. Who is the company's auditor? (See the Report of Independent Registered Public Accounting Firm.) What does the report indicate about the amounts reported in the company's financial statements?

The Buckle, Inc.

Financial Analysis

AP1–3 Financial information for **Buckle** is presented in **Appendix B** at the end of the book.

Required:

1. Determine the amounts Buckle reports for total assets, total liabilities, and total stockholders' equity in the balance sheet for the most recent year. Verify that the basic accounting equation balances.

2. Buckle refers to its income statement using another name. What is it?
3. Determine the amounts Buckle reports for net sales and net income in its income statement for the most recent year.
4. For investing activities, what are the largest inflows and largest outflows for the most recent year reported in the statement of cash flows? For financing activities, what are the largest inflows and largest outflows?
5. Who is the company's auditor? (See the Report of Independent Registered Public Accounting Firm.) What does the report indicate about the amounts reported in the company's financial statements?

Comparative Analysis

American Eagle Outfitters, Inc. vs. The Buckle, Inc.

AP1–4 Financial information for **American Eagle** is presented in **Appendix A** at the end of the book, and financial information for **Buckle** is presented in **Appendix B** at the end of the book.

Required:
1. Which company reports higher total assets?
2. Which company reports higher total liabilities? Does this always mean this company has a higher chance of not being able to repay its debt and declare bankruptcy? Explain.
3. What relevant information do total assets and total liabilities provide to creditors deciding whether to lend money to American Eagle versus Buckle?
4. Which company reports higher net income? Does this always mean this company's operations are more profitable? Explain.
5. What relevant information does net income provide to investors who are deciding whether to invest in American Eagle versus Buckle?

Ethics

AP1–5 Management has the responsibility of accurately preparing financial statements when communicating with investors and creditors. Another group, auditors, serves an independent role by helping to ensure that management has in fact appropriately applied GAAP in preparing the company's financial statements. Auditors examine (audit) financial statements to express a professional, independent opinion. The opinion reflects the auditors' assessment of the statements' fairness, which is determined by the extent to which they are prepared in compliance with GAAP.

Suppose an auditor is being paid $1,000,000 by the company to perform the audit. In addition, the company plans to pay the auditor $500,000 over the next year for business consulting advice and another $200,000 for preparing its tax returns. The auditor and management of the company have always shared a friendly relationship, which partly explains the company's willingness to give the auditor additional work for $700,000.

Required:
How might an auditor's ethics be challenged while performing an audit?

Internet Research

AP1–6 The purpose of this research case is to introduce you to the Internet home pages of the Securities and Exchange Commission (SEC) and the Financial Accounting Standards Board (FASB).

Required:
1. Access the SEC home page on the Internet (*www.sec.gov*). Under "About the SEC," choose "What We Do." What is the mission of the SEC? Why was the SEC created? What are the two objectives of the 1933 Securities Act? The 1934 Securities Exchange Act established the SEC. What does the 1934 Act empower the SEC to require?
2. Access *www.sec.gov/investor/pubs/begfinstmtguide.htm.* What are the four main financial statements discussed by the SEC? What does each report? What information is disclosed in the notes and management discussion and analysis (MD&A)?

3. Access the FASB home page on the Internet (*www.fasb.org*). Select "Facts About FASB." Describe the mission of the FASB. What is the relation between the SEC and the FASB?

4. Obtain a copy of the annual report of **Nike, Inc.** for the most recent year. You can find the annual report at the company's website (*www.nike.com*) in the investor information section or at the SEC's website (*www.sec.gov*) using EDGAR (Electronic Data Gathering, Analysis, and Retrieval). The SEC requires that Form 10-K, which includes the annual report, be filed on EDGAR. Answer the following questions:

   a. Did Nike prepare the four financial statements discussed by the SEC?

   b. In the MD&A section, how does the company describe its business environment?

   c. Find the note disclosures to the financial statements. What does the disclosure on operating segment information discuss?

Written Communication

AP1–7 Maria comes to you for investment advice. She asks, "Which company's stock should I buy? There are so many companies to choose from and I don't know anything about any of them."

Required:

Respond to Maria by explaining the two functions of financial accounting. Specifically address the four financial statements reported by companies and the information contained in each. Also explain the role of the auditor in the preparation of financial statements. What advice can you give her about finding a company's stock to buy?

Answers to the Self-Study Questions

1. b   2. d   3. d   4. b   5. a   6. c   7. b   8. d   9. d   10. a

CHAPTER 2

The Accounting Cycle: During the Period

Learning Objectives

AFTER STUDYING THIS CHAPTER, YOU SHOULD BE ABLE TO:

- **LO2–1** Identify the basic steps in measuring external transactions.
- **LO2–2** Analyze the impact of external transactions on the accounting equation.
- **LO2–3** Assess whether the impact of external transactions results in a debit or credit to an account balance.
- **LO2–4** Record transactions in a journal using debits and credits.
- **LO2–5** Post transactions to the general ledger.
- **LO2–6** Prepare a trial balance.

WALMART: SHELVES OF BUSINESS TRANSACTIONS

Walmart opened its first store in Rogers, Arkansas, in 1962. By 1967, the company had increased to 24 stores totaling $12,600,000 in sales, and the following year it expanded operations to Missouri and Oklahoma. Today, Wal-Mart Stores, Inc. (the parent company) is the world's largest retailer with nearly $500,000,000,000 in sales. (That's $500 billion!) With more than 2.2 million employees worldwide, it's the largest private employer in the United States and Mexico and one of the largest in Canada. Each year Walmart purchases from over 60,000 vendors merchandise totaling nearly $400 billion. More than 260 million customers visit Walmart stores each week.

With billions of transactions with customers, suppliers, employees, and government agencies, how does Walmart's management keep track of the company's financial position? How do investors know whether the company is profitable and whether management is efficiently running the company? How do creditors know whether they should lend money to the company and whether the company will be able to pay its financial obligations as they become due?

To answer these questions, a system must be in place that can measure billions of transactions of Walmart, summarize those measurements in an efficient way, and then communicate them to management and other decision makers. These are the roles of financial accounting.

In this chapter, we review the measurement process financial accountants use to identify, analyze, record, and summarize transactions. We'll see that financial accounting involves assessing the impact that business transactions have on the company's financial position. These effects are then recorded in accounts. For example, all of Walmart's cash transactions (increases and decreases) are recorded in the Cash account. We then summarize all of the increases and decreases in an account over the accounting period to calculate the account's balance. A list of all account balances provides a summary picture of the company's current financial position and performance during the year.

Without the measurement process of financial accounting, it would be nearly impossible to analyze a company's operations. Having a firm grasp of this measurement process is key to your understanding of financial accounting.

© AP Images/Reed Saxon

PART A

MEASURING BUSINESS ACTIVITIES

Recall from Chapter 1 that the two functions of financial accounting are to (1) measure business activities of the company and (2) communicate those measurements to external parties for decision-making purposes. The full set of procedures used to accomplish this two-step measurement/communication process is referred to as the accounting cycle. In this chapter, we'll focus on the procedures related to *measuring* business activities *during the accounting period.* In Chapter 3, we'll complete the accounting cycle by examining the remaining procedures that occur at the *end of the accounting period.* Although nearly every company accomplishes the accounting cycle using a computerized accounting system, this chapter shows a manual system to help you better understand the basic model underlying computerized programs.

External Transactions

■ **LO2–1**
Identify the basic steps in measuring external transactions.

The business activities, or transactions, we want to measure and communicate are classified as either external or internal. External transactions are transactions the firm conducts with a separate economic entity. Examples are selling products to a customer, purchasing supplies from a vendor, paying salaries to an employee, and borrowing money from a bank. Internal transactions are events that affect the financial position of the company but do not include an exchange with a separate company or individual. Examples are using supplies already purchased and earning revenues after having received cash in advance from a customer. In this chapter, we focus on the measurement of external transactions occurring during the period. Internal transactions are recorded at the end of the period, so we save those for Chapter 3.

In Part A of the chapter, we'll cover 10 basic business transactions to understand their effects on a company's financial position. Then, in Part B we'll cover those same 10 transactions and see how companies formally record those transactions in the accounting records. The 10 transactions are clearly labeled in Part A and Part B so you can compare the analysis of the transactions with the recording of the transactions.

 KEY POINT

External transactions are transactions between the company and a separate company or individual. Internal transactions do not include an exchange with a separate economic entity.

Measuring external transactions is a six-step process, as outlined in Illustration 2–1. **These steps are the foundation for the remaining chapters in this book.** Make sure you understand them before you proceed.

ILLUSTRATION 2–1

Six Steps in Measuring External Transactions

mhhe.com/4fa4

Step 1 Use source documents to identify **accounts** affected by an external transaction.
Step 2 Analyze the impact of the transaction on the **accounting equation.**
Step 3 Assess whether the transaction results in a **debit** or **credit** to account balances.
Step 4 Record the transaction in a **journal** using debits and credits.
Step 5 Post the transaction to the **general ledger.**
Step 6 Prepare a **trial balance.**

The first step in the measurement process involves gathering information about a transaction. Source documents such as sales invoices, bills from suppliers, and signed contracts provide information related to external transactions. These source documents usually identify the date and nature of each transaction, the participating parties, and the monetary terms. For example, a sales invoice might identify the date of sale, the customer, the specific items sold, the dollar amount of the sale, and the payment terms.

Steps 2–6 involve conventions used by accountants to capture the effects of transactions in accounts. An account summarizes all **transactions related to a particular item over a period of time.** For instance, *asset accounts* include Cash, Supplies, and Equipment. All transactions affecting cash are summarized in the Cash account. When a company receives cash, the balance of the Cash account increases. When the company pays cash, the balance of the Cash account decreases. This is the way that all accounts work. Examples of *liability accounts* include Accounts Payable, Salaries Payable, Utilities Payable, and Taxes Payable. Each of these accounts keeps a balance of amounts owed as a result of the related transactions. *Stockholders' equity accounts* include Common Stock and Retained Earnings. A list of all account names used to record transactions of a company is referred to as the chart of accounts. (Later in the chapter, we'll see a preliminary chart of accounts. **A representative chart of accounts can be found at the end of the book.** Keep it handy for reference throughout the course.)

In this chapter and throughout the remainder of the book, you'll learn how to compute the balance of each account and eventually use these account balances to prepare the financial statements introduced in Chapter 1. But first, let's work through steps 2–6 of the measurement process to see how external business transactions are summarized in account balances.

KEY POINT

The six-step measurement process (Illustration 2–1) is the foundation of financial accounting. To understand this process, it is important to realize in Step 2 that we analyze the effects of business transactions on the accounting equation (Part A of this chapter). Then, in Step 3 we begin the process of translating those effects into the accounting records (Part B of this chapter).

Effects of Transactions on the Basic Accounting Equation

The activities we want to record are those that affect the financial position of the company. That means they affect the accounting equation you learned about in Chapter 1. Remember, the basic accounting equation shows that assets equal liabilities plus stockholders' equity. In other words, resources of the company equal claims to those resources by creditors and owners.

■ **LO2–2**

Analyze the impact of external transactions on the accounting equation.

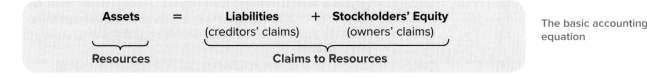

Assets	=	Liabilities	+	Stockholders' Equity
		(creditors' claims)		(owners' claims)
Resources		Claims to Resources		

The basic accounting equation

When **Walmart** borrows cash from a bank, its financial position is affected because assets (cash) increase and liabilities (the loan payable to the bank) increase. So, Walmart records that event in its accounting records. On the other hand, when Walmart hires Ralph as a front-door greeter, that action doesn't change the company's assets, liabilities, or stockholders' equity; Walmart's financial position is unaffected the day Ralph is hired, and until he begins work. Yes, Walmart hopes that hiring Ralph will favorably affect its financial position in the future, but the hiring itself does not.

The basic accounting equation must always remain in balance: The left side (assets) equals the right side (liabilities plus stockholders' equity). **Each transaction will have a dual effect.** If one side of the equation increases, then the other side of the equation increases by the same amount. That's what happens, for example, when Walmart borrows cash.

Sometimes, though, a transaction will not affect the *total* of either side. Let's say **Wendy's** buys new cash registers for its stores, paying cash. One asset (equipment) goes up; another asset (cash) goes down by the same amount. There's no change to assets *as a whole.* The accounting equation remains in balance. You can tell whether a transaction affects the accounting equation by considering its impact on the company's total resources—its total assets.

As the balance in an account changes, we record the increase or decrease in that specific account. Let's say we have $50,000 in cash. That's the *balance* in the Cash account. If we then collect $1,000 cash from a customer, the balance in the Cash account is now $51,000.

To see the effect of each transaction, ask yourself these questions:

1. **"What is one account in the accounting equation affected by the transaction? Does that account increase or decrease?"**

2. **"What is a second account in the accounting equation affected by the transaction? Does that account increase or decrease?"**

After noting the effects of the transaction on the accounting equation, ask yourself this:

3. **"Do assets equal liabilities plus stockholders' equity?"**

The answer to the third question must be "yes."

Most business transactions affect only two accounts.   However, there are some transactions that affect more than two accounts, and we'll cover those in later chapters. They are known as *compound transactions.*

The best way to understand the impact of a transaction on the accounting equation is to see it demonstrated by a few examples. Let's return to Eagle Golf Academy from Chapter 1. Illustration 2–2 summarizes the external transactions for Eagle in December, the first month of operations. (You may also want to refer back to the financial statements in Illustrations 1–5, 1–6, 1–7, and 1–8 to remind yourself how the transactions will eventually be reported.) We discuss the impact of these 10 transactions on the accounting equation later in this chapter.

ILLUSTRATION 2–2

External Transactions of Eagle Golf Academy

Transaction	Date	Description
(1)	Dec. 1	Sell shares of common stock for $25,000 to obtain the funds necessary to start the business.
(2)	Dec. 1	Borrow $10,000 from the local bank and sign a note promising to repay the full amount of the debt in three years.
(3)	Dec. 1	Purchase equipment necessary for giving golf training, $24,000 cash.
(4)	Dec. 1	Pay one year of rent in advance, $6,000 ($500 per month).
(5)	Dec. 6	Purchase supplies on account, $2,300.
(6)	Dec. 12	Provide golf training to customers for cash, $4,300.
(7)	Dec. 17	Provide golf training to customers on account, $2,000.
(8)	Dec. 23	Receive cash in advance for 12 golf training sessions to be given in the future, $600.
(9)	Dec. 28	Pay salaries to employees, $2,800.
(10)	Dec. 30	Pay cash dividends of $200 to shareholders.

TRANSACTION (1): ISSUE COMMON STOCK

To begin operations, Eagle Golf Academy needs cash. To generate cash from external sources, Eagle sells shares of common stock to investors for $25,000. In other words, the company receives cash of $25,000 from investors, who in turn become owners of the company by receiving shares of common stock.

Eagle Golf Academy

Stock Certificate

Investors

It's time to ask the three questions we asked earlier:

1. **"What is one account in the accounting equation affected by the transaction? Does that account increase or decrease?"**

   Answer: **Cash.** Cash is a resource owned by the company, which makes it an asset. The company receives cash from investors, so cash and total assets **increase** by $25,000.

2. **"What is a second account in the accounting equation affected by the transaction? Does that account increase or decrease?"**

   Answer: **Common Stock.** Common Stock is a stockholders' equity account. Issuing common stock to investors in exchange for $25,000 cash increases the amount of common stock owned by the company's stockholders, so common stock and total stockholders' equity both **increase.**

   Issuing common stock for cash increases both sides of the accounting equation:

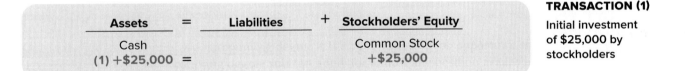

Assets	=	**Liabilities**	+	**Stockholders' Equity**
Cash				Common Stock
(1) +$25,000 =				+$25,000

TRANSACTION (1)

Initial investment of $25,000 by stockholders

3. **"Do assets equal liabilities plus stockholders' equity?"**

   Answer: **Yes.**

   Note that the accounting equation balances. If one side of the equation increases, so does the other side. We can use this same series of questions to understand the effect of *any* business transaction. Let's try another one.

 COMMON MISTAKE

It's sometimes tempting to *decrease* cash as a way of recording an investor's initial investment. However, we account for transactions *from the company's perspective,* and the company *received* cash from the stockholder—an increase in cash.

TRANSACTION (2): BORROW CASH FROM THE BANK

Seeking cash from another external source, Eagle borrows $10,000 from the bank and signs a note promising to repay it in three years.

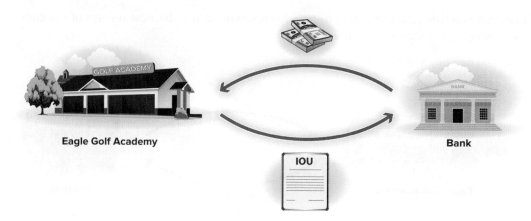

Eagle Golf Academy

Bank

IOU

1. **"What is one account in the accounting equation affected by the transaction? Does that account increase or decrease?"**

   Answer: **Cash.** Cash is a resource owned by the company, which makes it an asset. The company receives cash, so cash and total assets **increase.**

2. **"What is a second account in the accounting equation affected by the transaction? Does that account increase or decrease?"**

   Answer: **Notes Payable.** Notes payable represent amounts owed to creditors (the bank in this case), which makes them a liability. The company incurs debt when signing the note, so notes payable and total liabilities **increase.**

   Borrowing by signing a note causes both assets and liabilities to increase:

TRANSACTION (2)

Borrow $10,000 from the bank and sign a three-year note

Assets	=	Liabilities	+	Stockholders' Equity
Cash		Notes Payable		Common Stock
Bal. $ 25,000				$25,000
(2) +$10,000		+$10,000		
Bal. $ 35,000		$ 10,000		$25,000
$ 35,000	=		$35,000	

3. **"Do assets equal liabilities plus stockholders' equity?"**

   Answer: **Yes.**

   After these two transactions, the accounting equation remains in balance. Notice that the $10,000 cash collected on the note adds to the $25,000 cash received from stockholders. The total resources of the company equal $35,000. Creditors' claims to those resources total $10,000, and the remaining $25,000 in resources were provided by stockholders.

   Regardless of the number of transactions occurring during the period, the accounting equation always must remain in balance. For brevity, we do not address the three-question process for Eagle's remaining eight transactions, but you should ask yourself those questions until you feel comfortable with the process.

 KEY POINT

   After each transaction, the accounting equation must always remain in balance. In other words, assets must always equal liabilities plus stockholders' equity.

TRANSACTION (3): PURCHASE EQUIPMENT

Once Eagle obtains financing by issuing common stock and borrowing from the bank, the company can invest in long-term assets necessary to operate the business.

Eagle Golf Academy   Supplier

Buying equipment from a supplier causes one asset (equipment) to increase and another asset (cash) to decrease:

	Assets		=	Liabilities	+	Stockholders' Equity
	Cash	Equipment		Notes Payable		Common Stock
Bal.	$ 35,000			$10,000		$25,000
(3)	−$24,000	+$24,000				
Bal.	$ 11,000	$ 24,000		$10,000		$25,000
	$35,000		=		$35,000	

TRANSACTION (3)

Purchase equipment with cash, $24,000

Because purchasing one asset (equipment) with another asset (cash) has no effect on total assets, the accounting equation remains in balance.

TRANSACTION (4): PAY FOR RENT IN ADVANCE

On December 1, Eagle signs an agreement with a local golf course to rent space in the clubhouse and on the driving range to provide golf training to its customers. At the time the agreement is signed, Eagle pays one year of rent in advance, $6,000. Because the rent paid is for occupying space in the future, we record it as an asset representing a resource of the company. We call the asset *prepaid rent.* Other common examples of prepaid assets include prepaid insurance and prepaid advertising. These items often are purchased prior to their use.

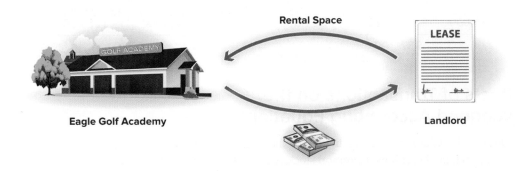

Rental Space

LEASE

Eagle Golf Academy   Landlord

Paying rent in advance causes one asset (prepaid rent) to increase and one asset (cash) to decrease:

TRANSACTION (4)

Pay one year of rent in advance, $6,000

	Assets			=	Liabilities	+	Stockholders' Equity
	Cash	Prepaid Rent	Equipment		Notes Payable		Common Stock
Bal.	$11,000		$24,000		$10,000		$25,000
(4)	−$ 6,000	+$6,000					
Bal.	$ 5,000	$6,000	$24,000		$10,000		$25,000
		$35,000		=		$35,000	

TRANSACTION (5): PURCHASE SUPPLIES ON ACCOUNT

On December 6, Eagle purchases supplies on account. The phrase *on account* indicates that the company does not pay cash immediately but promises to pay cash in the future. While supplies represent a resource of the company (an asset), the promise to pay later is an obligation (a liability). We refer to a liability of this type, in which we purchase something on account, as an *account payable*. The term *payable* means "to be paid in the future." Thus, the Accounts Payable account is a record of specific people and companies to whom we expect to pay cash in the future.

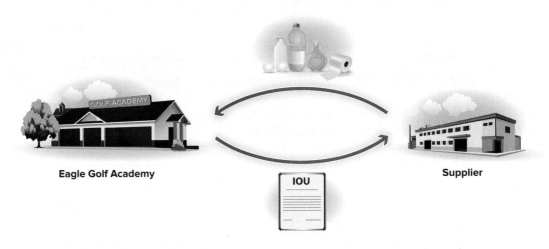

Eagle Golf Academy   IOU   Supplier

Purchasing supplies with the promise to pay cash in the future causes an asset (supplies) to increase and also causes a liability (accounts payable) to increase:

TRANSACTION (5)

Purchase supplies on account, $2,300

	Assets				=	Liabilities		+	Stockholders' Equity
	Cash	Supplies	Prepaid Rent	Equipment		Accounts Payable	Notes Payable		Common Stock
Bal.	$5,000		$6,000	$24,000			$10,000		$25,000
(5)		+$2,300				+$2,300			
Bal.	$5,000	$2,300	$6,000	$24,000		$ 2,300	$10,000		$25,000
		$37,300			=		$37,300		

Effects of Transactions on the Expanded Accounting Equation

As discussed in Chapter 1, we can divide stockholders' equity into its two components—common stock and retained earnings. Common stock represents investments by stockholders. Retained earnings represents net income reported over the life of the company that has *not* been distributed to stockholders as dividends. Both common stock and retained earnings represent stockholders' claims to the company's resources. Next, we can split retained earnings into its three components—revenues, expenses, and dividends. Illustration 2–3 presents the expanded accounting equation, which shows these components.

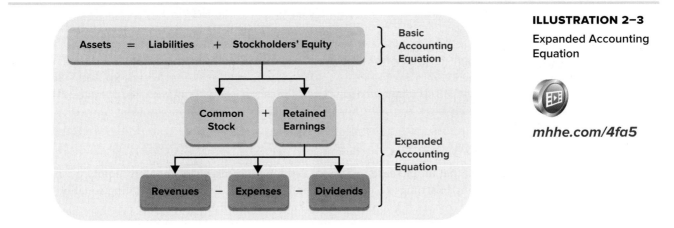

ILLUSTRATION 2–3

Expanded Accounting Equation

mhhe.com/4fa5

Be sure to notice the effects of revenues, expenses, and dividends on retained earnings (and therefore on total stockholders' equity) in the expanded accounting equation:

1. We *add* revenues to calculate retained earnings. That's because revenues increase net income, and net income increases stockholders' claims to resources. **Therefore, an** *increase* **in revenues has the effect of** *increasing* **stockholders' equity in the basic accounting equation.**

2. We *subtract* expenses and dividends to calculate retained earnings. Expenses reduce net income, and dividends represent a distribution of net income to stockholders. Both expenses and dividends reduce stockholders' claims to the company's resources. **Therefore, an** *increase* **in expenses or dividends has the effect of** *decreasing* **stockholders' equity in the basic accounting equation.**

KEY POINT

The expanded accounting equation demonstrates that revenues increase retained earnings while expenses and dividends decrease retained earnings. Retained earnings is a component of stockholders' equity.

TRANSACTION (6): PROVIDE SERVICES FOR CASH

To see an example of how revenue affects the expanded accounting equation, let's first consider the revenue recognition principle, which states that companies record revenue *at the time they provide goods and services to customers.* In transaction (6), Eagle provides golf training to customers who pay cash at the time of the service, $4,300. Because Eagle has provided services, it has revenues from customers.

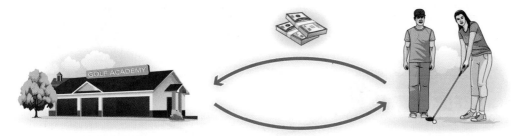

Eagle Golf Academy   Training   Customers

Providing services to customers for cash causes an asset (cash) and stockholders' equity (service revenue) to increase:

TRANSACTION (6)   Provide golf training to customers for cash, $4,300

	Assets				=	Liabilities		+	Stockholders' Equity	
	Cash	Supplies	Prepaid Rent	Equipment		Accounts Payable	Notes Payable		Common Stock	Retained Earnings
Bal.	$5,000	$2,300	$6,000	$24,000		$2,300	$10,000		$25,000	
(6)	+$4,300									+$4,300 Service Revenue
Bal.	$9,300	$2,300	$6,000	$24,000		$2,300	$10,000		$25,000	$4,300
			$41,600		=			$41,600		

Notice that an increase in Service Revenue increases stockholders' equity by increasing the Retained Earnings account (+$4,300). Therefore, the basic accounting equation remains in balance (Assets = Liabilities + Stockholders' Equity).

As shown in Illustration 2–3, revenues are a component of retained earnings. When a company records revenue, the amount of retained earnings (or net income) in the business increases. We can increase retained earnings by increasing its revenue component. Stated another way, an increase in revenues increases net income, which increases retained earnings, which increases total stockholders' equity:

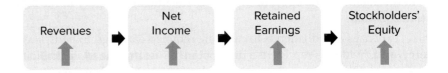

Revenues ➡ Net Income ➡ Retained Earnings ➡ Stockholders' Equity

TRANSACTION (7): PROVIDE SERVICES ON ACCOUNT

In transaction (7), other customers receive golf training but do not pay cash at the time of the service. Instead, these customers promise to pay $2,000 cash at some time in the future. Does failure to receive cash at the time of the service prevent Eagle from recording revenue? No. According to the revenue recognition principle discussed previously in transaction (6), Eagle has provided those services to customers and therefore has revenue. In addition, the *right* to receive cash from a customer is something of value the company owns, and therefore represents an asset. When a customer does not immediately pay for services with cash, we traditionally say the services are performed "on account," and we recognize an asset called *accounts receivable*. The term *receivable* means "to be received in the future." Thus, the Accounts Receivable account is a record of specific people and companies from whom we expect to receive cash in the future.

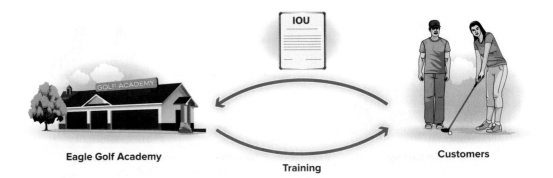

Eagle Golf Academy   Training   Customers

Providing services to customers on account causes an asset (accounts receivable) and stockholders' equity (service revenue) to increase:

TRANSACTION (7)   Provide golf training to customers on account, $2,000

		Assets				=	Liabilities		+ Stockholders' Equity		
	Cash	Accounts Receivable	Supplies	Prepaid Rent	Equipment		Accounts Payable	Notes Payable	Common Stock	Retained Earnings	
Bal.	$9,300		$2,300	$6,000	$24,000		$2,300	$10,000	$25,000	$ 4,300	
(7)		+$2,000								+$2,000	Service
Bal.	$9,300	$ 2,000	$2,300	$6,000	$24,000		$2,300	$10,000	$25,000	$ 6,300	Revenue
			$43,600			=			$43,600		

TRANSACTION (8): RECEIVE CASH IN ADVANCE FROM CUSTOMERS

Rather than providing services before receiving cash as in transaction (7), companies sometimes receive cash in advance from customers. In transaction (8), Eagle receives $600 from customers for golf training to be provided later. In this case, Eagle cannot report revenue from training at the time it receives this cash because it has yet to provide services to those customers. Recall that the *revenue recognition principle* states that revenue is recorded when goods and services are provided to customers. In the case of transaction (8), receiving cash in advance from customers creates an obligation for the company to perform services in the future. This future obligation is a liability (or debt), most commonly referred to as *deferred revenue*.[1]

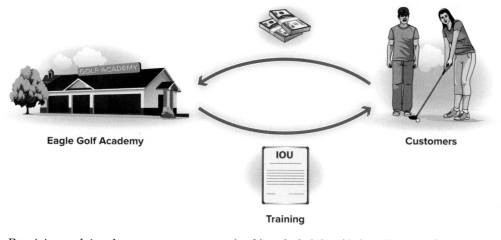

Eagle Golf Academy   Customers

IOU

Training

Receiving cash in advance causes an asset (cash) and a liability (deferred revenue) to increase:

TRANSACTION (8)   Receive cash in advance from customers, $600

		Assets				=	Liabilities			+ Stockholders' Equity	
	Cash	Accounts Receivable	Supplies	Prepaid Rent	Equipment		Accounts Payable	Deferred Revenue	Notes Payable	Common Stock	Retained Earnings
Bal.	$9,300	$2,000	$2,300	$6,000	$24,000		$2,300		$10,000	$25,000	$ 6,300
(8)	+$ 600							+$600			
Bal.	$9,900	$2,000	$2,300	$6,000	$24,000		$2,300	$600	$10,000	$25,000	$ 6,300
			$44,200			=			$44,200		

---

[1]Deferred revenue is sometimes referred to as the unearned revenue. The use of the term "deferred revenue" is increasingly popular in practice and is more consistent with the FASB's 2014 update of the revenue recognition principle (ASU No. 2014-09), which eliminates the "earnings" process in defining revenue. The term "deferred revenue" is also helpful in emphasizing that revenue is initially deferred but will be recorded eventually when the service is provided.

COMMON MISTAKE

Don't let the account name fool you. Even though the term *revenue* appears in the account title for *deferred revenue*, this is not a revenue account. *Deferred* indicates that the company has yet to provide services even though it has collected the customer's cash. The company owes the customer a service, which creates a liability.

TRANSACTION (9): PAY SALARIES TO EMPLOYEES

Companies incur a variety of costs in running the business. In transaction (9), Eagle pays salaries to employees for work in the current month. Because these salaries represent a cost of the current period, Eagle records them in the current month as salaries expense of $2,800.

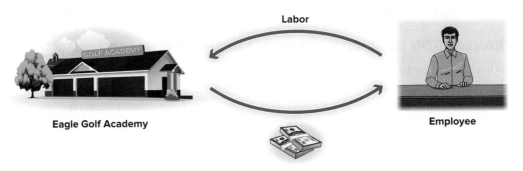

Labor

Eagle Golf Academy   Employee

Paying salaries for the current period causes an asset (cash) to decrease and stockholders' equity to decrease (and salaries expense to increase):

TRANSACTION (9)   Pay salaries to employees, $2,800

	Cash	Accounts Receivable	Supplies	Prepaid Rent	Equipment	=	Accounts Payable	Deferred Revenue	Notes Payable	+	Common Stock	Retained Earnings	
	Assets					=	**Liabilities**			+	**Stockholders' Equity**		
Bal.	$9,900	$2,000	$2,300	$6,000	$24,000		$2,300	$600	$10,000		$25,000	$6,300	
(9)	−$2,800											−$2,800	Salaries Expense
Bal.	$7,100	$2,000	$2,300	$6,000	$24,000		$2,300	$600	$10,000		$25,000	$3,500	
			$41,400			=			$41,400				

Notice that an *increase* in Salaries Expense results in a *decrease* in Retained Earnings (−$2,800). As a result, the accounting equation remains in balance, with both sides decreasing by $2,800. The concept of expenses flowing into retained earnings is the same concept that we see in transactions (6) and (7) where revenues also flow into retained earnings, but in the opposite direction.

Expenses *reduce* net income and therefore *reduce* the amount of retained earnings, a stockholders' equity account. Stated another way, an increase in expenses decreases net income, which decreases retained earnings, which decreases total stockholders' equity:

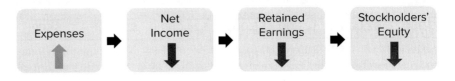

Expenses ➡ Net Income ➡ Retained Earnings ➡ Stockholders' Equity

Beyond salaries expense, companies have a number of other expenses. Most expense accounts are labeled with the word *expense* in the title. For instance, common expense accounts include Supplies Expense, Utilities Expense, Rent Expense, Advertising Expense, Interest Expense, and Insurance Expense.

When a company has a cost that benefits future periods, then we typically record an asset rather than an expense. For example, in transaction (3) we had the cost of equipment, in transaction (4) we had the cost of rent, and in transaction (5) we had the cost of supplies. In each of these transactions, the cost represented the purchase of a resource that will provide a benefit to the company beyond the date of the transaction, so we recorded each of these as assets.

TRANSACTION (10): PAY CASH DIVIDENDS

The final transaction of Eagle Golf Academy for the month is the payment of a $200 cash dividend to stockholders. Recall from the previous chapter that a dividend represents a payment of cash to the owners (stockholders) of the company. Normally a company wouldn't pay dividends after only a month in business, but we make this assumption here for purposes of illustration.

Reduced Claims to Company's Resources

Eagle Golf Academy

Investors

Paying dividends causes an asset (cash) to decrease and stockholders' equity to decrease (and dividends to increase):

TRANSACTION (10)   Pay dividends to stockholders, $200

		Assets			=		Liabilities		+	Stockholders' Equity	
	Cash	Accounts Receivable	Supplies	Prepaid Rent	Equipment	Accounts Payable	Deferred Revenue	Notes Payable	Common Stock	Retained Earnings	
Bal.	$7,100	$2,000	$2,300	$6,000	$24,000	$2,300	$600	$10,000	$25,000	$3,500	
(10)	−$ 200									−$ 200	Dividends
Bal.	$6,900	$2,000	$2,300	$6,000	$24,000	$2,300	$600	$10,000	$25,000	$3,300	
		$41,200				=			$41,200		

Like expenses, dividends reduce retained earnings, but dividends are *not* expenses. Instead, dividends are distributions of part of the company's net income to the owners, reducing the amount of earnings that have been retained in the business. Therefore, an *increase* in Dividends results in a *decrease* in Retained Earnings (−$200). The accounting equation remains in balance, with both sides decreasing by $200. Because retained earnings is a stockholders' equity account, when retained earnings decreases, so does stockholders' equity:

Dividends → Retained Earnings → Stockholders' Equity

COMMON MISTAKE

Students often believe a payment of dividends to owners increases stockholders' equity. Remember, you are accounting for the resources *of the company*. While stockholders have more personal cash after dividends have been paid, the company in which they own stock has *fewer* resources (less cash).

Illustration 2–4 summarizes all 10 of the month's transactions we just analyzed for Eagle Golf Academy. Notice that the accounting equation remains in balance.

ILLUSTRATION 2–4   Summary of All 10 External Transactions of Eagle Golf Academy

		Assets				=	Liabilities			+ Stockholders' Equity		
	Cash	Accounts Receivable	Supplies	Prepaid Rent	Equipment		Accounts Payable	Deferred Revenue	Notes Payable	Common Stock	Retained Earnings	
Dec. 1	$0	$0	$0	$0	$0		$0	$0	$0	$0	$0	
(1)	+25,000									+25,000		
(2)	+10,000								+10,000			
(3)	−24,000				+24,000							
(4)	−6,000			+6,000								
(5)			+2,300				+2,300					
(6)	+4,300										+4,300	Service Revenue
(7)		+2,000									+2,000	Service Revenue
(8)	+600							+600				
(9)	−2,800										−2,800	Salaries Expense
(10)	−200										−200	Dividends
Dec. 31	$6,900	$2,000	$2,300	$6,000	$24,000		$2,300	$600	$10,000	$25,000	$3,300	
			$41,200			=				$41,200		

Let's Review

mhhe.com/4fa6

Bogey Incorporated has the following transactions during May:

May 1   Purchase a storage building by obtaining a loan of $5,000.
May 6   Provide services to customers for cash, $1,800.
May 12   Pay $1,200 cash for advertising in May.
May 17   Repay $1,000 of the amount borrowed on May 1.
May 25   Purchase office supplies for $800 cash.

Required:

Indicate how each transaction affects the accounting equation.

Solution:

	Assets	=	Liabilities	+	Stockholders' Equity	
					Common Stock	Retained Earnings
May 1	+$5,000		+$5,000			
May 6	+$1,800					+$1,800
May 12	−$1,200					−$1,200
May 17	−$1,000		−$1,000			
May 25	+$ 800					
	−$ 800					
	+$4,600	=	+$4,000	+		+$ 600

Suggested Homework:
BE2–2, BE2–4;
E2–2, E2–3, E2–4;
P2–1A&B, P2–2A&B

DEBITS AND CREDITS

As we saw in the previous section, transactions have the effect of increasing or decreasing account balances. While the terms *increase* and *decrease* are well understood, accountants more often use the terms *debit* and *credit* to indicate whether an account balance has increased or decreased. Here, we introduce those terms, discuss their effect on account balances, and show how we record transactions using debits and credits.

Effects on Account Balances in the Basic Accounting Equation

You will need to learn how to increase and decrease account balances using the terms debit and credit because that's the language of accounting. Although debit and credit are derived from Latin terms, today **debit** simply means "left" and **credit** means "right." Their use dates back to 1494 and a Franciscan monk by the name of Luca Pacioli.

■ **LO2–3**

Assess whether the impact of external transactions results in a debit or credit to an account balance.

Let's start with the three account types in the basic accounting equation. Look at Illustration 2–5, which summarizes the effect of debits and credits on account balances.

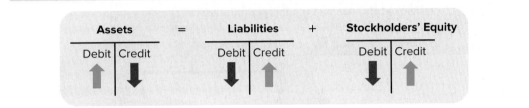

ILLUSTRATION 2–5

Debit and Credit Effects on Accounts in the Basic Accounting Equation

 COMMON MISTAKE

Some students think the term "debit" *always* means increase and "credit" *always* means decrease. While this is true for assets, it is *not* true for liabilities and stockholders' equity. Liabilities and stockholders' equity increase with a credit and decrease with a debit.

The balances of accounts in each of these categories can increase or decrease when a transaction occurs. For example, if a company receives cash (an asset), the balance of the Cash account increases. Likewise, when a company pays cash, the balance of the Cash account decreases. In accounting terminology, we refer to the increase in cash as a "debit to cash." We refer to the decrease in cash as a "credit to cash." This same approach is used for all asset accounts: **We refer to increases in assets as debits, and we refer to decreases in assets as credits.**

Just the opposite is true for accounts on the right-hand side of the accounting equation: **We refer to increases in liabilities and stockholders' equity as credits, and decreases in those accounts as debits.**

 KEY POINT

For the basic accounting equation (Assets = Liabilities + Stockholders' Equity), assets (left side) increase with *debits*. Liabilities and stockholders' equity (right side) increase with *credits*. The opposite is true to decrease any of these accounts.

Effects on Account Balances in the Expanded Accounting Equation

As we discussed previously in Illustration 2–3, we can expand the basic accounting equation to include the components of stockholders' equity (common stock and retained earnings)

and the components of retained earnings (revenues, expenses, and dividends). Because common stock and retained earnings are part of stockholders' equity, it follows directly that we increase both with a credit.

Revenues *increase* retained earnings ("there's more to keep"). Retained Earnings is a credit account, so we increase revenues with a credit. Expenses, on the other hand, *decrease* retained earnings ("there's less to keep"). Thus, we do the opposite of what we do with revenues: We increase expenses with a debit. **A debit to an expense is essentially a debit to Retained Earnings, decreasing the account.** Similarly, dividends *decrease* retained earnings, so we also record an increase in dividends with a debit. In Illustration 2–6 we show the effects of debits and credits on the components of stockholders' equity in the expanded accounting equation.

ILLUSTRATION 2–6

Debit and Credit Effects on Accounts in the Expanded Accounting Equation

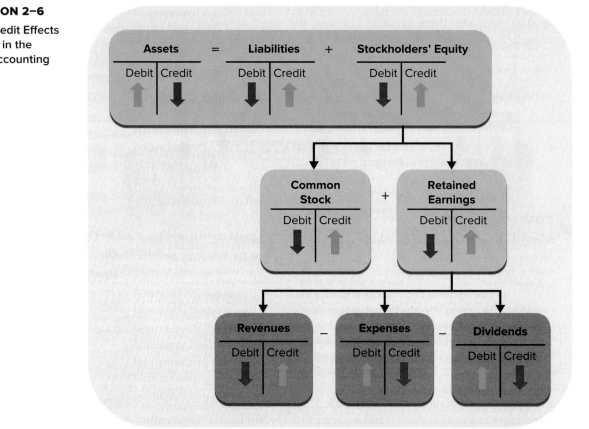

When a company earns revenues, we credit the revenue account because the amount of revenue increases. When a company incurs expenses, we debit the expense account because the amount of expense increases.

 KEY POINT

The Retained Earnings account is a stockholders' equity account that normally has a credit balance. The Retained Earnings account has three components—revenues, expenses, and dividends. Revenues (increased by credits) increase the balance of retained earnings. Expenses and dividends (increased by debits) decrease the balance of retained earnings.

Decision Point

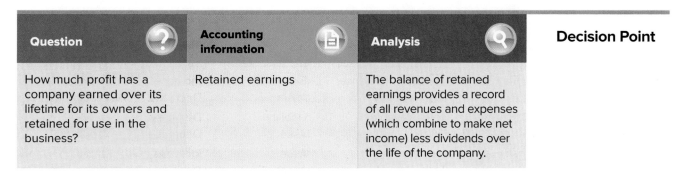

Question	Accounting information	Analysis
How much profit has a company earned over its lifetime for its owners and retained for use in the business?	Retained earnings	The balance of retained earnings provides a record of all revenues and expenses (which combine to make net income) less dividends over the life of the company.

Illustration 2–7 provides a simple memory aid that can help you remember debits and credits. Remember the acronym **DEALOR** and you'll be able to recall the effect that debits and credits have on account balances.

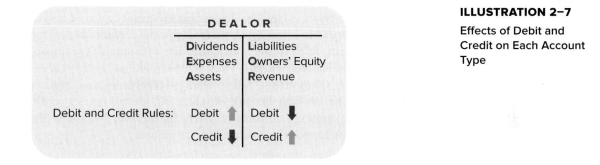

ILLUSTRATION 2–7

Effects of Debit and Credit on Each Account Type

The three accounts on the left, or debit, side of **DEALOR**—Dividends, Expenses, and Assets—increase with a debit and decrease with a credit. In contrast, the three accounts on the right, or credit, side—Liabilities, **O**wners' (stockholders') equity, and **R**evenues—increase with a credit and decrease with a debit.

Common Terms Another name for stockholders' equity is *owners' equity*, since stockholders are the owners of a company.

Let's Review

Bogey Incorporated has the following transactions during May:

May 1 Purchase a storage building by obtaining a loan of $5,000.
May 6 Provide services to customers for cash, $1,800.
May 12 Pay $1,200 cash for advertising in May.
May 17 Repay $1,000 of the amount borrowed on May 1.
May 25 Purchase office supplies for $800 cash.

Required:

For each transaction, (1) identify the two accounts involved, (2) the type of account, (3) whether the transaction increases or decreases the account balance, and (4) whether the increase or decrease would be recorded with a debit or credit.

Solution:

Date	(1) Accounts Involved	(2) Account Type	(3) Increase or Decrease	(4) Debit or Credit
May 1	Buildings	Asset	Increase	Debit
	Notes Payable	Liability	Increase	Credit
May 6	Cash	Asset	Increase	Debit
	Service Revenue	Revenue	Increase	Credit

(continued)

(concluded)

Date	(1) Accounts Involved	(2) Account Type	(3) Increase or Decrease	(4) Debit or Credit
May 12	Advertising Expense	Expense	Increase	Debit
	Cash	Asset	Decrease	Credit
May 17	Notes Payable	Liability	Decrease	Debit
	Cash	Asset	Decrease	Credit
May 25	Supplies	Asset	Increase	Debit
	Cash	Asset	Decrease	Credit

Suggested Homework:
BE2–5, BE2–6;
E2–6, E2–7;
P2–3A&B

Recording Transactions in a Journal

■ **LO2–4**

Record transactions in a journal using debits and credits.

We have just discussed whether the impact of an external transaction results in a debit or credit to an account balance. Next, we'll learn how to formally record transactions using those same debits and credits in a journal. A journal provides a chronological record of all transactions affecting a firm. Prior to the widespread use of computers, companies recorded their transactions in paper-based journals. Thus, the term journal entry was used to describe the format for recording a transaction. Today, nearly all companies have easy access to computers, and paper-based journals have become obsolete, but journal entries continue to be made in a computerized accounting information system. Illustration 2–8 shows the format we'll use throughout the book to record a company's transactions.

ILLUSTRATION 2–8

Format for Recording a Business Transaction, or Journal Entry

Date	Debit	Credit
Account Name	Amount	
Account Name		Amount
(Description of transaction)		

The entry that records a transaction has a place for the date of the transaction, the relevant account names, debit amounts, credit amounts, and a description of the transaction. We first list the account to be debited; below that, and indented to the right, we list the account to be credited. The entry has two amount columns—one for debits, one for credits. Because the amounts always represent dollar amounts (not number of units, for example), the dollar sign ($) is not used. As you might expect, the left-hand column is for debits, and the right-hand column is for credits. **For each journal entry, total debits must always equal total credits.** A brief description of the transaction is customarily included at the bottom to leave an information trail for later reference if necessary.

 COMMON MISTAKE

Many students forget to indent the credit account names. For the account credited, be sure to indent both the account name and the amount.

Think of recording a transaction as if you're writing a sentence form of the "accounting language." For example, recall in transaction (1) that "On December 1, Eagle Golf Academy sells shares of common stock to investors for cash of $25,000." Here is this same sentence about transaction (1) written in the language of accounting:

TRANSACTION (1)

Initial investment of $25,000 by stockholders

December 1	Debit	Credit
Cash *(+A)*..	**25,000**	
Common Stock *(+SE)*..		**25,000**
(Issue common stock for cash)		

Just as every English sentence uses at least one noun and one verb, every accounting sentence includes at least one debit and one credit. While not a formal part of recording transactions, we'll use a notation in parentheses beside the account name in Chapters 2 and 3 to help you get more familiar with the effect of debits and credits on the account balance. Thus, the entry shows that transaction (1) causes total assets to increase ($+A$) and total stockholders' equity to increase ($+SE$). Increases to assets are recorded with a debit, and increases to stockholders' equity are recorded with a credit. **You will need to learn to read and write in the language of accounting as this is the language used throughout the business world.**

KEY POINT

For each transaction, total debits must equal total credits.

COMMON MISTAKE

Students sometimes hear the phrase "assets are the debit accounts" and believe it indicates that assets can only be debited. This is incorrect! Assets, or any account, can be *either* debited or credited. Rather, this phrase indicates that debiting the asset account will increase the balance and that an asset account normally will have a debit balance. Similarly, the phrase "liabilities and stockholders' equity are the credit accounts" does *not* mean that these accounts cannot be debited. They will be debited when their balances decrease. Rather, the phrase means that crediting the liabilities and stockholders' equity accounts increases their balances, and they normally will have a credit balance.

The formal account names used to record transactions in the journal are listed in the *chart of accounts*. Illustration 2–9 provides the chart of accounts for Eagle Golf Academy based on the 10 transactions covered to this point. Later, we'll introduce other transactions and accounts for Eagle. **At the back of the book, you'll see a chart of accounts that includes all accounts used throughout the book.**

EAGLE GOLF ACADEMY
Chart of Accounts (preliminary)

Assets	Liabilities	Stockholders' Equity
Cash	Accounts Payable	Common Stock
Accounts Receivable	Deferred Revenue	Retained Earnings
Supplies	Notes Payable	**Dividends:**
Prepaid Rent		Dividends
Equipment		**Revenues:**
		Service Revenue
		Expenses:
		Salaries Expense

ILLUSTRATION 2–9

Preliminary Chart of Accounts for Eagle Golf Academy

Posting to the General Ledger

■ LO2–5
Post transactions to the general ledger.

As discussed in the previous section, a journal provides in a single location a chronological listing of every transaction affecting a company. As such, it serves as a handy way to review specific transactions and to locate any accounting errors at their original source. But it's not a convenient format for calculating account balances to use in preparing financial statements. You don't need to stretch your imagination too far to see that even for a very small company with few transactions, calculating account balances from a list of journal entries would very soon become unmanageable. Just imagine how lengthy the journal would be for

Walmart. If each sales transaction with a customer took about one inch of space, the journal would be over 150,000 miles long by the end of the year.

To make the calculation of account balances more efficient, we need to collect all transactions affecting an account in one location. We do this through a process called *posting*. Formally, posting is the process of transferring the debit and credit information from the journal to individual accounts in the general ledger. The general ledger provides in a single location the list of transactions affecting each account and the account's balance.

A general ledger account includes an account title, transaction date, transaction description, and columns for debits, credits, and the cumulative account balance. Illustration 2–10 presents the a basic format used for general ledger accounts.

ILLUSTRATION 2–10

General Ledger Account

Account: Title				
Date	Description	Debit	Credit	Balance

Computerized systems automatically and instantly post information from the journal to the general ledger accounts. Here, we will see the formal process of recording transactions in a journal and then posting them to the general ledger by working through the 10 transactions of Eagle Golf Academy listed in Illustration 2–2.

TRANSACTION (1): ISSUE COMMON STOCK

In transaction (1), Eagle issues common stock for $25,000 cash. As demonstrated in the previous section, Eagle records a debit to Cash and a credit to Common Stock in the journal. We debit Cash because it's an asset account, and asset balances increase with a debit. We credit Common Stock because it's a stockholders' equity account, and these balances increase with a credit.

Now, let's record the transaction in the journal and then post the debit and credit to the general ledger accounts.

TRANSACTION (1)

Initial investment of $25,000 by stockholders

December 1	Debit	Credit
Cash *(+A)*	25,000	
Common Stock *(+SE)*		25,000
(Issue common stock for cash)		

Account: Cash				
Date	Description	Debit	Credit	Balance
Dec. 1	Beginning balance			0
Dec. 1	Issue common stock for cash	25,000		25,000

Account: Common Stock				
Date	Description	Debit	Credit	Balance
Dec. 1	Beginning balance			0
Dec. 1	Issue common stock for cash		25,000	25,000

Notice that posting involves simply moving the debit to Cash from the journal entry to a debit (or left side) in the Cash general ledger account, increasing its balance by $25,000. The credit to Common Stock from the journal entry becomes a credit (or right side) in the Common Stock general ledger account, increasing its balance by $25,000.

The first row of the general ledger account is the balance at the beginning of the period. In this case, the balance is $0 for both accounts because Eagle is just beginning operations.

TRANSACTION (2): BORROW CASH FROM THE BANK

In transaction (2), Eagle borrows $10,000 cash from a bank. The company has an increase in cash (an asset) and an increase in the amount owed (a liability). Assets increase with a debit, so we debit Cash for $10,000. Liabilities increase with a credit, so we credit Notes Payable for $10,000. Let's record the transaction in the journal and then post the debit and credit to the general ledger accounts.

TRANSACTION (2)

Borrow $10,000 from the bank and sign a three-year note

December 1	Debit	Credit
Cash *(+A)*...	**10,000**	
Notes Payable *(+L)*..		**10,000**
(Borrow cash by signing three-year note)		

Account: Cash

Date	Description	Debit	Credit	Balance
Dec. 1	Beginning balance			0
Dec. 1	Issue common stock for cash	25,000		25,000
Dec. 1	Borrow cash by signing note	**10,000**		35,000

Account: Notes Payable

Date	Description	Debit	Credit	Balance
Dec. 1	Beginning balance			0
Dec. 1	Borrow cash by signing note		**10,000**	10,000

We see that the balance in both accounts increases by $10,000. The balance of the Cash account is now $35,000, which includes $25,000 cash received from stockholders in transaction (1) plus $10,000 cash received from the bank in transaction (2). The balance of the Notes Payable account increases from $0 to $10,000.

As we go through transactions (3)–(10) next, **notice how each individual transaction is recorded in the journal but then adds to or subtracts from the account's total balance in the general ledger.**

In addition, from this point forward we'll use a simplified version of the general ledger account, commonly referred to as a T-account. A T-account includes the account title at the top, one side for recording debits, and one side for recording credits. Consistent with our previous discussion of debits and credits, the left side of the T-account is the debit column, and the right side is the credit column. **You can see that the name *T-account* comes from the natural T shape formed in the general ledger by the debit and credit columns.** Shown next are the T-accounts for Cash and Notes Payable after posting transaction (2).

Cash			Notes Payable		
(1)	25,000			(2)	10,000
(2)	10,000				
Bal.	35,000			Bal.	10,000

TRANSACTION (3): PURCHASE EQUIPMENT

In transaction (3), Eagle purchases equipment with $24,000 cash. The company has an increase in equipment (an asset) and a decrease in cash (an asset). Assets increase with a debit, so we debit Equipment for $24,000. Assets decrease with a credit, so we credit Cash for $24,000.

TRANSACTION (3)

Purchase equipment with cash, $24,000

December 1	Debit	Credit
Equipment *(+A)*...	**24,000**	
Cash *(−A)*		**24,000**
(Purchase equipment with cash)		

Equipment			Cash				
(3)	**24,000**		(1)	25,000	(3)	**24,000**	
			(2)	10,000			
Bal.	24,000		Bal.	11,000			

For Cash (a *debit* account), notice that the $24,000 *credit* decreases the balance from $35,000 to $11,000.

TRANSACTION (4): PAY FOR RENT IN ADVANCE

In transaction (4), Eagle pays $6,000 cash for one year of rent. The company has an increase in prepaid rent (an asset) and a decrease in cash (an asset). Assets increase with a debit, so we debit Prepaid Rent for $6,000. Assets decrease with a credit, so we credit Cash for $6,000.

TRANSACTION (4)

Pay for one year of rent in advance, $6,000

December 1	Debit	Credit
Prepaid Rent *(+A)*..	**6,000**	
Cash *(−A)*		**6,000**
(Prepay rent with cash)		

Prepaid Rent			Cash				
(4)	**6,000**		(1)	25,000	(3)	24,000	
			(2)	10,000	(4)	**6,000**	
Bal.	6,000		Bal.	5,000			

TRANSACTION (5): PURCHASE SUPPLIES ON ACCOUNT

In transaction (5), Eagle purchases supplies on account for $2,300. The company has an increase in supplies (an asset) and an increase in amounts owed to suppliers (a liability). Assets increase with a debit, so we debit Supplies for $2,300. Liabilities increase with a credit, so we credit Accounts Payable for $2,300.

December 6	Debit	Credit
Supplies *(+A)*	**2,300**	
Accounts Payable *(+L)*..		**2,300**
(Purchase supplies on account)		

TRANSACTION (5)

Purchase supplies on account, $2,300

Supplies		Accounts Payable	
(5) 2,300			**(5) 2,300**
Bal. 2,300			Bal. 2,300

TRANSACTION (6): PROVIDE SERVICES FOR CASH

In transaction (6), Eagle provides golf training to customers for $4,300 cash. The company has an increase in cash (an asset) and an increase in service revenue (a revenue). Assets increase with a debit, so we debit Cash for $4,300. Revenues increase with a credit, so we credit Service Revenue for $4,300.

December 12	Debit	Credit
Cash *(+A)*..	**4,300**	
Service Revenue *(+R, +SE)*...................................		**4,300**
(Provide training to customers for cash)		

TRANSACTION (6)

Provide golf training to customers for cash, $4,300

Cash				Service Revenue	
(1) 25,000	(3) 24,000				**(6) 4,300**
(2) 10,000	(4) 6,000				
(6) 4,300					
Bal. 9,300					Bal. 4,300

TRANSACTION (7): PROVIDE SERVICES ON ACCOUNT

In transaction (7), Eagle provides golf training to customers on account for $2,000. The company has an increase in amounts expected to be received from customers (an asset) and an increase in service revenue (a revenue). Assets increase with a debit, so we debit Accounts Receivable for $2,000. Revenues increase with a credit, so we credit Service Revenue for $2,000.

December 17	Debit	Credit
Accounts Receivable *(+A)*	**2,000**	
Service Revenue *(+R, +SE)*		**2,000**
(Provide training to customers on account)		

TRANSACTION (7)

Provide golf training to customers on account, $2,000

Accounts Receivable		Service Revenue	
(7) 2,000			(6) 4,300
			(7) 2,000
Bal. 2,000			Bal. 6,300

TRANSACTION (8): RECEIVE CASH IN ADVANCE FROM CUSTOMERS

In transaction (8), Eagle receives $600 cash in advance from customers for golf training to be provided in the future. The company has an increase in cash (an asset) and an increase in obligations to provide future services (a liability). Assets increase with a debit, so we debit Cash for $600. Liabilities increase with a credit, so we credit Deferred Revenue for $600.

TRANSACTION (8)

Receive cash in advance from customers, $600

December 23	Debit	Credit
Cash *(+A)*..	**600**	
Deferred Revenue *(+L)*		**600**
(Receive cash in advance from customers)		

	Cash				Deferred Revenue	
(1)	25,000	(3)	24,000		(8)	600
(2)	10,000	(4)	6,000			
(6)	4,300					
(8)	**600**					
Bal.	9,900				Bal.	600

TRANSACTION (9): PAY SALARIES TO EMPLOYEES

In transaction (9), Eagle pays $2,800 cash for employee salaries during the month. The company has an increase in employee costs for work in the current period (an expense) and a decrease in cash (an asset). Expenses increase with a debit, so we debit Salaries Expense for $2,800. Assets decrease with a credit, so we credit Cash for $2,800.

TRANSACTION (9)

Pay salaries to employees, $2,800

December 28	Debit	Credit
Salaries Expense *(+E, −SE)*..	**2,800**	
Cash *(−A)*		**2,800**
(Pay salaries to employees)		

	Salaries Expense			Cash		
(9)	**2,800**		(1)	25,000	(3)	24,000
			(2)	10,000	(4)	6,000
			(6)	4,300	**(9)**	**2,800**
			(8)	600		
Bal.	2,800		Bal.	7,100		

TRANSACTION (10): PAY CASH DIVIDENDS

In transaction (10), Eagle pays $200 in cash dividends to stockholders. The company has an increase in the Dividends account and a decrease in cash (an asset). Dividends increase with a debit, so we debit Dividends for $200. Assets decrease with a credit, so we credit Cash for $200.

TRANSACTION (10)

Pay cash dividends to stockholders, $200

December 30	Debit	Credit
Dividends *(+D, −SE)*..	**200**	
Cash *(−A)*		**200**
(Pay cash dividends)		

	Dividends			Cash		
(10)	**200**		(1)	25,000	(3)	24,000
			(2)	10,000	(4)	6,000
			(6)	4,300	(9)	2,800
			(8)	600	**(10)**	**200**
Bal.	200		Bal.	6,900		

KEY POINT

Posting is the process of transferring the debit and credit information from transactions recorded in the journal to individual accounts in the general ledger.

A summary of the external transactions that have been recorded in a journal for Eagle Golf Academy is provided in Illustration 2–11.

ILLUSTRATION 2–11   Summary of Journal Entries Recorded for Transactions of Eagle Golf Academy

	Debit	Credit
(1) December 1		
Cash *(+A)*	25,000	
Common Stock *(+SE)*		25,000
(Issue common stock for cash)		
(2) December 1		
Cash *(+A)*	10,000	
Notes Payable *(+L)*		10,000
(Borrow cash by signing three-year note)		
(3) December 1		
Equipment *(+A)*	24,000	
Cash *(−A)*		24,000
(Purchase equipment for cash)		
(4) December 1		
Prepaid Rent *(+A)*	6,000	
Cash *(−A)*		6,000
(Prepay rent with cash)		
(5) December 6		
Supplies *(+A)*	2,300	
Accounts Payable *(+L)*		2,300
(Purchase supplies on account)		
(6) December 12		
Cash *(+A)*	4,300	
Service Revenue *(+R, +SE)*		4,300
(Provide training to customers for cash)		
(7) December 17		
Accounts Receivable *(+A)*	2,000	
Service Revenue *(+R, +SE)*		2,000
(Provide training to customers on account)		
(8) December 23		
Cash *(+A)*	600	
Deferred Revenue *(+L)*		600
(Receive cash in advance from customers)		
(9) December 28		
Salaries Expense *(+E, −SE)*	2,800	
Cash *(−A)*		2,800
(Pay salaries to employees)		
(10) December 30		
Dividends *(+D, −SE)*	200	
Cash *(−A)*		200
(Pay cash dividends)		

Illustration 2–12 provides the general ledger accounts after posting the journal entries summarized in Illustration 2–11. Account balances are in bold, and transaction numbers are shown in parentheses.

ILLUSTRATION 2–12   Posting of External Transactions of Eagle Golf Academy from Journal Entries to General Ledger Accounts

Assets	=	Liabilities	+	Stockholders' Equity

Assets

Cash

(1)	25,000	(3)	24,000
(2)	10,000	(4)	6,000
(6)	4,300	(9)	2,800
(8)	600	(10)	200
Bal. 6,900			

Accounts Receivable

(7)	2,000
Bal. 2,000	

Supplies

(5)	2,300
Bal. 2,300	

Prepaid Rent

(4)	6,000
Bal. 6,000	

Equipment

(3)	24,000
Bal. 24,000	

Liabilities

Accounts Payable

(5)	2,300
Bal. 2,300	

Deferred Revenue

(8)	600
Bal. 600	

Notes Payable

(2)	10,000
Bal. 10,000	

Stockholders' Equity

Common Stock

(1)	25,000
Bal. 25,000	

Retained Earnings

0
0

Service Revenue

(6)	4,300
(7)	2,000
Bal. 6,300	

Salaries Expense

(9)	2,800
Bal. 2,800	

Dividends

(10)	200
Bal. 200	

Transaction numbers are shown in parentheses. Account balances are in bold.

Let's Review

mhhe.com/4fa7

Bogey Incorporated has the following transactions during May:

May 1   Purchase a storage building by obtaining a loan of $5,000.
May 6   Provide services to customers for cash, $1,800.
May 12 Pay $1,200 cash for advertising in May.
May 17 Repay $1,000 of the amount borrowed on May 1.
May 25 Purchase office supplies for $800 cash.

Required:

1. Record each transaction.
2. Post the transactions to the Cash T-account, assuming a beginning balance of cash of $2,500 on May 1.

Solution:

1. Record each transaction.

May 1	Debit	Credit
Buildings (+A)	5,000	
Notes Payable (+L)		5,000
(Purchase building with note payable)		

May 6	Debit	Credit
Cash (+A)	1,800	
Service Revenue (+R, +SE)		1,800
(Provide services for cash)		

May 12	Debit	Credit
Advertising Expense (+E, −SE)	**1,200**	
Cash (−A)..		**1,200**
(Pay for advertising)		

May 17	Debit	Credit
Notes Payable (−L)	**1,000**	
Cash (−A)..		**1,000**
(Repay portion of note)		

May 25	Debit	Credit
Supplies (+A)	**800**	
Cash (−A)..		**800**
(Purchase supplies for cash)		

2. Post the transactions to the Cash T-account, assuming a beginning balance of cash of $2,500 on May 1.

	Cash			
Beginning balance	2,500			
May 6	1,800			
		1,200	May 12	
		1,000	May 17	
		800	May 25	
Ending balance	1,300			

Suggested Homework:
**BE2–7, BE2–8;
E2–8, E2–10, E2–11;
P2–4A&B, P2–5A&B**

Trial Balance

After we've posted journal entries to the general ledger accounts, **the sum of the accounts with debit balances should equal the sum of the accounts with credit balances.** This is expected because debits were equal to credits for every journal entry posted to those ledger accounts. To prove this and to check for any errors in posting, we prepare a trial balance. A trial balance is a list of all accounts and their balances at a particular date, showing that total debits equal total credits. Another purpose of the trial balance is to assist us in preparing adjusting entries (for *internal* transactions). We discuss adjusting entries in Chapter 3.

Using the account balances calculated in Illustration 2–12, we can now prepare the trial balance of Eagle Golf Academy. The trial balance appears in Illustration 2–13. Notice that accounts are listed with the debit balances in one column and the credit balances in another column. Asset, expense, and dividend accounts normally have debit balances. Liability, stockholders' equity, and revenue accounts normally have credit balances. As expected, total debits ($44,200) equal total credits ($44,200).

■ **LO2–6**
Prepare a trial balance.

COMMON MISTAKE

Just because the debits and credits are equal in a trial balance does not necessarily mean that all balances are correct. A trial balance could contain offsetting errors. For example, if we overstate cash and revenue each by $1,000, both accounts will be in error, but the trial balance will still balance, since the overstatement to cash increases debits by $1,000 and the overstatement to revenue increases credits by $1,000.

ILLUSTRATION 2–13

Trial Balance of Eagle
Golf Academy

EAGLE GOLF ACADEMY Trial Balance December 31		
Accounts	Debit	Credit
Cash	$ 6,900	
Accounts Receivable	2,000	
Supplies	2,300	
Prepaid Rent	6,000	
Equipment	24,000	
Accounts Payable		$ 2,300
Deferred Revenue		600
Notes Payable		10,000
Common Stock		25,000
Retained Earnings		0
Dividends	200	
Service Revenue		6,300
Salaries Expense	2,800	
Totals	$44,200	$44,200

Total debits equal total
credits.

As a final point, notice that the Retained Earnings account has a balance of $0. As we explained earlier, retained earnings is a composite of three other types of accounts—revenues, expenses, and dividends. Those three accounts have balances at this point, but those balances haven't yet been transferred to retained earnings. This transfer is known as the *closing process,* and we will discuss it in Chapter 3. Since this is the first period of the company's operations, retained earnings will start at $0. As time goes by, the retained earnings balance will be the accumulated net amount of revenues minus expenses and dividends.

Decision Point

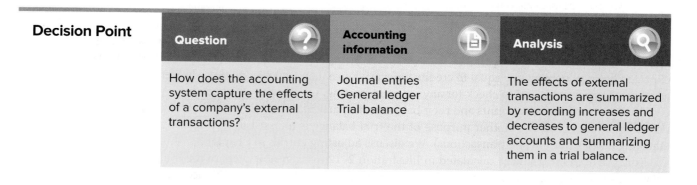

Question	Accounting information	Analysis
How does the accounting system capture the effects of a company's external transactions?	Journal entries General ledger Trial balance	The effects of external transactions are summarized by recording increases and decreases to general ledger accounts and summarizing them in a trial balance.

ORDER OF ACCOUNTS

The trial balance is used *for internal purposes only* and provides a check on the equality of the debits and credits. Because the trial balance is not a published financial statement to be used by external parties, there is no required order for listing accounts in the trial balance. However, most companies list accounts in the following order: assets, liabilities, stockholders' equity, dividends, revenues, and expenses. As we'll see in Chapter 3, the trial balance simplifies preparation of the published financial statements. Asset, liability, and stockholders' equity accounts are reported in the balance sheet. Dividends are reported in the statement of stockholders' equity. Revenue and expense accounts are reported in the income statement. Having the accounts listed in order of those classifications in the trial balance makes it easier to prepare the financial statements.

KEY POINT

A trial balance is a list of all accounts and their balances at a particular date. Debits must equal credits, but that doesn't necessarily mean that all account balances are correct.

 CAREER CORNER

The accuracy of account balances is essential for providing useful information to decision makers, such as investors and creditors. That's why the Securities and Exchange Commission (SEC) requires all companies with publicly traded stock to have their reported account balances verified by an independent audit firm. Auditors use their understanding of accounting principles and business practices to provide an opinion of reasonable assurance that account balances are free from material misstatements resulting from errors and fraud. Tens of thousands of audits are performed each year. Because of the huge demand for auditors and the valuable work experience it provides, many accounting majors begin their career as auditors.

© BananaStock/PictureQuest, RF

KEY POINTS BY LEARNING OBJECTIVE

LO2–1 Identify the basic steps in measuring external transactions.

External transactions are transactions between the company and a separate company or individual. Internal transactions do not include an exchange with a separate economic entity.

The six-step measurement process (Illustration 2–1) is the foundation of financial accounting. To understand this process, it is important to realize in Step 2 that we analyze the effects of business transactions on the accounting equation (Part A of this chapter). Then, in Step 3 we begin the process of translating those effects into the accounting records (Part B of this chapter).

LO2–2 Analyze the impact of external transactions on the accounting equation.

After each transaction, the accounting equation must always remain in balance. In other words, assets always must equal liabilities plus stockholders' equity.

The expanded accounting equation demonstrates that revenues increase retained earnings while expenses and dividends decrease retained earnings. Retained earnings is a component of stockholders' equity.

LO2–3 Assess whether the impact of external transactions results in a debit or credit to an account balance.

For the basic accounting equation (Assets = Liabilities + Stockholders' Equity), assets (left side) increase with *debits*. Liabilities and stockholders' equity (right side) increase with *credits*. The opposite is true to decrease any of these accounts.

The Retained Earnings account is a stockholders' equity account that normally has a credit balance. The Retained Earnings account has three components—revenues, expenses, and dividends. Revenues (increased by credits) increase the balance of Retained Earnings. Expenses and dividends (increased by debits) decrease the balance of Retained Earnings.

LO2–4 Record transactions in a journal using debits and credits.

For each transaction, total debits must equal total credits.

LO2–5 Post transactions to the general ledger.

Posting is the process of transferring the debit and credit information from transactions recorded in the journal to individual accounts in the general ledger.

LO2–6 Prepare a trial balance.

A trial balance is a list of all accounts and their balances at a particular date. Debits must equal credits, but that doesn't necessarily mean that all account balances are correct.

GLOSSARY

Account: A summary of the effects of all transactions related to a particular item over a period of time. **p. 55**

Accounting cycle: Full set of procedures used to accomplish the measurement/communication process of financial accounting. **p. 54**

Chart of accounts: A list of all account names used to record transactions of a company. **p. 55**

Credit: Right side of an account. Indicates a decrease to asset, expense, or dividend accounts, and an increase to liability, stockholders' equity, or revenue accounts. **p. 67**

Debit: Left side of an account. Indicates an increase to asset, expense, or dividend accounts, and a decrease to liability, stockholders' equity, or revenue accounts. **p. 67**

External transactions: Transactions the firm conducts with a separate economic entity. **p. 54**

General ledger: A single location that provides a list of transactions affecting each account and the account's balance. **p. 72**

Internal transactions: Events that affect the financial position of the company but do not include an exchange with a separate economic entity. **p. 54**

Journal: A chronological record of all transactions affecting a firm. **p. 70**

Journal entry: The format used for recording business transactions. **p. 70**

Posting: The process of transferring the debit and credit information from the journal to individual accounts in the general ledger. **p. 72**

Revenue recognition principle: Record revenue in the period in which we provide goods and services to customers. **p. 61**

T-account: A simplified form of a general ledger account with space at the top for the account title, one side for recording debits, and one side for recording credits. **p. 73**

Trial balance: A list of all accounts and their balances at a particular date, showing that total debits equal total credits. **p. 79**

SELF-STUDY QUESTIONS

1. Which of the following represents an external transaction? **(LO2–1)**
   a. Lapse of insurance due to passage of time.
   b. Use of office supplies by employees over time.
   c. Payment of utility bill.
   d. Salaries earned by employees but not yet paid.

2. Which of the following is *not* a step in the process of measuring external transactions? **(LO2–1)**
   a. Analyze the impact of the transaction on the accounting equation.
   b. Record the transaction using debits and credits.
   c. Post the transaction to the T-account in the general ledger.
   d. All of the above are steps in the measurement process of external transactions.

3. Which of the following transactions causes an increase in total assets? **(LO2–2)**
   a. Pay employee salaries for the current month.
   b. Pay dividends to stockholders.
   c. Issue common stock in exchange for cash.
   d. Purchase office equipment for cash.

4. Which of the following transactions causes an increase in stockholders' equity? **(LO2–2)**
   a. Pay dividends to stockholders.
   b. Obtain cash by borrowing from a local bank.
   c. Provide services to customers on account.
   d. Purchase advertising on a local radio station.

5. Which of the following causes the accounting equation *not* to balance? **(LO2–2)**
   a. Increase assets; increase liabilities.
   b. Decrease assets; increase expenses.
   c. Increase assets; increase dividends.
   d. Decrease liabilities; increase revenues.

6. A debit is used to increase which of the following accounts? **(LO2–3)**
   a. Utilities Expense.
   b. Accounts Payable.
   c. Service Revenue.
   d. Common Stock.

7. A credit is used to increase which of the following accounts? **(LO2–3)**
   a. Dividends.
   b. Insurance Expense.
   c. Cash.
   d. Service Revenue.

8. Providing services to customers on account for $100 is recorded as: **(LO2–4)**

   a. Accounts Receivable 100
       Service Revenue... 100
   b. Cash 100
       Accounts Receivable.................................... 100
   c. Service Revenue 100
       Accounts Receivable.................................... 100
   d. Service Expense 100
       Accounts Payable... 100

9. Posting is the process of: **(LO2–5)**
   a. Analyzing the impact of the transaction on the accounting equation.
   b. Obtaining information about external transactions from source documents.
   c. Transferring the debit and credit information from the journal to individual accounts in the general ledger.
   d. Listing all accounts and their balances at a particular date and showing the equality of total debits and total credits.

10. A trial balance can best be explained as a list of:
    a. The income statement accounts used to calculate net income. **(LO2–6)**

b. Revenue, expense, and dividend accounts used to show the balances of the components of retained earnings.
c. The balance sheet accounts used to show the equality of the accounting equation.
d. All accounts and their balances at a particular date.

Note: For answers, see the last page of the chapter.

For additional study materials, including 10 more multiple-choice Self-Study Questions, visit the Connect Library.

REVIEW QUESTIONS

1. Explain the difference between external transactions and internal transactions. If a company purchases supplies from a local vendor, would this be classified as an external or internal transaction? ■ **LO2–1**

2. List the steps we use to measure external transactions. ■ **LO2–1**

3. Each external transaction will have a dual effect on the accounting equation. Explain what this means. ■ **LO2–2**

4. Describe the impact of each of these external transactions on the accounting equation. ■ **LO2–2**
   a. Receive a loan from the bank.
   b. Pay employee salaries for the current period.
   c. Receive cash from customers for services provided in the current period.
   d. Purchase equipment by paying cash.

5. Jerry believes that "dual effect" indicates that, for all transactions, one account will increase and one account will decrease. Is Jerry correct? Explain. ■ **LO2–2**

6. What is the normal balance (debit or credit) of assets, liabilities, stockholders' equity, revenues, and expenses? ■ **LO2–3**

7. Jenny has learned that assets have debit balances, while liabilities have credit balances. Based on this, she believes that asset accounts can only be debited and liabilities can only be credited. Is Jenny correct? When would we credit an asset and when would we debit a liability? ■ **LO2–3**

8. For each of the following accounts, indicate whether we use a debit or a credit to *increase* the balance of the account. ■ **LO2–3**
   a. Cash.   c. Utilities Expense.
   b. Salaries Payable.   d. Service Revenue.

9. For each of the following accounts, indicate whether we use a debit or a credit to *decrease* the balance of the account. (Compare your answers to those for Question 8.) ■ **LO2–3**
   a. Cash.   c. Utilities Expense.
   b. Salaries Payable.   d. Service Revenue.

10. Suzanne knows that an increase to an expense reduces retained earnings (a stockholders' equity account). However, she also knows that expense accounts have a *debit* balance, while retained earnings normally has a *credit* balance. Are these two pieces of information consistent? Explain. ■ **LO2–3**

■ LO2–4   11. What is a journal? What is a journal entry?

■ LO2–4   12. Provide the proper format for recording a transaction.

■ LO2–4   13. Explain the phrase "debits equal credits" with regard to journal entries.

■ LO2–4   14. Record each of the following external transactions using debits and credits.
                   a. Receive cash of $1,200 for providing services to a customer.
                   b. Pay rent of $500 for the current month.
                   c. Purchase a building for $10,000 by signing a note with the bank.

■ LO2–4   15. Describe the events that correspond to the following transactions.

	Debit	Credit
a. Supplies..	20,000	
Cash..		20,000
b. Accounts Receivable	30,000	
Service Revenue...		30,000
c. Accounts Payable	10,000	
Cash..		10,000

■ LO2–5   16. What does a T-account represent? What is the left side of the T-account called? What is the right side called?

■ LO2–5   17. Describe what we mean by posting. Post the transactions in Question 15 to appropriate T-accounts.

■ LO2–5   18. What is a general ledger? How does it relate to the chart of accounts?

■ LO2–6   19. What is a trial balance? To what does the term "balance" refer?

■ LO2–6   20. If total debits equal total credits in the trial balance, does this indicate that all transactions have been properly accounted for? Explain.

BRIEF EXERCISES   Mc Graw Hill Education connect®

List steps in the measurement process (LO2–1)

BE2–1 Below are the steps in the measurement process of external transactions. Arrange them from first (1) to last (6).

_____ a. Post the transaction to the T-accounts in the general ledger.

_____ b. Assess whether the impact of the transaction results in a debit or credit to account balances.

_____ c. Use source documents to identify accounts affected by an external transaction.

_____ d. Analyze the impact of the transaction on the accounting equation.

_____ e. Prepare a trial balance.

_____ f. Record the transaction using debits and credits.

Balance the accounting equation (LO2–2)

BE2–2 Using the notion that the accounting equation (Assets = Liabilities + Stockholders' Equity) must remain in balance, indicate whether each of the following transactions is possible.

a. Cash increases; Accounts Payable decreases.

b. Service Revenue increases; Salaries Payable increases.

c. Advertising Expense increases; Cash decreases.

BE2-3 Suppose a local company has the following balance sheet accounts:

Balance the accounting equation (LO2–2)

Accounts	Balances
Land	$ 9,000
Equipment	?
Salaries Payable	4,300
Notes Payable	?
Supplies	2,100
Cash	7,200
Stockholders' Equity	13,500
Accounts Payable	1,700
Prepaid Rent	3,200

Calculate the missing amounts assuming the business has total assets of $37,500.

BE2-4 The following transactions occur for Badger Biking Company during the month of June:

a. Provide services to customers on account for $50,000.

b. Receive cash of $42,000 from customers in (a) above.

c. Purchase bike equipment by signing a note with the bank for $35,000.

d. Pay utilities of $5,000 for the current month.

Analyze the impact of transactions on the accounting equation (LO2–2)

Analyze each transaction and indicate the amount of increases and decreases in the accounting equation.

	Assets	=	Liabilities	+	Stockholders' Equity
(a)	_____		_____		_____
(b)	_____		_____		_____
(c)	_____		_____		_____
(d)	_____		_____		_____

BE2-5 For each of the following accounts, indicate whether a debit or credit is used to increase (+) or decrease (−) the balance of the account. The solution for the first one is provided as an example.

Understand the effect of debits and credits on accounts (LO2–3)

Account	Debit	Credit
Asset	+	−
Liability	_____	_____
Common Stock	_____	_____
Retained Earnings	_____	_____
Dividends	_____	_____
Revenue	_____	_____
Expense	_____	_____

BE2-6 Fill in the blanks below with the word "debit" or "credit."

Understand the effect of debits and credits on accounts (LO2–3)

a. The balance of an *asset* account increases with a _____ and decreases with a _____.

b. The balance of a *liability* account increases with a _____ and decreases with a _____.

c. The balance of a *stockholders' equity* account increases with a _____ and decreases with a _____.

d. The balance of a *revenue* account increases with a _____ and decreases with a _____.

e. The balance of an *expense* account increases with a _____ and decreases with a _____.

BE2-7 The following transactions occur for the Panther Detective Agency during the month of July:

a. Purchase a truck and sign a note payable, $15,000.

b. Purchase office supplies for cash, $600.

c. Pay $800 in rent for the current month.

Record transactions (LO2–4)

Record the transactions. The company uses the following accounts: Cash, Supplies, Equipment (for the truck), Notes Payable, and Rent Expense.

BE2–8 The following transactions occur for Cardinal Music Academy during the month of October:

a. Provide music lessons to students for $17,000 cash.

b. Purchase prepaid insurance to protect musical equipment over the next year for $4,200 cash.

c. Purchase musical equipment for $20,000 cash.

d. Obtain a loan from a bank by signing a note for $30,000.

Record the transactions. The company uses the following accounts: Cash, Prepaid Insurance, Equipment, Notes Payable, and Service Revenue.

BE2–9 Consider the following T-account for cash.

Cash	
13,000	8,200
4,400	1,900
3,500	5,500

1. Compute the balance of the Cash account.
2. Give some examples of transactions that would have resulted in the $4,400 posting to the account.
3. Give some examples of transactions that would have resulted in the $1,900 posting to the account.

BE2–10 The following transactions occur for the Wolfpack Shoe Company during the month of June:

a. Provide services to customers for $30,000 and receive cash.

b. Purchase office supplies on account for $20,000.

c. Pay $7,000 in salaries to employees for work performed during the month.

1. Analyze each transaction. For each transaction, indicate by how much each category in the accounting equation increases or decreases.

	Assets	=	Liabilities	+	Stockholders' Equity
(a)	_____		_____		_____
(b)	_____		_____		_____
(c)	_____		_____		_____
(d)	_____		_____		_____

2. Record the transactions. The company uses the following accounts: Cash, Supplies, Accounts Payable, Salaries Expense, and Service Revenue.
3. Post the transactions to T-accounts. Assume the opening balance in each of the accounts is zero.

BE2–11 Using the following information, prepare a trial balance. Assume all asset, dividend, and expense accounts have debit balances and all liability, stockholders' equity, and revenue accounts have credit balances. List the accounts in the following order: assets, liabilities, stockholders' equity, dividends, revenues, and expenses.

Cash	$6,100	Dividends	$ 500
Salaries Payable	700	Rent Expense	2,000
Prepaid Rent	900	Accounts Receivable	4,400
Accounts Payable	2,000	Common Stock	6,200
Retained Earnings	2,000	Service Revenue	7,100
Salaries Expense	3,000	Advertising Expense	1,100

Record transactions (LO2–4)

Analyze T-accounts (LO2–5)

Analyze the impact of transactions on the accounting equation, record transactions, and post (LO2–2, 2–3, 2–4, 2–5)

Prepare a trial balance (LO2–6)

BE2–12 Your study partner is having trouble getting total debits to equal total credits in the trial balance. Prepare a corrected trial balance by placing each account balance in the correct debit or credit column.

Correct a trial balance (LO2–6)

Trial Balance		
Accounts	**Debit**	**Credit**
Cash	$ 7,300	
Accounts Receivable		$ 2,100
Equipment	10,400	
Accounts Payable	3,900	
Deferred Revenue		1,100
Common Stock	11,000	
Retained Earnings		3,900
Dividends	600	
Service Revenue		4,500
Salaries Expense	3,200	
Utilities Expense		800
Total	$36,400	$12,400

EXERCISES

E2–1 Listed below are several terms and phrases associated with the measurement process for external transactions.

Identify terms associated with the measurement process (LO2–1)

List A	List B
_____ 1. Account	a. Record of all transactions affecting a company.
_____ 2. Analyze transactions	b. Determine the dual effect of business events on the accounting equation.
_____ 3. Journal	c. List of accounts and their balances.
_____ 4. Post	d. Summary of the effects of all transactions related to a particular item over a period of time.
_____ 5. Trial balance	e. Transfer balances from the journal to the general ledger.

Required:
Pair each item from List A with the item from List B to which it is most appropriately associated.

E2–2 Below are the external transactions for Shockers Incorporated.
1. Issue common stock in exchange for cash.
2. Purchase equipment by signing a note payable.
3. Provide services to customers on account.
4. Pay rent for the current month.
5. Pay insurance for the current month.
6. Collect cash from customers on account.

Analyze the impact of transactions on the accounting equation (LO2–2)

	Assets	=	Liabilities	+	Stockholders' Equity
1.	Increase	=	No effect	+	Increase
2.	_____		_____		_____
3.	_____		_____		_____
4.	_____		_____		_____
5.	_____		_____		_____
6.	_____		_____		_____

Required:

Analyze each transaction. Under each category in the accounting equation, indicate whether the transaction increases, decreases, or has no effect. The first item is provided as an example.

E2–3 Green Wave Company plans to own and operate a storage rental facility. For the first month of operations, the company had the following transactions.

1. Issue 10,000 shares of common stock in exchange for $32,000 in cash.
2. Purchase land for $19,000. A note payable is signed for the full amount.
3. Purchase storage container equipment for $8,000 cash.
4. Hire three employees for $2,000 per month.
5. Receive cash of $12,000 in rental fees for the current month.
6. Purchase office supplies for $2,000 on account.
7. Pay employees $6,000 for the first month's salaries.

Required:

For each transaction, describe the dual effect on the accounting equation. For example, in the first transaction, (1) assets increase and (2) stockholders' equity increases.

E2–4 Boilermaker House Painting Company incurs the following transactions for September.

1. Paint houses in the current month for $15,000 on account.
2. Purchase painting equipment for $16,000 cash.
3. Purchase office supplies on account for $2,500.
4. Pay employee salaries of $3,200 for the current month.
5. Purchase advertising to appear in the current month, $1,200.
6. Pay office rent of $4,400 for the current month.
7. Receive $10,000 from customers in (1) above.
8. Receive cash of $5,000 in advance from a customer who plans to have his house painted in the following month.

Required:

For each transaction, describe the dual effect on the accounting equation. For example, for the first transaction, (1) assets increase and (2) stockholders' equity increases.

E2–5 At the beginning of April, Owl Corporation has a balance of $13,000 in the Retained Earnings account. During the month of April, Owl had the following external transactions.

1. Issue common stock for cash, $11,000.
2. Provide services to customers on account, $8,500.
3. Provide services to customers in exchange for cash, $3,200.
4. Purchase equipment and pay cash, $7,600.
5. Pay rent for April, $1,100.
6. Pay employee salaries for April, $3,500.
7. Pay dividends to stockholders, $2,000.

Required:

Using the external transactions above, compute the balance of Retained Earnings at April 30.

E2–6 Below is a list of common accounts.

Accounts	Debit or Credit
Cash	1. _____
Service Revenue	2. _____
Salaries Expense	3. _____
Accounts Payable	4. _____
Equipment	5. _____
Retained Earnings	6. _____
Utilities Expense	7. _____
Accounts Receivable	8. _____

(continued)

(concluded)

Accounts	Debit or Credit
Dividends	9. _____
Common Stock	10. _____

Required:

Indicate whether the normal balance of each account is a debit or a credit.

E2–7 Below are several external transactions for Hokies Company.

Associate debits and credits with external transactions (LO2–3)

	Account Debited	Account Credited
Example: Purchase equipment in exchange for cash.	*Equipment*	*Cash*
1. Pay a cash dividend.	_____	_____
2. Pay rent in advance for the next three months.	_____	_____
3. Provide services to customers on account.	_____	_____
4. Purchase office supplies on account.	_____	_____
5. Pay salaries for the current month.	_____	_____
6. Issue common stock in exchange for cash.	_____	_____
7. Collect cash from customers for services provided in (3) above.	_____	_____
8. Borrow cash from the bank and sign a note.	_____	_____
9. Pay for the current month's utilities.	_____	_____
10. Pay for office supplies purchased in (4) above.	_____	_____

Hokies uses the following accounts:

Accounts Payable	Equipment	Accounts Receivable
Cash	Supplies	Utilities Expense
Prepaid Rent	Rent Expense	Service Revenue
Common Stock	Notes Payable	Retained Earnings
Salaries Payable	Salaries Expense	Dividends

Required:

Indicate which accounts should be debited and which should be credited.

E2–8 Terapin Company engages in the following external transactions for November.

Record transactions (LO2–4)

1. Purchase equipment in exchange for cash of $23,400.
2. Provide services to customers and receive cash of $6,800.
3. Pay the current month's rent of $1,300.
4. Purchase office supplies on account for $1,000.
5. Pay employee salaries of $2,100 for the current month.

Required:

Record the transactions. Terapin uses the following accounts: Cash, Supplies, Equipment, Accounts Payable, Service Revenue, Rent Expense, and Salaries Expense.

E2–9 Below are recorded transactions of Yellow Jacket Corporation for August.

Identify transactions (LO2–4)

	Debit	Credit
1. Equipment	8,800	
Cash		8,800
2. Accounts Receivable	3,200	
Service Revenue		3,200
3. Salaries Expense	1,900	
Cash		1,900
4. Cash	1,500	
Deferred Revenue		1,500
5. Dividends	900	
Cash		900

Required:

Provide an explanation for each transaction.

Record transactions (LO2–4)

E2–10 Sun Devil Hair Design has the following transactions during the month of February.

February 2	Pay $700 for radio advertising for February.
February 7	Purchase beauty supplies of $1,300 on account.
February 14	Provide beauty services of $2,900 to customers and receive cash.
February 15	Pay employee salaries for the current month of $900.
February 25	Provide beauty services of $1,000 to customers on account.
February 28	Pay utility bill for the current month of $300.

Required:

Record each transaction. Sun Devil uses the following accounts: Cash, Accounts Receivable, Supplies, Accounts Payable, Service Revenue, Advertising Expense, Salaries Expense, and Utilities Expense.

Record transactions (LO2–4)

E2–11 Bearcat Construction begins operations in March and has the following transactions.

March 1	Issue common stock for $21,000.
March 5	Obtain $9,000 loan from the bank by signing a note.
March 10	Purchase construction equipment for $25,000 cash.
March 15	Purchase advertising for the current month for $1,100 cash.
March 22	Provide construction services for $18,000 on account.
March 27	Receive $13,000 cash on account from March 22 services.
March 28	Pay salaries for the current month of $6,000.

Required:

Record each transaction. Bearcat uses the following accounts: Cash, Accounts Receivable, Equipment, Notes Payable, Common Stock, Service Revenue, Advertising Expense, and Salaries Expense.

Correct recorded transactions (LO2–4)

E2–12 Below are several transactions for Scarlet Knight Corporation. A junior accountant, recently employed by the company, proposes to record the following transactions.

External Transaction	Accounts	Debit	Credit
1. Owners invest $15,000 in the company and receive common stock.	Common Stock Cash	15,000	 15,000
2. Receive cash of $4,000 for services provided in the current period.	Cash Service Revenue	4,000	 4,000
3. Purchase office supplies on account, $300.	Supplies Cash	300	 300
4. Pay $600 for next month's rent.	Rent Expense Cash	600	 600
5. Purchase office equipment with cash of $2,200.	Cash Equipment	2,200	 2,200

Required:

Assess whether the junior accountant correctly proposes how to record each transaction. If incorrect, provide the correction.

Correct recorded transactions (LO2–4)

E2–13 Below are several transactions for Crimson Tide Corporation. A junior accountant, recently employed by the company, proposes to record the following transactions.

External Transaction	Accounts	Debit	Credit
1. Pay cash dividends of $800 to stockholders.	Cash Dividends	800	 800
2. Provide services on account for customers, $3,400.	Cash Service Revenue	3,400	 3,400

(concluded)

External Transaction	Accounts	Debit	Credit
3. Pay a $500 utilities bill for the current period.	Utilities Expense	500	
	Cash		500
4. Receive cash of $400 from previously billed customers.	Cash	400	
	Service Revenue		400
5. Pay for supplies previously purchased on account, $1,200.	Supplies Expense	1,200	
	Cash		1,200

Required:
Assess whether the junior accountant correctly proposes how to record each transaction. If incorrect, provide the correction.

E2–14 Consider the following transactions.

1. Receive cash from customers, $15,000.
2. Pay cash for employee salaries, $9,000.
3. Pay cash for rent, $3,000.
4. Receive cash from sale of equipment, $8,000.
5. Pay cash for utilities, $1,000.
6. Receive cash from a bank loan, $4,000.
7. Pay cash for advertising, $7,000.
8. Purchase supplies on account, $3,000.

Post transactions to Cash T-account (LO2–5)

Required:
Post transactions to the Cash T-account and calculate the ending balance. The beginning balance in the Cash T-account is $5,000.

E2–15 Consider the recorded transactions below.

Post transactions to T-accounts (LO2–5)

	Debit	Credit
1. Accounts Receivable	8,400	
Service Revenue		8,400
2. Supplies	2,300	
Accounts Payable		2,300
3. Cash	10,200	
Accounts Receivable		10,200
4. Advertising Expense	1,000	
Cash		1,000
5. Accounts Payable	3,700	
Cash		3,700
6. Cash	1,100	
Deferred Revenue		1,100

Required:
Post each transaction to T-accounts and compute the ending balance of each account. The beginning balance of each account before the transactions is: Cash, $3,400; Accounts Receivable, $4,200; Supplies, $400; Accounts Payable, $3,500; Deferred Revenue, $300. Service Revenue and Advertising Expense each have a beginning balance of zero.

E2–16 Below are T-accounts. The first row in each is the beginning balance, and the numbers in parentheses are transaction numbers.

Identify transactions (LO2–5)

	Cash				Accounts Receivable				Supplies	
	8,000				2,000				1,000	
(1)	20,000	14,000	(5)	(2)	5,000	4,000	(3)	(4)	6,000	
(3)	4,000	7,000	(6)							
	11,000				3,000				7,000	

	Accounts Payable			Service Revenue				Salaries Expense	
		2,000			0			0	
(6)	7,000	6,000	(4)		20,000	(1)	(5)	14,000	
					5,000	(2)			
		1,000			25,000			14,000	

Required:

Provide an explanation for each transaction.

Prepare a trial balance (LO2–6)

E2–17 Below is the complete list of accounts of Sooner Company and the related balance at the end of April. All accounts have their normal debit or credit balance. Cash, $3,900; Prepaid Rent, $7,400; Accounts Payable $4,300; Common Stock, $40,000; Service Revenue, $25,400; Salaries Expense, $8,200; Accounts Receivable, $6,100; Land, $60,000; Deferred Revenue, $2,300; Retained Earnings, $23,000; Supplies Expense, $9,400.

Required:

Prepare a trial balance with the list of accounts in the following order: assets, liabilities, stockholders' equity, revenues, and expenses.

Prepare a trial balance (LO2–6)

E2–18 Below is the complete list of accounts of Cobras Incorporated and the related balance at the end of March. All accounts have their normal debit or credit balance. Supplies, $1,000; Buildings, $55,000; Salaries Payable, $500; Common Stock, $35,000; Accounts Payable, $2,200; Utilities Expense, $3,700; Prepaid Insurance, $1,200; Service Revenue, $19,500; Accounts Receivable, $4,200; Cash, $3,500; Salaries Expense, $6,400; Retained Earnings, $17,800.

Required:

Prepare a trial balance with the list of accounts in the following order: assets, liabilities, stockholders' equity, revenues, and expenses.

Record transactions, post to T-accounts, and prepare a trial balance (LO2–4, 2–5, 2–6)

E2–19 Green Wave Company plans to own and operate a storage rental facility. For the first month of operations, the company has the following transactions.

1. January 1   Issue 10,000 shares of common stock in exchange for $42,000 in cash.
2. January 5   Purchase land for $24,000. A note payable is signed for the full amount.
3. January 9   Purchase storage container equipment for $9,000 cash.
4. January 12   Hire three employees for $3,000 per month.
5. January 18   Receive cash of $13,000 in rental fees for the current month.
6. January 23   Purchase office supplies for $3,000 on account.
7. January 31   Pay employees $9,000 for the first month's salaries.

Required:

1. Record each transaction. Green Wave uses the following accounts: Cash, Supplies, Land, Equipment, Common Stock, Accounts Payable, Notes Payable, Service Revenue, and Salaries Expense.
2. Post each transaction to T-accounts and compute the ending balance of each account. Since this is the first month of operations, all T-accounts have a beginning balance of zero.
3. After calculating the ending balance of each account, prepare a trial balance.

Record transactions, post to T-accounts, and prepare a trial balance (LO2–4, 2–5, 2–6)

E2–20 Boilermaker House Painting Company incurs the following transactions for September.

1. September 3   Paint houses in the current month for $20,000 on account.
2. September 8   Purchase painting equipment for $21,000 cash.
3. September 12   Purchase office supplies on account for $3,500.

4. September 15   Pay employee salaries of $4,200 for the current month.
5. September 19   Purchase advertising to appear in the current month for $1,000 cash.
6. September 22   Pay office rent of $5,400 for the current month.
7. September 26   Receive $15,000 from customers in (1) above.
8. September 30   Receive cash of $6,000 in advance from a customer who plans to have his house painted in the following month.

Required:

1. Record each transaction. Boilermaker uses the following accounts: Cash, Accounts Receivable, Supplies, Equipment, Accounts Payable, Deferred Revenue, Common Stock, Retained Earnings, Service Revenue, Salaries Expense, Advertising Expense, and Rent Expense.
2. Post each transaction to T-accounts and compute the ending balance of each account. At the beginning of September, the company had the following account balances: Cash, $46,100; Accounts Receivable, $1,700; Supplies, $500; Equipment, $7,400; Accounts Payable, $1,200; Common Stock, $25,000; Retained Earnings, $29,500. All other accounts had a beginning balance of zero.
3. After calculating the ending balance of each account, prepare a trial balance.

PROBLEMS: SET A

P2–1A Below is a list of activities for Jayhawk Corporation.

Analyze the impact of transactions on the accounting equation (LO2–2)

Transaction	Assets	=	Liabilities	+	Stockholders' Equity
1. *Issue common stock in exchange for cash.*	*Increase*	=	*No effect*	+	*Increase*
2. Purchase business supplies on account.	_____		_____		_____
3. Pay for legal services for the current month.	_____		_____		_____
4. Provide services to customers on account.	_____		_____		_____
5. Pay employee salaries for the current month.	_____		_____		_____
6. Provide services to customers for cash.	_____		_____		_____
7. Pay for advertising for the current month.	_____		_____		_____
8. Repay loan from the bank.	_____		_____		_____
9. Pay dividends to stockholders.	_____		_____		_____
10. Receive cash from customers in (4) above.	_____		_____		_____
11. Pay for supplies purchased in (2) above.	_____		_____		_____

Required:

For each activity, indicate whether the transaction increases, decreases, or has no effect on assets, liabilities, and stockholders' equity.

Analyze the impact
of transactions on
the accounting
equation (LO2–2)

P2–2A Below is a list of activities for Purple Cow Incorporated.

Transaction	Assets	=	Liabilities	+	Stockholders' Equity
1. *Provide services to customers on account, $1,600.*	*+$1,600*	*=*	*$0*	*+*	*+$1,600*
2. Pay $400 for current month's rent.	_____		_____		_____
3. Hire a new employee, who will be paid $500 at the end of each month.	_____		_____		_____
4. Pay $100 for advertising aired in the current period.	_____		_____		_____
5. Purchase office supplies for $400 cash.	_____		_____		_____
6. Receive cash of $1,000 from customers in (1) above.	_____		_____		_____
7. Obtain a loan from the bank for $7,000.	_____		_____		_____
8. Receive a bill of $200 for utility costs in the current period.	_____		_____		_____
9. Issue common stock for $10,000 cash.	_____		_____		_____
10. Pay $500 to employee in (3) above.	_____		_____		_____
Totals	_____	=	_____	+	_____

Required:

For each activity, indicate the impact on the accounting equation. After doing so for all transactions, ensure that the accounting equation remains in balance.

Identify the type
of account and its
normal debit or credit
balance (LO2–3)

P2–3A Below is a list of typical accounts.

Accounts	Type of Account	Normal Balance (Debit or Credit)
1. Salaries Payable	_____	_____
2. Common Stock	_____	_____
3. Prepaid Rent	_____	_____
4. Buildings	_____	_____
5. Utilities Expense	_____	_____
6. Equipment	_____	_____
7. Rent Expense	_____	_____
8. Notes Payable	_____	_____
9. Salaries Expense	_____	_____
10. Insurance Expense	_____	_____
11. Cash	_____	_____
12. Service Revenue	_____	_____

Required:

For each account, indicate (1) the type of account and (2) whether the normal account balance is a debit or credit. For the type of account, choose from asset, liability, stockholders' equity, dividend, revenue, or expense.

Record
transactions (LO2–4)

Flip Side of P2–5A

P2–4A Jake owns a lawn maintenance company, and Luke owns a machine repair shop. For the month of July, the following transactions occurred.

July 3   Jake provides lawn services to Luke's repair shop on account, $500.
July 6   One of Jake's mowers malfunctions. Luke provides repair services to Jake on account, $450.

July 9   Luke pays $500 to Jake for lawn services provided on July 3.
July 14   Luke borrows $600 from Jake by signing a note.
July 18   Jake purchases advertising in a local newspaper for the remainder of July and pays cash, $110.
July 20   Jake pays $450 to Luke for services provided on July 6.
July 27   Luke performs repair services for other customers for cash, $800.
July 30   Luke pays employee salaries for the month, $300.
July 31   Luke pays $600 to Jake for money borrowed on July 14.

Required:
Record the transactions for Jake's Lawn Maintenance Company.

P2–5A Refer to the transactions described in P2–4A. Keep in mind that Jake may not need to record all transactions.

Analyze the impact of transactions on the accounting equation and record transactions (LO2–2, 2–4)

Flip Side of P2–4A

Jake's Lawn Maintenance Company				Luke's Repair Shop		
	Assets	= Liabilities +	Stockholders' Equity	Assets	= Liabilities +	Stockholders' Equity
July 3	+$500 =	$0 +	+$500	$0	= +$500 +	−$500
6	___	___	___	___	___	___
9	___	___	___	___	___	___
14	___	___	___	___	___	___
18	___	___	___	___	___	___
20	___	___	___	___	___	___
27	___	___	___	___	___	___
30	___	___	___	___	___	___
31	___	___	___	___	___	___

Required:
1. Record each transaction for Luke's Repair Shop. Keep in mind that Luke may not need to record all transactions.
2. Using the format shown above, indicate the impact of each transaction on the accounting equation for each company.

P2–6A Below are the account balances of Bruins Company at the end of November.

Prepare a trial balance (LO2–6)

Accounts	Balances	Accounts	Balances
Cash	$40,000	Common Stock	$50,000
Accounts Receivable	50,000	Retained Earnings	35,000
Supplies	1,100	Dividends	1,100
Prepaid Rent	3,000	Service Revenue	65,000
Equipment	?	Salaries Expense	30,000
Accounts Payable	17,000	Rent Expense	12,000
Salaries Payable	5,000	Interest Expense	3,000
Interest Payable	3,000	Supplies Expense	7,000
Deferred Revenue	9,000	Utilities Expense	6,000
Notes Payable	30,000		

Complete the steps in the measurement of external transactions (LO2–4, 2–5, 2–6)

Required:
Prepare a trial balance by placing amounts in the appropriate debit or credit column and determining the balance of the Equipment account.

P2–7A Below are the transactions for Ute Sewing Shop for March, the first month of operations.

March   1   Issue common stock in exchange for cash of $3,000.
March   3   Purchase sewing equipment by signing a note with the local bank, $2,700.
March   5   Pay rent of $600 for March.
March   7   Martha, a customer, places an order for alterations to several dresses. Ute estimates that the alterations will cost Martha $800. Martha is not required to pay for the alterations until the work is complete.
March 12   Purchase sewing supplies for $130 on account. This material will be used to provide services to customers.
March 15   Ute delivers altered dresses to Martha and receives $800.
March 19   Ute agrees to alter 10 business suits for Bob, who has lost a significant amount of weight recently. Ute receives $700 from Bob and promises the suits to be completed by March 25.
March 25   Ute delivers 10 altered business suits to Bob.
March 30   Pay utilities of $95 for the current period.
March 31   Pay dividends of $150 to stockholders.

Required:

1. Record each transaction.
2. Post each transaction to the appropriate T-accounts.
3. Calculate the balance of each account at March 31.
4. Prepare a trial balance as of March 31.

Ute uses the following accounts: Cash, Supplies, Equipment, Accounts Payable, Deferred Revenue, Notes Payable, Common Stock, Dividends, Service Revenue, Rent Expense, and Utilities Expense.

Complete the steps in the measurement of external transactions
(LO2–4, 2–5, 2–6)

P2–8A Pirates Incorporated had the following balances at the beginning of September.

PIRATES INCORPORATED Trial Balance		
Accounts	**Debits**	**Credits**
Cash	$ 6,500	
Accounts Receivable	2,500	
Supplies	7,600	
Land	11,200	
Accounts Payable		$7,500
Notes Payable		3,000
Common Stock		9,000
Retained Earnings		8,300

The following transactions occur in September.

September   1   Provide services to customers for cash, $4,700.
September   2   Purchase land with a long-term note for $6,400 from Crimson Company.
September   4   Receive an invoice for $500 from the local newspaper for an advertisement that appeared on September 2.
September   8   Provide services to customers on account for $6,000.
September 10   Purchase supplies on account for $1,100.
September 13   Pay $4,000 to Crimson Company for a long-term note.
September 18   Receive $5,000 from customers on account.
September 20   Pay $900 for September's rent.
September 30   Pay September's utility bill of $2,000.
September 30   Pay employees $4,000 for salaries for the month of September.
September 30   Pay a cash dividend of $1,100 to shareholders.

Required:

1. Record each transaction.
2. Post each transaction to the appropriate T-accounts.

3. Calculate the balance of each account at September 30. (*Hint:* Be sure to include the balance at the beginning of September in each T-account.)
4. Prepare a trial balance as of September 30.

P2–9A RiverHawk Expeditions provides guided tours in scenic mountainous areas. After the first 11 months of operations in 2018, RiverHawk has the following account balances.

Complete the steps in the measurement of external transactions
(LO2–4, 2–5, 2–6)

RIVERHAWK EXPEDITIONS
Trial Balance
November 30, 2018

Accounts	Debits	Credits
Cash	$ 9,200	
Accounts Receivable	4,500	
Prepaid Insurance	400	
Equipment	24,100	
Land	170,000	
Accounts Payable		$ 3,300
Notes Payable		50,000
Common Stock		120,000
Retained Earnings		14,100
Dividends	5,000	
Service Revenue		75,000
Advertising Expense	11,000	
Salaries Expense	28,300	
Rent Expense	9,900	
Totals	$262,400	$262,400

The following transactions occur during December 2018:

December 1	Pay rent for mountain lodges the month of December, $900.
December 5	Provide guided tour to customers in Grand Teton National Park for cash, $2,800.
December 8	Borrow from a local bank by signing a note payable, $10,000. The note is due in one year with a 6% interest rate.
December 12	Receive cash from customers as payment for a guided tour that occurred on November 28, $3,500.
December 13	Issue additional shares of common stock for cash, $20,000.
December 15	Pay employee salaries for the first half of the month, $1,200.
December 17	Purchase advertising on several local radio stations to be aired during the following two weeks, $1,000.
December 22	Provide guided tour to customers in Yellowstone National Park on account, $3,200.
December 23	One of the customers from the December 22 tour claims to have seen the legendary creature Bigfoot. The company believes this exciting news will create additional revenue of $20,000 next year.
December 26	Purchase several pieces of hiking equipment to give customers a more enjoyable adventure, such as night-vision goggles, GPS, long-range binoculars, and video cameras, for cash, $28,500.
December 28	Pay cash on accounts payable, $1,500.
December 31	Pay dividends to stockholders, $2,000.

Required:

1. Record each transaction.
2. Post each transaction to the appropriate T-accounts.

3. Calculate the balance of each account at December 31. (*Hint:* Be sure to include the balance at the beginning of December in each T-account.)
4. Prepare a trial balance as of December 31.

PROBLEMS: SET B

Analyze the impact of transactions on the accounting equation (LO2–2)

P2–1B Below is a list of activities for Tigers Corporation.

Transaction	Assets	=	Liabilities	+	Stockholders' Equity
1. *Obtain a loan at the bank.*	*Increase*	=	*Increase*	+	*No effect*
2. Purchase a machine to use in operations for cash.	_____		_____		_____
3. Provide services to customers for cash.	_____		_____		_____
4. Pay employee salaries for the current month.	_____		_____		_____
5. Repay loan from the bank in (1) above.	_____		_____		_____
6. Customers pay cash in advance of services.	_____		_____		_____
7. Pay for maintenance costs in the current month.	_____		_____		_____
8. Pay for advertising in the current month.	_____		_____		_____
9. Purchase office supplies on account.	_____		_____		_____
10. Provide services to customers on account.	_____		_____		_____
11. Pay dividends to stockholders.	_____		_____		_____

Required:

For each activity, indicate whether the transaction increases, decreases, or has no effect on assets, liabilities, and stockholders' equity.

Analyze the impact of transactions on the accounting equation (LO2–2)

P2–2B Below is a list of activities for Vikings Incorporated.

Transaction	Assets	=	Liabilities	+	Stockholders' Equity
1. *Issue common stock in exchange for cash, $15,000.*	*+ $15,000*	=	*$0*	+	*+$15,000*
2. Obtain a loan from the bank for $9,000.	_____		_____		_____
3. Receive cash of $1,200 in advance from customers.	_____		_____		_____
4. Purchase supplies on account, $2,400.	_____		_____		_____
5. Pay one year of rent in advance, $12,000.	_____		_____		_____
6. Provide services to customers on account, $3,000.	_____		_____		_____
7. Repay $4,000 of the loan in (2) above.	_____		_____		_____
8. Pay the full amount for supplies purchased in (4) above.	_____		_____		_____
9. Provide services to customers in (3) above.	_____		_____		_____
10. Pay cash dividends of $1,000 to stockholders.	_____		_____		_____
Totals	_____	=	_____	+	_____

Required:

For each activity, indicate the impact on the accounting equation. After doing all the transactions, ensure that the accounting equation remains in balance.

P2–3B Below is a list of typical accounts.

Identify the type of account and its normal debit or credit balance **(LO2–3)**

Accounts	Type of Account	Normal Balance (Debit or Credit)
1. Supplies	_____	_____
2. Advertising Expense	_____	_____
3. Prepaid Insurance	_____	_____
4. Supplies Expense	_____	_____
5. Accounts Payable	_____	_____
6. Equipment	_____	_____
7. Dividends	_____	_____
8. Accounts Receivable	_____	_____
9. Retained Earnings	_____	_____
10. Deferred Revenue	_____	_____
11. Service Revenue	_____	_____
12. Utilities Payable	_____	_____

Required:

For each account, indicate (1) the type of account and (2) whether the normal account balance is a debit or credit. For type of account, choose from asset, liability, stockholders' equity, dividend, revenue, or expense.

P2–4B Eli owns an insurance office, while Olivia operates a maintenance service that provides basic custodial duties. For the month of May, the following transactions occurred.

Record transactions **(LO2–4)**

Flip Side of P2–5B

May 2	Olivia decides that she will need insurance for a one-day special event at the end of the month and pays Eli $300 in advance.
May 5	Olivia provides maintenance services to Eli's insurance offices on account, $425.
May 7	Eli borrows $500 from Olivia by signing a note.
May 14	Olivia purchases maintenance supplies from Spot Corporation, paying cash of $200.
May 19	Eli pays $425 to Olivia for maintenance services provided on May 5.
May 25	Eli pays the utility bill for the month of May, $135.
May 28	Olivia receives insurance services from Eli equaling the amount paid on May 2.
May 31	Eli pays $500 to Olivia for money borrowed on May 7.

Required:

Record each transaction for Eli's Insurance Services. Keep in mind that Eli may not need to record each transaction.

P2–5B Refer to the transactions described in P2–4B.

Analyze the impact of transactions on the accounting equation and record transactions **(LO2–2, 2–4)**

Flip Side of P2–4B

	Eli's Insurance Services				Olivia's Maintenance Services		
	Assets	= Liabilities +	Stockholders' Equity		Assets	= Liabilities +	Stockholders' Equity
May 2	+$300	= +$300 +	$0		+$300 −$300	= $0 +	$0
5	_____	_____	_____		_____	_____	_____
7	_____	_____	_____		_____	_____	_____

(continued)

(concluded)

	Eli's Insurance Services			Olivia's Maintenance Services		
	Assets	= Liabilities +	Stockholders' Equity	Assets	= Liabilities +	Stockholders' Equity
14	————	————	————	————	————	————
19	————	————	————	————	————	————
25	————	————	————	————	————	————
28	————	————	————	————	————	————
31	————	————	————	————	————	————

Required:

1. Record transactions for Olivia's Maintenance Services. Keep in mind that Olivia may not need to record each transaction.
2. Using the format shown, indicate the impact of each transaction on the accounting equation for each company.

Prepare a trial balance (LO2–6)

P2–6B Below are account balances of Ducks Company at the end of September.

Accounts	Balances	Accounts	Balances
Cash	$25,000	Retained Earnings	$13,000
Accounts Receivable	14,000	Dividends	4,000
Supplies	7,000	Service Revenue	?
Prepaid Insurance	5,000	Salaries Expense	9,000
Equipment	28,000	Insurance Expense	8,000
Accounts Payable	7,000	Advertising Expense	1,100
Salaries Payable	4,000	Supplies Expense	10,000
Utilities Payable	1,100	Entertainment Expense	6,000
Deferred Revenue	9,000	Utilities Expense	1,100
Common Stock	29,000		

Required:

Prepare a trial balance by placing amounts in the appropriate debit or credit column and determining the balance of the Service Revenue account.

Complete the steps in the measurement of external transactions (LO2–4, 2–5, 2–6)

P2–7B Below are the transactions for Salukis Car Cleaning for June, the first month of operations.

June 1	Obtain a loan of $70,000 from the bank by signing a note.
June 2	Issue common stock in exchange for cash of $40,000.
June 7	Purchase car wash equipment for $75,000 cash.
June 10	Purchase cleaning supplies of $8,000 on account.
June 12	Wash 500 cars for $10 each. All customers pay cash.
June 16	Pay employees $900 for work performed.
June 19	Pay for advertising in a local newspaper, costing $500.
June 23	Wash 600 cars for $10 each on account.
June 29	Pay employees $950 for work performed.
June 30	A utility bill of $1,400 for the current month is paid.
June 30	Pay dividends of $600 to stockholders.

Required:

1. Record each transaction.
2. Post each transaction to the appropriate T-accounts.
3. Calculate the balance of each account.
4. Prepare a trial balance for June.

Salukis uses the following accounts: Cash, Accounts Receivable, Supplies, Equipment, Accounts Payable, Notes Payable, Common Stock, Dividends, Service Revenue, Salaries Expense, Advertising Expense, and Utilities Expense.

P2–8B Buckeye Incorporated had the following balances at the beginning of November.

Complete the steps in the measurement of external transactions (LO2–4, 2–5, 2–6)

BUCKEYE INCORPORATED Trial Balance		
Accounts	**Debits**	**Credits**
Cash	$3,200	
Accounts Receivable	600	
Supplies	700	
Equipment	9,400	
Accounts Payable		$2,000
Notes Payable		4,000
Common Stock		7,000
Retained Earnings		900

The following transactions occur in November.

November 1	Issue common stock in exchange for $13,000 cash.
November 2	Purchase equipment with a long-term note for $3,500 from Spartan Corporation.
November 4	Purchase supplies for $1,000 on account.
November 10	Provide services to customers on account for $9,000.
November 15	Pay creditors on account, $1,100.
November 20	Pay employees $3,000 for the first half of the month.
November 22	Provide services to customers for $11,000 cash.
November 24	Pay $1,400 on the note from Spartan Corporation.
November 26	Collect $7,000 on account from customers.
November 28	Pay $1,100 to the local utility company for November gas and electricity.
November 30	Pay $5,000 rent for November.

Required:

1. Record each transaction.
2. Post each transaction to the appropriate T-accounts.
3. Calculate the balance of each account at November 30. (*Hint:* Be sure to include the balance at the beginning of November in each T-account.)
4. Prepare a trial balance as of November 30.

P2–9B Thunder Cat Services specializes in training and veterinary services to household pets, such as dogs, birds, lizards, fish, horses, and of course, cats. After the first 11 months of operations in 2018, Thunder Cat has the following account balances:

Complete the steps in the measurement of external transactions (LO2–4, 2–5, 2–6)

THUNDER CAT SERVICES Trial Balance November 30, 2018		
Accounts	**Debits**	**Credits**
Cash	$ 19,400	
Supplies	1,500	
Prepaid Rent	7,200	
Equipment	83,700	
Buildings	240,000	
Accounts Payable		$ 9,800
Deferred Revenue		2,000
Common Stock		125,000
Retained Earnings		75,500
Dividends	9,000	
Service Revenue		264,000
Salaries Expense	65,000	
Advertising Expense	18,200	
Utilities Expense	32,300	
Totals	$476,300	$476,300

The following transactions occur during December 2018:

December 1–31	Throughout the month, Thunder Cat provides services to customers for cash, $27,400. (*Hint:* Record the entire month's services in a single entry.)
December 4	Purchase pet supplies on account, $2,900.
December 8	Pay for fliers to be distributed to local residences to advertise the company's services, $3,200.
December 9	Pay for supplies purchased on December 4.
December 12	Issue additional shares of common stock for cash, $5,000.
December 16	Pay cash on accounts payable, $6,300.
December 19	Purchase equipment with cash, $7,700.
December 22	Pay utilities for December, $4,500.
December 24	Receive cash from customers for services to be provided next January, $2,300.
December 27	One of Thunder Cat's trainers takes a part-time job at the zoo and earns a salary of $1,200. The zoo and Thunder Cat Services are separate companies.
December 30	Pay employee salaries for the current month, $7,000.
December 31	Pay dividends to stockholders, $3,000.

Required:

1. Record each transaction.
2. Post each transaction to the appropriate T-accounts.
3. Calculate the balance of each account at December 31. (*Hint:* Be sure to include the balance at the beginning of December in each T-account.)
4. Prepare a trial balance as of December 31.

ADDITIONAL PERSPECTIVES

Great Adventures

Continuing Problem

(This is a continuation of the Great Adventures problem from Chapter 1.)

AP2–1 Tony and Suzie graduate from college in May 2018 and begin developing their new business. They begin by offering clinics for basic outdoor activities such as mountain biking or kayaking. Upon developing a customer base, they'll hold their first adventure races. These races will involve four-person teams that race from one checkpoint to the next using a combination of kayaking, mountain biking, orienteering, and trail running. In the long run, they plan to sell outdoor gear and develop a ropes course for outdoor enthusiasts.

On July 1, 2018, Tony and Suzie organize their new company as a corporation, Great Adventures Inc. The articles of incorporation state that the corporation will sell 20,000 shares of common stock for $1 each. Each share of stock represents a unit of ownership. Tony and Suzie will act as co-presidents of the company. The following business activities occur during July for Great Adventures.

July 1	Sell $10,000 of common stock to Suzie.
1	Sell $10,000 of common stock to Tony.
1	Purchase a one-year insurance policy for $4,800 ($400 per month) to cover injuries to participants during outdoor clinics.
2	Pay legal fees of $1,500 associated with incorporation.
4	Purchase office supplies of $1,800 on account.
7	Pay for advertising of $300 to a local newspaper for an upcoming mountain biking clinic to be held on July 15. Attendees will be charged $50 the day of the clinic.
8	Purchase 10 mountain bikes, paying $12,000 cash.
15	On the day of the clinic, Great Adventures receives cash of $2,000 from 40 bikers. Tony conducts the mountain biking clinic.
22	Because of the success of the first mountain biking clinic, Tony holds another mountain biking clinic and the company receives $2,300.
24	Pay for advertising of $700 to a local radio station for a kayaking clinic to be held on August 10. Attendees can pay $100 in advance or $150 on the day of the clinic.
30	Great Adventures receives cash of $4,000 in advance from 40 kayakers for the upcoming kayak clinic.

Required:
1. Record each transaction in July for Great Adventures. [Note: These same transactions can be assigned as part of a more complete accounting cycle in Chapter 3's AP3–1].
2. Post each transaction to T-accounts.
3. Prepare a trial balance.

American Eagle Outfitters, Inc.

Financial Analysis

AP2–2 Financial information for **American Eagle** is presented in **Appendix A** at the end of the book.

Required:
1. Is American Eagle's company size increasing? To answer, calculate the percentage change in total assets and percentage change in net sales for the most recent year.
2. Is American Eagle's total profitability increasing? Determine your answer by calculating the percentage change in net income for the most recent year.
3. Did American Eagle issue any common stock in the most recent year?
4. Do you see the term *debit* or *credit* listed in the balance sheet? Which account types in the balance sheet increase with a debit and which ones increase with a credit?
5. Do you see the term *debit* or *credit* listed in the income statement? Which account types in the income statement increase with a debit? Which increase with a credit?

The Buckle, Inc.

Financial Analysis

AP2–3 Financial information for **Buckle** is presented in **Appendix B** at the end of the book.

Required:
1. Is Buckle's company size increasing? Determine your answer by calculating the percentage change in total assets and percentage change in net sales for the most recent year.
2. Is Buckle's total profitability increasing? Determine your answer by calculating the percentage change in net income for the most recent year.
3. Did Buckle issue any common stock in the most recent year?
4. Do you see the term *debit* or *credit* listed in the balance sheet? Which account types in the balance sheet increase with a debit and which ones increase with a credit?
5. Do you see the term *debit* or *credit* listed in the income statement? Which account types in the income statement increase with a debit? Which increase with a credit?

American Eagle Outfitters, Inc. vs. The Buckle, Inc.

Comparative Analysis

AP2–4 Financial information for **American Eagle** is presented in **Appendix A** at the end of the book, and financial information for **Buckle** is presented in **Appendix B** at the end of the book.

Required:
Determine which company's growth rate in total assets, net sales, and net income is greater. Why do you think this might be the case?

Ethics

AP2–5 Larry has been the chief financial officer (CFO) of Maxima Auto Service for the past 10 years. The company has reported profits each year it's been in business. However, this year has been a tough one. Increased competition and the rising costs of labor have reduced the company's profits. On December 30, Larry informs Robert, the company's president and Larry's closest friend for the past 10 years, that it looks like the company will report a net loss (total expenses will be greater than total revenues) of about $50,000 this year.

The next day, December 31, while Larry is preparing the year-end reports, Robert stops by Larry's office to tell him that an additional $75,000 of revenues needs to be reported and that the company can now report a profit. When Larry asks about the source of the $75,000, Robert tells him, "Earlier in the month some customers paid for auto services with cash, and with this cash I bought additional assets for the company. That's why the $75,000 never showed up in the bank statement. I just forgot to tell you about this earlier." When Larry asks for more specifics about these transactions, Robert mumbles, "I can't recall where I placed the customer sales invoices or the purchase receipts for the assets, but don't worry; I know they're here. We've been friends for a lot of years and you can trust me. Now, let's hurry and finish those reports and I'll treat you to dinner tonight at the restaurant of your choice."

Required:

Discuss the ethical dilemma Larry faces: What is the issue? Who are the parties affected? What factors should Larry consider in making his decision?

Internet Research

AP2–6 Obtain a copy of the annual report of **Apple Inc.** for the most recent year. You can find the annual report at the company's website (*www.apple.com*) in the investor information section or at the Securities and Exchange Commission's website (*www.sec.gov*) using EDGAR (Electronic Data Gathering, Analysis, and Retrieval). Form 10-K, which includes the annual report, is required to be filed on EDGAR. Search or scroll within the annual report to find the financial statements.

Required:

Determine the following from the company's financial statements:
1. What amount does the company report for accounts receivable? What does this amount represent?
2. What amount does the company report for accounts payable? What does this amount represent?
3. The company reports a single amount for accrued expenses in the liability section of the balance sheet. What are some possible liabilities included in this amount?
4. What amount does the company report for common stock (including additional paid-in capital)? What does this amount represent?
5. Determine whether the company's total assets equal total liabilities plus total stockholders' (or shareholders') equity.
6. Apple refers to its income statement as the statement of operations. What amount does the company report for net sales? This amount represents sales of the company's products over what period of time?
7. What are some of the expenses listed in the income statement?
8. Do the company's total revenues exceed total expenses? By how much?

Written Communication

AP2–7 Barth Interior provides decorating advice to its clients. Three recent transactions of the company include:
a. Providing decorating services of $500 on account to one of its clients.
b. Paying $1,200 for an employee's salary in the current period.
c. Purchasing office equipment for $2,700 by paying cash.

Required:

Write a memo to your instructor describing each step of the six-step measurement process presented in Illustration 2–1 for each of the three transactions.

Answers to the Self-Study Questions
1. c   2. d   3. c   4. c   5. c   6. a   7. d   8. a   9. c   10. d

3

The Accounting Cycle: End of the Period

Learning Objectives

AFTER STUDYING THIS CHAPTER, YOU SHOULD BE ABLE TO:

- **LO3–1** Understand when revenues and expenses are recorded.
- **LO3–2** Distinguish between accrual-basis and cash-basis accounting.
- **LO3–3** Demonstrate the purposes and recording of adjusting entries.
- **LO3–4** Post adjusting entries and prepare an adjusted trial balance.
- **LO3–5** Prepare financial statements using the adjusted trial balance.
- **LO3–6** Demonstrate the purposes and recording of closing entries.
- **LO3–7** Post closing entries and prepare a post-closing trial balance.

FEDERAL EXPRESS: DELIVERING PROFITS TO INVESTORS

Wouldn't it be great to put $1,000 into the stock market and watch your investment really grow? Which stock should you buy? Where should you buy it? There are thousands of stocks listed on stock exchanges in the United States and thousands of others listed throughout the world. With so many choices, how do you tell the winning stocks from the losing stocks? The single piece of information that best distinguishes them is *net income.*

Recall that net income equals revenues minus expenses for each reporting period. It measures how profitable the business is. Stockholders are the owners of the business, and any profits of the company belong solely to them (and not to creditors). Therefore, as net income increases, so does the value of the company to its stockholders.

To see an example of the power of net income in explaining movements in stock prices, consider the following information for **FedEx Corporation (FedEx)**. Over the 20-year period from 1995–2014, FedEx's net income increased in 16 of 20 years. For the other four years, net income decreased. What happened to FedEx's stock price in each of these years? In the years that net income increased, FedEx's stock price *rose* an average of 20.5%. In contrast, in the years that net income decreased, FedEx's stock price *fell* an average of 8.8%. The goal is clear: Predict the direction of the change in net income and you'll predict the change in stock prices.

In this chapter, we discuss how revenues and expenses are measured to calculate a company's net income. We'll then look at how revenues and expenses are communicated in a financial statement referred to as the income statement. We'll also look at two other related statements—the statement of stockholders' equity and the balance sheet. The full set of financial statements provides a summary picture of the company's operations for the period and its current financial position. It is these financial statements and other related financial disclosures that investors use in deciding which company's stock to buy and sell.

© AP Images/Emile Wamsteker

PART A

ACCRUAL-BASIS ACCOUNTING

Net income, while certainly not the only consideration, is an essential aspect of good investment decisions. Investors know that any information they gather to help in predicting net income will lead to more profitable investments. Given the importance of net income to investors, standard setters have devoted considerable attention to the proper measurement of the two primary components of net income—revenues and expenses. In this section, we look at important principles behind reporting of revenues and expenses and at their effect on accounting.

Revenue and Expense Reporting

■ **LO3–1**
Understand when revenues and expenses are recorded.

If accounting information is to be useful in making decisions, accountants must measure and report revenues and expenses in a way that clearly reflects the ability of the company to create value for its owners, the stockholders. To do this, we use accrual-basis accounting, in which we record revenues when we provide goods and services to customers, and we record expenses with related revenues. We discuss these two ideas next.

REVENUE RECOGNITION

A company records revenues when it sells its products or services to a customer. For example, revenues are recorded when **FedEx** delivers a package, **American Eagle** sells a shirt, or **GEICO** provides insurance coverage. The overriding concept in understanding when to record revenue is the revenue recognition principle. The revenue recognition principle states that we record revenue in the period in which we provide goods and services to customers.[1] If a company sells products or services to a customer in 2018, the company should report the revenue in its 2018 income statement. If the company sells products or services to a customer in 2019, it should report the revenue in the 2019 income statement, and so on.

To demonstrate how the revenue recognition principle is applied, let's refer back to three of the transactions of Eagle Golf Academy discussed in Illustration 2–2 of Chapter 2. Restated below are Eagle's transactions (6), (7), and (8).

Transaction	Date	Description
(6)	Dec. 12	Provide golf training to customers for cash, $4,300.
(7)	Dec. 17	Provide golf training to customers on account, $2,000.
(8)	Dec. 23	Receive cash in advance for 12 golf training sessions to be given in the future, $600.

For which of these did Eagle provide a good or service at the time of the transaction? Answer: Transactions (6) and (7). **Therefore, Eagle recorded revenue for transaction (6) on December 12, and Eagle recorded revenue for transaction (7) on December 17.** You can refer back to Chapter 2 to see how we recorded revenue on these dates.

For transaction (8), however, notice that Eagle did not provide a service on December 23, even though it received cash from customers. Since Eagle simply received cash in advance and did not provide a service, **Eagle cannot record the revenue on December 23.** Instead, recall from Chapter 2 that Eagle records Deferred Revenue (a liability) on December 23, because we *owe* customers a service when they pay in advance. Eagle will wait to record the revenue until the services are provided at some later date. We'll look specifically at how this deferred revenue gets recorded as revenue in Part B of this chapter.

---

[1]The revenue recognition principle was recently revised by Accounting Standards Update No. 2014-09, "Revenues from Contracts with Customers," on May 28, 2014. Prior to this update, revenue recognition relied on the concepts of "revenue being earned" and "cash being collected or collectible." Our discussion of revenue recognition is based on the new standard.

KEY POINT

The revenue recognition principle states that we record revenue in the period in which we provide goods and services to customers, not necessarily in the period in which we receive cash.

EXPENSE RECOGNITION

Now let's discuss when we record expenses, the costs associated with producing the revenues. Common expenses include advertising, employees' salaries, utilities, office rent, and business supplies. Companies typically report expenses *in the same period as the revenues they help to generate* (a concept commonly referred to by accountants as the matching principle). Implied in this principle is a *cause-and-effect* relationship between revenue and expense recognition. In the same period we report revenues, we should also record all expenses incurred to generate those revenues. The result is a measure—net income—that matches current period accomplishments (revenues) and sacrifices (expenses).

To demonstrate expense recognition, let's again refer to three of the transactions of Eagle Golf Academy discussed in Illustration 2–2 of Chapter 2. Restated below are Eagle's transactions (4), (5), and (9).

Transaction	Date	Description
(4)	Dec. 1	Pay one year of rent in advance, $6,000 ($500 per month).
(5)	Dec. 6	Purchase supplies on account, $2,300.
(9)	Dec. 28	Pay salaries to employees, $2,800.

Rent, supplies, and salaries are all costs of running the business, but which of these transactions are recorded as an expense on the date it occurs?

For transaction (4), Eagle paid 12 months of rent on December 1. Even though a $6,000 cash payment for rent was made on December 1, the cost of this rent has not produced any revenue as of December 1. Therefore, no expense is recorded on December 1. Instead, Eagle records Prepaid Rent (an asset) for the future benefits to be received by the payment of rent in advance. When will the $6,000 cost of rent be expensed? As we'll see in Part B of this chapter, **we'll record $500 of rent expense at the end of December, and another $500 of rent expense at the end of each of the next 11 months.** The assumption is that the cost of rent for the month of December helps to produce revenue in December, the cost of rent in January helps to produce revenue in January, and so on. So, we expense one month of rent ($500) at the end of each month during the one-year rent period.

Transaction (5) did not involve cash, but Eagle did purchase supplies on account. When will the cost of supplies be recorded as an expense? Answer: when those supplies are used, because that's when they are assumed to help produce revenue. **By the end of December, the supplies used in December will have helped to produce revenue in December, and therefore that portion of the supplies will be recorded as supplies expense.** We'll see how to record the used supplies as an expense at the end of December in Part B of this chapter.

Finally, transaction (9) involves Eagle paying $2,800 for employees' salaries in December. As of December 28, what portion of the $2,800 represents a cost that helped to produce revenue as of December 28? Answer: all of it. Employees are assumed to produce revenue in the period that they work. In Chapter 2, **we saw that Eagle recorded Salaries Expense equal to $2,800 on December 28.** In Part B, we'll also see how to record salaries expense for the final three days in December.

Period Cost.   Some costs may be more difficult to match directly with the revenue they help to produce. These costs, commonly referred to as period costs, are expensed in the period they occur. For example, suppose Eagle had paid $100 in December for advertising. In theory, it would be ideal for Eagle to record the cost of advertising as an expense in the month that it records the revenue the advertising generates. However, it's difficult to determine when, how much, or even whether additional revenues occur as a result of advertising. Because of this, firms generally recognize advertising expenditures as expenses in the *period* the ads are provided, with no attempt made to match them with related revenues.

 KEY POINT

Most expenses are recorded in the same period as the revenues they help to generate. Other expenses indirectly related to producing revenues are recorded in the period they occur.

Decision Point

Question ?	Accounting information 📄	Analysis 🔍
Can the company generate revenues that exceed its expenses?	Revenues and expenses reported in the income statement	Revenues measure sales to customers during the year. Expenses measure the cost of those revenues. These two combine to measure net income, or profitability.

Accrual-Basis Compared with Cash-Basis Accounting

■ **LO3–2**
Distinguish between accrual-basis and cash-basis accounting.

In the preceding section, we discovered the following about accrual-basis accounting:

1. We record revenues when we provide goods and services to customers (the revenue recognition principle) and *not necessarily when we receive cash*.

2. We record expenses with related revenues and *not necessarily when we pay cash*.

An alternative to accrual-basis accounting is cash-basis accounting. Under cash-basis accounting:

1. We record revenues at the time we *receive cash*.

2. We record expenses at the time we *pay cash*.

Under cash-basis accounting, the timing of the cash flows of the company exactly matches the timing that revenues and expenses are recorded.

Illustration 3–1 summarizes revenue recognition for Eagle's transactions using accrual-basis and cash-basis accounting.

ILLUSTRATION 3–1   Accrual-Basis Revenue versus Cash-Basis Revenue

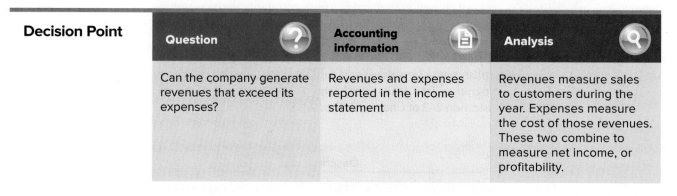

		Accrual-Basis		Cash-Basis	
Transaction	Description	Service Provided	Revenue Recorded	Cash Received	Revenue Recorded
(6) Dec. 12	Provide golf training to customers for cash, $4,300.	✓	$4,300	✓	$4,300
(7) Dec. 17	Provide golf training to customers on account. $2,000.	✓	$2,000	✗	$0 Defer revenue until cash received
(8) Dec. 23	Receive cash in advance for 12 golf training sessions to be given in the future, $600.	✗	$0 Defer revenue until service provided	✓	$600

Under accrual-basis accounting, revenue is recorded only at the time a service is provided. Under cash-basis accounting, the revenue equals the amount of cash received.

Illustration 3–2 summarizes expense recognition for Eagle's transactions using accrual-basis and cash-basis accounting.

ILLUSTRATION 3–2 Accrual-Basis Expense versus Cash-Basis Expense

		Accrual-Basis		Cash-Basis	
Transaction	Description	Cost Used	Expense Recorded	Cash Paid	Expense Recorded
(4) Dec. 1	Pay one year of rent in advance, $6,000 ($500 per month).	✗	$0 Defer expense until end of each month ($500/month)	✓	$6,000
(5) Dec. 6	Purchase supplies on account, $2,300.	✗	$0 Defer expense until supplies used	✗	$0 Defer expense until cash paid
(9) Dec. 28	Pay salaries to employees, $2,800.	✓	$2,800	✓	$2,800

Under accrual-basis accounting, an expense is recorded for the amount of the *cost used* to help produce revenue. In some cases (such as prepaid rent on December 1 or purchase of supplies on December 6), the cost is initially deferred in an asset account and later recorded as an expense as it helps in producing revenue. Under cash-basis accounting, the expense equals the amount of cash paid.

Under both accrual-basis and cash-basis accounting, all revenues and expenses are eventually recorded for the same amount. For example, the $2,300 of supplies purchased on December 6 will be fully expensed at some point under both accounting methods because all supplies will eventually be used (accrual-basis) and paid for (cash-basis). **The difference between the two methods is in the timing of when we record those revenues and expenses.** Under accrual-basis accounting, we record revenues when goods and services are provided to customers, and we record expenses when costs help to produce the related revenue. Under cash-basis accounting, we record revenues and expenses at the time we receive or pay cash.

Cash-basis accounting may seem appealing because it is essentially how we think about the inflow and outflow of cash from our bank accounts. However, **cash-basis accounting is not part of generally accepted accounting principles (GAAP).** Most major companies use accrual-basis accounting to properly record revenues when goods and services are provided and to properly record expenses in the same period as the revenue they help to generate. As we saw demonstrated above, revenues and expenses under accrual-basis accounting are not always recorded at the time the cash receipt or payment occurs. Because of the need to use accrual-basis accounting, companies must make adjustments to their accounting records at the end of the period to fully capture all revenue and expense transactions during the period. These period-end adjustments are known as *adjusting entries,* discussed next in Part B.

Cash-basis accounting is not part of generally accepted accounting principles (GAAP).

KEY POINT

The difference between accrual-basis accounting and cash-basis accounting is *timing.* Under accrual-basis accounting, we record revenues when we provide goods and services to customers, and we record expenses with the revenue they help to generate. Under cash-basis accounting, we record revenues when we receive cash, and we record expenses when we pay cash. Cash-basis accounting is not allowed for financial reporting purposes for most major companies.

Let's Review

Cavalier Company experienced the following set of events:

May: *Receives cash* from customers for services to be provided in June.
June: *Provides services* to customers who prepaid in May.
May: *Pays cash* for supplies but does not use them.
June: *Uses supplies* purchased in May.

Required:

1. Indicate in which month Cavalier records revenues under:
   a. Accrual-basis accounting
   b. Cash-basis accounting

2. Indicate in which month Cavalier records expenses under:
   a. Accrual-basis accounting
   b. Cash-basis accounting

Suggested Homework:
BE3–4, BE3–5;
E3–3, E3-4;
P3–1A&B; P3–2A&B

Solution:

1a. June   1b. May   2a. June   2b. May

PART B

THE MEASUREMENT PROCESS

In Chapter 2, we started the measurement process of the accounting cycle by recording and posting external transactions that occurred *during the period*. In this chapter, we will complete the accounting cycle process at the *end of the period* as summarized in Illustration 3–3. First we continue the measurement process by recording adjusting entries (or internal transactions). Following adjusting entries, we will prepare financial statements and then close the books.

ILLUSTRATION 3–3

The Accounting Cycle

mhhe.com/4fa8

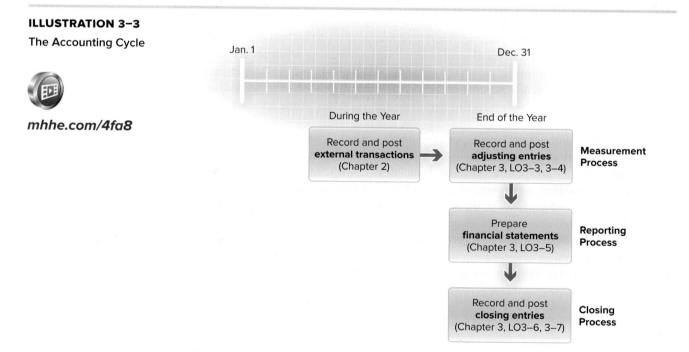

Adjusting Entries

■ **LO3–3**
Demonstrate the purposes and recording of adjusting entries.

At the end of a reporting period, even if we've accurately recorded every transaction that occurred during the period and accurately posted those transactions to appropriate accounts, our account balances are not updated for preparing financial statements. Before we can prepare the financial statements, we need to bring several of the account balances up-to-date.

That's the purpose of adjusting entries. We use adjusting entries to record events that have occurred but that we have not yet recorded.

To envision the process, think of your auto insurance. Insurance companies require you to pay for insurance in advance. On the day you purchased the insurance, you actually bought an *asset* representing insurance coverage over a future period. With each passing day, however, the length of your policy is lapsing, decreasing your insurance asset. Tomorrow you will have one day less insurance coverage than you do today.

The same holds true for a business and its insurance coverage. Although it's true that the company's asset is declining daily, it is unnecessary (and in fact impractical) to record the lapsing of the insurance coverage each day. Recording the expense is necessary, though, when it's time to prepare financial statements at the end of the reporting period. Thus, we use an end-of-period *adjusting entry*. In the case of the insurance coverage, the business adjusts downward the balance of the asset (prepaid insurance) and records insurance expense for the amount of the policy that has lapsed.

If we do not record the adjusting entry for the part of the insurance policy that has lapsed, then total assets will be overstated and expenses will be understated, causing net income to be overstated. Adjusting entries are a *necessary part of accrual-basis accounting*. They must be recorded at the end of each period before the company prepares its financial statements.

 KEY POINT

Adjusting entries are a necessary part of accrual-basis accounting. They help to update the balances of assets, liabilities, revenues, and expenses at the end of the accounting period for transactions that have occurred but have not yet been recorded.

It is useful to group adjusting entries into two broad categories—prepayments and accruals—that can be further divided into four subcategories: prepaid expenses, deferred revenues, accrued expenses, and accrued revenues. These four occur as shown in Illustration 3–4.

ILLUSTRATION 3–4

Types of Adjusting Entries

Prepayments / Deferrals

Prepaid Expenses—Pay cash (or have an obligation to pay cash) to purchase an asset in the current period that will be recorded as an expense in a future period.

Deferred Revenues—Receive cash in the current period that will be recorded as a revenue in a future period.

Accruals

Accrued Expenses—Record an expense in the current period that will be paid in cash in a future period.

Accrued Revenues—Record a revenue in the current period that will be collected in cash in a future period.

Let's consider each of these four types of adjusting entries by first looking back to the external transactions of Eagle Golf Academy from Chapter 2. For easy reference, we've restated these transactions in Illustration 3–5. We will prepare all adjusting entries on December 31, to account for other transactions that have occurred but not yet been recorded by the end of the period.

ILLUSTRATION 3–5

External Transactions of
Eagle Golf Academy

Transaction	Date	Description
(1)	Dec. 1	Sell shares of common stock for $25,000 to obtain the funds necessary to start the business.
(2)	Dec. 1	Borrow $10,000 from the local bank and sign a note promising to repay the full amount of the debt in three years.
(3)	Dec. 1	Purchase equipment necessary for giving golf training, $24,000 cash.
(4)	Dec. 1	Pay one year of rent in advance, $6,000 ($500 per month).
(5)	Dec. 6	Purchase supplies on account, $2,300.
(6)	Dec. 12	Provide golf training to customers for cash, $4,300.
(7)	Dec. 17	Provide golf training to customers on account, $2,000.
(8)	Dec. 23	Receive cash in advance for 12 golf training sessions to be given in the future, $600.
(9)	Dec. 28	Pay salaries to employees, $2,800.
(10)	Dec. 30	Pay cash dividends of $200 to shareholders.

PREPAID EXPENSES

Prepaid expenses are the costs of assets acquired in one period that will be recorded as an expense in a future period. Examples include the purchase of equipment or supplies and the payment of rent or insurance in advance. These payments *create future benefits,* so we initially record them as assets at the time of purchase. The benefits provided by these assets *expire in future periods,* so we need to expense their cost in those future periods. **The adjusting entry for a prepaid expense always includes a debit to an expense account (increase an expense) and a credit to an asset account (decrease an asset).**

Eagle Golf Academy had three prepaid expenses during December: It purchased equipment on December 1, rent on December 1, and supplies on December 6. Each of these items provides future benefits and was recorded as an asset at the time of purchase. *By the end of December,* the company has used a portion of each asset, and that portion no longer represents a future benefit. **The amount of the asset used is recorded as an expense, and the balance of the asset is reduced.** We'll look at each prepaid expense in turn.

Prepaid Rent.   Let's begin with transaction (4) in which Eagle Golf Academy purchases one year of rent in advance for $6,000 ($500 per month). The benefits from using the rented space occur evenly over time, with one month's cost attributable to December, one month's cost to next January, and so on. Therefore, we need to record one month of the asset's cost as an expense in December. At the same time, the asset account has one month's less benefit with each passing month, requiring us to reduce the balance of the asset.

The end-of-period **adjusting entry** for expiration of prepaid rent is below.

December 31	Debit	Credit
Rent Expense *(+E, −SE)*	**500**	
Prepaid Rent *(−A)*		**500**
(Reduce prepaid rent due to the passage of time)		

Notice that the adjusting entry includes a $500 expense (+E), which reduces net income and stockholders' equity (−SE). At the same time, the balance in the asset account, Prepaid Rent, decreases (−A) by $500 and will now have a balance of $5,500 (= $6,000 − $500). We adjust any other assets that expire over time (such as prepaid insurance) in a similar manner.

Supplies.   In transaction (5), Eagle purchases supplies for $2,300 on account on December 6. Even though cash will be paid later, the cost of supplies (or obligation to pay cash for supplies) is incurred on December 6. Suppose that at the end of December a count of supplies reveals that only $1,300 of supplies remains. What happened to the other $1,000 of supplies? Apparently, this is the amount of supplies used during the month. Since it's not cost-efficient to record the consumption of supplies every day, we make a single adjusting entry at the end of the period for the total amount used.

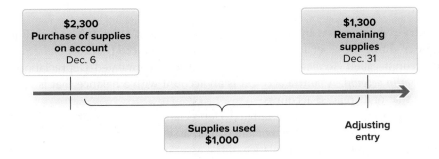

The end-of-period **adjusting entry** for supplies is below.

December 31	Debit	Credit
Supplies Expense *(+E, −SE)*	**1,000**	
Supplies *(−A)*		**1,000**
(Consume supplies during the current period)		

This entry simultaneously records the $1,000 of supplies used as an expense and reduces the balance of the Supplies account to the $1,300 amount that still remains.

Depreciable Assets.   In transaction (3), Eagle purchases equipment for $24,000 cash. Let's assume that, at the time of purchase, Eagle estimates the equipment will be useful for the next five years (60 months). Because one month (December) has passed since the purchase of this asset, Eagle has used one month of the asset's estimated 60-month useful life. In addition, the company has used one month of the asset's cost to produce revenue in December. Therefore, we should *match* the cost (expense) with the revenue it helps to produce. The cost of the equipment for one month's use is $400 (= $24,000 × 1/60). Although this creates a situation much like the expiration of prepaid rent or the use of supplies, we record the reduction in the cost of assets that have longer lives using a concept called *depreciation.*

Depreciation is the process of allocating the cost of an asset, such as equipment, to expense over the asset's useful life. We discuss this in detail in Chapter 7; here we will cover just the basics.

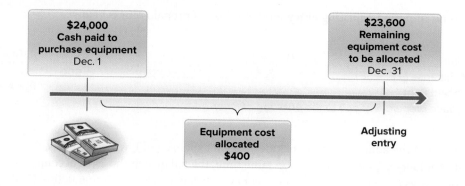

The end-of-period **adjusting entry** to record one month of depreciation for equipment is below.

December 31	Debit	Credit
Depreciation Expense *(+E, −SE)*	**400**	
Accumulated Depreciation *(−A)*		**400**
(Depreciate expense = $24,000 ÷ 60 months = $400 per month)		

This entry reduces assets by $400. Notice, however, that we didn't reduce Equipment directly, by crediting the asset account itself. Instead, we reduced the asset *indirectly* by crediting an account called *Accumulated Depreciation*. The Accumulated Depreciation account is called a *contra account.* A contra account is an account with a balance that is opposite, or "contra," to that of its related accounts.

Common Terms Another common name for *book value* is *carrying value* because this is the amount the asset is "carried" in the books.

The normal balance in the Accumulated Depreciation contra asset account is a *credit,* which is opposite to the normal *debit* balance in an asset account. The reason we use a contra account is to keep the original balance of the asset intact while reducing its current balance indirectly. In the balance sheet, we report equipment at its current book value, which equals its original cost less accumulated depreciation.

Illustration 3–6 shows how **Federal Express** records its property and equipment at original cost and then subtracts accumulated depreciation. As you will see in Chapter 7, depreciation is an *estimate* based on expected useful life and is an attempt to *allocate the cost of the asset over its useful life.* Depreciation is a calculation internal to the company and the cost of the asset less accumulated depreciation does not necessarily represent market value (what the asset could be sold for in the market).

ILLUSTRATION 3–6

Reporting Depreciation of Property and Equipment for Federal Express

FEDERAL EXPRESS Balance Sheet (partial) ($ in millions)	
Property and Equipment, at Cost	
Aircraft and related equipment	$15,632
Package handling and ground support equipment	7,196
Computer and electronic equipment	5,169
Vehicles	4,400
Facilities and other	8,294
	40,691
Less accumulated depreciation	(21,141)
Net property and equipment	$19,550

ETHICAL DILEMMA

© Eric Audras/PhotoAlto/
PictureQuest, RF

You have recently been employed by a large clothing retailer. One of your tasks is to help prepare financial statements for external distribution. The company's lender, National Savings & Loan, requires that financial statements be prepared according to generally accepted accounting principles (GAAP). During the months of November and December 2018, the company spent $1 million on a major TV advertising campaign. The $1 million included the costs of producing the commercials as well as the broadcast time purchased to run them. Because the advertising will be aired in 2018 only, you charge all the costs to advertising expense in 2018, in accordance with requirements of GAAP.

The company's chief financial officer (CFO), who hired you, asks you for a favor. Instead of charging the costs to advertising expense, he asks you to set up an asset called prepaid advertising and to wait until 2019 to record advertising expense. The CFO explains, "This ad campaign has produced significant sales in 2018; but I think it will continue to bring in customers throughout 2019. By recording the ad costs as an asset, we can match the cost of the advertising with the additional sales in 2019. Besides, if we expense the advertising in 2018, we will show an operating loss in our income statement. The bank requires that we continue to show profits in order to maintain our loan in good standing. Failure to remain in good standing could mean we'd have to lay off some of our recent hires." As an employee, should you knowingly record advertising costs incorrectly if asked to do so by your superior? Does your answer change if you believe that misreporting will save employee jobs?

DEFERRED REVENUES

We record deferred revenues when a company receives cash in advance from a customer for products or services to be provided in the future. When customers pay cash in advance, we debit cash and credit a liability. This liability reflects the company's obligation to provide goods or services to the customer in the future. Once it has provided these products or services, the company can record revenue and reduce its obligation to the customer. **The adjusting entry for a deferred revenue always includes a debit to a liability account (decrease a liability) and a credit to a revenue account (increase a revenue).**

In transaction (8), Eagle receives $600 in advance from customers who will be given 12 golf lessons ($50 per lesson) in the future. Later, as Eagle provides that training to customers, it reduces the liability to customers and can record the service revenue. Assume that by the end of December Eagle has provided 4 of the 12 training sessions paid for in advance ($50 × 4 sessions = $200).

The end-of-period **adjusting entry** to account for the services provided is below.

December 31	Debit	Credit
Deferred Revenue *(−L)*	**200**	
Service Revenue *(+R, +SE)*		**200**
(Provide services to customers who paid in advance)		

Illustration 3–7 shows an example of deferred revenue for **Netflix, Inc.**

ILLUSTRATION 3–7

Reporting Deferred Revenues and Other Current Liabilities for Netflix, Inc.

NETFLIX, INC.
Balance Sheet (partial)
($ in thousands)

Current liabilities:	
Accounts payable	$ 201,581
Deferred revenue	274,586
Other current liabilities*	2,186,987
Total current liabilities	$2,663,154

*Includes amounts owed for taxes, salaries, other operating costs, and short-term debt.

In its annual report, Netflix states: "Deferred revenue consists of membership fees billed to members that have not been recognized and gift and other prepaid memberships that have not been redeemed."[2]

Now that we've discussed prepaid expenses and deferred revenues, let's look at the two other categories of adjusting entries—accrued expenses and accrued revenues. Accruals are the opposite of prepayments. **With accruals, the cash flow occurs *after* either the expense or the revenue is recorded.** Walking through some examples using our Eagle Golf Academy illustration will demonstrate both types of accruals.

ACCRUED EXPENSES

When a company has a cost that helps to produce revenue but hasn't yet paid cash for that cost, it still should record the cost as an expense and also a liability for the amount owed. This is referred to as an accrued expense. **The adjusting entry for an accrued expense always includes a debit to an expense account (increase an expense) and a credit to a liability account (increase a liability).**

Accrued Salaries.   Eagle pays total salaries to its employees of $100 per day. For the first four weeks of December (28 days), Eagle pays $2,800 cash to employees. For simplicity, we combined each of these four weeks in transaction (9) in Illustration 3–5. For the remaining

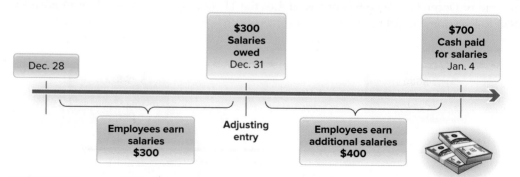

---

[2]The Deferred Revenue account is sometimes referred to as the Unearned Revenue account. The use of the term Deferred Revenue is increasingly popular in practice and is more consistent with the FASB's 2014 update of the revenue recognition principle (ASU No. 2014-09), which eliminates the "earnings" process in defining revenue. The term Deferred Revenue is also helpful in emphasizing that revenue is initially deferred but will be recorded eventually when the service is provided.

three days in December, employees earn additional salaries of $300, but Eagle doesn't plan to pay the employees until the end of the week, January 4. However, Eagle must record the $300 salaries expense in the month employees worked (December). Stated differently, the salaries expense *accrues* during December even though the company won't pay the expense until January.

The end-of-period **adjusting entry** for accrued salaries is below.

December 31	Debit	Credit
Salaries Expense *(+E, −SE)*	300	
Salaries Payable *(+L)*		300
(Salaries incurred, but not paid, in the current period)		

Accrued Utility Costs.   At the end of December, Eagle receives a utility bill for $900 associated with operations in December. Eagle plans to pay the bill on January 6. Even though it won't pay the cash until January, Eagle must record the utility costs for December as an expense in December. Eagle records the corresponding obligation to the utility company at the same time.

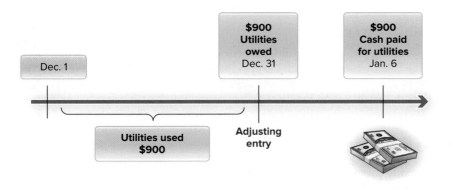

The end-of-period **adjusting entry** is below.

December 31	Debit	Credit
Utilities Expense *(+E, −SE)*	900	
Utilities Payable *(+L)*		900
(Utilities incurred, but not paid, in the current period)		

Accrued Interest.   In transaction (2), Eagle borrows $10,000 from the bank to begin operations. Assume the bank charges Eagle annual interest of 12% (or 1% per month) on the borrowed amount. Interest is due in one year, but repayment of the $10,000 borrowed is not due for three years. By the end of the first month, the loan has accrued interest of $100, calculated as follows:

Amount of note payable	×	Annual interest rate	×	Fraction of the year	=	Interest
$10,000	×	12%	×	1/12	=	$100

Notice that we multiplied by 1/12 to calculate the interest for one month (out of 12). If we had calculated interest for a two-month period, we would have multiplied by 2/12; for three months we would have multiplied by 3/12; and so on.

Although Eagle won't pay the $100 until one year later, it is a cost of using the borrowed funds during December and therefore is an expense for December.

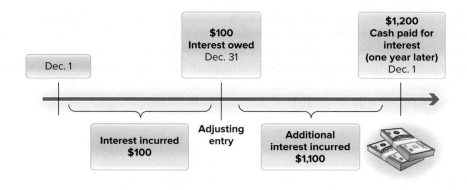

The end-of-period **adjusting entry** for interest payable is below.

December 31	Debit	Credit
Interest Expense *(+E, −SE)*	100	
Interest Payable *(+L)*		100
(Interest incurred, but not paid, in the current period)		

 COMMON MISTAKE

When recording the interest payable on a borrowed amount, students sometimes mistakenly credit the liability associated with the principal amount (Notes Payable). We record interest payable in a *separate account* (Interest Payable) to keep the balance owed for principal separate from the balance owed for interest.

ACCRUED REVENUES

When a company provides products or services to customers but hasn't yet received cash, it still should record the revenue and an asset for the amount expected to be received. This is referred to as an accrued revenue. **The adjusting entry for an accrued revenue always includes a debit to an asset account (increase an asset) and a credit to a revenue account (increase a revenue).**

Flip Side

Interest Receivable.   We can see an example of accrued revenues if we review the flip side of transaction (2), which we discussed in the previous section. The bank lends Eagle Golf Academy $10,000 and charges Eagle annual interest of 12% (or 1% per month) on the borrowed amount. By the end of the month, interest has been earned each day, but the bank has not yet recorded the interest because it is impractical to record interest on a daily basis. At the end of December, the bank records interest revenue of $100 (= $10,000 × 12% × 1/12). The bank's adjusting entry for December will include a debit to Interest Receivable and a credit to Interest Revenue for $100. Note that this is the same amount that Eagle Golf Academy, the borrower, records as Interest Expense.

The bank's end-of-period adjusting entry is presented below.

December 31	Debit	Credit
Interest Receivable *(+A)*	100	
Interest Revenue *(+R, +SE)*		100
(Interest earned in the current period)		

Accounts Receivable.   Revenue also accrues when a firm performs services but has not yet collected cash or billed the customer. Suppose, for instance, that Eagle provides $700 of golf training to customers from December 28 to December 31. However, it usually takes

Eagle one week to mail bills to customers and another week for customers to pay. Therefore, Eagle expects to receive cash from these customers during January 8–14. Because Eagle provided the service to customers in December (regardless of when cash receipt takes place), Eagle should recognize in December the service revenue and the amount receivable from those customers.

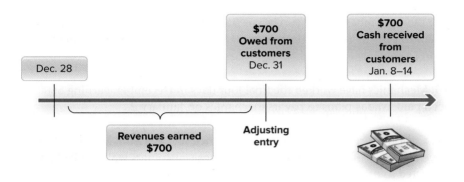

The end-of-period **adjusting entry** is below.

December 31	Debit	Credit
Accounts Receivable *(+A)*	**700**	
Service Revenue *(+R, +SE)*		**700**
(Bill customers for services provided during the current period)		

KEY POINT

Adjusting entries are needed when cash flows or obligations occur *before* the earnings-related activity (prepayment) or when cash flows occur *after* the earnings-related activity (accrual).

NO ADJUSTMENT NECESSARY

Notice that we did not make any adjusting entries associated with transaction (1) or (10) for Eagle Golf Academy. Transaction (1) is the sale of common stock, and transaction (10) is the payment of dividends to common stockholders. **Neither of these transactions involves the recognition of revenues or expenses and therefore will not require period-end adjusting entries.**

Similarly, transactions (6) and (9) did not require adjustment. **Transactions in which we receive cash at the same time we record revenue or pay cash at the same time we record an expense do *not* require adjusting entries.** For example, when Eagle provides golf training to customers for cash on December 12 [transaction (6)], the company records Service Revenue at the same time it records the cash received, and no corresponding period-end adjusting entry is needed. Similarly, when Eagle pays salaries to employees on December 28 [transaction (9)], the company records Salaries Expense at the same time it records cash paid, and no corresponding period-end adjusting entry is needed.

KEY POINT

Adjusting entries are *unnecessary* in two cases: (1) for transactions that do not involve revenue or expense activities and (2) for transactions that result in revenues or expenses being recorded at the same time as the cash flow.

Let's Review

mhhe.com/4fa9

Below are four scenarios for a local **Midas Muffler** shop for the month of December.

Scenario 1: On December 1, the balance of maintenance supplies totals $400. On December 15, the shop purchases an additional $200 of maintenance supplies with cash. By the end of December, only $100 of maintenance supplies remains.

Scenario 2: On December 4, Midas receives $6,000 cash from a local moving company in an agreement to provide truck maintenance of $1,000 each month for the next six months, beginning in December.

Scenario 3: Mechanics have worked the final four days in December, earning $600, but have not yet been paid. Midas plans to pay its mechanics on January 2.

Scenario 4: Customers receiving $250 of maintenance services from Midas on December 29 have not been billed as of the end of the month. These customers will be billed on January 3 and are expected to pay the full amount owed on January 6.

Required:
For each of the scenarios:
1. Indicate the type of adjusting entry needed.
2. Record the transaction described and the December 31 adjusting entry.

Solution:
Scenario 1: Adjusting entry type: Prepaid expense.

December 15 (external transaction)	Debit	Credit
Supplies *(+A)*	200	
Cash *(−A)*		200
(Purchase maintenance supplies with cash)		

December 31 (adjusting entry)	Debit	Credit
Supplies Expense *(+E, −SE)*	500	
Supplies *(−A)*		500
(Consume supplies)		
($400 + $200 − $100 = $500)		

Scenario 2: Adjusting entry type: Deferred revenue.

December 4 (external transaction)	Debit	Credit
Cash *(+A)*	6,000	
Deferred Revenue *(+L)*		6,000
(Receive cash in advance from customers)		

December 31 (adjusting entry)	Debit	Credit
Deferred Revenue *(−L)*	1,000	
Service Revenue *(+R, +SE)*		1,000
(Provide first of six months of services)		

Scenario 3: Adjusting entry type: Accrued expense.

December 31 (adjusting entry)	Debit	Credit
Salaries Expense (+E, −SE)	600	
Salaries Payable (+L)		600
(Owe for salaries earned by employees in the current period)		

January 2 (external transaction)	Debit	Credit
Salaries Payable (−L)	600	
Cash (−A)		600
(Pay salaries owed)		

Scenario 4: Adjusting entry type: Accrued revenue.

December 31 (adjusting entry)	Debit	Credit
Accounts Receivable (+A)	250	
Service Revenue (+R, +SE)		250
(Provide maintenance service on account)		

January 6 (external transaction)	Debit	Credit
Cash (+A)	250	
Accounts Receivable (−A)		250
(Collect cash from customers previously billed)		

Suggested Homework:
BE3–6, BE3–10;
E3–7, E3–8;
P3–3A&B, P3–4A&B

Adjusted Trial Balance

To complete the measurement process, we need to update balances of assets, liabilities, revenues, and expenses for adjusting entries. In Illustration 3–8, we summarize the eight adjusting entries of Eagle Golf Academy recorded earlier. (Note the adjusting entry for interest revenue is excluded as this entry is recorded by the bank, not Eagle Golf Academy.) To update balances, we post the adjustments to the appropriate accounts in the general ledger, as demonstrated in Illustration 3–9.

■ **LO3–4**
Post adjusting entries and prepare an adjusted trial balance.

ILLUSTRATION 3–8
Summary of Adjusting Entries for Eagle Golf Academy

December 31	Debit	Credit
(a) **Rent Expense** (+E, −SE)	500	
Prepaid Rent (−A)		500
(Reduce prepaid rent due to the passage of time)		
(b) **Supplies Expense** (+E, −SE)	1,000	
Supplies (−A)		1,000
(Consume supplies during the current period)		
(c) **Depreciation Expense** (+E, −SE)	400	
Accumulated Depreciation (−A)...		400
(Depreciate equipment)		
($24,000 ÷ 60 months = $400 per month)		
(d) **Deferred Revenue** (−L)	200	
Service Revenue (+R, +SE)		200
(Provide services to customers who paid in advance)		
(e) **Salaries Expense** (+E, −SE)	300	
Salaries Payable (+L)		300
(Owe for salaries earned by employees in the current period)		

(continued)

(concluded)

ILLUSTRATION 3–8

Summary of Adjusting Entries for Eagle Golf Academy *(continued)*

(f) **Utilities Expense** *(+E, −SE)*	900	
Utilities Payable *(+L)*		900
(Owe for utilities costs in the current period)		
(g) **Interest Expense** *(+E, −SE)*	100	
Interest Payable *(+L)*		100
(Owe for interest charges in the current period)		
(h) **Accounts Receivable** *(+A)*	700	
Service Revenue *(+R, +SE)*		700
(Bill customers for services provided during the month)		

mhhe.com/4fa10

ILLUSTRATION 3–9   Posting the Adjusting Entries (in red) of Eagle Golf Academy to General Ledger Accounts

Assets = **Liabilities** + **Stockholders' Equity**

Cash
(1)	25,000	(3)	24,000
(2)	10,000	(4)	6,000
(6)	4,300	(9)	2,800
(8)	600	(10)	200
Bal.	**6,900**		

Accounts Payable
		(5)	2,300
		Bal.	**2,300**

Common Stock
		(1)	25,000
		Bal.	**25,000**

Retained Earnings
		0
	Bal.	**0**

Accounts Receivable
(7)	2,000		
(h)	700		
Bal.	**2,700**		

Deferred Revenue
		(8)	600
(d)	200		
		Bal.	**400**

Dividends
(10)	200	
Bal.	**200**	

Service Revenue
		(6)	4,300
		(7)	2,000
		(d)	200
		(h)	700
		Bal.	**7,200**

Supplies
(5)	2,300		
		(b)	1,000
Bal.	**1,300**		

Salaries Payable
		(e)	300
		Bal.	**300**

Rent Expense
(a)	500	
Bal.	**500**	

Supplies Expense
(b)	1,000	
Bal.	**1,000**	

Prepaid Rent
(4)	6,000		
		(a)	500
Bal.	**5,500**		

Utilities Payable
		(f)	900
		Bal.	**900**

Depreciation Expense
(c)	400	
Bal.	**400**	

Salaries Expense
(9)	2,800	
(e)	300	
Bal.	**3,100**	

Equipment
(3)	24,000	
Bal.	**24,000**	

Interest Payable
		(g)	100
		Bal.	**100**

Utilities Expense
(f)	900	
Bal.	**900**	

Interest Expense
(g)	100	
Bal.	**100**	

Accumulated Depreciation
		(c)	400
		Bal.	**400**

Notes Payable
		(2)	10,000
		Bal.	**10,000**

- Amounts in black represent external transactions in December. Numbers in parentheses refer to transaction numbers in Illustration 3–5.
- Amounts in red represent period-end adjusting entries. Letters in parentheses refer to adjusting entries in Illustration 3–8.
- **Amounts in bold represent ending balances.**

COMMON MISTAKE

Students sometimes mistakenly include the Cash account in an adjusting entry. Typical adjusting entries will never include the Cash account. Note that no adjusting entries are posted to the Cash account in Illustration 3–9.

KEY POINT

We post adjusting entries to the general ledger to update the account balances.

After we have posted the adjusting entries to the general ledger accounts, we're ready to prepare an *adjusted* trial balance. An adjusted trial balance is a list of all accounts and their balances *after we have updated account balances for adjusting entries.* Illustration 3–10 shows the adjusted trial balance. Note that total debits equal total credits. The adjusted trial balance includes the adjusted balances of all general ledger accounts shown in Illustration 3–9.

EAGLE GOLF ACADEMY
Adjusted Trial Balance
December 31

Accounts	Debit	Credit
Cash	$ 6,900	
Accounts Receivable	2,700	
Supplies	1,300	
Prepaid Rent	5,500	
Equipment	24,000	
Accumulated Depreciation		$ 400
Accounts Payable		2,300
Salaries Payable		300
Utilities Payable		900
Deferred Revenue		400
Interest Payable		100
Notes Payable		10,000
Common Stock		25,000
Retained Earnings		0
Dividends	200	
Service Revenue		7,200
Rent Expense	500	
Supplies Expense	1,000	
Depreciation Expense	400	
Salaries Expense	3,100	
Utilities Expense	900	
Interest Expense	100	
Totals	$46,600	$46,600

ILLUSTRATION 3–10

Adjusted Trial Balance for Eagle Golf Academy

mhhe.com/4fa11

KEY POINT

An adjusted trial balance is a list of all accounts and their balances at a particular date, after we have updated account balances for adjusting entries.

PART C

■ LO3–5
Prepare financial
statements using the
adjusted trial balance.

THE REPORTING PROCESS: FINANCIAL STATEMENTS

Once the adjusted trial balance is complete, we prepare financial statements. Illustration 3–11 describes the relationship between the adjusted trial balance and the financial statements. Notice the color coding of the accounts, to indicate their relationships to the financial statements.

ILLUSTRATION 3–11

Relationship between
Adjusted Trial Balance and
Financial Statements

**STATEMENT OF
STOCKHOLDERS'
EQUITY**

**Common Stock
+
Retained Earnings
(= Beg. RE + NI − Div)
=
Stockholders' Equity**

EAGLE GOLF ACADEMY
Adjusted Trial Balance
December 31

Accounts	Debit	Credit
Cash	$ 6,900	
Accounts Receivable	2,700	
Supplies	1,300	
Prepaid Rent	5,500	
Equipment	24,000	
Accumulated Depreciation		$ 400
Accounts Payable		2,300
Salaries Payable		300
Utilities Payable		900
Deferred Revenue		400
Interest Payable		100
Notes Payable		10,000
Common Stock		25,000
Retained Earnings		0
Dividends	200	
Service Revenue		7,200
Rent Expense	500	
Supplies Expense	1,000	
Depreciation Expense	400	
Salaries Expense	3,100	
Utilities Expense	900	
Interest Expense	100	
Totals	$46,600	$46,600

BALANCE SHEET

Assets
=
Liabilities
+
**Stockholders'
Equity**

**INCOME
STATEMENT**

Revenues
−
Expenses
=
Net Income

Revenue and expense accounts are reported in the income statement. The difference between total revenues and total expenses equals net income. All asset, liability, and stockholders' equity accounts are reported in the balance sheet. The balance sheet confirms the equality of the basic accounting equation.

Income Statement

Illustration 3–12 shows the income statement of Eagle Golf Academy for the period ended December 31. The account names and amounts are those shown at the bottom of the adjusted trial balance in Illustration 3-11. The income statement demonstrates that Eagle Golf Academy earned revenues of $7,200 from providing training to customers. At the same time, the expenses of providing that training were $6,000. This means that Eagle made a profit of $1,200 for the period.

ILLUSTRATION 3–12

Income Statement for
Eagle Golf Academy

EAGLE GOLF ACADEMY
Income Statement
For the period ended December 31

Revenues	
Service revenue	$7,200
Expenses	
Rent expense	500
Supplies expense	1,000
Depreciation expense	400
Salaries expense	3,100
Utilities expense	900
Interest expense	100
Total expenses	6,000
Net income	**$1,200**

Statement of Stockholders' Equity

The statement of stockholders' equity summarizes the changes in each stockholders' equity account as well as in total stockholders' equity and the accounting value of the company to stockholders (owners). Illustration 3–13 shows the statement of stockholders' equity for Eagle Golf Academy.

ILLUSTRATION 3–13

Statement of
Stockholders' Equity for
Eagle Golf Academy

EAGLE GOLF ACADEMY
Statement of Stockholders' Equity
For the period ended December 31

	Common Stock	Retained Earnings	Total Stockholders' Equity
Beginning balance (Dec. 1)	$ -0-	$ -0-	$ -0-
Issuance of common stock	25,000		25,000
Add: Net income for the period		1,200	1,200
Less: Dividends		(200)	(200)
Ending balance (Dec. 31)	$25,000	$1,000	$26,000

Total stockholders' equity increases from **$0** at the beginning of December to **$26,000** by the end of December. The increase occurs as a result of a **$25,000** investment by the owners (stockholders) when they bought common stock plus an increase of **$1,000** when the company earned a profit of **$1,200** on behalf of its stockholders and distributed $200 of dividends.

You've seen that retained earnings has three components: revenues, expenses, and dividends. In the adjusted trial balance, the balance of the Retained Earnings account is its balance at the beginning of the accounting period—the balance *before* all revenue, expense, and dividend transactions. For Eagle Golf Academy, the beginning balance of Retained Earnings equals $0 since this is the first month of operations. Ending Retained Earnings equals its beginning balance of $0 plus the effects of all revenue and expense transactions (net income of **$1,200**) less dividends of **$200** paid to stockholders. Since dividends represent the payment of company resources (cash) to owners, they will have a negative effect on the stockholders' equity (retained earnings) of the company.

Balance Sheet

The balance sheet you saw in Chapter 1 contained the key asset, liability, and stockholders' equity accounts, presented as a rather simple list. Here, we introduce a slightly more complex form, called the classified balance sheet. A classified balance sheet groups a company's asset and liability accounts into current and long-term categories. We'll use the numbers from the adjusted trial balance to present the classified balance sheet for Eagle Golf Academy in Illustration 3–14.

ILLUSTRATION 3–14

Classified Balance Sheet for Eagle Golf Academy

EAGLE GOLF ACADEMY
Balance Sheet
December 31

Assets		Liabilities	
Current assets:		**Current liabilities:**	
Cash	$ 6,900	Accounts payable	$ 2,300
Accounts receivable	2,700	Salaries payable	300
Supplies	1,300	Utilities payable	900
Prepaid rent	5,500	Deferred revenue	400
Total current assets	16,400	Interest payable	100
		Total current liabilities	4,000
Long-term assets:			
Equipment	24,000	**Long-term liabilities:**	
Less: Accum. depr.	(400)	Notes payable	10,000
Total long-term assets	23,600	Total liabilities	14,000
		Stockholders' Equity	
		Common stock	25,000
		Retained earnings	1,000
		Total stockholders' equity	26,000
Total assets	$40,000	Total liabilities and stockholders' equity	$40,000

There are four items to note about the classified balance sheet.

1. **Total assets** equal current plus long-term assets.
2. **Total liabilities** equal current plus long-term liabilities.
3. **Total stockholders' equity** includes common stock and retained earnings from the statement of stockholders' equity.
4. Total assets must equal total liabilities plus stockholders equity.

We discuss each one of these items next.

The classified balance sheet separates assets into two major categories:

- *Current assets*—those that provide a benefit *within the next year.*
- *Long-term assets*—those that provide a benefit for *more than one year.*

In a few rare cases, companies that have *operating cycles* longer than one year will extend the definition of current assets to those that provide a benefit within the next operating cycle. For a service company (like Eagle Golf Academy), an **operating cycle** is the average time it takes to provide a service to a customer and then collect that customer's cash. For a company that sells products, an operating cycle would include the time it typically takes to purchase or manufacture those products to the time the company collects cash from selling those products to customers.

Current assets are typically listed in *order of liquidity.* The liquidity of an asset refers to how quickly it will be converted to cash. Recall that Eagle has borrowed $10,000 from a local bank. This bank wants to know the likelihood that Eagle will have enough cash to repay the borrowed amount plus the interest as they become due.

Cash is the most liquid of all assets, so it's listed first. *Accounts receivable* are amounts owed by customers to the company. They are generally collected within one month, so they are highly liquid assets and typically listed after cash. Next, we list prepaid expenses, such as *supplies* and *prepaid rent.* While these assets will not be converted to cash, they are expected to be consumed (or used up) within the next year, so they are included as current assets.

After current assets come long-term assets. These assets are expected to be converted to cash after one year or to be consumed for longer than one year. Long-term assets consist of the following types of assets:

- *Long-term investments*—investments in another company's debt or stock. We discuss long-term investments in debt and equity securities in **Appendix D** at the end of the book.
- *Property, plant, and equipment*—long-term productive assets used in the normal course of business, such as land, buildings, equipment, and machinery. Eagle's purchase of equipment is an example of a purchase of property, plant, and equipment. We discuss property, plant, and equipment in Chapter 7.
- *Intangible assets*—assets that lack physical substance but have long-term value to a company, such as patents, copyrights, trademarks, and franchises. We discuss intangible assets in Chapter 7.

After listing all of the assets, we see that total assets equal $40,000. This means that *in accounting terms* Eagle has resources of $40,000 that will provide benefits to the company in the future.

After assets, liabilities are listed next. They too are divided into two major categories:

- *Current liabilities*—those that are due *within the next year.*
- *Long-term liabilities*—those that are due in *more than one year.*

Like assets, liabilities are listed in this order to better help investors and creditors understand the company's liquidity. Eagle's bank wants to know not only the company's ability to convert assets into cash, but also whether the company has other obligations that will prevent full repayment of the amount borrowed. Investors of Eagle want to know whether the cash being generated by the assets will be enough to meet the company's obligations in the near future (current liabilities) as well as the longer term (long-term liabilities). Otherwise, operations may cease.

Eagle has many common current liabilities. *Accounts payable* are amounts owed for previous purchases of supplies on account. These amounts are typically required to be paid within one year. *Salaries payable* are amounts owed to employees; *utilities payable* are amounts owed to the utility company. These obligations are expected to be paid within one year.

Deferred revenue differs a little from the other liabilities. These amounts represent amounts received in advance from customers for services to be provided in the future. Therefore, though the company does not expect to pay cash within the next year, it does expect to provide those services within one year. By providing services, the company fulfills its current obligation to its customers. To the extent that Eagle does not provide those services, it will be required to repay customers.

Interest payable is the final current liability listed. As of December 31, the company owes one month of interest on the borrowing, but the bank will not require the interest to be paid until 11 months from now (next December 1). Nevertheless, for accounting purposes, this is an amount that is due within one year as of December 31, so it is listed as a current liability.

After current liabilities, Eagle lists long-term liabilities. These are amounts that are due in more than one year. Eagle only has one—bank borrowing of $10,000 that occurred on December 1. The borrowing was for three years, so as of December 31, the borrowing is due in two years and 11 months. Because the due date is longer than one year, the amount is listed as a long-term liability. Eagle's total liabilities include $4,000 of current liabilities plus $10,000 of long-term liabilities, for a total of $14,000.

Decision Maker's Perspective

Is the Balance Sheet Like a Photo or an MRI?

In Chapter 1, we mentioned that a balance sheet is like a photograph since it shows events at a point in time, whereas an income statement is like a video since it shows events over time. This is a common comparison used in describing the two primary financial statements.

However, rather than a photograph, maybe a better description of the balance sheet is an MRI (magnetic resonance imaging). MRIs are commonly used by physicians to diagnose and treat medical conditions. Whereas a photo conveys a clear image recognized by everyone, an MRI is a little more hazy and needs specialized medical training to utilize the full benefits of the image.

In the same way, items reported on the balance sheet are also a little hazy. As we will learn later, accounting numbers are subject to interpretation and companies have some leeway in reporting the numbers. Likewise, to utilize the full benefits of the balance sheet (and the other financial statements as well), users need specialized training in accounting and finance, beginning with the basic fundamentals obtained in this first accounting course.

The final section of the classified balance sheet is the stockholders' equity section. The amounts for the two stockholders' equity accounts—Common Stock and Retained Earnings—can be obtained directly from the statement of stockholders' equity. The balance of Common Stock is the total amount issued. The balance of Retained Earnings is the total net income over the life of the company (just the first month of operations in this example) less dividends.

It's also the case that the amount of total stockholders' equity confirms that total assets ($40,000) equal total liabilities plus stockholders' equity ($40,000). We achieve this equality only by including the correct balance of **$1,000** for Retained Earnings from the statement of stockholders' equity, not the balance of $0 from the adjusted trial balance.

 KEY POINT

We prepare the income statement, statement of stockholders' equity, and balance sheet from the adjusted trial balance. The income statement provides a measure of net income (profitability), calculated as revenues minus expenses. The balance sheet demonstrates that assets equal liabilities plus stockholders' equity (the basic accounting equation).

Statement of Cash Flows

The final financial statement we need to prepare is the statement of cash flows. As discussed in Chapter 1, the statement of cash flows measures activities involving cash receipts and cash payments, reflecting a company's operating, investing, and financing activities. We'll take another brief look at the statement of cash flows in Chapter 4 and then discuss it in detail in Chapter 11.

PART D

■ **LO3–6**
Demonstrate the purposes and recording of closing entries.

THE CLOSING PROCESS

Recall that revenues, expenses, and dividends are components of retained earnings. Notice that Eagle's balance sheet reports retained earnings of $1,000, as if all net income transactions (revenues and expenses) and dividend transactions had been recorded directly in Retained Earnings. However, instead of recording revenue, expense, and dividend transactions directly to the Retained Earnings account during the period, we recorded them to the three component accounts. This allows us to maintain individual measures of revenues, expenses, and dividends for preparing financial statements at the end of the period.

After we have reported revenues and expenses in the income statement and dividends in the statement of stockholders' equity, it's time to transfer these amounts to the Retained Earnings account itself. These three accounts—revenues, expenses, and dividends—are termed temporary accounts: We keep them for each period and then transfer the balances of revenues, expenses, and dividends to the Retained Earnings account. All accounts that appear in the balance sheet, including Retained Earnings, are permanent accounts, and we carry forward their balances from period to period. We treat only revenues, expenses, and dividends as temporary, *so it will appear as if we had recorded all these types of transactions directly in Retained Earnings* during the year. We accomplish this with closing entries.

Closing Entries

Closing entries **transfer the balances of all temporary accounts (revenues, expenses, and dividends) to the balance of the Retained Earnings account.** Here's how:

- All revenue accounts have credit balances. To transfer these balances to the Retained Earnings account, we debit each of these revenue accounts for its balance and credit Retained Earnings for the total.
- Similarly, all expense and dividend accounts have debit balances. So, we credit each of these accounts for its balance and debit Retained Earnings for the total.

By doing this, we accomplish two necessary tasks: First, we update the balance in the Retained Earnings account to reflect transactions related to revenues, expenses, and dividends in the current period. Second, we reduce the balances of all revenue, expense, and dividend accounts to zero so we can start from scratch in measuring those amounts in the next accounting period. After all, revenues, expenses, and dividends are temporary accounts, which means their balances each period must start at zero.

 KEY POINT

Closing entries serve two purposes: (1) to transfer the balances of temporary accounts (revenues, expenses, and dividends) to the Retained Earnings account, and (2) to reduce the balances of these temporary accounts to zero to prepare them for measuring activity in the next period.

For demonstration, refer back to Eagle Golf Academy. We can transfer the balances of all revenue, expense, and dividend accounts to the balance of the Retained Earnings account with the closing entries shown in Illustration 3–15.

Note that closing entries transfer the balances of the components of retained earnings (revenues, expenses, and dividends) to the balance of Retained Earnings itself. Retained Earnings is credited (increased) in the first entry and then debited (decreased) in the second

December 31	Debit	Credit
(a) **Service Revenue**	7,200	
Retained Earnings		7,200
(Close revenues to retained earnings)		
(b) **Retained Earnings**	6,000	
Rent Expense		500
Supplies Expense		1,000
Depreciation Expense		400
Salaries Expense		3,100
Utilities Expense		900
Interest Expense		100
(Close expenses to retained earnings)		
(c) **Retained Earnings**	200	
Dividends		200
(Close dividends to retained earnings)		

ILLUSTRATION 3–15

Closing Entries for Eagle Golf Academy

and third entries. Posting these amounts to the Retained Earnings account will result in the following ending balance:

	Retained Earnings	
		0 Beginning balance
		7,200 Total revenues
Total expenses	6,000	
Total dividends	200	
	1,000	Ending balance

The ending balance of Retained Earnings now includes all transactions affecting the components of the account. The ending balance of **$1,000** represents all revenues and expenses over the life of the company (just the first month of operations in this example) less dividends. Another way to think about the balance of Retained Earnings is that it's the amount of net income earned by the company for its owners but that has not been paid to owners in the form of dividends.

The ending balance of Retained Earnings on December 31 will be its beginning balance in the following period beginning January 1. Then we'll close revenues, expenses, and dividends in that period to Retained Earnings, and this cycle will continue each period.

Closing entries *do not affect the balances of permanent accounts* (assets, liabilities, and permanent stockholders' equity accounts) *other than retained earnings.* Permanent accounts carry a cumulative balance throughout the life of the company.

 COMMON MISTAKE

Students sometimes believe that closing entries are meant to reduce the balance of Retained Earnings to zero. Retained Earnings is a *permanent account,* representing the accumulation of all revenues, expenses, and dividends over the life of the company.

Illustration 3–16 shows retained earnings, net income, and dividends for **Coca-Cola** over a three-year period. Notice that the beginning balance each year equals the ending balance of the previous year. Then, the balance of retained earnings increases by the amount of net income less dividends for the year. **The ending balance of the Retained Earnings account represents the cumulative total of net income less dividends over the life of the company.** As of the end of 2014, Coca-Cola's total net income has exceeded total dividends by $63,408 million since the company first began operations in Atlanta, Georgia, on May 8, 1886.

ILLUSTRATION 3–16

Relation between Retained Earnings, Net Income, and Dividends for Coca-Cola

	THE COCA-COLA COMPANY ($ in millions)					
Year	Beginning Retained Earnings*	+	Net Income**	−	Dividends	= Ending Retained Earnings
2011						**$53,621**
2012	$53,621	+	$9,019	−	$4,595	= 58,045
2013	58,045	+	8,584	−	4,969	= 61,660
2014	61,660	+	7,098	−	5,350	= 63,408

*Beginning retained earnings is the ending retained earnings from the previous year.
**Net income equals total revenues minus total expenses.

 KEY POINT

Closing entries increase retained earnings by the amount of revenues for the period and decrease retained earnings by the amount of expenses and dividends for the period.

Post-Closing Trial Balance

■ LO3–7
Post closing entries and prepare a post-closing trial balance.

After we have prepared closing entries, we post amounts to the accounts in the general ledger. Illustration 3–17 demonstrates the process of posting the closing entries. The current balance of each account reflects transactions during the period (in black), adjusting entries (in red), and closing entries (in blue).

mhhe.com/4fa12

ILLUSTRATION 3–17   Posting the Closing Entries to Adjusted Balances of Ledger Accounts

| Assets | = | Liabilities | + | Stockholders' Equity |

Cash

(1)	25,000	(3)	24,000
(2)	10,000	(4)	6,000
(6)	4,300	(9)	2,800
(8)	600	(10)	200
Bal.	**6,900**		

Accounts Receivable

(7)	2,000		
(h)	700		
Bal.	**2,700**		

Supplies

(5)	2,300		
		(b)	1,000
Bal.	**1,300**		

Prepaid Rent

(4)	6,000		
		(a)	500
Bal.	**5,500**		

Equipment

| (3) | 24,000 | | |
| **Bal.** | **24,000** | | |

Accumulated Depreciation

| | | (c) | 400 |
| | | **Bal.** | **400** |

Accounts Payable

| | | (5) | 2,300 |
| | | **Bal.** | **2,300** |

Deferred Revenue

		(8)	600
(d)	200		
		Bal.	**400**

Salaries Payable

| | | (e) | 300 |
| | | **Bal.** | **300** |

Utilities Payable

| | | (f) | 900 |
| | | **Bal.** | **900** |

Interest Payable

| | | (g) | 100 |
| | | **Bal.** | **100** |

Notes Payable

| | | (2) | 10,000 |
| | | **Bal.** | **10,000** |

Common Stock

| | | (1) | 25,000 |
| | | **Bal.** | **25,000** |

Dividends

(10)	200		
		(c)	200
Bal.	**0**		

Rent Expense

(a)	500		
		(b)	500
Bal.	**0**		

Depreciation Expense

(c)	400		
		(b)	400
Bal.	**0**		

Utilities Expense

(f)	900		
		(b)	900
Bal.	**0**		

Retained Earnings

			0
		(a)	7,200
(b)	6,000		
(c)	200		
		Bal.	**1,000**

Service Revenue

		(6)	4,300
		(7)	2,000
		(d)	200
		(h)	700
(a)	7,200		
		Bal.	**0**

Supplies Expense

(b)	1,000		
		(b)	1,000
Bal.	**0**		

Salaries Expense

(9)	2,800		
(e)	300		
		(b)	3,100
Bal.	**0**		

Interest Expense

(g)	100		
		(b)	100
Bal.	**0**		

- Amounts in black represent external transactions during December. Numbers in parentheses refer to transaction numbers in Illustration 3–5.
- Amounts in red represent period-end adjusting entries. Letters in parentheses refer to adjusting entries in Illustration 3–8.
- Amounts in blue represent period-end closing entries. Letters in parentheses refer to closing entries in Illustration 3–15.
- Amounts in **bold** represent ending balances.

CAREER CORNER

In practice, accountants do not prepare closing entries. Virtually all companies have accounting software packages that automatically update the Retained Earnings account and Move the temporary accounts at the end of the year. Of course, accounting information systems go far beyond automatic closing entries. In today's competitive global environment, businesses demand information systems that can eliminate redundant tasks and quickly gather, process, and disseminate information to decision makers. Ordinary business processes—such as selling goods to customers, purchasing supplies, managing employees, and managing inventory—can be handled more efficiently with customized information systems. Employers recognize that individuals with strong information technology skills mixed with accounting knowledge add value to the company.

© George Doyle/Stockbyte/
Veer, RF

After we post the closing entries, the **$1,000** balance of Retained Earnings now equals the amount shown in the balance sheet. In addition, the ending balances of all revenue, expense, and dividend accounts are now zero and ready to begin the next period.

After we post the closing entries to the ledger accounts, we can prepare a post-closing trial balance. The post-closing trial balance is a list of all accounts and their balances at a particular date *after we have updated account balances for closing entries.* The post-closing trial balance helps to verify that we prepared and posted closing entries correctly and that the accounts are now ready for the next period's transactions.

Illustration 3–18 shows the post-closing trial balance for Eagle Golf Academy as of December 31.

Notice that the post-closing trial balance does not include any revenues, expenses, or dividends, because these accounts all have zero balances after closing entries. The balance of Retained Earnings has been updated from the adjusted trial balance to include all revenues, expenses, and dividends for the period.

ILLUSTRATION 3–18

Post-Closing Trial Balance for Eagle Golf Academy

EAGLE GOLF ACADEMY
Post-Closing Trial Balance
December 31

Accounts	Debit	Credit
Cash	$ 6,900	
Accounts Receivable	2,700	
Supplies	1,300	
Prepaid Rent	5,500	
Equipment	24,000	
Accumulated Depreciation		$ 400
Accounts Payable		2,300
Salaries Payable		300
Utilities Payable		900
Deferred Revenue		400
Interest Payable		100
Notes Payable		10,000
Common Stock		25,000
Retained Earnings		1,000
Totals	$40,400	$40,400

 KEY POINT

After we post the closing entries to the general ledger, the balance of Retained Earnings equals the amount shown in the balance sheet. The balances of all revenue, expense, and dividend accounts are zero at that point.

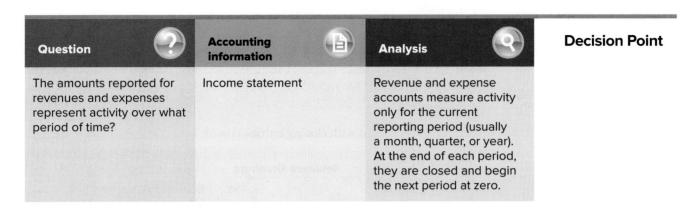

Decision Point

Question	Accounting information	Analysis
The amounts reported for revenues and expenses represent activity over what period of time?	Income statement	Revenue and expense accounts measure activity only for the current reporting period (usually a month, quarter, or year). At the end of each period, they are closed and begin the next period at zero.

Below is the adjusted trial balance of Beckham Soccer Academy for December 31.

Let's Review

mhhe.com/4fa13

BECKHAM SOCCER ACADEMY
Adjusted Trial Balance
December 31

Accounts	Debit	Credit
Cash	$ 2,600	
Supplies	3,900	
Accounts Payable		$ 1,000
Salaries Payable		300
Common Stock		3,000
Retained Earnings		1,700
Dividends	200	
Service Revenue		4,300
Salaries Expense	2,400	
Supplies Expense	700	
Rent Expense	500	
Totals	$10,300	$10,300

Required:

1. Prepare closing entries.
2. Post the closing entries to the Retained Earnings T-account.
3. Prepare a post-closing trial balance.

Solution:

1. Closing entries.

December 31	Debit	Credit
Service Revenue	4,300	
Retained Earnings		4,300
(Close revenues to retained earnings)		
Retained Earnings	3,600	
Salaries Expense		2,400
Supplies Expense		700
Rent Expense		500
(Close expenses to retained earnings)		

(continued)

(concluded)

December 31	Debit	Credit
Retained Earnings	200	
Dividends		200
(Close dividends to retained earnings)		

2. Retained Earnings T-account with closing entries posted.

Retained Earnings

		1,700	Beginning balance
		4,300	Total revenues
Total expenses	3,600		
Total dividends	200		
		2,200	Ending balance

3. Post-closing trial balance.

BECKHAM SOCCER ACADEMY
Post-Closing Trial Balance
December 31

Accounts	Debit	Credit
Cash	$2,600	
Supplies	3,900	
Accounts Payable		$1,000
Salaries Payable		300
Common Stock		3,000
Retained Earnings		2,200
Totals	$6,500	$6,500

Suggested Homework:
BE3–19, BE3–20;
E3–17, E3–18;
P3–7A&B; P3–8A&B

KEY POINTS BY LEARNING OBJECTIVE

LO3–1 Understand when revenues and expenses are recorded.

The revenue recognition principle states that we record revenue in the period in which we provide goods and services to customers, not necessarily in the period in which we receive cash.

Most expenses are recorded in the same period as the revenues they help to generate. Other expenses indirectly related to producing revenues are recorded in the period they occur.

LO3–2 Distinguish between accrual-basis and cash-basis accounting.

The difference between accrual-basis accounting and cash-basis accounting is *timing*. Under accrual-basis accounting, we record revenues when we provide goods and services to customers, and we record expenses with the revenue they help to generate. Under cash-basis accounting, we record revenues when we receive cash, and we record expenses when we pay cash. Cash-basis accounting is not allowed for financial reporting purposes for most major companies.

LO3–3 Demonstrate the purposes and recording of adjusting entries.

Adjusting entries are a necessary part of accrual-basis accounting. They help to update the balances of assets, liabilities, revenues, and expenses at the end of the accounting period for transactions that have occurred but have not yet been recorded.

Adjusting entries are needed when cash flows or obligations occur *before* the earnings-related activity (prepayment) or when cash flows occur *after* the earnings-related activity (accrual).

Adjusting entries are *unnecessary* in two cases: (1) for transactions that do not involve revenue or expense activities and (2) for transactions that result in revenues or expenses being recorded at the same time as the cash flow.

LO3–4 **Post adjusting entries and prepare an adjusted trial balance.**

We post adjusting entries to the general ledger to update the account balances.

An adjusted trial balance is a list of all accounts and their balances at a particular date, after we have updated account balances for adjusting entries.

LO3–5 **Prepare financial statements using the adjusted trial balance.**

We prepare the income statement, statement of stockholders' equity, and balance sheet from the adjusted trial balance. The income statement provides a measure of net income (profitability),

calculated as revenues minus expenses. The balance sheet demonstrates that assets equal liabilities plus stockholders' equity (the basic accounting equation).

LO3–6 **Demonstrate the purposes and recording of closing entries.**

Closing entries serve two purposes: (1) to transfer the balances of temporary accounts (revenues, expenses, and dividends) to the Retained Earnings account, and (2) to reduce the balances of these temporary accounts to zero to prepare them for measuring activity in the next period.

Closing entries increase retained earnings by the amount of revenues for the period and decrease retained earnings by the amount of expenses and dividends for the period.

LO3–7 **Post closing entries and prepare a post-closing trial balance.**

After we post the closing entries to the general ledger, the balance of Retained Earnings equals the amount shown in the balance sheet. The balances of all revenue, expense, and dividend accounts are zero at that point.

GLOSSARY

Accrual-basis accounting: Record revenues when goods and services are provided to customers, and record expenses with related revenues. **p. 108**

Accrued expense: When a company has incurred an expense but hasn't yet paid cash or recorded an obligation to pay. **p. 118**

Accrued revenue: When a company provides products or services to customers but hasn't yet received cash. **p. 120**

Adjusted trial balance: A list of all accounts and their balances after we have updated account balances for adjusting entries. **p. 125**

Adjusting entries: Entries used to record events that occur during the period but that have not yet been recorded by the end of the period. **p. 113**

Book value: An asset's original cost less accumulated depreciation. **p. 116**

Cash-basis accounting: Record revenues at the time cash is received and expenses at the time cash is paid. **p. 110**

Classified balance sheet: Balance sheet that groups a company's assets into current assets and long-term assets and that separates liabilities into current liabilities and long-term liabilities. **p. 128**

Closing entries: Entries that transfer the balances of all temporary accounts (revenues, expenses, and dividends) to the balance of the Retained Earnings account. **p. 131**

Contra account: An account with a balance that is opposite, or "contra," to that of its related accounts. **p. 116**

Deferred revenues: When a company receives cash in advance from a customer for products or services to be provided in the future. **p. 117**

Depreciation: The process of allocating the cost of a long-term asset to expense over its useful life. **p. 115**

Matching principle: Recognize expenses in the same period as the revenues they help to generate. **p. 109**

Permanent accounts: All accounts that appear in the balance sheet; account balances are carried forward from period to period. **p. 131**

Post-closing trial balance: A list of all accounts and their balances at a particular date after we have updated account balances for closing entries. **p. 134**

Prepaid expenses: The costs of assets acquired in one period that will be expensed in a future period. **p. 114**

Revenue recognition principle: Record revenue in the period in which we provide goods and services to customers. **p. 108**

Temporary accounts: All revenue, expense, and dividend accounts; account balances are maintained for a single period and then closed (or zeroed out) and transferred to the balance of the Retained Earnings account at the end of the period. **p. 131**

SELF-STUDY QUESTIONS

1. On May 5, Johnson Plumbing receives a phone call from a customer needing a new water heater and schedules a service visit for May 7. On May 7, Johnson installs the new water heater. The customer pays for services on May 10. According to the *revenue recognition principle,* on which date should Johnson record service revenue? **(LO3–1)**
   a. May 5 (date of phone call).
   b. May 7 (date of service).
   c. May 10 (date of cash receipt).
   d. Evenly over the three dates.

2. On January 17, Papa's Pizza signs a contract with Bug Zappers for exterminating services related to a recent sighting of cockroaches in the restaurant. Papa's pays for the extermination service on January 29, and Bug Zappers sprays for bugs on February 7. According to the *matching principle,* on which date should Papa's Pizza record the extermination expense? **(LO3–1)**
   a. January 17 (date of the contract).
   b. January 29 (date of cash payment).
   c. February 7 (date of extermination service).
   d. Evenly over the three dates.

3. Refer to the information in Self-Study Question 1. Using *cash-basis accounting,* on which date should Johnson record service revenue? **(LO3–2)**
   a. May 5 (date of phone call).
   b. May 7 (date of service).
   c. May 10 (date of cash receipt).
   d. Evenly over the three dates.

4. Refer to the information in Self-Study Question 2. Using *cash-basis accounting,* on which date should Papa's Pizza record the extermination expense? **(LO3–2)**
   a. January 17 (date of the contract).
   b. January 29 (date of cash payment).
   c. February 7 (date of extermination service).
   d. Evenly over the three dates.

5. Which of the following is *not* a characteristic of adjusting entries? **(LO3–3)**
   a. Reduce the balances of revenue, expense, and dividend accounts to zero.
   b. Allow for proper application of the revenue recognition principle (revenues) or the matching principle (expenses).
   c. Are part of accrual-basis accounting.
   d. Are recorded at the end of the accounting period.

6. Ambassador Hotels purchases one year of fire insurance coverage on December 1 for $24,000 ($2,000 per month), debiting Prepaid Insurance. On December 31, Ambassador would record the following year-end adjusting entry: **(LO3–3)**

	Debit	Credit
a. Insurance Expense............	24,000	
Prepaid Insurance..........		24,000
b. Insurance Expense............	2,000	
Prepaid Insurance..........		2,000
c. Insurance Expense............	22,000	
Prepaid Insurance..........		22,000

   d. No entry is required on December 31 because full cash payment was made on December 1 and the insurance does not expire until the following November 30.

7. An adjusted trial balance: **(LO3–4)**
   a. Lists all accounts and their balances at a particular date after updating account balances for adjusting entries.
   b. Is used to prepare the financial statements.
   c. Includes balances for revenues, expenses, and dividends.
   d. All the above.

8. Which of the following describes the information reported in the statement of stockholders' equity? **(LO3–5)**
   a. Net income for the period calculated as revenues minus expenses.
   b. Equality of total assets with total liabilities plus stockholders' equity.
   c. Change in stockholders' equity through changes in common stock and retained earnings.
   d. Net cash flows from operating, investing, and financing activities.

9. Which of the following describes the purpose(s) of closing entries? **(LO3–6)**
   a. Adjust the balances of asset and liability accounts for unrecorded activity during the period.
   b. Transfer the balances of temporary accounts (revenues, expenses, and dividends) to Retained Earnings.
   c. Reduce the balances of the temporary accounts to zero to prepare them for measuring activity in the next period.
   d. Both *b.* and *c.*

10. Which of the following accounts is *not* listed in a post-closing trial balance? **(LO3–7)**
    a. Prepaid Rent.
    b. Accounts Payable.
    c. Salaries Expense.
    d. Retained Earnings.

Note: For answers, see the last page of the chapter.

For additional study materials, including 10 more multiple-choice Self-Study Questions, visit Connect.

REVIEW QUESTIONS

1. Discuss the major principle that describes recording revenues.   ■ **LO3–1**

2. Discuss the major principle that describes recording expenses.   ■ **LO3–1**

3. Samantha is a first-year accounting student. She doesn't think it matters that expenses are reported in the same period's income statement with the related revenues (matching principle). She feels that "as long as revenues and expenses are recorded in any period, that's good enough." Help her understand why the matching principle is important.   ■ **LO3–1**

4. Describe when revenues and expenses are recognized using cash-basis accounting. How does this differ from accrual-basis accounting?   ■ **LO3–2**

5. Executive Lawn provides $100 of landscape maintenance to Peterson Law on April 10. Consider three scenarios: ■ **LO3–2**

   Flip Side of Question 7

   a. Peterson pays for the lawn service in advance on March 28.
   b. Peterson pays for the lawn service on April 10, the day of service.
   c. Peterson pays for the lawn service the following month on May 2.

   If Executive Lawn uses accrual-basis accounting, on which date would Executive Lawn record the $100 revenue for each scenario?

6. Consider the information in Question 5. Using cash-basis accounting, on which date would Executive Lawn record the $100 revenue for each scenario?   ■ **LO3–2**

   Flip Side of Question 8

7. Peterson Law asks Executive Lawn to provide $100 of landscape maintenance. Executive Lawn provides the service on April 10. Consider three scenarios:

   a. Peterson pays for the lawn service in advance on March 28.
   b. Peterson pays for the lawn service on April 10, the day of service.
   c. Peterson pays for the lawn service the following month on May 2.

   ■ **LO3–2**

   Flip Side of Question 5

   If Peterson Law uses accrual-basis accounting, on which date would Peterson Law record the $100 expense for each scenario?

8. Consider the information in Question 7. Using cash-basis accounting, on which date would Peterson Law record the $100 expense for each scenario?   ■ **LO3–2**

   Flip Side of Question 6

9. Why are adjusting entries necessary under accrual-basis accounting?   ■ **LO3–3**

10. There are two basic types of adjusting entries—prepayments and accruals. Describe each in terms of the timing of revenue and expense recognition versus the flow of cash.   ■ **LO3–3**

11. Provide an example of a prepaid expense. The adjusting entry associated with a prepaid expense always includes a debit and credit to which account classifications?   ■ **LO3–3**

12. Provide an example of a deferred revenue. The adjusting entry associated with a deferred revenue always includes a debit and credit to which account classifications?   ■ **LO3–3**

■ **LO3–3**

13. Provide an example of an accrued expense. The adjusting entry associated with an accrued expense always includes a debit and credit to which account classifications?

■ **LO3–3**

14. Provide an example of an accrued revenue. The adjusting entry associated with an accrued revenue always includes a debit and credit to which account classifications?

■ **LO3–3**

15. Sequoya Printing purchases office supplies for $75 on October 2. The staff uses the office supplies continually on a daily basis throughout the month. By the end of the month, office supplies of $25 remain. Record the month-end adjusting entry for office supplies (assuming the balance of Office Supplies at the beginning of October was $0).

■ **LO3–3**

16. Jackson Rental receives its September utility bill of $320 on September 30 but does not pay the bill until October 10. Jackson's accountant records the utility expense of $320 on October 10 at the time of payment. Will this cause any of Jackson's accounts to be misstated at the end of September? If so, indicate which ones and the direction of the misstatement.

■ **LO3–3**

17. Global Printing publishes several types of magazines. Customers are required to pay for magazines in advance. On November 5, Global receives cash of $120,000 for prepaid subscriptions. By the end of November, Global has distributed $20,000 of magazines to customers. Record the month-end adjusting entry.

■ **LO3–3**

18. At the end of May, Robertson Corporation has provided services to customers, but it has not yet billed these customers nor have any of them paid for those services. If Robertson makes no adjusting entry associated with these unpaid services provided, will any accounts be misstated? If so, indicate which ones and the direction of the misstatement.

■ **LO3–3**

19. Fill in the blank associated with each adjusting entry:
   a. *Prepaid expense:* Debit Supplies Expense; credit _____.
   b. *Deferred revenue:* Debit _____; credit Service Revenue.
   c. *Accrued expense:* Debit _____; credit Salaries Payable.
   d. *Accrued revenue:* Debit Accounts Receivable; credit _____.

■ **LO3–4**

20. What is the purpose of the adjusted trial balance? How do the adjusted trial balance and the (unadjusted) trial balance differ?

■ **LO3–5**

21. Explain what is meant by the term *classified* when referring to a balance sheet.

■ **LO3–5**

22. At the end of the period, Sanders Company reports the following amounts: Assets = $12,000; Liabilities = $8,000; Revenues = $5,000; Expenses = $3,000. Calculate stockholders' equity.

■ **LO3–6**

23. What are the two purposes of preparing closing entries?

■ **LO3–6**

24. What does it mean to close temporary accounts? Which of the following account types are closed: assets, liabilities, dividends, revenues, and expenses?

■ **LO3–6**

25. Describe the debits and credits for the three closing entries required at the end of a reporting period.

■ **LO3–6**

26. In its first four years of operations, Chance Communications reports net income of $300, $900, $1,500, and $2,400, respectively, and pays dividends of $200 per year. What would be the balance of Retained Earnings at the end of the fourth year?

■ **LO3–6**

27. Matt has been told by his instructor that dividends reduce retained earnings (and therefore stockholders' equity). However, since he knows that stockholders are receiving the dividends, Matt doesn't understand how paying dividends would *decrease* stockholders' equity. Explain this to Matt.

■ **LO3–7**

28. How do the adjusted trial balance and the post-closing trial balance differ? Which accounts are shown in the adjusted trial balance but not in the post-closing trial balance? Which account is shown in both trial balances but with a different balance on each?

BRIEF EXERCISES

BE3-1 Below are transactions for Lobos, Inc., during the month of December. Calculate the amount of revenue to recognize in December. If the transaction does not require the company to recognize a revenue, indicate how it would report the transaction.

a. Receive $1,200 cash from customers for services to be provided next month.

b. Perform $900 of services during the month and bill customers. Customers are expected to pay next month.

c. Perform $2,300 of services during the month and receive full cash payment from customers at the time of service.

Determine revenues to be recognized (LO3–1)

BE3-2 Below are transactions for Bronco Corporation during the month of June. Calculate the amount of expense to recognize in June. If the transaction does not require an expense to be recognized, indicate how the transaction would be reported.

a. Pay $600 cash to employees for work performed during June.

b. Receive a $200 telephone bill for the month of June, but Bronco does not plan to pay the bill until early next month.

c. Pay $500 on account for supplies purchased last month. All supplies were used last month.

Determine expenses to be recognized (LO3–1)

BE3-3 Hoya Corporation reports the following amounts: Assets = $18,000; Liabilities = $3,000; Stockholders' equity = $15,000; Dividends = $3,000; Revenues = $17,000; and Expenses = $12,000. What amount is reported for net income?

Calculate net income (LO3–1)

BE3-4 Consider the following set of transactions occurring during the month of May for Bison Consulting Company. For each transaction, indicate the impact on (1) the balance of cash, (2) cash-basis net income, and (3) accrual-basis net income for May. The first answer is provided as an example.

Analyze the impact of transactions on the balance of cash, cash-basis net income, and accrual-basis net income (LO3–1, 3–2)

Impact on:	Cash Balance	Cash-Basis Net Income	Accrual-Basis Net Income
(a) Receive $1,500 from customers who were billed for services in April.	+$1,500	+$1,500	$0
(b) Provide $3,200 of consulting services to a local business. Payment is not expected until June.			
(c) Purchase office supplies for $400 on account. All supplies are used by the end of May.			
(d) Pay $600 to workers. $400 is for work in May and $200 is for work in April.			
(e) Pay $200 to advertise in a local newspaper in May.			
Totals			

BE3-5 Rebel Technology maintains its records using cash-basis accounting. During the year, the company received cash from customers, $50,000, and paid cash for salaries, $21,900. At the beginning of the year, customers owe Rebel $1,100. By the end of the year, customers owe $8,000. At the beginning of the year, Rebel owes salaries of $7,000. At the end of the year, Rebel owes salaries of $4,000. Determine cash-basis net income and accrual-basis net income for the year.

Determine accrual-basis and cash-basis net income (LO3–1, 3–2)

BE3-6 At the beginning of May, Golden Gopher Company reports a balance in Supplies of $500. On May 15, Golden Gopher purchases an additional $3,300 of supplies for cash. By the end of May, only $300 of supplies remains. (1) Record the purchase of supplies on May 15. (2) Record the adjusting entry on May 31. (3) Calculate the balances after adjustment on May 31 of Supplies and Supplies Expense.

Record the adjusting entry for supplies (LO3–3)

Record the adjusting entry for prepaid rent (LO3–3)

BE3–7 Suppose Hoosiers, a specialty clothing store, rents space at a local mall for one year, paying $25,200 ($2,100/month) in advance on October 1. (1) Record the payment of rent in advance on October 1. (2) Record the adjusting entry on December 31. (3) Calculate the year-end adjusted balances of prepaid rent and rent expense (assuming the balance of Prepaid Rent at the beginning of the year is $0).

Record the adjusting entry for prepaid insurance (LO3–3)

BE3–8 Mountaineer Excavation operates in a low-lying area that is subject to heavy rains and flooding. Because of this, Mountaineer purchases one year of flood insurance in advance on March 1, paying $36,000 ($3,000/month). (1) Record the purchase of insurance in advance on March 1. (2) Record the adjusting entry on December 31. (3) Calculate the year-end adjusted balances of Prepaid Insurance and Insurance Expense (assuming the balance of Prepaid Insurance at the beginning of the year is $0).

Record the adjusting entry for depreciation (LO3–3)

BE3–9 Beaver Construction purchases new equipment for $50,400 cash on April 1, 2018. At the time of purchase, the equipment is expected to be used in operations for seven years (84 months) and have no resale or scrap value at the end. Beaver depreciates equipment evenly over the 84 months ($600/month). (1) Record the purchase of equipment on April 1. (2) Record the adjusting entry for depreciation on December 31, 2018. (3) Calculate the year-end adjusted balances of Accumulated Depreciation and Depreciation Expense (assuming the balance of Accumulated Depreciation at the beginning of 2018 is $0).

Record the adjusting entry for deferred revenue (LO3–3)

BE3–10 Suppose a customer rents a vehicle for three months from Commodores Rental on November 1, paying $6,000 ($2,000/month). (1) Record the rental for Commodores on November 1. (2) Record the adjusting entry on December 31. (3) Calculate the year-end adjusted balances of the Deferred Revenue and Service Revenue accounts (assuming the balance of Deferred Revenue at the beginning of the year is $0).

Record the adjusting entry for salaries payable (LO3–3)

BE3–11 Fighting Irish Incorporated pays its employees $5,600 every two weeks ($400/day). The current two-week pay period ends on December 28, 2018, and employees are paid $5,600. The next two-week pay period ends on January 11, 2019, and employees are paid $5,600. (1) Record the adjusting entry on December 31, 2018. (2) Record the payment of salaries on January 11, 2019. (3) Calculate the 2018 year-end adjusted balance of Salaries Payable (assuming the balance of Salaries Payable before adjustment in 2018 is $0).

Record the adjusting entry for interest payable (LO3–3)

Flip Side of BE3–13

BE3–12 Midshipmen Company borrows $15,000 from Falcon Company on July 1, 2018. Midshipmen repays the amount borrowed and pays interest of 12% (1%/month) on June 30, 2019. (1) Record the borrowing for Midshipmen on July 1, 2018. (2) Record the adjusting entry for Midshipmen on December 31, 2018. (3) Calculate the 2018 year-end adjusted balances of Interest Payable and Interest Expense (assuming the balance of Interest Payable at the beginning of the year is $0).

Record the adjusting entry for interest receivable (LO3–3)

Flip Side of BE3–12

BE3–13 Refer to the information in BE3–12. (1) Record the lending for Falcon on July 1, 2018. (2) Record the adjusting entry for Falcon on December 31, 2018. (3) Calculate the 2018 year-end adjusted balances of Interest Receivable and Interest Revenue (assuming the balance of Interest Receivable at the beginning of the year is $0).

Assign accounts to financial statements (LO3–5)

BE3–14 For each of the following accounts, indicate whether the account is shown in the income statement or the balance sheet:

Accounts	Financial Statement
1. Accounts Receivable	_____
2. Deferred Revenue	_____
3. Supplies Expense	_____
4. Salaries Payable	_____
5. Depreciation Expense	_____
6. Service Revenue	_____

BE3–15 Below are the four primary financial statements. Match each financial statement with its primary purpose to investors.

Understand the purpose of financial statements (LO3–5)

Financial Statements	Purposes
1. _____ Income statement	a. Provides measures of resources and claims to those resources at the end of the year.
2. _____ Statement of stockholders' equity	b. Provides an indication of the company's ability to make a profit during the current year.
3. _____ Balance sheet	c. Provides a measure of net increases and decreases in cash for the current year.
4. _____ Statement of cash flows	d. Shows changes in owners' claims to resources for the current year.

BE3–16 The following account balances appear in the 2018 adjusted trial balance of Beavers Corporation: Service Revenue, $275,000; Salaries Expense, $110,000; Supplies Expense, $20,000; Rent Expense, $26,000; Depreciation Expense, $44,000; and Delivery Expense, $18,000. Prepare an income statement for the year ended December 31, 2018.

Prepare an income statement (LO3–5)

BE3–17 The following account balances appear in the 2018 adjusted trial balance of Spiders Corporation: Common Stock, $30,000; Retained Earnings, $8,000; Dividends, $1,000; Service Revenue, $28,000; Salaries Expense, $16,000; and Rent Expense, $9,000. No common stock was issued during the year. Prepare the statement of stockholders' equity for the year ended December 31, 2018.

Prepare a statement of stockholders' equity (LO3–5)

BE3–18 The following account balances appear in the 2018 adjusted trial balance of Blue Devils Corporation: Cash, $5,000; Accounts Receivable, $9,000; Supplies, $19,000; Equipment, $120,000; Accumulated Depreciation, $45,000; Accounts Payable, $26,000; Salaries Payable, $16,000; Common Stock, $60,000; and Retained Earnings, _____. Prepare the December 31, 2018, classified balance sheet including the correct balance for retained earnings.

Prepare a classified balance sheet (LO3–5)

BE3–19 The year-end adjusted trial balance of Aggies Corporation included the following account balances: Retained Earnings, $230,000; Service Revenue, $900,000; Salaries Expense, $390,000; Rent Expense, $150,000; Interest Expense, $85,000; and Dividends, $60,000. Record the necessary closing entries.

Record closing entries (LO3–6)

BE3–20 The year-end adjusted trial balance of Hilltoppers Corporation included the following account balances: Cash, $5,000; Equipment, $17,000; Accounts Payable, $3,000; Common Stock, $11,000; Retained Earnings, $8,100; Dividends, $1,100; Service Revenue, $16,000; Salaries Expense, $11,000; and Utilities Expense, $4,000. Prepare the post-closing trial balance.

Prepare a post-closing trial balance (LO3–7)

EXERCISES

E3–1 Consider the following situations:
1. **American Airlines** collects cash on June 12 from the sale of a ticket to a customer. The flight occurs on August 16.
2. A customer purchases sunglasses from **Eddie Bauer** on January 27 on account. Eddie Bauer receives payment from the customer on February 2.
3. On March 30, a customer preorders 10 supreme pizzas (without onions) from **Pizza Hut** for a birthday party. The pizzas are prepared and delivered on April 2. The company receives cash at the time of delivery.
4. A customer pays in advance for a three-month subscription to **Sports Illustrated** on July 1. Issues are scheduled for delivery each week from July 1 through September 30.

Determine the timing of revenue recognition (LO3–1)

Required:

For each situation, determine the date for which the company recognizes the revenue under accrual-basis accounting.

Determine the timing of expense recognition (LO3–1)

E3–2 Consider the following situations:

1. **American Airlines** operates a flight from Dallas to Los Angeles on August 16. The pilots' salaries associated with the flight are paid on September 2.
2. **Eddie Bauer** pays cash on January 6 to purchase sunglasses from a wholesale distributor. The sunglasses are sold to customers on January 27.
3. On January 1, **Pizza Hut** pays for a one-year property insurance policy with coverage starting immediately.
4. **Sports Illustrated** signs an agreement with CBS on January 12 to provide television advertisements during the Super Bowl. Payment is due within 3 weeks after February 4, the day of the Super Bowl. Sports Illustrated makes the payment on February 23.

Required:

For each situation, determine the date for which the company recognizes the expense under accrual-basis accounting.

Differentiate cash-basis revenues from accrual-basis revenues (LO3–2)

E3–3 Refer to the situations discussed in E3–1.

Required:

For each situation, determine the date for which the company recognizes revenue using cash-basis accounting.

Differentiate cash-basis expenses from accrual-basis expenses (LO3–2)

E3–4 Refer to the situation discussed in E3–2.

Required:

For each situation, determine the date for which the company recognizes the expense using cash-basis accounting.

Determine the amount of net income (LO3–1)

E3–5 During the course of your examination of the financial statements of Trojan Corporation for the year ended December 31, 2018, you come across several items needing further consideration. Currently, net income is $100,000.

a. An insurance policy covering 12 months was purchased on October 1, 2018, for $24,000. The entire amount was debited to Prepaid Insurance and no adjusting entry was made for this item in 2018.

b. During 2018, the company received a $4,000 cash advance from a customer for services to be performed in 2019. The $4,000 was incorrectly credited to Service Revenue.

c. There were no supplies listed in the balance sheet under assets. However, you discover that supplies costing $2,750 were on hand at December 31, 2018.

d. Trojan borrowed $70,000 from a local bank on September 1, 2018. Principal and interest at 9% will be paid on August 31, 2019. No accrual was made for interest in 2018.

Required:

Using the information in *a* through *d* above, determine the proper amount of net income as of December 31, 2018.

Organize the steps in the accounting cycle (LO3–3, 3–4, 3–5, 3–6, 3–7)

E3–6 Listed below are all the steps in the accounting cycle.

(a) Record and post adjusting entries.
(b) Post the transaction to the T-account in the general ledger.
(c) Record the transaction.
(d) Prepare financial statements (income statement, statement of stockholders' equity, balance sheet, and statement of cash flows).
(e) Record and post closing entries.
(f) Prepare a trial balance.
(g) Analyze the impact of the transaction on the accounting equation.
(h) Assess whether the transaction results in a debit or a credit to the account balance.
(i) Use source documents to identify accounts affected by external transactions.

Required:

List the steps in proper order.

E3–7 Golden Eagle Company prepares monthly financial statements for its bank. The November 30 and December 31 adjusted trial balances include the following account information:

Record adjusting entries (LO3–3)

	November 30		December 31	
	Debit	**Credit**	**Debit**	**Credit**
Supplies	2,000		3,500	
Prepaid Insurance	8,000		6,000	
Salaries Payable		11,000		16,000
Deferred Revenue		3,000		1,500

The following information also is known:

a. Purchases of supplies in December total $4,500.

b. No insurance payments are made in December.

c. $11,000 is paid to employees during December for November salaries.

d. On November 1, a tenant pays Golden Eagle $4,500 in advance rent for the period November through January. Deferred Revenue is credited.

Required:

Show the adjusting entries that were made for supplies, prepaid insurance, salaries payable, and deferred revenue on December 31.

E3–8 Consider the following transactions for Huskies Insurance Company:

Record year-end adjusting entries (LO3–3)

a. Equipment costing $42,000 is purchased at the beginning of the year for cash. Depreciation on the equipment is $7,000 per year.

b. On June 30, the company lends its chief financial officer $50,000; principal and interest at 7% are due in one year.

c. On October 1, the company receives $16,000 from a customer for a one-year property insurance policy. Deferred Revenue is credited.

Required:

For each item, record the necessary adjusting entry for Huskies Insurance at its year-end of December 31. No adjusting entries were made during the year.

E3–9 Refer to the information in E3–8.

Calculate the effects of adjusting entries on net income (LO3–3)

Required:

For each of the adjustments in E3–8, indicate by how much net income in the income statement is higher or lower if the adjustment is not recorded.

E3–10 Consider the following situations for Shocker:

Record year-end adjusting entries (LO3–3)

a. On November 28, 2018, Shocker receives a $4,500 payment from a customer for services to be rendered evenly over the next three months. Deferred Revenue is credited.

b. On December 1, 2018, the company pays a local radio station $2,700 for 30 radio ads that were to be aired, 10 per month, throughout December, January, and February. Prepaid Advertising is debited.

c. Employee salaries for the month of December totaling $8,000 will be paid on January 7, 2019.

d. On August 31, 2018, Shocker borrows $70,000 from a local bank. A note is signed with principal and 9% interest to be paid on August 31, 2019.

Required:

Record the necessary adjusting entries for Shocker at December 31, 2018. No adjusting entries were made during the year.

E3–11 Refer to the information in E3–10.

Calculate the effects of adjusting entries on the accounting equation (LO3–3, 3–4)

Required:

For each of the adjustments recorded in E3–10, indicate by how much the assets, liabilities, and stockholders' equity in the December 31, 2018, balance sheet is higher or lower if the adjustment is not recorded.

Record year-end adjusting entries (LO3–3)

E3–12 Below are transactions for Wolverine Company during 2018.

a. On December 1, 2018, Wolverine receives $4,000 cash from a company that is renting office space from Wolverine. The payment, representing rent for December and January, is credited to Deferred Revenue.

b. Wolverine purchases a one-year property insurance policy on July 1, 2018, for $13,200. The payment is debited to Prepaid Insurance for the entire amount.

c. Employee salaries of $3,000 for the month of December will be paid in early January 2019.

d. On November 1, 2018, the company borrows $15,000 from a bank. The loan requires principal and interest at 10% to be paid on October 30, 2019.

e. Office supplies at the beginning of 2018 total $1,000. On August 15, Wolverine purchases an additional $3,400 of office supplies, debiting the Supplies account. By the end of the year, $500 of office supplies remains.

Required:

Record the necessary adjusting entries at December 31, 2018, for Wolverine Company. You do not need to record transactions made during the year. Assume that no financial statements were prepared during the year and no adjusting entries were recorded.

Record year-end adjusting entries (LO3–3)

E3–13 Below are transactions for Hurricane Company during 2018.

a. On October 1, 2018, Hurricane lends $9,000 to another company. The other company signs a note indicating principal and 12% interest will be paid to Hurricane on September 30, 2019.

b. On November 1, 2018, Hurricane pays its landlord $4,500 representing rent for the months of November through January. The payment is debited to Prepaid Rent for the entire amount.

c. On August 1, 2018, Hurricane collects $13,200 in advance from another company that is renting a portion of Hurricane's factory. The $13,200 represents one year's rent and the entire amount is credited to Deferred Revenue.

d. Depreciation on machinery is $5,500 for the year.

e. Salaries for the year earned by employees but not paid to them or recorded are $5,000.

f. Hurricane begins the year with $1,500 in supplies. During the year, the company purchases $5,500 in supplies and debits that amount to Supplies. At year-end, supplies costing $3,500 remain on hand.

Required:

Record the necessary adjusting entries at December 31, 2018, for Hurricane Company for each of the situations. Assume that no financial statements were prepared during the year and no adjusting entries were recorded.

Prepare an adjusted trial balance (LO3–3, 3–4)

E3–14 The December 31, 2018, unadjusted trial balance for Demon Deacons Corporation is presented below.

Accounts	Debit	Credit
Cash	$10,000	
Accounts Receivable	15,000	
Prepaid Rent	7,200	
Supplies	4,000	
Deferred Revenue		$ 3,000
Common Stock		11,000
Retained Earnings		6,000
Service Revenue		51,200
Salaries Expense	35,000	
	$71,200	$71,200

At year-end, the following additional information is available:

a. The balance of Prepaid Rent, $7,200, represents payment on October 31, 2018, for rent from November 1, 2018, to April 30, 2019.

b. The balance of Deferred Revenue, $3,000, represents payment in advance from a customer. By the end of the year, $750 of the services have been provided.

c. An additional $700 in salaries is owed to employees at the end of the year but will not be paid until January 4, 2019.

d. The balance of Supplies, $4,000, represents the amount of office supplies on hand at the beginning of the year of $1,700 plus an additional $2,300 purchased throughout 2018. By the end of 2018, only $800 of supplies remains.

Required:

1. Update account balances for the year-end information by recording any necessary adjusting entries. No prior adjustments have been made in 2018.
2. Prepare an adjusted trial balance as of December 31, 2018.

E3–15 Below are the restated amounts of net income and retained earnings for Volunteers Inc. and Raiders Inc. for the period 2009–2018. Volunteers began operations in 2010, while Raiders began several years earlier.

Calculate the balance of retained earnings (LO3–5)

	VOLUNTEERS INC. ($ in millions)		RAIDERS INC. ($ in millions)	
Year	Net Income (Loss)	Retained Earnings	Net Income (Loss)	Retained Earnings
2009	—	$0	$ 35	$11
2010	$ 30	_____	(43)	_____
2011	(7)	_____	63	_____
2012	41	_____	63	_____
2013	135	_____	102	_____
2014	30	_____	135	_____
2015	(131)	_____	(42)	_____
2016	577	_____	74	_____
2017	359	_____	110	_____
2018	360	_____	162	_____

Required:

Calculate the balance of retained earnings each year for each company. Neither company paid dividends during this time.

E3–16 The December 31, 2018, adjusted trial balance for Fightin' Blue Hens Corporation is presented below.

Prepare financial statements from an adjusted trial balance (LO3–5)

Accounts	Debit	Credit
Cash	$ 12,000	
Accounts Receivable	150,000	
Prepaid Rent	6,000	
Supplies	30,000	
Equipment	400,000	
Accumulated Depreciation		$135,000
Accounts Payable		12,000
Salaries Payable		11,000
Interest Payable		5,000
Notes Payable (due in two years)		40,000
Common Stock		300,000
Retained Earnings		60,000

(continued)

(concluded)

Accounts	Debit	Credit
Service Revenue		500,000
Salaries Expense	400,000	
Rent Expense	20,000	
Depreciation Expense	40,000	
Interest Expense	5,000	
Totals	$1,063,000	$1,063,000

Required:

1. Prepare an income statement for the year ended December 31, 2018.
2. Prepare a statement of stockholders' equity for the year ended December 31, 2018, assuming no common stock was issued during 2018.
3. Prepare a classified balance sheet as of December 31, 2018.

Record closing entries (LO3–6)

E3–17 Seminoles Corporation's fiscal year-end is December 31, 2018. The following is a partial adjusted trial balance as of December 31.

Accounts	Debit	Credit
Retained Earnings		$30,000
Dividends	$ 3,000	
Service Revenue		50,000
Interest Revenue		6,000
Salaries Expense	15,000	
Rent Expense	6,000	
Advertising Expense	3,000	
Depreciation Expense	11,000	
Interest Expense	5,000	

Required:

1. Prepare the necessary closing entries.
2. Calculate the ending balance of Retained Earnings.

Record closing entries and prepare a post-closing trial balance (LO3–6, 3–7)

E3–18 Laker Incorporated's fiscal year-end is December 31, 2018. The following is an adjusted trial balance as of December 31.

Accounts	Debit	Credit
Cash	$ 12,000	
Supplies	39,000	
Prepaid Rent	30,000	
Accounts Payable		$ 3,000
Notes Payable		30,000
Common Stock		40,000
Retained Earnings		9,000
Dividends	4,000	
Service Revenue		54,000
Salaries Expense	20,000	
Advertising Expense	13,000	
Rent Expense	10,000	
Utilities Expense	8,000	
Totals	$136,000	$136,000

Required:

1. Prepare the necessary closing entries.
2. Calculate the ending balance of Retained Earnings.
3. Prepare a post-closing trial balance.

E3–19 Refer to the adjusted trial balance in E3–16.

Record closing entries and prepare a post-closing trial balance (LO3–6, 3–7)

Required:

1. Record the necessary closing entries at December 31, 2018.
2. Prepare a post-closing trial balance.

E3–20 On January 1, 2018, Red Flash Photography had the following balances: Cash, $12,000; Supplies, $8,000; Land, $60,000; Deferred Revenue, $5,000; Common Stock $50,000; and Retained Earnings, $25,000. During 2018, the company had the following transactions:

1.	February 15	Issue additional shares of common stock, $20,000.
2.	May 20	Provide services to customers for cash, $35,000, and on account, $30,000.
3.	August 31	Pay salaries to employees for work in 2018, $23,000.
4.	October 1	Purchase rental space for one year, $12,000.
5.	November 17	Purchase supplies on account, $22,000.
6.	December 30	Pay dividends, $2,000.

Record transactions and prepare adjusting entries, adjusted trial balance, financial statements, and closing entries (LO3–3, 3–4, 3–5, 3–6, 3–7)

The following information is available on December 31, 2018:

1. Employees are owed an additional $4,000 in salaries.
2. Three months of the rental space has expired.
3. Supplies of $5,000 remain on hand.
4. All of the services associated with the beginning deferred revenue have been performed.

Required:

1. Record the transactions that occurred during the year.
2. Record the adjusting entries at the end of the year.
3. Prepare an adjusted trial balance.
4. Prepare an income statement, statement of stockholders' equity, and classified balance sheet.
5. Prepare closing entries.

E3–21 On January 1, 2018, the general ledger of Dynamite Fireworks includes the following account balances:

Complete the accounting cycle (LO3–3, 3–4, 3–5, 3–6)

Accounts	Debit	Credit
Cash	$23,800	
Accounts Receivable	5,200	
Supplies	3,100	
Land	50,000	
Accounts Payable		3,200
Common Stock		65,000
Retained Earnings		13,900
Totals	$82,100	$82,100

During January 2018, the following transactions occur:

January 2. Purchase rental space for one year in advance, $6,000 ($500/month).
January 9. Purchase additional supplies on account, $3,500
January 13. Provide services to customers on account, $25,500.
January 17. Receive cash in advance from customers for services to be provided in the future, $3,700.
January 20. Pay cash for salaries, $11,500.
January 22. Receive cash on accounts receivable, $24,100.
January 29. Pay cash on accounts payable, $4,000.

Required:

1. Record each of the transactions listed above.
2. Record adjusting entries on January 31.
   a. Rent for the month of January has expired.
   b. Supplies remaining at the end of January total $2,800.
   c. By the end of January, $3,200 of services has been provided to customers who paid in advance on January 17.
   d. Unpaid salaries at the end of January are $5,800.
3. Prepare an adjusted trial balance as of January 31, 2018, after updating beginning balances (above) for transactions during January (Requirement 1) and adjusting entries at the end of January (Requirement 2).
4. Prepare an income statement for the period ended January 31, 2018.
5. Prepare a classified balance sheet as of January 31, 2018.
6. Record closing entries.
7. Analyze the following features of Dynamite Fireworks' financial condition:
   a. What is the amount of profit reported for the month of January?
   b. Calculate the ratio of current assets to current liabilities at the end of January.
   c. Based on Dynamite Fireworks' profit and ratio of current assets to current liabilities, indicate whether Dynamite Fireworks appears to be in good or bad financial condition.

PROBLEMS: SET A

Determine accrual-basis and cash-basis revenues and expenses (LO3–1, 3–2)

P3–1A Consider the following transactions.

Transaction	Accrual-basis		Cash-basis	
	Revenue	Expense	Revenue	Expense
1. Receive cash from customers in advance, $600.	___	___	___	___
2. Pay utilities bill for the previous month, $150.	___	___	___	___
3. Pay for insurance one year in advance, $2,000.	___	___	___	___
4. Pay workers' salaries for the current month, $800.	___	___	___	___
5. Incur costs for employee salaries in the current month but do not pay, $1,000.	___	___	___	___
6. Receive cash from customers at the time of service, $1,700.	___	___	___	___
7. Purchase office supplies on account, $330.	___	___	___	___
8. Borrow cash from the bank, $4,000.	___	___	___	___
9. Receive cash from customers for services performed last month, $750.	___	___	___	___
10. Pay for advertising to appear in the current month, $450.	___	___	___	___

Required:

For each transaction, determine the amount of revenue or expense, if any, that is recorded under accrual-basis accounting and under cash-basis accounting in the current period.

Convert cash-basis accounting to accrual-basis accounting (LO3–1, 3–2)

P3–2A Minutemen Law Services maintains its books using cash-basis accounting. However, the company decides to borrow $100,000 from a local bank, and the bank requires Minutemen to provide annual financial statements prepared using accrual-basis accounting as part of the creditworthiness verification. During 2018, the company records the following cash flows:

Cash collected from customers		$70,000
Cash paid for:		
Salaries	$36,000	
Supplies	4,000	
Rent	5,000	
Insurance	7,000	
Utilities	3,000	55,000
Net cash flows		$15,000

You are able to determine the following information:

	January 1, 2018	December 31, 2018
Accounts Receivable	$21,000	$24,000
Prepaid Insurance	-0-	3,700
Supplies	5,000	2,000
Salaries Payable	2,700	4,400

Required:
Prepare an accrual-basis income statement for the year ended December 31, 2018, by calculating accrual-basis revenues and expenses.

P3–3A The information necessary for preparing the 2018 year-end adjusting entries for Gamecock Advertising Agency appears below. Gamecock's fiscal year-end is December 31.

Record adjusting entries (LO3–3)

a. On July 1, 2018, Gamecock receives $6,000 from a customer for advertising services to be given evenly over the next 10 months. Gamecock credits Deferred Revenue.

b. At the beginning of the year, Gamecock's depreciable equipment has a cost of $28,000, a four-year life, and no salvage value. The equipment is depreciated evenly (straight-line depreciation method) over the four years.

c. On May 1, 2018, the company pays $4,800 for a two-year fire and liability insurance policy and debits Prepaid Insurance.

d. On September 1, 2018, the company borrows $20,000 from a local bank and signs a note. Principal and interest at 12% will be paid on August 31, 2019.

e. At year-end there is a $2,700 debit balance in the Supplies (asset) account. Only $1,000 of supplies remains on hand.

Required:
Record the necessary adjusting entries on December 31, 2018. No prior adjustments have been made during 2018.

P3–4A Crimson Tide Music Academy offers lessons in playing a wide range of musical instruments. The *unadjusted* trial balance as of December 31, 2018, appears below. December 31 is the company's fiscal year-end.

Record adjusting entries (LO3–3)

Accounts	Debits	Credits
Cash	$ 10,300	
Accounts Receivable	9,500	
Supplies	2,000	
Prepaid Rent	7,200	
Equipment	90,000	

(continued)

(concluded)

Accumulated Depreciation		$ 12,000
Accounts Payable		7,700
Salaries Payable		-0-
Interest Payable		-0-
Utilities Payable		-0-
Notes Payable		20,000
Common Stock		45,000
Retained Earnings		19,000
Service Revenue		42,200
Salaries Expense	24,500	
Interest Expense	-0-	
Rent Expense	-0-	
Supplies Expense	-0-	
Utilities Expense	2,400	
Depreciation Expense	-0-	
Totals	$145,900	$145,900

Information necessary to prepare the year-end adjusting entries appears below.

a. Depreciation of equipment for the year is $6,000.

b. Accrued salaries at year-end should be $2,100.

c. Crimson Tide borrows $20,000 on September 1, 2018. The principal is due to be repaid in four years. Interest is payable each August 31 at an annual rate of 12%.

d. Unused supplies at year-end total $700. Crimson Tide debits Supplies at the time supplies are purchased.

e. Crimson Tide opens a second studio by paying for one year of rent in advance on April 1, 2018, for $7,200 ($600 per month) debiting Prepaid Rent.

f. Unpaid utilities for December total $200.

Required:

Record the necessary adjusting entries on December 31, 2018.

Prepare financial statements from an adjusted trial balance when net income is positive (LO3–5)

P3–5A Boilermaker Unlimited specializes in building new homes and remodeling existing homes. Remodeling projects include adding game rooms, changing kitchen cabinets and countertops, and updating bathrooms. Below is the year-end adjusted trial balance of Boilermaker Unlimited.

BOILERMAKER UNLIMITED
Adjusted Trial Balance
December 31, 2018 *(continued)*

Accounts	Debits	Credits
Cash	$ 16,000	
Accounts Receivable	25,000	
Supplies	32,000	
Prepaid Insurance	7,000	
Equipment	625,000	
Accumulated Depreciation		$ 200,000
Accounts Payable		31,000
Salaries Payable		28,000
Utilities Payable		5,000
Notes Payable (due in 5 years)		150,000

BOILERMAKER UNLIMITED
Adjusted Trial Balance
December 31, 2018 (concluded)

Common Stock		200,000
Retained Earnings		31,000
Dividends	26,000	
Service Revenue—new construction		450,000
Service Revenue—remodeling		280,000
Salaries Expense	160,000	
Supplies Expense	285,000	
Depreciation Expense	50,000	
Insurance Expense	25,000	
Utilities Expense	42,000	
Interest Expense	9,000	
Service Fee Expense	73,000	
Totals	$1,375,000	$1,375,000

Required:

Prepare an income statement, statement of stockholders' equity, and classified balance sheet. In preparing the statement of stockholders' equity, note that during the year the company issued additional common stock for $30,000. This amount is included in the amount for Common Stock in the adjusted trial balance.

P3–6A The year-end financial statements of Rattlers Tax Services are provided below.

Record closing entries and prepare a post-closing trial balance (LO3–6, 3–7)

RATTLERS TAX SERVICES
Income Statement

Service revenue		$77,500
Expenses:		
Salaries	$46,000	
Utilities	8,200	
Insurance	5,800	
Supplies	2,100	62,100
Net income		$15,400

RATTLERS TAX SERVICES
Statement of Stockholders' Equity

	Common Stock	Retained Earnings	Total S. Equity
Beg. bal., Jan. 1	$60,000	$24,500	$ 84,500
Issue stock	30,000		30,000
Net income		15,400	15,400
Dividends		(6,000)	(6,000)
Ending bal., Dec. 31	$90,000	$33,900	$123,900

RATTLERS TAX SERVICES
Balance Sheet

Assets		Liabilities	
Cash	$ 4,700	Accounts payable	$ 3,000
Accounts receivable	7,200	**Stockholders' Equity:**	
Land	115,000	Common stock	$90,000
		Retained earnings	33,900
			123,900
Total assets	$126,900	Total liabs. and equities	$126,900

Required:

1. Record year-end closing entries.
2. Prepare a post-closing trial balance. (*Hint:* The balance of Retained Earnings will be the amount shown in the balance sheet.)

Complete the accounting
cycle after adjusting
entries (LO3–4, 3–5, 3–6,
3–7)

P3–7A Refer to P3–4A.

Required:
Complete the following steps:
1. Enter the unadjusted balances from the trial balance into T-accounts.
2. Post the adjusting entries prepared in P3–4A to the accounts.
3. Prepare an adjusted trial balance.
4. Prepare an income statement and a statement of shareholders' equity for the year ended December 31, 2018, and a classified balance sheet as of December 31, 2018. Assume that no common stock is issued during the year.
5. Record closing entries.
6. Post closing entries to the accounts.
7. Prepare a post-closing trial balance.

Complete the full
accounting cycle (LO3–3,
3–4, 3–5, 3–6, 3–7)

P3–8A The general ledger of Red Storm Cleaners at January 1, 2018, includes the following account balances:

Accounts	Debits	Credits
Cash	$20,000	
Accounts Receivable	8,000	
Supplies	4,000	
Equipment	15,000	
Accumulated Depreciation		$ 5,000
Salaries Payable		7,500
Common Stock		25,000
Retained Earnings		9,500
Totals	$47,000	$47,000

The following is a summary of the transactions for the year:
a. March 12 Provide services to customers, $60,000, of which $21,000 is on account.
b. May 2 Collect on accounts receivable, $18,000.
c. June 30 Issue shares of common stock in exchange for $6,000 cash.
d. August 1 Pay salaries, $26,000 (of which $7,500 is for salaries payable in 2017).
e. September 25 Pay repairs and maintenance expenses, $13,000.
f. October 19 Purchase equipment for $8,000 cash.
g. December 30 Pay $1,100 cash dividends to stockholders.

Required:
1. Set up the necessary T-accounts and enter the beginning balances from the trial balance. In addition to the accounts shown, the company also has accounts for Dividends, Service Revenue, Salaries Expense, Repairs and Maintenance Expense, Depreciation Expense, and Supplies Expense.
2. Record each of the summary transactions listed above.
3. Post the transactions to the accounts.
4. Prepare an unadjusted trial balance.
5. Record adjusting entries. Accrued salaries at year-end amounted to $1,100. Depreciation for the year on the equipment is $5,000. Office supplies remaining on hand at the end of the year equal $1,200.
6. Post adjusting entries.
7. Prepare an adjusted trial balance.
8. Prepare an income statement for 2018 and a classified balance sheet as of December 31, 2018.
9. Record closing entries.
10. Post closing entries.
11. Prepare a post-closing trial balance.

P3–9A The general ledger of Zips Storage at January 1, 2018, includes the following account balances:

Complete the full accounting cycle (LO3–3, 3–4, 3–5, 3–6, 3–7)

Accounts	Debits	Credits
Cash	$ 24,600	
Accounts Receivable	15,400	
Prepaid Insurance	12,000	
Land	148,000	
Accounts Payable		$ 6,700
Deferred Revenue		5,800
Common Stock		143,000
Retained Earnings		44,500
Totals	$200,000	$200,000

The following is a summary of the transactions for the year:

a.	January	9	Provide storage services for cash, $134,100, and on account, $52,200.
b.	February	12	Collect on accounts receivable, $51,500.
c.	April	25	Receive cash in advance from customers, $12,900.
d.	May	6	Purchase supplies on account, $9,200.
e.	July	15	Pay property taxes, $8,500.
f.	September	10	Pay on accounts payable, $11,400.
g.	October	31	Pay salaries, $123,600.
h.	November	20	Issue shares of common stock in exchange for $27,000 cash.
i.	December	30	Pay $2,800 cash dividends to stockholders.

Required:

1. Set up the necessary T-accounts and enter the beginning balances from the trial balance. In addition to the accounts shown, the company has accounts for Supplies, Dividends, Service Revenue, Salaries Expense, Property Tax Expense, Supplies Expense, and Insurance Expense.
2. Record each of the summary transactions listed above.
3. Post the transactions to the accounts.
4. Prepare an unadjusted trial balance.
5. Record adjusting entries. Insurance expired during the year is $7,000. Supplies remaining on hand at the end of the year equal $2,900. Provide services of $11,800 related to cash paid in advance by customers.
6. Post adjusting entries.
7. Prepare an adjusted trial balance.
8. Prepare an income statement for 2018 and a classified balance sheet as of December 31, 2018.
9. Record closing entries.
10. Post closing entries.
11. Prepare a post-closing trial balance.

PROBLEMS: SET B

P3–1B Consider the following transactions.

Determine accrual-basis and cash-basis revenues and expenses (LO3–1, 3–2)

	Accrual-Basis		Cash-Basis	
Transaction	Revenue	Expense	Revenue	Expense
1. Receive cash from customers at the time of service, $3,700.				
2. Issue common stock for cash, $6,000.				

(continued)

(concluded)

3. Receive cash from customers who were previously billed, $1,700.

4. Incur utilities cost in the current month but do not pay, $600.

5. Pay workers' salaries for the current month, $700.

6. Pay for rent one year in advance, $3,600.

7. Repay a long-term note to the bank, $3,000.

8. Pay workers' salaries for the previous month, $850.

9. Pay dividends to stockholders, $500.

10. Purchase office supplies for cash, $540.

Required:

For each transaction, determine the amount of revenue or expense, if any, that is recorded under accrual-basis accounting and under cash-basis accounting.

Convert cash-basis accounting to accrual-basis accounting (LO3–1, 3–2)

P3–2B Horned Frogs Fine Cooking maintains its books using cash-basis accounting. However, the company recently borrowed $50,000 from a local bank, and the bank requires the company to provide annual financial statements prepared using accrual-basis accounting as part of the creditworthiness verification. During 2018, the company records the following cash flows:

Cash collected from customers		$65,000
Cash paid for:		
Salaries	$23,000	
Supplies	9,000	
Repairs and maintenance	8,000	
Insurance	4,000	
Advertising	6,000	50,000
Net cash flows		$15,000

You are able to determine the following information:

	January 1, 2018	December 31, 2018
Accounts Receivable	$18,000	$13,000
Prepaid Insurance	1,700	4,200
Supplies	-0-	2,000
Salaries Payable	4,200	2,800

Required:

Prepare an accrual-basis income statement for December 31, 2018, by calculating accrual-basis revenues and expenses.

Record adjusting entries (LO3–3)

P3–3B The information necessary for preparing the 2018 year-end adjusting entries for Bearcat Personal Training Academy appears below. Bearcat's fiscal year-end is December 31.

a. Depreciation on the equipment for the year is $7,000.

b. Salaries earned (but not paid) from December 16 through December 31, 2018, are $4,000.

c. On March 1, 2018, Bearcat lends an employee $20,000. The employee signs a note requiring principal and interest at 9% to be paid on February 28, 2019.

d. On April 1, 2018, Bearcat pays an insurance company $13,200 for a two-year fire insurance policy. The entire $13,200 is debited to Prepaid Insurance at the time of the purchase.

e. Bearcat uses $1,700 of supplies in 2018.

f. A customer pays Bearcat $2,700 on October 31, 2018, for three months of personal training to begin November 1, 2018. Bearcat credits Deferred Revenue at the time of cash receipt.

g. On December 1, 2018, Bearcat pays $6,000 rent to the owner of the building. The payment represents rent for December 2018 through February 2019, at $2,000 per month. Prepaid Rent is debited at the time of the payment.

Required:

Record the necessary adjusting entries at December 31, 2018. No prior adjustments have been made during 2018.

P3–4B Jaguar Auto Company provides general car maintenance to customers. The company's fiscal year-end is December 31. The December 31, 2018, trial balance (before any adjusting entries) appears below.

Record adjusting entries (LO3–3)

Accounts	Debits	Credits
Cash	$ 22,000	
Accounts Receivable	15,000	
Supplies	27,000	
Prepaid Insurance	24,000	
Equipment	95,000	
Accumulated Depreciation		$ 37,000
Accounts Payable		12,000
Salaries Payable		-0-
Utilities Payable		-0-
Interest Payable		-0-
Notes Payable		35,000
Common Stock		35,000
Retained Earnings		10,000
Dividends	3,000	
Service Revenue		227,000
Salaries Expense	158,000	
Depreciation Expense	-0-	
Insurance Expense	-0-	
Supplies Expense	-0-	
Utilities Expense	12,000	
Interest Expense	-0-	
Totals	$356,000	$356,000

Information necessary to prepare the year-end adjusting entries appears below.

a. Depreciation on the machines for the year is $10,000.

b. Employee salaries are paid every two weeks. The last pay period ended on December 23. Salaries earned from December 24 through December 31, 2018, are $4,000.

c. On September 1, 2018, Jaguar borrows $35,000 from a local bank and signs a note. The note requires interest to be paid annually on August 31 at 9%. The principal is due in five years.

d. On March 1, 2018, the company purchases insurance for $24,000 for a one-year policy to cover possible injury to mechanics. The entire $24,000 was debited to Prepaid Insurance at the time of the purchase.

e. $5,000 of supplies remains on hand at December 31, 2018.

f. On December 30, Jaguar receives a utility bill of $2,200 for the month. The bill will not be paid until early January 2019, and no entry was recorded when the bill was received.

Required:

Prepare the necessary adjusting entries on December 31, 2018.

Prepare financial
statements from
an adjusted trial
balance (LO3–5)

P3–5B Orange Designs provides consulting services related to home decoration. Orange Designs provides customers with recommendations for a full range of home décor, including window treatments, carpet and wood flooring, paint colors, furniture, and much more. Below is the year-end adjusted trial balance of Orange Designs.

ORANGE DESIGNS
Adjusted Trial Balance
December 31, 2018

Accounts	Debits	Credits
Cash	$ 6,000	
Accounts Receivable	5,000	
Supplies	3,000	
Prepaid Rent	7,000	
Buildings	120,000	
Accumulated Depreciation		$ 22,000
Accounts Payable		4,000
Salaries Payable		5,000
Utilities Payable		1,100
Notes Payable (due in four years)		30,000
Common Stock		60,000
Retained Earnings		16,000
Service Revenues		111,900
Salaries Expense	43,000	
Rent Expense	19,000	
Depreciation Expense	8,000	
Supplies Expense	9,000	
Advertising Expense	14,000	
Utilities Expense	13,000	
Interest Expense	3,000	
Totals	$250,000	$250,000

Required:

Prepare an income statement, statement of stockholders' equity, and classified balance sheet. In preparing the statement of stockholders' equity, note that during the year the company issued additional common stock of $11,000. This amount is included in the amount for Common Stock in the adjusted trial balance.

Record closing entries and
prepare a post-closing trial
balance (LO3–6, 3–7)

P3–6B The year-end financial statements of Fighting Illini Financial Services are provided below.

FIGHTING ILLINI
Income Statement

Service revenue		$89,700
Expenses:		
Salaries	$50,000	
Supplies	10,100	
Rent	8,500	
Delivery	4,700	73,300
Net income		$16,400

FIGHTING ILLINI
Statement of Stockholders' Equity

	Common Stock	Retained Earnings	Total S. Equity
Beg. bal., Jan. 1	$70,000	$33,300	$103,300
Issue stock	20,000		20,000
Net income		16,400	16,400
Dividends		(7,000)	(7,000)
Ending bal., Dec. 31	$90,000	$42,700	$132,700

FIGHTING ILLINI
Balance Sheet

Assets		Liabilities		
Cash	$ 7,600	Accounts payable		$ 5,100
Accounts receivable	10,200	**Stockholders' Equity**		
Land	120,000	Common stock	$90,000	
		Retained earnings	42,700	$132,700
Total assets	$137,800	Total liabs. and equities		$ 137,800

Required:
1. Record year-end closing entries.
2. Prepare a post-closing trial balance. (*Hint:* The balance of retained earnings will be the amount shown in the balance sheet.)

P3–7B Refer to P3–4B.

Required:
Complete the following steps:
1. Enter the unadjusted balances from the trial balance into T-accounts.
2. Post the adjusting entries prepared in P3–4B to the accounts.
3. Prepare an adjusted trial balance.
4. Prepare an income statement and a statement of shareholders' equity for the year ended December 31, 2018, and a classified balance sheet as of December 31, 2018. Assume that no common stock is issued during the year.
5. Record closing entries.
6. Post closing entries to the accounts.
7. Prepare a post-closing trial balance.

Complete the accounting cycle after adjusting entries (LO3–4, 3–5, 3–6, 3–7)

P3–8B The general ledger of Pipers Plumbing at January 1, 2018, includes the following account balances:

Complete the full accounting cycle (LO3–3, 3–4, 3–5, 3–6, 3–7)

Accounts	Debits	Credits
Cash	$ 4,500	
Accounts Receivable	9,500	
Supplies	3,500	
Equipment	36,000	
Accumulated Depreciation		$ 8,000
Accounts Payable		6,000
Utilities Payable		7,000
Deferred Revenue		-0-
Common Stock		23,000
Retained Earnings		9,500
Totals	$53,500	$53,500

The following is a summary of the transactions for the year:

a.	January	24	Provide plumbing services for cash, $20,000, and on account, $65,000.
b.	March	13	Collect on accounts receivable, $53,000.
c.	May	6	Issue shares of common stock in exchange for $11,000 cash.
d.	June	30	Pay salaries for the current year, $33,000.
e.	September 15		Pay for utilities expenses, $13,000, of which $7,000 represents costs for 2017.
f.	November 24		Receive cash in advance from customers, $10,000.
g.	December 30		Pay $3,000 cash dividends to stockholders.

Required:

1. Set up the necessary T-accounts and enter the beginning balances from the trial balance. In addition to the accounts shown, the company has accounts for Dividends, Service Revenue, Salaries Expense, Utilities Expense, Supplies Expense, and Depreciation Expense.
2. Record each of the summary transactions listed above.
3. Post the transactions to the accounts.
4. Prepare an unadjusted trial balance.
5. Record adjusting entries. Depreciation for the year on the machinery is $8,000. Plumbing supplies remaining on hand at the end of the year equal $1,100. Of the $10,000 paid in advance by customers, $7,000 of the work has been completed by the end of the year.
6. Post adjusting entries.
7. Prepare an adjusted trial balance.
8. Prepare an income statement for 2018 and a classified balance sheet as of December 31, 2018.
9. Record closing entries.
10. Post closing entries
11. Prepare a post-closing trial balance.

Complete the full accounting cycle (LO3–3, 3–4, 3–5, 3–6, 3–7)

P3–9B The general ledger of Jackrabbit Rentals at January 1, 2018, includes the following account balances:

Accounts	Debits	Credits
Cash	$ 41,500	
Accounts Receivable	25,700	
Land	110,800	
Accounts Payable		$ 15,300
Notes Payable		30,000
Common Stock		100,000
Retained Earnings		32,700
Totals	$178,000	$178,000

The following is a summary of the transactions for the year:

a.	January 12	Provide services to customers on account, $62,400.
b.	February 25	Provide services to customers for cash, $75,300.
c.	March 19	Collect on accounts receivable, $45,700.
d.	April 30	Issue shares of common stock in exchange for $30,000 cash.
e.	June 16	Purchase supplies on account, $12,100.
f.	July 7	Pay on accounts payable, $11,300.
g.	September 30	Pay salaries for employee work in the current year, $64,200.
h.	November 22	Pay advertising for the current year, $22,500.
i.	December 30	Pay $2,900 cash dividends to stockholders.

Required:

1. Set up the necessary T-accounts and enter the beginning balances from the trial balance. In addition to the accounts shown, the company also has accounts for Supplies, Salaries Payable, Interest Payable, Dividends, Service Revenue, Salaries Expense, Advertising Expense, Interest Expense, and Supplies Expense.
2. Record each of the summary transactions listed above.
3. Post the transactions to the accounts.
4. Prepare an unadjusted trial balance.
5. Record adjusting entries. Accrued interest on the notes payable at year-end amounted to $2,500. Accrued salaries at year-end amounted to $1,500. Supplies remaining on hand at the end of the year equal $2,300.
6. Post adjusting entries.

7. Prepare an adjusted trial balance.
8. Prepare an income statement for 2018 and a classified balance sheet as of December 31, 2018.
9. Record closing entries.
10. Post closing entries.
11. Prepare a post-closing trial balance.

ADDITIONAL PERSPECTIVES

Great Adventures

(This is a continuation of the Great Adventures problem from earlier chapters.)

AP3–1 You may refer to the opening story of Tony and Suzie and their decision to start Great Adventures in AP 1–1. More of their story and the first set of transactions for the company in July are presented in AP 2–1 and repeated here.

Continuing Problem

July 1	Sell $10,000 of common stock to Suzie.
1	Sell $10,000 of common stock to Tony.
1	Purchase a one-year insurance policy for $4,800 ($400 per month) to cover injuries to participants during outdoor clinics.
2	Pay legal fees of $1,500 associated with incorporation.
4	Purchase office supplies of $1,800 on account.
7	Pay for advertising of $300 to a local newspaper for an upcoming mountain biking clinic to be held on July 15. Attendees will be charged $50 the day of the clinic.
8	Purchase 10 mountain bikes, paying $12,000 cash.
15	On the day of the clinic, Great Adventures receives cash of $2,000 from 40 bikers. Tony conducts the mountain biking clinic.
22	Because of the success of the first mountain biking clinic, Tony holds another mountain biking clinic and the company receives $2,300.
24	Pay for advertising of $700 to a local radio station for a kayaking clinic to be held on August 10. Attendees can pay $100 in advance or $150 on the day of the clinic.
30	Great Adventures receives cash of $4,000 in advance from 40 kayakers for the upcoming kayak clinic.

The following transactions occur over the remainder of the year.

Aug. 1	Great Adventures obtains a $30,000 low-interest loan for the company from the city council, which has recently passed an initiative encouraging business development related to outdoor activities. The loan is due in three years, and 6% annual interest is due each year on July 31.
Aug. 4	The company purchases 14 kayaks, paying $28,000 cash.
Aug. 10	Twenty additional kayakers pay $3,000 ($150 each), in addition to the $4,000 that was paid in advance on July 30, on the day of the clinic. Tony conducts the first kayak clinic.
Aug. 17	Tony conducts a second kayak clinic, and the company receives $10,500 cash.
Aug. 24	Office supplies of $1,800 purchased on July 4 are paid in full.
Sep. 1	To provide better storage of mountain bikes and kayaks when not in use, the company rents a storage shed, purchasing a one-year rental policy for $2,400 ($200 per month).
Sep. 21	Tony conducts a rock-climbing clinic. The company receives $13,200 cash.
Oct. 17	Tony conducts an orienteering clinic. Participants practice how to understand a topographical map, read an altimeter, use a compass, and orient through heavily wooded areas. The company receives $17,900 cash.
Dec. 1	Tony decides to hold the company's first adventure race on December 15. Four-person teams will race from checkpoint to checkpoint using a combination of mountain biking, kayaking, orienteering, trail running, and rock-climbing skills. The first team in each category to complete all checkpoints in order wins. The entry fee for each team is $500.

(continued)

(concluded)

Dec. 5		To help organize and promote the race, Tony hires his college roommate, Victor. Victor will be paid $50 in salary for each team that competes in the race. His salary will be paid after the race.
Dec. 8		The company pays $1,200 to purchase a permit from a state park where the race will be held. The amount is recorded as a miscellaneous expense.
Dec. 12		The company purchases racing supplies for $2,800 on account due in 30 days. Supplies include trophies for the top-finishing teams in each category, promotional shirts, snack foods and drinks for participants, and field markers to prepare the racecourse.
Dec. 15		The company receives $20,000 cash from a total of forty teams, and the race is held.
Dec. 16		The company pays Victor's salary of $2,000.
Dec. 31		The company pays a dividend of $4,000 ($2,000 to Tony and $2,000 to Suzie).
Dec. 31		Using his personal money, Tony purchases a diamond ring for $4,500. Tony surprises Suzie by proposing that they get married. Suzie accepts and they get married!

The following information relates to year-end adjusting entries as of December 31, 2018.

a. Depreciation of the mountain bikes purchased on July 8 and kayaks purchased on August 4 totals $8,000.

b. Six months' of the one-year insurance policy purchased on July 1 has expired.

c. Four months' of the one-year rental policy purchased on September 1 has expired.

d. Of the $1,800 of office supplies purchased on July 4, $300 remains.

e. Interest expense on the $30,000 loan obtained from the city council on August 1 should be recorded.

f. Of the $2,800 of racing supplies purchased on December 12, $200 remains.

g. Suzie calculates that the company owes $14,000 in income taxes.

Required:

1. Record transactions from July 1 through December 31.
2. Record adjusting entries as of December 31, 2018.
3. Post transactions from July 1 through December 31 and adjusting entries on December 31 to T-accounts.
4. Prepare an adjusted trial balance as of December 31, 2018.
5. For the period July 1 to December 31, 2018, prepare an income statement and statement of stockholders' equity. Prepare a classified balance sheet as of December 31, 2018.
6. Record closing entries as of December 31, 2018.
7. Post closing entries to T-accounts.
8. Prepare a post-closing trial balance as of December 31, 2018.

Financial Analysis

American Eagle Outfitters, Inc.

AP3–2 Financial information for **American Eagle** is presented in **Appendix A** at the end of the book.

Required:

1. For the most recent year, what amount does American Eagle report for current assets? What assets are listed as current assets? What is the ratio of current assets to total assets?
2. For the most recent year, what amount does American Eagle report for current liabilities? What liabilities are listed as current liabilities? What is the ratio of current liabilities to total liabilities?
3. List any current assets or current liabilities that likely relate to adjusting entries.
4. What is the change in retained earnings reported in the balance sheet?
5. For the most recent year, what is the amount of net income reported in the income statement?
6. Using your answers in 4 and 5, calculate the amount of dividends paid during the year. Verify your answer by looking at the retained earnings column in the statement of stockholders' equity.

The Buckle, Inc.

AP3–3 Financial information for **Buckle** is presented in **Appendix B** at the end of the book.

Required:

1. For the most recent year, what amount does Buckle report for current assets? What assets are listed as current assets? What is the ratio of current assets to total assets?
2. For the most recent year, what amount does Buckle report for current liabilities? What liabilities are listed as current liabilities? What is the ratio of current liabilities to total liabilities?
3. List any current assets or current liabilities that likely relate to adjusting entries.
4. For the most recent year, what is the change in retained earnings reported in the balance sheet?
5. For the most recent year, what is the amount of net income reported in the income statement?
6. Using your answers in 4 and 5 above, calculate the amount of dividends paid during the year. Verify your answer by looking at the retained earnings column in the statement of stockholders' equity.

American Eagle Outfitters, Inc. vs. The Buckle, Inc.

AP3–4 Financial information for **American Eagle** is presented in **Appendix A** at the end of the book, and financial information for **Buckle** is presented in **Appendix B** at the end of the book.

Required:

1. Determine which company maintains a higher ratio of current assets to total assets. How might this be an advantage for the company?
2. Determine which company maintains a higher ratio of current liabilities to total liabilities. How might this be a disadvantage for the company?
3. The dividend payout ratio equals dividends paid during the year divided by net income. Determine which company has a higher dividend payout ratio. Why might this be the case?

Ethics

AP3–51 You have recently been hired as the assistant controller for Stanton Temperton Corporation, which rents building space in major metropolitan areas. Customers are required to pay six months of rent in advance. At the end of 2018, the company's president, Jim Temperton, notices that net income has fallen compared to last year. In 2017, the company reported before-tax profit of $330,000, but in 2018 the before-tax profit is only $280,000. This concerns Jim for two reasons. First, his year-end bonus is tied directly to before-tax profits. Second, shareholders may see a decline in profitability as a weakness in the company and begin to sell their stock. With the sell-off of stock, Jim's personal investment in the company's stock, as well as his company-operated retirement plan, will be in jeopardy of severe losses.

After close inspection of the financial statements, Jim notices that the balance of the Deferred Revenue account is $120,000. This amount represents payments in advance from long-term customers ($80,000) and from relatively new customers ($40,000). Jim comes to you, the company's accountant, and suggests that the firm should recognize as revenue in 2018 the $80,000 received in advance from long-term customers. He offers the following explanation: "First, we have received these customers' cash by the end of 2018, so there is no question about their ability to pay. Second, we have a long-term history of fulfilling our obligation to these customers. We have always stood by our commitments to our customers and we always will. We earned that money when we got them to sign the six-month contract."

Required:

Discuss the ethical dilemma you face. What is the issue? Who are the parties affected? What factors should you consider in making your decision?

Internet Research

AP3–6 Obtain a copy of the annual report of **McDonald's Corporation** for the most recent year. You can find the annual report at the company's website (*www.mcdonalds.com*) in the investor information section or at the Securities and Exchange Commission's website (*www.sec.gov*) using EDGAR (Electronic Data Gathering, Analysis, and Retrieval). Form 10-K, which includes the annual report, is required to be filed on EDGAR. Search or scroll within the annual report to find the financial statements.

Required:

Determine the following from the company's financial statements:
1. Do the company's revenues exceed expenses? What is the amount of net income?
2. Did net income increase in the most recent year compared to the previous year?
3. Which assets are listed as current assets? Why are other assets not listed as current assets?
4. Which liabilities are listed as current liabilities? Why are other liabilities not listed as current liabilities?
5. By how much did retained earnings increase/decrease in the most recent year compared to the previous year?
6. What is the amount of dividends paid to common stockholders? This information can be found in the statement of shareholders' equity or the statement of cash flows.
7. Explain the relationship between the change in retained earnings, net income, and dividends.

Written Communication

AP3–7 You are a tutor for introductory financial accounting. You tell the students, "Recording adjusting entries is a critical step in the accounting cycle, and the two major classifications of adjusting entries are prepayments and accruals." Chris, one of the students in the class, says, "I don't understand."

Required:

Respond to Chris.
1. When do prepayments occur? When do accruals occur?
2. Describe the appropriate adjusting entry for prepaid expenses and for deferred revenues. What is the effect on net income, assets, liabilities, and stockholders' equity of not recording a required adjusting entry for prepayments?
3. Describe the required adjusting entry for accrued expenses and for accrued revenues. What is the effect on net income, assets, liabilities, and shareholders' equity of not recording a required adjusting entry for accruals?

Answers to the Self-Study Questions
1. b   2. c   3. c   4. b   5. a   6. b   7. d   8. c   9. d   10. c

Cash and Internal Controls

4

Learning Objectives

AFTER STUDYING THIS CHAPTER, YOU SHOULD BE ABLE TO:

- ■ **LO4–1** Discuss the impact of accounting scandals and the passage of the Sarbanes-Oxley Act.
- ■ **LO4–2** Identify the components, responsibilities, and limitations of internal control.
- ■ **LO4–3** Define cash and cash equivalents.
- ■ **LO4–4** Understand controls over cash receipts and cash disbursements.
- ■ **LO4–5** Reconcile a bank statement.
- ■ **LO4–6** Account for employee purchases.
- ■ **LO4–7** Identify the major inflows and outflows of cash.

Analysis

- ■ **LO4–8** Assess cash holdings by comparing cash to noncash assets.

REGAL ENTERTAINMENT: INTERNAL CONTROLS ARE A BOX-OFFICE HIT

According to research conducted by the Association of Certified Fraud Examiners (ACFE, *www.acfe.com*), U.S. organizations lose an estimated $1 *trillion* (or about 5% of their total revenue) to employee fraud each year. This occurs despite increased corporate emphasis on antifraud controls and recent legislation to combat fraud. While some employees steal office supplies, inventory, and equipment, the asset most often targeted is cash. Cash fraud includes skimming cash receipts before they are recorded, stealing cash that has already been recorded, and falsely disbursing cash through fraudulent billing, expense reimbursement, or payroll.

Feature Story

Companies that rely heavily on cash transactions are especially susceptible to employee fraud. For example, consider a company like **Regal Entertainment Group** (NYSE: **RGC**), one of the world's largest motion picture providers. The company operates approximately 7,400 screens and sells about 220 million tickets per year, generating revenues each year of nearly $3 billion. The company often collects cash at the time it sells movie tickets or provides food and drinks at the concession. To minimize cash losses due to employee fraud, RGC establishes strong systems for internal control.

The revenue streams generated by admissions and concessions are fully supported by information systems to monitor cash flow and to detect fraud and inventory theft. Simpler approaches to internal control include *separation of duties:* For example, one person sells tickets, and another collects the tickets. This prevents the ticket seller from pocketing a moviegoer's cash and then allowing admission without a ticket being produced by the ticket machine. At the end of the day, the number of tickets produced by the machine should exactly match the cash collected.

In this chapter, we discuss much more about fraud and ways to prevent it. We will also examine specific internal controls related to cash. At the end of the chapter, we'll analyze the cash balances of **Regal Entertainment Group** versus **Cinemark Holdings**. You can apply your newly learned skills in preventing and detecting fraud at a movie theatre in Problem 4–1A.

© Altrendo Images/Getty Images

PART A

INTERNAL CONTROLS

As you saw in Chapters 1 through 3, the key roles of financial accounting are to measure business activities and to communicate those activities to external decision makers. It is important to the usefulness of this measurement/communication process that the numbers provided by financial accountants are *correct.* The decisions of investors and creditors rely on financial statements and other disclosed accounting information to *accurately* portray the activities of the company.

You might be surprised, though, to learn that some companies' published financial statements are *incorrect.* In recent years, well-known companies such as **Dell**, **Office Depot**, **Microsoft**, **Apple**, **Rite Aid**, and many others have issued incorrect financial statements. How could this happen? What can be done to help prevent it?

Companies issue incorrect financial statements for two reasons—errors and fraud. First, companies sometimes make accidental errors in recording (or failing to record) transactions or in applying accounting rules. When these errors are later discovered, companies often have to restate the financial statements affected. Even though these errors may be unintentional, they nevertheless can create confusion and weaken investors' and creditors' confidence in the important information role that accounting serves.

The second reason for incorrect financial accounting information relates to fraud. *Fraud* occurs when a person intentionally deceives another person for personal gain or to damage that person. Specifically related to business activities, the Association of Certified Fraud Examiners (ACFE) defines occupational fraud as the use of one's occupation for personal enrichment through the deliberate misuse or misapplication of the employer's resources.

The first source of occupational fraud is misuse of company resources. As discussed in the chapter-opening Feature Story, occupational fraud is a big business, with companies expecting to lose on average 5% of their total revenues to fraud each year. For a company like **Regal Entertainment Group**, 5% of total revenues would equal nearly $150 million lost to fraud in a single year. Cash is the asset most commonly involved with fraudulent activity. A significant portion of this chapter discusses the procedures businesses use to maintain control over cash receipts and cash disbursements.

The second source of occupational fraud involves financial statement manipulation. Here, those in charge of communicating financial accounting information falsify reports. You may have heard the phrase "cooking the books." The phrase implies that the accounting records ("books") have been presented in an altered form ("cooked"). Some managers are willing to cook the books for personal gain. Motives for such deception might be maximizing their compensation, increasing the company's stock price, and preserving their jobs.

The three elements necessary for every fraud are commonly referred to as the fraud triangle and are shown below in Illustration 4–1.

What can be done to help minimize fraud? At least one of the three elements of the fraud triangle must be eliminated. Of the three elements, companies have the greatest ability to eliminate *opportunity.* To eliminate opportunity, companies implement formal procedures known as internal controls. These represent a company's plan to (1) safeguard the

© Digital Vision/2007
Getty Images, Inc., RF

ILLUSTRATION 4–1

Fraud Triangle

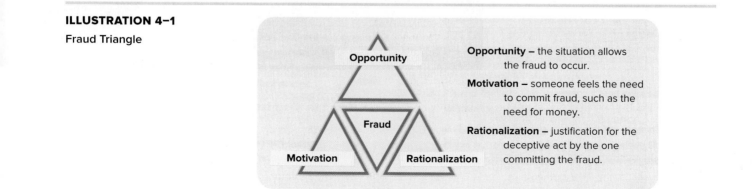

Opportunity – the situation allows the fraud to occur.

Motivation – someone feels the need to commit fraud, such as the need for money.

Rationalization – justification for the deceptive act by the one committing the fraud.

company's assets and (2) improve the accuracy and reliability of accounting information. In this chapter, we'll discuss the basic principles and procedures of companies' internal controls (with a deeper look at cash controls). The quality of internal controls directly affects the quality of financial accounting.

Accounting Scandals and Response by Congress

Managers are entrusted with the resources of both the company's lenders (liabilities) and its owners (stockholders' equity). In this sense, managers of the company act as stewards or caretakers of the company's assets. However, in recent years some managers shirked their ethical responsibilities and misused or misreported the company's funds. In many cases, top executives misreported accounting information to cover up their company's poor operating performance. Such fraudulent activity is costly: The ACFE reports that the median loss caused by fraudulent financial statement schemes, for example, is $1,000,000 per instance. As you become more familiar with specific accounting topics throughout the remainder of this book, you'll begin to understand how amounts reported in the financial statements can be manipulated by managers.

Two of the highest-profile cases of accounting fraud in U.S. history are the collapses of **Enron** and **WorldCom**. Enron used questionable accounting practices to avoid reporting billions in debt and losses in its financial statements. WorldCom misclassified certain expenditures to overstate assets and profitability by $11 billion. Both companies hoped to fool investors into overvaluing the company's stock. Other common types of financial statement fraud include creating fictitious revenues, improperly valuing assets, hiding liabilities, and mismatching revenues and expenses.

As the Enron and WorldCom frauds (as well as several others) were being uncovered in 2001 and 2002, the stock prices of these companies plummeted. Investors lost nearly $200 billion as a result. Employees of these companies also suffered. Both firms declared bankruptcy, resulting in employee termination; reduced salaries and increased workloads for those who were left; and loss of employee retirement funds, stock options, and health benefits.

■ **LO4–1**
Discuss the impact of accounting scandals and the passage of the Sarbanes-Oxley Act.

SARBANES-OXLEY ACT OF 2002

In response to these corporate accounting scandals and to public outrage over seemingly widespread unethical behavior of top executives, Congress passed the Sarbanes-Oxley Act, also known as the *Public Company Accounting Reform and Investor Protection Act of 2002* and commonly referred to as *SOX*. SOX applies to all companies that are required to file financial statements with the SEC and represents one of the greatest reforms in business practices in U.S. history. The act established a variety of guidelines related to auditor-client relations and internal control procedures. Illustration 4–2 provides an overview of the major provisions of SOX.

The last provision listed in Illustration 4–2, internal controls under Section 404, requires company management and auditors to document and assess the effectiveness of a company's internal controls—processes that could affect financial reporting. PCAOB chairman William McDonough explained the significance of this part of the law: "In the past, internal controls were merely considered by auditors; now they will have to be tested and examined in detail" (*PCAOBUS.org*, June 18, 2004). Whether you are an investor, an employee, a manager, or an auditor, understanding a company's internal controls is important.

 KEY POINT

The accounting scandals in the early 2000s prompted passage of the Sarbanes-Oxley Act (SOX). Among other stipulations, SOX sets forth a variety of guidelines related to auditor-client relations and additional internal controls. Section 404, in particular, requires company management and auditors to document and assess the effectiveness of a company's internal controls.

ILLUSTRATION 4–2

Major Provisions of the Sarbanes-Oxley Act of 2002

Oversight board	The Public Company Accounting Oversight Board (PCAOB) has the authority to establish standards dealing with auditing, quality control, ethics, independence, and other activities relating to the preparation of audited financial reports. The board consists of five members who are appointed by the Securities and Exchange Commission.
Corporate executive accountability	Corporate executives must personally certify the company's financial statements and financial disclosures. Severe financial penalties and the possibility of imprisonment are consequences of fraudulent misstatement.
Nonaudit services	It's unlawful for the auditors of public companies to also perform certain nonaudit services, such as investment advising, for their clients.
Retention of work papers	Auditors of public companies must retain all work papers for seven years or face a prison term for willful violation.
Auditor rotation	The lead auditor in charge of auditing a particular company (referred to as the *audit partner*) must rotate off that company within five years and allow a new audit partner to take the lead.
Conflicts of interest	Audit firms are not allowed to audit public companies whose chief executives worked for the audit firm and participated in that company's audit during the preceding year.
Hiring of auditor	Audit firms are hired by the audit committee of the board of directors of the company, not by company management.
Internal control	Section 404 of the act requires (a) that company management document and assess the effectiveness of all internal control processes that could affect financial reporting and (b) that company auditors express an opinion on whether management's assessment of the effectiveness of internal control is fairly stated. Smaller companies are exempt from requirement (b).

Framework for Internal Control

■ LO4–2

Identify the components, responsibilities, and limitations of internal control.

As noted earlier, internal control is a company's plan to (1) safeguard the company's assets and (2) improve the accuracy and reliability of accounting information. Effective internal control builds a wall to prevent misuse of company funds by employees and fraudulent or errant financial reporting. Strong internal control systems allow greater reliance by investors on reported financial statements.

COMPONENTS OF INTERNAL CONTROL

A framework for designing an internal control system was provided by the *Committee of Sponsoring Organizations (COSO)* of the Treadway Commission. COSO (*www.coso.org*) is dedicated to improving the quality of financial reporting through, among other things, effective internal controls. COSO suggests that internal control consists of five components, displayed in Illustration 4–3.

The components of internal control are built on the foundation of the ethical tone set by top management in its control environment. From there, management assesses risks, implements specific control activities, and continuously monitors all systems. Running throughout this structure is the need for timely information and communication. Employees at all levels must understand the importance of high-quality information. Lower-level employees must report information accurately and in a timely manner to those higher in the organization. Top executives of a company then must effectively communicate this information to external parties such as investors and creditors through financial statements.

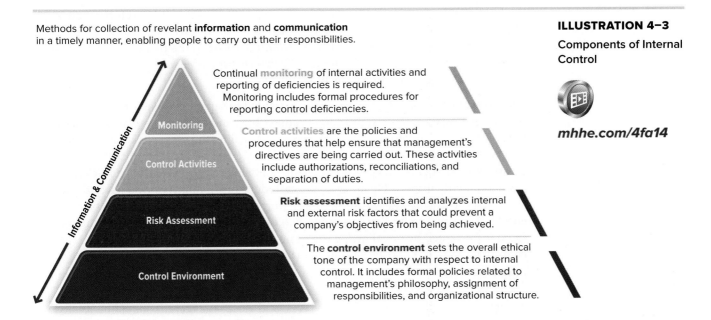

Methods for collection of revelant **information** and **communication** in a timely manner, enabling people to carry out their responsibilities.

Continual monitoring of internal activities and reporting of deficiencies is required. Monitoring includes formal procedures for reporting control deficiencies.

Control activities are the policies and procedures that help ensure that management's directives are being carried out. These activities include authorizations, reconciliations, and separation of duties.

Risk assessment identifies and analyzes internal and external risk factors that could prevent a company's objectives from being achieved.

The **control environment** sets the overall ethical tone of the company with respect to internal control. It includes formal policies related to management's philosophy, assignment of responsibilities, and organizational structure.

Monitoring
Control Activities
Risk Assessment
Control Environment
Information & Communication

ILLUSTRATION 4–3

Components of Internal Control

mhhe.com/4fa14

To see an example of how internal controls are linked to the information provided in financial statements, let's look at the description given by Regal Entertainment Group in its annual report (see Illustration 4–4).

REGAL ENTERTAINMENT GROUP
Notes to the Financial Statements (excerpt)

A company's internal control over financial reporting includes those policies and procedures that (1) pertain to the maintenance of records that, in reasonable detail, accurately and fairly reflect the transactions and dispositions of the assets of the company; (2) provide reasonable assurance that transactions are recorded as necessary to permit preparation of financial statements in accordance with generally accepted accounting principles, and that receipts and expenditures of the company are being made only in accordance with authorizations of management and directors of the company; and (3) provide reasonable assurance regarding prevention or timely detection of unauthorized acquisition, use, or disposition of the company's assets that could have a material effect on the financial statements.

ILLUSTRATION 4–4

Regal Entertainment's Discussion of Internal Controls over Financial Reporting

Movie Theatre Example.   Let's look at how the five components of internal control apply in actual practice. Here, we apply them to operating a movie theatre.

The overall attitudes and actions of management greatly affect the *control environment*. If employees notice unethical behavior or comments by management, they are more likely to behave in a similar manner, wasting the company's resources. Wouldn't you be more comfortable investing in or lending to a movie theatre if it were run by a highly ethical person, rather than someone of questionable character?

Risk assessment includes careful consideration of internal and external risk factors. Internal risks include issues such as unsafe lighting, faulty video projectors, unsanitary bathrooms, and employee incompetence with regard to food preparation. Common examples of external risks include a vendor supplying low-quality popcorn, moviegoers' security in the parking lot, or perhaps the decline in customer demand due to outside competition from DVD rentals or **Netflix**. These internal and external risk factors put the company's objectives in jeopardy.

Control activities include a variety of policies and procedures used to protect a company's assets. There are two general types of control activities: preventive and detective. *Preventive controls* are designed to keep errors or fraud from occurring in the first place. *Detective controls* are designed to detect errors or fraud that already have occurred.

Examples of preventive controls include:

1. **Separation of duties.** A set of procedures intended to separate duties among employees for authorizing transactions, recording transactions, and controlling related assets is referred to as separation of duties. The employee selling the movie ticket should not also be the employee in charge of collecting the tickets. The accountant at the movie theatre should not also have direct access to company cash by filling in as a ticket cashier or being responsible for the daily cash deposits. Employees who have physical control of theatre inventory (candy bars, T-shirts, and so on) should not also be in charge of accounting for that inventory. **You can see that in each of these examples, fraud is prevented by not allowing the same person to be responsible for both controlling the asset and accounting for the asset.**

2. **Physical controls** over assets and accounting records. Each night, money from ticket sales should be placed in the theatre's safe or deposited at the bank. Important documents should be kept in fireproof files, and electronic records should be backed up daily and require user-ID and password for access. Concession supplies should be kept in a locked room with access allowed only to authorized personnel.

3. **Proper authorization** to prevent improper use of the company's resources. The theatre should establish formal guidelines on how to handle cash receipts and make purchases. For example, only management should be authorized to make purchases over a certain amount.

4. **Employee management.** The company should provide employees with appropriate guidance to ensure they have the knowledge necessary to carry out their job duties. Employees should be made fully aware of the company's internal control procedures, ethical responsibilities, and channels for reporting irregular activities.

5. **E-commerce controls.** E-commerce refers to the wide range of electronic activities of a company, such as buying and selling over the Internet, digital information processing, and electronic communication. Given the tremendous growth of e-commerce activities in recent years, internal controls over these activities are becoming increasingly important. For example, only authorized personnel should have passwords to conduct electronic business transactions. The company should maintain and systematically check the firewall settings to prevent unauthorized access to accounts and credit card numbers. All employees should update the system's antivirus software periodically.

Examples of detective controls include:

1. **Reconciliations.** Management should periodically determine whether the amount of physical assets of the company (cash, supplies, inventory, and other property) agree with the accounting records. For example, accounting personnel should routinely reconcile the company's cash records with those of its bank, and any discrepancy should be investigated. Later in this chapter we'll see an example of how to prepare a bank reconciliation for Starlight Drive-In.

2. **Performance reviews.** The actual performance of individuals or processes should be checked against their expected performance. For example, the amount of concessions sold should be compared to the number of tickets sold over a period of time. If concession sales are lower than expected for a given number of tickets, employees could be wasting food, stealing snacks, or giving it to their friends for free. Alternatively, vendors may be supplying lower-quality food, driving down sales. Management may also wish to evaluate the overall performance of the theatre by comparing ticket sales for the current year with ticket sales for the previous year.

3. **Audits.** Many companies, such as those companies listed on a stock exchange, are required to have an independent auditor attest to the adequacy of their internal control

procedures. Other companies can voluntarily choose each year to have an auditor assess their internal control procedures to detect any deficiencies or fraudulent behavior of employees.

Monitoring of internal controls needs to occur on an ongoing basis. The theatre manager needs to actively review daily operations to ensure that control procedures work effectively. For instance, the manager should compare daily cash from ticket sales with the number of tickets issued, compare concession sales with units purchased, and make sure employees are paid only for actual hours worked.

Information and communication depend on the reliability of the accounting information system itself. If the accountant's office has papers scattered everywhere, and you learn the company still does all its accounting by hand without a computer, wouldn't you, as an investor or lender, be a bit worried? A system should be in place to ensure that current transactions of the company are reflected in current reports. Employees also should be aware of procedures in place to deal with any perceived internal control failures. For example, an anonymous tip hotline should be in place to encourage communication about unethical activities, such as an employee giving concession items for free to her friends. Employee tips historically have been the most common means of detecting employee fraud.

RESPONSIBILITIES FOR INTERNAL CONTROL

Everyone in a company has an impact on the operation and effectiveness of internal controls, but **the top executives are the ones who must take final responsibility for their establishment and success.** The CEO and CFO sign a report each year assessing whether the internal controls are adequate. Section 404 of SOX requires not only that companies document their internal controls and assess their adequacy, but that the company's auditors provide an opinion on management's assessment. A recent survey by Financial Executives International reports that the average total cost to a public company in complying with Section 404 is nearly $4 million.

The Public Company Accounting Oversight Board (PCAOB) further requires the auditor to express its own opinion on whether the company has maintained effective internal control over financial reporting. Illustration 4–5 provides an excerpt from Regal Entertainment's auditor's report.

REGAL ENTERTAINMENT GROUP
Auditor's Report (excerpt)

In our opinion, management's assessment that Regal Entertainment Group maintained effective internal control over financial reporting is fairly stated, in all material respects, based on criteria established in *Internal Control—Integrated Framework* issued by the Committee of Sponsoring Organizations of the Treadway Commission (COSO). Also, in our opinion, Regal Entertainment Group maintained, in all material respects, effective internal control over financial reporting, based on criteria established in *Internal Control—Integrated Framework* issued by the Committee of Sponsoring Organizations of the Treadway Commission (COSO).

ILLUSTRATION 4–5

Excerpt from Regal Entertainment's Auditor's Report Related to Effectiveness of Internal Controls

LIMITATIONS OF INTERNAL CONTROL

Unfortunately, even with the best internal control systems, financial misstatements can occur. While better internal control systems will more likely detect operating and reporting errors, no internal control system can turn a bad employee into a good one. No internal control system is perfect.

Internal control systems are especially susceptible to collusion. Collusion occurs when two or more people act in coordination to circumvent internal controls. Going back to our movie theatre example, if the ticket cashier and the ticket taker, or the ticket cashier and the accountant, decide to work together to steal cash, theft will be much more difficult to detect. Fraud cases that involve collusion are typically several times more severe than are fraud cases involving one person. This suggests that collusion is effective in circumventing control procedures.

Top-level employees who have the ability to override internal control features also have opportunity to commit fraud. For example, managers may be required to obtain approval from the chief financial officer (CFO) for all large purchases. However, if the CFO uses the company's funds to purchase a boat for personal use at a lake home, fewer controls are in place to detect this misappropriation. Even if lower-level employees suspect wrongdoing, they may be unwilling to confront their boss about the issue.

Finally, because there are natural risks to running any business, **effective internal controls and ethical employees alone cannot ensure a company's success, or even survival.** Regal Entertainment recognizes the limitations of internal controls and provides an explicit discussion of this issue in its annual report, as shown in Illustration 4–6.

ILLUSTRATION 4–6

Regal Entertainment's Discussion of Limitations of Internal Controls

> ### REGAL ENTERTAINMENT GROUP
> ### Management Discussion and Analysis (excerpt)
>
> Management recognizes that there are inherent limitations in the effectiveness of any internal control over financial reporting, including the possibility of human error and the circumvention or overriding of internal control. Accordingly, even effective internal control over financial reporting can provide only reasonable assurance with respect to financial statement preparation. Further, because of changes in conditions, the effectiveness of internal control over financial reporting may vary over time.

KEY POINT

Internal control refers to a company's plan to improve the accuracy and reliability of accounting information and safeguard the company's assets. Five key components to an internal control system are (1) control environment, (2) risk assessment, (3) control activities, (4) monitoring, and (5) information and communication. Control activities include those designed to prevent or detect fraudulent or erroneous behavior.

Decision Point

Question	Accounting information	Analysis
Does the company maintain adequate internal controls?	Management's discussion, auditor's opinion	If management or the auditor notes any deficiencies in internal controls, financial accounting information may be unreliable.

PART B

CASH

Among all of the company's assets, cash is the one most susceptible to employee fraud. The obvious way that employees steal cash is by physically removing it from the company, such as pulling it out of the cash register and walking out the door. However, there are other, less

Credit card companies earn revenues primarily in two ways. First, the cardholder has a specified grace period before he or she has to pay the credit card balance in full. If the balance is not paid by the end of the grace period, the issuing company will charge a fee (interest). Second, credit card companies charge the *retailer*, not the customer, for the use of the credit card. This charge generally ranges from 2% to 4% of the amount of the sale.

For example, suppose a movie theatre accepts MasterCard as payment for $2,000 worth of movie tickets, and MasterCard charges the movie theatre a service fee of 3% (or $60 on sales of $2,000). Moviegoers don't pay cash to the theatre at the time of sale, but MasterCard deposits cash, less the service fee expense, into the theatre's account usually within 24 hours. Therefore, the theatre records the $2,000 credit card transaction as $1,940 cash received and $60 service fee expense.

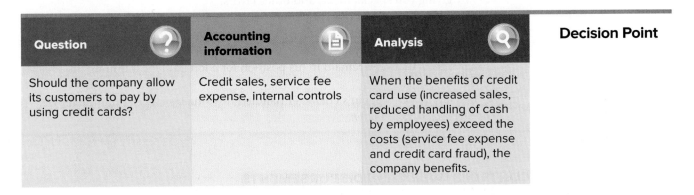

	Debit	Credit
Cash	1,940	
Service Fee Expense...	60	
Service Revenue..		2,000
(Sell tickets with credit card and 3% service fee)		

A = L + SE
+1,940
−60 Exp↑
+2,000 Rev↑

From the seller's perspective, the only difference between a cash sale and a credit card sale is that the seller must pay a fee to the credit card company for allowing the customer to use a credit card.

Decision Point

Question	Accounting information	Analysis
Should the company allow its customers to pay by using credit cards?	Credit sales, service fee expense, internal controls	When the benefits of credit card use (increased sales, reduced handling of cash by employees) exceed the costs (service fee expense and credit card fraud), the company benefits.

Acceptance of Debit Cards.   *Debit cards* also provide an additional control for cash receipts. Like credit cards, debit cards offer customers a way to purchase goods and services without a physical exchange of cash. They differ, however, in that most debit cards (sometimes referred to as *check cards*) work just like a check and withdraw funds directly from the cardholder's bank account at the time of use. (Recall that credit cards don't remove cash from the cardholder's account after each transaction.)

 COMMON MISTAKE

The term *debit card* can cause some confusion for someone in the first accounting course. Throughout this course, we refer to an increase in cash as a *debit* to cash. However, using your debit card will result in a decrease in your cash account. The term *debit card* refers to the bank's liability to the company being decreased (debited) when the company uses a debit card. Don't let this confuse you.

Similar to credit cards, the use of debit cards by customers results in a fee being charged to the retailer. However, the fees charged for debit cards are typically much lower than those charged for credit cards. Debit card transactions are recorded similar to credit card transactions.

ETHICAL DILEMMA

© Digital Vision LTD./SuperStock, RF

Suppose that you were sent to prison for a crime you did not commit. While in prison, the warden learns that you have taken financial accounting and are really good at "keeping the books." In fact, you are so good at accounting that you offer to teach other inmates basic financial skills that they'll use someday after being released.

However, the warden plans to use his position of authority at the prison to steal money. He uses prisoners as low-cost labor to do projects around town. Because other legitimate companies cannot compete with these low costs, they bribe the warden *not* to bid on jobs. The warden asks you to use your accounting skills to participate in a financial scam by falsifying documents and creating a false set of accounting records that will allow the warden's bribes to go undetected by state prison authorities. In other words, he wants you to "cook the books."

When you object to helping with this scam, the warden threatens to end your tutoring sessions with other inmates and sentence you to solitary confinement. To further sway your decision, he promises that if you'll help, he'll make your prison life easy by giving you special meals and other favors.

What would you do in this situation? If you help the warden steal money, you benefit personally and the other prisoners benefit by your continued tutoring sessions. However, the warden physically abuses some of the prisoners, and helping him steal money means that he'll remain in his position for a long time, continuing his abusive behavior.

To see how Tim Robbin's character handled this situation, check out the movie *The Shawshank Redemption.*

CONTROLS OVER CASH DISBURSEMENTS

Managers should design proper controls for cash disbursements to prevent any unauthorized payments and ensure proper recording. Consistent with our discussion of cash receipts, cash disbursements include not only disbursing physical cash, but also writing checks and using credit cards and debit cards to make payments. All these forms of payment constitute cash disbursement and require formal internal control procedures. Common controls over cash disbursements include:

1. Make all disbursements, other than very small ones, by check, debit card, or credit card. This provides a permanent record of all disbursements.

2. Authorize all expenditures before purchase and verify the accuracy of the purchase itself. The employee who authorizes payment should not also be the employee who prepares the check.

3. Make sure checks are serially numbered and signed only by authorized employees. Require two signatures for larger checks.

4. Periodically agree amounts shown in the debit card and credit card statements against purchase receipts. The employee verifying the accuracy of the debit card and credit card statements should not also be the employee responsible for actual purchases.

5. Set maximum purchase limits on debit cards and credit cards. Give approval to purchase above these amounts only to upper-level employees.

6. Employees responsible for making cash disbursements should not also be in charge of cash receipts.

When the movie theatre pays $1,000 to advertise its show times, it records the following transaction, regardless of whether it pays with cash, a check, or a debit card.

	Debit	Credit
Advertising Expense	1,000	
Cash		1,000
(Purchase advertising with cash, check, or debit card)		

A = L + SE

−1,000 Exp↑

−1,000

Because credit cards allow the purchaser to delay payment for several weeks or even months, if the theatre uses a credit card to pay for the $1,000 worth of advertising, it would record the purchase as follows.

	Debit	Credit
Advertising Expense	1,000	
Accounts Payable...		1,000
(Purchase advertising with credit card)		

A = L + SE

−1,000 Exp↑

+1,000

Smaller companies often use credit cards to make purchases, whereas larger companies buy on account (or on credit). Both result in payment by the company being somewhat delayed, and therefore both types of purchases result in Accounts Payable being recorded.

 KEY POINT

Because cash is the asset of a company most susceptible to employee fraud, controls over cash receipts and cash disbursements are an important part of a company's overall internal control system. Important controls over cash receipts include separation of duties for those who handle cash and independent verification of cash receipts. Important controls over cash disbursements include payment by check, credit card, or debit card, separation of duties, and various authorization and documentation procedures.

Bank Reconciliation

Another important control used by nearly all companies to help maintain control of cash is a bank reconciliation. A bank reconciliation matches the balance of cash in the bank account with the balance of cash in the company's own records. If you have your own checking account, you know that the balance of cash in your checkbook often does not equal the balance of cash in your bank account. Why is that? One possibility is that you (or your bank) made a recording error. More likely, though, you've written a check or have cash receipts that haven't yet reached the bank, or maybe the bank has made an adjustment you haven't yet recorded.

It's the same for a business. A company's cash balance as recorded in its books rarely equals the cash balance reported in the bank statement. The reasons for the differences are the same as those for your personal checking account: Differences in these balances most often occur because of either timing differences or errors. It is the *possibility* of these errors, or even outright fraudulent activities, that makes the bank reconciliation a useful cash control tool. A bank reconciliation connects the company's cash balance to the bank's cash balance by identifying differences due to timing and errors.

Timing differences *in cash occur when the company records transactions either before or after the bank records the same transactions.* For example, when a movie theatre pays its popcorn supplier $2,000 by check, the company records a decrease in cash immediately, but the bank doesn't record a decrease in cash until the popcorn supplier later deposits the

■ **LO4–5**
Reconcile a bank statement.

check. If the supplier waits a week before depositing the check, the balance of cash in the company's records will be reduced one week earlier than will the bank's.

Other times, it's the bank that is the first to record a transaction. For example, banks may charge service fees for a variety of items. These fees immediately reduce the bank's record of the company's balance for cash. However, the company may not be immediately aware of these fees. Only when inspecting the bank statement will the company become aware of the cash reduction. In this case, the bank's balance for cash reflects a cash transaction before the company's balance can reflect the same transaction.

***Errors* can be made either by the company or its bank and may be accidental or intentional.** An *accidental* error might occur if the company mistakenly were to record a check being written for $117 as $171 in its records, or if the bank improperly processed a deposit of $1,100 as a $1,010 deposit. An *intentional* error is the result of theft. If the company records a daily deposit of $5,000 but an employee deposits only $500 into the bank account and pockets the rest, the bank reconciliation will reveal the missing $4,500.

To see how a bank reconciliation is prepared, let's start by examining the bank statement of Starlight Drive-In. At the end of March, First Bank reports the bank statement in Illustration 4–8 for Starlight's account. Starlight's own record of cash activity over the same period is shown in Illustration 4–9.

First Bank's ending balance of cash ($4,100) differs from Starlight's ending balance of cash ($2,880). To understand why these two cash balances differ, we need to identify (1) timing differences created by cash activity reported by either First Bank or Starlight but not recorded by the other and (2) any errors.

ILLUSTRATION 4–8

Bank Statement

P.O. Box 26788
Odessa, TX 79760
(432) 799-BANK

First Bank
A Name You Can Trust

Member FDIC

| Account Holder: | Starlight Drive-In
221B Baker Street
Odessa, TX 79760 | Account Number: | 4061009619 |
| | | Statement Date: | March 31, 2018 |

Account Summary

Beginning Balance March 1, 2018	Deposits and Credits		Withdrawals and Debits		Ending Balance March 31, 2018
	No.	Total	No.	Total	
$3,800	4	$8,600	7	$8,300	$4,100

Account Details

Deposits and Credits			Withdrawals and Debits				Daily Balance	
Date	Amount	Desc.	Date	No.	Amount	Desc.	Date	Amount
3/5	$3,600	DEP	3/8	293	$2,100	CHK	3/5	$7,400
3/9	3,000	NOTE	3/12	294	2,900	CHK	3/8	5,300
3/22	1,980	DEP	3/15		400	EFT	3/9	8,300
3/31	20	INT	3/22		750	NSF	3/12	5,400
			3/26	296	1,900	CHK	3/15	5,000
			3/28		200	DC	3/22	6,230
			3/31		50	SF	3/26	4,330
							3/28	4,130
	$8,600				$8,300		3/31	$4,100

Desc.	**DEP** Customer deposit	**INT** Interest earned	**SF** Service fees
	NOTE Note collected	**CHK** Customer check	**NSF** Nonsufficient funds
	EFT Electronic funds transfer	**DC** Debit card	

ILLUSTRATION 4–9

Company Records of
Cash Activities

STARLIGHT DRIVE-IN
Cash Account Records
March 1, 2018, to March 31, 2018

Deposits			Checks			
Date	Description	Amount	Date	No.	Description	Amount
3/5	Sales receipts	$3,600	3/6	293	Salaries	$2,100
3/22	Sales receipts	1,980	3/11	294	Rent	2,600
3/31	Sales receipts	2,200	3/21	295	Utilities	1,200
			3/24	296	Insurance	1,900
			3/30	297	Supplies	900
		$7,780				$8,700

SUMMARY OF TRANSACTIONS

Beginning Cash Balance March 1, 2018	+	Deposits	−	Checks	=	Ending Cash Balance March 31, 2018
$3,800		$7,780		$8,700		$2,880

COMMON MISTAKE

Notice that bank statements refer to an increase (or deposit) in the cash balance as a *credit* and a decrease (or withdrawal) as a *debit*. This terminology is the opposite of that used in financial accounting, where *debit* refers to an increase in cash and *credit* refers to a decrease in cash. The reason for the difference in terminology is a difference in perspective. When a company makes a deposit, it views this as an increase to cash, so it records a debit to the Cash account. However, the bank views this same deposit as an increase in the amount owed to the company, or a liability, which is recorded as a credit. Similarly, a withdrawal of cash from the bank is viewed by the company as a decrease to its Cash account, so it is recorded with a credit, but the bank views this withdrawal as a decrease to the amount owed to the company, so it debits its liability.

Reconciling the bank account involves three steps:

1. Reconcile the **bank's** cash balance.
2. Reconcile the **company's** cash balance.
3. Update the company's Cash account by recording items identified in Step 2.

STEP 1: RECONCILE THE BANK'S CASH BALANCE

First, we consider cash transactions recorded by the company, but not yet recorded by its bank. These include deposits outstanding and checks outstanding. Deposits outstanding are cash receipts of the company that have not been added to the bank's record of the company's balance. Checks outstanding are checks the company has written that have not been subtracted from the bank's record of the company's balance.

Notice that Starlight reports three cash receipts of $3,600, $1,980, and $2,200 for the month of March (Illustration 4–9). The first two receipts are also reported as deposits in the bank statement (Illustration 4–8). The third one is not. Cash of $2,200 in Starlight's records is not yet reflected in the bank's cash balance by the end of March. This is a deposit outstanding.

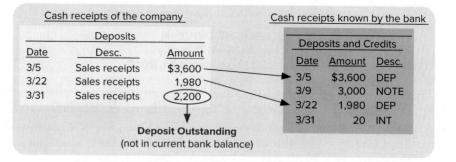

Now let's look at the five checks written by Starlight during the month of March (Illustration 4–9). Those five check numbers are listed below. Notice, however, that only checks #293, #294, and #296 are also reflected in the bank statement (Illustration 4–8). This means checks #295 (for $1,200) and #297 (for $900) remain outstanding and are not yet reflected in the bank's balance. These are checks outstanding. Notice also that check #294 was incorrectly recorded by the company for $2,600 instead of $2,900. We'll address this $300 company error in Step 2.

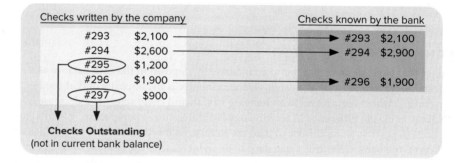

Starlight's bank reconciliation is shown in Illustration 4–10. On the left side, **we adjust the bank's cash balance by adding deposits outstanding and subtracting checks outstanding.** We would also need to look for and correct any bank errors, but there are none here.

ILLUSTRATION 4–10

Bank Reconciliation

mhhe.com/4fa15

STARLIGHT DRIVE-IN
Bank Reconciliation
March 31, 2018

Bank's Cash Balance		*Company's* Cash Balance	
Per bank statement	$4,100	Per general ledger	$2,880
Deposits outstanding:	+2,200	Note received	+2,800
3/31 = $2,200		Interest earned from note	+200
		Interest earned on bank account	+20
Checks outstanding:	−2,100	NSF check	−750
#295 = $1,200		Debit card for office equipment	−200
#297 = $ 900		EFT for advertising	−400
		Service fee	−50
		Corrected rent expense error	−300
Bank balance per reconciliation	$4,200	Company balance per reconciliation	$4,200

Reconciled

STEP 2: RECONCILE THE COMPANY'S CASH BALANCE

Next, we need to reconcile the company's cash balance. What are some examples of cash transactions recorded by the bank but not yet recorded by the company? Here are some common items that will *increase* the company's cash balance once the reconciliation occurs.

- **Bank collections** on the company's behalf offer a convenient and safer way for the company to collect cash. With the increase in electronic banking, these types of cash collections are becoming increasingly popular, especially in certain business settings such as recurring payments from customers, real estate transactions, collection agencies, and lending arrangements.
- Companies may also **earn interest** based on the average daily balance of their checking or savings account.

Other items in the reconciliation will *decrease* the company's cash balance.

- NSF checks occur when customers' checks are written on "nonsufficient funds." In other words, the company receives a customer's check and deposits that check, recording an increase in cash. However, the company later finds out from the bank statement that the customer's check was "bad," and the company then needs to decrease its cash balance to undo the initial increase.
- Employees sometimes use **debit cards** to make purchases. These purchases are immediately withdrawn from the bank account, but they may not be known by the company's accountant until examination of the bank statement.
- **Electronic funds transfers** (EFTs) are automatic transfers from one bank account to another (sometimes referred to as electronic checks or e-checks). For example, a company may pay its mortgage or utility bill by having it automatically withdrawn from its bank account.
- Banks charge **service fees** for various activities related to monthly maintenance, overdraft penalties, ATM use, wire transfers, foreign currency exchanges, automatic payments, and other account services. These fees may not be known by the company until examination of the bank statement.

Six cash transactions recorded by First Bank (Illustration 4–8) are not reported in Starlight's cash records (Illustration 4–9) by the end of March:

1. Note received by First Bank on Starlight's behalf ($3,000, which equals $2,800 plus related interest received of $200).
2. Interest earned by Starlight on its bank account ($20).
3. NSF check ($750).
4. Debit card purchase of office equipment by an employee ($200).
5. Electronic funds transfer (EFT) related to the payment of advertising ($400).
6. Service fee ($50).

 COMMON MISTAKE

Students sometimes mistake an NSF check as a bad check written *by* the company instead of one written *to* the company. When an NSF check occurs, the company has deposited a customer's check but the customer did not have enough funds to cover the check. The company must adjust its balance of cash downward to reverse the increase in cash it recorded at the time of deposit. The effect of this bounced customer check creates an account receivable for the company until the customer honors the funds it owes.

In addition to the amounts related to timing differences, we need to address one other reconciling item. Comparing Starlight's record of checks written to those in the bank statement reveals an error by Starlight. Check #294 for rent was written for $2,900, but Starlight's accountant recorded it incorrectly as $2,600. First Bank processed the check for the correct amount of $2,900. This means Starlight needs to reduce its cash balance by an additional

$300 for rent expense. In addition, the company may want to review its internal control procedures to identify the source of the error.

The company balance per reconciliation is calculated on the right side of Illustration 4–10. Once the company adjusts its balance for information revealed in the bank statement, its cash balance is $4,200. This reconciled balance matches the reconciled balance of the bank, providing some indication that cash is not being mishandled by employees.

Illustration 4–11 summarizes the basic items included in a bank reconciliation. **For the reconciliation to be complete, the reconciled bank balance must equal the reconciled company balance.**

ILLUSTRATION 4–11

Summary of Items Included in the Bank Reconciliation

		Bank's Cash Balance	Company's Cash Balance
		Per bank statement	Per general ledger
Timing Differences		+ Deposits outstanding − Checks outstanding	+ Notes received by bank + Interest received − NSF checks − Unrecorded debit cards − Unrecorded ETFs − Bank service fees
Errors		± Bank errors	± Company errors
		= **Bank balance per reconciliation**	= **Company balance per reconciliation**

STEP 3: UPDATE THE COMPANY'S CASH ACCOUNT

As a final step in the reconciliation process, a company must update the balance in its Cash account, to adjust for the items used to reconcile the *company's* cash balance (Step 2). We record these adjustments once the bank reconciliation is complete. Remember, these are amounts the company didn't know until it received the bank statement.

We record items that increase the company's cash with a debit to Cash. We credit Notes Receivable because the company has collected cash from the note, decreasing that asset account (−$2,800). We also credit Interest Revenue for interest earned from the note ($200) plus interest earned on its bank account ($20).

A = L + SE		March 31, 2018	Debit	Credit
+3,020		**Cash**	3,020	
−2,800		Notes Receivable...		2,800
+200 Rev↑		**Interest Revenue** (from note)...		200
+20 Rev↑		**Interest Revenue** (from bank account).................................		20
		(Record collection on note and interest earned)		

We record items that decrease the company's cash with a credit to Cash.

A = L + SE		March 31, 2018	Debit	Credit
+750		**Accounts Receivable**	750	
+200		**Equipment**	200	
−400 Exp↑		**Advertising Expense**	400	
−50 Exp↑		**Service Fee Expense**	50	
−300 Exp↑		**Rent Expense**	300	
−1,700		Cash		1,700
		(Record NSF check, equipment purchase, advertising payment, bank service fee, and check correction for rent)		

Accounts Receivable is debited in order to increase that asset account (+$750), to show that the customer who paid with an NSF check still owes the company money. The other debits are needed to record the items related to cash outflows—equipment purchased and expenses incurred.

COMMON MISTAKE

Some students try to update the Cash account for deposits outstanding, checks outstanding, or a bank error. The company does *not* need to adjust for these items related to reconciling the bank's balance because they are already properly recorded in the company's accounting records.

In the uncommon event that the two balances at the end of the bank reconciliation schedule are not equal, management investigates the discrepancy to check for wrongdoing or errors by company employees or the bank. If the company cannot resolve the discrepancy, it records the difference to either Miscellaneous Expense or Miscellaneous Revenue, depending on whether it has a debit or credit balance. For example, suppose a company is unable to account for $100 of missing cash. In this event, the company records the following transaction, increasing Miscellaneous Expense and decreasing Cash.

	Debit	Credit		A	=	L	+	SE	
Miscellaneous Expense	100							−100 Exp↑	
Cash		100		−100					
(Record loss of $100 cash)									

KEY POINT

In a bank reconciliation we reconcile the *bank's* cash balance for (1) cash transactions already recorded by the company but not yet recorded by the bank and (2) bank errors. Similarly, we reconcile the *company's* cash balance for (1) cash transactions already recorded by the bank but not yet recorded by the company and (2) company errors. After we complete the reconciliations, the amounts for the bank balance and the company balance should be equal. Any adjustments to the company's balance need to be recorded.

At the end of April 2018, Showtime Theatre's accounting records show a cash balance of $4,800. The April bank statement reports a cash balance of $3,700. The following information is gathered from the bank statement and company records:

Let's Review

mhhe.com/4fa16

Checks outstanding	$1,900	Customer's NSF check	$1,300
Deposits outstanding	1,600	Service fee	200
Interest earned	70		

In addition, Showtime discovered it correctly paid for advertising with a check for $220 but incorrectly recorded the check in the company's records for $250. The bank correctly processed the check for $220.

Required:

1. Prepare a bank reconciliation for the month of April 2018.
2. Prepare entries to update the balance of cash in the company's records.

Solution:

1. Bank reconciliation:

SHOWTIME THEATRE
Bank Reconciliation
April 30, 2018

Bank's Cash Balance		Company's Cash Balance	
Per bank statement	$3,700	Per general ledger	$4,800
Deposits outstanding	+1,600	Interest earned	+70
		Company error	+30
Checks outstanding	−1,900	Service fee	−200
		NSF check	−1,300
Bank balance per reconciliation	$3,400	Company balance per reconciliation	$3,400

2. Entries to update the company's balance of cash:

April 30, 2018	Debit	Credit
Cash	100	
Interest Revenue		70
Advertising Expense		30
(Record interest earned and error correction)		
Service Fee Expense	200	
Accounts Receivable	1,300	
Cash		1,500
(Record service fee and NSF check)		

Suggested Homework:
BE4–8, BE4–12;
E4–9, E4–10;
P4–2A&B, P4–3A&B

Employee Purchases

■ **LO4–6**
Account for employee purchases.

You probably pay for many of your purchases with a debit card, credit card, or check. For example, when you go out to eat with your friends at a local restaurant, you might use your debit card. You could also use your credit card for an online purchase, or maybe a check for a mail-in donation to your favorite charity. However, it's also nice to have a little cash in your wallet for quick expenditures. For example, you might decide to buy a soda from a machine or a hot dog at the game.

The same way you have multiple methods to make purchases, so do many employees on behalf of their company. For example, a traveling salesperson might be on the road and need to take a client to dinner, put gas in the car, or stay in a hotel that night. To do so, the salesperson can use a company-issued debit card or credit card (often referred to as purchase cards).

Similarly, an office manager might decide to have a lunch meeting for the staff and needs actual cash available to pay for pizza delivery. Cash on hand to pay for these minor purchases is referred to as a petty cash fund, and the employee responsible for the fund is often referred to as the *petty cash custodian*.

Employee purchases should be included in the accounting records by the end of the reporting period. Employee purchases made with debit cards and checks will be captured in the accounting records at the time the bank reconciliation is prepared, like we saw in the previous section. In this section, we discuss how to account for employee purchases using credit cards and the petty cash fund. Those expenditures typically are not immediately recorded in the accounting records, yet they are legitimate business transactions during the period.

Let's work through an example of Starlight Drive-In. In May, Starlight withdraws cash of $200 from the bank to have on hand in the petty cash fund. Starlight also issues credit cards to its purchasing manager and marketing manager. At the time these cards are issued, nothing is recorded because no expenditures have been made. However, for the petty cash fund, cash has been withdrawn from the bank, so we record the following entry that formally shows the transfer of cash from the bank to cash on hand in the petty cash fund:

May 1	Debit	Credit		A	=	L	+	SE
Petty Cash (on hand)	200			+200				
Cash (checking account)		200		−200				
(Establish the petty cash fund)								

During May, the petty cash custodian provides cash to employees for an office lunch and package delivery and places vouchers documenting the purposes of those expenditures in the petty cash fund. In addition, the purchasing manager and the marketing manager used their credit cards for expenditures related to their positions. Suppose the following items and amounts occur:

Petty Cash Fund (Cash)		Purchasing Manager (Credit Card)		Marketing Manager (Credit Card)	
Item	Amount	Item	Amount	Item	Amount
Lunch	$60	Supplies	$800	Advertising	$1,500
Delivery	$90	Supplies	$600	Postage	$1,200

At the end of May, the company's accountant collects vouchers from the petty cash fund and credit card receipts from the purchasing manager and marketing manager. The expenditures above are recorded in the company's records.

May 31	Debit	Credit		A	=	L	+	SE
Entertainment Expense	60							−60 Exp▲
Delivery Expense	90							−90 Exp▲
Supplies ($800 + $600)	1,400			+1,400				
Advertising Expense	1,500							−1,500 Exp▲
Postage Expense	1,200							−1,200 Exp▲
Petty Cash		150		−150				
Accounts Payable		4,100				+4,100		
(Recognize employee expenditures)								

The expenditures made with petty cash reduce the petty cash fund. The expenditures made with credit cards are not paid immediately, so they are recorded as Accounts Payable until paid. If the company's accountant decides to pay the credit card balance at the time of reconciliation, then the $4,100 credit would be to Cash.

Also at the end of the period, the $200 petty cash fund needs to be replenished. Cash of $150 has been disbursed during May ($60 for lunch and $90 for delivery). The fund has only $50 remaining, so management withdraws an additional $150 from the bank to place in the fund. The fund's physical balance will once again be $200.

May 31	Debit	Credit		A	=	L	+	SE
Petty Cash	150			+150				
Cash		150		−150				
(Replenish the petty cash fund)								

What if only $30 physically remains in the petty cash fund at the end of May, when there should be $50? It could be that $20 was stolen from the fund, or the fund could be missing a receipt for $20 to show where it was spent. If the question is not resolved, the firm will likely charge the $20 to Miscellaneous Expense.

 KEY POINT

To make purchases on behalf of the company, some employees are allowed to use debit cards and credit cards (purchase cards), write checks, and spend available cash on hand (petty cash fund). At the end of the period, all employee purchases are recorded, and the petty cash fund is replenished.

In addition to accounting for employee purchases, a system of internal control needs to be in place to ensure that all expenditures are legitimate and that company resources are not being wasted or stolen. Those controls include items such as the following.

- Employees should be required to provide receipts and justification for those receipts on a timely basis.
- A separate employee reviews receipts and supporting documents to ensure all expenditures are made appropriately.
- Credit card receipts are reconciled to credit card statements, just like we reconciled checks and debit card transactions to the bank statement.
- Spending limits are placed on employees who are authorized to use a company credit card or have access to company cash. Major expenditures require pre-approval through formal purchasing procedures.
- Only those employees that need to make timely business expenditures should receive authorization.

PART C

■ **LO4–7**
Identify the major inflows and outflows of cash.

STATEMENT OF CASH FLOWS

To this point, we've considered several internal controls related to cash. Here, we discuss how companies report cash activities to external parties. Companies report cash in two financial statements—in the balance sheet and in the statement of cash flows. As we discussed in Chapter 3, companies report cash as an asset in the balance sheet. The amount is typically reported as a current asset and represents cash *available* for spending at the end of the reporting period.

In addition, some companies separately report **restricted cash.** Restricted cash represents cash that is *not available* for current operations. Examples of restricted cash include cash set aside by the company for specific purposes such as repaying debt, purchasing equipment, or making investments in the future.

The balance sheet provides only the final balance for cash. It does not provide any details regarding cash receipts and cash payments. Companies report information about cash receipts and payments during the period in a statement of cash flows. **From the statement of cash flows, investors know a company's cash inflows and cash outflows related to (1) operating activities, (2) investing activities, and (3) financing activities.** We'll provide a complete discussion of the statement of cash flows in Chapter 11. Here, we briefly introduce the basics of the statement to help you understand that its purpose is to report activity related to the key topic of this chapter—cash.

Recall from Chapter 1 the three fundamental types of business activities relating to cash:

- *Operating activities* include cash transactions involving revenue and expense events during the period. In other words, operating activities include the cash effect of the same activities that are reported in the income statement to calculate net income.

- *Investing activities,* as the name implies, include cash investments in long-term assets and investment securities. When the firm later sells those assets, we consider those transactions investing activities also. So, investing activities tend to involve long-term assets.
- *Financing activities* include transactions designed to raise cash or finance the business. There are two ways to do this: borrow cash from lenders or raise cash from stockholders. We also consider cash outflows to repay debt and cash dividends to stockholders to be financing activities. So, financing activities involve liabilities and stockholders' equity.

It's easiest to understand cash flow information by looking at the underlying transactions. To do this, we'll refer back to the external transactions of Eagle Golf Academy introduced in Chapters 1 through 3. For convenience, Illustration 4–12 lists those transactions and analyzes their effects on the company's cash.

ILLUSTRATION 4–12

External Transactions of Eagle Golf Academy

Transaction	External Transactions in December	Type of Activity	Is Cash Involved?	Inflow or Outflow?
(1)	Sell shares of common stock for $25,000 to obtain the funds necessary to start the business.	Financing	YES	Inflow
(2)	Borrow $10,000 from the local bank and sign a note promising to repay the full amount of the debt in three years.	Financing	YES	Inflow
(3)	Purchase equipment necessary for giving golf training, $24,000 cash.	Investing	YES	Outflow
(4)	Pay one year of rent in advance, $6,000 ($500 per month).	Operating	YES	Outflow
(5)	Purchase supplies on account, $2,300.	Operating	NO	—
(6)	Provide golf training to customers for cash, $4,300.	Operating	YES	Inflow
(7)	Provide golf training to customers on account, $2,000.	Operating	NO	—
(8)	Receive cash in advance for 12 golf training sessions to be given in the future, $600.	Operating	YES	Inflow
(9)	Pay salaries to employees, $2,800.	Operating	YES	Outflow
(10)	Pay cash dividends of $200 to shareholders.	Financing	YES	Outflow

Which transactions involve the exchange of cash? All transactions except (5) and (7) involve either the receipt (inflow) or payment (outflow) of cash. **Only transactions involving cash affect a company's cash flows.**

Illustration 4–13 presents the statement of cash flows for Eagle Golf Academy using what's called the *direct method* of reporting operating activities. Corresponding transaction numbers are in brackets. (In Chapter 11 we'll discuss the *indirect method*.)

From the statement of cash flows, investors and creditors can see that the major source of cash inflow for Eagle is the issuance of common stock, a financing activity. Eagle has also received cash from bank borrowing, which must be repaid. The company is also investing in its future by purchasing equipment. Eagle reports this amount as an investing outflow.

With regard to the three types of business activities, the cash flow that's related most directly to the company's profitability is net cash flows from operating activities. For Eagle Golf Academy, net cash flows from operating activities are −$3,900. This means that cash *outflows* related to operating activities exceed inflows. Stated another way, cash outflows related to expense activities exceed cash inflows related to revenue activities. While Eagle reports net income of $1,200 in its income statement (see Illustration 3–12 in Chapter 3), these same

ILLUSTRATION 4–13

Statement of Cash Flows for Eagle Golf Academy

Numbers in brackets correspond to the external transaction numbers of Eagle Golf Academy in Illustration 4–12.

EAGLE GOLF ACADEMY		
Statement of Cash Flows		
For the period ended December 31, 2018		
Cash Flows from Operating Activities		
Cash inflows:		
From customers [6 and 8]	$ 4,900	
Cash outflows:		
For salaries [9]	(2,800)	
For rent [4]	(6,000)	
Net cash flows from operating activities		$ (3,900)
Cash Flows from Investing Activities		
Purchase equipment [3]	(24,000)	
Net cash flows from investing activities		(24,000)
Cash Flows from Financing Activities		
Issue common stock [1]	25,000	
Borrow from bank [2]	10,000	
Pay dividends [10]	(200)	
Net cash flows from financing activities		34,800
Net increase in cash		6,900
Cash at the beginning of the period		-0-
Cash at the end of the period		$ 6,900

activities are not able to generate positive cash flows for the company. Ultimately, companies must be able to generate positive operating cash flows to maintain long-term success.

The final amount reported in the statement of cash flows, **$6,900**, is the same amount of cash reported in the balance sheet. You can verify this is the case for Eagle Golf Academy by referring back to the balance sheet reported in Illustration 3–14 in Chapter 3.

KEY POINT

The statement of cash flows reports all cash activities for the period. *Operating activities* include those transactions involving revenue and expense activities. *Investing activities* include cash investments in long-term assets and investment securities. *Financing activities* include transactions designed to finance the business through borrowing and owner investment.

Decision Point

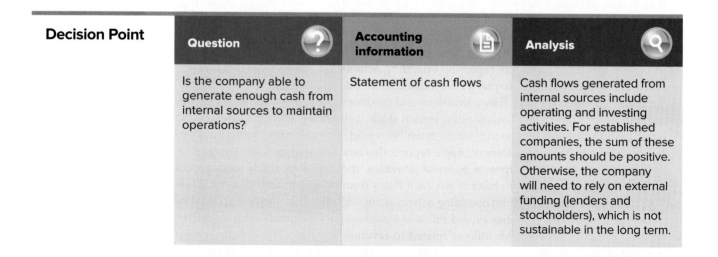

Question	Accounting information	Analysis
Is the company able to generate enough cash from internal sources to maintain operations?	Statement of cash flows	Cash flows generated from internal sources include operating and investing activities. For established companies, the sum of these amounts should be positive. Otherwise, the company will need to rely on external funding (lenders and stockholders), which is not sustainable in the long term.

Let's Review

A company reports in its current year each of the transactions listed below.

Required:

Indicate whether each transaction should be reported as an operating, investing, or financing cash flow in the company's statement of cash flows, and whether each is a cash inflow or outflow.

Transaction	Type of Cash Flow	Inflow or Outflow
1. Pay employees' salaries.	_____	_____
2. Obtain a loan at the bank.	_____	_____
3. Purchase a building with cash.	_____	_____
4. Purchase equipment with a note payable.	_____	_____

Solution:

1. Operating—outflow.

2. Financing—inflow.

3. Investing—outflow.

4. Not reported as a cash flow because no cash is involved in the transaction.

Suggested Homework:
BE4–14, BE4–15;
E4–14, E4–15;
P4–4A&B, P4–5A&B

CASH ANALYSIS
Regal Entertainment vs. Cinemark

ANALYSIS

■ **LO4–8**
Assess cash holdings by comparing cash to noncash assets.

In recent years, cash holdings of U.S. companies have increased enormously. At the end of 2014, total cash holdings of U.S. companies (excluding banks and other financial institutions) were estimated to be $1.7 trillion. Total cash holdings were less than half that amount just seven years earlier in 2007. At the end of 2014, the three companies with the largest cash holdings were **Apple, Microsoft, and Google**. Apple alone reported cash holdings of $178 billion, while Microsoft and Google had cash of $90 billion and $64 billion, respectively. Why are U.S. companies holding so much cash?

One reason for larger cash holdings is to ensure cash is available to prevent bankruptcy caused by short-term negative shocks in the business cycle. The financial crisis of 2008 caused some companies to enter bankruptcy, and many other companies struggled to meet their financial obligations on time. As a result, companies are keeping larger cash reserves as a precaution. To maintain normal operations, a company needs enough cash, or enough other assets that can quickly be converted to cash, to pay obligations as they become due. Having available cash also helps a company respond quickly to new, profitable opportunities. On the other hand, having too much cash represents idle resources that are not being used to produce revenues or that may be spent inefficiently. A company with too much cash may be a signal that management does not have additional opportunities for profitable expansion.

Let's examine the cash holdings of two of the largest movie theatre companies in the United States, **Regal Entertainment Group** and **Cinemark Holdings**.

RATIO OF CASH TO NONCASH ASSETS

Below is each company's ratio of cash and cash equivalents to noncash assets at the end of 2014. Noncash assets include total assets other than cash and cash equivalents.

($ in millions)	Cash and Cash Equivalents	Noncash Assets	Ratio
Regal Entertainment	$147.1	$2,392.4	6.1%
Cinemark Holdings	$638.9	$3,513.1	18.2%

CAREER CORNER

Financial analysts offer investment advice to their clients—banks, insurance companies, mutual funds, securities firms, and individual investors. This advice usually comes in the form of a formal recommendation (buy, hold, or sell). Before giving an opinion, analysts develop a detailed understanding of a company's operations through discussions with management, analysis of competitors, and projections of industry trends. They also develop a detailed understanding of a company's financial statements, including its cash holdings.

Understanding a company's cash balance involves knowing the trade-offs between having too much or too little cash. With too little cash, a company may not be able to pays its debts as they become due or may not be able to take advantage of profitable opportunities. Having too much cash can draw criticisms from analysts because management is not efficiently using stockholders' resources (idle cash). In that case, analysts often call for managers to return idle cash to stockholders by paying additional dividends. The importance of understanding these trade-offs is why many finance majors and MBA students, pursuing careers as financial analysts, take additional accounting-related courses when earning their degrees and even after graduation.

© Amos Morgan/Photodisc/
Getty Images, RF

Why is Cinemark's ratio of cash three times greater than Regal's? One reason is that management of Cinemark may be more cautious due to more volatile operations.

TREND IN OPERATING CASH FLOWS

Examining the trend in operating cash flows provides additional insight. Operating cash flows is the amount reported for net cash flows from operating activities in the statement of cash flows. Below is each company's trend in operating cash flows over the previous three years.

While the total amount of cash generated from operating activities over the three-year period is slightly greater for Cinemark, we can see that Cinemark's operations are more volatile. Volatility is a sign of risk. Cinemark states in its annual report to shareholders:

Our international operations are subject to certain political, economic and other uncertainties not encountered by our domestic operations, including risks of severe economic downturns and high inflation. We also face risks of currency fluctuations, hard currency shortages and controls of foreign currency exchange and transfers to the U.S., all of which could have an adverse effect on the results of our international operations.

($ in millions)	Operating Cash Flows	
Year	Regal Entertainment	Cinemark Holdings
2012	$346.6	$395.2
2013	$346.9	$309.7
2014	$349.1	$454.6

Cinemark generates more than one-fourth of its revenues from international operations, so a significant portion of its revenue stream faces additional risks. Regal does not have international operations and therefore does not face these similar risks.

In addition to increased operating risks, international operations also offer tax incentives to hold more cash. In the U.S., companies often are required to pay additional income taxes on foreign profits once those profits are returned as cash to the U.S. (called *repatriation taxes*). To avoid these additional taxes, companies with major international operations (such as Apple, Microsoft, and Google) often keep the cash from foreign profits in those foreign countries.

Another difference between the two companies' cash holdings relates to dividends. In 2014, Regal earned net income of $105 million but paid cash dividends of $295 million. The company states in its annual report that this extraordinary dividend was made to enhance shareholder value. On the other hand, Cinemark had net income of $171 million but returned only $96 million in cash dividends.

KEY POINT

A company's cash balance should be high enough to ensure that it can pay debts as they become due, but not so high that cash is idle and not being used effectively.

KEY POINTS BY LEARNING OBJECTIVE

LO4–1 Discuss the impact of accounting scandals and the passage of the Sarbanes-Oxley Act.

The accounting scandals in the early 2000s prompted passage of the Sarbanes-Oxley Act (SOX). Among other stipulations, SOX sets forth a variety of guidelines related to auditor-client relations and additional internal controls. Section 404, in particular, requires company management and auditors to document and assess the effectiveness of a company's internal controls.

LO4–2 Identify the components, responsibilities, and limitations of internal control.

Internal control refers to a company's plan to improve the accuracy and reliability of accounting information and safeguard the company's assets. Five key components to an internal control system are (1) control environment, (2) risk assessment, (3) control activities, (4) monitoring, and (5) information and communication. Control activities include those designed to prevent or detect fraudulent or erroneous behavior.

LO4–3 Define cash and cash equivalents.

Cash includes currency, coins, balances in savings and checking accounts, and checks and money orders received from customers. The cash balance also includes credit card and debit card sales, as well as cash equivalents, defined as investments that mature within three months from the date of purchase (such as money market funds, Treasury bills, and certificates of deposit).

LO4–4 Understand controls over cash receipts and cash disbursements.

Because cash is the asset of a company most susceptible to employee fraud, controls over cash receipts and cash disbursements are an important part of a company's overall internal control system. Important controls over cash receipts include segregation of duties for those who handle cash and independent verification of cash receipts. Important controls over cash disbursements include payment by check, credit card, or debit card, separation of duties, and various authorization and documentation procedures.

LO4–5 Reconcile a bank statement.

In a bank reconciliation we reconcile the *bank's* cash balance for (1) cash transactions already recorded by the company but not yet recorded by the bank and (2) bank errors. Similarly, we reconcile the *company's* cash balance for (1) cash transactions already recorded by the bank but not yet recorded by the company and (2) company errors. After we complete the reconciliations, the amounts for the bank balance and the company balance should be equal. Any adjustments to the company's balance need to be recorded.

LO4–6 Account for employee purchases.

To make purchases on behalf of the company, some employees are allowed to use debit cards and credit cards (purchase cards), write checks, and spend available cash on hand (petty cash fund). At the end of the period, all employee purchases are recorded, and the petty cash fund is replenished.

LO4–7 Identify the major inflows and outflows of cash.

The statement of cash flows reports all cash activities for the period. *Operating activities* include those transactions involving revenues and expenses. *Investing activities* include cash investments in long-term assets and investment securities. *Financing activities* include transactions designed to finance the business through borrowing and owner investment.

Analysis

LO4–8 Assess cash holdings by comparing cash to noncash assets.

A company's cash balance should be high enough to ensure that it can pay debts as they become due, but not so high that cash is idle and not being used effectively.

GLOSSARY

Bank reconciliation: Matching the balance of cash in the bank account with the balance of cash in the company's own records. **p. 179**

Cash: Currency, coins, balances in savings and checking accounts, items acceptable for deposit in these accounts (such as checks received from customers), credit card and debit card sales, and cash equivalents. **p. 175**

Cash equivalents: Short-term investments that have a maturity date no longer than three months from the date of purchase. **p. 175**

Checks outstanding: Checks the company has written that have not been subtracted from the bank's record of the company's balance. **p. 181**

Collusion: Two or more people acting in coordination to circumvent internal controls. **p. 173**

Deposits outstanding: Cash receipts of the company that have not been added to the bank's record of the company's balance. **p. 181**

Fraud triangle: The three elements present for every fraud—motivation, rationalization, and opportunity. **p. 168**

Internal controls: A company's plans to (1) safeguard the company's assets and (2) improve the accuracy and reliability of accounting information. **p. 168**

NSF checks: Checks drawn on nonsufficient funds, or "bad" checks from customers. **p. 183**

Occupational fraud: The use of one's occupation for personal enrichment through the deliberate misuse or misapplication of the employer's resources. **p. 168**

Petty cash fund: Small amount of cash kept on hand to pay for minor purchases. **p. 186**

Purchase cards: Company-issued debit cards or credit cards that allow authorized employees to make purchases on behalf of the company. **p. 186**

Sarbanes-Oxley Act: Known as the *Public Company Accounting Reform and Investor Protection Act of 2002* and commonly referred to as *SOX;* the act established a variety of guidelines related to auditor-client relations and internal control procedures. **p. 169**

Separation of duties: Authorizing transactions, recording transactions, and controlling related assets should be separated among employees. **p. 172**

SELF-STUDY QUESTIONS

1. Fraudulent reporting by management could include: **(LO4–1)**
   a. Fictitious revenues from a fake customer.
   b. Improper asset valuation.
   c. Mismatching revenues and expenses.
   d. All of the above.

2. The Sarbanes-Oxley Act (SOX) mandates which of the following? **(LO4–1)**
   a. Increased regulations related to auditor-client relations.
   b. Increased regulations related to internal control.
   c. Increased regulations related to corporate executive accountability.
   d. All of the above.

3. What is the concept behind *separation of duties* in establishing internal control? **(LO4–2)**
   a. Employee fraud is less likely to occur when access to assets and access to accounting records are separated.
   b. The company's financial accountant should not share information with the company's tax accountant.
   c. Duties of middle-level managers of the company should be clearly separated from those of top executives.
   d. The external auditors of the company should have no contact with managers while the audit is taking place.

4. Which of the following is considered cash for financial reporting purposes? **(LO4–3)**
   a. Accounts receivable.
   b. Investments with maturity dates greater than three months.
   c. Checks received from customers.
   d. Accounts payable.

5. Which of the following generally would *not* be considered good internal control of cash receipts? **(LO4–4)**
   a. Allowing customers to pay with a debit card.
   b. Requiring the employee receiving the cash from the customer to also deposit the cash into the company's bank account.
   c. Recording cash receipts as soon as they are received.
   d. Allowing customers to pay with a credit card.

6. Which of the following adjusts the bank's balance of cash in a bank reconciliation? **(LO4–5)**
   a. NSF checks.
   b. Service fees.
   c. An error by the company.
   d. Checks outstanding.

7. Which of the following adjusts the company's balance of cash in a bank reconciliation? **(LO4–5)**
   a. Interest earned.
   b. Checks outstanding.

c. Deposits outstanding.

d. An error by the bank.

c. Services provided to customers on account.

d. Payment for a new operating center.

8. The purpose of a petty cash fund is to: **(LO4–6)**
   a. Provide a convenient form of payment for the company's customers.
   b. Pay employee salaries at the end of each period.
   c. Provide cash on hand for minor expenditures.
   d. Allow the company to save cash for major future purchases.

9. Operating cash flows would include which of the following? **(LO4–7)**
   a. Repayment of borrowed money.
   b. Payment for employee salaries.

10. Which of the following could cause a company to have a high ratio of cash to noncash assets? **(LO4–8)**
    a. Highly volatile operations.
    b. Low dividend payments.
    c. Significant foreign operations.
    d. All of these factors could contribute to a high ratio of cash to noncash assets.

Note: For answers, see the last page of the chapter.

For additional study materials, including 10 more multiple-choice Self-Study Questions, visit Connect.

REVIEW QUESTIONS

1. Define occupational fraud. Describe two common means of occupational fraud. ■ **LO4–1**

2. What is internal control? Why should a company establish an internal control system? ■ **LO4–1**

3. "Managers are stewards of the company's assets." Discuss what this means. ■ **LO4–1**

4. Why are some managers motivated to manipulate amounts reported in the financial statements? ■ **LO4–1**

5. What is meant by the fraud triangle, and what can companies do to help prevent fraud? ■ **LO4–1**

6. What are some of the major provisions of the Sarbanes-Oxley Act? ■ **LO4–1**

7. Briefly describe the five components of internal control outlined by the Committee of Sponsoring Organizations (COSO). ■ **LO4–2**

8. Describe the difference between preventive controls and detective controls. What are examples of each? ■ **LO4–2**

9. What is meant by separation of duties? ■ **LO4–2**

10. Who has responsibility for internal control in an organization? According to guidelines set forth in Section 404 of the Sarbanes-Oxley Act, what role does the auditor play in internal control? ■ **LO4–2**

11. What are some limitations of internal control? ■ **LO4–2**

12. To what does collusion refer? ■ **LO4–2**

13. Is fraud more likely to occur when it is being committed by top-level employees? Explain. ■ **LO4–2**

14. Define cash and cash equivalents. ■ **LO4–3**

15. Describe how the purchase of items with a check is recorded. ■ **LO4–3**

16. Discuss basic controls for cash receipts. ■ **LO4–4**

17. What is a credit card? How are credit card sales reported? ■ **LO4–4**

18. What is a debit card? How are debit card sales reported? ■ **LO4–4**

19. Discuss basic controls for cash disbursements. ■ **LO4–4**

20. How are credit card purchases reported? ■ **LO4–4**

21. What is a bank reconciliation? How can it help in determining whether proper control of cash has been maintained? ■ **LO4–5**

■ **LO4–5**   22. What are two primary reasons that the company's balance of cash will differ between its own records and those of the bank?

■ **LO4–5**   23. Give some examples of timing differences in cash transactions that firms need to account for in a bank reconciliation.

■ **LO4–5**   24. After preparing a bank reconciliation, what adjustments does the company need to make to its records?

■ **LO4–6**   25. What are purchase cards and a petty cash fund?

■ **LO4–6**   26. Describe how management maintains control over employee purchases with credit cards and the petty cash fund.

■ **LO4–7**   27. The change in cash for the year can be calculated by comparing the balance of cash reported in this year's and last year's balance sheet. Why is the statement of cash flows needed?

■ **LO4–7**   28. Describe the operating, investing, and financing sections of the statement of cash flows.

■ **LO4–8**   29. Why is an analysis of the company's cash balance important?

■ **LO4–8**   30. We compared **Regal Entertainment** and **Cinemark** at the end of this chapter. What reasons were given for the differences in their cash balances?

BRIEF EXERCISES

 Mc Graw Hill Education **connect**®

Identify terms associated with the Sarbanes-Oxley Act **(LO4–1)**

BE4–1 Match each of the following provisions of the Sarbanes-Oxley Act (SOX) with its description.

Major Provisions of the Sarbanes-Oxley Act	Descriptions
_____ 1. Oversight board	a. Executives must personally certify the company's financial statements.
_____ 2. Corporate executive accountability	b. Audit firm cannot provide a variety of other services to its client, such as investment advising.
_____ 3. Auditor rotation	c. PCAOB establishes standards related to the preparation of audited financial reports.
_____ 4. Nonaudit services	d. Lead audit partners are required to change every five years.
_____ 5. Internal control	e. Management must document the effectiveness of procedures that could affect financial reporting.

Identify terms associated with components of internal control **(LO4–2)**

BE4–2 Match each of the following components of internal control with its description.

Components of Internal Control	Descriptions
_____ 1. Control environment	a. Procedures for maintaining separation of duties.
_____ 2. Risk assessment	b. Routine activities that are meant to continually observe internal control activities.
_____ 3. Control activities	c. Transfer of data from lower managers to top executives for accurate financial reporting.
_____ 4. Information and communication	d. Formal policies to evaluate internal and external threats to achieving company objectives.
_____ 5. Monitoring	e. Overall attitude of the company with respect to internal controls.

BE4–3 Match each of the following control activities with its definition.

Define control activities associated with internal control (LO4–2)

Control Activities	Definitions

Control Activities

_____ 1. Separation of duties
_____ 2. Physical controls
_____ 3. Proper authorization
_____ 4. Employee management
_____ 5. Reconciliations
_____ 6. Performance reviews

Definitions

a. The company should maintain security over assets and accounting records.
b. Management should periodically determine whether the amounts of physical assets of the company match the accounting records.
c. The company should provide employees with appropriate guidance to ensure they have the knowledge necessary to carry out their job duties.
d. The actual performance of individuals or processes should be checked against their expected performance.
e. Authorizing transactions, recording transactions, and maintaining control of the related assets should be separated among employees.
f. To prevent improper use of the company's resources, only certain employees are allowed to carry out certain business activities.

BE4–4 Determine whether the firm reports each of the following items as part of cash and cash equivalents in the balance sheet.

Identify cash and cash equivalents (LO4–3)

Item	Cash or Cash Equivalent? (yes/no)
1. Currency	_____
2. Inventory for sale to customers	_____
3. Balance in savings account	_____
4. Checks	_____
5. Accounts receivable	_____
6. Investments purchased with maturities of less than three months	_____

BE4–5 During the year, the following sales transactions occur. There is a charge of 3% on all credit card transactions and a 1% charge on all debit card transactions. Calculate the amount recorded as cash receipts from these transactions.

Determine cash sales (LO4–4)

1. Total cash sales = $500,000
2. Total check sales = $350,000
3. Total credit card sales = $600,000
4. Total debit card sales = $200,000

BE4–6 Record the following transactions.

Record cash expenditures (LO4–4)

1. Pay employee salaries of $600 by issuing checks.
2. Purchase computer equipment of $1,000 using a credit card.
3. Pay for maintenance of $400 for a company vehicle using a debit card.

BE4–7 Match each term associated with a bank reconciliation with its description.

Identify terms associated with a bank reconciliation (LO4–5)

Terms

_____ 1. Checks outstanding
_____ 2. NSF checks
_____ 3. Company error
_____ 4. Interest earned
_____ 5. Deposits outstanding
_____ 6. Bank service fees

Descriptions

a. Cash receipts received by the company but not yet recorded by the bank.
b. Fees imposed by the bank to the company for providing routine services.
c. Checks written to the company that are returned by the bank as not having adequate funds.
d. Checks written by the company but not yet recorded by the bank.
e. Money earned on the average daily balance of the checking account.
f. The company recorded a deposit twice.

Prepare a bank reconciliation (LO4–5)

BE4–8 Indicate whether the firm should add or subtract each item below from its balance of cash or the bank's balance of cash in preparing a bank reconciliation. The first answer is provided as an example. If an item is not a reconciling item, state "No entry."

Reconciliation Items	Bank Balance	Company Balance
1. Checks outstanding	Subtract	No entry
2. NSF checks	_____	_____
3. Deposit recorded twice by company	_____	_____
4. Interest earned	_____	_____
5. Deposits outstanding	_____	_____
6. Bank service fees	_____	_____

Reconcile timing differences in the bank's balance (LO4–5)

BE4–9 Damon Company receives its monthly bank statement, which reports a balance of $2,000. After comparing this to the company's cash records, Damon's accountants determine that deposits outstanding total $4,200 and checks outstanding total $4,450.

Required:

Calculate the reconciled bank balance for cash.

Reconcile timing differences in the company's balance (LO4–5)

BE4–10 Bourne Incorporated reports a cash balance at the end of the month of $2,620. A comparison of the company's cash records with the monthly bank statement reveals several additional cash transactions: bank service fees ($85), an NSF check from a customer ($350), a customer's note receivable collected by the bank ($1,000), and interest earned ($35).

Required:

Calculate the reconciled company balance for cash.

Record adjustments to the company's cash balance (LO4–5)

BE4–11 Refer to the information in **BE4–10**.

Required:

Record the necessary entries to adjust the balance of cash.

Prepare a bank reconciliation (LO4–5)

BE4–12 Brangelina Adoption Agency's general ledger shows a cash balance of $4,593. The balance of cash in the March-end bank statement is $7,345. A review of the bank statement reveals the following information: checks outstanding of $2,803, bank service fees of $85, and interest earned of $34. Calculate the correct balance of cash at the end of March.

Record employee purchases (LO4–6)

BE4–13 Clooney Corp. establishes a petty cash fund for $225 and issues a credit card to its office manager. By the end of the month, employees made one expenditure from the petty cash fund (entertainment, $25) and three expenditures with the credit card (postage, $60; delivery, $85; supplies expense, $50). Record all employee expenditures, and record the entry to replenish the petty cash fund. The credit card balance will be paid later.

Match types of cash flows with their definitions (LO4–7)

BE4–14 Match each type of cash flow to its definition.

Types of Cash Flows	Definitions
_____ 1. Operating cash flows	a. Cash flows related to long-term assets and investment securities.
_____ 2. Investing cash flows	b. Cash flows related to long-term liabilities and stockholders' equity.
_____ 3. Financing cash flows	c. Cash flows related to revenues and expenses.

Determine operating cash flows (LO4–7)

BE4–15 Eastwood Enterprises offers horseback riding lessons. During the month of June, the company provides lessons on account totaling $5,100. By the end of the month, the company received on account $4,500 of this amount. In addition, Eastwood received $500 on account from customers who were provided lessons in May. Determine the amount of operating cash flows Eastwood will report as received from customers in June.

Determine investing cash flows (LO4–7)

BE4–16 On January 12, Ferrell Incorporated obtains a permit to start a comedy club, which will operate only on Saturday nights. To prepare the club for the grand opening, Ferrell purchases tables, chairs, ovens, and other related equipment for $65,000 on January 16. Ferrell pays 20% of this amount (= $13,000) in cash at the time of purchase and signs a note with Live Bank for the remaining amount. Determine the amount of investing cash flows Ferrell would report in January.

BE4–17 Smith Law Firm specializes in the preparation of wills for estate planning. On October 1, 2018, the company begins operations by issuing stock for $11,000 and obtaining a loan from a local bank for $35,000. By the end of 2018, the company provides will preparation services of $42,000 cash and pays employee salaries of $33,000. In addition, Smith pays $3,000 in cash dividends to stockholders on December 31, 2018. Determine the amount of financing cash flows Smith would report in 2018.

Determine financing cash flows (LO4–7)

BE4–18 For each company, calculate the ratio of cash to noncash assets.

Calculate the ratio of cash to noncash assets (LO4–8)

	Cash	Total Assets	Total Liabilities
Tuohy Incorporated	$4,200	$23,400	$3,600
Oher Corporation	$3,500	$25,700	$6,200

EXERCISES

E4–1 Below are several statements about occupational fraud.
1. For most large companies, occupational fraud is minimal and internal control procedures are unnecessary.
2. Managers have a variety of reasons for manipulating the numbers in financial statements, such as maximizing their compensation, increasing the company's stock price, and preserving their jobs.
3. Internal control procedures include formal policies and procedures related to (1) safeguarding the company's assets and (2) improving the accuracy and reliability of accounting information.
4. "Cooking the books" is a phrase used by accountants to indicate the preparation of financial statements that are free of manipulation.
5. Most occupational fraud cases involve misuse of the company's resources.
6. Common types of financial statement fraud include creating fictitious revenues from a fake customer, improperly valuing assets, hiding liabilities, and mismatching revenues and expenses.

Answer true-or-false questions about occupational fraud (LO4–1)

Required:
State whether the answer to each of the statements is true or false.

E4–2 Below are several statements about the Sarbanes-Oxley Act (SOX).
1. SOX represents legislation passed in response to several accounting scandals in the early 2000s.
2. The requirements outlined in SOX apply only to those companies expected to have weak internal controls or to have manipulated financial statements in the past.
3. Section 404 of SOX requires both company management and auditors to document and assess the effectiveness of a company's internal control processes that could affect financial reporting.
4. Severe financial penalties and the possibility of imprisonment are consequences of fraudulent misstatement.
5. With the establishment of SOX, management now has primary responsibility for hiring an external audit firm.
6. The lead auditor in charge of auditing a particular company must rotate off that company only when occupational fraud is suspected.

Answer true-or-false questions about the Sarbanes-Oxley Act (LO4–1)

Required:
State whether the answer to each of the statements is true or false.

Answer true-or-false questions about internal controls (LO4–2)

E4–3 Below are several statements about internal controls.

1. The components of internal control are built on the foundation of the ethical tone set by top management.
2. Once every three months, managers need to review operations to ensure that control procedures work effectively.
3. Collusion refers to the act of a single individual circumventing internal control procedures.
4. Detective control procedures are designed to detect errors or fraud that have already occurred, while preventive control procedures are designed to keep errors or fraud from occurring in the first place.
5. Fraud committed by top-level employees is more difficult to detect because those employees more often have the ability to override internal control features.
6. A good example of separation of duties would be having one person collect cash from customers and account for it, while having another person order inventory and maintain control over it.
7. Employee tips historically have been the most common means of detecting employee fraud.
8. Detective controls include reconciling the physical assets of the company with the accounting records and comparing actual performance of individuals or processes against their expected performance.
9. Effective internal controls and ethical employees ensure a company's success.

Required:

State whether the answer to each of the statements is true or false.

Determine control activity violations (LO4–2)

E4–4 Below are several scenarios related to control activities of a company.

1. A manufacturing company compares total sales in the current year to those in the previous year but does not compare the cost of production.
2. So that employees can have easy access to office supplies, a company keeps supplies in unlocked cabinets in multiple locations.
3. At the end of each day, a single employee collects all cash received from customers, records the total, and makes the deposit at the bank.
4. At the end of the year only, the company compares its cash records to the bank's records of cash deposited and withdrawn during the year.
5. A company encourages employees to call an anonymous hotline if they believe other employees are circumventing internal control features.
6. All employees have the authority to refund a customer's money.

Required:

For each scenario, determine which control activity is violated. Control activities include separation of duties, physical controls, proper authorization, employee management, reconciliations, and performance reviews. If no control activity is violated, state "none."

Calculate the amount of cash to report (LO4–3)

E4–5 Below are several amounts reported at the end of the year.

Currency located at the company	$1,050
Supplies	3,200
Short-term investments that mature within three months	1,950
Accounts receivable	3,500
Balance in savings account	8,500
Checks received from customers but not yet deposited	650
Prepaid rent	1,450
Coins located at the company	110
Equipment	9,400
Balance in checking account	6,200

Required:

Calculate the amount of cash to report in the balance sheet.

E4–6 Douglas and Son, Inc., uses the following process for its cash receipts: The company typically receives cash and check sales each day and places them in a single drawer. Each Friday, the cash clerk records the amount of cash received and deposits the money in the bank account. Each quarter, the controller requests information from the bank necessary to prepare a bank reconciliation.

Discuss internal control procedures related to cash receipts (LO4–4)

Required:

Discuss Douglas and Son's internal control procedures related to cash receipts, noting both weaknesses and strengths.

E4–7 Goldie and Kate operate a small clothing store that has annual revenues of about $100,000. The company has established the following procedures related to cash disbursements: The petty cash fund consists of $10,000. Employees place a receipt in the fund when making expenditures from it and obtain the necessary cash. For any expenditure not made with the petty cash fund, the employee writes a check. Employees are not required to obtain permission to write a check but are asked to use good judgment. Any check written for more than $5,000 can be signed only by Goldie or Kate.

Discuss internal control procedures related to cash disbursements (LO4–4)

Required:

Discuss Goldie and Kate's internal control procedures related to cash disbursements, noting both weaknesses and strengths.

E4–8 Janice Dodds opens the mail for Ajax Plumbing Company. She lists all customer checks on a spreadsheet that includes the name of the customer and the check amount. The checks, along with the spreadsheet, are then sent to Jim Seymour in the accounting department, who records the checks and deposits them daily in the company's checking account.

Discuss internal control procedures related to cash receipts (LO4–4)

Required:

Describe how the company could improve its internal control procedure for the handling of its cash receipts.

E4–9 Spielberg Company's general ledger shows a checking account balance of $22,970 on July 31, 2018. The July cash receipts of $1,885, included in the general ledger balance, are placed in the night depository at the bank on July 31 and processed by the bank on August 1. The bank statement dated July 31 shows bank service fees of $55. The bank processes all checks written by the company by July 31 and lists them on the bank statement, except for one check totaling $1,460. The bank statement shows a balance of $22,490 on July 31.

Calculate the balance of cash using a bank reconciliation (LO4–5)

Required:

1. Prepare a bank reconciliation to calculate the correct ending balance of cash on July 31, 2018.
2. Record the necessary entry(ies) to adjust the balance for cash.

E4–10 On August 31, 2018, the general ledger of The Dean Acting Academy shows a balance for cash of $7,944. Cash receipts yet to be deposited into the checking account total $3,338, and checks written by the academy but not yet processed by the bank total $1,425. The company's balance of cash does not reflect a bank service fee of $35 and interest earned on the checking account of $46. These amounts are included in the balance of cash of $6,042 reported by the bank as of the end of August.

Calculate the balance of cash using a bank reconciliation (LO4–5)

Required:

1. Prepare a bank reconciliation to calculate the correct ending balance of cash on August 31, 2018.
2. Record the necessary entry(ies) to adjust the balance for cash.

E4–11 On October 31, 2018, Damon Company's general ledger shows a checking account balance of $8,397. The company's cash receipts for the month total $74,320, of which $71,295 has been deposited in the bank. In addition, the company has written checks for $72,467, of which $70,982 has been processed by the bank.

The bank statement reveals an ending balance of $11,727 and includes the following items not yet recorded by Damon: bank service fees of $150, note receivable collected by bank of

Calculate the balance of cash using a bank reconciliation (LO4–5)

$5,000, and interest earned on the account balance plus from the note of $320. After closer inspection, Damon realizes that the bank incorrectly charged the company's account $300 for an automatic withdrawal that should have been charged to another customer's account. The bank agrees to the error.

Required:
1. Prepare a bank reconciliation to calculate the correct ending balance of cash on October 31, 2018.
2. Record the necessary entries to adjust the balance for cash.

Record transactions for employee purchases (LO4–6)

E4–12 Halle's Berry Farm establishes a $200 petty cash fund on September 4 to pay for minor cash expenditures. The fund is replenished at the end of each month. At the end of September, the fund contains $30 in cash. The company has also issued a credit card and authorized its office manager to make purchases. Expenditures for the month include the following items:

Office party decorations (petty cash)	$170
Lawn maintenance (credit card)	420
Postage (credit card)	575
Fuel for delivery (credit card)	285

Required:
Record the establishment of the petty cash fund on September 4, all expenditures made during the month, and the replenishment of the petty cash fund on September 30. The credit card balance is not yet paid.

Record transactions for employee purchases (LO4–6)

E4–13 T. L. Jones Trucking Services establishes a petty cash fund on April 3 for $200. By the end of April, the fund has a cash balance of $97. The company has also issued a credit card and authorized its office manager to make purchases. Expenditures for the month include the following items:

Utilities (credit card)	$435
Entertainment (petty cash)	44
Stamps (petty cash)	59
Plumbing repair services (credit card)	630

Required:
Record the establishment of the petty cash fund on April 3, all expenditures made during the month, and the replenishment of the petty cash fund on April 30. The credit card balance is paid in full on April 30.

Classify cash flows (LO4–7)

E4–14 Below are several transactions for Witherspoon Incorporated, a small manufacturer of decorative glass designs.

Transaction	Cash Involved? (yes or no)	Operating, Investing, or Financing? (if cash involved)	Inflow or Outflow?
a. Borrow cash from the bank.			
b. Purchase supplies on account.			
c. Purchase equipment with cash.			
d. Provide services on account.			
e. Pay cash on account for b. above.			
f. Sell for cash a warehouse no longer in use.			
g. Receive cash on account for d. above.			
h. Pay cash to workers for salaries.			

Required:

For each transaction, indicate (1) whether cash is involved (yes or no), and, if cash is involved, (2) whether Witherspoon should classify it as operating, investing, or financing in a statement of cash flows, and (3) whether the cash is an inflow or outflow. Enter N/A if the question is not applicable to the statement.

E4–15 Below are several transactions for Meyers Corporation for 2018.

Calculate net cash flows (LO4–7)

Transaction	Cash Flows	Operating, Investing, or Financing?
a. Issue common stock for cash, $60,000.	_____	_____
b. Purchase building and land with cash, $45,000.	_____	_____
c. Provide services to customers on account, $8,000.	_____	_____
d. Pay utilities on building, $1,500.	_____	_____
e. Collect $6,000 on account from customers.	_____	_____
f. Pay employee salaries, $10,000.	_____	_____
g. Pay dividends to stockholders, $5,000.	_____	_____
Net cash flows for the year	_____	

Required:

1. For each transaction, determine the amount of cash flows (indicate inflows with a "+" and outflows with a "−"). If cash is involved in the transaction, indicate whether Meyers should classify it as operating, investing, or financing in a statement of cash flows. Enter N/A if the question is not applicable to the statement.
2. Calculate net cash flows for the year.
3. Assuming the balance of cash on January 1, 2018, equals $5,400, calculate the balance of cash on December 31, 2018.

E4–16 Below are cash transactions for Goldman Incorporated, which provides consulting services related to mining of precious metals.

Calculate operating cash flows (LO4–7)

a. Cash used for purchase of office supplies, $2,400.
b. Cash provided from consulting to customers, $50,600.
c. Cash used for purchase of mining equipment, $83,000.
d. Cash provided from long-term borrowing, $70,000.
e. Cash used for payment of employee salaries, $25,000.
f. Cash used for payment of office rent, $13,000.
g. Cash provided from sale of equipment purchased in *c.* above, $23,500.
h. Cash used to repay a portion of the long-term borrowing in *d.* above, $45,000.
i. Cash used to pay office utilities, $5,300.
j. Purchase of company vehicle, paying $11,000 cash and borrowing $16,000.

Required:

Calculate cash flows from operating activities.

E4–17 Refer to the information in E4–16.

Calculate investing cash flows (LO4–7)

Required:

Calculate cash flows from investing activities.

E4–18 Refer to the information in E4–16.

Calculate financing cash flows (LO4–7)

Required:

Calculate cash flows from financing activities.

E4–19 Consider the following information:

Compare operating cash flows to net income (LO4–7)

1. Service Revenue for the year = $80,000. Of this amount, $70,000 is collected during the year and $10,000 is expected to be collected next year.

2. Salaries Expense for the year = $40,000. Of this amount, $35,000 is paid during the year and $5,000 is expected to be paid next year.
3. Advertising Expense for the year = $10,000. All of this amount is paid during the year.
4. Supplies Expense for the year = $4,000. No supplies were purchased during the year.
5. Utilities Expense for the year = $12,000. Of this amount, $11,000 is paid during the year and $1,000 is expected to be paid next year.
6. Cash collected in advance from customers for services to be provided next year (Unearned Revenue) = $2,000.

Required:
1. Calculate operating cash flows.
2. Calculate net income.
3. Explain why these two amounts differ.

Analyze the ratio of cash to noncash assets (LO4–8)

E4–20 Below are amounts (in millions) for Glasco Company and Sullivan Company.

| | GLASCO COMPANY | | SULLIVAN COMPANY | |
Year	Operating Cash Flows	Foreign Revenues	Operating Cash Flows	Foreign Revenues
1	$450	$700	$280	$0
2	$130	$750	$300	$0
3	$320	$800	$320	$0

Both companies have total revenues of $2,500, $3,000, and $3,500 in each year.

Required:
Make a prediction as to which firm will have the higher ratio of cash to noncash assets at the end of year 3.

PROBLEMS: SET A

Discuss control procedures for cash receipts (LO4–4)

P4–1A The Carmike 8 Cinema is a modern theatre located close to a college campus. The cashier, located in a box office at the entrance to the theatre, receives cash from customers and operates a machine that ejects serially numbered tickets for each film. Customers then enter the theatre lobby where they can purchase refreshments at the concession stand. To gain admission to the movie, a customer hands the ticket to a ticket taker stationed some 50 feet from the box office at the entrance to the theatre lobby. The ticket taker tears the ticket in half, returns the stub to the customer, and allows the customer to enter the theatre hallway through a turnstile, which has an automatic counter of people entering. The ticket taker drops the other half of the ticket stub into a locked box.

Required:
1. What internal controls are present in the handling of cash receipts?
2. What steps should the theatre manager take regularly to give maximum effectiveness to these controls?
3. Assume the cashier and the ticket taker decide to work together in an effort to steal from the movie theatre. What action(s) might they take?
4. For each idea proposed in number 3 above, what additional control features could Carmike 8 Cinema add to catch the thieves and reduce the risk of future thefts?

Prepare the bank reconciliation and record cash adjustments (LO4–5)

P4–2A Oscar's Red Carpet Store maintains a checking account with Academy Bank. Oscar's sells carpet each day but makes bank deposits only once per week. The following provides information from the company's cash ledger for the month ending February 28, 2018.

	Date	Amount		No.	Date	Amount
Deposits:	2/4	$ 2,700	Checks:	321	2/2	$ 4,700
	2/11	2,300		322	2/8	400
	2/18	3,200		323	2/12	2,500
	2/25	4,100		324	2/19	2,200
Cash receipts:	2/26–2/28	1,600		325	2/27	200
		$13,900		326	2/28	700
				327	2/28	1,900
						$12,600

Balance on February 1	$ 6,800
Receipts	13,900
Disbursements	(12,600)
Balance on February 28	$ 8,100

Information from February's bank statement and company records reveals the following additional information:

a. The ending cash balance recorded in the bank statement is $13,145.

b. Cash receipts of $1,600 from 2/26–2/28 are outstanding.

c. Checks 325 and 327 are outstanding.

d. The deposit on 2/11 includes a customer's check for $200 that did not clear the bank (NSF check).

e. Check 323 was written for $2,800 for advertising in February. The bank properly recorded the check for this amount.

f. An automatic withdrawal for Oscar's February rent was made on February 4 for $1,100.

g. Oscar's checking account earns interest based on the average daily balance. The amount of interest earned for February is $20.

h. In January, one of Oscar's suppliers, Titanic Fabrics, borrowed $6,000 from Oscar. On February 24, Titanic paid $6,250 ($6,000 borrowed amount plus $250 interest) directly to Academy Bank in payment for January's borrowing.

i. Academy Bank charged service fees of $125 to Oscar's for the month.

Required:

1. Prepare a bank reconciliation for Oscar's checking account on February 28, 2018.
2. Record the necessary cash adjustments.

P4–3A The cash records and bank statement for the month of May for Diaz Entertainment are shown below.

Prepare the bank reconciliation and record cash adjustments (LO4–5)

DIAZ ENTERTAINMENT
Cash Account Records
May 1, 2018, to May 31, 2018

Cash Balance May 1, 2018		Deposits		Checks		Cash Balance May 31, 2018
$5,280	+	$12,040	–	$12,220	=	$5,100

Deposits				Checks			
Date	Desc.	Amount		Date	No.	Desc.	Amount
5/3	Sales	$ 1,460		5/7	471	Legal fees	$ 1,300
5/10	Sales	1,890		5/12	472	Property tax	1,670
5/17	Sales	2,520		5/15	473	Salaries	3,600
5/24	Sales	2,990		5/22	474	Advertising	1,500
5/31	Sales	3,180		5/30	475	Supplies	550
				5/31	476	Salaries	3,600
		$12,040					$12,220

P.O. Box 162647
Bowlegs, OK 74830
(405) 369-CASH

Midwest Bank
Looking Out For You

Member FDIC

Account Holder:	Diaz Entertainment	Account Number:	7772854360
	124 Saddle Blvd.		
	Bowlegs, OK 74830	Statement Date:	May 31, 2018

Account Summary

Beginning Balance May 1, 2018	Deposits and Credits No.	Total	Withdrawals and Debits No.	Total	Ending Balance May 31, 2018
$6,260	7	$10,050	9	$10,100	$6,210

Account Details

Deposits and Credits			Withdrawals and Debits				Daily Balance	
Date	Amount	Desc.	Date	No.	Amount	Desc.	Date	Amount
5/4	$1,460	DEP	5/1	469	$ 550	CHK	5/1	$5,710
5/11	1,890	DEP	5/2	470	430	CHK	5/2	5,280
5/18	2,520	DEP	5/9	471	1,300	CHK	5/4	6,740
5/20	1,100	NOTE	5/11		400	NSF	5/9	5,440
5/20	60	INT	5/12	472	1,670	CHK	5/11	6,930
5/25	2,990	DEP	5/18	473	3,600	CHK	5/12	5,260
5/31	30	INT	5/20		600	EFT	5/18	4,180
			5/25	474	1,500	CHK	5/20	4,740
			5/31		50	SF	5/25	6,230
	$10,050				$10,100		5/31	$6,210

Desc.	**DEP** Customer deposit	**INT** Interest earned	**SF** Service fees
	NOTE Note collected	**CHK** Customer check	**NSF** Nonsufficient funds
	EFT Electronic funds transfer		

Additional information:

a. The difference in the beginning balances in the company's records and the bank statement relates to checks #469 and #470, which are outstanding as of April 30, 2018 (prior month).

b. The bank made the EFT on May 20 in error. The bank accidentally charged Diaz for payment that should have been made on another account.

Required:

1. Prepare a bank reconciliation for Diaz's checking account on May 31, 2018.
2. Record the necessary cash adjustments.

Prepare the statement of cash flows (LO4–7)

P4–4A Below is a summary of all transactions of Pixar Toy Manufacturing for the month of August 2018.

Cash Transactions

Cash collections from:	
Customers	$ 93,500
Sale of unused warehouse	36,000
Bank borrowing	26,000
Cash payments for:	
Employee salaries	(65,300)
Office rent	(19,000)
Manufacturing equipment	(46,000)
Office utilities	(11,800)
Dividends to stockholders	(6,700)
Materials to make toys	(27,700)

Noncash Transactions

Sales to customers on account	16,400
Purchase of materials on account	13,900
Purchase equipment with promissory note to pay later	18,500

Required:

Prepare a statement of cash flows for the month of August 2018, properly classifying each of the transactions into operating, investing, and financing activities. The cash balance at the beginning of August is $25,500.

P4–5A Rocky owns and operates Balboa's Gym located in Philadelphia. The following transactions occur for the month of October:

Record transactions, post to the Cash T-account, and prepare the statement of cash flows **(LO4–7)**

October 2	Receive membership dues for the month of October totaling $8,500.
October 5	Issue common stock in exchange for cash, $12,000.
October 9	Purchase additional boxing equipment for $9,600, paying one-half of the amount in cash and the other one-half due by the end of the year.
October 12	Pay $1,500 for advertising regarding a special membership rate available during the month of October.
October 19	Pay dividends to stockholders, $4,400.
October 22	Pay liability insurance to cover accidents to members for the next six months, starting November 1, $6,900.
October 25	Receive cash in advance for November memberships, $5,600.
October 30	Receive, but do not pay, utilities bill for the month, $5,200.
October 31	Pay employees' salaries for the month, $7,300.

Required:

1. Record each transaction.
2. Identify the transactions involving cash.
3. Assuming the balance of cash at the beginning of October is $16,600, post each cash transaction to the Cash T-account and compute the ending cash balance.
4. Prepare a statement of cash flows for the month of October, properly classifying each of the cash transactions into operating, investing, and financing activities.
5. Verify that the net cash flows reported in the statement of cash flows equal the change in the cash balance for the month.

PROBLEMS: SET B

P4–1B At the end of February, Howard Productions' accounting records reveal a balance for cash equal to $19,225. However, the balance of cash in the bank at the end of February is only $735. Howard is concerned and asks the company's accountant to reconcile the two balances. Examination of the bank statement and company records at the end of February reveals the following information:

Prepare a bank reconciliation and discuss cash procedures **(LO4–4, 4–5)**

NSF checks	$5,278	Service fees	$159
Deposits outstanding	7,692	Checks outstanding	489

In addition, during February the company's accountant wrote a check to one of its suppliers for $150. The check was recorded correctly in the company's records for $150 but processed incorrectly by the bank for $1,500. Howard has contacted the bank, which has agreed to fix the error. Finally, a petty cash fund of $4,500 was established during February. This amount was withdrawn from the checking account but not recorded.

Required:

1. Calculate the correct ending balance of cash at the end of February.
2. Discuss any problems you see with the company's cash procedures.

P4–2B On October 31, 2018, the bank statement for the checking account of Blockwood Video shows a balance of $12,751, while the company's records show a balance of $12,381. Information that might be useful in preparing a bank reconciliation is as follows:

Prepare the bank reconciliation and record cash adjustments **(LO4–5)**

a. Outstanding checks are $1,280.

b. The October 31 cash receipts of $835 are not deposited in the bank until November 2.

c. One check written in payment of utilities for $147 is correctly recorded by the bank but is recorded by Blockwood as a disbursement of $174.

d. In accordance with prior authorization, the bank withdraws $560 directly from the checking account as payment on a note payable. The interest portion of that payment is $60 and the principal portion is $500. Blockwood has not recorded the direct withdrawal.

e. Bank service fees of $34 are listed on the bank statement.

f. A deposit of $577 is recorded by the bank on October 13, but it did not belong to Blockwood. The deposit should have been made to the checking account of Hollybuster Video, a separate company.

g. The bank statement includes a charge of $85 for an NSF check. The check is returned with the bank statement, and the company will seek payment from the customer.

Required:

1. Prepare a bank reconciliation for the Blockwood checking account on October 31, 2018.
2. Record the necessary cash adjustments.

Prepare the bank reconciliation and record cash adjustments (LO4–5)

P4–3B The cash records and bank statement for the month of July for Glover Incorporated are shown below.

GLOVER INCORPORATED
Cash Account Records
July 1, 2018, to July 31, 2018

Cash Balance July 1, 2018	+	Deposits	−	Checks	=	Cash Balance July 31, 2018
$7,510		$8,720		$10,560		$5,670

Deposits

Date	Desc.	Amount
7/9	Sales	$2,660
7/21	Sales	3,240
7/31	Sales	2,820
		$8,720

Checks

Date	No.	Desc.	Amount
7/7	531	Rent	$ 1,600
7/12	532	Salaries	2,060
7/19	533	Equipment	4,500
7/22	534	Utilities	1,000
7/30	535	Advertising	1,400
			$10,560

P.O. Box 123878
Gotebo, OK 73041
(580) 377-OKIE

Fidelity Union
You Can Bank On Us

Member FDIC

Account Holder: Glover Incorporated
519 Main Street
Gotebo, OK 73041

Account Number: 2252790471

Statement Date: July 31, 2018

Beginning Balance July 1, 2018	Deposits and Credits No.	Total	Withdrawals and Debits No.	Total	Ending Balance July 31, 2018
$8,200	3	$5,960	7	$10,410	$3,750

Deposits and Credits			Withdrawals and Debits				Daily Balance	
Date	Amount	Desc.	Date	No.	Amount	Desc.	Date	Amount
7/10	$2,660	DEP	7/2	530	$ 690	CHK	7/2	$7,510
7/22	3,240	DEP	7/10	531	1,600	CHK	7/10	8,570
7/31	60	INT	7/14	532	2,060	CHK	7/14	6,510
			7/18		500	NSF	7/18	6,010
			7/22	533	4,900	CHK	7/22	4,350
			7/26		600	EFT	7/26	3,750
			7/30		60	SF	7/30	3,690
	$5,960				$10,410		7/31	$3,750

Desc.   **DEP** Customer deposit   **INT** Interest earned   **SF** Service fees
NOTE Note collected   **CHK** Customer check   **NSF** Nonsufficient funds
EFT Electronic funds transfer

Additional information:

a. The difference in the beginning balances in the company's records and the bank statement relates to check #530, which is outstanding as of June 30, 2018.

b. Check #533 is correctly processed by the bank.

c. The EFT on July 26 relates to the purchase of office supplies.

Required:

1. Prepare a bank reconciliation for Glover's checking account on July 31, 2018.
2. Record the necessary cash adjustments.

P4–4B Below is a summary of all transactions of Dreamworks Bedding Supplies for the month of August 2018.

Prepare the statement of cash flows (LO4–7)

Cash Transactions	
Cash collections from:	
Customers	$ 80,400
Sale of unused land	15,700
Issuance of common stock	30,000
Interest earned on savings account	300
Cash payments for:	
Employee salaries	(47,100)
Delivery truck	(34,500)
Advertising expense	(5,900)
Office supplies	(3,800)
Repayment of borrowing	(9,000)
Bedding material	(13,000)
Noncash Transactions	
Sales to customers on account	12,300
Purchase of materials on account	8,400
Purchase equipment with promissory note to pay later	92,000

Required:

Prepare a statement of cash flows for the month of August, properly classifying each of the transactions into operating, investing, and financing activities. The cash balance at the beginning of August is $8,300.

P4–5B Peter loves dogs and cats. For the past several years, he has owned and operated Homeward Bound, which temporarily houses pets while their owners go on vacation. For the month of June, the company has the following transactions:

Record transactions, post to the Cash T-account, and prepare the statement of cash flows (LO4–7)

June 2	Obtain cash by borrowing $19,000 from the bank by signing a note.
June 3	Pay rent for the current month, $1,200.
June 7	Provide services to customers, $5,200 for cash and $3,500 on account.
June 11	Purchase cages and equipment necessary to maintain the animals, $8,400 cash.
June 17	Pay employees' salaries for the first half of the month, $6,500.
June 22	Pay dividends to stockholders, $1,550.
June 25	Receive cash in advance from a customer who wants to house his two dogs (Chance and Shadow) and cat (Sassy) while he goes on vacation the month of July, $2,100.
June 28	Pay utilities for the month, $3,300.
June 30	Record salaries earned by employees for the second half of the month, $6,500. Payment will be made on July 2.

Required:

1. Record each transaction.

2. Identify the transactions involving cash.
3. Assuming the balance of cash at the beginning of June is $14,700, post each cash transaction to the Cash T-account and compute the ending cash balance.
4. Prepare a statement of cash flows for the month of June, properly classifying each of the cash transactions into operating, investing, and financing activities.
5. Verify that the net cash flows reported in the statement of cash flows equal the change in the cash balance for the month.

ADDITIONAL PERSPECTIVES

Continuing Problem

Great Adventures

(This is a continuation of the Great Adventures problem from earlier chapters.)

AP4–1 An examination of the cash activities during the year shows the following.

GREAT ADVENTURES
Cash Account Records
July 1, 2018, to December 31, 2018

Deposits			Checks/Debit Cards			
Date	Desc.	Amount	Date	No.	Desc.	Amount
7/1	Stock sale	$ 20,000	7/1	101	Insurance	$ 4,800
7/15	Clinic receipts	2,000	7/2	102	Legal fees	1,500
7/22	Clinic receipts	2,300	7/7	DC	Advertising	300
7/30	Clinic receipts	4,000	7/8	103	Bikes	12,000
8/1	Borrowing	30,000	7/24	DC	Advertising	700
8/10	Clinic receipts	3,000	8/4	104	Kayaks	28,000
8/17	Clinic receipts	10,500	8/24	DC	Office supplies	1,800
9/21	Clinic receipts	13,200	9/1	105	Rent	2,400
10/17	Clinic receipts	17,900	12/8	106	Race permit	1,200
12/15	Race receipts	20,000	12/16	107	Salary	2,000
			12/31	108	Dividend	2,000
			12/31	109	Dividend	2,000
		$122,900				$58,700

SUMMARY OF TRANSACTIONS

Beginning Cash Balance July 1, 2018		Deposits		Checks		Ending Cash Balance December 31, 2018
$0	+	$122,900	−	$58,700	=	$64,200

Suzie has not reconciled the company's cash balance with that of the bank since the company was started. She asks Summit Bank to provide her with a six-month bank statement. To save time, Suzie makes deposits at the bank only on the first day of each month.

After comparing the two balances, Suzie has some concern because the bank's balance of $50,500 is substantially less than the company's balance of $64,200.

Required:
1. Discuss any problems you see with Great Adventures' internal control procedures related to cash.
2. Prepare Great Adventures' bank reconciliation for the six-month period ended December 31, 2018, and any necessary entries to adjust cash.
3. How did failure to reconcile the bank statement affect the reported amounts for assets, liabilities, stockholders' equity, revenues, and expenses?

Summit Bank
Leading You to the Top

Member FDIC

| Account Holder: | Great Adventures, Inc. | Account Number: | 1124537774 |
| | | Statement Date: | Dec. 31, 2018 |

Account Summary

Beginning Balance July 1, 2018	Deposits and Credits		Withdrawals and Debits		Ending Balance December 31, 2018
	No.	Total	No.	Total	
$0	8	$103,400	11	$52,900	$50,500

Account Details

Deposits and Credits			Withdrawals and Debits				Daily Balance	
Date	Amount	Desc.	Date	No.	Amount	Desc.	Date	Amount
7/1	$ 20,000	DEP	7/1	101	$ 4,800	CHK	7/1	$15,200
8/1	8,300	DEP	7/7	102	1,500	CHK	7/7	13,400
8/1	30,000	DEP	7/7		300	DC	7/14	1,400
9/1	13,500	DEP	7/14	103	12,000	CHK	7/24	700
9/30	200	INT	7/24		700	DC	8/1	39,000
10/1	13,200	DEP	8/9	104	28,000	CHK	8/9	11,000
11/1	17,900	DEP	8/24		1,800	DC	8/24	9,200
12/31	300	INT	9/2	105	2,400	CHK	9/1	22,700
			9/30		100	SF	9/2	20,300
			12/10	106	1,200	CHK	9/30	20,400
			12/31		100	SF	10/1	33,600
							11/1	51,500
							12/10	50,300
	$103,400				$52,900		12/31	$50,500

| Desc. | **DEP** Customer deposit | **INT** Interest earned | **SF** Service fees |
| | **CHK** Customer check | **DC** Debit card | |

American Eagle Outfitters, Inc.

Financial Analysis

AP4–2 Financial information for **American Eagle** is presented in **Appendix A** at the end of the book.

Required:
1. What does the Report of Independent Registered Public Accounting Firm indicate about American Eagle's internal controls?
2. In the summary of significant accounting policies, how does American Eagle define cash equivalents?
3. What is the amount of cash reported in the two most recent years? By how much has cash increased/decreased?
4. Determine the amounts American Eagle reports for net cash flows from operating activities, investing activities, and financing activities in its statement of cash flows for the most recent year. What are total cash flows for the year for continuing operations?
5. Compare your answers in Question 4 to the increase/decrease you calculated in Question 3. (Note: Include any effect of exchange rates and discontinued operations on cash as an additional cash flow in Question 4.)
6. What is American Eagle's ratio of cash to noncash assets?

Financial Analysis

The Buckle, Inc.

AP4–3 Financial information for **Buckle** is presented in **Appendix B** at the end of the book.

Required:

1. What does the Report of Independent Registered Public Accounting Firm indicate about Buckle's internal controls?
2. In the summary of significant accounting policies, how does Buckle define cash equivalents?
3. What is the amount of cash reported in the two most recent years? By how much has cash increased/decreased?
4. Determine the amounts Buckle reports for net cash flows from operating activities, investing activities, and financing activities in its statement of cash flows for the most recent year. What are total cash flows for the year?
5. Compare your answers in Question 4 to the increase/decrease you calculated in Question 3. (Note: Include any effect of exchange rates on cash as an additional cash flow in Question 4.)
6. What is Buckle's ratio of cash to noncash assets?

Comparative Analysis

American Eagle Outfitters, Inc., vs. The Buckle, Inc.

AP4–4 Financial information for **American Eagle** is presented in **Appendix A** at the end of the book, and financial information for **Buckle** is presented in **Appendix B** at the end of the book.

Required:

1. Which company has a higher ratio of cash to noncash assets? What might this mean about the two companies' operations?
2. Which company has a higher ratio of cash to current liabilities? What might this mean about the two companies' ability to pay debt?

Ethics

AP4–5 Between his freshman and sophomore years of college, Jack takes a job as ticket collector at a local movie theatre. Moviegoers purchase a ticket from a separate employee outside the theatre and then enter through a single set of doors. Jack takes half their ticket, and they proceed to the movie of their choice.

Besides trying to earn enough money for college the next year, Jack loves to watch movies. One of the perks of working for the movie theatre is that all employees are allowed to watch one free movie per day. However, in the employee handbook it states that friends and family of employees are not allowed to watch free movies. In addition, employees must pay full price for all concession items.

Soon after starting work at the theatre, Jack notices that most other employees regularly bring their friends and family to the movie without purchasing a ticket. When Jack stops them at the door to ask for their ticket, they say, "Jack, no one really follows that policy. Just be cool and let us in. You can do the same." Jack even notices that upper management does not follow the policy of no family and friends watching free movies. Furthermore, employees commonly bring their own cups to get free soft drinks and their own containers to eat free popcorn.

Jack considers whether he should also start bringing friends and family and enjoying the free popcorn and beverages. He reasons, "Why should I be the only one following the rules? If everyone else is doing it, including upper management, what harm would it be for me to do it too? After all, when you watch a movie you aren't really stealing anything, and popcorn and drinks cost hardly anything. Plus, I really need to save for college."

Required:

Discuss the ethical dilemma Jack faces. What is the issue? Who are the parties involved? What factors should Jack consider in making his decision?

Internet Research

AP4–6 Financial accounting information can often be found at financial websites. These websites are useful for collecting information about a company's stock price, analysts' forecasts, dividend history, historical financial accounting information, and much more. One such site is Yahoo! Finance (*finance.yahoo.com*).

Required:

1. Visit Yahoo! Finance and get a stock quote for **Exxon Mobil**. To do this, type "XOM" in the "Get Quotes" box. Under "Financials" click on the "Balance Sheet" link. Calculate Exxon Mobil's ratio of cash to noncash assets for the two most recent years.
2. Calculate **Linn Energy**'s ratio in the same way by typing "LINE" in the "Get Quotes" box.
3. Compare the ratios between the companies. What would explain the difference?
4. Click on "Historical Prices" and compare the trend in these companies' stock prices over the same two-year period used to calculate the ratio of cash to noncash assets.

Written Communication

AP4–7 Consider the following independent situations:

1. John Smith is the petty-cash custodian. John approves all requests for payment out of the $200 fund, which is replenished at the end of each month. At the end of each month, John submits a list of all accounts and amounts to be charged, and a check is written to him for the total amount. John is the only person ever to tally the fund.
2. All of the company's cash disbursements are made by check. Each check must be supported by an approved voucher, which is in turn supported by the appropriate invoice and, for purchases, a receiving document. The vouchers are approved by Dean Leiser, the chief accountant, after reviewing the supporting documentation. Betty Hanson prepares the checks for Leiser's signature. Leiser also maintains the company's check register (the cash disbursements journal) and reconciles the bank account at the end of each month.
3. Fran Jones opens the company's mail and lists all checks and cash received from customers. A copy of the list is sent to Jerry McDonald who maintains the general ledger accounts. Fran prepares and makes the daily deposit at the bank. Fran also maintains the subsidiary ledger for accounts receivable, which is used to generate monthly statements to customers.

Required:

Write a memo to your instructor indicating the apparent internal control weaknesses and suggest alternative procedures to eliminate the weaknesses.

Answers to the Self-Study Questions

1. d   2. d   3. a   4. c   5. b   6. d   7. a   8. c   9. b   10. d

CHAPTER 5

Receivables and Sales

Learning Objectives

AFTER STUDYING THIS CHAPTER, YOU SHOULD BE ABLE TO:

- ■ **LO5–1** Recognize accounts receivable.
- ■ **LO5–2** Calculate net revenues using discounts, returns, and allowances.
- ■ **LO5–3** Record an allowance for future uncollectible accounts.
- ■ **LO5–4** Use the aging method to estimate future uncollectible accounts.
- ■ **LO5–5** Apply the procedure to write off accounts receivable as uncollectible.
- ■ **LO5–6** Contrast the allowance method and direct write-off method when accounting for uncollectible accounts.
- ■ **LO5–7** Account for notes receivable and interest revenue.

Analysis

- ■ **LO5–8** Calculate key ratios investors use to monitor a company's effectiveness in managing receivables.

Appendix

- ■ **LO5–9** Estimate uncollectible accounts using the percentage-of-credit-sales method.

TENET HEALTHCARE: BAD DEBTS CAUSE PAIN TO INVESTORS

Tenet Healthcare Corporation is one of the largest hospital chains in the United States. The company operates 80 hospitals and 210 outpatient centers in 14 states, employs over 108,000 people, and sees millions of patients each year. For the period 2012–2014, the company reported net operating revenues of nearly $40 billion. Everything seems fine, right?

Wrong. Over this same period, Tenet reported pretax profits of only $323 million. That's a profit of less than one penny for every dollar of revenue. One of the key reasons for Tenet's poor operating performance was the cost of "uncompensated care." Uncompensated care occurs when patients receive services but are either unable or unwilling to pay. Though hospitals try to minimize these costs, federal law requires that patients not be denied emergency treatment due to inability to pay.

Feature Story

Tenet's uncompensated care includes (1) charity care, (2) discounted services, and (3) bad debts. Charity care refers to patients who are financially unable to pay for their health-care services. Discounted services are offered to patients who have no insurance or are underinsured. Bad debts occur when customers have been billed for services received but never pay.

Over the period 2012–2014, Tenet reported provisions for bad debts of more than $3 billion (7.5% of total revenue and nearly 10 times pretax profits), and this amount does not include additional costs for charity care and discounted services. Without the cost of uncompensated care, profits would have been dramatically higher.

In this chapter, we'll discuss how to record amounts receivable from customers. We'll also see how companies *estimate* the amount of receivables that are not expected to be collected (bad debts). Because bad debts negatively impact operating results, these amounts are important to investors and creditors.

At the end of the chapter, we'll analyze how well management of **Tenet Healthcare Corporation** collects cash from customers and compare the results with a close competitor, **LifePoint Hospitals**. Generally, the better a company is at collecting cash from customers, the more efficiently managers can run the business.

© Comstock Images/SuperStock, RF

PART A

RECOGNIZING ACCOUNTS RECEIVABLE

As we learned in Chapter 2, companies sometimes provide goods or services to customers, not for cash, but on account. Formally, accounts receivable represent the amount of cash owed to a company by its customers from the sale of products or services on account. To understand accounts receivable, we need to start with *credit sales,* from which accounts receivable originate.

Credit Sales and Accounts Receivable

■ **LO5–1**
Recognize accounts receivable.

Did you ever sell candy as part of a fund-raiser and have the person promise to pay you later? If so, you made a credit sale. Credit sales transfer products and services to a customer today while bearing the risk of collecting payment from that customer in the future. Credit sales transactions are also known as *sales on account.* Similarly, credit service transactions are also called *services on account.* Companies often combine total sales revenues with total service revenues in reporting total revenues on the income statement. As we saw in the opening story, Tenet Healthcare provides a considerable amount of healthcare–related sales and services on credit, but many of its credit customers never pay. In this chapter, we focus on recording sales or services on credit and dealing with the likelihood that some customers will not pay as promised.

Credit sales are common for many business transactions. Often, buyers find it more convenient to make multiple purchases using credit and then make a single payment to the seller at the end of the month. In other situations, buyers may not have sufficient cash available at the time of the purchase, or the transaction amount exceeds typical credit card limits. In such cases, the seller must be willing to allow a credit sale in order for the transaction to occur. The benefit of extending credit is that the seller makes it more convenient for the buyer to purchase goods and services. In the long term, credit sales should benefit the seller by increasing profitability of the company. The downside of extending credit is the delay in collecting cash from customers, and as already discussed, some customers may end up not paying at all. These disadvantages reduce the operating efficiency of the company and lead to lower profitability.

Credit sales typically include an informal credit agreement supported by an invoice. They require payment within 30 to 60 days after the sale, as indicated in the invoice. **Even though the seller does not receive cash at the time of the credit sale, the firm records revenue immediately once goods or services are provided to the customer and future collection from the customer is probable.**

Along with the recognized revenue, at the time of sale the seller also obtains a legal right to receive cash from the buyer. **The legal right to *receive* cash is valuable and represents an asset of the company.** This asset is referred to as accounts receivable (sometimes called *trade receivables*), and the firm records it at the time of a credit sale.

To see how companies record credit sales, consider an example. Suppose Link's Dental charges $500 for teeth whitening. Dee Kay decides to have her teeth whitened on March 1 but doesn't pay cash at the time of service. She promises to pay the $500 whitening fee to Link by March 31. Link's Dental records the following at the time of the whitening.

A = L + SE		March 1	Debit	Credit
+500		**Accounts Receivable**	500	
	+500 Rev ↑	**Service Revenue**		500
		(Provide services on account)		

Notice that instead of debiting Cash, as in a cash sale, Link's Dental debits another asset—Accounts Receivable—for the credit sale.

KEY POINT

Companies record an asset (accounts receivable) and revenue when they sell products and services to their customers on account, expecting payment in the future.

As you study receivables, realize that one company's right to *collect* cash corresponds to another company's (or individual's) obligation to *pay* cash. One company's account receivable is the flip side of another company's account payable. In Chapter 6 we discuss accounts payable in the context of inventory purchases on account. In Chapter 8 we again discuss accounts payable, but in the context of current liabilities.

Flip Side

OTHER TYPES OF RECEIVABLES

Other types of receivables are less common than accounts receivable. *Nontrade receivables* are receivables that originate from sources other than customers. They include tax refund claims, interest receivable, and loans by the company to other entities, including stockholders and employees. When receivables are accompanied by formal credit arrangements made with written debt instruments (or notes), we refer to them as *notes receivable*. We'll consider notes receivable later in this chapter.

Net Revenues

From time to time, companies offer discounts to customers. These discounts offer ways to quickly sell inventory, attract new customers, reward long-term loyal customers, and encourage customers to pay quickly on their accounts. However, while these discounts may be beneficial to the company's long-term success, they can reduce the amount of revenue reported in the current period. In addition, the company's revenues are reduced when customers return unsatisfactory products or demand allowances for inferior services or competitive pricing. Therefore, it is important for managers to consider not only their companies' total revenues, but also net revenues. Net revenues refer to a company's total revenues less any amounts for discounts, returns, and allowances. We discuss these items next.

■ **LO5–2**
Calculate net revenues using discounts, returns, and allowances.

Common Terms Net revenues are also often referred to as *net sales*.

TRADE DISCOUNTS

Trade discounts represent a reduction in the listed price of a product or service. Companies typically use trade discounts to provide incentives to larger customers or consumer groups to purchase from the company. Trade discounts also can be a way to change prices without publishing a new price list or to disguise real prices from competitors.

When recording a transaction, companies don't recognize trade discounts *directly*. Instead, they recognize trade discounts *indirectly* by recording the sale at the discounted price. For example, let's go back to Link's Dental, which typically charges $500 for teeth whitening. Assume that in order to entice more customers, Dr. Link offers a 20% discount on teeth whitening to any of his regular patients. Since Dee Kay is one of Dr. Link's regular patients, she can take advantage of the special discount and have her teeth whitened for only $400.

	Debit	Credit
March 1		
Accounts Receivable	400	
Service Revenue		400
(Make credit sale of $500 with a 20% trade discount)		

A	=	L	+	SE
+400				
				+400 Rev ↑

Notice that Link's Dental records the trade discount *indirectly* by simply recording revenue equal to the discounted price, which is $500 less the trade discount of $100 (= $500 × 20%).

SALES RETURNS AND SALES ALLOWANCES

In some cases, customers may not be satisfied with a product or service purchased. If a customer returns a product, we call that a sales return. After a sales return, (a) we reduce the customer's account balance if the sale was on account or (b) we issue a cash refund if the sale was for cash.

In other cases, the customer does not return the product or service, but the seller reduces the customer's balance owed to provide at least a partial adjustment of the amount the customer owes. This adjustment is called a sales allowance.

Suppose on March 5, after she gets her teeth whitened but before she pays, Dee notices that another local dentist is offering the same procedure for $350, which is $50 less than Link's discounted price of $400. Dee brings this to Dr. Link's attention and because his policy is to match any competitor's pricing, he offers to reduce Dee's account balance by $50. Link's Dental records the following sales allowance.

March 5	Debit	Credit
Sales Allowances	50	
Accounts Receivable		50
(Provide sales allowance for previous credit sale)		

The effects of the transaction on the financial statements are shown below.

Balance Sheet					Income Statement		
			Stockholders' Equity				
			Common	Retained			Net
Assets	=	**Liabilities** +	**Stock** +	**Earnings**	**Revenues** −	**Expenses** =	**Income**
−50	=			−50	−50		= −50

This transaction reduces accounts receivable (assets). Dr. Link has less receivable from Dee after the allowance—she now owes only $350.

This transaction also reduces Dr. Link's revenue. **Both sales returns and sales allowances are classified as contra revenues.** A contra revenue account is an account with a balance that is opposite, or "contra," to that of its related revenue account. The reason we use a contra revenue account is to keep a record of the total revenue earned separate from the reduction due to subsequent sales returns or sales allowances. Rather than analyze debits to the Service Revenue account, managers can more easily analyze debits to the Sales Returns or Sales Allowances accounts. Companies sometimes combine their sales returns and sales allowances in a single Sales Returns and Allowances account. For homework, use separate Sales Returns and Sales Allowances accounts.

 COMMON MISTAKE

Students sometimes misclassify contra revenue accounts—sales returns and sales allowances—as expenses. Like expenses, contra revenues have normal debit balances and reduce the reported amount of net income. However, contra revenues represent *reductions* of revenues, whereas expenses represent the separate costs of generating revenues.

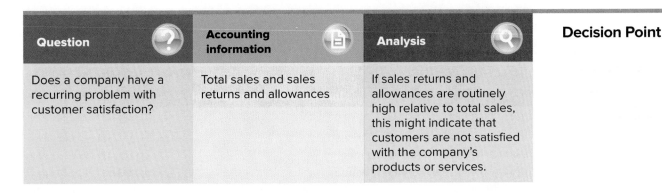

Question	Accounting information	Analysis
Does a company have a recurring problem with customer satisfaction?	Total sales and sales returns and allowances	If sales returns and allowances are routinely high relative to total sales, this might indicate that customers are not satisfied with the company's products or services.

SALES DISCOUNTS

Unlike a trade discount, a **sales discount** represents a reduction, not in the selling price of a product or service, but in the amount to be paid by a credit customer if payment is made within a specified period of time. It's a discount intended to provide incentive for quick payment.

Discount terms, such as 2/10, n/30, are a shorthand way to communicate the amount of the discount and the time period within which it's available. The term "2/10," pronounced "two ten," for example, indicates the customer will receive a 2% discount if the amount owed is paid within 10 days. The term "n/30," pronounced "net thirty," means that if the customer does *not* take the discount, full payment net of any returns or allowances is due within 30 days.

Assume Link's Dental wants Dee to pay quickly on her teeth-whitening bill and offers her terms of 2/10, n/30. This means that if Dee pays within 10 days, the amount due ($350 after the $100 trade discount and the $50 sales allowance) will be reduced by 2% (or $7 = $350 × 2%).

Collection During the Discount Period. Let's see what happens when Dee pays within 10 days: Assume that Dee pays on March 10, which is within the 10-day discount period. Link's Dental records the following entry when it receives payment.

March 10	Debit	Credit
Cash	343	
Sales Discounts	7	
Accounts Receivable		350
(Collect cash on account with a 2% sales discount)		

Balance Sheet					Income Statement			
			Stockholders' Equity					
			Common	**Retained**				**Net**
Assets	**=**	**Liabilities +**	**Stock**	**+ Earnings**	**Revenues**	**− Expenses**	**=**	**Income**
+343	=			−7	−7		=	−7
−350								
−7								

Notice that Link receives only $343 cash, the $350 amount owed less the 2% sales discount. Similar to sales returns and allowances, **we record sales discounts in a contra revenue account.** The reason we use a contra revenue account is to be able to keep the total revenue separate from the reduction in that revenue due to quick payment. In this case, Service Revenue has a credit balance of $400, and its related contra revenue account—Sales Discounts—has a debit balance of $7. The net effect is that sales discounts increase, reducing net revenues of the company.

It's easier to see the relationship between Service Revenue and related contra accounts by looking at the partial income statement of Link's Dental in Illustration 5–1.

ILLUSTRATION 5–1

Income Statement
Reporting Revenues
Net of Sales Discounts

LINK'S DENTAL Income Statement (partial)	
Service revenue	$400
Less: Sales allowances	(50)
Less: Sales discounts	(7)
Net service revenue	$343

Link provides a service with a normal price of $500. However, after the trade discount of $100, the sales allowance of $50, and the sales discount of $7, Link's income statement reports net revenue of $343.

Also notice that Link's Dental credits Accounts Receivable for $350, even though it receives only $343 cash. The reason is that the $350 balance in Accounts Receivable is "paid in full" by the combination of the $343 cash payment and the $7 sales discount. Dee owes $0 after paying $343. The balance of Accounts Receivable now equals $0, as demonstrated in Illustration 5–2.

ILLUSTRATION 5–2

Balance of Accounts
Receivable after Credit
Sale and Subsequent
Collection on Account

Credit sale of $500 with
$100 trade discount

Accounts Receivable			
Mar. 1 400			
	Mar. 5	50	Sales allowance of $50
	Mar. 10	350	Cash collection of $343 with $7 sales discount
Bal. 0			

Ending balance

Collection After the Discount Period.   For our second scenario, assume that Dee waits until March 31 to pay, which is *not* within the 10-day discount period. Link's Dental records the following transaction at the time it collects cash from Dee.

A = L + SE

+350
−350

March 31	Debit	Credit
Cash	**350**	
Accounts Receivable		**350**
(Collect cash on account)		

Notice that there is no indication in recording the transaction that the customer does not take the sales discount. This is the typical way to record a cash collection on account when no sales discounts are involved. Accounts Receivable is credited for $350 to reduce its balance to $0, representing the amount owed by the customer after payment.

KEY POINT

Sales discounts, returns, and allowances are contra revenue accounts. We subtract the balances in these accounts from total revenues when calculating net revenues.

Let's Review

Snap-Crackle-Pop (SCP) Chiropractic normally charges $120 for a full spinal adjustment. Currently, the company is offering a $20 discount to senior citizens. In addition, SCP offers terms 2/10, n/30 to all customers receiving services on account. The following events occur.

mhhe.com/4fa17

June 18   David, age 72, calls to set up an appointment.

June 20   David visits SCP and receives a spinal adjustment for the discounted price.

June 29   David pays for his office visit.

Required:

1. On what date should SCP record patient revenue?

2. Record patient revenue for SCP.

3. Record the cash collection for SCP assuming SCP receives David's payment in full on June 29 (within the discount period).

4. Calculate the balance of Accounts Receivable using a T-account format, and then calculate the balance of net revenue as shown in the income statement after the cash payment is received.

Solution:

1. SCP should record patient revenue on June 20—the date the service is provided.

2. Record patient revenue:

June 20	Debit	Credit
Accounts Receivable	**100**	
Service Revenue		**100**
(Provide services on account)		
(Revenue = $120 less $20 trade discount)		

3. Record receipt of David's payment in full within the discount period:

June 29	Debit	Credit
Cash	**98**	
Sales Discounts	**2**	
Accounts Receivable		**100**
(Collect cash on account with a 2% sales discount)		
(Sales discount = $100 × 2%)		

4. Balance of Accounts Receivable and calculation of net revenue after receipt of cash payment:

Accounts Receivable

Jun. 20	100		
		Jun. 29	100
Bal.	0		

Service revenue (from *Requirement* 2)	$100
Less: Sales discounts (from *Requirement* 3)	(2)
Net revenue	$ 98

Suggested Homework:
BE5–1, BE5–2;
E5–2, E5–3;
P5–2A&B

END-OF-PERIOD ADJUSTMENT FOR CONTRA REVENUES

The discussion above deals with how companies record contra revenues—sales discounts, sales returns, and sales allowances—*during the year*. However, companies also must adjust for these amounts at the *end of the year* using adjusting entries. The revenue recognition standard (ASU No. 2014-09) issued in 2014 requires a company to report revenues equal to the amount of cash the company "expects to be entitled to receive." Those expectations could change as new information becomes available.[1]

We can see how this works with a simple example. Suppose General Health sells medical parts and consultation services of $400,000 on account during 2018. Also during 2018, some customers receive sales discounts totaling $6,000 for quick payment, while others return unused parts of $10,000 and others receive allowances of $14,000. These contra revenue transactions reduce the amount of cash to be received from customers, so at the time they occur we need to reduce revenues. To reduce revenues, we debit Sales Discounts for $6,000, Sales Returns for $10,000, and Sales Allowances for $14,000. The procedure for recording these amounts was discussed earlier.

In addition, at the end of 2018 the company must *estimate* any additional discounts, returns, and allowances that will occur in 2019 *as a result of sales transactions in 2018.* The reason is that some activities associated with sales transactions in 2018 will not occur until 2019 but will affect the final amount of cash received from customers. Continuing our example, suppose the company estimates an additional $1,000 in sales discounts, $2,000 in sales returns, and $3,000 in sales allowances in 2019 associated with sales in 2018. These estimates represent the expectation of less cash to be received, so according to the revenue recognition standard, we need to reduce revenue in 2018 for their amounts as well.

As shown in Illustration 5–3, the amounts reported for contra revenues in the 2018 income statement include: (1) *actual* discounts, returns, and allowances during 2018 plus (2) *estimates* of discounts, returns, and allowances expected to occur in 2019 that relate to transactions in 2018. The result is net revenues for 2018 of $364,000.[2]

ILLUSTRATION 5–3

Income Statement Reporting Revenues Net of Sales Discounts, Returns, and Allowances

GENERAL HEALTH Income Statement (partial) For the year ended 2018	
Sales and service revenue	$ 400,000
Less: Sales discounts ($6,000 actual + $1,000 estimate)	(7,000)
Less: Sales returns ($10,000 actual + $2,000 estimate)	(12,000)
Less: Sales allowances ($14,000 actual + $3,000 estimate)	(17,000)
Net revenue	$364,000

The adjusting entries to record these estimated contra revenues at the end of the year can be somewhat complicated, so we leave them to a more advanced accounting course. For now, the important points to understand are:

1. Revenues are reported for the amount of cash a company expects to be entitled to receive from customers for providing goods and services.
2. Total revenues are reduced by sales discounts, sales returns, and sales allowances that occur during the year.
3. Total revenues are further reduced by an adjusting entry at the end of the year for the estimate of additional sales discounts, sales returns, and sales allowances expected to occur in the future but that relate to the current year.

PART B

VALUING ACCOUNTS RECEIVABLE

The right to receive cash from a customer is a valuable resource for the company. **This is why accounts receivable is an asset, reported in the company's balance sheet.** If the company expects to receive the cash within one year, it classifies the receivable as a current asset; otherwise it classifies the receivable as a long-term asset.

---

[1]The adjustment to revenues for expected cash to be received does not include the expectation that some customers will fail to pay amounts owed (bad debts). These amounts are reported as a separate expense (Bad Debt Expense), as we'll discuss in Part B of this chapter.
[2]Alternatively, a company could record estimates of total sales discounts, returns, and allowances at the time of the sale, and then revise that estimate downward at the end of the year based on actual amounts that have occurred. This alternate approach results in the same amount of net revenue being reported in the income statement. In practice, companies likely will find it easier to record sales discounts, returns, and allowances as they actually occur and then have a year-end adjustment for expected future amounts, as discussed in the text.

What, though, is the *value* of being owed $100? If you are confident the person will actually pay you $100 in the near future, then you might consider the right to receive the money to be worth $100. However, if the person is unable to pay you anything, then your right to collect $100 is worth $0. Of course there are many possibilities in between. To be useful to decision makers, accounts receivable should be reported at the amount of cash the firm *expects* to collect, an amount known as net realizable value.

KEY POINT

We recognize accounts receivable as assets in the balance sheet and report them at their *net realizable value*, that is, the amount of cash we expect to collect.

Allowance Method

We know that companies often are not able to collect all of their accounts receivable from customers. Rather than accept only cash payment at the time of sale, should companies extend credit to their customers by allowing them to purchase on account? **The *upside* of extending credit to customers is that it boosts sales by allowing customers the ability to purchase on account and pay cash later.** Just think of how many times you wanted to buy food, clothes, electronics, or other items, but you didn't have cash with you. You're not alone. Many customers may not have cash readily available to make a purchase or, for other reasons, simply prefer to buy on credit.

LO5–3
Record an allowance for future uncollectible accounts.

   The *downside* **of extending credit to customers is that not all customers will pay fully on their accounts.** Even the most well-meaning customers may find themselves in difficult financial circumstances beyond their control, limiting their ability to repay debt. Customers' accounts that we no longer consider collectible are uncollectible accounts, or *bad debts*.

   Generally Accepted Accounting Principles (GAAP) require that we account for uncollectible accounts using what's called the allowance method. This method involves *allowing for the possibility* that some accounts will be uncollectible at some point in the future.[3] Be sure to understand this key point. Using the allowance method, we account for events (customers' bad debts) that have *not yet* occurred but that are likely to occur. This is different from other transactions you've learned about to this point. Those earlier transactions involved recording events that have already occurred, such as purchasing supplies, paying employees, and providing services to customers. **Under the allowance method, companies are required to estimate *future* uncollectible accounts and record those estimates in the *current* year.**

   An account receivable we do not expect to collect has no value. Thus, we need to (1) reduce assets (accounts receivable) by an estimate of the amount we don't expect to collect. At the same time, failure to collect a customer's cash represents a cost inherent in using credit sales, so we also need to (2) increase expenses (bad debt expense) to reflect the cost of offering credit to customers. The bad debt expense will decrease net income. In the next section, we'll see how to use the allowance method to record estimated bad debts.

KEY POINT

Under the allowance method, companies are required to estimate *future* uncollectible accounts and record those estimates in the *current* year. Estimated uncollectible accounts reduce assets and increase expenses.

ESTIMATING UNCOLLECTIBLE ACCOUNTS

To use the allowance method, a company first estimates at the end of the *current* year how much in uncollectible accounts will occur in the *following* year. Consider an example of future uncollectible accounts for Kimzey Medical Clinic, which specializes in emergency outpatient care. Because it doesn't verify the patient's health insurance before administering

---

[3]Later in the chapter, we'll look at a second method—the direct write-off method. The direct write-off method is used for tax purposes but is generally not permitted for financial reporting.

care, Kimzey knows that a high proportion of fees for emergency care provided will not be collected.

In 2018, its first year of operations, Kimzey bills customers $50 million for emergency care services provided. By the end of the year, $20 million remains due from customers. Those receivables are assets of the company. But how much of the $20 million does Kimzey expect *not* to collect in the following year? **The receivables not expected to be collected should not be counted as assets.**

The credit manager at Kimzey estimates that approximately 30% of accounts receivable will not be collected. Estimating uncollectible accounts based on the percentage of accounts receivable expected not to be collected is known as the percentage-of-receivables method. This method sometimes is referred to as the *balance sheet method*, because we base the estimate of bad debts on a balance sheet amount—accounts receivable.[4]

Using the 30% estimate, Kimzey expects that $6 million of its accounts receivable (or 30% of $20 million) likely will never be collected. It makes the following year-end adjustment to allow for these future uncollectible accounts.

December 31, 2018 ($ in millions)	Debit	Credit
Bad Debt Expense	6	
Allowance for Uncollectible Accounts		6
(Estimate future bad debts)		
($20 million × 30% = $6 million)		

Balance Sheet						Income Statement		
			Stockholders' Equity					
			Common	**Retained**				**Net**
Assets	**=**	**Liabilities** **+**	**Stock**	**+ Earnings**		**Revenues −**	**Expenses =**	**Income**
−6	=			−6			+6	−6

The effect of the adjustment in the financial statements reflects the impact of the transaction on the financial position of the company. Because the nature of the accounts in this adjusting entry differs somewhat from those in other year-end adjusting entries we covered in Chapter 3, let's look closer.

Common Terms Bad debt expense sometimes is referred to as *uncollectible accounts expense* or *provision for doubtful accounts.*

Bad Debt Expense.   First, bad debt expense represents the cost of the estimated future bad debts. Kimzey estimates that it will not collect 30% of its accounts receivable, and so records Bad Debt Expense of $6 million. We include this expense in the income statement of the same period with which these bad debts are associated. By doing so, we properly "match" expenses (bad debts) with the revenues (credit sales) they help to generate. Illustration 5–4 shows the partial income statement for Kimzey Medical Clinic after estimating bad debt expense.

ILLUSTRATION 5–4

Partial Income Statement Showing Estimated Bad Debt Expense

KIMZEY MEDICAL CLINIC Income Statement (partial) For the year ended 2018	
($ in millions)	
Credit sales	$50
Bad debt expense	(6)
	$44

[4]In the appendix to this chapter, we'll consider a second method, the percentage-of-credit-sales method (also referred to as the income statement method). In practice, companies are required to follow the percentage-of-receivables method, so that will be our focus here.

In the 2018 income statement, we reduce the $50 million of revenue from credit sales by $6 million for estimated future bad debts. Even though the company reports credit sales of $50 million, the expected profit on these sales, after considering the cost of future bad debts, is only $44 million.

KEY POINT ⎯⎯⎯⎯⎯⎯⎯⎯⎯⎯⎯⎯⎯⎯⎯⎯⎯⎯⎯⎯⎯⎯⎯

Adjusting for estimates of future uncollectible accounts matches expenses (bad debts) in the same period as the revenues (credit sales) they help to generate.

Allowance for Uncollectible Accounts.   Second, we adjust for future bad debts by making an allowance for uncollectible accounts. The contra asset account Allowance for Uncollectible Accounts represents the amount of accounts receivable we do not expect to collect. Earlier in the chapter, we discussed *contra revenue* accounts—sales discounts, returns, and allowances. Recall that these accounts provide a way to *reduce revenue indirectly*. In the same way, the allowance account provides a way to *reduce accounts receivable* indirectly, rather than decreasing the accounts receivable balance itself.

Common Terms The allowance for uncollectible accounts is sometimes referred to as the *allowance for doubtful accounts.*

We report the allowance for uncollectible accounts in the asset section of the balance sheet, but it represents a reduction in the balance of accounts receivable. The difference between total accounts receivable and the allowance for uncollectible accounts is referred to as net accounts receivable, or net realizable value. Illustration 5–5 demonstrates the concept behind accounting for future uncollectible accounts and how the accounts receivable portion of Kimzey's year-end balance sheet appears.

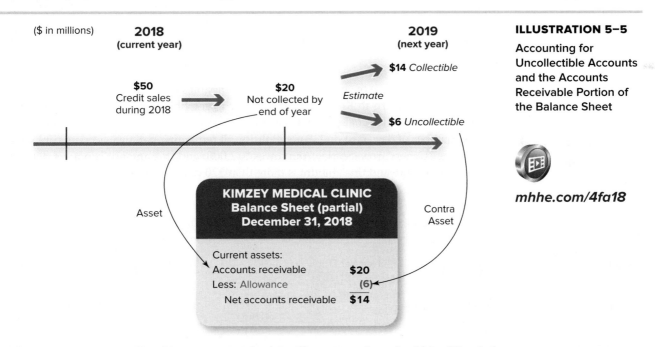

ILLUSTRATION 5–5

Accounting for Uncollectible Accounts and the Accounts Receivable Portion of the Balance Sheet

mhhe.com/4fa18

After we estimate uncollectible accounts to be $6 million, we reduce the $20 million balance of accounts receivable and report them at their net realizable value, or estimated collectible amount, of $14 million. But is this estimate correct? Only time will tell. Kimzey's prediction of $6 million for uncollectible accounts might be too high, or it might be too low. In either case, it's generally more informative than making no estimate at all. (Later in the chapter, we'll find out how close the estimate is.)

COMMON MISTAKE ⎯⎯⎯⎯⎯⎯⎯⎯⎯⎯⎯⎯⎯⎯⎯⎯⎯⎯

Because Allowance for Uncollectible Accounts has a normal credit balance, students sometimes misclassify this account as a liability, which also has a normal credit balance. Instead, a contra asset represents a reduction in a related asset.

KEY POINT

Recording an allowance for uncollectible accounts correctly reports accounts receivable at their net realizable value.

Decision Point

Question	Accounting information	Analysis
Are the company's credit sales policies too lenient?	Accounts receivable and the allowance for uncollectible accounts	A high ratio of the allowance for uncollectible accounts to total accounts receivable could be an indication that the company extends too much credit to high-risk customers.

AGING OF ACCOUNTS RECEIVABLE

■ LO5–4
Use the aging method to estimate future uncollectible accounts.

In our example for Kimzey Medical Clinic, we estimated future uncollectible accounts by applying a *single* estimated percentage to total accounts receivable (30%). Management can estimate this percentage using historical averages, current economic conditions, industry comparisons, or other analytical techniques. A more accurate method than assuming a single percentage uncollectible for all accounts is to consider the various *ages* of individual accounts receivable, using a higher percentage for "old" accounts than for "new" accounts. This is known as the aging method. For instance, accounts that are 120 days past due are older than accounts that are 60 days past due. **The older the account, the less likely it is to be collected.**

To determine the age of accounts receivable, companies must keep track of their individual customers. Let's return to Kimzey Medical Clinic to see how this looks. Illustration 5–6 lists eight of Kimzey's individual patients' accounts, including the amount owed by each patient and the number of days past due. For simplicity, all remaining patients' accounts are summarized in the "Others" row. Shirley Akin owes $12,000, and this amount is not yet due; Bruce Easley owes $4,000, and this amount is more than 120 days past due; and so on.

ILLUSTRATION 5–6

Kimzey's Accounts Receivable Aging Schedule

mhhe.com/4fa19

Patients	Not Yet Due	Days Past Due 1–60	Days Past Due 61–120	Days Past Due More than 120	Total
Shirley Akin	$ 12,000				$ 12,000
Bruce Easley				$ 4,000	4,000
Ben Greene		$ 5,000			5,000
Anita Hand			$ 7,000		7,000
Ima Hertz	9,000				9,000
Noah Luck		8,000			8,000
Phil Sikley	6,000				6,000
Justin Payne				10,000	10,000
Others	9,973,000	5,987,000	2,993,000	986,000	19,939,000
Total Accounts Receivable	$10,000,000	$ 6,000,000	$ 3,000,000	$1,000,000	$20,000,000
Estimated Percent Uncollectible	10%	30%	50%	70%	
Estimated Amount Uncollectible	$ 1,000,000	$1,800,000	$1,500,000	$ 700,000	$ 5,000,000

The estimated percent uncollectible increases with age

Notice that each age group has its own estimate of the percent uncollectible, and this percentage increases with the age of the account. The "Not Yet Due" column has an estimated 10% percent uncollectible because some of these patients will not pay; we just don't know which ones. The "1-60" days past due column has an estimated 30% uncollectible, since these accounts are older and less likely to be collected. The estimated percentage uncollectible continues to increase as the account becomes more past due.

Summing the estimated amount uncollectible for each age group results in a total estimate of **$5 million**. Using the aging method to estimate future uncollectible accounts should be more accurate than applying a single rate of 30% to the entire amount of accounts receivable, as was done previously. The reason is that accounting for the age of each account should more accurately predict the probability of the account balance not being collected. The adjusting entry at the end of 2018 to allow for future bad debts would instead be $5 million using the aging method.

December 31, 2018	Debit	Credit
Bad Debt Expense	5	
Allowance for Uncollectible Accounts		5
(Estimate future bad debts)		

A	=	L	+	SE
				−5 Exp ↑
−5				

Illustration 5–7 presents **Tenet Healthcare**'s policy of estimating uncollectible accounts.

ILLUSTRATION 5–7

Excerpt from Tenet Healthcare Corporation's Annual Report

TENET HEALTHCARE CORPORATION
Notes to the Financial Statements (excerpt)

We provide for an allowance against accounts receivable that could become uncollectible by establishing an allowance to reduce the carrying value of such receivables to their estimated net realizable value. We estimate this allowance based on the aging of our accounts receivable by hospital, our historical collection experience by hospital and for each type of payer over for a look-back period, and other relevant factors. There are various factors that can impact collection trends, such as changes in the economy, which in turn have an impact on unemployment rates and the number of uninsured and underinsured patients, the volume of patients through the emergency department, the increased burden of co-payments and deductibles to be made by patients with insurance, and business practices related to collection efforts. These factors continuously change and can have an impact on collection trends and our estimation process.

The following tables present the approximate aging by payer of our continuing operations' net accounts receivable.

Age	Medicare	Medicaid	Managed Care	Indemnity, Self-Pay, and Other	Total
0–60 days	$262	$ 67	$943	$ 158	$1,430
61–120 days	29	34	229	104	396
121–180 days	13	18	100	60	191
Over 180 days	19	34	157	225	435
Total	$323	$153	$1,429	$547	$2,452

KEY POINT

Using the aging method to estimate uncollectible accounts is more accurate than applying a single percentage to all accounts receivable. The aging method recognizes that the longer accounts are past due, the less likely they are to be collected.

Subsidiary Ledgers.   In practice, all companies maintain records for individual customer accounts to help in tracking amounts receivable and in estimating amounts uncollectible. This idea was demonstrated in Illustration 5–6. A subsidiary ledger contains a group of individual accounts associated with a particular general ledger control account. For example, the subsidiary ledger for accounts receivable keeps track of all increases and decreases to individual customers' accounts. The balances of all individual accounts then sum to the balance of total accounts receivable in the general ledger and reported in the balance sheet. Subsidiary ledgers are also used for accounts payable, property and equipment, investments, and other accounts.

Decision Point

Question	Accounting information	Analysis
How likely is it that the company's accounts receivable will be collected?	Notes to the financial statements detailing the age of individual accounts receivable	Older accounts are less likely to be collected.

WRITING OFF ACCOUNTS RECEIVABLE

■ LO5–5
Apply the procedure to write off accounts receivable as uncollectible.

To continue with our example of Kimzey Medical Clinic, let's suppose that on February 23, 2019 (the following year), Kimzey receives notice that one of its former patients, Bruce Easley, has filed for bankruptcy protection against all creditors. Based on this information, Kimzey believes it is unlikely Bruce will pay his account of $4,000. Remember, Kimzey previously allowed for the likelihood that *some* of its customers would not pay, though it didn't know which ones. Now that it *knows* a specific customer will not pay, it can adjust the allowance and reduce the accounts receivable balance itself. Upon receiving news of this *actual* bad debt, Kimzey records the following.

February 23, 2019	Debit	Credit
Allowance for Uncollectible Accounts	4,000	
Accounts Receivable		4,000
(Write off a customer's account)		

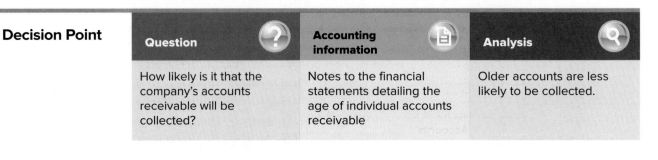

Balance Sheet				
			Stockholders' Equity	
			Common	**Retained**
Assets	**=**	**Liabilities +**	**Stock**	**+ Earnings**
+4,000	=			
−4,000				
0				

Income Statement		
		Net
Revenues	**− Expenses**	**= Income**

What is the effect in Kimzey's financial statements when writing off Bruce's account receivable? **Overall, the write-off of the account receivable has no effect on total amounts reported in the balance sheet or in the income statement.** Notice that there is no decrease in total assets and no decrease in net income with the write-off. Here's why: **We have already recorded the negative effects of the bad news.** Kimzey recorded those effects when it *estimated* future bad debts at the end of 2018 by recording a debit to bad debt expense and a credit to the allowance account. So, when Bruce declares bankruptcy in the following year, 2019, we had already established the allowance for this bad debt. The write-off on

February 23, 2019, reduces both an asset account (Accounts Receivable) and its contra asset account (Allowance for Uncollectible Accounts), leaving the *net* receivable unaffected. Thus, the entry to record the actual write-off results in no change to total assets and no change to net income.

 COMMON MISTAKE

Students often mistakenly record bad debt expense when they write off an uncollectible account. The bad debt expense was recorded in a prior year at the time of estimating uncollectible accounts.

COLLECTION OF ACCOUNTS PREVIOUSLY WRITTEN OFF

Later in 2019, on September 8, Bruce's bankruptcy proceedings are complete. Kimzey had expected to receive none of the $4,000 Bruce owed. However, after liquidating all assets, Bruce is able to pay each of his creditors 25% of the amount due them. So, when Kimzey receives payment of $1,000 (= $4,000 × 25%), it makes the following two entries.

September 8, 2019	Debit	Credit
Accounts Receivable	**1,000**	
Allowance for Uncollectible Accounts		**1,000**
(Reestablish portion of account previously written off)		
Cash	**1,000**	
Accounts Receivable		**1,000**
(Collect cash on account)		

Balance Sheet						Income Statement		
				Stockholders' Equity				
			Common	**Retained**				**Net**
Assets	**=**	**Liabilities** **+**	**Stock**	**+**	**Earnings**	**Revenues** **−**	**Expenses** **=**	**Income**
+1,000	=							
−1,000								
+1,000								
−1,000								
0								

The first entry simply reverses a portion of the previous entry that Kimzey made on February 23 to write off the account. The second entry records the collection of the account receivable. Notice that in both entries the debit entry increases total assets by the same amount that the credit entry decreases total assets. **Therefore, collecting cash on an account previously written off also has no effect on total assets and no effect on net income.**

Of course, the two entries above could have been recorded as a single entry by debiting Cash and crediting Allowance for Uncollectible Accounts. The debit to Accounts Receivable in the first entry and the credit to Accounts Receivable in the second entry exactly offset one another. Two entries are used here to help emphasize (1) the reversal of the prior write off and (2) the cash collection on account.

Continuing our example, suppose that by the end of 2019 total accounts written off by Kimzey equal $4 million. Because Kimzey allowed for bad debts by setting up the Allowance for Uncollectible Accounts for $5 million at the end of 2018, the write-offs in 2019 will have no effect on total assets or net income. But what about the remaining $1 million left in the balance of Allowance for Uncollectible Accounts? As we'll see next, the remaining balance of $1 million will affect our new adjustment in the following year.

KEY POINT

Writing off a customer's account as uncollectible reduces the balance of accounts receivable but also reduces the contra asset—allowance for uncollectible accounts. The net effect is that there is no change in the *net* receivable (accounts receivable less the allowance) or in total assets. We recorded the decrease to assets as a result of the bad debt when we established the allowance for uncollectible accounts in a prior year.

ESTIMATING UNCOLLECTIBLE ACCOUNTS IN THE FOLLOWING YEAR

At the end of 2019, Kimzey must once again estimate uncollectible accounts and make a year-end adjustment. Recall that Kimzey estimated bad debts in 2019 to be $5 million but only $4 million was actually written off. This means the balance of the allowance account at the end of 2019 prior to any year-end adjustment is $1 million.

Suppose that in 2019 Kimzey bills customers for services totaling $80 million, and $30 million are still receivable at the end of the year. Of the $30 million still receivable, let's say Kimzey again uses the aging method and estimates $8 million will not be collected. For what amount would Kimzey record the year-end adjusting entry for bad debts in 2019? Before answering, let's first examine the current balance of the allowance account, as shown in Illustration 5–8.

ILLUSTRATION 5–8

Balance of Kimzey's Allowance for Uncollectible Accounts

Allowance for Uncollectible Accounts
($ in millions)

Write-offs in 2019	4	5	Beginning balance for 2019
		1	Balance before adjustment
		?	Year-end adjustment
		8	Ending balance for 2019

Notice that the balance before the year-end adjustment in this example is a $1 million *credit*. **A *credit* balance before adjustment indicates that the estimate of uncollectible accounts at the beginning of the year (or end of last year) may have been too high.** However, it's possible that some of the estimated uncollectible accounts have not proven bad yet. **A *debit* balance before adjustment indicates that the estimate at the beginning of the year was too low.**

Based on all available information at the end of 2019, Kimzey estimates that the allowance for uncollectible accounts should be $8 million. This means the allowance account needs to increase from its current balance of $1 million credit to the estimated ending balance of $8 million credit. Kimzey can accomplish this by adjusting the account for $7 million as follows:

A = L + SE		December 31, 2019	Debit	Credit
	−7 Exp↑	**Bad Debt Expense**	7	
−7		**Allowance for Uncollectible Accounts**		7
		(Estimate future bad debts)		

In its 2019 income statement, Kimzey will report bad debt expense of $7 million along with other operating expenses of, say, $50 million. This is shown in Illustration 5–9.

In the 2019 balance sheet, Kimzey will report the allowance account at the best estimate of its appropriate balance, $8 million. This is shown in Illustration 5–10.

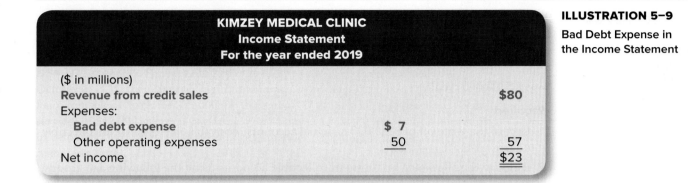

KIMZEY MEDICAL CLINIC
Income Statement
For the year ended 2019

($ in millions)		
Revenue from credit sales		$80
Expenses:		
Bad debt expense	$ 7	
Other operating expenses	50	57
Net income		$23

ILLUSTRATION 5–9
Bad Debt Expense in the Income Statement

KIMZEY MEDICAL CLINIC
Balance Sheet (partial)
December 31, 2019

Assets

Current assets ($ in millions):		
Accounts receivable	$30	
Less: Allowance for uncollectible accounts	(8)	
Net accounts receivable		$22

ILLUSTRATION 5–10
Accounts Receivable Portion of the Balance Sheet

The process of estimating an allowance for uncollectible accounts, writing off bad debts in the following period, and then reestimating the allowance at the end of the period is one that occurs throughout the company's life.

KEY POINT

The year-end adjustment for future uncollectible accounts is affected by the current balance of Allowance for Uncollectible Accounts before adjustment. The current balance before adjustment equals the estimate of uncollectible accounts at the beginning of the year (or end of last year) less actual write-offs in the current year.

Users of financial statements must realize that some of the amounts reported in financial statements are estimates, and estimating the future almost always results in some inaccuracy. Illustration 5–11 provides an excerpt from the annual report of **Tenet Healthcare Corporation**.

TENET HEALTHCARE CORPORATION
Notes to the Financial Statements (excerpt)

The preparation of financial statements, in conformity with accounting principles generally accepted in the United States of America, requires us to make estimates and assumptions that affect the amounts reported in the Consolidated Financial Statements and these accompanying notes. We regularly evaluate the accounting policies and estimates we use. In general, we base the estimates on historical experience and on assumptions that we believe to be reasonable given the particular circumstances in which we operate. Although we believe all adjustments considered necessary for fair presentation have been included, actual results may vary from those estimates.

ILLUSTRATION 5–11
Excerpt from Tenet Healthcare Corporation's Annual Report

Let's Review

mhhe.com/4fa20

Community Medical is an outpatient health facility that provides minor surgical and other health-related services to the local community. Many of the patients do not have medical insurance. These customers are required to pay for services within 30 days of receiving treatment. At the beginning of 2018, Community Medical's allowance for uncollectible accounts was a $100,000 credit.

Required:

1. Record the write-off of $120,000 of actual accounts receivable that became uncollectible during 2018.

2. Estimate the allowance for future uncollectible accounts using the following age groups, amount receivable, and estimated percent uncollectible at the end of 2018:

Age Group	Amount Receivable	Estimated Percent Uncollectible	Estimated Amount Uncollectible
Not yet due	$600,000	10%	
1–45 days past due	200,000	20%	
More than 45 days past due	50,000	60%	
Total	$850,000		

3. Use a T-account to determine the year-end adjustment to the allowance account.

4. Record the year-end adjustment for bad debt expense.

5. Prepare a partial balance sheet showing accounts receivable and the allowance for uncollectible accounts.

Solution:

1. Write-off of actual accounts receivable during 2018:

	Debit	Credit
Allowance for Uncollectible Accounts	120,000	
Accounts Receivable		120,000

2. Estimate of the allowance for future uncollectible accounts:

Age Group	Amount Receivable	Estimated Percent Uncollectible	Estimated Amount Uncollectible
Not yet due	$600,000	10%	$ 60,000
1–45 days past due	200,000	20%	40,000
More than 45 days past due	50,000	60%	30,000
Total	$850,000		$130,000

3. Year-end adjustment to the allowance account:

Allowance for Uncollectible Accounts

		100,000	Beginning balance
Write-offs	120,000		
Balance before adjustment	20,000		
		?	Year-end adjustment
		130,000	Estimated ending balance

4. Year-end adjustment for bad debt expense:

December 31, 2018	Debit	Credit
Bad Debt Expense	**150,000**	
Allowance for Uncollectible Accounts		**150,000***

*Notice from the T-account in *Requirement* 3 that the balance of the allowance account before adjustment is a $20,000 *debit*. Based on the estimated allowance of a $130,000 *credit*, we need a credit adjustment of $150,000. Of this adjustment, $20,000 is needed to get the allowance account to a zero balance, and the remaining $130,000 credit adjusts the account to the estimated ending balance.

COMMUNITY MEDICAL
Balance Sheet (partial)
December 31, 2018

Assets

Current assets:		
Accounts receivable	$850,000	
Less: Allowance for uncollectible accounts	(130,000)	
Net accounts receivable		$720,000

Suggested Homework:
BE5–9, BE5–10;
E5–10, E5–11;
P5–4A&B, P5–6A&B

Direct Write-Off Method

We've just seen how the *allowance method* for uncollectible accounts works. This is the method required for financial reporting by Generally Accepted Accounting Principles (GAAP). However, for tax reporting, companies use an alternative method commonly referred to as the *direct write-off method.* Under the the direct write-off method, we write off bad debts only at the time they actually become uncollectible, unlike the allowance method which requires estimation of uncollectible accounts before they even occur.

It is important to emphasize that the direct write-off method is not allowed for financial reporting under GAAP. It is only used in financial reporting if uncollectible accounts are not anticipated or are expected to be very small. **The direct write-off method is primarily used for tax reporting.** Companies do not report a tax deduction for bad debts until those bad debts are actually uncollectible.

To see how the direct write-off method works, suppose a company provides services on account for $100,000 in 2018, but makes no allowance for uncollectible accounts at the end of the year. Then, in the following year on September 17, 2019, an account of $2,000 becomes uncollectible. The company records the actual write-off as follows.

■ **LO5–6**
Contrast the allowance method and direct write-off method when accounting for uncollectible accounts.

September 17, 2019	Debit	Credit
Bad Debt Expense	**2,000**	
Accounts Receivable		**2,000**
(Write off uncollectible account directly)		

A	=	L	+	SE
				−2,000 Exp ↑
−2,000				

Notice that bad debt expense is recorded in the year of the write-off (2019) instead of the year of the service revenue (2018). Total assets are also reduced by crediting Accounts Receivable at the time of the actual write-off (2019). Compared to the allowance method, the direct write-off method causes assets to be overstated and operating expenses to be understated in 2018. **This is why the direct write-off method of accounting for uncollectible accounts is not permitted for financial reporting purposes except in limited circumstances.**

Illustration 5–12 highlights the timing difference between the allowance method and the direct write-off method for our example. For simplicity, assume that our *estimate* of uncollectible accounts of $2,000 at the end of 2018 turns out to be correct, and *actual* bad debts in 2019 are $2,000.

ILLUSTRATION 5–12   Comparing the Allowance Method and the Direct Write-off Method for Recording Uncollectible Accounts

2018	Allowance Method		Direct Write-off Method	
Year-end Adjustment (Estimate = $2,000)	**Bad Debt Expense** Allowance for Uncollectible Accounts	**2,000** 2,000	No adjustment	
2019				

Actual Write-offs (Actual = $2,000)	Allowance for Uncollectible Accounts
	    Accounts Receivable
		2,000
		2,000
			Bad Debt Expense
			    Accounts Receivable
				2,000
				2,000

Under the allowance method, future bad debts are *estimated* and recorded as an expense and a reduction in assets in 2018. Bad debt expense is recorded in the same period (2018) as the revenue it helps to create (also in 2018). Under the direct write-off method, though, we make no attempt to estimate future bad debts. We record bad debt expense in the period the account proves uncollectible. In this case, we report the bad debt expense and reduction in assets in 2019. The direct write-off method violates GAAP, since sales are recorded in one period (2018) and the related bad debt expense is recorded in the following period (2019).

 COMMON MISTAKE

Some students erroneously think firms should reduce total assets and record bad debt expense at the time the bad debt actually occurs. However, companies *anticipate* future bad debts and establish an allowance for those estimates.

Notice that, either way, the ultimate effect is a $2,000 debit to Bad Debt Expense and a $2,000 credit to Accounts Receivable. The balance of Allowance for Uncollectible Accounts cancels out; it initially increases with a credit for the estimate of bad debts and then decreases with a debit for actual bad debts. **The difference between the two methods is in the timing.**

 KEY POINT

The direct write-off method reduces accounts receivable and records bad debt expense at the time the account receivable proves uncollectible. If the credit sale occurs in a prior reporting period, bad debt expense is not properly matched with revenues (credit sales). Also, accounts receivable will be overstated in the prior period. The direct write-off method typically is not acceptable for financial reporting.

Decision Maker's Perspective

Managing Bad Debt Estimates

While the allowance method is conceptually superior to the direct write-off method and more accurately reports assets and matches revenues and expenses, it does have one disadvantage. This disadvantage arises from the fact that reported amounts under the allowance method represent management estimates. If so inclined, management could use these estimates to manipulate reported earnings. For example, if management wants to boost earnings in the current year, it can intentionally *underestimate* future uncollectible accounts. Similarly, if a company is having an especially good year and management wants to "reserve" earnings for the future, it can intentionally *overestimate* future uncollectible accounts. Having a large expense in the current year means there is less of a charge to bad debt expense in a future year, increasing future earnings. Other expenses, such as rent expense, are much more difficult to manipulate because their reported amounts don't rely on management estimates. These expenses are evidenced by past transactions, and their amounts are verifiable to the penny using a receipt or an invoice.

HealthSouth Corporation appears to have used estimates of uncollectible accounts to manipulate earnings. In the early 1990s, HealthSouth reported large amounts of bad debt expense, building large reserves in the allowance account. Then in the mid-1990s, as additional earnings were needed to meet analysts' expectations, HealthSouth was able to report low amounts for bad debt expense because of the previously inflated allowance account. In 1999, when it became apparent that HealthSouth's earnings were falling dramatically, the company took a "big bath" by reporting a very large charge to bad debt expense. Some companies feel that if they are going to have a bad year, they might as well release all the bad news at once. This makes it possible to report better news in future years.

ETHICAL DILEMMA

© Glow Images/Getty Images, RF

Philip Stanton, the executive manager of Thomson Pharmaceutical, receives a bonus if the company's net income in the current year exceeds net income in the past year. By the end of 2018, it appears that net income for 2018 will easily exceed net income for 2017. Philip has asked Mary Beth Williams, the company's controller, to try to reduce this year's income and "bank" some of the profits for future years. Mary Beth suggests that the company's bad debt expense as a percentage of accounts receivable for 2018 be increased from 10% to 15%. She believes 10% is the more accurate estimate but knows that both the corporation's internal and external auditors allow some flexibility in estimates. What is the effect of increasing the estimate of bad debts from 10% to 15% of accounts receivable? How does this "bank" income for future years? Why does Mary Beth's proposal present an ethical dilemma?

NOTES RECEIVABLE

Notes receivable are similar to accounts receivable but are more formal credit arrangements evidenced by a written debt instrument, or *note*. Notes receivable typically arise from loans to other entities (including affiliated companies); loans to stockholders and employees; and occasionally the sale of merchandise, other assets, or services.

Accounting for Notes Receivable

Like accounts receivable, notes receivable are assets and therefore have a normal debit balance. We classify notes receivable as either *current* or *noncurrent,* depending on the expected collection date. If the time to maturity is longer than one year, the note receivable is a long-term asset.

As an example, let's say that, on February 1, 2018, Kimzey Medical Clinic provides services of $10,000 to a patient, Justin Payne, who is not able to pay immediately. In place of payment, Justin offers Kimzey a six-month, 12% promissory note. Because of the large

PART C

■ **LO5–7**
Account for notes receivable and interest revenue.

amount of the receivable, Kimzey agrees to accept the promissory note as a way to increase the likelihood of eventually receiving payment. In addition, because of the delay in payment, Kimzey would like to charge interest on the outstanding balance. A formal promissory note provides an explicit statement of the interest charges. Illustration 5–13 shows an example of a typical note receivable.

ILLUSTRATION 5–13

Note Receivable

Face value ⟶ $ __10,000__   Date __February 1, 2018__

Due date ⟶ __Six months__   after date __I__   promise to pay to the
order of   __Kimzey Medical Clinic__

Payee ⟶   __Ten thousand and no/100__   dollars
                  for value received with interest at the rate of ⟶ __12%__ .

Interest rate ⟶   ⟶ *Justin Payne*
Maker ⟶

Kimzey records the note as follows.

A = L + SE

+10,000

+10,000 Rev ↑

February 1, 2018	Debit	Credit
Notes Receivable	**10,000**	
Service Revenue		**10,000**
(Accept a six-month, 12% note receivable for services provided)		

Another example of the use of notes receivable is to replace existing accounts receivable. For example, suppose that Justin received $10,000 of services on account, but Kimzey originally recorded the amount due as Accounts Receivable. Over time, it became apparent that Justin would not be able to pay quickly, so Kimzey required Justin to sign a six-month, 12% promissory note on February 1, 2018. When Justin signs the note, Kimzey records the following transaction to reclassify the existing account receivable as a note receivable.

A = L + SE

+10,000
−10,000

February 1, 2018	Debit	Credit
Notes Receivable	**10,000**	
Accounts Receivable		**10,000**
(Reclassify accounts receivable as notes receivable)		

Recognize that the transaction has no impact on the accounting equation; it is simply a matter of reclassifying assets. One asset (notes receivable) increases, while another asset (accounts receivable) decreases.

How would the patient, Justin Payne, record the previous transaction? By signing the note, Justin has an account payable that becomes reclassified as a note payable. He records the issuance of the note payable on February 1 as follows.

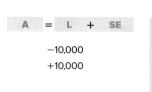

Flip Side

A = L + SE

−10,000
+10,000

February 1, 2018	Debit	Credit
Accounts Payable	**10,000**	
Notes Payable		**10,000**
(Reclassify accounts payable as notes payable)		

Flip Side

Just as one company's account payable is another company's account receivable, there is also a note payable for every note receivable. For every dollar a company earns in interest revenue, another company incurs a dollar of interest expense. We address notes payable in Chapter 8, but if you have a good understanding of notes receivable, then you have a head start with its flip side—notes payable.

KEY POINT

Notes receivable are similar to accounts receivable except that notes receivable are formal credit arrangements made with a written debt instrument, or *note*.

INTEREST CALCULATION

Many of the same issues we discussed concerning accounts receivable, such as allowing for uncollectible accounts, apply also to notes receivable. The one issue that usually applies to notes receivable but not to accounts receivable is interest. You're probably familiar with the concept of interest. You may be earning interest on money in a savings account or checking account, and you might be paying interest on student loans, a car loan, or a credit card.

In the previous example, Kimzey accepted a six-month, 12% promissory note. The "12%" indicates the *annual* interest rate charged by the payee. The terms of the six-month note mean that Kimzey will charge Justin Payne one-half year of interest, or 6%, on the face value. Interest on Kimzey's note receivable is calculated as follows.

		Face		Annual		Fraction
Interest	=	value	×	interest rate	×	of the year
$600	=	$10,000	×	12%	×	6/12

Interest calculation

KEY POINT

We calculate interest as the face value of the note multiplied by the stated annual interest rate multiplied by the appropriate fraction of the year that the note is outstanding.

COLLECTION OF NOTES RECEIVABLE

We record the collection of notes receivable the same way as collection of accounts receivable, except that we also record interest earned as interest revenue in the income statement.

Continuing the previous example, suppose that on August 1, 2018, the maturity date, Justin repays the note and interest in full as promised. Kimzey will record the following.

August 1, 2018	Debit	Credit	A = L + SE
Cash	10,600		+10,600
Notes Receivable		10,000	−10,000
Interest Revenue		600	+600 Rev ↑
(Collect note receivable and interest)			
(Interest revenue = $10,000 × 12% × 6/12)			

Over the six-month period, Kimzey earns interest revenue of $600. The credit to Notes Receivable reduces the balance in that account to $0, which is the amount Justin owes after payment to Kimzey.

ACCRUED INTEREST

It frequently happens that a note is issued in one year and the maturity date occurs in the following year. For example, what if Justin Payne issued the previous six-month note to Kimzey on November 1, 2018, instead of February 1, 2018? In that case, the $10,000 face value (principal) and $600 interest on the six-month note are not due until May 1, 2019. The length of the note (six months) and interest rate (12%) remain the same, and so the total interest of $600 charged to Justin remains the same. However, Kimzey will earn interest revenue in two separate accounting periods (assuming Kimzey uses a calendar year): for two months of the six-month note in 2018 (November and December), and for four months in the next year (January through April). Illustration 5–14 demonstrates the calculation of interest revenue over time. Interest receivable from Kimzey's six-month, $10,000, 12% note is $100 per month (= $10,000 × 12% × 1/12).

ILLUSTRATION 5–14

Calculating Interest Revenue over Time for Kimzey Medical Clinic

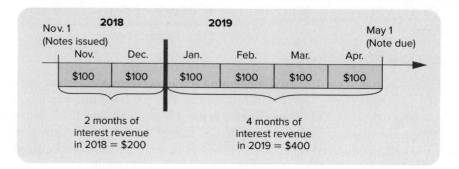

Because Kimzey earns two months of interest in 2018, it must accrue that interest as revenue on December 31, 2018 (even though no cash has been collected). The adjustment to accrue interest revenue follows.

A = L + SE	December 31, 2018	Debit	Credit
+200	**Interest Receivable**	200	
+200 Rev ↑	**Interest Revenue**		200
	(Accrue interest revenue)		
	(Interest revenue = $10,000 × 12% × 2/12)		

On May 1, 2019, the maturity date, Kimzey records the collection of the note receivable of $10,000 and interest of $600. Notice that the cash collected for interest includes $200 receivable from 2018, as well as $400 of additional interest revenue related to four months in 2019.

A = L + SE	May 1, 2019	Debit	Credit
+10,600	**Cash**	10,600	
−10,000	**Notes Receivable**		10,000
−200	**Interest Receivable** (from 2018)...........................		200
+400 Rev ↑	**Interest Revenue** (from 2019)............................		400
	(Collect note receivable and interest)		
	(Interest revenue = $10,000 × 12% × 4/12)		

The entry on May 1, 2019, eliminates the balances of the note receivable and interest receivable recorded in 2018.

 KEY POINT

We record interest earned on notes receivable but not yet collected by the end of the year as interest receivable and interest revenue.

Let's Review

mhhe.com/4fa21

General Hospital has a policy of lending any employee up to $3,000 for a period of 12 months at a fixed interest rate of 9%. Chevy Chase has worked for General Hospital for more than 10 years and wishes to take his family on a summer vacation. On May 1, 2018, he borrows $3,000 from General Hospital to be repaid in 12 months.

Required:

1. Record the loan of cash and acceptance of the note receivable by General Hospital.
2. Record General Hospital's year-end adjustment to accrue interest revenue.
3. Record the collection of the note with interest from Chevy Chase on May 1, 2019.

Solution:

1. Acceptance of the note receivable:

May 1, 2018	Debit	Credit
Notes Receivable	**3,000**	
Cash		**3,000**
(Accept note receivable)		

2. Year-end adjustment to accrue interest revenue:

December 31, 2018	Debit	Credit
Interest Receivable	**180**	
Interest Revenue (8 months' interest)		**180**
(Accrue interest revenue)		
(Interest revenue = $3,000 × 9% × 8/12)		

3. Collection of the note with interest:

May 1, 2019	Debit	Credit
Cash	**3,270**	
Notes Receivable		**3,000**
Interest Receivable		**180**
Interest Revenue (4 months' interest)		**90**
(Collect note receivable and interest)		
(Interest revenue = $3,000 × 9% × 4/12)		

Suggested Homework:
BE5–13, BE5–14;
E5–15, E5–17;
P5–8A&B

RECEIVABLES ANALYSIS
Tenet vs. LifePoint

ANALYSIS

The amount of a company's accounts receivable is influenced by a variety of factors, including the level of sales, the nature of the product or service sold, and credit and collection policies. These factors are, of course, related. For example, a change in credit policies could affect sales. More liberal credit policies—allowing customers a longer time to pay or offering cash discounts for early payment—often are initiated with the specific objective of increasing sales volume.

    Management's choice of credit and collection policies results in trade-offs. For example, when a company attempts to boost sales by allowing customers more time to pay, that policy also creates an increase in the required investment in receivables and may increase bad debts because older accounts are less likely to be collected. Offering discounts for early payment may increase sales volume, accelerate customer payment, and reduce bad debts, but at the same time it reduces the amount of cash collected from customers who take advantage of the discounts.

    Investors, creditors, and financial analysts can gain important insights by monitoring a company's investment in receivables. Two important ratios that help in understanding the company's effectiveness in managing receivables are the *receivables turnover ratio* and the *average collection period*. We discuss those measures and then compare them for **Tenet Healthcare Corporation** and **LifePoint Hospitals**.

RECEIVABLES TURNOVER RATIO

The receivables turnover ratio shows the *number of times* during a year that the average accounts receivable balance is collected (or "turns over"). We calculate it as follows:

■ **LO5–8**
Calculate key ratios investors use to monitor a company's effectiveness in managing receivables.

$$\text{Receivables turnover ratio} = \frac{\text{Net credit sales}}{\text{Average accounts receivable}}$$

Companies that make large amounts of credit sales often employ credit analysts. These analysts are responsible for deciding whether to extend credit to potential customers. To make this decision, credit analysts focus on the customer's credit history (such as delinquency in paying bills) and information about current financial position, generally found using amounts in the financial statements. When the credit risk is too high, the analyst will advise management to reject the customer's request for goods and services, or perhaps limit the amount of credit extended. Management must then face a difficult trade-off: the potential gains from additional customer revenues versus the risk of an eventual uncollectible account. Credit analysts are most commonly employed by financial institutions ranging from banks to credit rating agencies and investment companies.

© Brand X/JupiterImages/Getty Images, RF

The "net" in net credit sales refers to total credit sales net of discounts, returns, and allowances (similar to net revenues calculated earlier in the chapter). The amount for net credit sales is obtained from the current period's income statement; average accounts receivable equals the average of accounts receivable reported in this period's and last period's balance sheets. Last period's ending accounts receivable are this period's beginning accounts receivable. The more frequently a business is able to "turn over" its average accounts receivable, the more quickly it is receiving cash from its customers.

AVERAGE COLLECTION PERIOD

The average collection period is another way to express the same efficiency measure. This ratio shows the approximate *number of days* the average accounts receivable balance is outstanding. It is calculated as 365 days divided by the receivables turnover ratio.

$$\text{Average collection period} = \frac{365 \text{ days}}{\text{Receivables turnover ratio}}$$

Companies typically strive for a high receivables turnover ratio and a correspondingly low average collection period. As a company's sales increase, receivables also likely will increase. If the percentage increase in receivables is greater than the percentage increase in sales, the receivables turnover ratio will decline (and the average collection period will increase). This could indicate that customers are dissatisfied with the product or that the company's payment terms for attracting new customers are too generous, which, in turn, could increase sales returns and bad debts.

Of course, what's "high" and what's "low" for these ratios depends on the situation. Companies may wish to evaluate these ratios relative to the prior year's ratios, ratios of other firms in the same industry, or specific targets set by management.

As a practical matter, companies often do not separately report net credit sales versus net cash sales. They report only net sales as a total. Because of this, the receivables turnover ratio is most commonly calculated as net sales divided by average accounts receivable. This ratio can be interpreted as how well management collects cash from all sales to customers.

Let's compare **Tenet Healthcare Corporation** to **LifePoint Hospitals**. Below are relevant amounts for each company in 2014, along with their net income.

($ in millions)	Net Sales	Beginning Accounts Receivable	Ending Accounts Receivable	Bad Debt Expense
Tenet Healthcare	$17,920	$2,479	$3,256	$1,305
LifePoint Hospitals	5,301	1,337	1,462	818

To compute the receivables turnover ratio, we need the average accounts receivable, which is the beginning amount plus the ending amount, divided by 2.

Tenet Healthcare Average accounts receivable
= ($2,479 + $3,256) ÷ 2 = $2,867.5

LifePoint Hospitals Average accounts receivable
= ($1,337 + $1,462) ÷ 2 = $1,399.5

As shown in Illustration 5–15, we can divide net sales by average accounts receivable to compute the receivables turnover ratio. Then, we divide 365 days by the receivables turnover ratio to compute the average collection period.

	Receivables Turnover Ratio	Average Collection Period
Tenet Healthcare	$17,920 ÷ $2,867.5 = 6.2 times	365 ÷ 6.2 = 58.9 days
LifePoint Hospitals	$5,301 ÷ $1,399.5 = 3.8 times	365 ÷ 3.8 = 96.1 days

ILLUSTRATION 5–15

Comparison of Receivables Ratios between Tenet Healthcare Corporation and LifePoint Hospitals

From Illustration 5–15, we see that Tenet has a higher receivables turnover and a shorter collection period, indicating that the company more efficiently collects cash from patients than does LifePoint. The difference can be seen in the ratio of bad debt expense to net sales. For Tenet, bad debt expense represents a 7.3% reduction in net sales (= $1,305 ÷ $17,920). This same ratio for LifePoint is 15.4% (= $818 ÷ $5,301). Thus, LifePoint's less efficient cash collection causes a larger reduction in profitability.

Having enough cash is important to running any business. The more quickly a company can collect its receivables, the more quickly it can use that cash to generate even more cash by reinvesting in the business and generating additional sales.

 KEY POINT

The receivables turnover ratio and average collection period can provide an indication of management's ability to collect cash from customers in a timely manner.

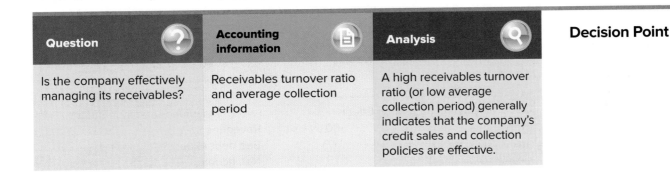

Decision Point

Question	Accounting information	Analysis
Is the company effectively managing its receivables?	Receivables turnover ratio and average collection period	A high receivables turnover ratio (or low average collection period) generally indicates that the company's credit sales and collection policies are effective.

PERCENTAGE-OF-CREDIT-SALES METHOD

APPENDIX

In the chapter, we estimated uncollectible accounts based on a percentage of accounts receivable at the end of the period. You learned that this method is the *percentage-of-receivables method* or the *balance sheet method,* because we base the estimate of bad debts on a balance sheet amount—accounts receivable. The estimated percentage could be a single percentage applied to the entire balance of accounts receivable, or it could vary based on the age of individual accounts receivable (the aging method).

As an alternative, we can estimate uncollectible accounts based on the percentage of credit sales for the year, aptly referred to as the *percentage-of-credit-sales method* or the *income statement method,* because we base the estimate of bad debts on an income statement amount—credit sales. In this appendix, we consider the percentage-of-credit-sales method.

Let's rework the example in the chapter for Kimzey Medical Clinic (see Illustrations 5–8 to Illustrations 5–10 and their discussion). During 2019, Kimzey bills customers $80 million for services, with $30 million in accounts receivable remaining at the end of the year. The balance of the allowance account, before adjustment, is a $1 million credit. For the percentage-of-receivables method, we'll use the estimate for uncollectible accounts used in

■ **LO5–9**

Estimate uncollectible accounts using the percentage-of-credit-sales method.

the chapter—$8 million based on the age of accounts receivable. For the percentage-of-credit-sales method, let's assume Kimzey expects 12.5% of credit sales to be uncollectible. Kimzey bases the 12.5% estimate on a number of factors, including current economic conditions and the average percentage of uncollectibles in the previous year, its first year of operations.

Illustration 5–16 demonstrates the differences in the two methods when adjusting for estimates of uncollectible accounts. **Notice that the two methods for estimating uncollectible accounts result in different adjustments.**

ILLUSTRATION 5–16

Adjusting for Estimates of Uncollectible Accounts

Percentage-of-Receivables Method (repeated from chapter)		Percentage-of-Credit Sales Method	
Estimate of Uncollectible Accounts		**Estimate of Uncollectible Accounts**	
• Varying percentage based on age of accounts receivable.		• 12.5% of credit sales in the current year will not be collected.	
• Allowance = $8 million.		• 12.5% of $80 million = $10 million.	
• Adjust from $1 million existing balance of allowance account.		• Ignore $1 million existing balance of allowance account.	
Adjustment ($ in millions)		**Adjustment ($ in millions)**	
Bad Debt Expense	7	Bad Debt Expense	10
Allowance for Uncoll. Accts.	7	Allowance for Uncoll. Accts.	10

Because the amounts of the adjustments differ, the effects on the financial statements differ. Recall that the balance of the allowance account before adjustment is a $1 million credit. After adjustment, the balance of the allowance account will differ between the two methods, as will the amount of bad debt expense. Illustration 5–17 summarizes the differences in financial statement effects.

ILLUSTRATION 5–17

Financial Statement Effects of Estimating Uncollectible Accounts

Percentage-of-Receivables Method ($ in millions)		Percentage-of-Credit-Sales Method ($ in millions)	
Income Statement Effect		**Income Statement Effect**	
Revenues	$80	Revenues	$80
Bad debt expense	(7)	Bad debt expense	(10)
Net income	$73	Net income	$70
Balance Sheet Effect		**Balance Sheet Effect**	
Accounts receivable	$30	Accounts receivable	$30
Less: Allowance	(8)*	Less: Allowance	(11)*
Net accounts receivable	$22	Net accounts receivable	$19
*$8 = $1 + $7 (adjustment)		*$11 = $1 + $10 (adjustment)	

From an income statement perspective, some argue that the percentage-of-credit-sales method provides a better method for estimating bad debts because expenses (bad debts) are better matched with revenues (credit sales). A better matching of expenses and revenues results in a more accurate measure of net income for the period. From a balance sheet perspective, though, the percentage-of-receivables method is preferable because assets (net accounts receivable) are reported closer to their net realizable value.

The current emphasis on better measurement of assets (balance sheet focus) outweighs the emphasis on better measurement of net income (income statement focus). **This is why the percentage-of-receivables method (balance sheet method) is the preferable method, while the percentage-of-credit-sales method (income statement method) is allowed only if amounts do not differ significantly from estimates using the percentage-of-receivables method.**

KEY POINT

When applying the percentage-of-credit-sales method, we adjust the allowance for uncollectible accounts for the current year's credit sales that we don't expect to collect (rather than adjusting at the end of the year for the percentage of accounts receivable we don't expect to collect).

KEY POINTS BY LEARNING OBJECTIVE

LO5–1   Recognize accounts receivable.

Companies record an asset (accounts receivable) and revenue when they sell products and services to their customers on account, expecting payment in the future.

LO5–2   Calculate net revenues using discounts, returns, and allowances.

Sales discounts, returns, and allowances are contra revenue accounts. We subtract the balances in these accounts from total revenues when calculating net revenues.

LO5–3   Record an allowance for future uncollectible accounts.

We recognize accounts receivable as assets in the balance sheet and record them at their *net realizable values,* that is, the amount of cash we expect to collect.

Under the allowance method, companies are required to estimate *future* uncollectible accounts and record those estimates in the *current* year. Estimated uncollectible accounts reduce assets and increase expenses.

Adjusting for estimates of future uncollectible accounts matches expenses (bad debts) in the same period as the revenues (credit sales) they help to generate.

Recording an allowance for uncollectible accounts correctly reports accounts receivable at their net realizable value.

LO5–4   Use the aging method to estimate future uncollectible accounts.

Using the aging method to estimate uncollectible accounts is more accurate than applying a single percentage to all accounts receivable. The aging method recognizes that the longer accounts are past due, the less likely they are to be collected.

LO5–5   Apply the procedure to write off accounts receivable as uncollectible.

Writing off a customer's account as uncollectible reduces the balance of accounts receivable but also reduces the contra asset—allowance for uncollectible accounts. The net effect is that there is no change in the *net* receivable (accounts receivable less the allowance) or in total assets. We recorded the decrease to assets as a result of the bad debt when we established the allowance for uncollectible accounts in a prior year.

The year-end adjustment for future uncollectible accounts is affected by the current balance of Allowance for Uncollectible Accounts before adjustment. The current balance before adjustment equals the estimate of uncollectible accounts at the beginning of the year (or end of last year) less actual write-offs in the current year.

LO5–6   Contrast the allowance method and direct write-off method when accounting for uncollectible accounts.

The direct write-off method reduces accounts receivable and records bad debt expense at the time the account receivable proves uncollectible. If the credit sale occurs in a prior reporting period, bad debt expense is not properly matched with revenues (credit sales). Also, accounts receivable will be overstated in the prior period. The direct write-off method typically is not acceptable for financial reporting.

LO5–7   Account for notes receivable and interest revenue.

Notes receivable are similar to accounts receivable except that notes receivable are formal credit arrangements made with a written debt instrument, or *note.*

We calculate interest as the face value of the note multiplied by the stated annual interest rate multiplied by the appropriate fraction of the year that the note is outstanding.

We record interest earned on notes receivable but not yet collected by the end of the year as interest receivable and interest revenue.

LO5–8   Calculate key ratios investors use to monitor a company's effectiveness in managing receivables.

The receivables turnover ratio and average collection period can provide an indication of management's ability to collect cash from customers in a timely manner.

Appendix

LO5–9   Estimate uncollectible accounts using the percentage-of-credit-sales method.

When applying the percentage-of-credit-sales method, we adjust the allowance for uncollectible accounts for the current year's credit sales that we don't expect to collect (rather than adjusting at the end of the year for the percentage of accounts receivable we don't expect to collect).

GLOSSARY

Accounts receivable: The amount of cash owed to the company by its customers from the sale of products or services on account. **p. 216**

Aging method: Basing the estimate of future bad debts on the various ages of individual accounts receivable, using a higher percentage for "old" accounts than for "new" accounts. **p. 226**

Allowance for uncollectible accounts: Contra asset account representing the amount of accounts receivable that we do not expect to collect. **p. 225**

Allowance method: Recording an adjustment at the end of each period to allow for the possibility of future uncollectible accounts. The adjustment has the effects of reducing assets and increasing expenses. **p. 223**

Average collection period: Approximate number of days the average accounts receivable balance is outstanding. It equals 365 divided by the receivables turnover ratio. **p. 240**

Bad debt expense: The amount of the adjustment to the allowance for uncollectible accounts, representing the cost of estimated future bad debts charged to the current period. **p. 224**

Contra revenue account: An account with a balance that is opposite, or "contra," to that of its related revenue account. **p. 218**

Credit sales: Transfer of products and services to a customer today while bearing the risk of collecting payment from that customer in the future. Also known as *sales on account* or *services on account.* **p. 216**

Direct write-off method: Recording bad debt expense at the time we know the account is actually uncollectible. **p. 233**

Net accounts receivable: The difference between total accounts receivable and the allowance for uncollectible accounts. **p. 225**

Net realizable value: The amount of cash the firm expects to collect. **p. 223**

Net revenues: A company's total revenues less any discounts, returns, and allowances. **p. 217**

Notes receivable: Formal credit arrangements evidenced by a written debt instrument, or *note.* **p. 235**

Percentage-of-receivables method: Method of estimating uncollectible accounts based on the percentage of accounts receivable expected not to be collected. **p. 224**

Receivables turnover ratio: Number of times during a year that the average accounts receivable balance is collected (or "turns over"). It equals net credit sales divided by average accounts receivable. **p. 239**

Sales allowance: Seller reduces the customer's balance owed or provides at least a partial refund because of some deficiency in the company's product or service. **p. 218**

Sales discount: Reduction in the amount to be paid by a credit customer if payment on account is made within a specified period of time. **p. 219**

Sales return: Customer returns a product. **p. 218**

Trade discount: Reduction in the listed price of a product or service. **p. 217**

Uncollectible accounts: Customers' accounts that no longer are considered collectible. **p. 223**

SELF-STUDY QUESTIONS

1. Accounts receivable are best described as: **(LO5–1)**
   a. Liabilities of the company that represent the amount owed to suppliers.
   b. Amounts that have previously been received from customers.
   c. Assets of the company representing the amount owed by customers.
   d. Amounts that have previously been paid to suppliers.

2. On March 17, Fox Lumber sells materials to Whitney Construction for $12,000, terms 2/10, n/30. Whitney pays for the materials on March 23. What amount would Fox record as revenue on March 17? **(LO5–2)**
   a. $12,400.
   b. $11,760.
   c. $12,000.
   d. $12,240.

3. Refer to the information in the previous question. What is the amount of net revenues (sales minus sales discounts) as of March 23? **(LO5–2)**
   a. $0.
   b. $11,760.
   c. $12,000.
   d. $12,240.

4. Suppose the balance of Allowance for Uncollectible Accounts at the end of the current year is $400 (*credit*) before any adjustment. The company estimates future uncollectible accounts to be $3,200. At what amount would bad debt expense be reported in the current year's income statement? **(LO5–3)**
   a. $400.
   b. $2,800.
   c. $3,200.
   d. $3,600.

5. Suppose the balance of Allowance for Uncollectible Accounts at the end of the current year is $400 (*debit*) before any adjustment. The company estimates future uncollectible accounts to be $3,200. At what amount would bad debt expense be reported in the current year's income statement? **(LO5–3)**
   a. $400.
   b. $2,800.
   c. $3,200.
   d. $3,600.

6. Kidz Incorporated reports the following aging schedule of its accounts receivable with the estimated percent uncollectible. What is the total estimate of uncollectible accounts using the aging method? **(LO5–4)**

Age Group	Amount Receivable	Estimated Percent Uncollectible
0–60 days	$20,000	2%
61–90 days	6,000	15%
More than 90 days past due	2,000	50%
Total	$28,000	

   a. $1,150.
   b. $1,900.
   c. $2,300.
   d. $5,900.

7. Using the allowance method, the entry to record a write-off of accounts receivable will include: **(LO5–5)**
   a. A debit to Bad Debt Expense.
   b. A debit to Allowance for Uncollectible Accounts.
   c. No entry because an allowance for uncollectible accounts was established in an earlier period.
   d. A debit to Service Revenue.

8. The direct write-off method is generally not permitted for financial reporting purposes because: **(LO5–6)**
   a. Compared to the allowance method, it would allow greater flexibility to managers in manipulating reported net income.
   b. This method is primarily used for tax purposes.
   c. It is too difficult to accurately estimate future bad debts.
   d. Expenses (bad debts) are not properly matched with the revenues (credit sales) they help to generate.

9. On January 1, 2018, Roberson Supply borrows $10,000 from Nees Manufacturing by signing a 9% note due in eight months. Calculate the amount of interest revenue Nees will record on September 1, 2018, the date that the note is due. **(LO5–7)**
   a. $300.
   b. $600.
   c. $900.
   d. $1,000.

10. At the beginning of 2018, Clay Ventures has total accounts receivable of $100,000. By the end of 2018, Clay reports net credit sales of $900,000 and total accounts receivable of $200,000. What is the receivables turnover ratio for Clay Ventures? **(LO5–8)**
   a. 2.0.
   b. 4.5.
   c. 6.0.
   d. 9.0.

Note: For answers, see the last page of the chapter.

For additional study materials, including 10 more Self-Study Questions, visit the Connect Library.

REVIEW QUESTIONS

1. When recording a credit sale, what account do we debit? Describe where this account is reported in the financial statements.   ■ **LO5–1**

2. What is the difference between a trade receivable and a nontrade receivable?   ■ **LO5–1**

3. Explain the difference between a trade discount and a sales discount. Where are sales discounts reported in the income statement?   ■ **LO5–2**

4. Briefly explain the accounting treatment for sales returns and allowances. Where are these accounts reported in the income statement?   ■ **LO5–2**

5. Revenue can be earned at one point or over a period. Provide an example of each.   ■ **LO5–2**

6. Explain the correct way companies should account for uncollectible accounts receivable (bad debts).   ■ **LO5–3**

7. What two purposes do firms achieve by estimating future uncollectible accounts?   ■ **LO5–3**

8. How does accounting for uncollectible accounts conform to the concept of the matching principle?   ■ **LO5–3**

■ **LO5–3**   9. What are the financial statement effects of establishing an allowance for uncollectible accounts?

■ **LO5–3**   10. Describe the year-end adjustment to record the allowance for uncollectible accounts.

■ **LO5–3**   11. Allowance for Uncollectible Accounts is a contra asset account, which means that its normal balance is a credit. However, it is possible for the account to have a debit balance before year-end adjustments are recorded. Explain how this could happen.

■ **LO5–3**   12. We report accounts receivable in the balance sheet at their *net realizable value.* Explain what this term means.

■ **LO5–4**   13. What does the *age* of accounts receivable refer to? How can we use an aging method to estimate uncollectible accounts receivable?

■ **LO5–5**   14. When we have established an allowance for uncollectible accounts, how do we write off an account receivable as uncollectible? What effect does this write-off have on the reported amount of total assets and net income at the time of the write-off?

■ **LO5–5**   15. If at the end of the year Allowance for Uncollectible Accounts has a credit balance before any adjustment, what might that tell us about last year's estimate of future uncollectible accounts?

■ **LO5–6**   16. Discuss the differences between the allowance method and the direct write-off method for recording uncollectible accounts. Which of the two is acceptable under financial accounting rules?

■ **LO5–7**   17. Notes receivable differ from accounts receivable in that notes receivable represent *written* debt instruments. What is one other common difference between notes receivable and accounts receivable?

■ **LO5–7**   18. With respect to notes receivable, explain what each of these represent: (a) face value, (b) annual interest rate, and (c) fraction of the year.

■ **LO5–7**   19. What will be the total interest earned on a 6%, $2,000 note receivable that is due in nine months?

■ **LO5–7**   20. Interest on a note receivable typically is due along with the face value at the note's maturity date. If the end of the accounting period occurs before the maturity date, how do we record interest earned but not yet collected?

■ **LO5–8**   21. How is the receivables turnover ratio measured? What does this ratio indicate? Is a higher or lower receivables turnover preferable?

■ **LO5–8**   22. How is the average collection period of receivables measured? What does this ratio indicate? Is a higher or lower average collection period preferable?

■ **LO5–8**   23. How can effectively managing receivables benefit a company?

■ **LO5–9**   24. Which method, the percentage-of-receivables method or the percentage-of-credit-sales method, is typically used in practice? Why?

■ **LO5–9**   25. Explain why the percentage-of-receivables method is referred to as the *balance sheet method* and the percentage-of-credit-sales method is referred to as the *income statement method.*

BRIEF EXERCISES   McGraw Hill Education **connect**

Record accounts receivable and trade discount (LO5–2)

BE5–1 The Giles Agency offers a 12% trade discount when providing advertising services of $1,000 or more to its customers. Audrey's Antiques decides to purchase advertising services of $3,500 (not including the trade discount), while Michael's Motors purchases only $700 of advertising. Both services are provided on account. Record both transactions for The Giles Agency, accounting for any trade discounts.

Calculate net sales (LO5–2)

BE5–2 Kelly's Jewelry has the following transactions during the year: total jewelry sales = $750,000; sales discounts = $20,000; sales returns = $50,000; sales allowances = $30,000. In addition, at the end of the year the company estimates the following transactions associated with jewelry sales in the current year will occur next year: sales discounts = $2,000; sales returns = $6,000; sales allowances = $4,000. Compute net sales.

BE5–3 At the end of the first year of operations, Mayberry Advertising had accounts receivable of $20,000. Management of the company estimates that 10% of the accounts will not be collected. What adjustment would Mayberry Advertising record for Allowance for Uncollectible Accounts?

Record the adjustment for uncollectible accounts (LO5–3)

BE5–4 At the end of the year, Mercy Cosmetics' balance of Allowance for Uncollectible Accounts is $600 (*credit*) before adjustment. The balance of Accounts Receivable is $25,000. The company estimates that 12% of accounts will not be collected over the next year. What adjustment would Mercy Cosmetics record for Allowance for Uncollectible Accounts?

Record the adjustment for uncollectible accounts (LO5–3)

BE5–5 Refer to the information in BE5–4, but now assume that the balance of Allowance for Uncollectible Accounts before adjustment is $600 (*debit*). The company still estimates future uncollectible accounts to be 12% of Accounts Receivable. What is the adjustment Mercy Cosmetics would record for Allowance for Uncollectible Accounts? Does the amount of the adjustment differ from BE5–4? If so, why?

Record the adjustment for uncollectible accounts (LO5–3)

BE5–6 At the end of the year, Dahir Incorporated's balance of Allowance for Uncollectible Accounts is $3,000 (*credit*) before adjustment. The company estimates future uncollectible accounts to be $15,000. What adjustment would Dahir record for Allowance for Uncollectible Accounts?

Record the adjustment for uncollectible accounts (LO5–3)

BE5–7 Refer to the information in BE5–6, but now assume that the balance of Allowance for Uncollectible Accounts before adjustment is $3,000 (*debit*). The company still estimates future uncollectible accounts to be $15,000. What is the adjustment Dahir would record for Allowance for Uncollectible Accounts? Does the amount of the adjustment differ from BE5–6? If so, why?

Record the adjustment for uncollectible accounts (LO5–3)

BE5–8 Williamson Distributors separates its accounts receivable into three age groups for purposes of estimating the percentage of uncollectible accounts.

Calculate uncollectible accounts using the aging method (LO5–4)

1. Accounts not yet due = $40,000; estimated uncollectible = 5%.
2. Accounts 1–30 days past due = $11,000; estimated uncollectible = 20%.
3. Accounts more than 30 days past due = $5,000; estimated uncollectible = 30%.

Compute the total estimated uncollectible accounts.

BE5–9 Trump Agency separates its accounts receivable into three age groups for purposes of estimating the percentage of uncollectible accounts.

Calculate uncollectible accounts using the aging method (LO5–4)

1. Accounts not yet due = $25,000; estimated uncollectible = 4%.
2. Accounts 1–60 days past due = $10,000; estimated uncollectible = 25%.
3. Accounts more than 60 days past due = $5,000; estimated uncollectible = 50%.

In addition, the balance of Allowance for Uncollectible Accounts before adjustment is $1,000 (*credit*). Compute the total estimated uncollectible accounts and record the year-end adjustment.

BE5–10 At the beginning of the year, Mitchum Enterprises allows for estimated uncollectible accounts of $15,000. By the end of the year, actual bad debts total $17,000. Record the write-off to uncollectible accounts. Following the write-off, what is the balance of Allowance for Uncollectible Accounts?

Record the write-off of uncollectible accounts (LO5–5)

BE5–11 Barnes Books allows for possible bad debts. On May 7, Barnes writes off a customer account of $7,000. On September 9, the customer unexpectedly pays the $7,000 balance. Record the cash collection on September 9.

Record collection of account previously written off (LO5–5)

BE5–12 At the end of 2018, Worthy Co.'s balance for Accounts Receivable is $20,000, while the company's total assets equal $1,500,000. In addition, the company expects to collect all of its receivables in 2019. In 2019, however, one customer owing $2,000 becomes a bad debt on March 14. Record the write off of this customer's account in 2019 using the direct write-off method.

Use the direct write-off method to account for uncollectible accounts (LO5–6)

Use the direct write-off method to account for uncollectible accounts (LO5–6)

BE5–13 Sanders Inc. is a small brick manufacturer that uses the direct write-off method to account for uncollectible accounts. At the end of 2018, its balance for Accounts Receivable is $35,000. The company estimates that of this amount, $4,000 is not likely to be collected in 2019. In 2019, the actual amount of bad debts is $3,000. Record, if necessary, an adjustment for estimated uncollectible accounts at the end of 2018 and the actual bad debts in 2019.

Use the direct write-off method to account for uncollectible accounts (LO5–6)

BE5–14 Brady is hired in 2018 to be the accountant for Anderson Manufacturing, a private company. At the end of 2018, the balance of Accounts Receivable is $29,000. In the past, Anderson has used only the direct write-off method to account for bad debts. Based on a detailed analysis of amounts owed, Brady believes the best estimate of future bad debts is $9,000. If Anderson continues to use the direct write-off method to account for uncollectible accounts, what adjustment, if any, would Brady record at the end of 2018? What adjustment, if any, would Brady record if Anderson instead uses the allowance method to account for uncollectible accounts?

Calculate amounts related to interest (LO5–7)

BE5–15 Calculate the missing amount for each of the following notes receivable.

Face Value	Annual Interest Rate	Fraction of the Year	Interest
$11,000	6%	4 months	(a)
$30,000	5%	(b)	$1,500
$35,000	(c)	6 months	$1,225
(d)	8%	6 months	$ 700

Calculate interest revenue on notes receivable (LO5–7)

BE5–16 On October 1, 2018, Oberley Corporation loans one of its employees $40,000 and accepts a 12-month, 9% note receivable. Calculate the amount of interest revenue Oberley will recognize in 2018 and 2019.

Use the percentage-of-credit-sales method to adjust for uncollectible accounts (LO5–9)

BE5–17 At the end of the year, Brinkley Incorporated's balance of Allowance for Uncollectible Accounts is $4,000 (*credit*) before adjustment. The company estimates future uncollectible accounts to be 3% of credit sales for the year. Credit sales for the year total $135,000. What is the adjustment Brinkley would record for Allowance for Uncollectible Accounts using the percentage-of-credit-sales method?

Use the percentage-of-credit-sales method to adjust for uncollectible accounts (LO5–9)

BE5–18 Refer to the information in BE5–17, but now assume that the balance of Allowance for Uncollectible Accounts before adjustment is $4,000 (*debit*). The company still estimates future uncollectible accounts to be 3% of credit sales for the year. What adjustment would Brinkley record for Allowance for Uncollectible Accounts using the percentage-of-credit-sales method?

Define terms related to receivables (LO5–1, 5–2, 5–3, 5–4, 5–5, 5–6, 5–7)

BE5–19 Match each of the following terms with its definition.

Terms	Definitions
_____ 1. Accounts receivable	a. Reductions in amount owed by customers because of deficiency in products or services.
_____ 2. Credit sales	
_____ 3. Sales allowances	b. Formal credit arrangements evidenced by a written debt instrument.
_____ 4. Allowance method	
_____ 5. Notes receivable	c. Amount of cash owed to the company by customers from the sale of products or services on account.
_____ 6. Direct write-off method	
	d. Recording bad debt expense at the time the account is known to be uncollectible.
_____ 7. Net revenues	
_____ 8. Sales discounts	e. Sales on account to customers.
_____ 9. Aging method	f. Reductions in amount owed by customers if payment on account is made within a specified period of time.
	g. Total revenues less discounts, returns, and allowances.
	h. Recording an adjustment at the end of each period for the estimate of future uncollectible accounts.
	i. Estimated percentage of uncollectible accounts is greater for "old" accounts than for "new" accounts.

EXERCISES

Mc Graw Hill Education **connect**

E5–1 On May 7, Juanita Construction provides services on account to Michael Wolfe for $4,000. Michael pays for those services on May 13.

Record credit sale (LO5–1)

Required:
For Juanita Construction, record the service on account on May 7 and the collection of cash on May 13.

E5–2 Merry Maidens Cleaning generally charges $300 for a detailed cleaning of a normal-size home. However, to generate additional business, Merry Maidens is offering a new-customer discount of 10%. On May 1, Ms. E. Pearson has Merry Maidens clean her house and pays cash equal to the discounted price.

Record cash sales with a trade discount (LO5–2)

Required:
Record the revenue earned by Merry Maidens Cleaning on May 1.

E5–3 On March 12, Medical Waste Services provides services on account to Grace Hospital for $11,000, terms 2/10, n/30. Grace pays for those services on March 20.

Record credit sale and cash collection with a sales discount (LO5–1, 5–2)

Required:
For Medical Waste Services, record the service on account on March 12 and the collection of cash on March 20.

E5–4 Refer to the information in E5–3, but now assume that Grace does not pay for services until March 31, missing the 2% sales discount.

Record credit sale and cash collection (LO5–1, 5–2)

Flip Side of E5–5

Required:
For Medical Waste Services, record the service on account on March 12 and the collection of cash on March 31.

E5–5 Refer to the information in E5–4.

Record credit purchase and cash payment (LO5–1, 5–2)

Flip Side of E5–4

Required:
For Grace Hospital, record the purchase of services on account on March 12 and the payment of cash on March 31.

E5–6 On April 25, Foreman Electric installs wiring in a new home for $3,500 on account. However, on April 27, Foreman's electrical work does not pass inspection, and Foreman grants the customer an allowance of $600 because of the problem. The customer makes full payment of the balance owed, excluding the allowance, on April 30.

Record credit sales with a sales allowance (LO5–1, 5–2)

Required:
1. Record the credit sale on April 25.
2. Record the sales allowance on April 27.
3. Record the cash collection on April 30.
4. Calculate net sales associated with these transactions.

E5–7 During 2018, its first year of operations, Pave Construction provides services on account of $160,000. By the end of 2018, cash collections on these accounts total $110,000. Pave estimates that 25% of the uncollected accounts will be bad debts.

Record the adjustment for uncollectible accounts and calculate net realizable value (LO5–3)

Required:
1. Record the adjustment for uncollectible accounts on December 31, 2018.
2. Calculate the net realizable value of accounts receivable.

E5–8 Physicians' Hospital has the following balances on December 31, 2018, before any adjustment: Accounts Receivable = $60,000; Allowance for Uncollectible Accounts = $1,100 *(credit)*. On December 31, 2018, Physicians' estimates uncollectible accounts to be 15% of accounts receivable.

Record the adjustment for uncollectible accounts and calculate net realizable value (LO5–3)

Required:
1. Record the adjustment for uncollectible accounts on December 31, 2018.

2. Determine the amount at which bad debt expense is reported in the income statement and the allowance for uncollectible accounts is reported in the balance sheet.

3. Calculate the net realizable value of accounts receivable.

Record the adjustment for uncollectible accounts and calculate net realizable value (LO5–3)

E5–9 Southwest Pediatrics has the following balances on December 31, 2018, before any adjustment: Accounts Receivable = $130,000; Allowance for Uncollectible Accounts = $2,100 (*debit*). On December 31, 2018, Southwest estimates uncollectible accounts to be 20% of accounts receivable.

Required:

1. Record the adjustment for uncollectible accounts on December 31, 2018.

2. Determine the amount at which bad debt expense is reported in the income statement and the allowance for uncollectible accounts is reported in the balance sheet.

3. Calculate the net realizable value of accounts receivable.

Record the adjustment for uncollectible accounts using the aging method (LO5–4)

E5–10 Mercy Hospital has the following balances on December 31, 2018, before any adjustment: Accounts Receivable = $70,000; Allowance for Uncollectible Accounts = $1,400 (*credit*). Mercy estimates uncollectible accounts based on an aging of accounts receivable as shown below.

Age Group	Amount Receivable	Estimated Percent Uncollectible
Not yet due	$50,000	15%
0–30 days past due	11,000	20%
31–90 days past due	8,000	45%
More than 90 days past due	1,000	85%
Total	$70,000	

Required:

1. Estimate the amount of uncollectible receivables.

2. Record the adjustment for uncollectible accounts on December 31, 2018.

3. Calculate the net realizable value of accounts receivable.

Record the adjustment for uncollectible accounts using the aging method (LO5–4)

E5–11 The Physical Therapy Center specializes in helping patients regain motor skills after serious accidents. The center has the following balances on December 31, 2018, before any adjustment: Accounts Receivable = $110,000; Allowance for Uncollectible Accounts = $4,000 (*debit*). The center estimates uncollectible accounts based on an aging of accounts receivable as shown below.

Age Group	Amount Receivable	Estimated Percent Uncollectible
Not yet due	$ 60,000	4%
0–60 days past due	26,000	20%
61–120 days past due	16,000	30%
More than 120 days past due	8,000	85%
Total	$110,000	

Required:

1. Estimate the amount of uncollectible receivables.

2. Record the adjustment for uncollectible accounts on December 31, 2018.

3. Calculate the net realizable value of accounts receivable.

Identify the financial statement effects of transactions related to accounts receivable and allowance for uncollectible accounts (LO5–3, 5–5)

E5–12 Consider the following transactions associated with accounts receivable and the allowance for uncollectible accounts.

Credit Sales Transaction Cycle	Assets	Liabilities	Stockholders' Equity	Revenues	Expenses
1. Provide services on account					
2. Estimate uncollectible accounts					
3. Write off accounts as uncollectible					
4. Collect on account previously written off					

Required:
For each transaction, indicate whether it would increase (I), decrease (D), or have no effect (NE) on the account totals. (*Hint:* Make sure the accounting equation, Assets = Liabilities + Stockholders' Equity, remains in balance after each transaction.)

E5–13 At the beginning of 2018, Brad's Heating & Air (BHA) has a balance of $26,000 in accounts receivable. Because BHA is a privately owned company, the company has used only the direct write-off method to account for uncollectible accounts. However, at the end of 2018, BHA wishes to obtain a loan at the local bank, which requires the preparation of proper financial statements. This means that BHA now will need to use the allowance method. The following transactions occur during 2018 and 2019.

Compare the allowance method and the direct write-off method (LO5–6)

a. During 2018, install air conditioning systems on account, $190,000.
b. During 2018, collect $185,000 from customers on account.
c. At the end of 2018, estimate that uncollectible accounts total 15% of ending accounts receivable.
d. In 2019, customers' accounts totaling $8,000 are written off as uncollectible.

Required:
1. Record each transaction using the allowance method.
2. Record each transaction using the direct write-off method.
3. Calculate the difference in net income (before taxes) in 2018 and 2019 between the two methods.

E5–14 During 2018, LeBron Corporation accepts the following notes receivable.
a. On April 1, LeBron provides services to a customer on account. The customer signs a four-month, 9% note for $7,000.
b. On June 1, LeBron lends cash to one of the company's vendors by accepting a six-month, 10% note for $11,000.
c. On November 1, LeBron accepts payment for prior services by having a customer with a past-due account receivable sign a three-month, 8% note for $6,000.

Record notes receivable (LO5–7)

Required:
Record the acceptance of each of the notes receivable.

E5–15 On March 1, Terrell & Associates provides legal services to Whole Grain Bakery regarding some recent food poisoning complaints. Legal services total $11,000. In payment for the services, Whole Grain Bakery signs a 9% note requiring the payment of the face amount and interest to Terrell & Associates on September 1.

Record notes receivable and interest revenue (LO5–7)
Flip Side of E5–16

Required:
For Terrell & Associates, record the acceptance of the note receivable on March 1 and the cash collection on September 1.

E5–16 Refer to the information in E5–15.

Record notes payable and interest expense (LO5–7)

Flip Side of E5–15

Record notes receivable and interest revenue (LO5–7)

Required:

For Whole Grain Bakery, record the issuance of the note payable on March 1 and the cash payment on September 1.

E5–17 On April 1, 2018, Shoemaker Corporation realizes that one of its main suppliers is having difficulty meeting delivery schedules, which is hurting Shoemaker's business. The supplier explains that it has a temporary lack of funds that is slowing its production cycle. Shoemaker agrees to lend $600,000 to its supplier using a 12-month, 11% note.

Required:

Record the following transactions for Shoemaker Corporation.
1. The loan of $600,000 and acceptance of the note receivable on April 1, 2018.
2. The adjustment for accrued interest on December 31, 2018.
3. Cash collection of the note and interest on April 1, 2019.

Calculate receivables ratios (LO5–8)

E5–18 Below are amounts (in millions) from three companies' annual reports.

	Beginning Accounts Receivable	Ending Accounts Receivable	Net Sales
WalCo	$1,815	$2,762	$322,427
TarMart	$6,166	$6,694	$ 67,878
CostGet	$ 629	$ 665	$ 68,963

Required:

For each company, calculate the receivables turnover ratio and the average collection period (rounded to one decimal place). Which company appears most efficient in collecting cash from sales?

Compare the percentage-of-receivables method and the percentage-of-credit-sales method (LO5–9)

E5–19 Suzuki Supply reports the following amounts at the end of 2018 (before adjustment).

Credit Sales for 2018	$260,000	
Accounts Receivable, December 31, 2018	55,000	
Allowance for Uncollectible Accounts, December 31, 2018	1,100	(credit)

Required:
1. Record the adjustment for uncollectible accounts using the percentage-of-receivables method. Suzuki estimates 12% of receivables will not be collected.
2. Record the adjustment for uncollectible accounts using the percentage-of-credit-sales method. Suzuki estimates 3% of credit sales will not be collected.
3. Calculate the effect on net income (before taxes) and total assets in 2018 for each method.

Compare the percentage-of-receivables method and the percentage-of-credit-sales method (LO5–9)

E5–20 Refer to the information in E5–19, but now assume that the balance of the Allowance for Uncollectible Accounts on December 31, 2018, is $1,100 (*debit*) (before adjustment).

Required:
1. Record the adjustment for uncollectible accounts using the percentage-of-receivables method. Suzuki estimates 12% of receivables will not be collected.
2. Record the adjustment for uncollectible accounts using the percentage-of-credit-sales method. Suzuki estimates 3% of credit sales will not be collected.
3. Calculate the effect on net income (before taxes) and total assets in 2018 for each method.

E5–21 On January 1, 2018, the general ledger of 3D Family Fireworks includes the following account balances:

Complete the accounting cycle using receivable transactions (LO5–1, 5–3, 5–4, 5–5, 5–7, 5–8)

Accounts	Debit	Credit
Cash	$ 23,900	
Accounts Receivable	13,600	
Allowance for Uncollectible Accounts		$ 1,400
Supplies	2,500	
Notes Receivable (6%, due in 2 years)	20,000	
Land	77,000	
Accounts Payable		7,200
Common Stock		96,000
Retained Earnings		32,400
Totals	$137,000	$137,000

During January 2018, the following transactions occur:

January 2	Provide services to customers for cash, $35,100.
January 6	Provide services to customers on account, $72,400.
January 15	Write off accounts receivable as uncollectible, $1,000.
January 20	Pay cash for salaries, $31,400.
January 22	Receive cash on accounts receivable, $70,000.
January 25	Pay cash on accounts payable, $5,500.
January 30	Pay cash for utilities during January, $13,700.

Required:

1. Record each of the transactions listed above.
2. Record adjusting entries on January 31.
   a. At the end of January, $5,000 of accounts receivable are past due, and the company estimates that 20% of these accounts will not be collected. Of the remaining accounts receivable, the company estimates that 5% will not be collected. The note receivable of $20,000 is considered fully collectible and therefore is not included in the estimate of uncollectible accounts.
   b. Supplies at the end of January total $700.
   c. Accrued interest revenue on notes receivable for January. Interest is expected to be received each December 31.
   d. Unpaid salaries at the end of January are $33,500.
3. Prepare an adjusted trial balance as of January 31, 2018, after updating beginning balances (above) for transactions during January (*Requirement* 1) and adjusting entries at the end of January (*Requirement* 2).
4. Prepare an income statement for the period ended January 31, 2018.
5. Prepare a classified balance sheet as of January 31, 2018.
6. Record closing entries.
7. Analyze how well 3D Family Fireworks manages its receivables:
   a. Calculate the receivables turnover ratio for the month of January (*Hint:* For the numerator, use total services provided to customers on account). If the industry average of the receivables turnover ratios for the month of January is 4.2 times, is the company collecting cash from customers *more* or *less* efficiently than other companies in the same industry?
   b. Calculate the ratio of Allowance for Uncollectible Accounts to Accounts Receivable at the end of January. Based on a comparison of this ratio to the same ratio at the beginning of January, does the company expect an *improvement* or *worsening* in cash collections from customers on credit sales?

PROBLEMS: SET A   connect

Calculate the amount of revenue to recognize (LO5–1)

P5–1A Assume the following scenarios.

Scenario 1:   During 2018, **IBM** provides consulting services on its mainframe computer for $11,000 on account. The customer does not pay for those services until 2019.

Scenario 2:   On January 1, 2018, **Gold's Gym** sells a one-year membership for $1,200 cash. Normally, this type of membership would cost $1,600, but the company is offering a 25% "New Year's Resolution" discount.

Scenario 3:   During 2018, **The Manitowoc Company** provides shipbuilding services to the U.S. Navy for $450,000. The U.S. Navy will pay $150,000 at the end of each year for the next three years, beginning in 2018.

Scenario 4:   During 2018, **Goodyear** sells tires to customers on account for $35,000. By the end of the year, collections total $30,000. At the end of 2019, it becomes apparent that the remaining $5,000 will never be collected from customers.

Required:

For each scenario, calculate the amount of revenue to be recognized in 2018.

Record transactions related to credit sales and contra revenues (LO5–1, 5–2)

P5–2A Outdoor Expo provides guided fishing tours. The company charges $300 per person but offers a 20% discount to parties of four or more. Consider the following transactions during the month of May.

May 2   Charlene books a fishing tour with Outdoor Expo for herself and four friends at the group discount price ($1,200 = $240 × 5). The tour is scheduled for May 7.

May 7   The fishing tour occurs. Outdoor Expo asks that payment be made within 30 days of the tour and offers a 6% discount for payment within 15 days.

May 9   Charlene is upset that no one caught a single fish and asks management for a discount. Outdoor Expo has a strict policy of no discounts related to number of fish caught.

May 15   Upon deeper investigation, management of Outdoor Expo discovers that Charlene's tour was led by a new guide who did not take the group to some of the better fishing spots. In concession, management offers a sales allowance of 30% of the amount due.

May 20   Charlene pays for the tour after deducting the sales allowance.

Required:

1. Record the necessary transaction(s) for Outdoor Expo on each date.
2. Show how Outdoor Expo would present net revenues in its income statement.

Record transactions related to accounts receivable (LO5–3, 5–5)

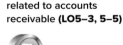

P5–3A The following events occur for The Underwood Corporation during 2018 and 2019, its first two years of operations.

June 12, 2018	Provide services to customers on account for $41,000.
September 17, 2018	Receive $25,000 from customers on account.
December 31, 2018	Estimate that 45% of accounts receivable at the end of the year will not be received.
March 4, 2019	Provide services to customers on account for $56,000.
May 20, 2019	Receive $10,000 from customers for services provided in 2018.
July 2, 2019	Write off the remaining amounts owed from services provided in 2018.
October 19, 2019	Receive $45,000 from customers for services provided in 2019.
December 31, 2019	Estimate that 45% of accounts receivable at the end of the year will not be received.

Required:

1. Record transactions for each date.
2. Post transactions to the following accounts: Cash, Accounts Receivable, and Allowance for Uncollectible Accounts.
3. Calculate the net realizable value of accounts receivable at the end of 2018 and 2019.

P5–4A Pearl E. White Orthodontist specializes in correcting misaligned teeth. During 2018, Pearl provides services on account of $590,000. Of this amount, $80,000 remains receivable at the end of the year. An aging schedule as of December 31, 2018, is provided below.

Record transactions related to uncollectible accounts (LO5–4, 5–5)

Age Group	Amount Receivable	Estimated Percent Uncollectible
Not yet due	$40,000	4%
0–90 days past due	16,000	20%
91–180 days past due	11,000	25%
More than 180 days past due	13,000	80%
Total	$80,000	

Required:
1. Calculate the allowance for uncollectible accounts.
2. Record the December 31, 2018, adjustment, assuming the balance of Allowance for Uncollectible Accounts before adjustment is $5,000 (*credit*).
3. On July 19, 2019, a customer's account balance of $8,000 is written off as uncollectible. Record the write-off.
4. On September 30, 2019, the customer whose account was written off in *Requirement* 3 unexpectedly pays the full amount. Record the cash collection.

P5–5A In an effort to boost sales in the current year, Roy's Gym has implemented a new program where members do not have to pay for their annual membership until the end of the year. The program seems to have substantially increased membership and revenues. Below are year-end amounts.

Compare the direct write-off method to the allowance method (LO5–3, 5–6)

	Membership Revenues	Accounts Receivable
Last year	$150,000	$ 6,000
Current year	450,000	170,000

Arnold, the owner, realizes that many members have not paid their annual membership fees by the end of the year. However, Arnold believes that no allowance for uncollectible accounts should be reported in the current year because none of the nonpaying members' accounts have proven uncollectible. Arnold wants to use the direct write-off method to record bad debts, waiting until the end of next year before writing off any accounts.

Required:
1. Do you agree with Arnold's reasoning for not reporting any allowance for future uncollectible accounts? Explain.
2. Suppose that similar programs in the past have resulted in uncollectible accounts of approximately 70%. If Arnold uses the allowance method, what should be the balance of Allowance for Uncollectible Accounts at the end of the current year?
3. Based on your answer in *Requirement* 2, for what amount will total assets and expenses be misstated in the current year if Arnold uses the direct write-off method? Ignore tax effects.

P5–6A Willie Cheetum is the CEO of Happy Foods, a distributor of produce to grocery store chains throughout the Midwest. At the end of the year, the company's accounting manager provides Willie with the following information, before any adjustment.

Using estimates of uncollectible accounts to overstate income (LO5–3)

Accounts receivable	$1,100,000
Estimated percentage uncollectible	9%
Allowance for uncollectible accounts	$40,000 (credit)
Operating income	$260,000

Willie's compensation contract states that if the company generates operating income of at least $210,000, he will get a salary bonus early next year.

Required:

1. Record the adjustment for uncollectible accounts using the accountant's estimate of 9% of accounts receivable.
2. After the adjustment is recorded in *Requirement* 1, what is the revised amount of operating income? Will Willie get his salary bonus?
3. Willie instructs the accountant to record the adjustment for uncollectible accounts using 6% rather than 9% of accounts receivable. Now will Willie get his salary bonus? Explain.
4. By how much would total assets and operating income be misstated using the 6% amount?

Overestimating future uncollectible accounts (LO5–3, 5–5)

P5–7A Humanity International sells medical and food supplies to those in need in underdeveloped countries. Customers in these countries are often very poor and must purchase items on account. At the end of 2018, total accounts receivable equal $1,300,000. The company understands that it's dealing with high credit risk clients. These countries are often in the middle of a financial crisis, civil war, severe drought, or some other difficult circumstance. Because of this, Humanity International typically estimates the percentage of uncollectible accounts to be 35% (= $455,000). Actual write-offs in 2019 total only $300,000, which means that the company significantly overestimated uncollectible accounts in 2018. It appears that efforts by the International Monetary Fund (IMF) and the United Nations (UN), and a mild winter mixed with adequate spring rains, have provided for more stable economic conditions than were expected, helping customers to pay on their accounts.

Required:

1. Record the adjustment for uncollectible accounts at the end of 2018, assuming there is no balance in Allowance for Uncollectible Accounts at the end of 2018 before any adjustment.
2. By the end of 2019, Humanity International has the benefit of hindsight to know that estimates of uncollectible accounts in 2018 were too high. How did this overestimation affect the reported amounts of total assets and expenses at the end of 2018? Ignore tax effects.
3. Should Humanity International prepare new financial statements for 2018 to show the correct amount of uncollectible accounts? Explain.

Record long-term notes receivable and interest revenue (LO5–7)

P5–8A On December 1, 2018, Liang Chemical provides services to a customer for $90,000. In payment for the services, the customer signs a three-year, 10% note. The face amount is due at the end of the third year, while annual interest is due each December 1.

Required:

1. Record the acceptance of the note on December 1, 2018.
2. Record the interest collected on December 1 for 2019 and 2020, and the adjustment for interest revenue on December 31 for 2018, 2019, and 2020.
3. Record the cash collection on December 1, 2021.

Calculate and analyze ratios (LO5–8)

P5–9A Assume selected financial data for **Walmart** and **Target**, two close competitors in the retail industry, are as follows:

($ in millions)	Net Sales	Beginning Accounts Receivable	Ending Accounts Receivable
Walmart	$443,854	$5,089	$5,937
Target	68,466	6,153	5,927

Required:

1. Calculate the receivables turnover ratio and average collection period for Walmart and Target. Round your answers to one decimal place. Which company has better ratios? Compare your calculations with those for **Tenet Healthcare** and **LifePoint Hospitals** reported in the chapter text. Which industry maintains a higher receivables turnover?
2. Because most companies do not separately report cash sales and credit sales, the calculations used here and in the chapter text use companies' reported amount of net sales, which is a combination of cash sales and credit sales. How would including cash sales affect the receivables turnover ratio? How does this help to explain your answer in *Requirement* 1 above?

PROBLEMS: SET B

P5–1B Assume the following scenarios.

Calculate the amount of revenue to recognize (LO5–1)

Scenario 1:   During 2018, **The Hubbard Group** provides services of $900,000 for repair of a state highway. The company receives an initial payment of $300,000 with the balance to be received the following year.

Scenario 2:   **Rolling Stone** magazine typically charges $80 for a one-year subscription. On January 1, 2018, Herman, age 72, purchases a one-year subscription to the magazine and receives a 15% senior citizen discount.

Scenario 3:   During 2018, **Waste Management** provides services on account for $30,000. The customer pays for those services in 2019.

Scenario 4:   During 2018, **Sysco Corporation** sells grocery items to one of its customers for $260,000 on account. Cash collections on those sales are $180,000 in 2018 and $60,000 in 2019. The remaining $20,000 is written off as uncollectible in 2019.

Required:

For each scenario, calculate the amount of revenue to be recognized in 2018.

P5–2B Data Recovery Services (DRS) specializes in data recovery from crashed hard drives. The price charged varies based on the extent of damage and the amount of data being recovered. DRS offers a 10% discount to students and faculty at educational institutions. Consider the following transactions during the month of June.

Record transactions related to credit sales and contra revenues (LO5–1, 5–2)

June 10   Rashid's hard drive crashes and he sends it to DRS.

June 12   After initial evaluation, DRS e-mails Rashid to let him know that full data recovery will cost $3,000.

June 13   Rashid informs DRS that he would like them to recover the data and that he is a student at UCLA, qualifying him for a 10% educational discount and reducing the cost by $300 (= $3,000 × 10%).

June 16   DRS performs the work and claims to be successful in recovering all data. DRS asks Rashid to pay within 30 days of today's date, offering a 2% discount for payment within 10 days.

June 19   When Rashid receives the hard drive, he notices that DRS did not successfully recover all data. Approximately 30% of the data has not been recovered and he informs DRS.

June 20   DRS reduces the amount Rashid owes by 30%.

June 30   Rashid pays the amount owed.

Required:

1. Record the necessary transaction(s) for Data Recovery Services on each date.
2. Show how net revenues would be presented in the income statement.
3. Calculate net revenues if Rashid had paid his bill on June 25.

P5–3B The following events occur for Morris Engineering during 2018 and 2019, its first two years of operations.

Record transactions related to accounts receivable (LO5–3, 5–5)

February 2, 2018	Provide services to customers on account for $38,000.
July 23, 2018	Receive $27,000 from customers on account.
December 31, 2018	Estimate that 25% of uncollected accounts will not be received.
April 12, 2019	Provide services to customers on account for $51,000.
June 28, 2019	Receive $6,000 from customers for services provided in 2018.
September 13, 2019	Write off the remaining amounts owed from services provided in 2018.
October 5, 2019	Receive $45,000 from customers for services provided in 2019.
December 31, 2019	Estimate that 25% of uncollected accounts will not be received.

Required:

1. Record transactions for each date.
2. Post transactions to the following accounts: Cash, Accounts Receivable, and Allowance for Uncollectible Accounts.
3. Calculate the net realizable value of accounts receivable at the end of 2018 and 2019.

P5–4B Facial Cosmetics provides plastic surgery primarily to hide the appearance of unwanted scars and other blemishes. During 2018, the company provides services of $410,000 on account. Of this amount, $60,000 remains uncollected at the end of the year. An aging schedule as of December 31, 2018, is provided below.

Age Group	Amount Receivable	Estimated Percent Uncollectible
Not yet due	$40,000	3%
0–30 days past due	11,000	4%
31–60 days past due	8,000	11%
More than 60 days past due	1,000	25%
Total	$60,000	

Required:
1. Calculate the allowance for uncollectible accounts.
2. Record the December 31, 2018, adjustment, assuming the balance of Allowance for Uncollectible Accounts before adjustment is $400 (*debit*).
3. On April 3, 2019, a customer's account balance of $500 is written off as uncollectible. Record the write-off.
4. On July 17, 2019, the customer whose account was written off in *Requirement* 3 unexpectedly pays $100 of the amount but does not expect to pay any additional amounts. Record the cash collection.

P5–5B Letni Corporation engages in the manufacture and sale of semiconductor chips for the computing and communications industries. During the past year, operating revenues remained relatively flat compared to the prior year but management notices a big increase in accounts receivable. The increase in receivables is largely due to the recent economic slowdown in the computing and telecommunications industries. Many of the company's customers are having financial difficulty, lengthening the period of time it takes to collect on accounts. Below are year-end amounts.

Age Group	Operating Revenue	Accounts Receivable	Average Age	Accounts Written Off
Two years ago	$1,300,000	$150,000	5 days	$ 0
Last year	1,600,000	160,000	7 days	1,000
Current year	1,700,000	330,000	40 days	0

Paul, the CEO of Letni, notices that accounts written off over the past three years have been minimal and, therefore, suggests that no allowance for uncollectible accounts be established in the current year. Any account proving uncollectible can be charged to next year's financial statements (the direct write-off method).

Required:
1. Do you agree with Paul's reasoning? Explain.
2. Suppose that other companies in these industries have had similar increasing trends in accounts receivable aging. These companies also had very successful collections in the past but now estimate uncollectible accounts to be 25% because of the significant downturn in the industries. If Letni uses the allowance method estimated at 25% of accounts receivable, what should be the balance of Allowance for Uncollectible Accounts at the end of the current year?
3. Based on your answer in *Requirement* 2, for what amount will total assets and expenses be misstated in the current year if Letni uses the direct write-off method? Ignore tax effects.

P5–6B Wanda B. Rich is the CEO of Outlet Flooring, a discount provider of carpet, tile, wood, and laminate flooring. At the end of the year, the company's accountant provides Wanda with the following information, before any adjustment.

Accounts receivable	$11,000,000
Estimated percentage uncollectible	4%
Allowance for uncollectible accounts	$110,000 (*credit*)
Operating income	$2,900,000

Wanda has significant stock ownership in the company and, therefore, would like to keep the stock price high. Analysts on Wall Street expect the company to have operating income of $2,200,000. The fact that actual operating income is well above this amount will make investors happy and help maintain a high stock price. Meeting analysts' expectations will also help Wanda keep her job.

Required:

1. Record the adjustment for uncollectible accounts using the accountant's estimate of 4% of accounts receivable.
2. After the adjustment is recorded in *Requirement 1*, what is the revised amount of operating income? Will Outlet Flooring still meet analysts' expectations?
3. Wanda instructs the accountant to instead record $700,000 as bad debt expense so that operating income will exactly meet analysts' expectations. By how much would total assets and operating income be misstated if the accountant records this amount?
4. Why would Wanda be motivated to manage operating income in this way?

P5–7B By the end of its first year of operations, Previts Corporation has credit sales of $750,000 and accounts receivable of $350,000. Given it's the first year of operations, Previts' management is unsure how much allowance for uncollectible accounts it should establish. One of the company's competitors, which has been in the same industry for an extended period, estimates uncollectible accounts to be 2% of ending accounts receivable, so Previts decides to use that same amount. However, actual write-offs in the following year were 25% of the $350,000 (= $87,500). Previts' inexperience in the industry led to making sales to high credit risk customers.

Underestimating future uncollectible accounts (LO5–3, 5–5)

Required:

1. Record the adjustment for uncollectible accounts at the end of the first year of operations using the 2% estimate of accounts receivable.
2. By the end of the second year, Previts has the benefit of hindsight to know that estimates of uncollectible accounts in the first year were too low. By how much did Previts underestimate uncollectible accounts in the first year? How did this underestimation affect the reported amounts of total assets and expenses at the end of the first year? Ignore tax effects.
3. Should Previts prepare new financial statements for the first year of operations to show the correct amount of uncollectible accounts? Explain.

P5–8B On April 15, 2018, Sampson Consulting provides services to a customer for $110,000. To pay for the services, the customer signs a three-year, 12% note. The face amount is due at the end of the third year, while annual interest is due each April 15. (*Hint:* Because the note is accepted during the middle of the month, Sampson plans to recognize one-half month of interest revenue in April 2018, and one-half month of interest revenue in April 2021.)

Record long-term notes receivable and interest revenue (LO5–7)

Required:

1. Record the acceptance of the note on April 15, 2018.
2. Record the interest collected on April 15 for 2019 and 2020, and the adjustment for interest revenue on December 31, 2018, 2019, and 2020.
3. Record the cash collection on April 15, 2021.

P5–9B Assume selected financial data for **Sun Health Group** and **Select Medical Corporation**, two companies in the health-care industry, are as follows:

Calculate and analyze ratios (LO5–8)

($ in millions)	Net Sales	Beginning Accounts Receivable	Ending Accounts Receivable
Sun Health	$1,930	$215	$202
Select Medical	2,240	414	353

Required:

1. Calculate the receivables turnover ratio and average collection period for Sun Health and Select Medical. Round your answers to one decimal place. Compare your calculations with those for **Tenet Healthcare** and **LifePoint Hospitals** reported in the chapter text. Which of the four companies maintains a higher receivables turnover?
2. How does the receivables turnover ratio reflect the efficiency of management? Discuss factors that affect the receivables turnover ratio.

ADDITIONAL PERSPECTIVES

Continuing Problem

Great Adventures

(This is a continuation of the Great Adventures problem from earlier chapters.)

P5–1 Tony and Suzie are ready to expand Great Adventures even further in 2019. Tony believes that many groups in the community (for example, Boy Scouts, church groups, civic groups, and local businesses) would like to hold one-day outings for their members. Groups would engage in outdoor activities such as rock climbing, fishing, capture the flag, paintball, treasure hunts, scavenger hunts, nature hikes, and so on. The purpose of these one-day events would be for each member of the group to learn the importance of TEAM (Together Everyone Achieves More).

Tony knows that most people are not familiar with these types of activities, so to encourage business he allows groups to participate in the event before paying. He offers a 5% quick-payment discount to those that pay within 10 days after the event. He also guarantees that at least eight hours of outdoor activities will be provided or the customer will receive a 20% discount. For the first six months of the year, the following activities occur for TEAM operations.

Jan.	24	Great Adventures purchases outdoor gear such as ropes, helmets, harnesses, compasses, and other miscellaneous equipment for $5,000 cash.
Feb.	25	Mr. Kendall's Boy Scout troop participates in a one-day TEAM adventure. Normally, Tony would charge a group of this size $3,500, but he wants to encourage kids to exercise more and enjoy the outdoors so he charges the group only $3,000. Great Adventures provides these services on account.
Feb.	28	The Boy Scout troop pays the full amount owed, less the 5% quick-payment discount.
Mar.	19	Reynold's Management has its employees participate in a one-day TEAM adventure. Great Adventures provides services on account for $4,000, and Reynold's agrees to pay within 30 days.
Mar.	27	Reynold's pays the full amount owed, less the 5% quick-payment discount.
Apr.	7	Several men from the Elks Lodge decide to participate in a TEAM adventure. They pay $7,500, and the event is scheduled for the following week.
Apr.	14	The TEAM adventure is held for members of the Elks Lodge.
May	9	Myers Manufacturing participates in a TEAM adventure. Great Adventures provides services on account for $6,000, and Myers agrees to pay within 30 days.
Jun.	1–30	Several MBA groups participate in TEAM adventures during June. Great Adventures provides services on account for $24,000 to these groups, with payment due in July.
Jun.	30	Myers Manufacturing fails to pay the amount owed within the specified period and agrees to sign a three-month, 8% note receivable to replace the existing account receivable.

Required:

1. Record TEAM adventure transactions occurring during the first six months of 2019.
2. As of June 30, 2019, Great Adventures finishes its first 12 months of operations. If Suzie wants to prepare financial statements, part of the process would involve allowing for uncollectible accounts receivable.

   a. Suppose Suzie estimates uncollectible accounts to be 10% of accounts receivable (which does not include the $6,000 note receivable from Myers Manufacturing). Record the adjustment for uncollectible accounts on June 30, 2019.

   b. Prepare a partial balance sheet showing the net accounts receivable section.

American Eagle Outfitters, Inc.

Financial Analysis

AP5–2 Financial information for **American Eagle** is presented in **Appendix A** at the end of the book.

Required:
1. Determine whether the trend in net sales has been increasing or decreasing for the past three years.
2. Where is accounts receivable reported? Explain why using net sales to calculate the receivables turnover ratio might not be a good indicator of a company's ability to efficiently manage receivables for a retail company like American Eagle, which typically sells clothing for cash.
3. Does American Eagle report an allowance for uncollectible accounts in the balance sheet? If so, how much is reported for the most recent year?

The Buckle, Inc.

Financial Analysis

AP5–3 Financial information for **Buckle** is presented in **Appendix B** at the end of the book.

Required:
1. Determine whether the trend in net sales has been increasing or decreasing for the past three years.
2. Where is accounts receivable reported? Explain why using net sales to calculate the receivables turnover ratio might not be a good indicator of a company's ability to efficiently manage receivables for a retail company like Buckle, which typically sells clothing for cash.
3. Does Buckle report an allowance for uncollectible accounts in the balance sheet? If so, how much is reported for the most recent year?

American Eagle Outfitters, Inc. vs. The Buckle, Inc.

Comparative Analysis

AP5–4 Financial information for **American Eagle** is presented in **Appendix A** at the end of the book, and financial information for **Buckle** is presented in **Appendix B** at the end of the book.

Required:
Try to estimate each company's ratio of total current receivables to total current assets. Do you see problems with either company's management of receivables?

Ethics

AP5–5 You have recently been hired as the assistant controller for Stanton Industries. Your immediate superior is the controller who, in turn, reports to the vice president of finance.

The controller has assigned you the task of preparing the year-end adjustments. For receivables, you have prepared an aging of accounts receivable and have applied historical percentages to the balances of each of the age categories. The analysis indicates that an appropriate balance for Allowance for Uncollectible Accounts is $180,000. The existing balance in the allowance account prior to any adjustment is a $20,000 credit balance.

After showing your analysis to the controller, he tells you to change the aging category of a large account from over 120 days to current status and to prepare a new invoice to the customer with a revised date that agrees with the new aging category. This will change the required allowance for uncollectible accounts from $180,000 to $135,000. Tactfully, you ask the controller for an explanation for the change and he tells you, "We need the extra income; the bottom line is too low."

Required:
1. What is the effect on income before taxes of the change requested by the controller?
2. Discuss the ethical dilemma you face. Consider your options and responsibilities along with the possible consequences of any action you might take. Who are the parties affected? What factors should you consider in making your decision?

Internet Research

AP5–6 Obtain a copy of the annual report of **Avon Products, Inc.**, for the most recent year. You can find the annual report at the company's website (*www.avon.com*) in the investor information section or at the Securities and Exchange Commission's website (*www.sec.gov*) using EDGAR (Electronic Data Gathering, Analysis, and Retrieval). Form 10-K, which includes the annual report, is required to be filed on EDGAR. Search or scroll within the annual report to find the financial statements.

Required:

Answer the following questions related to the company's accounts receivable and bad debts:
1. What is the amount of net accounts receivable at the end of the year? What is the amount of total accounts receivable?
2. What is the amount of bad debt expense for the year? (*Hint:* Check the statement of cash flows.)
3. Determine the amount of actual bad debt write-offs made during the year. Assume that all bad debts relate only to trade accounts receivable. Did the company underestimate or overestimate bad debts?
4. Calculate the receivables turnover ratio and average collection period for the most recent year. Round your answers to one decimal place. Assuming the industry averages for the receivables turnover ratio and average collection period are 10.5 times and 34.8 days, respectively, what do you conclude about the receivables of Avon?

Written Communication

AP5–7 You have been hired as a consultant by a parts manufacturing firm to provide advice as to the proper accounting methods the company should use in some key areas. In the area of receivables, the company president does not understand your recommendation to use the allowance method for uncollectible accounts. She stated, "Financial statements should be based on objective data rather than the guesswork required for the allowance method. Besides, since my uncollectibles are fairly constant from period to period, with significant variations occurring infrequently, the direct write-off method is just as good as the allowance method."

Required:

Draft a one-page response in the form of a memo to the president in support of your recommendation for the company to use the allowance method.

Earnings Management

AP5–8 Ernie Upshaw is the supervising manager of Sleep Tight Bedding. At the end of the year, the company's accounting manager provides Ernie with the following information, before any adjustment.

Accounts receivable	$500,000
Estimated percent uncollectible	9%
Allowance for uncollectible accounts	$20,000 (*debit*)
Operating income	$320,000

In the previous year, Sleep Tight Bedding reported operating income (after adjustment) of $275,000. Ernie knows that it's important to report an upward trend in earnings. This is important not only for Ernie's compensation and employment, but also for the company's stock price. If investors see a decline in earnings, the stock price could drop significantly, and Ernie owns a large amount of the company's stock. This has caused Ernie many sleepless nights.

Required:

1. Record the adjustment for uncollectible accounts using the accounting manager's estimate of 9% of accounts receivable.

2. After the adjustment is recorded in *Requirement* 1, what is the revised amount of operating income? Does operating income increase or decrease compared to the previous year?
3. Ernie instructs the accounting manager to record the adjustment for uncollectible accounts using 4% rather than 9% of accounts receivable. After this adjustment, does operating income increase or decrease compared to the previous year?
4. By how much would total assets and expenses be misstated using the 4% amount?

Answers to the Self-Study Questions

1. c   2. c   3. b   4. b   5. d   6. c   7. b   8. d   9. b   10. c

Inventory and Cost of Goods Sold

Learning Objectives

AFTER STUDYING THIS CHAPTER, YOU SHOULD BE ABLE TO:

- **LO6–1** Trace the flow of inventory costs from manufacturing companies to merchandising companies.
- **LO6–2** Understand how cost of goods sold is reported in a multiple-step income statement.
- **LO6–3** Determine the cost of goods sold and ending inventory using different inventory cost methods.
- **LO6–4** Explain the financial statement effects and tax effects of inventory cost methods.
- **LO6–5** Record inventory transactions using a perpetual inventory system.
- **LO6–6** Apply the lower of cost and net realizable value rule for inventories.

Analysis

- **LO6–7** Analyze management of inventory using the inventory turnover ratio and gross profit ratio.

Appendix

- **LO6–8** Record inventory transactions using a periodic inventory system.
- **LO6–9** Determine the financial statement effects of inventory errors.

BEST BUY: TAKING INVENTORY OF ELECTRONICS SOLD

Best Buy Co., Inc., is the largest consumer electronics retailer in the United States. You are probably familiar with most of the products offered by Best Buy—computers, computer software, TVs, video games, music, mobile phones, digital and video cameras, home appliances (washing machines, dryers, and refrigerators), and other related merchandise.

Merchandise inventory for sale to customers is the single largest asset owned by Best Buy, as it is for many retail companies. At any given time, Best Buy holds more than $5 billion in inventory, or about 34% of the company's total assets. Proper management of inventory is key to the company's success.

Management of Best Buy knows there is a fine line between having too little and too much inventory. Having too little inventory reduces the selection of products available to customers, ultimately reducing sales revenue. On the other hand, in a technology-based industry where changes occur rapidly, having too much inventory can leave the store holding outdated inventory. Just think of what happens to the value of computers when the next generation becomes available. Managers don't want to get stuck with old inventory that is decreasing in value. Besides obsolescence, other costs associated with holding large inventories are storage, insurance, and shrinkage (theft). Holding less inventory also provides access to money that can be invested elsewhere within the company.

For now, Best Buy seems to be taking the right steps with its inventory. Look below at the company's revenues from sales of inventory compared to the cost of the inventory sold. These amounts are reported in the company's income statement ($ in millions). The difference between net sales (a revenue) and cost of goods sold (an expense) is called *gross profit*, and it has averaged more than $9 billion over the period 2013–2015.

	2013	2014	2015
Net sales	$38,252	$40,611	$40,339
Cost of goods sold	29,229	31,212	31,292
Gross profit	$ 9,023	$ 9,399	$ 9,047

In this chapter, we explore how to account for the purchase and sale of inventory items. We'll see how inventory (an asset in the balance sheet) turns into cost of goods sold (an expense in the income statement) once it is sold, and how these amounts can affect business decisions. At the end of the chapter, we'll analyze inventory transactions of **Best Buy** versus **Tiffany's**.

© Susan Van Etten/PhotoEdit

PART A

UNDERSTANDING INVENTORY AND COST OF GOODS SOLD

In preceding chapters, we dealt with companies that provide a service. **Service companies** such as **FedEx**, **United Healthcare**, **Allstate Insurance**, and **Marriott Hotels** earn revenues by providing services to their customers. FedEx delivers your packages, United Healthcare treats your medical needs, Allstate provides insurance coverage, and Marriott offers you a place to stay the night. Many companies, though, earn revenues by selling inventory rather than a service.

Part A of this chapter introduces the concept of inventory and demonstrates the different methods used to calculate the cost of inventory for external reporting. Once you understand this, then you're ready to see, in Part B and Part C, how companies actually maintain their own (internal) records of inventory transactions and the adjustments that are sometimes needed to prepare financial statements.

Inventory

■ **LO6–1**
Trace the flow of inventory costs from manufacturing companies to merchandising companies.

Companies that earn revenue by selling inventory are either *manufacturing* or *merchandising companies*. Inventory includes items a company intends for sale to customers. You already are familiar with several types of inventory—clothes at **The Limited**, shoes at **Payless ShoeSource**, grocery items at **Publix Super Markets**, digital equipment at **Best Buy**, building supplies at **The Home Depot**, and so on. Inventory also includes items that are not yet finished products. For instance, lumber at a cabinet manufacturer, steel at a construction firm, and rubber at a tire manufacturer are part of inventory because the firm will use them to make a finished product for sale to customers.

We report inventory as a current asset in the balance sheet—an *asset* because it represents a valuable resource to the company, and *current* because the company expects to convert it to cash in the near term. At the end of the period, the amount the company reports for inventory is the cost of inventory *not yet sold*. But what happens to the cost of the inventory sold during the period? The company reports the cost of the inventory it sold as cost of goods sold in the income statement.

Common Terms
Cost of goods sold is also referred to as *cost of sales, cost of merchandise sold,* or *cost of products sold.*

Determining the amount of ending inventory and cost of goods sold is a critical task in accounting for inventory. For companies that earn revenues by selling inventory, ending inventory is often the largest asset in the balance sheet, and cost of goods sold often is the largest expense in the income statement. Before we explore how companies calculate these amounts, we first need to consider the different types of inventory between merchandising and manufacturing companies.

MERCHANDISING COMPANIES

Merchandising companies purchase inventories that are primarily in finished form for resale to customers. These companies may assemble, sort, repackage, redistribute, store, refrigerate, deliver, or install the inventory, but they do not manufacture it. They simply serve as intermediaries in the process of moving inventory from the manufacturer, the company that actually makes the inventory, to the end user.

We can broadly classify merchandising companies as wholesalers or retailers. *Wholesalers* resell inventory to retail companies or to professional users. For example, a wholesale food service company like **Sysco Corporation** supplies food to restaurants, schools, and sporting events but generally does not sell food directly to the public. Also, Sysco does not transform the food prior to sale; it just stores the food, repackages it as necessary, and delivers it.

Common Terms
Inventory is also referred to as *merchandise inventory.*

Retailers purchase inventory from manufacturers or wholesalers and then sell this inventory to end users. You probably are more familiar with retail companies because these are the companies from which you buy products. **Best Buy**, **Target**, **Lowe's**, **Macy's**, **Gap**, **Sears**, and **McDonald's** are retailers. Merchandising companies typically hold their inventories in a single category simply called *inventory*.

MANUFACTURING COMPANIES

Manufacturing companies manufacture the inventories they sell, rather than buying them in finished form from suppliers. **Apple Inc.**, **Coca-Cola**, **Harley-Davidson**, **ExxonMobil**, **Ford**, **Sony**, and **Intel** are manufacturers. Manufacturing companies buy the inputs for the products they manufacture. Thus, we classify inventory for a manufacturer into three categories: (1) raw materials, (2) work in process, and (3) finished goods:

- *Raw materials* inventory includes the cost of components that will become part of the finished product but have not yet been used in production.
- *Work-in-process* inventory refers to the products that have been started in the production process but are not yet complete at the end of the period. The total costs include raw materials, direct labor, and indirect manufacturing costs called *overhead*.
- *Finished goods* inventory consists of items for which the manufacturing process is complete.

Intel manufactures the components that are used to build computers. At any given time, Intel's inventory includes the cost of materials that will be used to build computer components (raw materials), partially manufactured components (work-in-process), and fully assembled but unsold components (finished goods). These separate inventory accounts are added together and reported by Intel as total inventories. Other companies, such as **Best Buy**, don't manufacture computers or their components. Instead, Best Buy purchases finished computers from manufacturers. These computers represent merchandise ready for sale to customers like you. Illustration 6–1 shows the different inventory accounts for Intel and Best Buy as reported in their balance sheets.

ILLUSTRATION 6–1

Inventory Amounts for a Manufacturing Company (Intel) Versus a Merchandising Company (Best Buy)

INVENTORY (from balance sheets)		
Inventory accounts ($ in millions)	Intel	Best Buy
Raw materials	$ 462	
Work in process	2,375	
Finished goods	1,436	
Merchandise inventories		$5,174
Total inventories	$4,273	$5,174

KEY POINT

Service companies record revenues when providing services to customers. Merchandising and manufacturing companies record revenues when selling inventory to customers.

FLOW OF INVENTORY COSTS

Illustration 6–2 shows the flow of inventory costs for the three types of companies—service, merchandising, and manufacturing.

Inventory's journey begins when manufacturing companies purchase raw materials, hire workers, and incur manufacturing overhead during production. Once the products are finished, manufacturers normally pass inventories to merchandising companies, whether wholesalers or retailers. Merchandising companies then sell inventories to you, the end user. In some cases, manufacturers may sell directly to end users.

Some companies sell goods and also provide services to customers. For example, **IBM** generates about half its revenues from selling its inventories of hardware and software, and the other half from providing services like consulting, systems maintenance, and financing.

In this chapter, we focus on merchandising companies, both wholesalers and retailers. Still, most of the accounting principles and procedures discussed here also apply to

ILLUSTRATION 6–2

Types of Companies and Flow of Inventory Costs

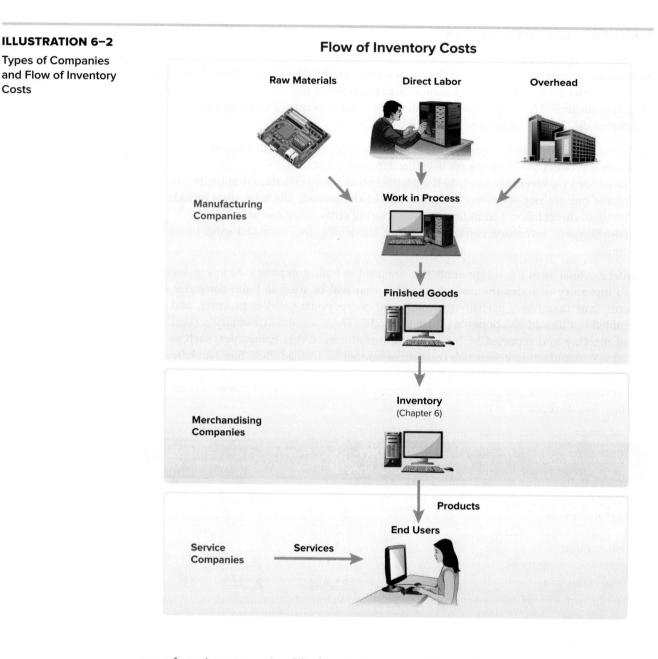

manufacturing companies. We do not attempt to address all the unique problems of accumulating the direct costs of raw materials and labor and allocating manufacturing overhead. We leave those details for managerial and cost accounting courses. In this course, we focus on the financial reporting implications of inventory cost flows.

Cost of Goods Sold

■ **LO6–2**

Understand how cost of goods sold is reported in a multiple-step income statement.

Let's think a little more about the relationship between ending inventory in the balance sheet and cost of goods sold in the income statement. To do this, we'll use a simple example for a local **Best Buy**, depicted in Illustration 6–3. Assume the store begins the year with $20,000 of DVD player inventory. That amount represents how much Best Buy spent to purchase the inventory of DVD players on hand at the beginning of the year. During the year, the company purchases additional DVD players for $90,000. The total cost of inventory (DVD players) available for sale is $110,000 (= $20,000 + $90,000).

Now, here's where we'll see the direct relationship between ending inventory and cost of goods sold. Of the $110,000 in inventory available for sale, assume that by the end of the year the purchase cost of the remaining DVD players *not sold* equals $30,000. This is the amount reported for ending inventory. What is the amount reported for cost of goods *sold?* If $30,000

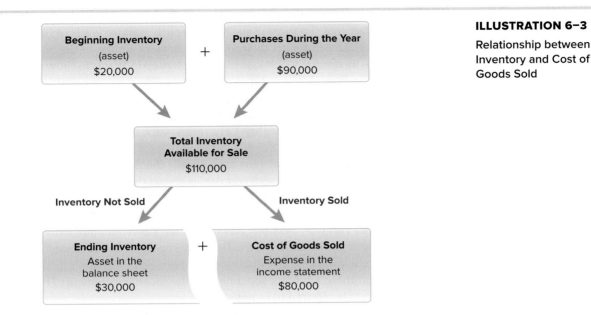

ILLUSTRATION 6–3

Relationship between Inventory and Cost of Goods Sold

of the inventory available for sale was not sold, then the remaining portion of $80,000 (= $110,000 − $30,000) was sold. This is the amount reported for cost of goods sold.

KEY POINT

Inventory is a current asset reported in the balance sheet and represents the cost of inventory *not yet sold* at the end of the period. Cost of goods sold is an expense reported in the income statement and represents the cost of inventory *sold*.

MULTIPLE-STEP INCOME STATEMENT

To see how **Best Buy** actually reports its cost of goods sold as an expense, as well as its other income statement items, let's look at Illustration 6–4.

ILLUSTRATION 6–4

Multiple-Step Income Statement for Best Buy

Best Buy Co., Inc. Multiple-Step Income Statement For the year ended January 31, 2015 ($ in millions)	
Revenues (net of returns, allowances, and discounts)	$40,339
Cost of goods sold	31,292
Gross profit	9,047
Selling, general, and administrative expenses (includes advertising, salaries, rent, utilities, supplies, depreciation, and other operating expenses)	7,597
Operating income	1,450
Other income (expense):	
Gain on sale of investment	13
Investment income and other	14
Interest expense	(90)
Income before income taxes	1,387
Income tax expense	141
Net income*	$ 1,246

Multiple levels of profit

*Amounts include those from Best Buy's actual income statement excluding small adjustments for discontinued operations and noncontrolling interest.

The format of Best Buy's income statement is called the multiple-step income statement, referring to the fact that the income statement reports *multiple* levels of income (or profit). Most companies choose to report their income statement similar to the one shown for Best Buy. The reason why companies choose the multiple-step format is to show the revenues and expenses that arise from different types of activities. By separating revenues and expenses into their different types, investors and creditors are better able to determine the source of a company's profitability. Understanding the source of current profitability often enables a better prediction of future profitability. Let's review each level of profitability.

Gross Profit.   Inventory transactions are typically the most important activities of a merchandising company. For this reason, companies report the revenues and expenses directly associated with these transactions in the top section of a multiple-step income statement.

Sales of inventory are commonly reported as sales revenue, while services provided are recorded as service revenue. Best Buy has mostly sales revenue, but some service revenue, and reports them together as *Revenues.* Best Buy reports these revenues after subtracting customer returns, allowances, and discounts, as discussed in Chapter 5, although the company does not list these amounts separately in the income statement. The net amount of revenues is commonly referred to as **net sales.**

Next, the cost of inventory sold is reported as an expense called *Cost of goods sold.* Best Buy's cost of goods sold includes not only the cost of the physical merchandise purchased from suppliers, but also costs related to getting inventory ready for sale, such as shipping and other costs for its distribution network.

Net revenues (or net sales) minus cost of goods sold equals gross profit. Gross profit is the first level of profit shown in the multiple-step income statement. Gross profit provides a key measure of profitability for the company's primary business activities. Best Buy's gross profit is just over $9 billion for approximately $40 billion in sales.

Operating Income.   After gross profit, the next items reported are *Selling, general, and administrative expenses,* often referred to as **operating expenses.** We discussed several types of operating expenses in earlier chapters—advertising, salaries, rent, utilities, supplies, and depreciation. These costs are normal for operating most companies. Best Buy has total operating expenses of $7,597 million, and like most companies, does not list individual operating expense amounts in the income statement.

Gross profit reduced by these operating expenses is referred to as operating income (or sometimes referred to as *income from operations*). It measures profitability from *normal* operations, a key performance measure for predicting the future profit-generating ability of the company.

Income Before Income Taxes.   After operating income, a company reports *nonoperating* revenues and expenses. Best Buy refers to these items as *Other income (expense).* Other income items are shown as positive amounts, and other expense items are shown as negative amounts (in parentheses). Nonoperating revenues and expenses arise from activities that are *not* part of the company's primary operations.

Best Buy reports two nonoperating revenues—gain on the sale of investments and investment income. Gains on the sale of long-term assets (such as investments, land, equipment, and buildings) occur when assets are sold for more than their recorded amounts. Investment income includes earnings from dividends and interest. Nonoperating revenues are not typical operating activities, but they do represent a source of profitability, so they are included in the income statement.

Nonoperating expenses most commonly include interest expense. Best Buy reports interest expense of $90 million. Nonoperating expenses could also include losses on the sale of investments or long-term assets. Investors focus less on nonoperating revenues and expenses than on income from operations, because nonoperating activities often do not have long-term implications on the company's profitability.

Combining operating income with nonoperating revenues and expenses yields income before income taxes. For Best Buy, the amount of nonoperating expenses exceeds the amount of nonoperating revenues, so income before income taxes is lower than operating income.

Net Income.   Next, a company subtracts *income tax expense* to find its bottom-line net income. Income tax expense is reported separately because it represents a significant expense. It's also the case that most major corporations (formally referred to as C corporations) are tax-paying entities, while income taxes of sole proprietorships and partnerships are paid at the individual owner level. By separately reporting income tax expense, the income statement clearly labels the difference in profitability associated with the income taxes of a corporation.

Best Buy's income tax expense equals 10.2% of income before taxes (= $141 ÷ $1,387). The actual corporate tax rate for Best Buy's level of income is 35%. The reason Best Buy's income tax expense is only 10.2% is because companies sometimes operate in foreign jurisdictions with lower tax rates or because tax rules differ from financial reporting rules. Differences in reporting rules can result in financial income differing from taxable income in any particular year. A more realistic tax expense for Best Buy can be calculated by looking at amounts over the three-year period ending January 31, 2015. Best Buy's cumulative tax expense divided by cumulative income before income taxes for 2013, 2014, and 2015 equaled 32.0%.

KEY POINT

A multiple-step income statement reports multiple levels of profitability. **Gross profit equals net revenues (or net sales) minus cost of goods sold. Operating income equals gross profit minus operating expenses. Income before income taxes equals operating income plus nonoperating revenues and minus nonoperating expenses. Net income equals all revenues minus all expenses.**

Decision Maker's Perspective

Investors Understand One-Time Gains

Investors typically take a close look at the components of a company's profits. For example, **Ford Motor Company** announced that it had earned a net income for the fourth quarter (the final three months of the year) of $13.6 billion. Analysts had expected Ford to earn only $1.7 to $2.0 billion for that period. The day that Ford announced this earnings news, its stock price *fell* about 4.5%.

Why would Ford's stock price fall on a day when the company reported these seemingly high profits? A closer inspection of Ford's income statement shows that it included a one-time gain of $12.4 billion for the fourth quarter. After subtracting this one-time gain, Ford actually earned only about $1.2 billion from normal operations, easily missing analysts' expectations. This disappointing earnings performance is the reason the company's stock price fell.

Inventory Cost Methods

To this point, we've discussed the cost of inventory without considering how we determine that cost. We do that now by considering four methods for inventory costing:

1. Specific identification
2. First-in, first-out (FIFO)
3. Last-in, first-out (LIFO)
4. Weighted-average cost

■ **LO6–3**
Determine the cost of goods sold and ending inventory using different inventory cost methods.

SPECIFIC IDENTIFICATION

The specific identification method is the method you might think of as the most logical. It matches—identifies—each unit of inventory with its actual cost. For example, an automobile has a unique serial number that we can match to an invoice identifying the actual purchase price. Fine jewelry and pieces of art are other possibilities. Specific identification works well in such cases.

However, the specific identification method is practicable only for companies selling unique, expensive products. Consider the inventory at **The Home Depot** or **Macy's**: large stores and numerous items, many of which are relatively inexpensive. Specific identification would be very difficult for such merchandisers. Although bar codes and RFID tags now make it possible to identify and track each unit of inventory, the costs of doing so outweigh the benefits for multiple, small inventory items. For that reason, the specific identification method is used primarily by companies with unique, expensive products with low sales volume.

FIRST-IN, FIRST-OUT

For practical reasons, most companies use one of the three inventory cost flow assumptions—FIFO, LIFO, or weighted-average cost—to determine cost of goods sold and inventory. Note the use of the word *assumptions:* Each of these three inventory cost methods *assumes* a particular pattern of inventory cost flows. However, the *actual* flow of inventory does not need to match the *assumed* cost flow in order for the company to use a particular method.

To see how the three cost flow assumptions work, let's begin with FIFO. We'll examine the inventory transactions in Illustration 6–5 for Mario's Game Shop, which sells video game controllers. Mario has 100 units of inventory at the beginning of the year and then makes two purchases during the year—one on April 25 and one on October 19. (Note the different unit costs at the time of each purchase.) There are **1,000** game controllers available for sale.

ILLUSTRATION 6–5

Inventory Transactions for Mario's Game Shop

Date	Transaction	Number of Units	Unit Cost	Total Cost
Jan. 1	Beginning inventory	100	$ 7	$ 700
Apr. 25	Purchase	300	9	2,700
Oct. 19	Purchase	600	11	6,600
	Total goods available for sale	1,000		$10,000
Jan. 1–Dec. 31	Total sales to customers	800		
Dec. 31	Ending inventory	200		

During the year, Mario sells **800** video game controllers for $15 each. This means that **200** controllers remain in ending inventory at the end of the year. But which 200? Do they include some of the $7 units from beginning inventory? Are they 200 of the $9 units from the April 25 purchase? Or, do they include some $11 units from the October 19 purchase? We consider these questions below.

Using the first-in, first-out (FIFO) method, we assume that the first units purchased (the first in) are the first ones sold (the first out). We assume that beginning inventory sells first, followed by the inventory from the first purchase during the year, followed by the inventory from the second purchase during the year, and so on.

In our example, which 800 units did Mario's Game Shop sell? Using the FIFO method, we *assume* they were the *first* 800 units purchased, and that all other units remain in ending inventory. These calculations are shown in Illustration 6–6.

We assume that all units from beginning inventory (100 units) and the April 25 purchase (300 units) were sold. For the final 400 units sold, we split the October 19 purchase of 600 units into two groups—400 units assumed sold and 200 units assumed not sold. We calculate cost of goods sold as the units of inventory assumed sold times their respective unit costs. [That is: (100 × $7) + (300 × $9) + (400 × $11) in our example.] Similarly, ending inventory equals the units assumed not sold times *their* respective unit costs (200 × $11 in our

Inventory Transactions for Mario's Game Shop—FIFO METHOD

Beginning Inventory and Purchases	Cost of Goods Available for Sale			=	Cost of Goods Sold	+	Ending Inventory
	Number of Units	× Unit Cost	= Total Cost				
Jan. 1	100	$ 7	$ 700		Sold first	$ 700	
Apr. 25	300	9	2,700		800	2,700	
Oct. 19	400	11	4,400		units	4,400	
	200	11	2,200		Not sold		$2,200
	1,000		$10,000	=		$7,800	+ $2,200

ILLUSTRATION 6–6

Inventory Calculation Using the FIFO Method

mhhe.com/4fa22

example). The amount of cost of goods sold Mario reports in the income statement will be $7,800. The amount of ending inventory in the balance sheet will be $2,200.

You may have noticed that we don't actually need to directly calculate both cost of goods sold and inventory. Once we calculate one, the other is apparent. Because the two amounts always add up to the cost of goods available for sale (**$10,000** in our example), knowing either amount allows us to subtract to find the other.

Realize, too, that the amounts reported for ending inventory and cost of goods sold do *not* represent the actual cost of inventory sold and not sold. That's okay. **Companies are allowed to report inventory costs by** *assuming* **which units of inventory are sold and not sold, even if this does not match the** *actual* **flow.** This is another example of using estimates in financial accounting.

LAST-IN, FIRST-OUT

Using the last-in, first-out (LIFO) method, we assume that the last units purchased (the last in) are the first ones sold (the first out). If Mario sold 800 units, we assume all the 600 units purchased on October 19 (the last purchase) were sold, along with 200 units from the April 25 purchase. That leaves 100 of the units from the April 25 purchase and all 100 units from beginning inventory assumed to remain in ending inventory (not sold). Illustration 6–7 shows calculations of cost of goods sold and ending inventory for the LIFO method.

Inventory Transactions for Mario's Game Shop—LIFO METHOD

Beginning Inventory and Purchases	Cost of Goods Available for Sale			=	Cost of Goods Sold	+	Ending Inventory
	Number of Units	× Unit Cost	= Total Cost				
Jan. 1	100	$ 7	$ 700		Not sold		$ 700
Apr. 25	100	9	900				900
	200	9	1,800		Sold last 800 units	$1,800	
Oct. 19	600	11	6,600			6,600	
	1,000		$10,000			$8,400	+ $1,600

ILLUSTRATION 6–7

Inventory Calculation Using the LIFO Method

mhhe.com/4fa23

COMMON MISTAKE

Many students find it surprising that companies are allowed to report inventory costs using assumed amounts rather than actual amounts. Nearly all companies sell their actual inventory in a FIFO manner, but they are allowed to report it as if they sold it in a LIFO manner. Later, we'll see why that's advantageous.

WEIGHTED-AVERAGE COST

Using the weighted-average cost method, we assume that both cost of goods sold and ending inventory consist of a random mixture of all the goods available for sale. We assume each unit of inventory has a cost equal to the weighted-average unit cost of all inventory items. We calculate that cost at the end of the year as:

$$\text{Weighted-average unit cost} = \frac{\text{Cost of goods available for sale}}{\text{Number of units available for sale}}$$

Illustration 6–8 demonstrates the calculation of cost of goods sold and ending inventory using the weighted-average cost method. Notice that the weighted-average cost of each game controller is $10, even though none of the game controllers actually cost $10. However, on average, all the game controllers cost $10, and this is the amount we use to calculate cost of goods sold and ending inventory under the weighted-average cost method.

ILLUSTRATION 6–8

Inventory Calculation Using the Weighted-Average Cost Method

Inventory Transactions for Mario's Game Shop—
WEIGHTED-AVERAGE COST METHOD

		Cost of Goods Available for Sale					
Date	Transaction	Number of Units	×	Unit Cost	=	Total Cost	
Jan. 1	Beginning inventory	100		$ 7		$ 700	
Apr. 25	Purchase	300		9		2,700	
Oct. 19	Purchase	600		11		6,600	
		1,000				$10,000	

Weighted-average unit cost $= \dfrac{\$10,000}{1,000 \text{ units}} =$ $10 per unit

Cost of goods sold	=	800 sold	×	$10	=	$ 8,000
Ending inventory	=	200 not sold	×	10	=	2,000
						$10,000

 COMMON MISTAKE

In calculating the weighted-average unit cost, be sure to use a *weighted* average of the unit cost instead of the *simple* average. In the example above, there are three unit costs: $7, $9, and $11. A simple average of these amounts is $9 [= (7 + 9 + 11) ÷ 3]. The simple average, though, fails to take into account that more units were purchased at $11 than at $7 or $9. So we need to *weight* the unit costs by the number of units purchased. We do that by taking the total cost of goods available for sale ($10,000) divided by the total number of units available for sale (1,000) for a weighted average of $10.

Illustration 6–9 depicts the concept behind the three inventory cost flow assumptions for Mario's Game Shop. Mario begins the year with 100 units previously purchased for $7 per unit. During the year Mario makes two additional purchases with unit costs of $9 and $11.

ILLUSTRATION 6–9 Comparison of Cost of Goods Sold and Ending Inventory under the Three Inventory Cost Flow Assumptions for Mario's Game Shop

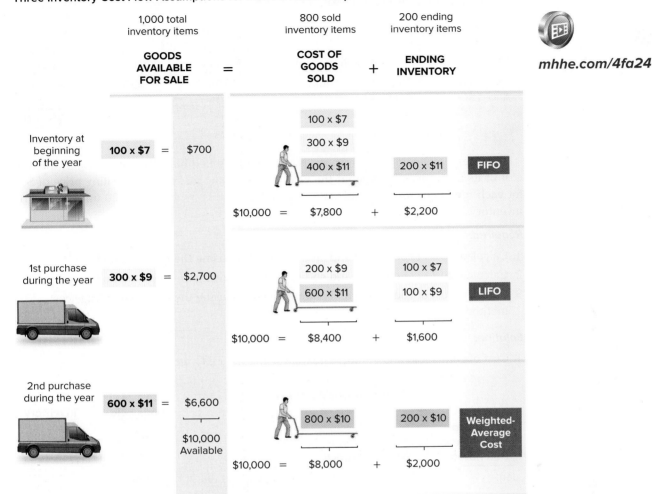

mhhe.com/4fa24

The total inventory available for sale is $10,000. If Mario sells 800 units of inventory, which 800 are they? Using FIFO, we assume inventory is sold in the order purchased: Beginning inventory is sold first, the first purchase during the year is sold second, and part of the second purchase during the year is sold third. Using LIFO, we assume inventory is sold in the *opposite* order that we purchased it: The last purchase is sold first, and part of the second-to-last purchase is sold second. Using average cost, we assume inventory is sold using an average of all inventory purchased, including the beginning inventory.

 COMMON MISTAKE

FIFO and LIFO describe more directly the calculation of *cost of goods sold*, rather than ending inventory. For example, FIFO (first-in, first-out) directly suggests which inventory units are assumed sold (the first ones in) and therefore used to calculate cost of goods sold. It is implicit under FIFO that the inventory units *not* sold are the last ones in and are used to calculate ending inventory.

KEY POINT

Companies are allowed to report inventory costs by *assuming* which specific units of inventory are sold and not sold, even if this does not match the *actual* flow. The three major inventory cost flow assumptions are FIFO (first-in, first-out), LIFO (last-in, first-out), and weighted-average cost.

Let's Review

mhhe.com/4fa25

NASCAR Unlimited sells remote-control cars. The company has the following beginning inventory and purchase for the year.

Date	Transaction	Number of Units	Unit Cost	Total Cost
Jan. 1	Beginning inventory	120	$20	$2,400
Aug. 15	Purchase	180	15	2,700
	Total	300		$5,100

Because of technological advances, NASCAR Unlimited has seen a decrease in the unit cost of its inventory. Throughout the year, the company maintained a selling price of $30 for each remote-control car and sold a total of 280 units, which leaves 20 units in ending inventory.

Required:

1. Calculate cost of goods sold and ending inventory using the FIFO method.
2. Calculate cost of goods sold and ending inventory using the LIFO method.
3. Calculate cost of goods sold and ending inventory using the weighted-average cost method.

Solution:

1. Cost of goods sold and ending inventory using the **FIFO method:**

Beginning Inventory and Purchases	Cost of Goods Available for Sale			=	Cost of Goods Sold	+	Ending Inventory
	Number of Units	× Unit Cost	= Total Cost				
Jan. 1	120	$20	$2,400 ⎤	Sold first 280 units	$2,400		
Aug. 15 {	160	15	2,400 ⎦		2,400		
	20	15	300 }	Not sold			$300
	300		$5,100	=	$4,800	+	$300

2. Cost of goods sold and ending inventory using the **LIFO method:**

Beginning Inventory and Purchases	Cost of Goods Available for Sale			=	Cost of Goods Sold	+	Ending Inventory
	Number of Units	× Unit Cost	= Total Cost				
Jan. 1 {	20	$20	$ 400 }	Not sold			$400
	100	20	2,000 ⎤	Sold last 280 units	$2,000		
Aug. 15	180	15	2,700 ⎦		2,700		
	300		$5,100	=	$4,700	+	$400

3. Cost of goods sold and ending inventory using the **weighted-average cost method:**

$$\text{Weighted-average unit cost} = \frac{\$5,100}{300} = \$17$$

Cost of goods sold	= 280 sold	× $17	=	$4,760
Ending inventory	= 20 not sold	× 17	=	340
	300			$5,100

Suggested Homework:
BE6–5, BE6–6;
E6–4, E6–5;
P6–1A&B, P6–2A&B

Effects of Inventory Cost Methods

Companies are free to choose FIFO, LIFO, or weighted-average cost to report inventory and cost of goods sold. However, because inventory costs generally change over time, the reported amounts for ending inventory and cost of goods sold will not be the same across inventory reporting methods. These differences could cause investors and creditors to make bad decisions if they are not aware of differences in inventory assumptions.

■ **LO6–4**
Explain the financial statement effects and tax effects of inventory cost methods.

Illustration 6–10 compares the FIFO, LIFO, and weighted-average cost methods for Mario's Game Shop (assuming rising costs). (Recall from earlier discussion in this chapter that *gross profit* is a key measure of profitability, calculated as the difference between revenues and cost of goods sold.)

	FIFO	LIFO	Weighted-Average
Balance sheet:			
Ending inventory	$ 2,200	$ 1,600	$ 2,000
Income statement:			
Sales revenue (800 × $15)	$12,000	$12,000	$12,000
Cost of goods sold	7,800	8,400	8,000
Gross profit	$ 4,200	$ 3,600	$ 4,000

ILLUSTRATION 6–10
Comparison of Inventory Cost Methods, When Costs Are Rising

When inventory costs are rising, Mario's Game Shop will report both higher inventory in the balance sheet and higher gross profit in the income statement if it chooses FIFO. The reason is that FIFO assumes the lower costs of the earlier purchases become cost of goods sold first, leaving the higher costs of the later purchases in ending inventory. Under the same assumption (rising inventory costs), LIFO will produce the *opposite* effect: LIFO will report both the lowest inventory and the lowest gross profit. The weighted-average cost method typically produces amounts that fall between the FIFO and LIFO amounts for both cost of goods sold and ending inventory.

Accountants often call FIFO the *balance-sheet approach:* The amount it reports for ending inventory (which appears in the *balance sheet*) better approximates the current cost of inventory. The ending inventory amount reported under LIFO, in contrast, generally includes "old" inventory costs that do not realistically represent the cost of today's inventory.

FIFO has a balance-sheet focus.

Accountants often call LIFO the *income-statement approach:* The amount it reports for cost of goods sold (which appears in the *income statement*) more realistically matches the current costs of inventory needed to produce current revenues. Recall that LIFO assumes the last purchases are sold first, reporting the most recent inventory cost in cost of goods sold. However, also note that the most recent cost is not the same as the actual cost. FIFO better approximates actual cost of goods sold for most companies, since most companies' actual physical flow follows FIFO.

LIFO has an income-statement focus.

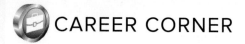

CAREER CORNER

Many career opportunities are available in tax accounting. Because tax laws constantly change and are complex, tax accountants provide services to their clients not only through income tax statement preparation but also by formulating tax strategies to minimize tax payments. The choice of LIFO versus FIFO is one such example.

Tax accountants need a thorough understanding of legal matters, business transactions, and the tax code. Large corporations increasingly are looking to hire individuals with both an accounting and a legal background in tax. For example, someone who is a Certified Public Accountant (CPA) and has a law degree is especially desirable in the job market. In addition, people in nonaccounting positions also benefit greatly from an understanding of tax accounting. Whether you work in a large corporation or own a small business, virtually all business decisions have tax consequences.

© BananaStock/JupiterImages, RF

FIFO matches physical flow for most companies.

FIFO generally results in higher assets and higher net income when inventory costs are rising.

LIFO generally results in greater tax savings.

Decision Maker's Perspective

FIFO or LIFO?

Management must weigh the benefits of FIFO and LIFO when deciding which inventory cost flow assumption will produce a better outcome for the company. Here we review the logic behind that decision.

Why Choose FIFO?

Most companies' actual physical flow follows FIFO. Think about a supermarket, sporting goods store, clothing shop, electronics store, or just about any company you're familiar with. These companies generally sell their oldest inventory first (first-in, first-out). If a company wants to choose an inventory method that most closely approximates its *actual physical flow* of inventory, then for most companies FIFO makes the most sense.

Another reason managers may want to use FIFO relates to its effect on the financial statements. **During periods of rising costs, which is the case for most companies (including our example for Mario's Game Shop), FIFO results in a (1)** *higher* **ending inventory, (2)** *lower* **cost of goods sold, and (3)** *higher* **reported profit than does LIFO.** Managers may want to report higher assets and profitability to increase their bonus compensation, decrease unemployment risk, satisfy shareholders, meet lending agreements, or increase stock price.

Why Choose LIFO?

If FIFO results in higher total assets and higher net income and produces amounts that most closely follow the actual flow of inventory, why would any company choose LIFO? **The primary benefit of choosing LIFO is tax savings.** LIFO results in the lowest amount of reported profits (when inventory costs are rising). While that might not look so good in the income statement, it's a welcome outcome in the tax return. When taxable income is lower, the company owes less in taxes to the Internal Revenue Service (IRS).

Can a company have its cake and eat it too by using FIFO for financial reporting and LIFO for the tax return? No. The IRS established the LIFO conformity rule, which requires a company that uses LIFO for tax reporting to also use LIFO for financial reporting.

REPORTING THE LIFO DIFFERENCE

As Mario's Game Shop demonstrates, the choice between FIFO and LIFO results in different amounts for ending inventory in the balance sheet and cost of goods sold in the income statement. This complicates the way we compare financial statements: One company may be using FIFO, while a competing company may be using LIFO. To determine which of the two companies is more profitable, investors must adjust for the fact that managers' choice of inventory method has an effect on reported performance.

Because of the financial statement effects of different inventory methods, companies that choose LIFO must report the difference in the amount of inventory a company would report *if* it used FIFO instead of LIFO. (This difference is sometimes referred to as the LIFO reserve.) For some companies that have been using LIFO for a long time or for companies that have seen dramatic increases in inventory costs, the LIFO difference can be substantial. For example, Illustration 6–11 shows the effect of the LIFO difference reported by **Rite Aid Corporation**, which uses LIFO to account for most of its inventory.

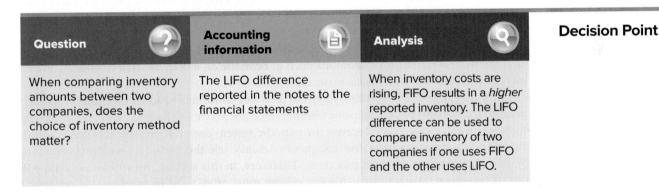

RITE AID CORPORATION
Notes to the Financial Statements (partial)

($ in millions)	2015	2014
Reported inventory under LIFO	$2,883	$2,994
LIFO difference	998	1,019
Inventory assuming FIFO	$3,881	$4,013

ILLUSTRATION 6–11

Impact of the LIFO Difference on Reported Inventory of Rite Aid Corporation

If Rite Aid had used FIFO instead of LIFO, reported inventory amounts would have been $998 million greater and $1,019 million greater in 2015 and 2014, respectively. The magnitude of these effects can have a significant influence on investors' decisions.

Question	Accounting information	Analysis
When comparing inventory amounts between two companies, does the choice of inventory method matter?	The LIFO difference reported in the notes to the financial statements	When inventory costs are rising, FIFO results in a *higher* reported inventory. The LIFO difference can be used to compare inventory of two companies if one uses FIFO and the other uses LIFO.

Decision Point

CONSISTENCY IN REPORTING

Companies can choose which inventory method they prefer, even if the method does not match the actual physical flow of goods. However, once the company chooses a method, it is not allowed to frequently change to another one.[1] For example, a retail store cannot use FIFO in the current year because inventory costs are rising and then switch to LIFO in the following year because inventory costs are now falling.

However, a company need not use the same method for all its inventory. **International Paper Company**, for instance, uses LIFO for its raw materials and finished pulp and paper products, and both FIFO and weighted-average cost for other inventories. Because of the importance of inventories and the possible differential effects of different methods on the financial statements, a company informs its stockholders of the inventory method(s) being used in a note to the financial statements.

KEY POINT

Generally, FIFO more closely resembles the actual physical flow of inventory. When inventory costs are rising, FIFO results in higher reported inventory in the balance sheet and higher reported income in the income statement. Conversely, LIFO results in a lower reported inventory and net income, reducing the company's income tax obligation.

---

[1]When a company changes from LIFO for tax purposes, it cannot change back to LIFO until it has filed five tax returns using the non-LIFO method.

INTERNATIONAL FINANCIAL REPORTING STANDARDS (IFRS)

SHOULD LIFO BE ELIMINATED?

LIFO is *not* allowed under IFRS because it tends not to match the actual physical flow of inventory. FIFO and weighted-average cost are allowable inventory cost methods under IFRS. This distinction will become increasingly important as the United States continues to consider whether to accept IFRS for financial reporting. Will LIFO eventually disappear as a permitted inventory cost flow method? Perhaps so . . . stay tuned.

For more discussion, see Appendix E.

PART B

RECORDING INVENTORY TRANSACTIONS

So far, we've talked about purchases and sales of inventories and how to track their costs. We have not yet discussed how to *record* inventory transactions. We turn to that topic now.

To maintain a record of inventory transactions, in practice nearly all companies use a perpetual inventory system. This system involves recording inventory purchases and sales on a *perpetual* (continual) basis. Managers know that to make good decisions they need to keep track each day of which inventory is selling and which is not. This information will affect decisions related to purchase orders, pricing, product development, and employee management. Because these decisions need to be made on a daily basis, maintaining inventory records on a continual basis is necessary.

In contrast, a periodic inventory system does not continually record inventory amounts. Instead, it calculates the balance of inventory once per *period,* at the end, based on a physical count of inventory on hand. Because the periodic system does not provide a useful, continuing record of inventory, very few companies actually use the periodic inventory system in practice to record inventory transactions. **Therefore, in this section, we will focus on how to record inventory transactions using the system most often used in practice—the perpetual inventory system.** Appendix A to the chapter shows how to record transactions using the periodic inventory system.

Perpetual Inventory System

■ **LO6–5**
Record inventory transactions using a perpetual inventory system.

To see how to record inventory transactions using a perpetual inventory system, we will look again at the inventory transactions for Mario's Game Shop. Recall that from January 1 through December 31, Mario sold 800 controllers. Now let's modify the example by giving exact dates for the sale of the 800 controllers—300 on July 17 and 500 on December 15. Illustration 6–12 shows the order of inventory transactions for Mario's Game Shop, including the total cost of the inventory and the total revenue from the sale of the 800 controllers.

ILLUSTRATION 6–12

Inventory Transactions for Mario's Game Shop

Date	Transaction	Details	Total Cost	Total Revenue
Jan. 1	Beginning inventory	100 units for $7 each	$ 700	
Apr. 25	Purchase	300 units for $9 each	2,700	
Jul. 17	Sale	300 units for $15 each		$ 4,500
Oct. 19	Purchase	600 units for $11 each	6,600	
Dec. 15	Sale	500 units for $15 each		7,500
	Totals		$10,000	$12,000

Using this information, let's see how Mario would record purchases and sales of inventory.

INVENTORY PURCHASES AND SALES

To record the purchase of new inventory, we debit Inventory (an asset) to show that the company's balance of this asset account has increased. At the same time, if the purchase was paid in cash, we credit Cash. Or more likely, if the company made the purchase on account, we credit Accounts Payable, increasing total liabilities. Thus, Mario records the first purchase of 300 units for $2,700 on April 25 as:

April 25	Debit	Credit
Inventory	**2,700**	
Accounts Payable		**2,700**
(Purchase inventory on account)		

Balance Sheet					Income Statement		
			Stockholders' Equity				
			Common	**Retained**			**Net**
Assets	**=**	**Liabilities +**	**Stock +**	**Earnings**	**Revenues −**	**Expenses =**	**Income**
+2,700	=	+2,700					

On July 17, Mario sold 300 units of inventory on account for $15 each, resulting in total sales of $4,500. We make two entries to record the sale: (1) The first entry shows an increase to the asset account (in this case, Accounts Receivable) and an increase to Sales Revenue. (2) The second entry reduces the Inventory account as it records cost of goods sold.

Mario records as revenue the $4,500 from the July 17 sale. That amount is the price Mario charges to customers, but what did that inventory *cost* Mario? (That is, what is the cost of the goods sold?) Because Mario's Game Shop, like nearly all companies, actually sells its oldest inventory first (FIFO), the cost of the *first* 300 units purchased is $2,500, which is $700 of beginning inventory (100 units × $7) plus $1,800 of the April 25 purchase (200 units × $9). We record this amount as the cost of goods sold for the July 17 sale. At the same time, we maintain a continual (perpetual) record of inventory by reducing the Inventory balance by the cost of the amount sold, $2,500, as shown below.

July 17	Debit	Credit
Accounts Receivable	**4,500**	
Sales Revenue		**4,500**
(Sell inventory on account)		
($4,500 = 300 units × $15)		
Cost of Goods Sold	**2,500**	
Inventory		**2,500**
(Record cost of inventory sold)		
($2,500 = [100 units × $7] + [200 units × $9])		

Balance Sheet					Income Statement		
			Stockholders' Equity				
			Common	**Retained**			**Net**
Assets	**=**	**Liabilities +**	**Stock +**	**Earnings**	**Revenues −**	**Expenses =**	**Income**
+4,500	=			+2,000	+4,500	− +2,500	= +2,000
−2,500							
+2,000							

By recording the sales revenue and the cost of goods sold at the same time, we can see that Mario's profit on the sale is $2,000.

On October 19, Mario purchased 600 additional units of inventory for $6,600 on account. We record that purchase as:

A = L + SE		Debit	Credit
+6,600	**October 19**		
	Inventory	**6,600**	
+6,600	**Accounts Payable**		**6,600**
	(Purchase inventory on account)		

On December 15, Mario sold another 500 units for $15 each on account. Again, we make two entries to record the sale. The first entry increases Accounts Receivable and Sales Revenue. The second entry adjusts the Cost of Goods Sold and Inventory accounts. What did the inventory sold on December 15 cost Mario? On the FIFO basis, the cost of goods sold is $5,300 (100 units × $9 plus 400 units × $11). Mario increases Cost of Goods Sold and decreases Inventory by that amount. Thus, we record the sale on December 15 as:

A = L + SE		Debit	Credit
+7,500	**December 15**		
	Accounts Receivable	**7,500**	
+7,500 Rev ↑	**Sales Revenue**		**7,500**
	(Sell inventory on account)		
	($7,500 = 500 units × $15)		
A = L + SE			
−5,300 Exp ↑	**Cost of Goods Sold**	**5,300**	
−5,300	**Inventory**		**5,300**
	(Record cost of inventory sold)		
	($5,300 = [100 units × $9] + [400 units × $11])		

After recording all purchases and sales of inventory for the year, we can determine the ending balance of Inventory by examining the postings to the account. Thus, Mario's ending Inventory balance is $2,200, as shown in Illustration 6–13. Refer back to Illustration 6–6 to verify the ending balance of inventory using FIFO.

ILLUSTRATION 6–13

Inventory Account for Mario's Game Shop

	Inventory		
Jan. 1 Beginning	700		
Apr. 25 Purchase	2,700	2,500	Jul. 17 Sale
Oct. 19 Purchase	6,600	5,300	Dec. 15 Sale
	10,000	7,800	
Dec. 31 Ending			
FIFO amount	Bal. 2,200		

 KEY POINT

The perpetual inventory system maintains a continual—or *perpetual*—record of inventory purchased and sold. When companies *purchase* inventory using a perpetual inventory system, they increase the Inventory account and either decrease Cash or increase Accounts Payable. When companies *sell* inventory, they make two entries: (1) They increase an asset account (Cash or Accounts Receivable) and increase Sales Revenue, and (2) they increase Cost of Goods Sold and decrease Inventory.

Simple Adjustment from FIFO to LIFO. In the example above, we recorded inventory transactions using the FIFO assumption. Thus, Mario assumed that the 800 units sold during the year came from the first 800 units purchased. **In practice, virtually all companies maintain their own inventory records using the FIFO assumption, because that's how they typically sell their actual inventory.**[2] However, as discussed earlier in the chapter, for preparing financial statements, many companies choose to report their inventory using the LIFO assumption. So, how does a company adjust its own inventory records maintained on a FIFO basis to a LIFO basis for preparing financial statements? The adjustment is referred to as the LIFO adjustment, and you'll see that this involves a *simple* adjusting entry at the end of the year.

To see how easy the LIFO adjustment can be, let's refer back to our example involving Mario's Game Shop. As summarized in Illustration 6–13, Mario's ending balance of Inventory using FIFO is $2,200. Under LIFO, it is only $1,600 (see Illustration 6–7). As a result, if Mario's Game Shop wants to adjust its FIFO inventory records to LIFO for preparing financial statements, it needs to adjust Inventory downward by $600 (decreasing the balance from $2,200 to $1,600). In this case, we record the LIFO adjustment at the end of the period through a decrease to Inventory and an increase to Cost of Goods Sold:

December 31	Debit	Credit
Cost of Goods Sold	600	
Inventory		600
(Record the LIFO adjustment)		

A	=	L	+	SE
				−600 Exp ↑
−600				

In rare situations where the LIFO Inventory balance is *greater* than the FIFO Inventory balance (such as when inventory costs are declining), the entry for the LIFO adjustment would be reversed.

Illustration 6–14 shows the Inventory account for Mario's Game Shop after the LIFO adjustment. Notice that the balance of Inventory has decreased to reflect the amount reported under the LIFO method.

The difference in reported inventory when using LIFO instead of FIFO is commonly referred to as the *LIFO reserve*.

ILLUSTRATION 6–14

Inventory Account for Mario's Game Shop, after LIFO Adjustment

	Inventory			
Jan. 1 Beginning	700			
Apr. 25 Purchase	2,700	2,500	Jul. 17 Sale	
Oct. 19 Purchase	6,600	5,300	Dec. 15 Sale	
	10,000	7,800		
Dec. 31 FIFO amount	2,200			
		600	Dec. 31 LIFO adjustment	
Dec. 31 Ending LIFO amount	Bal. 1,600			

KEY POINT

Nearly all companies maintain their own inventory records on a FIFO basis, and then some prepare financial statements on a LIFO basis. To adjust their FIFO inventory records to LIFO for financial reporting, companies use a LIFO adjustment at the end of the period.

---

[2]Some companies use the weighted-average method with a perpetual inventory system for their inventory records. This means the company must recalculate the average cost of remaining inventory each time a new purchase is made during the year. Each sale could then potentially be assigned a different average cost—unlike our example in Illustration 6–8, which assumes a periodic system (a single average cost for the entire period). For this reason, the weighted-average method using a perpetual inventory system is often referred to as the *moving-average* method. With the help of computers and electronic scanners, such tedious calculations throughout the period are possible. However, for this introductory course we focus on conceptual understanding from the weighted-average method and leave the moving-average method for more advanced accounting classes.

ADDITIONAL INVENTORY TRANSACTIONS

To this point, we've recorded inventory purchases and inventory sales transactions. Let's add three more inventory-related transactions to our Mario's example. Let's assume Mario also:

1. On April 25, pays freight charges of $300 for inventory purchased on April 25.
2. On April 30, pays for the units purchased on April 25, less a 2% purchase discount.
3. On October 22, returns 50 defective units from the October 19 purchase.

Next, we discuss how to record each of these three transactions.

Freight Charges.   A significant cost associated with inventory for most merchandising companies includes freight (also called shipping or delivery) charges. This includes the cost of shipments of inventory from suppliers, as well as the cost of shipments to customers. When goods are shipped, they are shipped with terms *FOB shipping point* or *FOB destination.* FOB stands for "free on board" and indicates *when* title (ownership) passes from the seller to the buyer. FOB *shipping point* means title passes when the seller *ships* the inventory, not when the buyer receives it. In contrast, if the seller ships the inventory FOB *destination,* then title transfers to the buyer when the inventory reaches its destination.

For example, suppose that when Mario purchased 300 units for $2,700 ($9 per unit) on April 25, the terms of the purchase were FOB shipping point. The inventory was shipped from the supplier's warehouse on April 25 but did not arrive at Mario's location until April 29. Mario would record the purchase when title passes—April 25—even though Mario does not have actual physical possession of the inventory until April 29. If, instead, the terms of the purchase were FOB destination, Mario would have waited until the inventory was received on April 29 to record the purchase. This idea is demonstrated in Illustration 6–15.

ILLUSTRATION 6–15

Shipping Terms

Freight charges on incoming shipments from suppliers are commonly referred to as freight-in. **We add the cost of freight-in to the balance of Inventory.** In this case, the cost of freight is considered a cost of the purchased inventory. When Mario pays $300 for freight charges associated with the purchase of inventory on April 25, those charges would be recorded as part of the inventory cost.

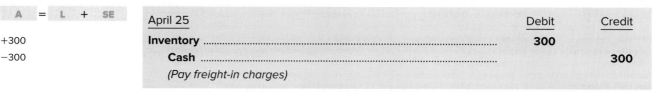

A = L + SE		April 25	Debit	Credit
+300		**Inventory**	**300**	
−300		**Cash**		**300**
		(Pay freight-in charges)		

Later, when that inventory is sold, those freight charges become part of the cost of goods sold. In Mario's case, all of the units purchased on April 25 are sold by the end of the year, so the $300 freight charge would be reported as part of cost of goods sold in the income statement at the end of the year.

The cost of freight on shipments *to* customers is called freight-out. Shipping charges for outgoing inventory are reported in the income statement either as part of cost of goods sold or as an operating expense, usually among selling expenses. If a company adopts a policy of not including shipping charges in cost of goods sold, both the amounts incurred during the period as well as the income statement classification of the expense must be disclosed.[3]

To see an example of how **Amazon.com** accounts for freight charges, look at Illustration 6–16.

ILLUSTRATION 6–16

Accounting for
Shipping Costs by
Amazon.com

AMAZON.COM, INC.
Notes to the Financial Statements (excerpt)

Cost of sales consists of the purchase price of consumer products and . . . **inbound and outbound shipping costs.** Outbound shipping costs (net of shipping revenue) in 2014, 2013, and 2012 were $4.2 billion, $3.5 billion, and $2.9 billion.

Purchase Discounts.   As discussed in Chapter 5, sellers often encourage prompt payment by offering *discounts* to buyers. From the seller's point of view, these are sales discounts; from the buyer's point of view, they are *purchase discounts*. Purchase discounts allow buyers to trim a portion of the cost of the purchase in exchange for payment within a certain period of time. Buyers are not required to take purchase discounts, but many find it advantageous to do so.

Let's assume that Mario's supplier, Luigi Software, Inc., offers terms 2/10, n/30 for the April 25 purchase on account. This means that Mario can receive a 2% discount if payment is made within 10 days, but the total invoice is due within 30 days. Mario's policy is to take advantage of discounts offered.

Recall that on April 25 Mario purchased 300 units on account for $9 each (or $2,700 total). When Mario makes payment on April 30, the discount would be $54 (= $2,700 × 2%). Mario has to pay only $2,646 (= $2,700 − $54) to eliminate the $2,700 amount owed. To account for the purchase discount, we subtract the discount from the balance in the Inventory account:

April 30	Debit	Credit	A	=	L	+	SE
Accounts Payable	**2,700**				−2,700		
Inventory		**54**	−54				
Cash		**2,646**	−2,646				
(Pay on account with a 2% purchase discount of $54)							
($54 = $2,700 × 2%)							

Just as freight charges *add* to the cost of inventory and therefore increase the cost of goods sold once those items are sold, purchase discounts *subtract* from the cost of inventory and therefore reduce cost of goods sold once those items are sold. When Mario sells the 300 units purchased on April 25, the cost of goods sold associated with those items will be the cost of the actual units ($2,700) plus freight charges ($300) less the purchase discount ($54), totaling $2,946.

---

[3]FASB ASC 605-45-50-2: Revenue Recognition-Principal Agent Considerations-Disclosure-Shipping and Handling Fees and Costs (previously "Accounting for Shipping and Handling Fees and Costs," *EITF Issue No 00-10* [Norwalk, Conn.: FASB, 2000] par. 6).

Purchase Returns.   Occasionally, a company will find inventory items to be unacceptable for some reason—perhaps they are damaged or are different from what was ordered. In those cases, the company returns the items to the supplier and records the purchase return as a reduction in both Inventory and Accounts Payable. For example, when Mario decides on October 22 to return 50 defective units from the 600 units purchased on October 19 for $11 each, the company would record the following transaction:

A	=	L	+	SE
		−550		
−550				

October 22	Debit	Credit
Accounts Payable	**550**	
Inventory		**550**
(Return inventory previously purchased on account)		
($550 = 50 defective units × $11)		

Let's recalculate Mario's gross profit after accounting for the additional inventory transactions related to freight charges and the purchase discount. The calculations are demonstrated in Illustration 6–17. Recall that Mario sold 800 units during the year for $15 each (or $12,000 total). This is the amount reported as sales revenue. From sales revenue, we subtract the cost of the 800 units sold. To calculate this amount, we need to look back at transactions related to the purchase cost of those 800 units, including the cost of freight charges and the purchase discount associated with the purchase on April 25. Mario would report $8,046 as the cost of goods sold, resulting in a gross profit of $3,954.

ILLUSTRATION 6–17

Gross Profit for Mario's Game Shop after Additional Inventory Transactions

	Units	Unit Price	Total
Sales revenue	800	$15	$12,000

	Units	Unit Cost	Total
Cost of goods sold:			
Beginning inventory	100	$ 7	$ 700
Purchase on April 25	300	9	2,700
Freight charges			300
Purchase discount			(54)
Purchase on October 19	400	11	4,400
	800		$ 8,046
Gross profit			$ 3,954

KEY POINT

For most companies, freight charges are added to the cost of inventory, whereas purchase returns and purchase discounts are deducted from the cost of inventory. Some companies choose to report freight charges on outgoing shipments as part of selling expenses instead of cost of goods sold.

Let's Review

mhhe.com/4fa26

Camcorder Central sells high-end **Sony** camcorders and accounts for its inventory using FIFO with a perpetual system. At the beginning of March, the company has camcorder inventory of $24,000 (= $240 × 100 units).

Required:

Record the following inventory transactions for Camcorder Central.
1. On March 7, Camcorder Central purchases on account 210 camcorders from Sony Corporation for $250 each, terms 2/10, n/30.

2. On March 8, Camcorder Central pays $2,000 for freight charges associated with the 210 camcorders purchased on March 7.

3. On March 10, Camcorder Central returns to Sony 10 defective camcorders from the March 7 purchase, receiving a credit of $250 for each camcorder.

4. On March 16, Camcorder Central makes full payment for inventory purchased on March 7, excluding the 10 defective camcorders returned and the 2% discount received.

5. On March 20, Camcorder Central sells 300 camcorders for $90,000 ($300 each). All sales are for cash.

Solution:

1. Camcorder Central's March 7 purchase on account of 210 camcorders from Sony Corporation for $250 each, terms 2/10, n/30:

March 7	Debit	Credit
Inventory	**52,500**	
Accounts Payable		**52,500**
(Purchase camcorders on account)		
($52,500 = $250 × 210 camcorders)		

2. Camcorder's March 8 payment for freight charges associated with the camcorders purchased on March 7:

March 8	Debit	Credit
Inventory	**2,000**	
Cash		**2,000**
(Pay for freight charges)		

3. Camcorder's March 10 return of 10 defective camcorders from the March 7 purchase, for a credit of $250 per camcorder:

March 10	Debit	Credit
Accounts Payable	**2,500**	
Inventory		**2,500**
(Return defective camcorders)		

4. Camcorder's March 16 payment for inventory purchased on March 7, excluding the returned camcorders and less the 2% discount:

March 16	Debit	Credit
Accounts Payable	**50,000**	
Inventory		**1,000**
Cash		**49,000**
(Make full payment for March 7 purchase)		
($1,000 = $50,000 × 2%)		

5. Camcorder's cash sale on March 20 of 300 camcorders for $300 each:

March 20	Debit	Credit
Cash	**90,000**	
Sales Revenue		**90,000**
(Sell 300 camcorders for cash)		
($90,000 = $300 × 300 camcorders)		

| Cost of Goods Sold .... | **75,000** | |
| Inventory .... | | **75,000** |

(Record cost of camcorders sold)
(Cost of 100 camcorders in beginning inventory = $24,000)
(Cost of 200 camcorders purchased = $52,500 + $2,000 − $2,500 − $1,000 = $51,000)

Suggested Homework:
BE6–10, BE6–12;
E6–9, E6–10;
P6–3A&B, P6–6A&B

Flip Side

SALES TRANSACTIONS: THE OTHER SIDE OF PURCHASE TRANSACTIONS

For every purchase transaction, there is a sales transaction for another party. Sometimes, seeing the other side of the transaction helps us understand the economic events we are recording. In the Let's Review exercise above, Camcorder Central made a $52,500 purchase of inventory on account from Sony Corporation. Camcorder Central then returned inventory of $2,500 and received a $1,000 purchase discount for quick payment. Camcorder Central is the purchaser and Sony is the seller. We discussed returns and discounts from the seller's viewpoint in Chapter 5; here, let's briefly reexamine the transactions between Sony and Camcorder Central so we can see a side-by-side comparison of purchase and sales transactions. Illustration 6–18 shows these entries.

ILLUSTRATION 6–18

Comparison of Purchase and Sale of Inventory Transactions

Purchaser			Seller		
Camcorder Central			**Sony Corporation**		
Purchase on Account			**Sale on Account***		
Inventory	52,500		Accounts Receivable	52,500	
Accounts Payable		52,500	Sales Revenue		52,500
Purchase Return			**Sales Return**		
Accounts Payable	2,500		Sales Return	2,500	
Inventory		2,500	Accounts Receivable		2,500
Payment on Account with Discount			**Receipt on Account with Discount**		
Accounts Payable	50,000		Cash	49,000	
Inventory		1,000	Sales Discounts	1,000	
Cash		49,000	Accounts Receivable		50,000

*In practice, Sony also records the cost of inventory sold at the time of the sale. For simplicity, we omit this part of the transaction since Camcorder Central has no comparable transaction. We have also omitted Camcorder Central's March 20 sale of camcorders, since Sony is not party to that transaction.

PART C

LOWER OF COST AND NET REALIZABLE VALUE

■ **LO6–6**

Apply the lower of cost and net realizable value rule for inventories.

Think about the store where you usually buy your clothes. You've probably noticed the store selling leftover inventory at deeply discounted prices after the end of each selling season to make room for the next season's clothing line. The value of the company's old clothing inventory has likely fallen below its original cost. Is it appropriate to still report the reduced-value inventory at its original cost?

When the value of inventory falls below its original cost, companies are required to report inventory at the lower net realizable value of that inventory. Net realizable value is the estimated selling price of the inventory in the ordinary course of business less any costs of completion, disposal, and transportation. In other words, it's the *net* amount a company expects to *realize* in cash from the sale of the inventory.

Once a company has determined both the cost and the net realizable value of inventory, it reports ending inventory in the balance sheet at the *lower* of the two amounts. This method of recording inventory is lower of cost and net realizable value.[4]

---

[4]The discussion here is based on the last ruling of the FASB (May 13, 2015) at the time this book went to print. The method of reporting inventory using the lower of cost and net realizable value applies to companies that use FIFO and weighted-average, but not LIFO. For LIFO, companies report inventory using the lower of cost or market, where market is typically defined as replacement cost. Market value is never greater than net realizable value.

Illustration 6–19 demonstrates the concept behind the lower of cost and net realizable value (NRV).

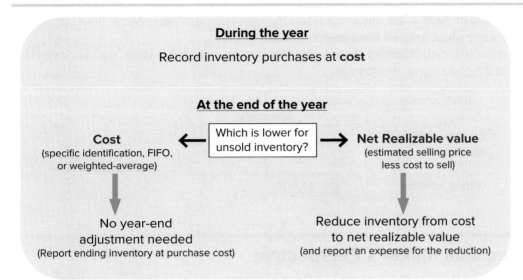

ILLUSTRATION 6–19
Lower of Cost and Net Realizable Value

To see how we apply the lower of cost and net realizable value to inventory amounts, assume Mario's Game Shop sells FunStation 2 and FunStation 3. Illustration 6–20 shows information related to ending inventory at the end of the year.

ILLUSTRATION 6–20
Calculating the Lower of Cost and Net Realizable Value

Inventory Items	Quantity	Cost Per unit	Cost Total	NRV Per unit	NRV Total	Lower of Cost and NRV	Year-end Adjustment Needed*
FunStation 2	15	$300	$ 4,500	$200	$3,000	= $ 3,000	$1,500
FunStation 3	20	400	8,000	450	9,000	= 8,000	0
			$12,500			$11,000	$1,500
			Recorded Cost			**Ending Inventory**	

* The year-end adjustment is recorded when NRV is below cost. The adjustment equals the difference between cost and net realizable value.

Mario reports the FunStation 2 in ending inventory at net realizable value ($200 per unit) because that's lower than its original cost ($300 per unit). The 15 FunStation 2s were originally reported in inventory at their cost of $4,500 (= 15 × $300). To reduce the inventory from that original cost of $4,500 to its lower net realizable value of $3,000 (= 15 × $200), Mario records a $1,500 reduction in inventory with the following year-end adjustment.

December 31	Debit	Credit
Cost of Goods Sold (expense)	1,500	
Inventory		1,500
(Adjust inventory down to net realizable value)		

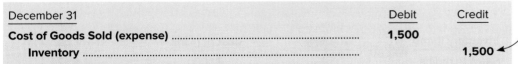

Balance Sheet					Income Statement		
			Stockholders' Equity				
			Common	**Retained**			**Net**
Assets	**=**	**Liabilities +**	**Stock +**	**Earnings**	**Revenues −**	**Expenses =**	**Income**
−1,500	=			−1,500		+1,500	= −1,500

Notice that the write-down of inventory has the effect not only of reducing total assets, but also of reducing net income and retained earnings.

The FunStation 3 inventory, on the other hand, remains on the books at its original cost of $8,000 (= $400 × 20), since cost is less than net realizable value. Mario does not need to make any adjustment for these inventory items.

After adjusting inventory to the lower of cost and net realizable value, the store calculates its ending balance of inventory as:

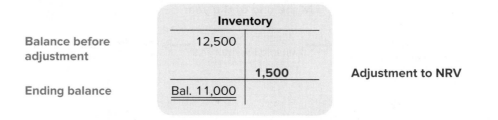

	Inventory		
Balance before adjustment	12,500		
		1,500	**Adjustment to NRV**
Ending balance	Bal. 11,000		

Decision Maker's Perspective

Conservatism and the Lower of Cost and Net Realizable Value Method

Firms are required to report the falling value of inventory, but they are not allowed to report any increasing value of inventory. Why is this? The answer lies in the conservative nature of some accounting procedures. A *conservative* approach in accounting implies that there is more potential harm to users of financial statements if estimated *gains* turn out to be wrong than if estimated *losses* turn out to be wrong. It also guides companies, when faced with a choice, to select accounting methods that are less likely to overstate assets and net income. Therefore, companies typically do not report estimated gains.

KEY POINT

We report inventory at the lower of cost and net realizable value; that is, at cost (specific identification, FIFO, or weighted-average cost) or net realizable value (selling price minus cost of completion, disposal, and transportation), whichever is lower. When net realizable value falls below cost, we adjust downward the balance of inventory from cost to net realizable value.

Let's Review

mhhe.com/4fa27

Auto Adrenaline provides specialty car products—satellite radios, GPS navigation systems, and subwoofers. At the end of the year, the company's records show the following amounts in ending inventory.

Inventory Items	Quantity	Cost per Unit	NRV per Unit
Satellite radios	10	$100	$120
GPS navigators	20	300	350
Subwoofers	40	70	50

Required:

1. Determine ending inventory using the lower of cost and net realizable value method.
2. Record any necessary year-end adjustment entry associated with the lower of cost and net realizable value.

Solution:

1. Ending inventory, lower of cost and net realizable value:

Inventory Items	Quantity	Cost Per unit	Cost Total	NRV Per unit	NRV Total	Lower of Cost and NRV	Year-end Adjustment Needed
Satellite radios	10	$100	$1,000	$120	$1,200	= $1,000	$ 0
GPS navigators	20	300	6,000	350	7,000	= 6,000	0
Subwoofers	40	70	2,800	50	2,000	= 2,000	800
			$9,800			$9,000	$800
			Recorded Cost			Ending Inventory	

Cost is lower than net realizable value for satellite radios and GPS navigators. We get lower of cost and net realizable value by multiplying the *cost* per unit times the quantity. However, net realizable value is lower than cost for subwoofers. In that case, we get lower of cost and net realizable by multiplying the *net realizable value* per unit times quantity.

2. Year-end adjustment associated with the lower of cost and net realizable value:

December 31	Debit	Credit
Cost of Goods Sold	800	
Inventory		800
(Adjust inventory down to net realizable value)		
($800 = 40 subwoofers × $20 decline in net realizable value below cost)		

We need the $800 adjustment to reduce the reported Inventory balance of the 40 subwoofers by $20 each (from $70 to $50).

Suggested Homework:
BE6–14, BE6–15;
E6–13, E6–14;
P6–4A&B

ETHICAL DILEMMA

© Goodshoot/PictureQuest

Diamond Computers, which is owned and operated by Dale Diamond, manufactures and sells different types of computers. The company has reported profits every year since its inception in 2000 and has applied for a bank loan near the end of 2018 to upgrade manufacturing facilities. These upgrades should significantly boost future productivity and profitability.

In preparing the financial statements for the year, the chief accountant, Sandy Walters, mentions to Dale that approximately $80,000 of computer inventory has become obsolete and a write-down of inventory should be recorded in 2018.

Dale understands that the write-down would result in a net loss being reported for company operations in 2018. This could jeopardize the company's application for the bank loan, which would lead to employee layoffs. Dale is a very kind, older gentleman who cares little for his personal wealth but who is deeply devoted to his employees' well-being. He truly believes the loan is necessary for the company's sustained viability. Dale suggests Sandy wait until 2019 to write down the inventory so that profitable financial statements can be presented to the bank this year.

Explain how failing to record the write-down in 2018 inflates profit in that year. How would this type of financial accounting manipulation potentially harm the bank? Can Sandy justify the manipulation based on Dale's kind heart for his employees?

ANALYSIS

■ LO6–7
Analyze management of inventory using the inventory turnover ratio and gross profit ratio.

INVENTORY ANALYSIS
Best Buy vs. Tiffany's

As discussed in the previous section, if managers purchase too much inventory, the company runs the risk of the inventory becoming outdated, resulting in inventory write-downs. Outside analysts as well as managers often use the *inventory turnover ratio* to evaluate a company's effectiveness in managing its investment in inventory. In addition, investors often rely on the *gross profit ratio* to determine the core profitability of a merchandising company's operations. We discuss these ratios next.

INVENTORY TURNOVER RATIO

The inventory turnover ratio shows the *number of times* the firm sells its average inventory balance during a reporting period. It is calculated as cost of goods sold divided by average inventory.

$$\text{Inventory turnover ratio} = \frac{\text{Cost of goods sold}}{\text{Average inventory}}$$

The amount for cost of goods sold is obtained from the current period's income statement; average inventory equals the average of inventory reported in this period's and last period's balance sheets. Last period's ending inventory is this period's beginning inventory. The more frequently a business is able to sell or "turn over" its average inventory balance, the less the company needs to invest in inventory for a given level of sales. Other things equal, a higher ratio indicates greater effectiveness of a company in managing its investment in inventory.

AVERAGE DAYS IN INVENTORY

Another way to measure the same activity is to calculate the average days in inventory. This ratio indicates the approximate *number of days* the average inventory is held. It is calculated as 365 days divided by the inventory turnover ratio.

$$\text{Average days in inventory} = \frac{365}{\text{Inventory turnover ratio}}$$

We can analyze the inventory of **Best Buy** and **Tiffany's** by calculating these ratios for both companies. Best Buy sells a large volume of commonly purchased products. In contrast, Tiffany's is a specialty retailer of luxury jewelry, watches, and other accessories. Below are relevant amounts for each company.

($ in millions)	Cost of Goods Sold	Beginning Inventory	Ending Inventory
Best Buy	$31,292	$5,376	$5,174
Tiffany's	1,713	2,326	2,362

To compute the inventory turnover ratio we need the *average* inventory, which is the beginning amount of inventory plus the ending amount, divided by 2.

Best Buy   Average inventory = ($5,376 + $5,174) ÷ 2 = $5,275
Tiffany's   Average inventory = ($2,326 + $2,362) ÷ 2 = $2,344

We put average inventory in the denominator to compute the inventory turnover ratio, as shown in Illustration 6–21.

	Inventory Turnover Ratio	Average Days in Inventory
Best Buy	$31,292 ÷ $5,275 = 5.9 times	$\dfrac{365}{5.8}$ = 62 days
Tiffany's	$1,713 ÷ $2,344 = 0.7 times	$\dfrac{365}{0.7}$ = 521 days

ILLUSTRATION 6–21

Inventory Turnover Ratios for Best Buy and Tiffany's

The turnover ratio is much higher for Best Buy. On average, each dollar of inventory is sold in 62 days. In contrast, each dollar of inventory at Tiffany's is sold every 521 days. If the two companies had the same business strategies, this would indicate that Best Buy is better at managing inventory. In this case, though, the difference in inventory turnover relates to the products the two companies sell. Best Buy sells mostly common household electronics and accessories, while Tiffany's has some very expensive jewelry (like engagement rings) that takes time to sell to the right customer. As we see in the next section, Tiffany's offsets its low inventory turnover with a higher profit margin.

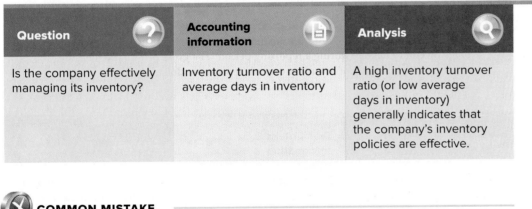

Decision Point

Question	Accounting information	Analysis
Is the company effectively managing its inventory?	Inventory turnover ratio and average days in inventory	A high inventory turnover ratio (or low average days in inventory) generally indicates that the company's inventory policies are effective.

⊗ COMMON MISTAKE

Many students use ending inventory rather than average inventory in calculating the inventory turnover ratio. Generally, when you calculate a ratio that includes an income statement item (an amount generated over a period) with a balance sheet item (an amount at a particular date), the balance sheet item needs to be converted to an amount *over the same period*. This is done by averaging the beginning and ending balances of the balance sheet item.

GROSS PROFIT RATIO

Another important indicator of the company's successful management of inventory is the gross profit ratio (also called *gross profit percentage*). It measures the amount by which the sale of inventory exceeds its cost per dollar of sales. We calculate the gross profit ratio as gross profit divided by net sales. (Net sales equal total sales revenue less sales discounts, returns, and allowances.)

$$\text{Gross profit ratio} = \frac{\text{Gross profit}}{\text{Net sales}}$$

The higher the gross profit ratio, the higher is the "markup" a company is able to achieve on its inventories. Best Buy and Tiffany's report the following information.

($ in millions)	Net Sales	−	Cost of Goods Sold	=	Gross Profit
Best Buy	$40,339		$31,292		$9,047
Tiffany's	4,250		1,713		2,537

Illustration 6–22 shows calculation of the gross profit ratio for Best Buy and Tiffany's.

ILLUSTRATION 6–22

Gross Profit Ratios for Best Buy and Tiffany's

	Gross Profit/Net Sales	=	Gross Profit Ratio
Best Buy	$9,047/$40,339	=	22%
Tiffany's	$2,537/$4,250	=	60%

For Best Buy, this means that for every $1 of net sales, the company spends $0.78 on inventory, resulting in a gross profit of $0.22. In contrast, the gross profit ratio for Tiffany's is 60%. We saw earlier that Tiffany's inventory turnover is much lower than that of Best Buy. But, we see now that Tiffany's makes up for that lower turnover with a much higher gross profit margin. The products Best Buy sells are familiar goods, and competition from companies like **Walmart**, **Target**, and **Sears** for these high-volume items keeps sale prices low compared to costs. Because Tiffany's specializes in custom jewelry and other expensive accessories, there is less competition, allowing greater price markups.

 KEY POINT

The inventory turnover ratio indicates the number of times the firm sells, or turns over, its average inventory balance during a reporting period. The gross profit ratio measures the amount by which the sale of inventory exceeds its cost per dollar of sales.

Decision Point

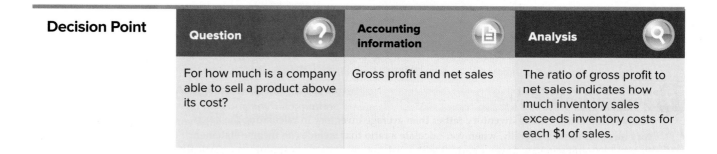

Question	Accounting information	Analysis
For how much is a company able to sell a product above its cost?	Gross profit and net sales	The ratio of gross profit to net sales indicates how much inventory sales exceeds inventory costs for each $1 of sales.

APPENDIX A

RECORDING INVENTORY TRANSACTIONS USING A PERIODIC INVENTORY SYSTEM

■ **LO6–8**

Record inventory transactions using a periodic inventory system.

In this chapter, we discussed how to record inventory transactions using a *perpetual* inventory system. Here we discuss how to record inventory transactions using a *periodic* inventory system.

Recall that under a **perpetual inventory system** we maintain a continual—or *perpetual*—record of inventory purchased and sold. In contrast, using a **periodic inventory system** we do not continually modify inventory amounts. Instead, we *periodically* adjust for purchases and sales of inventory at the end of the reporting period, based on a physical count of inventory on hand.

To demonstrate the differences in these two systems, let's record inventory transactions under the periodic system using the same information (from Illustration 6–12) that we used to demonstrate the perpetual inventory system. We repeat those transactions in Illustration 6–23.

Date	Transaction	Details	Total Cost	Total Revenue
Jan. 1	Beginning inventory	100 units for $7 each	$ 700	
Apr. 25	Purchase	300 units for $9 each	2,700	
Jul. 17	Sale	300 units for $15 each		$ 4,500
Oct. 19	Purchase	600 units for $11 each	6,600	
Dec. 15	Sale	500 units for $15 each		7,500
	Totals		$10,000	$12,000

ILLUSTRATION 6–23

Inventory Transactions for Mario's Game Shop

To make the distinction between the perpetual system and the periodic system easier, in the next section we look at side-by-side comparisons. The perpetual entries are repeated from those in the chapter and shown on the left side of each comparison.

INVENTORY PURCHASES AND SALES

The first transaction on April 25 involves the purchase of $2,700 of inventory on account. Under the periodic system, instead of debiting the Inventory account, we debit a Purchases account. Remember, we're not continually adjusting the Inventory account under the periodic method. We use the Purchases account to temporarily track increases in inventory.

Perpetual System			Periodic System		
Inventory	2,700		Purchases	2,700	
Accounts Payable		2,700	Accounts Payable		2,700

The transaction on July 17 involves the sale on account of 300 units of inventory for $4,500. We record that transaction as follows.

Perpetual System			Periodic System		
Accounts Receivable	4,500		Accounts Receivable	4,500	
Sales Revenue		4,500	Sales Revenue		4,500
Cost of Goods Sold	2,500				
Inventory		2,500	No entry for cost of goods sold		

Notice that under the periodic system, we record the sales revenue, but we don't record the reduction in inventory or the increase in cost of goods sold at the time of the sale. Instead, we will record these at the end of the period.

The final two transactions are (1) the purchase of 600 additional units of inventory for $6,600 on account on October 19 and (2) the sale of 500 units for $7,500 on account on December 15. We record that transaction as follows.

Perpetual System			Periodic System		
Inventory	6,600		Purchases	6,600	
Accounts Payable		6,600	Accounts Payable		6,600

Perpetual System			Periodic System		
Accounts Receivable	7,500		Accounts Receivable	7,500	
Sales Revenue		7,500	Sales Revenue		7,500
Cost of Goods Sold	5,300				
Inventory		5,300	No entry for cost of goods sold		

In addition to purchases and sales of inventory, we also looked at additional inventory transactions for Mario's Game Shop that related to freight charges, purchase discounts, and purchase returns:

1. On April 25, Mario pays freight charges of $300 for inventory purchased on April 25.
2. On April 30, Mario pays for the units purchased on April 25, less a 2% purchase discount.
3. On October 22, Mario returns 50 defective units from the October 19 purchase.

Next, let's also compare the perpetual system and periodic system for these transactions.

FREIGHT CHARGES

Under the perpetual system discussed in the chapter, we saw that freight charges are included as an additional cost of inventory. Here we'll see that under the periodic system, we record these charges in a separate account called Freight-in. That account will later be closed in a period-end adjustment. For freight charges of $300 associated with the April 25 purchase, we record the following transaction.

Perpetual System			Periodic System		
Inventory	300		Freight-in	300	
Cash		300	Cash		300

PURCHASE DISCOUNTS AND RETURNS

Under the perpetual system, purchase discounts and purchase returns are recorded as a reduction in inventory cost. Under the periodic system, these transactions are recorded in separate accounts—Purchase Discounts and Purchase Returns. In the perpetual system, we credit purchase returns and purchase discounts to Inventory. The Purchase Returns and Purchase Discounts accounts used in the periodic system are referred to as *contra purchases accounts*.

For our examples in the chapter, Mario (1) makes payment on April 30 for inventory purchased on April 25 for $2,700, receiving a $54 discount and (2) returns 50 defective units on October 22 from the 600 units purchased on account on October 19 for $11 each.

Perpetual System			Periodic System		
Accounts Payable	2,700		Accounts Payable	2,700	
Inventory		54	Purchase Discounts		54
Cash		2,646	Cash		2,646

Perpetual System			Periodic System		
Accounts Payable	550		Accounts Payable	550	
Inventory		550	Purchase Returns		550

PERIOD-END ADJUSTMENT

A period-end adjustment is needed only under the periodic system. The adjustment serves the following purposes:

1. Adjusts the balance of inventory to its proper ending balance.
2. Records the cost of goods sold for the period, to match inventory costs with the related sales revenue.
3. Closes (or zeros out) the temporary purchases accounts (Purchases, Freight-in, Purchase Discounts, and Purchase Returns).

Let's see what the period-end adjustment would look like for Mario's Game Shop using the transactions described in this appendix. In addition, recall that beginning inventory equals $700 (= 100 units × $7 unit cost) and ending inventory equals $1,650 (= 150 units × $11 unit cost).

Perpetual System	Periodic System		
No entry	Inventory (ending)	1,650	
	Cost of Goods Sold	8,046	
	Purchase Discounts	54	
	Purchase Returns	550	
	Purchases		9,300
	Freight-in		300
	Inventory (beginning)		700

(Temporary accounts closed)

Notice that (1) the balance of Inventory is updated for its ending amount of $1,650, while its beginning balance of $700 is eliminated, (2) Cost of Goods Sold is recorded for $8,046, and (3) temporary accounts related to purchases are closed to zero. Purchase Discounts and Purchase Returns are credit balance accounts so they need to be debited to close them. Likewise, Purchases and Freight-in are debit balance accounts so they need to credited to close them.

If you look carefully, you may notice that the amount of cost of goods sold above calculated under the periodic system is exactly the same as that calculated under the perpetual system (in Illustration 6–17). To see a detailed example of this, let's examine the first section of the multiple-step income statement, shown again in Illustration 6–24.

ILLUSTRATION 6–24

Calculation of Gross Profit in a Multiple-Step Income Statement

MARIO'S GAME SHOP
Multiple-Step Income Statement (partial)
For the year ended December 31, 2018

Sales revenue		$12,000
Cost of goods sold:		
Beginning inventory	$ 700	
Add: Purchases	9,300	
Freight-in	300	
Less: Purchase discounts	(54)	
Purchase returns	(550)	
Cost of goods available for sale	9,696	
Less: Ending inventory	(1,650)	
Cost of goods sold		8,046
Gross profit		$ 3,954

The periodic system and perpetual system will always produce the same amounts for cost of goods sold (and therefore also ending inventory) when the FIFO inventory method is used.

However, when using LIFO or weighted-average, the amounts for cost of goods sold may differ between the periodic system and perpetual system. The reason for this difference is discussed further in more advanced accounting courses; it happens because determining which units of inventory are assumed sold occurs at the time of each sale throughout the period using a perpetual system but just once at the end of the period using a periodic system. For those interested, the book's online resources include additional discussion and problems related to FIFO, LIFO, and weighted–average using the perpetual inventory system.

As discussed in Part B of the chapter, most companies maintain their own records on a FIFO basis and then adjust for the LIFO or weighted-average difference in preparing financial statements. **The inventory recording and reporting procedures discussed in Part B of the chapter most closely reflect those used in actual practice.**

KEY POINT

Using the periodic inventory system, we record purchases, freight-in, purchase returns, and purchase discounts to *temporary accounts* rather than directly to Inventory. These temporary accounts are closed in a period-end adjustment. In addition, at the time inventory is sold, we do not record a decrease in inventory sold; instead, we update the balance of Inventory in the period-end adjustment.

APPENDIX B

■ LO6–9
Determine the financial statement effects of inventory errors.

INVENTORY ERRORS

Nobody's perfect, and even accountants make mistakes. When we discover accounting errors, we correct them. However, we don't always know when we've made an error. Errors can unknowingly occur in inventory amounts if there are mistakes in a physical count of inventory or in the pricing of inventory quantities.

EFFECTS IN THE CURRENT YEAR

To understand the effects of an inventory error in the financial statements, let's think again about the formula for cost of goods sold, shown in Illustration 6–25.

ILLUSTRATION 6–25

Calculation of Cost of Goods Sold

	Beginning Inventory	
+	Purchases	
−	Ending Inventory	→ Asset; Balance sheet
	Cost of Goods Sold	→ Expense; Income statement

Notice that an error in calculating ending inventory (an asset in the balance sheet) causes an error in calculating cost of goods sold (an expense in the income statement). If cost of goods sold is misstated, gross profit will be misstated as well, but in the opposite direction. This is true because gross profit equals sales *minus* cost of goods sold. The effect of the inventory error in the current year is summarized in Illustration 6–26.

ILLUSTRATION 6–26

Summary of Effects of Inventory Error in the Current Year

Inventory Error	Ending Inventory	Cost of Goods Sold	Gross Profit
Overstate ending inventory	Overstate	Understate	Overstate
Understate ending inventory	Understate	Overstate	Understate

EFFECTS IN THE FOLLOWING YEAR

To understand the effects of a current-year inventory error on financial statements in the following year, remember that the amount of ending inventory this year is the amount of beginning inventory next year. An error in ending inventory this year will create an error in beginning inventory next year. This is demonstrated in Illustration 6–27.

ILLUSTRATION 6–27

Relationship between Cost of Goods Sold in the Current Year and the Following Year

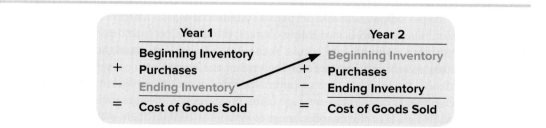

Notice that ending inventory is *subtracted* in calculating cost of goods sold in year 1 (the year of the inventory error). That same amount becomes beginning inventory in the following year and is *added* in calculating cost of goods sold. Because of this, **an error in calculating ending inventory in the current year will automatically affect cost of goods sold in the following year** *in the opposite direction.*

Consider a simple example to see how this works. Illustration 6–28 shows the correct inventory amounts for 2018 and 2019.

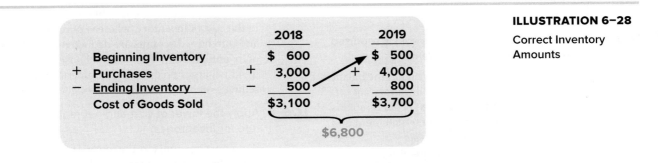

ILLUSTRATION 6–28

Correct Inventory
Amounts

	2018	2019
Beginning Inventory	$ 600	$ 500
+ Purchases	+ 3,000	+ 4,000
– Ending Inventory	– 500	– 800
Cost of Goods Sold	$3,100	$3,700

$6,800

Now, assume the company mistakenly reports ending inventory in 2018 as $400, instead of $500. The effect of the mistake is shown in Illustration 6–29.

ILLUSTRATION 6–29

Incorrect Inventory
Amounts

	2018	2019
Beginning Inventory	$ 600	$ 400
+ Purchases	+ 3,000	+ 4,000
– Ending Inventory	– 400	– 800
Cost of Goods Sold	$3,200	$3,600

$6,800

Notice three things: First, the amount reported for inventory is correct by the end of the second year, $800. This is true *even if the company had never discovered its inventory mistake in 2018.*

Second, the total amount reported for cost of goods sold over the two-year period from 2018 to 2019 is the same ($6,800) whether the error occurs or not. That's because the overstatement to cost of goods sold of $100 in 2018 is offset by an understatement to cost of goods sold of $100 in 2019. This also means that the inventory error affects gross profit in each of the two years, but the combined two-year gross profit amount is unaffected.

Third, if the combined two-year gross profit is correct, then retained earnings will also be correct by the end of 2019. Thus, the inventory error in 2018 has no effect on the accounting equation at the end of 2019. Assets (inventory) and stockholders' equity (retained earnings) are correctly stated.

KEY POINT

In the current year, inventory errors affect the amounts reported for inventory and retained earnings in the balance sheet and amounts reported for cost of goods sold and gross profit in the income statement. At the end of the following year, the error has no effect on ending inventory or retained earnings but reverses for cost of goods sold and gross profit.

KEY POINTS BY LEARNING OBJECTIVE

LO6–1 Trace the flow of inventory costs from manufacturing companies to merchandising companies.

Service companies record revenues when providing services to customers. Merchandising and manufacturing companies record revenues when selling inventory to customers.

LO6–2 Understand how cost of goods sold is reported in a multiple-step income statement.

Inventory is a current asset reported in the balance sheet and represents the cost of inventory *not yet sold* at the end of the period. Cost of goods sold is an expense reported in the income statement and represents the cost of inventory *sold*.

A multiple-step income statement reports multiple levels of profitability. **Gross profit** equals net revenues (or net sales) minus cost of goods sold. **Operating income** equals gross profit minus operating expenses. **Income before income taxes** equals operating income plus nonoperating revenues and minus nonoperating expenses. **Net income** equals all revenues minus all expenses.

LO6–3 Determine the cost of goods sold and ending inventory using different inventory cost methods.

Companies are allowed to report inventory costs by *assuming* which specific units of inventory are sold and not sold, even if this does not match the *actual* flow. The three major inventory cost flow assumptions are FIFO (first-in, first-out), LIFO (last-in, first-out), and weighted-average cost.

LO6–4 Explain the financial statement effects and tax effects of inventory cost methods.

Generally, FIFO more closely resembles the actual physical flow of inventory. When inventory costs are rising, FIFO results in higher reported inventory in the balance sheet and higher reported income in the income statement. Conversely, LIFO results in a lower reported inventory and net income, reducing the company's income tax obligation.

LO6–5 Record inventory transactions using a perpetual inventory system.

The perpetual inventory system maintains a continual—or *perpetual*—record of inventory purchased and sold. When companies *purchase* inventory using a perpetual inventory system, they increase the Inventory account and either decrease Cash or increase Accounts Payable. When companies *sell* inventory, they make two entries: (1) They increase an asset account (Cash or Accounts Receivable) and increase Sales Revenue, and (2) they increase Cost of Goods Sold and decrease Inventory.

Nearly all companies maintain their own inventory records on a FIFO basis, and then some prepare financial statements on a LIFO basis. To adjust their FIFO inventory records to LIFO for financial reporting, companies use a LIFO adjustment at the end of the period.

For most companies, freight charges are added to the cost of inventory, whereas purchase returns and purchase discounts are deducted from the cost of inventory. Some companies choose to report freight charges on outgoing shipments as part of selling expenses instead of cost of goods sold.

LO6–6 Apply the lower of cost and net realizable value rule for inventories.

We report inventory at the lower of cost and net realizable value; that is, at cost (specific identification, FIFO, or weighted-average cost) or net realizable value (selling price minus cost of completion, disposal, and transportation), whichever is lower. When net realizable value falls below cost, we adjust downward the balance of inventory from cost to net realizable value.

Analysis

LO6–7 Analyze management of inventory using the inventory turnover ratio and gross profit ratio.

The inventory turnover ratio indicates the number of times the firm sells, or turns over, its average inventory balance during a reporting period. The gross profit ratio measures the amount by which the sale of inventory exceeds its cost per dollar of sales.

Appendixes

LO6–8 Record inventory transactions using a periodic inventory system.

Using the periodic inventory system, we record purchases, freight-in, purchase returns, and purchase discounts to *temporary accounts* rather than directly to Inventory. These temporary accounts are closed in a period-end adjustment. In addition, at the time inventory is sold, we do not record a decrease in inventory sold; instead, we update the balance of Inventory in the period-end adjustment.

LO6–9 Determine the financial statement effects of inventory errors.

In the current year, inventory errors affect the amounts reported for inventory and retained earnings in the balance sheet and amounts reported for cost of goods sold and gross profit in the income statement. At the end of the following year, the error has no effect on ending inventory or retained earnings but reverses for cost of goods sold and gross profit.

GLOSSARY

Average days in inventory: Approximate number of days the average inventory is held. It equals 365 days divided by the inventory turnover ratio. **p. 292**

Cost of goods sold: Cost of the inventory that was sold during the period. **p. 266**

First-in, first-out method (FIFO): Inventory costing method that assumes the first units purchased (the first in) are the first ones sold (the first out). **p. 272**

Freight-in: Cost to transport inventory to the company, which is included as part of inventory cost. **p. 284**

Freight-out: Cost of freight on shipments to customers, which is included in the income statement either as part of cost of goods sold or as a selling expense. **p. 285**

Gross profit: The difference between net sales and cost of goods sold. **p. 270**

Gross profit ratio: Measure of the amount by which the sale of inventory exceeds its cost per dollar of sales. It equals gross profit divided by net sales. **p. 293**

Income before income taxes: Operating income plus non-operating revenues less nonoperating expenses. **p. 270**

Inventory: Items a company intends for sale to customers. **p. 266**

Inventory turnover ratio: The number of times a firm sells its average inventory balance during a reporting period. It equals cost of goods sold divided by average inventory. **p. 292**

Last-in, first-out method (LIFO): Inventory costing method that assumes the last units purchased (the last in) are the first ones sold (the first out). **p. 273**

LIFO adjustment: An adjustment used to convert a company's own inventory records maintained on a FIFO basis to LIFO basis for preparing financial statements. **p. 283**

LIFO conformity rule: IRS rule requiring a company that uses LIFO for tax reporting to also use LIFO for financial reporting. **p. 278**

Lower of cost and net realizable value: Method where companies report inventory in the balance sheet at the lower of cost and net realizable value, where net realizable value equals estimated selling price of the inventory in the ordinary course of business less any costs of completion, disposal, and transportation. **p. 288**

Multiple-step income statement: An income statement that reports *multiple* levels of income (or profitability). **p. 270**

Net income: Difference between all revenues and all expenses for the period. **p. 271**

Net realizable value: Estimated selling price of the inventory in the ordinary course of business less any costs of completion, disposal, and transportation. **p. 288**

Operating income: Profitability from normal operations that equals gross profit less operating expenses. **p. 270**

Periodic inventory system: Inventory system that periodically adjusts for purchases and sales of inventory at the end of the reporting period based on a physical count of inventory on hand. **p. 280**

Perpetual inventory system: Inventory system that maintains a continual record of inventory purchased and sold. **p. 280**

Specific identification method: Inventory costing method that matches or identifies each unit of inventory with its actual cost. **p. 271**

Weighted-average cost method: Inventory costing method that assumes both cost of goods sold and ending inventory consist of a random mixture of all the goods available for sale. **p. 274**

SELF-STUDY QUESTIONS

1. Which of following companies record revenues when selling inventory? **(LO6–1)**
   a. Service companies.
   b. Manufacturing companies.
   c. Merchandising companies.
   d. Both manufacturing and merchandising companies.

2. At the beginning of the year, Bennett Supply has inventory of $3,500. During the year, the company purchases an additional $12,000 of inventory. An inventory count at the end of the year reveals remaining inventory of $4,000. What amount will Bennett report for cost of goods sold? **(LO6–2)**
   a. $11,000.
   b. $11,500.
   c. $12,000.
   d. $12,500.

3. Which of the following levels of profitability in a multiple-step income statement represents revenues from the sale of inventory less the cost of that inventory? **(LO6–2)**
   a. Gross profit.
   b. Operating income.
   c. Income before income taxes.
   d. Net income.

4. Madison Outlet has the following inventory transactions for the year: **(LO6–3)**

Date	Transaction	Number of Units	Unit Cost	Total Cost
Jan. 1	Beginning inventory	10	$200	$2,000
Mar. 14	Purchase	15	300	4,500
				$6,500
Jan. 1–Dec. 31	Total sales to customers	12		

What amount would Madison report for *cost of goods sold* using FIFO?

a. $2,600.
b. $2,900.
c. $3,600.
d. $3,900.

5. Which inventory cost flow assumption generally results in the lowest reported amount for cost of goods sold when inventory costs are rising? **(LO6–4)**
a. Lower of cost and net realizable value.
b. First-in, first-out (FIFO).
c. Last-in, first-out (LIFO).
d. Weighted-average cost.

6. Using a *perpetual* inventory system, the purchase of inventory on account would be recorded as: **(LO6–5)**
a. Debit Cost of Goods Sold; credit Inventory.
b. Debit Inventory; credit Sales Revenue.
c. Debit Purchases; credit Accounts Payable.
d. Debit Inventory; credit Accounts Payable.

7. At the end of a reporting period, Maxwell Corporation determines that its ending inventory has a cost of $1,000 and a net realizable value of $800. What would be the effect(s) of the adjustment to write down inventory to net realizable value? **(LO6–6)**
a. Decrease total assets.
b. Decrease net income.
c. Decrease retained earnings.
d. All of these answer choices are correct.

8. For the year, Simmons Incorporated reports net sales of $100,000, cost of goods sold of $80,000, and an average inventory balance of $40,000. What is Simmons' gross profit ratio? **(LO6–7)**
a. 20%.
b. 25%.
c. 40%.
d. 50%.

9. Using a *periodic* inventory system, the purchase of inventory on account would be recorded as: **(LO6–8)**
a. Debit Cost of Goods Sold; credit Inventory.
b. Debit Inventory; credit Sales Revenue.
c. Debit Purchases; credit Accounts Payable.
d. Debit Inventory; credit Accounts Payable.

10. Suppose Ajax Corporation overstates its ending inventory amount. What effect will this have on the reported amount of cost of goods sold in the year of the error? **(LO6–9)**
a. Overstate cost of goods sold.
b. Understate cost of goods sold.
c. Have no effect on cost of goods sold.
d. Not possible to determine with information given.

Note: For answers, see the last page of the chapter.

For additional study materials, including 10 more multiple-choice Self-Study Questions, visit Connect.

REVIEW QUESTIONS

■ **LO6–1**   1. What is inventory? Where in the financial statements is inventory reported?

■ **LO6–1**   2. What is the primary distinction between a service company and a manufacturing or merchandising company?

■ **LO6–1**   3. What is the difference among raw materials inventory, work-in-process inventory, and finished goods inventory?

■ **LO6–2**   4. Define the cost of goods available for sale. How does it relate to cost of goods sold and ending inventory?

■ **LO6–2**   5. For a company like **Best Buy**, what does the balance of Cost of Goods Sold in the income statement represent? What does the balance of Inventory in the balance sheet represent?

■ **LO6–2**   6. What is a multiple-step income statement? What information does it provide beyond "bottom-line" net income?

■ **LO6–3**   7. Cheryl believes that companies report cost of goods sold and ending inventory based on *actual* units sold and not sold. Her accounting instructor explains that most companies account for cost of goods sold and ending inventory based on *assumed* units sold and not sold. Help her understand why companies are allowed to do this.

■ **LO6–3**   8. What are the three primary cost flow assumptions? How does the specific identification method differ from these three primary cost flow assumptions?

■ **LO6–4**   9. Which cost flow assumption generally results in the highest reported amount for ending inventory when inventory costs are rising? Explain.

10. Which cost flow assumption generally results in the highest reported amount of net income when inventory costs are rising? Explain.   ■ **LO6–4**

11. What does it mean that FIFO has a balance-sheet focus and LIFO has an income-statement focus?   ■ **LO6–4**

12. Explain how LIFO generally results in lower income taxes payable when inventory costs are increasing. What is the LIFO conformity rule?   ■ **LO6–4**

13. What is the difference between the *timing* of recording inventory transactions under the perpetual and periodic inventory systems?   ■ **LO6–5**

14. Explain how freight charges, purchase returns, and purchase discounts affect the cost of inventory.   ■ **LO6–5**

15. Explain the method of reporting inventory at lower of cost and net realizable value.   ■ **LO6–6**

16. How is cost of inventory determined? How is net realizable value determined?   ■ **LO6–6**

17. Describe the entry to adjust from cost to net realizable value for inventory write-downs. What effects does this adjustment have on (a) assets, (b) liabilities, (c) stockholders' equity (or retained earnings), (d) revenues, (e) expenses, and (f) net income?   ■ **LO6–6**

18. What is meant by the assertion that an example of conservatism in accounting is recording inventory at the lower of cost and net realizable value?   ■ **LO6–6**

19. What is the inventory turnover ratio? What is it designed to measure?   ■ **LO6–7**

20. How is gross profit calculated? What is the gross profit ratio? What is it designed to measure?   ■ **LO6–7**

21. Explain how the sale of inventory on account is recorded under a periodic system. How does this differ from the recording under a perpetual system?   ■ **LO6–8**

22. What are the purposes of the period-end adjustment under the periodic inventory system?   ■ **LO6–8**

23. Jeff is the new inventory manager for Alan Company. During the year-end inventory count, Jeff forgets that the company stores additional inventory in a back room, causing his final ending inventory count to be understated.
Explain what effect this error will have on the reported amounts for (a) assets, (b) liabilities, (c) stockholders' equity (or retained earnings), (d) revenues, (e) expenses, and (f) net income in the current year.   ■ **LO6–9**

24. Refer to the inventory error in Question 23. Explain what effect Jeff's error will have on reported amounts at the end of the following year, assuming the mistake is not corrected and no further mistakes are made.   ■ **LO6–9**

BRIEF EXERCISES

connect

BE6–1 Match each of the following types of companies with its definition.

Understand terms related to types of companies (LO6–1)

Types of Companies	Definitions
1. _____ Service company	a. Purchases goods that are primarily in finished form for resale to customers.
2. _____ Merchandising company	b. Records revenues when providing services to customers.
3. _____ Manufacturing company	c. Produces the goods they sell to customers.

BE6–2 Match each of the following inventory classifications with its definition.

Understand terms related to inventory (LO6–1)

Inventory Classifications	Definitions
1. _____ Raw materials	a. Cost of items not yet complete by the end of the period.
2. _____ Work-in-process	b. Inventory that has been substantially completed.
3. _____ Finished goods	c. Basic components used to build a product.

Calculate cost of goods sold (LO6–2)

BE6–3 At the beginning of the year, Bryers Incorporated reports inventory of $8,000. During the year, the company purchases additional inventory for $23,000. At the end of the year, the cost of inventory remaining is $10,000. Calculate cost of goods sold for for the year.

Calculate amounts related to the multiple-step income statement (LO6–2)

BE6–4 For each company, calculate the missing amount.

Company	Sales Revenue	Cost of Goods Sold	Gross Profit	Operating Expenses	Net Income
Lennon	$18,000	(a)	$8,000	$3,500	$4,500
Harrison	20,000	$11,000	(b)	6,000	3,000
McCartney	13,000	9,000	4,000	(c)	1,500
Starr	16,000	6,000	10,000	6,500	(d)

Calculate ending inventory and cost of goods sold using FIFO (LO6–3)

BE6–5 During the year, Wright Company sells 470 remote-control airplanes for $110 each. The company has the following inventory purchase transactions for the year.

Date	Transaction	Number of Units	Unit Cost	Total Cost
Jan. 1	Beginning inventory	60	$82	$ 4,920
May 5	Purchase	250	85	21,250
Nov. 3	Purchase	200	90	18,000
		510		$44,170

Calculate ending inventory and cost of goods sold for the year, assuming the company uses FIFO.

Calculate ending inventory and cost of goods sold using LIFO (LO6–3)

BE6–6 Refer to the information in BE6–5. Calculate ending inventory and cost of goods sold for the year, assuming the company uses LIFO.

Calculate ending inventory and cost of goods sold using weighted-average cost (LO6–3)

BE6–7 Refer to the information in BE6–5. Calculate ending inventory and cost of goods sold for the year, assuming the company uses weighted-average cost.

Calculate ending inventory and cost of goods sold using specific identification (LO6–3)

BE6–8 Refer to the information in BE6–5. Calculate ending inventory and cost of goods sold for the year, assuming the company uses specific identification. Actual sales by the company include its entire beginning inventory, 230 units of inventory from the May 5 purchase, and 180 units from the November 3 purchase.

Identify financial statement effects of FIFO and LIFO (LO6–4)

BE6–9 For each item below, indicate whether FIFO or LIFO will generally result in a higher reported amount when inventory costs are rising versus falling. The first answer is provided as an example.

Inventory Costs	Higher Total Assets	Higher Cost of Goods Sold	Higher Net Income
Rising	FIFO		
Declining			

Record inventory purchases and sales using a perpetual system (LO6–5)

BE6–10 Shankar Company uses a perpetual system to record inventory transactions. The company purchases inventory on account on February 2 for $40,000 and then sells this inventory on account on March 17 for $60,000. Record transactions for the purchase and sale of inventory.

Record freight charges for inventory using a perpetual system (LO6–5)

BE6–11 Shankar Company uses a perpetual system to record inventory transactions. The company purchases inventory on account on February 2 for $40,000.

In addition to the cost of inventory, the company also pays $600 for freight charges associated with the purchase on the same day. Record the purchase of inventory on February 2, including the freight charges.

BE6–12 Shankar Company uses a perpetual system to record inventory transactions. The company purchases 1,500 units of inventory on account on February 2 for $60,000 ($40 per unit) but then returns 100 defective units on February 5. Record the inventory purchase on February 2 and the inventory return on February 5.

Record purchase returns of inventory using a perpetual system (LO6–5)

BE6–13 Shankar Company uses a perpetual system to record inventory transactions. The company purchases inventory on account on February 2 for $40,000, with terms 3/10, n/30. On February 10, the company pays on account for the inventory. Record the inventory purchase on February 2 and the payment on February 10.

Record purchase discounts of inventory using a perpetual system (LO6–5)

BE6–14 Powder Ski Shop reports inventory using the lower of cost and net realizable value (NRV). Information related to its year-end inventory appears on the next page. Calculate the amount to be reported for ending inventory.

Calculate ending inventory using lower of cost and net realizable value (LO6–6)

Inventory	Quantity	Cost	NRV
Ski jackets	20	$115	$ 95
Skis	25	300	350

BE6–15 Creative Technology reports inventory using the lower of cost and net realizable value (NRV). Below is information related to its year-end inventory. Calculate the amount to be reported for ending inventory.

Calculate ending inventory using the lower of cost and net realizable value (LO6–6)

Inventory	Quantity	Cost	NRV
Optima cameras	110	$45	$75
Inspire speakers	50	55	45

BE6–16 Using the amounts below, calculate the inventory turnover ratio, average days in inventory, and gross profit ratio.

Calculate inventory ratios (LO6–7)

Net sales	$250,000
Cost of goods sold	180,000
Beginning inventory	55,000
Ending inventory	45,000

BE6–17 Refer to the information in BE6–10, but now assume that Shankar uses a periodic system to record inventory transactions. Record transactions for the purchase and sale of inventory.

Record inventory purchases and sales using a periodic system (LO6–8)

BE6–18 Refer to the information in BE6–11, but now assume that Shankar uses a periodic system to record inventory transactions. Record the purchase of inventory on February 2, including the freight charges.

Record freight charges for inventory using a periodic system (LO6–8)

BE6–19 Refer to the information in BE6–12, but now assume that Shankar uses a periodic system to record inventory transactions. Record the inventory purchase on February 2 and the inventory return on February 5.

Record purchase returns of inventory using a periodic system (LO6–8)

BE6–20 Refer to the information in BE6–13, but now assume that Shankar uses a periodic system to record inventory transactions. Record the inventory purchase on February 2 and the payment on February 10.

Record purchase discounts of inventory using a periodic system (LO6–8)

BE6–21 Ebbers Corporation overstated its ending inventory balance by $15,000 in 2018. What impact will this error have on cost of goods sold and gross profit in 2018 and 2019?

Find income statement effects of overstatement in ending inventory (LO6–9)

BE6–22 Refer to the information in BE6–21. What impact will this error have on ending inventory and retained earnings in 2018 and 2019? Ignore any tax effects.

Find balance sheet effects of overstatement in ending inventory (LO6–9)

EXERCISES

Mc Graw Hill Education **connect**

Calculate cost of goods sold (LO6–2)

E6–1 Russell Retail Group begins the year with inventory of $55,000 and ends the year with inventory of $45,000. During the year, the company has four purchases for the following amounts.

Purchase on February 17	$210,000
Purchase on May 6	130,000
Purchase on September 8	160,000
Purchase on December 4	410,000

Required:
Calculate cost of goods sold for the year.

Prepare a multiple-step income statement (LO6–2)

E6–2 Wayman Corporation reports the following amounts in its December 31, 2018, income statement.

Sales revenue	$390,000	Income tax expense	$ 50,000
Interest expense	20,000	Cost of goods sold	130,000
Salaries expense	40,000	Advertising expense	30,000
Utilities expense	50,000		

Required:
Prepare a multiple-step income statement.

Prepare a multiple-step income statement and analyze profitability (LO6–2)

E6–3 Tisdale Incorporated reports the following amount in its December 31, 2018, income statement.

Sales revenue	$300,000	Income tax expense	$ 30,000
Nonoperating revenue	110,000	Cost of goods sold	190,000
Selling expenses	60,000	Administrative expenses	40,000
General expenses	50,000		

Required:
1. Prepare a multiple-step income statement.
2. Explain how analyzing the multiple levels of profitability can help in understanding the future profit-generating potential of Tisdale Incorporated.

Calculate inventory amounts when costs are rising (LO6–3)

E6–4 During the year, TRC Corporation has the following inventory transactions.

Date	Transaction	Number of Units	Unit Cost	Total Cost
Jan. 1	Beginning inventory	50	$42	$ 2,100
Apr. 7	Purchase	130	44	5,720
Jul. 16	Purchase	200	47	9,400
Oct. 6	Purchase	110	48	5,280
		490		$22,500

For the entire year, the company sells 440 units of inventory for $60 each.

Required:
1. Using FIFO, calculate (a) ending inventory, (b) cost of goods sold, (c) sales revenue, and (d) gross profit.
2. Using LIFO, calculate (a) ending inventory, (b) cost of goods sold, (c) sales revenue, and (d) gross profit.

3. Using weighted-average cost, calculate (a) ending inventory, (b) cost of goods sold, (c) sales revenue, and (d) gross profit.
4. Determine which method will result in higher profitability when inventory costs are rising.

E6–5 During the year, Trombley Incorporated has the following inventory transactions.

Calculate inventory amounts when costs are declining (LO6–3)

Date	Transaction	Number of Units	Unit Cost	Total Cost
Jan. 1	Beginning inventory	20	$22	$ 440
Mar. 4	Purchase	25	21	525
Jun. 9	Purchase	30	20	600
Nov. 11	Purchase	30	18	540
		105		$2,105

For the entire year, the company sells 81 units of inventory for $30 each.

Required:

1. Using FIFO, calculate (a) ending inventory, (b) cost of goods sold, (c) sales revenue, and (d) gross profit.
2. Using LIFO, calculate (a) ending inventory, (b) cost of goods sold, (c) sales revenue, and (d) gross profit.
3. Using weighted-average cost, calculate (a) ending inventory, (b) cost of goods sold, (c) sales revenue, and (d) gross profit.
4. Determine which method will result in higher profitability when inventory costs are declining.

E6–6 Bingerton Industries began the year with inventory of $85,000. Purchases of inventory on account during the year totaled $310,000. Inventory costing $335,000 was sold on account for $520,000.

Record inventory transactions using a perpetual system (LO6–5)

Required:

Record transactions for the purchase and sale of inventory using a perpetual system.

E6–7 On June 5, Staley Electronics purchases 200 units of inventory on account for $20 each. After closer examination, Staley determines 40 units are defective and returns them to its supplier for full credit on June 9. All remaining inventory is sold on account on June 16 for $35 each.

Record inventory purchase and purchase return using a perpetual system (LO6–5)

Required:

Record transactions for the purchase, return, and sale of inventory using a perpetual system.

E6–8 On June 5, Staley Electronics purchases 200 units of inventory on account for $19 each, with terms 2/10, n/30. Staley pays for the inventory on June 12.

Record inventory purchase and purchase discount using a perpetual system (LO6–5)

Required:

1. Record transactions for the purchase of inventory and payment on account using a perpetual system.
2. Now assume payment is made on June 22. Record the payment on account.

E6–9 Littleton Books has the following transactions during May.

Record transactions using a perpetual system (LO6–5)

May 2	Purchases books on account from Readers Wholesale for $3,300, terms 1/10, n/30.
May 3	Pays cash for freight costs of $200 on books purchased from Readers.
May 5	Returns books with a cost of $400 to Readers because part of the order is incorrect.
May 10	Pays the full amount due to Readers.
May 30	Sells all books purchased on May 2 (less those returned on May 5) for $4,000 on account.

Required:

1. Record the transactions of Littleton Books, assuming the company uses a perpetual inventory system.
2. Assume that payment to Readers is made on May 24 instead of May 10. Record this payment.

Record transactions using a perpetual system (LO6–5)

E6–10 Sundance Systems has the following transactions during July.

July 5 Purchases 40 LCD televisions on account from Red River Supplies for $2,500 each, terms 3/10, n/30.
July 8 Returns to Red River two televisions that had defective sound.
July 13 Pays the full amount due to Red River.
July 28 Sells remaining 38 televisions from July 5 for $3,000 each on account.

Required:

Record the transactions of Sundance Systems, assuming the company uses a perpetual inventory system.

Record transactions using a perpetual system (LO6–5)

Flip Side of E6–12

E6–11 DS Unlimited has the following transactions during August.

August 6 Purchases 70 handheld game devices on account from GameGirl, Inc., for $200 each, terms 1/10, n/60.
August 7 Pays $400 to Sure Shipping for freight charges associated with the August 6 purchase.
August 10 Returns to GameGirl six game devices that were defective.
August 14 Pays the full amount due to GameGirl.
August 23 Sells 50 game devices purchased on August 6 for $220 each to customers on account. The total cost of the 50 game devices sold is $10,212.50.

Required:

Record the transactions of DS Unlimited, assuming the company uses a perpetual inventory system.

Record transactions using a perpetual system (LO6–5)

Flip Side of E6–11

E6–12 Refer to the transactions in E6–11.

Required:

Prepare the transactions for GameGirl, Inc., assuming the company uses a perpetual inventory system. Assume the 70 game devices sold on August 6 to DS Unlimited had a cost to GameGirl of $180 each. The items returned on August 10 were considered worthless to GameGirl and were discarded.

Calculate inventory using lower of cost and net realizable value (LO6–6)

E6–13 Home Furnishings reports inventory using the lower of cost and net realizable value (NRV). Below is information related to its year-end inventory.

Inventory	Quantity	Cost	NRV
Furniture	200	$ 85	$100
Electronics	50	400	300

Required:

1. Calculate ending inventory using the lower of cost and net realizable value.
2. Record any necessary adjustment to inventory.
3. Explain the impact of the adjustment in the financial statements.

Calculate inventory using lower of cost and net realizable value (LO6–6)

E6–14 A company like **Golf USA** that sells golf-related inventory typically will have inventory items such as golf clothing and golf equipment. As technology advances the design and performance of the next generation of drivers, the older models become less marketable and therefore decline in value. Suppose that in the current year, **Ping** (a manufacturer of golf clubs) introduces the MegaDriver II, the new and improved version of the MegaDriver. Below are amounts related to Golf USA's inventory at the end of the year.

Inventory	Quantity	Cost	NRV
Shirts	35	$ 60	$ 70
MegaDriver	15	360	250
MegaDriver II	30	350	420

Required:

1. Calculate ending inventory using the lower of cost and net realizable value.
2. Record any necessary adjustment to inventory.
3. Explain the impact of the adjustment in the financial statements.

E6–15 Lewis Incorporated and Clark Enterprises report the following amounts for the year.

Calculate cost of goods sold, the inventory turnover ratio, and average days in inventory (LO6–2, 6–7)

	Lewis	Clark
Inventory (beginning)	$ 24,000	$ 50,000
Inventory (ending)	18,000	60,000
Purchases	261,000	235,000
Purchase returns	15,000	60,000

Required:

1. Calculate cost of goods sold for each company.
2. Calculate the inventory turnover ratio for each company.
3. Calculate the average days in inventory for each company.
4. Explain which company appears to be managing its inventory more efficiently.

E6–16 Below are amounts found in the income statements of three companies.

Calculate levels of profitability for a multiple-step income statement and the gross profit ratio (LO6–2, 6–7)

Company	Sales Revenue	Cost of Goods Sold	Operating Expenses	Nonoperating Expenses	Income Tax Expense
Henry	$32,000	$ 4,800	$ 5,000	$2,000	$2,000
Grace	35,000	24,500	13,100	7,000	0
James	40,000	24,800	3,000	0	3,000

Required:

1. For each company, calculate (a) gross profit, (b) operating income, (c) income before income taxes, and (d) net income.
2. For each company, calculate the gross profit ratio and indicate which company has the most favorable ratio.

E6–17 Refer to the transactions in E6–9.

Record transactions using a periodic system (LO6–8)

Required:

1. Record the transactions of Littleton Books, assuming the company uses a periodic inventory system.
2. Record the period-end adjustment to cost of goods sold on May 31, assuming the company has no beginning or ending inventory.

E6–18 Refer to the transactions in E6–10.

Record transactions using a periodic system (LO6–8)

Required:

1. Record the transactions of Sundance Systems, assuming the company uses a periodic inventory system.
2. Record the period-end adjustment to cost of goods sold on July 31, assuming the company has no beginning inventory.

E6–19 Refer to the transactions in E6–11.

Record inventory purchases and sales using a periodic system (LO6–8)

Required:

1. Record the transactions of DS Unlimited, assuming the company uses a periodic inventory system.
2. Record the period-end adjustment to cost of goods sold on August 31, assuming the company has no beginning inventory and ending inventory has a cost of $2,859.50.

Find financial statement effects of understatement in ending inventory (LO6–9)

E6–20 Mulligan Corporation purchases inventory on account with terms FOB shipping point. The goods are shipped on December 30, 2018, but do not reach Mulligan until January 5, 2019. Mulligan correctly records accounts payable associated with the purchase but does not include this inventory in its 2018 ending inventory count.

Required:
1. If an error has been made, explain why.
2. If an error has been made, indicate whether there is an understatement (U), overstatement (O), or no effect (N) on the reported amount of each financial statement element in the current year and following year. Ignore any tax effects.

	Balance Sheet			Income Statement		
Year	Assets	Liabilities	Stockholders' Equity	Revenues	Cost of Goods Sold	Gross Profit
Current						
Following						

Complete the accounting cycle using inventory transactions (LO6–2, 6–3, 6–5, 6–6, 6–7)

E6–21 On January 1, 2018, the general ledger of Big Blast Fireworks includes the following account balances:

Accounts	Debit	Credit
Cash	$ 21,900	
Accounts Receivable	36,500	
Allowance for Uncollectible Accounts		$ 3,100
Inventory	30,000	
Land	61,600	
Accounts Payable		32,400
Notes Payable (8%, due in 3 years)		30,000
Common Stock		56,000
Retained Earnings		28,500
Totals	$150,000	$150,000

The $30,000 beginning balance of inventory consists of 300 units, each costing $100. During January 2018, Big Blast Fireworks had the following inventory transactions:

January	3	Purchase 1,200 units for $126,000 on account ($105 each).
January	8	Purchase 1,300 units for $143,000 on account ($110 each).
January	12	Purchase 1,400 units for $161,000 on account ($115 each).
January	15	Return 100 of the units purchased on January 12 because of defects.
January	19	Sell 4,000 units on account for $600,000. The cost of the units sold is determined using a FIFO perpetual inventory system.
January	22	Receive $580,000 from customers on accounts receivable.
January	24	Pay $410,000 to inventory suppliers on accounts payable.
January	27	Write off accounts receivable as uncollectible, $2,500.
January	31	Pay cash for salaries during January, $128,000.

Required:
1. Record each of the transactions listed above, assuming a FIFO perpetual inventory system.
2. Record adjusting entries on January 31.
   a. At the end of January, the company estimates that the remaining units of inventory are expected to sell in February for only $100 each.

b. At the end of January, $4,000 of accounts receivable are past due, and the company estimates that 40% of these accounts will not be collected. Of the remaining accounts receivable, the company estimates that 4% will not be collected.

c. Accrued interest expense on notes payable for January. Interest is expected to be paid each December 31.

d. Accrued income taxes at the end of January are $12,300.

3. Prepare an adjusted trial balance as of January 31, 2018, after updating beginning balances (above) for transactions during January (*Requirement* 1) and adjusting entries at the end of January (*Requirement* 2).

4. Prepare a multiple-step income statement for the period ended January 31, 2018.

5. Prepare a classified balance sheet as of January 31, 2018.

6. Record closing entries.

7. Analyze how well Big Blast Fireworks' manages its inventory:

a. Calculate the inventory turnover ratio for the month of January. If the industry average of the inventory turnover ratio for the month of January is 18.5 times, is the company managing its inventory *more* or *less* efficiently than other companies in the same industry?

b. Calculate the gross profit ratio for the month of January. If the industry average gross profit ratio is 33%, is the company *more* or *less* profitable per dollar of sales than other companies in the same industry?

c. Used together, what might the inventory turnover ratio and gross profit ratio suggest about Big Blast Fireworks' business strategy? Is the company's strategy to sell a *higher volume of less expensive* items or does the company appear to be selling a *lower volume of more expensive* items?

PROBLEMS: SET A

P6–1A Sandra's Purse Boutique has the following transactions related to its top-selling Gucci purse for the month of October.

Date	Transactions	Units	Cost per Unit	Total Cost
October 1	Beginning inventory	6	$900	$ 5,400
October 4	Sale	4		
October 10	Purchase	5	910	4,550
October 13	Sale	3		
October 20	Purchase	4	920	3,680
October 28	Sale	7		
October 30	Purchase	7	930	6,510
				$20,140

Calculate ending inventory and cost of goods sold for four inventory methods (LO6–3)

Required:

1. Calculate ending inventory and cost of goods sold at October 31, using the specific identification method. The October 4 sale consists of purses from beginning inventory, the October 13 sale consists of one purse from beginning inventory and two purses from the October 10 purchase, and the October 28 sale consists of three purses from the October 10 purchase and four purses from the October 20 purchase.

2. Using FIFO, calculate ending inventory and cost of goods sold at October 31.

3. Using LIFO, calculate ending inventory and cost of goods sold at October 31.

4. Using weighted-average cost, calculate ending inventory and cost of goods sold at October 31.

P6–2A Greg's Bicycle Shop has the following transactions related to its top-selling Mongoose mountain bike for the month of March:

Calculate ending inventory, cost of goods sold, sales revenue, and gross profit for four inventory methods (LO6–3, 6–4, 6–5)

Date	Transactions	Units	Cost per Unit	Total Cost
March 1	Beginning inventory	20	$250	$ 5,000
March 5	Sale ($400 each)	15		
March 9	Purchase	10	270	2,700
March 17	Sale ($450 each)	8		
March 22	Purchase	10	280	2,800
March 27	Sale ($475 each)	12		
March 30	Purchase	9	300	2,700
				$13,200

Required:

1. Calculate ending inventory and cost of goods sold at March 31, using the specific identification method. The March 5 sale consists of bikes from beginning inventory, the March 17 sale consists of bikes from the March 9 purchase, and the March 27 sale consists of four bikes from beginning inventory and eight bikes from the March 22 purchase.
2. Using FIFO, calculate ending inventory and cost of goods sold at March 31.
3. Using LIFO, calculate ending inventory and cost of goods sold at March 31.
4. Using weighted-average cost, calculate ending inventory and cost of goods sold at March 31.
5. Calculate sales revenue and gross profit under each of the four methods.
6. Comparing FIFO and LIFO, which one provides the more meaningful measure of ending inventory? Explain.
7. If Greg's Bicycle Shop chooses to report inventory using LIFO instead of FIFO, record the LIFO adjustment.

Record transactions and prepare a partial income statement using a perpetual inventory system (LO6–2, 6–5)

P6–3A At the beginning of July, CD City has a balance in inventory of $3,400. The following transactions occur during the month of July.

July 3	Purchase CDs on account from Wholesale Music for $2,300, terms 1/10, n/30.
July 4	Pay cash for freight charges related to the July 3 purchase from Wholesale Music, $110.
July 9	Return incorrectly ordered CDs to Wholesale Music and receive credit, $200.
July 11	Pay Wholesale Music in full.
July 12	Sell CDs to customers on account, $5,800, that had a cost of $3,000.
July 15	Receive full payment from customers related to the sale on July 12.
July 18	Purchase CDs on account from Music Supply for $3,100, terms 1/10, n/30.
July 22	Sell CDs to customers for cash, $4,200, that had a cost of $2,500.
July 28	Return CDs to Music Supply and receive credit of $300.
July 30	Pay Music Supply in full.

Required:

1. Assuming that CD City uses a perpetual inventory system, record the transactions.
2. Prepare the top section of the multiple-step income statement through gross profit for the month of July.

Report inventory using lower of cost and net realizable value (LO6–6)

P6–4A A local **Chevrolet** dealership carries the following types of vehicles:

Inventory Items	Quantity	Cost per Unit	NRV per Unit	Lower of Cost and NRV
Vans	4	$27,000	$25,000	_____
Trucks	7	18,000	17,000	_____
2-door sedans	3	13,000	15,000	_____
4-door sedans	5	17,000	20,000	_____
Sports cars	1	37,000	40,000	_____
SUVs	6	30,000	28,000	_____

Because of recent increases in gasoline prices, the car dealership has noticed a reduced demand for its SUVs, vans, and trucks.

Required:
1. Compute the total cost of the entire inventory.
2. Determine whether each inventory item would be reported at cost or net realizable value (NRV). Multiply the quantity of each inventory item by the appropriate cost or NRV amount and place the total in the "Lower of Cost and NRV" column. Then determine the total for that column.
3. Compare your answers in *Requirement* 1 and *Requirement* 2 and then record any necessary adjustment to write down inventory from cost to net realizable value.
4. Discuss the financial statement effects of using lower of cost and net realizable value to report inventory.

P6–5A For the current year, Parker Games has the following inventory transactions related to its traditional board games.

Calculate ending inventory and cost of goods sold using FIFO and LIFO and adjust inventory using lower of cost and net realizable value (LO6–3, 6–6)

Date	Transaction	Units	Cost	Total Cost
Jan. 1	Beginning inventory	120	$21	$2,520
Mar. 12	Purchase	90	16	1,440
Sep. 17	Purchase	60	9	540
		270		$4,500
Jan. 1–Dec. 31	Sales	170		

Because of the increasing popularity of electronic video games, Parker Games continues to see a decline in the demand for board games. Sales prices have decreased by over 50% during the year. At the end of the year, Parker estimates the net realizable value of the 100 units of unsold inventory to be $500.

Required:
1. Using FIFO, calculate ending inventory and cost of goods sold.
2. Using LIFO, calculate ending inventory and cost of goods sold.
3. Determine the amount of ending inventory to report using lower of cost and net realizable value under FIFO. Record any necessary adjustment.

P6–6A At the beginning of October, Bowser Co.'s inventory consists of 50 units with a cost per unit of $50. The following transactions occur during the month of October.

Record transactions using a perpetual system, prepare a partial income statement, and adjust for the lower of cost and net realizable value (LO6–2, 6–3, 6–4, 6–5, 6–6)

October 4	Purchase 130 units of inventory on account from Waluigi Co. for $50 per unit, terms 2/10, n/30.
October 5	Pay cash for freight charges related to the October 4 purchase, $600.
October 9	Return 10 defective units from the October 4 purchase and receive credit.
October 12	Pay Waluigi Co. in full.
October 15	Sell 160 units of inventory to customers on account, $12,800. (*Hint*: The cost of units sold from the October 4 purchase includes $50 unit cost plus $5 per unit for freight less $1 per unit for the purchase discount, or $54 per unit.)
October 19	Receive full payment from customers related to the sale on October 15.
October 20	Purchase 100 units of inventory from Waluigi Co. for $70 per unit, terms 2/10, n/30.
October 22	Sell 100 units of inventory to customers for cash, $8,000.

Required:
1. Assuming that Bowser Co. uses a FIFO perpetual inventory system to maintain its inventory records, record the transactions.
2. Suppose by the end of October that the remaining inventory is estimated to have a net realizable value per unit of $35. Record any necessary adjustment for lower of cost and net realizable value.
3. Prepare the top section of the multiple-step income statement through gross profit for the month of October after the adjustment for lower of cost and net realizable value.

Prepare a multiple-step income statement and calculate the inventory turnover ratio and gross profit ratio (LO6–2, 6–7)

P6–7A Baskin-Robbins is one of the world's largest specialty ice cream shops. The company offers dozens of different flavors, from Very Berry Strawberry to lowfat Espresso 'n Cream. Assume that a local Baskin-Robbins in Raleigh, North Carolina, has the following amounts for the month of July 2018.

Salaries expense	$13,700	Sales revenue	$69,800
Inventory (July 1, 2018)	2,300	Interest income	3,300
Sales returns	1,100	Cost of goods sold	28,700
Utilities expense	3,600	Rent expense	6,700
Income tax expense	6,000	Interest expense	400
		Inventory (July 31, 2018)	1,100

Required:
1. Prepare a multiple-step income statement for the month ended July 31, 2018.
2. Calculate the inventory turnover ratio for the month of July. Would you expect this ratio to be higher or lower in December 2018? Explain.
3. Calculate the gross profit ratio for the month of July.

Use the inventory turnover ratio and gross profit ratio to analyze companies (LO6–7)

P6–8A Wawa Food Markets is a convenience store chain located primarily in the Northeast. The company sells gas, candy bars, drinks, and other grocery-related items. **St. Jude Medical Incorporated** sells medical devices related to cardiovascular needs. Suppose a local Wawa Food Market and St. Jude sales office report the following amounts in the same year (company names are disguised):

	Company 1	Company 2
Net sales	$400,000	$400,000
Cost of goods sold	180,000	330,000
Gross profit	$220,000	$ 70,000
Average inventory	$ 40,000	$ 30,000

Required:
1. For Company 1 and Company 2, calculate the inventory turnover ratio.
2. For Company 1 and Company 2, calculate the gross profit ratio.
3. After comparing the inventory turnover ratios and gross profit ratios, which company do you think is Wawa and which is St. Jude? Explain.

Record transactions and prepare a partial income statement using a periodic inventory system (LO6–8)

P6–9A Refer to the transactions of CD City in P6–3A.

Required:
1. Assuming that CD City uses a periodic inventory system, record the transactions.
2. Record the month-end adjustment to inventory, assuming that a final count reveals ending inventory with a cost of $2,889.
3. Prepare the top section of the multiple-step income statement through gross profit for the month of July.

Correct inventory understatement and calculate gross profit ratio (LO6–7, 6–9)

P6–10A Over a four-year period, Jackie Corporation reported the following series of gross profits.

	2015	2016	2017	2018
Net sales	$60,000	$66,000	$74,000	$90,000
Cost of goods sold	32,000	46,000	28,000	48,000
Gross profit	$28,000	$20,000	$46,000	$42,000

In 2018, the company performed a comprehensive review of its inventory accounting procedures. Based on this review, company records reveal that ending inventory was understated by $11,000 in 2016. Inventory in all other years is correct.

Required:

1. Calculate the gross profit ratio for each of the four years based on amounts originally reported.
2. Calculate the gross profit ratio for each of the four years based on corrected amounts. Describe the trend in the gross profit ratios based on the original amounts versus the corrected amounts.
3. Total gross profit over the four-year period based on the amounts originally reported equals $136,000 (= $28,000 + $20,000 + $46,000 + $42,000). Compare this amount to total gross profit over the four-year period based on the corrected amounts.

PROBLEMS: SET B

P6–1B Jimmie's Fishing Hole has the following transactions related to its top-selling **Shimano** fishing reel for the month of June:

Calculate ending inventory and cost of goods sold for four inventory methods (LO6–3)

Date	Transactions	Units	Cost per Unit	Total Cost
June 1	Beginning inventory	16	$350	$ 5,600
June 7	Sale	11		
June 12	Purchase	10	340	3,400
June 15	Sale	12		
June 24	Purchase	10	330	3,300
June 27	Sale	8		
June 29	Purchase	9	320	2,880
				$15,180

Required:

1. Calculate ending inventory and cost of goods sold at June 30, using the specific identification method. The June 7 sale consists of fishing reels from beginning inventory, the June 15 sale consists of three fishing reels from beginning inventory and nine fishing reels from the June 12 purchase, and the June 27 sale consists of one fishing reel from beginning inventory and seven fishing reels from the June 24 purchase.
2. Using FIFO, calculate ending inventory and cost of goods sold at June 30.
3. Using LIFO, calculate ending inventory and cost of goods sold at June 30.
4. Using weighted-average cost, calculate ending inventory and cost of goods sold at June 30.

P6–2B Pete's Tennis Shop has the following transactions related to its top-selling **Wilson** tennis racket for the month of August:

Calculate ending inventory, cost of goods sold, sales revenue, and gross profit for four inventory methods (LO6–3, 6–4, 6–5)

Date	Transactions	Units	Cost per Unit	Total Cost
August 1	Beginning inventory	8	$160	$1,280
August 4	Sale ($225 each)	5		
August 11	Purchase	10	150	1,500
August 13	Sale ($240 each)	8		
August 20	Purchase	10	140	1,400
August 26	Sale ($250 each)	11		
August 29	Purchase	11	130	1,430
				$5,610

Required:

1. Calculate ending inventory and cost of goods sold at August 31, using the specific identification method. The August 4 sale consists of rackets from beginning inventory, the August 13 sale consists of rackets from the August 11 purchase, and the August 26 sale consists of one racket from beginning inventory and 10 rackets from the August 20 purchase.

2. Using FIFO, calculate ending inventory and cost of goods sold at August 31.
3. Using LIFO, calculate ending inventory and cost of goods sold at August 31.
4. Using weighted-average cost, calculate ending inventory and cost of goods sold at August 31.
5. Calculate sales revenue and gross profit under each of the four methods.
6. Comparing FIFO and LIFO, which one provides the more meaningful measure of ending inventory? Explain.
7. If Pete's chooses to report inventory using LIFO, record the LIFO adjustment.

Record transactions and prepare a partial income statement using a perpetual inventory system (LO6–2, 6–5)

P6–3B At the beginning of June, Circuit Country has a balance in inventory of $3,000. The following transactions occur during the month of June.

June 2	Purchase radios on account from Radio World for $2,700, terms 1/15, n/45.
June 4	Pay cash for freight charges related to the June 2 purchase from Radio World, $400.
June 8	Return defective radios to Radio World and receive credit, $400.
June 10	Pay Radio World in full.
June 11	Sell radios to customers on account, $5,000, that had a cost of $3,200.
June 18	Receive payment on account from customers, $4,000.
June 20	Purchase radios on account from Sound Unlimited for $3,800, terms 3/10, n/30.
June 23	Sell radios to customers for cash, $5,300, that had a cost of $3,600.
June 26	Return damaged radios to Sound Unlimited and receive credit of $500.
June 28	Pay Sound Unlimited in full.

Required:
1. Assuming that Circuit Country uses a perpetual inventory system, record the transactions.
2. Prepare the top section of the multiple-step income statement through gross profit for the month of June.

Report inventory using lower of cost and net realizable value (LO6–6)

P6–4B A home improvement store, like Lowe's, carries the following items:

Inventory Items	Quantity	Cost per Unit	NRV per Unit	Lower of Cost and NRV
Hammers	110	$ 8.00	$ 8.50	_____
Saws	60	11.00	10.00	_____
Screwdrivers	140	3.00	3.60	_____
Drills	50	26.00	24.00	_____
1-gallon paint cans	170	6.50	6.00	_____
Paintbrushes	190	7.00	7.50	_____

Required:
1. Compute the total cost of inventory.
2. Determine whether each inventory item would be reported at cost or net realizable value. Multiply the quantity of each inventory item by the appropriate cost or NRV amount and place the total in the "Lower of Cost and NRV" column. Then determine the total of that column.
3. Compare your answers in *Requirement* 1 and *Requirement* 2 and then record any necessary adjustment to write down inventory from cost to net realizable value.
4. Discuss the financial statement effects of using lower of cost and net realizable value to report inventory.

Calculate ending inventory and cost of goods sold using FIFO and LIFO and adjust inventory using lower of cost and net realizable value (LO6–3, 6–6)

P6–5B Trends by Tiffany sells high-end leather purses. The company has the following inventory transactions for the year.

Date	Transaction	Units	Cost	Total Cost
Jan. 1	Beginning inventory	20	$500	$ 10,000
Apr. 9	Purchase	30	520	15,600
Oct. 4	Purchase	11	550	6,050
		61		$31,650
Jan. 1–Dec. 31	Sales	52		

Because trends in purses change frequently, Trends by Tiffany estimates that the remaining nine purses have a net realizable value at December 31 of only $350 each.

Required:

1. Using FIFO, calculate ending inventory and cost of goods sold.
2. Using LIFO, calculate ending inventory and cost of goods sold.
3. Determine the amount of ending inventory to report using lower of cost and net realizable value under FIFO. Record any necessary adjustment.

P6–6B At the beginning of November, Yoshi Inc.'s inventory consists of 60 units with a cost per unit of $94. The following transactions occur during the month of November.

November 2   Purchase 90 units of inventory on account from Toad Inc. for $100 per unit, terms 3/10, n/30.
November 3   Pay cash for freight charges related to the November 2 purchase, $231.
November 9   Return 13 defective units from the November 2 purchase and receive credit.
November 11   Pay Toad Inc. in full.
November 16   Sell 100 units of inventory to customers on account, $14,000. (*Hint*: The cost of units sold from the November 2 purchase includes $100 unit cost plus $3 per unit for freight less $3 per unit for the purchase discount, or $100 per unit.)
November 20   Receive full payment from customers related to the sale on November 16.
November 21   Purchase 70 units of inventory from Toad Inc. for $104 per unit, terms 2/10, n/30.
November 24   Sell 90 units of inventory to customers for cash, $12,600.

Record transactions using a perpetual system, prepare a partial income statement, and adjust for the lower of cost and net realizable value (LO6–2, 6–3, 6–4, 6–5, 6–6)

Required:

1. Assuming that Yoshi Inc. uses a FIFO perpetual inventory system to maintain its internal inventory records, record the transactions.
2. Suppose by the end of November that the remaining inventory is estimated to have a net realizable value per unit of $81, record any necessary adjustment for the lower of cost and net realizable value.
3. Prepare the top section of the multiple-step income statement through gross profit for the month of November after the adjustment for lower of cost and net realizable value.

P6–7B Toys "R" Us sells a variety of children's toys, games, books, and accessories. Assume that a local store has the following amounts for the month of March 2018.

Prepare a multiple-step income statement and calculate the inventory turnover ratio and gross profit ratio (LO6–2, 6–7)

Sales revenue	$77,300	Inventory (Mar. 31, 2018)	$1,000
Advertising expense	6,400	Insurance expense	2,300
Rent expense	4,300	Sales discounts	3,000
Gain on sale of building	7,500	Salaries expense	9,400
Inventory (Mar. 1, 2018)	2,800	Income tax expense	4,200
Cost of goods sold	35,800		

Required:

1. Prepare a multiple-step income statement for the month ended March 31, 2018.
2. Calculate the inventory turnover ratio for the month of March. Would you expect this ratio to be higher or lower in December 2018? Explain.
3. Calculate the gross profit ratio for the month of March.

Use the inventory turnover ratio and gross profit ratio to analyze companies (LO6–7)

P6–8B Payless ShoeSource and Dillard's both offer men's formal footwear. Payless offers lower- to middle-priced footwear, whereas Dillard's offers more specialized, higher-end footwear. The average price for a pair of shoes in Payless may be about $50, whereas the average price in Dillard's may be about $175. The types of shoes offered by Dillard's are not sold by many other stores. Suppose a Payless store and a Dillard's store report the following amounts for men's shoes in the same year (company names are disguised):

	Company 1	Company 2
Net sales	$200,000	$200,000
Cost of goods sold	130,000	165,000
Gross profit	$ 70,000	$ 35,000
Average inventory	$ 35,000	$ 20,000

Required:
1. For Company 1 and Company 2, calculate the inventory turnover ratio.
2. For Company 1 and Company 2, calculate the gross profit ratio.
3. After comparing the inventory turnover ratios and gross profit ratios, which company do you think is Payless and which is Dillard's? Explain.

Record transactions and prepare a partial income statement using a periodic inventory system (LO6–8)

P6–9B Refer to the transactions of Circuit Country in P6–3B.

Required:
1. Assuming that Circuit Country uses a periodic inventory system, record the transactions.
2. Record the month-end adjustment to inventory, assuming that a final count reveals ending inventory with a cost of $2,078.
3. Prepare the top section of the multiple-step income statement through gross profit for the month of June.

Determine the effects of inventory errors using FIFO (LO6–3, 6–9)

P6–10B Sylvester has a bird shop that sells canaries. Sylvester maintains accurate records on the number of birds purchased from its suppliers and the number sold to customers. The records show the following purchases and sales during 2018.

Date	Transactions	Units	Cost per Unit	Total Cost
January 1	Beginning inventory	35	$40	$ 1,400
April 14	Purchase	80	42	3,360
August 22	Purchase	130	44	5,720
October 29	Purchase	95	46	4,370
		340		$14,850
Jan. 1–Dec. 31	Sales ($60 each)	280		

Sylvester uses a periodic inventory system and believes there are 60 birds remaining in ending inventory. However, Sylvester neglects to make a final inventory count at the end of the year. An employee accidentally left one of the cages open one night and 10 birds flew away, leaving only 50 birds in ending inventory. Sylvester is not aware of the lost canaries.

Required:
1. What amount will Sylvester calculate for ending inventory and cost of goods sold using FIFO, assuming he erroneously believes 60 canaries remain in ending inventory?
2. What amount would Sylvester calculate for ending inventory and cost of goods sold using FIFO if he knew that only 50 canaries remain in ending inventory?
3. What effect will the inventory error have on reported amounts for (a) ending inventory, (b) retained earnings, (c) cost of goods sold, and (d) net income (ignoring tax effects) in 2018?
4. Assuming that ending inventory is correctly counted at the end of 2019, what effect will the inventory error in 2018 have on reported amounts for (a) ending inventory, (b) retained earnings, (c) cost of goods sold, and (d) net income (ignoring tax effects) in 2019?

ADDITIONAL PERSPECTIVES

Great Adventures

(This is a continuation of the Great Adventures problem from earlier chapters.)

AP6–1 Now that operations for outdoor clinics and TEAM events are running smoothly, Suzie thinks of another area for business expansion. She notices that a few clinic participants wear multiuse (MU) watches. Beyond the normal timekeeping features of most watches, MU watches are able to report temperature, altitude, and barometric pressure. MU watches are waterproof, so moisture from kayaking, rain, fishing, or even diving up to 100 feet won't damage them. Suzie decides to have MU watches available for sale at the start of each clinic. The following transactions relate to purchases and sales of watches during the second half of 2019. All watches are sold for $300 each.

Continuing Problem

Jul.	17	Purchased 50 watches for $7,500 ($150 per watch) on account.
Jul.	31	Sold 40 watches for $12,000 cash.
Aug.	12	Purchased 40 watches for $6,400 ($160 per watch) cash.
Aug.	22	Sold 30 watches for $9,000 on account.
Sep.	19	Paid for watches ordered on July 17.
Sep.	27	Received full payment for watches sold on account on August 22.
Oct.	27	Purchased 80 watches for $13,600 ($170 per watch) cash.
Nov.	20	Sold 90 watches for $27,000 cash.
Dec.	4	Purchased 100 watches for $18,000 ($180 per watch) cash.
Dec.	8	Sold 40 watches for $12,000 on account.

Required:

1. (a) Calculate sales revenue, cost of goods sold, and ending inventory as of December 31, 2019, assuming Suzie uses FIFO to account for inventory.
   (b) Prepare the gross profit section of a partial income statement for transactions related to MU watches.
2. Late in December, the next generation of multiuse (MU II) watches is released. In addition to all of the features of the MU watch, the MU II watches are equipped with a global positioning system (GPS) and have the ability to download and play songs and videos off the Internet. The demand for the original MU watches is greatly reduced. As of December 31, the estimated net realizable value of MU watches is only $100 per watch.
   (a) Record any necessary adjustment on December 31, 2019, related to this information.
   (b) For what amount would MU inventory be reported in the December 31, 2019, balance sheet?
   (c) Prepare an updated gross profit section of a partial income statement accounting for this additional information. Compare your answer to *Requirement* 1(b).

American Eagle Outfitters, Inc.

Financial Analysis

AP6–2 Financial information for **American Eagle** is presented in **Appendix A** at the end of the book.

Required:

1. For the most recent year, what is the amount of inventory in the balance sheet? What does this amount represent?
2. American Eagle refers to its cost of goods sold using a different name. What is it?
3. For the most recent year, what is the amount of cost of goods sold in the income statement? What does this amount represent?
4. Calculate American Eagle's inventory turnover ratio and average days in inventory for the most recent year.
5. Calculate American Eagle's gross profit ratio for each of the three years. Do you notice any trend?
6. For the most recent year, calculate American Eagle's ratio of operating expenses to net sales.

Financial Analysis

The Buckle, Inc.

AP6–3 Financial information for **Buckle** is presented in **Appendix B** at the end of the book.

Required:

1. For the most recent year, what is the amount of inventory in the balance sheet? What does this amount represent?
2. Buckle refers to its cost of goods sold using a different name. What is it?
3. For the most recent year, what is the amount of cost of goods sold in the income statement? What does this amount represent?
4. Calculate Buckle's inventory turnover ratio and average days in inventory for the most recent year.
5. Calculate Buckle's gross profit ratio for each of the three years. Do you notice any trend?
6. For the most recent year, calculate Buckle's ratio of operating expenses to net sales.

Comparative Analysis

American Eagle Outfitters, Inc. vs. The Buckle, Inc.

AP6–4 Financial information for **American Eagle** is presented in **Appendix A** at the end of the book, and financial information for **Buckle** is presented in **Appendix B** at the end of the book.

Required:

1. Which company carries a greater inventory balance as a percentage of total assets?
2. Analyze each company's inventory using the inventory turnover ratio and average days in inventory.
3. Determine which company's operations are more profitable using the gross profit ratio.
4. Considering the companies' ratio of operating expenses to net sales, does your answer to *Requirement* 3 change? Explain.

Ethics

AP6–5 Horizon Corporation manufactures personal computers. The company began operations in 2009 and reported profits for the years 2009 through 2016. Due primarily to increased competition and price slashing in the industry, 2017's income statement reported a loss of $20 million. Just before the end of the 2018 fiscal year, a memo from the company's chief financial officer to Jim Fielding, the company controller, included the following comments:

> If we don't do something about the large amount of unsold computers already manufactured, our auditors will require us to record a write down. The resulting loss for 2018 will cause a violation of our debt covenants and force the company into bankruptcy. I suggest that you ship half of our inventory to J.B. Sales, Inc., in Oklahoma City. I know the company's president, and he will accept the inventory and acknowledge the shipment as a purchase. We can record the sale in 2018 which will boost our loss to a profit. Then J.B. Sales will simply return the inventory in 2019 after the financial statements have been issued.

Required:

Discuss the ethical dilemma faced by Jim Fielding. What is the issue? Who are the parties involved? What factors should Jim consider in making his decision?

Internet Research

AP6–6 Obtain copies of the annual reports of **The Coca-Cola Company** and **PepsiCo** for the most recent year. You can find the annual reports at the companies' websites (*www.coca-cola.com* and *www.pepsico.com*) in the investor information section or at the Securities and Exchange Commission's website (*www.sec.gov*) using EDGAR (Electronic Data Gathering, Analysis, and Retrieval). The SEC requires Form 10-K, which includes the annual report, to be filed on EDGAR. Search or scroll within the annual reports to find the financial statements.

Required:
1. For each company, calculate the gross profit ratio, inventory turnover ratio, and average days in inventory.
2. Compare the management of each company's investment in inventory.

Written Communication

AP6–7 You have just been hired as a consultant to Gilbert Industries, a newly formed company. The company president, Mindy Grayson, is seeking your advice as to the appropriate inventory method Gilbert should use to value its inventory and cost of goods sold. Ms. Grayson has narrowed the choice to LIFO and FIFO. She has heard that LIFO might be better for tax purposes, but FIFO has certain advantages for financial reporting to investors and creditors. You have been told that the company will be profitable in its first year and for the foreseeable future.

Required:
Prepare a report for the president describing the factors that should be considered by Gilbert in choosing between LIFO and FIFO.

Earnings Management

AP6–8 Eddie's Galleria sells billiard tables. The company has the following purchases and sales for 2018.

Date	Transactions	Units	Cost per Unit	Total Cost
January 1	Beginning inventory	150	$540	$ 81,000
March 8	Purchase	120	570	68,400
August 22	Purchase	100	600	60,000
October 29	Purchase	80	640	51,200
		450		$260,600
Jan. 1–Dec. 31	Sales ($700 each)	400		

Eddie is worried about the company's financial performance. He has noticed an increase in the purchase cost of billiard tables, but at the same time, competition from other billiard table stores and other entertainment choices have prevented him from increasing the sales price. Eddie is worried that if the company's profitability is too low, stockholders will demand he be replaced. Eddie does not want to lose his job. Since 60 of the 400 billiard tables sold have not yet been picked up by the customers as of December 31, 2018, Eddie decides incorrectly to include these tables in ending inventory. He appropriately includes the sale of these 60 tables as part of total revenues in 2018.

Required:
1. What amount will Eddie calculate for ending inventory and cost of goods sold using FIFO, assuming he erroneously reports that 110 tables remain in ending inventory?
2. What amount would Eddie calculate for cost of goods sold using FIFO if he correctly reports that only 50 tables remain in ending inventory?
3. What effect will the inventory error have on reported amounts for (a) ending inventory, (b) retained earnings, (c) cost of goods sold, and (d) net income (ignoring tax effects) in 2018?
4. Assuming that ending inventory is correctly counted at the end of 2019, what effect will the inventory error in 2018 have on reported amounts for (a) ending inventory, (b) retained earnings, (c) cost of goods sold, and (d) net income (ignoring tax effects) in 2019?

Answers to the Self-Study Questions
  1. d   2. b   3. a   4. a   5. b   6. d   7. d   8. a   9. c   10. b

Long-Term Assets

Learning Objectives

AFTER STUDYING THIS CHAPTER, YOU SHOULD BE ABLE TO:

- **LO7–1**   Identify the major types of property, plant, and equipment.
- **LO7–2**   Identify the major types of intangible assets.
- **LO7–3**   Describe the accounting treatment of expenditures after acquisition.
- **LO7–4**   Calculate depreciation of property, plant, and equipment.
- **LO7–5**   Calculate amortization of intangible assets.
- **LO7–6**   Account for the disposal of long-term assets.

Analysis

- **LO7–7**   Describe the links among return on assets, profit margin, and asset turnover.

Appendix

- **LO7–8**   Identify impairment situations and describe the two-step impairment process.

WORLDCOM: EXPENSES CALLED ASSETS

WorldCom was the leading telecommunications company in North America. Then in 2002, a routine internal audit uncovered massive accounting fraud. The firm had recorded assets in the balance sheet that should have been recorded as expenses in the income statement. Although this kind of fraudulent reporting was not new, the size of the fraud set new records. By failing to properly record these expenses, WorldCom overstated its income and assets by nearly $11 billion (not $11 million, but $11 *billion!*). Estimates of investor losses from the resulting bankruptcy exceeded $100 billion.

Feature Story

How was the fraud accomplished? When WorldCom used the telecommunication lines of another company, it paid a fee. This fee is part of normal operating costs, and it should have been recorded in the income statement as an operating expense. Instead, WorldCom recorded these operating expenses in the balance sheet as **long-term assets.** Failure to report these operating expenses caused net income to be overstated by billions; operating expenses were purposely misstated as assets.

What motivated WorldCom's management to commit this fraud? It appears the intention was to hide operating losses and maintain a strong stock price. If investors had known the true operating performance of WorldCom, the stock price would have tumbled.

For his role in the accounting scandal that led to the largest bankruptcy in U.S. history, Bernard Ebbers, the 63-year-old CEO of WorldCom, was sentenced to 25 years in a low-security federal prison.[1] Ebbers, who took the stand in his own defense, insisted that he knew nothing of WorldCom's fraudulent accounting, but had left the accounting to Scott Sullivan, the company's chief financial officer (CFO). The jury did not buy Ebbers's hands-off defense. They concluded that the CEO, as head of the company, is ultimately responsible for the firm's accounting.

In this chapter, we discuss how to record the acquisition of long-term assets; allocate the cost of long-term assets through depreciation or amortization; and how to record the sale, retirement, or exchange of long-term assets at the end of their useful life.

At the end of the chapter, we compare the return on assets for **Walmart** and **Costco.** We separate return on assets into two parts: profit margin (how much a company makes for each dollar in sales) and asset turnover (how much sales a company generates for each dollar in assets). We then examine whether the ratios support our expectations regarding Walmart and Costco, two close competitors in the discount retail market.

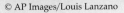

© AP Images/Louis Lanzano

[1]J. Sandberg, D. Solomon, and R. Blumenstein. "Inside WorldCom's Unearthing of a Vast Accounting Scandal." *The Wall Street Journal* (June 27, 2002); K. Eichenwald and S. Romero. "Inquiry Finds Effort to Delay at WorldCom." *The New York Times* (July 4, 2002); K. Crawford. "Ex-WorldCom CEO Ebbers Guilty." *CNNMoney.com* (March 15, 2005); and "Bernard Ebbers Given 25-year Prison Sentence." CBC News (July 13, 2005).

Krispy Kreme cannot make doughnuts without its manufacturing facilities and the equipment in those facilities. In contrast, it's not physical assets but copyrights on its computer software that give **Google** the ability to generate billions of dollars in revenue each year. Both of these types of revenue-producing assets are considered *long-term assets,* the topic of this chapter.

We classify long-term assets into two major categories:

1. **Tangible assets.** Assets in this category include land, land improvements, buildings, equipment, and natural resources. Krispy Kreme's land, buildings, and equipment fall into this category.

2. **Intangible assets.** Assets in this category include patents, trademarks, copyrights, franchises, and goodwill. We distinguish these assets from property, plant, and equipment by their lack of physical substance. The evidence of their existence often is based on a legal contract. Google's copyrights are intangible assets.

Long-term assets often represent a significant portion of the total assets of a company. Illustration 7–1 presents a breakdown of the total assets for **Darden Restaurants**, a publicly traded company that owns and operates restaurant chains such as **Olive Garden**, **Longhorn Steakhouse**, and **Bahama Breeze**. Notice that current assets represent only about 28% of total assets, and long-term assets make up the remaining 72%. Accounting for long-term assets, both tangible (property, plant, and equipment) and intangible, is important and is the primary focus in this chapter.

ILLUSTRATION 7–1

Balance Sheet for Darden Restaurants

DARDEN RESTAURANTS Balance Sheet (partial) ($ in thousands)	
Cash	$ 98,300
Receivables	207,800
Inventory	196,800
Other current assets	1,473,500
Total current assets	1,976,400
Property, plant, and equipment	3,381,000
Intangible assets	1,447,100
Other long-term assets and investments	296,200
Total assets	**$7,100,700**

To properly report both tangible and intangible assets, we need to address a variety of issues including (1) which amounts to include in their initial cost, (2) how to expense their costs while using them, and (3) how to record their sale or disposal at the end of their useful life. These three issues are the basis for the three major parts of the chapter.

PART A

ACQUISITIONS

The first issue to consider in accounting for long-term assets is how to record their cost at the time of acquisition. To do this, we need to understand the major types of tangible and intangible assets. We begin with tangible assets, also referred to as property, plant, and equipment.

■ **LO7–1**

Identify the major types of property, plant, and equipment.

Property, Plant, and Equipment

The property, plant, and equipment category consists of land, land improvements, buildings, equipment, and natural resources. The general rule for recording all such long-term assets can be simply stated as: **We record a long-term asset at its cost** *plus* **all expenditures necessary to get the asset ready for use.** Thus, the initial cost of a long-term asset might be more than just its purchase price; it also will include any additional amounts the firm paid to bring the asset to its desired condition and location for use. We use the term capitalize to describe recording an expenditure as an asset.

When we make an expenditure, we have the choice of recording it as an expense of the current period or recording it as an asset and then allocating that cost as an expense over future periods. The choice depends on when the company benefits from having the asset: in the current period or over future periods. Determining which costs to record as expenses and which to record as long-term assets is crucial. Several infamous accounting frauds, like **WorldCom**, were the result of inflating net income by improperly recording current expenses as long-term assets.

We look at land, land improvements, buildings, equipment, basket purchases, and natural resources next.

LAND

The Land account represents land a company is using in its operations. (In contrast, land purchased for investment purposes is recorded in a separate investment account.) We capitalize to Land all expenditures necessary to get the land ready for its intended use.

Such capitalized costs include the purchase price of the land plus closing costs such as fees for the attorney, real estate agent commissions, title, title search, and recording fees. If the property is subject to back taxes or other obligations, we include these amounts as well. In fact, any additional expenditure such as clearing, filling, and leveling the land, or even removing existing buildings to prepare the land for its intended use, become part of the land's capitalized cost. If we receive any cash from selling salvaged building materials, we reduce the cost of land by that amount.

Assume, for instance, that **Olive Garden**, a restaurant chain owned by **Darden Restaurants** purchases a two-acre tract of land and an existing building for $500,000. The company plans to remove the existing building and construct a new Olive Garden restaurant on the site. In addition to the purchase price, the company pays a sales commission of $30,000 to the real estate agent and title insurance of $3,000. Olive Garden also pays $8,000 in property taxes, which includes $6,000 of back taxes (unpaid taxes from previous years) paid by Olive Garden on behalf of the seller and $2,000 due for the current fiscal year after the purchase date. Shortly after closing, the company pays a contractor $50,000 to tear down the old building and remove it from the site. Olive Garden is able to sell salvaged materials from the building for $5,000 and pays an additional $6,000 to level the land.

Using the guideline of **cost** *plus* **all expenditures necessary to get the asset ready for use,** at what amount should Olive Garden record as the total cost of the land? Illustration 7–2 provides the details in computing the cost of the land.

Purchase price of land (and existing building)	$500,000
Commissions	30,000
Back property taxes	6,000
Title insurance	3,000
Cost of removing existing building	50,000
Less: Salvaged materials from existing building	(5,000)
Cost of leveling the land	6,000
Total cost of land	$590,000

ILLUSTRATION 7–2

Computation of the Cost of Land

© Alistair Berg/Lifesize/ Getty Images, RF

You may wonder why Olive Garden recorded only $6,000 for property taxes. That was the amount required to get the asset ready for use—Olive Garden could not use the land until it paid the back taxes. The additional $2,000 in property taxes, though, relates only to the current period, so Olive Garden records that amount as an expense in the current period. All of the other costs, including the $6,000 in back property taxes, are necessary to acquire the land, so Olive Garden capitalizes them. Note that the salvaged materials sold for $5,000 reduce the overall cost of the land.

COMMON MISTAKE

Many students incorrectly add or ignore the cash received from the sale of salvaged materials. Cash received from the sale of salvaged materials *reduces* the total cost of land.

LAND IMPROVEMENTS

Beyond the cost of the land, **Olive Garden** likely will spend additional amounts to improve the land by adding a parking lot, sidewalks, driveways, landscaping, lighting systems, fences, sprinklers, and similar additions. These are land improvements. Because land improvements have limited useful lives (parking lots eventually wear out), and land has an unlimited useful life, we record land improvements separately from the land itself.

BUILDINGS

Buildings include administrative offices, retail stores, manufacturing facilities, and storage warehouses. **The cost of acquiring a building usually includes realtor commissions and legal fees in addition to the purchase price.** The new owner sometimes needs to remodel or otherwise modify the building to suit its needs. These additional costs are part of the building's acquisition cost.

Unique accounting issues arise when a firm constructs a building rather than purchasing it. Of course the cost of construction includes architect fees, material costs, and construction labor. New building construction likely also includes costs such as manager supervision, overhead (costs indirectly related to the construction), and interest costs incurred during construction.

EQUIPMENT

Equipment is a broad term that includes machinery used in manufacturing, computers and other office equipment, vehicles, furniture, and fixtures. **The cost of equipment is the actual purchase price plus all other costs necessary to prepare the asset for use.** These can be any of a variety of other costs including sales tax, shipping, delivery insurance, assembly, installation, testing, and even legal fees incurred to establish title.

What about recurring costs related to equipment, such as annual property insurance and annual property taxes on vehicles? Rather than including recurring costs as part of the cost of the equipment, we expense them as we incur them. The question to ask yourself when deciding whether to add a cost to the asset account or record it as an expense of the current period is, *"Is this a cost of acquiring the asset and getting it ready for use, or is it a recurring cost that benefits the company in the current period?"*

Assume that **Olive Garden** purchases new restaurant equipment for $82,000 plus $6,500 in sales tax. It pays a freight company $800 to transport the equipment and $200 shipping insurance. The firm pays $1,600 for one year of liability insurance on the equipment in advance. The equipment was also installed at an additional cost of $1,500. Illustration 7–3

© Comstock Images/ Jupiterimages, RF

ILLUSTRATION 7–3

Computation of the Cost of Equipment

Purchase price	$82,000
Sales tax	6,500
Transportation	800
Shipping insurance	200
Installation	1,500
Total cost of equipment	$91,000

shows the calculation of the amount at which Olive Garden should record the cost of the equipment.

Thus, Olive Garden should record the equipment at a total cost of $91,000. With the exception of the $1,600 annual insurance on the equipment, each of the expenditures described was necessary to bring the equipment to its condition and location for use. Olive Garden will report the $1,600 for one year of liability insurance as prepaid insurance and allocate the $1,600 to insurance expense over the first year of coverage.

BASKET PURCHASES

Sometimes companies purchase more than one asset at the same time for one purchase price. This is known as a basket purchase. For example, assume **Olive Garden** purchases land, building, and equipment together for $900,000. We need to record land, building, and equipment in separate accounts. How much should we record in the separate accounts for land, building, and equipment? The simple answer is that we allocate the total purchase price of $900,000 based on the estimated fair values of each of the individual assets. Estimated fair values are estimates of what the separate assets are worth.

The difficulty, though, is that the estimated fair values of the individual assets often exceed the total purchase price, in this case, $900,000. Let's say the estimated fair values of land, building, and equipment are $200,000, $700,000, and $100,000, respectively, for a total estimated fair value of $1 million. In that case, Olive Garden's total purchase of $900,000 will be allocated to the separate accounts for Land, Building, and Equipment based on their relative fair values as shown in Illustration 7–4.

ILLUSTRATION 7–4

Allocation of Cost in a Basket Purchase

	Estimated Fair Value	Allocation Percentage		Amount of Basket Purchase	Recorded Amount
Land	$ 200,000	$200,000/$1,000,000 = 20%	×	$900,000	$180,000
Building	700,000	$700,000/$1,000,000 = 70%	×	$900,000	630,000
Equipment	100,000	$100,000/$1,000,000 = 10%	×	$900,000	90,000
Total	$1,000,000		100%		$900,000

NATURAL RESOURCES

Many companies depend heavily on natural resources, such as oil, natural gas, timber, and even salt. **ExxonMobil**, for example, maintains oil and natural gas deposits on six of the world's seven continents. **Weyerhaeuser** is one of the largest pulp and paper companies in the world with major investments in timber forests. Even salt is a natural resource, with the largest supply in the United States mined under the Great Lakes of North America.

We can distinguish natural resources from other property, plant, and equipment by the fact that we can physically use up, or *deplete,* natural resources. ExxonMobil's oil reserves are a natural resource that decreases as the firm extracts oil. Similarly, timber land is used up to produce materials in the construction industry and salt is extracted from salt mines for use in cooking and melting icy roads.

 KEY POINT

Tangible assets such as land, land improvements, buildings, equipment, and natural resources are recorded at cost plus all costs necessary to get the asset ready for its intended use.

Intangible Assets

The other major category of long-term assets, intangible assets, have no physical substance. Assets in this category include patents, trademarks, copyrights, franchises, and goodwill.

■ **LO7–2**

Identify the major types of intangible assets.

Despite their lack of physical substance, intangible assets can be very valuable indeed. One of the most valuable intangible assets for many companies is their trademark or brand. *Interbrand* publishes an annual list of the 100 most valuable brands. Illustration 7–5 summarizes the top 10 most valuable brands. As you can see, the **Apple** brand has an estimated value of $118.9 billion. Despite this value, Apple reports total intangible assets on its balance sheet at less than $10 billion. Later, we'll see why many intangible assets are *not* recorded in the balance sheet at their estimated values.

ILLUSTRATION 7–5   World's Top 10 Brands

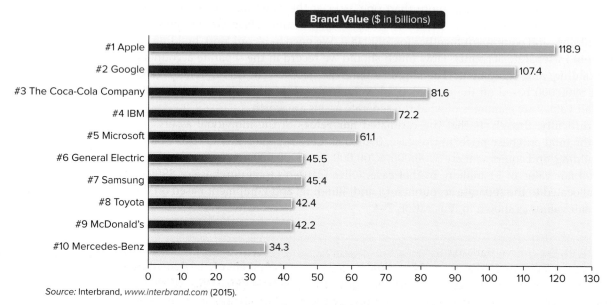

Brand Value ($ in billions)

#1	Apple	118.9
#2	Google	107.4
#3	The Coca-Cola Company	81.6
#4	IBM	72.2
#5	Microsoft	61.1
#6	General Electric	45.5
#7	Samsung	45.4
#8	Toyota	42.4
#9	McDonald's	42.2
#10	Mercedes-Benz	34.3

Source: Interbrand, *www.interbrand.com* (2015).

Companies acquire intangible assets in two ways:

1. They *purchase* intangible assets like patents, copyrights, trademarks, or franchise rights from other companies.
2. They *develop* intangible assets internally, for instance by developing a new product or process and obtaining a protective patent.

The reporting rules for intangible assets vary depending on whether the company purchased the asset or developed it internally. Reporting *purchased* intangibles is similar to reporting purchased property, plant, and equipment. **We record purchased intangible assets at their original cost plus all other costs, such as legal fees, necessary to get the asset ready for use.**

Reporting intangible assets that are *developed internally* is quite different. Rather than reporting these in the balance sheet as intangible assets, **we expense in the income statement most of the costs for internally developed intangible assets in the period we incur those costs.** For example, the research and development (R&D) costs incurred in developing a patent internally are not recorded as an intangible asset in the balance sheet. Instead, they are expensed directly in the income statement. The reason we expense all R&D costs is the difficulty in determining the portion of R&D that benefits future periods. Conceptually, we should record as an intangible asset the portion that benefits future periods. Due to the difficulties in arriving at this estimate, current U.S. accounting rules require firms to expense all R&D costs as incurred.

A similar argument about the difficulty of estimating benefits in future periods can be made for advertising expenses. Advertising at Apple clearly has made its trademark more valuable. Because we cannot tell what portion of today's advertising benefits future periods and how many periods it might benefit, advertising costs are not reported as an intangible asset in the balance sheet. Instead, advertising costs are recorded as expenses and are reported in the income statement in the period incurred.

INTERNATIONAL FINANCIAL REPORTING STANDARDS (IFRS)

SHOULD R&D BE CLASSIFIED AS AN ASSET OR AN EXPENSE?

International accounting standards differ from U.S. accounting standards in the treatment of R&D costs. U.S. GAAP requires that we expense all research and development expenditures in the period incurred. IFRS makes a distinction between *research* activities and *development* activities. Under IFRS, research expenditures are expensed in the period incurred, consistent with U.S. GAAP. However, development costs that benefit future periods can be recorded as an intangible asset.

For more discussion, see Appendix E.

KEY POINT

We record purchased intangibles as long-term assets at their purchase price plus all costs necessary to get the asset ready for use. We expense internally generated intangibles, such as R&D and advertising costs, as we incur them.

Let's look in more detail at some specific types of intangible assets.

PATENTS

A patent is an exclusive right to manufacture a product or to use a process. The U.S. Patent and Trademark Office grants this right for a period of 20 years. **When a firm *purchases* a patent, it records the patent as an intangible asset at its purchase price plus other costs such as legal and filing fees to secure the patent.** Filing fees include items such as the fee to record a patent with the U.S. Patent and Trademark Office.

In contrast, when a firm *develops a patent internally,* it expenses the research and development costs as it incurs them. For example, major pharmaceutical companies like **Amgen** and **Gilead Sciences** spend over a billion dollars each year developing new drug patents. Most of these research and development costs are recorded as operating expenses in the income statement. An exception to this rule is legal fees. The firm will record in the Patent asset account the legal and filing fees to secure the patent, even if it developed the patented item or process internally.

Holders of patents often need to defend their exclusive rights in court. For example, **The J.M. Smucker Company** obtained a patent on a round, crustless, frozen peanut butter and jelly sandwich sealed in an airtight foil wrapper, marketed under the name "Uncrustables." Smucker's later had to defend its patent by attempting to stop another company from making similar sandwiches. The costs of successfully defending a patent, including attorneys' fees, are added to the Patent account.

COPYRIGHTS

A copyright is an exclusive right of protection given by the U.S. Copyright Office to the creator of a published work such as a song, film, painting, photograph, book, or computer software. Copyrights are protected by law and give the creator (and his or her heirs) the exclusive right to reproduce and sell the artistic or published work for the life of the creator plus 70 years. A copyright also allows the copyright holder to pursue legal action against anyone who attempts to infringe the copyright. Accounting for the costs of copyrights is virtually identical to that of patents.

TRADEMARKS

A trademark, like the name **Apple**, is a word, slogan, or symbol that distinctively identifies a company, product, or service. The firm can register its trademark with the U.S. Patent and

Trademark Office to protect it from use by others for a period of 10 years. The registration can be renewed for an indefinite number of 10-year periods, so a trademark is an example of an intangible asset whose useful life can be indefinite.

Firms often acquire trademarks through acquisition. As an example, **Hewlett-Packard (HP)** acquired all the outstanding stock of **Compaq Computer Corporation** for $24 billion, of which $1.4 billion was assigned to the Compaq trademark.

Advertising costs can factor into the value of a trademark in a big way. For example, Apple has aired commercials featuring each new iPhone release. Certainly these ads benefited Apple. But what was the value to the company of the advertising? And for how many years will Apple receive that value? Since these items are so difficult to estimate, when a firm develops a trademark internally through advertising, it doesn't record the advertising costs as part of the cost of the intangible asset. Instead, it expenses the advertising costs in the income statement. Even though some advertising costs meet the definition of an asset by providing future benefits, due to the difficulty in estimating these amounts, financial accounting rules require advertising costs to be expensed as incurred.

A firm can record attorney fees, registration fees, design costs, successful legal defense, and other costs directly related to securing the trademark as an intangible asset in the Trademark asset account. This is how Apple Inc. can have a trademark valued at $118.9 billion, but reported in the balance sheet for much less. The estimated value of the trademark is not recorded in the Trademarks account; instead, only the legal, registration, and design fees are recorded. The advertising costs that help create value for the trademark are recorded as advertising expense.

FRANCHISES

Subway, McDonald's, and **KFC** are three of the world's largest franchises. Many popular retail businesses such as restaurants, auto dealerships, and hotels are set up as franchises. These are local outlets that pay for the exclusive right to use the franchisor company's name and to sell its products within a specified geographical area. Many franchisors provide other benefits to the franchisee, such as participating in the construction of the retail outlet, training employees, and purchasing national advertising.

To record the cost of a franchise, the franchisee records the initial fee as an intangible asset. Additional periodic payments to the franchisor usually are for services the franchisor provides on a continuing basis, and the franchisee will expense them as incurred.

GOODWILL

Goodwill often is the largest (and the most unique) intangible asset in the balance sheet. **It is recorded *only* when one company acquires another company.** Goodwill is recorded by the acquiring company for the amount that the purchase price exceeds the fair value of the acquired company's identifiable net assets.

The calculation of goodwill is easiest to see with a simple example. Assume that Allied Foods acquires Ritz Produce by paying $36 million in cash. The fair values of Ritz Produce's identifiable assets and liabilities are as follows ($ in millions):

Accounts receivable	$10	Accounts payable	$ 9
Equipment	32	Long-term notes payable	15
Patent	8		
Total fair value of assets	$50	Total fair value of liabilities	$24

In this example, Ritz Produce has identifiable net assets of $26 million (= $50 million − $24 million). Why is Allied Foods willing to pay $36 million to acquire a company that has *identifiable* net assets of only $26 million? Allied Foods must believe that there are other benefits worth $10 million in the acquisition, but these benefits are *not identified* as assets in the balance sheet of Ritz Produce. Allied Food will record these unidentified assets as goodwill

© Jacek Lasa/Alamy Images, RF

at the time it pays $36 million. Illustration 7–6 summarizes the calculation of goodwill ($10 million) that Allied Foods would report in its balance sheet.

ILLUSTRATION 7–6

Business Acquisition with Goodwill

($ in millions)		
Purchase price		$36
Less:		
Fair value of assets acquired	$ 50	
Less: Fair value of liabilities assumed	(24)	
Fair value of identifiable net assets		(26)
Goodwill		**$10**

Allied Foods records the acquisition as follows:

	Debit	Credit	A	=	L	+	SE
Accounts Receivable (at fair value)	10		+10				
Equipment (at fair value)	32		+32				
Patent (at fair value)	8		+8				
Goodwill (remaining purchase price)	10		+10				
Accounts Payable (at fair value)		9			+9		
Notes Payable (at fair value)		15			+15		
Cash (at purchase price)		36	−36				
(Acquire assets and liabilities of Ritz Produce)							

Most companies also create goodwill to some extent through advertising, training, and other efforts. However, as it does for other internally generated intangibles, a company must *expense* costs incurred in the internal generation of goodwill. Imagine how difficult it would be to estimate the amount and future benefits of internally generated goodwill. Due to this difficulty, we record goodwill only when it is part of the acquisition of another business.

 KEY POINT

Intangible assets include patents, copyrights, trademarks, franchises, and goodwill.

Expenditures after Acquisition

Over the life of a long-term asset, the owners often incur additional expenditures for repairs and maintenance, additions, improvements, or litigation costs. We credit these costs to Cash or perhaps to Accounts Payable or Notes Payable, but what account do we debit? The choice is to debit either an asset or an expense. Recall that an asset is a prob-able future benefit. **We capitalize an expenditure as an asset if it increases future benefits. We expense an expenditure if it benefits only the current period.** To see the choice more clearly, let's look at repairs and maintenance, additions, improvements, and litigation costs in more detail.

■ **LO7–3**
Describe the accounting treatment of expenditures after acquisition.

REPAIRS AND MAINTENANCE

The cost of an engine tune-up or the repair of an engine part for a delivery truck allows the truck to continue its productive activity. We expense repairs and maintenance expenditures like these in the period incurred because they maintain a given level of benefits. We capital-ize as assets more extensive repairs that *increase* the future benefits of the delivery truck, such as a new transmission or an engine overhaul.

CAREER CORNER

The legal defense of intangible asset rights often requires the services of a lawyer. Accounting and law actually have a lot in common. Some business professionals (such as those specializing in tax law) have both a CPA license and a law degree. If you are considering a career in law, don't shy away from accounting and other business courses. The skills developed in accounting and related business courses are valuable in analyzing many of the challenging research questions addressed in law school. While the most traditional career path to law is through a liberal arts degree such as political science, many law students enter law school with an undergraduate degree in business.

© Fancy Photography/
Veer, RF

ADDITIONS

An **addition** occurs when we add a new major component to an existing asset. We should capitalize the cost of additions if they increase, rather than maintain, the future benefits from the expenditure. For example, adding a refrigeration unit to a delivery truck increases the capability of the truck beyond that originally anticipated, thus increasing its future benefits.

IMPROVEMENTS

An improvement is the cost of replacing a major component of an asset. The replacement can be a new component with the same characteristics as the old component, or a new component with enhanced operating capabilities. For example, we could replace an existing refrigeration unit in a delivery truck with a new but similar unit or with a new and improved refrigeration unit. In either case, the cost of the improvement usually increases future benefits, and we should capitalize it to the Equipment account.

LEGAL DEFENSE OF INTANGIBLE ASSETS

The expenditures after acquisition mentioned so far—repairs and maintenance, additions, and improvements—generally relate to property, plant, and equipment. Intangible assets, though, also can require expenditures after their acquisition, the most frequent being the cost of legally defending the right that gives the asset its value. For example, when The J.M. Smucker Company attempted to prevent another company from copying its peanut butter and jelly sandwich patent, it incurred legal costs. If a firm successfully defends an intangible right, it should capitalize the litigation costs. However, if the defense of an intangible right is unsuccessful, then the firm should expense the litigation costs as incurred because they provide no future benefit.

MATERIALITY

Materiality relates to the size of an item that is likely to influence a decision. An item is said to be material if it is large enough to influence a decision. Materiality is an important consideration in the "capitalize versus expense" decision. There often are practical problems in capitalizing small expenditures. For example, a stapler may have a 20-year service life, but it would not be practical to capitalize such a small amount. Companies generally expense all costs under a certain dollar amount, say $1,000, regardless of whether future benefits are increased. It's important for a company to establish a policy for treating these expenditures and apply the policy consistently.

Illustration 7–7 provides a summary of expenditures after acquisition.

 KEY POINT

We capitalize (record as an asset) expenditures that benefit *future* periods. We expense items that benefit only the *current* period.

Let's Review

Lincoln Driving Academy purchased a pre-owned car for use in its driver's education program. Lincoln incurred the following expenses related to the car.

1. Replaced the car's transmission at a cost of $4,100. The repairs are considered extensive and increase future benefits.

2. Installed a passenger side brake to be used by the instructor, if necessary, at a cost of $1,100.

3. Paid the annual registration fees of $185.

4. Changed the oil and had an engine tune-up at a cost of $350.

5. Overhauled the engine at a cost $2,200, increasing the service life of the car by an estimated four years.

Required:

Indicate whether Lincoln should capitalize or expense each of these expenditures. How could Lincoln fraudulently use expenditures like these to increase reported earnings?

Solution:

1. Capitalize. It benefits future periods.

2. Capitalize. It benefits future periods.

3. Expense. It benefits only the current period.

4. Expense. It benefits only the current period.

5. Capitalize. It benefits future periods.

Lincoln could increase reported earnings by improperly recording expenses as assets. For example, Lincoln could record maintenance and repair expense (like item 4.) to the equipment asset account. This would lower expenses and increase earnings reported in the current year.

Type of Expenditure	Definition	Period Benefited	Usual Accounting Treatment
Repairs and maintenance	Maintaining a given level of benefits	Current	Expense
Repairs and maintenance	Making major repairs that increase future benefits	Future	Capitalize
Additions	Adding a new major component	Future	Capitalize
Improvements	Replacing a major component	Future	Capitalize
Legal defense of intangible assets	Incurring litigation costs to defend the legal right to the asset	Future	Capitalize (Expense if defense is unsuccessful)

ILLUSTRATION 7–7

Expenditures after Acquisition

COST ALLOCATION

PART B

When people talk about a car depreciating, they usually are talking about how much the value of the car has decreased. Depreciation in accounting, though, is different. The primary dictionary definition of depreciation differs from the definition of depreciation used in accounting:

> **Dictionary definition** = Decrease in value (or selling price) of an asset.
> **Accounting definition** = Allocation of an asset's cost to an expense over time.

If depreciation were calculated based on the dictionary definition, we would need to estimate the value of each long-term asset each period. Due to the difficulty and subjectivity involved, long-term assets are not adjusted to fair value each period. Rather, long-term assets are recorded at their cost, and then this cost is allocated to expense over time. We use the term *depreciation* to describe that process when it applies to property, plant, and equipment. For intangible assets, the cost allocation process is called *amortization*.

Depreciation of Property, Plant, and Equipment

■ **LO7–4**
Calculate depreciation of property, plant, and equipment.

Depreciation in accounting is allocating the cost of an asset to an expense over its service life. An asset provides benefits (revenues) to a company in future periods. We allocate a portion of the asset's cost to depreciation expense in each year the asset provides a benefit. If the asset will provide benefits to the company for four years, for example, then we allocate a portion of the asset's cost to depreciation expense in each year for four years. Illustration 7–8 portrays this concept of depreciating an asset's original purchase cost over the periods benefited.

ILLUSTRATION 7–8

Depreciation of Long-Term Assets

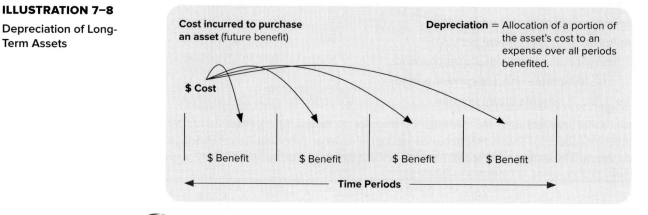

 COMMON MISTAKE

Students sometimes mistake accounting depreciation as recording the decrease in value of an asset. Depreciation in accounting is *not* a valuation process. Rather, depreciation in accounting is an allocation of an asset's cost to expense over time.

For demonstration, let's assume the local **Starbucks** pays $1,200 for equipment—say, an espresso machine. The machine is expected to have a service life of four years. We record annual depreciation as shown below.

A = L + SE		Debit	Credit
−300 Exp ↑	Depreciation Expense	300	
−300	Accumulated Depreciation		300
	(Depreciate equipment)		
	($300 = $1,200 ÷ 4 years)		

The credit side of the entry requires some explanation. Accumulated Depreciation is a contra asset account, meaning that it reduces an asset account. Rather than credit the Equipment account directly, we instead credit its contra account, which we offset against the Equipment account in the balance sheet. In this manner, a company can keep track of the amount originally paid for the equipment and the amount of depreciation taken on the asset so far.

Most companies have separate accumulated depreciation accounts for each specific asset or asset class. For simplicity, we use one general account called Accumulated Depreciation. The name of the account comes from the fact that the depreciation we record each period *accumulates* in the account. After one year, for instance, we have:

Equipment (cost)	$1,200
Less: Accumulated depreciation ($300 × 1 year)	(300)
= Book value	$ 900

Book value, also referred to as carrying value, equals the original cost of the asset minus the current balance in Accumulated Depreciation. Note that by increasing accumulated depreciation each period, we are reducing the book value of equipment. The Accumulated Depreciation account allows us to reduce the book value of assets through depreciation, while maintaining the original cost of each asset in the accounting records.

After two years, we have:

Equipment (cost)	$1,200
Less: Accumulated depreciation ($300 × 2 years)	(600)
= Book value	$ 600

Each year the Accumulated Depreciation account increases by $300 and the book value decreases by $300. By the end of the fourth year, Accumulated Depreciation will be $1,200 and the book value will be $0.

KEY POINT

Depreciation refers to the allocation of the asset's original cost to an expense during the periods benefited. Depreciation does *not* refer to the change in value or selling price.

Recording depreciation requires accountants to estimate the *service life* of the asset, as well as its residual value at the end of that life. The service life, or useful life, is how long the company expects to receive benefits from the asset before disposing of it. We can measure service life in units of time or in units of activity. For example, the estimated service life of a delivery truck might be either five years or 100,000 miles. We use the terms service life and useful life interchangeably, because both terms are used in practice.

Common Terms Service life often is called useful life.

The depreciation process also requires accountants to estimate what an asset's value will be at the end of its service life. Called residual value, or *salvage value*, this value is the amount the company expects to receive from selling the asset at the end of its service life. A company might estimate residual value from prior experience or by researching the resale values of similar types of assets. Due to the difficulty in estimating residual value, it's not uncommon to assume a residual value of zero.

Common Terms Residual value often is called salvage value

Remember: We record depreciation for land improvements, buildings, and equipment, but we *don't* record depreciation for land. Unlike other long-term assets, land is not "used up" over time.

COMMON MISTAKE

Some students want to depreciate land. Land is *not* depreciated, because its service life never ends.

In the following sections, we illustrate the three most common depreciation methods used in practice: straight-line, declining-balance, and activity-based.[2] These three methods illustrate the basic differences in how depreciation estimates are made. They are important for different reasons.

1. **Straight-line.** This method simply takes an equal amount of depreciation each year. It is by far the most common depreciation method used in financial accounting.
2. **Declining-balance.** This method is an accelerated method, meaning that more depreciation expense is taken in the early years than in the later years of an asset's life.

---

[2]Some introductory financial accounting textbooks illustrate a fourth depreciation method called *sum-of-the-years'-digits*. However, use of this method has decreased dramatically over the years to the point that this method is now rarely seen in actual practice. A recent survey of depreciation methods used by large public companies is provided in Illustration 7–18.

The concepts behind declining-balance are also used in calculating depreciation for tax purposes.

3. **Activity-based.** This method calculates depreciation based on the use of the asset. For example, a vehicle can be depreciated based on the miles driven. It is commonly used to allocate the cost of natural resources.

All three illustrations are based on the same business situation: Little King Sandwiches, a local submarine sandwich restaurant, purchased a new delivery truck. The specific details of that purchase are described in Illustration 7–9.

ILLUSTRATION 7–9

Data to Illustrate Depreciation Methods

Cost of the new truck	$40,000
Estimated residual value	$5,000
Estimated service life	5 years or 100,000 miles

STRAIGHT-LINE DEPRECIATION

By far the most easily understood and widely used depreciation method is straight-line. With the straight-line method we allocate an *equal* amount of the depreciable cost to each year of the asset's service life. The *depreciable cost* is the asset's cost minus its estimated residual value. Depreciable cost represents the total depreciation to be taken over the asset's useful life. To calculate depreciation expense for a given year, we simply divide the depreciable cost by the number of years in the asset's life, as shown in Illustration 7–10.

ILLUSTRATION 7–10

Formula for Straight-Line Depreciation

$$\text{Depreciation expense} = \frac{\text{Asset's cost} - \text{Residual value}}{\text{Service life}} = \frac{\text{Depreciable cost}}{\text{Service life}}$$

$$\text{Depreciation expense} = \frac{\$40,000 - \$5,000}{5 \text{ years}} = \$7,000 \text{ per year}$$

Note that dividing the depreciable cost each year by five is the same as multiplying the depreciable cost each year by 20% ($1/5 = 0.20$).

Illustration 7–11 provides a depreciation schedule using the straight-line method.

ILLUSTRATION 7–11

Straight-Line Depreciation Schedule

mhhe.com/4fa28

	LITTLE KING SANDWICHES					
	Depreciation Schedule—Straight-Line					
	Calculation				**End-of-Year Amounts**	
Year	Depreciable Cost	×	Depreciation Rate	=	Depreciation Expense	Accumulated Depreciation	Book Value*
							$40,000
1	$35,000		0.20		$ 7,000	$ 7,000	33,000
2	35,000		0.20		7,000	14,000	26,000
3	35,000		0.20		7,000	21,000	19,000
4	35,000		0.20		7,000	28,000	12,000
5	35,000		0.20		7,000	35,000	**5,000**
Total					**$35,000**		

*Book value is the original cost of the asset ($40,000) minus accumulated depreciation. Book value of $33,000 at the end of year 1, for example, is $40,000 minus $7,000 in accumulated depreciation.

Partial-Year Depreciation. We assume Little King Sandwiches bought the delivery truck at the beginning of year 1. What if it bought the truck sometime during the year instead? Then, the company will record depreciation for only the portion of the first year that it owned the truck. For example, if Little King bought the truck on November 1 and its year-end is December 31, it will record depreciation for only two of the 12 months in year 1. So, depreciation expense in year 1 is $1,167 (= $7,000 × 2/12). If instead Little King bought the truck earlier, on March 1, it will record depreciation for 10 of the 12 months in year 1. In that case, depreciation expense in year 1 is $5,833 (= $7,000 × 10/12).

In both cases, depreciation for the second, third, fourth, and fifth years still is $7,000. The partial-year depreciation for the first year does not affect depreciation in those subsequent years. However, it does affect depreciation in the asset's final year of service life: Since the firm didn't take a full year of depreciation in year 1, it needs to record a partial year of depreciation in year 6 in order to fully depreciate the truck from its cost of $40,000 down to its residual value of $5,000. Depreciation in year 6 is $5,833 for the truck purchased on November 1 (= $7,000 − $1,167). If the truck was purchased on March 1, depreciation in year 6 is $1,167 (= $7,000 − $5,833).

⊗ COMMON MISTAKE

Many students think March 1 to the end of the year is nine months because December is the twelfth month and March is the third month. March 1 to the end of the year is actually *ten* months; it is every month except January and February.

Change in Depreciation Estimate. Depreciation is an *estimate*. Remember that the amount of depreciation allocated to each period is based on management's estimates of service life and of residual value—as well as the depreciation method chosen. Management needs to periodically review these estimates. If a change in estimate is required, the company changes depreciation in current and future years, but not in prior periods.

For example, assume that after three years Little King Sandwiches estimates the remaining service life of the delivery truck to be four more years, for a total service life of seven years rather than the original five. At this time, Little King also changes the estimated residual value to $3,000 from the original estimate of $5,000. How much should Little King record each year for depreciation in years 4 to 7? Take the book value at the end of year 3 ($19,000), subtract the new estimated residual value ($3,000), and then divide by the new remaining service life (four more years). Little King Sandwiches will record depreciation in years 4 to 7 as $4,000 per year. Illustration 7–12 shows the calculations.

Book value, end of year 3	$19,000
− New residual value	(3,000)
New depreciable cost	16,000
÷ New remaining service life	4
Annual depreciation in years 4 to 7	$ 4,000

ILLUSTRATION 7–12

Change in Depreciation Estimate

Notice that Little King Sandwiches makes all the changes in years 4 to 7. The company does not go back and change the calculations for depreciation already recorded during the first three years.

Straight-line depreciation assumes that the benefits we derive from the use of an asset are the same each year. In some situations it might be more reasonable to assume that the asset will provide greater benefits in the earlier years of its life than in the later years. In these cases, we achieve a better matching of depreciation with revenues by using an accelerated depreciation method, with higher depreciation in the earlier years of the asset's life and lower depreciation in later years. We look at one such method next.

ETHICAL DILEMMA

© Stockbyte/Punchstock Images, RF

James Wright is the chief financial officer (CFO) for The Butcher Block, a major steakhouse restaurant chain. As CFO, James has the final responsibility for all aspects of financial reporting. James tells investors that The Butcher Block should post earnings of at least $1 million.

In examining the preliminary year-end numbers, James notices that earnings are coming in at $950,000. He also is aware that The Butcher Block has been depreciating most of its restaurant equipment over a five-year useful life. He proposes to change the estimated useful life for a subset of the equipment to a useful life of seven, rather than five, years. By depreciating over a longer useful life, depreciation expense will be lower in the current year, increasing earnings to just over $1 million. It looks like The Butcher Block is going to exceed earnings of $1 million after all.

Do you think James Wright's change in the depreciable life of assets is ethical? What concerns might you have?

DECLINING-BALANCE DEPRECIATION

The declining-balance method is an accelerated depreciation method. Declining-balance depreciation will be higher than straight-line depreciation in earlier years, but lower in later years. **However, both declining-balance and straight-line will result in the same total depreciation over the asset's service life.** No matter what allocation method we use, total depreciation over the asset's service life will be equal to the depreciable cost (asset cost minus residual value).

The depreciation rate we use under the declining-balance method is a multiple of the straight-line rate, such as 125%, 150%, or 200% of the straight-line rate. The most common declining-balance rate is 200%, which we refer to as the *double*-declining-balance method since the rate is double the straight-line rate. In our illustration for Little King Sandwiches, the double-declining-balance rate would be 40% (double the straight-line rate of 20%). Illustration 7–13 provides a depreciation schedule using the double-declining-balance method.

ILLUSTRATION 7–13

Double-Declining-Balance Depreciation Schedule

mhhe.com/4fa29

			LITTLE KING SANDWICHES			
			Depreciation Schedule—Double-Declining-Balance			
		Calculation			End-of-Year Amounts	
Year	Beginning Book Value	×	Depreciation Rate	= Depreciation Expense	Accumulated Depreciation	Book Value*
						$40,000
1	$40,000		0.40	**$16,000**	$16,000	24,000
2	24,000		0.40	9,600	25,600	14,400
3	14,400		0.40	5,760	31,360	8,640
4	8,640		0.40	3,456	34,816	5,184
5	5,184			184**	35,000	**5,000**
Total				**$35,000**		

*Book value is the original cost of the asset minus accumulated depreciation. Book value at the end of year 1 is $24,000, equal to the cost of $40,000 minus accumulated depreciation of $16,000. Book value at the end of **year 1** in the last column is equal to book value at the beginning of **year 2** in the second column of the schedule.
**Amount necessary to reduce book value to residual value.

A simple way to get the depreciation rate for double-declining-balance is to divide the number 2 by the estimated service life (2/5 year service life = 0.40). The depreciation rate for double-declining-balance depreciation is determined by the following general equation:

$$\textbf{Double-declining depreciation rate = 2/Estimated service life}$$

If the service life had been four years instead of five, what depreciation rates would we use under straight-line and under double-declining-balance? The straight-line rate is 1 divided by the four-year service life, or 1/4 = 0.25. The double-declining-balance rate is 2 divided by the four-year service life, or 2/4 = 0.50.

Notice two unusual features of declining-balance depreciation.

1. We multiply the rate by *book value* (cost minus accumulated depreciation), rather than by the depreciable cost (cost minus residual value).

2. In year 5, we are not able to record depreciation expense for the entire $5,184 times 0.40, because doing so would cause the book value to fall below the expected residual value. Instead, depreciation expense in the final year is the amount that reduces book value to the estimated residual value (book value beginning of year, $5,184, minus estimated residual value, $5,000, = $184).

If the estimated residual value is high enough, the asset will reach its residual value in fewer years than its expected service life. For instance, if the estimated residual value had been $10,000 rather than $5,000, the delivery truck would be fully depreciated under the double-declining-balance method in only three years, even though we used a five-year life in determining the depreciation rate.

 COMMON MISTAKE

When using the declining-balance method, mistakes are commonly made in the first and last year of the calculation. In the first year, students sometimes calculate depreciation incorrectly as cost minus residual value times the depreciation rate. The correct way in the first year is to simply multiply cost times the depreciation rate. In the final year, some students incorrectly calculate depreciation expense in the same manner as in earlier years, multiplying book value by the depreciation rate. However, under the declining-balance method, depreciation expense in the final year is the amount necessary to reduce book value down to residual value.

ACTIVITY-BASED DEPRECIATION

Straight-line and declining-balance methods measure depreciation based on time. In an activity-based method, we instead allocate an asset's cost based on its *use*. For example, we could measure the service life of a machine in terms of its output (units, pounds, barrels). This method also works for vehicles such as our delivery truck, whose use we measure in miles.

We first compute the average *depreciation rate per unit* by dividing the depreciable cost (cost minus residual value) by the number of units expected to be produced. In our illustration, the depreciation rate is $0.35 per mile, calculated as shown in Illustration 7–14.

Common Terms Activity-based depreciation is also called *units of production* or *units of output.*

$$\text{Depreciation rate per unit} = \frac{\textbf{Depreciable cost}}{\textbf{Total units expected to be produced}}$$

$$\text{Depreciation rate} = \frac{\$40,000 - \$5,000}{100,000 \text{ expected miles}} = \$0.35 \text{ per mile}$$

ILLUSTRATION 7–14

Formula for Activity-Based Depreciation

To calculate the depreciation expense for the reporting period, we then multiply the per unit rate by the number of units of activity each period. Illustration 7–15 shows a depreciation schedule using the activity-based method. The actual miles driven in years 1 to 5 were

30,000, 22,000, 15,000, 20,000, and 13,000. Notice that the activity-based method is very similar to the straight-line method, except that rather than dividing the depreciable cost by the service life in years, we divide it by the service life in expected miles.

ILLUSTRATION 7–15

Activity-Based Depreciation Schedule

mhhe.com/4fa30

			LITTLE KING SANDWICHES **Depreciation Schedule—Activity-Based**			
	Calculation				End-of-Year Amounts	
Year	Miles Driven	×	Depreciation Rate =	Depreciation Expense	Accumulated Depreciation	Book Value*
						$40,000
1	30,000		$0.35	$10,500	$10,500	29,500
2	22,000		0.35	7,700	18,200	21,800
3	15,000		0.35	5,250	23,450	16,550
4	20,000		0.35	7,000	30,450	9,550
5	13,000		0.35	4,550	35,000	5,000
Total				$35,000		

*Book value is the original cost of the asset ($40,000) minus accumulated depreciation. Book value of $29,500 in year 1 is $40,000 minus $10,500 in accumulated depreciation.

In our illustration, the delivery truck is driven exactly 100,000 miles over the five years. What if we drive the delivery truck *less than* 100,000 miles by the end of the fifth year? Then we will continue to depreciate the truck past five years until we reach 100,000 miles. Similarly, if we drive the delivery truck more than 100,000 miles by the end of the fifth year, we will stop depreciating the truck at 100,000 miles before the five years are up. In either case, we need to depreciate the asset until the book value (cost minus accumulated depreciation) declines to the estimated residual value.

Decision Maker's Perspective

Selecting a Depreciation Method

Assume you are the chief financial officer (CFO) responsible for your company's accounting and reporting policies. Which depreciation method would you choose? Illustration 7–16 compares annual depreciation under the three alternatives we discussed.

ILLUSTRATION 7–16

Comparison of Depreciation Methods

Year	Straight-Line	Double-Declining-Balance	Activity-Based
1	$ 7,000	$16,000	$10,500
2	7,000	9,600	7,700
3	7,000	5,760	5,250
4	7,000	3,456	7,000
5	7,000	184	4,550
Total	$35,000	$35,000	$35,000

Comparing methods, we see that all three alternatives result in total depreciation of $35,000 ($40,000 cost minus $5,000 residual value). Straight-line creates an equal amount of depreciation each year. Double-declining-balance creates more depreciation in earlier years and less depreciation in later years. Activity-based depreciation varies depending on the miles driven each year. Illustration 7–17 provides a graph that shows depreciation expense over time for each of these three methods.

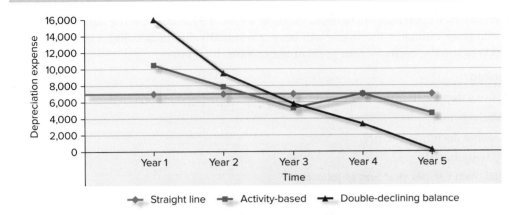

Companies are free to choose the depreciation method they believe best reflects the pattern of an asset's use and the revenues it creates. Illustration 7–18 shows the results of a recent survey of depreciation methods used by large public companies.

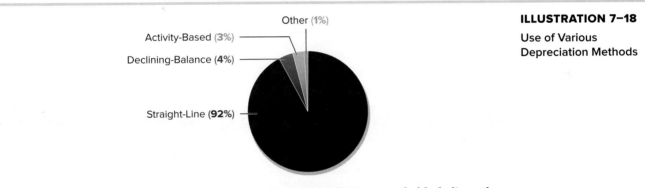

ILLUSTRATION 7–18

**Use of Various
Depreciation Methods**

Why do so many companies use the straight-line method? Many probably believe they realize benefits from their plant assets approximately evenly over these assets' service lives. Certainly another motivating factor is that straight-line is the easiest method to apply. One more important motivation is straight-line's positive effect on reported income. Straight-line produces a higher net income than accelerated methods in the earlier years of an asset's life. Higher net income can improve bonuses paid to management, increase stock prices, and reduce the likelihood of violating debt agreements with lenders.

TAX DEPRECIATION

Conflicting with the desire to report higher net income is the desire to reduce taxes by *reducing* taxable income. An accelerated method serves this objective by reducing taxable income more in the earlier years of an asset's life than does straight-line. As a result, most companies use the straight-line method for financial reporting and the Internal Revenue Service's prescribed accelerated method (called MACRS[3]) for income tax purposes. Thus, companies record higher net income using straight-line depreciation and lower taxable income using MACRS depreciation. MACRS combines declining-balance methods in earlier years with straight-line in later years to allow for a more advantageous tax depreciation deduction. Congress, not accountants, approved MACRS rules to encourage greater investment in long-term assets by U.S. companies.

 KEY POINT

Straight-line, declining-balance, and activity-based depreciation all are acceptable depreciation methods for financial reporting. Most companies use straight-line depreciation for financial reporting and an accelerated method called MACRS for tax reporting.

[3]Modified Accelerated Cost Recovery System.

Let's Review

mhhe.com/4fa31

University Hero purchases new bread ovens at a cost of $110,000. On the date of purchase, the company estimates the ovens will have a residual value of $20,000. University Hero expects to use the ovens for four years or about 9,000 total hours.

Required:

Prepare a depreciation schedule using each of the following methods:

1. Straight-line.
2. Double-declining-balance.
3. Activity-based.

Actual oven use per year was as follows:

Year	Hours Used
1	2,200
2	2,600
3	2,300
4	2,100
Total	9,200

Solution:

1. Straight-line:

UNIVERSITY HERO
Depreciation Schedule—Straight-Line

	Calculation				End-of-Year Amounts	
Year	Depreciable Cost	×	Depreciation Rate*	=	Depreciation Expense	Accumulated Depreciation	Book Value**
1	$90,000		0.25		**$22,500**	$22,500	$87,500
2	90,000		0.25		**22,500**	45,000	65,000
3	90,000		0.25		**22,500**	67,500	42,500
4	90,000		0.25		**22,500**	90,000	**20,000**
Total					**$90,000**		

*1 ÷ 4 years = 0.25 per year
**$110,000 cost minus accumulated depreciation.

2. Double-declining-balance:

UNIVERSITY HERO
Depreciation Schedule—Double-Declining-Balance

	Calculation				End-of-Year Amounts	
Year	Beginning Book Value	×	Depreciation Rate*	=	Depreciation Expense	Accumulated Depreciation	Book Value**
1	$110,000		0.50		**$55,000**	$55,000	$55,000
2	55,000		0.50		**27,500**	82,500	27,500
3	27,500		0.50		**7,500***	90,000	**20,000**
4					**0**	90,000	**20,000**
Total					**$90,000**		

*2 ÷ 4 years = 0.50 per year
**$110,000 cost minus accumulated depreciation.
***Amount needed to reduce book value to residual value.

3. Activity-based:

			UNIVERSITY HERO — Depreciation Schedule—Activity-Based			
		Calculation			End-of-Year Amounts	
Year	Hours Used	× Depreciation Rate*	= Depreciation Expense		Accumulated Depreciation	Book Value**
1	2,200	$10	**$22,000**		$22,000	$88,000
2	2,600	10	**26,000**		48,000	62,000
3	2,300	10	**23,000**		71,000	39,000
4	2,100		**19,000*****		90,000	**20,000**
Total	9,200		**$90,000**			

*$90,000 ÷ 9,000 hours = $10/hour
**$110,000 cost minus accumulated depreciation.
***Amount needed to reduce book value to residual value.

Suggested Homework:
BE7–7, BE7–8;
E7–10, E7–11;
P7–5A&B, P7–7A&B

Amortization of Intangible Assets

Allocating the cost of property, plant, and equipment to expense is called depreciation. Similarly, allocating the cost of *intangible* assets to expense is called amortization.

INTANGIBLE ASSETS SUBJECT TO AMORTIZATION

Most intangible assets have a finite useful life that we can estimate. The service life of an intangible asset usually is limited by legal, regulatory, or contractual provisions. For example, the legal life of a patent is 20 years. However, the estimated useful life of a patent often is less than 20 years if the benefits are not expected to continue for the patent's entire legal life. The patent for the Apple Watch, for example, is amortized over fewer than 20 years, since new technology will cause the watch to become outdated in a shorter period.

The expected residual value of most intangible assets is zero. This might not be the case, though, if at the end of its useful life to the reporting entity the asset will benefit another entity. For example, if **Apple** has a commitment from another company to purchase one of its patents at the end of the patent's useful life at a determinable price, we use that price as the patent's residual value.

Most companies use *straight-line amortization* for intangibles. Also, many companies credit amortization to the intangible asset account itself rather than to accumulated amortization. That's the approach illustrated in the chapter and the approach to be used for homework in Connect. However, using a contra account such as Accumulated Amortization is also acceptable in practice.

Let's look at an example: In early January, Little King Sandwiches acquires franchise rights from University Hero for $800,000. The franchise agreement is for a period of 20 years. In addition, Little King purchases a patent for a meat-slicing process for $72,000. The original legal life of the patent was 20 years, and there are 12 years remaining. However, due to expected technological obsolescence, the company estimates that the useful life of the patent is only 8 more years. Little King uses straight-line amortization for all intangible assets. The company's fiscal year-end is December 31. Little King records the amortization expense for the franchise and the patent as follows.

■ **LO7–5**
Calculate amortization of intangible assets.

	Debit	Credit
Amortization Expense	**40,000**	
Franchises		**40,000**
(Amortize franchise)		
($40,000 = $800,000 / 20 years)		

A = L + SE
−40,000 Exp ↑
−40,000

A	=	L	+	SE		

−9,000 Exp ↑

−9,000

Amortization Expense	9,000	
Patents		9,000

(Amortize patent)
($9,000 = $72,000 / 8 years)

INTANGIBLE ASSETS NOT SUBJECT TO AMORTIZATION

We don't depreciate land because it has an unlimited life. Similarly, we do *not* amortize intangible assets with indefinite (unknown or not determinable) useful lives. Illustration 7–19 provides a summary of intangible assets that are amortized and those that are not amortized. An asset's useful life is indefinite if there is no foreseeable limit on the period of time over which we expect it to contribute to the cash flows of the entity. For example, suppose Little King acquired a trademark for its name. Registered trademarks have a legal life of 10 years, but the trademark registration is renewable for an indefinite number of 10-year periods. We consider the life of Little King's trademark for its name to be indefinite, so we don't amortize it.

ILLUSTRATION 7–19

Amortization Treatment of Intangible Assets

Intangible Assets Subject to Amortization (those with finite useful life)	Intangible Assets Not Subject to Amortization (those with indefinite useful life)
• Patents	• Goodwill
• Copyrights	• Trademarks (with indefinite life)
• Trademarks (with finite life)	
• Franchises	

Goodwill is the most common intangible asset with an indefinite useful life. Recall that we measure goodwill as the difference between the purchase price of a company and the fair value of all its identifiable net assets (tangible and intangible assets minus the liabilities assumed). Does this mean that goodwill and other intangible assets with indefinite useful lives will remain on a company's balance sheet at their original cost forever? Probably not. **Management must review long-term assets for a potential write-down when events or changes in circumstances indicate the asset's "recoverable amount" is *less than* its "recorded amount" in the accounting records.** The recoverable amount is the cash expected to be received from using the asset over its remaining useful life. All long-term assets are subject to these impairment rules, which we discuss in more detail in the appendix to this chapter.

KEY POINT

Amortization is a process, similar to depreciation, in which we allocate the cost of intangible assets over their estimated service lives. Intangible assets with an indefinite useful life (goodwill and most trademarks) are *not* amortized.

PART C

■ **LO7–6**

Account for the disposal of long-term assets.

ASSET DISPOSITION: SALE, RETIREMENT, OR EXCHANGE

Few things last forever. In this section we discuss what to do when we no longer use a long-term asset. Illustration 7–20 shows three different ways an asset can be disposed of. A *sale* is the most common method to dispose of an asset. When a long-term asset is no longer useful but cannot be sold, we have a *retirement*. For example, Little King Sandwiches might physically remove a baking oven that no longer works and also remove it from the accounting records through a retirement entry. An *exchange* occurs when two companies trade assets. In an exchange, we often use cash to make up for any difference in fair value between the assets.

ILLUSTRATION 7–20

Three Methods of Asset Disposal

Sale of Long-Term Assets

Selling a long-term asset can result in either a gain or a loss. We record a *gain* if we sell the asset for *more* than its book value. Similarly, we record a *loss* if we sell the asset for *less* than its book value. A gain is a credit balance account like other revenue accounts; a loss is a debit balance account like other expense accounts. Gains and losses, along with items such as interest revenue and interest expense, are recorded on the income statement as nonoperating revenues and expenses. Remember, book value is the cost of the asset minus accumulated depreciation. In order to have the correct book value, it's important to record depreciation up to the date of the sale.

 COMMON MISTAKE

Some students forget to update depreciation prior to recording the disposal of the asset. Depreciation must be recorded up to the date of the sale, retirement, or exchange. Otherwise, the book value will be overstated, and the resulting gain or loss on disposal will be in error as well.

To illustrate the recording of disposals, let's return to our delivery truck example for Little King Sandwiches. Assume Little King uses straight-line depreciation and records the delivery truck in the Equipment account. The specific details are summarized again in Illustration 7–21.

Original cost of the truck	$40,000
Estimated residual value	$5,000
Estimated service life	5 years

ILLUSTRATION 7–21

Data to Illustrate Long-Term Asset Disposals

If we assume that Little King sells the delivery truck at the end of year 3 for $22,000, we can calculate the gain as $3,000. The gain is equal to the sale amount of $22,000 less the truck's book value of $19,000. Illustration 7–22 shows the calculation.

ILLUSTRATION 7–22

Gain on Sale

Sale amount		$22,000
Less:		
Original cost of the truck	$40,000	
Less: Accumulated depreciation (3 years × $7,000/year)	(21,000)	
Book value at the end of year 3		19,000
Gain		**$ 3,000**

We record the sale by removing the delivery truck (Equipment) and its accumulated depreciation from the accounting records and recording the cash collected. The gain is the difference between the sale amount and the book value of the asset.

A = L + SE		Debit	Credit
+22,000	**Cash**	**22,000**	
+21,000	**Accumulated Depreciation**	**21,000**	
−40,000	**Equipment**		**40,000**
+3,000 Rev ↑	**Gain**		**3,000**
	(Sell equipment for a gain)		

COMMON MISTAKE

Be careful not to combine the delivery truck ($40,000) and accumulated depreciation ($21,000) and credit the $19,000 difference to the Equipment account. Instead, remove the delivery truck and accumulated depreciation from the accounting records separately. Otherwise, the Equipment and the Accumulated Depreciation accounts will incorrectly have a remaining balance after the asset has been sold.

If we assume that Little King sells the delivery truck at the end of year 3 for only $17,000 instead of $22,000, we have a $2,000 loss as calculated in Illustration 7–23. In this case, the sale amount is less than the truck's book value.

ILLUSTRATION 7–23

Loss on Sale

Sale amount		$17,000
Less:		
Original cost of the truck	$40,000	
Less: Accumulated depreciation (3 years × $7,000/year)	(21,000)	
Book value at the end of year 3		19,000
Loss		**$(2,000)**

We record the loss on sale as:

A = L + SE		Debit	Credit
+17,000			
+21,000	**Cash**	**17,000**	
	Accumulated Depreciation	**21,000**	
−2,000 Exp ↑	**Loss**	**2,000**	
−40,000	**Equipment**		**40,000**
	(Sell equipment for a loss)		

Decision Point

Question ❓	Accounting information 📄	Analysis 🔍
How different is the asset's recorded book value from its actual fair value?	Gain or loss on sale	A gain on sale indicates the actual fair value is more than the recorded book value. A loss on sale indicates the opposite.

Retirement of Long-Term Assets

Now assume that Little King retires the delivery truck instead of selling it. If, for example, the truck is totaled in an accident at the end of year 3, we have a $19,000 loss on retirement as calculated in Illustration 7–24.

ILLUSTRATION 7–24

Loss on Retirement

Sale amount		$ 0
Less:		
Original cost of the truck	$40,000	
Less: Accumulated depreciation (3 years × $7,000/year)	(21,000)	
Book value at the end of year 3		19,000
Loss		$(19,000)

We record the loss on retirement as:

	Debit	Credit		A	=	L	+	SE
Accumulated Depreciation	21,000			+21,000				
Loss	19,000							−19,000 Exp ↑
Equipment		40,000		−40,000				
(Retire equipment for a loss)								

The above entry assumes Little King did not have collision insurance coverage. If Little King had insured the truck and collected $17,000 in insurance money for the totaled vehicle, the entry would be identical to the sale for $17,000 in Illustration 7–23.

Exchange of Long-Term Assets

Now assume that Little King exchanges the delivery truck at the end of year 3 for a new truck valued at $45,000. The dealership gives Little King a trade-in allowance of $23,000 on the exchange, with the remaining $22,000 paid in cash. We have a $4,000 gain, as calculated in Illustration 7–25.[4]

ILLUSTRATION 7–25

Gain on Exchange

Trade-in allowance		$23,000
Less:		
Original cost of the truck	$40,000	
Less: Accumulated depreciation (3 years × $7,000/year)	(21,000)	
Book value at the end of year 3		19,000
Gain		$ 4,000

We record the gain on exchange as:

	Debit	Credit		A	=	L	+	SE
Equipment (new)	45,000			+45,000				
Accumulated Depreciation	21,000			+21,000				
Cash		22,000		−22,000				
Equipment (old)		40,000		−40,000				
Gain		4,000						+4,000 Rev ↑
(Exchange equipment for a gain)								

---

[4]In 2005, a new accounting standard (FASB ASC 845: Nonmonetary Transactions) simplified accounting for exchanges by requiring the new asset acquired in an exchange be recorded at fair value. This eliminates the deferred gain on exchange recorded under previous standards.

KEY POINT

If we dispose of an asset for *more* than book value, we record a gain. If we dispose of an asset for *less* than book value, we record a loss.

ANALYSIS

ASSET ANALYSIS
Walmart vs. Costco

■ LO 7–7
Describe the links among return on assets, profit margin, and asset turnover.

We have discussed the purchase, depreciation, and disposal of long-term assets. In this final section, we see how to use actual financial statement information to analyze the profitability of a company's assets. Illustration 7–26 provides selected financial data reported from **Walmart** and **Costco** for use in our analysis. These two companies are close competitors in the discount retail industry.

ILLUSTRATION 7–26

Selected Financial Data for Walmart and Costco

($ in millions)	
Walmart	
Net sales	$485,651
Net income	16,363
Total assets, beginning	204,751
Total assets, ending	203,706
Costco	
Net sales	$112,640
Net income	2,058
Total assets, beginning	30,283
Total assets	33,024

RETURN ON ASSETS

Walmart had net income of $16.4 billion and Costco had net income of $2.1 billion. Since Walmart's net income is so much larger, is Walmart more profitable? Not necessarily. Walmart is also a much larger company as indicated by total assets. Walmart's total assets were $203.7 billion compared to $33.0 billion for Costco. A more comparable measure of profitability than income is return on assets, or ROA for short, which equals net income divided by *average* total assets.

$$\text{Return on Assets} = \frac{\text{Net income}}{\text{Average total assets}}$$

The average is calculated as the beginning amount plus the ending amount, divided by 2. Dividing net income by average total assets adjusts net income for differences in company size.

COMMON MISTAKE

Students sometimes divide by ending total assets rather than by *average* total assets. We measure net income over time, whereas we measure total assets at a *point* in time. Therefore, whenever we divide a number in the income statement by a number in the balance sheet, it's more meaningful to use an *average* balance sheet number.

The return on assets ratio is calculated for Walmart and Costco in Illustration 7–27.

($ in millions)	Net Income	÷	Average Total Assets	=	Return on Assets
Walmart	$16,363	÷	($204,751 + $203,706)/2	=	8.0%
Costco	$ 2,058	÷	($30,283 + $33,024)/2	=	6.5%

ILLUSTRATION 7–27

Return on Assets for Walmart and Costco

Return on assets indicates the amount of net income generated for each dollar invested in assets. With an ROA of 8.0%, Walmart generates 8 cents of profit for every dollar of assets. Costco's 6.5% ROA indicates that it generates 6.5 cents of profit for every dollar of assets. Even after adjusting for company size, Walmart is more profitable than Costco.

Decision Point

Question	Accounting information	Analysis
How effectively is the company using its assets?	Return on assets ratio	A higher return on assets generally indicates a more effective use of assets.

PROFIT MARGIN AND ASSET TURNOVER

We can explore profitability further by separating return on assets into two components: profit margin and asset turnover, as shown in Illustration 7–28.

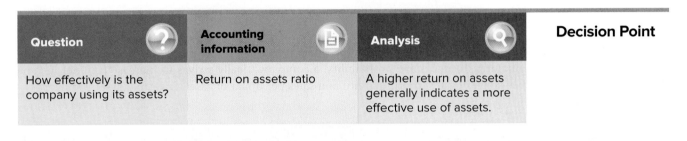

$$\text{Return on assets} = \text{Profit margin} \times \text{Asset turnover}$$

$$\frac{\text{Net income}}{\text{Average total assets}} = \frac{\text{Net income}}{\text{Net sales}} \times \frac{\text{Net sales}}{\text{Average total assets}}$$

ILLUSTRATION 7–28

Components of Return on Assets

As the second row in Illustration 7–28 indicates, profit margin is calculated as net income divided by net sales. This ratio indicates the earnings per dollar of sales. Asset turnover is calculated as net sales divided by average total assets. This ratio measures the sales per dollar of assets invested.

Decision Maker's Perspective

Strategies for Increasing Return on Assets

Companies have two primary strategies for increasing their return on assets: increasing profit margin and increasing asset turnover. Some companies pursue a higher profit margin through *product differentiation* and *premium pricing*. They set higher selling prices, giving them more profit per dollar of sales. Other companies pursue a higher asset turnover by charging *lower prices*. They increase sales volume, giving them more sales per dollar invested in assets.

Comparing Walmart and Costco, we might expect Walmart to have a higher profit margin and a lower asset turnover than Costco. Walmart's operating results include both traditional Walmart stores and their wholesale stores (Sam's Clubs). Costco focuses solely on wholesale stores, specifically designed to offer lower prices to customers with higher sales volume than traditional retail stores. In Illustrations 7–29 and 7–30 we calculate profit margin and asset turnover for both companies. We then can see if the data support our expectations regarding Walmart and Costco.

ILLUSTRATION 7–29

Profit Margin for Walmart and Costco

($ in millions)	Net Income	÷	Net Sales	=	Profit Margin
Walmart	$16,363	÷	$485,651	=	3.4%
Costco	$ 2,058	÷	$112,640	=	1.8%

ILLUSTRATION 7–30

Asset Turnover for Walmart and Costco

($ in millions)	Net Sales	÷	Average Total Assets	=	Asset Turnover
Walmart	$485,651	÷	($204,751 + $203,706)/2	=	2.4 times
Costco	$112,640	÷	($30,283 + $33,024)/2	=	3.6 times

Illustration 7–29 indicates that Walmart's profit margin is higher than Costco's. Illustration 7–30, however, shows that Costco has the higher asset turnover. These accounting ratios support our expectations regarding the business strategies Walmart and Costco are pursuing. To maximize profitability, a company ideally strives to increase *both* net income per dollar of sales (profit margin) and sales per dollar of assets invested (asset turnover).

Decision Point

Question ?	Accounting information 🗎	Analysis 🔍
How much profit is being generated from sales?	Profit margin	A higher profit margin indicates a company generates a higher net income per dollar of sales.
Is the company effectively generating sales from its assets?	Asset turnover ratio	A higher asset turnover indicates a company generates a higher sales volume per dollar of assets invested.

KEY POINT

Return on assets indicates the amount of net income generated for each dollar invested in assets. Return on assets can be separated to examine two important business strategies: profit margin and asset turnover.

APPENDIX

■ **LO7–8**

Identify impairment situations and describe the two-step impairment process.

ASSET IMPAIRMENT

Depreciation and amortization represent a gradual consumption of the benefits inherent in property, plant, and equipment and intangible assets. Situations can arise, however, that cause a significant decline or impairment of the total benefits or service potential of specific long-term assets. For example, if a retail chain closed several stores and no longer used them in operations, the buildings and equipment may be subject to impairment. **Sears Holding Corporation**, the parent company of **Sears** and **Kmart**, recorded impairment charges of $220 million in a recent year related to the write-down of buildings and other fixed assets associated with a closing of selected stores.

Management must review long-term assets for impairment. Impairment occurs when the expected future cash flows (expected future benefits) generated for a long-term asset fall below its book value (original cost minus accumulated depreciation).

Reporting for impairment losses is a two-step process summarized in Illustration 7–31.

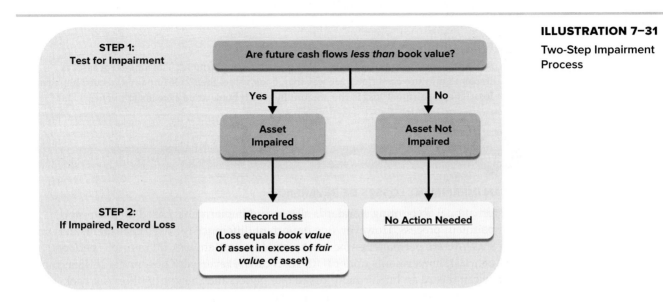

ILLUSTRATION 7–31

Two-Step Impairment Process

To illustrate asset impairment, suppose Little King pays $60,000 for the trademark rights to a line of specialty sandwiches. After several years, the book value is now $50,000, based on the initial cost of $60,000 less $10,000 in accumulated amortization. Unfortunately, sales for this line of specialty sandwiches are disappointing, and management estimates the total future cash flows from sales will be only $20,000. Due to the disappointing sales, the estimated fair value of the trademark is now only about $12,000. Here's how Little King determines and records the impairment loss.

STEP 1: TEST FOR IMPAIRMENT

The long-term asset is impaired since future cash flows ($20,000) are less than book value ($50,000).

STEP 2: IF IMPAIRED, RECORD THE LOSS

The loss is $38,000, calculated as the amount by which book value ($50,000) exceeds fair value ($12,000). We record the impairment loss as follows:

	Debit	Credit				
			A	=	L	+ SE
Loss	38,000					−38,000 Exp ↑
Trademarks		38,000	−38,000			
(Record impairment of trademark)						

COMMON MISTAKE

Some students forget step 1 when considering impairment. Record an impairment loss only when book value exceeds *both* future cash flows and fair value.

What is the overall financial statement effect of an impairment loss? The impairment entry reduces net income in the income statement by $38,000 and reduces total assets in the balance sheet by $38,000. The new balance in the Trademarks account is $12,000, which equals its current fair value. We can write down the trademark further through impairment in future years, but we cannot write it back up under current accounting rules.

We covered the basic impairment rules in this appendix. The two-step impairment process applies to property, plant, and equipment and intangible assets subject to amortization.

Impairment calculations for intangible assets not subject to amortization, like goodwill, are covered in more advanced accounting courses.

KEY POINT

Impairment is a two-step process: **Step 1: Test for impairment:** The long-term asset is impaired if future cash flows are less than book value. **Step 2: If impaired, record impairment loss:** The impairment loss is the amount by which book value exceeds fair value.

INTERNATIONAL FINANCIAL REPORTING STANDARDS (IFRS)

CAN IMPAIRMENT LOSSES BE REVERSED?

International accounting standards also record impairments based on a two-step impairment process. However, one important difference is this: Impairments under U.S. GAAP are permanent—the asset cannot be written back up in future periods. In contrast, impairments under IFRS rules can be reversed. Thus, under IFRS a company can record an impairment loss in one period and then write the asset back up with a corresponding gain in a later period.

For more discussion, see Appendix E.

Decision Maker's Perspective

Taking a Big Bath

In practice, determining impairment losses can be subjective. Accounting research suggests that managers sometimes use the recording of impairment losses to their advantage. Some companies time their impairment losses with other one-time losses such as losses on sales of assets, inventory write-downs, and restructuring charges, to record a big loss in one year. We refer to this practice as taking a big bath—recording all losses in one year to make a bad year even worse. Management thus cleans its slate and is able to report higher earnings in future years. Future earnings are higher because the write-down of assets in this year results in lower depreciation and amortization charges in the future. When analyzing financial statements, investors should be alert to this kind of manipulation.

KEY POINTS BY LEARNING OBJECTIVE

LO7–1   Identify the major types of property, plant, and equipment.

Tangible assets such as land, land improvements, buildings, equipment, and natural resources are recorded at cost plus all costs necessary to get the asset ready for its intended use.

LO7–2   Identify the major types of intangible assets.

We record purchased intangibles as long-term assets at their purchase price plus all costs necessary to get the asset ready for use. We expense internally generated intangibles, such as R&D and advertising costs, as we incur those costs.

Intangible assets include patents, copyrights, trademarks, franchises, and goodwill.

LO7–3   Describe the accounting treatment of expenditures after acquisition.

We capitalize (record as an asset) expenditures that benefit *future* periods. We expense items that benefit only the *current* period.

LO7–4   Calculate depreciation of property, plant, and equipment.

Depreciation refers to the allocation of an asset's original cost to an expense during the periods benefited. Depreciation does *not* refer to the change in value or selling price.

Straight-line, declining-balance, and activity-based depreciation all are acceptable depreciation methods for financial reporting. Most companies use straight-line depreciation for financial reporting and an accelerated method called MACRS for tax reporting.

LO7–5 Calculate amortization of intangible assets.

Amortization is a process, similar to depreciation, in which we allocate the cost of intangible assets over their estimated service life. Intangible assets with an indefinite useful life (goodwill and most trademarks) are *not* amortized.

LO7–6 Account for the disposal of long-term assets.

If we dispose of an asset for *more* than book value, we record a gain. If we dispose of an asset for *less* than book value, we record a loss.

Analysis

LO7–7 Describe the links among return on assets, profit margin, and asset turnover.

Return on assets indicates the amount of net income generated for each dollar invested in assets. Return on assets can be separated to examine two important business strategies: profit margin and asset turnover.

Appendix

LO7–8 Identify impairment situations and describe the two-step impairment process.

Impairment is a two-step process. **Step 1: Test for impairment:** The long-term asset is impaired if future cash flows are less than book value. **Step 2: If impaired, record loss:** The impairment loss is the amount by which book value exceeds fair value.

GLOSSARY

Accelerated depreciation method: Allocates a higher depreciation in the earlier years of the asset's life and lower depreciation in later years. **p. 337**

Accumulated Depreciation: A contra asset account representing the total depreciation taken to date. **p. 334**

Activity-based method: Allocates an asset's cost based on its use. **p. 339**

Addition: Occurs when a new major component is added to an existing asset. **p. 332**

Amortization: Allocation of the cost of an intangible asset over its service life. **p. 343**

Asset turnover: Net sales divided by average total assets, which measures the sales per dollar of assets invested. **p. 349**

Basket purchase: Purchase of more than one asset at the same time for one purchase price. **p. 327**

Big bath: Recording all losses in one year to make a bad year even worse. **p. 352**

Book value: An asset's original cost less accumulated depreciation. **p. 335**

Capitalize: Record an expenditure as an asset. **p. 325**

Copyright: An exclusive right of protection given to the creator of a published work such as a song, film, painting, photograph, book, or computer software. **p. 329**

Declining-balance method: An accelerated depreciation method that records more depreciation in earlier years and less depreciation in later years. **p. 338**

Depreciation: Allocating the cost of a long-term asset to an expense over its service life. **p. 334**

Franchise: Local outlets that pay for the exclusive right to use the franchisor company's name and to sell its products within a specified geographical area. **p. 330**

Goodwill: Goodwill equals the purchase price less the fair value of the net assets acquired. **p. 330**

Impairment: Occurs when the future cash flows (future benefits) generated for a long-term asset fall below its book value (cost minus accumulated depreciation). **p. 350**

Improvement: The cost of replacing a major component of an asset. **p. 332**

Intangible assets: Long-term assets that lack physical substance, and whose existence is often based on a legal contract. **p. 327**

Land improvements: Improvements to land such as paving, lighting, and landscaping that, unlike land itself, are subject to depreciation. **p. 326**

Material: Large enough to influence a decision. **p. 332**

Natural resources: Assets like oil, natural gas, and timber that we can physically use up or deplete. **p. 327**

Patent: An exclusive right to manufacture a product or to use a process. **p. 329**

Profit margin: Net income divided by net sales; indicates the earnings per dollar of sales. **p. 349**

Repairs and maintenance: Expenses that maintain a given level of benefits in the period incurred. **p. 331**

Residual value: The amount the company expects to receive from selling the asset at the end of its service life; also referred to as *salvage value.* **p. 335**

Return on assets: Net income divided by average total assets; measures the amount of net income generated for each dollar invested in assets. **p. 348**

Service life: How long the company expects to receive benefits from the asset before disposing of it; also referred to as *useful life.* **p. 335**

Straight-line method: Allocates an equal amount of depreciation to each year of the asset's service life. **p. 336**

Trademark: A word, slogan, or symbol that distinctively identifies a company, product, or service. **p. 329**

SELF-STUDY QUESTIONS

1. We normally record a long-term asset at the: **(LO7–1)**
   a. Cost of the asset only.
   b. Cost of the asset plus all costs necessary to get the asset ready for use.
   c. Appraised value.
   d. Cost of the asset, but subsequently adjust it up or down to appraised value.

2. Sandwich Express incurred the following costs related to its purchase of a bread machine. **(LO7–1)**

Cost of the equipment	$20,000
Sales tax (8%)	1,600
Shipping	2,200
Installation	1,400
Total costs	$25,200

   At what amount should Sandwich Express record the bread machine?
   a. $20,000.
   b. $21,600.
   c. $23,800.
   d. $25,200.

3. Research and development costs generated internally: **(LO7–2)**
   a. Are recorded as research and development assets.
   b. Are capitalized and then amortized.
   c. Should be included in the cost of the patent they relate to.
   d. Should be expensed.

4. Which of the following expenditures should be recorded as an expense? **(LO7–3)**
   a. Repairs and maintenance that maintain current benefits.
   b. Adding a major new component to an existing asset.
   c. Replacing a major component of an existing asset.
   d. Successful legal defense of an intangible asset.

5. Which of the following will maximize net income by minimizing depreciation expense in the first year of the asset's life? **(LO7–4)**
   a. Short service life, high residual value, and straight-line depreciation.
   b. Long service life, high residual value, and straight-line depreciation.
   c. Short service life, low residual value, and double-declining-balance depreciation.
   d. Long service life, high residual value, and double-declining-balance depreciation.

6. The book value of an asset is equal to the: **(LO7–4)**
   a. Replacement cost.
   b. Asset's cost less accumulated depreciation.
   c. Asset's fair value less its historical cost.
   d. Historical cost plus accumulated depreciation.

7. The balance in the Accumulated Depreciation account represents: **(LO7–4)**
   a. The amount charged to expense in the current period.
   b. A contra expense account.
   c. A cash fund to be used to replace plant assets.
   d. The amount charged to depreciation expense since the acquisition of the plant asset.

8. Which of the following statements is *true* regarding the amortization of intangible assets? **(LO7–5)**
   a. Intangible assets with a limited useful life are not amortized.
   b. The service life of an intangible asset is always equal to its legal life.
   c. The expected residual value of most intangible assets is zero.
   d. In recording amortization, Accumulated Amortization is always credited.

9. Equipment originally costing $95,000 has accumulated depreciation of $30,000. If it sells the equipment for $55,000, the company should record: **(LO7–6)**
   a. No gain or loss.
   b. A gain of $10,000.
   c. A loss of $10,000.
   d. A loss of $40,000.

10. The return on assets is equal to the: **(LO7–7)**
    a. Profit margin plus asset turnover.
    b. Profit margin minus asset turnover.
    c. Profit margin times asset turnover.
    d. Profit margin divided by asset turnover.

Note: For answers, see the last page of the chapter.

For additional study materials, including 10 more multiple-choice Self-Study Questions, visit Connect.

REVIEW QUESTIONS

1. **WorldCom** committed the largest fraud in U.S. history. What was the primary method WorldCom's management used to carry out the fraud?   ■ **LO7–1**

2. What are the two major categories of long-term assets? How do these two categories differ?   ■ **LO7–1**

3. Explain how we initially record a long-term asset.   ■ **LO7–1**

4. If University Hero initially records an expense incorrectly as an asset, how does this mistake affect the income statement and the balance sheet?   ■ **LO7–1**

5. Little King acquires land and an old building across the street from Northwestern State University. Little King intends to remove the old building and build a new sandwich shop on the land. What costs might the firm incur to make the land ready for its intended use?   ■ **LO7–1**

6. Why don't we depreciate land? What are land improvements? Why do we record land and land improvements separately?   ■ **LO7–1**

7. Equipment includes machinery used in manufacturing, computers and other office equipment, vehicles, furniture, and fixtures. What costs might we incur to get equipment ready for use?   ■ **LO7–1**

8. Where in the balance sheet do we report natural resources? Provide three examples of natural resource assets.   ■ **LO7–1**

9. Explain how the accounting treatment differs between purchased and internally developed intangible assets.   ■ **LO7–2**

10. What are the differences among a patent, a copyright, and a trademark?   ■ **LO7–2**

11. What is goodwill and how do we measure it? Can we sell goodwill separately from the business?   ■ **LO7–2**

12. How do we decide whether to capitalize (record as an asset) or expense a particular cost?   ■ **LO7–3**

13. Explain the usual accounting treatment for repairs and maintenance, additions, and improvements.   ■ **LO7–3**

14. Are litigation costs to defend an intangible asset capitalized or expensed? Explain your answer.   ■ **LO7–3**

15. How is the dictionary definition different from the accounting definition of depreciation?   ■ **LO7–4**

16. What factors must we estimate in allocating the cost of a long-term asset over its service life?   ■ **LO7–4**

17. What is the service life of an asset? How do we determine service life under the straight-line and the activity-based depreciation methods?   ■ **LO7–4**

18. What is residual value? How do we use residual value in calculating depreciation under the straight-line method?   ■ **LO7–4**

19. Contrast the effects of the straight-line, declining-balance, and activity-based methods on annual depreciation expense.   ■ **LO7–4**

20. Assume that Little King Sandwiches uses straight-line depreciation and University Hero uses double-declining-balance depreciation. Explain the difficulties in comparing the income statements and balance sheets of the two companies.   ■ **LO7–4**

21. Assume Little King Sandwiches depreciates a building over 40 years and University Hero depreciates a similar building over 20 years, and both companies use the straight-line depreciation method. Explain the difficulties in comparing the income statements and balance sheets of the two companies.   ■ **LO7–4**

- LO7-4   22. Which depreciation method is most common for financial reporting? Which depreciation method is most common for tax reporting? Why do companies choose these methods?

- LO7-5   23. Justin Time is confident that firms amortize all intangible assets. Is he right? If amortized, are intangible assets always amortized over their legal life? Explain.

- LO7-6   24. What is book value? How do we compute the gain or loss on the sale of long-term assets?

- LO7-7   25. Describe return on assets, profit margin, and asset turnover.

- LO7-7   26. Provide an example of a company with a high profit margin. Provide an example of a company with a high asset turnover.

- LO7-8   27. What is an asset impairment? Describe the two-step process for recording impairments. How does recording an impairment loss affect the income statement and the balance sheet?

- LO7-8   28. How do companies take a *big bath*? Explain the effect of a big bath on the current year's and future years' net income.

BRIEF EXERCISES

Determine the initial cost of land (LO7–1)

BE7–1 Fresh Veggies, Inc. (FVI), purchases land and a warehouse for $490,000. In addition to the purchase price, FVI makes the following expenditures related to the acquisition: broker's commission, $29,000; title insurance, $1,900; and miscellaneous closing costs, $6,000. The warehouse is immediately demolished at a cost of $29,000 in anticipation of building a new warehouse. Determine the amount FVI should record as the cost of the land.

Determine the initial cost of equipment (LO7–1)

BE7–2 Whole Grain Bakery purchases an industrial bread machine for $30,000. In addition to the purchase price, the company makes the following expenditures: freight, $2,000; installation, $4,000; testing, $1,500; and property tax on the machine for the first year, $600. What is the initial cost of the bread machine?

Calculate goodwill (LO7–2)

BE7–3 Kosher Pickle Company acquires all the outstanding stock of Midwest Produce for $19 million. The fair value of Midwest's assets is $14.3 million. The fair value of Midwest's liabilities is $2.5 million. Calculate the amount paid for goodwill.

Compute research and development expense (LO7–2)

BE7–4 West Coast Growers incurs the following costs during the year related to the creation of a new disease-resistant tomato plant.

Salaries for R&D	$540,000
Depreciation on R&D facilities and equipment	145,000
Utilities incurred for the R&D facilities	7,000
Patent filing and related legal costs	27,000
Payment to another company for part of the development work	13,000

What amount should West Coast Growers report as research and development (R&D) expense in its income statement?

Account for expenditures after acquisition (LO7–3)

BE7–5 Hanoi Foods incurs the following expenditures during the current fiscal year: (1) annual maintenance on its machinery, $8,900; (2) remodeling of offices, $42,000; (3) improvement of the shipping and receiving area, resulting in an increase in productivity, $25,000; and (4) addition of a security system to the manufacturing facility, $35,000. How should Hanoi account for each of these expenditures?

Explain the accounting definition of depreciation (LO7–4)

BE7–6 Early in the fiscal year, The Beanery purchases a delivery vehicle for $40,000. At the end of the year, the machine has a fair value of $33,000. The company controller records depreciation expense of $7,000 for the year, the decline in the vehicle's value. Explain why the controller's approach to recording depreciation expense is not correct.

BE7–7 El Tapitio purchased restaurant furniture on September 1, 2018, for $45,000. Residual value at the end of an estimated 10-year service life is expected to be $6,000. Calculate depreciation expense for 2018 and 2019, using the straight-line method, and assuming a December 31 year-end.

Calculate partial-year depreciation (LO7–4)

BE7–8 Hawaiian Specialty Foods purchased equipment for $30,000. Residual value at the end of an estimated four-year service life is expected to be $3,000. The machine operated for 3,100 hours in the first year, and the company expects the machine to operate for a total of 20,000 hours. Calculate depreciation expense for the first year using each of the following depreciation methods: (1) straight-line, (2) double-declining-balance, and (3) activity-based.

Calculate depreciation (LO7–4)

BE7–9 In early January, Burger Mania acquired 100% of the common stock of the Crispy Taco restaurant chain. The purchase price allocation included the following items: $4 million, patent; $5 million, trademark considered to have an indefinite useful life; and $6 million, goodwill. Burger Mania's policy is to amortize intangible assets with finite useful lives using the straight-line method, no residual value, and a five-year service life. What is the total amount of amortization expense that would appear in Burger Mania's income statement for the first year ended December 31 related to these items?

Calculate amortization expense (LO7–5)

BE7–10 Granite Stone Creamery sold ice cream equipment for $16,000. Granite Stone originally purchased the equipment for $90,000, and depreciation through the date of sale totaled $71,000. What was the gain or loss on the sale of the equipment?

Account for the sale of long-term assets (LO7–6)

BE7–11 China Inn and Midwest Chicken exchanged assets. China Inn received a delivery truck and gave equipment. The fair value and book value of the equipment were $22,000 and $12,000 (original cost of $45,000 less accumulated depreciation of $33,000), respectively. To equalize market values of the exchanged assets, China Inn paid $9,000 in cash to Midwest Chicken. At what amount did China Inn record the delivery truck? How much gain or loss did China Inn recognize on the exchange?

Account for the exchange of long-term assets (LO7–6)

Flip Side of BE7–12

BE7–12 China Inn and Midwest Chicken exchanged assets. Midwest Chicken received equipment and gave a delivery truck. The fair value and book value of the delivery truck given were $31,000 and $32,600 (original cost of $37,000 less accumulated depreciation of $4,400), respectively. To equalize market values of the exchanged assets, Midwest Chicken received $9,000 in cash from China Inn. At what amount did Midwest Chicken record the equipment? How much gain or loss did Midwest Chicken recognize on the exchange?

Account for the exchange of long-term assets (LO7–6)

Flip Side of BE7–11

BE7–13 The balance sheet of Cedar Crest Resort reports total assets of $840,000 and $930,000 at the beginning and end of the year, respectively. The return on assets for the year is 20%. Calculate Cedar Crest's net income for the year.

Use the return on assets ratio (LO7–7)

BE7–14 Vegetarian Delights has been experiencing declining market conditions for its specialty foods division. Management decided to test the operational assets of the division for possible impairment. The test revealed the following: book value of division's assets, $33.5 million; fair value of division's assets, $30 million; sum of estimated future cash flows generated from the division's assets, $38 million. What amount of impairment loss, if any, should Vegetarian Delights record?

Determine the impairment loss (LO7–8)

BE7–15 Refer to the situation described in BE7–14. Assume the sum of estimated future cash flows is $32 million instead of $38 million. What amount of impairment loss should Vegetarian Delights record?

Determine the impairment loss (LO7–8)

EXERCISES

E7–1 McCoy's Fish House purchases a tract of land and an existing building for $1,000,000. The company plans to remove the old building and construct a new restaurant on the site. In addition to the purchase price, McCoy pays closing costs, including title insurance of $3,000. The company also pays $14,000 in property taxes, which includes $9,000 of back taxes (unpaid taxes from previous years) paid by McCoy on behalf of the seller and $5,000 due for the current fiscal year after the purchase date. Shortly after closing, the company pays a contractor $50,000 to tear down the old building and remove it from the site. McCoy is able to sell salvaged materials from the old building for $5,000 and pays an additional $11,000 to level the land.

Record purchase of land (LO7–1)

Required:

Determine the amount McCoy's Fish House should record as the cost of the land.

Record purchase of equipment (LO7–1)

E7–2 Orion Flour Mills purchased a new machine and made the following expenditures:

Purchase price	$75,000
Sales tax	6,000
Shipment of machine	1,000
Insurance on the machine for the first year	700
Installation of machine	2,000

The machine, including sales tax, was purchased on account, with payment due in 30 days. The other expenditures listed above were paid in cash.

Required:

Record the above expenditures for the new machine.

Allocate costs in a basket purchase (LO7–1)

E7–3 Red Rock Bakery purchases land, building, and equipment for a single purchase price of $600,000. However, the estimated fair values of the land, building, and equipment are $175,000, $455,000, and $70,000, respectively, for a total estimated fair value of $700,000.

Required:

Determine the amounts Red Rock should record in the separate accounts for the land, the building, and the equipment.

Ethical dilemma in a basket purchase (LO7–1, 7–4)

E7–4 The Donut Stop purchased land and a building for $2 million. To maximize the company's tax deduction for depreciation, management allocated only 10% of the purchase price to land and 90% of the purchase price to the building. A more reasonable allocation would have been 20% to the land and 80% to the building.

Required:

1. Explain the tax benefits of allocating less to the land and more to the building.
2. Is the allocation made by Donut Stop's management ethical? Why or why not? Who, if anyone, was harmed?

Reporting intangible assets (LO7–2)

E7–5 Brick Oven Corporation made the following expenditures during the first month of operations:

Attorneys' fees to organize the corporation	$ 9,000
Purchase of a patent	40,000
Legal and other fees for transfer of the patent	2,500
Preopening employee salaries	80,000
Total	$131,500

Required:

Record the $131,500 in cash expenditures.

Calculate the amount of goodwill (LO7–2)

E7–6 Mainline Produce Corporation acquired all the outstanding common stock of Iceberg Lettuce Corporation for $30,000,000 in cash. The book values and fair values of Iceberg's assets and liabilities were as follows:

	Book Value	Fair Value
Current assets	$11,400,000	$14,400,000
Property, plant, and equipment	20,200,000	26,200,000
Other assets	3,400,000	4,400,000
Current liabilities	7,800,000	7,800,000
Long-term liabilities	13,200,000	12,200,000

Required:

Calculate the amount paid for goodwill.

E7–7 Satellite Systems modified its model Z2 satellite to incorporate a new communication device. The company made the following expenditures:

Basic research to develop the technology	$3,900,000
Engineering design work	1,180,000
Development of a prototype device	590,000
Testing and modification of the prototype	390,000
Legal fees for patent application	79,000
Legal fees for successful defense of the new patent	39,000
Total	$6,178,000

During your year-end review of the accounts related to intangibles, you discover that the company has capitalized all the above as costs of the patent. Management contends that the device represents an improvement of the existing communication system of the satellite and, therefore, should be capitalized.

Required:

1. Which of the above costs should Satellite Systems capitalize to the Patent account in the balance sheet?
2. Which of the above costs should Satellite Systems report as research and development expense in the income statement?
3. What are the basic criteria for determining whether to capitalize or expense intangible related costs?

E7–8 Listed below are several terms and phrases associated with operational assets. Pair each item from List A (by letter) with the item from List B that is most appropriately associated with it.

List A	List B
_____ 1. Depreciation	a. Exclusive right to display a word, a symbol, or an emblem.
_____ 2. Goodwill	
_____ 3. Amortization	b. Exclusive right to benefit from a creative work.
_____ 4. Natural resources	c. Assets that represent contractual rights.
_____ 5. Intangible assets	d. Oil and gas deposits, timber tracts, and mineral deposits.
_____ 6. Copyright	
_____ 7. Trademark	e. Purchase price less fair value of net identifiable assets.
	f. The allocation of cost for plant and equipment.
	g. The allocation of cost for intangible assets.

E7–9 Sub Sandwiches of America made the following expenditures related to its restaurant:

1. Replaced the heating equipment at a cost of $250,000.
2. Covered the patio area with a clear plastic dome and enclosed it with glass for use during the winter months. The total cost of the project was $750,000.
3. Performed annual building maintenance at a cost of $24,000.
4. Paid for annual insurance for the facility at $8,800.
5. Built a new sign above the restaurant, putting the company name in bright neon lights, for $9,900.
6. Paved a gravel parking lot at a cost of $65,000.

Required:

Sub Sandwiches of America credits Cash for each of these expenditures. Indicate the account it debits for each.

E7–10 Super Saver Groceries purchased store equipment for $29,500. Super Saver estimates that at the end of its 10-year service life, the equipment will be worth $3,500. During the 10-year period, the company expects to use the equipment for a total of 13,000 hours. Super Saver used the equipment for 1,700 hours the first year.

Required:

Calculate depreciation expense for the first year, using each of the following methods. Round all amounts to the nearest dollar.
1. Straight-line.
2. Double-declining-balance.
3. Activity-based.

E7–11 Speedy Delivery Company purchases a delivery van for $36,000. Speedy estimates that at the end of its four-year service life, the van will be worth $6,400. During the four-year period, the company expects to drive the van 148,000 miles.

Required:

Calculate annual depreciation for the first two years using each of the following methods. Round all amounts to the nearest dollar.
1. Straight-line.
2. Double-declining-balance.
3. Activity-based.

Actual miles driven each year were 40,000 miles in year 1 and 46,000 miles in year 2.

E7–12 Togo's Sandwiches acquired equipment on April 1, 2018, for $18,000. The company estimates a residual value of $2,000 and a five-year service life.

Required:

Calculate depreciation expense using the straight-line method for 2018 and 2019, assuming a December 31 year-end.

E7–13 Tasty Subs acquired a delivery truck on October 1, 2018, for $21,600. The company estimates a residual value of $1,200 and a six-year service life.

Required:

Calculate depreciation expense using the straight-line method for 2018 and 2019, assuming a December 31 year-end.

E7–14 The Donut Stop acquired equipment for $19,000. The company uses straight-line depreciation and estimates a residual value of $3,000 and a four-year service life. At the end of the second year, the company estimates that the equipment will be useful for four additional years, for a total service life of six years rather than the original four. At the same time, the company also changed the estimated residual value to $1,200 from the original estimate of $3,000.

Required:

Calculate how much The Donut Stop should record each year for depreciation in years 3 to 6.

E7–15 Tasty Subs acquired a delivery truck on October 1, 2018, for $21,500. The company estimates a residual value of $2,500 and a six-year service life. It expects to drive the truck 100,000 miles. Actual mileage was 5,000 miles in 2018 and 19,000 miles in 2019.

Required:

Calculate depreciation expense using the activity-based method for 2018 and 2019, assuming a December 31 year-end.

E7–16 On January 1, 2018, Weaver Corporation purchased a patent for $237,000. The remaining legal life is 20 years, but the company estimates the patent will be useful for only six more years. In January 2020, the company incurred legal fees of $57,000 in successfully defending a patent infringement suit. The successful defense did not change the company's estimate of useful life. Weaver Corporation's year-end is December 31.

Required:

1. Record the purchase in 2018; amortization in 2018; amortization in 2019; legal fees in 2020; and amortization in 2020.
2. What is the balance in the Patent account at the end of 2020?

E7–17 Abbott Landscaping purchased a tractor at a cost of $42,000 and sold it three years later for $21,600. Abbott recorded depreciation using the straight-line method, a five-year service life, and a $3,000 residual value. Tractors are included in the Equipment account.

Record the sale of
equipment **(LO7–6)**

Required:
1. Record the sale.
2. Assume the tractor was sold for $13,600 instead of $21,600. Record the sale.

E7–18 Salad Express exchanged land it had been holding for future plant expansion for a more suitable parcel of land along distribution routes. Salad Express reported the old land on the previously issued balance sheet at its original cost of $70,000. According to an independent appraisal, the old land currently is worth $132,000. Salad Express paid $19,000 in cash to complete the transaction.

Record an exchange of
land **(LO7–6)**

Required:
1. What is the fair value of the new parcel of land received by Salad Express?
2. Record the exchange.

E7–19 Brad's BBQ reported sales of $735,000 and net income of $28,000. Brad's also reported ending total assets of $496,000 and beginning total assets of $389,000.

Calculate ratios **(LO7–7)**

Required:
Calculate the return on assets, the profit margin, and the asset turnover ratio for Brad's BBQ.

E7–20 Midwest Services, Inc., operates several restaurant chains throughout the Midwest. One restaurant chain has experienced sharply declining profits. The company's management has decided to test the operational assets of the restaurants for possible impairment. The relevant information for these assets is presented below.

Calculate impairment
loss **(LO7–8)**

Book value	$8.6 million
Estimated total future cash flows	7.1 million
Fair value	5.9 million

Required:
1. Determine the amount of the impairment loss, if any.
2. Repeat *Requirement* 1 assuming that the estimated total future cash flows are $10 million and the fair value is $8.2 million.

E7–21 On January 1, 2018, the general ledger of TNT Fireworks includes the following account balances:

Complete the accounting
cycle using long-term
asset transactions
(LO 7–4, 7–7)

Accounts	Debit	Credit
Cash	$ 58,700	
Accounts Receivable	25,000	
Allowance for Uncollectible Accounts		$ 2,200
Inventory	36,300	
Notes Receivable (5%, due in 2 years)	12,000	
Land	155,000	
Accounts Payable		14,800
Common Stock		220,000
Retained Earnings		50,000
Totals	$287,000	$287,000

During January 2018, the following transactions occur:

January 1 Purchase equipment for $19,500. The company estimates a residual value of $1,500 and a five-year service life.

January 4 Pay cash on accounts payable, $9,500.

January 8 Purchase additional inventory on account, $82,900.

January 15	Receive cash on accounts receivable, $22,000
January 19	Pay cash for salaries, $29,800.
January 28	Pay cash for January utilities, $16,500.
January 30	Firework sales for January total $220,000. All of these sales are on account. The cost of the units sold is $115,000.

Required:

1. Record each of the transactions listed above.
2. Record adjusting entries on January 31.
   a. Depreciation on the equipment for the month of January is calculated using the straight-line method.
   b. At the end of January, $3,000 of accounts receivable are past due, and the company estimates that 50% of these accounts will not be collected. Of the remaining accounts receivable, the company estimates that 3% will not be collected. The note receivable of $12,000 is considered fully collectible and therefore is not included in the estimate of uncollectible accounts.
   c. Accrued interest revenue on notes receivable for January.
   d. Unpaid salaries at the end of January are $32,600.
   e. Accrued income taxes at the end of January are $9,000.
3. Prepare an adjusted trial balance as of January 31, 2018, after updating beginning balances (above) for transactions during January (*Requirement* 1) and adjusting entries at the end of January (*Requirement* 2).
4. Prepare a multiple-step income statement for the period ended January 31, 2018.
5. Prepare a classified balance sheet as of January 31, 2018.
6. Record closing entries.
7. Analyze how well TNT Fireworks manages its assets:
   a. Calculate the return on assets ratio for the month of January. If the average return on assets for the industry in January is 2%, is the company *more* or *less* profitable than other companies in the same industry?
   b. Calculate the profit margin for the month of January. If the industry average profit margin is 4%, is the company *more* or *less* efficient at converting sales to profit than other companies in the same industry?
   c. Calculate the asset turnover ratio for the month of January. If the industry average asset turnover is 0.5 times per month, is the company more or less efficient at producing revenues with its assets than other companies in the same industry?

PROBLEMS: SET A

Mc Graw Hill Education **connect**

Determine the acquisition cost of land and building (LO7–1)

P7–1A The Italian Bread Company purchased land as a factory site for $70,000. An old building on the property was demolished, and construction began on a new building. Costs incurred during the first year are listed as follows:

Demolition of old building	$ 9,000
Sale of salvaged materials	(1,100)
Architect fees (for new building)	20,000
Legal fees (for title investigation of land)	3,000
Property taxes on the land (for the first year)	4,000
Building construction costs	600,000
Interest costs related to the construction	23,000

Required:

Determine the acquisition cost of equipment (LO7–1)

Determine the amounts that the company should record in the Land and the Building accounts.

P7–2A Great Harvest Bakery purchased bread ovens from New Morning Bakery. New Morning Bakery was closing its bakery business and sold its two-year-old ovens at a discount for $700,000. Great Harvest incurred and paid freight costs of $35,000, and its employees ran special electrical connections to the ovens at a cost of $5,000. Labor costs were $37,800. Unfortunately, one of the ovens was damaged during installation, and repairs cost $4,000. Great Harvest then consumed $900 of bread dough in testing the ovens. It installed safety guards on the ovens at a cost of $1,500 and placed the machines in operation.

Flip Side of P7–8A

Required:
1. Prepare a schedule showing the amount at which the ovens should be recorded in Great Harvest's Equipment account.
2. Indicate where any amounts not included in the Equipment account should be recorded.

P7–3A Fresh Cut Corporation purchased all the outstanding common stock of Premium Meats for $12,000,000 in cash. The book values and fair values of Premium Meats' assets and liabilities were:

Calculate and record goodwill (LO7–2)

	Book Value	**Fair Value**
Accounts Receivable	$1,800,000	$ 1,600,000
Equipment	8,500,000	9,900,000
Patents	300,000	1,700,000
Notes Payable	(2,700,000)	(2,700,000)
Net assets	$7,900,000	$10,500,000

Required:
1. Calculate the amount Fresh Cut should report for goodwill.
2. Record Fresh Cut's acquisition of Premium Meats.

P7–4A Several years ago, Health Services acquired a helicopter for use in emergency situations. Health Services incurred the following expenditures related to the helicopter delivery operations in the current year:

Record expenditures after acquisition (LO7–3)

1. Overhauled the engine at a cost of $7,500. Health Services estimated the work would increase the service life for an additional five years.
2. Cleaned, repacked, and sealed the bearings on the helicopter at a cost of $800. This repair is performed annually.
3. Added new emergency health equipment to the helicopter for $25,000.
4. Modified the helicopter to reduce cabin noise by installing new sound barrier technology at a cost of $15,000.
5. Paid insurance on the helicopter for the current year, which increased 15% over the prior year to $9,000.
6. Performed annual maintenance and repairs at a cost of $39,000.

Required:
Indicate whether Health Services should capitalize or expense each of these expenditures. How could Health Services use expenditures like these to increase reported earnings?

P7–5A University Car Wash built a deluxe car wash across the street from campus. The new machines cost $270,000 including installation. The company estimates that the equipment will have a residual value of $24,000. University Car Wash also estimates it will use the machine for six years or about 12,000 total hours.

Determine depreciation under three methods (LO7–4)

Required:
Prepare a depreciation schedule for six years using the following methods:
1. Straight-line.
2. Double-declining-balance.
3. Activity-based.

Actual use per year was as follows:

Year	Hours Used
1	3,100
2	1,100
3	1,200
4	2,800
5	2,600
6	1,200

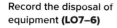

Record amortization and prepare the intangible assets section (LO7–5)

P7–6A The following information relates to the intangible assets of University Testing Services (UTS):

a. On January 1, 2018, UTS completed the purchase of Heinrich Corporation for $3,510,000 in cash. The fair value of the net identifiable assets of Heinrich was $3,200,000.

b. Included in the assets purchased from Heinrich was a patent valued at $82,250. The original legal life of the patent was 20 years; there are 12 years remaining, but UTS believes the patent will be useful for only seven more years.

c. UTS acquired a franchise on July 1, 2018, by paying an initial franchise fee of $333,000. The contractual life of the franchise is 9 years.

Required:

1. Record amortization expense for the intangible assets at December 31, 2018.
2. Prepare the intangible asset section of the December 31, 2018, balance sheet.

Compute depreciation, amortization, and book value of long-term assets (LO7–4, 7–5)

P7–7A Solich Sandwich Shop had the following long-term asset balances as of December 31, 2018:

	Cost	Accumulated Depreciation	Book Value
Land	$ 95,000	–	$ 95,000
Building	460,000	$(165,600)	294,400
Equipment	235,000	(50,000)	185,000
Patent	250,000	(100,000)	150,000

Solich purchased all the assets at the beginning of 2016 (3 years ago). The building is depreciated over a 10-year service life using the double-declining-balance method and estimating no residual value. The equipment is depreciated over a nine-year useful life using the straight-line method with an estimated residual value of $10,000. The patent is estimated to have a five-year service life with no residual value and is amortized using the straight-line method. Depreciation and amortization have been recorded for 2016 and 2017.

Required:

1. For the year ended December 31, 2018, record depreciation expense for buildings and equipment. Land is not depreciated.
2. For the year ended December 31, 2018, record amortization expense for the patent.
3. Calculate the book value for each of the four long-term assets at December 31, 2018.

Record the disposal of equipment (LO7–6)

Flip Side of P7–2A

P7–8A New Morning Bakery is in the process of closing its operations. It sold its two-year-old bakery ovens to Great Harvest Bakery for $700,000. The ovens originally cost $910,000, had an estimated service life of 10 years, and an estimated residual value of $60,000. New Morning Bakery uses the straight-line depreciation method for all equipment.

Required:

1. Calculate the balance in the Accumulated Depreciation account at the end of the second year.
2. Calculate the book value of the ovens at the end of the second year.

3. What is the gain or loss on the sale of the ovens at the end of the second year?
4. Record the sale of the ovens at the end of the second year.

P7–9A Sub Station and Planet Sub reported the following selected financial data ($ in thousands). Sub Station's business strategy is to sell the best tasting sandwich with the highest quality ingredients. Planet Sub's business strategy is to sell the lowest cost sub on the planet.

Calculate and interpret ratios (LO7–7)

	Sub Station	Planet Sub
Net sales	$108,249	$62,071
Net income	25,922	3,492
Total assets, beginning	75,183	38,599
Total assets, ending	116,371	44,533

Required:
1. Calculate Sub Station's return on assets, profit margin, and asset turnover ratio.
2. Calculate Planet Sub's return on assets, profit margin, and asset turnover ratio.
3. Which company has the higher profit margin and which company has the higher asset turnover? Is this consistent with the primary business strategies of these two companies?

P7–10A University Hero is considering expanding operations beyond its healthy sandwiches. Jim Axelrod, vice president of marketing, would like to add a line of smoothies with a similar health emphasis. Each smoothie would include two free health supplements such as vitamins, antioxidants, and protein. Jim believes smoothie sales should help fill the slow mid-afternoon period. Adding the line of smoothies would require purchasing additional freezer space, machinery, and equipment. Jim provides the following projections of net sales, net income, and average total assets in support of his proposal.

Calculate and interpret ratios (LO7–7)

	Sandwiches Only	Sandwiches and Smoothies
Net sales	$900,000	$1,500,000
Net income	170,000	260,000
Average total assets	500,000	900,000

Required:
1. Calculate University Hero's return on assets, profit margin, and asset turnover for sandwiches only.
2. Calculate University Hero's return on assets, profit margin, and asset turnover for sandwiches and smoothies.
3. Based on these ratios, what recommendation would you make?

PROBLEMS: SET B

P7–1B The Italian Pizza Company purchased land as a factory site for $90,000. Prior to construction of the new building, the land had to be cleared of trees and brush. Construction costs incurred during the first year are listed below:

Determine the acquisition cost of land and building (LO7–1)

Land clearing costs	$ 5,000
Sale of firewood to a worker	(400)
Architect fees (for new building)	30,000
Title investigation of land	3,500
Property taxes on land (for the first year)	3,000
Building construction costs	400,000

Required:

Determine the amounts that the company should record in the Land and the New Building accounts.

Determine the acquisition
cost of equipment **(LO7–1)**

Flip Side of P7–8B

P7–2B Sicily Pizza purchased baking ovens from New World Deli. New World Deli was closing its bakery business and sold its three-year-old ovens for $341,000. In addition to the purchase price, Sicily Pizza paid shipping costs of $16,000. Employees of Sicily Pizza installed the ovens; labor costs were $17,000. An outside contractor performed some of the electrical work for $3,800. Sicily Pizza consumed pizza dough with a cost of $1,300 in testing the ovens. It then installed new timers on the ovens at a cost of $800 and placed the machines in operation.

Required:

1. Prepare a schedule showing the amount at which Sicily Pizza should record the ovens in the Equipment account.
2. Indicate where any amounts not included in the Equipment account should be recorded.

Calculate and record
goodwill **(LO7–2)**

P7–3B Northern Equipment Corporation purchased all the outstanding common stock of Pioneer Equipment Rental for $5,600,000 in cash. The book values and fair values of Pioneer's assets and liabilities were:

	Book Value	Fair Value
Accounts Receivable	$ 750,000	$ 650,000
Buildings	4,100,000	4,800,000
Equipment	110,000	200,000
Accounts Payable	(750,000)	(750,000)
Net assets	$4,210,000	$4,900,000

Required:

1. Calculate the amount Northern Equipment should report for goodwill.
2. Record Northern Equipment's acquisition of Pioneer Equipment Rental.

Record expenditures after
acquisition **(LO7–3)**

P7–4B Stillwater Youth Programs (SYP) purchased a used school bus to transport children for its after-school program. SYP incurred the following expenses related to the bus for the current year:

1. Replaced a blown tire on the bus for $175.
2. Installed new seats on the bus at a cost of $5,000.
3. Installed a DVD player and sound system to entertain the children in-transit and announce upcoming events at a cost of $1,000.
4. Paid insurance on the school bus for the current year, which increased 10% over the prior year to an annual premium of $2,800.
5. Performed annual maintenance and repairs for $1,400.
6. Overhauled the engine at a cost of $6,500, increasing the service life of the bus by an estimated three years.

Required:

Indicate whether SYP should capitalize or expense each of these expenditures. How could SYP use expenditures like these to increase reported earnings?

Determine depreciation
under three
methods **(LO7–4)**

P7–5B Cheetah Copy purchased a new copy machine. The new machine cost $140,000 including installation. The company estimates the equipment will have a residual value of $35,000. Cheetah Copy also estimates it will use the machine for four years or about 8,000 total hours.

Required:

Prepare a depreciation schedule for four years using the following methods:
1. Straight-line.
2. Double-declining-balance. (Hint: The asset will be depreciated in only two years.)
3. Activity-based.

Actual use per year was as follows:

Year	Hours Used
1	3,000
2	2,000
3	2,000
4	2,000

P7–6B The following information relates to the intangible assets of Lettuce Express:

a. On January 1, 2018, Lettuce Express completed the purchase of Farmers Produce, Inc., for $1,600,000 in cash. The fair value of the identifiable net assets of Farmers Produce was $1,440,000.

b. Included in the assets purchased from Farmers Produce was a patent for a method of processing lettuce valued at $49,500. The original legal life of the patent was 20 years. There are still 17 years left on the patent, but Lettuce Express estimates the patent will be useful for only 9 more years.

c. Lettuce Express acquired a franchise on July 1, 2018, by paying an initial franchise fee of $216,000. The contractual life of the franchise is eight years.

Required:
1. Record amortization expense for the intangible assets at December 31, 2018.
2. Prepare the intangible asset section of the December 31, 2018, balance sheet.

P7–7B Togo's Sandwich Shop had the following long-term asset balances as of January 1, 2018:

	Cost	Accumulated Depreciation	Book Value
Land	$ 85,000	–	$ 85,000
Building	560,000	$(201,600)	358,400
Equipment	145,000	(30,000)	115,000
Patent	125,000	(50,000)	75,000

Togo's purchased all the assets at the beginning of 2016 (3 years ago). The building is depreciated over a 10-year service life using the double-declining-balance method and estimating no residual value. The equipment is depreciated over a nine-year useful life using the straight-line method with an estimated residual value of $10,000. The patent is estimated to have a five-year service life with no residual value and is amortized using the straight-line method. Depreciation and amortization have been recorded for 2016 and 2017.

Required:
1. For the year ended December 31, 2018, record depreciation expense for buildings and equipment. Land is not depreciated.
2. For the year ended December 31, 2018, record amortization expense for the patent.
3. Calculate the book value for each of the four long-term assets at December 31, 2018.

P7–8B New Deli is in the process of closing its operations. It sold its three-year-old ovens to Sicily Pizza for $341,000. The ovens originally cost $455,000 and had an estimated service life of 10 years and an estimated residual value of $30,000. New Deli uses straight-line depreciation for all equipment.

Required:
1. Calculate the balance in the Accumulated Depreciation account at the end of the third year.
2. Calculate the book value of the ovens at the end of the third year.
3. What is the gain or loss on the sale of the ovens at the end of the third year?
4. Record the sale of the ovens at the end of the third year.

Record amortization and prepare the intangible assets section (LO7–5)

Compute depreciation, amortization, and book value of long-term assets (LO7–4, 7–5)

Record the disposal of equipment (LO7–6)

Flip Side of P7–2B

Calculate and interpret ratios (LO7–7)

P7–9B Papa's Pizza is the market leader and Pizza Prince is an up-and-coming player in the highly competitive delivery pizza business. The companies reported the following selected financial data ($ in thousands):

	Papa's Pizza	Pizza Prince
Net sales	$24,128	$1,835
Net income	2,223	129
Total assets, beginning	14,998	919
Total assets, ending	15,465	1,157

Required:
1. Calculate the return on assets, profit margin, and asset turnover ratio for Papa's Pizza.
2. Calculate the return on assets, profit margin, and asset turnover ratio for Pizza Prince.
3. Which company has the higher profit margin and which company has the higher asset turnover?

Calculate and interpret ratios (LO7–7)

P7–10B Barry Sanders, likely the best running back to ever play football, has opened a successful used-car dealership. He has noted a higher than normal percentage of sales for trucks and SUVs with hauling capacity at his dealership. He is also aware that several of the best recreational lakes in the state are located nearby. Barry is considering expanding his dealership to include the sale of recreational boats. Barry provides the following projections of net sales, net income, and average total assets in support of his proposal.

	Cars Only	Cars and Boats
Net sales	$6,500,000	$7,700,000
Net income	500,000	700,000
Average total assets	1,700,000	1,900,000

Required:
1. Calculate Barry's return on assets, profit margin, and asset turnover for cars only.
2. Calculate Barry's return on assets, profit margin, and asset turnover for cars and boats.
3. Based on these ratios, what recommendation would you make?

ADDITIONAL PERSPECTIVES

Great Adventures

(This is a continuation of the Great Adventures problem from earlier chapters.)

Continuing Problem

AP7–1 Tony and Suzie see the need for a rugged all-terrain vehicle to transport participants and supplies. They decide to purchase a used Suburban. The cost of the Suburban is $12,000. The vehicle is purchased in late June and will be put into use on July 1, 2019. Annual insurance from **GEICO** runs $1,800 per year. The paint is starting to fade, so they spend an extra $3,000 to repaint the vehicle, placing the Great Adventures logo on the front hood, back, and both sides. An additional $2,000 is spent on a deluxe roof rack and a trailer hitch. The painting, roof rack, and hitch are all expected to increase the future benefits of the vehicle for Great Adventures. They expect to use the Suburban for five years and then sell the vehicle for $4,500.

Required:
1. Determine the amount that should be recorded for the new vehicle.
2. Indicate where any amounts not included in the Equipment account should be recorded.
3. Prepare a depreciation schedule using the straight-line method. Follow the example in Illustration 7–11, except the first and last years will have a half-year of depreciation to reflect the beginning of its service life on July 1, 2019.
4. Record the sale of the vehicle two years later on July 1, 2021, for $10,000.

American Eagle Outfitters, Inc.

Financial Analysis

AP7–2 Financial information for **American Eagle** is presented in **Appendix A** at the end of the book.

Required:
1. The summary of significant accounting policies is located in note 2 to the financial statements. Locate the section on property and equipment. What depreciation method does American Eagle use? What are the estimated useful lives for buildings, leasehold improvements, and fixtures and equipment?
2. Find note 7 entitled Property and Equipment. What are the cost and the book value of property and equipment? What is the trend in depreciation expense for the past three years?
3. Find note 10 entitled Leases. Retail stores, like American Eagle, tend to lease rather than buy their stores. What is the most common term for the store leases? What are the future minimum lease obligations under operating leases at January 31, 2015?

The Buckle, Inc.

Financial Analysis

AP7–3 Financial information for **Buckle** is presented in **Appendix B** at the end of the book.

Required:
1. The summary of significant accounting policies is located in note A to the financial statements. Locate the section on property and equipment. What depreciation method does Buckle use? What are the estimated useful lives for property and equipment? What are the estimated useful lives for buildings?
2. Find note D entitled Property and Equipment. What is the cost of property and equipment? What is the trend in property and equipment for the past two years?
3. Find note H entitled Commitments. Retail stores, like Buckle, tend to lease rather than buy their stores. What is the most common term for the leases? What are the future minimum rental commitments under operating leases as of January 31, 2015?

American Eagle Outfitters, Inc. vs. The Buckle, Inc.

Comparative Analysis

AP7–4 Financial information for **American Eagle** is presented in **Appendix A** at the end of the book, and financial information for **Buckle** is presented in **Appendix B** at the end of the book.

Required:
1. Calculate American Eagle's return on assets, profit margin, and asset turnover ratio.
2. Calculate Buckle's return on assets, profit margin, and asset turnover ratio.
3. Which company is doing better based on return on assets? Which company has the higher profit margin? Which company has the higher asset turnover?

Ethics

AP7–5 Companies often are under pressure to meet or beat Wall Street earnings projections in order to increase stock prices and also to increase the value of stock options. Some resort to earnings management practices to artificially create desired results.

Required:
1. How can a company increase earnings by changing its depreciation method?
2. How can a company increase earnings by changing the estimated service lives of depreciable assets?
3. How can a company increase earnings by changing the estimated residual value of depreciable assets?

Internet Research

AP7–6 Companies are increasingly making their accounting information, especially their annual reports, available through their websites. Select a well-known publicly traded company and go to its website. Look for the investment section, and then click on annual reports.

Select the most recent annual report. If you have difficulty, try another company. Answer the following questions based on the company's most recent annual report.

Required:

1. What is the official name of the company?
2. What is its fiscal year-end?
3. At the end of the year, what is the net balance in property, plant, and equipment? (*Hint: Requirements* 3 and 4 are reported in the balance sheet.)
4. Does the company have any intangible assets? If so, how much is reported for intangible assets?
5. What is the balance in accumulated depreciation? (*Hint:* This is either in the balance sheet or in a note about property, plant, and equipment.)
6. Which method of depreciation is used? (*Hint:* It's usually disclosed in the notes under summary of accounting policies.)

Written Communication

AP7–7 At a recent luncheon, you were seated next to Mr. Fogle, the president of a local company that manufactures food processors. He heard that you were in a financial accounting class and asked:

> "Why is it that I'm forced to record depreciation expense on my property when I could sell it for more than I originally paid? I thought that the purpose of the balance sheet is to reflect the value of my business and that the purpose of the income statement is to report the net change in value or wealth of a company. It just doesn't make sense to penalize my profits when the building hasn't lost any value."

At the conclusion of the luncheon, you promised to send him a short explanation of the rationale for current depreciation practices.

Required:

Prepare a memo to Mr. Fogle. Explain the accounting concept of depreciation and contrast this with the dictionary definition of depreciation.

Earnings Management

AP7–8 Edward L. Vincent is CFO of Energy Resources, Inc. The company specializes in the exploration and development of natural gas. It's near year-end, and Edward is feeling terrific. Natural gas prices have risen throughout the year, and Energy Resources is set to report record-breaking performance that will greatly exceed analysts' expectations. However, during an executive meeting this morning, management agreed to "tone down" profits due to concerns that reporting excess profits could encourage additional government regulations in the industry, hindering future profitability.

Edward decides to adjust the estimated service life of development equipment from 10 years to 6 years. He also plans to adjust estimated residual values on development equipment to zero as it is nearly impossible to accurately estimate residual values on equipment like this anyway.

Required:

1. Explain how the adjustment of estimated service life from 10 years to 6 years will affect depreciation expense and net income.
2. Explain how the adjustment of estimated residual values to zero will affect depreciation expense and net income.
3. In addition to heading off additional government regulations, why might Energy Resources have an incentive to report lower profits in the current period?

Answers to the Self-Study Questions

1. b   2. d   3. d   4. a   5. b   6. b   7. d   8. c   9. c   10. c

Current Liabilities

Learning Objectives

AFTER STUDYING THIS CHAPTER, YOU SHOULD BE ABLE TO:

- **LO8–1** Distinguish between current and long-term liabilities.
- **LO8–2** Account for notes payable and interest expense.
- **LO8–3** Account for employee and employer payroll liabilities.
- **LO8–4** Explain the accounting for other current liabilities.
- **LO8–5** Apply the appropriate accounting treatment for contingencies.

Analysis

- **LO8–6** Assess liquidity using current liability ratios.

UNITED AIRLINES: A FUTURE UP IN THE AIR

Do you think airlines like **American**, **Delta**, or **United** would be a good investment? Warren Buffett, a self-made billionaire based in Omaha, Nebraska, is regarded as one of the world's top investors. Years ago, he observed that the airline industry had not made a dime for investors in a century of manned flight. Buffett acknowledged his mistake in buying stock in **US Airways**, which later filed for Chapter 11 bankruptcy. In fact, American, Delta, and United Airlines have all filed for bankruptcy over the years and all three airlines have successfully emerged out of bankruptcy. In recent years, airlines have been a great investment providing returns exceeding the market average.

Companies must file for bankruptcy protection when they no longer are able to pay their liabilities as they become due. By carefully examining information in financial statements, investors and creditors can assess a company's profitability and its *liquidity*—its ability to pay currently maturing debt. Both profitability and liquidity help indicate a company's risk of filing for bankruptcy. Wise investors, like Warren Buffett, pay careful attention to these warning signs.

What are some of the current liabilities reported by companies in the airline industry? The airline industry is very labor-intensive, resulting in extensive payroll liabilities. Another substantial current liability for airlines is advance ticket sales. This liability, representing tickets sold for future flights, is in the billions of dollars for several major U.S. airlines. Airlines are also well known for their frequent-flyer programs. These programs have created liabilities for frequent-flyer incentives exceeding $100 million. Finally, a somewhat different type of liability airlines face is contingent liabilities. A *contingent liability* is a possible liability for which payment is contingent upon another event. An example is pending litigation. All of the major airlines report contingent liabilities related to unsettled litigation. With airlines incurring so many types of liabilities, it is no wonder many airlines have filed for bankruptcy.

In this chapter, we adopt an airline and travel theme in exploring current liabilities such as notes payable, payroll liabilities, other current liabilities, and contingent liabilities. At the end of the chapter, we compare liquidity ratios between **United Airlines** and **American Airlines**, to explore whether United or American is in a better position to pay their current liabilities as they come due.

© Bloomberg/Getty Images

CURRENT LIABILITIES

In the four preceding chapters, we worked our way down the asset side of the balance sheet, examining cash, accounts receivable, inventory, and long-term assets. We now turn to the other half of the balance sheet. In these next three chapters, we look at current liabilities (Chapter 8), long-term liabilities (Chapter 9), and stockholders' equity (Chapter 10).

Liabilities have three essential characteristics. Liabilities are: (1) probable *future* sacrifices of economic benefits, (2) arising from *present* obligations to other entities, (3) resulting from *past* transactions or events.[1] The definition of liabilities touches on the present, the future, and the past: A liability is a present responsibility to sacrifice assets in the future due to a transaction or other event that happened in the past.

Recall that assets represent probable future *benefits.* In contrast, liabilities represent probable future *sacrifices* of benefits. What benefits are sacrificed? Most liabilities require the future sacrifice of cash. For instance, accounts payable, notes payable, and salaries payable usually are paid in cash.

Can you think of a liability that requires paying something other than cash? One such liability is deferred revenue. Remember (from Chapter 3) that this liability arises when a company receives payment in advance of providing the product or service it's selling. This obligation requires giving up inventory or services rather than cash to satisfy the liability.

Current vs. Long-Term Classification

In a classified balance sheet, we categorize liabilities as either current or long-term. **In most cases, current liabilities are payable within one year, and long-term liabilities are payable more than one year from now.**

Current liabilities are *usually,* but not always, due within one year. But for some companies (a winery, for example), it takes longer than a year to perform the activities that produce revenue. We call the time it takes to produce revenue the *operating cycle.* If a company has an operating cycle longer than one year, its current liabilities are defined by the operating cycle rather than by the length of a year. For now, remember that in most cases (but not all) current liabilities are due within one year.

Distinguishing between current and long-term liabilities is important in helping investors and creditors assess risk. Given a choice, most companies would prefer to report a liability as long-term rather than current, because doing so may cause the firm to appear less risky. In turn, less-risky firms may enjoy lower interest rates on borrowing and command higher stock prices for new stock listings.

The Feature Story at the beginning of this chapter pointed out that the U.S. airline industry has experienced financial difficulties over the years, resulting in greater risk to investors. Several major airlines were forced into bankruptcy because they were unable to pay current liabilities as they became due. In Illustration 8–1 an excerpt from the annual report of **United Airlines** discusses the problem.

■ **LO8–1**
Distinguish between current and long-term liabilities.

Common Terms Current liabilities are also sometimes called *short-term liabilities* or *short-term debt.*

ILLUSTRATION 8–1
Bankruptcy of United Airlines

> **UNITED AIRLINES**
> **Management Discussion and Analysis (excerpt)**
>
> Over the past several years, United and indeed the entire airline industry have faced severe business challenges and fundamental industry changes which have produced material adverse impacts on earnings, financial position and liquidity.
> Operating revenues for the airline industry in general, as well as for United, have been adversely impacted by several factors. The growth of low cost carriers; excess seat capacity; pricing transparency; reduced demand for high-yield business travel; global events such as the war in Iraq, the outbreak of disease as well as the fear of terrorist attacks since September 11, 2001; and the enactment of federal taxes on ticket sales to fund additional airport security measures, have caused earnings to decline.

---

[1]"Elements of Financial Statements." 1985. *Statement of Financial Accounting Concepts No. 6* (Stamford, Conn.: FASB), par. 38.

What obligations do firms most frequently report as current liabilities? Notes payable, accounts payable, and payroll liabilities are three main categories. In addition, companies report a variety of other current liabilities, including deferred revenue, sales tax payable, and the current portion of long-term debt.

There is no prescribed order for presenting accounts within the current liabilities section of the balance sheet. Illustration 8–2 presents the current liabilities section for **Southwest Airlines**.

ILLUSTRATION 8–2

Current Liabilities Section for Southwest Airlines

SOUTHWEST AIRLINES Balance Sheet (partial) ($ in millions)	
Current liabilities:	
Current debt	$ 258
Accounts payable and accrued liabilities	2,768
Other current liabilities	2,897
Total current liabilities	$5,923

Like Southwest Airlines, many companies first list notes payable (which Southwest calls "current debt"), followed by accounts payable, and then other current liabilities. In keeping with this order, we discuss notes payable in the next section.

KEY POINT

In most cases, current liabilities are payable within one year, and long-term liabilities are payable more than one year from now.

Notes Payable

In Chapter 5, we saw how companies account for notes receivable. Here, we discuss the flip side—notes payable. Recall that notes receivable is an asset that creates interest revenue. In contrast, notes payable is a *liability* that creates interest *expense*.

When a company borrows cash from a bank, the bank requires the company to sign a note promising to repay the amount borrowed plus interest. The borrower reports its liability as notes payable. About two-thirds of bank loans are short-term. Companies often use short-term debt because it usually offers lower interest rates than long-term debt.

Assume **Southwest Airlines** borrows $100,000 from **Bank of America** on September 1, 2018, signing a 6%, six-month note for the amount borrowed plus accrued interest due six months later on March 1, 2019. On September 1, 2018, Southwest will receive $100,000 in cash and record the following:

■ **LO8–2**
Account for notes payable and interest expense.

September 1, 2018	Debit	Credit
Cash	**100,000**	
Notes Payable		**100,000**
(*Issue notes payable*)		

A	=	L	+	SE
+100,000				
		+100,000		

When a company borrows money, it pays the lender **interest** in return for using the lender's money during the term of the loan. Interest is stated in terms of an annual percentage rate to be applied to the face value of the loan. Because the stated interest rate is an *annual* rate, when calculating interest for a current note payable we must adjust for the fraction of the year the loan spans. We calculate interest on notes as:

$$\text{Interest} = \frac{\text{Face}}{\text{value}} \times \frac{\text{Annual}}{\text{interest rate}} \times \frac{\text{Fraction}}{\text{of the year}}$$

In the example above, how much interest cost does Southwest incur for the six-month period of the note from September 1, 2018, to March 1, 2019?

$$\$3,000 = \$100,000 \times 6\% \times 6/12$$

However, if Southwest's reporting period ends on December 31, 2018, the company should not wait until March 1, 2019, to record interest. Instead, the company records the four months' interest incurred during 2018 in an adjustment prior to preparing the 2018 financial statements. Since the firm will not pay the 2018 interest until the note becomes due (March 1, 2019), it records **interest payable,** as follows:

A = L + SE	December 31, 2018	Debit	Credit
−2,000 Exp ↑	**Interest Expense** (= $100,000 × 6% × 4/12)	**2,000**	
+2,000	**Interest Payable**		**2,000**
	(Record interest incurred, but not paid)		

> **COMMON MISTAKE**
>
> When calculating the number of months of interest, students sometimes mistakenly subtract December (month 12) from September (month 9) and get three months. However, the time from September 1 to December 31 includes both September and December, so there are four months. If you are ever in doubt, count out the months on your fingers. Your fingers never lie.

The purpose of the adjusting entry is to report four months' interest (September, October, November, and December) in 2018. Southwest will report the remaining $1,000 of interest (for January and February) in 2019. Since the firm won't actually pay the 2018 interest until March 1, 2019, its financial statements for the year ended December 31, 2018, will show interest payable of $2,000 along with notes payable of $100,000 as current liabilities in the balance sheet, and the "other expenses" section of the income statement will report interest expense of $2,000.

When the note comes due on March 1, 2019, Southwest Airlines will pay the face value of the loan ($100,000) plus the entire $3,000 interest incurred ($100,000 × 6% × 6/12). The $3,000 represents six months of interest—the four months of interest ($2,000) in 2018 previously recorded as interest payable and two months of interest ($1,000) in 2019. Southwest records these transactions on March 1, 2019, as follows:

A = L + SE	March 1, 2019	Debit	Credit
−100,000	**Notes Payable** (face value)	**100,000**	
−1,000 Exp ↑	**Interest Expense** (= $100,000 × 6% × 2/12)	**1,000**	
−2,000	**Interest Payable** (= $100,000 × 6% × 4/12)	**2,000**	
−103,000	**Cash**		**103,000**
	(Pay notes payable and interest)		

The entry on March 1 does the following:

- Removes the note payable ($100,000).
- Records interest expense for January and February 2019 ($1,000).
- Removes the interest payable recorded in the December 31, 2018 entry ($2,000).
- Reduces cash ($103,000).

Notice that we record interest expense incurred for four months in 2018 and two months in 2019, rather than recording all six months' interest expense in 2019 when we pay it.

KEY POINT

We record interest expense in the period in which we *incur* it, rather than in the period in which we pay it.

Flip Side

How would the lender, Bank of America, record this note? For the bank it's a **note receivable** rather than a note payable, and it generates **interest revenue** rather than interest expense. (You may want to review the discussion of notes receivable in Chapter 5.) The entries for Bank of America's loan are as follows:

September 1, 2018	Debit	Credit	A	=	L	+	SE
Notes Receivable	100,000		+100,000				
Cash		100,000	−100,000				
(Issue notes receivable)							

December 31, 2018	Debit	Credit	A	=	L	+	SE
Interest Receivable	2,000		+2,000				
Interest Revenue (= $100,000 × 6% × 4/12)		2,000					+2,000 Rev ↑
(Record interest earned, but not received)							

March 1, 2019	Debit	Credit	A	=	L	+	SE
Cash	103,000		+103,000				
Interest Revenue (= $100,000 × 6% × 2/12)		1,000					+1,000 Rev ↑
Interest Receivable (= $100,000 × 6% × 4/12)		2,000	−2,000				
Notes Receivable (face value)		100,000	−100,000				
(Collect notes receivable and interest)							

Assume **Delta Airlines** borrows $500,000 from **Chase Bank** on November 1, 2018, signing a 9%, six-month note payable.

Let's Review

mhhe.com/4fa32

Required:

1. Record the issuance of the note payable.
2. Record the adjustment for interest payable on December 31, 2018.
3. Record the payment of the note and interest at maturity.

Solution:

1. Record the issuance of the note payable.

November 1, 2018	Debit	Credit
Cash	500,000	
Notes Payable		500,000
(Issue note payable)		

2. Record the adjustment for interest payable on December 31, 2018.

December 31, 2018	Debit	Credit
Interest Expense (= $500,000 × 9% × 2/12)	**7,500**	
Interest Payable		**7,500**
(*Record interest incurred, but not paid*)		

3. Record the payment of the note and interest at maturity.

Suggested Homework:
BE8–1, BE8–2;
E8–2, E8–3;
P8–2A&B

May 1, 2019	Debit	Credit
Notes Payable	**500,000**	
Interest Expense (= $500,000 × 9% × 4/12)	**15,000**	
Interest Payable (= $500,000 × 9% × 2/12)	**7,500**	
Cash		**522,500**
(*Pay note payable and interest*)		

Many companies prearrange the terms of a note payable by establishing a line of credit with a bank. A line of credit is an informal agreement that permits a company to borrow up to a prearranged limit without having to follow formal loan procedures and prepare paperwork. Notes payable is recorded each time the company borrows money under the line of credit. However, no entry is made up front when the line of credit is first negotiated, since no money has yet been borrowed.

Decision Point

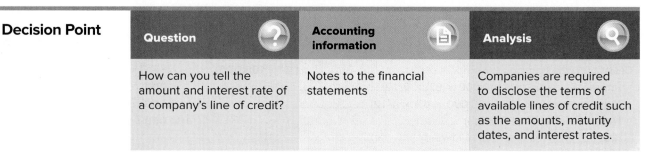

Question		Accounting information		Analysis	
How can you tell the amount and interest rate of a company's line of credit?		Notes to the financial statements		Companies are required to disclose the terms of available lines of credit such as the amounts, maturity dates, and interest rates.	

If a company borrows from another company rather than from a bank, the note is referred to as commercial paper. The recording for commercial paper is exactly the same as the recording for notes payable described earlier. Commercial paper is sold with maturities normally ranging from 30 to 270 days. Since a company is borrowing directly from another company, the interest rate on commercial paper is usually lower than on a bank loan. Because of this, commercial paper has thus become an increasingly popular way for large companies to raise funds.

 KEY POINT

Many short-term loans are arranged under an existing line of credit with a bank, or for larger corporations in the form of commercial paper, a loan from one company to another.

Accounts Payable

Accounts payable, sometimes called *trade accounts payable,* are amounts the company owes to suppliers of merchandise or services that it has bought on credit. We previously discussed accounts payable when we studied inventory purchases in Chapter 6. Briefly, recall that when a company purchases inventory on account (if it does not pay immediately with cash), it increases Inventory and Accounts Payable. Later, when the company pays the amount owed, it decreases both Cash and Accounts Payable. Most accounts are payable within one year and are therefore classified as current liabilities. Any accounts payable in more than one year would be classified as long-term liabilities.

Payroll Liabilities

Many companies, including those in the airline industry, are very labor-intensive. Payroll liabilities make up a significant portion of current liabilities for these companies. Here, we will look at how payroll is calculated for both the employee and the employer.

■ **LO8–3**
Account for employee and employer payroll liabilities.

Let's assume you are hired at a $60,000 annual salary with salary payments of $5,000 per month. Before making any spending plans, though, you need to realize that your paycheck will be much *less* than $5,000 a month. For instance, your employer will "withhold" amounts for (1) federal and state income taxes; (2) Social Security and Medicare; (3) health, dental, disability, and life insurance premiums; and (4) *employee* investments to retirement or savings plans. Realistically, then, your $5,000 monthly salary translates to much less in actual take-home pay as summarized next.

Monthly salary	$5,000
Less:	
Federal income taxes	(750)
State income taxes	(300)
Social Security and Medicare	(383)
Employee contributions for health insurance	(197)
Employee investments in retirement plan	(220)
= Actual take-home pay	$3,150

Now assume you hire an employee at a starting annual salary of $60,000. Your costs for this employee will be much *more* than $5,000 per month. Besides the $5,000 monthly salary, you will incur significant costs for (1) federal and state unemployment taxes; (2) the *employer* portion of Social Security and Medicare; (3) *employer* contributions for health, dental, disability, and life insurance; and (4) *employer* contributions to retirement or savings plans. With these additional costs, a $5,000 monthly salary could very easily create total costs in excess of $6,000 per month. Illustration 8–3 summarizes payroll costs for employees and employers. We discuss these costs next.

ILLUSTRATION 8–3
Payroll Costs for Employees and Employers

Employee Costs	**Employer Costs**
• Federal and state income taxes	• Federal and state unemployment taxes
• Employee portion of Social Security and Medicare	• Employer matching portion of Social Security and Medicare
• Employee contributions for health, dental, disability, and life insurance	• Employer contributions for health, dental, disability, and life insurance
• Employee investments in retirement or savings plans	• Employer contributions to retirement or savings plans

EMPLOYEE COSTS

Companies are required by law to withhold federal and state income taxes from employees' paychecks and remit these taxes to the government. The amount withheld varies according to the amount the employee earns and the number of exemptions the employee claims.

When comparing compensation among different career opportunities, don't base your final decision on salary alone. Various employers offer *fringe benefits*—also called "perquisites," or "perks"—that catch the attention of would-be employees: a pound of coffee every month at Starbucks, free skiing for employees at Vail Ski Resort, or scuba and kayaking in the pool at Nike's Athletic Village in Beaverton, Oregon. More common fringe benefits include employer coverage of family health insurance, educational benefits, and contributions to retirement or savings plans.

However, even more important than either salary *or* benefits are the training and experience the position offers. Training and experience can provide you with the skills necessary to land that big promotion or dream job in the future.

© Jim Arbogast/Photodisc/Getty Images, RF

IRS Publication 15, also called Circular E, is a valuable tool for employers, answering important payroll tax withholding questions as well as providing the individual tax tables. If you are able to claim more exemptions, you will have less tax withheld from your paycheck. Not all states require the payment of personal income taxes: Alaska, Florida, Nevada, South Dakota, Texas, Washington, and Wyoming have no state income tax. Two others, New Hampshire and Tennessee, tax only dividend and interest income.

Employers also withhold Social Security and Medicare taxes from employees' paychecks. Collectively, Social Security and Medicare taxes are referred to as FICA taxes, named for the Federal Insurance Contributions Act (FICA). This act requires employers to withhold a 6.2% Social Security tax up to a maximum base amount plus a 1.45% Medicare tax with no maximum. Therefore, the total FICA tax is 7.65% (6.2% + 1.45%) on income up to a base amount ($118,500 in 2015) and 1.45% on all income above the base amount. For example, if you earn less than $118,500, you will have 7.65% withheld from your check all year. However, if you earn, let's say, $168,500, you would have 7.65% withheld for FICA on the first $118,500 of your annual salary and then only 1.45% withheld on the remaining $50,000 earned during the rest of the year.[2]

Besides the required deductions for income tax and FICA taxes, employees may opt to have additional amounts withheld from their paychecks. These might include the employee portion of insurance premiums, employee investments in retirement or savings plans, and contributions to charitable organizations such as **United Way**. The employer records the amounts deducted from employee payroll as liabilities until it pays them to the appropriate organizations.

EMPLOYER COSTS

By law, the employer pays an additional (matching) FICA tax on behalf of the employee. The employer's limits on FICA tax are the same as the employee's. Thus, the government actually collects 15.3% (7.65% employee + 7.65% employer) on each employee's salary.

In addition to FICA, the employer also must pay federal and state unemployment taxes on behalf of its employees. The *Federal Unemployment Tax Act* (FUTA) requires a tax of 6.2% on the first $7,000 earned by each employee. This amount is reduced by a 5.4% (maximum) credit for contributions to state unemployment programs, so the net federal rate often is 0.8%. Under the *State Unemployment Tax Act* (SUTA), in many states the maximum state unemployment tax rate is 5.4%, but many companies pay a lower rate based on past employment history.[3]

 **COMMON MISTAKE**

Many people think FICA taxes are paid only by the employee. The employer is required to match the amount withheld for each employee, effectively doubling the amount paid into Social Security.

---

[2]High income earners pay an additional 0.9% for Medicare taxes above a certain income threshold. The threshold for this additional amount depends on the taxpayer's filing status. This additional amount is not matched by the employer.
[3]Employers also pay workers' comp (workers' compensation), a form of insurance providing wage replacement and medical benefits to employees injured on the job. Workers' comp is recorded as Insurance Expense.

Additional employee benefits paid for by the employer are referred to as fringe benefits. Employers often pay all or part of employees' insurance premiums and make contributions to retirement or savings plans. Many companies provide additional fringe benefits specific to the company or the industry. For instance, a fringe benefit in the airline industry is free flights for employees and their families. Some fringe benefits, like free skiing for employees of a ski resort, are usually not recorded in the accounting records.

To understand how employee and employer payroll costs are recorded, assume that Hawaiian Travel Agency has a total payroll for the month of January of $100,000 for its 20 employees. Its withholdings and payroll taxes are shown in Illustration 8–4.

Federal and state income tax withheld	$24,000
Health insurance premiums (Blue Cross) paid by employer	5,000
Contribution to retirement plan (Fidelity) paid by employer	10,000
FICA tax rate (Social Security and Medicare)	7.65%
Federal and state unemployment tax rate	6.2%

ILLUSTRATION 8–4

Payroll Example, Hawaiian Travel Agency

Hawaiian Travel Agency records the *employee* salary expense, withholdings, and salaries payable on January 31 as follows:

January 31	Debit	Credit		A = L + SE
Salaries Expense	100,000			−100,000 Exp ↑
Income Tax Payable		24,000		+24,000
FICA Tax Payable (= 0.0765 × $100,000)		7,650		+7,650
Salaries Payable (to balance)		68,350		+68,350
(*Record employee salary expense and withholdings*)				

Hawaiian Travel Agency also records its employer-provided fringe benefits as Salaries Expense and records the related credit balances to Accounts Payable:

January 31	Debit	Credit		A = L + SE
Salaries Expense (fringe benefits)	15,000			−15,000 Exp ↑
Accounts Payable (to Blue Cross)		5,000		+5,000
Accounts Payable (to Fidelity)		10,000		+10,000
(*Record employer-provided fringe benefits*)				

Hawaiian Travel Agency pays employer's FICA taxes at the same rate that the employees pay (7.65%) and also pays unemployment taxes at the rate of 6.2%. The agency records its *employer's* payroll taxes as follows:

January 31	Debit	Credit		A = L + SE
Payroll Tax Expense (total)	13,850			−13,850 Exp ↑
FICA Tax Payable (= 0.0765 × $100,000)		7,650		+7,650
Unemployment Tax Payable (= 0.062 × $100,000)		6,200		+6,200
(*Record employer payroll taxes*)				

Hawaiian Travel Agency incurred an additional $28,850 in expenses ($15,000 for fringe benefits plus $13,850 for employer payroll taxes) beyond the $100,000 salary expense. Also notice that the FICA tax payable in the *employee* withholding is the same amount recorded for *employer* payroll tax. That's because the employee pays 7.65% and the employer matches this amount with an additional 7.65%. The amounts withheld are then transferred at regular intervals, monthly or quarterly, to their designated recipients. Income taxes, FICA taxes, and unemployment taxes are transferred to various government agencies, and fringe benefits are paid to the company's contractual suppliers.

 KEY POINT

> Employee salaries are reduced by withholdings for federal and state income taxes, FICA taxes, and the employee portion of insurance and retirement contributions. The employer, too, incurs additional payroll expenses for unemployment taxes, the employer portion of FICA taxes, and employer insurance and retirement contributions.

Other Current Liabilities

■ **LO8–4**
Explain the accounting for other current liabilities.

Additional current liabilities companies might report include deferred revenues, sales tax payable, and the current portion of long-term debt. We explore each of these in more detail next.

DEFERRED REVENUES

United Airlines sells tickets and collects the cash price several days, weeks, or sometimes months before the actual flight. When does United Airlines record the revenue—when it sells the ticket, or when the flight actually takes place? Illustration 8–5 provides the answer, in United's disclosure of its revenue recognition policies.

ILLUSTRATION 8–5

Revenue Recognition Policy of United Airlines

UNITED AIRLINES
Notes to the Financial Statements (excerpt)

Airline Revenues—We record passenger fares and cargo revenues as operating revenues when the transportation is provided. The value of unused passenger tickets is included in current liabilities as advance ticket sales. We periodically evaluate the balance in advance ticket sales and record any adjustments in the period the evaluation is completed.

As you can see, United waits until the actual flight occurs to record the revenues. Since the flights have not taken place, the airline has not yet earned the revenue.

United's situation is not unique. It's not uncommon for companies to require advance payments from customers that will be applied to the purchase price when they deliver goods or provide services. You've likely been one of these customers. Examples of advance payments are gift cards from clothing stores like **American Eagle** or restaurants like **Chili's**, movie tickets from **Fandango**, room deposits at hotels like **Holiday Inn Express**, and subscriptions for magazines like *Sports Illustrated*.

How do these companies account for the cash they receive in advance? We initially discussed deferred revenue in Chapter 3, but let's review with an example. Assume **Apple Inc.** sells an iTunes gift card to a customer for $100. Apple records the sale of the gift card as follows:

A = L + SE		Debit	Credit
+100	Cash	100	
+100	Deferred Revenue		100
	(Receive cash for gift card)		

As you can see, Apple records the receipt of cash, but does not credit Sales Revenue. Rather, since the music has not been downloaded yet, the company credits Deferred Revenue, a liability account. While it may seem unusual for an account called Deferred Revenue to be a liability, think of it this way: Having already collected the cash, the company now has the *obligation* to provide a good or service.

COMMON MISTAKE

Some students incorrectly think the Deferred Revenue account is a revenue account, since the account has the word "Revenue" in the title. As indicated above, Deferred Revenue is a liability account, not a revenue account.

When the customer purchases and downloads, say, $15 worth of music, Apple records the following:

	Debit	Credit
Deferred Revenue	15	
Sales Revenue		15
(Record revenue from music downloaded)		

A = L + SE
−15
+15 Rev ↑

As the company earns revenue from music downloads, it decreases (debits) Deferred Revenue and increases (credits) Sales Revenue. The customer has a balance of $85 on his gift card, and Apple has a balance in Deferred Revenue, a liability account, of $85 for future music downloads.

KEY POINT

When a company receives cash in advance, it debits Cash and credits Deferred Revenue, a current liability account. When it earns the revenue, the company debits Deferred Revenue and credits Sales Revenue.

Let's Review

mhhe.com/4fa33

The **Dallas Cowboys** football stadium has a seating capacity of 80,000, expandable to 111,000 with standing-room-only capacity. The new stadium cost $1.15 billion, making it one of the most expensive sports stadiums ever built. The Cowboys hold eight regular season games at home; an average ticket sells for about $100 a game. Assume the Cowboys collect $48 million in season ticket sales prior to the beginning of the season. For eight home games, that's $6 million per game ($48 million ÷ 8 games).

Required:

1. Record the sale of $48 million in season tickets prior to the beginning of the season.
2. Record the $6 million in revenue recognized after the first game.

Solution:

1. Sale of $48 million in season ticket sales:

($ in millions)	Debit	Credit
Cash	48	
Deferred Revenue		48
(Sell season tickets prior to the beginning of the season)		

2. $6 million in revenue recognized after the first game:

($ in millions)	Debit	Credit
Deferred Revenue	6	
Sales Revenue		6
(Earn revenue for each home game played)		

Suggested Homework:
BE8–6,
E8–10;
P8–5A&B

The Cowboys would make similar entries after each home game.

SALES TAX PAYABLE

Most states impose a state sales tax, and many areas include a local sales tax as well. Yet, some states do not have a sales tax. Upon arriving in Oregon for the first time, Don ordered lunch at a fast-food restaurant. His meal cost $4.99. When the employee at the counter said, "You're not from Oregon, are you?", Don wondered aloud how the sales clerk could tell. The clerk politely replied, "You have five dollars and some change in your hand, but in Oregon there's no sales tax." States that currently don't impose a general state sales tax are Alaska, Delaware, Montana, New Hampshire, and Oregon. However, many cities in Alaska have *local* sales taxes. The other four states impose sales-type taxes on specific transactions such as lodging, tobacco, or gasoline sales.

Each company selling products subject to sales tax is responsible for collecting the sales tax directly from customers and periodically sending the sales taxes collected to the state and local governments. The selling company records sales revenue in one account and sales tax payable in another. **When the company collects the sales taxes, it increases (debits) Cash and increases (credits) Sales Tax Payable.**

 COMMON MISTAKE

Some students want to debit Sales Tax Expense. Note that a Sales Tax Expense account does not even exist. That's because, while sales tax is an expense for the consumer, it is not an expense for the company selling the goods or service. For the company, sales taxes are simply additional cash collected for taxes owed to the local or state government.

Let's look at an example. Suppose you buy lunch in the airport for $15 plus 10% sales tax. The airport restaurant records the transaction this way:

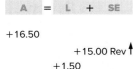

		Debit	Credit
Cash		**16.50**	
Sales Revenue			**15.00**
Sales Tax Payable (= $15 × 10%)			**1.50**
(Record sales and sales tax)			

A = L + SE
+16.50
        +15.00 Rev ↑
        +1.50

The amount of sales tax can also be computed by knowing the total cash for the transaction and the sales tax rate. For example, when the cashier at the airport asked you to pay $16.50 for lunch, you could have figured the amount of the sale versus the amount of the sales taxes if you knew the sales tax rate was 10%. If we divide the total cash of $16.50 by 1.10 (1 + 10% sales tax rate), we get $15 (= $16.50 ÷ 1.10) for the actual sale, leaving $1.50 as sales tax. In this situation, the general formula to determine sales tax can be stated as:

$$\text{Sales tax} = \text{Total cash paid} - \frac{\text{Total cash paid}}{1 + \text{Sales tax rate}}$$

 KEY POINT

Sales taxes collected from customers by the seller are not an expense. Instead, they represent current liabilities payable to the government.

CURRENT PORTION OF LONG-TERM DEBT

The current portion of long-term debt is the amount that will be paid within the next year. Management needs to know this amount in order to budget the cash flow necessary to pay the current portion as it comes due. Investors and lenders also pay attention to current debt because it provides information about a company's bankruptcy risk.

Long-term obligations (notes, mortgages, bonds) usually are reclassified and reported as current liabilities when they become payable within the upcoming year (or operating cycle, if longer than a year). For example, a firm reports a 10-year note payable as a long-term liability for nine years but as a current liability in the balance sheet prepared during the tenth year of its term to maturity.

As another example, **Southwest Airlines** had total borrowings of $2,692 million. Of that amount, $258 million is due in the next year and the remaining $2,434 million is recorded as long-term debt. In its balance sheet, the company records the $2,692 million in current and long-term debt, as shown in Illustration 8–6.

ILLUSTRATION 8–6
Current Portion of Long-Term Debt

SOUTHWEST AIRLINES
Balance Sheet (partial)
($ in millions)

Current liabilities:	
Current portion of long-term debt	$ 258
Long-term liabilities:	
Long-term debt	2,434
Total borrowings	$2,692

KEY POINT

We report the currently maturing portion of a long-term debt as a current liability in the balance sheet.

Decision Maker's Perspective

Current or Long-Term?

Given a choice, do you suppose management would prefer to report an obligation as a current liability or a long-term liability? Other things being equal, most managers would choose the long-term classification. The reason is that outsiders such as banks, bondholders, and shareholders usually consider debt that is due currently to be riskier than debt that is not due for some time. Riskier debt means paying higher interest rates for borrowing. So, be aware that management has incentives to report current obligations as long-term.

CONTINGENCIES

PART B

Many companies are involved in litigation disputes, in which the final outcome is uncertain. In its financial statements, does the company wait until the lawsuit is settled, or does it go ahead and report the details of the unsettled case? In this section, we discuss how to report these uncertain situations, which are broadly called contingencies. We look at contingent liabilities first and then their flip side, contingent gains.

■ **LO8–5**
Apply the appropriate accounting treatment for contingencies.

Contingent Liabilities

A contingent liability is an existing uncertain situation that *might* result in a loss depending on the outcome of a future event. Examples include lawsuits, product warranties, environmental problems, and premium offers. **Philip Morris**'s tobacco litigation, **Motorola**'s cell phone warranties, **BP**'s environmental obligations, and **United**'s frequent-flyer program are all contingent liabilities. Let's consider a litigation example.

LITIGATION AND OTHER CAUSES

Deloitte was the auditor for a client we'll call Jeeps, Inc. The client sold accessories for jeeps, such as tops, lights, cargo carriers, and hitches. One of the major issues that appeared in Deloitte's audit of Jeeps, Inc., was outstanding litigation. Several lawsuits against the company alleged that the jeep top (made of vinyl) did not hold in a major collision. The jeep manufacturer, **Chrysler**, also was named in the lawsuits. The damages claimed were quite large, about $100 million. Although the company had litigation insurance, there was some question whether the insurance company could pay because the insurance carrier was undergoing financial difficulty. The auditor discussed the situation with the outside legal counsel representing Jeeps, Inc.

What, if anything, should the auditor require Jeeps, Inc., to report because of the litigation? The outcome of the litigation was not settled by the end of the year, so no amount is yet legally owed. There are three options to consider for Jeeps, Inc.

1. Report a liability in the balance sheet for the full $100 million (or perhaps some lesser amount that is more likely to be owed),
2. Do not report a liability in the balance sheet, but provide full disclosure of the litigation in a note to the financial statements, or
3. Do not report a liability in the balance sheet and provide no disclosure in a note.

The option we choose depends on (1) the likelihood of payment and (2) the ability to estimate the amount of payment. Illustration 8–7 provides details for each of these criteria.

ILLUSTRATION 8–7

Criteria for Reporting a Contingent Liability

1. **The likelihood of payment is**
   a. *Probable*—likely to occur;
   b. *Reasonably possible*—more than remote but less than probable; or
   c. *Remote*—the chance is slight.

2. **The amount of payment is**
   a. *Reasonably estimable*; or
   b. *Not reasonably estimable.*

A contingent liability is recorded only if a loss is probable *and* the amount is reasonably estimable. In the case of Jeeps, Inc., above, if the auditor believes it is probable that Jeeps, Inc., will lose the $100 million lawsuit at some point in the future, Jeeps, Inc., would report a contingent liability for $100 million at the end of the year.

December 31 ($ in millions)	Debit	Credit
Loss	**100**	
Contingent Liability		**100**
(Record a contingent liability)		

The loss is reported in the income statement as either an operating or a nonoperating expense. The contingent liability is reported in the balance sheet as either a current or a long-term liability depending on when management expects the probable loss to be paid.

If the likelihood of payment is probable and if one amount within a range appears more likely, we record that amount. When no amount within the range appears more likely than others, we record the *minimum* amount and disclose the range of potential loss.

If the likelihood of payment is only *reasonably possible* rather than probable, we record no entry but make full disclosure in a note to the financial statements to describe the contingency. Finally, if the likelihood of payment is *remote*, disclosure usually is not required. Illustration 8–8 provides a summary of the accounting for contingent liabilities.

INTERNATIONAL FINANCIAL REPORTING STANDARDS (IFRS)

WHEN SHOULD CONTINGENT LIABILITIES BE REPORTED?

We record a contingent liability under U.S. GAAP if it's both probable and the amount is reasonably estimable. IFRS rules are similar, but the threshold is "more likely than not." This is a lower threshold than "probable," and thus, contingent liabilities are more likely to be recorded under IFRS rules than under U.S. GAAP.

For more discussion, see Appendix E.

ILLUSTRATION 8–8

Accounting Treatment of Contingent Liabilities

	Amount of payment is:	
Likelihood of payment is:	*Reasonably Estimable*	*Not Reasonably Estimable*
Probable	Liability recorded	Disclosure required
Reasonably possible	Disclosure required	Disclosure required
Remote	Disclosure not required	Disclosure not required

KEY POINT

A contingent liability is recorded only if a loss is **probable** *and* the amount is **reasonably estimatable**.

Back to the example of Jeeps, Inc.: How do you think Deloitte, as the auditor of Jeeps, Inc., treated the litigation described earlier? Based on the response of legal counsel, the likelihood of the payment occurring was considered to be remote, so disclosure was not required. Although this additional disclosure may not be required, it still may prove useful to investors and creditors evaluating the financial stability of a company involved in litigation. Since the amount was so large, and because there were concerns about the firm's primary insurance carrier undergoing financial difficulty, Deloitte insisted on full disclosure of the litigation in the notes to the financial statements.

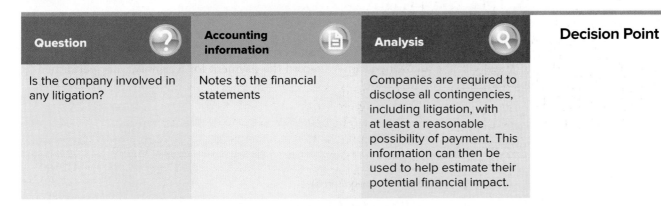

Decision Point

Question	Accounting information	Analysis
Is the company involved in any litigation?	Notes to the financial statements	Companies are required to disclose all contingencies, including litigation, with at least a reasonable possibility of payment. This information can then be used to help estimate their potential financial impact.

Illustration 8–9 provides excerpts from the disclosure of contingencies made by **United Airlines**.

WARRANTIES

Warranties are perhaps the most common example of contingent liabilities. When you buy a new **Dell** laptop, it comes with a warranty covering the hardware from defect for either a

ILLUSTRATION 8–9

Disclosure of
Contingencies by
United Airlines

UNITED AIRLINES
Notes to the Financial Statements (excerpts)

Legal and Environmental Contingencies. United Airlines has certain contingencies resulting from litigation and claims (including environmental issues) incident to the ordinary course of business. Management believes, after considering a number of factors, including (but not limited to) the views of legal counsel, the nature of contingencies to which we are subject and prior experience, that the ultimate disposition of these contingencies will not materially affect the Company's consolidated financial position or results of operations.

Contingency for Frequent-Flyer Program Awards. United's MileagePlus frequent-flyer program awards mileage credits to passengers who fly on United, United Express, and certain other airlines that participate in the program. When a travel award level is attained by a MileagePlus member, we record a liability for the estimated cost of such awards.

90-day, one-year, or two-year period depending on the product. Why does Dell offer a warranty? To increase sales, of course.

A company needs to record warranty expense in the same accounting period it sells you a product. The warranty for the computer represents an expense and a liability for Dell at the time of the sale because it meets the criteria for recording a contingent liability: Because warranties almost always entail an eventual expenditure, it's *probable* that a cost will be incurred. And even though Dell doesn't know exactly what that cost will be, it can, based on experience, *reasonably estimate* the amount. Let's look at a warranty example in more detail.

Dell introduces a new laptop computer in December that carries a one-year warranty against manufacturer's defects. Based on industry experience with similar product introductions, Dell expects warranty costs will be an amount equal to approximately 3% of sales. New laptop sales for the month of December are $1.5 million. Dell records the warranty liability on December 31 as follows:

A	=	L	+	SE		Debit	Credit
				−45,000 Exp ↑	**December 31**		
		+45,000			**Warranty Expense** ($1.5 million × 3%)	**45,000**	
					Warranty Liability		**45,000**
					(*Record liability for warranties*)		

When customers make warranty claims and Dell incurs costs to satisfy those claims, the liability is reduced. Let's say that customers make warranty claims costing Dell $12,000 in January of the following year. We record the payment for warranty work performed as follows:

A	=	L	+	SE		Debit	Credit
		−12,000			**January 31**		
−12,000					**Warranty Liability**	**12,000**	
					Cash		**12,000**
					(*Record actual warranty expenditures*)		

The entry above assumes Dell pays for all warranty costs with cash to simplify the transaction. Companies may also use employee labor hours, parts from inventory, or supplies in satisfying warranty claims. In that more complex case, we might credit Salaries Payable, Inventory, or Supplies rather than Cash.

Any time you need to calculate a balance, it's often helpful to make a T-account and record the transactions. Remember, journal entries show the transaction, while T-accounts give you the balance. The balance in the Warranty Liability account at the end of January is $33,000 as follows:

	Warranty Liability	
Actual payment	12,000	45,000	Estimated expense
		33,000	Final balance

COMMON MISTAKE

Some students think the balance in the Warranty Liability account is always equal to Warranty Expense. Remember, the Warranty Liability account is increased when the estimated warranty liability is recorded, but then is reduced over time by actual warranty expenditures.

Contingent Gains

A contingent gain is an existing uncertain situation that might result in a gain, which often is the flip side of contingent liabilities. In a pending lawsuit, one side—the defendant—faces a contingent liability, while the other side—the plaintiff—has a contingent gain. For example, **Polaroid** sued **Kodak** for patent infringement of its instant photography technology. Polaroid had a contingent gain, while Kodak faced a contingent loss.

As discussed earlier, we record contingent liabilities when the loss is probable and the amount is reasonably estimable. However, **we do not record contingent gains until the gain is certain.** The nonparallel treatment of contingent gains follows the same conservative reasoning that motivates reporting some assets (like inventory) at lower of cost and net realizable value. Specifically, it's desirable to anticipate losses, but recognizing gains should await their final settlement. Though firms do not record contingent gains in the accounts, they sometimes disclose them in notes to the financial statements.

KEY POINT

Unlike contingent liabilities, contingent gains are not recorded until the gain is certain and no longer a contingency.

Flip Side

© AP Images/David Parry

ANALYSIS

LIQUIDITY ANALYSIS
United Airlines vs. American Airlines

Liquidity refers to having sufficient cash (or other current assets convertible to cash in a relatively short time) to pay currently maturing debts. Because a lack of liquidity can result in financial difficulties or even bankruptcy, it is critical that managers as well as outside investors and lenders maintain close watch on this aspect of a company's well-being. Here we look at three liquidity measures: working capital, the current ratio, and the acid-test ratio. All three measures are calculated using current assets and current liabilities.

■ **LO8–6**
Assess liquidity using current liability ratios.

WORKING CAPITAL

The concept of working capital is straightforward. It is simply the difference between current assets and current liabilities:

$$\text{Working capital} = \text{Current assets} - \text{Current liabilities}$$

Working capital answers the question, "After paying our current obligations, how much will we have to work with?" For example, if you have $20 in your pocket and you know that you still owe $10 to your friend and $3 for parking, your working capital is $7. A large positive working capital is an indicator of liquidity—whether a company will be able to pay its current debts on time.

However, working capital is not the best measure of liquidity when comparing one company with another, because it does not control for the relative size of each company. In comparing companies, the current ratio and the acid-test ratio are better measures of a company's ability to pay its debts on time.

CURRENT RATIO

We calculate the current ratio by dividing current assets by current liabilities:

$$\text{Current ratio} = \frac{\text{Current assets}}{\text{Current liabilities}}$$

A current ratio greater than 1 indicates that there are more current assets than current liabilities. Recall that current assets include cash, current investments, accounts receivable, inventories, and prepaid expenses. As a rule of thumb, a current ratio of 1 or higher often reflects an acceptable level of liquidity. A current ratio of, say, 1.5 indicates that for every $1 of current liabilities, the company has $1.50 of current assets.

In general, the higher the current ratio, the greater the company's liquidity. But we should evaluate the current ratio, like other ratios, in the context of the industry in which the company operates. Keep in mind, though, that not all current assets are equally liquid, which leads us to another, more specific ratio for measuring liquidity.

 ETHICAL DILEMMA

© AP Images/David Parry

Airport Accessories (AA) has several loans outstanding with a local bank. The loan contract contains an agreement that AA must maintain a current ratio of at least 0.90. Micah, the assistant controller, estimates that the year-end current assets and current liabilities will be $2,100,000 and $2,400,000, respectively. These estimates provide a current ratio of only 0.875. Violation of the debt agreement will increase AA's borrowing costs because the loans will be renegotiated at higher interest rates.

Micah proposes that AA purchase inventory of $600,000 on credit before year-end. This will cause both current assets and current liabilities to increase by the same amount, but the current ratio will increase to 0.90. The extra $600,000 in inventory will be used over the next year. However, the purchase will cause warehousing costs and financing costs to increase.

Micah is concerned about the ethics of his proposal. What do you think?

ACID-TEST RATIO

Common Terms The acid-test ratio is also called the quick ratio.

The acid-test ratio, or *quick ratio,* is similar to the current ratio but is based on a more conservative measure of current assets available to pay current liabilities. We calculate it by dividing "quick assets" by current liabilities. Quick assets include only cash, current investments, and accounts receivable. By eliminating other current assets, such as inventory and prepaid expenses, that are less readily convertible into cash, the acid-test ratio may provide a better indication of a company's liquidity than does the current ratio.

$$\text{Acid-test ratio} = \frac{\text{Cash} + \text{Current investments} + \text{Accounts receivable}}{\text{Current liabilities}}$$

We interpret the acid-test ratio much like the current ratio, with one difference: We know that the current assets in the top half of the ratio are only those that can be quickly converted to cash. Thus, an acid-test ratio of, say, 1.5 would indicate that for every $1 of current liabilities, the company has $1.50 of current assets that are easily convertible to cash that might be used to help pay the current liabilities as they come due. As is true for other ratios, be sure to evaluate the acid-test ratio in the context of the industry in which the company operates.

KEY POINT

Working capital is the difference between current assets and current liabilities. The current ratio is equal to current assets divided by current liabilities. The acid-test ratio is equal to quick assets (cash, current investments, and accounts receivable) divided by current liabilities. Each measures a company's liquidity, its ability to pay currently maturing debts.

Decision Point

Question	Accounting information	Analysis
Does the company have enough cash to pay current liabilities as they come due?	Working capital, current ratio, and acid-test ratio	A high working capital, current ratio, or acid-test ratio generally indicates the ability to pay current liabilities on a timely basis.

Many companies in the airline industry struggle to maintain adequate liquidity. United Airlines declared bankruptcy in 2002 and emerged from bankruptcy in 2006. Similarly, American Airlines declared bankruptcy in 2011 and came out of bankruptcy two years later in late 2013. The recovery by American Airlines has been remarkable. Their share price increased from around $25 per share when they first came out of bankruptcy in December 2013 to over $50 per share, just one year later.

Let's Review

Let's compare **United Airlines'** liquidity ratios to those of **American Airlines** and see if the recovery from bankruptcy of American Airlines is reflected in stronger liquidity ratios. Selected financial data regarding current assets and current liabilities for United and American Airlines[4] are as follows.

mhhe.com/4fa34

($ in millions)	United	American
Current assets:		
Cash and cash equivalents	$ 2,623	$ 1,768
Current investments	2,382	6,309
Net receivables	1,737	1,771
Inventory	666	1,004
Other current assets	730	1,260
Total current assets	$ 8,138	$12,112
Current liabilities:		
Current debt	$ 2,117	$ 1,708
Accounts payable and accrued liabilities	7,401	4,668
Other current liabilities	2,990	7,059
Total current liabilities	$12,508	$13,435

---

[4]American Airlines Group (Ticker AAL) includes American Airlines, US Airways and Envoy Aviation.

Required:

1. Calculate and compare working capital for United Airlines and American Airlines.
2. Calculate the current ratio for United Airlines and American Airlines. Which company has a higher current ratio?
3. Calculate the acid-test (quick) ratio for United Airlines and American Airlines. Which company has a higher acid-test ratio?

Solution:

1. Working capital:

($ in millions)	Current Assets	−	Current Liabilities	=	Working Capital
United	$ 8,138	−	$12,508	=	$(4,370)
American	$12,112	−	$13,435	=	$(1,323)

Both companies have a negative working capital, in which current liabilities exceed current assets. United has a large negative working capital of $4,370 million; American has a smaller negative working capital of $1,323 million. That's about a $3 billion difference and likely a contributing factor to American Airlines' recovery in share price.

2. Current ratio:

($ in millions)	Current Assets	÷	Current Liabilities	=	Current Ratio
United	$ 8,138	÷	$12,508	=	0.65
American	$12,112	÷	$13,435	=	0.90

American has a higher current ratio, which would indicate better liquidity than United. American's current ratio is just below 1, indicating current assets are just a little less than current liabilities. On the other hand, United's current ratio is much lower indicating worse liquidity.

3. Acid-test (quick) ratio:

($ in millions)	Quick Assets	÷	Current Liabilities	=	Acid-Test Ratio
United	$6,742	÷	$12,508	=	0.54
American	$9,848	÷	$13,435	=	0.73

Remember that *quick assets* equal cash + current investments + net receivables.

By eliminating less-liquid current assets such as inventory and other current assets, the acid-test ratio often provides a better indicator of liquidity. Again, American Airlines has a higher acid-test ratio of 0.73, compared to only 0.54 for United Airlines.

We should be careful to evaluate liquidity measures in the context of an industry. The airlines have faced tough times and many airlines have struggled to maintain adequate liquidity. So, while American's current ratio and acid-test ratio exceed those for United Airlines, the liquidity for both companies likely does not compare well with companies in most other industries.

Suggested Homework:
BE8–15;
E8–16;
P8–9A&B

Decision Maker's Perspective

Indicators of Liquidity

If the firm's current ratio or acid-test ratio is lower than that of the industry as a whole, does that mean liquidity is a problem? Perhaps, but perhaps not. It does, though, raise a red flag that suggests caution when assessing other aspects of the company.

It's important to remember that each ratio is but one piece of the puzzle. For example, profitability is probably the best long-run indicator of liquidity. It is difficult to maintain liquidity over a string of consecutive loss years. Another consideration is that management may be very efficient in managing current assets so that some current assets—receivables or inventory—remain at minimum amounts. This is good for the company overall, but it may result in less-impressive current and acid-test ratios. The turnover ratios we discussed in Chapters 5 and 6, such as receivables turnover and inventory turnover, help measure the efficiency of asset management in this regard.

 COMMON MISTAKE

As a general rule, a higher current ratio is better. However, a high current ratio is not always a positive signal. Companies having difficulty collecting receivables or holding excessive inventory will also have a higher current ratio. Managers must balance the incentive for strong liquidity (yielding a higher current ratio) with the need to minimize levels of receivables and inventory (yielding a lower current ratio).

Effect of Transactions on Liquidity Ratios

It also is important to understand the effect of specific transactions on the current ratio and acid-test ratio. Both ratios have the same denominator, current liabilities, so a decrease in current liabilities will increase the ratios (dividing by a smaller number makes the ratio bigger). Likewise, an increase in current liabilities will decrease the ratios (dividing by a bigger number makes the ratio smaller).

How are the ratios affected by changes in current assets? It depends on which current asset changes. Both ratios include cash, current investments, and accounts receivable. An increase in any of those will increase *both* ratios. However, only the current ratio includes inventory and other current assets. An increase in inventory or other current assets will increase the current ratio, but not the acid-test ratio.

What about changes in current liabilities? Current liabilities are in the bottom half of the fraction (the denominator) for both ratios. Therefore, an increase in current liabilities will decrease both ratios, since we are dividing by a larger amount. Illustration 8–10 summarizes the effect of changes in current assets and current liabilities on the liquidity ratios.

	Changes that Increase the Ratio	Changes that Decrease the Ratio
Current Ratio	• Increase in current assets • Decrease in current liabilities	• Decrease in current assets • Increase in current liabilities
Acid-Test Ratio	• Increase in quick assets • Decrease in current liabilities	• Decrease in quick assets • Increase in current liabilities

ILLUSTRATION 8–10

Effect of Various Changes on the Liquidity Ratios

LIQUIDITY MANAGEMENT

Can management influence the ratios that measure liquidity? Yes, at least to some extent. A company can influence the timing of inventory and accounts payable recognition by asking suppliers to change their delivery schedules. For instance, a large airplane manufacturer like **Boeing** might delay the shipment and billing of certain inventory parts to receive them in early January rather than late December, reducing inventory and accounts payable at year-end. It can also choose to make additional purchases in late December, increasing inventory and accounts payable at year-end. Let's see how changes in the delivery of inventory affect the current ratio.

Assume a company with a current ratio of 1.25 (current assets of $5 million and current liabilities of $4 million) has a *debt covenant* with its bank that requires a minimum current ratio exceeding 1.25. A debt covenant is an agreement between a borrower and a lender that requires certain minimum financial measures be met or the lender can recall the debt. By delaying the receipt of $1 million in goods until early January, inventory and accounts payable would both be lower by $1 million than they would be without the delay. This, in turn, increases the current ratio to 1.33 (current assets of $4 million and current liabilities of $3 million), and the requirement of the debt covenant is met.

Now, let's look at what happens when the current ratio is less than 1.00. Assume the company has a current ratio of 0.75 (current assets of $3 million and current liabilities of $4 million) and has a *debt covenant* with its bank that requires a minimum current ratio exceeding 0.75. In this situation, delaying the delivery of $1 million decreases the current ratio even further to 0.67 (current assets of $2 million and current liabilities of $3 million).

Rather than delay delivery, the company could choose instead to purchase $1 million in additional inventory on credit. Then, inventory and accounts payable both increase by $1 million, raising the current ratio from 0.75 to 0.80 (current assets of $4 million and current liabilities of $5 million). This is what was proposed in the ethical dilemma presented earlier in the chapter. Investors and creditors should be aware of managerial activities that increase liquidity ratios, such as large fluctuations in inventory purchases near year-end or unusual variations in accounts payable balances.

KEY POINTS BY LEARNING OBJECTIVE

LO8–1   **Distinguish between current and long-term liabilities.**

In most cases, current liabilities are payable within one year and long-term liabilities are payable more than one year from now.

LO8–2   **Account for notes payable and interest expense.**

We record interest expense in the period we incur it, rather than in the period in which we pay it.

Many short-term loans are arranged under an existing line of credit with a bank, or for larger corporations in the form of commercial paper, a loan from one company to another.

LO8–3   **Account for employee and employer payroll liabilities.**

Employee salaries are reduced by withholdings for federal and state income taxes, FICA taxes, and the employee portion of insurance and retirement contributions. The employer, too, incurs additional payroll expenses for unemployment taxes, the employer portion of FICA taxes, and employer insurance and retirement contributions.

LO8–4   **Explain the accounting for other current liabilities.**

When a company receives cash in advance, it debits Cash and credits Deferred Revenue, a current liability account. When it earns the revenue, the company debits Deferred Revenue and credits Sales Revenue.

Sales taxes collected from customers by the seller are not an expense. Instead, they represent current liabilities payable to the government.

We report the currently maturing portion of a long-term debt as a current liability in the balance sheet.

LO8–5   **Apply the appropriate accounting treatment for contingencies.**

A contingent liability is recorded only if a loss is **probable** *and* the amount is **reasonably estimatable**.

Unlike contingent liabilities, contingent gains are not recorded until the gain is certain and no longer a contingency.

Analysis

LO8–6   Assess liquidity using current liability ratios.

Working capital is the difference between current assets and current liabilities. The current ratio is equal to current assets divided by current liabilities. The acid-test ratio is equal to quick assets (cash, short-term investments, and accounts receivable) divided by current liabilities. Each measures a company's liquidity, its ability to pay currently maturing debts.

GLOSSARY

Acid-test ratio: Cash, current investments, and accounts receivable divided by current liabilities; measures the availability of liquid current assets to pay current liabilities. **p. 390**

Commercial paper: Borrowing from another company rather than from a bank. **p. 378**

Contingencies: Uncertain situations that can result in a gain or a loss for a company. **p. 385**

Contingent gain: An existing uncertain situation that might result in a gain. **p. 389**

Contingent liability: An existing uncertain situation that might result in a loss. **p. 385**

Current liabilities: Debts that, in most cases, are due within one year. However, when a company has an operating cycle of longer than a year, its current liabilities are defined by the length of the operating cycle, rather than by the length of one year. **p. 374**

Current portion of long-term debt: Debt that will be paid within the next year. **p. 384**

Current ratio: Current assets divided by current liabilities; measures the availability of current assets to pay current liabilities. **p. 390**

Debt covenant: An agreement between a borrower and a lender requiring certain minimum financial measures be met or the lender can recall the debt. **p. 394**

Deferred revenue: Cash received in advance from a customer for products or services to be provided in the future. **p. 382**

FICA taxes: Based on the Federal Insurance Contributions Act; tax withheld from employees' paychecks and matched by employers for Social Security and Medicare. **p. 380**

Fringe benefits: Additional employee benefits paid for by the employer. **p. 381**

Liability: A present responsibility to sacrifice assets in the future due to a transaction or other event that happened in the past. **p. 374**

Line of credit: An informal agreement that permits a company to borrow up to a prearranged limit without having to follow formal loan procedures and prepare paperwork. **p. 378**

Liquidity: Having sufficient cash (or other assets convertible to cash in a relatively short time) to pay currently maturing debts. **p. 389**

Notes payable: Written promises to repay amounts borrowed plus interest. **p. 375**

Quick assets: Includes only cash, current investments, and accounts receivable. **p. 390**

Sales tax payable: Sales tax collected from customers by the seller, representing current liabilities payable to the government. **p. 384**

Unemployment taxes: A tax to cover federal and state unemployment costs paid by the employer on behalf of its employees. **p. 380**

Working capital: The difference between current assets and current liabilities. **p. 389**

SELF-STUDY QUESTIONS

1. Which of the following statements regarding liabilities is *not* true? **(LO8–1)**
   a. Liabilities can be for services rather than cash.
   b. Liabilities are reported in the balance sheet for almost every business.
   c. Liabilities result from future transactions.
   d. Liabilities represent probable future sacrifices of benefits.

2. Current liabilities: **(LO8–1)**
   a. May include contingent liabilities.
   b. Include obligations payable within one year or one operating cycle, whichever is shorter.

   c. Can be satisfied only with the payment of cash.
   d. Are preferred by most companies over long-term liabilities.

3. If Express Jet borrows $100 million on October 1, 2018, for one year at 6% interest, how much interest expense does it record for the year ended December 31, 2018? **(LO8–2)**
   a. $0.
   b. $1 million.
   c. $1.5 million.
   d. $6 million.

4. We record interest expense on a note payable in the period in which: **(LO8–2)**
   a. We pay cash for interest.
   b. We incur interest.
   c. We pay cash and incur interest.
   d. We pay cash or incur interest.

5. Which of the following is *not* deducted from an employee's salary? **(LO8–3)**
   a. FICA taxes.
   b. Unemployment taxes.
   c. Income taxes.
   d. Employee portion of insurance and retirement payments.

6. The seller collects sales taxes from the customer at the time of sale and reports the sales taxes as: **(LO8–4)**
   a. Sales tax expense.
   b. Sales tax revenue.
   c. Sales tax receivable.
   d. Sales tax payable.

7. Management can estimate the amount of loss that will occur due to litigation against the company. If the likelihood of loss is reasonably possible, a contingent liability should be: **(LO8–5)**
   a. Disclosed but not reported as a liability.
   b. Disclosed and reported as a liability.
   c. Neither disclosed nor reported as a liability.
   d. Reported as a liability but not disclosed.

8. Smith Co. filed suit against Western, Inc., seeking damages for patent infringement. Western's legal counsel believes it is probable that Western will settle the lawsuit for an estimated amount in the range of $75,000 to $175,000, with all amounts in the range considered equally likely. How should Western report this litigation? **(LO8–5)**
   a. As a liability for $75,000 with disclosure of the range.
   b. As a liability for $125,000 with disclosure of the range.
   c. As a liability for $175,000 with disclosure of the range.
   d. As a disclosure only. No liability is reported.

9. The acid-test ratio is: **(LO8–6)**
   a. Current assets divided by current liabilities.
   b. Cash and current investments divided by current liabilities.
   c. Cash, current investments, and accounts receivable divided by current liabilities.
   d. Cash, current investments, accounts receivable, and inventory divided by current liabilities.

10. Assuming a current ratio of 1.00 and an acid-test ratio of 0.75, how will the purchase of inventory with cash affect each ratio? **(LO8–6)**
   a. Increase the current ratio and increase the acid-test ratio.
   b. No change to the current ratio and decrease the acid-test ratio.
   c. Decrease the current ratio and decrease the acid-test ratio.
   d. Increase the current ratio and decrease the acid-test ratio.

Note: For answers, see the last page of the chapter.

For additional study materials, including 10 more multiple-choice Self-Study Questions, visit Connect.

REVIEW QUESTIONS

■ **LO8–1**　1. What are the essential characteristics of liabilities for purposes of financial reporting?

■ **LO8–1**　2. How do we define current liabilities? Long-term liabilities?

■ **LO8–1**　3. Why is it important to distinguish between current and long-term liabilities?

■ **LO8–1**　4. Provide examples of current liabilities in the airline industry.

■ **LO8–2**　5. Explain why we record interest in the period in which we incur it rather than in the period in which we pay it.

■ **LO8–2**　6. Bank loans often are arranged under existing lines of credit. What is a line of credit? How does a line of credit work?

■ **LO8–2**　7. How does commercial paper differ from a normal bank loan? Why is the interest rate often less for commercial paper?

■ **LO8–3**　8. Name at least four items withheld from employee payroll checks. Which deductions are required by law and which are voluntary?

■ **LO8–3**　9. Name at least four employer costs in addition to the employee's salary. Which costs are required by law and which are voluntary?

10. Who pays Social Security taxes: the employer, the employee, or both? How is the deduction for Social Security and Medicare (FICA) computed?   ■ **LO8–3**

11. How do retailers like **McDonald's**, **American Eagle**, and **Apple Inc.** account for the sale of gift cards?   ■ **LO8–4**

12. *Sports Illustrated* sells magazine subscriptions in advance of their distribution. (a) What journal entry would the company make at the time it sells subscriptions? (b) What journal entry would the company make each time it distributes a magazine?   ■ **LO8–4**

13. Like all retailers, **Hollister** is required to collect sales tax to be remitted to state and local government authorities. Assume a local store has cash proceeds from sales of $5,325, including $325 in sales tax. What is the sales tax rate? Provide the journal entry to record the proceeds.   ■ **LO8–4**

14. If $10 million of **Dell Inc.**'s $130 million notes payable is due in the next year, how will the firm present this debt within the current and long-term liabilities sections of the current year's balance sheet?   ■ **LO8–4**

15. Define contingent liability. Provide three common examples.   ■ **LO8–5**

16. List and briefly describe the three categories of likelihood that a payment for a contingent liability will need to be made.   ■ **LO8–5**

17. Under what circumstances should a firm report a contingent liability?   ■ **LO8–5**

18. Suppose the firm's analysis of a contingent liability indicates that an obligation is not probable. What accounting treatment, if any, is warranted?   ■ **LO8–5**

19. If a contingent liability is probable but estimable only within a range, what amount, if any, should the firm report?   ■ **LO8–5**

20. Your company is the plaintiff in a lawsuit. Legal counsel advises you that your eventual victory is inevitable. "You will be awarded $2 million," your attorney confidently asserts. Describe the appropriate accounting treatment.   ■ **LO8–5**

21. Current liabilities affect a company's liquidity. What is liquidity, and how do we evaluate it?   ■ **LO8–6**

22. Explain the differences among working capital, the current ratio, and the acid-test ratio.   ■ **LO8–6**

23. How would the following transactions affect the current ratio and the acid-test ratio? (a) Purchase of inventory with cash; and (b) sale of inventory for more than its cost. Assume that prior to these transactions the current ratio and acid-test ratio are both less than one.   ■ **LO8–6**

BRIEF EXERCISES

BE8–1 On November 1, Bahama Cruise Lines borrows $4 million and issues a six-month, 6% note payable. Interest is payable at maturity. Record the issuance of the note and the appropriate adjustment for interest expense at December 31, the end of the reporting period.

Record notes payable (LO8–2)
Flip Side of BE8–2

BE8–2 On November 1, Bahama National Bank lends $4 million and accepts a six-month, 6% note receivable. Interest is due at maturity. Record the acceptance of the note and the appropriate adjustment for interest revenue at December 31, the end of the reporting period.

Record notes receivable (LO8–2)
Flip Side of BE8–1

BE8–3 On July 1, Alaskan Adventures issues a $160,000, eight-month, 6% note. Interest is payable at maturity. What is the amount of interest expense that the company would record in a year-end adjustment on December 31?

Determine interest expense (LO8–2)

BE8–4 On April 1, Online Travel issues $13 million of commercial paper with a maturity on December 31 and a 9% interest rate. Record the issuance of the commercial paper and its repayment at maturity.

Record commercial paper (LO8–2)

McGraw Hill Education **connect**

Calculate FICA taxes (LO8–3)

BE8–5 Mike Samson is a college football coach making a base salary of $652,800 a year ($54,400 per month). Employers are required to withhold a 6.2% Social Security tax up to a maximum base amount and a 1.45% Medicare tax with no maximum. Assuming the FICA base amount is $118,500, compute how much will be withheld during the year for Coach Samson's Social Security and Medicare. What additional amount will the employer need to contribute?

Record deferred revenues (LO8–4)

BE8–6 On December 18, Intel receives $260,000 from a customer toward a cash sale of $2.6 million for computer chips to be completed on January 23. The computer chips had a total production cost of $1.6 million. What journal entries should Intel record on December 18 and January 23? Assume Intel uses the perpetual inventory system.

Record sales tax (LO8–4)

BE8–7 During December, Far West Services makes a $3,200 credit sale. The state sales tax rate is 6% and the local sales tax rate is 2.5%. Record sales and sales tax payable.

Report current portion of long-term debt (LO8–4)

BE8–8 On September 1, 2018, Southwest Airlines borrows $41 million, of which $10 million is due next year. Show how Southwest Airlines would record the $41 million debt on its December 31, 2018, balance sheet.

Calculate warranty liability (LO8–5)

BE8–9 Sony introduces a new compact music player to compete with Apple's iPod that carries a two-year warranty against manufacturer's defects. Based on industry experience with similar product introductions, warranty costs are expected to be approximately 3% of sales. By the end of the first year of selling the product, total sales are $31 million, and actual warranty expenditures are $300,000. What amount (if any) should Sony report as a liability at the end of the year?

Determine the financial statement effect of a contingent liability (LO8–5)

BE8–10 Consultants notify management of Discount Pharmaceuticals that a stroke medication poses a potential health hazard. Counsel indicates that a product recall is probable and is estimated to cost the company $8 million. How will this affect the company's income statement and balance sheet this period?

Account for a contingent liability (LO8–5)
Flip Side of BE8–12

BE8–11 Electronic Innovators is the defendant in a $10 million lawsuit filed by one of its customers, Aviation Systems. The litigation is in final appeal, and legal counsel advises that it is probable that Electronic Innovators will lose the lawsuit. The estimated amount is somewhere between $6 and $10 million. How should Electronic Innovators account for this event?

Account for a contingent gain (LO8–5)
Flip Side of BE8–11

BE8–12 Aviation Systems is involved in a $10 million lawsuit filed against one of its suppliers, Electronic Innovators. The litigation is in final appeal, and legal counsel advises that it is probable that Aviation Systems will win the lawsuit and be awarded somewhere between $6 and $10 million. How should Aviation Systems account for this event?

Determine the financial statement effect of a contingent liability (LO8–5)

BE8–13 The Environmental Protection Agency (EPA) is in the process of investigating a possible water contamination issue at the manufacturing facility of Northwest Forest Products. The EPA has not yet proposed a penalty assessment. Management feels an assessment is reasonably possible, and if an assessment is made, an unfavorable settlement is estimated between $20 and $30 million. How should Northwest Forest Products report this situation in its current financial statements?

Account for contingent liabilities (LO8–5)

BE8–14 Motorola is a world leader in the development of cellular phone technology. During the year, the company becomes aware of potential costs due to (1) a product defect that is reasonably possible and is reasonably estimable, (2) a safety hazard that is probable and cannot be reasonably estimated, and (3) a new product warranty that is probable and can be reasonably estimated. Which of these potential costs, if any, should Motorola record?

Calculate current and acid-test ratios (LO8–6)

BE8–15 Airline Accessories has the following current assets: cash, $112 million; receivables, $104 million; inventory, $192 million; and other current assets, $28 million. Airline Accessories has the following liabilities: accounts payable, $118 million; current portion of long-term debt, $45 million; and long-term debt, $33 million. Based on these amounts, calculate the current ratio and the acid-test ratio for Airline Accessories.

EXERCISES

E8–1 Match (by letter) the correct reporting method for each of the items listed below.

Determine proper classification of liabilities (LO8–1)

Reporting Method

C = Current liability
L = Long-term liability
D = Disclosure note only
N = Not reported

Item

_____ 1. Accounts payable.
_____ 2. Current portion of long-term debt.
_____ 3. Sales tax collected from customers.
_____ 4. Notes payable due next year.
_____ 5. Notes payable due in two years.
_____ 6. Advance payments from customers.
_____ 7. Commercial paper.
_____ 8. Unused line of credit.
_____ 9. A contingent liability with a *probable* likelihood of occurring within the next year and can be estimated.
_____ 10. A contingent liability with a *reasonably possible* likelihood of occurring within the next year and can be estimated.

E8–2 On November 1, 2018, Aviation Training Corp. borrows $60,000 cash from Community Savings and Loan. Aviation Training signs a three-month, 7% note payable. Interest is payable at maturity. Aviation's year-end is December 31.

Record notes payable (LO8–2)

Required:

1. Record the note payable by Aviation Training.
2. Record the appropriate adjustment for the note by Aviation Training on December 31, 2018.
3. Record the payment of the note at maturity.

E8–3 On August 1, 2018, Trico Technologies, an aeronautic electronics company, borrows $21 million cash to expand operations. The loan is made by FirstBanc Corp. under a short-term line of credit arrangement. Trico signs a six-month, 9% promissory note. Interest is payable at maturity. Trico's year-end is December 31.

Record notes payable (LO8–2)

Flip Side of E8–4

Required:

1. Record the issuance of the note by Trico Technologies.
2. Record the appropriate adjustment for the note by Trico on December 31, 2018.
3. Record the payment of the note by Trico at maturity.

E8–4 On August 1, 2018, Trico Technologies, an aeronautic electronics company, borrows $21 million cash to expand operations. The loan is made by FirstBanc Corp. under a short-term line of credit arrangement. Trico signs a six-month, 9% promissory note. Interest is payable at maturity. FirstBanc Corp.'s year-end is December 31.

Record notes receivable (LO8–2)

Flip Side of E8–3

Required:

1. Record the acceptance of the note by FirstBanc Corp.
2. Record the appropriate adjustment for the note by FirstBanc Corp. on December 31, 2018.
3. Record the receipt of cash by FirstBanc Corp. at maturity.

E8–5 OS Environmental provides cost-effective solutions for managing regulatory requirements and environmental needs specific to the airline industry. Assume that on July 1 the company issues a one-year note for the amount of $6 million. Interest is payable at maturity.

Determine interest expense (LO8–2)

Required:

Determine the amount of interest expense that should be recorded in a year-end adjusting entry under each of the following independent assumptions:

Interest Rate	Fiscal Year-End
1. 11%	December 31
2. 9%	September 30
3. 10%	October 31
4. 7%	January 31

Record a line of credit (LO8–2)

E8–6 The following selected transactions relate to liabilities of Rocky Mountain Adventures. Rocky Mountain's fiscal year ends on December 31.

January 13	Negotiate a revolving credit agreement with First Bank that can be renewed annually upon bank approval. The amount available under the line of credit is $10 million at the banks prime rate.
February 1	Arrange a three-month bank loan of $5 million with First Bank under the line of credit agreement. Interest at the prime rate of 7% is payable at maturity.
May 1	Pay the 7% note at maturity.

Required:

Record the appropriate entries, if any, on January 13, February 1, and May 1.

Calculate payroll withholdings and payroll taxes (LO8–3)

E8–7 Aspen Ski Resorts has 100 employees, each working 40 hours per week and earning $20 an hour. Although the company does not pay any health or retirement benefits, one of the perks of working at Aspen is that employees are allowed free skiing on their days off. Federal income taxes are withheld at 15% and state income taxes at 5%. FICA taxes are 7.65% of the first $118,500 earned per employee and 1.45% thereafter. Unemployment taxes are 6.2% of the first $7,000 earned per employee.

Required:

1. Compute the total salary expense, the total withholdings from employee salaries, and the actual direct deposit of payroll for the first week of January.
2. Compute the total payroll tax expense Aspen Ski Resorts will pay for the first week of January in addition to the total salary expense and employee withholdings calculated in *Requirement* 1.
3. How should Aspen Ski Resorts account for the free skiing given to employees on their days off?

Record payroll (LO8–3)

E8–8 During January, Luxury Cruise Lines incurs employee salaries of $3 million. Withholdings in January are $229,500 for the employee portion of FICA, $450,000 for federal income tax, $187,500 for state income tax, and $30,000 for the employee portion of health insurance (payable to **Blue Cross Blue Shield**). The company incurs an additional $186,000 for federal and state unemployment tax and $90,000 for the employer portion of health insurance.

Required:

1. Record the employee salary expense, withholdings, and salaries payable.
2. Record the employer-provided fringe benefits.
3. Record the employer payroll taxes.

Record payroll (LO8–3)

E8–9 Airline Temporary Services (ATS) pays employees monthly. Payroll information is listed below for January, the first month of ATS's fiscal year. Assume that none of the employees exceeds the federal unemployment tax maximum salary of $7,000 in January.

Salaries expense	$600,000
Federal and state income tax withheld	120,000
Federal unemployment tax rate	0.80%
State unemployment tax rate (after FUTA deduction)	5.40%
Social Security (FICA) tax rate	7.65%

Required:

Record salaries expense and payroll tax expense for the January pay period.

E8–10 **Apple Inc.** is the number one online music retailer through its iTunes music store. Apple sells iTunes gift cards in $15, $25, and $50 increments. Assume Apple sells $21 million in iTunes gift cards in November, and customers redeem $14 million of the gift cards in December.

Analyze and record deferred revenues (LO8–4)

Required:

1. Record the advance collection of $21 million for iTunes gift cards in November.
2. Record the revenue earned when $14 million in gift cards is redeemed in December.
3. What is the ending balance in the Deferred Revenue account?

E8–11 Top Sound International designs and sells high-end stereo equipment for auto and home use. Engineers notified management in December 2018 of a circuit flaw in an amplifier that poses a potential fire hazard. Further investigation indicates that a product recall is probable, estimated to cost the company $4 million. The fiscal year ends on December 31.

Analyze and record a contingent liability (LO8–5)

Required:

1. Should this contingent liability be reported, disclosed in a note only, or neither? Explain.
2. What loss, if any, should Top Sound report in its 2018 income statement?
3. What liability, if any, should Top Sound report in its 2018 balance sheet?
4. What entry, if any, should be recorded?

E8–12 Pacific Cruise Lines is a defendant in litigation involving a swimming accident on one of its three cruise ships.

Determine proper treatment of a contingent liability (LO8–5)

Required:

For each of the following scenarios, determine the appropriate way to report the situation. Explain your reasoning and record any necessary entry.

1. The likelihood of a payment occurring is probable, and the estimated amount is $1.3 million.
2. The likelihood of a payment occurring is probable, and the amount is estimated to be in the range of $1.1 to $1.6 million.
3. The likelihood of a payment occurring is reasonably possible, and the estimated amount is $1.3 million.
4. The likelihood of a payment occurring is remote, while the estimated potential amount is $1.3 million.

E8–13 Computer Wholesalers restores and resells notebook computers. It originally acquires the notebook computers from corporations upgrading their computer systems, and it backs each notebook it sells with a 90-day warranty against defects. Based on previous experience, Computer Wholesalers expects warranty costs to be approximately 6% of sales. Sales for the month of December are $600,000. Actual warranty expenditures in January of the following year were $13,000.

Record warranties (LO8–5)

Required:

1. Does this situation represent a contingent liability? Why or why not?
2. Record warranty expense and warranty liability for the month of December based on 6% of sales.
3. Record the payment of the actual warranty expenditures of $13,000 in January of the following year.
4. What is the balance in the Warranty Liability account after the entries in *Requirements* 2 and 3?

E8–14 **Dow Chemical Company** provides chemical, plastic, and agricultural products and services to various consumer markets. The following excerpt is taken from the disclosure notes of Dow's annual report.

Analyze disclosure of contingent liabilities (LO8–5)

> ### DOW CHEMICAL
> #### Notes to the Financial Statements (excerpt)
>
> Dow Chemical had accrued obligations of $381 million for environmental remediation and restoration costs, including $40 million for the remediation of Superfund sites. This is management's best estimate of the costs for remediation and restoration with respect to environmental matters for which the Company has accrued liabilities, although the ultimate cost with respect to these particular matters could range up to twice that amount. Inherent uncertainties exist in these estimates primarily due to unknown conditions, changing governmental regulations and legal standards regarding liability, and evolving technologies for handling site remediation and restoration.

Required:

1. Does the excerpt describe a contingent liability?
2. Under what conditions would Dow record such a contingency?
3. How did Dow record the $381 million?

Calculate and analyze liquidity ratios (LO8–6)

E8–15 Selected financial data regarding current assets and current liabilities for Queen's Line, a competitor in the cruise line industry, is provided:

($ in millions)	
Current assets:	
Cash and cash equivalents	$ 331
Current investments	63
Net receivables	230
Inventory	116
Other current assets	135
Total current assets	$ 875
Current liabilities:	
Accounts payable	$1,025
Short-term debt	694
Other current liabilities	919
Total current liabilities	$2,638

Required:

1. Calculate the current ratio and the acid-test ratio for Queen's Line.
2. Compare your calculations with those for United Airlines and American Airlines reported in the chapter text. Which company appears more likely to have difficulty paying its currently maturing debts?

Complete the accounting cycle using current liability transactions (LO 8-1, 8-2, 8-4, 8-6)

E8–16 On January 1, 2018, the general ledger of ACME Fireworks includes the following account balances:

Accounts	Debit	Credit
Cash	$ 25,100	
Accounts Receivable	46,200	
Allowance for Uncollectible Accounts		$ 4,200
Inventory	20,000	
Land	46,000	
Equipment	15,000	
Accumulated Depreciation		1,500
Accounts Payable		28,500
Notes Payable (6%, due April 1, 2019)		50,000
Common Stock		35,000
Retained Earnings		33,100
Totals	$152,300	$152,300

During January 2018, the following transactions occur:

January   2   Sold gift cards totaling $8,000. The cards are redeemable for merchandise within one year of the purchase date.

January   6   Purchase additional inventory on account, $147,000.

January   15   Firework sales for the first half of the month total $135,000. All of these sales are on account. The cost of the units sold is $73,800.

January   23   Receive $125,400 from customers on accounts receivable.

January   25   Pay $90,000 to inventory suppliers on accounts payable.

January   28   Write off accounts receivable as uncollectible, $4,800.

January   30   Firework sales for the second half of the month total $143,000. Sales include $11,000 for cash and $132,000 on account. The cost of the units sold is $79,500.

January   31   Pay cash for monthly salaries, $52,000.

Required:

1. Record each of the transactions listed above.
2. Record adjusting entries on January 31.
   a. Depreciation on the equipment for the month of January is calculated using the straight-line method. At the time the equipment was purchased, the company estimated a residual value of $3,000 and a two-year service life.
   b. At the end of January, $11,000 of accounts receivable are past due, and the company estimates that 30% of these accounts will not be collected. Of the remaining accounts receivable, the company estimates that 5% will not be collected.
   c. Accrued interest expense on notes payable for January.
   d. Accrued income taxes at the end of January are $13,000.
   e. By the end of January, $3,000 of the gift cards sold on January 2 have been redeemed.
3. Prepare an adjusted trial balance as of January 31, 2018, after updating beginning balances (above) for transactions during January (*Requirement* 1) and adjusting entries at the end of January (*Requirement* 2).
4. Prepare a multiple-step income statement for the period ended January 31, 2018.
5. Prepare a classified balance sheet as of January 31, 2018.
6. Record closing entries.
7. Analyze the following for ACME Fireworks:
   a. Calculate the current ratio at the end of January. If the average current ratio for the industry is 1.8, is ACME Fireworks more or less liquid than the industry average?
   b. Calculate the acid-test ratio at the end of January. If the average acid-test ratio for the industry is 1.5, is ACME Fireworks more or less likely to have difficulty paying its currently maturing debts (compared to the industry average)?
   c. Assume the notes payable were due on April 1, 2018, rather than April 1, 2019. Calculate the revised current ratio at the end of January, and indicate whether the revised ratio would *increase, decrease,* or remain *unchanged* compared to your answer in (a).

PROBLEMS: SET A

P8–1A Listed below are several terms and phrases associated with current liabilities. Pair each item from List A (by letter) with the item from List B that is most appropriately associated with it.

Review current liability terms and concepts (LO8–1)

List A	List B
_____ 1. An IOU promising to repay the amount borrowed plus interest.	a. Recording of a contingent liability.
_____ 2. Payment amount is reasonably possible and is reasonably estimable.	b. Deferred revenue.
_____ 3. Mixture of liabilities and equity a business uses.	c. The riskiness of a business's obligations.
_____ 4. Payment amount is probable and is reasonably estimable.	d. Disclosure of a contingent liability.

(continued)

(concluded)

_____ 5. A liability that requires the sacrifice of something other than cash.

_____ 6. Long-term debt maturing within one year.

_____ 7. FICA and FUTA.

_____ 8. Informal agreement that permits a company to borrow up to a prearranged limit.

_____ 9. Classifying liabilities as either current or long-term helps investors and creditors assess this.

_____ 10. Amount of note payable × annual interest rate × fraction of the year.

e. Interest on debt.
f. Payroll taxes.
g. Line of credit.
h. Capital structure.
i. Note payable.
j. Current portion of long-term debt.

Record notes payable and notes receivable (LO8–2)

P8–2A Precision Castparts, a manufacturer of processed engine parts in the automotive and airline industries, borrows $41 million cash on October 1, 2018, to provide working capital for anticipated expansion. Precision signs a one-year, 9% promissory note to Midwest Bank under a prearranged short-term line of credit. Interest on the note is payable at maturity. Each firm has a December 31 year-end.

Required:

1. Prepare the journal entries on October 1, 2018, to record (a) the notes payable for Precision Castparts and (b) the notes receivable for Midwest Bank.
2. Record the adjustments on December 31, 2018, for (a) Precision Castparts and (b) Midwest Bank.
3. Prepare the journal entries on September 30, 2019, to record payment of (a) the notes payable for Precision Castparts and (b) the notes receivable for Midwest Bank.

Record payroll (LO8–3)

P8–3A Caribbean Tours' total payroll for the month of January was $600,000. The following withholdings, fringe benefits, and payroll taxes apply:

Federal and state income tax withheld	$60,000
Health insurance premiums paid by employer (payable to **Blue Cross**)	10,800
Contribution to retirement plan paid by employer (payable to **Fidelity**)	24,000
FICA tax rate (Social Security and Medicare)	7.65%
Federal and state unemployment tax rate	6.20%

Assume that none of the withholdings or payroll taxes has been paid by the end of January (record them as payables), and no employee's cumulative wages exceed the relevant wage bases.

Required:

1. Record the employee salary expense, withholdings, and salaries payable.
2. Record the employer-provided fringe benefits.
3. Record the employer payroll taxes.

Record payroll (LO8–3)

P8–4A Vacation Destinations offers its employees the option of contributing up to 7% of their salaries to a voluntary retirement plan, with the employer matching their contribution. The company also pays 100% of medical and life insurance premiums. Assume that no employee's cumulative wages exceed the relevant wage bases. Payroll information for the first biweekly payroll period ending February 14 is listed below.

Wages and salaries	$1,500,000
Employee contribution to voluntary retirement plan	63,000
Medical insurance premiums paid by employer	31,500
Life insurance premiums paid by employer	6,000
Federal and state income tax withheld	375,000
Social Security tax rate	6.20%
Medicare tax rate	1.45%
Federal and state unemployment tax rate	6.20%

Required:
1. Record the employee salary expense, withholdings, and salaries payable.
2. Record the employer-provided fringe benefits.
3. Record the employer payroll taxes.

P8–5A The University of Michigan football stadium, built in 1927, is the largest college stadium in America, with a seating capacity of 114,000 fans. Assume the stadium sells out all six home games before the season begins, and the athletic department collects $102.6 million in ticket sales.

Record deferred revenues (LO8–4)

Required:
1. What is the average price per season ticket and average price per individual game ticket sold?
2. Record the advance collection of $102.6 million in ticket sales.
3. Record the revenue earned after the first home game is completed.

P8–6A Texas Roadhouse opened a new restaurant in October. During its first three months of operation, the restaurant sold gift cards in various amounts totaling $3,500. The cards are redeemable for meals within one year of the purchase date. Gift cards totaling $728 were presented for redemption during the first three months of operation prior to year-end on December 31. The sales tax rate on restaurant sales is 4%, assessed at the time meals (not gift cards) are purchased. Texas Roadhouse will remit sales taxes in January.

Record deferred revenues and sales taxes (LO8–4)

Required:
1. Record (in summary form) the $3,500 in gift cards sold (keeping in mind that, in actuality, the firm would record each sale of a gift card individually).
2. Record the $728 in gift cards redeemed. (*Hint:* The $728 includes a 4% sales tax of $28.)
3. Determine the balance in the Deferred Revenue account (remaining liability for gift cards) Texas Roadhouse will report on the December 31 balance sheet.

P8–7A The ink-jet printing division of Environmental Printing has grown tremendously in recent years. Assume the following transactions related to the ink-jet division occur during the year ended December 31, 2018.

Record contingencies (LO8–5)

Required:
Record any amounts as a result of each of these contingencies.
1. Environmental Printing is being sued for $11 million by Addamax. Plaintiff alleges that the defendants formed an unlawful joint venture and drove it out of business. The case is expected to go to trial later this year. The likelihood of payment is reasonably possible.
2. Environmental Printing is the plaintiff in an $9 million lawsuit filed against a competitor in the high-end color-printer market. Environmental Printing expects to win the case and be awarded between $6.5 and $9 million.
3. Environmental Printing recently became aware of a design flaw in one of its ink-jet printers. A product recall appears probable. Such an action would likely cost the company between $500,000 and $900,000.

P8–8A Dinoco Petroleum faces three potential contingency situations, described below. Dinoco's fiscal year ends December 31, 2018, and it issues its 2018 financial statements on March 15, 2019.

Record contingencies (LO8–5)

Required:
Determine the appropriate means of reporting each situation for the year ended December 31, 2018, and record any necessary entries. Explain your reasoning.
1. In the initial trial, Dinoco lost a $130 million lawsuit resulting from a dispute with a supplier. The case is under appeal. Although Dinoco is unable to predict the outcome, it does not expect the case to have a material adverse effect on the company.
2. In November 2017, the state of Texas filed suit against Dinoco, seeking civil penalties and injunctive relief for violations of environmental laws regulating hazardous waste. On January 12, 2019, Dinoco reached a settlement with state authorities. Based upon discussions with legal counsel, it is probable that Dinoco will require $150 million to cover the cost of violations.

3. Dinoco is the plaintiff in a $300 million lawsuit filed against a customer for damages due to lost profits from rejected contracts and for unpaid receivables. The case is in final appeal, and legal counsel advises that it is probable Dinoco will prevail and be awarded $150 million.

Calculate and analyze ratios (LO8–6)

P8–9A Selected financial data regarding current assets and current liabilities for ACME Corporation and Wayne Enterprises, are as follows:

($ in millions)	ACME Corporation	Wayne Enterprises
Current assets:		
Cash and cash equivalents	$ 2,494	$ 541
Current investments		125
Net receivables	1,395	217
Inventory	10,710	8,600
Other current assets	773	301
Total current assets	$15,372	$9,784
Current liabilities		
Current debt	$ 1,321	$ 47
Accounts payable and accrued liabilities	8,871	5,327
Other current liabilities	1,270	2,334
Total current liabilities	$11,462	$7,708

Required:
1. Calculate the current ratio for ACME Corporation and Wayne Enterprises. Which company has the better ratio?
2. Calculate the acid-test (quick) ratio for ACME Corporation and Wayne Enterprises. Which company has the better ratio?
3. How would the purchase of additional inventory on credit affect the current ratio? How would it affect the acid-test ratio?

PROBLEMS: SET B   connect

Review current liability terms and concepts (LO8–1)

P8–1B Listed below are several terms and phrases associated with current liabilities. Pair each item from List A (by letter) with the item from List B that is most appropriately associated with it.

List A	List B
_____ 1. Interest expense is recorded in the period interest is incurred rather than in the period interest is paid.	a. The riskiness of a business's obligations.
_____ 2. Payment is reasonably possible and is reasonably estimable.	b. Current portion of long-term debt.
_____ 3. Cash, current investments, and accounts receivable all divided by current liabilities.	c. Recording a contingent liability.
_____ 4. Payment is probable and is reasonably estimable.	d. Disclosure of a contingent liability.
_____ 5. Gift cards.	e. Interest expense.
_____ 6. Long-term debt maturing within one year.	f. FICA.
_____ 7. Social Security and Medicare.	g. Commercial paper.
_____ 8. Unsecured notes sold in minimum denominations of $25,000 with maturities up to 270 days.	h. Acid-test ratio.
	i. Accrual accounting.
_____ 9. Classifying liabilities as either current or long-term helps investors and creditors assess this.	j. Deferred revenue.
_____ 10. Incurred on notes payable.	

P8–2B Eskimo Joe's, designer of the world's second best-selling T-shirt (just behind **Hard Rock Cafe**), borrows $21 million cash on November 1, 2018. Eskimo Joe's signs a six-month, 7% promissory note to Stillwater National Bank under a prearranged short-term line of credit. Interest on the note is payable at maturity. Each firm has a December 31 year-end.

Record notes payable and notes receivable (LO8–2)

Required:
1. Prepare the journal entries on November 1, 2018, to record (a) the notes payable for Eskimo Joe's and (b) the notes receivable for Stillwater National Bank.
2. Record the adjustment on December 31, 2018, for (a) Eskimo Joe's and (b) Stillwater National Bank.
3. Prepare the journal entries on April 30, 2019, to record payment of (a) the notes payable for Eskimo Joe's and (b) the notes receivable for Stillwater National Bank.

P8–3B Kashi Sales, L.L.C., produces healthy, whole-grain foods such as breakfast cereals, frozen dinners, and granola bars. Assume payroll for the month of January was $500,000 and the following withholdings, fringe benefits, and payroll taxes apply:

Record payroll (LO8–3)

Federal and state income tax withheld	$135,000
Health insurance premiums (**Blue Cross**) paid by employer	13,000
Contribution to retirement plan (**Fidelity**) paid by employer	60,000
FICA tax rate (Social Security and Medicare)	7.65%
Federal and state unemployment tax rate	6.20%

Assume that Kashi has paid none of the withholdings or payroll taxes by the end of January (record them as payables), and no employee's cumulative wages exceed the relevant wage bases.

Required:
1. Record the employee salary expense, withholdings, and salaries payable.
2. Record the employer-provided fringe benefits.
3. Record the employer payroll taxes.

P8–4B Emily Turnbull, president of Aerobic Equipment Corporation, is concerned about her employees' well-being. The company offers its employees free medical, dental, and life insurance coverage. It also matches employee contributions to a voluntary retirement plan up to 6% of their salaries. Assume that no employee's cumulative wages exceed the relevant wage bases. Payroll information for the biweekly payroll period ending January 24 is listed below.

Record payroll (LO8–3)

Wages and salaries	$2,500,000
Employee contribution to voluntary retirement plan	125,000
Medical insurance premiums paid by employer	50,000
Dental insurance premiums paid by employer	17,500
Life insurance premiums paid by employer	8,750
Federal and state income tax withheld	537,500
FICA tax rate	7.65%
Federal and state unemployment tax rate	6.20%

Required:
1. Record the employee salary expense, withholdings, and salaries payable.
2. Record the employer-provided fringe benefits.
3. Record the employer payroll taxes.

P8–5B Named in honor of the late Dr. F. C. "Phog" Allen, the Kansas Jayhawks' head coach for 39 years, Allen Fieldhouse is labeled by many as one of the best places in America to watch a college basketball game. Allen Fieldhouse has a seating capacity of 16,300. Assume

Record deferred revenues (LO8–4)

the basketball arena sells out all 16 home games before the season begins, and the athletic department collects $9,128,000 in ticket sales.

Required:

1. What is the average price per season ticket and average price per individual game ticket sold?
2. Record the advance collection of $9,128,000 in ticket sales.
3. Record the revenue earned after the first home game is completed.

Record deferred revenues and sales taxes (LO8–4)

P8–6B **Logan's Roadhouse** opened a new restaurant in November. During its first two months of operation, the restaurant sold gift cards in various amounts totaling $2,300. The cards are redeemable for meals within one year of the purchase date. Gift cards totaling $742 were presented for redemption during the first two months of operation prior to year-end on December 31. The sales tax rate on restaurant sales is 6%, assessed at the time meals (not gift cards) are purchased. Logan's will remit sales taxes in January.

Required:

1. Record (in summary form) the $2,300 in gift cards sold (keeping in mind that, in actuality, each sale of a gift card or a meal would be recorded individually).
2. Record the $742 in gift cards redeemed. (*Hint:* The $742 includes a 6% sales tax of $42.)
3. Determine the balance in the Deferred Revenue account (remaining liability for gift cards) to be reported on the December 31 balance sheet.

Record contingencies (LO8–5)

P8–7B Compact Electronics is a leading manufacturer of digital camera equipment. Assume the following transactions occur during the year ended December 31, 2018.

Required:

Record any amounts as a result of each of these contingencies.

1. Accounts receivable were $29 million (all credit) at the end of 2018. Although no specific customer accounts have been shown to be uncollectible, the company estimates that 3% of accounts receivable will eventually prove uncollectible.
2. Compact Electronics is the plaintiff in a $5 million lawsuit filed against a supplier. The suit is in final appeal, and attorneys advise it is virtually certain that Compact Electronics will win and be awarded $3.5 million.
3. In November 2018, Compact Electronics became aware of a design flaw in one of its digital camera models. A product recall appears probable and would likely cost the company $600,000.
4. Compact Electronics is the defendant in a patent infringement lawsuit brought by a competitor. It appears reasonably likely Compact Electronics will lose the case, and potential losses are estimated to be in the range of $2.5 to $3.5 million.

Record contingencies (LO8–5)

P8–8B Authors Academic Press faces three potential contingency situations, described below. Authors' fiscal year ends December 31, 2018.

Required:

Determine the appropriate means of reporting each situation for the year ended December 31, 2018, and record any necessary entries. Explain your reasoning.

1. In August 2018, a worker was injured in an accident, partially as a result of his own negligence. The worker has sued the company for $1.2 million. Legal counsel believes it is reasonably possible that the outcome of the suit will be unfavorable, and that the settlement would cost the company from $300,000 to $600,000.
2. A suit for breach of contract seeking damages of $3 million was filed by an author on October 4, 2018. Legal counsel believes an unfavorable outcome is probable. A reasonable estimate of the award to the plaintiff is between $1.5 million and $2.25 million. No amount within this range is a better estimate of potential damages than any other amount.
3. Authors is the plaintiff in a pending court case. Its lawyers believe it is probable that Authors will be awarded damages of $3 million.

P8–9B Selected financial data regarding current assets and current liabilities for Ferris Air and Oceanic Airlines are provided as follows:

Calculate and analyze ratios (LO8–6)

($ in millions)	Ferris Air	Oceanic Airlines
Current assets:		
Cash and cash equivalents	$1,113	$ 2,791
Current investments	1,857	958
Net receivables	578	2,156
Inventory	469	1,023
Other current assets	210	1,344
Total current assets	$4,227	$ 8,272
Current liabilities:		
Current debt	$ 271	$ 1,627
Accounts payable and accrued liabilities	2,209	5,686
Other current liabilities	2,170	5,957
Total current liabilities	$4,650	$13,270

Required:
1. Calculate the current ratio for Ferris Air and Oceanic Airlines. Which company has the better current ratio?
2. Calculate the acid-test (quick) ratio for Ferris Air and Oceanic Airlines. Which company has the better acid-test ratio?
3. How would the purchase of additional inventory with cash affect the current ratio? How would it affect the acid-test ratio?

ADDITIONAL PERSPECTIVES

Great Adventures

(This is a continuation of the Great Adventures problem from earlier chapters.)

AP8–1 Great Adventures is a defendant in litigation involving a biking accident during one of its adventure races. The front tire on one of the bikes came off during the race, resulting in serious injury to the rider. However, Great Adventures can document that each bike was carefully inspected prior to the race. It may have been that the rider loosened the wheel during the race and then forgot to tighten the quick-release mechanism.

Continuing Problem

Required:
For each of the following scenarios, determine the appropriate way to report the situation. Explain your reasoning and record any necessary entry.
1. The likelihood of a payment occurring is probable, and the estimated amount is $120,000.
2. The likelihood of a payment occurring is probable, and the amount is estimated to be in the range of $100,000 to $150,000.
3. The likelihood of a payment occurring is reasonably possible, and the estimated amount is $120,000.
4. The likelihood of a payment occurring is remote, while the estimated potential amount is $120,000.

American Eagle Outfitters, Inc.

Financial Analysis

AP8–2 Financial information for **American Eagle** is presented in **Appendix A** at the end of the book.

Required:

1. Calculate the current ratio for the past two years. Did the current ratio improve or weaken in the more recent year?
2. Calculate the acid-test (quick) ratio for the past two years. Did the acid-test ratio improve or weaken in the more recent year?
3. If American Eagle used $100 million in cash to pay $100 million in accounts payable, how would its current ratio and acid-test ratio change? Show your calculations.

Financial Analysis

The Buckle, Inc.

AP8–3 Financial information for **Buckle** is presented in **Appendix B** at the end of the book.

Required:

1. Calculate the current ratio for the past two years. Did the current ratio improve or weaken in the more recent year?
2. Calculate the acid-test (quick) ratio for the past two years. Did the acid-test ratio improve or weaken in the more recent year?
3. If Buckle purchased $50 million of inventory by debiting Inventory and crediting Accounts Payable, how would its current ratio and acid-test ratio change? Show your calculations.

Comparative Analysis

American Eagle Outfitters, Inc. vs. The Buckle, Inc.

AP8–4 Financial information for **American Eagle** is presented in **Appendix A** at the end of the book, and financial information for **Buckle** is presented in **Appendix B** at the end of the book.

Required:

1. Calculate the current ratio for both companies for the year ended January 31, 2015. Which company has the better ratio? Compare your calculations with those for **United Airlines** and **American Airlines** reported in the chapter text. Which industry maintains a higher current ratio?
2. Calculate the acid-test (quick) ratio for both companies for the year ended January 31, 2015. Which company has the better ratio? Compare your calculations with those for United Airlines and American Airlines reported in the chapter text. Which industry maintains a higher acid-test ratio?
3. How would the purchase of additional inventory with accounts payable affect the current ratio for these two companies?

Ethics

AP8–5 Eugene Wright is CFO of Caribbean Cruise Lines. The company designs and manufactures luxury boats. It's near year-end, and Eugene is feeling kind of queasy. The economy is in a recession, and demand for luxury boats is way down. Eugene did some preliminary liquidity analysis and noted the company's current ratio is slightly below the 1.2 minimum stated in its debt covenant with First Federal Bank. Eugene realizes that if the company reports a current ratio below 1.2 at year-end, the company runs the risk that First Federal will call its $10 million loan. He just cannot let that happen.

Caribbean Cruise Lines has current assets of $12 million and current liabilities of $10.1 million. Eugene decides to delay the delivery of $1 million in inventory purchased on account from the originally scheduled date of December 26 to a new arrival date of January 3. This maneuver will decrease inventory and accounts payable by $1 million at December year-end. Eugene believes the company can somehow get by without the added inventory, as manufacturing slows down some during the holiday season.

Required:

1. How will the delay in the delivery of $1 million in inventory purchased on account affect the company's current ratio on December 31? Provide supporting calculations of the current ratio before and after this proposed delivery delay.
2. Is this practice ethical? Provide arguments both for and against.

Internet Research

AP8–6 A very helpful site to learn about individual publicly traded companies is *finance. yahoo.com*. Go to this website and look up a well-known publicly traded company. Once you find the company page, perform the following tasks.

Required:
1. Click on "Basic Chart." How has the stock price changed over the past year?
2. Click on "Profile." In what industry does the company operate?
3. Click on "Key Statistics." What is the current ratio for the company?
4. Click on "SEC Filings." When was the most recent 10-K, also called the annual report, submitted?
5. Click on "Competitors." Who are the company's primary competitors?

Written Communication

AP8–7 Western Manufacturing is involved with several potential contingent liabilities. Your assignment is to draft the appropriate accounting treatment for each situation described below. Western's fiscal year-end is December 31, 2018, and the financial statements will be issued in early February 2019.

a. During 2018, Western experienced labor disputes at three of its plants. Management hopes an agreement will soon be reached. However, negotiations between the company and the unions have not produced an acceptable settlement, and employee strikes are currently under way. It is virtually certain that material costs will be incurred, but the amount of possible costs cannot be reasonably estimated.

b. Western warrants most products it sells against defects in materials and workmanship for a period of a year. Based on its experience with previous product introductions, warranty costs are expected to approximate 2% of sales. A new product introduced in 2018 had sales of $2 million, and actual warranty expenditures incurred so far on the product are $25,000. The only entry made so far relating to warranties on this new product was to debit Warranty Expense $25,000 and credit Cash $25,000.

c. Western is involved in a suit filed in January 2019 by Crump Holdings seeking $88 million, as an adjustment to the purchase price in connection with the company's sale of its textile business in 2018. The suit alleges that Western misstated the assets and liabilities used to calculate the purchase price for the textile division. Legal counsel advises that it is reasonably possible that Western could lose up to $88 million.

Required:
In a memo, describe the appropriate means of reporting each situation and explain your reasoning.

Earnings Management

AP8–8 Quattro Technologies, a hydraulic manufacturer in the aeronautics industry, has reported steadily increasing earnings over the past few years. The company reported net income of $120 million in 2016 and $140 million in 2017. The stock is receiving increasing analyst attention because many investors expect the steady earnings growth to continue well into the future.

One of the factors increasing sales is the superior warranty Quattro offers. Based on experience, warranty expense in 2018 should be around $40 million. However, in a recent executive meeting it was suggested that the CFO report a larger, more conservative, estimate of warranty expense. Income before warranty expense in 2018 is $210 million. By recording a warranty expense of $50 million this year, Quattro could maintain its steady earnings growth and be in a better position to maintain earnings growth again next year.

Required:
1. Can Quattro use warranty expense to manage its earnings? How?
2. Assume income before warranty expense is $210 million in 2018 and 2019, and total warranty expense over the two years is $80 million. What is the impact of the executive meeting suggestion on income in 2018? In 2019?
3. Is the executive meeting suggestion ethical? What would you do if you were the CFO?

Answers to the Self-Study Questions
1. c   2. a   3. c   4. b   5. b   6. d   7. a   8. a   9. c   10. b

Long-Term Liabilities

Learning Objectives

AFTER STUDYING THIS CHAPTER, YOU SHOULD BE ABLE TO:

- **LO9–1** Explain financing alternatives.
- **LO9–2** Account for installment notes payable.
- **LO9–3** Understand the balance sheet effects of operating and capital leases.
- **LO9–4** Identify the characteristics of bonds.
- **LO9–5** Determine the price of a bond issue.
- **LO9–6** Account for the issuance of bonds.
- **LO9–7** Record the retirement of bonds.

Analysis

- **LO9–8** Make financial decisions using long-term liability ratios.

SIX FLAGS: THE UPS AND DOWNS OF BORROWING

Can you name the largest chain of amusement parks in the world? Would you guess **Disney**? **Six Flags** actually is larger, with 18 amusement and water parks across North America. The first Six Flags amusement park, *Six Flags Over Texas,* was built in 1961 in Arlington, between Dallas and Fort Worth. The park is named for the six different flags that have flown over the state of Texas during its history—the flags of Spain, France, Mexico, the Republic of Texas, the United States, and the Confederate States of America.

What is the top-rated amusement park in the world? Six Flags? Disney? Guess again. Cedar Point, in Sandusky, Ohio, is known as the roller-coaster capital of the world. With a lineup that includes three of the top 10 steel roller coasters, Cedar Point is a coaster lover's dream come true. Its parent firm, **Cedar Fair Entertainment Company**, owns and operates 15 amusement parks and 7 water parks across North America.

Both Six Flags and Cedar Fair are listed on the New York Stock Exchange, Six Flags under the ticker symbol SIX and Cedar Fair under the ticker symbol FUN. Both carry a very high level of long-term debt, increasing their risk of bankruptcy. In fact, Six Flags entered into bankruptcy in 2009 and successfully restructured the company, coming out of bankruptcy in 2010. In recent years, both companies have been excellent investments with share prices worth almost 5 times what the price was just 5 years earlier. However, investors must pay careful attention to company performance, especially with the added risk associated with higher levels of long-term liabilities.

Assuming more debt can be either good or bad. If a company earns a rate of return higher than the interest rate on its debt, borrowing additional funds can increase overall profitability. On the other hand, if a company earns a rate of return lower than the interest rate on its debt, borrowing additional funds will further reduce profitability and may even result in bankruptcy proceedings.

In this chapter, we focus on long-term liabilities such as installment notes, leases, and bonds. At the end of the chapter, we look at at how debt affects the riskiness and profitability of **Coca-Cola** and **Pepsi**.

© Thinkstock/Getty Images, RF

PART A

LONG-TERM DEBT

Suppose you are the chief financial officer (CFO) for California Coasters, a company that designs, manufactures, and installs roller coasters. The executives at your company have an idea for a new ride that could revolutionize the amusement park industry. A ride like this could spur a huge increase in sales volume and create the opportunity to expand the idea to amusement parks around the world. But growth requires funding. Let's consider the financing alternatives available.

Financing Alternatives

■ **LO9–1**
Explain financing alternatives.

Some of the funds needed to pay for a company's growth can come from the profits generated by operations. Profits generated by the company are a source of *internal financing*. Frequently, though, companies must rely on funds from those outside the company to pay for operations. Funds coming from those outside of the company are sources of *external financing*. Let's look back at the basic accounting equation:

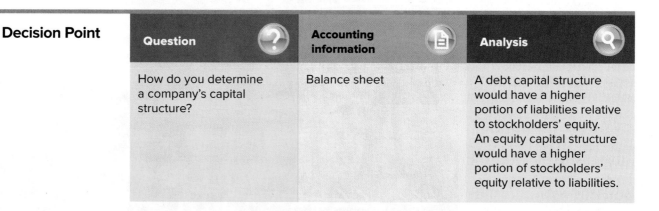

Assets =	**Liabilities** +	**Stockholders' Equity**
(resources)	(creditors' claims)	(owners' claims)

The right side of the accounting equation reveals the two sources of external financing—debt financing and equity financing. Debt financing refers to borrowing money from creditors (liabilities). Equity financing refers to obtaining investment from stockholders (stockholders' equity).

Amusement parks, like **Six Flags** or **Cedar Fair**, typically use debt financing to a greater extent for their financing. High-tech companies, like **Google** or **Microsoft**, use equity financing to a greater extent to finance their asset growth. The mixture of liabilities and stockholders' equity a business uses is called its capital structure.

Decision Point

Question ❓	Accounting information 📄	Analysis 🔍
How do you determine a company's capital structure?	Balance sheet	A debt capital structure would have a higher portion of liabilities relative to stockholders' equity. An equity capital structure would have a higher portion of stockholders' equity relative to liabilities.

Why would a company choose to borrow money rather than issue additional stock in the company? One of the primary reasons relates to taxes. **Interest expense incurred when borrowing money is tax-deductible, whereas dividends paid to stockholders are *not* tax-deductible.** Interest expense incurred on debt reduces taxable income; paying dividends to stockholders does not reduce taxable income because dividends are not an expense. Therefore, debt can be a less costly source of external financing.

 KEY POINT

Companies obtain external funds through debt financing (liabilities) and equity financing (stockholders' equity). One advantage of debt financing is that interest on borrowed funds is tax-deductible.

Companies have three primary sources of long-term debt financing: notes, leases, and bonds. We discuss each of these sources of long-term debt financing next, beginning with installment notes.

Installment Notes

You may have purchased a car, or maybe even a house. If so, unless you paid cash, you signed a note promising to pay the purchase price over, say, 4 years for the car or 30 years for the house. Car loans and home loans usually call for payment in monthly installments rather than by a single amount at maturity. Companies, too, often borrow cash using installment notes. **Each installment payment includes both an amount that represents interest and an amount that represents a reduction of the outstanding loan balance.** The periodic reduction of the balance is enough that at maturity the note is completely paid.

To illustrate, assume that California Coasters obtains a $25,000, 6%, four-year loan for a new delivery truck on January 1, 2018. Payments of $587.13 are required at the end of each month for 48 months.[1] An amortization schedule provides a summary of the cash paid, interest expense, and decrease in carrying value for each monthly payment. Illustration 9–1 provides a partial amortization schedule for the loan.

■ **LO9–2**
Account for installment notes payable.

ILLUSTRATION 9–1
Amortization Schedule for an Installment Note

mhhe.com/4fa35

(1)	(2)	(3) Interest Expense	(4) Decrease in Carrying Value	(5) Carrying Value
Date	Cash Paid	Carrying Value × Market Rate	(2) − (3)	Prior Carrying Value − (4)
1/1/18				$25,000.00
1/31/18	$587.13	$125.00	$462.13	24,537.87
2/28/18	587.13	122.69	464.44	24,073.43
*	*	*	*	*
*	*	*	*	*
11/30/21	587.13	5.83	581.30	584.21
12/31/21	587.13	2.92	584.21	0

First calculate interest expense as the carrying value times the market rate (6% × 1/12 = 0.5% per month in this example). The difference between the cash paid and interest expense each month equals the decrease in carrying value. Finally, the prior carrying value less the decrease in carrying value equals the new balance in carrying value. Notice the following features of the amortization schedule:

1. The carrying value (also referred to as the principal) begins at $25,000, the original amount of the loan.
2. The carrying value decreases with each monthly payment, but only for a portion of the cash paid. By the end of the four-year loan, the carrying value equals $0.
3. With each monthly cash payment, the portion assigned to interest expense becomes less and the portion that reduces the carrying value becomes more.
4. Interest expense equals a constant percentage of the prior month's carrying value. Since carrying value decreases over time, interest expense also decreases over time.

California Coasters records the note of $25,000 and the first two monthly payments of $587.13 as follows:

January 1, 2018	Debit	Credit		A	=	L	+	SE
Cash	**25,000**			+25,000				
Notes Payable		**25,000**				+25,000		
(Issue a note payable)								

---

[1]The monthly payment of $587.13 is based on the following financial calculator inputs: future value, $0; present value, $25,000; market interest rate, 0.5% (6% ÷ 12 periods each year); periods to maturity, 48 (4 years × 12 periods each year)—and solving for the monthly payment (PMT).

A	=	L	+	SE

−125.00 Exp ↑
−462.13
−587.13

January 31, 2018

Interest Expense (= $25,000 × 6% × 1/12)	**125.00**	
Notes Payable (difference)	**462.13**	
Cash (monthly payment)		**587.13**
(Pay monthly installment on note)		

A	=	L	+	SE

−122.69 Exp ↑
−464.44
−587.13

February 28, 2018

Interest Expense (= $24,537.87 × 6% × 1/12)	**122.69**	
Notes Payable (difference)	**464.44**	
Cash (monthly payment)		**587.13**
(Pay monthly installment on note)		

Notice that the amounts used in recording the monthly payments come directly from the amortization schedule.

KEY POINT

Most notes payable require periodic installment payments. Each installment payment includes an amount that represents interest expense and an amount that represents a reduction of the outstanding loan balance.

Leases

■ LO9–3
Understand the balance sheet effects of operating and capital leases.

If you have ever leased a car or an apartment, you are familiar with leasing. A lease is a contractual arrangement by which the *lessor* (owner) provides the *lessee* (user) the right to use an asset for a specified period of time.

Leasing has grown to be the most popular method of external financing of corporate assets in America. The airplane in which you last flew probably was leased, as was the gate from which it departed. Your favorite clothing store at the local shopping mall likely leases the space it operates. In fact, many financing companies exist for the sole purpose of acquiring assets and leasing them to others.

Decision Maker's Perspective

Why Do Many Companies Lease Rather Than Buy?

1. *Leasing improves cash flows through up to 100% financing.* In a purchase, most lenders require a down payment up to 20%. In contrast, leasing may allow you to finance up to the entire purchase price, freeing cash for other uses.

2. *Leasing improves the balance sheet by reducing long-term debt.* If the lease is an operating lease, the lessee reports only rent expense, avoiding the reporting of long-term debt on the balance sheet.

3. *Leasing can lower income taxes.* Many companies today find that purchasing equipment causes them to be faced with an extra income tax burden under the alternative minimum tax (AMT) calculations. Leasing can help avoid these additional taxes.

For accounting purposes, we have two basic types of leases: operating leases and capital leases. Operating leases are like rentals. If you lease a car for a week, you really have no intention of owning the car. The lessor owns the asset, and the lessee simply uses the asset temporarily. Over the lease term, the lessee records rent expense and the lessor records rent revenue.

Illustration 9–2 presents **Six Flags**'s disclosure of operating leases. Note that Six Flags has over $163 million in expected future payments under operating lease contracts.

ILLUSTRATION 9–2

Six Flags's Disclosure
of Operating Leases

SIX FLAGS, INC.
Notes to the Financial Statements

Future minimum obligations under operating leases, including site leases, at December 31, 2014, are summarized as follows (in thousands):

Year ending December 31, 2014

2015	$ 6,002
2016	6,033
2017	5,888
2018	3,514
2019	3,478
2020 and thereafter	138,134
Total	$163,049

However, not all leases are simply rentals. Capital leases occur when the lessee essentially buys an asset and borrows the money through a lease to pay for the asset. For example, let's say California Coasters leases rather than buys the delivery truck, signing a four-year lease at 6% interest that automatically transfers ownership of the truck to California Coasters at the end of the lease term. The dealership (the lessor) calculates the lease payments to cover the purchase price of the truck plus 6% interest. In substance, California Coasters (the lessee) bought the truck and borrowed the money at 6% interest to pay for it, even though the company signed a so-called lease agreement. California Coasters would record the lease just as if it had bought the truck and borrowed the money from the dealer under an installment note—except "notes payable" would be labeled "lease payable."

Do companies acquiring assets through a lease prefer operating leases or capital leases? Let's look at the effect of both operating and capital leases on the balance sheet to help us decide. Assume a company has assets of $100 million, liabilities of $60 million, and stockholders' equity of $40 million. The company then signs a new lease to purchase long-term assets valued at $10 million. Illustration 9–3 compares the balance sheet effects between the two methods.

ILLUSTRATION 9–3

Balance Sheet Effects
of Operating and
Capital Leases

	Assuming the lease is a(n)	
($ in millions)	**Operating Lease**	**Capital Lease**
Total assets	$100	$100 + $10 = $110
Total liabilities	$ 60	$ 60 + $10 = $ 70
Stockholders' equity	40	40 + $ 0 = $ 40
Total liabilities and equity	$100	$100 + $10 = $110
Total liabilities / Stockholders' equity	$ 60 / 40 = 1.5	$ 70 / 40 = 1.75

Under an operating lease, the $10 million lease is not reported in the balance sheet. The company simply records rent expense as the payments are made, and this expense is reported in the income statement. Under a capital lease, the $10 million lease is added to both assets and liabilities, to recognize the purchase of an asset and the incurrence of an additional lease liability. While stockholders' equity remains the same for both types of leases, the relationship between total liabilities and stockholders' equity differs. Under an operating lease, the ratio of total liabilities to stockholders' equity is lower, making the company appear less risky to investors and lenders from the standpoint of potential bankruptcy. That's why most companies prefer operating leases.[2]

---

[2]At the time this book went to print, the FASB was still deliberating whether all leases should be reported as assets and liabilities, eliminating the reporting differences of a capital lease versus an operating lease in the balance sheet. For FASB updates, please refer to Connect.

KEY POINT

An operating lease is recorded just like a rental. In a capital lease, the lessee essentially "buys" the asset and borrows the money to pay for it.

Decision Point

Question	Accounting information	Analysis
Does the company have significant obligations related to operating leases?	Disclosure of lease commitments in the notes to the financial statements	Operating lease commitments are not reported as liabilities on the balance sheet, but are disclosed in the notes to the financial statements. They need to be considered when calculating important debt ratios such as the debt to equity ratio.

Bonds

■ LO9–4
Identify the characteristics of bonds.

A **bond** is a formal debt instrument that obligates the borrower to repay a stated amount, referred to as the *principal* or *face amount,* at a specified maturity date. Bonds are very similar to notes. Bonds, though, usually are issued to many lenders, while notes most often are issued to a single lender such as a bank. Traditionally, interest on bonds is paid twice a year (semiannually) on designated interest dates, beginning six months after the original bond issue date.

Perhaps your local school board issued bonds to build a new football stadium for the high school, or maybe your hometown issued bonds to build a new library. To build the stadium or library, a city needs external financing, so it borrows money from people in the community. In return, those investing in the bonds receive interest over the life of the bonds, say 20 years, and repayment of the principal amount at the end of the bonds' life.

For most large corporations, bonds are sold, or *underwritten,* by investment houses. The three largest bond underwriters are **JPMorgan Chase**, **Citigroup**, and **Bank of America**.

The issuing company—the borrower—pays a fee for these underwriting services. Other costs include legal, accounting, registration, and printing fees. To keep costs down, the issuing company may choose to sell the debt securities directly to a single investor, such as a large investment fund or an insurance company. This is referred to as a **private placement**.

Why do some companies issue bonds rather than borrow money directly from a bank? A company that borrows by issuing bonds is effectively bypassing the bank and borrowing directly from the investing public—usually at a lower interest rate than it would in a bank loan. However, issuing bonds entails significant bond issue costs that can exceed 5% of the amount borrowed. For smaller loans, the additional bond issuance costs exceed the savings from a lower interest rate, making it more economical to borrow from a bank. For loans of $20 million or more, the interest rate savings often exceed the additional bond issuance costs, making a bond issue more attractive.

Bonds may be secured or unsecured, term or serial, callable, or convertible. Illustration 9–4 provides a summary. We'll discuss each of these characteristics next.

SECURED AND UNSECURED BONDS

When you buy a house and finance your purchase with a bank loan, you sign a mortgage agreement assigning your house as collateral. If later you are unable to make the

© AP Images/Bebeto Matthews

payments, the bank is entitled to take your house. Secured bonds are similar. They are supported by specific assets the issuer has pledged as collateral. If the borrower defaults on the payments, the lender is entitled to the assets pledged as collateral.

However, **most bonds are unsecured.** Unsecured bonds, also referred to as *debentures,* are not backed by a specific asset. These bonds are secured only by the "full faith and credit" of the borrower.

TERM AND SERIAL BONDS

Term bonds require payment of the full principal amount of the bond at the end of the loan term. Most bonds have this characteristic. To ensure that sufficient funds are available to pay back the bonds at the end of the loan term, the borrower usually sets aside money in a "sinking fund." A sinking fund is an investment fund to which an organization makes payments each year over the life of its outstanding debt. For example, say a company borrows $20 million by issuing term bonds due in 10 years. The company might put $2 million each year into a sinking fund, so that at the end of 10 years, $20 million is available to pay back the bonds on the due date.

CAREER CORNER

Financing alternatives, capital structure, notes, leases, and bonds are topics covered in both accounting and finance. How do you decide whether to major in accounting or finance? Some students choose finance because they consider accounting more of a "desk job" and finance more "people-oriented." This just isn't true! Both accounting and finance positions require strong communication skills. Other students avoid accounting because they heard it was more difficult. Although an accounting degree is not easy, remember **Nike**'s famous slogan "No pain, no gain." Accounting majors can apply for most entry-level finance positions, while finance majors do not have the accounting coursework to apply for most entry-level accounting positions.

© Charles Gullung/Comet/ Corbis

Bond Characteristic	Definition
Secured	Bonds are backed by collateral.
Unsecured	Bonds are not backed by collateral.
Term	Bond issue matures on a single date.
Serial	Bond issue matures in installments.
Callable	Borrower can pay off bonds early.
Convertible	Lender can convert bonds to common stock.

ILLUSTRATION 9–4

Summary of Bond Characteristics

Serial bonds require payments in installments over a series of years. Rather than issuing $20 million in bonds that will be due at the *end* of the 10th year, the company may issue $20 million in serial bonds, of which $2 million is due *each year* for the next 10 years. This makes it easier to meet its bond obligations as they become due. Since **most bonds are term bonds,** we focus on term bonds in this chapter.

CALLABLE BONDS

Suppose your company issued bonds a few years ago that pay 10% interest. Now market interest rates have declined to 6%, but you're obligated to pay 10% interest for the remaining time to maturity. How can you avoid this unfortunate situation?

Most corporate bonds are callable, or redeemable. This feature allows the borrower to repay the bonds before their scheduled maturity date at a specified call price, usually at an amount just above face value. Callable bonds protect the borrower against future decreases in interest rates. If interest rates decline, the borrower can buy back the high-interest-rate bonds at a fixed price and issue new bonds at the new, lower interest rate.

CONVERTIBLE BONDS

While a bond could be both callable and convertible, **a call feature is more common than a conversion feature.** Another important distinction is that callable bonds benefit the borrower, whereas convertible bonds benefit both the borrower and the lender. Convertible bonds allow the lender (the investor) to convert each bond into a specified number of shares of common stock. For example, let's say a $1,000 convertible bond can be converted into 20 shares of common stock. In this case, convertible bondholders benefit if the market price of the common stock goes above $50 per share (= $1,000 ÷ 20 shares), assuming the current market price of the bond is $1,000. If the company's stock price goes to $60 per share, the convertible bondholder can trade the $1,000 bond for 20 shares of stock worth $60 per share (or $1,200). Prior to conversion, the bondholder still receives interest on the convertible bond. The borrower also benefits. Convertible bonds sell at a higher price and require a lower interest rate than bonds without a conversion feature.

INTERNATIONAL FINANCIAL REPORTING STANDARDS (IFRS)

DOES CONVERTIBLE DEBT HAVE AN EQUITY COMPONENT?

Using IFRS, we separate the issue price of convertible debt into its liability (bonds) and equity (conversion option) components. Under U.S. GAAP, the entire issue price is recorded as a liability.

For more discussion, see Appendix E.

KEY POINT

The distinguishing characteristics of bonds include whether they are backed by collateral (secured or unsecured), become due at a single specified date or over a series of years (term or serial), can be redeemed prior to maturity (callable), or can be converted into common stock (convertible).

Corporations normally issue bonds in the millions of dollars. However, to simplify the illustrations in this chapter, we drop three digits and illustrate the issuance of bonds in thousands rather than in millions. We begin with the following example and build upon it as we progress through the chapter.

Assume that on January 1, 2018, California Coasters decides to raise money for development of its new roller coaster by issuing $100,000 of bonds paying interest of 7% each year. The bonds are due in 10 years, with interest payable semiannually on June 30 and December 31 each year. **In practice, most corporate bonds pay interest semiannually (every six months) rather than paying interest monthly, quarterly, or annually.** Thus, investors in Calfornia Coasters' bonds will receive (1) the *face amount* of $100,000 at the end of 10 years and (2) *interest payments* of $3,500 (= $100,000 × 7% × 1/2 year) every six months for 10 years. That's a total of 20 interest payments of $3,500 each (= $70,000). Illustration 9–5 provides a timeline of the cash flows related to the bond issue.

Over the 10-year period, bondholders will receive a total of $170,000, which is the face amount of $100,000 due at maturity plus 20 semiannual interest payments of $3,500, totaling $70,000. How much are investors willing to pay today for the right to receive $170,000 over the next 10 years? Certainly less than $170,000, because the cash flows are in the future. In the next section we see how to determine that price.

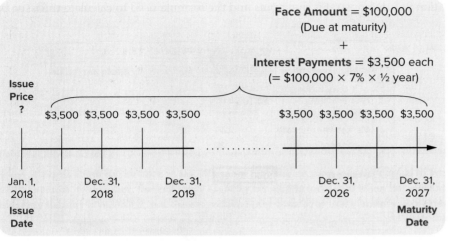

ILLUSTRATION 9–5

Timeline of a Bond Issue

PRICING A BOND

PART B*

We can calculate the issue price of a bond as the present value of the face amount *plus* the present value of the periodic interest payments. To calculate the issue price of California Coasters' $100,000 bonds, we need to determine the face amount of the bonds, the interest payment each period, the market interest rate per period, and the number of periods to maturity.

■ **LO9–5**
Determine the price of a bond issue.

Bonds Issued at Face Amount

The face amount equals $100,000. The interest payment every six months is $3,500 (= $100,000 × 7% × 1/2 year). The stated interest rate is the rate quoted in the bond contract used to calculate the cash payments for interest. The market interest rate represents the true interest rate used by investors to value the bond issue. The market rate can be equal to, less than, or greater than the stated 7% interest rate paid to investors. As we will see later, the market rate is determined for each bond issue by the forces of supply and demand.

Common Terms The market rate is also known as the *effective-interest rate* or *yield rate.*

Let's first assume the market interest rate is 7%, the same as the stated interest rate. (Later we will calculate the bond issue price when the market interest rate is less than or greater than the stated interest rate.) The number of periods to maturity is the number of years to maturity multiplied by the number of interest payments per year. Since the bonds pay interest semiannually (twice per year) for 10 years, there are 20 periods to maturity.

One way to determine the issue price of bonds is to use your financial calculator. Illustration 9–6 shows the calculator inputs used to obtain an issue price at the face amount of $100,000.

ILLUSTRATION 9–6

Pricing Bonds Issued at Face Amount Using a Financial Calculator

Bond Characteristics	Key	Amount
CALCULATOR INPUT		
1. Face amount	FV	$100,000
2. Interest payment	PMT	$3,500 = 100,000 × 7% × 1/2 year
3. Market interest rate	I	3.5 = 7% ÷ 2 periods per year
4. Periods to maturity	N	20 = 10 years × 2 periods each year
CALCULATOR OUTPUT		
Issue price	PV	$100,000

*Note: Part B on pricing a bond is designed to be a stand-alone section. Instructors can choose whether or not to cover the material in this section. Some instructors choose to save this material for intermediate accounting or the first finance course. Other instructors emphasize this material right after covering Appendix C on the time value of money. Pricing a bond represents an excellent application of the present value concepts discussed in Appendix C.

An alternative to using a financial calculator is to calculate the price of bonds in Excel. Illustration 9–7 demonstrates the inputs and the formula used to calculate the issue price.

ILLUSTRATION 9–7

Pricing Bonds Issued at Face Amount Using Excel

	C7			f_x	=-PV(C4, C5, C3, C2, 0)	
	A	B	C	D	E	F
1						
2	Face amount		$100,000.00			
3	Interest payment		$3,500.00			
4	Market interest rate		.035			
5	Number of periods		20			
6						
7	Issue price		$100,000.00			
8						
9						

Sheet1 Sheet2 Sheet3

Ready   100%

A third alternative is to calculate the price of the bonds using present value tables. In Illustration 9–8 we calculate the price of the bonds using the present value tables provided at the back of this textbook.

ILLUSTRATION 9–8

Pricing Bonds Issued at Face Amount Using Present Value Tables

Present value of face amount	= $100,000 × 0.50257*	=	$ 50,257
Present value of interest payments	= $3,500[1] × 14.21240**	=	49,743
Issue price of the bonds			$100,000

[1]$100,000 × 7% × 1/2 year = $3,500
*Table 2, i = 3.5%, n = 20
**Table 4, i = 3.5%, n = 20

We use Table 2, the present value of $1, to calculate the present value of the face amount since it's just one amount ($100,000) due at maturity. We use Table 4, the present value of an ordinary annuity of $1, to calculate the present value of the interest payments since they are a series of equal amounts ($3,500 each) paid every semiannual interest period. A series of equal amounts over equal time periods is called an annuity.

Using any of these three alternatives, the issue price of the bonds is equal to $100,000. All three methods have their advantages. A financial calculator and Excel are simple to use and provide greater flexibility regarding the choice of different interest rates and time periods. On the other hand, present value tables provide a more detailed understanding of how bond prices are determined.

We assumed a market rate of 7%, which is exactly equal to the 7% stated rate of interest on the bond contract. The market rate is the interest rate investors determine for each bond issue through the forces of supply and demand. Market rates change continuously. Announcements by the Federal Reserve regarding its intentions to increase the federal funds rate (the interest rate the Federal Reserve charges to banks), political unrest, and fears of growing inflation, to name a few, can cause an increase in market interest rates.

Another important point to remember is that the market rate is not the same for all companies issuing bonds. Market rates vary based on the default risk of the company issuing the bonds. Default risk refers to the possibility that a company will be unable to pay the bond's face amount or interest payments as they become due. As a company's default risk increases, investors demand a higher market interest rate on their bond investments. **The higher the market interest rate, the lower the bond issue price will be.**

Bonds Issued at a Discount

Now let's assume that California Coasters issues the same $100,000 of 7% bonds when other bonds of similar risk and maturity are paying the market rate of 8%. California Coasters' bonds are less attractive to investors, because investors can purchase bonds of similar risk that are paying the higher 8% rate. Because of this, to make the bonds more attractive, California Coasters will have to issue its 7% bonds *below* its $100,000 face amount. Bonds issued *below* face amount are said to be issued at a discount.

In this instance, the bonds will be issued for less than the $100,000 face amount. How much less? Let's calculate the bond issue price using I = 4% (= 8% ÷ 2) rather than the 3.5% used in the previous example. In Illustration 9–9 we recalculate the issue price of the bonds, assuming the market rate of interest is now 8% per year (4% every semiannual period).

ILLUSTRATION 9–9

Pricing Bonds Issued at a Discount Using a Financial Calculator

CALCULATOR INPUT

Bond Characteristics	Key	Amount
1. Face amount	FV	$100,000
2. Interest payment	PMT	$3,500 = $100,000 × 7% × 1/2 year
3. Market interest rate	I	4 = 8% ÷ 2 periods per year
4. Periods to maturity	N	20 = 10 years × 2 periods each year

CALCULATOR OUTPUT

Issue price	PV	$93,205

Illustration 9–10 demonstrates how to use Excel to determine the issue price.

ILLUSTRATION 9–10

Pricing Bonds Issued at a Discount Using Excel

	C7		f_x =-PV(C4, C5, C3, C2, 0)			
	A	B	C	D	E	F
1						
2	Face amount		$100,000.00			
3	Interest payment		$3,500.00			
4	Market interest rate		.04			
5	Number of periods		20			
6						
7	Issue price		$93,205.00			
8						
9						

Sheet1 Sheet2 Sheet3
Ready   100%

In Illustration 9–11 we calculate the price of the bonds using the present value tables provided at the back of this textbook, assuming the market rate of interest is 8% per year, or 4% every semiannual period.

ILLUSTRATION 9–11

Pricing Bonds Issued at a Discount Using Present Value Tables

Present value of principal	= $100,000 × 0.45639*	=	$45,639
Present value of interest payments	= $3,500[1] × 13.59033**	=	47,566
Issue price of the bonds			$93,205

[1]$100,000 × 7% × 1/2 year = $3,500
*Table 2, i = 4%, n = 20
**Table 4, i = 4%, n = 20

In practice, investors refer to the bonds as being "issued at 93.2." This means the bonds were issued at approximately 93.2% of the $100,000 face value, or $93,200 (rounded). We see that in this instance the bond issue price is below the face amount of $100,000, but the issuer is still required to pay back the full $100,000 principal amount when the bond matures in 10 years, as well as the 20 semiannual interest payments of $3,500 each.

Why did California Coasters receive less than $100,000 for the issuance of the bonds? The reason is that the bonds pay only 7% interest but other companies' bonds with similar risk and maturity length are paying 8% interest (market rate). Therefore, the 7% interest offered by California Coasters is less attractive to investors who could choose a similar bond that pays 8% interest. These investors will not pay full price for California Coasters' bonds, and the bonds will issue at a discount. By issuing the bonds for only $93,205, the interest payments of $3,500 *effectively* become equal the market rate of 8%. **In other words, an investor paying $93,205 for the 7% bonds will earn the same rate of return (8%) as an investor paying $100,000 for 8% bonds.**

 COMMON MISTAKE

The interest rate we use to calculate the bond issue price is always the *market* rate, never the stated rate. Some students get confused and incorrectly use the stated rate to calculate present value. Use the stated rate to calculate the interest payment each period, but use the market rate to calculate the present value of the cash flows.

Bonds Issued at a Premium

Now let's assume that California Coasters issues $100,000 of 7% bonds when other bonds of similar risk and maturity are paying a market rate of only 6%. Investors will pay *more* than $100,000 for these 7% bonds since they look relatively attractive compared with bonds paying only 6%. These bonds will sell at a premium. A premium occurs when the issue price of a bond is *above* its face amount. In this case, the bonds will sell for more than $100,000. How much more? In Illustration 9–12 we recalculate the issue price using a market rate of 6% (3% semiannually).

ILLUSTRATION 9–12

Pricing Bonds Issued at a Premium Using a Financial Calculator

CALCULATOR INPUT

Bond Characteristics	Key	Amount
1. Face amount	FV	$100,000
2. Interest payment	PMT	$3,500 = $100,000 × 7% × 1/2 year
3. Market interest rate	I	3 = 6% ÷ 2 semiannual periods
4. Periods to maturity	N	20 = 10 years × 2 periods each year

CALCULATOR OUTPUT

Issue price	PV	$107,439

Illustration 9–13 demonstrates how to use Excel to determine the issue price.

ILLUSTRATION 9–13

Pricing Bonds Issued at a Premium Using Excel

	C7		f_x	=-PV(C4, C5, C3, C2, 0)		
	A	B	C	D	E	F
1						
2	Face amount		$100,000.00			
3	Interest payment		$3,500.00			
4	Market interest rate		.03			
5	Number of periods		20			
6						
7	Issue price		$107,439.00			
8						
9						

Sheet1 / Sheet2 / Sheet3

Ready 100%

Illustration 9–14 calculates the price of the bonds using the present value tables provided at the back of this textbook, again assuming the market rate of interest is 6% (3% semiannually).

ILLUSTRATION 9–14

Pricing Bonds Issued at a Premium Using Present Value Tables

Present value of principal	= $100,000 × 0.55368*	=	$ 55,368
Present value of interest payments	= $3,500[1] × 14.87747**	=	52,071
Issue price of the bonds			$107,439

[1]$100,000 × 7% × 1/2 year = $3,500
*Table 2, $i = 3\%$, $n = 20$
**Table 4, $i = 3\%$, $n = 20$

ILLUSTRATION 9–14

Pricing Bonds Issued at a Premium Using Present Value Tables

In practice, investors might refer to these bonds as being "issued at 107.4." This means the bonds were issued at approximately 107.4% of the $100,000 face value, or $107,400 (rounded).

Here, we see that the bond issue price is above the face amount of $100,000. California Coasters receives $107,439 from investors, but will need to pay back only $100,000 when the bonds mature in 10 years, as well as the 20 semiannual interest payments of $3,500 each. Why did the bonds issue at a premium? Because the bonds pay 7% interest when the interest rate for bonds of similar risk and maturity length is only 6% (market rate). Investors are willing to pay more for bonds that offer the more attractive 7% rate. However, by issuing the bonds for $107,439, the company is effectively lowering the interest earned by investors from the stated rate of 7% to the market rate of 6%.

Illustration 9–15 shows the relation between the stated interest rate, the market interest rate, and the bond issue price.

ILLUSTRATION 9–15

Stated Rate, Market Rate, and the Bond Issue Price

Bonds Issued at a Discount	Bonds Issued at Face Amount	Bonds Issued at a Premium
Stated rate (7%)	Stated rate (7%)	Stated rate (7%)
<	=	>
Market rate (8%)	Market rate (7%)	Market rate (6%)

If the bonds' stated interest rate is less than the market interest rate, then the bonds will issue below face amount (discount). If the bonds' stated interest rate equals the market interest rate, then the bonds will issue at face amount. Finally, if the bonds' stated interest rate is more than the market interest rate, the bonds will issue above face amount (premium).

Which is most common in practice—bonds issued at face amount, a discount, or a premium? Most bonds initially are issued at a slight discount. Because there is a delay between when the company determines the characteristics of the bonds and when the bonds actually are issued, the company must estimate the market rate of interest. Bond issuers usually adopt a stated interest rate that is close to, but just under, the expected market interest rate. However, in future periods, the bonds may trade at either a discount or a premium depending on changes in market interest rates.

 KEY POINT

The issue price of a bond is equal to the present value of the face amount (principal) payable at maturity, plus the present value of the periodic interest payments. Bonds can be issued at face amount, below face amount (at a discount), or above face amount (at a premium).

Let's Review

mhhe.com/4fa36

Assume that on January 1, 2018, Water World issues $200,000 of 9% bonds, due in 10 years, with interest payable semiannually on June 30 and December 31 each year.

Required:

1. If the market rate is 9%, will the bonds issue at face amount, a discount, or a premium? Calculate the issue price.

2. If the market rate is 10%, will the bonds issue at face amount, a discount, or a premium? Calculate the issue price.

3. If the market rate is 8%, will the bonds issue at face amount, a discount, or a premium? Calculate the issue price.

Solution:

1. If the market rate is 9%, the bonds will issue at face amount.

CALCULATOR INPUT		
Bond Characteristics	**Key**	**Amount**
1. Face amount	FV	$200,000
2. Interest payment	PMT	$9,000 = $200,000 × 9% × 1/2 year
3. Market interest rate	I	4.5 = 9% ÷ 2 semiannual periods
4. Periods to maturity	N	20 = 10 years × 2 periods each year
CALCULATOR OUTPUT		
Issue price	PV	$200,000

	C7	▼	f_x	=-PV(C4, C5, C3, C2, 0)		
	A	B	C	D	E	F
1						
2	Face amount		$200,000.00			
3	Interest payment		$9,000.00			
4	Market interest rate		.045			
5	Number of periods		20			
6						
7	Issue price		$200,000.00			
8						
9						

Sheet1 / Sheet2 / Sheet3

Ready   100%

PRESENT VALUE TABLES			
Present value of principal	= $200,000 × 0.41464*	=	$ 82,928
Present value of interest payments	= $9,000[1] × 13.00794**	=	117,072
Issue price of the bonds			$200,000

[1]$200,000 × 9% × 1/2 year = $9,000
*Table 2, i = 4.5%, n = 20
**Table 4, i = 4.5%, n = 20

2. If the market rate is 10%, the bonds will issue at a discount. The only change we make in the calculation is that now I = 5 rather than 4.5.

CALCULATOR INPUT

Bond Characteristics	Key	Amount
1. Face amount	FV	$200,000
2. Interest payment	PMT	$9,000 = $200,000 × 9% × 1/2 year
3. Market interest rate	I	5 = 10% ÷ 2 semiannual periods
4. Periods to maturity	N	20 = 10 years × 2 periods each year

CALCULATOR OUTPUT

Issue price	PV	$187,538

	C7			f_x =-PV(C4, C5, C3, C2, 0)		
	A	B	C	D	E	F
1						
2	Face amount		$200,000.00			
3	Interest payment		$9,000.00			
4	Market interest rate		.05			
5	Number of periods		20			
6						
7	Issue price		$187,538.00			
8						
9						

Sheet1 / Sheet2 / Sheet3

Ready   100%

PRESENT VALUE TABLES

Present value of principal	= $200,000 × 0.37689*	=	$ 75,378
Present value of interest payments	= $9,000[1] × 12.46221**	=	112,160
Issue price of the bonds			$187,538

[1]$200,000 × 9% × 1/2 year = $9,000
*Table 2, i = 5%, n = 20
**Table 4, i = 5%, n = 20

3. If the market rate is 8%, the bonds will issue at a premium. The only change we make in the calculation is that now I = 4.

CALCULATOR INPUT

Bond Characteristics	Key	Amount
1. Face amount	FV	$200,000
2. Interest payment	PMT	$9,000 = $200,000 × 9% × 1/2 year
3. Market interest rate	I	4 = 8% ÷ 2 semiannual periods
4. Periods to maturity	N	20 = 10 years × 2 periods each year

CALCULATOR OUTPUT

Issue price	PV	$213,590

	A	B	C	D	E	F
			fx	=-PV(C4, C5, C3, C2, 0)		
1						
2	Face amount		$200,000.00			
3	Interest payment		$9,000.00			
4	Market interest rate		.04			
5	Number of periods		20			
6						
7	Issue price		$213,590.00			
8						
9						

Sheet1 Sheet2 Sheet3

Suggested Homework:
BE9–4, BE9–5;
E9–5, E9–6;
P9–3A&B

PRESENT VALUE TABLES

Present value of principal	= $200,000 × 0.45639* =	$ 91,278
Present value of interest payments	= $9,000[1] × 13.59033** =	122,312
Issue price of the bonds		$213,590

[1]$200,000 × 9% × 1/2 year = $9,000
*Table 2, $i = 4\%$, $n = 20$
**Table 4, $i = 4\%$, $n = 20$

PART C

RECORDING BONDS PAYABLE

■ **LO9–6**
Account for the issuance of bonds.

To see how to record the issuance of bonds and the related interest, let's return to our initial example. On January 1, 2018, California Coasters issues $100,000 of 7% bonds, due in 10 years, with interest payable semiannually on June 30 and December 31 each year.

Bonds Issued at Face Value

The bonds issue for exactly $100,000, assuming a 7% market interest rate. California Coasters records the bond issue as:

A = L + SE
+100,000
          +100,000

January 1, 2018	Debit	Credit
Cash	**100,000**	
Bonds Payable		**100,000**
(Issue bonds at face amount)		

California Coasters reports bonds payable in the long-term liabilities section of the balance sheet. Nine years from now, when the bonds are within one year of maturity, the firm will reclassify the bonds as current liabilities.

On June 30, 2018, California Coasters records the first semiannual interest payment:

A = L + SE
          −3,500 Exp ↑
−3,500

June 30, 2018	Debit	Credit
Interest Expense	**3,500**	
Cash		**3,500**
(Pay semiannual interest)		
($3,500 = $100,000 × 7% × 1/2)		

The firm will record another semiannual interest payment on December 31, 2018. In fact, it will record this same semiannual interest payment at the end of every six-month period for the next 10 years.

Bonds Issued at a Discount

In the preceding example we assumed the stated interest rate (7%) and the market interest rate (7%) were the same. How will the entries differ if the stated interest rate is 7% and the market rate is, say, 8%? The bonds will issue at only $93,205. This is less than $100,000 because the bonds are paying only 7%, while investors can purchase bonds of similar risk paying 8%. When bonds issue at less than face value, we say they issue at a discount. California Coasters records the bond issue as:

January 1, 2018	Debit	Credit		A	=	L	+	SE
Cash	93,205			+93,205				
Discount on Bonds Payable	6,795					−6,795		
Bonds Payable		100,000				+100,000		
(*Issue bonds at a discount*)								

We debit Cash for the issue price of $93,205, and we credit Bonds Payable for the $100,000 principal amount to be paid in 10 years. The difference between these two amounts is debited to Discount on Bonds Payable. The Discount account is a contra-liability, which is deducted from Bonds Payable in the balance sheet as shown below:

Long-term liabilities:	
Bonds payable	$100,000
Less: Discount on bonds payable	(6,795)
Carrying value	$ 93,205

The difference between the Bonds Payable account and the Discount on Bonds Payable account is called carrying value. The carrying value will increase from the amount originally borrowed ($93,205) to the amount due at maturity ($100,000) over the 10-year life of the bonds.

We calculate each period's interest expense as the carrying value (the amount actually owed during that period) times the market rate (4% semiannually or 8% annually, in our example). This method of calculating interest is referred to as the *effective-interest method*.[3] For the first interest payment, interest expense is:

$$\begin{array}{ccc} \text{Interest} \\ \text{expense} \\ \$3,728 \end{array} = \begin{array}{c} \text{Carrying value} \\ \text{of bond} \\ \$93,205 \end{array} \times \begin{array}{c} \text{Market interest} \\ \text{rate per period} \\ 8\% \times 1/2 \end{array}$$

However, the bond agreement specifies that cash paid for interest is equal to the face amount times the stated rate (3.5% semiannually or 7% annually, in our example):

$$\begin{array}{ccc} \text{Cash paid for} \\ \text{interest} \\ \$3,500 \end{array} = \begin{array}{c} \text{Face amount} \\ \text{of bond} \\ \$100,000 \end{array} \times \begin{array}{c} \text{Stated interest} \\ \text{rate per period} \\ 7\% \times 1/2 \end{array}$$

Notice that when the bond sells at a discount, interest expense ($3,728) is *more* than the cash paid for interest ($3,500). (Later, we'll see that the opposite is true when the bond sells at a premium.) On June 30, 2018, California Coasters records interest expense, a decrease

---

[3]We cover the effective-interest method, as this is the generally accepted method under both U.S. GAAP and IFRS. The straight-line amortization method, which is allowed only if it does not materially differ from the effective-interest method, is discussed as an alternative approach in intermediate accounting.

in the discount on bonds payable (which actually increases the carrying value of bonds payable), and the cash paid for interest as follows:

A = L + SE

−3,728 Exp ↑

+228

−3,500

June 30, 2018	Debit	Credit
Interest Expense (= $93,205 × 8% × 1/2)............................	**3,728**	
Discount on Bonds Payable (difference)............................		**228**
Cash (= $100,000 × 7% × 1/2)...		**3,500**
(*Pay semiannual interest*)		

✖ COMMON MISTAKE

Students sometimes incorrectly record interest expense using the stated rate rather than the market rate. Remember that interest expense is the carrying value times the market rate, while the cash paid for interest is the face amount times the stated rate.

Because the carrying value of debt issued at a discount increases over time, interest expense also will increase each semiannual interest period. We record interest for the next semiannual interest period on December 31, 2018, as:

A = L + SE

−3,737 Exp ↑

+237

−3,500

December 31, 2018	Debit	Credit
Interest Expense (= [$93,205 + $228] × 8% × 1/2).......................	**3,737**	
Discount on Bonds Payable (difference)............................		**237**
Cash (= $100,000 × 7% × 1/2)...		**3,500**
(*Pay semiannual interest*)		

A bond amortiation schedule summarizes the cash paid, interest expense, and changes in carrying value for each semiannual interest period. Illustration 9–16 provides an amortization schedule for the bonds issued at a discount. Note that the amounts for the June 30, 2018, and the December 31, 2018, semiannual interest payments shown above can be taken directly from the amortization schedule.

ILLUSTRATION 9–16

Amortization Schedule for Bonds Issued at a Discount

mhhe.com/4fa37

(1) Date	(2) Cash Paid	(3) Interest Expense	(4) Increase in Carrying Value	(5) Carrying Value
	Face Amount × Stated Rate	Carrying Value × Market Rate	(3)−(2)	Prior Carrying Value + (4)
1/1/18				$ 93,205
6/30/18	$3,500	$3,728	$228	93,433
12/31/18	3,500	3,737	237	93,670
*	*	*	*	*
*	*	*	*	99,057
6/30/27	3,500	3,962	462	99,519
12/31/27	3,500	3,981	481	100,000

The amortization schedule shows interest calculations every six months because interest is paid semiannually. The entire amortization schedule would include 20 more rows (10 years × 2 periods per year) after the initial balance on January 1, 2018. To save space, we show only the amortization for the first and last years. The eight years in the middle are represented by asterisks. Cash paid is $3,500 (= $100,000 × 7% × 1/2) every six months. Interest expense is the carrying value times the market rate. Interest expense for the six months ended June 30, 2018, is $3,728 (= $93,205 × 4%). The difference between interest expense and the cash paid increases the carrying value of the bonds. At the maturity date, the carrying value will equal the face amount of $100,000.

Decision Maker's Perspective

Carrying Value and Market Value

Is the carrying value of bonds payable reported in the balance sheet really what the bonds are worth? Yes, but only on the date issued and on the final maturity date. Between these two dates, the carrying value of bonds payable reported in the balance sheet can vary considerably from the true underlying market value of the liability. The reason is that the market interest rate is constantly changing. The market value of bonds moves in the opposite direction of interest rates: When market interest rates go up, the market value of bonds goes down. However, the carrying value of bonds is not adjusted for changes in market interest rates after the issue date.

Refer back to the amortization schedule for the bonds issued at a discount by California Coasters. The carrying value of $93,205 on the date of issue equals the market value of the bonds. However, the carrying value one year later on December 31, 2018 ($93,670), will equal market value *only* if the market rate of interest continues to be 8%. If market interest rates go up during the year, the value of bonds payable will fall. Similarly, if market rates go down during the year, the value of bonds payable will increase.

Current generally accepted accounting principles allow the option to report some or all of a company's financial assets and liabilities at fair value. If a company chooses to report bonds payable at fair value, then it reports changes in fair value as gains and losses in the income statement.

Bonds Issued at a Premium

Now assume California Coasters issues $100,000 of 7% bonds when other bonds of similar risk are paying a market rate of only 6%. The bonds will issue at $107,439. Investors will pay more than $100,000 for these 7% bonds because bonds of similar risk are paying only 6% interest. When bonds issue at more than face value, we say they issue at a premium. California Coasters records the bond issue as:

January 1, 2018	Debit	Credit	A	=	L	+	SE
Cash	**107,439**		+107,439				
Bonds Payable		**100,000**			+100,000		
Premium on Bonds Payable		**7,439**			+7,439		
(*Issue bonds at a premium*)							

We debit Cash for the issue price of $107,439. We credit Bonds Payable for the face value of $100,000. The difference is credited to Premium on Bonds Payable. The balance of Premium on Bonds Payable is added to Bonds Payable in the balance sheet as shown below:

Long-term liabilities:	
Bonds payable	$100,000
Add: Premium on bonds payable	7,439
Carrying value	$107,439

Initially, the carrying value is $107,439. However, California Coasters will need to pay back only $100,000 when the bonds mature in 10 years. Therefore, the carrying value will decrease from $107,439 (issue price) to $100,000 (face amount) over the 10-year life of the bonds. We still calculate interest expense as the carrying value times the market rate

(3% semiannually). On June 30, 2018, California Coasters records an interest payment, assuming the bonds were issued at a premium, as follows:

A = L + SE	
−3,223 Exp ↑	
−277	
−3,500	

June 30, 2018	Debit	Credit
Interest Expense (= $107,439 × 6% × 1/2)...........................	**3,223**	
Premium on Bonds Payable (difference)................................	**277**	
Cash (= $100,000 × 7% × 1/2)..		**3,500**
(*Pay semiannual interest*)		

When bonds are issued at a premium, the carrying value of the debt decreases over time. That's why we *debit* Premium on Bonds Payable, because the premium is decreasing over time. Since the carrying value of the debt decreases over time, interest expense will also decrease each semiannual interest period. California Coasters records interest for the next semiannual interest period on December 31, 2018, as:

A = L + SE	
−3,215 Exp ↑	
−285	
−3,500	

December 31, 2018	Debit	Credit
Interest Expense (= [$107,439 − $277] × 6% × 1/2).....................	**3,215**	
Premium on Bonds Payable (difference)................................	**285**	
Cash (= $100,000 × 7% × 1/2)..		**3,500**
(*Pay semiannual interest*)		

The amortization schedule in Illustration 9–17 summarizes the recording of interest expense for the bonds issued at a premium.

ILLUSTRATION 9–17

Amortization Schedule for Bonds Issued at a Premium

mhhe.com/4fa38

(1)	(2)	(3)	(4)	(5)
		Interest	Decrease in	Carrying
Date	Cash Paid	Expense	Carrying Value	Value
	Face Amount × Stated Rate	Carrying Value × Market Rate	(2)−(3)	Prior Carrying Value − (4)
1/1/18				$107,439
6/30/18	$3,500	$3,223	$277	107,162
12/31/18	3,500	3,215	285	106,877
*	*	*	*	*
*	*	*	*	100,956
6/30/27	3,500	3,029	471	100,485
12/31/27	3,500	3,015	485	100,000

Just as in the discount example, the amounts for the June 30, 2018, and the December 31, 2018, semiannual interest payments can be obtained directly from the amortization schedule. Now, however, with a bond premium, the difference between cash paid and interest expense *decreases* the carrying value each period from $107,439 at bond issue down to $100,000 (the face amount) at bond maturity.

Illustration 9–18 shows how carrying value changes as a bond approaches its maturity date.

KEY POINT

When bonds issue at face amount, the carrying value and the corresponding interest expense *remain constant* over time. When bonds issue at a discount (below face amount), the carrying value and the corresponding interest expense *increase* over time. When bonds issue at a premium (above face amount), the carrying value and the corresponding interest expense *decrease* over time.

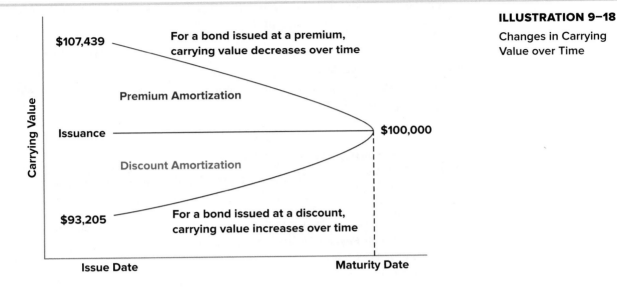

ILLUSTRATION 9–18

Changes in Carrying Value over Time

Assume that on January 1, 2018, Water World issues $200,000 of 9% bonds, due in 10 years, with interest payable semiannually on June 30 and December 31 each year.

Let's Review

Required:

1. If the market rate is 9%, the bonds will issue at $200,000. Record the bond issue on January 1, 2018, and the first two semiannual interest payments on June 30, 2018, and December 31, 2018.

2. If the market rate is 10%, the bonds will issue at $187,538. Record the bond issue on January 1, 2018, and the first two semiannual interest payments on June 30, 2018, and December 31, 2018.

3. If the market rate is 8%, the bonds will issue at $213,590. Record the bond issue on January 1, 2018, and the first two semiannual interest payments on June 30, 2018, and December 31, 2018.

mhhe.com/4fa39

Solution:

1. Record the bonds issued at face amount and the first two semiannual interest payments:

January 1, 2018	Debit	Credit
Cash	**200,000**	
Bonds Payable		**200,000**
(*Issue bonds at face amount*)		
June 30, 2018		
Interest Expense	**9,000**	
Cash (= $200,000 × 9% × 1/2)		**9,000**
(*Pay semiannual interest*)		
December 31, 2018		
Interest Expense	**9,000**	
Cash (= $200,000 × 9% × 1/2)		**9,000**
(*Pay semiannual interest*)		

2. Record the bonds issued at a discount and the first two semiannual interest payments:

January 1, 2018	Debit	Credit
Cash	187,538	
Discount on Bonds Payable..	12,462	
Bonds Payable		200,000
(Issue bonds at a discount)		
June 30, 2018		
Interest Expense (= $187,538 × 10% × 1/2)	9,377	
Discount on Bonds Payable (difference)		377
Cash (= $200,000 × 9% × 1/2)		9,000
(Pay semiannual interest)		
December 31, 2018		
Interest Expense (= [$187,538 + $377] × 10% × 1/2)	9,396	
Discount on Bonds Payable (difference)		396
Cash (= $200,000 × 9% × 1/2)		9,000
(Pay semiannual interest)		

3. Record the bonds issued at a premium and the first two semiannual interest payments:

January 1, 2018	Debit	Credit
Cash	213,590	
Bonds Payable		200,000
Premium on Bonds Payable..		13,590
(Issue bonds at a premium)		
June 30, 2018		
Interest Expense (= $213,590 × 8% × 1/2)	8,544	
Premium on Bonds Payable (difference)	456	
Cash (= $200,000 × 9% × 1/2)		9,000
(Pay semiannual interest)		
December 31, 2018		
Interest Expense (= [$213,590 − $456] × 8% × 1/2).......................	8,525	
Premium on Bonds Payable (difference)	475	
Cash (= $200,000 × 9% × 1/2)		9,000
(Pay semiannual interest)		

Suggested Homework:
BE9–7, BE9–8;
E9–8, E9–9;
P9–4A&B, P9–6A&B

Accounting for Bond Retirements

■ **LO9–7**
Record the retirement of bonds.

When the issuing corporation buys back its bonds from the investors, we say the company has **retired** those bonds. The corporation can wait until the bonds mature to retire them, or frequently (for reasons we describe below), the issuer will choose to buy the bonds back from the bondholders early.

BOND RETIREMENTS AT MATURITY

Regardless of whether bonds are issued at face amount, a discount, or a premium, **their carrying value at maturity will equal their face amount.** California Coasters records the retirement of its bonds at maturity (December 31, 2027) as:

A = L + SE

−100,000

−100,000

December 31, 2027	Debit	Credit
Bonds Payable	100,000	
Cash		100,000
(Retire bonds at maturity)		

BOND RETIREMENTS BEFORE MATURITY

Earlier we noted that a call feature accompanies most bonds, allowing the issuer to buy back bonds at a fixed price. Even when bonds are not callable in this way, the issuing company can retire bonds early by purchasing them on the open market. Regardless of the method, when the issuer retires debt of any type before its scheduled maturity date, the transaction is an early extinguishment of debt.

A simple example of an early extinguishment of debt is paying off your car loan early. If you owe $5,000 on your car loan and you have to pay $5,200 to pay it off early, we would record a $200 loss on the early retirement of your debt. If you have to pay only $4,700, we would record a $300 gain on the early retirement of your debt. The same scenario holds true for bonds.

Let's return to our example of California Coasters issuing $100,000 of 7% bonds maturing in 10 years when other bonds of similar risk are paying 6%. The bonds were issued on January 1, 2018, above face amount (at a premium) at $107,439. The carrying value of the bonds one year later on December 31, 2018 is $106,877 (see the amortization table in Illustration 9–17).

When interest rates go down, bond prices go up. If the market rate drops to 5%, it will now cost $114,353 to retire the bonds on December 31, 2018.[4] The bonds have a carrying value on December 31, 2018, of $106,877 but it will cost the issuing company $114,353 to retire them. California Coasters will record a loss for the difference between the price paid to repurchase the bonds and the bonds' carrying value. California Coasters records the retirement as:

December 31, 2018	Debit	Credit		A	=	L	+	SE
Bonds Payable (account balance)...	**100,000**					−100,000		
Premium on Bonds Payable..	**6,877**					−6,877		
Loss (difference)	**7,476**							−7,476 Exp ↑
Cash (amount paid)		**114,353**		−114,353				
(*Retire bonds before maturity*)								

If California Coasters paid less than $106,877 to retire the bonds, a gain would have been recorded instead of a loss. Gains and losses on the early extinguishment of debt are reported as nonoperating items in the income statement. This is similar to gains and losses on the sale of long-term assets, discussed in Chapter 7.

Decision Maker's Perspective

Why Buy Back Debt Early?

In the example above, California Coasters recorded a loss of $7,476 due to a decrease in market interest rates of 1%. One way a company can protect itself from decreases in interest rates is to include a call feature allowing the company to repurchase bonds at a fixed price (such as 2% over face amount, which in our example would be $102,000). When interest rates decrease, companies with a call feature are more likely to repurchase higher-cost debt and then reissue debt at new, lower interest rates. This type of buyback and reissue lowers future interest expense.

Another reason to repay debt early is to improve the company's debt ratios (discussed later in the chapter). **Six Flags** sold seven amusement parks for just over $300 million and used the proceeds to reduce its overall debt.

---

[4]The repurchase price of $114,353 is based on the following financial calculator inputs: future value, $100,000; interest payment each period, $3,500; market interest rate each period, 2.5% (5% ÷ 2 semiannual periods); and periods to maturity, 18 (9 years left × 2 periods each year).

Early extinguishment of debt can also be timed to manage reported earnings. Since bonds payable are reported at carrying values and not market values, firms can time their repurchase of bonds to help meet earnings expectations. For instance, when interest rates go up, bond prices go down. In this case, California Coasters will record a gain rather than a loss on early extinguishment.

KEY POINT

No gain or loss is recorded on bonds retired at maturity. For bonds retired before maturity, we record a gain or loss on early extinguishment equal to the difference between the price paid to repurchase the bonds and the bonds' carrying value.

ETHICAL DILEMMA

© Tom Stoddart Archive/Getty Images

On January 1, 2017, West-Tex Oil issued $50 million of 8% bonds maturing in 10 years. The market interest rate on the issue date was 9%, which resulted in the bonds being issued at a discount. In December 2018, Tex Winters, the company CFO, notes that in the two years since the bonds were issued, interest rates have fallen almost 3%. Tex suggests that West-Tex might consider repurchasing the 8% bonds and reissuing new bonds at the lower current interest rates.

Another executive, Will Bright, asks, "Won't the repurchase result in a large loss to our financial statements?" Tex agrees, indicating that West-Tex is likely to just meet earnings targets for 2018. The company would probably not meet its targets with a multimillion-dollar loss on a bond repurchase. However, 2019 looks to be a record-breaking year. They decide that maybe they should wait until 2019 to repurchase the bonds.

How could the repurchase of debt cause a loss to be reported in net income? Explain how the repurchase of debt might be timed to manage reported earnings. Is it ethical to time the repurchase of bonds to help meet earnings targets?

ANALYSIS

■ LO9–8
Make financial decisions using long-term liability ratios.

DEBT ANALYSIS
Coca-Cola vs. PepsiCo

Business decisions include risk. Failure to properly consider risk is one of the most costly, yet most common, mistakes investors and creditors make. Long-term debt is one of the first places decision makers look when trying to get a handle on risk. As stated in the feature story at the beginning of the chapter, **Six Flags** went into bankruptcy due to difficulties in repaying its long-term debt. Illustration 9–19 describes steps taken by Six Flags to reduce its long-term debt.

Here, we look at two ratios frequently used to measure financial risk related to long-term liabilities: (1) debt to equity and (2) times interest earned.

DEBT TO EQUITY RATIO

To measure a company's risk, we often calculate the debt to equity ratio:

$$\text{Debt to equity ratio} = \frac{\text{Total liabilities}}{\text{Stockholders' equity}}$$

ILLUSTRATION 9–19

Six Flags's Notes to the Financial Statements (excerpt)

> **SIX FLAGS, INC.**
> **Notes to the Financial Statements (excerpt)**
>
> Six Flags, Inc., entered into an agreement to sell three of its water parks and four of its theme parks to PARC 7F-Operations Corporation (PARC) of Jacksonville, Florida, for $312 million, consisting of $275 million in cash and a note receivable for $37 million.
>   The disposition of these seven parks is a key component of the Company's overall strategy to reduce debt and enhance operational and financial flexibility. Company management stated that its intent was to reduce debt by several hundred million dollars over the next several years.

Debt requires payment on specific dates. Failure to repay debt or the interest associated with the debt on a timely basis may result in default and perhaps even bankruptcy for a company. Other things being equal, the higher the debt to equity ratio, the higher the risk of bankruptcy. When a company assumes more debt, risk increases.

Debt also can be an advantage. It can enhance the return to stockholders. If a company earns a return in excess of the cost of borrowing the funds, shareholders are provided with a total return greater than what could have been earned with equity funds alone. Unfortunately, borrowing is not always favorable. Sometimes the cost of borrowing the funds exceeds the returns they generate. This illustrates the risk–reward trade-off faced by shareholders.

Have you ever ordered a Pepsi and then found out the place serves only Coke products? Amusement parks often have exclusive contracts for soft drinks. The official soft drink of **Six Flags** is Coca-Cola. **Cedar Point** used to serve only Pepsi products, but has recently also signed an exclusive deal with Coca-Cola. Illustration 9–20 provides selected financial data for **Coca-Cola** and **PepsiCo**.

ILLUSTRATION 9–20

Financial Information for Coca-Cola and PepsiCo

Selected Balance Sheet Data
December 31, 2014 and 2013
($ in millions)

	Coca-Cola		PepsiCo	
	2014	**2013**	**2014**	**2013**
Total assets	$92,023	$90,055	$70,509	$77,478
Total liabilities	$61,703	$56,882	$52,961	$53,089
Stockholders' equity	30,320	33,173	17,548	24,389
Total liabilities and equity	$92,023	$90,055	$70,509	$77,478

Income Statements
For the year ended December 31, 2014
($ in millions)

	Coca-Cola	PepsiCo
Net sales	$45,998	$66,683
Cost of goods sold	17,889	30,884
Gross profit	28,109	35,799
Operating expenses	18,301	26,178
Interest expense	483	909
Tax expense	2,201	2,199
Net income	$ 7,124	$ 6,513

Illustration 9–21 compares the debt to equity ratio for Coca-Cola and PepsiCo.

ILLUSTRATION 9–21

Debt to Equity Ratio for Coca-Cola and PepsiCo

($ in millions)	Total Liabilities	÷	Stockholders' Equity	=	Debt to Equity Ratio
Coca-Cola	$61,703	÷	$30,320	=	2.04
PepsiCo	$52,961	÷	$17,548	=	3.02

The debt to equity ratio is higher for PepsiCo. Debt to equity is a measure of financial leverage. Thus, PepsiCo has higher leverage than Coca-Cola. Leverage enables a company to earn a higher return using debt than without debt, in the same way a person can lift more weight with a lever than without it.

Decision Point

Question	Accounting information	Analysis
Which company has higher leverage?	Debt to equity ratio	Debt to equity is a measure of financial leverage. Companies with more debt will have a higher debt to equity ratio and higher leverage.

PepsiCo is assuming more debt, and therefore its investors are assuming more risk. Remember, this added debt could be good or bad depending on whether the company earns a return in excess of the cost of borrowed funds. Let's explore this further by revisiting the return on assets introduced in Chapter 7. Recall that return on assets measures the amount of income generated for each dollar of assets. In Illustration 9–22 we calculate the return on assets for Coca-Cola and PepsiCo.

$$\text{Return on assets} = \frac{\text{Net income}}{\text{Average total assets}}$$

ILLUSTRATION 9–22

Return on Assets for Coca-Cola and PepsiCo

($ in millions)	Net Income	÷	Average Total Assets	=	Return on Assets
Coca-Cola	$7,124	÷	$91,039*	=	7.8%
PepsiCo	$6,513	÷	$73,994**	=	8.8%

*($92,023 + $90,055)/2
**($70,509 + 77,478)/2

Coca-Cola returns 7.8 cents for each dollar of assets, compared with 8.8 cents for PepsiCo. For both companies, the return on assets exceeds the cost of borrowing (each company's borrowing rate is less than 4%). Therefore, both companies increase their total return by borrowing at a low rate and then earning a higher return on those borrowed funds. This illustrates the power of leverage to increase a company's profits. This is especially true for PepsiCo because its return on assets is higher than Coca-Cola. However, if return on assets should fall below the rate charged on borrowed funds, PepsiCo's greater leverage will result in a lower overall return to shareholders. That's where the risk comes in.

TIMES INTEREST EARNED RATIO

Lenders require interest payments in return for the use of their money. Failure to pay interest when it is due may invoke penalties, possibly leading to bankruptcy. A ratio often used to measure this risk is the times interest earned ratio. This ratio provides an indication to creditors of how many "times" greater earnings are than interest expense. A company's earnings (or profitability) provide an indication of its ability to generate cash from operations in the current year and in future years, and its cash that will be used to pay interest payments. So, **the higher a company's earnings relative to its interest expense, the more likely it will be able to make current and future interest payments.**

At first glance, you might think we can calculate the times interest earned ratio as net income divided by interest expense. But remember, interest is one of the expenses subtracted in determining net income. So, to measure how many times greater earnings are than interest expense, we need to add interest expense back to net income. Similarly, because interest is deductible for income tax purposes, we also need to add back income tax expense to get a measure of earnings *before* the effects of interest and taxes. We compute the times interest earned ratio as:

$$\text{Times interest earned ratio} = \frac{\text{Net income} + \text{Interest expense} + \text{Tax expense}}{\text{Interest expense}}$$

To further understand why we need to add back interest expense and income tax expense to net income, assume a company has the following income statement:

Income before interest and taxes	$100,000
Interest expense	**(20,000)**
Income before taxes	80,000
Income tax expense (40%)	(32,000)
Net income	$ 48,000

How many times greater is the company's earnings than interest expense? Is it 2.4 times greater (= $48,000 ÷ $20,000)? No, it's 5.0 times greater (= $100,000 ÷ $20,000). If current earnings provide an indication of the ability of a company to generate cash from operations in the current year and in future years, then a ratio of 5.0 suggests that the company will have plenty of cash available to pay current and future interest payments.

Illustration 9–23 computes the times interest earned ratios for Coca-Cola and PepsiCo to compare the companies' ability to make interest payments.

($ in millions)	Net Income + Interest Expense + Tax Expense	÷	Interest Expense	=	Times Interest Earned Ratio
Coca-Cola	$9,808	÷	$483	=	20.3
PepsiCo	$9,621	÷	$909	=	10.6

ILLUSTRATION 9–23

Times Interest Earned Ratio for Coca-Cola and PepsiCo

Coca-Cola has a higher times interest earned ratio than PepsiCo, indicating Coca-Cola is better able to meet its long-term interest obligations. However, both companies exhibit strong earnings in relation to their interest expense, and both companies appear well able to meet interest payments as they become due.

 KEY POINT

The debt to equity ratio is a measure of financial leverage. Taking on more debt (higher leverage) can be good or bad depending on whether the company earns a return in excess of the cost of borrowed funds. The times interest earned ratio measures a company's ability to meet interest payments as they become due.

Decision Point

Question	Accounting information 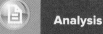	Analysis
Can a company meet its interest obligations?	Times interest earned ratio	A high times interest earned ratio indicates the ability of a company to meet its interest obligations.

KEY POINTS BY LEARNING OBJECTIVE

LO9–1 Explain financing alternatives.

Companies obtain external funds through debt financing (liabilities) and equity financing (stockholders' equity). One advantage of debt financing is that interest on borrowed funds is tax-deductible.

LO9–2 Account for installment notes payable.

Most notes payable require periodic installment payments. Each installment payment includes an amount that represents interest expense and an amount that represents a reduction of the outstanding loan balance.

LO9–3 Understand the balance sheet effects of operating and capital leases.

An operating lease is recorded just like a rental. In a capital lease, the lessee essentially "buys" the asset and borrows the money to pay for it.

LO9–4 Identify the characteristics of bonds.

The distinguishing characteristics of bonds include whether they are backed by collateral (secured or unsecured), become due at a single specified date or over a series of years (term or serial), can be redeemed prior to maturity (callable), or can be converted into common stock (convertible).

LO9–5 Determine the price of a bond issue.

The issue price of a bond is equal to the present value of the face amount (principal) payable at maturity, plus the present value of the periodic interest payments. Bonds can be issued at face amount, below face amount (at a discount), or above face amount (at a premium).

LO9–6 Account for the issuance of bonds.

When bonds issue at face amount, the carrying value and the corresponding interest expense *remain constant* over time. When bonds issue at a discount (below face amount), the carrying value and the corresponding interest expense *increase* over time. When bonds issue at a premium (above face amount), the carrying value and the corresponding interest expense *decrease* over time.

LO9–7 Record the retirement of bonds.

No gain or loss is recorded on bonds retired at maturity. For bonds retired before maturity, we record a gain or loss on early extinguishment equal to the difference between the price paid to repurchase the bonds and the bonds' carrying value.

Analysis

LO9–8 Make financial decisions using long-term liability ratios.

The debt to equity ratio is a measure of financial leverage. Assuming more debt (higher leverage) can be good or bad depending on whether the company earns a return in excess of the cost of borrowed funds. The times interest earned ratio measures a company's ability to meet interest payments as they become due.

GLOSSARY

Amortization schedule: Provides a summary of the cash interest payments, interest expense, and changes in carrying value for debt instruments. **p. 415**

Annuity: Cash payments of equal amounts over equal time periods. **p. 422**

Bond: A formal debt instrument that obligates the borrower to repay a stated amount, referred to as the principal or face amount, at a specified maturity date. **p. 418**

Callable: A bond feature that allows the borrower to repay the bonds before their scheduled maturity date at a specified call price. **p. 419**

Capital lease: Contract in which the lessee essentially buys an asset and borrows the money through a lease to pay for the asset. **p. 417**

Capital structure: The mixture of liabilities and stockholders' equity in a business. **p. 414**

Carrying value: The balance in the bonds payable account, which equals the face value of bonds payable minus the discount or the face value plus the premium. **p. 429**

Convertible: A bond feature that allows the lender (or investor) to convert each bond into a specified number of shares of common stock. **p. 420**

Debt financing: Borrowing money from creditors. **p. 414**

Debt to equity ratio: Total liabilities divided by total stockholders' equity; measures a company's risk. **p. 436**

Default risk: The risk that a company will be unable to pay the bond's face amount or interest payments as it becomes due. **p. 422**

Discount: A bond's issue price is below the face amount. **p. 423**

Early extinguishment of debt: The issuer retires debt before its scheduled maturity date. **p. 435**

Equity financing: Obtaining investment from stockholders. **p. 414**

Installment payment: Includes both an amount that represents interest and an amount that represents a reduction of the outstanding balance. **p. 415**

Lease: A contractual arrangement by which the lessor (owner) provides the lessee (user) the right to use an asset for a specified period of time. **p. 416**

Market interest rate: Represents the true interest rate used by investors to value a bond. **p. 421**

Operating lease: Contract in which the lessor owns the asset and the lessee uses the asset temporarily. **p. 416**

Premium: A bond's issue price is above the face amount. **p. 424**

Private placement: Sale of debt securities directly to a single investor. **p. 418**

Return on assets: Net income divided by average total assets; measures the amount of net income generated for each dollar invested in assets. **p. 438**

Secured bonds: Bonds that are supported by specific assets pledged as collateral. **p. 419**

Serial bonds: Bonds that require payment of the principal amount of the bond over a series of maturity dates. **p. 419**

Sinking fund: An investment fund used to set aside money to be used to pay debts as they come due. **p. 419**

Stated interest rate: The rate quoted in the bond contract used to calculate the cash payments for interest. **p. 421**

Term bonds: Bonds that require payment of the full principal amount at the end of the loan term. **p. 419**

Times interest earned ratio: Ratio that compares interest expense with income available to pay those charges. **p. 438**

Unsecured bonds: Bonds that are *not* supported by specific assets pledged as collateral. **p. 419**

SELF-STUDY QUESTIONS

1. Which of the following is *not* a primary source of corporate debt financing? **LO9–1**
   a. Bonds.
   b. Notes.
   c. Leases.
   d. Receivables.

2. Which of the following leases is essentially the purchase of an asset with debt financing? **LO9–3**
   a. An operating lease.
   b. A capital lease.
   c. Both an operating lease and a capital lease.
   d. Neither an operating lease nor a capital lease.

3. Serial bonds are: **LO9–4**
   a. Bonds backed by collateral.
   b. Bonds that mature in installments.
   c. Bonds the issuer can repurchase at a fixed price.
   d. Bonds issued below the face amount.

4. Convertible bonds: **LO9–4**
   a. Provide potential benefits only to the issuer.
   b. Provide potential benefits only to the investor.
   c. Provide potential benefits to both the issuer and the investor.
   d. Provide no potential benefits.

5. The price of a bond is equal to: **LO9–5**
   a. The present value of the face amount plus the present value of the stated interest payments.
   b. The future value of the face amount plus the future value of the stated interest payments.
   c. The present value of the face amount only.
   d. The present value of the interest only.

6. Which of the following is true for bonds issued at a discount? **LO9–6**
   a. The stated interest rate is greater than the market interest rate.
   b. The market interest rate is greater than the stated interest rate.
   c. The stated interest rate and the market interest rate are equal.
   d. The stated interest rate and the market interest rate are unrelated.

7. Interest expense on bonds payable is calculated as: **LO9–6**
   a. Face amount times the stated interest rate.
   b. Carrying value times the market interest rate.
   c. Face amount times the market interest rate.
   d. Carrying value times the stated interest rate.

8. When bonds are issued at a discount, what happens to the carrying value and interest expense over the life of the bonds? **LO9–6**
   a. Carrying value and interest expense increase.
   b. Carrying value and interest expense decrease.
   c. Carrying value decreases and interest expense increases.
   d. Carrying value increases and interest expense decreases.

9. Lincoln County retires a $50 million bond issue when the carrying value of the bonds is $48 million, but the market value of the bonds is $54 million. Lincoln County will record the retirement as: **LO9–7**
   a. A debit of $6 million to Loss due to early extinguishment.
   b. A credit of $6 million to Gain due to early extinguishment.
   c. No gain or loss on retirement.
   d. A debit to Cash for $54 million.

10. Which of the following ratios measures financial leverage? **LO9–8**
    a. The return on assets ratio.
    b. The inventory turnover ratio.
    c. The times interest earned ratio.
    d. The debt to equity ratio.

Note: For answers, see the last page of the chapter.

For additional study materials, including 10 more multiple-choice Self-Study Questions, visit Connect.

REVIEW QUESTIONS

■ **LO9–1**   1. What is capital structure? How do the capital structures of **Ford** and **Microsoft** differ?

■ **LO9–1**   2. Why would a company choose to borrow money rather than issue additional stock?

■ **LO9–2**   3. How do interest expense and the carrying value of the note change over time for an installment note with fixed monthly loan payments?

■ **LO9–3**   4. Explain the difference between an operating lease and a capital lease.

■ **LO9–4**   5. What are bond issue costs? What is an underwriter?

■ **LO9–4**   6. Why do some companies issue bonds rather than borrow money directly from a bank?

■ **LO9–4**   7. Contrast the following types of bonds:
   a. Secured and unsecured.
   b. Term and serial.
   c. Callable and convertible.

■ **LO9–4**   8. What are convertible bonds? How do they benefit both the investor and the issuer?

■ **LO9–5**   9. How do we calculate the issue price of bonds? Is it equal to the present value of the principal? Explain.

■ **LO9–5**   10. Explain the difference in each of these terms used for bonds:
   a. Face amount and carrying value.
   b. Stated interest rate and market interest rate.

■ **LO9–5**   11. If bonds issue at a *discount*, is the stated interest rate less than, equal to, or more than the market interest rate? Explain.

■ **LO9–5**   12. If bonds issue at a *premium*, is the stated interest rate less than, equal to, or more than the market interest rate? Explain.

■ **LO9–5**   13. Extreme Motion issues $500,000 of 6% bonds due in 20 years with interest payable semiannually on June 30 and December 31. What is the amount of the cash payment for interest every six months? How many interest payments will there be?

■ **LO9–5**   14. Extreme Motion issues $500,000 of 6% bonds due in 20 years with interest payable semiannually on June 30 and December 31. Calculate the issue price of the bonds assuming a market interest rate of:
   a. 5%
   b. 6%
   c. 7%

15. If bonds issue at a *discount,* what happens to the carrying value of bonds payable and the amount recorded for interest expense over time? ■ LO9–6

16. If bonds issue at a *premium,* what happens to the carrying value of bonds payable and the amount recorded for interest expense over time? ■ LO9–6

17. Explain how each of the columns in an amortization schedule is calculated, assuming the bonds are issued at a discount. How is the amortization schedule different if bonds are issued at a premium? ■ LO9–6

18. Why would a company choose to buy back bonds before their maturity date? ■ LO9–7

19. If bonds with a face value of $250,000 and a carrying value of $280,000 are retired early at a cost of $330,000, is a gain or loss recorded by the issuer retiring the bonds? How does the issuer record the retirement? ■ LO9–7

20. What are the potential risks and rewards of carrying additional debt? ■ LO9–8

BRIEF EXERCISES

BE9–1 On January 1, 2018, Corvallis Carnivals borrows $30,000 to purchase a delivery truck by agreeing to a 5%, five-year loan with the bank. Payments of $566.14 are due at the end of each month, with the first installment due on January 31, 2018. Record the issuance of the note payable and the first monthly payment.

Record installment notes (LO9–2)

BE9–2 Water Emporium issues $20 million of 4% convertible bonds that mature in 10 years. Each $1,000 bond is convertible into 20 shares of common stock. The current market price of Water Emporium stock is $40 per share.
1. Explain why Water Emporium might choose to issue convertible bonds.
2. Explain why investors might choose Water Emporium's convertible bonds.

Explain the conversion feature of bonds (LO9–4)

BE9–3 Ultimate Butter Popcorn issues 7%, 10-year bonds with a face amount of $60,000. The market interest rate for bonds of similar risk and maturity is 7%. Interest is paid semiannually. At what price will the bonds issue?

Calculate the issue price of bonds (LO9–5)

BE9–4 Ultimate Butter Popcorn issues 7%, 15-year bonds with a face amount of $60,000. The market interest rate for bonds of similar risk and maturity is 8%. Interest is paid semiannually. At what price will the bonds issue?

Calculate the issue price of bonds (LO9–5)

BE9–5 Ultimate Butter Popcorn issues 7%, 20-year bonds with a face amount of $60,000. The market interest rate for bonds of similar risk and maturity is 6%. Interest is paid semiannually. At what price will the bonds issue?

Calculate the issue price of bonds (LO9–5)

BE9–6 Pretzelmania, Inc., issues 7%, 10-year bonds with a face amount of $70,000 for $70,000 on January 1, 2018. The market interest rate for bonds of similar risk and maturity is 7%. Interest is paid semiannually on June 30 and December 31.
1. Record the bond issue.
2. Record the first interest payment on June 30, 2018.

Record bond issue and related semiannual interest (LO9–6)

BE9–7 Pretzelmania, Inc., issues 7%, 15-year bonds with a face amount of $70,000 for $63,948 on January 1, 2018. The market interest rate for bonds of similar risk and maturity is 8%. Interest is paid semiannually on June 30 and December 31.
1. Record the bond issue.
2. Record the first interest payment on June 30, 2018.

Record bond issue and related semiannual interest (LO9–6)

BE9–8 Pretzelmania, Inc., issues 7%, 15-year bonds with a face amount of $70,000 for $76,860 on January 1, 2018. The market interest rate for bonds of similar risk and maturity is 6%. Interest is paid semiannually on June 30 and December 31.
1. Record the bond issue.
2. Record the first interest payment on June 30, 2018.

Record bond issue and related semiannual interest (LO9–6)

BE9–9 Pretzelmania, Inc., issues 7%, 10-year bonds with a face amount of $70,000 for $70,000 on January 1, 2018. The market interest rate for bonds of similar risk and maturity is 7%. Interest is paid *annually* on December 31.
1. Record the bond issue.
2. Record the first interest payment on December 31, 2018.

BE9–10 Pretzelmania, Inc., issues 7%, 15-year bonds with a face amount of $70,000 for $64,008 on January 1, 2018. The market interest rate for bonds of similar risk and maturity is 8%. Interest is paid *annually* on December 31.
1. Record the bond issue.
2. Record the first interest payment on December 31, 2018. (Hint: Interest expense is 8% times the carrying value of $64,008.)

BE9–11 Pretzelmania, Inc., issues 7%, 15-year bonds with a face amount of $70,000 for $76,799 on January 1, 2018. The market interest rate for bonds of similar risk and maturity is 6%. Interest is paid *annually* on December 31.
1. Record the bond issue.
2. Record the first interest payment on December 31, 2018. (*Hint:* Interest expense is 6% times the carrying value of $76,799.)

BE9–12 On January 1, 2018, Lizzy's Lemonade issues 5%, 20-year bonds with a face amount of $100,000 for $88,443, priced to yield 6%. Interest is paid semiannually. What amount of interest expense will be recorded on June 30, 2018, the first interest payment date?

BE9–13 On January 1, 2018, Lyle's Limeade issues 4%, 10-year bonds with a face amount of $90,000 for $82,985, priced to yield 5%. Interest is paid semiannually. What amount of interest expense will be recorded in the December 31, 2018, annual income statement?

BE9–14 Presented below is a partial amortization schedule for Discount Pizza.

(1) Period	(2) Cash Paid for Interest	(3) Interest Expense	(4) Increase in Carrying Value	(5) Carrying Value
Issue date				$63,948
1	$2,450	$2,558	$108	64,056
2	2,450	2,562	112	64,168

1. Record the bond issue assuming the face value of bonds payable is $70,000.
2. Record the first interest payment.
3. Explain why interest expense increases each period.

BE9–15 Presented below is a partial amortization schedule for Premium Pizza.

(1) Period	(2) Cash Paid for Interest	(3) Interest Expense	(4) Decrease in Carrying Value	(5) Carrying Value
Issue date				$76,860
1	$2,450	$2,306	$144	76,716
2	2,450	2,301	149	76,567

1. Record the bond issue assuming the face value of bonds payable is $70,000.
2. Record the first interest payment.
3. Explain why interest expense decreases each period.

BE9–16 Discount Pizza retires its 7% bonds for $68,000 before their scheduled maturity. At the time, the bonds have a face value of $70,000 and a carrying value of $64,168. Record the early retirement of the bonds.

BE9–17 Premium Pizza retires its 7% bonds for $72,000 before their scheduled maturity. At the time, the bonds have a face value of $70,000 and a carrying value of $76,567. Record the early retirement of the bonds.

Record early retirement of bonds issued at a premium (LO9–7)

BE9–18 Surf's Up, a manufacturer of surfing supplies and training equipment, has the following selected data ($ in millions):

Calculate ratios (LO9–8)

SURF'S UP Selected Balance Sheet Data		
	2018	**2017**
Total assets	$727	$718
Total liabilities	628	530
Total stockholders' equity	99	188

SURF'S UP Selected Income Statement Data	
	2018
Sales revenue	$795
Interest expense	15
Tax expense	44
Net income	66

Based on these amounts, calculate the following ratios for 2018:
1. Debt to equity ratio.
2. Return on assets ratio.
3. Times interest earned ratio.

EXERCISES

E9–1 Penny Arcades, Inc., is trying to decide between the following two alternatives to finance its new $35 million gaming center:

Compare financing alternatives (LO9–1)

a. Issue $35 million of 7% bonds at face amount.
b. Issue 1 million shares of common stock for $35 per share.

	Issue Bonds	Issue Stock
Operating income	$11,000,000	$11,000,000
Interest expense (bonds only)		
Income before tax		
Income tax expense (35%)		
Net income	$	$
Number of shares	4,000,000	5,000,000
Earnings per share (Net income/# of shares)	$	$

Required:
1. Assuming bonds or shares of stock are issued at the beginning of the year, complete the income statement for each alternative.
2. Which alternative results in the highest earnings per share?

E9–2 On January 1, 2018, Tropical Paradise borrows $50,000 by agreeing to a 6%, six-year note with the bank. The funds will be used to purchase a new BMW convertible for use in promoting resort properties to potential customers. Loan payments of $828.64 are due at the end of each month with the first installment due on January 31, 2018.

Record installment notes (LO9–2)

Required:
Record the issuance of the installment note payable and the first two monthly payments.

E9–3 Coney Island enters into a lease agreement for a new ride valued at $2 million. Prior to this agreement, the company's total assets are $25 million and its total liabilities are $15 million.

Compare operating and capital leases (LO9–3, LO9–8)

Required:
1. Calculate total stockholders' equity prior to the lease agreement.
2. Assuming an operating lease, calculate the debt to equity ratio.

3. Assuming a capital lease, calculate the debt to equity ratio.

4. Why might Coney Island prefer an operating lease?

Match bond terms with their definitions (LO9–4)

E9–4 Listed below are terms and definitions associated with bonds.

Terms

———— 1. Sinking fund.

———— 2. Secured bond.

———— 3. Unsecured bond.

———— 4. Term bond.

———— 5. Serial bond.

———— 6. Callable bond.

———— 7. Convertible bond.

———— 8. Bond issue costs.

Definitions

a. Allows the issuer to pay off the bonds early at a fixed price.

b. Matures in installments.

c. Secured only by the "full faith and credit" of the issuing corporation.

d. Allows the investor to transfer each bond into shares of common stock.

e. Money set aside to pay debts as they come due.

f. Matures on a single date.

g. Supported by specific assets pledged as collateral by the issuer.

h. Includes underwriting, legal, accounting, registration, and printing fees.

Required:

Match (by letter) the bond terms with their definitions. Each letter is used only once.

Calculate the issue price of bonds (LO9–5)

E9–5 On January 1, 2018, Frontier World issues $41 million of 9% bonds, due in 20 years, with interest payable semiannually on June 30 and December 31 each year. The proceeds will be used to build a new ride that combines a roller coaster, a water ride, a dark tunnel, and the great smell of outdoor barbeque, all in one ride.

Required:

1. If the market rate is 8%, will the bonds issue at face amount, a discount, or a premium? Calculate the issue price.

2. If the market rate is 9%, will the bonds issue at face amount, a discount, or a premium? Calculate the issue price.

3. If the market rate is 10%, will the bonds issue at face amount, a discount, or a premium? Calculate the issue price.

Calculate the issue price of bonds (LO9–5)

E9–6 On January 1, 2018, Water World issues $26 million of 7% bonds, due in 10 years, with interest payable semiannually on June 30 and December 31 each year. Water World intends to use the funds to build the world's largest water avalanche and the "tornado"—a giant outdoor vortex in which riders spin in progressively smaller and faster circles until they drop through a small tunnel at the bottom.

Required:

1. If the market rate is 6%, will the bonds issue at face amount, a discount, or a premium? Calculate the issue price.

2. If the market rate is 7%, will the bonds issue at face amount, a discount, or a premium? Calculate the issue price.

3. If the market rate is 8%, will the bonds issue at face amount, a discount, or a premium? Calculate the issue price.

Record bonds issued at face amount (LO9–6)

E9–7 On January 1, 2018, Splash City issues $500,000 of 9% bonds, due in 20 years, with interest payable semiannually on June 30 and December 31 each year.

Required:

Assuming the market interest rate on the issue date is 9%, the bonds will issue at $500,000. Record the bond issue on January 1, 2018, and the first two semiannual interest payments on June 30, 2018, and December 31, 2018.

E9–8 On January 1, 2018, Splash City issues $500,000 of 9% bonds, due in 20 years, with interest payable semiannually on June 30 and December 31 each year.

Record bonds issued at a discount (LO9–6)

Required:

Assuming the market interest rate on the issue date is 10%, the bonds will issue at $457,102.

1. Complete the first three rows of an amortization table.
2. Record the bond issue on January 1, 2018, and the first two semiannual interest payments on June 30, 2018, and December 31, 2018.

E9–9 On January 1, 2018, Splash City issues $500,000 of 9% bonds, due in 20 years, with interest payable semiannually on June 30 and December 31 each year.

Record bonds issued at a premium (LO9–6)

Required:

Assuming the market interest rate on the issue date is 8%, the bonds will issue at $549,482.

1. Complete the first three rows of an amortization table.
2. Record the bond issue on January 1, 2018, and the first two semiannual interest payments on June 30, 2018, and December 31, 2018.

E9–10 On January 1, 2018, White Water issues $600,000 of 7% bonds, due in 10 years, with interest payable semiannually on June 30 and December 31 each year.

Record bonds issued at face amount (LO9–6)

Required:

Assuming the market interest rate on the issue date is 7%, the bonds will issue at $600,000. Record the bond issue on January 1, 2018, and the first two semiannual interest payments on June 30, 2018, and December 31, 2018.

E9–11 On January 1, 2018, White Water issues $600,000 of 7% bonds, due in 10 years, with interest payable semiannually on June 30 and December 31 each year.

Record bonds issued at a discount (LO9–6)

Required:

Assuming the market interest rate on the issue date is 8%, the bonds will issue at $559,229.

1. Complete the first three rows of an amortization table.
2. Record the bond issue on January 1, 2018, and the first two semiannual interest payments on June 30, 2018, and December 31, 2018.

E9–12 On January 1, 2018, White Water issues $600,000 of 7% bonds, due in 10 years, with interest payable semiannually on June 30 and December 31 each year.

Record bonds issued at a premium (LO9–6)

Required:

Assuming the market interest rate on the issue date is 6%, the bonds will issue at $644,632.

1. Complete the first three rows of an amortization table.
2. Record the bond issue on January 1, 2018, and the first two semiannual interest payments on June 30, 2018, and December 31, 2018.

E9–13 On January 1, 2018, White Water issues $600,000 of 7% bonds, due in 10 years, with interest payable annually on December 31 each year.

Record bonds issued at face amount with interest payable annually (LO9–6)

Required:

Assuming the market interest rate on the issue date is 7%, the bonds will issue at $600,000. Record the bond issue on January 1, 2018, and the first two interest payments on December 31, 2018, and December 31, 2019.

E9–14 On January 1, 2018, White Water issues $600,000 of 7% bonds, due in 10 years, with interest payable annually on December 31 each year.

Record bonds issued at a discount with interest payable annually (LO9–6)

Required:

Assuming the market interest rate on the issue date is 8%, the bonds will issue at $559,740.

1. Complete the first three rows of an amortization table. (*Hint:* Use Illustration 9–16, except the dates for the first three rows will be 1/1/18, 12/31/18, and 12/31/19 since interest is payable *annually* rather than semiannually. Interest expense for the period ended December 31, 2018, is calculated as the carrying value of $559,740 times the market rate of 8%.)

2. Record the bond issue on January 1, 2018, and the first two interest payments on December 31, 2018, and December 31, 2019.

Record bonds issued at a premium with interest payable *annually* (LO9–6)

E9–15 On January 1, 2018, White Water issues $600,000 of 7% bonds, due in 10 years, with interest payable annually on December 31 each year.

Required:
Assuming the market interest rate on the issue date is 6%, the bonds will issue at $644,161.
1. Complete the first three rows of an amortization table. (*Hint:* Use Illustration 9–17, except the dates for the first three rows will be 1/1/18, 12/31/18, and 12/31/19 since interest is payable *annually* rather than semiannually. Interest expense for the period ended December 31, 2018, is calculated as the carrying value of $644,161 times the market rate of 6%.)
2. Record the bond issue on January 1, 2018, and the first two interest payments on December 31, 2018, and December 31, 2019.

Record the retirement of bonds (LO9–7)

E9–16 On January 1, 2018, Splash City issues $500,000 of 9% bonds, due in 20 years, with interest payable semiannually on June 30 and December 31 each year. The market interest rate on the issue date is 10% and the bonds issued at $457,102.

Required:
1. Using an amortization schedule, show that the bonds have a carrying value of $458,633 on December 31, 2019.
2. If the market interest rate drops to 7% on December 31, 2019, it will cost $601,452 to retire the bonds. Record the retirement of the bonds on December 31, 2019.

Record the retirement of bonds (LO9–7)

E9–17 On January 1, 2018, White Water issues $600,000 of 7% bonds, due in 10 years, with interest payable semiannually on June 30 and December 31 each year. The market interest rate on the issue date is 6% and the bonds issued at $644,632.

Required:
1. Using an amortization schedule, show that the bonds have a carrying value of $633,887 on December 31, 2020.
2. If the market interest rate increases to 8% on December 31, 2020, it will cost $568,311 to retire the bonds. Record the retirement of the bonds on December 31, 2020.

Calculate and analyze ratios (LO9–8)

E9–18 Two online travel companies, E-Travel and Pricecheck, provide the following selected financial data:

($ in thousands)	E-Travel	Pricecheck
Total assets	$7,437,156	$2,094,224
Total liabilities	4,254,475	486,610
Total stockholders' equity	3,182,681	1,607,614
Sales revenue	$3,455,426	$2,838,212
Interest expense	94,233	34,084
Tax expense	174,400	57,168
Net income	319,526	509,472

Required:
1. Calculate the debt to equity ratio for E-Travel and Pricecheck. Which company has the higher ratio?
2. Calculate the times interest earned ratio for E-Travel and Pricecheck. Which company is better able to meet interest payments as they become due?

E9–19 On January 1, 2018, the general ledger of Freedom Fireworks includes the following account balances: **(LO9-2, LO9-8)**

Accounts	Debit	Credit
Cash	$ 11,200	
Accounts Receivable	34,000	
Allowance for Uncollectible Accounts		$ 1,800
Inventory	152,000	
Land	67,300	
Buildings	120,000	
Accumulated Depreciation		9,600
Accounts Payable		17,700
Common Stock		200,000
Retained Earnings		155,400
Totals	$384,500	$384,500

During January 2018, the following transactions occur:

January 1 Borrow $100,000 from Captive Credit Corporation. The installment note bears interest at 7% annually and matures in 5 years. Payments of $1,980 are required at the end of each month for 60 months.

January 4 Receive $31,000 from customers on accounts receivable.

January 10 Pay cash on accounts payable, $11,000.

January 15 Pay cash for salaries, $28,900.

January 30 Firework sales for the month total $195,000. Sales include $65,000 for cash and $130,000 on account. The cost of the units sold is $112,500.

January 31 Pay the first monthly installment of $1,980 related to the $100,000 borrowed on January 1. Round your interest calculation to the nearest dollar.

Required:
1. Record each of the transactions listed above.
2. Record adjusting entries on January 31.
   a. Depreciation on the building for the month of January is calculated using the straight-line method. At the time the equipment was purchased, the company estimated a service life of 10 years and a residual value of $24,000.
   b. At the end of January, $3,000 of accounts receivable are past due, and the company estimates that 50% of these accounts will not be collected. Of the remaining accounts receivable, the company estimates that 2% will not be collected. No accounts were written off as uncollectible in January.
   c. Unpaid salaries at the end of January are $26,100.
   d. Accrued income taxes at the end of January are $8,000.
3. Prepare an adjusted trial balance as of January 31, 2018, after updating beginning balances (above) for transactions during January (*Requirement* 1) and adjusting entries at the end of January (*Requirement* 2).
4. Prepare a multiple-step income statement for the period ended January 31, 2018.
5. Prepare a classified balance sheet as of January 31, 2018. (Hint: The carrying value of notes payable on January 31, 2018 is $98,603; $17,411 is reported as notes payable in the current liabilities section and $81,192 is reported as notes payable in the long-term liabilities section ($17, 411 + $81,192 = $98,603).
6. Record closing entries.
7. Analyze the following for Freedom Fireworks:
   a. Calculate the debt to equity ratio. If the average debt to equity ratio for the industry is 1.0, is Freedom Fireworks more or less leveraged than other companies in the same industry?

b. Calculate the times interest earned ratio. If the average times interest earned ratio for the industry is 20 times, is the company more or less able to meet interest payments than other companies in the same industry?

c. Based on the ratios calculated in (a) and (b), would Freedom Fireworks be more likely to receive a higher or lower interest rate than the average borrowing rate in the industry?

PROBLEMS: SET A

■ connect

Record and analyze installment notes (LO9–2)

P9–1A On January 1, 2018, Gundy Enterprises purchases an office for $360,000, paying $60,000 down and borrowing the remaining $300,000, signing a 7%, 10-year mortgage. Installment payments of $3,483.25 are due at the end of each month, with the first payment due on January 31, 2018.

Required:
1. Record the purchase of the building on January 1, 2018.
2. Complete the first three rows of an amortization schedule similar to Illustration 9–1.
3. Record the first monthly mortgage payment on January 31, 2018. How much of the first payment goes to interest expense and how much goes to reducing the carrying value of the loan?
4. Total payments over the 10 years are $417,990 ($3,483.25 × 120 monthly payments). How much of this is interest expense and how much is actual payment of the loan?

Explore the impact of leases on the debt to equity ratio (LO9–3, LO9–8)

P9–2A Thrillville has $41 million in bonds payable. One of the contractual agreements in the bond indenture is that the debt to equity ratio cannot exceed 2.0. Thrillville's total assets are $81 million, and its liabilities other than the bonds payable are $11 million. The company is considering some additional financing through leasing.

Required:
1. Calculate total stockholders' equity using the balance sheet equation.
2. Calculate the debt to equity ratio.
3. Explain the difference between an operating lease and a capital lease.
4. The company enters a lease agreement requiring lease payments with a present value of $16 million. Will this lease agreement affect the debt to equity ratio differently if the lease is recorded as an operating lease versus a capital lease?
5. Will entering into the lease cause the debt to equity ratio to be in violation of the contractual agreement in the bond indenture? Show your calculations (a) assuming an operating lease and (b) assuming a capital lease.

Calculate the issue price of a bond and prepare amortization schedules (LO9–5, LO9–6)

P9–3A Coney Island Entertainment issues $1,300,000 of 7% bonds, due in 15 years, with interest payable semiannually on June 30 and December 31 each year.

Required:
Calculate the issue price of a bond and complete the first three rows of an amortization schedule when:
1. The market interest rate is 7% and the bonds issue at face amount.
2. The market interest rate is 8% and the bonds issue at a discount.
3. The market interest rate is 6% and the bonds issue at a premium.

Record bond issue and related interest (LO9–6)

P9–4A On January 1, 2018, Twister Enterprises, a manufacturer of a variety of transportable spin rides, issues $600,000 of 8% bonds, due in 20 years, with interest payable semiannually on June 30 and December 31 each year.

Required:
1. If the market interest rate is 8%, the bonds will issue at $600,000. Record the bond issue on January 1, 2018, and the first two semiannual interest payments on June 30, 2018, and December 31, 2018.
2. If the market interest rate is 9%, the bonds will issue at $544,795. Record the bond issue on January 1, 2018, and the first two semiannual interest payments on June 30, 2018, and December 31, 2018.
3. If the market interest rate is 7%, the bonds will issue at $664,065. Record the bond issue on January 1, 2018, and the first two semiannual interest payments on June 30, 2018, and December 31, 2018.

P9–5A On January 1, 2018, Vacation Destinations issues $40 million of bonds that pay interest semiannually on June 30 and December 31. Portions of the bond amortization schedule appear below:

Understand a bond amortization schedule (LO9–6)

(1) Date	(2) Cash Paid for Interest	(3) Interest Expense	(4) Increase in Carrying Value	(5) Carrying Value
1/1/2018				$37,281,935
6/30/2018	$1,400,000	$1,491,277	$91,277	37,373,212
12/31/2018	1,400,000	1,494,928	94,928	37,468,140

Required:

1. Were the bonds issued at face amount, a discount, or a premium?
2. What is the original issue price of the bonds?
3. What is the face amount of the bonds?
4. What is the stated annual interest rate?
5. What is the market annual interest rate?
6. What is the total cash paid for interest assuming the bonds mature in 10 years?

P9–6A On January 1, 2018, Universe of Fun issues $900,000, 8% bonds that mature in 10 years. The market interest rate for bonds of similar risk and maturity is 9%, and the bonds issue for $841,464. Interest is paid semiannually on June 30 and December 31.

Prepare a bond amortization schedule and record transactions for the bond issuer (LO9–6)

Required:

1. Complete the first three rows of an amortization schedule.
2. Record the issuance of the bonds on January 1, 2018.
3. Record the interest payments on June 30, 2018, and December 31, 2018.

P9–7A Selected financial data for Bahama Bay and Caribbean Key are as follows:

Calculate and analyze ratios (LO9–8)

($ in millions)	Bahama Bay		Caribbean Key	
	2018	2017	2018	2017
Total assets	$8,861	$9,560	$7,640	$7,507
Total liabilities	5,724	6,606	2,819	2,689
Total stockholders' equity	3,137	2,954	4,821	4,818
Sales revenue	$6,321		$3,949	
Interest expense	170		70	
Tax expense	148		8	
Net income	562		88	

Required:

1. Calculate the debt to equity ratio for Bahama Bay and Caribbean Key for the most recent year. Which company has the higher ratio?
2. Calculate the return on assets for Bahama Bay and Caribbean Key. Which company appears more profitable?
3. Calculate the times interest earned ratio for Bahama Bay and Caribbean Key. Which company is better able to meet interest payments as they become due?

PROBLEMS: SET B

P9–1B On January 1, 2018, Stoops Entertainment purchases a building for $610,000, paying $110,000 down and borrowing the remaining $500,000, signing a 9%, 15-year mortgage.

Record and analyze installment notes (LO9–2)

Installment payments of $5,071.33 are due at the end of each month, with the first payment due on January 31, 2018.

Required:
1. Record the purchase of the building on January 1, 2018.
2. Complete the first three rows of an amortization schedule similar to Illustration 9–1.
3. Record the first monthly mortgage payment on January 31, 2018. How much of the first payment goes to interest expense and how much goes to reducing the carrying value of the loan?
4. Total payments over the 15 years are $912,839 ($5,071.33 × 180 monthly payments). How much of this is interest expense and how much is actual payment of the loan?

Explore the impact of leases on the debt to equity ratio (LO9–3, LO9–8)

P9–2B Chunky Cheese Pizza has $61 million in bonds payable. The bond indenture states that the debt to equity ratio cannot exceed 3.25. Chunky's total assets are $201 million, and its liabilities other than the bonds payable are $91 million. The company is considering some additional financing through leasing.

Required:
1. Calculate total stockholders' equity using the balance sheet equation.
2. Calculate the debt to equity ratio.
3. Explain the difference between an operating and a capital lease.
4. The company enters a lease agreement requiring lease payments with a present value of $26 million. Will this lease agreement affect the debt to equity ratio differently if the lease is recorded as an operating lease versus a capital lease?
5. Will entering into the lease cause the debt to equity ratio to be in violation of the contractual agreement in the bond indenture? Show your calculations (a) assuming an operating lease and (b) assuming a capital lease.

Calculate the issue price of a bond and prepare amortization schedules (LO9–5, LO9–6)

P9–3B Christmas Anytime issues $850,000 of 6% bonds, due in 10 years, with interest payable semiannually on June 30 and December 31 each year.

Required:
Calculate the issue price of a bond and complete the first three rows of an amortization schedule when:
1. The market interest rate is 6% and the bonds issue at face amount.
2. The market interest rate is 7% and the bonds issue at a discount.
3. The market interest rate is 5% and the bonds issue at a premium.

Record bond issue and related interest (LO9–6)

P9–4B Viking Voyager specializes in the design and production of replica Viking boats. On January 1, 2018, the company issues $3,000,000 of 9% bonds, due in 10 years, with interest payable semiannually on June 30 and December 31 each year.

Required:
1. If the market interest rate is 9%, the bonds will issue at $3,000,000. Record the bond issue on January 1, 2018, and the first two semiannual interest payments on June 30, 2018, and December 31, 2018.
2. If the market interest rate is 10%, the bonds will issue at $2,813,067. Record the bond issue on January 1, 2018, and the first two semiannual interest payments on June 30, 2018, and December 31, 2018.
3. If the market interest rate is 8%, the bonds will issue at $3,203,855. Record the bond issue on January 1, 2018, and the first two semiannual interest payments on June 30, 2018, and December 31, 2018.

Understand a bond amortization schedule (LO9–6)

P9–5B Temptation Vacations issues $60 million in bonds on January 1, 2018, that pay interest semiannually on June 30 and December 31. Portions of the bond amortization schedule appear below:

(1) Date	(2) Cash Paid for Interest	(3) Interest Expense	(4) Decrease in Carrying Value	(5) Carrying Value
1/1/2018				$66,934,432
6/30/2018	$2,100,000	$2,008,033	$91,967	$66,842,465
12/31/2018	2,100,000	2,005,274	94,726	66,747,739

Required:
1. Were the bonds issued at face amount, a discount, or a premium?
2. What is the original issue price of the bonds?
3. What is the face amount of the bonds?
4. What is the stated annual interest rate?
5. What is the market annual interest rate?
6. What is the total cash paid for interest assuming the bonds mature in 20 years?

P9–6B Super Splash issues $1,000,000, 7% bonds on January 1, 2018, that mature in 15 years. The market interest rate for bonds of similar risk and maturity is 6%, and the bonds issue for $1,098,002. Interest is paid semiannually on June 30 and December 31.

Prepare a bond amortization schedule and record transactions for the bond issuer (LO9–6)

Required:
1. Complete the first three rows of an amortization schedule.
2. Record the issuance of the bonds on January 1, 2018.
3. Record the interest payments on June 30, 2018, and December 31, 2018.

P9–7B Selected financial data for Surf City and Paradise Falls are as follows:

Calculate and analyze ratios (LO9–8)

($ in millions)	Surf City		Paradise Falls	
	2018	**2017**	**2018**	**2017**
Total assets	$19,828	$19,804	$39,161	$38,637
Total liabilities	11,519	11,396	15,232	14,805
Total stockholders' equity	8,309	8,408	23,929	23,832
Sales revenue	$ 7,688		$15,382	
Interest expense	356		336	
Tax expense	–		4	
Net income	18		1,298	

Required:
1. Calculate the debt to equity ratio for Surf City and Paradise Falls for the most recent year. Which company has the higher ratio?
2. Calculate the return on assets for Surf City and Paradise Falls. Which company appears more profitable?
3. Calculate the times interest earned ratio for Surf City and Paradise Falls. Which company is better able to meet interest payments as they become due?

ADDITIONAL PERSPECTIVES

Great Adventures

(This is a continuation of the Great Adventures problem from earlier chapters.)

AP9–1 Tony's favorite memories of his childhood were the times he spent with his dad at camp. Tony was daydreaming of those days a bit as he and Suzie jogged along a nature trail and came across a wonderful piece of property for sale. He turned to Suzie and said, "I've always wanted to start a camp where families could get away and spend some quality time together. If we just had the money, I know this would be the perfect place." They called several banks and on January 1, 2020, Great Adventures obtained a $500,000, 6%, 10-year installment loan from Summit Bank. Payments of $5,551 are required at the end of each month over the life of the 10-year loan. Each monthly payment of $5,551 includes both interest expense and principal payments (i.e., reduction of the loan amount).

Continuing Problem

Late that night Tony exclaimed, "$500,000 for our new camp, this has to be the best news ever." Suzie snuggled close and said, "There's something else I need to tell you. Tony, I'm expecting!" They decided right then, if it was a boy, they would name him Venture.

Required:

1. Complete the first three rows of an amortization table.
2. Record the note payable on January 1, 2020, and the first two payments on January 31, 2020, and February 28, 2020.

Financial Analysis

American Eagle Outfitters, Inc.

AP9–2 Financial information for **American Eagle** is presented in **Appendix A** at the end of the book.

Required:

1. Calculate the debt to equity ratio for the past two years. Did the ratio improve or weaken in the more recent year?
2. Calculate the return on assets for the most recent year. Does the return on assets exceed the cost of borrowing?
3. *Review the balance sheet and note 9 to the financial statements.* Based on this information, how would you rate the bankruptcy risk of American Eagle?

Financial Analysis

The Buckle, Inc.

AP9–3 Financial information for **Buckle** is presented in **Appendix B** at the end of the book.

Required:

1. Calculate the debt to equity ratio for the past two years. Did the ratio improve or weaken in the more recent year?
2. Calculate the return on assets for the most recent year. Does the return on assets exceed the cost of borrowing?
3. *Review the balance sheet and note E to the financial statements.* Based on this information, how would you rate the bankruptcy risk of Buckle?

Comparative Analysis

American Eagle Outfitters, Inc., vs. The Buckle, Inc.

AP9–4 Financial information for **American Eagle** is presented in **Appendix A** at the end of the book, and financial information for **Buckle** is presented in **Appendix B** at the end of the book.

Required:

1. Calculate the debt to equity ratio for American Eagle and Buckle for the most recent year. Which company has the better ratio? Compare your calculations with those for **Coca-Cola** and **PepsiCo** reported earlier in the chapter. Which industry maintains a higher debt to equity ratio?
2. Calculate the return on assets for American Eagle and Buckle for the most recent year. Which company appears more profitable?

Ethics

AP9–5 The Tony Hawk Skate Park was built in early 2016. The construction was financed by $10 million of 5% bonds issued at face value, due in 10 years, with interest payable on June 30 and December 31 each year. The park did well initially, reporting net income in both 2016 and 2017. However, the discussion at the executive board meeting in late 2018 focused on falling skate-park revenues and increasing maintenance expenses. While several ideas were proposed, Jim Trost, the VP of finance, had an intriguing short-term solution. Jim stated, "Interest rates have steadily climbed the past three years. At the current market interest rate of 9%, we could repurchase our bonds for just under $8 million, recording a gain of over $2 million on the repurchase. We could then reissue new bonds at the current 9% rate."

Required:

1. Calculate the actual repurchase price on December 31, 2018, assuming the 10-year, 5% bonds paying interest semiannually were initially issued at a face value of $10 million three years earlier on January 1, 2016. (*Hint:* The periods to maturity (*n*) will now be 14, calculated as 7 years remaining times 2 periods each year.)

2. Record the bond retirement on December 31, 2018.
3. Is it ethical to time the repurchase of bonds in 2018 in order to include a $2 million gain on repurchase in a bad year? What if the transaction is fully disclosed?
4. From a business standpoint, is the retirement of 5% bonds and the reissue of 9% bonds a good idea? Explain why or why not.

Internet Research

AP9–6 Standard & Poor's is a global leader in credit ratings and credit risk analysis. Go to its website at **standardandpoors.com**.

Required:

1. Click on "ABOUT US" then "Key Statistics" under "S&P Rating Services." About how much debt is covered by Standard & Poor's credit ratings?
2. Go back to the home page. Click on "RATINGS." Click on "HOT TOPICS IN CREDIT FINANCE" at the top right of the page. Briefly summarize an item in the news today.
3. Go back to the home page. Click on "S&P INDICES." Click on "S&P 500." When did the S&P 500 begin?
4. Go back to standardandpoors.com. Click on the three products and services provided by McGraw Hill Financial. Briefly summarize one of the products.

Written Communication

AP9–7 Western Entertainment is considering issuing bonds to finance its business expansion. The company contacts you, a business consultant charging $200 an hour, to answer the following questions.
1. What are the advantages of issuing bonds over borrowing funds from a bank?
2. What are the advantages of issuing bonds over issuing common stock?
3. How is a bond price determined?

Required:

Write a memo providing answers worthy of your billing rate.

Earnings Management

AP9–8 Adrenaline Entertainment is struggling financially and its CFO, David Plesko, is starting to feel the heat. Back on January 1, 2014, Adrenaline Entertainment issued $100 million of 6% bonds, due in 15 years, with interest payable semiannually on June 30 and December 31 each year. The market interest rate on the date of issue was 5%.

It is now the end of 2018, and David has a plan to increase reported net income in 2018. The market interest rate has risen to 9% by the end of 2018. David wants to retire the $100 million, 6% bonds and reissue new 9% bonds instead.

Required:

1. Show that the bonds originally were issued on January 1, 2014, for $110,465,146.
2. Calculate the carrying value of the bonds five years later on December 31, 2018. (*Hint:* Use a market rate of 2.5% (5% ÷ 2), and the number of periods is now 20 semiannual periods.)
3. Calculate the market value of the bonds five years later on December 31, 2018. (*Hint:* The market rate is now 4.5% (9% ÷ 2) rather than 2.5% (5% ÷ 2), and the number of periods is now 20 semiannual periods.)
4. Record the early retirement of the bonds on December 31, 2018. Does the transaction increase net income? By how much (ignoring any tax effect)?
5. Is David Plesko's plan ethical? Do you think investors would agree with David Plesko that the retirement of the 6% bonds and the reissue of 9% bonds is a good idea? Explain why or why not.

Answers to the Self-Study Questions

1. d   2. b   3. b   4. c   5. a   6. b   7. b   8. a   9. a   10. d

10

Stockholders' Equity

RALPH LAUREN: TAKING POLO TO THE TOP TEN?

David Letterman made the "Top Ten" list famous. His top ten things you *don't* want to hear from your accountant include, "Listen, I'm not good with math," "Do you have any dedemptions or exuptions or whatever?," and "Relax, everything here will be fine—I used to work for Enron."

Wouldn't it be nice to know the top ten best stock investments for the future? Although we can't predict the future, we can learn from the past. The 10 best stock investments and their investment return over the past 10 years were:

Feature Story

Rank	Company	10-Year Total Return (%)
1	Keurig Green Mountain	7,729
2	Monster Beverage	6,570
3	Priceline Group	6,278
4	Apple	4,420
5	Alexion Pharmaceuticals	4,265
6	Regeneron Pharmaceuticals	4,167
7	Netflix	2,840
8	Intuitive Surgical	1,797
9	Salesforce.com	1,687
10	Western Digital	1,306

The first-place finisher, **Keurig Green Mountain**, produces and sells specialty coffee, coffee makers, teas, and other beverages. If you had invested $1,000 in the company, your investment would have grown to $77,290 in 10 years. Scanning the top 10, you see beverages, technology, and the medical field as hot investment areas.

In this chapter, we discuss stockholders' equity using the clothing industry as an example. Shopping mall staples like **Ralph Lauren**, **Abercrombie**, and **American Eagle** have been great companies to invest in over the years, but have performed below average in recent years. Some reasons include increasing competition in the clothing industry and a consumer trend toward purchasing more clothing online.

Are clothing companies like Ralph Lauren going to make a comeback? At the end of the chapter, we'll compare equity ratios between Ralph Lauren (known for their Polo shirts) with Abercrombie (also known for their Hollister clothing brand) to provide us with some additional clues.

© Bloomberg/Getty Images

Recall from the accounting equation that assets equal liabilities plus stockholders' equity.

Assets	**=**	**Liabilities**	**+**	**Stockholders' Equity**
(resources)		(creditors' claims)		(owners' claims)

In Chapters 4–7 we focused on assets and in Chapters 8–9 on liabilities. Here, in Chapter 10, we focus on the third component of the accounting equation—stockholders' equity. Because assets represent resources of the company and liabilities are creditors' claims to those resources, equity represents the owners' residual claim to those resources. Stated another way, equity is equal to what we own (assets) minus what we owe (liabilities). We use the term *stockholders'* equity (as opposed to *owners'* equity) because our focus is on corporations and stockholders are the owners of a corporation.

Common Terms
Stockholders' equity sometimes is referred to as *shareholders' equity*.

Stockholders' equity consists of three primary classifications: paid-in capital, retained earnings, and treasury stock. Paid-in capital is the amount stockholders have invested in the company. Retained earnings is the amount of earnings the corporation has kept or retained—that is, the earnings not paid out in dividends. Treasury stock is the corporation's own stock that it has reacquired. Illustration 10–1 shows those components in the stockholders' equity section of the balance sheet for **American Eagle**.

ILLUSTRATION 10–1

Stockholders' Equity Section for American Eagle

AMERICAN EAGLE OUTFITTERS, INC.
Balance Sheet
January 31, 2015

($ and shares in thousands)	
Stockholders' equity:	
Preferred stock, $0.01 par value	$ –0–
Common stock, $0.01 par value	2,496
Additional paid-in capital	559,731
Total paid-in capital	562,227
Retained earnings	1,543,085
Less: **Treasury stock,** 55,050 (thousand) shares	(965,566)
Total stockholders' equity	**$1,139,746**

At this point, simply note that total stockholders' equity for American Eagle consists of total paid-in capital, retained earnings, and treasury stock. Stockholders' equity is increased by paid-in capital and retained earnings and reduced by treasury stock. We'll fill in the details as we progress through the chapter.

In Part A of the chapter, we discuss transactions involving paid-in capital. A better description might be "invested capital" since it's the amount stockholders invest when they purchase a company's stock. In Part B, we examine transactions involving retained earnings. A better description might be "earned capital," since it's the amount the company has *earned* for the stockholders. In Part C, we look at the reporting of stockholders' equity.

PART A

INVESTED CAPITAL

Invested capital is the amount of money paid into a company by its owners. Recall from Chapter 1 that a company can be formed as a sole proprietorship, a partnership, or a corporation. A sole proprietorship is a business owned by one person, whereas a partnership is a business owned by two or more persons. A **corporation** is an entity that is legally separate from its owners and even pays its own income taxes. Most corporations are owned by many stockholders, although some corporations are owned entirely by one individual. While sole proprietorships are the most common form of business, corporations dominate in terms of total sales, assets, earnings, and employees.

Corporations

Corporations are formed in accordance with the laws of individual states. The state incorporation laws guide corporations as they write their articles of incorporation (sometimes called the *corporate charter*). The articles of incorporation describe (a) the nature of the firm's business activities, (b) the shares of stock to be issued, and (c) the initial board of directors. The board of directors establishes corporate policies and appoints officers who manage the corporation. Illustration 10–2 presents an organization chart tracing the line of authority for a typical corporation.

■ **LO10–1**
Identify the advantages and disadvantages of the corporate form of ownership.

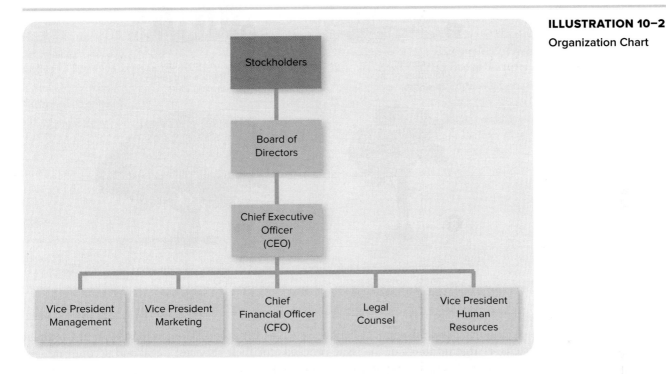

ILLUSTRATION 10–2
Organization Chart

Ultimately, a corporation's stockholders control the company. They are the owners of the corporation. By voting their shares, stockholders determine the makeup of the board of directors—which in turn appoints the management to run the company.

STAGES OF EQUITY FINANCING

Most corporations that end up selling stock on a major stock exchange don't begin that way. Instead, there's usually a progression of equity financing stages leading to a public offering, as summarized in Illustration 10–3.

Most corporations first raise money by selling stock to the founders of the business and to their friends and family. As the equity financing needs of the corporation grow, companies prepare a business plan and seek outside investment from "angel" investors and venture capital firms. Angel investors are wealthy individuals in the business community, like those featured in the television show *Shark Tank,* willing to risk investment funds on a promising business venture. Individual angel investors may invest from a few thousand dollars to millions of dollars in the corporation. Venture capital firms provide additional financing, often in the millions, for a percentage ownership in the company. Many venture capital firms look to invest in promising companies to which they can add value through business contacts, financial expertise, or marketing channels. Most corporations do not consider issuing stock to the general public ("going public") until their equity financing needs exceed $20 million.

The first time a corporation issues stock to the public is called an initial public offering (IPO). Like the issuance of bonds in Chapter 9, the public issuance of stock is a major event requiring the assistance of an investment banking firm (underwriter), lawyers, and public

ILLUSTRATION 10–3

Stages of Equity
Financing

Stages of Equity Financing

The progression leading to a public offering
might include some or all of these steps:

Investment by the
founders of the
business.

Investment by
friends and family of
the founders.

Outside investment by
"angel" investors and
venture capital firms.

Initial public offering
(IPO).

accountants. Major investment bankers, such as **Citigroup, Morgan Stanley**, and **Goldman Sachs**, charge up to 6% of the issue proceeds for their services. Legal and accounting fees also are not cheap, costing several hundred dollars an hour for services performed in preparation for a public stock offering.

PUBLIC OR PRIVATE

Corporations may be either public or private. The stock of a publicly held corporation trades on the New York Stock Exchange (NYSE) or National Association of Securities Dealers Automated Quotations (NASDAQ), or by over-the-counter (OTC) trading. Many of the largest companies in the world such as **Walmart, ExxonMobil**, and **General Electric** are traded on the NYSE. The NASDAQ is home to many of the largest high-tech companies, including **Apple, Microsoft**, and **Intel**. Over-the-counter trading takes place outside one of the major stock exchanges. All publicly held corporations are regulated by the Securities and Exchange Commission (SEC), resulting in significant additional reporting and filing requirements.

A privately held corporation does not allow investment by the general public and normally has fewer stockholders than a public corporation. Three of the largest private corporations in the United States are **Cargill** (agricultural commodities), **Koch Industries** (oil and gas), and **Mars** (food and candy). Generally, corporations whose stock is privately held do not need to file financial statements with the SEC.

Frequently, companies begin as smaller, privately held corporations. Then, as success broadens opportunities for expansion, the corporation goes public. For example, **Facebook** was a private corporation until it went public in May 2012 and raised $16 billion of outside investment funds. Similarly, **Ali Baba** (a Chinese online commerce company similar to **eBay** in the United States) went public in September 2014 and raised $25 billion of outside investment funds. The result was the largest technology IPO ever.

STOCKHOLDER RIGHTS

Whether public or private, stockholders are the owners of the corporation and have certain rights: the right to vote (including electing the board of directors), the right to receive dividends, and the right to share in the distribution of assets if the company is dissolved. Illustration 10–4 further explains these stockholder rights.

ILLUSTRATION 10–4

Stockholder Rights

Right to Vote
Stockholders *vote* on matters, including the election of corporate directors.

Right to Receive Dividends
Stockholders share in profits when the company declares *dividends*. The percentage of shares a stockholder owns determines his or her share of the dividends distributed.

Dividends

Right to Share in the Distribution of Assets
Stockholders share in *the distribution of assets* if the company is dissolved. The percentage of shares a stockholder owns determines his or her share of the assets, which are distributed after creditors and preferred stockholders are paid.

ADVANTAGES OF A CORPORATION

A corporation offers two primary advantages over sole proprietorships and partnerships: limited liability and the ability to raise capital and transfer ownership.

Limited Liability. Limited liability guarantees that stockholders in a corporation can lose no more than the amount they invested in the company, even in the event of bankruptcy. In contrast, owners in a sole proprietorship or a partnership can be held personally liable for debts the company has incurred, above and beyond the investment they have made.

Ability to Raise Capital and Transfer Ownership. Because corporations sell ownership interest in the form of shares of stock, ownership rights are easily transferred. An investor can sell his or her ownership interest (shares of stock) at any time and without affecting the structure of the corporation or its operations. As a result, attracting outside investment is easier for a corporation than for a sole proprietorship or a partnership.

DISADVANTAGES OF A CORPORATION

A corporation has two primary disadvantages relative to sole proprietorships and partnerships: additional taxes and more paperwork.

Additional Taxes. Owners of sole proprietorships and partnerships are taxed once, when they include their share of earnings in their personal income tax returns. However, corporations have double taxation: As a legal entity separate from its owners, a corporation pays income taxes on its earnings. Then, when it distributes the earnings to stockholders in dividends, the stockholders—the company's owners—pay taxes a second time on the corporate dividends they receive. In other words, corporate income is taxed once on earnings at the corporate level and again on dividends at the individual level.

More Paperwork. To protect the rights of those who buy a corporation's stock or who lend money to a corporation, the federal and state governments impose extensive reporting requirements on the company. The additional paperwork is intended to ensure adequate disclosure of the information investors and creditors need.

Illustration 10–5 summarizes the primary advantages and disadvantages of a corporation compared to a sole proprietorship or partnership.

ILLUSTRATION 10–5

Advantages and Disadvantages of a Corporation

Advantages	Disadvantages
Limited liability A stockholder can lose no more than the amount invested.	**Additional taxes** Corporate earnings are taxed twice—at the corporate level and individual stockholder level.
Ability to raise capital and transfer ownership Attracting outside investment and transferring ownership is easier for a corporation.	**More paperwork** Federal and state governments impose additional reporting requirements.

Decision Maker's Perspective

Limited Liability *and* Beneficial Tax Treatment

Wouldn't it be nice to get the best of both worlds—enjoy the limited liability of a corporation and the tax benefits of a sole proprietorship or partnership? An S corporation allows a company to enjoy limited liability as a corporation, but tax treatment as a partnership. Because of these benefits, many companies that qualify choose to incorporate as S corporations. One of the major restrictions is that the corporation cannot have more than 100 stockholders, so S corporations appeal more to smaller, less widely held businesses.

Two additional business forms have evolved in response to liability issues and tax treatment—*limited liability companies* (LLCs) and *limited liability partnerships* (LLPs). Most accounting firms in the United States adopt one of these two business forms because they offer limited liability and avoid double taxation, but with no limits on the number of owners as in an S corporation.

KEY POINT

The primary advantages of the corporate form of business are limited liability and the ability to raise capital. The primary disadvantages are additional taxes and more paperwork.

Common Stock

■ **LO10–2**

Record the issuance of common stock.

We can think of the common stockholders as the "true owners" of the business. The number of shares of common stock in a corporation are described as being authorized, issued, or outstanding.

AUTHORIZED, ISSUED, AND OUTSTANDING STOCK

Authorized stock is the total number of shares available to sell, stated in the company's articles of incorporation. The authorization of stock is not recorded in the accounting records.

However, the corporation is required to disclose in the financial statements the number of shares authorized. Issued stock is the number of shares that have been sold to investors. A company usually does not issue all its authorized stock. Outstanding stock is the number of shares held *by investors*. Issued and outstanding shares are the same as long as the corporation has not repurchased any of its own shares. Repurchased shares, called *treasury stock,* are included as part of shares issued, but excluded from shares outstanding. We discuss treasury stock in more detail later in the chapter. Illustration 10–6 summarizes the differences between authorized, issued, and outstanding shares.

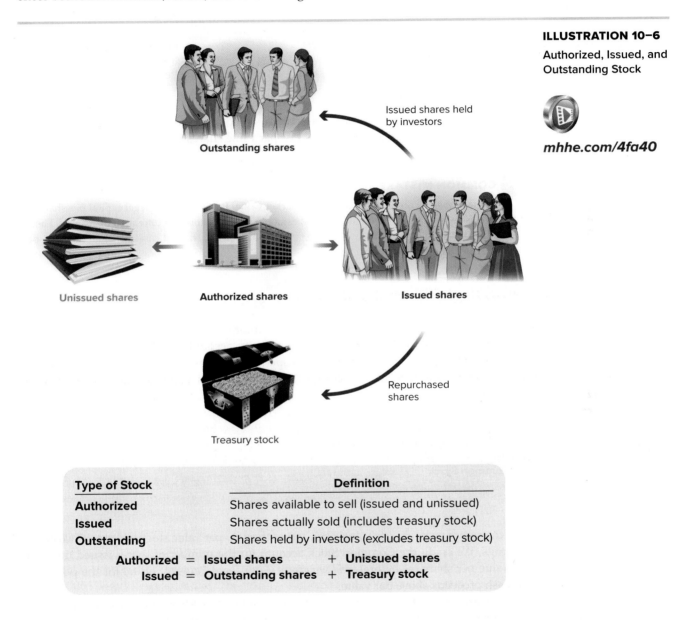

ILLUSTRATION 10–6

Authorized, Issued, and Outstanding Stock

mhhe.com/4fa40

Issued shares held by investors

Outstanding shares

Unissued shares   **Authorized shares**   **Issued shares**

Repurchased shares

Treasury stock

Type of Stock	Definition
Authorized	Shares available to sell (issued and unissued)
Issued	Shares actually sold (includes treasury stock)
Outstanding	Shares held by investors (excludes treasury stock)

$$\text{Authorized} = \text{Issued shares} + \text{Unissued shares}$$
$$\text{Issued} = \text{Outstanding shares} + \text{Treasury stock}$$

PAR VALUE

Par value is the legal capital per share of stock that's assigned when the corporation is first established. Par value originally indicated the real value of a company's shares of stock. Today, **par value has no relationship to the market value of the common stock.** For instance, **American Eagle**'s common stock has a par value of $0.01 per share but a market value that has ranged, over the past five years, between $10 and $22 per share.

Laws in most states permit corporations to issue no-par stock. No-par value stock is common stock that has not been assigned a par value. Most new corporations, and even some established corporations such as **Nike** or **Procter & Gamble**, issue no-par value common

Decision Point

Question		Accounting information		Analysis	
How many of a company's shares are authorized, issued, and outstanding?		Balance sheet		The number of authorized, issued, and outstanding shares is normally reported in the stockholders' equity section of the balance sheet. If the number of issued and outstanding shares differs, look for a separate line in the equity section called *treasury stock*.	

stock. In some cases, a corporation assigns a stated value to the shares. Stated value is treated and recorded in the same manner as par value shares.

 COMMON MISTAKE

Some students confuse par value with market value. Par value is the legal capital per share that is set when the corporation is first established and actually is unrelated to "value." The market value per share is equal to the current share price. In most cases, the market value per share will far exceed the par value.

ACCOUNTING FOR COMMON STOCK ISSUES

When a company receives cash from issuing common stock, it debits Cash. If it issues no-par value stock, the corporation credits the equity account entitled Common Stock. For example, let's assume Canadian Falcon, a specialty retailer of casual apparel and accessories, issues 1,000 shares of no-par value common stock at $30 per share. We record this transaction as:

A = L + SE			Debit	Credit
+30,000		Cash (= 1,000 shares × $30)	30,000	
	+30,000	Common Stock		30,000
		(Issue no-par value common stock)		

If the company issues par value stock rather than no-par value stock, we credit two equity accounts. We credit the Common Stock account for the number of shares issued times the par value per share (as before), *and* we credit Additional Paid-in Capital for the portion of the cash proceeds above par value.

Common Terms
Additional paid-in capital is simply the amount paid for stock over par value. It is also called paid-in *capital in excess of par.*

For example, assume that Canadian Falcon issues 1,000 shares of $0.01 par value common stock at $30 per share. The company credits the Common Stock account for par value. One thousand shares issued times $0.01 per share is $10. The company credits Additional Paid-in Capital for the portion of the cash proceeds above par value.

A = L + SE			Debit	Credit
+30,000		Cash (= 1,000 shares × $30)	30,000	
	+10	Common Stock (= 1,000 shares × $0.01)		10
	+29,990	Additional Paid-in Capital (difference)		29,990
		(Issue common stock above par)		

What if the common stock had a *stated value* of $0.01, rather than a *par value* of $0.01? We would record the same entry as in the par value example. For accounting purposes, **stated value is treated in the same manner as par value.**

Occasionally, a company will issue shares of stock in exchange for noncash goods or services. For example, what if 1,000 shares of common stock were issued to an attorney in payment for $30,000 in legal services? We would record the transaction in the same way as above, except we debit Legal Fees Expense, rather than Cash, for $30,000. The noncash exchange of stock, in this case for legal services, must be recorded at the fair value of the goods or services received.

 KEY POINT

If no-par value stock is issued, the corporation debits Cash and credits Common Stock. If par value or stated value stock is issued, the corporation debits Cash and credits two equity accounts—Common Stock at the par value or stated value per share and Additional Paid-in Capital for the portion above par or stated value.

Preferred Stock

In order to attract wider investment, some corporations issue preferred stock in addition to common stock. **American Eagle** has been authorized to issue 5 million shares of preferred stock, but the company has yet to issue any of these shares. Preferred stock is "preferred" over common stock in two ways:

■ **LO10–3**
Contrast preferred stock with common stock and bonds payable.

1. Preferred stockholders usually have first rights to a specified amount of dividends (a stated dollar amount per share or a percentage of par value per share). If the board of directors declares dividends, preferred shareholders will receive the designated dividend before common shareholders receive any.
2. Preferred stockholders receive preference over common stockholders in the distribution of assets in the event the corporation is dissolved.

About 20% of the largest U.S. companies have preferred stock outstanding.

However, unlike common stock, most preferred stock does not have voting rights, leaving control of the company to common stockholders.

COMPARISON OF FINANCING ALTERNATIVES

Preferred stock actually has a mixture of attributes somewhere between common stock (equity) and bonds (liabilities). Investors in common stock are the owners of the corporation because they have voting rights. Investors in bonds are creditors who have loaned money to the corporation. Preferred stockholders have characteristics of both. Illustration 10–7 provides a comparison of common stock, preferred stock, and bonds along several dimensions. Note that preferred stock falls in the middle between common stock and bonds for each of these factors.

ILLUSTRATION 10–7
Comparison of Financing Alternatives

Factor	Common Stock	Preferred Stock	Bonds
Voting rights	Yes	Usually no	No
Risk to the investor	Highest	Middle	Lowest
Expected return to the investor	Highest	Middle	Lowest
Preference for dividends/interest	Lowest	Middle	Highest
Preference in distribution of assets	Lowest	Middle	Highest
Tax deductibility of payments	No	Usually no	Yes

FEATURES OF PREFERRED STOCK

Preferred stock is especially interesting due to the flexibility allowed in its contractual provisions. For instance, preferred stock might be convertible, redeemable, and/or cumulative:

Convertible	Shares can be converted into common stock
Redeemable	Shares can be returned to (or redeemed by) the corporation at a fixed price.
Cumulative	Shares receive priority for future dividends, if dividends are not paid in a given year.

Preferred stock may be convertible, which allows the stockholder to exchange shares of preferred stock for common stock at a specified conversion ratio. Occasionally, preferred stock is redeemable at the option of either stockholders or the corporation. A redemption privilege might allow preferred stockholders the option, under specified conditions, to return their shares for a predetermined redemption price. Similarly, shares may be redeemable at the option of the issuing corporation.

INTERNATIONAL FINANCIAL REPORTING STANDARDS (IFRS)

SHOULD PREFERRED STOCK BE CLASSIFIED AS DEBT RATHER THAN EQUITY?

Under U.S. accounting rules, we usually record preferred stock in the stockholders' equity section of the balance sheet just above common stock. However, sometimes preferred stock shares features with debt. Redeemable preferred stock with a fixed redemption date (called *mandatorily redeemable*) is reported, like bonds payable, in the liability section of the balance sheet.[1] However, under IFRS, most preferred stock is reported as debt, with the dividends reported in the income statement as interest expense. Under U.S. GAAP, that's the case only for "mandatorily redeemable" preferred stock.

For more discussion, see Appendix E.

Preferred stock usually is cumulative. If the specified dividend is not paid in a given year, unpaid dividends (called dividends in arrears) accumulate, and the firm must pay them in a later year before paying any dividends on common stock. Let's look at an example. Assume that a company issues 1,000 shares of 8%, $30 par value preferred stock and 1,000 shares of $1 par value common stock at the beginning of 2016. If the preferred stock is cumulative, the company owes a dividend on the preferred stock of $2,400 each year (= 1,000 shares × 8% × $30 par value). If the dividend is not paid in 2016 or 2017, dividends in arrears for the two years will total $4,800.

Now, let's say the company declares a total dividend of $10,000 in 2018. How will the total dividend of $10,000 be allocated between preferred stockholders and common stockholders? It depends on whether the preferred stock is cumulative or noncumulative as outlined in Illustration 10–8.

Before the company can pay dividends to common stockholders, if the preferred stock is cumulative, the company must pay the $4,800 in unpaid dividends for 2016 and 2017 and then the current dividend on preferred stock of $2,400 in 2018. After paying the preferred stock dividends, the company can pay the remaining balance of $2,800 (= $10,000 − $4,800 − $2,400) in dividends on common stock. However, if the preferred stock is noncumulative, any dividends in arrears are lost. The dividend of $10,000 in 2018 will be split, with $2,400 paid to preferred stockholders for the current year and the remaining $7,600 paid to common stockholders.

---

[1]FASB ASC Topic 480: Distinguishing Liabilities from Equity.

ILLUSTRATION 10–8

Allocate Dividends between Preferred and Common Stock

If the preferred stock is cumulative:

Preferred dividends in arrears for 2016 and 2017	$ 4,800
Preferred dividends for 2018 (1,000 shares × 8% × $30 par value)	2,400
Remaining dividends to common stockholders	2,800
Total dividends	$10,000

If the preferred stock is noncumulative:

Preferred dividends in arrears for 2016 and 2017	$ 0
Preferred dividends for 2018 (1,000 shares × 8% × $30 par value)	2,400
Remaining dividends to common stockholders	7,600
Total dividends	$10,000

Because dividends are not an actual liability until they are declared by the board of directors, dividends in arrears are not reported as a liability in the balance sheet. However, information regarding any dividends in arrears is disclosed in the notes to the financial statements.

ACCOUNTING FOR PREFERRED STOCK ISSUES

We record the issuance of preferred stock similar to the way we did for the issue of common stock. Assume that Canadian Falcon issues 1,000 shares of $30 par value preferred stock for $40 per share. We record the transaction as:

	Debit	Credit	A	=	L	+	SE
Cash (= 1,000 shares × $40)	**40,000**		+40,000				
Preferred Stock (= 1,000 shares × $30)		**30,000**					+30,000
Additional Paid-in Capital (difference)..................................		**10,000**					+10,000
(Issue preferred stock above par)							

Illustration 10–9 displays the stockholders' equity section of the balance sheet for Canadian Falcon following the issuance of both common and preferred stock. We discuss the retained earnings balance later in the chapter.

ILLUSTRATION 10–9

Stockholders' Equity Section

CANADIAN FALCON	
Balance Sheet (partial)	

Stockholders' equity:	
Preferred stock, $30 par value; 100,000 shares authorized; 1,000 shares issued and outstanding	$ 30,000
Common stock, $0.01 par value; 1 million shares authorized; 1,000 shares issued and outstanding	10
Additional paid-in capital	39,990
Total paid-in capital	70,000
Retained earnings	30,000
Total stockholders' equity	$100,000

KEY POINT

Preferred stock has features of both common stock and bonds and is usually included in stockholders' equity. However, some preferred stock (mandatorily redeemable) is so similar to bonds that we include it with bonds payable in the liability section of the balance sheet.

Treasury Stock

■ **LO10–4**
Account for treasury stock.

We just examined the issuance of common and preferred stock. Next, we look at what happens when companies acquire shares they have previously issued. Treasury stock is the name given to a corporation's own stock that it has acquired.

Over two-thirds of all publicly traded companies report treasury stock in their balance sheets. Illustration 10–10 provides a summary of cash dividends and stock repurchases for the 1,000 largest companies in the U.S.

ILLUSTRATION 10–10   Cash Dividends versus Stock Repurchases

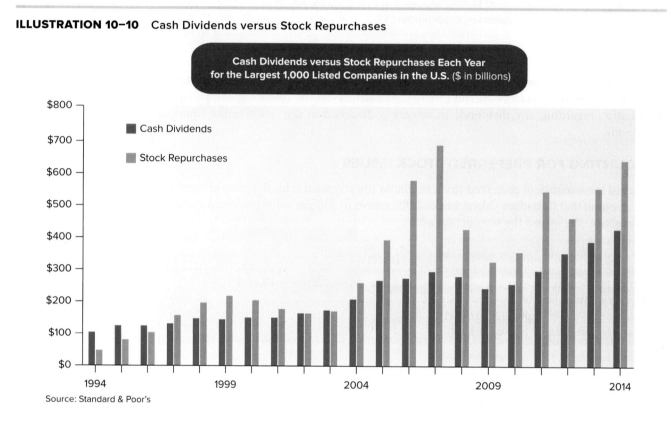

Source: Standard & Poor's

For the 1,000 largest U.S. companies, stock repurchases are larger than cash dividends paid in recent years. In addition, cash dividends are relatively steady over time, while stock repurchases are more volatile. Both cash dividends and stock repurchases return cash to investors, but companies have different reasons for choosing which method to return that cash.

Decision Maker's Perspective

Why Corporations Repurchase Their Stock

What would motivate a company to buy back its own stock? Companies buy back their own stock for various reasons:

1. **To boost underpriced stock.** When company management feels the market price of its stock is too low, it may attempt to support the price by decreasing the supply of stock in the marketplace. An announcement by **Johnson & Johnson** that it planned to buy up to $5 billion of its outstanding shares triggered a public buying spree that pushed the stock price up by more than 3%.

2. **To distribute surplus cash without paying dividends.** While dividends usually are a good thing, investors do pay personal income tax on them. Another way for a firm to distribute surplus cash to shareholders without giving them taxable *dividend* income is to use the excess cash to repurchase its own stock. Under a stock repurchase, only shareholders selling back their stock to the company at a profit incur taxable income.

3. **To boost earnings per share.** Earnings per share is calculated as earnings divided by the number of shares outstanding. Stock repurchases reduce the number of shares outstanding, thereby increasing earnings per share. However, with less cash in the company, it's more difficult for companies to maintain the same level of earnings following a share repurchase.

4. **To satisfy employee stock ownership plans.** Another motivation for stock repurchases is to acquire shares used in employee stock award and stock option compensation programs. **Microsoft**, for example, reported that its board of directors had approved a program to repurchase shares of its common stock to offset the increase in shares from stock option and stock purchase plans.

ACCOUNTING FOR TREASURY STOCK

Treasury stock is the repurchase of a company's own issued stock. **Just as issuing shares increases stockholders' equity, buying back those shares decreases stockholders' equity.** Rather than reducing the stock accounts directly, though, we record treasury stock as a "negative" or "contra" account. Recall that stockholders' equity accounts normally have credit balances. So, treasury stock is included in the stockholders' equity section of the balance sheet with an opposite, or debit, balance. When a corporation repurchases its own stock, it increases (debits) Treasury Stock, while it decreases (credits) Cash.

⊗ COMMON MISTAKE

Sometimes students confuse the purchase of treasury stock with investments in another company. An equity investment is the purchase of stock *in another corporation,* and we record it as an increase in assets. Treasury stock is the repurchase of a *corporation's own stock,* and we record it as a reduction in stockholders' equity. It is not an asset; a company cannot invest in itself.

We record treasury stock at the *cost* of the shares reacquired. For example, let's assume that Canadian Falcon repurchases 100 shares of its own $0.01 par value common stock at $30 per share. We record this transaction as:

	Debit	Credit
Treasury Stock (= 100 shares × $30)	**3,000**	
Cash		**3,000**
(Repurchase treasury stock)		

A	=	L	+	SE
				−3,000
−3,000				

Notice that the stock's par value has no effect on the entry to record treasury stock. We record treasury stock at its cost, which is $30 per share in this example. The debit to Treasury Stock reduces stockholders' equity. Illustration 10–11 displays the stockholders' equity section of the balance sheet before and after the repurchase of treasury stock.

ILLUSTRATION 10–11

Stockholders' Equity before and after Purchase of Treasury Stock

CANADIAN FALCON Balance Sheet (partial)		
Stockholders' equity:	**Before**	**After**
Preferred stock, $30 par value; 100,000 shares authorized; 1,000 shares issued and outstanding	$ 30,000	$30,000
Common stock, $0.01 par value; 1 million shares authorized; 1,000 shares issued and 900 shares outstanding	10	10
Additional paid-in capital	39,990	39,990
Total paid-in capital	70,000	70,000
Retained earnings	30,000	30,000
Treasury stock, 100 shares	0	(3,000)
Total stockholders' equity	$100,000	$97,000

Treasury stock is reported as a contra equity, or negative amount, because treasury stock reduces total stockholders' equity.

Now let's assume that Canadian Falcon reissues the 100 shares of treasury stock for $35. Recall that these shares originally were purchased for $30 per share, so the $35 reissue price represents a $5 per share increase in additional paid-in capital. It's *not* recorded as a $5 per share gain in the income statement, as we would for the sale of an investment in another company, since the company is reissuing its own stock. We record this transaction as:

A	=	L	+	SE		Debit	Credit
+3,500					**Cash** (= 100 shares × $35)..........	**3,500**	
				+3,000	**Treasury Stock** (= 100 shares × $30)............		**3,000**
				+500	**Additional Paid-in Capital**[2] (= 100 shares × $5)		**500**
					(Reissue treasury stock above cost)		

We debit Cash for $35 per share to record the inflow of cash from reissuing treasury stock. We recorded the 100 shares of treasury stock in the accounting records at a cost of $30 per share at the time of purchase. Now, when we reissue the treasury shares, we must reduce the Treasury Stock account at the same $30 per share. We record the $500 difference (= 100 shares × $5 per share) as Additional Paid-in Capital. Illustration 10–12 presents the stockholders' equity section of the balance sheet before and immediately after the sale of treasury stock.

ILLUSTRATION 10–12

Stockholders' Equity before and after Sale of Treasury Stock

CANADIAN FALCON Balance Sheet (partial)		
Stockholders' equity:	**Before**	**After**
Preferred stock, $30 par value; 100,000 shares authorized; 1,000 shares issued and outstanding	$30,000	$30,000
Common stock, $0.01 par value; 1 million shares authorized; 1,000 shares issued and 900 shares outstanding	10	10
Additional paid-in capital	39,990	40,490
Total paid-in capital	70,000	70,500
Retained earnings	30,000	30,000
Treasury stock, 100 shares	(3,000)	0
Total stockholders' equity	$97,000	$100,500

What if the stock price goes down, and we reissue the treasury stock for less than we paid to buy back the shares? Let's assume Canadian Falcon later purchases and reissues the 100 shares of treasury stock for only $25 rather than $35. It records the reissue as:

A	=	L	+	SE		Debit	Credit
+2,500					**Cash** (= 100 × $25)	**2,500**	
				−500	**Additional Paid-in Capital**[3] (= 100 × $5)	**500**	
				+3,000	**Treasury Stock** (= 100 × $30)............		**3,000**
					(Reissue treasury stock below cost)		

By purchasing 100 shares of its own stock for $30 per share and reselling them for only $25 per share, Canadian Falcon experienced a decrease in additional paid-in capital. This is reflected in the entry as a debit to the Additional Paid-in Capital account. It's not recorded

---

[2]Some companies credit "Additional Paid-in Capital from Treasury Stock Transactions" as a separate account from "Additional Paid-in Capital from Common Stock Transactions." We combine all additional paid-in capital entries into one "Additional Paid-in Capital" account, similar to how most companies report additional paid-in capital on the balance sheet.

[3]Companies debit Retained Earnings rather than Additional Paid-in Capital if there is not a sufficient prior credit balance in Additional Paid-in Capital from treasury stock transactions. The details are covered in intermediate financial accounting courses.

as a $5 per share loss in the income statement, as we would for the sale of an investment in another company, because the company is reissuing its own stock.

KEY POINT

We include treasury stock in the stockholders' equity section of the balance sheet as a reduction in stockholders' equity. When we reissue treasury stock, we report the difference between its cost and the cash received as an increase or decrease in additional paid-in capital.

EARNED CAPITAL

PART B

In Part A of the chapter, we discussed transactions involving "invested capital," because when investors buy a corporation's stock, they are investing in the company. Here, in Part B, we examine transactions involving retained earnings. Similarly, we might refer to this source of stockholders' equity as "earned capital," because it represents the net assets of the company that have been *earned* for the stockholders rather than *invested* by the stockholders.

■ **LO10–5**
Describe retained earnings and record cash dividends.

Retained Earnings

As noted at the beginning of the chapter, retained earnings represent the earnings retained in the corporation—earnings not paid out as dividends to stockholders. In other words, the balance in retained earnings equals all net income, less all dividends, since the company began operations.

$$\text{Retained Earnings} = \text{All net income since the company began} - \text{All dividends since the company began}$$

Let's look at an example. Illustration 10-13 shows how net income and dividends impact the balance in retained earnings over a four year period.

	Net Income (Net Loss)	Dividends	Balance in Retained Earnings
Year 1	$ (1,000)	$ 0	$ (1,000)
Year 2	3,000	0	2,000
Year 3	4,000	1,000	5,000
Year 4	10,000	3,000	12,000

ILLUSTRATION 10–13
Retained Earnings Over a Four-Year Period

In year 1, the first year of operations, the company reports a net loss of $1,000. It is quite common for companies not to be profitable in the start-up phase of the business. The net loss results in a balance of $ −1,000 in retained earnings. In year 2, the company reports net income of $3,000. This means that by the end of year 2, all net incomes ($ −1,000 in year 1 and $3,000 in year 2) minus all dividends ($0 in years 1 and 2) results in a cumulative balance in retained earnings of $2,000.

In year 3, the difference between net income and dividends is $3,000 (= $4,000 − $1,000), and this amount adds to the cumulative balance of retained earnings. In year 4, the difference between net income and dividends is $7,000, once again adding to the cumulative balance of retained earnings. **This process of adding net income and subtracting dividends each year to calculate the cumulative balance of retained earnings continues over the life of the company.**

COMMON MISTAKE

Some students think, incorrectly, that retained earnings represents a *cash* balance set aside by the company. In fact, the size of retained earnings can differ greatly from the balance in the Cash account. American Eagle reported $1.5 billion in retained earnings, but only $410 million in cash.

In a company's early years, the balance in retained earnings tends to be small, and total paid-in capital—money invested into the corporation—tends to be large. As the years go by, the earnings retained in the business continue to grow and, for many profitable companies, can exceed the total amount originally invested in the corporation. Unfortunately, for some companies, expenses sometimes are more than revenues, so a net loss rather than net income is recorded. Just as net income increases retained earnings, a net loss *decreases* retained earnings.

Retained Earnings has a normal credit balance, consistent with other stockholders' equity accounts. However, if losses exceed income since the company began, Retained Earnings will have a debit balance. A debit balance in Retained Earnings is called an accumulated deficit. In Illustration 10-13, we saw an example of an accumulated deficit in year 1. We subtract an accumulated deficit from total paid-in capital in the balance sheet to arrive at total stockholders' equity. Many companies in the start-up phase or when experiencing financial difficulties report an accumulated deficit.

Cash Dividends

Dividends are distributions by a corporation to its stockholders. Investors pay careful attention to cash dividends. A change in the quarterly or annual cash dividend paid by a company can provide useful information about its future prospects. For instance, an increase in dividends often is perceived as good news. Companies tend to increase dividends when the company is doing well and future prospects look bright.

Decision Maker's Perspective

Why Don't Some Companies Pay Dividends?

Some companies are unprofitable and, therefore, unable to pay cash dividends. However, many profitable companies *choose* not to pay cash dividends. Companies with large expansion plans, called *growth companies,* prefer to reinvest earnings in the growth of the company rather than distribute earnings back to investors in the form of cash dividends. **Starbucks** is a nice example. As companies mature and their growth opportunities diminish, they tend to pay out more dividends. **Microsoft** and **Walmart** did not pay dividends in their early growth years, but have been paying them in more recent years.

Why do investors buy stock in companies like **Starbucks** if they do not receive dividends? Investors also make money when a company's share price increases. For instance, **American Eagle** has experienced tremendous increases in share price over the years. Illustration 10–14 presents the disclosure of American Eagle's dividend policy.

ILLUSTRATION 10–14

American Eagle's Dividend Policy

> **AMERICAN EAGLE OUTFITTERS, INC.**
> **Notes to the Financial Statements (excerpt)**
>
> On December 4, the board of directors of American Eagle Outfitters, Inc., declared a dividend of $0.11 per share payable on December 28, to shareholders of record as of December 19. The payment of future dividends is at the discretion of our Board and is based on future earnings, cash flow, financial condition, capital requirements, changes in U.S. taxation and other relevant factors. It is anticipated that any future dividends paid will be declared on a quarterly basis.

Note that it is the board of directors that declares the cash dividend to be paid. The day this occurs is known as the declaration date. The declaration of a dividend creates a binding legal obligation for the company declaring the dividend. On that date, we (a) increase Dividends, a temporary account that is closed into Retained Earnings at the end of each period, and (b) increase a liability account, Dividends Payable. The board of directors also indicates a specific date on which the company will determine the registered owners of stock and therefore who will receive the dividend. This date is called the record date. Investors who own stock on the date of record are entitled to receive the dividend. The date of the actual distribution is the payment date.

Dividends are paid only on shares outstanding. **Dividends are not paid on treasury shares.** To illustrate the payment of a cash dividend, assume that on March 15 Canadian Falcon declares a $0.25 per share dividend on its 2,000 outstanding shares—1,000 shares of common stock and 1,000 shares of preferred stock. We record the declaration of cash dividends as:

March 15 (declaration date)	Debit	Credit	A	=	L	+	SE
Dividends (= 2,000 shares × $0.25)	**500**						−500
Dividends Payable		**500**			+500		
(Declare cash dividends)							

The Dividends account is a *temporary* stockholders' equity account that is closed into Retained Earnings at the end of each period. Dividends are legally payable, once declared by the board of directors, so Dividends Payable is credited.

COMMON MISTAKE

Some students incorrectly calculate dividends based on the number of issued shares. Dividends are based on the number of outstanding shares since dividends are not paid on treasury stock.

Let's continue our example and assume that the dividend declared by Canadian Falcon is paid on April 15 to stockholders of record at March 31. We make no entry on March 31, the date of record. We record the payment of cash dividends on April 15 as:

April 15 (payment date)	Debit	Credit	A	=	L	+	SE
Dividends Payable (= 2,000 shares × $0.25)	**500**				−500		
Cash		**500**	−500				
(Pay cash dividends)							

Because cash is the asset most easily distributed to stockholders, most corporate dividends are cash dividends. In concept, though, any asset can be distributed to stockholders as a dividend. When a noncash asset is distributed to stockholders, it is referred to as a property dividend. Securities held as investments are the assets most often distributed in a property dividend. The actual recording of property dividends is covered in intermediate accounting.

KEY POINT

The declaration of cash dividends decreases Retained Earnings and increases Dividends Payable. The payment of cash dividends decreases Dividends Payable and decreases Cash. The net effect, then, is a reduction in both Retained Earnings and Cash.

Decision Point

Question	Accounting information	Analysis
How much profit has the company made for its shareholders that has not been paid back to them in dividends?	Balance in Retained Earnings	The balance in Retained Earnings shows all net income less dividends since the company began operations.

Let's Review

mhhe.com/4fa41

Slacks 5th Avenue has two classes of stock authorized: $100 par preferred and $1 par common. As of the beginning of the year, 1,000 shares of common stock and no preferred shares have been issued. The following transactions affect stockholders' equity during the year:

January	15	Issue 2,000 additional shares of common stock for $20 per share.
February	1	Issue 100 shares of preferred stock for $110 per share.
June	1	Declare a cash dividend of $5 per share on preferred stock and $1 per share on common stock to all stockholders of record on June 15.
June	30	Pay the cash dividend declared on June 1.
October	1	Purchase 200 shares of treasury stock for $25 per share.
November	1	Reissue 100 shares of the treasury stock purchased on October 1 for $28 per share.

Slacks 5th Avenue has the following beginning balances in its stockholders' equity accounts: Preferred Stock, $0: Common Stock, $1,000; Paid-in Capital, $14,000; and Retained Earnings, $5,000.

Required:

1. Record each transaction.
2. Indicate whether each transaction increases (+), decreases (−), or has no effect (NE), on total assets, total liabilities, and total stockholders' equity.

Solution:

1. Entries to record each transaction:

January 15	Debit	Credit
Cash (= 2,000 × $20)..	40,000	
Common Stock (= 2,000 × $1)...		2,000
Additional Paid-in Capital (difference)............................		38,000
(Issue common stock above par)		
February 1		
Cash (= 100 × $110)	11,000	
Preferred Stock (= 100 × $100)......................................		10,000
Additional Paid-in Capital (difference)		1,000
(Issue preferred stock above par)		
June 1		
Dividends*	3,500	
Dividends Payable		3,500
(Declare cash dividends)		
*=(100 preferred shares × $5) + (3,000 common shares × $1)		

June 30	Debit	Credit
Dividends Payable	3,500	
Cash		3,500
(Pay cash dividends)		
October 1		
Treasury Stock (= 200 shares × $25)	5,000	
Cash		5,000
(Purchase treasury stock)		
November 1		
Cash (= 100 shares × $28)	2,800	
Treasury Stock (= 100 shares × $25)		2,500
Additional Paid-in Capital (= 100 × $3)		300
(Reissue treasury stock above cost)		

2. Effects of transactions on the components of the accounting equation:

Transaction	Total Assets	Total Liabilities	Total Stockholders' Equity
Issue common stock	+	NE	+
Issue preferred stock	+	NE	+
Declare cash dividends	NE	+	−
Pay cash dividends	−	−	NE
Purchase treasury stock	−	NE	−
Reissue treasury stock	+	NE	+

Suggested Homework:
BE10–3, BE10–4;
E10–5, E10–6;
P10–2A&B

Stock Dividends and Stock Splits

Sometimes corporations distribute to shareholders additional shares of the companies' own stock rather than cash. These are known as stock dividends or stock splits depending on the size of the stock distribution. Suppose you own 100 shares of stock. Assuming a 10% stock dividend, you'll get 10 additional shares. A 100% stock dividend, equivalent to a 2-for-1 stock split, means 100 more shares.

Large stock dividends (25% or more of the shares outstanding) and stock splits are declared primarily due to the effect they have on stock prices. Let's say that before the 100% stock dividend, your shares are trading at $40 a share, so your 100 shares are worth $4,000. After the 100% stock dividend, you will have twice as many shares. It sounds good, but let's look closer. Since the company as a whole still has the same value, each share of stock is now worth one-half what it was worth before the stock dividend. Your 200 shares still have a value of $4,000, the same as your 100 shares before the stock dividend. However, now each share is worth half as much—$20 rather than $40 per share.

Think of the company as a pizza. A 100% stock dividend is like changing an 8-slice pizza into 16 slices by cutting each slice in half. You are no better off with 16 half-slices than with the original 8 slices. Whether it's cut in 8 large slices or 16 smaller slices, it's still the same-sized pizza. Whether a company is represented by 1 million shares worth $40 each or 2 million shares worth $20 each, it's the same $40 million company. **Total assets, total liabilities, and total stockholders' equity do not change as a result of a stock dividend.**

■ **LO10–6**
Explain the effect of stock dividends and stock splits.

© Royalty-Free/Digital Stock/Corbis, RF

Decision Maker's Perspective

Why Declare a Stock Split?

Why would a company declare a 2-for-1 stock split when the stockholders are not really receiving anything of substance? The primary reason is to lower the trading price of the stock to a more acceptable trading range, making it attractive to a larger number of potential investors. Many companies like their stock to trade under $100 per share—$20 to $40 per share is common. For instance, after a company declares a 2-for-1 stock split with a per share market price of $80, it then has twice the number of shares outstanding, each with an approximate market value reduced to a more marketable trading range of $40.

However, there are exceptions to the normal trading range. **Google**'s stock traded at over $500 per share in 2015. **Berkshire Hathaway**'s "A" shares traded at over $200,000 per share in 2015, making it accessible only to wealthier investors. Berkshire Hathaway is founded by billionaire investor Warren Buffett. While still an outspoken critic of stock dividends and stock splits, even Warren Buffett is giving in a little. Berkshire Hathaway's "B" shares, designed for general public investment, were split 50 to 1 and have split again to trade in a more acceptable trading range, making the stock more accessible to the general public.

Accounting standards distinguish between stock splits, large stock dividends, and small stock dividends. We look first at the accounting for stock splits and large stock dividends because they are more common in practice.

STOCK SPLITS/LARGE STOCK DIVIDENDS

When a company declares a stock split, we do not record a transaction. After a 2-for-1 stock split, the Common Stock account balance (total par value) represents twice as many shares. For instance, assume Canadian Falcon declares a 2-for-1 stock split on its 1,000 shares of $0.01 par value common stock. The balance in the Common Stock account is 1,000 shares times $0.01 par value per share, which equals $10. With no journal entry, the balance remains $10 despite the number of shares doubling. As a result, the par value *per share* is reduced by one-half to $0.005 (2,000 shares times $0.005 par per share still equals $10).

As you might expect, having the par value per share change in this way is cumbersome and expensive. All records, printed or electronic, that refer to the previous amount must be changed to reflect the new amount. To avoid changing the par value per share, most companies report stock splits in the same way as a large stock dividend. We account for a large stock dividend by recording an increase in the Common Stock account in the amount of the par value of the additional shares distributed, as presented below:

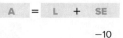

		Debit	Credit
Stock Dividends (= 1,000 shares × $0.01)		**10**	
Common Stock			**10**
(Record 100% [large] stock dividend)			

−10 (to Stock Dividends)
+10 (to Common Stock)

Similar to cash dividends, the Stock Dividends account is a temporary stockholders' equity account that is closed into Retained Earnings. The debit to Stock Dividends reduces Retained Earnings. So, a stock dividend entry decreases one equity account, Retained Earnings, and increases another equity account, Common Stock. **Note that the above entry does not change total assets, total liabilities, or total stockholders' equity.** Illustration 10–15 presents the stockholders' equity section of the balance sheet for Canadian Falcon before and after the 2-for-1 stock split accounted for as a 100% stock dividend.

Notice that total stockholders' equity remains at $100,000 before and after the stock distribution. Common stock increased by $10, while retained earnings decreased by $10. Illustration 10–16 summarizes the effects of a stock split and a stock dividend.

CANADIAN FALCON
Balance Sheet (partial)

	Before 100% Stock Dividend	After 100% Stock Dividend
Stockholders' equity:		
Preferred stock, $30 par value	$ 30,000	$ 30,000
Common stock, $0.01 par value	10	20
Additional paid-in capital	40,490	40,490
Total paid-in capital	70,500	70,510
Retained earnings	29,500	29,490
Total stockholders' equity	$100,000	$100,000
Common shares outstanding	1,000	2,000
Par value per share	$ 0.01	$ 0.01
Share price	$ 30	$ 15

ILLUSTRATION 10–16

Effects of a Stock Split and a Stock Dividend

	Stock Split	Stock Dividend
Total stockholders' equity	No change	No change
Common stock	No change	Increase
Retained earnings	No change	Decrease
Par value per share	Decrease	No change

Illustration 10–17 presents the disclosure of American Eagle's 3-for-2 stock split.

ILLUSTRATION 10–17

American Eagle's Stock Split

AMERICAN EAGLE OUTFITTERS, INC.
Notes to the Financial Statements

On November 13, the Company's Board approved a 3-for-2 stock split. This stock split was distributed on December 18, to stockholders of record on November 24. All share amounts and per share data presented herein have been restated to reflect this stock split.

SMALL STOCK DIVIDENDS

Recall that we record large stock dividends at the *par value* per share. We record small stock dividends at the *market value,* rather than the par value per share. Assume, for example, the market value of Canadian Falcon common stock is $30 per share when Canadian Falcon declares a 10% dividend on its 1,000 shares outstanding of $0.01 par value common stock. After the 10% stock dividend, Canadian Falcon will have an additional 100 shares outstanding. The company records this small stock dividend as:

	Debit	Credit	A	=	L	+	SE
Stock Dividends (= 1,000 × 10% × $30)	3,000						−3,000
Common Stock (= 1,000 × 10% × $0.01)		1					+1
Additional Paid-in Capital (difference)		2,999					+2,999
(Pay 10% [small] stock dividend)							

So, small stock dividends are recorded at the market value per new share, while large stock dividends are recorded at the par value per share. Why the inconsistency? Some believe that a small stock dividend will have little impact on the market price of shares currently outstanding, arguing for the recording of small stock dividends at market value. However, this reasoning is contrary to research evidence, which finds the market price adjusts for both large and small stock dividends.[4] A 10% stock dividend will result in 10% more shares, but each share will be worth 10% less, so the investor is no better off. **Note that the above entry still does not change total assets, total liabilities, or total stockholders' equity.** The debit to Stock Dividends simply decreases one equity account, Retained Earnings, while the credits increase two other equity accounts, Common Stock and Additional Paid-in Capital.

 ETHICAL DILEMMA

© Fuse/Getty Images, RF

Intercontinental Clothing Distributors has paid cash dividends every year since the company was founded in 1990. The dividends have steadily increased from $0.05 per share to the latest dividend declaration of $1.00 per share. The board of directors is eager to continue this trend despite the fact that earnings fell significantly during the recent quarter. The chair of the board proposes a solution. He suggests a 5% stock dividend in lieu of a cash dividend, to be accompanied by the following press announcement: "In place of our regular $1.00 per share cash dividend, Intercontinental will distribute a 5% stock dividend on its common shares, currently trading at $20 per share. Changing the form of the dividend will permit the company to direct available cash resources to the modernization of facilities and other capital improvements.

Is a 5% stock dividend on shares trading at $20 per share equivalent to a $1.00 per share cash dividend? Is the chair's suggestion ethical?

 KEY POINT

Declaring stock dividends and stock splits is like cutting a pizza into more slices. Everyone has more shares, but each share is worth proportionately less than before.

PART C

■ **LO10–7**
Prepare and analyze the stockholders' equity section of a balance sheet and the statement of stockholders' equity.

REPORTING STOCKHOLDERS' EQUITY

We now can apply what we've learned so far in the chapter to analyze the stockholders' equity of an actual company—**American Eagle**. In this section, we show the financial statement presentation of stockholders' equity in the balance sheet and differentiate it from the statement of stockholders' equity.

Stockholders' Equity in the Balance Sheet

Illustration 10–18 presents the stockholders' equity section of the balance sheet for **American Eagle**, introduced briefly at the beginning of the chapter.

---

[4]Taylor W. Foster and Don Vickrey. 1978. "The Information Content of Stock Dividend Announcements." *Accounting Review* 53, no. 2 (April), pp. 360–70; and J. David Spiceland and Alan J. Winters. 1986. "The Market Reaction to Stock Distributions: The Effect of Market Anticipation and Cash Returns." *Accounting and Business Research* 16, no. 63 (Summer), pp. 211–25.

ILLUSTRATION 10–18

Stockholders' Equity
Section for American
Eagle

AMERICAN EAGLE OUTFITTERS, INC.
Balance Sheet
January 31, 2015

($ and shares in thousands)	
Stockholders' equity:	
Preferred stock, $0.01 par value	$ –0–
Common stock, $0.01 par value	2,496
Additional paid-in capital	559,731
Total paid-in capital	562,227
Retained earnings	1,543,085
Less: **Treasury stock,** 55,050 (thousand) shares	(965,566)
Total stockholders' equity	**$1,139,746**

Preferred stock is usually listed before common stock in the balance sheet. American Eagle has 5 million shares of preferred stock authorized but has not yet issued any preferred shares. Can you determine how many shares of common stock the company has issued? Common stock is reported at its par value of $0.01 per share. If we take the Common Stock account balance of $2,496,000 ($2,496 in thousands) and divide it by $0.01 per share, we find that the company has issued just under 250 million shares (249,600,000). The number of shares outstanding is equal to the number of shares issued (249,600,000) minus the number of shares bought back (the 55,050,000 treasury shares), or 194,550,000 shares.

Notice that the Additional Paid-in Capital account balance is much larger than the Common Stock account balance. This is to be expected. Remember, American Eagle has a par value of only $0.01 per share, so most of the money invested in the company was credited to Additional Paid-in Capital rather than Common Stock.

Now look at retained earnings. When a company is started, most of the equity is in the paid-in capital section because that's the amount invested by stockholders. But then, if a company is profitable, like American Eagle, and pays little in dividends, the retained earnings section of equity grows and often exceeds the amount invested by stockholders. For American Eagle, the balance in retained earnings is so large that it actually exceeds total stockholders' equity. How can this happen? American Eagle has been very profitable over the years, building retained earnings. It has used a portion of cash generated from earnings to buy back treasury shares, which decreases stockholders' equity. American Eagle has applied this strategy to such an extent that the balance in treasury stock (representing the cost of shares repurchased by the company) now exceeds total paid-in capital (representing the total cost of shares originally issued).

American Eagle has been very active in acquiring treasury shares. Has it benefited from the treasury stock repurchase? Dividing the treasury stock balance of $965,566 by the 55,050 shares repurchased, we can estimate an average purchase cost of $17.54 per share. That average purchase price is higher than the trading price of $14.04 per share at January 31, 2015. Thus, at this point in time, it looks like American Eagle has not benefited from the treasury stock repurchase. However, if stock prices should again rise above $17.54 per share, the company could sell the treasury shares for more than the average purchase price.

Decision Maker's Perspective

Why Doesn't Stockholders' Equity Equal the Market Value of Equity?

The *market* value of equity is the price investors are willing to pay for a company's stock. The market value of equity equals the stock price times the number of shares outstanding. On the other hand, the *book* value of equity equals total stockholders' equity reported in the balance sheet. Market value and book value generally are not the same, and often are vastly different. For example, American Eagle reported total stockholders' equity of about $1.1 billion ($1,139,746,000 specifically), yet its market value at this same time was over $2.7 billion. Why?

Keep in mind that stockholders' equity is equal to assets minus liabilities. An asset's book value usually equals its market value *on the date it's purchased.* However, the two aren't necessarily the same after that. For instance, an asset such as a building often increases in value over time, but it continues to be reported in the balance sheet at historical cost minus accumulated depreciation. Consider another example. American Eagle creates brand awareness and increases market value through advertising, but under accounting rules, it expenses all its advertising costs as it incurs them. This causes the true market value of assets and stockholders' equity to be greater than the amount recorded for assets and stockholders' equity in the accounting records.

Statement of Stockholders' Equity

The stockholders' equity section of the balance sheet, like the one we just examined for American Eagle, shows the balance in each equity account *at a point in time.* In contrast, the statement of stockholders' equity summarizes the *changes* in the balance in each stockholders' equity account *over a period of time.*

To contrast the stockholders' equity section of the balance sheet and the statement of stockholders' equity, let's compare both statements for Canadian Falcon. Illustration 10–19 shows the stockholders' equity section reported in Canadian Falcon's balance sheet.

ILLUSTRATION 10–19

Stockholders' Equity Section—Canadian Falcon

CANADIAN FALCON Balance Sheet (partial) December 31, 2018	
Stockholders' equity:	
Preferred stock, $30 par value; 100,000 shares authorized;	
1,000 shares issued and outstanding	$ 30,000
Common stock, $0.01 par value; 1 million shares authorized;	
2,000 shares issued and outstanding	20
Additional paid-in capital	40,490
Total paid-in capital	70,510
Retained earnings	29,490
Treasury stock	–0–
Total stockholders' equity	$100,000

Compare that snapshot of stockholders' equity at the end of 2018 with Illustration 10–20, showing the statement of stockholders' equity for Canadian Falcon.

Each of the beginning balances in Illustration 10–20 is zero because this is the first year of operations. (The beginning balances for the following year, January 1, 2019, are the same as the ending balance this year, December 31, 2018.)

The statement of stockholders' equity reports how each equity account changed during the year. For instance, the Common Stock account increased because Canadian Falcon issued common stock and declared a 100% stock dividend. The Additional Paid-in Capital account increased from the issuance of common stock, the issuance of preferred stock, and the sale of treasury stock for more than its original cost. Retained Earnings increased due to net income and decreased due to both cash and stock dividends. The retained earnings column is sometimes shown separately and referred to as a *statement of retained earnings.* The repurchase of treasury stock is shown as a reduction because treasury stock reduces total stockholders' equity. The ending balance in Treasury Stock is zero, since all the treasury stock purchased was resold by the end of the year.

ILLUSTRATION 10–20

Statement of Stockholders' Equity— Canadian Falcon

CANADIAN FALCON
Statement of Stockholders' Equity
For the year ended December 31, 2018

	Preferred Stock	Common Stock	Additional Paid-in Capital	Retained Earnings	Treasury Stock	Total Stockholders' Equity
Balance, January 1	$ –0–	$–0–	$ –0–	$ –0–	$ –0–	$ –0–
Issue common stock		10	29,990			30,000
Issue preferred stock	30,000		10,000			40,000
Repurchase treasury stock					(3,000)	(3,000)
Sale of treasury stock			500		3,000	3,500
Cash dividends				(500)		(500)
100% stock dividend		10		(10)		–0–
Net income				30,000		30,000
Balance, December 31	$30,000	$ 20	$40,490	$29,490	$ –0–	$100,000

mhhe.com/4fa42

 KEY POINT

The stockholders' equity section of the balance sheet presents the balance of each equity account *at a point in time*. The statement of stockholders' equity shows the change in each equity account balance *over time*.

This is a continuation of the Let's Review exercise presented earlier in the chapter. Recall that Slacks 5th Avenue has two classes of stock authorized: $100 par preferred and $1 par value common. As of the beginning of 2018, 1,000 shares of common stock have been issued and no shares of preferred stock have been issued. The following transactions affect stockholders' equity during 2018:

Let's Review

mhhe.com/4fa43

January   15   Issue 2,000 additional shares of common stock for $20 per share.
February   1   Issue 100 shares of preferred stock for $110 per share.
June   1   Declare a cash dividend of $5 per share on preferred stock and $1 per share on common stock to all stockholders of record on June 15.
June   30   Pay the cash dividend declared on June 1.
October   1   Purchase 200 shares of common treasury stock for $25 per share.
November 1   Reissue 100 shares of treasury stock purchased on October 1 for $28 per share.

Slacks 5th Avenue has the following beginning balances in its stockholders' equity accounts on January 1, 2018: Preferred Stock, $0; Common Stock, $1,000; Paid-in Capital, $14,000; and Retained Earnings, $5,000. Net income for the year ended December 31, 2018, is $4,000.

Required:

Taking into consideration the beginning balances and all of the transactions during 2018, prepare the following for Slacks 5th Avenue:

1. The stockholders' equity section as of December 31, 2018.
2. The statement of stockholders' equity for the year ended December 31, 2018.

Solution:

1. Stockholders' equity section:

SLACKS 5TH AVENUE Balance Sheet (partial) December 31, 2018	
Stockholders' equity:	
Preferred stock, $100 par value	$10,000
Common stock, $1 par value	3,000
Additional paid-in capital	53,300
Total paid-in capital	66,300
Retained earnings	5,500
Treasury stock	(2,500)
Total stockholders' equity	$69,300

2. Statement of stockholders' equity:

SLACKS 5TH AVENUE Statement of Stockholders' Equity For the year ended December 31, 2018						
	Preferred Stock	Common Stock	Additional Paid-in Capital	Retained Earnings	Treasury Stock	Total Stockholders' Equity
Balance, January 1	$ –0–	$1,000	$14,000	$5,000	$ –0–	$20,000
Issue of common stock		2,000	38,000			40,000
Issue of preferred stock	10,000		1,000			11,000
Cash dividends				(3,500)		(3,500)
Repurchase of treasury stock					(5,000)	(5,000)
Sale of treasury stock			300		2,500	2,800
Net income				4,000		4,000
Balance, December 31	$10,000	$3,000	$53,300	$5,500	$(2,500)	$69,300

Suggested Homework:
BE10–13, BE10–14;
E10–11, E10–12;
P10–5A&B

ANALYSIS

EQUITY ANALYSIS
Ralph Lauren vs. Abercrombie & Fitch

■ **LO10–8**
Evaluate company performance using information on stockholders' equity.

Earnings are the key to a company's long-run survival. However, we need to evaluate earnings in comparison to the size of the investment. For instance, earnings of $500,000 may be quite large for a small business but would be a rather disappointing outcome for a major corporation like **American Eagle**. A useful summary measure of earnings that considers the relative size of the business is the return on equity.

RETURN ON EQUITY

The **return on equity** (ROE) measures the ability of company management to generate earnings from the resources that owners provide. We compute the ratio by dividing net income by average stockholders' equity.

$$\text{Return on equity} = \frac{\text{Net income}}{\text{Average stockholders' equity}}$$

Ralph Lauren is probably best known for its Polo clothing line. We can compare its profitability with a competitor in the clothing industry, **Abercrombie & Fitch** (Abercrombie for short), that owns both the more expensive Abercrombie label and the relatively less expensive Hollister line of clothing. As mentioned in the feature story, the clothing industry has been struggling in the face of higher competition. Lower-cost clothing chains like **Forever 21** and **H&M** have further increased competition in an already crowded clothing market. Illustration 10–21 provides selected financial data for Ralph Lauren and Abercrombie.

($ in millions)	Ralph Lauren	Abercrombie
Net sales	$ 7,620	$3,744
Net income	$ 691	$ 52
Stockholders' equity, beginning	$ 4,034	$1,729
Stockholders' equity, ending	$ 3,891	$1,390
Stock price, ending	$131.22	$25.52
Dividends per share	$ 1.83	$ 0.82
Average shares outstanding	86.3 million	69.4 million

ILLUSTRATION 10–21

Selected Financial Data for Ralph Lauren and Abercrombie

The return on equity for both companies is calculated in Illustration 10–22.

($ in millions)	Net Income	÷	Average Stockholders' Equity	=	Return on Equity
Ralph Lauren	$691	÷	($4,034 + $3,891)/2	=	17.4%
Abercrombie	$ 52	÷	($1,729 + $1,390)/2	=	3.3%

ILLUSTRATION 10–22

Return on Equity for Ralph Lauren and Abercrombie

Ralph Lauren has a very respectable return on equity of 17.4%, compared to only 3.3% for Abercrombie. A return on equity of 17.4% suggests that for every $1 of investors' resources, the company has earned an additional $0.17 in the current period for its investors. In contrast, Abercrombie's return on equity of only 3.3% is reflective of the struggles experienced during this period by the clothing industry as a whole. Ralph Lauren's continued popularity has allowed it to rise a bit above the competition.

DIVIDEND YIELD

Investors are also interested in knowing how much a company pays out in dividends relative to its share price. The dividend yield is computed as dividends per share divided by the stock price.

$$\text{Dividend yield} = \frac{\text{Dividends per share}}{\text{Stock price}}$$

Dividend yield for Ralph Lauren and Abercrombie is shown in Illustration 10–23.

($ in millions)	Dividends Per Share	÷	Stock Price	=	Dividend Yield
Ralph Lauren	$1.83	÷	$131.22	=	1.4%
Abercrombie	$0.82	÷	$ 25.52	=	3.2%

ILLUSTRATION 10–23

Dividend Yield for Ralph Lauren and Abercrombie

Ralph Lauren's dividend yield at 1.4% is less than half the dividend yield for Abercrombie at 3.2%. Dividend yield is an extremely common ratio used by investors. Investors who want to acquire a portfolio of companies providing the highest dividend yield can simply invest in an investment fund such as the **Vanguard High Dividend Yield Index Fund**.

EARNINGS PER SHARE

Earnings per share (EPS) measures the net income earned per share of common stock. We calculate earnings per share as net income minus preferred stock dividends divided by the average shares outstanding during the period:

$$\text{Earnings per share} = \frac{\text{Net income} - \text{Dividends on preferred stock}}{\text{Average shares of common stock outstanding}}$$

The upper half of the fraction measures the income available to common stockholders. We subtract any dividends paid to preferred stockholders from net income to arrive at the income available to the true owners of the company—the common stockholders. If a company does not issue preferred stock, the top half of the fraction is simply net income. We then divide income available to common stockholders by the average shares outstanding during the period to calculate earnings per share.

Earnings per share is useful in comparing earnings performance for the same company over time.   It is *not* useful for comparing earnings performance of one company with another because of wide differences in the number of shares outstanding among companies. For instance, assume two companies, Alpha and Beta, both report net income of $1 million and are valued by the market at $20 million. Quite comparable, right? Not if we are talking about their earnings per share. If Alpha has one million shares outstanding and Beta has two million shares outstanding, their earnings per share amounts will not be comparable. Alpha will have a share price of $20 (= $20 million ÷ 1 million shares) and an EPS of $1.00 (= $1 million in earnings ÷ 1 million shares). Beta, on the other hand, will have a share price of $10 ($20 million ÷ 2 million shares) and an EPS of $0.50 ($1 million in earnings ÷ 2 million shares). Is the earnings performance for Alpha better than that for Beta? Of course not. They both earned $1 million. Alpha's earnings per share is higher simply because it has half as many shares outstanding. (Same pizza, fewer slices.)

If Alpha declared a 2-for-1 stock split, its earnings per share would match Beta's exactly. The key point is that earnings per share is useful in comparing either Alpha's earnings over time or Beta's earnings over time, but it is not useful in comparing the companies with each other.

Investors use earnings per share extensively in evaluating the earnings performance of a company over time. Investors are looking for companies with the potential to increase earnings per share. Analysts also forecast earnings on a per share basis. If reported earnings per share fall short of analysts' forecasts, this is considered negative news, usually resulting in a decline in a company's stock price.

PRICE-EARNINGS RATIO

Another measure widely used by analysts is the price-earnings ratio (PE ratio). It indicates how the stock is trading relative to current earnings. We calculate the PE ratio as the stock price divided by earnings per share, so that both stock price and earnings are expressed on a per share basis:

$$\text{Price-earnings ratio} = \frac{\text{Stock price}}{\text{Earnings per share}}$$

Price-earnings ratios commonly are in the range of 15 to 20. A high PE ratio indicates that the market has high hopes for a company's stock and has bid up the price. Growth stocks are stocks whose future earnings investors expect to be higher. Their stock prices are high in relation to current earnings because investors expect future earnings to be higher. On the other hand, value stocks are stocks that are priced low in relation to current earnings. The low price in relation to earnings may be justified due to poor future prospects, or it might suggest an underpriced stock that could boom in the future. Illustration 10–24 calculates the price-earnings ratios for Ralph Lauren and Abercrombie.

($ in thousands)	Stock Price	÷	Earnings per Share	=	Price-Earnings Ratio
Ralph Lauren	$131.22	÷	$691 / 86.3	=	16.4
Abercrombie	$ 25.52	÷	$ 52 / 69.4	=	34.1

ILLUSTRATION 10–24

Price-Earnings Ratios for Ralph Lauren and Abercrombie

The price-earnings ratios for Ralph Lauren and Abercrombie are 16.4 and 34.1, respectively. A low price-earnings ratio indicates to investors that a stock is priced low in relation to its current earnings. Ralph Lauren's PE ratio is in the common range of 15 to 20, while Abercrombie's is much higher at 34.1 indicating that investors expect future earnings to be higher.

KEY POINT

The return on equity measures the ability to generate earnings from the owners' investment. It is calculated as net income divided by average stockholders' equity. The dividend yield measures how much a company pays out in dividends in relation to its stock price. Earnings per share measures the net income earned per share of common stock. The price-earnings ratio indicates how the stock is trading relative to current earnings.

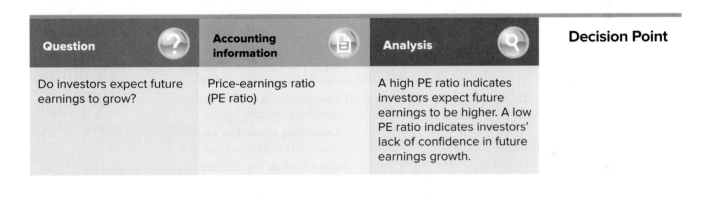

Decision Point

Question	Accounting information	Analysis
Do investors expect future earnings to grow?	Price-earnings ratio (PE ratio)	A high PE ratio indicates investors expect future earnings to be higher. A low PE ratio indicates investors' lack of confidence in future earnings growth.

KEY POINTS BY LEARNING OBJECTIVE

LO10–1 Identify the advantages and disadvantages of the corporate form of ownership.

The primary advantages of the corporate form of business are limited liability and the ability to raise capital. The primary disadvantages are additional taxes and more paperwork.

LO10–2 Record the issuance of common stock.

If no-par value stock is issued, the corporation debits Cash and credits Common Stock. If par value or stated value stock is issued, the corporation debits Cash and credits two equity accounts—Common Stock at the par value or stated value per share and Additional Paid-in Capital for the portion above par or stated value.

LO10–3 Contrast preferred stock with common stock and bonds payable.

Preferred stock has features of both common stock and bonds and is usually included in stockholders' equity. However, some preferred stock (mandatorily redeemable) is so similar to bonds that we include it with bonds payable in the liability section of the balance sheet.

LO10–4 Account for treasury stock.

We include treasury stock in the stockholders' equity section of the balance sheet as a reduction in stockholders' equity. When we reissue treasury stock, we report the difference between its cost and the cash received as an increase or decrease in additional paid-in capital.

LO10–5 Describe retained earnings and record cash dividends.

The declaration of cash dividends decreases Retained Earnings and increases Dividends Payable. The payment of cash dividends decreases Dividends Payable and decreases Cash. The net effect, then, is a reduction in both Retained Earnings and Cash.

LO10–6 Explain the effect of stock dividends and stock splits.

Declaring stock dividends and stock splits is like cutting a pizza into more slices. Everyone has more shares, but each share is worth proportionately less than before.

LO10–7 Prepare and analyze the stockholders' equity section of a balance sheet and the statement of stockholders' equity.

The stockholders' equity section of the balance sheet presents the balance of each equity account *at a point in time.* The statement of stockholders' equity shows the change in each equity account balance *over time.*

Analysis

LO10–8 Evaluate company performance using information on stockholders' equity.

The return on equity measures the ability to generate earnings from the owners' investment. It is calculated as net income divided by average stockholders' equity. The dividend yield measures how much a company pays out in dividends in relation to its stock price. Earnings per share measures the net income earned per share of common stock. The price-earnings ratio indicates how the stock is trading relative to current earnings.

GLOSSARY

Accumulated deficit: A debit balance in Retained Earnings. **p. 472**

Additional paid-in capital: The portion of the cash proceeds above par value. **p. 464**

Angel investors: Wealthy individuals in the business community willing to risk investment funds on a promising business venture. **p. 459**

Articles of incorporation: Describes the nature of the firm's business activities, the shares to be issued, and the composition of the initial board of directors. **p. 459**

Authorized stock: The total number of shares available to sell, stated in the company's articles of incorporation. **p. 462**

Convertible: Shares can be exchanged for common stock. **p. 466**

Cumulative: Preferred stock shares receive priority for future dividends, if dividends are not paid in a given year. **p. 466**

Declaration date: The day on which the board of directors declares the dividend to be paid. **p. 472**

Dividends: Distributions by a corporation to its stockholders. **p. 472**

Dividends in arrears: Unpaid dividends on cumulative preferred stock. **p. 466**

Dividend yield: Dividends per share divided by the stock price. **p. 483**

Double taxation: Corporate income is taxed once on earnings at the corporate level and again on dividends at the individual level. **p. 461**

Earnings per share: Measures the net income earned per share of common stock. **p. 484**

Growth stocks: Stocks that tend to have higher price-earnings ratios and are expected to have higher future earnings. **p. 484**

Initial public offering (IPO): The first time a corporation issues stock to the public. **p. 459**

Issued stock: The number of shares sold to investors; includes treasury shares. **p. 463**

Limited liability: Stockholders in a corporation can lose no more than the amount they invested in the company. **p. 461**

No-par value stock: Common stock that has not been assigned a par value. **p. 463**

Organization chart: Traces the line of authority within the corporation. **p. 459**

Outstanding stock: The number of shares held by investors; excludes treasury shares. **p. 463**

Paid-in capital: The amount stockholders have invested in the company. **p. 458**

Par value: The legal capital assigned per share of stock. **p. 463**

Payment date: The date of the actual distribution of dividends. **p. 473**

Preferred stock: Stock with preference over common stock in the payment of dividends and the distribution of assets. **p. 465**

Price-earnings ratio: The stock price divided by earnings per share so that both stock price and earnings are expressed on a per share basis. **p. 484**

Privately held corporation: Does not allow investment by the general public and normally has fewer stockholders. **p. 460**

Property dividend: The distribution of a noncash asset to stockholders. **p. 473**

Publicly held corporation: Allows investment by the general public and is regulated by the Securities and Exchange Commission. **p. 460**

Record date: A specific date on which the company will determine the registered owners of stock and, therefore, who will receive the dividend. **p. 473**

Redeemable: Shares can be returned to the corporation at a fixed price. **p. 466**

Retained earnings: Represents all net income, less all dividends, since the company began. **pp. 458, 471**

Return on equity: Net income divided by average stockholders' equity; measures the income generated per dollar of equity. **p. 482**

S corporation: Allows a company to enjoy limited liability as a corporation, but tax treatment as a partnership. **p. 462**

Stated value: The legal capital assigned per share to no-par stock. **p. 464**

Statement of stockholders' equity: Summarizes the changes in the balance in each stockholders' equity account over a period of time. **p. 480**

Stock dividends: Additional shares of a company's own stock given to stockholders. **p. 475**

Stock split: A large stock dividend that includes a reduction in the par or stated value per share. **p. 475**

Treasury stock: A corporation's own stock that it has acquired. **pp. 458, 468**

Value stocks: Stocks that tend to have lower price-earnings ratios and are priced low in relation to current earnings. **p. 484**

Venture capital firms: Provide additional financing, often in the millions, for a percentage ownership in the company. **p. 459**

SELF-STUDY QUESTIONS

1. Which of the following is a publicly traded company? **(LO10–1)**
   a. American Eagle.
   b. Cargill.
   c. Ernst & Young.
   d. Koch Industries.

2. The advantages of owning a corporation include: **(LO10–1)**
   a. Difficulty in transferring ownership.
   b. Limited liability.
   c. Lower taxes.
   d. Less paperwork.

3. The correct order from the smallest number of shares to the largest number of shares is: **(LO10–2)**
   a. Authorized, issued, and outstanding.
   b. Outstanding, issued, and authorized.
   c. Issued, outstanding, and authorized.
   d. Issued, authorized, and outstanding.

4. Preferred stock: **(LO10–3)**
   a. Is always recorded as a liability.
   b. Is always recorded as part of stockholders' equity.
   c. Can have features of both liabilities and stockholders' equity.
   d. Is not included in either liabilities or stockholders' equity.

5. Treasury stock: **(LO10–4)**
   a. Has a normal credit balance.
   b. Decreases stockholders' equity.
   c. Is recorded as an investment.
   d. Increases stockholders' equity.

6. Retained earnings: **(LO10–5)**
   a. Has a normal debit balance.
   b. Decreases stockholders' equity.
   c. Is equal to the balance in cash.
   d. Increases stockholders' equity.

7. We record cash dividends on the: **(LO10–5)**
   a. Declaration date, record date, and payment date.
   b. Record date and payment date.
   c. Declaration date and payment date.
   d. Declaration date and record date.

8. Both cash dividends and stock dividends: **(LO10–6)**
   a. Reduce total assets.
   b. Reduce total liabilities.
   c. Reduce total stockholders' equity.
   d. Reduce retained earnings.

9. How does the stockholders' equity section in the balance sheet differ from the statement of stockholders' equity? **(LO10–7)**
   a. The stockholders' equity section shows balances at a point in time, whereas the statement of stockholders' equity shows activity over a period of time.
   b. The stockholders' equity section shows activity over a period of time, whereas the statement of stockholders' equity is at a point in time.
   c. There are no differences between them.
   d. The stockholders' equity section is more detailed than the statement of stockholders' equity.

10. The PE ratio: **(LO10–8)**
   a. Tends to be lower for growth stocks.
   b. Tends to be higher for value stocks.
   c. Indicates how a stock is trading in relation to current earnings.
   d. Typically is less than 1.

Note: For answers, see the last page of the chapter.

For additional study materials, including 10 more multiple-choice Self-Study questions, visit Connect.

REVIEW QUESTIONS

■ LO10–1   1. Corporations typically do not first raise capital by issuing stock to the general public. What are the common stages of equity financing leading to an initial public offering (IPO)?

■ LO10–1   2. What is the difference between a public and a private corporation? Provide an example of each.

■ LO10–1   3. What are the basic ownership rights of common stockholders?

■ LO10–1   4. Which form of business organization is most common? Which form of business organization is larger in terms of total sales, total assets, earnings, and number of employees?

■ LO10–1   5. Describe the primary advantages and disadvantages of a corporation.

■ LO10–1   6. Explain how an LLC or an S corporation represents the "best of both worlds" in terms of business ownership.

■ LO10–2   7. Explain the difference between authorized, issued, and outstanding shares.

■ LO10–2   8. The articles of incorporation allow for the issuance of 1 million shares of common stock. During its first year, California Clothing issued 100,000 shares and reacquired 10,000 shares it held as treasury stock. At the end of the first year, how many shares are authorized, issued, and outstanding?

■ LO10–2   9. What is par value? How is it related to market value? How is it used in recording the issuance of stock?

■ LO10–3   10. What are the three potential features of preferred stock? Indicate whether each feature makes the preferred stock appear more like stockholders' equity or more like long-term liabilities.

■ LO10–3   11. Explain why preferred stock often is said to be a mixture of attributes somewhere between common stock and bonds.

■ LO10–4   12. What would motivate a company to buy back its own stock?

■ LO10–4   13. How is the accounting for a repurchase of a company's own stock (treasury stock) different from the purchase of stock in another corporation?

■ LO10–5   14. Explain why some companies choose not to pay cash dividends. Why do investors purchase stock in companies that do not pay cash dividends?

■ LO10–5   15. Describe the declaration date, record date, and payment date for a cash dividend.

■ LO10–6   16. How does a 100% stock dividend or a 2-for-1 stock split affect total assets, total liabilities, and total stockholders' equity?

■ LO10–6   17. Contrast the effects of a cash dividend and a stock dividend on total assets, total liabilities, and total stockholders' equity.

■ LO10–6   18. What happens to the par value, the share's trading price, and the number of shares outstanding in a 2-for-1 stock split?

■ LO10–7   19. Indicate the correct order in which to report the following accounts in the stockholders' equity section of the balance sheet: Additional Paid-in Capital, Common Stock, Preferred Stock, Treasury Stock, and Retained Earnings.

■ LO10–7   20. How is the stockholders' equity section of the balance sheet different from the statement of stockholders' equity?

■ LO10–7   21. Why doesn't total stockholders' equity equal the market value of the firm?

■ LO10–8   22. Explain why earnings per share is useful for comparing earnings performance for the same company over time, but is not useful for comparing earnings performance between two competing companies.

■ LO10–8   23. What does "PE" stand for in the PE ratio, and how do investors use this ratio?

BRIEF EXERCISES

BE10–1 Waldo is planning to start a clothing store helping big and tall men blend in with the crowd. Explain to Waldo the advantages and disadvantages of a corporation in comparison to a sole proprietorship or partnership.

Cite advantages and disadvantages of a corporation (LO10–1)

BE10–2 Renaldo heard that an S corporation combines the benefits of a corporation with the benefits of a partnership. Explain to Renaldo the specific benefits of an S corporation and any drawbacks to organizing as an S corporation.

Understand an S corporation (LO10–1)

BE10–3 Western Wear Clothing issues 3,000 shares of its $0.01 par value common stock to provide funds for further expansion. Assuming the issue price is $11 per share, record the issuance of common stock.

Record issuance of common stock (LO10–2)

BE10–4 Gothic Architecture is a new chain of clothing stores specializing in the color black. Gothic issues 1,000 shares of its $1 par value common stock at $30 per share. Record the issuance of the stock. How would the entry differ if Gothic issued no-par value stock?

Record issuance of common stock (LO10–2)

BE10–5 Equinox Outdoor Wear issues 1,000 shares of its $0.01 par value preferred stock for cash at $32 per share. Record the issuance of the preferred shares.

Record issuance of preferred stock (LO10–3)

BE10–6 Match each of the following preferred stock features with its description.

Recognize preferred stock features (LO10–3)

Preferred Stock Features	Description
1. Convertible	a. Prior unpaid dividends receive priority.
2. Redeemable	b. Shares can be sold at a predetermined price.
3. Cumulative	c. Shares can be exchanged for common stock.

BE10–7 Rachel's Designs has 2,000 shares of 7%, $50 par value cumulative preferred stock issued at the beginning of 2016. All remaining shares are common stock. Due to cash flow difficulties, the company was not able to pay dividends in 2016 or 2017. The company plans to pay total dividends of $23,000 in 2018. How much of the $23,000 dividend will be paid to preferred stockholders and how much will be paid to common stockholders?

Determine the amount of preferred stock dividends (LO10–3)

BE10–8 California Surf Clothing Company issues 1,000 shares of $1 par value common stock at $35 per share. Later in the year, the company decides to repurchase 100 shares at a cost of $38 per share. Record the purchase of treasury stock.

Record purchase of treasury stock (LO10–4)

BE10–9 Refer to the situation described in BE10–8. Record the transaction if California Surf reissues the 100 shares of treasury stock at $40 per share.

Record sale of treasury stock (LO10–4)

BE10–10 Divine Apparel has 4,000 shares of common stock outstanding. On October 1, the company declares a $0.75 per share dividend to stockholders of record on October 15. The dividend is paid on October 31. Record all transactions on the appropriate dates for cash dividends.

Record cash dividends (LO10–5)

BE10–11 On June 30, the board of directors of Sandals, Inc., declares a 100% stock dividend on its 30,000, $1 par, common shares. The market price of Sandals common stock is $35 on June 30. Record the stock dividend.

Record stock dividends (LO10–6)

BE10–12 Refer to the situation described in BE10–11, but assume a 2-for-1 stock split instead of the 100% stock dividend. Explain why Sandals did not record a 2-for-1 stock split. What are the number of shares, par value per share, and market price per share immediately after the 2-for-1 stock split?

Analyze a stock split (LO10–6)

BE10–13 Indicate whether each of the following transactions increases (+), decreases (−), or has no effect (NE) on total assets, total liabilities, and total stockholders' equity. The first transaction is completed as an example.

Indicate effects on total stockholders' equity (LO10–7)

Transaction	Total Assets	Total Liabilities	Total Stockholders' Equity
Issue common stock	+	NE	+
Issue preferred stock			
Purchase treasury stock			
Sale of treasury stock			

Prepare the stockholders' equity section (LO10–7)

BE10–14 Summit Apparel has the following accounts at December 31: Common Stock, $1 par value, 2,000,000 shares issued; Paid-in Capital, $18 million; Retained Earnings, $11 million; and Treasury Stock, 60,000 shares, $1.32 million. Prepare the stockholders' equity section of the balance sheet.

Calculate the return on equity (LO10–8)

BE10–15 The financial statements of Colorado Outfitters include the following selected data ($ in millions): sales, $9,543; net income, $320; beginning stockholders' equity, $3,219; and ending stockholders' equity, $2,374. Calculate the return on equity.

EXERCISES

McGraw Hill Education **connect**

Match terms with their definitions (LO10–1)

E10–1 Match (by letter) the following terms with their definitions. Each letter is used only once.

Terms

_____ 1. Publicly held corporation.
_____ 2. Organization chart.
_____ 3. Articles of incorporation.
_____ 4. Limited liability.
_____ 5. Initial public offering.
_____ 6. Double taxation.
_____ 7. S corporation.
_____ 8. Limited liability company.

Definitions

a. Shareholders can lose no more than the amount they invest in the company.
b. Corporate earnings are taxed twice—at the corporate level and individual shareholder level.
c. Like an S corporation, but there are no limitations on the number of owners as in an S corporation.
d. Traces the line of authority within the corporation.
e. Allows for legal treatment as a corporation, but tax treatment as a partnership.
f. Has stock traded on a stock exchange such as the New York Stock Exchange (NYSE).
g. The first time a corporation issues stock to the public.
h. Describes (a) the nature of the firm's business activities, (b) the shares to be issued, and (c) the composition of the initial board of directors.

Explain the meaning of terms used in stockholders' equity (LO10–2, 10–3, 10–4)

E10–2 Your friend, Jonathon Fain, is an engineering major with an entrepreneurial spirit. He wants to start his own corporation and needs your accounting expertise. He has no idea what the following terms mean: (1) authorized stock, (2) issued stock, (3) outstanding stock, (4) preferred stock, and (5) treasury stock.

Required:
Write a note to Jonathon carefully explaining what each term means and how they are different from each other.

Record the issuance of common stock (LO10–2)

E10–3 Clothing Frontiers began operations on January 1 and engages in the following transactions during the year related to stockholders' equity.

January 1   Issues 700 shares of common stock for $50 per share.
April   1   Issues 110 additional shares of common stock for $54 per share.

Required:
1. Record the transactions, assuming Clothing Frontiers has no-par common stock.
2. Record the transactions, assuming Clothing Frontiers has either $1 par value or $1 stated value common stock.

E10–4 Nathan's Athletic Apparel has 2,000 shares of 5%, $100 par value preferred stock the company issued at the beginning of 2017. All remaining shares are common stock. The company was not able to pay dividends in 2017, but plans to pay dividends of $22,000 in 2018.

Determine the amount of preferred stock dividends (LO10–3)

Required:
1. Assuming the preferred stock is cumulative, how much of the $22,000 dividend will be paid to preferred stockholders and how much will be paid to common stockholders in 2018?
2. Assuming the preferred stock is noncumulative, how much of the $22,000 dividend will be paid to preferred stockholders and how much will be paid to common stockholders in 2018?

E10–5 Italian Stallion has the following transactions during the year related to stockholders' equity.

February 1   Issues 6,000 shares of no-par common stock for $16 per share.
May   15   Issues 700 shares of $10 par value preferred stock for $13 per share.
October   1   Declares a cash dividend of $1.25 per share to all stockholders of record (both common and preferred) on October 15.
October 15   Date of record.
October 31   Pays the cash dividend declared on October 1.

Record common stock, preferred stock, and dividend transactions (LO10–2, 10–3, 10–5)

Required:
Record each of these transactions.

E10–6 Finishing Touches has two classes of stock authorized: 8%, $10 par preferred, and $1 par value common. The following transactions affect stockholders' equity during 2018, its first year of operations:

Record issuance of stock and treasury stock transactions (LO10–2, 10–3, 10–4)

January   2   Issues 100,000 shares of common stock for $35 per share.
February   6   Issues 3,000 shares of 8% preferred stock for $11 per share.
September 10   Repurchases 11,000 shares of its own common stock for $40 per share.
December 15   Reissues 5,500 shares of treasury stock at $45 per share.

Required:
Record each of these transactions.

E10–7 Refer to the information in E10–6. In its first year of operations, Finishing Touches has net income of $160,000 and pays dividends at the end of the year of $94,500 ($1 per share) on all common shares outstanding and $2,400 on all preferred shares outstanding.

Prepare the stockholders' equity section (LO10–7)

Required:
Prepare the stockholders' equity section of the balance sheet for Finishing Touches as of December 31, 2018.

E10–8 On March 15, **American Eagle** declares a quarterly cash dividend of $0.125 per share payable on April 13 to all stockholders of record on March 30.

Record cash dividends (LO10–5)

Required:
Record American Eagle's declaration and payment of cash dividends for its 210 million shares.

E10–9 Power Drive Corporation designs and produces a line of golf equipment and golf apparel. Power Drive has 100,000 shares of common stock outstanding as of the beginning of 2018. Power Drive has the following transactions affecting stockholders' equity in 2018.

Record common stock, treasury stock, and cash dividends (LO10–2, 10–4, 10–5)

March   1   Issues 65,000 additional shares of $1 par value common stock for $62 per share.
May   10   Repurchases 6,000 shares of treasury stock for $65 per share.
June   1   Declares a cash dividend of $2.00 per share to all stockholders of record on June 15. (Hint: Dividends are not paid on treasury stock.)
July   1   Pays the cash dividend declared on June 1.
October 21   Reissues 3,000 shares of treasury stock purchased on May 10 for $70 per share.

Required:

Record each of these transactions.

Record stock dividends and stock splits (LO10–6)

E10–10 On September 1, the board of directors of Colorado Outfitters, Inc., declares a stock dividend on its 10,000, $1 par, common shares. The market price of the common stock is $30 on this date.

Required:

1. Record the stock dividend assuming a small (10%) stock dividend.
2. Record the stock dividend assuming a large (100%) stock dividend.
3. Record the transaction assuming a 2-for-1 stock split.

Prepare the stockholders' equity section (LO10–7)

E10–11 Refer to the information in E10–9. Power Drive Corporation has the following beginning balances in its stockholders' equity accounts on January 1, 2018: Common Stock, $100,000; Additional Paid-in Capital, $5,500,000; and Retained Earnings, $3,000,000. Net income for the year ended December 31, 2018, is $700,000.

Required:

Taking into consideration all of the transactions recorded in E10–9, prepare the stockholders' equity section of the balance sheet for Power Drive Corporation as of December 31, 2018.

Prepare a statement of stockholders' equity (LO10–7)

E10–12 Refer to the information in E10–9. Power Drive Corporation has the following beginning balances in its stockholders' equity accounts on January 1, 2018: Common Stock, $100,000; Additional Paid-in Capital, $5,500,000; and Retained Earnings, $3,000,000. Net income for the year ended December 31, 2018, is $700,000.

Required:

Taking into consideration all the transactions recorded in E10–9, prepare the statement of stockholders' equity for Power Drive Corporation for the year ended December 31, 2018, using the format provided.

POWER DRIVE CORPORATION
Statement of Stockholders' Equity
For the year ended December 31, 2018

	Common Stock	Additional Paid-in Capital	Retained Earnings	Treasury Stock	Total Stockholders' Equity
Balance, January 1	$100,000	$5,500,000	$3,000,000	$ -0-	$8,600,000
Issue common stock					
Purchase treasury stock					
Cash dividends					
Sale of treasury stock					
Net income					
Balance, December 31					

Indicate effects on total stockholders' equity (LO10–7)

E10–13 Indicate whether each of the following transactions increases (+), decreases (−), or has no effect (NE) on total assets, total liabilities, and total stockholders' equity. The first transaction is completed as an example.

Transaction	Total Assets	Total Liabilities	Total Stockholders' Equity
Issue common stock	+	NE	+
Issue preferred stock			
Purchase treasury stock			
Sale of treasury stock			
Declare cash dividend			
Pay cash dividend			
100% stock dividend			
2-for-1 stock split			

E10–14 United Apparel has the following balances in its stockholders' equity accounts on December 31, 2018: Treasury Stock, $850,000; Common Stock, $600,000; Preferred Stock, $3,600,000; Retained Earnings, $2,200,000; and Additional Paid-in Capital, $8,800,000.

Prepare the stockholders' equity section (LO10–7)

Required:

Prepare the stockholders' equity section of the balance sheet for United Apparel as of December 31, 2018.

E10–15 The financial statements of Friendly Fashions include the following selected data (in millions):

Calculate and analyze ratios (LO10–8)

($ in millions)	2018	2017
Sales	$10,043	$11,134
Net income	$ 312	$ 818
Stockholders' equity	$ 1,850	$ 2,310
Average shares outstanding (in millions)	675	–
Dividends per share	$ 0.31	
Stock price	$ 6.20	–

Required:

1. Calculate the return on equity in 2018.
2. Calculate the dividend yield in 2018.
3. Calculate earnings per share in 2018.
4. Calculate the price-earnings ratio in 2018.

E10–16 Financial information for Forever 18 includes the following selected data:

Calculate and analyze ratios (LO10–8)

($ in millions)	2018	2017
Net income	$ 129	$ 308
Dividends on preferred stock	$ 20	$ 15
Average shares outstanding (in millions)	150	400
Stock price	$12.02	$10.97

Required:

1. Calculate earnings per share in 2017 and 2018. Did earnings per share increase in 2018?
2. Calculate the price-earnings ratio in 2017 and 2018. In which year is the stock priced lower in relation to reported earnings?

E10–17 On January 1, 2018, the general ledger of Grand Finale Fireworks includes the following account balances:

(LO 10–2, 10–4, 10–5, 10–8)

Accounts	Debit	Credit
Cash	$ 42,700	
Accounts Receivable	44,500	
Supplies	7,500	
Equipment	64,000	
Accumulated Depreciation		$ 9,000
Accounts Payable		14,600
Common Stock, $1 par value		10,000
Additional Paid-in Capital		80,000
Retained Earnings		45,100
Totals	$158,700	$158,700

During January 2018, the following transactions occur:

January 2   Issue an additional 2,000 shares of $1 par value common stock for $40,000.
January 9   Provide services to customers on account, $14,300.
January 10   Purchase additional supplies on account, $4,900.
January 12   Repurchase 1,000 shares of treasury stock for $18 per share.
January 15   Pay cash on accounts payable, $16,500.
January 21   Provide services to customers for cash, $49,100.
January 22   Receive cash on accounts receivable, $16,600.
January 29   Declare a cash dividend of $0.30 per share to all shares outstanding on January 29. The dividend is payable on February 15.

          (*Hint:* Grand Finale Fireworks had 10,000 shares outstanding on January 1, 2018 and dividends are not paid on treasury stock.)

January 30   Reissue 600 shares of treasury stock for $20 per share.
January 31   Pay cash for salaries during January, $42,000.

Required:

1. Record each of the transactions listed above.
2. Record adjusting entries on January 31.

   a. Unpaid utilities for the month of January are $6,200.

   b. Supplies at the end of January total $5,100.

   c. Depreciation on the equipment for the month of January is calculated using the straight-line method. At the time the equipment was purchased, the company estimated a service life of three years and a residual value of $10,000.

   d. Accrued income taxes at the end of January are $2,000.

3. Prepare an adjusted trial balance as of January 31, 2018, after updating beginning balances (above) for transactions during January (*Requirement* 1) and adjusting entries at the end of January (*Requirement* 2).
4. Prepare a multiple-step income statement for the period ended January 31, 2018.
5. Prepare a classified balance sheet as of January 31, 2018.
6. Record closing entries.
7. Analyze the following for Grand Finale Fireworks:

   a. Calculate the return on equity for the month of January. If the average return on equity for the industry for January is 2.5%, is the company *more* or *less* profitable than other companies in the same industry?

   b. How many shares of common stock are outstanding as of January 31, 2018?

   c. Calculate earnings per share for the month of January. (*Hint:* To calculate average shares of common stock outstanding take the beginning shares outstanding plus the ending shares outstanding and divide the total by 2.) If earnings per share was $3.60 last year (i.e., an average of $0.30 per month), is earnings per share for January 2018 *better* or *worse* than last year's average?

PROBLEMS: SET A

Match terms with their definitions (LO10–1)

P10–1A Match (by letter) the following terms with their definitions. Each letter is used only once.

Terms

_____ 1. Cumulative.
_____ 2. Retained earnings.
_____ 3. Outstanding stock.
_____ 4. Limited liability.
_____ 5. Treasury stock.
_____ 6. Issued stock.
_____ 7. Angel investors.
_____ 8. Paid-in capital.
_____ 9. Authorized stock.
_____ 10. Redeemable.

Definitions

a. The amount invested by stockholders.

b. Shares available to sell.

c. Shares can be returned to the corporation at a predetermined price.

d. The earnings not paid out in dividends.

e. Shares actually sold.

f. Shares receive priority for future dividends if dividends are not paid in a given year.

g. Shares held by investors.

h. Shareholders can lose no more than the amount they invested in the company.

i. Wealthy individuals in the business community willing to risk investment funds on a promising business venture.

j. The corporation's own stock that it acquired.

P10–2A Donnie Hilfiger has two classes of stock authorized: $1 par preferred and $0.01 par value common. As of the beginning of 2018, 300 shares of preferred stock and 4,000 shares of common stock have been issued. The following transactions affect stockholders' equity during 2018:

Record equity transactions and indicate the effect on the balance sheet equation (LO10–2, 10–3, 10–4, 10–5)

March	1	Issue 1,100 shares of common stock for $42 per share.
May	15	Purchase 400 shares of treasury stock for $35 per share.
July	10	Reissue 200 shares of treasury stock purchased on May 15 for $40 per share.
October	15	Issue 200 shares of preferred stock for $45 per share.
December	1	Declare a cash dividend on both common and preferred stock of $0.50 per share to all stockholders of record on December 15. (Hint: Dividends are not paid on treasury stock.)
December	31	Pay the cash dividends declared on December 1.

Donnie Hilfiger has the following beginning balances in its stockholders' equity accounts on January 1, 2018: Preferred Stock, $300; Common Stock, $40; Additional Paid-in Capital, $76,000; and Retained Earnings, $30,500. Net income for the year ended December 31, 2018, is $10,800.

Required:

1. Record each of these transactions.

2. Indicate whether each of these transactions would increase (+), decrease (−), or have no effect (NE) on total assets, total liabilities, and total stockholders' equity by completing the following chart.

Transaction	Total Assets	Total Liabilities	Total Stockholders' Equity
Issue common stock			
Purchase treasury stock			
Reissue treasury stock			
Issue preferred stock			
Declare cash dividends			
Pay cash dividends			

P10–3A Sammy's Sportshops has been very profitable in recent years and has seen its stock price steadily increase to over $100 per share. The CFO thinks the company should consider either a 100% stock dividend or a 2-for-1 stock split.

Indicate effect of stock dividends and stock splits (LO10–6)

Required:

1. Complete the following chart comparing the effects of a 100% stock dividend versus a 2-for-1 stock split on the stockholders' equity accounts, shares outstanding, par value, and share price.

	Before	After 100% Stock Dividend	After 2-for-1 Stock Split
Common stock, $1 par value	$ 1,100		
Additional paid-in capital	59,000		
Total paid-in capital	60,100		
Retained earnings	23,850		
Total stockholders' equity	$83,950		
Shares outstanding	1,100		
Par value per share	$ 1		
Share price	$ 130		

2. What is the primary reason companies declare a large stock dividend or a stock split?

Analyze the stockholders' equity section (LO10–7)

P10–4A The stockholders' equity section of Velcro World is presented here.

VELCRO WORLD
Balance Sheet (partial)

($ and shares in thousands)
Stockholders' equity:

Preferred stock, $1 par value	$ 6,000
Common stock, $1 par value	30,000
Additional paid-in capital	1,164,000
Total paid-in capital	1,200,000
Retained earnings	288,000
Treasury stock, 11,000 common shares	(352,000)
Total stockholders' equity	$1,136,000

Required:

Based on the stockholders' equity section of Velcro World, answer the following questions. Remember that all amounts are presented in thousands.
1. How many shares of preferred stock have been issued?
2. How many shares of common stock have been issued?
3. If the common shares were issued at $30 per share, at what average price per share were the preferred shares issued?
4. If retained earnings at the beginning of the period was $250 million and $30 million was paid in dividends during the year, what was the net income for the year?
5. What was the average cost per share of the treasury stock acquired?

Understand stockholders' equity and the statement of stockholders' equity (LO10–7)

P10–5A Refer to the information provided in P10–2A.

Required:

Taking into consideration the beginning balances on January 1, 2018 and all the transactions during 2018, respond to the following for Donnie Hilfiger:
1. Prepare the stockholders' equity section of the balance sheet as of December 31, 2018.
2. Prepare the statement of stockholders' equity for the year ended December 31, 2018.
3. Explain how *Requirements* 1 and 2 are similar and how they are different.

Record equity transactions and prepare the stockholders' equity section (LO10–2, 10–3, 10–4, 10–5, 10–7)

P10–6A Major League Apparel has two classes of stock authorized: 6%, $10 par preferred, and $1 par value common. The following transactions affect stockholders' equity during 2018, its first year of operations:

January	2	Issue 110,000 shares of common stock for $70 per share.
February	14	Issue 60,000 shares of preferred stock for $12 per share.
May	8	Repurchase 11,000 shares of its own common stock for $60 per share.

May	31	Reissue 5,500 shares of treasury stock for $65 per share.
December	1	Declare a cash dividend on its common stock of $0.25 per share and a $36,000 (6% of par value) cash dividend on its preferred stock payable to all stockholders of record on December 15. The dividend is payable on December 30. (*Hint:* Dividends are not paid on treasury stock.)
December	30	Pay the cash dividends declared on December 1.

Required:

1. Record each of these transactions.
2. Prepare the stockholders' equity section of the balance sheet as of December 31, 2018. Net income for the year was $490,000.

P10–7A Khaki Republic sells clothing and accessories through premium outlet locations and online. Selected financial data for Khaki Republic is provided as follows:

Calculate and analyze ratios (LO10–8)

($ in millions)	
Sales	$4,158
Net income	$ 144
Stockholders' equity, beginning	$1,890
Stockholders' equity, ending	$1,931
Average shares outstanding (in millions)	85.6
Dividends per share	$ 0.75
Stock price, ending	$47.23

Required:

1. Calculate the return on equity for Khaki Republic. How does it compare with the return on equity for Ralph Lauren and Abercrombie reported in the chapter?
2. Calculate the dividend yield for Khaki Republic. How does it compare with the dividend yield for Ralph Lauren and Abercrombie reported in the chapter?
3. Calculate the price-earnings ratio for Khaki Republic. How does it compare with the price-earnings ratio for Ralph Lauren and Abercrombie reported in the chapter?

PROBLEMS: SET B

P10–1B Match (by letter) the following terms with their definitions. Each letter is used only once.

Match terms with their definitions (LO10–1 to 10–8)

Terms

_____ 1. PE ratio.
_____ 2. Stockholders' equity section of the balance sheet.
_____ 3. Accumulated deficit.
_____ 4. Growth stocks.
_____ 5. 100% stock dividend.
_____ 6. Statement of stockholders' equity.
_____ 7. Treasury stock.
_____ 8. Value stocks.
_____ 9. Return on equity.
_____ 10. Retained earnings.

Definitions

a. A debit balance in Retained Earnings.
b. Priced high in relation to current earnings as investors expect future earnings to be higher.
c. Effectively the same as a 2-for-1 stock split.
d. The earnings not paid out in dividends.
e. The stock price divided by earnings per share.
f. Summarizes the *changes* in the balance in each stockholders' equity account *over a period of time.*
g. Priced low in relation to current earnings.

h. Measures the ability of company management to generate earnings from the resources that owners provide.

i. Shows the balance in each equity account *at a point in time.*

j. The corporation's own stock that it acquired.

Record equity transactions and indicate the effect on the balance sheet equation (LO10–2, 10–3, 10–4, 10–5)

P10–2B Nautical has two classes of stock authorized: $10 par preferred, and $1 par value common. As of the beginning of 2018, 125 shares of preferred stock and 3,000 shares of common stock have been issued. The following transactions affect stockholders' equity during 2018:

March	1	Issue 3,000 additional shares of common stock for $10 per share.
April	1	Issue 175 additional shares of preferred stock for $40 per share.
June	1	Declare a cash dividend on both common and preferred stock of $0.25 per share to all stockholders of record on June 15.
June	30	Pay the cash dividends declared on June 1.
August	1	Purchase 175 shares of common treasury stock for $7 per share.
October	1	Reissue 125 shares of treasury stock purchased on August 1 for $9 per share.

Nautical has the following beginning balances in its stockholders' equity accounts on January 1, 2018: Preferred Stock, $1,250; Common Stock, $3,000; Additional Paid-in Capital, $19,500; and Retained Earnings, $11,500. Net income for the year ended December 31, 2018, is $7,650.

Required:

1. Record each of these transactions.

2. Indicate whether each of these transactions would increase (+), decrease (−), or have no effect (NE) on total assets, total liabilities, and total stockholders' equity by completing the following chart.

Transaction	Total Assets	Total Liabilities	Total Stockholders' Equity
Issue common stock			
Issue preferred stock			
Declare cash dividends			
Pay cash dividends			
Purchase treasury stock			
Reissue treasury stock			

Indicate effect of stock dividends and stock splits (LO10–6)

P10–3B The Athletic Village has done very well the past year, and its stock price is now trading at $102 per share. Management is considering either a 100% stock dividend or a 2-for-1 stock split.

Required:

Complete the following chart comparing the effects of a 100% stock dividend versus a 2-for-1 stock split on the stockholders' equity accounts, shares outstanding, par value, and share price.

	Before	After 100% Stock Dividend	After 2-for-1 Stock Split
Common stock, $0.01 par value	$ 11		
Additional paid-in capital	34,990		
Total paid-in capital	35,001		
Retained earnings	16,000		
Total stockholders' equity	$51,001		
Shares outstanding	1,100		
Par value per share	$ 0.01		
Share price	$ 102		

P10–4B The stockholders' equity section of The Seventies Shop is presented here.

Analyze the stockholders' equity section (LO10–7)

THE SEVENTIES SHOP
Balance Sheet (partial)

($ in thousands)	
Stockholders' equity:	
Preferred stock, $50 par value	$ –0–
Common stock, $5 par value	20,000
Additional paid-in capital	100,000
Total paid-in capital	120,000
Retained earnings	53,000
Treasury stock	(3,700)
Total stockholders' equity	$169,300

Required:
Based on the stockholders' equity section of The Seventies Shop, answer the following questions. Remember that all amounts are presented in thousands.
1. How many shares of preferred stock have been issued?
2. How many shares of common stock have been issued?
3. Total paid-in capital is $120 million. At what average price per share were the common shares issued?
4. If retained earnings at the beginning of the period was $45 million and net income during the year was $9,907,500, how much was paid in dividends for the year?
5. If the treasury stock was reacquired at $20 per share, how many shares were reacquired?
6. How much was the dividend per share? (*Hint:* Dividends are not paid on treasury stock.)

P10–5B Refer to the information provided in P10–2B.

Understand stockholders' equity and the statement of stockholders' equity (LO10–7)

Required:
Taking into consideration the beginning balances on January 1, 2018 and all the transactions during 2018, respond to the following for Nautical:
1. Prepare the stockholders' equity section of the balance sheet as of December 31, 2018.
2. Prepare the statement of stockholders' equity for the year ended December 31, 2018.
3. Explain how *Requirements* 1 and 2 are similar and how they are different.

P10–6B National League Gear has two classes of stock authorized: 4%, $20 par preferred, and $5 par value common. The following transactions affect stockholders' equity during 2018, National League's first year of operations:

Record equity transactions and prepare the stockholders' equity section (LO10–2, 10–3, 10–4, 10–5, 10–7)

February	2	Issue 1.5 million shares of common stock for $35 per share.
February	4	Issue 600,000 shares of preferred stock for $23 per share.
June	15	Repurchase 150,000 shares of its own common stock for $30 per share.
August	15	Reissue 112,500 shares of treasury stock for $45 per share.
November	1	Declare a cash dividend on its common stock of $1.50 per share and a $480,000 (4% of par value) cash dividend on its preferred stock payable to all stockholders of record on November 15. (*Hint:* Dividends are not paid on treasury stock.)
November	30	Pay the dividends declared on November 1.

Required:
1. Record each of these transactions.
2. Prepare the stockholders' equity section of the balance sheet as of December 31, 2018. Net income for the year was $4,900,000.

Calculate and analyze
ratios (LO10–8)

P10–7B Selected financial data for DC Menswear is provided as follows:

($ in millions)	
Sales	$14,549
Net income	$ 833
Stockholders' equity, beginning	$ 4,080
Stockholders' equity, ending	$ 2,755
Average shares outstanding (in millions)	485
Dividends per share	$ 1.00
Stock price, ending	$ 18.93

Required:

1. Calculate the return on equity for DC Menswear. How does it compare with the return on equity for Ralph Lauren and Abercrombie reported in the chapter?
2. Calculate the dividend yield for DC Menswear. How does it compare with the dividend yield for Ralph Lauren and Abercrombie reported in the chapter?
3. Calculate the price-earnings ratio for DC Menswear. How does it compare with the price-earnings ratio for Ralph Lauren and Abercrombie reported in the chapter?

ADDITIONAL PERSPECTIVES

Great Adventures

(This is a continuation of the Great Adventures problem from earlier chapters.)

**Continuing
Problem**

AP10–1 Tony and Suzie purchased land costing $500,000 for a new camp in January 2020. Now they need money to build the cabins, dining facility, a ropes course, and an outdoor swimming pool. Tony and Suzie first checked with Summit Bank to see if they could borrow another million dollars, but unfortunately the bank turned them down as too risky. Undeterred, they promoted their idea to close friends they had made through the outdoor clinics and TEAM events. They decided to go ahead and sell shares of stock in the company to raise the additional funds for the camp. Great Adventures has two classes of stock authorized: 8%, $10 par preferred, and $1 par value common.

When the company began on July 1, 2018, Tony and Suzie each purchased 10,000 shares of $1 par value common stock at $1 per share. The following transactions affect stockholders' equity during 2020, its third year of operations:

July	2	Issue an additional 100,000 shares of common stock for $12 per share.
September 10		Repurchase 10,000 shares of its own common stock (i.e., treasury stock) for $15 per share.
November 15		Reissue 5,000 shares of treasury stock at $16 per share.
December 1		Declare a cash dividend on its common stock of $115,000 ($1 per share) to all stockholders of record on December 15.
December 31		Pay the cash dividend declared on December 1.

Required:

1. Record each of these transactions.
2. Great Adventures has net income of $150,000 in 2020. Retained earnings at the beginning of 2020 was $140,000. Prepare the stockholders' equity section of the balance sheet for Great Adventures as of December 31, 2020.

Financial Analysis

American Eagle Outfitters, Inc.

AP10–2 Financial information for **American Eagle** is presented in **Appendix A** at the end of the book. Using the financial information presented in **Appendix A,** answer the following.

Required:

1. What is the par value per share for the common stock?

2. How many common shares were issued at the end of the most recent year?
3. Did the company have any treasury stock? How many shares?
4. How much did the company pay in cash dividends in the most recent year? (Hint: Look in the statement of stockholders' equity in the retained earnings column.)

The Buckle, Inc.

Financial Analysis

AP10–3 Financial information for **Buckle** is presented in **Appendix B** at the end of the book.

Required:
1. What is the par value per share for the common stock?
2. How many common shares were issued at the end of the most recent year?
3. Did the company have any treasury stock? How many shares?
4. How much did the company pay in cash dividends in the most recent year? (Hint: Look in the statement of stockholders' equity in the retained earnings column.)

American Eagle Outfitters, Inc. vs. The Buckle, Inc.

Comparative Analysis

AP10–4 Financial information for **American Eagle** is presented in **Appendix A** at the end of the book, and financial information for **Buckle** is presented in **Appendix B** at the end of the book. The stock prices as of January 31, 2015, for American Eagle and Buckle were $14.04 and $50.79, respectively.

Required:
1. Calculate the return on equity for American Eagle and Buckle for the year ended January 31, 2015. Which company has a higher return on equity?
2. Calculate the dividend yield for American Eagle and Buckle for the year ended January 31, 2015. Which company has a higher dividend yield?
3. Calculate the price-earnings ratio on January 31, 2015, for American Eagle and Buckle. Basic earnings per share are provided for each company near the bottom of the income statement. Which is trading at a lower price per dollar of earnings?

Ethics

AP10–5 Put yourself in the shoes of a company president: The extremely successful launch of a new product has resulted in an additional $5 million in unexpected operating cash flows. You can think of several ways to use the extra $5 million.

One alternative is to pay out a special dividend to the shareholders. As president, you are accountable to the board of directors, which is elected by the shareholders. Rather than pay a dividend, you could repurchase shares of the company's own stock. The stock seems currently to be underpriced, and by purchasing treasury shares you are distributing surplus cash to shareholders without giving them taxable dividend income.

You could also pay a special year-end bonus to your employees. With 500 employees, that would average $10,000 per employee, quite a nice holiday bonus. After all, it was the employees' hard work and dedication that earned the money in the first place.

Or you could use the money to reinvest in the company. By reinvesting the money, it might be easier to continue the upward earnings trend in the future.

Finally, you could approach the board of directors for a compensation adjustment of your own. It's been a great year, and you are the president of the company. Shouldn't you at least share in the success?

Required:
Determine how you would allocate the additional $5 million. Are there other areas in which to spend the money not mentioned in the above case? Is it ethical for the president to be directly compensated based on the company's performance each year?

Internet Research

AP10–6 EDGAR, the Electronic Data Gathering, Analysis, and Retrieval system, is a giant database of documents the U.S. Securities and Exchange Commission (SEC) requires that companies submit. All publicly traded domestic companies use EDGAR to make the majority of their filings. (Filings by foreign companies are not required to be filed on EDGAR, but many of these companies do so voluntarily.) Form 10-K, which includes the annual report, is an important document required to be filed on EDGAR. The SEC makes this information available, free to the public, on the Internet.

Required:
1. Access EDGAR on the Internet. The web address is *www.sec.gov*.
2. Search for a public company with which you are familiar. Access its most recent 10-K filing, and search or scroll to find the statement of stockholders' equity.
3. Determine from the statement the transactions that affected common stock during the past year.
4. Determine from the statement the transactions that affected retained earnings during the past year.
5. Explain how the totals on the statement of stockholders' equity agree with the amounts reported in the stockholders' equity section in the balance sheet.

Written Communication

AP10–7 Preferred stock has characteristics of both liabilities and stockholders' equity. Convertible bonds are another example of a financing arrangement that blurs the line between liabilities and stockholders' equity. Items like these have led some to conclude that the present distinction between liabilities and equity should be eliminated. Under this approach, liabilities and equity would be combined into one category that includes both creditor and owner claims to resources.

Required:
1. Define liabilities and stockholders' equity.
2. Provide arguments in support of maintaining the distinction between liabilities and stockholders' equity in the balance sheet.
3. Provide arguments in support of eliminating the distinction between liabilities and stockholders' equity in the balance sheet.
4. Which do you recommend? Why?

Earnings Management

AP10–8 Renegade Clothing is struggling to meet analysts' forecasts. It's early December 2018, and the year-end projections are in. Listed below are the projections for the year ended 2018 and the comparable actual amounts for 2017.

	Projected 2018	Actual 2017
Sales	$14,000,000	$16,023,000
Net income	878,000	1,113,000
Total assets	$ 6,500,000	$ 6,821,000
Total liabilities	$ 2,500,000	$ 2,396,000
Stockholders' equity	4,000,000	4,425,000
Total liabilities and stockholders' equity	$ 6,500,000	$ 6,821,000
Shares outstanding at year-end	950,000	950,000

Analysts forecast earnings per share for 2018 to be $0.95 per share. It looks like earnings per share will fall short of expectations in 2018.

Ronald Outlaw, the director of marketing, has a creative idea to improve earnings per share and the return on equity. He proposes the company borrow additional funds and use the proceeds to repurchase some of its own stock—treasury shares. Is this a good idea?

Required:

1. Calculate the projected earnings per share and return on equity for 2018 before any repurchase of stock.

Now assume Renegade Clothing borrows $1 million and uses the money to purchase 100,000 shares of its own stock at $10 per share. The projections for 2018 will change as follows:

	2018	2017
Sales	$14,000,000	$16,023,000
Net income	878,000	1,113,000
Total assets	$ 6,500,000	$ 6,821,000
Total liabilities	$ 3,500,000	$ 2,396,000
Stockholders' equity	3,000,000	4,425,000
Total liabilities and stockholders' equity	$ 6,500,000	$ 6,821,000
Shares outstanding at year-end	850,000	950,000

2. Calculate the new projected earnings per share and return on equity for 2018, assuming the company goes through with the treasury stock repurchase. (*Hint:* In computing earnings per share, average shares outstanding is now 900,000 = (850,000 + 950,000) / 2.)
3. Explain how the repurchase of treasury stock near year-end improves earnings per share and the return on equity ratio.

Answers to the Self-Study Questions

1. a   2. b   3. b   4. c   5. b   6. d   7. c   8. d   9. a   10. c

CHAPTER 11

Statement of Cash Flows

Learning Objectives

AFTER STUDYING THIS CHAPTER, YOU SHOULD BE ABLE TO:

- **LO11–1** Classify cash transactions as operating, investing, or financing activities.
- **LO11–2** Prepare the operating activities section of the statement of cash flows using the indirect method.
- **LO11–3** Prepare the investing activities section and the financing activities section of the statement of cash flows.

Analysis

- **LO11–4** Perform financial analysis using the statement of cash flows.

Appendix

- **LO11–5** Prepare the operating activities section of the statement of cash flows using the direct method.

APPLE INC.: CASH FLOWS AT THE CORE

Net income represents all revenues less expenses of a company during a reporting period. Operating cash flows represent the cash inflows less cash outflows related to the very same revenue and expense activities. Although you might expect these two amounts to be similar, fairly large differences can occur. Below are the net income (loss) and operating cash flows for three well-known companies in the technology industry ($ in millions):

Company Name	Net Income	Operating Cash Flows
Apple	$39,510	$59,713
Google	14,444	22,376
Amazon	(241)	6,842

All three companies report much higher operating cash flows than net income. **Amazon** demonstrates that a company can report a loss and still generate large positive operating cash flows. One reason that operating cash flows are often higher than net income is that certain items, like depreciation expense, decrease net income but have no effect on operating cash flows. Both net income and operating cash flows are important indicators in explaining stock prices, but which is more important to investors?

In comparing net income with operating cash flows, research consistently finds that net income is more important. Net income works better than operating cash flow in forecasting not only future net income, but also future cash flow.[1] Research also finds that stock returns (the change in stock price plus dividends) are more closely related to net income than to operating cash flow.[2] Net income helps smooth out the unevenness or lumpiness in year-to-year operating cash flow, producing a better estimate of ongoing profitability.

It's important to remember that both net income and operating cash flow provide important information. An investor or creditor who analyzes both net income and operating cash flow will do better than one who focuses solely on net income. In this chapter, we will learn how to prepare and analyze the operating, investing, and financing sections of the statement of cash flows. At the end of the chapter, we'll perform a cash flow analysis for **Apple** vs. **Google**.

© AP Images/Rex Features

---

[1]M. Barth, C. Cram, and K. Nelson. 2001. "Accruals and the Prediction of Future Cash Flows." *The Accounting Review 76* (January), pp. 27–58; and C. Finger. 1994. "The Ability of Earnings to Predict Future Earnings and Cash Flow." *Journal of Accounting Research* 32 (Autumn), pp. 210–23.

[2]P. Dechow. 1994. "Accounting Earnings and Cash Flow as Measures of Firm Performance: The Role of Accounting Accruals." *Journal of Accounting and Economics* (July), pp. 3–42.

PART A

FORMATTING THE STATEMENT OF CASH FLOWS

A statement of cash flows provides a summary of cash inflows and cash outflows during the reporting period. A cash *inflow* simply means cash received by the company during the period. Similarly, a cash *outflow* is cash paid by the company during the period. The difference between cash inflows and cash outflows is called *net cash flows* (or the change in cash) during the period. Illustration 11–1 presents the statement of cash flows for E-Games, Inc.

ILLUSTRATION 11–1

Statement of
Cash Flows

E-GAMES, INC.
Statement of Cash Flows
For the year ended December 31, 2018

Cash Flows from Operating Activities		
Net income	$42,000	
Adjustments to reconcile net income to net cash flows from operating activities:		
Depreciation expense	9,000	
Loss on sale of land	4,000	
Increase in accounts receivable	(7,000)	
Decrease in inventory	10,000	
Increase in prepaid rent	(2,000)	
Decrease in accounts payable	(5,000)	
Increase in interest payable	1,000	
Decrease in income tax payable	(2,000)	
Net cash flows from operating activities		$50,000
Cash Flows from Investing Activities		
Purchase of investments	(35,000)	
Sale of land	6,000	
Net cash flows from investing activities		(29,000)
Cash Flows from Financing Activities		
Issuance of common stock	5,000	
Payment of cash dividends	(12,000)	
Net cash flows from financing activities		(7,000)
Net increase (decrease) in cash		14,000
Cash at the beginning of the period		48,000
Cash at the end of the period		$62,000
Note: Noncash Activities		
Purchased equipment by issuing a note payable		$20,000

We will use this statement as an example throughout the chapter. Don't be concerned about the details yet. That's what the rest of the chapter is all about.

Classification of Transactions

■ **LO11–1**

Classify cash transactions as operating, investing, or financing activities.

The three primary categories of cash flows are (1) cash flows from operating activities, (2) cash flows from investing activities, and (3) cash flows from financing activities. Classifying each cash flow by source (operating, investing, or financing activities) is more informative than simply listing the various cash flows.

CASH FLOW ACTIVITIES

Operating activities include cash receipts and cash payments for transactions relating to revenue and expense activities. These are essentially the very same activities reported in the income statement. In other words, cash flows from operating activities include the elements of net income, but reported on a cash basis. Common examples of operating activities include the collection of cash from customers or the payment of cash for inventory, salaries, and rent.

Investing activities include cash transactions involving the purchase and sale of long-term assets and current investments. Companies periodically invest cash to replace or expand productive facilities such as buildings, land, and equipment. They might also invest in other assets, such as stocks or bonds of other companies, with the expectation of a return on those investments. Eventually, many of these assets are sold. The purchase and sale of long-term assets and investments are common examples of investing activities.

Financing activities are both inflows and outflows of cash resulting from the external financing of a business. A major portion of financing for many companies comes from external sources, specifically stockholders and lenders. Common financing activities are borrowing and repaying debt, issuing and repurchasing stock, and paying dividends.

INTERNATIONAL FINANCIAL REPORTING STANDARDS (IFRS)

SHOULD ALL FINANCIAL STATEMENTS INCLUDE OPERATING, INVESTING, AND FINANCING CLASSIFICATIONS?

In a joint project on financial reporting presentation with the FASB, the IASB recently proposed extending the operating, investing, and financing classifications used in the statement of cash flows to the income statement and the balance sheet. If the proposal goes through, all the major financial statements will be organized along the lines of operating, investing, and financing activities.

For more discussion, see Appendix E.

Illustration 11–2 lists common cash receipts and cash payments for operating, investing, and financing activities. **Review this illustration carefully** (you may even want to bookmark it); it will come in handy in solving many of the homework problems at the end of the chapter.

ILLUSTRATION 11–2

Operating, Investing, and Financing Activities

Cash Flows from Operating Activities	
Cash Inflows	**Cash Outflows**
Sale of goods or services	For inventory
Collection of interest and dividends	For operating expenses
	For interest
	For income taxes

Cash Flows from Investing Activities	
Cash Inflows	**Cash Outflows**
Sale of investments	Purchase of investments
Sale of long-term assets	Purchase of long-term assets
Collection of notes receivable	Lending with notes receivable

Cash Flows from Financing Activities	
Cash Inflows	**Cash Outflows**
Issuance of bonds or notes payable	Repayment of bonds or notes payable
Issuance of stock	Acquisition of treasury stock
	Payment of dividends

Let's look at a few of the cash flows. For example, we report interest and dividends received from investments with operating activities rather than investing activities.

Similarly, we report interest paid on bonds or notes payable with operating activities rather than financing activities. Why are these classified as operating activities? They are included in operating activities because each is a cash flow from an activity reported in the income statement—interest revenue, dividend revenue, and interest expense. As we discussed earlier, operating activities are those we report in the income statement.

On the other hand, we record dividends paid as a financing activity. Recall that dividends are not an expense and, therefore, paying dividends has no effect on net income. The payment of dividends simply reduces assets (cash) and stockholders' equity (retained earnings).

 COMMON MISTAKE

Students sometimes misclassify dividends in preparing the statement of cash flows. Dividends *received* are included in operating activities. Dividends *paid* are included in financing activities.

As we saw in Chapter 3, we prepare the income statement, the statement of stockholders' equity, and the balance sheet directly from the adjusted trial balance. Unfortunately, though, the accounts listed on the adjusted trial balance do not directly provide the cash inflows and cash outflows we report in the statement of cash flows. We need to rely on other information sources to determine the amounts necessary to prepare the statement of cash flows. Illustration 11–3 outlines the three primary sources.

ILLUSTRATION 11–3

Information Sources for Preparing the Statement of Cash Flows

Information Sources	Explanation
1. Income statement	Revenues and expenses provide information in determining cash flows from operating activities.
2. Balance sheet	Changes in assets, liabilities, and stockholders' equity from the end of the last period to the end of this period help to identify cash flows from operating, investing, and financing activities.
3. Detailed accounting records	Sometimes additional information from the accounting records is needed to determine specific cash inflows or cash outflows for the period.

Illustration 11–4 summarizes the relationship of the income statement and balance sheet to the operating, investing, and financing sections in the statement of cash flows.

 KEY POINT

Operating activities generally relate to income statement items and changes in current assets and current liabilities. Investing activities primarily involve changes in long-term assets. Financing activities primarily involve changes in long-term liabilities and stockholders' equity.

NONCASH ACTIVITIES

Suppose a company borrows $200,000 in cash from a bank, issuing a long-term note payable for that amount. The firm reports this transaction in a statement of cash flows as a *financing activity*. Now suppose the company uses that cash to purchase new equipment. It reports this second transaction as an *investing activity*. But what if, instead of two separate transactions, the company acquired $200,000 of new equipment by issuing a $200,000 long-term note payable in a *single transaction*? Since this transaction does not affect cash, it is excluded from the statement of cash flows.

However, undertaking a significant investing activity and a significant financing activity as two parts of a single transaction does not lessen the value of reporting these activities. For

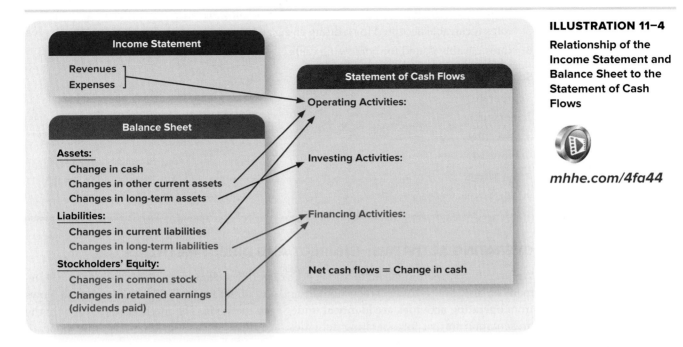

ILLUSTRATION 11–4

Relationship of the Income Statement and Balance Sheet to the Statement of Cash Flows

mhhe.com/4fa44

that reason, transactions that do not increase or decrease cash, but that result in significant investing and financing activities, are reported as noncash activities either directly after the cash flow statement or in a note to the financial statements. Examples of significant noncash investing and financing activities include:

1. Purchase of long-term assets by issuing debt.
2. Purchase of long-term assets by issuing stock.
3. Conversion of bonds payable into common stock.
4. Exchange of long-term assets.

Having a better overall picture of total investing and financing activities is important for investors and creditors. Thus, they should consider both the investing and financing activities reported in the statement of cash flows and the noncash investing and financing activities reported directly after the cash flow statement or in the notes to the financial statements.

Decision Point

Question ?	Accounting information	Analysis
Did the company have any significant noncash investing and financing activities?	Noncash activities are reported either directly after the cash flow statement or in a note to the financial statements	The disclosure of noncash investing and financing activities can be combined with information reported in the statement of cash flows to provide a better overall picture of total investing and financing activities.

Indicate whether each of the following items is classified as an operating activity, investing activity, financing activity, or a significant noncash activity.

1. Dividends received from an investment.
2. Dividends paid to shareholders.
3. Property, plant, and equipment purchased for cash.

Let's Review

mhhe.com/4fa44

4. Property, plant, and equipment purchased by issuing stock.

5. Notes receivable accepted for lending cash.

6. Notes payable issued for borrowing cash.

Suggested Homework:
BE11–1, BE11–2;
E11–3, E11–4;
P11–1A&B

Solution:

1. Operating.

2. Financing.

3. Investing.

4. Noncash.

5. Investing.

6. Financing.

OPERATING ACTIVITIES—INDIRECT AND DIRECT METHODS

We have two ways to determine and report cash flows from operating activities in a statement of cash flows—the indirect method and the direct method. **The total net cash flows from operating activities are identical under both methods.** The methods differ only in the presentation format for operating activities. We report investing, financing, and noncash activities identically under both methods.

Using the indirect method, we begin with net income and then list adjustments to net income, in order to arrive at operating cash flows. An example of the indirect method was presented in Illustration 11–1. The indirect method is more popular because it is generally easier and less costly to prepare. In fact, nearly all major companies in the United States (about 99%) prepare the statement of cash flows using the indirect method.[3] For this reason, we emphasize the indirect method.

Using the direct method, we adjust the items in the income statement to directly show the cash inflows and outflows from operations such as cash received from customers and cash paid for inventory, salaries, rent, interest, and taxes. If a company decides to use the direct method to report operating activities, it must also report the indirect method either along with the statement of cash flows or in a separate note to the financial statements.

We discuss the indirect method in the next section. We present the direct method using the same example in an appendix to this chapter.

 KEY POINT

Companies choose between the indirect method and the direct method in reporting operating activities in the statement of cash flows. The indirect method is less costly to prepare and is used in practice by the majority of companies. The direct method more logically presents the cash inflows and outflows from operations. The investing and financing sections of the statement of cash flows are identical under both methods.

PART B

PREPARING THE STATEMENT OF CASH FLOWS

In this section, we first look at the steps involved in preparing the statement of cash flows, and its basic format. Then we work through these steps in preparing the operating, investing, and financing sections of the statement of cash flows.

Steps in Preparing the Statement of Cash Flows

Illustration 11–5 summarizes the four basic steps in preparing the statement of cash flows.

---

[3]*Accounting Trends and Techniques—2011* (New York: American Institute of Certified Public Accountants).

Step 1. Calculate net cash flows from *operating activities*, using information from the income statement and changes in current assets (other than cash) and current liabilities from the balance sheet.

Step 2. Determine the net cash flows from *investing activities*, by analyzing changes in long-term asset accounts from the balance sheet.

Step 3. Determine the net cash flows from *financing activities*, by analyzing changes in long-term liabilities and stockholders' equity accounts from the balance sheet.

Step 4. Combine the operating, investing, and financing activities, and make sure the total from these three activities equals the amount of cash reported in the balance sheet this year versus last year (the change in cash).

ILLUSTRATION 11–5

Steps in Preparing the Statement of Cash Flows

Illustration 11–6 provides the income statement, balance sheets, and additional information for E-Games, Inc. We will use this information to prepare the statement of cash flows following the four basic steps.

ILLUSTRATION 11–6

Income Statement, Balance Sheets, and Additional Information for E-Games, Inc.

E-GAMES, INC.
Income Statement
For the year ended December 31, 2018

Net sales		$1,012,000
Expenses:		
Cost of goods sold	$650,000	
Operating expenses (salaries, rent, utilities)	286,000	
Depreciation expense	9,000	
Loss on sale of land	4,000	
Interest expense	5,000	
Income tax expense	16,000	
Total expenses		970,000
Net income		$ 42,000

E-GAMES, INC.
Balance Sheets
December 31, 2018 and 2017

	2018	2017	Increase (I) or Decrease (D)
Assets			
Current assets:			
Cash	$ 62,000	$ 48,000	$14,000 (I)
Accounts receivable	27,000	20,000	7,000 (I)
Inventory	35,000	45,000	10,000 (D)
Prepaid rent	4,000	2,000	2,000 (I)
Long-term assets:			
Investments	35,000	0	35,000 (I)
Land	70,000	80,000	10,000 (D)
Equipment	90,000	70,000	20,000 (I)
Accumulated depreciation	(23,000)	(14,000)	9,000 (I)
Total assets	$300,000	$251,000	

(continued)

ILLUSTRATION 11–6
(*concluded*)

	2018	2017	Increase (I) or Decrease (D)
Liabilities and Stockholders' Equity			
Current liabilities:			
Accounts payable	$ 22,000	$ 27,000	$ 5,000 (D)
Interest payable	2,000	1,000	1,000 (I)
Income tax payable	5,000	7,000	2,000 (D)
Long-term liabilities:			
Notes payable	95,000	75,000	20,000 (I)
Stockholders' equity:			
Common stock	105,000	100,000	5,000 (I)
Retained earnings	71,000	41,000	30,000 (I)
Total liabilities and stockholders' equity	$300,000	$251,000	

Additional Information for 2018:

1. Purchased stock in Intendo Corporation for $35,000.
2. Sold land originally costing $10,000 for only $6,000, resulting in a $4,000 loss on sale of land.
3. Purchased $20,000 in equipment by issuing a $20,000 note payable due in three years. No cash was exchanged in the transaction.
4. Issued common stock for $5,000 cash.
5. Declared and paid a cash dividend of $12,000.

Notice the first line of the balance sheets in 2017 and 2018. Cash increased from $48,000 in 2017 to $62,000 in 2018. **The purpose of the statement of cash flows is to report the activities that caused the $14,000 increase in cash.** Those activities are listed by type—operating, investing, or financing.

Basic Format

In preparing the statement of cash flows, it's helpful to first set up the basic format. As Illustration 11–7 shows, the last three lines of the statement of cash flows include amounts for the net increase (decrease) in cash, cash at the beginning of the period, and cash at the end of the period obtained from the E-Games balance sheet. The $14,000 change in the cash balance will be our "check figure," which means the cash inflows and cash outflows we identify must net to this amount.

Operating Activities—Indirect Method

■ LO11–2
Prepare the operating activities section of the statement of cash flows using the indirect method.

As summarized in Illustration 11–5, the first step in preparing the statement of cash flows is to calculate net cash flows from *operating activities* using information from the income statement and changes in current assets (other than cash) and current liabilities from the balance sheet.

Under the indirect method, we calculate net cash flows from operating activities by starting with net income from the income statement. Net income includes all revenue and expense activities reported on an *accrual basis.* That is, we report revenues when we provide goods and services to customers and expenses when we incur them, regardless of when the related cash flows occur. But what are the cash flows from those same revenue and expense activities? That amount equals net cash flows from operating activities. In other words, net cash flows from operating activities include all revenue and expense activities reported on a *cash basis.*

To provide a reconciliation from net income (accrual basis) to net cash flows from operating activities (cash basis), we need to remove noncash activities from net income, so that

ILLUSTRATION 11–7

Basic Format for the Statement of Cash Flows

E-GAMES, INC.
Statement of Cash Flows
For the year ended December 31, 2018

Cash Flows from Operating Activities		
Net income	$42,000	
Adjustments to reconcile net income to net cash flows from operating activities:		
(List individual reconciling items)	_____	
Net cash flows from operating activities		$ XXX
Cash Flows from Investing Activities		
(List individual inflows and outflows)	_____	
Net cash flows from investing activities		XXX
Cash Flows from Financing Activities		
(List individual inflows and outflows)	_____	
Net cash flows from financing activities		XXX
Net increase (decrease) in cash		**14,000**
Cash at the beginning of the period		48,000
Cash at the end of the period		$62,000

ILLUSTRATION 11–7

Basic Format for the Statement of Cash Flows

what's left is operating cash flows only. Adjustments to net income in calculating operating cash flows include:

1. **Noncash items.** These items include revenues and expenses that never affect cash. Common examples are depreciation expense and amortization expense.

2. **Nonoperating items.** These items include gains and losses on the sale of long-term assets that do not affect *operating* cash flows. Common examples are gains and losses on the sale of land, buildings, and equipment.

3. **Changes in current assets and current liabilities.** These changes represent the noncash portion of some revenues and expenses. They occur when the cash flow for the year does not equal the related amount reported in the income statement. For example, all sales to customers are reported as revenues in the income statement, but only cash collected from customers represents an operating cash inflow. The amount of revenue not collected in cash will equal the increase in accounts receivable.

Illustration 11–8 provides a summary of the adjustments we make to convert net income to net cash flows from operating activities. The first two items represent noncash expenses, the second two items are nonoperating items, and the final four are changes in current assets and current liabilities.

ILLUSTRATION 11–8

Summary of Adjustments to Net Income

Cash Flows from Operating Activities

Net income
Adjustments to reconcile net income to net cash flows from operating activities:
  + Depreciation expense
  + Amortization expense

  + Loss on sale of assets
  − Gain on sale of assets
  − Increase in a current asset
  + Decrease in a current asset
  + Increase in a current liability
  − Decrease in a current liability
  = Net cash flows from operating activities

This illustration is a helpful reference when completing the homework at the end of the chapter. We look at each of these adjustments in the sections that follow.

NONCASH ITEMS

Using the indirect method, we first adjust net income for depreciation expense.

Depreciation Expense. Depreciation expense reduces net income. Remember, though, depreciation expense is not a cash outflow in the current period. It is recorded with a debit to Depreciation Expense and a credit to Accumulated Depreciation; the Cash account is not involved. Because we *deducted* this noncash expense in the determination of net income, we need to add it back in calculating operating cash flows. This is part of the reconciliation from net income to operating cash flows. Amortization of intangible assets is treated the same way as depreciation of tangible assets. We add back both depreciation expense and amortization expense to net income in arriving at cash flows from operating activities.

E-Games, Inc., reports net income of $42,000 and depreciation expense of $9,000 in its income statement. Because depreciation expense reduces net income by $9,000, E-Games will add the $9,000 back to net income in arriving at net cash flows from operations. Illustration 11–9 shows how E-Games reports depreciation expense in the statement of cash flows under the indirect method.

ILLUSTRATION 11–9

Adjustment for
Depreciation Expense

E-GAMES, INC. Statement of Cash Flows (partial)	
Cash Flows from Operating Activities	
Net income	$42,000
Adjustments to reconcile net income to net *cash flows from operating activities:*	
Depreciation expense	**9,000**

NONOPERATING ITEMS

Next, we adjust for gains and losses that do not affect operating cash flows (adjustments for nonoperating effects, such as a loss on sale of land).

Loss on Sale of Land. Losses on the sale of long-term assets decrease net income, while gains on the sale of those assets increase net income. E-Games reports a $4,000 loss on sale of land in its income statement. The loss is not an *operating* cash inflow or cash outflow. (The actual sale of land is an *investing* activity discussed later in the chapter.) And yet, we subtracted the $4,000 loss in the income statement in the determination of net income, so we need to add it back in order to eliminate this nonoperating component of net income. Illustration 11–10 shows how E-Games adds back the loss on sale of land to net income in arriving at net cash flows from operating activities.

ILLUSTRATION 11–10

Adjustment for Loss on
Sale of Land

E-GAMES, INC. Statement of Cash Flows (partial)	
Cash Flows from Operating Activities	
Net income	$42,000
Adjustments to reconcile net income to net cash *flows from operating activities:*	
Depreciation expense	9,000
Loss on sale of land	**4,000**

What if E-Games, Inc., had a gain of $4,000, rather than a loss, on the sale of land? Because we would have added the $4,000 gain in the determination of net income, we would need to subtract it from net income to eliminate it.

COMMON MISTAKE

Students sometimes are unsure whether to add or subtract a loss on the sale of assets. Just remember that a loss is like an expense—both reduce net income. Treat a loss on the sale of assets like depreciation expense and add it back to net income. A gain on the sale of long-term assets is the opposite of an expense, so we subtract it from net income to arrive at net cash flows from operating activities.

CHANGES IN CURRENT ASSETS AND CURRENT LIABILITIES

For components of net income that increase or decrease cash, but *by an amount different from that reported in the income statement,* we adjust net income for changes in the balances of related balance sheet accounts to convert the effects of those items to a cash basis.

For example, E-Games reports sales revenue of $1,012,000 in its income statement. This does not mean, however, that E-Games collected $1,012,000 cash from its customers during the reporting period. Because accounts receivable increased during the year, some of the sales revenue the company earned must not yet have been collected. We need, then, to make an adjustment to net income for the change in accounts receivable to convert sales revenue to a cash basis. To similarly convert other income statement components from accrual basis to cash basis, we adjust net income for changes in all current assets (other than cash) and current liabilities. Let's look at the changes in current assets and current liabilities for E-Games to see how this works.

Increase in Accounts Receivable.   E-Games' accounts receivable increased $7,000 during the year (from $20,000 in 2017 to $27,000 in 2018). This tells us that the company must have collected less cash than its $1,012,000 in sales revenue. Why? Because customers owe the company $7,000 more than before. Here's a summary;

Sales Revenue	$1,012,000
−Increase in Accounts Receivable	− 7,000
=Cash inflow	$1,005,000

The $7,000 increase in accounts receivable represents $7,000 of sales that E-Games reported as part of net income but that did not result in operating cash inflows. Therefore, to adjust net income (accrual basis) to operating cash flows (cash basis), we need to eliminate $7,000 from net income, as shown in Illustration 11–11.

E-GAMES, INC. Statement of Cash Flows (partial)	
Cash Flows from Operating Activities	
Net income	$42,000
Adjustments to reconcile net income to net cash flows from operating activities:	
Depreciation expense	9,000
Loss on sale of land	4,000
Increase in accounts receivable	**(7,000)**

ILLUSTRATION 11–11

Adjustment for Change in Accounts Receivable

A decrease in accounts receivable would have the opposite effect. We would *add* a decrease in accounts receivable to net income to arrive at net cash flows from operating activities. A decrease in accounts receivable indicates that we collected more cash from customers than we recorded as sales revenue.

Decrease in Inventory.   E-Games' inventory balance decreased by $10,000 during the year. This tells us that the company sold $10,000 of inventory that it did not replace. This $10,000 is reported as cost of goods sold (an expense) in the income statement, reducing net income, but it has no effect on cash. To adjust for cash being greater by $10,000, we add the decrease in inventory to net income. Illustration 11–12 shows this adjustment.

ILLUSTRATION 11–12

Adjustment for Change in Inventory

E-GAMES, INC. Statement of Cash Flows (partial)	
Cash Flows from Operating Activities	
Net income	$42,000
Adjustments to reconcile net income to net cash flows from operating activities:	
Depreciation expense	9,000
Loss on sale of land	4,000
Increase in accounts receivable	(7,000)
Decrease in inventory	**10,000**

Increase in Prepaid Rent.   E-Games' prepaid rent increased $2,000 during the year. The company paid $2,000 cash for an asset (prepaid rent) for which there is no corresponding expense (rent expense). In other words, the cash outflow for prepaid rent caused cash to decrease by $2,000, but net income remained unaffected. To adjust for cash being lower by $2,000, we subtract the increase in prepaid rent from net income. Illustration 11–13 shows this adjustment.

ILLUSTRATION 11–13

Adjustment for Change in Prepaid Rent

E-GAMES, INC. Statement of Cash Flows (partial)	
Cash Flows from Operating Activities	
Net income	$42,000
Adjustments to reconcile net income to net cash flows from operating activities:	
Depreciation expense	9,000
Loss on sale of land	4,000
Increase in accounts receivable	(7,000)
Decrease in inventory	10,000
Increase in prepaid rent	**(2,000)**

Decrease in Accounts Payable.   E-Games' accounts payable decreased $5,000 during the year. The decrease in accounts payable indicates that the company paid $5,000 cash to reduce its liability (accounts payable) but reported no corresponding expense (cost of goods sold) during the period. In other words, the cash outflow to reduce accounts payable caused cash to decrease by $5,000, but net income remained unaffected. To adjust for cash being lower by $5,000, we subtract the decrease in accounts payable from net income, as shown in Illustration 11–14.

ILLUSTRATION 11–14

Adjustment for Change in Accounts Payable

E-GAMES, INC.
Statement of Cash Flows (partial)

Cash Flows from Operating Activities

Net income	$42,000
Adjustments to reconcile net income to net cash flows from operating activities:	
Depreciation expense	9,000
Loss on sale of land	4,000
Increase in accounts receivable	(7,000)
Decrease in inventory	10,000
Increase in prepaid rent	(2,000)
Decrease in accounts payable	**(5,000)**

Increase in Interest Payable.   E-Games' interest payable increased $1,000 during the year. An increase in interest payable indicates that the company recorded interest expense of $1,000 for which it did not pay cash. In other words, the $1,000 increase in interest payable reduces net income (because of interest expense) but has no effect on cash. To adjust for cash being greater by $1,000, we add the increase in interest payable to net income. This is shown in Illustration 11–15.

ILLUSTRATION 11–15

Adjustment for Change in Interest Payable

E-GAMES, INC.
Statement of Cash Flows (partial)

Cash Flows from Operating Activities

Net income	$42,000
Adjustments to reconcile net income to net cash flows from operating activities:	
Depreciation expense	9,000
Loss on sale of land	4,000
Increase in accounts receivable	(7,000)
Decrease in inventory	10,000
Increase in prepaid rent	(2,000)
Decrease in accounts payable	(5,000)
Increase in interest payable	**1,000**

Decrease in Income Tax Payable.   E-Games' income tax payable decreased $2,000 during the year. The decrease in income tax payable indicates that the company paid $2,000 cash to reduce its liability (income tax payable) but reported no corresponding expense (income tax expense) during the period. In other words, the cash outflow to reduce income tax payable caused cash to decrease by $2,000, but net income remained unaffected. To adjust for cash being lower by $2,000, we subtract the decrease in income tax payable from net income. Illustration 11–16 shows this adjustment and calculates total net cash flows from operating activities of $50,000.

KEY POINT

Using the indirect method, we start with net income and adjust this number for (1) revenue and expense items that do not affect cash, (2) gains and losses that do not affect operating cash flows, and (3) changes in current assets and current liabilities.

ILLUSTRATION 11–16

Adjustment for Change in Income Tax Payable

E-GAMES, INC.
Statement of Cash Flows (partial)

Cash Flows from Operating Activities

Net income	$42,000
Adjustments to reconcile net income to net cash flows from operating activities:	
Depreciation expense	9,000
Loss on sale of land	4,000
Increase in accounts receivable	(7,000)
Decrease in inventory	10,000
Increase in prepaid rent	(2,000)
Decrease in accounts payable	(5,000)
Increase in interest payable	1,000
Decrease in income tax payable	**(2,000)**
Net cash flows from operating activities	$50,000

Decision Point

Question	Accounting information	Analysis
Is a company's net income supported by strong operating cash flows?	Operating activities section of the statement of cash flows using the indirect method	The operating activities section using the indirect method reconciles net income to operating cash flows. Net income is considered to be of higher quality when backed by strong operating cash flows.

Let's Review

mhhe.com/4fa45

Provided below are the income statement, balance sheets, and additional information for E-Phones, Inc.

E-PHONES, INC.
Income Statement
For the year ended December 31, 2018

Net sales		$2,200,000
Gain on sale of investment		5,000
Expenses:		
Cost of goods sold	$1,100,000	
Operating expenses	450,000	
Depreciation expense	25,000	
Income tax expense	217,000	
Total expenses		1,792,000
Net income		$ 413,000

E-PHONES, INC.
Balance Sheets
December 31, 2018 and 2017

	2018	2017	Increase (I) or Decrease (D)
Assets			
Current assets:			
Cash	$ 32,000	$ 48,000	$ 16,000 (D)
Accounts receivable	32,000	40,000	8,000 (D)
Inventory	100,000	70,000	30,000 (I)
Long-term assets:			
Investments	0	50,000	50,000 (D)
Land	280,000	180,000	100,000 (I)
Equipment	200,000	140,000	60,000 (I)
Accumulated depreciation	(53,000)	(28,000)	25,000 (I)
Total assets	$591,000	$500,000	
Liabilities and Stockholders' Equity			
Current liabilities:			
Accounts payable	$ 52,000	$ 62,000	$ 10,000 (D)
Income tax payable	55,000	12,000	43,000 (I)
Long-term liabilities:			
Bonds payable	0	200,000	200,000 (D)
Stockholders' equity:			
Common stock	200,000	100,000	100,000 (I)
Retained earnings	284,000	126,000	158,000 (I)
Total liabilities and stockholders' equity	$591,000	$500,000	

Additional Information for 2018:

Sold an investment in stock costing $50,000 for $55,000, resulting in a $5,000 gain on sale of investment.

Required:

Prepare the operating activities section of statement of cash flows for E-Phones using the *indirect method*.

Solution:

E-PHONES, INC.
Statement of Cash Flows—Indirect Method
For the year ended December 31, 2018

Cash Flows from Operating Activities	
Net income	$413,000
Adjustments to reconcile net income to net cash flows from operating activities:	
Depreciation expense	25,000
Gain on sale of investment	(5,000)
Decrease in accounts receivable	8,000
Increase in inventory	(30,000)
Decrease in accounts payable	(10,000)
Increase in income tax payable	43,000
Net cash flows from operating activities	$444,000

Suggested Homework:
BE11–4, BE11–5;
E11–8, E11–9, E11–11;
P11–3A&B

Investing and Financing Activities

■ **LO11–3**

Prepare the investing activities section and the financing activities section of the statement of cash flows.

As noted earlier, we prepare the investing and financing activities in the statement of cash flows the same whether we use the indirect or the direct method. Here, we take a detailed look at how investing and financing activities are determined, continuing our example of E-Games, Inc.

INVESTING ACTIVITIES

The second step in preparing the statement of cash flows is to determine the net cash flows from *investing* activities. Companies periodically invest cash to replace or expand productive facilities such as property, plant, and equipment. Information concerning these investing activities can provide valuable insight to decision makers regarding the nature and amount of assets being acquired for future use, as well as provide clues concerning the company's ambitions for the future.

We can find a firm's investing activities by analyzing changes in long-term asset accounts from the balance sheet.[4] Looking at that section of E-Games' balance sheet, we determine the following cash flows from investing activities.

Increase in Investments.   Investments increased $35,000 during the year (from $0 in 2017 to $35,000 in 2018). In the absence of contrary evidence, it's logical to assume the increase is due to the purchase of investments during the year. Additional-information item (1) in Illustration 11–6 confirms this assumption. As Illustration 11–17 shows, we report the purchase of investments as a cash outflow of $35,000 from investing activities.

Decrease in Land.   The Land account decreased $10,000 during the year, indicating that E-Games sold land costing $10,000. Additional-information item (2) in Illustration 11–6 indicates that we originally recorded the land at a cost of $10,000 but sold it for only $6,000 (resulting in a loss on the sale of land of $4,000, as recorded in the operating activities section). We report $6,000 as a cash inflow from investing activities—the *actual* amount of cash proceeds received from the sale. (See Illustration 11–17 below.)

ILLUSTRATION 11–17

Cash Flows from Investing Activities

E-GAMES, INC. Statement of Cash Flows (partial)	
Cash Flows from Investing Activities	
Purchase of investments	$(35,000)
Sale of land	6,000
Net cash flows from investing activities	$ (29,000)
Note: Noncash Activities	
Purchased equipment by issuing a note payable	$ 20,000

 COMMON MISTAKE

Some students mistakenly record a cash inflow from investing activities, like the sale of land for $6,000, at an amount that equals the change in the asset account, $10,000 in this case. Remember that the investing activities section reports the *actual* cash received or paid for an asset, which is usually not the same as the change in the asset account reported in the balance sheet.

Increase in Equipment.   E-Games' Equipment account increased by $20,000 during the year. If E-Games purchased the equipment with cash, we would record a cash outflow from investing activities of $20,000. However, additional-information item (3) in Illustration 11–6 indicates

---

[4]Although not used as an example in this chapter, it's also possible to have investing activities related to changes in current investments or current notes receivable.

that the firm paid for the equipment by issuing a $20,000 note payable. No cash was exchanged in the transaction. The increase in equipment therefore represents a noncash activity, which is disclosed either directly after the cash flow statement or in a note to the financial statements. Illustration 11–17 provides a summary of the cash flows from investing activities and disclosure of the noncash activity.

FINANCING ACTIVITIES

The third step in preparing the statement of cash flows is to determine the net cash flows from *financing* activities. To fund its operating and investing activities, a company must often rely on external financing from two sources—creditors and shareholders. Cash transactions (inflows and outflows) with creditors and shareholders are reported in the financing activities section of the statement of cash flows.

We can find a firm's financing activities by examining changes in long-term liabilities and stockholders' equity accounts from the balance sheet.[5] Referring back to E-Games' balance sheet, we find the following cash flows from financing activities.

CAREER CORNER

Are you good at analysis? If so, you might consider a career as a financial analyst. A career in this field involves understanding the operations of companies, assessing the reasonableness of their stock price, and predicting their future performance. Analysts rely heavily on financial statements as a source of information in predicting stock price movements. Because financial statements, including the cash flow statement covered in this chapter, are learned in accounting, it is no surprise that a strong background in accounting is necessary for a career as a financial analyst. A background in accounting is useful, not only in preparing accounting information, but analyzing and interpreting that information as well.

© Thinkstock/Jupiterimages, RF

Increase in Notes Payable.   E-Games has only one long-term liability. The company reports an increase in notes payable of $20,000. As we saw earlier, this was in payment for equipment and represents a noncash activity disclosed in a note to the financial statements.

Increase in Common Stock.   Common stock increased by $5,000 during the year. Item (4) of the additional information in Illustration 11–6 confirms that this was the result of issuing $5,000 of common stock. As Illustration 11–18 shows, the $5,000 inflow of cash is reported as a financing activity.

ILLUSTRATION 11–18

Cash Flows from Financing Activities

E-GAMES, INC. Statement of Cash Flows (partial)	
Cash Flows from Financing Activities	
Issuance of common stock	$ 5,000
Payment of cash dividends	(12,000)
Net cash flows from financing activities	(7,000)

Increase in Retained Earnings.   E-Games' Retained Earnings balance increased by $30,000 during the year. Recall from earlier chapters that the balance of Retained Earnings increases with net income and decreases with dividends:

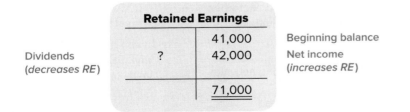

	Retained Earnings	
		41,000	Beginning balance
Dividends (*decreases RE*)	?	42,000	Net income (*increases RE*)
		71,000	

---

[5]Although not used as an example in this chapter, it is also possible for financing activities to be indicated by changes in current liability accounts, such as current notes payable.

Since net income is $42,000 and retained earnings increased by only $30,000, the company must have declared dividends of $12,000 during the year:

Retained earnings, beginning balance	$41,000
+ Net income	42,000
− Dividends	(12,000)
Retained earnings, ending balance	$71,000

Item (5), listed as additional information at the end of Illustration 11–6, confirms that E-Games declared and paid dividends of $12,000 during the year. As shown in Illustration 11–18, we report the payment of cash dividends as a cash outflow from financing activities.

Only the dividends actually paid in cash during the year are reported in the statement of cash flows. If the company declares dividends in 2018 but does not pay them until 2019, it will report the dividends paid as a cash outflow in 2019, not in 2018.

 KEY POINT

Most investing activities can be explained by changes in long-term asset accounts. Most financing activities can be explained by changes in long-term liability and stockholders' equity accounts.

The fourth and final step in preparing the statement of cash flows is to combine the operating, investing, and financing activities and make sure the total of these three activities equals the net increase (decrease) in cash in the balance sheet. Illustration 11–19 shows

ILLUSTRATION 11–19

Complete Statement of Cash Flows for E-Games, Inc.

mhhe.com/4fa45

E-GAMES, INC. Statement of Cash Flows For the year ended December 31, 2018		
Cash Flows from Operating Activities		
Net income		$42,000
Adjustments to reconcile net income to net cash flows *from operating activities:*		
Depreciation expense		9,000
Loss on sale of land		4,000
Increase in accounts receivable		(7,000)
Decrease in inventory		10,000
Increase in prepaid rent		(2,000)
Decrease in accounts payable		(5,000)
Increase in interest payable		1,000
Decrease in income tax payable		(2,000)
Net cash flows from operating activities		$50,000
Cash Flows from Investing Activities		
Purchase of investments		(35,000)
Sale of land		6,000
Net cash flows from investing activities		(29,000)
Cash Flows from Financing Activities		
Issuance of common stock		5,000
Payment of cash dividends		(12,000)
Net cash flows from financing activities		(7,000)
Net increase (decrease) in cash		**14,000**
Cash at the beginning of the period		48,000
Cash at the end of the period		$62,000
Note: Noncash Activities		
Purchased equipment by issuing a note payable		$20,000

the complete statement of cash flows for E-Games, with all three sections—operating, investing, and financing—included along with the note for noncash activities.

This is the moment of truth. The sum of the net cash flows from operating, investing, and financing activities should equal the net increase (decrease) in cash for the period. In Illustration 11–19, we see that the total of the cash flows from operating (+$50,000), investing (−$29,000), and financing (−$7,000) activities equals the net increase in cash of $14,000 reconciling cash from the two consecutive balance sheets originally reported in Illustration 11–6.

This is a continuation of the Let's Review exercise presented earlier in the chapter. Provided below are the income statement, balance sheets, and additional information for E-Phones, Inc.

Let's Review

mhhe.com/4fa46

E-PHONES, INC. Income Statement For the year ended December 31, 2018		
Net sales		$2,200,000
Gain on sale of investment		5,000
Expenses:		
Cost of goods sold	$1,100,000	
Operating expenses	450,000	
Depreciation expense	25,000	
Income tax expense	217,000	
Total expenses		1,792,000
Net income		$ 413,000

E-PHONES, INC. Balance Sheets December 31, 2018 and 2017			
	2018	**2017**	**Increase (I) or Decrease (D)**
Assets			
Current assets:			
Cash	$ 32,000	$ 48,000	$ 16,000 (D)
Accounts receivable	32,000	40,000	8,000 (D)
Inventory	100,000	70,000	30,000 (I)
Long-term assets:			
Investments	0	50,000	50,000 (D)
Land	280,000	180,000	100,000 (I)
Equipment	200,000	140,000	60,000 (I)
Accumulated depreciation	(53,000)	(28,000)	25,000 (I)
Total assets	$591,000	$500,000	
Liabilities and Stockholders' Equity			
Current liabilities:			
Accounts payable	$ 52,000	$ 62,000	$ 10,000 (D)
Income tax payable	55,000	12,000	43,000 (I)
Long-term liabilities:			
Bonds payable	0	200,000	200,000 (D)
Stockholders' equity:			
Common stock	200,000	100,000	100,000 (I)
Retained earnings	284,000	126,000	158,000 (I)
Total liabilities and stockholders' equity	$591,000	$500,000	

Additional Information for 2018:

1. Sold an investment in stock costing $50,000 for $55,000, resulting in a $5,000 gain on sale of investment.
2. Purchased $100,000 in land, issuing $100,000 of common stock as payment. No cash was exchanged in the transaction.
3. Purchased equipment for $60,000 cash.
4. Retired the $200,000 balance in bonds payable at the beginning of the year.
5. Declared and paid a cash dividend of $255,000.

Required:

Prepare the statement of cash flows using the *indirect method*. Disclose any noncash transactions in an accompanying note.

Solution:

E-PHONES, INC.
Statement of Cash Flows—Indirect Method
For the year ended December 31, 2018

Cash Flows from Operating Activities		
Net income	$413,000	
Adjustments to reconcile net income to net cash flows from operating activities:		
Depreciation expense	25,000	
Gain on sale of investment	(5,000)	
Decrease in accounts receivable	8,000	
Increase in inventory	(30,000)	
Decrease in accounts payable	(10,000)	
Increase in income tax payable	43,000	
Net cash flows from operating activities		$444,000
Cash Flows from Investing Activities		
Sale of investment	55,000	
Purchase of equipment	(60,000)	
Net cash flows from investing activities		(5,000)
Cash Flows from Financing Activities		
Retirement of bonds payable	(200,000)	
Payment of cash dividends	(255,000)	
Net cash flows from financing activities		(455,000)
Net increase (decrease) in cash		(16,000)
Cash at the beginning of the period		48,000
Cash at the end of the period		$ 32,000
Note: Noncash Activities		
Purchased land by issuing common stock		$100,000

Suggested Homework:
E11–10;
P11–2A&B; P11–4A&B

ANALYSIS

CASH FLOW ANALYSIS
Apple vs. Google

■ **LO11–4**
Perform financial analysis using the statement of cash flows.

Throughout this text, we have emphasized the analysis of financial statements from a decision maker's perspective. Often that analysis includes the development and comparison of financial ratios. The ratios discussed in Chapters 5 through 10 are all based on income statement and balance sheet amounts.

Decision Maker's Perspective

Cash Flow Ratios

Analysts often supplement their investigation of income statement and balance sheet amounts with cash flow ratios. Some cash flow ratios are derived by substituting net cash flows from operating activities in place of net income—not to replace those ratios but to complement them. Substituting cash flow from operations in place of net income offers additional insight in the evaluation of a company's profitability and financial strength.[6] Positive cash flow from operations is important to a company's survival in the long run.

Now we reexamine the financial ratios introduced in Chapter 7—return on assets, profit margin, and asset turnover—substituting net cash flows from operating activities, also called **operating cash flows,** in place of net income. Illustration 11–20 provides selected financial data for **Apple** and **Google**.

ILLUSTRATION 11–20

Selected Financial Data

($ in millions)	Apple	Google
Net sales	$182,795	$ 66,001
Net income	39,510	14,444
Operating cash flows	59,713	22,376
Total assets, beginning	207,000	110,920
Total assets, ending	231,839	131,133

RETURN ON ASSETS

Return on assets, introduced in Chapter 7, is calculated as net income divided by average total assets. Illustration 11–21 presents return on assets for Apple and Google.

ILLUSTRATION 11–21

Return on Assets for Apple and Google

($ in millions)	Net Income	÷	Average Total Assets	=	Return on Assets
Apple	$39,510	÷	($207,000 + $231,839)/2	=	18.0%
Google	$14,444	÷	($110,920 + $131,133)/2	=	11.9%

The return on assets for Apple is very high at 18.0%, while Google reports a respectable return on assets of 11.9%. Thus, Apple generated more income for each dollar invested in assets.

CASH RETURN ON ASSETS

We can gain additional insights by examining a similar measure called the cash return on assets. We calculate it as:

Cash return on assets = Operating cash flows ÷ Average total assets

Illustration 11–22 presents the cash return on assets for Apple and Google.

ILLUSTRATION 11–22

Cash Return on Assets for Apple and Google

($ in millions)	Operating Cash Flows	÷	Average Total Assets	=	Cash Return on Assets
Apple	$59,713	÷	($207,000 + $231,839)/2	=	27.2%
Google	$22,376	÷	($110,920 + $131,133)/2	=	18.5%

[6]Proposals for informative sets of cash flow ratios are offered by Charles A. Carslaw and John R. Mills. 1991. "Developing Ratios for Effective Cash Flow Statement Analysis." *Journal of Accountancy 172* (November), pp. 63–70; Don E. Giacomino and David E. Mielke. 1993. "Cash Flows: Another Approach to Ratio Analysis." *Journal of Accountancy 174* (March), pp. 55–58; and John Mills and Jeanne H. Yamamura. 1998. "The Power of Cash Flow Ratios." *Journal of Accountancy 186* (October), pp. 53–61.

Apple's cash return on assets of 27.2% is much higher than Google's cash return on assets of 18.5%. Note that, as discussed in the Feature Story, operating cash flows exceed net income for both Apple and Google. Do you think Apple's higher cash return on assets is due to higher pricing strategies or greater sales volume? We examine this question next.

COMPONENTS OF CASH RETURN ON ASSETS

Let's explore the cash return on assets further by separating the ratio into two separate parts, as shown in Illustration 11–23.

ILLUSTRATION 11–23

Components of Cash Return on Assets

Cash return on assets	=	Cash flow to sales	×	Asset turnover
$\dfrac{\text{Operating cash flows}}{\text{Average total assets}}$	=	$\dfrac{\text{Operating cash flows}}{\text{Net sales}}$	×	$\dfrac{\text{Net sales}}{\text{Average total assets}}$

Cash return on assets can be separated into cash flow to sales and asset turnover. Cash flow to sales measures the operating cash flows generated for each dollar of sales. (It is the cash flow equivalent to profit margin, introduced in Chapter 7.) Asset turnover, also covered in Chapter 7, measures the sales revenue generated per dollar of assets. Cash flow to sales and asset turnover represent two primary strategies that companies have for increasing their cash return on assets. One strategy, pursued by both Apple and Google, is to sell highly innovative products that yield very high cash inflows from customers in relationship to the cash outflows to produce their products. Another strategy is to pursue high asset turnover by selling at lower prices than the competition. In Illustrations 11–24 and 11–25, we calculate cash flow to sales and asset turnover for both companies.

ILLUSTRATION 11–24

Cash Flow to Sales for Apple and Google

($ in millions)	Operating Cash Flows	÷	Net Sales	=	Cash Flow to Sales
Apple	$59,713	÷	$182,795	=	32.7%
Google	$22,376	÷	$ 66,001	=	33.9%

ILLUSTRATION 11–25

Asset Turnover for Apple and Google

($ in millions)	Net Sales	÷	Average Total Assets	=	Asset Turnover
Apple	$182,795	÷	($207,000 + $231,839)/2	=	0.8 times
Google	$ 66,001	÷	($110,920 + $131,133)/2	=	0.5 times

The cash flow to sales ratios support our expectations regarding the business strategies of Apple and Google. Both Apple and Google report high cash flow to sales ratios of 32.7% and 33.9%, respectively. Both companies also report asset turnover below one, indicating a high margin rather than a high turnover strategy. However, Apple generates a slightly higher asset turnover than Google, as Illustration 11–25 shows, helping to explain why Apple's overall cash return on assets is higher than Google's. To maximize cash flow from operations, a company strives to increase *both* cash flow per dollar of sales (cash flow to sales) and sales per dollar of assets invested (asset turnover).

 KEY POINT

Cash return on assets indicates the amount of operating cash flow generated for each dollar invested in assets. We can separate cash return on assets into two components—cash flow to sales and asset turnover—to examine two important business strategies.

Question 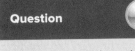	Accounting information	Analysis
Are the company's cash flows based more on selling at higher prices or on increasing sales volume?	Cash flow to sales and asset turnover ratios	Companies with high cash flow to sales ratios obtain high cash inflows from sales to customers in relation to the cash outflows to produce the products. Companies with high asset turnover ratios may not make as much on each sale, but they make money through higher sales volume.

ETHICAL DILEMMA

© Digital Stock/Corbis, RF

Ebenezer is CEO of a successful small business. One day he stops by to see Tim Cratchit, the new branch manager at First National Bank. Ebenezer and his partner Marley would like to double the size of their loan with the bank from $500,000 to $1 million. Ebenezer explains, "Business is booming, sales and earnings are up each of the past three years, and we could certainly use the funds for further business expansion." Tim Cratchit has a big heart, and Ebenezer has been a close friend of the family. He thinks to himself this loan decision will be easy, but he asks Ebenezer to e-mail the past three years' financial statements as required by bank policy.

In looking over the financial statements sent by Ebenezer, Tim becomes concerned. Sales and earnings have increased just as Ebenezer said. However, receivables, inventory, and accounts payable have grown at a much faster rate than sales. Further, he notices a steady decrease in operating cash flows over the past three years, with negative operating cash flows in each of the past two years.

Who are the stakeholders, and what is the ethical dilemma? Do you think Tim should go ahead and approve the loan?

OPERATING ACTIVITIES—DIRECT METHOD

APPENDIX

■ **LO11–5**
Prepare the operating activities section of the statement of cash flows using the direct method.

There are two acceptable alternatives in reporting operating activities—the indirect method and the direct method. The presentation of operating activities in the main body of the chapter is referred to as the indirect method. By this method, we begin with reported net income and work backward to convert to a cash basis.

An alternative is the direct method, by which we report the cash inflows and cash outflows from operating activities directly in the statement of cash flows. For instance, we report *cash received from customers* as the cash effect of sales, and *cash paid to suppliers* as the cash effect of cost of goods sold. Income statement items that have *no* cash effect—such as depreciation expense or gains and losses on the sale of assets—are simply not reported under the direct method.

Here, we repeat the example for E-Games, Inc., this time presenting cash flows from operating activities using the direct method. For convenience, the income statement, balance sheets, and additional information for E-Games, Inc., are repeated in Illustration 11–26.

ILLUSTRATION 11–26

Income Statement, Balance Sheets, and Additional Information for E-Games, Inc.

E-GAMES, INC.
Income Statement
For the year ended December 31, 2018

Net sales		$1,012,000
Expenses:		
Cost of goods sold	$650,000	
Operating expenses (salaries, rent, utilities)	286,000	
Depreciation expense	9,000	
Loss on sale of land	4,000	
Interest expense	5,000	
Income tax expense	16,000	
Total expenses		970,000
Net income		$ 42,000

E-GAMES, INC.
Balance Sheets
December 31, 2018 and 2017

	2018	2017	Increase (I) or Decrease (D)
Assets			
Current assets:			
Cash	$ 62,000	$ 48,000	$14,000 (I)
Accounts receivable	27,000	20,000	7,000 (I)
Inventory	35,000	45,000	10,000 (D)
Prepaid rent	4,000	2,000	2,000 (I)
Long-term assets:			
Investments	35,000	0	35,000 (I)
Land	70,000	80,000	10,000 (D)
Equipment	90,000	70,000	20,000 (I)
Accumulated depreciation	(23,000)	(14,000)	9,000 (I)
Total assets	$300,000	$251,000	
Liabilities and Stockholders' Equity			
Current liabilities:			
Accounts payable	$ 22,000	$ 27,000	$ 5,000 (D)
Interest payable	2,000	1,000	1,000 (I)
Income tax payable	5,000	7,000	2,000 (D)
Long-term liabilities:			
Notes payable	95,000	75,000	20,000 (I)
Stockholders' equity:			
Common stock	105,000	100,000	5,000 (I)
Retained earnings	71,000	41,000	30,000 (I)
Total liabilities and stockholders' equity	$300,000	$251,000	

(continued)

ILLUSTRATION 11–26

(concluded)

Additional Information for 2018:

1. Purchased stock in Intendo Corporation for $35,000.
2. Sold land originally costing $10,000 for only $6,000, resulting in a $4,000 loss on sale of land.
3. Purchased $20,000 in equipment by issuing a $20,000 note payable due in three years. No cash was exchanged in the transaction.
4. Issued common stock for $5,000 cash.
5. Declared and paid a cash dividend of $12,000.

Remember from Illustration 11–5 that the first step in preparing the statement of cash flows is to calculate net cash flows from *operating* activities using information from the income statement and changes in current assets and current liabilities from the balance sheet.

The income statement reports revenues earned during the year, *regardless of when cash is received,* and the expenses incurred in generating those revenues, *regardless of when cash is paid.* This is the *accrual concept* of accounting that we've discussed throughout the book. Cash flows from operating activities, on the other hand, are both inflows and outflows of cash that result from activities reported in the income statement. In other words, it's the elements of net income, but **reported on a cash basis.** Using the direct method, we examine each account in the income statement and convert it from an accrual amount to a cash amount. We directly report the cash inflows and cash outflows from operating activities as shown in Illustration 11–27.

ILLUSTRATION 11–27

Operating Activities Using the Direct Method

Cash Flows from Operating Activities
Cash inflows:
    Cash received from customers
    Cash received from interest
    Cash received from dividends
Cash outflows:
    Cash paid to suppliers
    Cash paid for operating expenses
    Cash paid for interest
    Cash paid for income taxes
= Net cash flows from operating activities

The best way to apply the direct method is to convert each revenue and expense item to its cash-basis amount. We do this by considering how each income statement account is affected by related changes in current asset and current liability accounts.

Cash Received from Customers. E-Games reports net sales of $1,012,000 as the first item in its income statement. Did E-Games receive $1,012,000 in cash from those sales? We can answer this by looking at the change in accounts receivable. If accounts receivable increases, this indicates that net sales exceed cash receipts from customers. That's why customers owe more than they did before. If accounts receivable decreases, the opposite will be true. Recall that accounts receivable increased $7,000. Therefore, we deduct the $7,000 increase in accounts receivable from net sales to obtain cash received from customers of $1,005,000, as shown in Illustration 11–28.

Let's consider this again from a couple of different perspectives. Accounts receivable increases when customers buy on credit and decreases when we receive cash from

ILLUSTRATION 11–28

Cash Received from
Customers

Net sales	$ 1,012,000
− Increase in accounts receivable	(7,000)
= **Cash received from customers**	**$1,005,000**

customers. We can compare sales and the change in accounts receivable during the year to determine the amount of cash we received from customers. In T-account format the relationship looks like this:

Accounts Receivable

Beginning balance	20,000		
Credit sales	1,012,000	?	Cash received
(*increase A/R*)			(*decreases A/R*)
Ending balance	27,000		

We see from this analysis that *cash received from customers* must have been $1,005,000. Still another way to view the situation is to think about how E-Games recorded these selling and collection activities during the year:

	Debit	Credit
Cash (to balance)	1,005,000	
Accounts Receivable (= $27,000 − $20,000)	7,000	
Sales Revenue (from income statement)		1,012,000
(*Receive cash from customers*)		

We record an increase in Sales Revenue with a credit and an increase in Accounts Receivable with a debit. Cash received from customers must be $1,005,000 for debits to equal credits.

Cash Paid to Suppliers.   Moving down the income statement, we see that E-Games reports cost of goods sold of $650,000. Did E-Games pay cash of $650,000 to suppliers of those goods during the year? To answer this, we look to the two current balance sheet accounts affected by merchandise purchases—Inventory and Accounts Payable.

First, compare cost of goods sold with the change in inventory to determine the cost of goods purchased (not necessarily cash paid) during the year. Inventory decreased by $10,000. We can visualize the relationship in T-account format:

Inventory

Beginning balance	45,000		
Cost of goods purchased	?	650,000	Cost of goods sold
(*increases inventory*)			(*decreases inventory*)
Ending balance	35,000		

The number needed to explain the change is $640,000. That's the cost of goods *purchased* during the year. It's not necessarily true, though, that E-Games paid $640,000 cash to suppliers of these goods. We need to look at the change in accounts payable to determine the cash paid to suppliers:

Accounts Payable

		27,000	Beginning balance
Cash paid to suppliers	?	640,000	Cost of goods purchased
(*decreases A/P*)			(*increases A/P*)
		22,000	Ending balance

We now see that cash paid to suppliers must be $645,000. We can confirm this by looking at how E-Games recorded inventory purchases and sales during the year:

	Debit	Credit
Cost of Goods Sold (from income statement)......................................	**650,000**	
Accounts Payable (= $27,000 − $22,000)..	**5,000**	
Inventory (= $45,000 − $35,000)..		**10,000**
Cash (to balance)...		**645,000**
(Pay cash for inventory)		

We record an increase in Cost of Goods Sold with a debit, a decrease in Inventory with a credit, and a decrease in Accounts Payable with a debit. Cash paid to suppliers is the "plug" figure we need for debits to equal credits in the journal entry.

Alternatively, we can analyze the situation this way: Inventory decreased $10,000 for the year, so E-Games needed to purchase only $640,000 of goods in order to sell $650,000 of goods; $10,000 came from existing inventory. Because accounts payable decreased by $5,000, cash paid to suppliers must have been $5,000 more than purchases, so we add the decrease in accounts payable to purchases of $640,000 to arrive at cash paid to suppliers of $645,000, as shown in Illustration 11–29.

Cost of goods sold	$ 650,000
− Decrease in inventory	(10,000)
= Purchases	640,000
+ Decrease in accounts payable	5,000
= Cash paid to suppliers	**$645,000**

ILLUSTRATION 11–29

Cash Paid to Suppliers

Cash Paid for Operating Expenses.   Operating expenses of $286,000 appear next in the income statement. We examine the changes in current assets and current liabilities for any accounts related to operating expenses. Rent expense is included in operating expenses, so we must consider the change in prepaid rent. Increasing prepaid rent takes additional cash. Prepaid rent increased by $2,000, so we need to add this change to operating expenses to determine the cash paid for operating expenses, as shown in Illustration 11–30.

Operating expenses	$ 286,000
+ Increase in prepaid rent	2,000
= Cash paid for operating expenses	**$288,000**

ILLUSTRATION 11–30

Cash Paid for Operating Expenses

We see no current assets or current liabilities associated with other operating expenses such as salaries expense or utilities expense, so we make no adjustments to these operating expenses. Therefore, the amounts we report for these operating expenses in the income statement must equal the amount of cash we paid for these items.

Let's check our calculation by recording the payment for operating expenses during the year:

	Debit	Credit
Operating Expenses (from the income statement).............................	**286,000**	
Prepaid Rent (= $4,000 − $2,000)...	**2,000**	
Cash (to balance)...		**288,000**
(Pay operating expenses)		

Depreciation Expense and Loss on Sale of Land.   The next expense listed in the income statement is depreciation expense of $9,000. Depreciation expense has no effect on cash flows. It is merely an allocation in the current period of a prior cash expenditure (to acquire the depreciable asset). Therefore, unlike the other expenses to this point, depreciation is *not* reported on the statement of cash flows under the direct method.

Similar to depreciation expense, the loss on sale of land is *not* reported because it, too, has no effect on *operating* cash flows. Additional-information item (2) in Illustration 11–26 indicates that land we originally purchased at a cost of $10,000 was sold for $6,000, resulting in a loss on the sale of land of $4,000. E-Games records the sale as:

	Debit	Credit
Cash (selling price)..	**6,000**	
Loss (difference)	**4,000**	
Land (cost)		**10,000**
(Receive cash from sale of land)		

As we discussed previously, we report the $6,000 cash inflow as an investing activity, because both investing in land and later selling it are considered investing activities. The original cost of the land, and thus the loss, has no effect on operating cash flows.

Cash Paid for Interest.   E-Games next reports interest expense of $5,000 in the income statement. The related current asset or current liability in the balance sheet is interest payable. If interest payable increases, interest expense exceeds cash paid for interest. Interest payable increases $1,000. As shown in Illustration 11–31, we deduct the increase in interest payable from interest expense to arrive at cash paid for interest.

ILLUSTRATION 11–31

Cash Paid for Interest

Interest expense	$5,000
− Increase in interest payable	(1,000)
= Cash paid for interest	**$4,000**

We can check our calculation by recording the payment for interest during the year:

	Debit	Credit
Interest Expense (from income statement)..	**5,000**	
Interest Payable (= $2,000 − $1,000)		**1,000**
Cash (to balance)...		**4,000**
(Pay interest)		

Cash Paid for Income Taxes.   The final item reported in the income statement is income tax expense of $16,000. The related current asset or current liability in the balance sheet is income tax payable. Income tax payable decreased $2,000. This means that E-Games paid $2,000 more than the income tax expense recorded. As shown in Illustration 11–32, we add the decrease in income tax payable to income tax expense to calculate cash paid for income taxes.

ILLUSTRATION 11–32

Cash Paid for Income Taxes

Income tax expense	$16,000
+ Decrease in income tax payable	2,000
= Cash paid for income taxes	**$18,000**

Recording the payment of taxes during the year confirms this:

	Debit	Credit
Income Tax Expense (from income statement)...................................	**16,000**	
Income Tax Payable (= $7,000 − $5,000)	**2,000**	
Cash (to balance)...		**18,000**
(Pay income taxes)		

Illustration 11–33 shows the completed operating activities section using the direct method.

E-GAMES, INC.
Statement of Cash Flows (partial)—Direct Method

Cash Flows from Operating Activities

Cash received from customers	$1,005,000
Cash paid to suppliers	(645,000)
Cash paid for operating expenses	(288,000)
Cash paid for interest	(4,000)
Cash paid for income taxes	(18,000)
Net cash flows from operating activities	$50,000

ILLUSTRATION 11–33

Operating Activities Using the Direct Method

Note that the net cash flows from operating activities is $50,000—**the same amount we calculated earlier in Illustration 11–16 using the indirect method.** This will always be the case. The indirect method begins with net income, whereas the direct method considers each of the individual accounts that make up net income. Both methods take into consideration the *same changes* in current asset and current liability accounts.

KEY POINT

The indirect method and direct method differ only in the presentation of operating activities. In the indirect method, we start with net income and make adjustments to arrive at net cash flows from operating activities. In the direct method, we convert each individual line item in the income statement to its cash basis and directly list the cash inflows and cash outflows from operating activities. The net cash flows from operating activities are *the same under both methods.*

The income statement, balance sheets, and additional information from the accounting records of E-Phones, Inc., are provided below.

Let's Review

mhhe.com/4fa47

E-PHONES, INC.
Income Statement
For the year ended December 31, 2018

Net sales		$2,200,000
Gain on sale of investment		5,000
Expenses:		
Cost of goods sold	$1,100,000	
Operating expenses	450,000	
Depreciation expense	25,000	
Income tax expense	217,000	
Total expenses		1,792,000
Net income		$ 413,000

E-PHONES, INC.
Balance Sheets
December 31, 2018 and 2017

	2018	2017	Increase (I) or Decrease (D)
Assets			
Current assets:			
Cash	$ 32,000	$ 48,000	$ 16,000 (D)
Accounts receivable	32,000	40,000	8,000 (D)
Inventory	100,000	70,000	30,000 (I)
Long-term assets:			
Investments	0	50,000	50,000 (D)
Land	280,000	180,000	100,000 (I)
Equipment	200,000	140,000	60,000 (I)
Accumulated depreciation	(53,000)	(28,000)	25,000 (I)
Total assets	$591,000	$500,000	
Liabilities and Stockholders' Equity			
Current liabilities:			
Accounts payable	$ 52,000	$ 62,000	$ 10,000 (D)
Income tax payable	55,000	12,000	43,000 (I)
Long-term liabilities:			
Bonds payable	0	200,000	200,000 (D)
Stockholders' equity:			
Common stock	200,000	100,000	100,000 (I)
Retained earnings	284,000	126,000	158,000 (I)
Total liabilities and stockholders' equity	$591,000	$500,000	

Additional Information for 2018:

1. Sold an investment in stock costing $50,000 for $55,000, resulting in a $5,000 gain on sale of investment.
2. Purchased $100,000 in land, issuing $100,000 of common stock as payment. No cash was exchanged in the transaction.
3. Purchased equipment for $60,000 cash.
4. Retired the $200,000 balance in bonds payable at the beginning of the year.
5. Declared and paid a cash dividend of $255,000.

Required:

Prepare the statement of cash flows using the *direct method* for reporting operating activities. Disclose any noncash transactions in a note to the statement of cash flows.

Solution:

E-PHONES, INC. Statement of Cash Flows—Direct Method For the year ended December 31, 2018		
Cash Flows from Operating Activities		
Cash received from customers	$2,208,000	
Cash paid to suppliers	(1,140,000)	
Cash paid for operating expenses	(450,000)	
Cash paid for income taxes	(174,000)	
Net cash flows from operating activities		$444,000
Cash Flows from Investing Activities		
Sale of investment	55,000	
Purchase of equipment	(60,000)	
Net cash flows from investing activities		(5,000)
Cash Flows from Financing Activities		
Retire bonds payable	(200,000)	
Payment of cash dividends	(255,000)	
Net cash flows from financing activities		(455,000)
Net increase (decrease) in cash		(16,000)
Cash at the beginning of the period		48,000
Cash at the end of the period		$ 32,000
Note: Noncash Activities		
Purchased land by issuing common stock		$100,000

Here are the supporting calculations for cash flows from operating activities under the direct method:

Net sales	$ 2,200,000
+ Decrease in accounts receivable	8,000
= **Cash received from customers**	**$2,208,000**
Cost of goods sold	$ 1,100,000
+ Increase in inventory	30,000
= Purchases	1,130,000
+ Decrease in accounts payable	10,000
= **Cash paid to suppliers**	**$1,140,000**
Cash paid for operating expenses	**$ 450,000**
Income tax expense	$ 217,000
− Increase in income tax payable	(43,000)
= **Cash paid for income taxes**	**$ 174,000**

Suggested Homework:
BE11–12, BE11–13;
E11–13, E11–14;
P11–6A&B; P11–7A&B

KEY POINTS BY LEARNING OBJECTIVE

LO11–1 Classify cash transactions as operating, investing, or financing activities.

Operating activities generally relate to income statement items and changes in current assets and current liabilities. Investing activities primarily involve changes in long-term assets. Financing activities primarily involve changes in long-term liabilities and stockholders' equity.

Companies choose between the indirect method and the direct method in reporting operating activities in the statement of cash flows. The indirect method is less costly to prepare and is used in practice by the majority of companies. The direct method more logically presents the cash inflows and outflows from operations. The investing and financing sections of the statement of cash flows are identical under both methods.

LO11–2 Prepare the operating activities section of the statement of cash flows using the indirect method.

Using the indirect method, we start with net income and adjust this number for (1) revenue and expense items that do not affect cash, (2) gains and losses that do not affect operating cash flows, and (3) changes in current assets and current liabilities.

LO11–3 Prepare the investing activities section and the financing activities section of the statement of cash flows.

Most investing activities can be explained by changes in long-term asset accounts. Most financing activities can be explained by changes in long-term liability and stockholders' equity accounts.

Analysis

LO11–4 Perform financial analysis using the statement of cash flows.

Cash return on assets indicates the amount of operating cash flow generated for each dollar invested in assets. We can separate cash return on assets into two components—cash flow to sales and asset turnover—to examine two important business strategies.

Appendix

LO11–5 Prepare the operating activities section of the statement of cash flows using the direct method.

The indirect method and direct method differ only in the presentation of operating activities. In the indirect method, we start with net income and make adjustments to arrive at net cash flows from operating activities. In the direct method, we convert each individual line item in the income statement to its cash basis and directly list the cash inflows and cash outflows from operating activities. The net cash flows from operating activities are *the same under both methods.*

GLOSSARY

Asset turnover: Net sales divided by average total assets, which measures the sales per dollar of assets invested. **p. 526**

Cash flow to sales: Net cash flows from operating activities divided by sales revenue; measures the operating cash flow generated per dollar of sales. **p. 526**

Cash return on assets: Net cash flows from operating activities divided by average total assets; measures the operating cash flow generated per dollar of assets. **p. 525**

Direct method: Adjusts the items on the income statement to directly show the cash inflows and outflows from operations, such as cash received from customers and cash paid for inventory, salaries, rent, interest, and taxes. **p. 510**

Financing activities: Includes cash transactions resulting from the external financing of a business. **p. 507**

Indirect method: Begins with net income and then lists adjustments to net income in order to arrive at operating cash flows. **p. 510**

Investing activities: Includes cash transactions involving the purchase and sale of long-term assets and current investments. **p. 507**

Noncash activities: Significant investing and financing activities that do not affect cash. **p. 509**

Operating activities: Includes cash receipts and cash payments for transactions relating to revenue and expense activities. **p. 506**

Statement of cash flows A financial statement that measures activities involving cash receipts and cash payments over a period of time. **p. 506**

SELF-STUDY QUESTIONS

1. The purchase of a long-term asset is classified in the statement of cash flows as a(n): **(LO11–1)**
   a. Operating activity.
   b. Investing activity.
   c. Financing activity.
   d. Noncash activity.

2. The issuance of common stock is classified in the statement of cash flows as a(n): **(LO11–1)**
   a. Operating activity.
   b. Investing activity.
   c. Financing activity.
   d. Noncash activity.

3. The issuance of bonds payable is classified in the statement of cash flows as a(n): **(LO11–1)**
   a. Operating activity.
   b. Investing activity.
   c. Financing activity.
   d. Noncash activity.

4. Which of the following is an example of a noncash activity? **(LO11–1)**
   a. Sale of land for more than its cost.
   b. Purchase of land by issuing common stock.
   c. Sale of land for less than its cost.
   d. Purchase of land using cash proceeds from issuance of common stock.

5. We can identify operating activities from income statement information and changes in: **(LO11–2)**
   a. Current asset and current liability accounts.
   b. Long-term asset accounts.
   c. Long-term liability accounts.
   d. Stockholders' equity accounts.

6. The indirect and direct methods: **(LO11–2)**
   a. Are used by companies about equally in actual practice.
   b. Affect the presentations of operating, investing, and financing activities.
   c. Arrive at different amounts for net cash flows from operating activities.
   d. Are two allowable methods to present operating activities in the statement of cash flows.

7. Which of the following is an example of a cash inflow from an investing activity? **(LO11–3)**
   a. Receipt of cash from the issuance of common stock.
   b. Receipt of cash from the sale of equipment.
   c. Receipt of cash from the issuance of a note payable.
   d. Receipt of cash from the sale of inventory.

8. Which of the following is an example of a cash outflow from a financing activity? **(LO11–3)**
   a. Payment of interest.
   b. Purchase of an intangible asset.
   c. Payment of cash dividends.
   d. Purchase of land.

9. We can separate cash return on assets into: **(LO11–4)**
   a. Cash flow to sales and return on assets.
   b. Profit margin and asset turnover.
   c. Cash flow to sales and profit margin.
   d. Cash flow to sales and asset turnover.

10. Which of the following items do we report in the statement of cash flows using the direct method? **(LO11–5)**
    a. Depreciation expense.
    b. Gain on sale of an asset.
    c. Cash paid to suppliers.
    d. Loss on sale of an asset.

Note: For answers, see the last page of the chapter.

For additional study materials, including 10 more multiple-choice Self-Study Questions, visit Connect.

REVIEW QUESTIONS

1. Identify and briefly describe the three categories of cash flows reported in the statement of cash flows.   ■ **LO11–1**

2. Changes in current assets and current liabilities are used in determining net cash flows from operating activities. Changes in which balance sheet accounts are used in determining net cash flows from investing activities? Changes in which balance sheet accounts are used in determining net cash flows from financing activities?   ■ **LO11–1**

3. Explain what we mean by noncash activities and provide an example.   ■ **LO11–1**

■ **LO11–1**   4. Why is it necessary to use an income statement, balance sheet, and additional information to prepare a statement of cash flows?

■ **LO11–1**   5. Describe the basic format used in preparing a statement of cash flows, including the heading, the three major categories, and what is included in the last three lines of the statement.

■ **LO11–1**   6. Briefly describe the four steps outlined in the text for preparing a statement of cash flows.

■ **LO11–1**   7. Distinguish between the indirect method and the direct method for reporting net cash flows from operating activities. Which method is more common in practice? Which method provides a more logical presentation of cash flows?

■ **LO11–2**   8. Describe the most common adjustments we use to convert net income to net cash flows from operations under the indirect method.

■ **LO11–2**   9. The executives at Peach, Inc., are confused. The company reports a net loss of $200,000, and yet its net cash flow from operating activities increased $300,000 during the same period. Is this possible? Explain.

■ **LO11–2**   10. Explain how we report depreciation expense in the statement of cash flows using the indirect method. Why do we report it this way?

■ **LO11–2**   11. Describe how we report a gain or loss on the sale of an asset in the statement of cash flows using the indirect method. Why do we report it this way?

■ **LO11–2**   12. Indicate whether we add or subtract each of the following items from net income in preparing the statement of cash flows using the indirect method: (a) an increase in current assets, (b) a decrease in current assets, (c) an increase in current liabilities, and (d) a decrease in current liabilities.

■ **LO11–2**   13. How does an increase in accounts receivable affect net income in relation to operating cash flows? Why? How does a decrease in accounts receivable affect net income in relation to operating cash flows? Why?

■ **LO11–3**   14. Bell Corporation purchases land by issuing its own common stock. How do we report this transaction, if at all?

■ **LO11–2, 11–3**   15. A $10,000 investment on the books of a company is sold for $9,000. Under the indirect method, how does this transaction affect operating, investing, and financing activities?

■ **LO11–3**   16. Provide three examples of financing activities reported in the statement of cash flows.

■ **LO11–4**   17. Explain the difference between the calculation of return on assets and cash return on assets. How can cash-based ratios supplement the analysis of ratios based on income statement and balance sheet information?

■ **LO11–4**   18. Describe the two primary strategies firms use to increase cash return on assets. Which strategy does **Apple** use, and which does **Google** use?

■ **LO11–5**   19. What are the primary cash inflows and cash outflows under the direct method for determining net cash flows from operating activities?

■ **LO11–5**   20. Why do we exclude depreciation expense and the gain or loss on sale of an asset from the operating activities section of the statement of cash flows under the direct method?

BRIEF EXERCISES

Determine proper classification **(LO11–1)**

BE11–1 Classify each of the following items as an operating, investing, or financing activity.
1. Dividends paid.
2. Repayment of notes payable.
3. Payment for inventory.
4. Purchase of equipment.
5. Interest paid.

BE11–2 The following selected transactions occur during the first year of operations. Determine how each should be reported in the statement of cash flows.
1. Issued one million shares of common stock at $20 per share.
2. Paid $75,000 to suppliers for inventory.
3. Paid a dividend of $1 per share to common stockholders.
4. Loaned $50,000 to an employee and accepted a note receivable.

Determine proper classification (LO11–1)

BE11–3 Place the following items in the correct order as they would appear in the statement of cash flows.
Financing activities.
Net increase (decrease) in cash.
Operating activities.
Beginning cash balance.
Ending cash balance.
Investing activities.

Understand the basic format for the statement of cash flows (LO11–2)

BE11–4 Laser World reports net income of $650,000. Depreciation expense is $50,000, accounts receivable increases $11,000, and accounts payable decreases $30,000. Calculate net cash flows from operating activities using the indirect method.

Calculate operating activities—indirect method (LO11–2)

BE11–5 Macrosoft Company reports net income of $75,000. The accounting records reveal depreciation expense of $90,000 as well as increases in prepaid rent, accounts payable, and income tax payable of $70,000, $10,000, and $23,000, respectively. Prepare the operating activities section of Macrosoft's statement of cash flows using the indirect method.

Calculate operating activities—indirect method (LO11–2)

BE11–6 Hi-Tech, Inc., reports net income of $70 million. Included in that number are depreciation expense of $6 million and a loss on the sale of equipment of $2 million. Records reveal increases in accounts receivable, accounts payable, and inventory of $3 million, $4 million, and $5 million, respectively. What are Hi-Tech's net cash flows from operating activities?

Calculate operating activities—indirect method (LO11–2)

BE11–7 Engineering Wonders reports net income of $70 million. Included in that number is building depreciation expense of $6 million and a gain on the sale of land of $2 million. Records reveal decreases in accounts receivable, accounts payable, and inventory of $3 million, $4 million, and $5 million, respectively. What are Engineering Wonders' net cash flows from operating activities?

Calculate operating activities—indirect method (LO11–2)

BE11–8 Creative Sound Systems sold investments, land, and its own common stock for $40 million, $16 million, and $42 million, respectively. Creative Sound Systems also purchased treasury stock, equipment, and a patent for $22 million, $26 million, and $13 million, respectively. What amount should the company report as net cash flows from investing activities?

Calculate net cash flows from investing activities (LO11–3)

BE11–9 Refer to the situation described in BE11–8. What amount should Creative Sound Systems report as net cash flows from financing activities?

Calculate net cash flows from financing activities (LO11–3)

BE11–10 The balance sheet of Cranium Gaming reports total assets of $500,000 and $800,000 at the beginning and end of the year, respectively. Sales revenues are $2.10 million, net income is $75,000, and operating cash flows are $60,000. Calculate the cash return on assets, cash flow to sales, and asset turnover for Cranium Gaming.

Calculate the cash return on assets (LO11–4)

BE11–11 The balance sheet of Innovative Products reports total assets of $620,000 and $820,000 at the beginning and end of the year, respectively. The cash return on assets for the year is 25%. Calculate Innovative Products' net cash flows from operating activities (operating cash flows) for the year.

Calculate the net cash flows from operating activities (LO11–4)

BE11–12 Video Shack's accounts receivable decreases during the year by $9 million. What is the amount of cash received from customers during the reporting period if its net sales are $73 million?

Determine cash received from customers (LO11–5)

BE11–13 Electronic Superstore's inventory increases during the year by $5 million, and its accounts payable to suppliers increases by $7 million during the same period. What is the amount of cash paid to suppliers of merchandise during the reporting period if its cost of goods sold is $45 million?

Determine cash paid to suppliers (LO11–5)

Determine cash paid for operating expenses (LO11–5)

BE11–14 Wireless Solutions reports operating expenses of $985,000. Operating expenses include both rent expense and salaries expense. Prepaid rent increases during the year by $30,000 and salaries payable increases by $20,000. What is the cash paid for operating expenses during the year?

Determine cash paid for income taxes (LO11–5)

BE11–15 Computer World reports income tax expense of $340,000. Income taxes payable at the beginning and end of the year are $60,000 and $75,000, respectively. What is the cash paid for income taxes during the year?

EXERCISES

Match terms with their definitions (LO11–1, 11–2, 11–3, 11–4, 11–5)

E11–1 Match (by letter) the following items with the description or example that best fits. Each letter is used only once.

Terms

_____ 1. Operating activities.
_____ 2. Investing activities.
_____ 3. Financing activities.
_____ 4. Noncash activities.
_____ 5. Indirect method.
_____ 6. Direct method.
_____ 7. Depreciation expense.
_____ 8. Cash return on assets.

Descriptions

a. Begins with net income and then lists adjustments to net income in order to arrive at operating cash flows.
b. Item included in net income, but excluded from net operating cash flows.
c. Net cash flows from operating activities divided by average total assets.
d. Cash transactions involving lenders and investors.
e. Cash transactions involving net income.
f. Cash transactions for the purchase and sale of long-term assets.
g. Purchase of long-term assets by issuing stock.
h. Shows the cash inflows and outflows from operations such as cash received from customers and cash paid for inventory, salaries, rent, interest, and taxes.

Determine proper classification (LO11–1)

E11–2 Discount Computers is in its second year of business providing computer repair services in the local community and reselling used computers on the Internet. The company is owned by 10 investors, each investing $100,000. Justin Lake was hired as president and CEO, with one stipulation: He would receive no salary unless the company achieved annual operating cash flows exceeding $200,000. If the $200,000 was achieved, Justin would receive a $100,000 bonus, and each of the 10 investors would receive a dividend of $10,000.

At the end of the year, Justin had Nicole Roberts, one of the business interns from the local college, calculate a preliminary statement of cash flows. Operating cash flows were $185,000. Justin carefully looked over the calculations that night and then met with Nicole in the morning. Justin starts out: "Nicole, you did an excellent job in preparing the statement of cash flows. The only change I could find is that we need to move the $25,000 increase in notes payable to the bank from financing activities to operating activities. We borrowed that money three months ago and plan to pay it back within a year. After you finish the changes, round up the rest of the interns. Lunch is on me."

Required:

Do you agree with the change recommended by Justin Lake? Is there anything unethical about his actions? What should Nicole do in this situation?

E11–3 Analysis of an income statement, balance sheet, and additional information from the accounting records of Gadgets, Inc., reveals the following items.

1. Purchase of a patent.
2. Depreciation expense.
3. Decrease in accounts receivable.
4. Issuance of a note payable.
5. Increase in inventory.
6. Collection of notes receivable.
7. Purchase of equipment.
8. Exchange of long-term assets.
9. Decrease in accounts payable.
10. Payment of dividends.

Determine proper classification (LO11–1)

Required:

Indicate in which section of the statement of cash flows each of these items would be reported: operating activities (indirect method), investing activities, financing activities, or a separate noncash activities note.

E11–4 Wi-Fi, Inc., has the following selected transactions during the year.

1. Issues $20 million in bonds.
2. Purchases equipment for $80,000.
3. Pays a $20,000 account payable.
4. Collects a $15,000 account receivable.
5. Exchanges land for a new patent. Both are valued at $300,000.
6. Declares and pays a cash dividend of $100,000.
7. Loans $50,000 to a customer, accepting a note receivable.
8. Pays $75,000 to suppliers for inventory.

Determine proper classification (LO11–1)

Required:

Indicate in which section of the statement of cash flows each of these items would be reported: operating activities (indirect method), investing activities, financing activities, or a separate noncash activities note.

E11–5 Ernie's Electronics had the following transactions with Bert's Bargain House:

1. Ernie sold Bert land, originally purchased for $180,000, at a sales price of $195,000, resulting in a gain on sale of land of $15,000.
2. Ernie borrowed $100,000 from Bert, signing a three-year note payable.
3. Ernie purchased $1 million in common stock in Bert's Bargain House through a private placement.
4. Ernie received a dividend of $40,000 from the common stock investment in Bert's Bargain House.

Determine proper classification (LO11–1)

Flip Side of E11–6

Required:

Analyze each of the four transactions from the perspective of Ernie's Electronics. Indicate in which section of the statement of cash flows each of these items would be reported for Ernie's Electronics: operating activities (indirect method), investing activities, financing activities, or a separate noncash activities note.

E11–6 Refer to the transactions between Ernie's Electronics and Bert's Bargain House recorded in E11–5.

Determine proper classification (LO11–1)

Flip Side of E11–5

Required:

Analyze each of the four transactions from the perspective of Bert's Bargain House. Indicate in which section of the statement of cash flows each of these items would be reported for Bert's Bargain House: operating activities (indirect method), investing activities, financing activities, or a separate noncash activities note.

Prepare the basic format for the statement of cash flows (LO11–2, 11–3)

E11–7 Technology Solutions' format for the statement of cash flows was corrupted by a computer virus, as follows:

TECHNOLOGY SOLUTIONS
Statement of Cash Flows
For the year ended December 31, 2018

Cash at the beginning of the period	$$$
Cash at the end of the period	$$$
Net increase (decrease) in cash	$$$
Cash Flows from Financing Activities	
List of cash inflows and outflows from financing activities	
Net cash flows from financing activities	$$$
Noncash Activities	
List of noncash transactions	$$$
Cash Flows from Investing Activities	
List of cash inflows and outflows from investing activities	
Net cash flows from investing activities	$$$
Cash Flows from Operating Activities	
List of items adjusting net income to operating cash flows	
Adjustments to reconcile net income to net cash flows from operating activities	
Net income	
Net cash flows from operating activities	$$$

Required:

Prepare a correct format for Technology Solutions to use in preparing the statement of cash flows.

Calculate operating activities—indirect method (LO11–2)

E11–8 Hardware Suppliers reports net income of $165,000. Included in net income is a gain on the sale of land of $20,000. A comparison of this year's and last year's balance sheets reveals an increase in accounts receivable of $35,000, an increase in inventory of $20,000, and a decrease in accounts payable of $55,000.

Required:

Prepare the operating activities section of the statement of cash flows using the indirect method. Do you see a pattern in Hardware Suppliers' adjustments to net income to arrive at operating cash flows? What might this imply?

Calculate operating activities—indirect method (LO11–2)

E11–9 Software Distributors reports net income of $65,000. Included in that number is depreciation expense of $15,000 and a loss on the sale of land of $6,000. A comparison of this year's and last year's balance sheets reveals a decrease in accounts receivable of $28,000, a decrease in inventory of $37,000, and an increase in accounts payable of $45,000.

Required:

Prepare the operating activities section of the statement of cash flows using the indirect method. Do you see a pattern in Software Distributors' adjustments to net income to arrive at operating cash flows? What might this imply?

E11–10 The balance sheets for Plasma Screens Corporation, along with additional information, are provided below:

Prepare a statement of cash flows—indirect method (LO11–2, 11–3)

PLASMA SCREENS CORPORATION
Balance Sheets
December 31, 2018 and 2017

	2018	2017
Assets		
Current assets:		
Cash	$ 108,900	$ 126,800
Accounts receivable	82,000	97,000
Inventory	105,000	89,000
Prepaid rent	6,000	3,000
Long-term assets:		
Land	530,000	530,000
Equipment	830,000	720,000
Accumulated depreciation	(438,000)	(288,000)
Total assets	$1,223,900	$1,277,800
Liabilities and Stockholders' Equity		
Current liabilities:		
Accounts payable	$ 109,000	$ 94,000
Interest payable	6,900	13,800
Income tax payable	10,000	6,000
Long-term liabilities:		
Notes payable	115,000	230,000
Stockholders' equity:		
Common stock	750,000	750,000
Retained earnings	233,000	184,000
Total liabilities and stockholders' equity	$1,223,900	$1,277,800

Additional Information for 2018:

1. Net income is $79,000.
2. The company purchases $110,000 in equipment.
3. Depreciation expense is $150,000.
4. The company repays $115,000 in notes payable.
5. The company declares and pays a cash dividend of $30,000.

Required:

Prepare the statement of cash flows using the indirect method.

E11–11 Portions of the financial statements for Peach Computer are provided below.

Calculate operating activities—indirect method (LO11–2)

PEACH COMPUTER
Income Statement
For the year ended December 31, 2018

Net sales		$2,050,000
Expenses:		
Cost of goods sold	$1,150,000	
Operating expenses	660,000	
Depreciation expense	60,000	
Income tax expense	50,000	
Total expenses		1,920,000
Net income		$ 130,000

	PEACH COMPUTER **Selected Balance Sheet Data** **December 31**		
	2018	**2017**	**Increase (I) or Decrease (D)**
Cash	$112,000	$90,000	$22,000 (I)
Accounts receivable	46,000	54,000	8,000 (D)
Inventory	85,000	60,000	25,000 (I)
Prepaid rent	4,000	7,000	3,000 (D)
Accounts payable	55,000	42,000	13,000 (I)
Income tax payable	6,000	15,000	9,000 (D)

Required:

Prepare the operating activities section of the statement of cash flows for Peach Computer using the *indirect* method.

Calculate financial ratios (LO11–4)

E11–12 Zoogle has the following selected data ($ in millions):

Net sales	$24,651
Net income	6,620
Operating cash flows	9,326
Total assets, beginning	41,768
Total assets, ending	50,497

Required:

1. Calculate the return on assets.
2. Calculate the cash return on assets.
3. Calculate the cash flow to sales ratio and the asset turnover ratio.

Calculate operating activities—direct method (LO11–5)

E11–13 Refer to the information provided for Peach Computer in E11–11.

Required:

Prepare the operating activities section of the statement of cash flows for Peach Computer using the *direct* method.

Calculate operating activities—direct method (LO11–5)

E11–14 Mega Screens, Inc., reports net sales of $3,200,000, cost of goods sold of $2,000,000, and income tax expense of $150,000 for the year ended December 31, 2018. Selected balance sheet accounts are as follows:

	MEGA SCREENS, INC. **Selected Balance Sheet Data** **December 31**		
	2018	**2017**	**Increase (I) or Decrease (D)**
Cash	$150,000	$195,000	$45,000 (D)
Accounts receivable	285,000	230,000	55,000 (I)
Inventory	125,000	165,000	40,000 (D)
Accounts payable	120,000	137,000	17,000 (D)
Income tax payable	25,000	16,000	9,000 (I)

Required:

Calculate cash received from customers, cash paid to suppliers, and cash paid for income taxes.

Calculate operating activities—direct method (LO11–5)

E11–15 The income statement for Electronic Wonders reports net sales of $91,758 million and cost of goods sold of $69,278 million. An examination of balance sheet amounts indicates accounts receivable increased $1,733 million, inventory increased $883 million, and accounts payable to suppliers decreased $1,967 million.

Required:

Using the direct method, calculate (1) cash received from customers and (2) cash paid to suppliers.

PROBLEMS: SET A

connect

P11–1A Listed below are several transactions. For each transaction, indicate by letter whether the cash effect of each transaction is reported in a statement of cash flows as an operating (O), investing (I), financing (F), or noncash (NC) activity. Also, indicate whether the transaction is a cash inflow (CI) or cash outflow (CO), or has no effect on cash (NE). The first answer is provided as an example.

Determine proper classification **(LO11–1)**

Transaction	Type of Activity	Cash Inflow or Outflow
1. *Payment of employee salaries.*	*O*	*CO*
2. Sale of land for cash.		
3. Purchase of rent in advance.		
4. Collection of an account receivable.		
5. Issuance of common stock.		
6. Purchase of inventory.		
7. Collection of notes receivable.		
8. Payment of income taxes.		
9. Sale of equipment for a note receivable.		
10. Issuance of bonds.		
11. Loan to another firm.		
12. Payment of a long-term note payable.		
13. Purchase of treasury stock.		
14. Payment of an account payable.		
15. Sale of equipment for cash.		

P11–2A Seth Erkenbeck, a recent college graduate, has just completed the basic format to be used in preparing the statement of cash flows (indirect method) for ATM Software Developers. All amounts are in thousands (000s).

Basic format for the statement of cash flows **(LO11–2, 11–3)**

ATM SOFTWARE DEVELOPERS Statement of Cash Flows For the year ended December 31, 2018	
Cash Flows from Operating Activities	
Net income	$
Adjustments to reconcile net income to net cash flows from operating activities:	
Net cash flows from operating activities	
Cash Flows from Investing Activities	
Net cash flows from investing activities	
Cash Flows from Financing Activities	
Net cash flows from financing activities	
Net increase (decrease) in cash	$ 3,765
Cash at the beginning of the period	7,510
Cash at the end of the period	$11,275

Listed below in random order are line items to be included in the statement of cash flows.

Cash received from the sale of land	$ 8,650
Issuance of common stock	13,075
Depreciation expense	5,465
Increase in accounts receivable	4,090
Decrease in accounts payable	1,760
Issuance of long-term notes payable	16,495
Purchase of equipment	39,865
Decrease in inventory	1,475
Decrease in prepaid rent	905
Payment of dividends	6,370
Net income	12,400
Purchase of treasury stock	2,615

Required:

Prepare the statement of cash flows for ATM Software Developers using the *indirect* method.

Calculate operating activities—indirect method (LO11–2)

P11–3A Portions of the financial statements for Alliance Technologies are provided below.

ALLIANCE TECHNOLOGIES
Income Statement
For the year ended December 31, 2018

Net sales		$405,000
Expenses:		
Cost of goods sold	$235,000	
Operating expenses	70,000	
Depreciation expense	17,000	
Income tax expense	27,000	
Total expenses		349,000
Net income		$ 56,000

ALLIANCE TECHNOLOGIES
Selected Balance Sheet Data
December 31, 2018, compared to December 31, 2017

Decrease in accounts receivable	$ 7,000
Increase in inventory	14,000
Decrease in prepaid rent	10,000
Increase in salaries payable	6,000
Decrease in accounts payable	9,000
Increase in income tax payable	24,000

Required:

Prepare the operating activities section of the statement of cash flows for Alliance Technologies using the *indirect* method.

P11–4A The income statement, balance sheets, and additional information for Video Phones, Inc., are provided.

Prepare a statement of cash flows—indirect method (LO11–2, 11–3)

VIDEO PHONES, INC.
Income Statement
For the year ended December 31, 2018

Net sales		$3,636,000
Expenses:		
Cost of goods sold	$2,450,000	
Operating expenses	958,000	
Depreciation expense	37,000	
Loss on sale of land	9,000	
Interest expense	20,000	
Income tax expense	58,000	
Total expenses		3,532,000
Net income		$ 104,000

VIDEO PHONES, INC.
Balance Sheets
December 31

	2018	2017
Assets		
Current assets:		
Cash	$ 254,600	$227,800
Accounts receivable	92,000	70,000
Inventory	105,000	145,000
Prepaid rent	14,400	7,200
Long-term assets:		
Investments	115,000	0
Land	220,000	260,000
Equipment	290,000	220,000
Accumulated depreciation	(81,000)	(44,000)
Total assets	$1,010,000	$886,000
Liabilities and Stockholders' Equity		
Current liabilities:		
Accounts payable	$ 75,000	$ 91,000
Interest payable	7,000	12,000
Income tax payable	16,000	15,000
Long-term liabilities:		
Notes payable	305,000	235,000
Stockholders' equity:		
Common stock	400,000	400,000
Retained earnings	207,000	133,000
Total liabilities and stockholders' equity	$1,010,000	$886,000

Additional Information for 2018:

1. Purchase investment in bonds for $115,000.
2. Sell land costing $40,000 for only $31,000, resulting in a $9,000 loss on sale of land.
3. Purchase $70,000 in equipment by borrowing $70,000 with a note payable due in three years. No cash is exchanged in the transaction.
4. Declare and pay a cash dividend of $30,000.

Required:

Prepare the statement of cash flows using the *indirect* method. Disclose any noncash transactions in an accompanying note.

Calculate and analyze
ratios (LO11–4)

P11–5A Cyberdyne Systems and Virtucon are competitors focusing on the latest technologies. Selected financial data is provided below:

($ in millions)	Cyberdyne	Virtucon
Net sales	$37,905	$ 4,984
Net income	9,737	1,049
Operating cash flows	14,565	1,324
Total assets, beginning	57,851	14,928
Total assets, ending	72,574	14,783

Required:
1. Calculate the return on assets for both companies.
2. Calculate the cash return on assets for both companies.
3. Calculate the cash flow to sales ratio and the asset turnover ratio for both companies.
4. Which company has the more favorable ratios?

Calculate operating
activities—direct
method (LO11–5)

P11–6A Refer to the information provided in P11–3A for Alliance Technologies.

Required:
Prepare the operating activities section of the statement of cash flows for Alliance Technologies using the *direct* method.

Calculate operating
activities—direct
method (LO11–5)

P11–7A Data for Video Phones, Inc., are provided in P11–4A.

Required:
Prepare the statement of cash flows for Video Phones, Inc., using the *direct* method. Disclose any noncash transactions in an accompanying note.

Prepare an income
statement using operating
cash flow information—
indirect and direct
methods (LO11–2, 11–5)

P11–8A Cash flows from operating activities for both the indirect and direct methods are presented for Reverse Logic. All amounts are in thousands (000s).

Cash Flows from Operating Activities (Indirect method)		
Net income	$ 174	
Adjustments to reconcile net income to net cash flows from operating activities:		
Depreciation expense	62	
Increase in accounts receivable	(38)	
Decrease in inventory	50	
Increase in prepaid rent	(5)	
Decrease in accounts payable	(11)	
Decrease in income tax payable	(9)	
Net cash flows from operating activities		$223
Cash Flows from Operating Activities (Direct method)		
Cash received from customers	$ 4,070	
Cash paid to suppliers	(2,585)	
Cash paid for operating expenses	(1,163)	
Cash paid for income taxes	(99)	
Net cash flows from operating activities		$223

Required:
Complete the following income statement for Reverse Logic. Assume all accounts payable are to suppliers.

REVERSE LOGIC
Income Statement
For the year ended December 31, 2018

Net sales		$?
Expenses:		
Cost of goods sold	$?	
Operating expenses	?	
Depreciation expense	62	
Income tax expense	?	
Total expenses		?
Net income		$174

[*Hint:* Use the following calculations and work backwards from bottom (in red) to top for each item.]

Net sales	
± Change in accounts receivable	_____
= **Cash received from customers**	=========
Cost of goods sold	
± Change in inventory	_____
= Purchases	
± Change in accounts payable	_____
= **Cash paid to suppliers**	=========
Operating expenses	
± Change in prepaid rent	_____
= **Cash paid for operating expenses**	=========
Income tax expense	
± Change in income tax payable	_____
= **Cash paid for income taxes**	=========

PROBLEMS: SET B

P11–1B Listed below are several transactions. For each transaction, indicate by letter whether the cash effect of each transaction is reported in a statement of cash flows as an operating (O), investing (I), financing (F), or noncash (NC) activity. Also, indicate whether the transaction is a cash inflow (CI) or cash outflow (CO), or has no effect on cash (NE). The first answer is provided as an example.

Determine proper classification (LO11–1)

Transaction	Type of Activity	Cash Inflow or Outflow
1. *Issuance of common stock.*	*F*	*CI*
2. Sale of land for cash.		
3. Purchase of treasury stock.		
4. Collection of an account receivable.		

(continued)

(concluded)

Transaction	Type of Activity	Cash Inflow or Outflow
5. Issuance of a note payable.		
6. Purchase of inventory.		
7. Repayment of a note payable.		
8. Payment of employee salaries.		
9. Sale of equipment for a note receivable.		
10. Issuance of bonds.		
11. Investment in bonds.		
12. Payment of interest on bonds payable.		
13. Payment of a cash dividend.		
14. Purchase of a building.		
15. Collection of a note receivable.		

Basic format for the statement of cash flows (LO11–2, 11–3)

P11–2B Natalie King has completed the basic format to be used in preparing the statement of cash flows (indirect method) for CPU Hardware Designers. All amounts are in thousands (000s).

CPU HARDWARE DESIGNERS
Statement of Cash Flows
For the year ended December 31, 2018

Cash Flows from Operating Activities
Net income
Adjustments to reconcile net income to net cash flows from operating activities:

Net cash flows from operating activities   _____

Cash Flows from Investing Activities

Net cash flows from investing activities   _____

Cash Flows from Financing Activities

Net cash flows from financing activities   _____

Net increase (decrease) in cash	$(28,000)
Cash at the beginning of the period	90,000
Cash at the end of the period	$ 62,000

Below, in random order, are line items to be included in the statement of cash flows.

Cash received from the sale of land	$ 4,000
Issuance of common stock	300,000
Depreciation expense	30,000
Increase in accounts receivable	70,000
Increase in accounts payable	11,000
Loss on sale of land	8,000
Purchase of equipment	230,000
Increase in inventory	40,000
Increase in prepaid rent	11,000
Payment of dividends	50,000
Net income	80,000
Repayment of notes payable	60,000

Required:

Prepare the statement of cash flows for CPU Hardware Designers using the *indirect* method.

P11–3B Portions of the financial statements for Software Associates are provided below.

Calculate operating activities—indirect method (LO11–2)

SOFTWARE ASSOCIATES
Income Statement
For the year ended December 31, 2018

Net sales		$710,000
Expenses:		
Cost of goods sold	$420,000	
Operating expenses	130,000	
Depreciation expense	33,000	
Income tax expense	49,000	
Total expenses		632,000
Net income		$ 78,000

SOFTWARE ASSOCIATES
Selected Balance Sheet Data
December 31, 2018, compared to December 31, 2017

Decrease in accounts receivable	$10,000
Decrease in inventory	13,000
Increase in prepaid rent	3,000
Decrease in salaries payable	4,000
Increase in accounts payable	7,000
Increase in income tax payable	8,000

Required:

Prepare the operating activities section of the statement of cash flows for Software Associates using the *indirect* method.

P11–4B The income statement, balance sheets, and additional information for Virtual Gaming Systems are provided.

Prepare a statement of cash flows—indirect method (LO11–2, 11–3)

VIRTUAL GAMING SYSTEMS
Income Statement
For the year ended December 31, 2018

Net sales		$2,600,000
Gain on sale of land		7,000
Total revenues		2,607,000
Expenses:		
Cost of goods sold	$1,650,000	
Operating expenses	615,000	
Depreciation expense	33,000	
Interest expense	34,000	
Income tax expense	80,000	
Total expenses		2,412,000
Net income		$ 195,000

VIRTUAL GAMING SYSTEMS
Balance Sheets
December 31

	2018	2017
Assets		
Current assets:		
Cash	$ 409,500	$ 343,800
Accounts receivable	64,000	80,000
Inventory	160,000	145,000
Prepaid rent	4,600	7,200
Long-term assets:		
Investments	205,000	110,000
Land	215,000	270,000
Equipment	250,000	220,000
Accumulated depreciation	(143,000)	(110,000)
Total assets	$1,165,100	$1,066,000
Liabilities and Stockholders' Equity		
Current liabilities:		
Accounts payable	$ 35,000	$ 98,000
Interest payable	5,100	4,000
Income tax payable	25,000	29,000
Long-term liabilities:		
Notes payable	265,000	235,000
Stockholders' equity:		
Common stock	460,000	400,000
Retained earnings	375,000	300,000
Total liabilities and stockholders' equity	$1,165,100	$1,066,000

Additional Information for 2018:
1. Purchase additional investment in stocks for $95,000.
2. Sell land costing $55,000 for $62,000, resulting in a $7,000 gain on sale of land.
3. Purchase $30,000 in equipment by borrowing $30,000 with a note payable due in three years. No cash is exchanged in the transaction.
4. Declare and pay a cash dividend of $120,000.
5. Issue common stock for $60,000.

Required:

Prepare the statement of cash flows using the *indirect* method. Disclose any noncash transactions in an accompanying note.

Calculate and analyze ratios (LO11–4)

P11–5B International Genetic Technologies (InGen) and The Resources Development Association (RDA) are companies involved in cutting-edge genetics research. Selected financial data are provided below:

($ in millions)	InGen	RDA
Net sales	$127,245	$106,916
Net income	7,074	15,855
Operating cash flows	12,639	19,846
Total assets, beginning	124,503	113,452
Total assets, ending	129,517	116,433

Required:

1. Calculate the return on assets for both companies.
2. Calculate the cash return on assets for both companies.
3. Calculate the cash flow to sales ratio and the asset turnover ratio for both companies.
4. Which company has the more favorable ratios?

P11–6B Refer to the information provided in P11–3B for Software Associates.

Required:

Prepare the operating activities section of the statement of cash flows for Software Associates using the *direct* method.

P11–7B Data for Virtual Gaming Systems are provided in P11–4B.

Required:

Prepare the statement of cash flows for Virtual Gaming Systems using the *direct* method. Disclose any noncash transactions in an accompanying note.

P11–8B Cash flows from operating activities for both the indirect and direct methods are presented for Electronic Transformations.

Calculate operating activities—direct method (LO11–5)

Calculate operating activities—direct method (LO11–5)

Prepare an income statement using operating cash flow information—indirect and direct methods (LO11–2, 11–5)

Cash Flows from Operating Activities (Indirect method)

Net income	$36,000	
Adjustments to reconcile net income to net cash flows from operating activities:		
Depreciation expense	9,000	
Increase in accounts receivable	(13,000)	
Increase in accounts payable	8,000	
Increase in income tax payable	6,000	
Net cash flows from operating activities		$46,000

Cash Flows from Operating Activities (Direct method)

Cash received from customers	$83,000	
Cash paid for operating expenses	(26,000)	
Cash paid for income taxes	(11,000)	
Net cash flows from operating activities		$46,000

Required:

Complete the following income statement for Electronic Transformations. Assume all accounts payable are to suppliers.

ELECTRONIC TRANSFORMATIONS
Income Statement
For the year ended December 31, 2018

Net sales		$?
Expenses:		
Operating expenses	$?	
Depreciation expense	9,000	
Income tax expense	?	
Total expenses		?
Net income		$36,000

[*Hint:* Use the following calculations and work backwards from bottom (in red) to top for each item.]

Net sales
± Change in accounts receivable
= **Cash received from customers**
_____

Operating expenses
± Change in accounts payable
= **Cash paid for operating expenses**
_____

Income tax expense
± Change in income tax payable
= **Cash paid for income taxes**
_____

ADDITIONAL PERSPECTIVES

Great Adventures

(This is a continuation of the Great Adventures problem from earlier chapters.)

Continuing Problem

AP11–1 The income statement, balance sheets, and additional information for Great Adventures, Inc., are provided below.

GREAT ADVENTURES, INC.
Income Statement
For the year ended December 31, 2020

Revenues:		
Service revenue (clinic, racing, TEAM)	$543,000	
Sales revenue (MU watches)	118,000	
Total revenues		$661,000
Expenses:		
Cost of goods sold (watches)	70,000	
Operating expenses	304,276	
Depreciation expense	50,000	
Interest expense	29,724	
Income tax expense	57,000	
Total expenses		511,000
Net income		$150,000

GREAT ADVENTURES, INC.
Balance Sheets
December 31, 2020 and 2019

	2020	2019	Increase (I) or Decrease (D)
Assets			
Current assets:			
Cash	$ 322,362	$138,000	$ 184,362 (I)
Accounts receivable	45,000	35,000	10,000 (I)
Inventory	17,000	14,000	3,000 (I)
Other current assets	13,000	11,000	2,000 (I)

(continued)

(concluded)

GREAT ADVENTURES, INC.
Balance Sheets
December 31, 2020 and 2019

	2020	2019	Increase (I) or Decrease (D)
Long-term assets:			
Land	$ 500,000	$ 0	$ 500,000 (I)
Buildings	1,000,000	0	1,000,000 (I)
Equipment	65,000	65,000	
Accumulated depreciation	(75,250)	(25,250)	50,000 (I)
Total assets	$1,887,112	$ 237,750	
Liabilities and Stockholders' Equity			
Current liabilities:			
Accounts payable	$ 12,000	$ 9,000	$ 3,000 (I)
Interest payable	750	750	
Income tax payable	57,000	38,000	19,000 (I)
Long-term liabilities:			
Notes payable	492,362	30,000	462,362 (I)
Stockholders' equity:			
Common stock	120,000	20,000	100,000 (I)
Paid-in capital	1,105,000	0	1,105,000 (I)
Retained earnings	175,000	140,000	35,000 (I)
Treasury stock	(75,000)	0	(75,000) (I)
Total liabilities and stockholders' equity	$1,887,112	$237,750	

Additional Information for 2020:

1. Borrowed $500,000 in January 2020. Made 12 monthly payments during the year, reducing the balance of the loan by $37,638.
2. Issued common stock for $1,200,000.
3. Purchased 10,000 shares of treasury stock for $15 per share.
4. Reissued 5,000 shares of treasury stock at $16 per share.
5. Declared and paid a cash dividend of $115,000.

Required:
Prepare the statement of cash flows for the year ended December 31, 2020, using the *indirect* method.

American Eagle Outfitters, Inc.

Financial Analysis

AP11–2 Financial information for **American Eagle** is presented in **Appendix A** at the end of the book.

Required:
1. What was the amount of increase or decrease in cash and cash equivalents for the most recent year?
2. What was net cash from operating activities for the most recent year? Is net cash from operating activities increasing each year? What is the largest reconciling item between net income and net operating cash flows during the most recent year?

3. What was net cash from investing activities for the most recent year? Is it positive or negative? What is the largest investing activity during the most recent year?
4. What was net cash from financing activities for the most recent year? Is negative financing activities a good sign or a bad sign? What is the largest financing activity during the most recent year?

Financial Analysis

The Buckle, Inc.

AP11–3 Financial information for **Buckle** is presented in **Appendix B** at the end of the book.

Required:
1. What was the amount of increase or decrease in cash and cash equivalents for the most recent year?
2. What was net cash from operating activities for the most recent year? Is net cash from operating activities increasing each year? What is the largest reconciling item between net income and net operating cash flows during the most recent year?
3. What was net cash from investing activities for the most recent year? Is it positive or negative? What is the largest investing activity during the most recent year?
4. What was net cash from financing activities for the most recent year? Is negative financing activities a good sign or a bad sign? What is the largest financing activity during the most recent year?

Comparative Analysis

American Eagle Outfitters, Inc. vs. The Buckle, Inc.

AP11–4 Financial information for **American Eagle** is presented in **Appendix A** at the end of the book, and financial information for **Buckle** is presented in **Appendix B** at the end of the book.

Required:
1. Calculate American Eagle's cash return on assets, cash flow to sales, and asset turnover ratio.
2. Calculate Buckle's cash return on assets, cash flow to sales, and asset turnover ratio.
3. Which company is doing better based on cash return on assets? Which company has the higher cash flow to sales? Which company has the higher asset turnover?

Ethics

AP11–5 Aggressive Corporation approaches Matt Taylor, a loan officer for Oklahoma State Bank, seeking to increase the company's borrowings with the bank from $100,000 to $150,000. Matt has an uneasy feeling as he examines the loan application from Aggressive Corporation, which just completed its first year of operations. The application included the following financial statements.

AGGRESSIVE CORPORATION		
Income Statement		
For the year ended December 31, 2018		
Net sales		$200,000
Expenses:		
Cost of goods sold	$110,000	
Operating expenses	50,000	
Depreciation expense	10,000	
Total expenses		170,000
Net income		$ 30,000

AGGRESSIVE CORPORATION
Balance Sheets
December 31

	2018	2017
Assets		
Current assets:		
Cash	$ 10,000	$0
Accounts receivable	60,000	0
Inventory	40,000	0
Long-term assets:		
Equipment	100,000	0
Accumulated depreciation	(10,000)	0
Total assets	$200,000	$0
Liabilities and Stockholders' Equity		
Current liabilities:		
Accounts payable	$ 20,000	$0
Interest payable	10,000	0
Long-term liabilities:		
Note payable	100,000	0
Stockholders' equity:		
Common stock	40,000	0
Retained earnings	30,000	0
Total liabilities and stockholders' equity	$200,000	$0

The income statement submitted with the application shows net income of $30,000 in the first year of operations. Referring to the balance sheet, this net income represents a more-than-acceptable 15% rate of return on assets of $200,000.

Matt's concern stems from his recollection that the $100,000 note payable reported on the balance sheet is a three-year loan from his bank, approved earlier this year. He recalls another promising new company that, just recently, defaulted on its loan due to its inability to generate sufficient cash flows to meet its loan obligations.

Seeing Matt's hesitation, Larry Bling, the CEO of Aggressive Corporation, closes the door to the conference room and shares with Matt that he owns several other businesses. He says he will be looking for a new CFO in another year to run Aggressive Corporation along with his other businesses and Matt is just the kind of guy he is looking for. Larry mentions that as CFO, Matt would receive a significant salary. Matt is flattered and says he will look over the loan application and get back to Larry concerning the $50,000 loan increase by the end of the week.

Required:
1. Prepare a statement of cash flows for Aggressive Corporation.
2. Explain how Aggressive Corporation can have positive net income but negative operating cash flows. How does the finding of negative operating cash flows affect your confidence in the reliability of the net income amount?
3. Why do you think Larry mentioned the potential employment position? Should the potential employment position with Aggressive Corporation have any influence on the loan decision?

Internet Research

AP11–6 EDGAR, the Electronic Data Gathering, Analysis, and Retrieval system, is a giant database of documents required to be submitted to the U.S. Securities and Exchange Commission (SEC). All publicly traded domestic companies use EDGAR to make the majority of their filings. (Filings by foreign companies are not required to be filed on EDGAR, but many of these companies do so voluntarily.) Form 10-K, which includes the annual report, is an important document required to be filed on EDGAR. The SEC makes this information available, free to the public, on the Internet.

Required:

1. Access EDGAR on the Internet. The web address is ***www.sec.gov.***
2. Search for a public company with which you are familiar. Access its most recent 10-K filing. Search or scroll to find the statement of cash flows.
3. Is the direct or indirect method used to report operating activities? What is the largest adjustment to net income in reconciling net income and cash flows from operations in the most recent year?
4. What has been the most significant investing activity for the company in the most recent three years?
5. What has been the most significant financing activity for the company in the most recent three years?

Written Communication

AP11–7 "Why can't we pay our shareholders a dividend?" shouts your new boss at Polar Opposites. "This income statement you prepared for me says we earned $5 million in our first year!" You recently prepared the financial statements below.

POLAR OPPOSITES
Income Statement
For the year ended December 31, 2018

	($ in millions)
Net sales	$65
Cost of goods sold	(35)
Depreciation expense	(4)
Operating expenses	(21)
Net income	$ 5

POLAR OPPOSITES
Balance Sheet
December 31, 2018

	($ in millions)
Cash	$ 1
Accounts receivable (net)	16
Merchandise inventory	14
Machinery (net)	44
Total assets	$75
Accounts payable	$ 7
Accrued expenses payable	9
Notes payable	29
Common stock	25
Retained earnings	5
Total liabilities and stockholders' equity	$75

Although net income was $5 million, cash flow from operating activities was a negative $5 million. This just didn't make any sense to your boss.

Required:

Prepare a memo explaining how net income could be positive and operating cash flows negative. Include in your report a determination of operating cash flows of negative $5 million using the *indirect* method.

Earnings Management

AP11–8 Bryan Eubank began his accounting career as an auditor for a Big 4 CPA firm. He focused on clients in the high-technology sector, becoming an expert on topics such as inventory write-downs, stock options, and business acquisitions. Impressed with his technical skills and experience, General Electronics, a large consumer electronics chain, hired Bryan as the company controller responsible for all of the accounting functions within the corporation. Bryan was excited about his new position—for about a week, until he took the first careful look at General Electronics' financial statements.

The cause of Bryan's change in attitude is the set of financial statements he's been staring at for the past few hours. For some time prior to his recruitment, he had been aware that his new employer had experienced a long trend of moderate profitability. The reports on his desk confirm the slight but steady improvements in net income in recent years. The disturbing trend Bryan is now noticing, though, is a decline in cash flows from operations. Bryan has sketched out the following comparison ($ in millions):

	2018	2017	2016	2015
Operating income	$1,400	$1,320	$1,275	$1,270
Net income	385	350	345	295
Cash flows from operations	16	110	120	155

Profits? Yes. Increasing profits? Yes. So what is the cause of his distress? The trend in cash flows from operations, which is going in the opposite direction of net income. Upon closer review, Bryan noticed a couple events that, unfortunately, seem related:

a. The company's credit policy has been loosened, credit terms relaxed, and payment periods lengthened. This has resulted in a large increase in accounts receivable.

b. Several of the company's salary arrangements, including that of the CEO and CFO, are based on reported net income.

Required:

1. What is likely causing the increase in accounts receivable? How does an increase in accounts receivable affect net income differently than operating cash flows?
2. Explain why salary arrangements for officers, such as the CEO and CFO, might increase the risk of earnings management.
3. Why is the trend in cash flows from operations, combined with the additional events, such a concern for Bryan?
4. What course of action, if any, should Bryan take?

Answers to the Self-Study Questions

1. b 2. c 3. c 4. b 5. a 6. d 7. b 8. c 9. d 10. c

Financial Statement Analysis

Learning Objectives

AFTER STUDYING THIS CHAPTER, YOU SHOULD BE ABLE TO:

- **LO12–1** Perform vertical analysis.
- **LO12–2** Perform horizontal analysis.
- **LO12–3** Use ratios to analyze a company's risk.
- **LO12–4** Use ratios to analyze a company's profitability.
- **LO12–5** Distinguish persistent earnings from one-time items.
- **LO12–6** Distinguish between conservative and aggressive accounting practices.

UNDER ARMOUR: MAKING THE COMPETITION SWEAT

It started with a simple plan to make a superior T-shirt—a shirt that provides compression and removes perspiration from your skin rather than absorbs it. Founded in 1996 by former University of Maryland football player Kevin Plank, **Under Armour** is now widely recognized for its performance apparel—clothing designed to keep athletes cool, dry, and light. With its introduction of football cleats, Under Armour has joined **Nike** and **Reebok** as one of only three authorized footwear suppliers for the National Football League.

The company has expanded beyond football to supply athletic apparel for nearly every major sport. Under Armour has endorsement contracts with top professional athletes such as Tom Brady and Dez Bryant (football), Stephen Curry (basketball), Bryce Harper (baseball), Jordan Spieth (golf), Michael Phelps (swimming), and Lyndsey Vonn (skiing). The Under Armour name is even stretching overseas with a strong market presence in the United Kingdom, Canada, Europe, Japan, Australia, New Zealand, and South Africa.

Investors are very enthusiastic about Under Armour's growth potential. Many think the company is poised to become the next Nike. Why has Under Armour performed so well? Will it continue that success? What are the risks of investing in a company like Under Armour?

In this chapter, we use financial analysis tools to analyze financial statements—the same statements you've learned to prepare in the preceding chapters. The techniques we introduce here—such as vertical analysis, horizontal analysis, and ratio analysis—help in evaluating the riskiness and profitability of companies such as Under Armour and comparing them to industry leaders like Nike.

At the end of the chapter, we provide examples of conservative and aggressive accounting practices. Accounting is not black and white. Many accounting decisions fall into a gray area subject to potential earnings management.

Feature Story

© Tim Casey

© Rim Light/PhotoLink/
Photodisc/Getty Images, RF

PART A

COMPARISON OF FINANCIAL ACCOUNTING INFORMATION

We use ratios to make comparisons every day. Consider major sports. Batting averages provide feedback in baseball about how well a player is hitting. Basketball and football use points per game to compare teams' offensive and defensive performance. In each case, the ratio is more meaningful than a single number by itself. For example, are 100 hits in baseball a good number? It depends on the number of at-bats.

Likewise, we can use ratios to help evaluate a firm's performance and financial position. Is net income of $10 million a cause for shareholders to celebrate? Probably not, if shareholders' equity is $1 billion, because $10 million is then only a 1% return on equity. But if shareholders' equity is $20 million, net income of $10 million is a 50% return on equity and definitely something to celebrate. Ratios are most useful when compared to some standard. That standard of comparison may be the performance of another company, last year's performance by the same company, or the average performance of companies in the same industry. Illustration 12–1 provides a summary of these three different types of comparisons.

ILLUSTRATION 12–1   Three Types of Comparisons

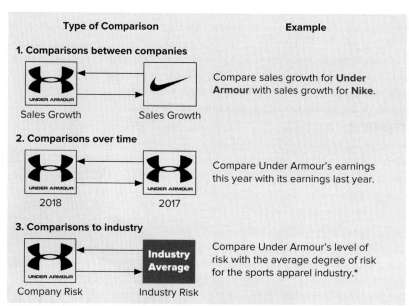

*Industry averages can be obtained from websites such as Yahoo! Finance or from financial ratings agencies such as Dun & Bradstreet, Moody's, and Standard & Poor's.

Vertical Analysis

■ **LO12–1**
Perform vertical analysis.

Common Terms Vertical analysis is also known as *common-size analysis.*

In performing vertical analysis, we express each item in a financial statement as a percentage of the same base amount. For instance, we can express each line item in an income statement as a percentage of sales. In a balance sheet, we can express each item as a percentage of total assets. Let's look at an example to see the benefits of vertical analysis.

VERTICAL ANALYSIS OF THE INCOME STATEMENT

Illustration 12–2 provides common-size income statements for **Under Armour** and **Nike**. Notice that the two companies end their fiscal years on different dates. Under Armour's year-end is December 31 while Nike's is May 31. Even though the year-ends do not exactly match, we can still make meaningful comparisons between the two companies.

ILLUSTRATION 12–2

Common-Size Income Statements

UNDER ARMOUR AND NIKE
Common-Size Income Statements
For the years ended December 31, 2014, and May 31, 2014
($ in millions)

	UNDER ARMOUR		NIKE	
	Amount	%	Amount	%
Net sales	$3,084	100.0	$27,799	100.0
Cost of goods sold	1,572	51.0	15,353	55.2
Gross profit	1,512	49.0	12,446	44.8
Operating expenses	1,158	37.5	8,766	31.5
Operating income	354	11.5	3,680	13.3
Other expense	12	0.4	136	0.5
Income before tax	342	11.1	3,544	12.8
Income tax expense	134	4.4	851	3.1
Net income	$ 208	6.7	$ 2,693	9.7

The red arrow indicates the direction in which to read this statement.

What do we learn from this comparison? Nike reports net income of almost $2.7 billion while Under Armour reports only $208 million. Does this mean Nike's operations are much more profitable than Under Armour's? Not necessarily. Nike is a much larger company, reporting sales over $27 billion compared to $3 billion for Under Armour. Because of its greater size, we expect Nike to report a greater *amount* of net income. To better compare the performance of the two companies, we use vertical analysis to express each income statement item as a *percentage of sales.*

Under Armour's gross profit equals 49.0% of sales ($1,512 ÷ $3,084) compared to Nike's 44.8%. This means that Under Armour earns a slightly higher gross profit for each dollar of sales, consistent with its business strategy of focusing on high-quality performance apparel. However, Under Armour's higher gross profit is offset by its proportionately higher operating expenses, 37.5% of sales compared to 31.5% for Nike. The net result is that operating income, as a percentage of sales, is slightly lower for Under Armour. Finally, Nike's net income, as a percentage of sales, exceeds Under Armour's by 3%. This is explained by Nike's slightly better operating income as a percentage of sales, and it appears Nike has a lower portion of income reduced for income tax expense.

Decision Point

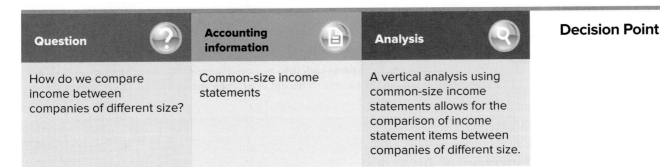

Question	Accounting information	Analysis
How do we compare income between companies of different size?	Common-size income statements	A vertical analysis using common-size income statements allows for the comparison of income statement items between companies of different size.

VERTICAL ANALYSIS OF THE BALANCE SHEET

Vertical analysis of the balance sheet is useful, too. For this, we divide each balance sheet item by total assets to get an idea of its relative significance. Illustration 12–3 provides common-size balance sheets for **Under Armour** and **Nike**.

What can we learn by analyzing the common-size balance sheets? Focusing on the asset portion of the balance sheet, we discover that Under Armour has a higher percentage of

ILLUSTRATION 12–3

Common-Size Balance Sheets

The red arrow indicates the direction in which to read this statement.

		UNDER ARMOUR		NIKE	
		Amount	**%**	**Amount**	**%**
UNDER ARMOUR AND NIKE					
Common-Size Balance Sheets					
December 31, 2014, and May 31, 2014					
($ in millions)					
Assets					
Current assets		$1,549	73.9	$13,696	73.7
Property and equipment		306	14.6	2,834	15.2
Intangible assets		149	7.1	413	2.2
Other assets		91	4.4	1,651	8.9
Total assets		$2,095	100.0	$18,594	100.0
Liabilities and Stockholders' Equity					
Current liabilities		$ 422	20.2	$ 5,027	27.0
Long-term liabilities		323	15.4	2,743	14.8
Common stock		493	23.5	5,953	32.0
Retained earnings		857	40.9	4,871	26.2
Total liabilities and stockholders' equity		$2,095	100.0	$18,594	100.0

intangible assets than Nike and a slightly lower share of assets invested in property and equipment. Nike has a higher percentage of other assets.

Looking at liabilities and stockholders' equity, we see that Nike has a slightly higher portion of current liabilities. As we will see later in the ratio analysis in Part B, Nike's higher current liabilities will result in a less favorable current ratio and acid-test ratio. Both companies maintain similar proportions of long-term liabilities (15.4% and 14.8%) and are financed to a greater extent by equity than by debt.

Finally, it's interesting to note the relative contributions of common stock and retained earnings for the two companies. For Under Armour, the balance in retained earnings exceeds the balance in common stock, indicating the profits retained in the company exceed the amounts originally invested in the company. For Nike, the balance in common stock exceeds the balance in retained earnings, indicating the amounts invested by shareholders exceed the profits retained.

KEY POINT

With vertical analysis, we express each item as a percentage of the same base amount, such as a percentage of sales in the income statement or as a percentage of total assets in the balance sheet.

Horizontal Analysis

■ **LO12–2**

Perform horizontal analysis.

Common Terms
Horizontal analysis is also known as *trend analysis* or *time-series analysis*.

We use horizontal analysis to analyze trends in financial statement data for a single company over time. With horizontal analysis, we calculate the amount and percentage change in an account from last year to this year. This data can then be used to compare rates of change across accounts. Are sales growing faster than cost of goods sold? Are operating expenses growing faster than sales? Are any specific expenses increasing at a greater rate than others? Questions such as these can help identify areas of concern or, perhaps, indications of better things to come.

HORIZONTAL ANALYSIS OF THE INCOME STATEMENT

Illustration 12–4 provides income statements over two years for Under Armour. The final two columns show the dollar amount and percentage changes.

ILLUSTRATION 12–4

Horizontal Analysis of Under Armour's Income Statements

UNDER ARMOUR Income Statements For the years ended December 31 ($ in millions)				
	Year		**Increase (Decrease)**	
	2014	**2013**	**Amount**	**%**
Net sales	$3,084	$2,332	$752	32.2
Cost of goods sold	1,572	1,195	377	31.5
Gross profit	1,512	1,137	375	33.0
Operating expenses	1,158	872	286	32.8
Operating income	354	265	89	33.6
Other expense	12	4	8	200.0
Income before tax	342	261	81	31.0
Income tax expense	134	99	35	35.4
Net income	$ 208	$ 162	$ 46	28.4

The red arrow indicates the direction in which to read this statement.

We calculate the *amount* of the increases or decreases by simply subtracting the 2013 balance from the 2014 balance. A positive difference indicates the amount increased in 2014. A negative amount represents a decrease, which we record in parentheses. We calculate the *percentage* increase or decrease based on the following formula:

$$\% \text{ Increase (Decrease)} = \frac{\text{Current-year amount} - \text{Prior-year amount}}{\text{Prior-year amount}}$$

In our example, the calculation would be:

$$\% \text{ Increase (Decrease)} = \frac{2014 \text{ amount} - 2013 \text{ amount}}{2013 \text{ amount}}$$

For example, the *amount* of sales increased $752 million—equal to sales of $3,084 million in 2014 minus sales of $2,332 million in 2013. We calculate the *percentage* increase of 32.2% by dividing the $752 million increase in sales by 2013 sales of $2,332 million. If the base-year amount (2013 in our example) is ever zero, we can't calculate a percentage for that item.

The horizontal analysis of Under Armour's income statement demonstrates strong, steady growth in company operations. Gross profit increased 33.0% ($375 ÷ $1,137), operating income increased 33.6% ($89 ÷ $265), income before tax increased 31.0% ($81 ÷ $261), and net income increased 28.4% ($46 ÷ $162). The growth in these income measures definitely is impressive.

HORIZONTAL ANALYSIS OF THE BALANCE SHEET

Illustration 12–5 provides balance sheet information for Under Armour for 2014 and 2013, with amount and percentage changes in the final two columns.

The horizontal analysis of Under Armour's balance sheet further reflects its growth in operations during the year. Each of the categories increased, with the exception of a slight decrease in current liabilities. Besides reinvesting profits in the company, Under Armour is funding its growth with both long-term debt and issuing additional shares. Long-term liabilities increased by $226 million and Under Armour had a stock offering again in 2014,

ILLUSTRATION 12–5

Horizontal Analysis
of Under Armour's
Balance Sheets

UNDER ARMOUR Balance Sheets December 31 ($ in millions)				
	Year		**Increase (Decrease)**	
	2014	**2013**	**Amount**	**%**
Assets				
Current assets	$1,549	$1,129	$420	37.2
Property and equipment	306	224	82	36.6
Intangible assets	149	146	3	2.1
Other assets	91	79	12	15.2
Total assets	$2,095	$1,578	$517	32.8
Liabilities and Stockholders' Equity				
Current liabilities	$ 422	$ 427	$ (5)	(1.2)
Long-term liabilities	323	97	226	233.0
Common stock	493	400	93	23.3
Retained earnings	857	654	203	31.0
Total liabilities and stockholders' equity	$2,095	$1,578	$517	32.8

The red arrow indicates
the direction in which to
read this statement.

as reflected in the $93 million increase in common stock. Retained earnings increased $203 million, or 31.0%, due primarily to net income of $208 million during the year.

 **KEY POINT**

We use horizontal analysis to analyze trends in financial statement data, such as the amount of change and the percentage change, for one company over time.

Let's Review

mhhe.com/4fa48

The income statements for **Nike** for the years ending May 31, 2014 and 2013, are as follows:

NIKE Income Statements For the years ended May 31 ($ in millions)				
			Increase (Decrease)	
	2014	**2013**	**Amount**	**%**
Net sales	$27,799	$25,313		
Cost of goods sold	15,353	14,279		
Gross profit	12,446	11,034		
Operating expenses	8,766	7,796		
Operating income	3,680	3,238		
Other income (expense)	(136)	39		
Income before tax	3,544	3,277		
Income tax expense	851	805		
Net income	$ 2,693	$ 2,472		

Required:

Complete the "Amount" and "%" columns in a horizontal analysis of Nike's income statements. Discuss the meaning of the major fluctuations during the year.

Solution:

NIKE Income Statements For the years ended May 31 ($ in millions)				
			Increase (Decrease)	
	2014	**2013**	**Amount**	**%**
Net sales	$27,799	$25,313	$2,486	9.8
Cost of goods sold	15,353	14,279	1,074	7.5
Gross profit	12,446	11,034	1,412	12.8
Operating expenses	8,766	7,796	970	12.4
Operating income	3,680	3,238	442	13.7
Other income (expense)	(136)	39	(175)	N/A
Income before tax	3,544	3,277	267	8.1
Income tax expense	851	805	46	5.7
Net income	$ 2,693	$ 2,472	$ 221	8.9

Nike's sales and cost of goods sold increased 9.8% and 7.5%, respectively, over the previous year. These changes resulted in a 12.8% increase in gross profit in comparison to the previous year. Operating expenses increased 12.4% and operating income increased 13.7%. Nike reported other income of $39 million in 2013, but recorded other expense of $136 million in 2014. This increase in other expenses of $175 million helps explain why the percentage increases in income before tax (8.1%) and net income (8.9%) are less than the percentage increase in operating income (13.7%) for the year. Note that Nike's net income growth of 8.9% is good, but falls way short of Under Armour's net income growth of 28.4% for the same year.

Suggested Homework:
BE12–1, BE12–2;
E12–2, E12–3;
P12–2A&B, P12–3A&B

USING RATIOS TO ASSESS RISK AND PROFITABILITY

Beginning in Chapter 4, we provided an example of ratio analysis between two competing companies at the end of each chapter. Let's now apply what we learned in those separate ratio analyses in a detailed examination of **Under Armour**, comparing the results to the sports apparel industry leader—**Nike**. The income statement and balance sheet for Under Armour are presented in Illustration 12–6.

We'll review 14 ratios classified into two categories: risk ratios and profitability ratios. When calculating ratios, remember how income statement accounts differ from balance sheet accounts: We measure income statement accounts over a *period* of time (like a video).

 COMMON MISTAKE

In comparing an income statement account with a balance sheet account, some students incorrectly use the balance sheet account's ending balance, rather than the *average* of its beginning and ending balances. Since income statement accounts are measured over a period of time, comparisons to related balance sheet accounts also need to be over time by taking the average of the beginning and ending balances.

ILLUSTRATION 12–6

Under Armour's
Financial Statements

UNDER ARMOUR Income Statement For the year ended December 31, 2014 ($ in millions)	
	2014
Net sales	$3,084
Cost of goods sold	1,572
Gross profit	1,512
Operating expenses	1,158
Operating income	354
Other expense	12*
Income before tax	342
Income tax expense	134
Net income	$ 208

*Other expense includes interest expense of $5 million

UNDER ARMOUR Balance Sheets December 31 ($ in millions)		
	2014	**2013**
Assets		
Current assets:		
Cash	$ 593	$ 348
Net receivables	332	248
Inventory	537	469
Other current assets	87	64
Total current assets	1,549	1,129
Property and equipment	306	224
Intangible assets	149	146
Other assets	91	79
Total assets	$2,095	$1,578
Liabilities and Stockholders' Equity		
Current liabilities	$ 422	$ 427
Long-term liabilities	323	97
Stockholders' equity	1,350	1,054
Total liabilities and stockholders' equity	$2,095	$1,578

We measure balance sheet accounts at a *point* in time (like a photograph). Therefore, ratios that compare an income statement account with a balance sheet account should express the balance sheet account as an *average* of the beginning and ending balances.

Risk Analysis

■ **LO12–3**

Use ratios to analyze a company's risk.

Illustration 12–7 summarizes eight risk ratios, the chapters in which we discussed them, and how they're calculated. We divide the eight risk ratios into six liquidity ratios and two solvency ratios. Liquidity refers to having sufficient cash (or other assets readily convertible into cash) to pay its *current* liabilities. The accounts used to calculate liquidity ratios are located in the current assets and current liabilities sections of the balance sheet. Solvency refers to a company's ability to pay its *long-term* liabilities as well.

Let's calculate each of the eight risk ratios for Under Armour and then compare the results with Nike's. **We show the detailed calculations for Nike in a review problem at the end of this section.**

RECEIVABLES TURNOVER RATIO

The receivables turnover ratio measures how many times, on average, a company collects its receivables during the year. A low receivables turnover ratio may indicate that the company is having trouble collecting its accounts receivable. A high receivables turnover ratio is a positive sign that a company can quickly turn its receivables into cash. Illustration 12–8 shows the calculation of the receivables turnover ratio for Under Armour and compares it to Nike's.

CAREER CORNER

Investors and creditors, as well as suppliers, customers, employees, and the government among others, rely heavily on financial accounting information. Who checks big companies like Under Armour and Nike to make sure they are reporting accurately? Auditors. Many accounting majors begin their careers in auditing. They then use the experience they gain in auditing to obtain management and accounting positions in private industry, sometimes even with a company they previously audited.

However, auditing is not just for accounting majors. Finance majors are hired as auditors in the banking and insurance industries. Management information systems (MIS) majors are hired to audit computer systems. Management majors are hired to audit the effectiveness and efficiency of management operations. There even are marketing auditors, who identify strengths and weaknesses in marketing strategy and overall marketing structures.[1] Analysis skills, like those covered in this chapter, are the types of skills necessary for a successful career in auditing, and for that matter, in almost any career in business.

© BananaStock Ltd/Imagine, RF

ILLUSTRATION 12–7 Risk Ratios

Risk Ratios	Chapter	Calculations
Liquidity		
Receivables turnover ratio	5	$\dfrac{\text{Net credit sales}}{\text{Average accounts receivable}}$
Average collection period	5	$\dfrac{365 \text{ days}}{\text{Receivables turnover ratio}}$
Inventory turnover ratio	6	$\dfrac{\text{Cost of goods sold}}{\text{Average inventory}}$
Average days in inventory	6	$\dfrac{365 \text{ days}}{\text{Inventory turnover ratio}}$
Current ratio	8	$\dfrac{\text{Current assets}}{\text{Current liabilities}}$
Acid-test ratio	8	$\dfrac{\text{Cash} + \text{Current investments} + \text{Accounts receivable}}{\text{Current liabilities}}$
Solvency		
Debt to equity ratio	9	$\dfrac{\text{Total liabilities}}{\text{Stockholders' equity}}$
Times interest earned ratio	9	$\dfrac{\text{Net income} + \text{Interest expense} + \text{Tax expense}}{\text{Interest expense}}$

Receivables Turnover Ratio	Under Armour	Nike
$\dfrac{\text{Net credit sales}}{\text{Average accounts receivable}}$	$\dfrac{\$3,084}{(\$248 + \$332)/2} = 10.6 \text{ times}$	7.7 times

ILLUSTRATION 12–8

Receivables Turnover Ratio

---

[1] J. Mylonakis. 2003. "Functions and Responsibilities of Marketing Auditors in Measuring Organizational Performance." *International Journal of Technology Management 25*, no. 8, pp. 814–25.

In calculating the receivables turnover ratio, we have assumed that Under Armour's sales are all credit sales. (Under Armour does not usually sell directly to customers, but to retailers such as **Dick's Sporting Goods**.) The bottom half of the fraction is the *average* accounts receivable during the year, calculated as beginning receivables plus ending receivables divided by two. Under Armour's receivables turnover ratio is 10.6, indicating that receivables turn over (are collected) 10.6 times per year. This is much higher than Nike's receivables turnover ratio of 7.7.

AVERAGE COLLECTION PERIOD

We often convert the receivables turnover ratio into days and call it the average collection period. The shorter the average collection period, the better. Illustration 12–9 displays the average collection period for Under Armour and Nike.

ILLUSTRATION 12–9

Average Collection Period

Average Collection Period	Under Armour	Nike
$\dfrac{365 \text{ days}}{\text{Receivables turnover ratio}}$	$\dfrac{365}{10.6} = 34.4 \text{ days}$	47.4 days

Under Armour's average collection period of 34.4 days is 365 days divided by the receivables turnover ratio of 10.6. It takes Under Armour an average of over one month (34.4 days) to collect its accounts receivable. Nike's average collection period, at 47.4 days, is almost two weeks longer.

INVENTORY TURNOVER RATIO

The inventory turnover ratio measures how many times, on average, a company sells its entire inventory during the year. A high inventory turnover ratio usually is a positive sign. It indicates that inventory is selling quickly, less cash is tied up in inventory, and the risk of outdated inventory is lower. However, an extremely high inventory turnover ratio might be a signal that the company is losing sales due to inventory shortages. Illustration 12–10 provides the inventory turnover ratios for Under Armour and Nike.

ILLUSTRATION 12–10

Inventory Turnover Ratio

Inventory Turnover Ratio	Under Armour	Nike
$\dfrac{\text{Cost of goods sold}}{\text{Average inventory}}$	$\dfrac{\$1,572}{(\$469 + \$537)/2} = 3.1 \text{ times}$	4.1 times

Inventory at Under Armour turns over, on average, 3.1 times per year compared to 4.1 times per year at Nike. The slower inventory turnover at Under Armour is a negative sign, indicating a greater risk of slow-moving inventory items.

AVERAGE DAYS IN INVENTORY

We can convert the inventory turnover ratio into days and call it the average days in inventory. As you can imagine, companies try to minimize the number of days they hold inventory. We calculate the average days in inventory in Illustration 12–11.

ILLUSTRATION 12–11

Average Days in Inventory

Average Days in Inventory	Under Armour	Nike
$\dfrac{365 \text{ days}}{\text{Inventory turnover ratio}}$	$\dfrac{365}{3.1} = 117.7 \text{ days}$	89.0 days

Under Armour's average days in inventory is 117.7 days, calculated as 365 days divided by the inventory turnover ratio of 3.1. In comparison, Nike's average days in inventory is much lower at 89.0 days.

Inventory turnover ratios and the resulting average days in inventory vary significantly by industry. For example, compared with the sporting goods apparel industry, the dairy industry with its perishable products has a much higher inventory turnover, and car dealerships have a lower inventory turnover. Inventory turnover might even vary by product within the same industry. For instance, within the dairy industry, the inventory turnover for milk is much higher than that for aged cheddar cheese. Similarly, within the auto industry, the inventory turnover for cars like the Toyota Corolla is much higher than for the higher-priced Toyota Land Cruiser.

CURRENT RATIO

The current ratio compares current assets to current liabilities. It's probably the most widely used of all liquidity ratios. A high current ratio indicates that a company has sufficient current assets to pay current liabilities as they become due. Illustration 12–12 presents the current ratios for Under Armour and Nike.

Current Ratio	Under Armour	Nike
Current assets	$\dfrac{\$1,549}{\$422} = 3.7$ to 1	2.7 to 1
Current liabilities		

ILLUSTRATION 12–12

Current Ratio

Under Armour's current ratio of 3.7 means the firm has $3.70 in current assets for each $1 in current liabilities. Under Armour's current ratio is higher than Nike's current ratio of 2.7. A company needs to maintain sufficient current assets to pay current liabilities as they become due. Thus, a higher current ratio usually indicates less risk.

However, a high current ratio is not always a good signal. A high current ratio might occur when a company has difficulty collecting receivables or carries too much inventory. Analysts become concerned if a company reports an increasing current ratio combined with either a lower receivables turnover ratio or a lower inventory turnover ratio.

ETHICAL DILEMMA

© Ian M Butterfield [004 MKY]/Alamy

Michael Hechtner was recently hired as an assistant controller for Athletic Persuasions, a recognized leader in the promotion of athletic events. However, the past year has been a difficult one for the company's operations. In order to help with slowing sales, the company has extended credit to more customers and accepted payment over longer time periods, resulting in a significant increase in accounts receivable. Similarly, with slowing sales, its inventory of promotional supplies has increased dramatically.

One afternoon, Michael joined the controller, J.P. Sloan, for a visit with their primary lender, First National Bank. Athletic Persuasions had used up its line of credit and was looking to borrow additional funds. In meeting with the loan officer at the bank, Michael was surprised at the positive spin J.P. Sloan put on the company operations. J.P. exclaimed, "Athletic Persuasions continues to prosper in a difficult environment. Our current assets have significantly increased in relation to current liabilities, resulting in a much improved current ratio over the prior year. It seems wherever I look, the company has been successful."

Is there anything unethical in the controller's statement to the banker? What should Michael do in this situation? Is it acceptable for Michael just to keep quiet?

ACID-TEST RATIO

The acid-test ratio is similar to the current ratio but is a more conservative measure of current assets available to pay current liabilities. Specifically, the top part of the fraction includes only cash, current investments, and accounts receivable. Because it eliminates current assets such as inventories and prepaid expenses that are less readily convertible into cash, the acid-test ratio often provides a better indication of a company's liquidity than does the current ratio. We calculate the acid-test ratio in Illustration 12–13.

ILLUSTRATION 12–13
Acid-Test Ratio

Acid-Test Ratio	Under Armour	Nike
$\dfrac{\text{Cash + Current investments + Accounts receivable}}{\text{Current liabilities}}$	$\dfrac{\$593 + \$0 + \$332}{\$422} = 2.2 \text{ to } 1$	1.8 to 1

Under Armour did not report any current investments, so a $0 is recorded for current investments in the top part of the fraction. Under Armour's acid-test ratio is 2.2 to 1 and compares favorably with Nike's ratio of 1.8 to 1. Both companies appear to have more than enough liquid assets available to pay current liabilities as they become due.

DEBT TO EQUITY RATIO

The first six ratios we covered relate to liquidity, or a company's ability to pay its current liabilities. The final two ratios we cover (debt to equity and times interest earned) relate to solvency, or a company's ability to pay its long-term liabilities as well.

Other things being equal, the higher the debt to equity ratio, the higher the risk of bankruptcy. The reason is that, unlike shareholders, debt holders have the ability to force a company into bankruptcy for failing to pay interest or repay the debt in a timely manner. Illustration 12–14 shows the calculation of the debt to equity ratio for Under Armour and Nike.

ILLUSTRATION 12–14
Debt to Equity Ratio

Debt to Equity Ratio	Under Armour	Nike
$\dfrac{\text{Total liabilities}}{\text{Stockholders' equity}}$	$\dfrac{\$422 + \$323}{\$1,350} = 55.2\%$	71.8%

Under Armour has a debt to equity ratio of 55.2%, or about $0.55 in liabilities for each $1 in stockholders' equity. Nike's debt to equity ratio is higher, at 71.8%.

Additional debt can be good for investors, as long as a company earns a return on borrowed funds in excess of interest costs. However, taking on additional debt can also be bad for investors, if interest costs exceed a company's return on borrowed funds. This highlights the risk-return trade-off of debt. More debt increases the risk of bankruptcy, but it also increases the potential returns investors can enjoy.

TIMES INTEREST EARNED RATIO

We use the times interest earned ratio to compare interest payments with a company's income available to pay those charges. Interest payments are more often associated with long-term liabilities than with current liabilities such as wages, taxes, and utilities. That's why we classify this ratio as a solvency ratio rather than a liquidity ratio.

We calculate the times interest earned ratio by dividing net income *before* interest expense and income taxes by interest expense. To get to this amount, we just add interest expense and tax expense back to net income. We use net income before interest expense and income taxes as a reliable indicator of the amount available to pay the interest. Illustration 12–15 shows how the ratio is calculated.

Under Armour's interest expense of $5 million is not listed separately on the income statement, but rather, is obtained from the notes to the financial statements. The times

Times Interest Earned Ratio	Under Armour	Nike
$\dfrac{\text{Net income} + \text{Interest expense} + \text{Tax expense}}{\text{Interest expense}}$	$\dfrac{\$208 + \$5 + \$134}{\$5} = 69.4$ times	108.4 times

ILLUSTRATION 12–15

Times Interest Earned Ratio

interest earned ratio for Under Armour is 69.4. That means Under Armour's net income before interest and taxes was 69.4 times the amount it needed for interest expense alone. In comparison, Nike has an even better times interest earned ratio of 108.4. Both Under Armour and Nike generate more than enough income to cover their interest payments.

KEY POINT

We categorize risk ratios into liquidity ratios and solvency ratios. Liquidity ratios focus on the company's ability to pay *current* liabilities, whereas solvency ratios focus more on *long-term* liabilities.

The income statement and balance sheets for **Nike** are shown below.

Let's Review

mhhe.com/4fa49

NIKE
Income Statement
For the year ended May 31, 2014
($ in millions)

Net sales	$27,799
Cost of goods sold	15,353
Gross profit	12,446
Operating expenses	8,766
Operating income	3,680
Other income (expense)	(136)*
Income before tax	3,544
Income tax expense	851
Net income	$ 2,693

*Includes interest expense of $33 million

NIKE
Balance Sheets
May 31
($ in millions)

	2014	2013
Assets		
Current assets:		
Cash	$ 2,220	$ 3,337
Current investments	2,922	2,628
Net receivables	3,789	3,425
Inventory	3,947	3,484
Other current assets	818	756
Total current assets	13,696	13,630
Property and equipment	2,834	2,452
Intangible assets	413	420
Other assets	1,651	1,043
Total assets	$18,594	$17,545

(*continued*)

(concluded)

NIKE Balance Sheets May 31 ($ in millions)		
	2014	**2013**
Liabilities and Stockholders' Equity		
Current liabilities	$ 5,027	$ 3,962
Long-term liabilities	2,743	2,502
Stockholders' equity	10,824	11,081
Total liabilities and stockholders' equity	$18,594	$17,545

Required:

Calculate the eight risk ratios we've discussed for Nike for the year ended May 31, 2014.

Solution:

Risk Ratios	Calculations	
Liquidity		
Receivables turnover ratio	$$\frac{\$27,799}{(\$3,425 + \$3,789)/2}$$	= 7.7 times
Average collection period	$$\frac{365}{7.7}$$	= 47.4 days
Inventory turnover ratio	$$\frac{\$15,353}{(\$3,484 + \$3,947)/2}$$	= 4.1 times
Average days in inventory	$$\frac{365}{4.1}$$	= 89.0 days
Current ratio	$$\frac{\$13,696}{\$5,027}$$	= 2.7 to 1
Acid-test ratio	$$\frac{\$2,220 + \$2,922 + \$3,789}{\$5,027}$$	= 1.8 to 1
Solvency		
Debt to equity ratio	$$\frac{\$5,027 + \$2,743}{\$10,824}$$	= 71.8%
Times interest earned ratio	$$\frac{\$2,693 + \$33 + \$851}{\$33}$$	= 108.4 times

Suggested Homework:
BE12–6, BE12–7;
E12–5, E12–7;
P12–4A&B, P12–6A&B

Profitability Analysis

■ **LO12–4**
Use ratios to analyze a company's profitability.

Our next six ratios focus on profitability, the primary measure of company success. Profitability ratios measure the earnings or operating effectiveness of a company. Not only is profitability necessary just to survive as a company, it's the primary indicator used by investors and creditors in making financial decisions. Illustration 12–16 summarizes the six profitability ratios we have examined, the chapters in which we discussed them, and how we calculate them.

ILLUSTRATION 12–16

Profitability Ratios

Profitability Ratios	Chapter	Calculations
Gross profit ratio	6	$\dfrac{\text{Gross profit}}{\text{Net sales}}$
Return on assets	7	$\dfrac{\text{Net income}}{\text{Average total assets}}$
Profit margin	7	$\dfrac{\text{Net income}}{\text{Net sales}}$
Asset turnover	7	$\dfrac{\text{Net sales}}{\text{Average total assets}}$
Return on equity	10	$\dfrac{\text{Net income}}{\text{Average stockholders' equity}}$
Price-earnings ratio	10	$\dfrac{\text{Stock price}}{\text{Earnings per share}}$

GROSS PROFIT RATIO

The gross profit ratio indicates the portion of each dollar of sales above its cost of goods sold. We calculate this ratio as gross profit (net sales minus cost of goods sold) divided by net sales. Gross profit ratios vary by industry. For example, consider the average gross profit ratio for the following major industries: retail grocery stores (27%), apparel stores (35%), and major drug manufacturers (68%). Illustration 12–17 presents the calculation of the gross profit ratio for Under Armour and a comparison with Nike. **We'll calculate Nike's profitability ratios in a review problem at the end of this section.**

Common Terms Gross profit is also called *gross margin* or *gross profit margin.*

ILLUSTRATION 12–17

Gross Profit Ratio

Gross Profit Ratio	Under Armour	Nike
$\dfrac{\text{Gross profit}}{\text{Net sales}}$	$\dfrac{\$1,512}{\$3,084} = 49.0\%$	44.8%

With a gross profit ratio of 49.0%, Under Armour sells its merchandise for about twice what it costs to produce. In comparison, Nike has a gross profit ratio of 44.8%. Nike's gross profit is still quite high, but not as high as Under Armour's.

Gross profit ratios normally decline as competition increases. For example, a patented drug can sell for many times its production cost. However, when the patent expires, competition from generic drug companies drives down selling prices, resulting in lower gross profit ratios.

Decision Maker's Perspective

How Warren Buffett Interprets Financial Statements

Warren Buffett is one of the world's wealthiest individuals, with investments in the billions. As founder and CEO of **Berkshire Hathaway**, an investment company located in Omaha, Nebraska, he is also highly regarded as one of the world's top investment advisors. So, what's the secret to his success? Warren Buffett is best known for his attention to details, carefully examining each line in the financial statements.

Warren Buffett seeks to invest in companies with a "durable competitive advantage." That means he is looking for profitable companies that can maintain their profitability over time. To find these companies, he carefully studies their income statements for evidence of above-average profits that can be sustained despite actions taken by competing companies. He also studies their balance sheets looking for financially healthy companies. Some of his major investments include **GEICO, Burlington Northern, Coca-Cola, Dairy Queen, Duracell, Heinz, See's Candies,** and **Fruit of the Loom.** Warren Buffett uses ratios just like the ones covered in this chapter, but it's his unique ability to interpret those ratios in selecting the best possible investments that sets him apart.

RETURN ON ASSETS

Common Terms Return on assets is referred to as *ROA*.

Return on assets measures the income the company earns on each dollar invested in assets. We calculate it as net income divided by *average* (not *ending*) total assets. Average total assets are calculated as beginning total assets plus ending total assets divided by 2. Illustration 12–18 provides the calculation of return on assets for Under Armour and a comparison to Nike.

ILLUSTRATION 12–18

Return on Assets

Return on Assets	Under Armour	Nike
$\dfrac{\text{Net income}}{\text{Average total assets}}$	$\dfrac{\$208}{(\$1,578 + \$2,095)/2} = 11.3\%$	14.9%

Under Armour earned a return on assets of 11.3%, which is lower than Nike's return on assets of 14.9%. As we learned in Chapter 7, we can further separate return on assets into two ratios: profit margin and asset turnover. Illustration 12–19 shows the calculations.

ILLUSTRATION 12–19

Components of Return on Assets

Return on Assets	=	Profit margin	×	Asset turnover
$\dfrac{\text{Net income}}{\text{Average total assets}}$	$=$	$\dfrac{\text{Net income}}{\text{Net sales}}$	$\times$	$\dfrac{\text{Net sales}}{\text{Average total assets}}$

Some companies, like **Saks Fifth Avenue**, rely more on high profit margins, while other companies, like **Dollar General**, rely more on asset turnover. Investors are especially intrigued by companies that can obtain both—high profit margins and high asset turnover. For example, **Apple Inc.** introduced several extremely popular products such as the iPhone and the Apple watch that generate both high profit margin and high asset turnover for the company.

PROFIT MARGIN

Profit margin measures the income earned on each dollar of sales. We calculate it by dividing net income by net sales. Illustration 12–20 provides the calculation of profit margin for Under Armour and Nike.

ILLUSTRATION 12–20

Profit Margin

Profit Margin	Under Armour	Nike
$\dfrac{\text{Net income}}{\text{Net sales}}$	$\dfrac{\$208}{\$3,084} = 6.7\%$	9.7%

Under Armour has a profit margin of 6.7%, meaning that for every dollar of sales, almost 7 cents goes toward net income. Nike has a higher profit margin of 9.7%. Now let's look at asset turnover, the second factor influencing return on assets.

ASSET TURNOVER

Asset turnover measures sales volume in relation to the investment in assets. We calculate asset turnover as sales divided by *average* (not *ending*) total assets. Illustration 12–21 presents the calculation of asset turnover.

ILLUSTRATION 12–21

Asset Turnover

Asset Turnover	Under Armour	Nike
$\dfrac{\text{Net sales}}{\text{Average total assets}}$	$\dfrac{\$3,084}{(\$1,578 + \$2,095)/2} = 1.7$ times	1.5 times

Under Armour's asset turnover is 1.7. Under Armour generates $1.70 in annual sales for every dollar it invests in assets. Nike's asset turnover is just slightly lower at 1.5.

RETURN ON EQUITY

Return on equity measures the income earned for each dollar in stockholders' equity. Return on equity relates net income to the investment made by owners of the business. The ratio is calculated by dividing net income by *average* stockholders' equity. Average stockholders' equity is calculated as beginning stockholders' equity plus ending stockholders' equity divided by 2. Illustration 12–22 shows the calculation of return on equity.

Common Terms Return on equity is referred to as *ROE*.

ILLUSTRATION 12–22

Return on Equity

Return on Equity	Under Armour	Nike
$\dfrac{\text{Net income}}{\text{Average stockholders' equity}}$	$\dfrac{\$208}{(\$1,054 + \$1,350)/2} = 17.3\%$	24.6%

Under Armour has a return on equity of 17.3%. Its net income is 17.3 cents for every dollar invested in equity. Nike has an even higher return on equity of 24.6%.

Why is Nike's return on assets 3.6 percentage points higher than Under Armour's, while its return on equity is 7.3 percentage points higher than Under Armour's? The answer relates to *financial leverage*—the amount of debt each company carries. Recall that Nike has a higher debt to equity ratio. Remember, too, that debt can be good for the company as long as the return on investment exceeds the interest cost of borrowing. Both Under Armour and Nike enjoy returns well in excess of the interest cost on borrowed funds. By carrying greater debt, Nike is able to provide a higher return on equity in relationship to its return on assets, further benefiting the investors in the company.

PRICE-EARNINGS RATIO

The price-earnings (PE) ratio compares a company's share price with its earnings per share. The PE ratio is an indication of investors' expectations of future earnings for the company. Illustration 12–23 presents the PE ratios for Under Armour and Nike.

ILLUSTRATION 12–23

Price-Earnings Ratio

Price-Earnings Ratio	Under Armour	Nike
$\dfrac{\text{Stock price}}{\text{Earnings per share}}$	$\dfrac{\$67.90}{\$0.98} = 69.3$	25.2

At the end of 2014, Under Armour's closing stock price was $67.90, and the company reported earnings per share for 2014 of $0.98. This represents a PE ratio of 69.3. The stock price is trading at 69 times earnings. In contrast, the PE ratio for Nike is 25.2. Stocks commonly trade at a PE ratio somewhere between 15 and 20. At 69.3, Under Armour has a very high PE ratio. It appears that, at least at this point in time, investors are more optimistic about Under Armour's future earnings potential than Nike's, as shown by the price they are willing to pay for Under Armour stock.

As we discussed in Chapter 10, investors pursue two basic types of stock investments: growth stocks and value stocks. Growth stocks, like Under Armour, have high expectations of future earnings growth and therefore usually trade at higher PE ratios. Growth stocks are said to be *great* stocks at a *good* price. Value stocks have lower share prices in relationship to their fundamental ratios and therefore trade at lower (bargain) PE ratios. Value stocks are said to be *good* stocks at a *great* price. Some investors take the strategy of picking the stocks with the best future potential (growth stocks); other investors shop for the best bargains (value stocks). Most investors take a combined approach, searching for stocks based on both future potential and current stock price.

KEY POINT

Profitability ratios measure the earnings or operating effectiveness of a company over a period of time, such as a year. Investors view profitability as the number one measure of company success.

Let's Review

The income statement and balance sheets for **Nike** follow. In addition, Nike reported earnings per share for the year ended May 31, 2014, of $3.05, and the closing stock price on May 31, 2014, was $76.91.

mhhe.com/4fa50

Required:

Calculate the six profitability ratios we've discussed for Nike for the year ended May 31, 2014.

NIKE Income Statement For the year ended May 31, 2014 ($ in millions)	
Net sales	$27,799
Cost of goods sold	15,353
Gross profit	12,446
Operating expenses	8,766
Operating income	3,680
Other income (expense)	(136)*
Income before tax	3,544
Income tax expense	851
Net income	$ 2,693

*Includes interest expense of $33 million.

NIKE Balance Sheets May 31 ($ in millions)	2014	2013
Assets		
Current assets:		
Cash	$ 2,220	$ 3,337
Current investments	2,922	2,628
Net receivables	3,789	3,425
Inventory	3,947	3,484
Other current assets	818	756
Total current assets	13,696	13,630
Property and equipment	2,834	2,452
Intangible assets	413	420
Other assets	1,651	1,043
Total assets	$18,594	$17,545

(continued)

(concluded)

NIKE
Balance Sheets
MAY 31
($ in millions)

Liabilities and Stockholders' Equity	2014	2013
Current liabilities	$ 5,027	$ 3,962
Long-term liabilities	2,743	2,502
Stockholders' equity	10,824	11,081
Total liabilities and stockholders' equity	$18,594	$17,545

Solution:

Profitability Ratios	Calculations	
Gross profit ratio	$\dfrac{\$12,446}{\$27,799}$	= 44.8%
Return on assets	$\dfrac{\$2,693}{(\$17,545 + \$18,594)/2}$	= 14.9%
Profit margin	$\dfrac{\$2,693}{\$27,799}$	= 9.7%
Asset turnover	$\dfrac{\$27,799}{(\$17,545 + \$18,594)/2}$	= 1.5 times
Return on equity	$\dfrac{\$2,693}{(\$11,081 + \$10,824)/2}$	= 24.6%
Price-earnings ratio	$\dfrac{\$76.91}{\$3.05}$	= 25.2

Suggested Homework:
BE12–10, BE12–11;
E12–6, E12–8;
P12–5A&B, P12–6A&B

EARNINGS PERSISTENCE AND EARNINGS QUALITY

■ **PART C**

As we just saw when analyzing the PE ratio, investors expect **Under Armour**'s earnings will grow at a faster rate than **Nike**'s. That's why Under Armour's stock price is higher relative to its current earnings. If for some reason investors see Under Armour's growth in earnings begin to slow, the stock price will fall. Investors are interested in whether earnings will remain strong and in the quality of those earnings. We look at those topics in this section.

Earnings Persistence and One-Time Income Items

To make predictions of future earnings, investors look for current earnings that will continue or *persist* into future years. Some items that are part of net income in the current year are not expected to persist. We refer to these as *one-time income items*. Discontinued operations, discussed below, is a prime example.

■ **LO12–5**
Distinguish persistent earnings from one-time items.

DISCONTINUED OPERATIONS

A discontinued operation is a business, or a component of a business, that the organization has already discontinued or plans to discontinue. For example, Nike reported a $21 million gain on discontinued operations in a previous year related to the sale of **Cole Haan** (footwear, handbags, and accessories) to **Apax Partners**. **We report any gains or losses**

on discontinued operations in the current year, separately from gains and losses on the portion of the business that will continue. This allows investors the opportunity to exclude discontinued operations in their estimate of income that will persist into future years.

Based on a recent FASB standard, only disposals of businesses representing strategic shifts that have a major effect on an organization's operations and financial results are reported in discontinued operations. Examples include a disposal of a major geographical area, a major line of business, or a major investment in which the company has significant influence.

As an example, let's consider Federer Sports Apparel, which has two business activities: a very profitable line of tennis apparel and a less profitable line of tennis shoes. Let's say that during 2018, the company decides to sell the tennis shoe business to a competitor, and the total gain from discontinued operations is $1.5 million. We report the gain "net of tax." This means the $1.5 million gain (before tax), less $500,000 in related taxes, is reported on the income statement as a $1 million gain. Illustration 12–24 shows the income statement presentation of discontinued operations for Federer Sports Apparel.

© Ahmed Jadallah/Reuters/Landov

ILLUSTRATION 12–24

Presentation of a Discontinued Operation

FEDERER SPORTS APPAREL Income Statement For the year ended December 31, 2018	
Net sales	$15,500,000
Cost of goods sold	7,000,000
Gross profit	8,500,000
Operating expenses	1,200,000
Depreciation expense	1,000,000
Other revenues and expenses	300,000
Income before tax	6,000,000
Income tax expense	2,000,000
Income from continuing operations	4,000,000
Discontinued operation:	
Gain from disposal of tennis shoe segment, net of tax	1,000,000
Net income	$ 5,000,000

With discontinued operations reported separately in the income statement, investors can clearly see the reported net income *excluding* the effects of the discontinued tennis shoe segment, $4.0 million in this situation. Investors then can use the income excluding discontinued operations, $4.0 million, to estimate income that persists into future periods.

Decision Point

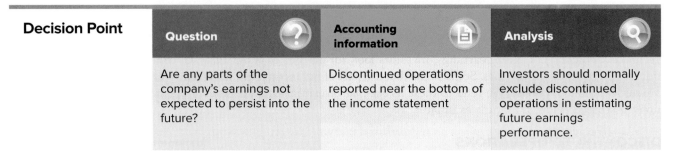

Question	Accounting information	Analysis
Are any parts of the company's earnings not expected to persist into the future?	Discontinued operations reported near the bottom of the income statement	Investors should normally exclude discontinued operations in estimating future earnings performance.

OTHER REVENUES AND EXPENSES

The sale or disposal of a significant component of a company's operations (i.e., a component having a major effect on the company's operations and financial results) is recorded as

INTERNATIONAL FINANCIAL REPORTING STANDARDS (IFRS)

DO INTERNATIONAL STANDARDS INFLUENCE THE FASB?

The FASB and the IASB work closely together in developing new standards. Discontinued operations are a good example. Rather than coming up with separate rules, the IASB reviewed the FASB's extensive work in the area and adopted nearly identical standards for the reporting of discontinued operations. Recently, the FASB simplified their definition of discontinued operations to match the broader definitions used by international standards.

Extraordinary items are another example. The FASB used to require companies to report extraordinary items at the bottom of the income statement in a manner similar to how we report discontinued operations. However, the IASB does not allow the reporting of extraordinary items. Recently, the FASB also eliminated the reporting of extraordinary items, consistent with international standards.

For more discussion, see Appendix E.

discontinued operations. However, the sale or disposal of most assets is reported, not as discontinued operations, but rather as other revenues and expenses. For example, as mentioned previously, Nike's sale of Cole Haan (footwear, handbags, and accessories) to Apax Partners was recorded as discontinued operations. Similarly, Nike owns Converse and tracks it as a separate operating segment. If Nike sold Converse, it could record the sale as discontinued operations. On the other hand, the sale of a Nike store, manufacturing plant, or distribution center to another company would not be recorded as discontinued operations. Rather, the gain or loss on the sale would be included as "other revenues and expenses" (just below operating expenses) in the income statement.

Common examples of "other revenues and expenses" are listed in Illustration 12–25.

ILLUSTRATION 12–25

Other Revenues and Expenses

Other Revenues and Expenses

Examples

1. Losses due to the write-down of receivables, inventory, or long-term assets.
2. Gains or losses on the sale of long-term assets.
3. Losses due to an employee strike.
4. Losses due to business restructuring.
5. Uninsured losses from a natural disaster such as a flood, earthquake, or hurricane.

Decision Maker's Perspective

Does Location in the Income Statement Matter?

As manager of a company, would you prefer to show a loss as part of other expenses or as a discontinued operation? Your first response might be that it really doesn't matter, since the choice affects only the location in the income statement and has no effect on the final net income number. True, yet many managers still prefer to show a loss near the bottom of the income statement, rather than placing it higher on the income statement as part of other expenses. Why?

One use of an income statement by investors is to estimate income that will persist into future years. Understandably, a manager might want to report a discontinued operation as a way to signal to investors that it is a one-time item and they should exclude it in estimating income for future years. Doing so would result in the appearance of higher recurring income, potentially boosting the company's stock price. So, at least in some situations, it's not just the final net income number that matters, but also the location of the item in the income statement that matters as well.

 KEY POINT

When using a company's current earnings to estimate future earnings performance, investors normally should exclude discontinued operations.

Quality of Earnings

■ LO12–6
Distinguish between conservative and aggressive accounting practices.

Quality of earnings refers to the ability of reported earnings to reflect the company's true earnings, as well as the usefulness of reported earnings to predict future earnings. To illustrate the concept, we continue our example of Federer Sports Apparel.

Let's move one year forward to 2019 for our example company, Federer Sports Apparel. Mr. Nadal, as chief financial officer (CFO), is responsible for all the accounting, finance, and MIS operations of the business. He has developed a reputation for his conservative, yet powerful management style. Illustration 12–26 presents the preliminary financial statements for 2019, prepared under the supervision of Mr. Nadal.

ILLUSTRATION 12–26

Financial Statements Prepared by Mr. Nadal

FEDERER SPORTS APPAREL
Income Statement
For the year ended December 31, 2019

Net sales	$18,800,000
Cost of goods sold	13,200,000
Gross profit	5,600,000
Operating expenses	1,600,000
Depreciation expense	1,000,000
Inventory write-down	200,000
Loss (litigation)	1,500,000
Income before tax	1,300,000
Income tax expense	450,000
Net income	$ 850,000

FEDERER SPORTS APPAREL
Balance Sheets
December 31

	2019	2018
Cash	$ 2,300,000	$ 800,000
Accounts receivable	1,500,000	1,200,000
Inventory	2,800,000	1,700,000
Buildings	11,000,000	11,000,000
Less: Accumulated depreciation	(2,000,000)	(1,000,000)
Total assets	$15,600,000	$13,700,000
Accounts payable	$ 1,450,000	$ 1,700,000
Contingent liability	1,500,000	0
Common stock	8,000,000	8,000,000
Retained earnings	4,650,000	4,000,000
Total liabilities and stockholders' equity	$15,600,000	$13,700,000

(continued)

ILLUSTRATION 12–26

(*concluded*)

FEDERER SPORTS APPAREL
Statement of Cash Flows
For the year ended December 31, 2019

Cash Flows from Operating Activities

Net income	$ 850,000	
Adjustments to reconcile net income to net cash flows from operating activities:		
Depreciation expense	1,000,000	
Increase in accounts receivable	(300,000)	
Increase in inventory	(1,100,000)	
Decrease in accounts payable	(250,000)	
Increase in contingent liability	1,500,000	
Net cash flows from operating activities		$1,700,000
Cash Flows from Investing Activities		
Net cash flows from investing activities		0
Cash Flows from Financing Activities		
Payment of cash dividends	(200,000)	
Net cash flows from financing activities		(200,000)
Net increase (decrease) in cash		1,500,000
Cash at the beginning of the period		800,000
Cash at the end of the period		$2,300,000

NADAL RETIRES AND DJOKOVIC IS HIRED

After completing the preliminary financial statements for 2019, Mr. Nadal retires, and the company hires a new CFO, Mr. Djokovic. In contrast to Mr. Nadal, Mr. Djokovic has a more aggressive, quick-hitting management style. Mr. Djokovic has made it clear that he is now in charge and changes will be made. Illustration 12–27 outlines four accounting changes Mr. Djokovic proposes. They are based on accounting topics we discussed in Chapters 5, 6, 7, and 8.

ILLUSTRATION 12–27

Mr. Djokovic's Proposed Changes

Mr. Djokovic's Proposed Changes

1. **Estimate of bad debts.** At the end of 2019, Mr. Nadal estimated that future bad debts will be 6% to 10% of current accounts receivable. He decided to play it safe and recorded an allowance equal to 10% of accounts receivable, or $150,000. Mr. Djokovic proposes changing the estimate to be 6% of accounts receivable, or $90,000. This change would increase net accounts receivable and decrease bad debt expense by $60,000.

2. **Write-down of inventory.** Mr. Nadal recorded a $200,000 write-down of inventory as follows:

December 31, 2019	Debit	Credit
Loss	200,000	
Inventory		200,000
(Write-down inventory)		

Mr. Djokovic insists the write-down was not necessary because the decline in inventory value was only temporary. Therefore, he proposes eliminating this entry, which would increase inventory and decrease loss on inventory write-down by $200,000.

3. **Change in depreciation estimate.** For the building purchased for $11 million at the beginning of 2018, Mr. Nadal recorded depreciation expense of $1 million in 2018 and 2019, using the straight-line method over 10 years with an estimated salvage value of $1 million. Beginning in 2019, Mr. Djokovic proposes calculating depreciation over a total

(*continued*)

ILLUSTRATION 12–27

(*concluded*)

of 20 years instead of 10 and using an estimated salvage value of $500,000. That change decreases accumulated depreciation and depreciation expense in 2019 by $500,000.

4. **Loss contingency.** At the end of 2019, the company's lawyer advised Mr. Nadal that there was a 70% chance of losing a litigation suit of $1,500,000 filed against the company. Mr. Nadal recorded the possible loss as follows:

December 31, 2019	Debit	Credit
Loss	1,500,000	
Contingent Liability		1,500,000
(*Record litigation against the company*)		

Mr. Djokovic argues that the likelihood of losing the litigation is reasonably possible, but not probable. Therefore, he proposes removing the litigation entry from the accounting records. The change would remove the loss and decrease liabilities by $1,500,000.

How will the proposed accounting changes affect net income? Illustration 12–28 presents the preliminary income statement prepared by Mr. Nadal, the effect of the accounting changes, and the updated income statement prepared by Mr. Djokovic.

ILLUSTRATION 12–28

Income Statement
Revised by
Mr. Djokovic

FEDERER SPORTS APPAREL Income Statement For the year ended December 31, 2019			
	Nadal	**Changes**	**Djokovic**
Net sales	$18,800,000		$18,800,000
Cost of goods sold	13,200,000		13,200,000
Gross profit	5,600,000		5,600,000
Operating expenses	1,600,000	$ (60,000)	1,540,000
Depreciation expense	1,000,000	(500,000)	500,000
Inventory write-down	200,000	(200,000)	0
Loss (litigation)	1,500,000	(1,500,000)	0
Income before tax	1,300,000	2,260,000	3,560,000
Income tax expense	450,000		450,000
Net income	$ 850,000	$2,260,000	$ 3,110,000

The four proposed accounting changes cause net income to more than triple, from $850,000 to $3,110,000. Notice that all four changes proposed by Mr. Djokovic increase net income: The reduction in the estimated allowance for uncollectible accounts increases net income $60,000; the elimination of the inventory write-down increases net income $200,000; the reduction in depreciation estimate increases net income $500,000; and the elimination of the contingent litigation liability increases net income $1,500,000. **Note that income tax expense did not change because all of these changes affect financial income but not taxable income.**

How do positive changes to net income affect the balance sheet? Illustration 12–29 presents the balance sheet originally prepared by Mr. Nadal, the effect of the four accounting changes, and the updated balance sheet prepared by Mr. Djokovic.

The balance sheet also improves from the proposed adjustments. Total assets increase due to increases in receivables and inventory plus a decrease in accumulated depreciation. Total liabilities decrease due to the elimination of the $1.5 million litigation liability. Stockholders' equity also goes up, due to the increase in retained earnings caused by the increase in reported net income for the year.

Decision Maker's Perspective

Look Out for Earnings Management at Year-End

Let's assume you're an auditor and all four of the final changes to the accounting records near year-end increase income. Wouldn't you be just a little concerned? It may be that all four adjustments are perfectly legitimate, but it also may be an indication management is inflating earnings. Year-end adjustments, especially those with an increasing or decreasing pattern, should be investigated with greater skepticism.

ILLUSTRATION 12–29

Balance Sheet Revised by Mr. Djokovic

FEDERER SPORTS APPAREL
Balance Sheet
December 31, 2019

	Nadal	Changes	Djokovic
Assets			
Cash	$ 2,300,000		$ 2,300,000
Accounts receivable	1,500,000	$ 60,000	1,560,000
Inventory	2,800,000	200,000	3,000,000
Buildings	11,000,000		11,000,000
Less: Accumulated depreciation	(2,000,000)	500,000	(1,500,000)
Total assets	$15,600,000	$ 760,000	$16,360,000
Liabilities and Stockholders' Equity			
Accounts payable	$ 1,450,000		$ 1,450,000
Contingent liability	1,500,000	(1,500,000)	0
Common stock	8,000,000		8,000,000
Retained earnings	4,650,000	2,260,000	6,910,000
Total liabilities and stockholders' equity	$15,600,000	$ 760,000	$16,360,000

What about the effects of the proposed adjustments on the statement of cash flows? Illustration 12–30 provides the statement of cash flows as revised by Mr. Djokovic.

Interestingly, the proposed changes have **no effect at all on total operating cash flows or on the overall change in cash.** Net cash flows from operating activities remain at $1,700,000 after the four proposed transactions. The net increase in cash remains at $1,500,000. None of the proposed changes affects the underlying cash flows of the company. **Rather, each proposed change improves the *appearance* of amounts reported in the income statement and the balance sheet.**

SYMBOLISM REVEALED

By now you've probably recognized that Mr. Nadal and Mr. Djokovic are names of famous tennis players. However, they are also used here to symbolize an important accounting concept. Mr. Nadal represents conservative accounting practices. Conservative accounting practices are those that result in reporting lower income, lower assets, and higher liabilities. The larger estimation of the allowance for uncollectible accounts, the write-down of over-valued inventory, the use of a shorter useful life for depreciation, and the recording of a contingent litigation loss are all examples of conservative accounting.

In contrast, Mr. Djokovic represents aggressive accounting practices. Aggressive accounting practices result in reporting higher income, higher assets, and lower liabilities. Mr. Djokovic's lower estimation of the allowance for uncollectible accounts, waiting to report an inventory write-down, choosing a longer useful life for depreciation, and waiting

ILLUSTRATION 12–30

Statement of Cash
Flows Revised by
Mr. Djokovic

FEDERER SPORTS APPAREL
Statement of Cash Flows
For the year ended December 31, 2019

	Nadal	Changes	Djokovic
Operating Activities			
Net income	$ 850,000	$2,260,000	$3,110,000
Adjustments to reconcile net income to net cash flows from operating activities:			
Depreciation expense	1,000,000	(500,000)	500,000
Increase in accounts receivable	(300,000)	(60,000)	(360,000)
Increase in inventory	(1,100,000)	(200,000)	(1,300,000)
Decrease in accounts payable	(250,000)		(250,000)
Increase in contingent liability	1,500,000	(1,500,000)	0
Net cash flows from operating activities	1,700,000	0	1,700,000
Investing Activities	0		0
Financing Activities			
Payment of cash dividends	(200,000)		(200,000)
Net cash flows from financing activities	(200,000)		(200,000)
Net increase (decrease) in cash	1,500,000		1,500,000
Cash at the beginning of the period	800,000		800,000
Cash at the end of the period	$2,300,000		$2,300,000

to record a litigation loss all are examples of more aggressive accounting. Being able to distinguish between conservative and aggressive accounting practices is important. Everyone involved in business, not just accountants, needs to recognize that accounting is not just black and white. There are actually many gray areas in accounting, requiring management judgment in the application of accounting principles.

 KEY POINT

Changes in accounting estimates and practices alter the appearance of amounts reported in the income statement and the balance sheet. However, changes in accounting estimates and practices usually have no effect on a company's underlying cash flows.

Let's Review

Classify each of the following accounting practices as conservative or aggressive.

1. Increase the allowance for uncollectible accounts.
2. When costs are going up, change from LIFO to FIFO.
3. Increase the useful life for calculating depreciation.
4. Record a larger expense for warranties.
5. Wait to record revenue until the cash is collected.

Solution:

1. Conservative.
2. Aggressive.
3. Aggressive.
4. Conservative.
5. Conservative.

Suggested Homework:
BE12–14, BE12–15;
E12–14, E12–15

KEY POINTS BY LEARNING OBJECTIVE

LO12–1 Perform vertical analysis.

For vertical analysis, we express each item as a percentage of the same base amount, such as a percentage of sales in the income statement or as a percentage of total assets in the balance sheet.

LO12–2 Perform horizontal analysis.

We use horizontal analysis to analyze trends in financial statement data, such as the amount of change and the percentage change, for one company over time.

LO12–3 Use ratios to analyze a company's risk.

We categorize risk ratios into liquidity ratios and solvency ratios. Liquidity ratios focus on the company's ability to pay *current* liabilities, whereas solvency ratios focus more on *long-term* liabilities.

LO12–4 Use ratios to analyze a company's profitability.

Profitability ratios measure the earnings or operating effectiveness of a company over a period of time, such as a year. Investors view profitability as the number one measure of company success.

LO12–5 Distinguish persistent earnings from one-time items.

When using a company's current earnings to estimate future earnings performance, investors normally should exclude discontinued operations.

LO12–6 Distinguish between conservative and aggressive accounting practices.

Changes in accounting estimates and practices alter the appearance of amounts reported in the income statement and the balance sheet. However, changes in accounting estimates and practices usually have no effect on a company's underlying cash flows.

GLOSSARY

Acid-test ratio: Cash, current investments, and accounts receivable divided by current liabilities; measures the availability of liquid current assets to pay current liabilities. **p. 572**

Aggressive accounting practices: Practices that result in reporting higher income, higher assets, and lower liabilities. **p. 585**

Asset turnover: Net sales divided by average total assets, which measures the sales per dollar of assets invested. **p. 576**

Average collection period: Approximate number of days the average accounts receivable balance is outstanding. It equals 365 days divided by the receivables turnover ratio. **p. 570**

Average days in inventory: Approximate number of days the average inventory is held. It equals 365 days divided by the inventory turnover ratio. **p. 570**

Conservative accounting practices: Practices that result in reporting lower income, lower assets, and higher liabilities. **p. 585**

Current ratio: Current assets divided by current liabilities; measures the availability of current assets to pay current liabilities. **p. 571**

Debt to equity ratio: Total liabilities divided by stockholders' equity; measures a company's risk. **p. 572**

Discontinued operation: The sale or disposal of a significant component of a company's operations. **p. 579**

Gross profit ratio: Measure of the amount by which the sale of inventory exceeds its cost per dollar of sales. It equals gross profit divided by net sales. **p. 575**

Growth stocks: Stocks that tend to have higher price-earnings ratios and are expected to have higher future earnings. **p. 577**

Horizontal analysis: Analyzes trends in financial statement data for a single company over time. **p. 564**

Inventory turnover ratio: The number of times a firm sells its average inventory balance during a reporting period. It equals cost of goods sold divided by average inventory. **p. 570**

Liquidity: Having sufficient cash (or other assets convertible to cash in a relatively short time) to pay currently maturing debts. **p. 568**

Price-earnings (PE) ratio: Compares a company's share price with its earnings per share. **p. 577**

Profit margin: Net income divided by net sales; indicates the earnings per dollar of sales. **p. 576**

Profitability ratios: Measure the earnings or operating effectiveness of a company. **p. 574**

Quality of earnings: Refers to the ability of reported earnings to reflect the company's true earnings, as well as the usefulness of reported earnings to predict future earnings. **p. 582**

Receivables turnover ratio: Number of times during a year that the average accounts receivable balance is collected (or "turns over"). It equals net credit sales divided by average accounts receivable. **p. 569**

Return on assets: Net income divided by average total assets; measures the amount of net income generated for each dollar invested in assets. **p. 576**

Return on equity: Net income divided by average stockholders' equity; measures the income generated per dollar of equity. **p. 577**

Solvency: Refers to a company's ability to pay its long-term liabilities. **p. 569**

Times interest earned ratio: Ratio that compares interest expense with income available to pay those charges. **p. 572**

Value stocks: Stocks that tend to have lower price-earnings ratios and are priced low in relation to current earnings. **p. 577**

Vertical analysis: Expresses each item in a financial statement as a percentage of the same base amount. **p. 562**

SELF-STUDY QUESTIONS

1. When using vertical analysis, we express income statement accounts as a percentage of: **LO12–1**
   a. Net income.
   b. Sales.
   c. Gross profit.
   d. Total assets.

2. When using vertical analysis, we express balance sheet accounts as a percentage of: **LO12–1**
   a. Total assets.
   b. Total liabilities.
   c. Total stockholders' equity.
   d. Sales.

3. Horizontal analysis examines trends in a company: **LO12–2**
   a. Between income statement accounts in the same year.
   b. Between balance sheet accounts in the same year.
   c. Between income statement and balance sheet accounts in the same year.
   d. Over time.

4. Which of the following is an example of horizontal analysis? **LO12–2**
   a. Comparing operating expenses with sales.
   b. Comparing the growth in sales with the growth in cost of goods sold.
   c. Comparing property, plant, and equipment with total assets.
   d. Comparing gross profit across companies.

5. Which of the following ratios is most useful in evaluating solvency? **LO12–3**
   a. Receivables turnover ratio.
   b. Inventory turnover ratio.
   c. Debt to equity ratio.
   d. Current ratio.

6. Which of the following is a positive sign that a company can quickly turn its receivables into cash? **LO12–3**
   a. A low receivables turnover ratio.
   b. A high receivables turnover ratio.
   c. A low average collection period.
   d. Both a high receivables turnover ratio and a low average collection period.

7. The Sports Shack reports net income of $120,000, sales of $1,200,000, and average assets of $960,000. The profit margin is: **LO12–4**
   a. 10%.
   b. 12.5%.
   c. 80%.
   d. 125%.

8. The Sports Shack reports net income of $120,000, sales of $1,200,000, and average assets of $960,000. The asset turnover is: **LO12–4**
   a. 0.10 times.
   b. 0.80 times.
   c. 8 times.
   d. 1.25 times.

9. Which of the following items would we report at the very bottom of the income statement just before net income? **LO12–5**
   a. Losses due to the write-down of inventory.
   b. Gain on the sale of long-term assets.
   c. Discontinued operations.
   d. Losses due to restructuring.

10. Which of the following is an example of a conservative accounting practice? **LO12–6**
    a. Adjust the allowance for uncollectible accounts to a larger amount.
    b. Record inventory at market rather than lower-of-cost-or-market.

c. Change from double-declining-balance to straight-line depreciation.

d. Record sales revenue before it is actually earned.

Note: For answers, see the last page of the chapter.

For additional study materials, including 10 more multiple-choice Self-Study Questions, visit **Connect.**

REVIEW QUESTIONS

1. Identify the three types of comparisons commonly used in financial statement analysis.   ■ **LO12–1, 12–2**

2. Explain the difference between vertical and horizontal analysis.   ■ **LO12–1, 12–2**

3. In performing vertical analysis, we express each item in a financial statement as a percentage of a base amount. What base amount is commonly used for income statement accounts? For balance sheet accounts?   ■ **LO12–1**

4. Two profitable companies in the same industry have similar total stockholders' equity. However, one company has most of its equity balance in common stock, while the other company has most of its equity balance in retained earnings. Neither company has ever paid a dividend. Which one is more likely to be an older and more established company? Why?   ■ **LO12–1**

5. In performing horizontal analysis, why is it important to look at both the amount and the percentage change?   ■ **LO12–2**

6. Explain why ratios that compare an income statement account with a balance sheet account should express the balance sheet account as an average of the beginning and ending balances.   ■ **LO12–3**

7. What is the difference between liquidity and solvency?   ■ **LO12–3**

8. Which risk ratios best answer each of the following financial questions?
   a. How quickly is a company able to collect its receivables?
   b. How quickly is a company able to sell its inventory?
   c. Is the company able to make interest payments as they become due?

9. Determine whether each of the following changes in risk ratios is good news or bad news about a company.   ■ **LO12–3**
   a. Increase in receivables turnover.
   b. Decrease in inventory turnover.
   c. Increase in the current ratio.
   d. Increase in the debt to equity ratio.

10. Pro Leather, a supplier to sporting goods manufacturers, has a current ratio of 0.90, based on current assets of $450,000 and current liabilities of $500,000. How, if at all, will a $100,000 purchase of inventory on account affect the current ratio?   ■ **LO12–3**

11. Which profitability ratios best answer each of the following financial questions?   ■ **LO12–4**
    a. What is the income earned for each dollar invested in assets?
    b. What is the income earned for each dollar of sales?
    c. What is the amount of sales for each dollar invested in assets?

12. Determine whether each of the following changes in profitability ratios normally is good news or bad news about a company.   ■ **LO12–4**
    a. Increase in profit margin.
    b. Decrease in asset turnover.
    c. Decrease in return on equity.
    d. Increase in the price-earnings ratio.

■ LO12–4

13. Hash Mark, Inc., reports a return on assets of 8% and a return on equity of 12%. Why do the two rates differ?

■ LO12–5

14. Define earnings persistence. How does earnings persistence relate to the reporting of discontinued operations?

■ LO12–5

15. Shifting Formations, Inc., reports earnings per share of $1.30. In the following year, it reports bottom-line earnings per share of $1.25 but earnings per share on income before discontinued operations of $1.50. Is this trend in earnings per share favorable or unfavorable? Explain why.

■ LO12–6

16. Explain the difference between conservative and aggressive accounting practices.

■ LO12–6

17. Provide an example of a conservative accounting practice. Why is this practice conservative?

■ LO12–6

18. Provide an example of an aggressive accounting practice. Why is this practice aggressive?

■ LO12–6

19. Goal Line Products makes several year-end adjustments, including an increase in the allowance for uncollectible accounts, a write-down of inventory, a decrease in the estimated useful life for depreciation, and an increase in the liability reported for litigation. What, if anything, do all these adjustments have in common?

■ LO12–6

20. Provide an example of an adjustment that improves the income statement and the balance sheet, but has no effect on cash flows.

BRIEF EXERCISES

Prepare vertical analysis (LO12–1)

BE12–1 Perform a vertical analysis on the following information.

	2018	2017
Cash	$ 420,000	$1,050,000
Accounts receivable	660,000	300,000
Inventory	1,020,000	925,000
Long-term assets	3,900,000	2,725,000
Total assets	$6,000,000	$5,000,000

Prepare horizontal analysis (LO12–2)

BE12–2 Using the information presented in BE12–1, perform a horizontal analysis providing both the amount and percentage change.

Understand vertical analysis (LO12–1)

BE12–3 Athletic World reports the following vertical analysis percentages.

	2018	2017
Sales	100%	100%
Cost of goods sold	48%	56%
Operating expenses	35%	30%

Did Athletic World's income before tax as a percentage of sales increase, decrease, or stay the same? If net income as a percentage of sales increases, does that mean net income also increases? Explain.

Understand horizontal analysis (LO12–2)

BE12–4 Sales are $2.6 million in 2017, $2.7 million in 2018, and $2.5 million in 2019. What is the percentage change from 2017 to 2018? What is the percentage change from 2018 to 2019? Be sure to indicate whether the percentage change is an increase or a decrease.

BE12–5 If sales are $1,150,000 in 2019 and this represents a 15% increase over sales in 2018, what were sales in 2018?

Understand percentage change (LO12–2)

BE12–6 Universal Sports Supply began the year with an accounts receivable balance of $200,000 and a year-end balance of $220,000. Credit sales of $750,000 generate a gross profit of $250,000. Calculate the receivables turnover ratio for the year.

Calculate receivables turnover (LO12–3)

BE12–7 Universal Sports Supply began the year with an inventory balance of $65,000 and a year-end balance of $75,000. Sales of $750,000 generate a gross profit of $250,000. Calculate the inventory turnover ratio for the year.

Calculate inventory turnover (LO12–3)

BE12–8 The Intramural Sports Club reports sales revenue of $1,140,000. Inventory at both the beginning and end of the year totals $200,000. The inventory turnover ratio for the year is 4.9. What amount of gross profit does the company report in its income statement?

Understand inventory turnover (LO12–3)

BE12–9 Dungy Training Company has a current ratio of 0.70 to 1, based on current assets of $3.43 million and current liabilities of $4.90 million. How, if at all, will a $900,000 cash purchase of inventory affect the current ratio? How, if at all, will a $900,000 purchase of inventory on account affect the current ratio?

Understand the current ratio (LO12–3)

BE12–10 Peyton's Palace has net income of $15 million on sales revenue of $130 million. Total assets were $96 million at the beginning of the year and $104 million at the end of the year. Calculate Peyton's return on assets, profit margin, and asset turnover ratios.

Calculate profitability ratios (LO12–4)

BE12–11 LaDanion's Limos reports net income of $130,000, average total assets of $700,000, and average total liabilities of $340,000. Calculate LaDanion's return on assets and return on equity ratios.

Calculate profitability ratios (LO12–4)

BE12–12 Kobe's Clinics provides health services and career counseling. Net income from the health services business this year is $32 million after tax. During the year, Kobe's Clinics sold the career counseling side of the business at a loss after tax of $7.5 million. Show how Kobe's Clinics would report this loss in the income statement, beginning with income from continuing operations of $32 million.

Record discontinued operations (LO12–5)

BE12–13 Game Time Sports owns a recreational facility with basketball courts, pitching machines, and athletic fields. Determine whether the firm should report each of the following items as discontinued operations, other revenues, or other expenses.
1. Due to insurance concerns, Game Time sells a trampoline basketball game for a loss of $1,500.
2. Game Time experiences water damage due to a flood from a recent heavy storm. The company replaces the basketball floors at a cost of $75,000. Unfortunately, Game Time does not carry flood insurance.
3. Game Time has revenues from three sources: basketball, baseball, and football. It sells the baseball operations for a loss of $55,000 to focus on the more profitable basketball and football operations.
4. Game Time sells one of the buildings used for basketball operations at a gain of $250,000. The company has two other buildings for basketball and plans to build a new facility for basketball in another year or two.

Classify income statement items (LO12–5)

BE12–14 Classify each of the following accounting practices as conservative or aggressive.
1. Increase the allowance for uncollectible accounts.
2. When costs are rising, change from LIFO to FIFO.
3. Change from declining-balance to straight-line depreciation in the second year of an asset depreciated over 20 years.

Distinguish between conservative and aggressive accounting practices (LO12–6)

BE12–15 Classify each of the following accepted accounting practices as conservative or aggressive.
1. Use lower-of-cost-or-market to value inventory.
2. Expense all research and development costs rather than recording some research and development costs as an asset.
3. Record loss contingencies when they are probable and can be reasonably estimated, but do not record gain contingencies until they are certain.

Distinguish between conservative and aggressive accounting practices (LO12–6)

EXERCISES   Mc Graw Hill Education **connect**®

Match terms with their
definitions (LO12–1, 12–2,
12–3, 12–4, 12–5, 12–6)

E12–1 Match (by letter) the following items with the description or example that best fits. Each letter is used only once.

Terms

_____ 1. Vertical analysis.
_____ 2. Horizontal analysis.
_____ 3. Liquidity.
_____ 4. Solvency.
_____ 5. Discontinued operations.
_____ 6. Quality of earnings.
_____ 7. Conservative accounting practices.
_____ 8. Aggressive accounting practices.

Descriptions

a. A company's ability to pay its current liabilities.
b. Accounting choices that result in reporting lower income, lower assets, and higher liabilities.
c. Accounting choices that result in reporting higher income, higher assets, and lower liabilities.
d. The ability of reported earnings to reflect the company's true earnings as well as the usefulness of reported earnings to help investors predict future earnings.
e. A tool to analyze trends in financial statement data for a single company over time.
f. The sale or disposal of a significant component of a company's operations.
g. A means to express each item in a financial statement as a percentage of a base amount.
h. A company's ability to pay its long-term liabilities.

Prepare vertical
analysis (LO12–1)

E12–2 The income statements for Federer Sports Apparel for 2019 and 2018 are presented below.

FEDERER SPORTS APPAREL Income Statements For the years ended December 31		
	2019	**2018**
Net sales	$18,800,000	$15,500,000
Cost of goods sold	13,200,000	7,000,000
Gross profit	5,600,000	8,500,000
Operating expenses	1,600,000	1,200,000
Depreciation expense	1,000,000	1,000,000
Inventory write-down	200,000	
Loss (litigation)	1,500,000	300,000
Income before tax	1,300,000	6,000,000
Income tax expense	450,000	2,000,000
Net income	$ 850,000	$ 4,000,000

Required:
Prepare a vertical analysis of the data for 2019 and 2018.

Prepare horizontal
analysis (LO12–2)

E12–3 Refer to the information provided in E12–2.

Required:
Prepare a horizontal analysis for 2019 using 2018 as the base year.

Prepare vertical
and horizontal
analyses (LO12–1, 12–2)

E12–4 The balance sheets for Federer Sports Apparel for 2019 and 2018 are presented below.

FEDERER SPORTS APPAREL
Balance Sheets
December 31

	2019	2018
Assets		
Cash	$ 2,300,000	$ 800,000
Accounts receivable	1,500,000	1,200,000
Inventory	2,800,000	1,700,000
Buildings	11,000,000	11,000,000
Less: Accumulated depreciation	(2,000,000)	(1,000,000)
Total assets	$15,600,000	$13,700,000
Liabilities and Stockholders' Equity		
Accounts payable	$ 1,450,000	$ 1,700,000
Contingent liability	1,500,000	0
Common stock	8,000,000	8,000,000
Retained earnings	4,650,000	4,000,000
Total liabilities and stockholders' equity	$15,600,000	$13,700,000

Required:

1. Prepare a vertical analysis of the balance sheet data for 2019 and 2018. Express each amount as a percentage of total assets.
2. Prepare a horizontal analysis for 2019 using 2018 as the base year.

E12–5 The 2018 income statement of Adrian Express reports sales of $19,310,000, cost of goods sold of $12,250,000, and net income of $1,700,000. Balance sheet information is provided in the following table.

Evaluate risk
ratios (LO12–3)

ADRIAN EXPRESS
Balance Sheets
December 31, 2018 and 2017

	2018	2017
Assets		
Current assets:		
Cash	$ 700,000	$ 860,000
Accounts receivable	1,600,000	1,100,000
Inventory	2,000,000	1,500,000
Long-term assets	4,900,000	4,340,000
Total assets	$9,200,000	$7,800,000
Liabilities and Stockholders' Equity		
Current liabilities	$1,920,000	$1,760,000
Long-term liabilities	2,400,000	2,500,000
Common stock	1,900,000	1,900,000
Retained earnings	2,980,000	1,640,000
Total liabilities and stockholders' equity	$9,200,000	$7,800,000

Industry averages for the following four risk ratios are as follows:

Average collection period	25 days
Average days in inventory	60 days
Current ratio	2 to 1
Debt to equity ratio	50%

Required:

1. Calculate the four risk ratios listed above for Adrian Express in 2018.
2. Do you think the company is more risky or less risky than the industry average? Explain your answer.

Evaluate profitability ratios (LO12–4)

E12–6 Refer to the information for Adrian Express in E12–5. Industry averages for the following profitability ratios are as follows:

Gross profit ratio	45%
Return on assets	25%
Profit margin	15%
Asset turnover	2.5 times
Return on equity	35%

Required:

1. Calculate the five profitability ratios listed above for Adrian Express.
2. Do you think the company is more profitable or less profitable than the industry average? Explain your answer.

Calculate risk ratios (LO12–3)

E12–7 The balance sheets for Plasma Screens Corporation and additional information are provided below.

PLASMA SCREENS CORPORATION Balance Sheets December 31, 2018 and 2017		
	2018	**2017**
Assets		
Current assets:		
Cash	$ 242,000	$ 130,000
Accounts receivable	98,000	102,000
Inventory	105,000	90,000
Investments	5,000	3,000
Long-term assets:		
Land	580,000	580,000
Equipment	890,000	770,000
Less: Accumulated depreciation	(528,000)	(368,000)
Total assets	$1,392,000	$1,307,000
Liabilities and Stockholders' Equity		
Current liabilities:		
Accounts payable	$ 109,000	$ 95,000
Interest payable	7,000	13,000
Income tax payable	9,000	6,000
Long-term liabilities:		
Notes payable	110,000	220,000
Stockholders' equity:		
Common stock	800,000	800,000
Retained earnings	357,000	173,000
Total liabilities and stockholders' equity	$1,392,000	$1,307,000

Additional Information for 2018:
1. Net income is $184,000.
2. Sales on account are $1,890,000.
3. Cost of goods sold is $1,394,250.

Required:
1. Calculate the following risk ratios for 2018:
   a. Receivables turnover ratio.
   b. Inventory turnover ratio.
   c. Current ratio.
   d. Acid-test ratio.
   e. Debt to equity ratio.
2. When we compare two companies, can one have a higher current ratio while the other has a higher acid-test ratio? Explain your answer.

E12–8 Refer to the information provided for Plasma Screens Corporation in E12–7.

Calculate profitability ratios (LO12–4)

Required:
1. Calculate the following profitability ratios for 2018:
   a. Gross profit ratio.
   b. Return on assets.
   c. Profit margin.
   d. Asset turnover.
   e. Return on equity.
2. When we compare two companies, can one have a higher return on assets while the other has a higher return on equity? Explain your answer.

E12–9 The following condensed information is reported by Sporting Collectibles.

Calculate profitability ratios (LO12–4)

	2018	2017
Income Statement Information		
Sales revenue	$14,820,000	$9,400,000
Cost of goods sold	9,544,080	6,900,000
Net income	418,000	348,000
Balance Sheet Information		
Current assets	$ 1,700,000	$1,600,000
Long-term assets	2,300,000	2,000,000
Total assets	$ 4,000,000	$3,600,000
Current liabilities	$ 1,300,000	$1,000,000
Long-term liabilities	1,400,000	1,400,000
Common stock	900,000	900,000
Retained earnings	400,000	300,000
Total liabilities and stockholders' equity	$ 4,000,000	$3,600,000

Required:
1. Calculate the following profitability ratios for 2018:
   a. Gross profit ratio.
   b. Return on assets.

      c. Profit margin.

      d. Asset turnover.

      e. Return on equity.

  2. Determine the amount of dividends paid to shareholders in 2018.

Calculate profitability ratios (LO12–4)

E12–10 The income statement for Stretch-Tape Corporation reports net sales of $540,000 and net income of $65,700. Average total assets for the year are $900,000. Stockholders' equity at the beginning of the year was $600,000, and $30,000 was paid to stockholders as dividends during the year. There were no other stockholders' equity transactions that occurred during the year.

Required:

Calculate the return on assets, profit margin, asset turnover, and return on equity ratios.

Classify income statement items (LO12–5)

E12–11 As an auditor for Bernard and Thomas, you are responsible for determining the proper classification of income statement items in the audit of California Sports Grill.

  a. One of the company's restaurants was destroyed in a forest fire that raged through Southern California. Uninsured losses from the fire are estimated to be $450,000.

  b. California Sports Grill has three operating divisions: restaurants, catering, and frozen retail foods. The company sells the frozen retail foods division of the business for a profit of $2.4 million in order to focus more on the restaurant and catering business.

  c. An employee strike to increase wages and benefits shut down operations for several days at an estimated cost of $200,000.

  d. A restaurant waiter slipped on a wet floor and sued the company. The employee won a settlement for $100,000, but California Sports Grill has not yet paid the settlement.

  e. The company owns and operates over 40 restaurants but sold one restaurant this year at a gain of $650,000.

Required:

Indicate whether each item should be classified as discontinued operations, other revenues, or other expenses.

Record discontinued operations (LO12–5)

E12–12 LeBron's Bookstores has two divisions: books and electronics. The electronics division had another great year in 2018 with net sales of $11 million, cost of goods sold of $6.5 million, operating expenses of $3 million, and income tax expense of $375,000. The book division did not do as well and was sold during the year. The loss from operations and sale of the book division was $900,000 before taxes and $675,000 after taxes.

Required:

Prepare the multiple-step income statement for LeBron's Bookstores, including the proper reporting for the discontinued book division.

Record discontinued operations and other expenses (LO12–5)

E12–13 Shaquille Corporation has operating income of $1.7 million, a loss on write-down of inventory of $200,000, and income tax expense of $425,000 for the year ended December 31, 2018, before considering the following item: a $275,000 gain, after tax, from the disposal of an operating segment.

Required:

Prepare the 2018 multiple step income statement for Shaquille Corporation beginning with operating income.

Distinguish between conservative and aggressive accounting practices (LO12–6)

E12–14 Dwight's Trophy Shop is considering the following accounting changes:

  a. Increase the allowance for uncollectible accounts.

  b. When costs are going up, change from LIFO to FIFO.

  c. Change from the straight-line method of depreciation to declining-balance in the second year of equipment with a 10-year life.

  d. Record a smaller expense for warranties.

Required:
Classify each accounting change as either conservative or aggressive.

E12–15 Attached is a schedule of five proposed changes at the end of the year.

Distinguish between conservative and aggressive accounting practices (LO12–6)

($ in 000s)	Before the Change	Proposed Change		After the Change
Net sales	$18,800,000	(a)	$200,000	$19,000,000
Cost of goods sold	13,200,000	(b)	400,000	13,600,000
Operating expenses	1,600,000	(c)	(100,000)	1,500,000
Other revenue	500,000	(d)	50,000	550,000
Other expense	450,000	(e)	(50,000)	400,000
Net income	$ 4,050,000			$ 4,050,000

Required:
1. Indicate whether each of the proposed changes is conservative, aggressive, or neutral.
2. Indicate whether the total effect of all the changes is conservative, aggressive, or neutral.

PROBLEMS: SET A

P12–1A Sports Emporium has two operating segments: sporting goods and sports apparel. The income statement for each operating segment is presented below.

Perform vertical analysis (LO12–1)

	SPORTS EMPORIUM Income Statement For the year ended December 31, 2018			
	Sporting Goods		**Sports Apparel**	
	Amount	%	Amount	%
Net sales	$1,800,000		$970,000	
Cost of goods sold	1,040,000		440,000	
Gross profit	760,000		530,000	
Operating expenses	450,000		340,000	
Operating income	310,000		190,000	
Other income (expense)	20,000		(15,000)	
Income before tax	330,000		175,000	
Income tax expense	80,000		70,000	
Net income	$ 250,000		$105,000	

Required:
1. Complete the "%" columns to be used in a vertical analysis of Sports Emporium's two operating segments. Express each amount as a percentage of sales.
2. Use vertical analysis to compare the profitability of the two operating segments. Which segment is more profitable?

P12–2A The income statements for Anything Tennis for the years ending December 31, 2018 and 2017, are provided below.

Perform horizontal analysis (LO12–2)

ANYTHING TENNIS **Income Statements** **For the years ended December 31**				
			Increase (Decrease)	
	2018	**2017**	**Amount**	**%**
Net sales	$3,500,000	$2,620,000		
Cost of goods sold	2,150,000	1,380,000		
Gross profit	1,350,000	1,240,000		
Operating expenses	810,000	630,000		
Operating income	540,000	610,000		
Other income (expense)	10,000	6,000		
Income before tax	550,000	616,000		
Income tax expense	100,000	140,000		
Net income	$ 450,000	$ 476,000		

Required:

1. Complete the "Amount" and "%" columns to be used in a horizontal analysis of the income statements for Anything Tennis.
2. Discuss the major fluctuations in income statement items during the year.

Perform vertical and horizontal analysis (LO12–1, 12–2)

P12–3A The balance sheets for Sports Unlimited for 2018 and 2017 are provided below.

SPORTS UNLIMITED **Balance Sheets** **For the years ended December 31**		
	2018	**2017**
Assets		
Current assets:		
Cash	$103,500	$ 70,400
Accounts receivable	46,800	32,000
Inventory	44,550	71,200
Prepaid rent	7,200	3,600
Long-term assets:		
Investment in bonds	54,900	0
Land	117,450	141,600
Equipment	106,200	102,000
Less: Accumulated depreciation	(30,600)	(20,800)
Total assets	$450,000	$400,000
Liabilities and Stockholders' Equity		
Current liabilities:		
Accounts payable	$ 30,150	$ 46,800
Interest payable	7,200	3,600
Income tax payable	12,150	10,000
Long-term liabilities:		
Notes payable	138,150	127,600
Stockholders' equity:		
Common stock	144,000	144,000
Retained earnings	118,350	68,000
Total liabilities and stockholders' equity	$450,000	$400,000

Required:

1. Prepare a vertical analysis of Sports Unlimited's 2018 and 2017 balance sheets. Express each amount as a percentage of total assets for that year.

2. Prepare a horizontal analysis of Sports Unlimited's 2018 balance sheet using 2017 as the base year.

P12–4A The following income statement and balance sheets for Virtual Gaming Systems are provided.

Calculate risk ratios (LO12–3)

VIRTUAL GAMING SYSTEMS
Income Statement
For the year ended December 31, 2018

Net sales		$3,086,000
Cost of goods sold		1,960,000
Gross profit		1,126,000
Expenses:		
Operating expenses	$868,000	
Depreciation expense	32,000	
Loss on sale of land	9,000	
Interest expense	20,000	
Income tax expense	58,000	
Total expenses		987,000
Net income		$ 139,000

VIRTUAL GAMING SYSTEMS
Balance Sheets
December 31

	2018	2017
Assets		
Current assets:		
Cash	$196,000	$154,000
Accounts receivable	91,000	70,000
Inventory	115,000	145,000
Prepaid rent	13,000	7,200
Long-term assets:		
Investment in bonds	115,000	0
Land	220,000	250,000
Equipment	280,000	220,000
Less: Accumulated depreciation	(84,000)	(52,000)
Total assets	$946,000	$794,200
Liabilities and Stockholders' Equity		
Current liabilities:		
Accounts payable	$ 76,000	$ 91,000
Interest payable	8,000	4,000
Income tax payable	20,000	15,000
Long-term liabilities:		
Notes payable	295,000	235,000
Stockholders' equity:		
Common stock	310,000	310,000
Retained earnings	237,000	139,200
Total liabilities and stockholders' equity	$946,000	$794,200

Required:

Assuming that all sales were on account, calculate the following risk ratios for 2018.

1. Receivables turnover ratio.
2. Average collection period.
3. Inventory turnover ratio.

4. Average days in inventory.
5. Current ratio.
6. Acid-test ratio.
7. Debt to equity ratio.
8. Times interest earned ratio.

Calculate profitability
ratios (LO12–4)

P12–5A Data for Virtual Gaming Systems are provided in P12–4A. Earnings per share for the year ended December 31, 2018, are $1.40. The closing stock price on December 31, 2018, is $28.30.

Required:
Calculate the following profitability ratios for 2018.
1. Gross profit ratio.
2. Return on assets.
3. Profit margin.
4. Asset turnover.
5. Return on equity.
6. Price-earnings ratio.

Use ratios to analyze risk
and profitability (LO12–3,
12–4)

P12–6A Income statement and balance sheet data for Virtual Gaming Systems are provided below.

VIRTUAL GAMING SYSTEMS
Income Statements
For the years ended December 31

	2019	2018
Net sales	$3,560,000	$3,086,000
Cost of goods sold	2,490,000	1,960,000
Gross profit	1,070,000	1,126,000
Expenses:		
Operating expenses	965,000	868,000
Depreciation expense	40,000	32,000
Loss on sale of land	0	9,000
Interest expense	23,000	20,000
Income tax expense	9,000	58,000
Total expenses	1,037,000	987,000
Net income	$ 33,000	$ 139,000

VIRTUAL GAMING SYSTEMS
Balance Sheets
December 31

	2019	2018	2017
Assets			
Current assets:			
Cash	$ 216,000	$196,000	$154,000
Accounts receivable	90,000	91,000	70,000
Inventory	140,000	115,000	145,000
Prepaid rent	15,000	13,000	7,200
Long-term assets:			
Investment in bonds	115,000	115,000	0
Land	310,000	220,000	250,000
Equipment	310,000	280,000	220,000
Less: Accumulated depreciation	(124,000)	(84,000)	(52,000)
Total assets	$1,072,000	$946,000	$794,200

(continued)

(concluded)

VIRTUAL GAMING SYSTEMS
Balance Sheets
December 31

	2019	2018	2017
Liabilities and Stockholders' Equity			
Current liabilities:			
Accounts payable	$ 161,000	$ 76,000	$ 91,000
Interest payable	12,000	8,000	4,000
Income tax payable	13,000	20,000	15,000
Long-term liabilities:			
Notes payable	450,000	295,000	235,000
Stockholders' equity:			
Common stock	310,000	310,000	310,000
Retained earnings	126,000	237,000	139,200
Total liabilities and stockholders' equity	$1,072,000	$946,000	$794,200

Required:

1. Calculate the following risk ratios for 2018 and 2019:
   a. Receivables turnover ratio.   c. Current ratio.
   b. Inventory turnover ratio.   d. Debt to equity ratio.
2. Calculate the following profitability ratios for 2018 and 2019:
   a. Gross profit ratio.   c. Profit margin.
   b. Return on assets.   d. Asset turnover.
3. Based on the ratios calculated, determine whether overall risk and profitability improved from 2018 to 2019.

PROBLEMS: SET B

connect

P12–1B Game-On Sports operates in two distinct segments: athletic equipment and accessories. The income statement for each operating segment is presented below.

Perform vertical analysis (LO12–1)

GAME-ON SPORTS
Income Statement
For the year ended December 31, 2018

	Athletic Equipment		Accessories	
	Amount	%	Amount	%
Net sales	$3,050,000		$3,500,000	
Cost of goods sold	1,350,000		1,670,000	
Gross profit	1,700,000		1,830,000	
Operating expenses	750,000		800,000	
Operating income	950,000		1,030,000	
Other income (expense)	80,000		(15,000)	
Income before tax	1,030,000		1,015,000	
Income tax expense	235,000		210,000	
Net income	$ 795,000		$ 805,000	

Required:

1. Complete the "%" columns to be used in a vertical analysis of Game-On Sports' two operating segments. Express each amount as a percentage of sales.
2. Use vertical analysis to compare the profitability of the two operating segments. Which segment is more profitable?

Perform horizontal
analysis (LO12–2)

P12–2B The income statements for Galaxy Tennis for the years ending December 31, 2018 and 2017, are provided below.

GALAXY TENNIS
Income Statements
For the years ended December 31

	2018	2017	Increase (Decrease) Amount	%
Net sales	$6,150,000	$6,250,000		
Cost of goods sold	2,850,000	2,920,000		
Gross profit	3,300,000	3,330,000		
Operating expenses	1,510,000	1,390,000		
Operating income	1,790,000	1,940,000		
Other income (expense)	60,000	85,000		
Income before tax	1,850,000	2,025,000		
Income tax expense	390,000	435,000		
Net income	$1,460,000	$1,590,000		

Required:
1. Complete the "Amount" and "%" columns to be used in a horizontal analysis of Galaxy Tennis income statement.
2. Discuss the major fluctuations in income statement items during the year.

Perform vertical and
horizontal analysis
(LO12–1, 12–2)

P12–3B The balance sheets for Fantasy Football for 2018 and 2017 are provided below.

FANTASY FOOTBALL
Balance Sheets
December 31

	2018	2017
Assets		
Current assets:		
Cash	$ 208,000	$ 262,200
Accounts receivable	856,000	999,400
Inventory	1,900,000	1,349,000
Supplies	124,000	87,400
Long-term assets:		
Equipment	1,292,000	1,292,000
Less: Accumulated depreciation	(380,000)	(190,000)
Total assets	$4,000,000	$3,800,000
Liabilities and Stockholders' Equity		
Current liabilities:		
Accounts payable	$ 168,000	$ 129,200
Interest payable	0	3,800
Income tax payable	76,000	76,000
Long-term liabilities:		
Notes payable	760,000	760,000
Stockholders' equity:		
Common stock	786,600	786,600
Retained earnings	2,209,400	2,044,400
Total liabilities and stockholders' equity	$4,000,000	$3,800,000

Required:
1. Prepare a vertical analysis of Fantasy Football's 2018 and 2017 balance sheets. Express each amount as a percentage of total assets for that year.
2. Prepare a horizontal analysis of Fantasy Football's 2018 balance sheet using 2017 as the base year.

P12–4B The following income statement and balance sheets for The Athletic Attic are provided.   **Calculate risk ratios (LO12–3)**

THE ATHLETIC ATTIC
Income Statement
For the year ended December 31, 2018

Net sales		$8,900,000
Cost of goods sold		5,450,000
Gross profit		3,450,000
Expenses:		
Operating expenses	$1,600,000	
Depreciation expense	210,000	
Interest expense	50,000	
Income tax expense	360,000	
Total expenses		2,220,000
Net income		$1,230,000

THE ATHLETIC ATTIC
Balance Sheets
December 31

	2018	2017
Assets		
Current assets:		
Cash	$ 164,000	$ 214,000
Accounts receivable	790,000	810,000
Inventory	1,405,000	1,075,000
Supplies	110,000	85,000
Long-term assets:		
Equipment	1,150,000	1,150,000
Less: Accumulated depreciation	(420,000)	(210,000)
Total assets	$3,199,000	$3,124,000
Liabilities and Stockholders' Equity		
Current liabilities:		
Accounts payable	$ 115,000	$ 91,000
Interest payable	0	5,000
Income tax payable	40,000	31,000
Long-term liabilities:		
Notes payable	600,000	600,000
Stockholders' equity:		
Common stock	700,000	700,000
Retained earnings	1,744,000	1,697,000
Total liabilities and stockholders' equity	$3,199,000	$3,124,000

Required:
Assuming that all sales were on account, calculate the following risk ratios for 2018:
1. Receivables turnover ratio.
2. Average collection period.
3. Inventory turnover ratio.
4. Average days in inventory.
5. Current ratio.
6. Acid-test ratio.

7. Debt to equity ratio.

8. Times interest earned ratio.

Calculate profitability ratios (LO12–4)

P12–5B Data for The Athletic Attic are provided in P12–4B. Earnings per share for the year ended December 31, 2018, are $1.36. The closing stock price on December 31, 2018, is $22.42.

Required:

Calculate the following profitability ratios for 2018:

1. Gross profit ratio.

2. Return on assets.

3. Profit margin.

4. Asset turnover.

5. Return on equity.

6. Price-earnings ratio.

Use ratios to analyze risk and profitability (LO12–3, 12–4)

P12–6B Income statement and balance sheet data for The Athletic Attic are provided below.

THE ATHLETIC ATTIC
Income Statements
For the years ended December 31

	2019	2018
Net sales	$10,400,000	$8,900,000
Cost of goods sold	6,800,000	5,450,000
Gross profit	3,600,000	3,450,000
Expenses:		
Operating expenses	1,600,000	1,600,000
Depreciation expense	200,000	210,000
Interest expense	40,000	50,000
Income tax expense	400,000	360,000
Total expenses	2,240,000	2,220,000
Net income	$ 1,360,000	$1,230,000

THE ATHLETIC ATTIC
Balance Sheets
December 31

	2019	2018	2017
Assets			
Current assets:			
Cash	$ 225,000	$ 164,000	$ 214,000
Accounts receivable	990,000	790,000	810,000
Inventory	1,725,000	1,405,000	1,075,000
Supplies	130,000	110,000	85,000
Long-term assets:			
Equipment	1,100,000	1,150,000	1,150,000
Less: Accumulated depreciation	(600,000)	(420,000)	(210,000)
Total assets	$3,570,000	$3,199,000	$3,124,000
Liabilities and Stockholders' Equity			
Current liabilities:			
Accounts payable	$ 175,000	$ 115,000	$ 91,000
Interest payable	4,000	0	5,000
Income tax payable	40,000	40,000	31,000
Long-term liabilities:			
Notes payable	500,000	600,000	600,000
Stockholders' equity:			
Common stock	600,000	700,000	700,000
Retained earnings	2,251,000	1,744,000	1,697,000
Total liabilities and stockholders' equity	$3,570,000	$3,199,000	$3,124,000

Required:

1. Calculate the following risk ratios for 2018 and 2019:
   a. Receivables turnover ratio.
   c. Current ratio.
   b. Inventory turnover ratio.
   d. Debt to equity ratio.
2. Calculate the following profitability ratios for 2018 and 2019:
   a. Gross profit ratio.
   c. Profit margin.
   b. Return on assets.
   d. Asset turnover.
3. Based on the ratios calculated, determine whether overall risk and profitability improved from 2018 to 2019.

ADDITIONAL PERSPECTIVES

Great Adventures

(This is the conclusion of the Great Adventures problem from earlier chapters.)

AP12–1 Income statement and balance sheet data for Great Adventures, Inc., are provided below.

Continuing Problem

GREAT ADVENTURES, INC.
Income Statement
For the year ended December 31, 2020

Revenues:		
Service revenue (clinic, racing, TEAM)	$543,000	
Sales revenue (MU watches)	118,000	
Total revenues		$661,000
Expenses:		
Cost of goods sold (MU watches)	70,000	
Operating expenses	304,276	
Depreciation expense	50,000	
Interest expense	29,724	
Income tax expense	57,000	
Total expenses		511,000
Net income		$150,000

GREAT ADVENTURES, INC.
Balance Sheets
December 31, 2020 and 2019

	2020	2019	Increase (I) or Decrease (D)
Assets			
Current assets:			
Cash	$ 322,362	$138,000	$ 184,362 (I)
Accounts receivable	45,000	35,000	10,000 (I)
Inventory	17,000	14,000	3,000 (I)
Other current assets	13,000	11,000	2,000 (I)
Long-term assets:			
Land	500,000	0	500,000 (I)
Buildings	1,000,000	0	1,000,000 (I)
Equipment	65,000	65,000	
Less: Accumulated depreciation	(75,250)	(25,250)	50,000 (I)
Total assets	$1,887,112	$ 237,750	

(*continued*)

(concluded)

GREAT ADVENTURES, INC.
Balance Sheets
December 31, 2020 and 2019

	2020	2019	Increase (I) or Decrease (D)
Liabilities and Stockholders' Equity			
Current liabilities:			
Accounts payable	$ 12,000	$ 9,000	$ 3,000 (I)
Interest payable	750	750	
Income tax payable	57,000	38,000	19,000 (I)
Long-term liabilities:			
Notes payable	492,362	30,000	462,362 (I)
Stockholders' equity:			
Common stock	120,000	20,000	100,000 (I)
Paid-in capital	1,105,000	0	1,105,000 (I)
Retained earnings	175,000	140,000	35,000 (I)
Treasury stock	(75,000)	0	(75,000) (I)
Total liabilities and stockholders' equity	$1,887,112	$237,750	

As you can tell from the financial statements, 2020 was an especially busy year. Tony and Suzie were able to use the $1.2 million received from the issuance of 100,000 shares of stock to hire a construction company for $1 million to build the cabins, dining facilities, ropes course, and the outdoor swimming pool. They even put in a baby pool to celebrate the birth of their firstborn son, little Venture Matheson.

Required:

1. Calculate the following risk ratios for 2020.
   a. Receivables turnover ratio. (*Hint:* Use total revenues for net credit sales)
   b. Average collection period.
   c. Inventory turnover ratio.
   d. Average days in inventory.
   e. Current ratio.
   f. Acid-test ratio. (*Hint:* There are no current investments)
   g. Debt to equity ratio.
   h. Times interest earned ratio.
2. Calculate the following profitability ratios for 2020.
   a. Gross profit ratio (on the MU watches).
   b. Return on assets.
   c. Profit margin.
   d. Asset turnover.
   e. Return on equity.
   Note: In calculating profit margin and asset turnover, net sales should include both service revenue and sales revenue.
3. Briefly comment on Great Adventures' risk and profitability in 2020.

Financial Analysis   **American Eagle Outfitters, Inc.**

AP12–2 Financial information for **American Eagle** is presented in **Appendix A** at the end of the book.

Required:

1. Calculate the following risk ratios for the year ended January 31, 2015:
   a. Receivables turnover ratio.
   b. Average collection period.

   c. Inventory turnover ratio.

   d. Average days in inventory.

   e. Current ratio.

   f. Acid-test ratio.

   g. Debt to equity ratio.

2. Calculate the following profitability ratios for the year ended January 31, 2015:

   a. Gross profit ratio.

   b. Return on assets.

   c. Profit margin.

   d. Asset turnover.

   e. Return on equity.

The Buckle, Inc.   **Financial Analysis**

AP12–3 Financial information for **Buckle** is presented in **Appendix B** at the end of the book.

Required:

1. Calculate the following risk ratios for the year ended January 31, 2015:

   a. Receivables turnover ratio.

   b. Average collection period.

   c. Inventory turnover ratio.

   d. Average days in inventory.

   e. Current ratio.

   f. Acid-test ratio.

   g. Debt to equity ratio.

2. Calculate the following profitability ratios for the year ended January 31, 2015:

   a. Gross profit ratio.

   b. Return on assets.

   c. Profit margin.

   d. Asset turnover.

   e. Return on equity.

American Eagle Outfitters, Inc., vs. The Buckle, Inc.   **Comparative Analysis**

AP12–4 Financial information for **American Eagle** is presented in **Appendix A** at the end of the book, and financial information for **Buckle** is presented in **Appendix B** at the end of the book.

Required:

1. Calculate the following risk ratios for both companies for the year ended January 31, 2015. Based on these calculations, which company appears to be more risky?

   a. Receivables turnover ratio.

   b. Average collection period.

   c. Inventory turnover ratio.

   d. Average days in inventory.

   e. Current ratio.

   f. Acid-test ratio.

   g. Debt to equity ratio.

2. Calculate the following profitability ratios for both companies for the year ended January 31, 2015. Based on these calculations, which company appears to be more profitable?

   a. Gross profit ratio.

   b. Return on assets.

   c. Profit margin.

   d. Asset turnover.

   e. Return on equity.

Ethics

AP12–5 After years of steady growth in net income, The Performance Drug Company sustained a loss of $1.6 million in 2018. The loss was primarily due to a $2 million loss on the write-down of inventory near year-end.

The CFO, Joe Mammoth, suggests the company wait to record the write-down of inventory until early 2019. "If we wait and report the loss next year, net income for 2018 will still be positive, similar to previous years. Investors will appreciate the continued profitability and we can take the loss on inventory write-down next year when operations are better." Joe further notes that executive bonuses are tied to income and if we don't show a profit this year, there will be no bonuses.

The CEO, John Stackhouse, asks Joe to justify this treatment. "I know we record an inventory write-down each year," Joe replies, "but just this once, I think we can wait and record the write-down next year."

Required:

Discuss the ethical dilemma faced by the CFO and the CEO. Who are the stakeholders and how are they affected?

Internet Research

AP12–6 Did you know that you can get lots of financial information free of charge? Go to **finance.yahoo.com.** Use the quote lookup located on the left side to get financial information about any publicly traded company.

Required:

1. For your company of choice, obtain the most recent income statement and balance sheet information by clicking on the financials in the bottom left hand corner.
2. Click on competitors to obtain a direct competitor comparison with your company of choice. Select a competing company and obtain their most recent income statement and balance sheet information.
3. Calculate the following risk ratios for both companies for the most recent year. Based on these calculations, which company appears to be more risky?
   a. Receivables turnover ratio.
   b. Inventory turnover ratio.
   c. Current ratio.
   d. Acid-test ratio.
   e. Debt to equity ratio.
4. Calculate the following profitability ratios for both companies for the most recent year. Based on these calculations, which company appears to be more profitable?
   a. Gross profit ratio.
   b. Return on assets.
   c. Profit margin.
   d. Asset turnover.
   e. Return on equity.

Written Communication

AP12–7 Roseburg Corporation manufactures cardboard containers. In 2014, the company purchased several large tracts of timber for $20 million with the intention of harvesting its own timber rather than buying timber from outside suppliers. However, in 2018, Roseburg abandoned the idea, and sold all of the timber tracts for $30 million. Net income for 2018, before considering this event, was $12 million.

Required:

Write a memo providing your recommended income statement presentation of the gain on the sale of the timber tracts. Be sure to include a discussion of the alternatives that might be considered.

Earnings Management

AP12–8 Major League Products provides merchandise carrying the logos of each fan's favorite major league team. In recent years, the company has struggled to compete against new Internet-based companies selling products at much lower prices. Andrew Ransom, in his second year out of college, was assigned to audit the financial statements of Major League Products. One of the steps in the auditing process is to examine the nature of year-end adjustments. Andrew's investigation reveals that the company has made several year-end adjustments, including (a) a decrease in the allowance for uncollectible accounts, (b) a reversal in the previous write-down of inventory, (c) an increase in the estimated useful life used to calculate depreciation expense, and (d) a decrease in the liability reported for litigation.

Required:
1. Classify each adjustment as conservative or aggressive.
2. What, if anything, do all these adjustments have in common?
3. How do these adjustments affect the company's cash balance?
4. Why might these year-end adjustments, taken together, raise concerns about earnings management?

Answers to the Self-Study Questions
1. b   2. a   3. d   4. b   5. c   6. d   7. a   8. d   9. c   10. a

American Eagle Outfitters, Inc., 2014 Annual Report

For the complete annual report, go online to http://investors.ae.com/sec-filings/annual-report-10-K/default.aspx.

UNITED STATES SECURITIES AND EXCHANGE COMMISSION
Washington, D.C. 20549

Form 10-K

☑ **ANNUAL REPORT PURSUANT TO SECTION 13 OR 15(d) OF THE SECURITIES EXCHANGE ACT OF 1934**

For the Fiscal Year Ended January 31, 2015

OR

☐ **TRANSITION REPORT PURSUANT TO SECTION 13 OR 15(d) OF THE SECURITIES EXCHANGE ACT OF 1934**

Commission File Number: 1-33338

American Eagle Outfitters, Inc.

(Exact name of registrant as specified in its charter)

Delaware	**No. 13-2721761**
(State or other jurisdiction of incorporation or organization)	*(I.R.S. Employer Identification No.)*
77 Hot Metal Street, Pittsburgh, PA	**15203-2329**
(Address of principal executive offices)	*(Zip Code)*

Registrant's telephone number, including area code: (412) 432-3300

Securities registered pursuant to Section 12(b) of the Act:

Common Shares, $0.01 par value	New York Stock Exchange
(Title of class)	*(Name of each exchange on which registered)*

Securities registered pursuant to Section 12(g) of the Act:
None

Indicate by check mark if the registrant is a well-known seasoned issuer, as defined in Rule 405 of the Securities Act.   YES ☑ NO ☐

Indicate by check mark if the registrant is not required to file reports pursuant to Section 13 or Sections 15(d) of the Act.   YES ☐ NO ☑

Indicate by check mark whether the registrant (1) has filed all reports required to be filed by Section 13 or 15(d) of the Securities Exchange Act of 1934 during the preceding 12 months (or for such shorter period that the registrant was required to file such reports), and (2) has been subject to the filing requirements for at the past 90 days.   YES ☑   NO ☐

Indicate by check mark whether the registrant has submitted electronically and posted on its corporate Web site, if any, every Interactive Data File required to be submitted and posted pursuant to Rule 405 of Regulation S-T (§232.405 of this chapter) during the preceding 12 months (or for such shorter period that the registrant was required to submit and post such files).   YES ☑   NO ☐

Indicate by check mark if disclosure of delinquent filers pursuant to Item 405 of Regulation S-K (§229.405 of this chapter) is not contained herein, and will not be contained, to the best of registrant's knowledge, in definitive proxy or information statements incorporated by reference in Part III of this Form 10-K or any amendment to this Form 10-K.   ☐

Indicate by check mark whether the registrant is a large accelerated filer, an accelerated filer, a non-accelerated filer, or a smaller reporting company. See the definitions of "large accelerated filer," "accelerated filer" and "smaller reporting company" in Rule 12b-2 of the Exchange Act. (Check one):

Large accelerated filer ☑   Accelerated filer ☐   Non-accelerated filer ☐   Smaller reporting company ☐
(Do not check if a smaller reporting company)

Indicate by check mark whether the registrant is a shell company (as defined in Rule 12b-2 of the Act).   YES ☐   NO ☑

The aggregate market value of voting and non-voting common equity held by non-affiliates of the registrant as of August 2, 2014 was $1,874,117,608.

Indicate the number of shares outstanding of each of the registrant's classes of common stock, as of the latest practicable date: 195,022,073 Common Shares were outstanding at March 9, 2015.

DOCUMENTS INCORPORATED BY REFERENCE

Part III — Proxy Statement for 2015 Annual Meeting of Stockholders, in part, as indicated.

Report of Independent Registered Public Accounting Firm

The Board of Directors and Stockholders of
American Eagle Outfitters, Inc.

We have audited the accompanying consolidated balance sheets of American Eagle Outfitters, Inc. as of January 31, 2015 and February 1, 2014, and the related consolidated statements of operations, comprehensive income, stockholders' equity, and cash flows for each of the three years in the period ended January 31, 2015. These financial statements are the responsibility of the Company's management. Our responsibility is to express an opinion on these financial statements based on our audits.

We conducted our audits in accordance with the standards of the Public Company Accounting Oversight Board (United States). Those standards require that we plan and perform the audit to obtain reasonable assurance about whether the financial statements are free of material misstatement. An audit includes examining, on a test basis, evidence supporting the amounts and disclosures in the financial statements. An audit also includes assessing the accounting principles used and significant estimates made by management, as well as evaluating the overall financial statement presentation. We believe that our audits provide a reasonable basis for our opinion.

In our opinion, the financial statements referred to above present fairly, in all material respects, the consolidated financial position of American Eagle Outfitters, Inc. at January 31, 2015 and February 1, 2014, and the consolidated results of its operations and its cash flows for each of the three years in the period ended January 31, 2015, in conformity with U.S. generally accepted accounting principles.

We also have audited, in accordance with the standards of the Public Company Accounting Oversight Board (United States), American Eagle Outfitters, Inc.'s internal control over financial reporting as of January 31, 2015, based on criteria established in Internal Control — Integrated Framework issued by the Committee of Sponsoring Organizations of the Treadway Commission (2013 framework) and our report dated March 11, 2015 expressed an unqualified opinion thereon.

/s/   Ernst & Young LLP

Pittsburgh, Pennsylvania
March 11, 2015

AMERICAN EAGLE OUTFITTERS, INC.
CONSOLIDATED BALANCE SHEETS

(In thousands, except per share amounts)	January 31, 2015	February 1, 2014
Assets		
Current assets:		
Cash and cash equivalents	$ 410,697	$ 418,933
Short-term investments	—	10,002
Merchandise inventory	278,972	291,541
Accounts receivable	67,894	73,882
Prepaid expenses and other	73,848	88,155
Deferred income taxes	59,102	45,478
Total current assets	890,513	927,991
Property and equipment, at cost, net of accumulated depreciation	694,856	632,986
Intangible assets, at cost, net of accumulated amortization	47,206	49,271
Goodwill	13,096	13,530
Non-current deferred income taxes	14,035	24,835
Other assets	37,202	45,551
Total assets	$1,696,908	$1,694,164
Liabilities and Stockholders' Equity		
Current liabilities:		
Accounts payable	$ 191,146	$ 203,872
Accrued compensation and payroll taxes	44,884	23,560
Accrued rent	78,567	76,397
Accrued income and other taxes	33,110	5,778
Unredeemed gift cards and gift certificates	47,888	47,194
Current portion of deferred lease credits	12,969	13,293
Other liabilities and accrued expenses	50,529	45,384
Total current liabilities	459,093	415,478
Non-current liabilities:		
Deferred lease credits	54,516	59,510
Non-current accrued income taxes	10,456	16,543
Other non-current liabilities	33,097	36,455
Total non-current liabilities	98,069	112,508
Commitments and contingencies	—	—
Stockholders' equity:		
Preferred stock, $0.01 par value; 5,000 shares authorized; none issued and outstanding	—	—
Common stock, $0.01 par value; 600,000 shares authorized; 249,566 shares issued; 194,516 and 193,149 shares outstanding, respectively	2,496	2,496
Contributed capital	569,675	573,008
Accumulated other comprehensive income	(9,944)	12,157
Retained earnings	1,543,085	1,569,851
Treasury stock, 55,050 and 56,417 shares, respectively, at cost	(965,566)	(991,334)
Total stockholders' equity	1,139,746	1,166,178
Total liabilities and stockholders' equity	$1,696,908	$1,694,164

Refer to Notes to Consolidated Financial Statements

AMERICAN EAGLE OUTFITTERS, INC.
CONSOLIDATED STATEMENTS OF OPERATIONS

| | For the Years Ended | | |
| | January 31, 2015 | February 1, 2014 | February 2, 2013 |
(In thousands, except per share amounts)			
Total net revenue	$3,282,867	$3,305,802	$3,475,802
Cost of sales, including certain buying, occupancy and warehousing expenses	2,128,193	2,191,803	2,085,480
Gross profit	1,154,674	1,113,999	1,390,322
Selling, general and administrative expenses	806,498	796,505	834,601
Restructuring charges	17,752		
Loss on impairment of assets	33,468	44,465	34,869
Depreciation and amortization expense	141,191	131,974	126,246
Operating income	155,765	141,055	394,606
Other income, net	3,737	1,022	7,432
Income before income taxes	159,502	142,077	402,038
Provision for income taxes	70,715	59,094	137,940
Income from continuing operations	88,787	82,983	264,098
Loss from discontinued operations, net of tax	(8,465)	—	(31,990)
Net income	$ 80,322	$ 82,983	$ 232,108
Basic income per common share:			
Income from continuing operations	$ 0.46	$ 0.43	$ 1.35
Loss from discontinued operations	(0.04)	—	(0.16)
Basic net income per common share	$ 0.42	$ 0.43	$ 1.19
Diluted income per common share:			
Income from continuing operations	$ 0.46	$ 0.43	$ 1.32
Loss from discontinued operations	(0.04)	—	(0.16)
Diluted net income per common share	$ 0.42	$ 0.43	$ 1.16
Weighted average common shares outstanding — basic	194,437	192,802	196,211
Weighted average common shares outstanding — diluted	195,135	194,475	200,665

Refer to Notes to Consolidated Financial Statements

AMERICAN EAGLE OUTFITTERS, INC.
CONSOLIDATED STATEMENTS OF COMPREHENSIVE INCOME

(In thousands)	For the Years Ended		
	January 31, 2015	February 1, 2014	February 2, 2013
Net income	$ 80,322	$ 82,983	$232,108
Other comprehensive (loss) income:			
Foreign currency translation (loss) gain	(22,101)	(17,140)	638
Other comprehensive (loss) income	(22,101)	(17,140)	638
Comprehensive income	$ 58,221	$ 65,843	$232,746

Refer to Notes to Consolidated Financial Statements

AMERICAN EAGLE OUTFITTERS, INC.
CONSOLIDATED STATEMENTS OF STOCKHOLDERS' EQUITY

(In thousands, except per share amounts)	Shares Outstanding (1)	Common Stock	Contributed Capital	Retained Earnings	Treasury Stock(2)	Accumulated Other Comprehensive Income (Loss)	Stockholders' Equity
Balance at January 28, 2012	193,848	$ 2,496	$ 552,797	$1,771,464	$(938,565)	$ 28,659	$1,416,851
Stock awards	—	—	76,108	—	—	—	76,108
Repurchase of common stock as part of publicly announced programs	(8,407)	—	—	—	(173,554)	—	(173,554)
Repurchase of common stock from employees	(280)	—	—	—	(4,125)	—	(4,125)
Reissuance of treasury stock	7,443	—	(11,054)	(36,213)	125,515	—	78,248
Net income	—	—	—	232,108	—	—	232,108
Other comprehensive income	—	—	—	—	—	638	638
Cash dividends and dividend equivalents ($2.05 per share)	—	—	9,214	(414,301)	—	—	(405,087)
Balance at February 2, 2013	192,604	$ 2,496	$ 627,065	$1,553,058	$(990,729)	$ 29,297	$1,221,187
Stock awards	—	—	1,184	—	—	—	1,184
Repurchase of common stock as part of publicly announced programs	(1,600)	—	—	—	(33,051)	—	(33,051)
Repurchase of common stock from employees	(1,059)	—	—	—	(23,385)	—	(23,385)
Reissuance of treasury stock	3,204	—	(56,706)	6,090	55,831	—	5,215
Net income	—	—	—	82,983	—	—	82,983
Other comprehensive income	—	—	—	—	—	(17,140)	(17,140)
Cash dividends and dividend equivalents ($0.375 per share)	—	—	1,465	(72,280)	—	—	(70,815)
Balance at February 1, 2014	193,149	$ 2,496	$ 573,008	$1,569,851	$(991,334)	$ 12,157	$1,166,178
Stock awards	—	—	12,372	—	—	—	12,372
Repurchase of common stock from employees	(517)	—	—	—	(7,464)	—	(7,464)
Reissuance of treasury stock	1,884	—	(17,988)	(7,503)	33,232	—	7,741
Net income	—	—	—	80,322	—	—	80,322
Other comprehensive income	—	—	—	—	—	(22,101)	(22,101)
Cash dividends and dividend equivalents ($0.50 per share)	—	—	2,283	(99,585)	—	—	(97,302)
Balance at January 31, 2015	194,516	$ 2,496	$ 569,675	$1,543,085	$(965,566)	$ (9,944)	$1,139,746

(1)   600,000 authorized, 249,566 issued and 194,516 outstanding, $0.01 par value common stock at January 31, 2015; 600,000 authorized, 249,566 issued and 193,149 outstanding, $0.01 par value common stock at February 1, 2014; 600,000 authorized, 249,566 issued and 192,604 outstanding, $0.01 par value common stock at February 2, 2013. The Company has 5,000 authorized, with none issued or outstanding, $0.01 par value preferred stock at January 31, 2015, February 1, 2014 and February 2, 2013.

(2)   55,050 shares, 56,417 shares, and 56,962 shares at January 31, 2015, February 1, 2014 and February 2, 2013, respectively. During Fiscal 2014, Fiscal 2013, and Fiscal 2012, 1,884 shares, 3,204 shares, and 7,443 shares, respectively, were reissued from treasury stock for the issuance of share-based payments.

Refer to Notes to Consolidated Financial Statements

AMERICAN EAGLE OUTFITTERS, INC.
CONSOLIDATED STATEMENTS OF CASH FLOWS

	For the Years Ended		
	January 31,	February 1,	February 2,
(In thousands)	2015	2014	2013
Operating activities:			
Net income	$ 80,322	$ 82,983	$ 232,108
Loss from discontinued operations, net of tax	8,465	—	31,990
Income from continuing operations	$ 88,787	$ 82,983	$ 264,098
Adjustments to reconcile net income to net cash provided by operating activities			
Depreciation and amortization	142,351	134,047	128,397
Share-based compensation	16,070	(6,541)	66,349
Deferred income taxes	(2,279)	20,100	(30,647)
Foreign currency transaction loss (gain)	(495)	1,378	100
Loss on impairment of assets	33,468	44,465	34,869
Changes in assets and liabilities:			
Merchandise inventory	8,586	40,148	35,202
Accounts receivable	3,084	(29,511)	(6,664)
Prepaid expenses and other	14,282	(10,844)	404
Other assets	6,612	(36,089)	(8,165)
Accounts payable	(5,280)	28,568	(10,468)
Unredeemed gift cards and gift certificates	1,238	1,269	1,473
Deferred lease credits	(4,528)	583	(11,073)
Accrued compensation and payroll taxes	20,716	(42,465)	23,018
Accrued income and other taxes	24,826	(25,840)	(7,408)
Accrued liabilities	(9,012)	27,605	20,186
Total adjustments	249,639	146,873	235,573
Net cash provided by operating activities from continuing operations	**338,426**	**229,856**	**499,671**
Investing activities:			
Capital expenditures for property and equipment	(245,002)	(278,499)	(93,939)
Purchase of long-lived assets in a business combination	—	(20,751)	—
Acquisition of intangible assets	(1,264)	(6,835)	(1,125)
Purchase of available-for-sale securities	—	(52,065)	(111,086)
Sale of available-for-sale securities	10,002	162,785	15,500
Net cash (used for) provided by investing activities from continuing operations	**(236,264)**	**(195,365)**	**(190,650)**
Financing activities:			
Payments on capital leases and other	(7,143)	(2,839)	(3,066)
Repurchase of common stock as part of publicly announced programs	—	(33,051)	(173,554)
Repurchase of common stock from employees	(7,464)	(23,386)	(4,125)
Net proceeds from stock options exercised	7,305	6,197	76,401
Excess tax benefit from share-based payments	742	8,833	13,279
Cash used to net settle equity awards	—	—	—
Cash dividends paid	(97,224)	(72,280)	(403,490)
Net cash used for financing activities from continuing operations	**(103,784)**	**(116,526)**	**(494,555)**
Effect of exchange rates on cash	(7,578)	(8,151)	504
Cash flows of discontinued operations			
Net cash provided by (used for) operating activities	963	—	(24,616)
Net cash used for investing activities	—	—	(780)
Net cash used for financing activities	—	—	—
Effect of exchange rates on cash	—	—	—
Net cash provided by (used for) discontinued operations	**963**	**—**	**(25,396)**
Net decrease in cash and cash equivalents	**(8,237)**	**(90,186)**	**(210,426)**
Cash and cash equivalents — beginning of period	$ 418,933	$ 509,119	719,545
Cash and cash equivalents — end of period	$ 410,697	$ 418,933	$ 509,119

Refer to Notes to Consolidated Financial Statements

AMERICAN EAGLE OUTFITTERS, INC.
NOTES TO CONSOLIDATED FINANCIAL STATEMENTS
FOR THE YEAR ENDED JANUARY 31, 2015

1.   Business Operations

American Eagle Outfitters, Inc. (the "Company"), a Delaware corporation, operates under the American Eagle Outfitters ® ("AEO") and aerie ® by American Eagle Outfitters ® ("aerie") brands. The Company operated 77kids by American Eagle Outfitters ® ("77kids") until its exit in Fiscal 2012.

Founded in 1977, American Eagle Outfitters is a leading apparel and accessories retailer that operates more than 1,000 retail stores in the U.S. and internationally, online at ae.com and aerie.com and international store locations managed by third-party operators. Through its brands, the Company offers high quality, on-trend clothing, accessories and personal care products at affordable prices. The Company's online business, AEO Direct, ships to 81 countries worldwide.

Merchandise Mix

The following table sets forth the approximate consolidated percentage of total net revenue from continuing operations attributable to each merchandise group for each of the periods indicated:

	For the Years Ended		
	January 31, 2015	February 1, 2014	February 2, 2013
Men's apparel and accessories	39%	40%	39%
Women's apparel and accessories (excluding aerie)	53%	52%	52%
aerie	8%	8%	9%
Total	100%	100%	100%

2.   Summary of Significant Accounting Policies

Fiscal Year

Our financial year is a 52/53 week year that ends on the Saturday nearest to January 31. As used herein, "Fiscal 2015" refers to the 52 week period ending January 30, 2016. "Fiscal 2014" and "Fiscal 2013" refer to the 52 week period ended January 31, 2015 and February 1, 2014, respectively. "Fiscal 2012" refers to the 53 week period ended February 2, 2013. "Fiscal 2011" and "Fiscal 2010" refer to the 52 week periods ended January 28, 2012 and January 29, 2011, respectively.

Estimates

The preparation of financial statements in conformity with accounting principles generally accepted in the United States of America ("GAAP") requires the Company's management to make estimates and assumptions that affect the reported amounts of assets and liabilities and disclosure of contingent assets and liabilities at the date of the financial statements and the reported amounts of revenues and expenses during the reporting period. Actual results could differ from those estimates. On an ongoing basis, our management reviews its estimates based on currently available information. Changes in facts and circumstances may result in revised estimates.

Cash and Cash Equivalents, Short-term Investments and Long-term Investments

Cash includes cash equivalents. The Company considers all highly liquid investments purchased with a remaining maturity of three months or less to be cash equivalents.

As of February 1, 2014, short-term investments include treasury bills and term-deposits purchased with a maturity of greater than three months, but less than one year.

Long-term investments are included within other assets on the Company's Consolidated Balance Sheets. As of January 31, 2015 and February 1, 2014, the Company held no long-term investments.

Refer to Note 3 to the Consolidated Financial Statements for information regarding cash and cash equivalents and investments.

Merchandise Inventory

Merchandise inventory is valued at the lower of average cost or market, utilizing the retail method. Average cost includes merchandise design and sourcing costs and related expenses. The Company records merchandise receipts at the time which both title and risk of loss for the merchandise transfers to the Company.

The Company reviews its inventory levels to identify slow-moving merchandise and generally uses markdowns to clear merchandise. Additionally, the Company estimates a markdown reserve for future planned permanent markdowns related to current inventory. Markdowns may occur when inventory exceeds customer demand for reasons of style, seasonal adaptation, changes in customer preference, lack of consumer acceptance of fashion items, competition, or if it is determined that the inventory in stock will not sell at its currently ticketed price. Such markdowns may have a material adverse impact on earnings, depending on the extent and amount of inventory affected. The Company also estimates a shrinkage reserve for the period between the last physical count and the balance sheet date. The estimate for the shrinkage reserve, based on historical results, can be affected by changes in merchandise mix and changes in actual shrinkage trends.

AMERICAN EAGLE OUTFITTERS, INC.

NOTES TO CONSOLIDATED FINANCIAL STATEMENTS — (Continued)

Property and Equipment

Property and equipment is recorded on the basis of cost with depreciation computed utilizing the straight-line method over the assets' estimated useful lives. The useful lives of our major classes of assets are as follows:

Buildings	25 years
Leasehold improvements	Lesser of 10 years or the term of the lease
Fixtures and equipment	5 years

In accordance with ASC 360, *Property, Plant, and Equipment* , the Company's management evaluates the value of leasehold improvements and store fixtures associated with retail stores, which have been open for a period of time sufficient to reach maturity. The Company evaluates long-lived assets for impairment at the individual store level, which is the lowest level at which individual cash flows can be identified. Impairment losses are recorded on long-lived assets used in operations when events and circumstances indicate that the assets might be impaired and the undiscounted cash flows estimated to be generated by those assets are less than the carrying amounts of the assets. When events such as these occur, the impaired assets are adjusted to their estimated fair value and an impairment loss is recorded separately as a component of operating income under loss on impairment of assets.

During Fiscal 2014, the Company recorded pre-tax asset impairment charges of $33.5 million that includes $25.1 million for the impairment of 79 retail stores recorded as a loss on impairment of assets in the Consolidated Statements of Operations. Based on the Company's evaluation of current and future projected performance, it was determined that these stores would not be able to generate sufficient cash flow over the expected remaining lease term to recover the carrying value of the respective stores' assets. Additionally, the Company recorded $8.4 million of impairment charges related to corporate assets.

During Fiscal 2013, the Company recorded asset impairment charges of $44.5 million consisting of $25.2 million for the impairment of 69 retail stores and $19.3 million for the Company's Warrendale, Pennsylvania Distribution Center, recorded as a loss on impairment of assets in the Consolidated Statements of Operations. The retail store impairments were recorded based on the results of the Company's evaluation of stores that considered performance during the holiday selling season and a significant portfolio review in the fourth quarter of Fiscal 2013 that considered current and future performance projections and strategic real estate initiatives. The Company determined that these stores would not be able to generate sufficient cash flow over the expected remaining lease term to recover the carrying value of the respective stores assets.

During Fiscal 2012, the Company recorded asset impairment charges of $34.9 million consisting of the impairment of 52 retail stores, which is recorded as a loss on impairment of assets in the Consolidated Statements of Operations. This impairment was recorded based on the results of the Company's evaluation of stores that considered performance during the holiday selling season and strategic decisions made in the fourth quarter of Fiscal 2012 regarding the rebalancing of our store fleet. The Company determined that these stores would not be able to generate sufficient cash flow over the expected remaining lease term to recover the carrying value of the respective stores assets. Additionally, the Company recorded $16.6 million of store asset impairment charges related to 77kids stores, which is included in Discontinued Operations.

Refer to Note 15 to the Consolidated Financial Statements for additional information regarding the discontinued operations for 77kids.

When the Company closes, remodels or relocates a store prior to the end of its lease term, the remaining net book value of the assets related to the store is recorded as a write-off of assets within depreciation and amortization expense.

Refer to Note 7 to the Consolidated Financial Statements for additional information regarding property and equipment.

Revenue Recognition

Revenue is recorded for store sales upon the purchase of merchandise by customers. The Company's e-commerce operation records revenue upon the estimated customer receipt date of the merchandise. Shipping and handling revenues are included in total net revenue. Sales tax collected from customers is excluded from revenue and is included as part of accrued income and other taxes on the Company's Consolidated Balance Sheets.

Revenue is recorded net of estimated and actual sales returns and deductions for coupon redemptions and other promotions. The Company records the impact of adjustments to its sales return reserve quarterly within total net revenue and cost of sales. The sales return reserve reflects an estimate of sales returns based on projected merchandise returns determined through the use of historical average return percentages.

| | For the Years Ended | | |
(In thousands)	January 31, 2015	February 1, 2014	February 2, 2013
Beginning balance	$ 2,205	$ 4,481	$ 2,929
Returns	(79,813)	(85,871)	(86,895)
Provisions	80,857	83,595	88,447
Ending balance	$ 3,249	$ 2,205	$ 4,481

AMERICAN EAGLE OUTFITTERS, INC.

NOTES TO CONSOLIDATED FINANCIAL STATEMENTS — (Continued)

Revenue is not recorded on the purchase of gift cards. A current liability is recorded upon purchase, and revenue is recognized when the gift card is redeemed for merchandise. Additionally, the Company recognizes revenue on unredeemed gift cards based on an estimate of the amounts that will not be redeemed ("gift card breakage"), determined through historical redemption trends. Gift card breakage revenue is recognized in proportion to actual gift card redemptions as a component of total net revenue. For further information on the Company's gift card program, refer to the Gift Cards caption below.

The Company recognizes royalty revenue generated from its franchise agreements based upon a percentage of merchandise sales by the franchisee. This revenue is recorded as a component of total net revenue when earned.

Cost of Sales, Including Certain Buying, Occupancy and Warehousing Expenses

Cost of sales consists of merchandise costs, including design, sourcing, importing and inbound freight costs, as well as markdowns, shrinkage and certain promotional costs (collectively "merchandise costs") and buying, occupancy and warehousing costs.

Design costs are related to the Company's Design Center operations and include compensation, travel, supplies and samples for our design teams, as well as rent and depreciation for the Company's Design Center. These costs are included in cost of sales as the respective inventory is sold.

Buying, occupancy and warehousing costs consist of compensation, employee benefit expenses and travel for the Company's buyers and certain senior merchandising executives; rent and utilities related to the Company's stores, corporate headquarters, distribution centers and other office space; freight from the Company's distribution centers to the stores; compensation and supplies for the Company's distribution centers, including purchasing, receiving and inspection costs; and shipping and handling costs related to our e-commerce operation. Gross profit is the difference between total net revenue and cost of sales.

Selling, General and Administrative Expenses

Selling, general and administrative expenses consist of compensation and employee benefit expenses, including salaries, incentives and related benefits associated with the Company's stores and corporate headquarters. Selling, general and administrative expenses also include advertising costs, supplies for our stores and home office, communication costs, travel and entertainment, leasing costs and services purchased. Selling, general and administrative expenses do not include compensation, employee benefit expenses and travel for the Company's design, sourcing and importing teams, the Company's buyers and the Company's distribution centers as these amounts are recorded in cost of sales.

Advertising Costs

Certain advertising costs, including direct mail, in-store photographs and other promotional costs are expensed when the marketing campaign commences. As of January 31, 2015 and February 1, 2014, the Company had prepaid advertising expense of $6.6 million and $9.0 million, respectively. All other advertising costs are expensed as incurred. The Company recognized $94.2 million, $87.0 million and $90.0 million in advertising expense during Fiscal 2014, Fiscal 2013 and Fiscal 2012, respectively.

Store Pre-Opening Costs

Store pre-opening costs consist primarily of rent, advertising, supplies and payroll expenses. These costs are expensed as incurred.

Other Income, Net

Other income, net consists primarily of interest income/expense, foreign currency transaction gain/loss and realized investment gains/losses.

Gift Cards

The value of a gift card is recorded as a current liability upon purchase and revenue is recognized when the gift card is redeemed for merchandise. The Company estimates gift card breakage and recognizes revenue in proportion to actual gift card redemptions as a component of total net revenue. The Company determines an estimated gift card breakage rate by continuously evaluating historical redemption data and the time when there is a remote likelihood that a gift card will be redeemed. The Company recorded gift card breakage of $7.0 million, $7.3 million and $8.9 million during Fiscal 2014, Fiscal 2013 and Fiscal 2012, respectively.

AMERICAN EAGLE OUTFITTERS, INC.

NOTES TO CONSOLIDATED FINANCIAL STATEMENTS — (Continued)

3.   Cash and Cash Equivalents, Short-term Investments and Long-term Investments

The following table summarizes the fair market value of our cash and marketable securities, which are recorded on the Consolidated Balance Sheets:

(In thousands)	January 31, 2015	February 1, 2014
Cash and cash equivalents:		
Cash	370,692	$330,013
Money-market	40,005	25,696
Treasury bills	—	63,224
Total cash and cash equivalents	410,697	$418,933
Short-term investments:		
Treasury bills	—	$ 10,002
Total short-term investments	—	$ 10,002
Total	410,697	$428,935

Proceeds from the sale of available-for-sale securities were $10.0 million, $162.8 million and $15.5 million for Fiscal 2014, Fiscal 2013 and Fiscal 2012, respectively. Purchases of available-for-sale securities for Fiscal 2013 and Fiscal 2012 were $52.1 million and $111.1 million, respectively. At January 31, 2015 and February 1, 2014, the fair value of all available for sale securities approximated par, with no gross unrealized holding gains or losses.

4.   Fair Value Measurements

ASC 820, *Fair Value Measurement Disclosures* ("ASC 820"), defines fair value, establishes a framework for measuring fair value in accordance with GAAP, and expands disclosures about fair value measurements. Fair value is defined under ASC 820 as the exit price associated with the sale of an asset or transfer of a liability in an orderly transaction between market participants at the measurement date.

Financial Instruments

Valuation techniques used to measure fair value under ASC 820 must maximize the use of observable inputs and minimize the use of unobservable inputs. In addition, ASC 820 establishes this three-tier fair value hierarchy, which prioritizes the inputs used in measuring fair value. These tiers include:

- *Level 1* — Quoted prices in active markets for identical assets or liabilities.

- *Level 2* — Inputs other than Level 1 that are observable, either directly or indirectly, such as quoted prices for similar assets or liabilities; quoted prices in markets that are not active; or other inputs that are observable or can be corroborated by observable market data for substantially the full term of the assets or liabilities.

- *Level 3* — Unobservable inputs (i.e., projections, estimates, interpretations, etc.) that are supported by little or no market activity and that are significant to the fair value of the assets or liabilities.

As of January 31, 2015 and February 1, 2014, the Company held certain assets that are required to be measured at fair value on a recurring basis. These include cash equivalents and investments.

In accordance with ASC 820, the following tables represent the fair value hierarchy for the Company's financial assets (cash equivalents and investments) measured at fair value on a recurring basis as of January 31, 2015 and February 1, 2014:

| | | Fair Value Measurements at January 31, 2015 | | |
| | | Quoted Market Prices in Active Markets for Identical Assets | Significant Other | Significant Unobservable |
(In thousands)	Carrying Amount	(Level 1)	Observable Inputs (Level 2)	Inputs (Level 3)
Cash and cash equivalents				
Cash	$370,692	$ 370,692	$ —	$ —
Money-market	40,005	40,005	—	—
Total cash and cash equivalents	$410,697	$ 410,697	$ —	$ —
Total short-term investments	—	—	—	—
Total	$410,697	$ 410,697	$ —	$ —

AMERICAN EAGLE OUTFITTERS, INC.

NOTES TO CONSOLIDATED FINANCIAL STATEMENTS — (Continued)

(In thousands)	Carrying Amount	Fair Value Measurements at February 1, 2014		
		Quoted Market Prices in Active Markets for Identical Assets (Level 1)	Significant Other Observable Inputs (Level 2)	Significant Unobservable Inputs (Level 3)
Cash and cash equivalents				
Cash	$330,013	$ 330,013	$ —	$ —
Treasury bills	63,224	63,224	—	—
Money-market	25,696	25,696	—	—
Total cash and cash equivalents	$418,933	$ 418,933	$ —	$ —
Short-term investments				
Treasury bills	$ 10,002	$ 10,002	$ —	$ —
Total short-term investments	$ 10,002	$ 10,002	$ —	$ —
Total	$428,935	$ 428,935	$ —	$ —

In the event the Company holds Level 3 investments, a discounted cash flow model is used to value those investments. There were no Level 3 investments at January 31, 2015 or February 1, 2014.

Non-Financial Assets

The Company's non-financial assets, which include goodwill, intangible assets and property and equipment, are not required to be measured at fair value on a recurring basis. However, if certain triggering events occur, or if an annual impairment test is required and the Company is required to evaluate the non-financial instrument for impairment, a resulting asset impairment would require that the non-financial asset be recorded at the estimated fair value. As a result of the Company's annual goodwill impairment test performed as of January 31, 2015, the Company concluded that its goodwill was not impaired.

Certain long-lived assets were measured at fair value on a nonrecurring basis using Level 3 inputs as defined in ASC 820. During Fiscal 2014 and Fiscal 2013, certain long-lived assets related to the Company's retail stores and corporate assets were determined to be unable to recover their respective carrying values and were written down to their fair value, resulting in a loss of $33.5 million and $44.5 million, respectively, which is recorded as a loss on impairment of assets within the Consolidated Statements of Operations. The fair value of the impaired assets after the recorded loss is an immaterial amount.

The fair value of the Company's stores were determined by estimating the amount and timing of net future cash flows and discounting them using a risk-adjusted rate of interest. The Company estimates future cash flows based on its experience and knowledge of the market in which the store is located.

5.   Earnings per Share

The following is a reconciliation between basic and diluted weighted average shares outstanding:

(In thousands, except per share amounts)	For the Years Ended		
	January 31, 2015	February 1, 2014	February 2, 2013
Weighted average common shares outstanding:			
Basic number of common shares outstanding	194,437	192,802	196,211
Dilutive effect of stock options and non-vested restricted stock	698	1,673	4,454
Dilutive number of common shares outstanding	195,135	194,475	200,665

Equity awards to purchase approximately 2.3 million, 1.7 million and 1.5 million shares of common stock during the Fiscal 2014, Fiscal 2013 and Fiscal 2012, respectively, were outstanding, but were not included in the computation of weighted average diluted common share amounts as the effect of doing so would have been anti-dilutive.

Additionally, for Fiscal 2014, approximately 1.9 million of performance-based restricted stock awards were not included in the computation of weighted average diluted common share amounts because the number of shares ultimately issued is contingent on the Company's performance compared to pre-established performance goals. For Fiscal 2013, approximately 1.8 million of performance-based restricted stock awards were not included in the computation of weighted average diluted common share amounts because the number of shares ultimately issued is contingent on the Company's performance compared to pre-established performance goals.

Refer to Note 12 to the Consolidated Financial Statements for additional information regarding share-based compensation.

AMERICAN EAGLE OUTFITTERS, INC.

NOTES TO CONSOLIDATED FINANCIAL STATEMENTS — (Continued)

6.   Accounts Receivable

Accounts receivable are comprised of the following:

(In thousands)	January 31, 2015	February 1, 2014
Franchise and license receivable	$ 24,945	$ 22,943
Merchandise sell-offs and vendor receivables	12,953	16,106
Credit card program receivable	9,637	15,000
Marketing cost reimbursements	4,640	6,063
Gift card receivable	4,453	986
Landlord construction allowances	3,354	11,626
Other Items	7,912	1,158
Total	$ 67,894	$ 73,882

7.   Property and Equipment

Property and equipment consists of the following:

(In thousands)	January 31, 2015	February 1, 2014
Land	$ 17,495	$ 17,986
Buildings	201,024	140,600
Leasehold improvements	571,312	600,572
Fixtures and equipment	852,408	732,228
Construction in progress	42,470	102,974
Property and equipment, at cost	$1,684,709	$1,594,360
Less: Accumulated depreciation	(989,853)	(961,374)
Property and equipment, net	$ 694,856	$ 632,986

Depreciation expense is summarized as follows:

	For the Years Ended		
(In thousands)	January 31, 2015	February 1, 2014	February 2, 2013
Depreciation expense	$132,529	$116,761	$122,756

Additionally, during Fiscal 2014, Fiscal 2013 and Fiscal 2012, the Company recorded $6.4 million, $14.6 million and $3.7 million, respectively, related to asset write-offs within depreciation and amortization expense.

8.   Intangible Assets

Intangible assets include costs to acquire and register the Company's trademark assets. The following table represents intangible assets as of January 31, 2015 and February 1, 2014:

(In thousands)	January 31, 2015	February 1, 2014
Trademarks, at cost	$ 59,385	$ 58,121
Less: Accumulated amortization	(12,179)	(8,850)
Intangible assets, net	$ 47,206	$ 49,271

Amortization expense is summarized as follows:

	For the Years Ended		
(In thousands)	January 31, 2015	February 1, 2014	February 2, 2013
Amortization expense	$ 3,465	$ 2,714	$ 1,952

AMERICAN EAGLE OUTFITTERS, INC.

NOTES TO CONSOLIDATED FINANCIAL STATEMENTS — (Continued)

The table below summarizes the estimated future amortization expense for intangible assets existing as of January 31, 2015 for the next five Fiscal Years:

(In thousands)	Future Amortization
2015	3,404
2016	3,473
2017	3,472
2018	3,452
2019	3,433

9.   Other Credit Arrangements

In December 2014, the Company entered into a new Credit Agreement ("Credit Agreement") for five-year, syndicated, asset-based revolving credit facilities (the "Credit Facilities"). The Credit Agreement provides senior secured revolving credit for loans and letters of credit up to $400 million, subject to customary borrowing base limitations. The Credit Facilities provide increased financial flexibility and take advantage of a favorable credit environment.

All obligations under the Credit Facilities are unconditionally guaranteed by certain subsidiaries. The obligations under the Credit Agreement are secured by a first-priority security interest in certain working capital assets of the borrowers and guarantors, consisting primarily of cash, receivables, inventory and certain other assets, and will be further secured by first-priority mortgages on certain real property.

As of January 31, 2015, the Company was in compliance with the terms of the Credit Agreement and had $8.1 million outstanding in stand-by letters of credit. No loans were outstanding under the Credit Agreement on January 31, 2015.

The Credit Facilities replace the Company's syndicated, unsecured, revolving credit facility in the amount of $150.0 million.

Additionally, the Company has borrowing agreements with two separate financial institutions under which it may borrow an aggregate of $155.0 million USD for the purposes of trade letter of credit issuances. The availability of any future borrowings under the trade letter of credit facilities is subject to acceptance by the respective financial institutions.

As of January 31, 2015, the Company had outstanding trade letters of credit of $13.7 million.

10.   Leases

The Company leases all store premises, some of its office space and certain information technology and office equipment. The store leases generally have initial terms of 10 years and are classified as operating leases. Most of these store leases provide for base rentals and the payment of a percentage of sales as additional contingent rent when sales exceed specified levels. Additionally, most leases contain construction allowances and/or rent holidays. In recognizing landlord incentives and minimum rent expense, the Company amortizes the items on a straight-line basis over the lease term (including the pre-opening build-out period).

A summary of fixed minimum and contingent rent expense for all operating leases follows:

	For the Years Ended		
(In thousands)	January 31, 2015	February 1, 2014	February 2, 2013
Store rent:			
Fixed minimum	$279,640	$260,668	$250,844
Contingent	6,733	6,576	9,758
Total store rent, excluding common area maintenance charges, real estate taxes and certain other expenses	$286,373	$267,244	$260,602
Offices, distribution facilities, equipment and other	15,449	17,153	14,960
Total rent expense	$301,822	$284,397	$275,562

In addition, the Company is typically responsible under its store, office and distribution center leases for tenant occupancy costs, including maintenance costs, common area charges, real estate taxes and certain other expenses.

AMERICAN EAGLE OUTFITTERS, INC.
NOTES TO CONSOLIDATED FINANCIAL STATEMENTS — (Continued)

The table below summarizes future minimum lease obligations, consisting of fixed minimum rent, under operating leases in effect at January 31, 2015:

(In thousands)	Future Minimum Lease Obligations
Fiscal years:	
2015	287,091
2016	259,106
2017	229,489
2018	199,208
2019	173,388
Thereafter	549,046
Total	1,697,328

ITEM 9.   *IN AND DISAGREEMENTS WITH ACCOUNTANTS ON ACCOUNTING AND FINANCIAL DISCLOSURE.*
**   *CHANGES***

None.

ITEM 9A.   *CONTROLS AND PROCEDURES.*

Disclosure Controls and Procedures

We maintain disclosure controls and procedures that are designed to provide reasonable assurance that information required to be disclosed in our reports under the Securities Exchange Act of 1934, as amended (the "Exchange Act"), is recorded, processed, summarized and reported within the time periods specified in the SEC's rules and forms, and that such information is accumulated and communicated to the management of American Eagle Outfitters, Inc. (the "Management"), including our Principal Executive Officer and our Principal Financial Officer, as appropriate, to allow timely decisions regarding required disclosure. In designing and evaluating the disclosure controls and procedures, Management recognized that any controls and procedures, no matter how well designed and operated, can provide only reasonable assurance of achieving the desired control objectives.

In connection with the preparation of this Annual Report on Form 10-K as of January 31, 2015, an evaluation was performed under the supervision and with the participation of our Management, including the Principal Executive Officer and Principal Financial Officer, of the effectiveness of the design and operation of the Company's disclosure controls and procedures (as defined in Rule 13a-15(e) under the Exchange Act). Based upon that evaluation, our Principal Executive Officer and our Principal Financial Officer have concluded that our disclosure controls and procedures were effective at the reasonable assurance level as of the end of the period covered by this Annual Report on Form 10-K.

Management's Annual Report on Internal Control Over Financial Reporting

Our Management is responsible for establishing and maintaining adequate internal control over financial reporting (as defined in Rule 13a-15(f) under the Exchange Act). Our internal control over financial reporting is designed to provide a reasonable assurance to our Management and our Board regarding the preparation and fair presentation of published financial statements.

All internal control systems, no matter how well designed, have inherent limitations. Therefore, even those systems determined to be effective can provide only reasonable assurance with respect to financial statement preparation and presentation.

Our Management assessed the effectiveness of our internal control over financial reporting as of January 31, 2015. In making this assessment, our Management used the criteria set forth by the Committee of Sponsoring Organizations of the Treadway Commission (COSO) in Internal Control — Integrated Framework (2013). Based on this assessment, our Management concluded that we maintained effective internal control over financial reporting as of January 31, 2015.

The Company's independent registered public accounting firm that audited the financial statements included in this Annual Report issued an attestation report on the Company's internal control over financial reporting.

Changes in Internal Control Over Financial Reporting

There were no changes in our internal control over financial reporting during the three months ended January 31, 2015 that have materially affected, or are reasonably likely to materially affect, our internal control over financial reporting.

Report of Independent Registered Public Accounting Firm

The Board of Directors and Stockholders of American Eagle Outfitters, Inc.

We have audited American Eagle Outfitters, Inc.'s internal control over financial reporting as of January 31, 2015, based on criteria established in Internal Control — Integrated Framework issued by the Committee of Sponsoring Organizations of the Treadway Commission (2013 framework) (the COSO criteria). American Eagle Outfitters, Inc.'s management is responsible for maintaining effective internal control over financial reporting, and for its assessment of the effectiveness of internal control over financial reporting included in the accompanying Management's Annual Report on Internal Control over Financial Reporting. Our responsibility is to express an opinion on the Company's internal control over financial reporting based on our audit.

We conducted our audit in accordance with the standards of the Public Company Accounting Oversight Board (United States). Those standards require that we plan and perform the audit to obtain reasonable assurance about whether effective internal control over financial reporting was maintained in all material respects. Our audit included obtaining an understanding of internal control over financial reporting, assessing the risk that a material weakness exists, testing and evaluating the design and operating effectiveness of internal control based on the assessed risk, and performing such other procedures as we considered necessary in the circumstances. We believe that our audit provides a reasonable basis for our opinion.

A company's internal control over financial reporting is a process designed to provide reasonable assurance regarding the reliability of financial reporting and the preparation of financial statements for external purposes in accordance with generally accepted accounting principles. A company's internal control over financial reporting includes those policies and procedures that (1) pertain to the maintenance of records that, in reasonable detail, accurately and fairly reflect the transactions and dispositions of the assets of the company; (2) provide reasonable assurance that transactions are recorded as necessary to permit preparation of financial statements in accordance with generally accepted accounting principles, and that receipts and expenditures of the company are being made only in accordance with authorizations of management and directors of the company; and (3) provide reasonable assurance regarding prevention or timely detection of unauthorized acquisition, use or disposition of the company's assets that could have a material effect on the financial statements.

Because of its inherent limitations, internal control over financial reporting may not prevent or detect misstatements. Also, projections of any evaluation of effectiveness to future periods are subject to the risk that controls may become inadequate because of changes in conditions, or that the degree of compliance with the policies or procedures may deteriorate.

In our opinion, American Eagle Outfitters, Inc. maintained, in all material respects, effective internal control over financial reporting as of January 31, 2015, based on the COSO criteria.

We also have audited, in accordance with the standards of the Public Company Accounting Oversight Board (United States), the consolidated balance sheets of American Eagle Outfitters, Inc. as of January 31, 2015 and February 1, 2014 and the related consolidated statements of operations, comprehensive income, stockholders' equity, and cash flows for each of the three years in the period ended January 31, 2015 of American Eagle Outfitters, Inc. and our report dated March 11, 2015 expressed an unqualified opinion thereon.

/s/   Ernst & Young LLP

Pittsburgh, Pennsylvania
March 11, 2015

For the complete annual report, go online to http://corporate.buckle.com/investors/annual-reports

FINANCIAL HIGHLIGHTS

(DOLLAR AMOUNTS IN THOUSANDS EXCEPT PER SHARE AMOUNTS AND SELECTED OPERATING DATA)

Buckle

	JANUARY 31, 2015	FEBRUARY 1, 2014	FEBRUARY 2, 2013 (a)
INCOME STATEMENT DATA			
NET SALES	$ 1,153,142	$ 1,128,001	$ 1,124,007
INCOME BEFORE INCOME TAXES	$ 259,696	$ 260,456	$ 261,699
PROVISION FOR INCOME TAXES	$ 97,132	$ 97,872	$ 97,394
NET INCOME	$ 162,564	$ 162,584	$ 164,305
DILUTED EARNINGS PER SHARE	$ 3.38	$ 3.39	$ 3.44
NET INCOME AS A PERCENTAGE OF NET SALES	14.1%	14.4%	14.6%
BALANCE SHEET DATA			
WORKING CAPITAL	$ 202,318	$ 218,756	$ 147,917
LONG-TERM INVESTMENTS	$ 43,698	$ 43,436	$ 35,735
TOTAL ASSETS	$ 542,993	$ 546,293	$ 477,974
LONG-TERM DEBT	$ –	$ –	$ –
STOCKHOLDERS' EQUITY	$ 355,278	$ 361,930	$ 289,649
SELECTED OPERATING DATA			
NUMBER OF STORES OPEN AT YEAR END	460	450	440
AVERAGE SALES PER SQUARE FOOT	$ 459	$ 461	$ 475
AVERAGE SALES PER STORE (000'S)	$ 2,321	$ 2,318	$ 2,380
COMPARABLE STORE SALES CHANGE	–%	–%	2.1%

(a) CONSISTS OF 53 WEEKS.

NET SALES (AMOUNTS IN MILLIONS)

2005	$501
2006	$530
2007	$620
2008	$792
2009	$898
2010	$950
2011	$1,063
2012	$1,124
2013	$1,128
2014	$1,153

DILUTED EARNINGS PER SHARE

2005	$1.13
2006	$1.24
2007	$1.63
2008	$2.24
2009	$2.73
2010	$2.86
2011	$3.20
2012	$3.44
2013	$3.39
2014	$3.38

DEAR SHAREHOLDERS:

Thanks to the commitment to excellence by Buckle's nearly 9,000 teammates, fiscal 2014 was another strong year. Net sales increased 2.2% to a record $1.153 billion – our 13th consecutive year of growth in total net sales – and our comparable store sales were even with fiscal 2013. Net income was essentially flat at $162.6 million or $3.38 per diluted share in 2014 compared to $162.6 million or $3.39 per diluted share in 2013. Our gross margin for the year was 44.0% compared 44.2% in 2013 and our operating margin was 22.3% compared to 22.8% for 2013 – marking our 6th consecutive year with a gross margin over 44.0% and an operating margin above 22.0%.

Our consistent and high level of profitability has given us the opportunity to reward our loyal shareholders, and 2014 was no exception. In January, we paid a $2.77 per share special cash dividend – our 7th consecutive fiscal year with a special dividend and 8th out of the last 9 years. We also increased our quarterly dividend 4.5% from $0.22 per share to $0.23 per share in January 2015. The $176.6 million we paid in dividends during fiscal 2014 brings our total cash returned to shareholders over the past 10 years to $1.336 billion, including $1.188 billion in dividends and $148.0 million in share repurchases. Additionally, our year-end balance sheet remains strong with $203.3 million of total cash and investments, stockholders' equity of $355.3 million, and no long term debt as of January 31, 2015.

The secret to our continued success truly is the talent, longevity, and dedication of our many outstanding teammates. Everything we do is focused on our mission of *CREATING THE MOST ENJOYABLE SHOPPING EXPERIENCE POSSIBLE FOR OUR GUESTS*. Led by Kari Smith, Michelle Hoffman, and our 21 district leaders, the sales team is *UNSTOPPABLE* in their quest to continually enhance our reputation for service by making the in-store experience special and earning the loyalty of our guests every day. Pat Whisler and Bob Carlberg do an outstanding job of leading our merchandising teams with their excitement for both our merchandise and our guests. Their teams do a tremendous job of identifying trends and working with our vendors to deliver constant newness in terms of exclusive brands, styles, fits, finishes, and details. Teammates in the corporate office are also vital to our success as they support both our stores and our continued growth with their expertise across many disciplines.

Our strong financial position also enables us to invest for the future. During the year, we opened 16 new stores, completed 18 full remodels, and closed 6 stores to end the year with 460 stores in 44 states. Plans for 2015 include 9 new stores and 11 full remodels. We also continued construction during the year on a new 80,000 square foot office building in Kearney, Nebraska, which we expect to be completed in the first quarter of fiscal 2015.

In closing, I would like to take this opportunity to thank each of our teammates for their continued hard work and dedication to serving our guests and fulfilling our mission. I would also like to thank our shareholders, business partners, and guests for their loyalty and support.

Sincerely,

Dennis H. Nelson
PRESIDENT AND CHIEF EXECUTIVE OFFICER

STEADY GROWTH

At Buckle, we are always seeking opportunities to continue our growth. In 2014, we opened 16 new stores, including our first store in Alaska, and completed 18 full remodels. As of January 31, 2015, 365 of our 460 stores featured our signature store design. Plans for 2015 include 9 new store openings and 11 full remodels.

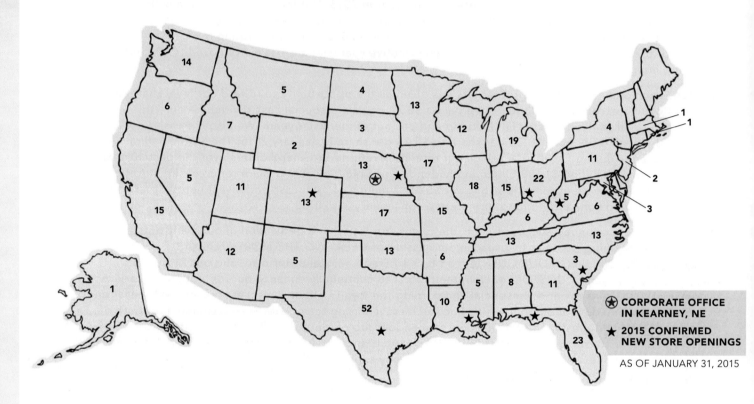

⊛ CORPORATE OFFICE IN KEARNEY, NE

★ 2015 CONFIRMED NEW STORE OPENINGS

AS OF JANUARY 31, 2015

2015 CONFIRMED NEW STORE OPENINGS

BRADLEY, WV
Crossroads Mall

MOUNT PLEASANT, SC
Mount Pleasant Towne Centre

PANAMA CITY BEACH, FL
Pier Park

SLIDELL, LA
Fremaux Town Center

LAKEWOOD (DENVER), CO
Colorado Mills

OMAHA, NE
Village Pointe

SAN ANTONIO, TX
Rivercenter

WEST CHESTER (CINCINNATI), OH
Liberty Center

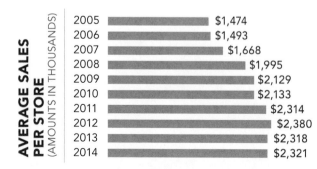

AVERAGE SALES PER STORE (AMOUNTS IN THOUSANDS)

Year	Sales
2005	$1,474
2006	$1,493
2007	$1,668
2008	$1,995
2009	$2,129
2010	$2,133
2011	$2,314
2012	$2,380
2013	$2,318
2014	$2,321

AVERAGE SALES PER SQUARE FOOT

Year	Sales
2005	$298
2006	$302
2007	$335
2008	$401
2009	$428
2010	$428
2011	$462
2012	$475
2013	$461
2014	$459

UNITED STATES
SECURITIES AND EXCHANGE COMMISSION
WASHINGTON, D.C. 20549

FORM 10-K

☒ **ANNUAL REPORT PURSUANT TO SECTION 13 OR 15(d) OF**
THE SECURITIES EXCHANGE ACT OF 1934

For the Fiscal Year Ended **January 31, 2015**

☐ **TRANSITION REPORT PURSUANT TO SECTION 13 OR 15(d) OF**
THE SECURITIES EXCHANGE ACT OF 1934

For the Transition Period from _____ to _____

Commission File Number: 001-12951

THE BUCKLE, INC.

(Exact name of Registrant as specified in its charter)

Nebraska	**47-0366193**
(State or other jurisdiction of incorporation or organization)	(I.R.S. Employer Identification No.)

2407 West 24th Street, Kearney, Nebraska 68845-4915
(Address of principal executive offices)   (Zip Code)

Registrant's telephone number, including area code: **(308) 236-8491**

Securities registered pursuant to Section 12(b) of the Act:

<u>Title of class</u>	<u>Name of Each Exchange on Which Registered</u>
Common Stock, $.01 par value	New York Stock Exchange

Securities registered pursuant to Section 12(g) of the Act: None

Indicate by check mark if the registrant is a well-known seasoned issuer, as defined in Rule 405 of the Securities Act. Yes ☑ No ☐

Indicate by check mark if the registrant is not required to file reports pursuant to Section 13 or 15(d) of the Act. Yes ☐ No ☑

Indicate by check mark whether the registrant (1) has filed all reports required to be filed by Section 13 or 15(d) of the Securities Exchange Act of 1934 during the preceding 12 months (or for such shorter period that the Registrant was required to file such reports) and (2) has been subject to such filing requirements for the past 90 days. Yes ☑ No ☐

Indicate by check mark whether the registrant has submitted electronically and posted on its corporate Web site, if any, every Interactive Data File required to be submitted and posted pursuant to Rule 405 of Regulation S-T during the preceding 12 months (or for a shorter period that the registrant was required to submit and post such files). Yes ☑ No ☐

Indicate by check mark if disclosure of delinquent filers pursuant to Item 405 of Regulation S-K is not contained herein, and will not be contained, to the best of the Registrant's knowledge, in definitive proxy or information statements incorporated by reference in Part III of this Form 10-K or any amendment to this Form 10-K. ☐

Indicate by check mark whether the registrant is a large accelerated filer, accelerated filer, non-accelerated filer, or smaller reporting company. (See definition of "large accelerated filer," "accelerated filer," and "smaller reporting company" in Rule 12b-2 of the Exchange Act). Check one.

☑ Large accelerated filer; ☐ Accelerated filer; ☐ Non-accelerated filer; ☐ Smaller Reporting Company

Indicate by check mark whether the registrant is a shell company (as defined in Rule 12b-2 of the Act). Yes ☐ No ☑

The aggregate market value (based on the closing price of the New York Stock Exchange) of the common stock of the registrant held by non-affiliates of the registrant was $1,254,762,760 on August 2, 2014. For purposes of this response, executive officers and directors are deemed to be the affiliates of the Registrant and the holdings by non-affiliates was computed as 27,877,422 shares.

The number of shares outstanding of the Registrant's Common Stock, as of March 26, 2015, was 48,532,963.

DOCUMENTS INCORPORATED BY REFERENCE

Portions of the definitive Proxy Statement for the registrant's 2015 Annual Meeting of Shareholders to be held May 29, 2015 are incorporated by reference in Part III.

Source: BUCKLE INC, 10-K, April 01, 2015

Powered by Morningstar® Document Research℠

The information contained herein may not be copied, adapted or distributed and is not warranted to be accurate, complete or timely. The user assumes all risks for any damages or losses arising from any use of this information, except to the extent such damages or losses cannot be limited or excluded by applicable law. Past financial performance is no guarantee of future results.

ITEM 8 - FINANCIAL STATEMENTS AND SUPPLEMENTARY DATA

REPORT OF INDEPENDENT REGISTERED PUBLIC ACCOUNTING FIRM

To the Board of Directors and Stockholders of
The Buckle, Inc.
Kearney, Nebraska

We have audited the accompanying consolidated balance sheets of The Buckle, Inc. and subsidiary (the "Company") as of January 31, 2015 and February 1, 2014, and the related consolidated statements of income, comprehensive income, stockholders' equity, and cash flows for each of the three fiscal years in the period ended January 31, 2015. Our audits also included the financial statement schedule listed in the Index at Item 15. These financial statements and financial statement schedule are the responsibility of the Company's management. Our responsibility is to express an opinion on the financial statements and financial statement schedule based on our audits.

We conducted our audits in accordance with the standards of the Public Company Accounting Oversight Board (United States). Those standards require that we plan and perform the audit to obtain reasonable assurance about whether the financial statements are free of material misstatement. An audit includes examining, on a test basis, evidence supporting the amounts and disclosures in the financial statements. An audit also includes assessing the accounting principles used and significant estimates made by management, as well as evaluating the overall financial statement presentation. We believe that our audits provide a reasonable basis for our opinion.

In our opinion, such consolidated financial statements present fairly, in all material respects, the financial position of The Buckle, Inc. and subsidiary as of January 31, 2015 and February 1, 2014, and the results of their operations and their cash flows for each of the three fiscal years in the period ended January 31, 2015, in conformity with accounting principles generally accepted in the United States of America. Also, in our opinion, such financial statement schedule, when considered in relation to the basic consolidated financial statements taken as a whole, presents fairly, in all material respects, the information set forth therein.

We have also audited, in accordance with the standards of the Public Company Accounting Oversight Board (United States), the Company's internal control over financial reporting as of January 31, 2015, based on the criteria established in *Internal Control - Integrated Framework (2013)* issued by the Committee of Sponsoring Organizations of the Treadway Commission and our report dated April 1, 2015 expressed an unqualified opinion on the Company's internal control over financial reporting.

/s/ Deloitte & Touche LLP

DELOITTE & TOUCHE LLP
Omaha, Nebraska
April 1, 2015

Source: BUCKLE INC, 10-K, April 01, 2015

Powered by Morningstar® Document Research℠

The information contained herein may not be copied, adapted or distributed and is not warranted to be accurate, complete or timely. The user assumes all risks for any damages or losses arising from any use of this information, except to the extent such damages or losses cannot be limited or excluded by applicable law. Past financial performance is no guarantee of future results.

THE BUCKLE, INC.

CONSOLIDATED BALANCE SHEETS
(Amounts in Thousands Except Share and Per Share Amounts)

ASSETS		January 31, 2015		February 1, 2014
CURRENT ASSETS:				
Cash and cash equivalents	$	133,708	$	164,868
Short-term investments (Notes A, B, and C)		25,857		20,197
Receivables		8,567		4,318
Inventory		129,921		124,141
Prepaid expenses and other assets (Note F)		26,536		28,613
Total current assets		324,589		342,137
PROPERTY AND EQUIPMENT (Note D)		427,915		393,656
Less accumulated depreciation and amortization		(255,252)		(235,087)
		172,663		158,569
LONG-TERM INVESTMENTS (Notes A, B, and C)		43,698		43,436
OTHER ASSETS (Note G)		2,043		2,151
	$	542,993	$	546,293

LIABILITIES AND STOCKHOLDERS' EQUITY

CURRENT LIABILITIES:				
Accounts payable	$	35,714	$	37,147
Accrued employee compensation		36,920		36,933
Accrued store operating expenses		9,984		9,983
Gift certificates redeemable		23,992		23,131
Income taxes payable		15,661		16,187
Total current liabilities		122,271		123,381
DEFERRED COMPENSATION (Note I)		14,261		12,797
DEFERRED RENT LIABILITY		40,566		37,564
OTHER LIABILITIES (Note F)		10,617		10,621
Total liabilities		187,715		184,363
COMMITMENTS (Notes E and H)				
STOCKHOLDERS' EQUITY (Note J):				
Common stock, authorized 100,000,000 shares of $.01 par value; 48,379,613 and 48,336,392 shares issued and outstanding at January 31, 2015 and February 1, 2014, respectively		484		483
Additional paid-in capital		131,112		124,134
Retained earnings		224,111		238,151
Accumulated other comprehensive loss		(429)		(838)
Total stockholders' equity		355,278		361,930
	$	542,993	$	546,293

See notes to consolidated financial statements.

Source: BUCKLE INC, 10-K, April 01, 2015

Powered by Morningstar® Document Research℠

The information contained herein may not be copied, adapted or distributed and is not warranted to be accurate, complete or timely. The user assumes all risks for any damages or losses arising from any use of this information, except to the extent such damages or losses cannot be limited or excluded by applicable law. Past financial performance is no guarantee of future results.

THE BUCKLE, INC.

CONSOLIDATED STATEMENTS OF INCOME
(Amounts in Thousands Except Per Share Amounts)

	Fiscal Years Ended		
	January 31, 2015	February 1, 2014	February 2, 2013
SALES, Net of returns and allowances of $110,793, $108,851, and $106,612, respectively	$ 1,153,142	$ 1,128,001	$ 1,124,007
COST OF SALES (Including buying, distribution, and occupancy costs)	645,810	628,856	624,692
Gross profit	507,332	499,145	499,315
OPERATING EXPENSES:			
Selling	212,688	206,893	201,963
General and administrative	37,671	35,258	39,177
	250,359	242,151	241,140
INCOME FROM OPERATIONS	256,973	256,994	258,175
OTHER INCOME, Net (Note A)	2,723	3,462	3,524
INCOME BEFORE INCOME TAXES	259,696	260,456	261,699
PROVISION FOR INCOME TAXES (Note F)	97,132	97,872	97,394
NET INCOME	$ 162,564	$ 162,584	$ 164,305
EARNINGS PER SHARE (Note K):			
Basic	$ 3.39	$ 3.41	$ 3.47
Diluted	$ 3.38	$ 3.39	$ 3.44

See notes to consolidated financial statements.

Source: BUCKLE INC, 10-K, April 01, 2015

Powered by Morningstar® Document Research℠

The information contained herein may not be copied, adapted or distributed and is not warranted to be accurate, complete or timely. The user assumes all risks for any damages or losses arising from any use of this information, except to the extent such damages or losses cannot be limited or excluded by applicable law. Past financial performance is no guarantee of future results.

THE BUCKLE, INC.

CONSOLIDATED STATEMENTS OF COMPREHENSIVE INCOME
(Amounts in Thousands)

	Fiscal Years Ended		
	January 31, 2015	February 1, 2014	February 2, 2013
NET INCOME	$ 162,564	$ 162,584	$ 164,305
OTHER COMPREHENSIVE INCOME, NET OF TAX:			
Change in unrealized loss on investments, net of tax of $240, $56, and $(138), respectively	409	96	(235)
Other comprehensive income	409	96	(235)
COMPREHENSIVE INCOME	$ 162,973	$ 162,680	$ 164,070

See notes to consolidated financial statements.

Source: BUCKLE INC, 10-K, April 01, 2015

Powered by Morningstar® Document Research℠

The information contained herein may not be copied, adapted or distributed and is not warranted to be accurate, complete or timely. The user assumes all risks for any damages or losses arising from any use of this information, except to the extent such damages or losses cannot be limited or excluded by applicable law. Past financial performance is no guarantee of future results.

THE BUCKLE, INC.

CONSOLIDATED STATEMENTS OF STOCKHOLDERS' EQUITY
(Amounts in Thousands Except Share and Per Share Amounts)

	Number of Shares	Common Stock	Additional Paid-in Capital	Retained Earnings	Accumulated Other Comprehensive Loss	Total
BALANCE, January 28, 2012	47,432,089	$ 474	$ 100,333	$ 263,039	$ (699)	$ 363,147
Net income	—	—	—	164,305	—	164,305
Dividends paid on common stock, ($5.30 per share)	—	—	—	(254,633)	—	(254,633)
Common stock issued on exercise of stock options	377,520	4	842	—	—	846
Issuance of non-vested stock, net of forfeitures	249,660	3	(3)	—	—	—
Amortization of non-vested stock grants, net of forfeitures	—	—	8,388	—	—	8,388
Income tax benefit related to exercise of stock options	—	—	7,831	—	—	7,831
Change in unrealized loss on investments, net of tax	—	—	—	—	(235)	(235)
BALANCE, February 2, 2013	48,059,269	$ 481	$ 117,391	$ 172,711	$ (934)	$ 289,649
Net income	—	—	—	162,584	—	162,584
Dividends paid on common stock, ($2.02 per share)	—	—	—	(97,144)	—	(97,144)
Common stock issued on exercise of stock options	25,555	—	—	—	—	—
Issuance of non-vested stock, net of forfeitures	251,568	2	(2)	—	—	—
Amortization of non-vested stock grants, net of forfeitures	—	—	5,066	—	—	5,066
Income tax benefit related to exercise of stock options	—	—	1,679	—	—	1,679
Change in unrealized loss on investments, net of tax	—	—	—	—	96	96
BALANCE, February 1, 2014	48,336,392	$ 483	$ 124,134	$ 238,151	$ (838)	$ 361,930
Net income	—	—	—	162,564	—	162,564
Dividends paid on common stock, ($3.66 per share)	—	—	—	(176,604)	—	(176,604)
Common stock issued on exercise of stock options	17,091	—	70	—	—	70
Issuance of non-vested stock, net of forfeitures	26,130	1	(1)	—	—	—
Amortization of non-vested stock grants, net of forfeitures	—	—	6,013	—	—	6,013
Income tax benefit related to exercise of stock options	—	—	896	—	—	896
Change in unrealized loss on investments, net of tax	—	—	—	—	409	409
BALANCE, January 31, 2015	48,379,613	$ 484	$ 131,112	$ 224,111	$ (429)	$ 355,278

See notes to consolidated financial statements.

Source: BUCKLE INC, 10-K, April 01, 2015

Powered by Morningstar® Document Research℠

The information contained herein may not be copied, adapted or distributed and is not warranted to be accurate, complete or timely. The user assumes all risks for any damages or losses arising from any use of this information, except to the extent such damages or losses cannot be limited or excluded by applicable law. Past financial performance is no guarantee of future results.

THE BUCKLE, INC.

CONSOLIDATED STATEMENTS OF CASH FLOWS
(Amounts in Thousands)

	Fiscal Years Ended		
	January 31, 2015	February 1, 2014	February 2, 2013
CASH FLOWS FROM OPERATING ACTIVITIES:			
Net income	$ 162,564	$ 162,584	$ 164,305
Adjustments to reconcile net income to net cash flows from operating activities:			
Depreciation and amortization	31,679	32,631	33,834
Amortization of non-vested stock grants, net of forfeitures	6,013	5,066	8,388
Deferred income taxes	(1,675)	(2,086)	(1,939)
Other	1,163	988	1,528
Changes in operating assets and liabilities:			
Receivables	(2,134)	(989)	596
Inventory	(5,780)	(20,288)	356
Prepaid expenses and other assets	3,508	(2,255)	(10,281)
Accounts payable	(2,915)	2,738	6,534
Accrued employee compensation	(13)	(5,250)	(671)
Accrued store operating expenses	1	(138)	(1,004)
Gift certificates redeemable	861	910	1,935
Income taxes payable	(1,970)	(2,699)	14,897
Deferred rent liabilities and deferred compensation	4,466	2,814	2,463
Net cash flows from operating activities	195,768	174,026	220,941
CASH FLOWS FROM INVESTING ACTIVITIES:			
Purchases of property and equipment	(45,454)	(28,811)	(30,297)
Proceeds from sale of property and equipment	—	11	1,140
Other	108	112	130
Purchases of investments	(43,404)	(32,314)	(29,933)
Proceeds from sales/maturities of investments	38,131	30,981	37,294
Net cash flows from investing activities	(50,619)	(30,021)	(21,666)
CASH FLOWS FROM FINANCING ACTIVITIES:			
Proceeds from the exercise of stock options	70	—	846
Excess tax benefit from stock option exercises	225	399	5,609
Payment of dividends	(176,604)	(97,144)	(254,633)
Net cash flows from financing activities	(176,309)	(96,745)	(248,178)
NET INCREASE (DECREASE) IN CASH AND CASH EQUIVALENTS	(31,160)	47,260	(48,903)
CASH AND CASH EQUIVALENTS, Beginning of year	164,868	117,608	166,511
CASH AND CASH EQUIVALENTS, End of year	$ 133,708	$ 164,868	$ 117,608

See notes to consolidated financial statements.

Source: BUCKLE INC, 10-K, April 01, 2015

Powered by Morningstar® Document Research℠

The information contained herein may not be copied, adapted or distributed and is not warranted to be accurate, complete or timely. The user assumes all risks for any damages or losses arising from any use of this information, except to the extent such damages or losses cannot be limited or excluded by applicable law. Past financial performance is no guarantee of future results.

THE BUCKLE, INC.
NOTES TO CONSOLIDATED FINANCIAL STATEMENTS
(Dollar Amounts in Thousands Except Share and Per Share Amounts)

A. SUMMARY OF SIGNIFICANT ACCOUNTING POLICIES

Fiscal Year - The Buckle, Inc. (the "Company") has its fiscal year end on the Saturday nearest January 31. All references in these consolidated financial statements to fiscal years are to the calendar year in which the fiscal year begins. Fiscal 2014 represents the 52-week period ended January 31, 2015, fiscal 2013 represents the 52-week period ended February 1, 2014, and fiscal 2012 represents the 53-week period ended February 2, 2013.

Nature of Operations - The Company is a retailer of medium to better-priced casual apparel, footwear, and accessories for fashion-conscious young men and women operating 460 stores located in 44 states throughout the United States as of January 31, 2015.

During fiscal 2014, the Company opened 16 new stores, substantially remodeled 18 stores, and closed 6 stores. During fiscal 2013, the Company opened 13 new stores, substantially remodeled 8 stores, and closed 3 stores. During fiscal 2012, the Company opened 10 new stores, substantially remodeled 21 stores, and closed 1 store.

Principles of Consolidation - The consolidated financial statements include the accounts of The Buckle, Inc. and its wholly-owned subsidiary. All intercompany accounts and transactions have been eliminated in consolidation.

Revenue Recognition - Retail store sales are recorded upon the purchase of merchandise by customers. Online sales are recorded when merchandise is delivered to the customer, with the time of delivery being based on estimated shipping time from the Company's distribution center to the customer. Shipping fees charged to customers are included in revenue and shipping costs are included in selling expenses. Shipping costs were $6,549, $6,223, and $6,477 during fiscal 2014, 2013, and 2012, respectively. Merchandise returns are estimated based upon the historical average sales return percentage and accrued at the end of the period. The reserve for merchandise returns was $943 and $750 as of January 31, 2015 and February 1, 2014, respectively. The Company recognizes revenue from sales made under its layaway program upon delivery of the merchandise to the customer.

The Company records the sale of gift cards and gift certificates as a current liability and recognizes a sale when a customer redeems the gift card or gift certificate. The amount of the gift certificate liability is determined using the outstanding balances from the prior three years of issuance and the gift card liability is determined using the outstanding balances from the prior four years of issuance. The Company records breakage as other income when the probability of redemption is remote, based on historical issuance and redemption patterns. Breakage recorded for the fiscal years ended January 31, 2015, February 1, 2014, and February 2, 2013 was $860, $1,146, and $755, respectively. The Company recognizes a current liability for the down payment and subsequent installment payments made when merchandise is placed on layaway and recognizes layaways as a sale at the time the customer makes final payment and picks up the merchandise.

Cash and Cash Equivalents - The Company considers all highly liquid debt instruments with an original maturity of three months or less when purchased to be cash equivalents.

Inventory - Inventory is stated at the lower of cost or market. Cost is determined using the average cost method. Management makes adjustments to inventory and cost of goods sold to account for merchandise obsolescence and markdowns based on assumptions using calculations applied to current inventory levels by department within each different markdown level. Management also reviews the levels of inventory in each markdown group, and the overall aging of inventory, versus the estimated future demand for such product and the current market conditions. The calculation for estimated markdowns and/or obsolescence reduced the Company's inventory valuation by $7,970 and $7,415 as of January 31, 2015 and February 1, 2014, respectively. The amount charged (credited) to cost of goods sold, resulting from adjustments for estimated markdowns and/or obsolescence, was $555, $1,129, and $1,382, for fiscal years 2014, 2013, and 2012, respectively.

Property and Equipment - Property and equipment are stated on the basis of historical cost. Depreciation is provided using a combination of accelerated and straight-line methods based upon the estimated useful lives of the assets. The majority of property and equipment have useful lives of five to ten years with the exception of buildings, which have estimated useful lives of 31.5 to 39 years. Leasehold improvements are stated on the basis of historical cost and are amortized over the shorter of the life of the lease or the estimated economic life of the assets. When circumstances indicate the carrying values of long-lived assets may be impaired, an evaluation is performed on current net book value amounts. Judgments made by the Company related to the expected useful lives of property and equipment and the ability to realize cash flows in excess of carrying amounts of such assets are affected by factors such as changes in economic conditions and changes in operating performance. As the Company assesses the expected cash flows and carrying amounts of long-lived assets, adjustments are made to such carrying values.

Advertising Costs - Advertising costs are expensed as incurred and were $12,041, $11,088 and $10,214 for fiscal years 2014, 2013, and 2012, respectively.

Other Income - The Company's other income is derived primarily from interest and dividends received on cash and investments.

The information contained herein may not be copied, adapted or distributed and is not warranted to be accurate, complete or timely. The user assumes all risks for any damages or losses arising from any use of this information, except to the extent such damages or losses cannot be limited or excluded by applicable law. Past financial performance is no guarantee of future results.

D.   PROPERTY AND EQUIPMENT

	January 31, 2015	February 1, 2014
Land	$ 2,165	$ 2,165
Building and improvements	28,033	28,006
Office equipment	10,080	9,357
Transportation equipment	20,790	20,782
Leasehold improvements	154,441	146,655
Furniture and fixtures	167,575	157,771
Shipping/receiving equipment	27,172	26,392
Screenprinting equipment	111	111
Construction-in-progress	17,548	2,417
Total	$ 427,915	$ 393,656

E.   FINANCING ARRANGEMENTS

The Company has available an unsecured line of credit of $25,000 with Wells Fargo Bank, N.A. for operating needs and letters of credit. The line of credit provides that outstanding letters of credit cannot exceed $20,000. Borrowings under the line of credit provide for interest to be paid at a rate based on LIBOR. The Company has, from time to time, borrowed against these lines during periods of peak inventory build-up. There were no bank borrowings as of January 31, 2015 and February 1, 2014. There were no bank borrowings during fiscal 2014, 2013, and 2012. The Company had outstanding letters of credit totaling $2,026 and $3,226 as of January 31, 2015 and February 1, 2014, respectively. The line of credit agreement was amended effective February 16, 2015, subsequent to the end of the fiscal year. The amended agreement extended the expiration date of the note from July 31, 2015 to July 31, 2017 and reduced the amount available for letters of credit from $20,000 to $10,000.

H.   COMMITMENTS

Leases - The Company conducts its operations in leased facilities under numerous non-cancelable operating leases expiring at various dates through fiscal 2025. Most of the Company's stores have lease terms of approximately ten years and generally do not contain renewal options. Most lease agreements contain tenant improvement allowances, rent holidays, rent escalation clauses, and/or contingent rent provisions. For purposes of recognizing lease incentives and minimum rental expenses on a straight-line basis over the terms of the leases, the Company uses the date of initial possession to begin amortization, which is generally when the Company enters the space and begins to make improvements in preparation of intended use. For tenant improvement allowances and rent holidays, the Company records a deferred rent liability on the consolidated balance sheets and amortizes the deferred rent over the terms of the leases as reductions to rent expense on the consolidated statements of income. For scheduled rent escalation clauses during the lease terms or for rental payments commencing at a date other than the date of initial occupancy, the Company records minimum rental expenses on a straight-line basis over the terms of the leases on the consolidated statements of income. Certain leases provide for contingent rents, which are determined as a percentage of gross sales in excess of specified levels. The Company records a contingent rent liability on the consolidated balance sheets and the corresponding rent expense when specified levels have been achieved or are reasonably probable to be achieved. Operating lease base rental expense for fiscal 2014, 2013, and 2012 was $65,712, $61,640, and $58,683, respectively. Most of the rental payments are based on a minimum annual rental plus a percentage of sales in excess of a specified amount. Percentage rents for fiscal 2014, 2013, and 2012 were $4,434, $5,080, and $5,163, respectively.

Total future minimum rental commitments under these operating leases with remaining lease terms in excess of one year as of January 31, 2015 are as follows:

Fiscal Year	Minimum Rental Commitments
2015	$ 66,147
2016	61,388
2017	56,020
2018	48,842
2019	41,355
Thereafter	92,540
Total minimum rental commitments	$ 366,292

Litigation - From time to time, the Company is involved in litigation relating to claims arising out of its operations in the normal course of business. As of the date of these consolidated financial statements, the Company was not engaged in any legal proceedings that are expected, individually or in the aggregate, to have a material effect on the Company.

Source: BUCKLE INC, 10-K, April 01, 2015

Powered by Morningstar® Document Research℠

The information contained herein may not be copied, adapted or distributed and is not warranted to be accurate, complete or timely. The user assumes all risks for any damages or losses arising from any use of this information, except to the extent such damages or losses cannot be limited or excluded by applicable law. Past financial performance is no guarantee of future results.

K. EARNINGS PER SHARE

The following table provides reconciliation between basic and diluted earnings per share:

| | Fiscal Years Ended | | | | | | | | |
| | January 31, 2015 | | | February 1, 2014 | | | February 2, 2013 | | |
	Income	Weighted Average Shares	Per Share Amount	Income	Weighted Average Shares	Per Share Amount	Income	Weighted Average Shares	Per Share Amount
Basic EPS	$ 162,564	47,927	$ 3.39	$ 162,584	47,744	$ 3.41	$ 164,305	47,383	$ 3.47
Effect of Dilutive Securities:									
Stock options and non-vested shares	—	163	(0.01)	—	232	(0.02)	—	327	(0.03)
Diluted EPS	$ 162,564	48,090	$ 3.38	$ 162,584	47,976	$ 3.39	$ 164,305	47,710	$ 3.44

No stock options were deemed anti-dilutive and excluded from the computation of diluted earnings per share for fiscal 2014, 2013 or 2012.

L. SEGMENT INFORMATION

The Company is a retailer of medium to better priced casual apparel, footwear, and accessories. The Company operates its business as one reportable segment. The Company operated 460 stores located in 44 states throughout the United States as of January 31, 2015.

The following is information regarding the Company's major product lines, stated as a percentage of the Company's net sales:

| | Fiscal Years Ended | | |
Merchandise Group	January 31, 2015	February 1, 2014	February 2, 2013
Denims	43.7%	45.3%	46.4%
Tops (including sweaters)	30.8	30.2	30.9
Accessories	8.6	8.5	8.4
Sportswear/Fashions	6.2	6.0	5.7
Footwear	5.9	5.8	5.3
Outerwear	2.3	2.3	2.2
Casual bottoms	1.2	0.9	0.8
Other	1.3	1.0	0.3
Total	100.0%	100.0%	100.0%

Source: BUCKLE INC, 10-K, April 01, 2015

Powered by Morningstar® Document Research℠

The information contained herein may not be copied, adapted or distributed and is not warranted to be accurate, complete or timely. The user assumes all risks for any damages or losses arising from any use of this information, except to the extent such damages or losses cannot be limited or excluded by applicable law. Past financial performance is no guarantee of future results.

ITEM 9 - CHANGES IN AND DISAGREEMENTS WITH ACCOUNTANTS ON ACCOUNTING AND FINANCIAL DISCLOSURE

None.

ITEM 9A – CONTROLS AND PROCEDURES

The Company maintains a system of disclosure controls and procedures that are designed to provide reasonable assurance that material information, which is required to be timely disclosed, is accumulated and communicated to management in a timely manner. An evaluation of the effectiveness of the design and operation of the Company's disclosure controls and procedures (as defined in Rules 13a-15(e) of the Securities Exchange Act of 1934 (the "Exchange Act")) was performed as of the end of the period covered by this report. This evaluation was performed under the supervision and with the participation of the Company's Chief Executive Officer and Chief Financial Officer. Based upon that evaluation, the Chief Executive Officer and Chief Financial Officer concluded that the Company's disclosure controls and procedures as of the end of the period covered by this report were effective to provide reasonable assurance that information required to be disclosed by the Company in the Company's reports that it files or submits under the Exchange Act is accumulated and communicated to management, including its Chief Executive Officer and Chief Financial Officer, as appropriate, to allow timely decisions regarding required disclosure and are effective to provide reasonable assurance that such information is recorded, processed, summarized, and reported within the time periods specified by the SEC's rules and forms.

Change in Internal Control Over Financial Reporting - There were no changes in the Company's internal control over financial reporting that occurred during the Company's last fiscal quarter that have materially affected, or are reasonably likely to materially affect, the Company's internal control over financial reporting.

Management's Report on Internal Control Over Financial Reporting - Management of the Company is responsible for establishing and maintaining adequate internal control over financial reporting as defined in Rules 13a-15(f) and 15d-15(f) under the Securities Exchange Act of 1934. The Company's internal control over financial reporting is designed to provide reasonable assurance regarding the reliability of financial reporting and the preparation of financial statements for external purposes in accordance with accounting principles generally accepted in the United State of America ("GAAP").

All internal control systems, no matter how well designed, have inherent limitations. Therefore, even those systems determined to be effective can provide only reasonable assurance with respect to financial statement preparation and presentation. Because of its inherent limitations, internal control over financial reporting may not prevent or detect misstatements.

Management has assessed the effectiveness of the Company's internal control over financial reporting as of January 31, 2015, based on the criteria set forth by the Committee of Sponsoring Organizations ("COSO") of the Treadway Commission in their *Internal Control-Integrated Framework (2013)*. In making its assessment of internal control over financial reporting, management has concluded that the Company's internal control over financial reporting was effective as of January 31, 2015.

The Company's independent registered public accounting firm, Deloitte & Touche LLP, has audited the effectiveness of the Company's internal control over financial reporting. Their report appears herein.

Source: BUCKLE INC, 10-K, April 01, 2015

Powered by Morningstar® Document Research℠

The information contained herein may not be copied, adapted or distributed and is not warranted to be accurate, complete or timely. The user assumes all risks for any damages or losses arising from any use of this information, except to the extent such damages or losses cannot be limited or excluded by applicable law. Past financial performance is no guarantee of future results.

REPORT OF INDEPENDENT REGISTERED PUBLIC ACCOUNTING FIRM

To the Board of Directors and Stockholders of
The Buckle, Inc.
Kearney, Nebraska

We have audited the internal control over financial reporting of The Buckle, Inc. and subsidiary (the "Company") as of January 31, 2015, based on criteria established in *Internal Control - Integrated Framework (2013)* issued by the Committee of Sponsoring Organizations of the Treadway Commission. The Company's management is responsible for maintaining effective internal control over financial reporting and for its assessment of the effectiveness of internal control over financial reporting, included in the accompanying *Management's Report on Internal Control Over Financial Reporting*. Our responsibility is to express an opinion on the Company's internal control over financial reporting based on our audit.

We conducted our audit in accordance with the standards of the Public Company Accounting Oversight Board (United States). Those standards require that we plan and perform the audit to obtain reasonable assurance about whether effective internal control over financial reporting was maintained in all material respects. Our audit included obtaining an understanding of internal control over financial reporting, assessing the risk that a material weakness exists, testing and evaluating the design and operating effectiveness of internal control based on the assessed risk, and performing such other procedures as we considered necessary in the circumstances. We believe that our audit provides a reasonable basis for our opinion.

A company's internal control over financial reporting is a process designed by, or under the supervision of, the company's principal executive and principal financial officers, or persons performing similar functions, and effected by the company's board of directors, management, and other personnel to provide reasonable assurance regarding the reliability of financial reporting and the preparation of financial statements for external purposes in accordance with generally accepted accounting principles. A company's internal control over financial reporting includes those policies and procedures that (1) pertain to the maintenance of records that, in reasonable detail, accurately and fairly reflect the transactions and dispositions of the assets of the company; (2) provide reasonable assurance that transactions are recorded as necessary to permit preparation of financial statements in accordance with generally accepted accounting principles, and that receipts and expenditures of the company are being made only in accordance with authorizations of management and directors of the company; and (3) provide reasonable assurance regarding prevention or timely detection of unauthorized acquisition, use, or disposition of the company's assets that could have a material effect on the financial statements.

Because of the inherent limitations of internal control over financial reporting, including the possibility of collusion or improper management override of controls, material misstatements due to error or fraud may not be prevented or detected on a timely basis. Also, projections of any evaluation of the effectiveness of the internal control over financial reporting to future periods are subject to the risk that the controls may become inadequate because of changes in conditions, or that the degree of compliance with the policies or procedures may deteriorate.

In our opinion, the Company maintained, in all material respects, effective internal control over financial reporting as of January 31, 2015, based on the criteria established in *Internal Control - Integrated Framework (2013)* issued by the Committee of Sponsoring Organizations of the Treadway Commission.

We have also audited, in accordance with the standards of the Public Company Accounting Oversight Board (United States), the consolidated financial statements and financial statement schedule as of and for the fiscal year ended January 31, 2015 of the Company and our report dated April 1, 2015 expressed an unqualified opinion on those financial statements and financial statement schedule.

/s/ Deloitte & Touche LLP

DELOITTE & TOUCHE LLP
Omaha, Nebraska
April 1, 2015

Source: BUCKLE INC, 10-K, April 01, 2015   Powered by Morningstar® Document Research℠

*The information contained herein may not be copied, adapted or distributed and is not warranted to be accurate, complete or timely. The user assumes all risks for any damages or losses arising from any use of this information,
except to the extent such damages or losses cannot be limited or excluded by applicable law. Past financial performance is no guarantee of future results.*

Learning Objectives

AFTER STUDYING THIS APPENDIX, YOU SHOULD BE ABLE TO:

- **LO C–1** Contrast simple and compound interest.
- **LO C–2** Calculate the future value and present value of a single amount.
- **LO C–3** Calculate the future value and present value of an annuity.

Congratulations! While at a local convenience store, you bought a lottery ticket and won $1,000. The ticket gives you the option of receiving (a) $1,000 today or (b) $1,000 one year from now. Which do you choose?

Probably, all of us would choose $1,000 today. Choosing to take the money today instead of one year from now just makes common sense. It also makes good economic sense. You could take your $1,000 winnings today, put it in a savings account, earn interest on it for one year, and have an amount greater than $1,000 a year from now. So, $1,000 today is not equal to $1,000 a year from now. This simple example demonstrates the time value of money, which means that interest causes the value of money received today to be greater than the value of that same amount of money received in the future.

Time value of money concepts are useful—in fact, essential—in solving many business decisions. These decisions include valuing assets and liabilities, making investment decisions, paying off debts, and establishing a retirement plan, to name just a few. We'll discuss some of these next.

Simple versus Compound Interest

Interest is the cost of borrowing money. If you borrow $1,000 today and agree to pay 10% interest, you will pay back $1,100 a year from now. It is this interest that gives money its time value. Simple interest is interest you earn on the initial investment only. Calculate it as the initial investment times the applicable interest rate times the period of the investment or loan:

■ LO C–1
Contrast simple and compound interest.

$$\text{Simple interest} = \text{Initial investment} \times \text{Interest rate} \times \text{Time}$$

For example, suppose you put $1,000 into a savings account that pays simple interest of 10% and then withdraw the money at the end of three years. Illustration C–1 demonstrates that the amount of simple interest you earned on your $1,000 in each of the three years is $100 (= $1,000 × 10%).

With simple interest at 10% annually, the $1,000 initial investment generates $100 of interest each year and grows to **$1,300** by the end of the third year.

ILLUSTRATION C–1

Calculation of Simple Interest

Time	Simple Interest (= Initial investment × Interest rate)	Outstanding Balance
Initial investment		$1,000
End of year 1	$1,000 × 10% = $100	$1,100
End of year 2	$1,000 × 10% = $100	$1,200
End of year 3	$1,000 × 10% = $100	**$1,300**

Compound interest works differently. Compound interest is interest you earn on the initial investment *and on previous interest.* Because you are earning "interest on interest" each period, compound interest yields increasingly larger amounts of interest earnings for each period of the investment (unlike simple interest, which yielded the same $100 in each year of our example above). Illustration C–2 shows calculations of compound interest for a $1,000, three-year investment that earns 10%.

ILLUSTRATION C–2

Calculation of Compound Interest

Time	Compound Interest (= Outstanding balance × Interest rate)	Outstanding Balance
Initial investment		$1,000
End of year 1	$1,000 × 10% = $100	$1,100
End of year 2	$1,100 × 10% = $110	$1,210
End of year 3	$1,210 × 10% = $121	**$1,331**

With compound interest at 10% annually, the $1,000 initial investment grows to **$1,331** at the end of three years. This compares to only **$1,300** for simple interest. The extra $31 represents *compounding,* or interest earned on interest. Nearly all business applications use compound interest, and compound interest is what we use in calculating the time value of money.

KEY POINT

Simple interest is interest we earn on the initial investment only. Compound interest is the interest we earn on the initial investment plus previous interest. We use compound interest in calculating the time value of money.

Time Value of a Single Amount

■ LO C–2
Calculate the future value and present value of a single amount.

To better understand how compound interest affects the time value of money, we'll examine this topic from two perspectives. First, we'll calculate how much an amount today will grow to be at some point in the future (*future value*), and then we'll take the opposite perspective and examine how much an amount in the future is worth today (*present value*).

FUTURE VALUE

In the example above, in which we invested $1,000 for three years at 10% compounded annually, we call $1,331 the future value. Future value is how much an amount today will grow to be in the future. The timeline in Illustration C–3 provides a useful way to visualize future values. Time $n = 0$ indicates today, the date of the initial investment.

ILLUSTRATION C–3

Future Value of a Single Amount

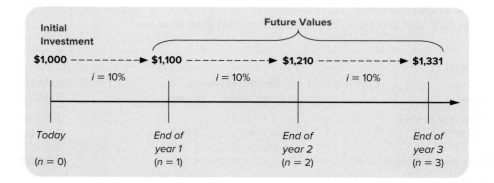

Notice that at the end of each year, the investment grows by 10%. The future value at the end of the first year is **$1,100** (= $1,000 × 1.10). After three years, the investment has a future value of **$1,331** (= $1,000 × 1.10 × 1.10 × 1.10), representing 10% growth of a growing base amount each year.

To calculate future value, we can use a mathematical formula, time value of money tables, a calculator, or a computer spreadsheet. We show all four methods below.

Formula.   We can determine the future value of any amount with a formula, as follows:

$$FV = I\,(1 + i)^n$$

where:

FV = future value of the invested amount
I = initial investment
i = interest rate
n = number of compounding periods

Table 1.   Instead of using a formula, we can also determine future value by using time value of money tables. Table 1, Future Value of $1, located at the end of this book, contains the future value of $1 invested for various periods of time, n, and various interest rates, i. With this table, it's easy to determine the future value of any invested amount. To do so, simply multiply the invested amount by the table value you find at the intersection of the *column* for the desired interest rate and the *row* for the number of periods. Illustration C–4 contains an excerpt from Table 1.

ILLUSTRATION C–4
Future Value of $1
(excerpt from Table 1)

Interest Rates (i)

Periods (n)	7%	8%	9%	10%	11%	12%
1	1.07000	1.08000	1.09000	1.10000	1.11000	1.12000
2	1.14490	1.16640	1.18810	1.21000	1.23210	1.25440
3	1.22504	1.25971	1.29503	1.33100	1.36763	1.40493
4	1.31080	1.36049	1.41158	1.46410	1.51807	1.57352
5	1.40255	1.46933	1.53862	1.61051	1.68506	1.76234
6	1.50073	1.58687	1.67710	1.77156	1.87041	1.97382
7	1.60578	1.71382	1.82804	1.94872	2.07616	2.21068
8	1.71819	1.85093	1.99256	2.14359	2.30454	2.47596

The table shows various values of $(1 + i)^n$ for different combinations of i and n. From the table you can find the future value factor for three periods ($n = 3$) at 10% interest to be 1.33100. This means that $1 invested at 10% compounded annually will grow to $1.331 (= $1 × 1.331) in three years. The table uses $1 as the initial investment, whereas our example used $1,000. Therefore, we need to multiply the future value factor by $1,000.

$$FV = I \times FV \text{ factor}$$
$$FV = \$1,000 \times 1.33100^* = \$1,331$$
*Future value of $1; $n = 3$, $i = 10\%$

Calculator.   Of course, you can do the same future value calculations by using a calculator. Future values are automatically stored in the memory of financial calculators. To compute a future value, you input three amounts: (1) initial investment, (2) interest rate per period, and (3) number of periods. Illustration C–5 shows the inputs and output using a financial calculator.

Excel.   Another option is to use an Excel spreadsheet, which has automatically stored the time value factors. To see how this is performed, see Illustration C–6.

ILLUSTRATION C–5

Calculate the Future Value of a Single Amount Using a Financial Calculator

The key symbols used to input the interest rate and number of periods differ across calculators, so be sure to check which key is appropriate for your calculator.

CALCULATOR INPUTS

Inputs	Key	Amount
1. Present value (initial investment)	PV	$1,000
2. Interest rate per period	i	10%
3. Number of periods	n	3

CALCULATOR OUTPUT

Future value	FV	$1,331

ILLUSTRATION C–6

Calculate the Future Value of a Single Amount Using Excel

	C7			f_x	=-FV(C4, C5, 0, C3, 0)	
	A	B	C	D	E	
1						
2						
3	Amount		$1,000.00			
4	Rate		10%			
5	Number of periods		3			
6						
7	FV		$1,331.00			
8						

Sheet1 Sheet2 Sheet3

Ready   Scroll Lock   100%

Interest Compounding More Than Annually. In our example, interest was compounded annually (once per year). Remember that the n in the future value formula refers to the number of compounding *periods*—which is not necessarily the number of years. For example, suppose the three-year, $1,000 investment earns 10% compounded *semiannually*, or twice per year. The number of periods over three years is now six (= 3 years × 2 semiannual periods per year). The interest rate per period is 5% (= 10% annual rate ÷ 2).[1] The future value of the three-year, $1,000 investment that earns 10% compounded semiannually is calculated below.

$$FV = I \times FV \text{ factor}$$
$$FV = \$1,000 \times 1.34010^* = \$1,340$$
$$^*\text{Future value of } \$1; n = 6, i = 5\%$$

Notice that the future amount is slightly higher for semiannual compounding ($1,340) compared to annual compounding ($1,331). **The more frequent the rate of compounding, the more interest we earn on previous interest, resulting in a higher future value.**

To confirm your understanding, let's look at a couple of examples of how to calculate the future value of a single amount.

Example 1. Suppose a company's top executive, Shirley McDaniel, currently owns stock in the company worth $800,000. Shirley is ready to retire but will not do so until her stock is worth at least $1,000,000. Over the next three years, the company's stock is expected to grow 8% annually. Will Shirley be ready to retire in three years?

The future value of $800,000 in three years with an annual interest rate of 8% equals $1,007,768 (= $800,000 × 1.25971, time value factor from Table 1, Future Value of $1, with $n = 3$ and $i = 8\%$). With 8% growth, Shirley *will* be ready to retire in three years.

---

[1]The rate of compounding can be broken into any number of periods. For example, if we instead assume *quarterly* compounding (four times per year), the number of periods over three years would be 12 (= 3 years × 4 quarters) and the interest rate per period would be 2.5% (= 10% ÷ 4 quarters).

Example 2.   Now suppose you are 20 years old and would like to retire by age 60. A goal of yours has always been to retire as a millionaire. You don't have any money to invest, but you do have a pretty nice car. If you sold your car for $28,000, bought a six-year-old car for $5,000, and invested the difference of $23,000 earning a 10% annual return, how much would you have at retirement?

The future value of $23,000 in 40 years (your proposed retirement age minus your present age) with an annual interest rate of 10% equals $1,040,963 (= $23,000 × 45.25926, time value factor from Table 1, Future Value of $1, with $n = 40$ and $i = 10\%$). With a 10% annual return, just $23,000 today will grow to over one million dollars in 40 years. If you swap your expensive wheels, you'll have that million-dollar nest egg.

PRESENT VALUE

Present value is precisely the opposite of future value. Instead of telling us how much some amount today will grow to be in the future, present value tells us the value today of receiving some larger amount in the future. What is it worth today to receive $1,331 in three years? To answer this, we need to determine the discount rate. The discount rate is the rate at which we would be willing to give up current dollars for future dollars. If you would be willing to give up $100 today to receive $108 in one year, then your discount rate, or time value of money, equals 8%.

Continuing with our example, let's assume that your discount rate is 10%. In this case, the present value of receiving $1,331 in three years is $1,000. We could have figured this from Illustration C–3 by working backwards from the future value. The timeline in Illustration C–7 depicts this relationship between present value and future value.

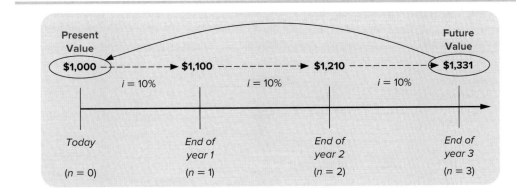

ILLUSTRATION C–7

Present Value of a Single Amount

To calculate present value, we can use a formula, time value of money tables, a calculator, or a computer spreadsheet. We show all four methods below.

Formula.   We can calculate present values with the following formula:

$$PV = \frac{FV}{(1 + i)^n}$$

Table 2.   Alternatively, we can use Table 2, Present Value of $1, located at the end of this book. Illustration C–8 shows an excerpt of Table 2.

From the table you can find the present value factor for three periods ($n = 3$) at 10% is 0.75131. This means that $1 received in three years where there is interest of 10% compounded annually is worth about $0.75 today. So, the present value of $1,331 is approximately $1,000.

$$PV = FV \times PV \text{ factor}$$
$$PV = \$1,331 \times 0.75131 = \$1,000^*$$
*Rounded to the nearest whole dollar

ILLUSTRATION C–8

Present Value of $1
(excerpt from Table 2)

Periods (n)	Interest Rates (i)					
	7%	8%	9%	10%	11%	12%
1	0.93458	0.92593	0.91743	0.90909	0.90090	0.89286
2	0.87344	0.85734	0.84168	0.82645	0.81162	0.79719
3	0.81630	0.79383	0.77218	0.75131	0.73119	0.71178
4	0.76290	0.73503	0.70843	0.68301	0.65873	0.63552
5	0.71299	0.68058	0.64993	0.62092	0.59345	0.56743
6	0.66634	0.63017	0.59627	0.56447	0.53464	0.50663
7	0.62275	0.58349	0.54703	0.51316	0.48166	0.45235
8	0.58201	0.54027	0.50187	0.46651	0.43393	0.40388

Calculator.   Illustration C–9 shows the same example worked out with a financial calculator.

ILLUSTRATION C–9

Calculate the Present
Value of a Single
Amount Using a
Financial Calculator

CALCULATOR INPUTS

Inputs	Key	Amount
1. Future value	FV	$1,331
2. Interest rate per period	i	10%
3. Number of periods	n	3

CALCULATOR OUTPUT

Present value	PV	$1,000

Excel.   In Illustration C–10, we see the same example worked out using an Excel spreadsheet.

ILLUSTRATION C–10

Calculate the Present
Value of a Single
Amount Using Excel

To confirm your understanding, let's look at a couple of examples of how to calculate the present value of a single amount.

Example 1.   Suppose Fisher Realtors lists for sale a 2,500-square-foot business building for $500,000. Someone offers to purchase the building, taking occupancy today, and then pay $575,000 in two years. If Fisher's discount rate is 7% compounded annually, should it accept the customer's offer?

The present value of receiving $575,000 in two years with an annual interest rate of 7% equals $502,228 (= $575,000 × 0.87344, time value factor from Table 2, Present Value of $1, with $n = 2$ and $i = 7\%$). The present value of the future $575,000 payment is $502,228, which is greater than the $500,000 listed selling price, so Fisher should accept the offer.

Example 2.   Let's assume you would like to be a millionaire in 40 years. Investing aggressively in higher-risk securities, you are pretty confident you can earn an average return of 12% a year. How much do you need to invest today to have $1,000,000 in 40 years?

The present value of $1,000,000 in 40 years with an annual interest rate of 12% equals $10,750 (= $1,000,000 × 0.01075, time value factor from Table 2, Present Value of $1, with

$n = 40$ and $i = 12\%$). An investment of only $10,750 today would grow to $1,000,000 in 40 years, assuming a 12% annual interest rate.

If you could earn only 6% annually rather than 12%, you would have to invest quite a bit more. The present value of $1,000,000 in 40 years with an interest rate of 6% equals $97,220 (= $1,000,000 × 0.09722, time value factor from Table 2, Present Value of $1, with $n = 40$ and $i = 6\%$). Over longer periods, the investment return you can achieve really makes a difference in the wealth you can accumulate.

KEY POINT

The *future value* of a single amount is how much that amount today will grow to be in the future. The *present value* of a single amount is the value today of receiving that amount in the future.

Let's Review

Below are four scenarios related to the future value and present value of a single amount.

1. Manuel is saving for a new car. He puts $10,000 into an investment account today. He expects the account to earn 12% annually. How much will Manuel have in five years?

2. Ingrid would like to take her family to Disney World in three years. She expects the trip to cost $4,500 at that time. If she can earn 9% annually, how much should she set aside today so that she can pay for the trip in three years?

3. John puts $6,000 in a savings account today that earns 8% interest compounded semiannually. How much will John have in six years?

4. Anna purchases a ring with a selling price of $4,000 today but doesn't have to pay cash until one year from the purchase date. Assuming a discount rate of 16% compounded quarterly, what is Anna's actual cost of the ring today?

Required:

Calculate the time value of money for each scenario.

Solution:

(Rounded to the nearest whole dollar)
1. $10,000 × 1.76234 (FV of $1, $n = 5$, $i = 12\%$) = $17,623
2. $4,500 × 0.77218 (PV of $1, $n = 3$, $i = 9\%$) = $3,475
3. $6,000 × 1.60103 (FV of $1, $n = 12$, $i = 4\%$) = $9,606
4. $4,000 × 0.85480 (PV of $1, $n = 4$, $i = 4\%$) = $3,419

Suggested Homework:
BEC–2, BEC–4;
EC–1, EC–3;
PC–1A&B

Time Value of an Annuity

Up to now, we've focused on calculating the future value and present value of a *single* amount. However, many business transactions are structured as a series of receipts and payments of cash rather than a single amount. If we are to receive or pay the same amount each period, we refer to the cash flows as an annuity. Familiar examples of annuities are monthly payments for a car loan, house loan, or apartment rent. Of course, payments need not be monthly. They could be quarterly, semiannually, annually, or any interval. **As long as the cash payments are of equal amounts over equal time intervals, we refer to the cash payments as an annuity.**

As with single amounts, we can calculate both the future value and the present value of an annuity.

■ **LO C–3**
Calculate the future value and present value of an annuity.

FUTURE VALUE

Let's suppose that you decide to invest $1,000 at the end of *each year* for the next three years, earning 10% compounded annually. What will the value of these three $1,000 payments be at the end of the third year? The timeline in Illustration C–11 demonstrates how to calculate the future value of this annuity.

ILLUSTRATION C–11

Future Value of an Annuity

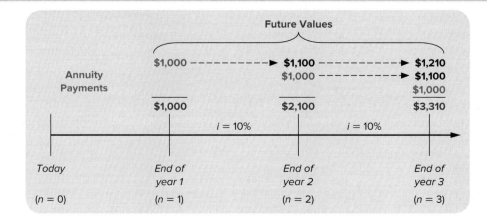

By the end of year 1, the investment's future value equals the $1,000 annuity payment. No interest has been earned because you invest the $1,000 at the *end* of the year. By the end of year 2, though, the first annuity payment has grown by 10% ($1,100 = $1,000 × 1.10), and you make the second $1,000 annuity payment. Adding these together, your total investment has grown to **$2,100**. By the end of the third year, the first annuity payment has grown by another 10% ($1,210 = $1,100 × 1.10), the second annuity payment has grown by 10% ($1,100 = $1,000 × 1.10), and you make the final $1,000 annuity payment. Add these together to find that the total investment has grown to **$3,310**. This is the future value of a $1,000 annuity for three years at 10% interest compounded annually.

Table 3.   Since annuities consist of multiple payments, calculating the future value of an annuity can be time-consuming, especially as the length of the annuity increases. To make this task more efficient, we can calculate the future value of an annuity using the time value of money tables located at the end of this book, a financial calculator, or a computer spreadsheet.[2]

Illustration C–12 shows an excerpt of Table 3, Future Value of an Annuity of $1.

ILLUSTRATION C–12

Future Value of an Annuity of $1 (excerpt from Table 3)

Periods (n)	Interest Rates (i)					
	7%	**8%**	**9%**	**10%**	**11%**	**12%**
1	1.0000	1.0000	1.0000	1.0000	1.0000	1.0000
2	2.0700	2.0800	2.0900	2.1000	2.1100	2.1200
3	3.2149	3.2464	3.2781	3.3100	3.3421	3.3744
4	4.4399	4.5061	4.5731	4.6410	4.7097	4.7793
5	5.7507	5.8666	5.9847	6.1051	6.2278	6.3528
6	7.1533	7.3359	7.5233	7.7156	7.9129	8.1152
7	8.6540	8.9228	9.2004	9.4872	9.7833	10.0890
8	10.2598	10.6366	11.0285	11.4359	11.8594	12.2997

We calculate the future value of an annuity (FVA) by multiplying the annuity payment by the factor corresponding to three periods and 10% interest:

$$\text{FVA} = \$1,000 \times 3.3100 = \$3,310$$

Calculator.   You can also calculate the future value of an annuity using a financial calculator. To compute the future value of an annuity, you simply input three amounts: (1) payment amount, (2) interest rate per period, and (3) number of periods. Make sure the present value (PV) is set equal to zero. Illustration C–13 presents the inputs and output using a financial calculator.

---

[2]The mathematical formula for calculating the future value of an annuity is a bit more complicated than are these other methods, so we'll focus on those.

CALCULATOR INPUTS

Inputs	Key	Amount
1. Payment amount	PMT	$1,000
2. Interest rate per period	i	10%
3. Number of periods	n	3

CALCULATOR OUTPUT

Future value	FV	$3,310

Excel. Illustration C–14 shows the Excel method for calculating the future value of an annuity.

ILLUSTRATION C–14

Calculate the Future Value of an Annuity Using Excel

	C7			f_x =-FV(C4, C5, C3, 0, 0)		
	A	B	C	D	E	
1						
2						
3	Amount		$1,000.00			
4	Rate		10%			
5	Number of periods		3			
6						
7	FV		$3,310.00			
8						

Sheet1 / Sheet2 / Sheet3

Ready   Scroll Lock   100%

Again, let's look at two examples.

Example 1. Suppose **Warner Bros.** borrows $300 million to produce another *Batman* movie and is required to pay back this amount in five years. If, at the end of each of the next five years, Warner Bros. puts $50 million in an account that is expected to earn 12% interest compounded annually, will the company have enough cash set aside to pay its debt?

The future value of a $50 million annuity over five years that earns 12% annually equals $317,640,000 (= $50,000,000 × 6.3528, time value factor from Table 3, Future Value of an Annuity of $1, with $n = 5$ and $i = 12\%$). Warner Bros. will have enough cash to pay its $300 million debt.

Example 2. You still have aspirations of being a millionaire in 40 years, but you do not have much money to invest right now. If you set aside just $2,500 at the end of each year with an average annual return of 10%, how much will you have at the end of 40 years?

The future value of a $2,500 annuity over 40 years that earns 10% annually equals $1,106,482 (= $2,500 × 442.5926, time value factor from Table 3, Future Value of an Annuity of $1, with $n = 40$ and $i = 10\%$). You will have quite a bit less assuming an average annual return of 8% ($647,641) and quite a bit more if you can achieve an average annual return of 12% ($1,917,729). Interest rates matter!

PRESENT VALUE

One application of the present value of an annuity relates back to Chapter 9. There, you learned that we report certain liabilities in financial statements at their present values. Most of these liabilities specify that the borrower must pay the lender periodic interest payments (or an annuity) over the life of the loan. As a result, we use the present value of an annuity to determine what portion of these future interest payments the borrower must report as a liability today.

To understand the idea behind the present value of an annuity, you need to realize that each annuity payment represents a single future amount. We calculate the present value of *each* of these future amounts and then add them together to determine the present value of an annuity. This idea is depicted in the timeline in Illustration C–15.

ILLUSTRATION C–15

Present Value of an Annuity

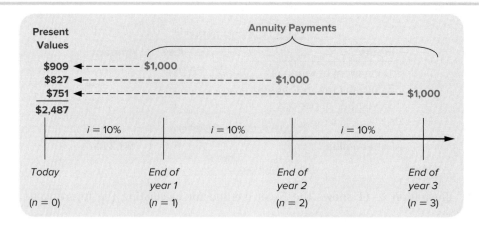

The present value of three **$1,000** annual payments discounted at 10% equals the present value of the first payment (**$909**), plus the present value of the second payment (**$827**), plus the present value of the third payment (**$751**). You can verify these amounts by looking at the present value factors in Table 2, Present Value of $1, with $n = 1, 2$, and 3 and $i = 10\%$. The total present value of the annuity is **$2,487**.

Table 4. Instead of calculating the present value of each annuity payment, a more efficient method is to use time value of money tables. An excerpt of Table 4, Present Value of an Annuity of $1, located at the end of this book, is shown in Illustration C–16.

ILLUSTRATION C–16

Present Value of an Annuity of $1 (excerpt from Table 4)

Periods (n)	Interest Rates (i)					
	7%	8%	9%	10%	11%	12%
1	0.93458	0.92593	0.91743	0.90909	0.90090	0.89286
2	1.80802	1.78326	1.75911	1.73554	1.71252	1.69005
3	2.62432	2.57710	2.53129	2.48685	2.44371	2.40183
4	3.38721	3.31213	3.23972	3.16987	3.10245	3.03735
5	4.10020	3.99271	3.88965	3.79079	3.69590	3.60478
6	4.76654	4.62288	4.48592	4.35526	4.23054	4.11141
7	5.38929	5.20637	5.03295	4.86842	4.71220	4.56376
8	5.97130	5.74664	5.53482	5.33493	5.14612	4.96764

We calculate the present value of an annuity (PVA) by multiplying the annuity payment by the factor corresponding to three periods and 10% interest:

$$\text{PVA} = \$1,000 \times 2.48685 = \$2,487$$

Calculator. Illustration C–17 shows the calculator solution.

ILLUSTRATION C–17

Calculate the Present Value of an Annuity Using a Financial Calculator

CALCULATOR INPUTS		
Inputs	Key	Amount
1. Payment amount	PMT	$1,000
2. Interest rate per period	i	10%
3. Number of periods	n	3
CALCULATOR OUTPUT		
Present value	PV	$2,487

Excel.   Illustration C–18 shows the Excel solution.

C7	▼	f_x =-PV(C4, C5, C3, 0, 0)			
	A	B	C	D	E
1					
2					
3	Amount		$1,000.00		
4	Rate		10%		
5	Number of periods		3		
6					
7	PV		$2,486.85		
8					

Sheet1 Sheet2 Sheet3

Ready   Scroll Lock   100%

ILLUSTRATION C–18

Calculate the Present Value of an Annuity Using Excel

Again, let's look at some examples.

Example 1.   A movie theatre considers upgrading its concessions area at a cost of $10,000. The upgrades are expected to produce additional cash flows from concession sales of $2,000 per year over the next six years. Should the movie theatre upgrade its concessions area if its discount rate is 8% annually?

The present value of a $2,000 annuity over six years at 8% interest is $9,245.76 (= $2,000 × 4.62288, time value factor from Table 4, Present Value of an Annuity of $1, with $n = 6$ and $i = 8\%$). The $10,000 cost of the upgrade is greater than the present value of the future cash flows of $9,245.76 generated. The theatre will be better off *not* making the investment.

Example 2.   Each year you play the Monopoly game at **McDonald's**. This is your year: As you peel back the sticker, you realize you have both Park Place and Boardwalk. You have just won a million dollars payable in $50,000 installments over the next 20 years. Assuming a discount rate of 10%, how much did you really win?

The present value of a $50,000 annuity over 20 periods at 10% is $425,678 (= $50,000 × 8.51356, time value factor from Table 4, Present Value of an Annuity of $1, with $n = 20$ and $i = 10\%$). The value today of $50,000 per year for the next 20 years is actually less than half a million dollars, though you'd probably not be too disappointed with these winnings.

KEY POINT

Cash payments of equal amounts over equal time intervals are called an annuity. The *future* value of an annuity is the sum of the future values of a series of cash payments. Similarly, the *present* value of an annuity is the sum of the present values of a series of cash payments.

Below are four scenarios related to the future value and present value of an annuity.

Let's Review

1. Manuel is saving for a new car. He puts $2,000 into an investment account at the end of each year for the next five years. He expects the account to earn 12% annually. How much will Manuel have in five years?

2. Ingrid would like to take her family to Disney World in three years. She decides to purchase a vacation package that requires her to make three annual payments of $1,500 at the end of each year for the next three years. If she can earn 9% annually, how much should she set aside today so that the three annual payments can be made?

3. John puts $500 in a savings account at the end of each six months for the next six years that earns 8% interest compounded semiannually. How much will John have in six years?

4. Anna purchases a ring with a selling price of $4,000 and will make four payments of $1,000 at the end of each quarter for the next four quarters. Assuming a discount rate of 16% compounded quarterly, what is Anna's actual cost of the ring today?

Required:

Calculate the time value of money for each scenario.

Solution:

(Rounded to the nearest whole dollar)

Suggested Homework:
BEC–8, BEC–11;
EC–6, EC–8;
PC–3A&B

1. $2,000 × 6.3528 (FV of Annuity of $1, $n = 5$, $i = 12\%$) = $12,706
2. $1,500 × 2.53129 (PV of Annuity of $1, $n = 3$, $i = 9\%$) = $3,797
3. $500 × 15.0258 (FV of Annuity of $1, $n = 12$, $i = 4\%$) = $7,513
4. $1,000 × 3.62990 (PV of Annuity of $1, $n = 4$, $i = 4\%$) = $3,630

KEY POINTS BY LEARNING OBJECTIVE

LO C–1 Contrast simple and compound interest.

Simple interest is interest we earn on the initial investment only. Compound interest is the interest we earn on the initial investment plus previous interest. We use compound interest in calculating the time value of money.

LO C–2 Calculate the future value and present value of a single amount.

The *future value* of a single amount is how much that amount today will grow to be in the future.

The *present value* of a single amount is the value today of receiving that amount in the future.

LO C–3 Calculate the future value and present value of an annuity.

Cash payments of equal amounts over equal time intervals are called an annuity. The *future* value of an annuity is the sum of the future values of a series of cash payments. Similarly, the *present* value of an annuity is the sum of the present values of a series of cash payments.

GLOSSARY

Annuity: Cash payments of equal amounts over equal time intervals. **p. C–7**

Compound interest: Interest earned on the initial investment and on previous interest. **p. C–2**

Discount rate: The rate at which someone would be willing to give up current dollars for future dollars. **p. C–5**

Future value: How much an amount today will grow to be in the future. **p. C–2**

Present value: The value today of receiving some amount in the future. **p. C–5**

Simple interest: Interest earned on the initial investment only. **p. C–1**

Time value of money: The value of money today is greater than the value of that same amount of money in the future. **p. C–1**

SELF-STUDY QUESTIONS

1. How does simple interest differ from compound interest? **(LO C–1)**
   a. Simple interest includes interest earned on the initial investment plus interest earned on previous interest.
   b. Simple interest includes interest earned on the initial investment only.
   c. Simple interest is for a shorter time interval.
   d. Simple interest is for a longer time interval.

2. What is the future value of $100 invested in an account for eight years that earns 10% annual interest, compounded semiannually (rounded to the nearest whole dollar)? **(LO C–2)**

   a. $214.
   b. $216.
   c. $218.
   d. $220.

3. Present value represents: **(LO C–2)**
   a. The value today of receiving money in the future.
   b. The amount that an investment today will grow to be in the future.
   c. The difference between the initial investment and the growth of that investment over time.
   d. A series of equal payments.

4. Cooper wants to save for college. Assuming he puts $5,000 into an account at the end of each year for five years and earns 12% compounded annually, how much will he have saved by the end of the fifth year (rounded to the nearest whole dollar)? **(LO C–3)**

a. $25,000.
b. $31,764.
c. $18,024.
d. $14,096.

Note: For answers, see the last page of the chapter.

REVIEW QUESTIONS

1. Define interest. Explain the difference between simple interest and compound interest ■ **LO C–1**

2. Identify the three items of information necessary to calculate the future value of a single amount ■ **LO C–2**

3. Define the present value of a single amount. What is the discount rate? ■ **LO C–2**

4. What is an annuity? ■ **LO C–3**

5. What is the relationship between the present value of a single amount and the present value of an annuity? ■ **LO C–3**

BRIEF EXERCISES

BEC–1 Oprah is deciding between investment options. Both investments earn an interest rate of 7%, but interest on the first investment is compounded annually, while interest on the second investment is compounded semiannually. Which investment would you advise Oprah to choose? Why?

Understand simple versus compound interest (LO C–1)

BEC–2 Dusty would like to buy a new car in six years. He currently has $15,000 saved. He's considering buying a car for around $19,000 but would like to add a Turbo engine to increase the car's performance. This would increase the price of the car to $23,000. If Dusty can earn 9% interest, compounded annually, will he be able to get a car with a Turbo engine in six years?

Calculate the future value of a single amount (LO C–2)

BEC–3 Arnold and Helene would like to visit Austria in two years to celebrate their 25th wedding anniversary. Currently, the couple has saved $27,000, but they expect the trip to cost $31,000. If they put $27,000 in an account that earns 7% interest, compounded annually, will they be able to pay for the trip in two years?

Calculate the future value of a single amount (LO C–2)

BEC–4 Calculate the future value of the following single amounts.

Calculate the future value of a single amount (LO C–2)

	Initial Investment	Annual Rate	Interest Compounded	Period Invested
1.	$8,000	10%	Annually	7 years
2.	6,000	12	Semiannually	4 years
3.	9,000	8	Quarterly	3 years

BEC–5 Maddy works at Burgers R Us. Her boss tells her that if she stays with the company for five years, she will receive a bonus of $6,000. With an annual discount rate of 8%, calculate the value today of receiving $6,000 in five years.

Calculate the present value of a single amount (LO C–2)

BEC–6 Ronald has an investment opportunity that promises to pay him $55,000 in three years. He could earn a 6% annual return investing his money elsewhere. What is the most he would be willing to invest today in this opportunity?

Understand simple versus compound interest (LO C–2)

BEC–7 Calculate the present value of the following single amounts.

Calculate the present value of a single amount (LO C–2)

	Future Value	Annual Rate	Interest Compounded	Period Invested
1.	$10,000	6%	Annually	5 years
2.	7,000	8	Semiannually	8 years
3.	6,000	12	Quarterly	4 years

Calculate the future value
of an annuity (LO C–3)

BEC–8 Tom and Suri decide to take a worldwide cruise. To do so, they need to save $30,000. They plan to invest $4,000 at the end of each year for the next seven years to earn 8% compounded annually. Determine whether Tom and Suri will reach their goal of $30,000 in seven years.

Calculate the future value
of an annuity (LO C–3)

BEC–9 Matt plans to start his own business once he graduates from college. He plans to save $3,000 every six months for the next five years. If his savings earn 10% annually (or 5% every six months), determine how much he will save by the end of the fifth year.

Calculate the future value
of an annuity (LO C–3)

BEC–10 Calculate the future value of the following annuities, assuming each annuity payment is made at the end of each compounding period.

	Annuity Payment	Annual Rate	Interest Compounded	Period Invested
1.	$3,000	7%	Annually	6 years
2.	6,000	8	Semiannually	9 years
3.	5,000	12	Quarterly	5 years

Calculate the present
value of an annuity
(LO C–3)

BEC–11 Tatsuo has just been awarded a four-year scholarship to attend the university of his choice. The scholarship will pay $8,000 each year for the next four years to reimburse normal school-related expenditures. Each $8,000 payment will be made at the end of the year, contingent on Tatsuo maintaining good grades in his classes for that year. Assuming an annual interest rate of 6%, determine the value today of receiving this scholarship if Tatsuo maintains good grades.

Calculate the present
value of an annuity
(LO C–3)

BEC–12 Monroe Corporation is considering the purchase of new equipment. The equipment will cost $35,000 today. However, due to its greater operating capacity, Monroe expects the new equipment to earn additional revenues of $5,000 by the end of each year for the next 10 years. Assuming a discount rate of 10% compounded annually, determine whether Monroe should make the purchase.

Calculate the present
value of an annuity
(LO C–3)

BEC–13 Calculate the present value of the following annuities, assuming each annuity payment is made at the end of each compounding period.

	Annuity Payment	Annual Rate	Interest Compounded	Period Invested
1.	$4,000	7%	Annually	5 years
2.	9,000	8	Semiannually	3 years
3.	3,000	8	Quarterly	2 years

EXERCISES

Calculate the future value
of a single amount
(LO C–2)

EC–1 The four people below have the following investments.

	Invested Amount	Interest Rate	Compounding
Jerry	$13,000	12%	Quarterly
Elaine	16,000	6	Semiannually
George	23,000	8	Annually
Kramer	19,000	10	Annually

Required:
Determine which of the four people will have the greatest investment accumulation in six years.

Calculate the future value of
a single amount (LO C–2)

EC–2 You want to save for retirement. Assuming you are now 25 years old and you want to retire at age 55, you have 30 years to watch your investment grow. You decide to invest in the stock market, which has earned about 13% per year over the past 80 years and is expected to continue at this rate. You decide to invest $2,000 today.

Required:

How much do you expect to have in 40 years?

EC–3 The four actors below have just signed a contract to star in a dramatic movie about relationships among hospital doctors. Each person signs independent contracts with the following terms:

Calculate the present value of a single amount (LO C–2)

Contract Terms		
	Contract Amount	**Payment Date**
Derek	$600,000	2 years
Isabel	640,000	3 years
Meredith	500,000	Today
George	500,000	1 year

Required:

Assuming an annual discount rate of 9%, which of the four actors is actually being paid the most?

EC–4 Ray and Rachel are considering the purchase of two deluxe kitchen ovens. The first store offers the two ovens for $3,500 with payment due today. The second store offers the two ovens for $3,700 due in one year.

Calculate the present value of a single amount (LO C–2)

Required:

Assuming an annual discount rate of 9%, from which store should Ray and Rachel buy their ovens?

EC–5 Lights, Camera, and More sells filmmaking equipment. The company offers three purchase options: (1) pay full cash today, (2) pay one-half down and the remaining one-half plus 10% in one year, or (3) pay nothing down and the full amount plus 15% in one year. George is considering buying equipment from Lights, Camera, and More for $150,000 and therefore has the following payment options:

Calculate the present value of a single amount (LO C–2)

	Payment Today	**Payment in One Year**	**Total Payment**
Option 1	$150,000	$ 0	$150,000
Option 2	75,000	82,500	157,500
Option 3	0	172,500	172,500

Required:

Assuming an annual discount rate of 11%, calculate which option has the lowest total cost in present value terms.

EC–6 GMG Studios plans to invest $60,000 at the end of each year for the next three years. There are three investment options available.

Calculate the future value of an annuity (LO C–3)

	Annual Rate	**Interest Compounded**	**Period Invested**
Option 1	7%	Annually	3 years
Option 2	9	Annually	3 years
Option 3	11	Annually	3 years

Required:

Determine the accumulated investment amount by the end of the third year for each of the options.

Calculate the future value of an annuity (LO C–3)

EC–7 You would like to start saving for retirement. Assuming you are now 25 years old and you want to retire at age 55, you have 30 years to watch your investment grow. You decide to invest in the stock market, which has earned about 13% per year over the past 80 years and is expected to continue at this rate. You decide to invest $2,000 at the end of each year for the next 30 years.

Required:

Calculate how much your accumulated investment is expected to be in 30 years.

Calculate the present value of an annuity (LO C–3)

EC–8 Denzel needs a new car. At the dealership, he finds the car that he likes. The dealership gives him two payment options:
1. Pay $35,000 for the car today.
2. Pay $4,000 at the end of each quarter for three years.

Required:

Assuming Denzel uses a discount rate of 12% (or 3% quarterly), determine which option gives him the lower cost.

PROBLEMS: SET A ■ connect

Calculate the future value of a single amount (LO C–2)

PC–1A Alec, Daniel, William, and Stephen decide today to save for retirement. Each person wants to retire by age 65 and puts $11,000 into an account earning 10% compounded annually.

Person	Age	Initial Investment	Accumulated Investment by Retirement (age 65)
Alec	55	$11,000	$_____
Daniel	45	11,000	$_____
William	35	11,000	$_____
Stephen	25	11,000	$_____

Required:

Calculate how much each person will have accumulated by the age of 65.

Consider present value (LO C–2, LO C–3)

PC–2A Bruce is considering the purchase of a restaurant named Hard Rock Hollywood. The restaurant is listed for sale at $1,000,000. With the help of his accountant, Bruce projects the net cash flows (cash inflows less cash outflows) from the restaurant to be the following amounts over the next 10 years:

Years	Amount
1–6	$100,000 (each year)
7	110,000
8	120,000
9	130,000
10	140,000

Bruce expects to sell the restaurant after 10 years for an estimated $1,300,000.

Required:

If Bruce wants to make at least 11% annually on his investment, should he purchase the restaurant? (Assume all cash flows occur at the end of each year.)

Determine present value alternatives (LO C–2, C–3)

PC–3A Hollywood Tabloid needs a new state-of-the-art camera to produce its monthly magazine. The company is looking at two cameras that are both capable of doing the job and has determined the following:

Camera 1 costs $6,000. It should last for eight years and have annual maintenance costs of $300 per year. After eight years, the magazine can sell the camera for $300.

Camera 2 costs $5,500. It will also last for eight years and have maintenance costs of $900 in year three, $900 in year five, and $1,000 in year seven. After eight years, the camera will have no resale value.

Required:

Determine which camera Hollywood Tabloid should purchase. Assume that an interest rate of 9% properly reflects the discount rate in this situation and that maintenance costs are paid at the end of each year.

PROBLEMS: SET B

PC–1B Mary Kate, Ashley, Dakota, and Elle each want to buy a new home. Each needs to save enough to make a 25% down payment. For example, to buy a $100,000 home, a person would need to save $25,000. At the end of each year for four years, the women make the following investments:

Calculate the future value of an annuity (LO C–3)

Person	Annuity Payment	Type of Account	Expected Annual Return	Four-Year Accumulated Investment	Maximum Home Purchase
Mary Kate	$4,000	Savings	2%	$_____	$_____
Ashley	5,000	CDs	4	$_____	$_____
Dakota	6,000	Bonds	7	$_____	$_____
Elle	6,000	Stocks	11	$_____	$_____

Required:

1. Calculate how much each woman is expected to accumulate in the investment account by the end of the fourth year.
2. What is the maximum amount each woman can spend on a home, assuming she uses her accumulated investment account to make a 25% down payment?

PC–2B Woody Lightyear is considering the purchase of a toy store from Andy Enterprises. Woody expects the store will generate net cash flows (cash inflows less cash outflows) of $60,000 per year for 20 years. At the end of the 20 years, he intends to sell the store for $600,000. To finance the purchase, Woody will borrow using a 20-year note that requires 9% interest.

Consider the present value of investments (LO C–2, C–3)

Required:

What is the maximum amount Woody should offer Andy for the toy store? (Assume all cash flows occur at the end of each year.)

PC–3B Star Studios is looking to purchase a new building for its upcoming film productions. The company finds a suitable location that has a list price of $1,600,000. The seller gives Star Studios the following purchase options:

Determine present value alternatives (LO C–2, C–3)

1. Pay $1,600,000 immediately.
2. Pay $600,000 immediately and then pay $150,000 each year over the next 10 years, with the first payment due in one year.
3. Make 10 annual installments of $250,000, with the first payment due in one year.
4. Make a single payment of $2,300,000 at the end of five years.

Required:

Determine the lowest-cost alternative for Star Studios, assuming that the company can borrow funds to finance the purchase at 8%.

Answers to the Self-Study Questions

1. b   2. c   3. a   4. b

Learning Objectives

AFTER STUDYING THIS APPENDIX, YOU SHOULD BE ABLE TO:

- ■ **LO D–1** Explain why companies invest in other companies.
- ■ **LO D–2** Account for investments in equity securities when the investor has *insignificant* influence.
- ■ **LO D–3** Account for investments in equity securities when the investor has *significant* influence.
- ■ **LO D–4** Account for investments in equity securities when the investor has *controlling* influence.
- ■ **LO D–5** Account for investments in debt securities.

Why Companies Invest in Other Companies

To finance growing operations, a company raises additional funds either by issuing *equity securities,* such as the common and preferred stock we discussed in Chapter 10, or by issuing *debt securities,* such as the bonds we discussed in Chapter 9. These equity and debt securities are purchased by individual investors, by mutual funds, and also by other companies. In this appendix, we focus on investments by companies in equity and debt securities issued by other companies. Companies invest in other companies for a variety of reasons, primarily those indicated in Illustration D–1.

■ **LO D–1**
Explain why companies invest in other companies.

ILLUSTRATION D–1

Why Companies Invest in Other Companies

1. To receive dividends, earn interest, and gain from the increase in the value of their investment.

2. To temporarily invest excess cash created by operating in seasonal industries.

3. To build strategic alliances, increase market share, or enter new industries.

Companies purchase *equity securities* for dividend income and for appreciation in the value of the stock. Many companies pay a stable dividend stream to their investors. Historically, **General Electric** has been one of the most reliable, highest-dividend-paying stocks on the New York Stock Exchange. In contrast, some companies pay little or no dividends. Companies with large expansion plans, called *growth companies,* prefer to reinvest earnings in the growth of the company rather than distribute earnings to investors in the form of cash dividends. For example, **Starbucks,** founded in 1987, did not pay a cash dividend until March 2010. Even without receiving dividends, investors still benefit when companies reinvest earnings, leading to even more profits in the future and eventually higher stock prices.

Companies purchase *debt securities* primarily for the interest revenue they provide, although investment returns also are affected when the values of debt securities change over time. As we discussed in Chapter 9, the value of a debt security with fixed interest payments changes in the opposite direction of interest rates. For example, when general market interest rates decrease, the market value of a bond with fixed interest payments goes up because the fixed interest payments are now more attractive to investors.

The seasonal nature of some companies' operations also influences their investment balances. *Seasonal* refers to the revenue activities of a company varying based on the time (or season) of the year. For instance, agricultural and construction companies enjoy more revenues in the summer, and ski resorts earn most of their revenues in the winter. Most retail companies see their sales revenues increase dramatically during the holiday season. As a result of having seasonal operations, companies save excess cash generated during the busy part of the year to maintain operations during the slower time of the year. With this excess cash, companies tend to purchase low-risk investments such as money market funds (savings accounts), government bonds, or highly rated corporate bonds. These low-risk investments enable companies to earn some interest, while ensuring the funds will be available when needed during the slow season. Investing excess cash in stocks is more risky because the value of stocks varies more than the value of bonds. Stocks typically have greater upside potential, providing a higher average return to their investors than do bonds over the long run. However, stocks can lose value in the short run, making them a better choice for investments that are more long-term in nature.

Companies also can make sizeable long-run stock investments in other companies for strategic purposes. For instance, **AT&T** acquired **Cingular Wireless** to gain a stronger presence in the market for cell phones. **Coca-Cola** acquired **Minute Maid,** and **PepsiCo** purchased **Tropicana,** in order to diversify beyond soft drinks. Sometimes, a company will remove competition and increase market share by purchasing a controlling interest (more than 50% of its voting stock) in a competing company. Companies also might purchase a controlling interest in an established company in a *different* industry to expand into that industry and avoid many of the start-up costs associated with beginning a new business from scratch.

 KEY POINT

Companies invest in other companies primarily to receive dividends, earn interest, and gain from the increase in the value of their investment. Companies in seasonal industries often invest excess funds generated during the busy season and draw on these funds in the slow season. Many companies also make investments for strategic purposes to develop closer business ties, increase market share, or expand into new industries.

PART A

EQUITY INVESTMENTS

Equity investments are the "flip side" of issuing stock. One company issues stock, and another company invests by purchasing that stock. We discussed the issuance of stock in Chapter 10. Here, we discuss how companies that purchase stock account for their investment.

The way we account for equity investments is determined by the *degree of influence* an investor has over the company in which it invests. **A guideline for determining the degree of influence is the percentage of stock held by the investor.** Illustration D–2 summarizes the reporting methods for equity investments.

When one company (the investor) purchases more than 50% of the voting stock of another company (the investee), the investor has *controlling influence;* by voting those shares, the investor actually can *control* the investee's operations. Companies account for their controlling investments using the consolidation method. Under this method, both companies continue to operate as separate legal entities, but the investing company uses *consolidated* financial statements to report operations, as if the two companies were operating as a single combined company. We'll discuss consolidated statements in more detail later in this appendix.

ILLUSTRATION D–2 Accounting for Equity Investments

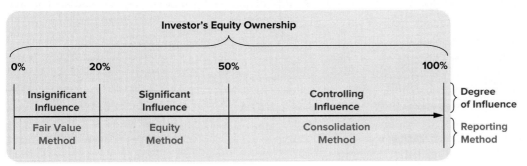

When ownership is below 50% of the voting shares, the investor still might be able to exercise *significant influence* over the investee. This would be the case if the investor owns a large percentage of the outstanding shares *relative to other shareholders.* By voting all those shares with a single intent, the purchasing company can sway decisions in the direction it desires. When significant influence exists, we account for the investment using the equity method. In the absence of evidence to the contrary, an investor exercises significant influence when it owns between 20% and 50% of the voting shares.

In the most common investment scenario, a corporate investor has *insignificant* influence, often indicated by ownership of less than 20% of the voting shares. In this case, we use the *fair value method.* Fair value is the amount an investment could be bought or sold for in a current transaction between willing parties. For example, when you purchased your car, you and the car dealership (or whomever you bought the car from) came to an agreement on the purchase price, or fair value, of the car. What could you sell that car for today? That's the car's current fair value. When an investor has insignificant influence, we report the investment at fair value. We discuss accounting for equity securities with insignificant influence in more detail next.

Equity Investments with Insignificant Influence

As mentioned above, when the purchasing company has insignificant influence, we use the fair value method. Under the fair value method, equity investments are classified as either trading securities or available-for-sale securities. Trading securities are securities that the investor expects to sell (trade) in the near future and are classified as current assets. Available-for-sale securities are securities held for reasons other than attempting to profit from trading in the near future and are classified as either current or long-term assets.

We first discuss some basic investment transactions, including the purchase of an investment, the receipt of cash dividends, and the sale of an investment. We then address how companies actually adjust their investments to fair value; that adjustment will depend on whether the investment is classified as trading securities or available-for-sale securities.

■ **LO D–2**
Account for investments in equity securities when the investor has *insignificant* influence.

PURCHASE EQUITY INVESTMENTS

To see how a company accounts for the purchase of an equity investment, let's assume Nathan's Sportswear purchases 100 shares of Canadian Falcon common stock for $30 per share on December 6. Nathan's Sportswear records the investment as follows:

December 6	Debit	Credit	A	=	L	+	SE
Investments	3,000		+3,000				
Cash		3,000	−3,000				
(Purchase common stock)							
($3,000 = 100 shares × $30)							

RECEIVE CASH DIVIDENDS

If Canadian Falcon pays cash dividends of $0.50 per share on December 15, Nathan's Sportswear records the cash receipt on its 100 shares of stock as follows:

+50

+50 Rev ↑

December 15	Debit	Credit
Cash...	**50**	
Dividend Revenue		**50**
(Receive cash dividends)		
($50 = 100 shares × $0.50)		

SELL EQUITY INVESTMENTS

Now let's assume that Nathan's Sportswear wants to sell its shares of Canadian Falcon. We record the sale of equity investments similar to the sale of many other assets, such as land (discussed in Chapter 7). If the investment sells for *more* than its recorded amount, we record a *gain* on the sale of investments. If the investment sells for *less* than its recorded amount, we record a *loss* on the sale of investments. Gains and losses on the sale of investments are reported in the income statement, with gains being reported as part of other revenues and losses as part of other expenses.

If Nathan's Sportswear sells 10 shares for $36 per share on December 18, we record the following:

A = L + SE

+360
−300

+60 Rev ↑

December 18	Debit	Credit
Cash *(10 shares × $36)*..	**360**	
Investments *(10 shares × $30)*		**300**
Gain *(difference)*		**60**
(Sell investments above recorded amount)		

The difference between the selling price of $36 per share and the currently recorded amount of $30 per share represents a $6 gain on each of the 10 shares. If Nathan's Sportswear then decides on December 26 to sell another 10 shares for only $28 per share, we record the following:

A = L + SE

+280

−20 Exp ↑

−300

December 26	Debit	Credit
Cash *(10 shares × $28)*..	**280**	
Loss *(difference)*..	**20**	
Investments *(10 shares × $30)*		**300**
(Sell investments below recorded amount)		

ADJUST TO FAIR VALUE: TRADING SECURITIES

At the end of each period, we adjust equity investments to fair value. For example, after selling 20 shares, Nathan's Sportswear still owns 80 shares of Canadian Falcon, originally purchased for $30 per share. If Canadian Falcon's stock at the end of the year has a current price of $32 per share, then Nathan's Sportswear needs to adjust the recorded amount of the investment ($30 per share) to its current fair value ($32 per share). This requires a $2 per share upward adjustment to the Investments account.[1]

---

[1]Many companies increase the investment indirectly with a debit to a Fair Value Adjustment allowance rather than to the Investments account itself. We record the fair value adjustment directly to the Investments account, as this is simpler and reinforces the concept that the adjustment to fair value directly affects the Investments account.

December 31	Debit	Credit		A	=	L	+	SE
Investments	**160**			+160				
Unrealized Holding Gain—Net Income		**160**						+160 Rev ↑
(Increase investments to fair value)								
($160 = 80 shares × $2)								

Recording the adjustment to fair value involves an account we've not yet discussed, called *Unrealized Holding Gain–Net Income.* The term *unrealized* means the gain has not been realized (has not been obtained) in the form of actual cash (or the right to receive cash). The gain is *realized* when the investment has been sold and the gain is "locked in." **Because Nathan's Sportswear classifies this investment as a trading security, it reports the unrealized holding gain in the current year's income statement when calculating net income.** Even though the gain is unrealized, reporting it as part of current net income is appropriate because trading securities are actively managed for the purpose of profiting from short-term market price changes. Thus, gains and losses that result from holding trading securities represent measures of success or lack of success in managing investments, and these gains and losses are properly included as part of net income.

ADJUST TO FAIR VALUE: AVAILABLE-FOR-SALE SECURITIES

Unlike trading securities, available-for-sale securities are *not* acquired for the purpose of profiting from short-term price changes. Thus, unrealized gains and losses from holding available-for-sale securities are not considered current measures of performance to be included in net income. Instead, unrealized gains and losses from changes in the fair value of available-for-sale securities are reported as *other comprehensive income,* which we discuss next.[2]

Referring to our previous example, if Nathan's Sportswear accounts for its investment in Canadian Falcon as available-for-sale securities, it will report the $2 per share increase in fair value at the end of the year as part of other comprehensive income rather than as part of net income:

December 31	Debit	Credit		A	=	L	+	SE
Investments	**160**			+160				
Unrealized Holding Gain—Other Comprehensive Income		**160**						+160 Rev ↑
(Increase investments to fair value)								
($160 = 80 shares × $2)								

Revenues, expenses, gains, and losses are included in net income and reported in the income statement. Comprehensive income is a broader measure of income in which we report all changes in stockholders' equity other than investment by stockholders and payment of dividends. Comprehensive income includes all of the typical income statement items plus other comprehensive income items, such as unrealized holding gains and losses on available-for-sale securities:

Comprehensive income = Net income + Other comprehensive income

Illustration D–3 shows an example of the income statement and the statement of comprehensive income for Nathan's Sportswear. To complete the statement of comprehensive income, we assume sales revenue totals $2,000 and operating expenses are $1,500. The statement also includes:

- $50 in dividend revenue on December 15.
- a $60 realized gain on the sale of 10 shares of stock on December 18.
- a $20 realized loss on the sale of 10 shares on December 26.
- a $160 unrealized holding gain resulting from the upward fair value adjustment on December 31, the end of the year.

---

[2]At the time this book went to print, the FASB was considering whether unrealized gains and losses on available-for-sale securities should be reported in income similar to the treatment for trading securities. Please refer to Connect for any FASB updates in this area.

ILLUSTRATION D–3

Income Statement and Statement of Comprehensive Income

NATHAN'S SPORTSWEAR
Statement of Comprehensive Income (condensed)

Sales revenue	$2,000	⎫
Operating expenses	1,500	
Operating income	500	
Dividend revenue	50	**Income**
Gain on sale of investments	60	**Statement**
Loss on sale of investments	(20)	
Net income	590	⎭
Unrealized holding gain	**160**	
Comprehensive income	$ 750	

Statement of Comprehensive Income

KEY POINT

We report investments at fair value when a company has an insignificant influence over another company in which it invests, often indicated by an ownership interest of less than 20%. For investments classified as trading securities, unrealized holding gains and losses are included in net income. For investments classified as available-for-sale securities, unrealized holding gains and losses are included as other comprehensive income.

Let's Review

Flip Side

This problem is the flip side of a Let's Review problem presented in Chapter 10. Sheer Designs, a custom clothing designer, has heard great things about Slacks 5th Avenue and has decided to make a small investment (insignificant influence) in the corporation's common stock. Sheer Designs has the following transactions relating to its investment in Slacks 5th Avenue.

January	15	Purchase 500 shares of common stock for $20 per share.
June	30	Receive a cash dividend of $1 per share.
October	1	Sell 100 shares of common stock for $25 per share.
December	31	The fair value of Slacks 5th Avenue's stock equals $23 per share.

Required:

1. Record each of these transactions, including the fair value adjustment on December 31. Assume the investment is classified as available-for-sale securities.
2. Calculate the balance in the Investments account on December 31.

Solution:

1. Record transactions:

January 15	Debit	Credit
Investments	**10,000**	
Cash		**10,000**
(Purchase common stock)		
($10,000 = 500 shares × $20)		

June 30		
Cash	**500**	
Dividend Revenue		**500**
(Receive cash dividends)		
($500 = 500 shares × $1)		

October 1		
Cash *(100 shares × $25)*...	**2,500**	
Investments *(100 shares × $20)*......................................		**2,000**
Gain *(difference)*		**500**
(Sell investments above recorded amount)		
December 31		
Investments	**1,200**	
Unrealized Holding Gain—Other Comprehensive Income		**1,200**
(Adjust investments to fair value)		
($1,200 = 400 shares × $3)		

2. The balance in the Investments account on December 31 is $9,200, which equals the 400 remaining shares times $23 per share fair value. The balance in the Investments account can be verified by posting all transactions to a T-account, as follows.

Investments	
10,000	
	2,000
1,200	
Bal. 9,200	

Suggested Homework:
BED–3, BED–4;
ED–2, ED–3;
PD–1A&B

INTERNATIONAL FINANCIAL REPORTING STANDARDS (IFRS)

International accounting standards differ from U.S. accounting standards in the classification of investments. Under IFRS, the default classification for investments in equity securities is called FVTPL (Fair Value through Profit and Loss). Accounting for FVTPL is similar to that for trading securities under U.S. GAAP. Investments in equity securities classified as FVTOCI (Fair Value through Other Comprehensive Income) are treated similar to available-for-sale securities under U.S. GAAP. Investments in the FVTOCI category have *unrealized* gains and losses included in other comprehensive income.

Equity Investments with Significant Influence

When a company owns between 20% and 50% of the common stock in another company, it is presumed that the investing company exercises significant influence over the investee. Share ownership provides voting rights, and by voting these shares, the investing company can sway decisions in the direction it desires, such as the selection of members of the board of directors. This significant influence changes the accounting for the investment. When a company has significant influence over an investee, the company is required to use the equity method. **Under the equity method, the investor accounts for the investment as if the investee is a part of the investor company.** Let's discuss some specific transactions using the equity method.

■ **LO D–3**
Account for investments in equity securities when the investor has *significant* influence.

PURCHASE EQUITY INVESTMENTS

Assume that, on January 2, Nathan's Sportswear purchases 25% of Canadian Falcon's common stock for $25,000. By holding 25% of the stock, Nathan's Sportswear can now exert significant influence over the operations of Canadian Falcon. Nathan's Sportswear records this equity investment as:

A	=	L	+	SE
+25,000				
−25,000				

January 2	Debit	Credit
Investments	**25,000**	
Cash		**25,000**
(Purchase common stock)		

RECOGNIZE EQUITY INCOME

Under the equity method, the investor (Nathan's Sportswear) includes in net income its portion of the investee's (Canadian Falcon's) net income. Assume that on December 31, Canadian Falcon reports net income of $30,000 for the year. Nathan's Sportswear records $7,500 of equity income, which represents its 25% share of Canadian Falcon's net income of $30,000.

A	=	L	+	SE
+7,500				
				+7,500 Rev ↑

December 31	Debit	Credit
Investments	**7,500**	
Equity Income		**7,500**
(Earn equity income)		
($7,500 = $30,000 × 25%)		

Equity Income is a revenue account included in the "other revenue" portion of the income statement. The reason Nathan's Sportswear can record a portion of Canadian Falcon's net income as its own is that significant ownership essentially eliminates the independent operations of the two companies. Nathan's Sportswear can significantly influence the operations of Canadian Falcon. **Therefore, the success (or failure) of Canadian Falcon's operations should partially be assigned to Nathan's Sportswear and recognized as income (or loss) in its income statement, based on its portion of ownership.**

RECEIVE CASH DIVIDENDS

Because we record equity income when the investee reports net income (as in the transaction above), it would be inappropriate to record equity income again when the investee distributes that same net income as dividends to the investor. To do so would be to double-count equity income. Instead, the investor records dividend payments received from the investee as a *reduction* in the Investments account. Assuming Canadian Falcon pays total dividends of $500 to all shareholders on December 31, Nathan's Sportswear receives its share of $125 (=$500 × 25%) and records the following:

A	=	L	+	SE
+125				
−125				

December 31	Debit	Credit
Cash	**125**	
Investments		**125**
(Receive cash dividends)		
($125 = $500 × 25%)		

The rationale for this accounting is that the investee is distributing cash in the form of dividends. This distribution of assets by the investee reduces that company's equity. To account for the investee's decrease in equity, the investor decreases its Investments account based on its portion of ownership.

We can see the balances in the Investments and Equity Income accounts for Nathan's Sportswear after posting the three transactions above.

Investments

Initial investment	25,000
25% of net income	7,500	125	25% of dividends
Bal. 32,375	

Equity Income

	7,500	25% of net income
	Bal. 7,500

The Investments account increases by the initial investment and the investor's share of the investee's net income, and it decreases by the investor's share of the investee's dividends. The Equity Income account reflects the investor's share of net income rather than its share of dividends.

KEY POINT

We initially record equity investments at cost. Under the equity method, the balance of the Investments account increases for the investor's share of the investee's net income and decreases for the investor's share of the investee's cash dividends. Equity Income reflects the investor's share of the investee's net income.

The equity method can differ significantly from recording investments under the fair value method. Under the fair value method, the investment by Nathan's Sportswear would be recorded at the purchase price of $25,000 and then be adjusted to fair value at the end of each period. Under the equity method, no adjustment is made to fair value.[2] In addition, Nathan's Sportswear would record only $125 of dividend revenue under the fair value method, rather than the $7,500 of equity income recorded using the equity method.

Let's Review

Sheer Designs, a custom clothing designer, has heard great things about Slacks 5th Avenue and has decided to make a 40% investment (significant influence) in the corporation's common stock. Sheer Designs has the following transactions relating to its investment in Slacks 5th Avenue.

January	1	Purchase 500 shares of common stock for $20 per share.
June	30	Receive a cash dividend of $500 (or $1 per share), representing its 40% share of Slacks 5th Avenue's total dividend distribution of $1,250.
December 31		Slacks 5th Avenue reports total net income of $5,000 for the year.
December 31		The fair value of Slacks 5th Avenue's stock equals $23 per share.

Required:

1. Record each of these transactions.
2. Calculate the balance of the Investments account on December 31.

---

[2]Adjustment to fair value is an allowable alternative under the equity method but is not common in practice.

Solution:

1. Record transactions:

January 1	Debit	Credit
Investments	**10,000**	
Cash		**10,000**
(Purchase common stock)		
June 30		
Cash	**500**	
Investments		**500**
(Receive cash dividends)		
($500 = 500 shares × $1)		
December 31		
Investments	**2,000**	
Equity Income		**2,000**
(Earn equity income)		
($2,000 = $5,000 × 40%)		

December 31

No adjustments are recorded for fair value changes when using the equity method.

2. The balance of the Investments account on December 31 is $11,500. The balance of the Investments account can be verified by posting all transactions to a T-account.

Suggested Homework:
BED–7, BED–8;
ED–6, ED–7;
PD–2A&B

Investments	
10,000	
	500
2,000	
Bal. 11,500	

INTERNATIONAL FINANCIAL REPORTING STANDARDS (IFRS)

Like U.S. GAAP, international accounting standards require the equity method when the investor exerts significant influence over investees (which they call "associates"). A difference, though, is that IFRS requires that the accounting policies of investees be adjusted to match those of the investor when applying the equity method. U.S. GAAP has no such requirement.

Equity Investments with Controlling Influence

■ **LO D–4**

Account for investments in equity securities when the investor has *controlling* influence.

If a company purchases more than 50% of the voting stock of another company, it's said to have a *controlling influence.* By voting these shares, the investor actually can control the acquired company. The investor is referred to as the *parent;* the investee is the *subsidiary.* Investments involving the purchase of more than 50% of the voting stock are accounted for by the parent using the consolidation method.

Under the consolidation method, the parent company prepares consolidated financial statements. These statements combine the parent's and subsidiary's operating activities as if the two companies were a *single* reporting company, even though both companies continue to operate as separate legal entities. Illustration D–4 demonstrates the concept of consolidation.

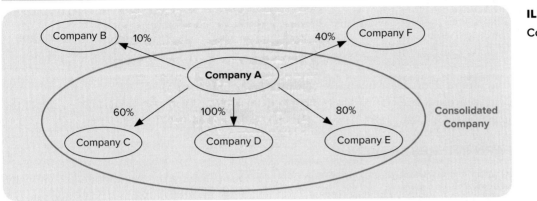

ILLUSTRATION D–4
Consolidation Method

Suppose Company A owns common stock in five other companies. When preparing financial statements, Company A combines its financial statement results with all companies in which it has greater than 50% ownership (in this instance, Companies C, D, and E). For example, if Company A has $10 million cash and Companies C, D, and E have $2 million, $4 million, and $6 million, respectively, the consolidated balance sheet would report cash of $22 million.[3] The cash balances for Companies B and F are not included in the consolidated financial statements of Company A. The 10% ownership (insignificant influence) in Company B is accounted for using the fair value method, while the 40% ownership (significant influence) in Company F is accounted for using the equity method.

KEY POINT

We account for investments involving the purchase of more than 50% of the voting stock of another company using the consolidation method. Under the consolidation method, the parent company prepares consolidated financial statements, in which the companies are combined as if they were a single company.

DEBT INVESTMENTS

Debt investments are the "flip side" of long-term debt: One party *borrows* by issuing a debt instrument, while another party *lends* by investing in the debt instrument. In Chapter 9, we discussed how to record the issuance of bonds (a specific type of debt instrument). Here, we discuss how to record an investment in bonds.

PURCHASE DEBT INVESTMENTS

Assume that on January 1, 2018, Nathan's Sportswear purchases $100,000 of 7%, 10-year bonds issued by California Coasters, with interest receivable semiannually on June 30 and December 31 each year. If the market rate of interest is 8%, Nathan's Sportswear will purchase the bonds at a discount, paying only $93,205 for the bonds.[4] Because the bonds pay only 7% compared to the prevailing market rate of 8%, we know that Nathan's Sportswear

PART B

■ **LO D–5**
Account for investments in debt securities.

Flip Side

---

[3]Any transactions between Companies A, C, D, and E are eliminated from consolidated reporting because these transactions are not with external parties. This avoids "double-counting" those amounts in the consolidated statements. For example, we report amounts owed by Company C to Company D as accounts payable in Company C's balance sheet and as accounts receivable in Company D's balance sheet. However, these amounts are not included in the consolidated balance sheet because a company can't owe money to itself, and the consolidated company is treated as a single company for financial reporting purposes.
[4]The bond price of $93,205 is calculated in Illustration 9–8.

will buy them at less than the face amount of $100,000. Nathan's Sportswear records this bond investment as:

A	=	L	+	SE
+93,205				
−93,205				

January 1, 2018	Debit	Credit
Investments	93,205	
Cash		93,205
(Purchase bonds)		

Nathan's Sportswear initially records the investment at $93,205. The carrying value will increase from $93,205 (purchase price) to $100,000 (face value) over the 10-year life of the bonds. Let's see why.

EARN INTEREST REVENUE

Interest revenue is the carrying value ($93,205 to start) times the market rate (8% annually, or 4% semiannually). The cash received is the face value ($100,000) times the stated rate (7% annually, or 3.5% semiannually). On June 30, 2018, six months after the initial bond investment, Nathan's Sportswear records interest revenue and cash received as follows:

A	=	L	+	SE
+3,500				
+228				
			+3,728 Rev ↑	

June 30, 2018	Debit	Credit
Cash (= $100,000 × 7% × ½)	3,500	
Investments (difference)	228	
Interest Revenue (= $93,205 × 8% × ½)		3,728
(Receive semiannual interest revenue)		

The investment earned interest revenue of $3,728, but the investor received cash of only $3,500. Therefore, Nathan's Sportswear is entitled to receive the remaining $228 when the bond matures. That's why the investment's carrying value increases by that amount. Because the carrying value of the bonds increases over time, interest revenue will also increase each semiannual interest period because it's calculated as a constant rate (8% × ½ in this example) times the carrying value. On December 31, 2018, Nathan's Sportswear records cash received and interest revenue for the second six-month period as:

A	=	L	+	SE
+3,500				
+237				
			+3,737 Rev ↑	

December 31, 2018	Debit	Credit
Cash (= $100,000 × 7% × ½)	3,500	
Investments (difference)	237	
Interest Revenue (= [$93,205 + 228] × 8% × ½)		3,737
(Receive semiannual interest revenue)		

The amortization schedule in Illustration D–5 demonstrates how the carrying amount of the bond investment would increase until it reaches maturity. Notice that the amounts in the amortization schedule are identical to those in the schedule we used for *bonds payable* in Chapter 9, Illustration 9–16.

Flip Side

SELL DEBT INVESTMENTS

Let's assume that market interest rates have dropped from 8% to 6% during 2018. Nathan's Sportswear decides to sell the bonds on December 31, 2018, when their carrying value is $93,670 (see amortization schedule in Illustration D–5). When interest rates go down, the investment value of bonds goes up. If the market rate drops to 6%, the value of the bonds will increase to $106,877.[5] The bonds have a carrying value on December 31, 2018, of only $93,670, but Nathan's Sportswear sells them for $106,877 and records a gain for the difference.

---

[5]The $106,877 is based on the following inputs: future value, $100,000; interest payment each semiannual period, $3,500; market interest rate each semiannual period, 3% (6% ÷ 2 semiannual periods); and periods to maturity, 18 (9 years left × 2 semiannual periods each year).

(1) Date	(2) Cash Received	(3) Interest Revenue	(4) Increase in Carrying Value	(5) Carrying Value
	Face Amount × Stated Rate	Carrying Value × Market Rate	(3) − (2)	Prior Carrying Value + (4)
1/1/18				$ 93,205
6/30/18	$3,500	$3,728	$228	93,433
12/31/18	3,500	3,737	237	93,670
*	*	*	*	*
*	*	*	*	99,057
6/30/27	3,500	3,962	462	99,519
12/31/27	3,500	3,981	481	$100,000

December 31, 2018	Debit	Credit
Cash..	**106,877**	
Investments		**93,670**
Gain (difference)		**13,207**
(Sell bonds before maturity)		

A = L + SE

+106,877
−93,670
+13,207 Rev ↑

The gain on the sale of bonds is reported in the income statement as part of other revenue. Of course, if the bond was sold for a loss, it would be reported in the income statement as part of other expense.

ADJUST TO FAIR VALUE

We classify debt investments as either (1) held-to-maturity securities, (2) trading securities, or (3) available-for-sale securities. Held-to-maturity securities are debt securities that the company expects to hold until they *mature,* which means until they become payable.[6] Since we do not expect to sell these securities until they mature, companies are not required to adjust held-to-maturity securities to fair value.[7]

The accounting for debt investments classified as trading securities or available-for-sale securities is nearly identical to that already discussed for equity securities. Recall that *trading securities* are securities that the investor expects to sell (trade) in the near future. These investments are adjusted to fair value with the unrealized gain or loss included in net income. *Available-for-sale securities* are investments that do not fit the other two categories; they are not expected to be sold in the near future, yet they are not expected to be held to maturity either. These investments are adjusted to fair value with the unrealized gain or loss included in comprehensive income.

KEY POINT

Bond investments are the "flip side" of bonds payable. Bond investments are long-term assets that earn interest revenue, while bonds payable are long-term liabilities that incur interest expense.

---

[6]Equity securities do not have a held-to-maturity classification because equity securities do not have a maturity date.
[7]However, U.S. GAAP does allow companies to elect a fair value option. Under this option, companies may report held-to-maturity securities at fair value, with unrealized gains and losses recognized in income in the period in which they occur—the same approach we use to account for trading securities.

Let's Review

Assume that on January 1, 2018, Wally World issues $200,000 of 9% bonds, due in 10 years, with interest payable semiannually on June 30 and December 31 each year. American Life Insurance Company (ALICO) purchases all of the bonds.

Required:

1. If the market rate is 9%, the bonds will sell for $200,000. Record the investment in bonds by ALICO on January 1, 2018, and receipt of the first semiannual interest payment on June 30, 2018.

2. If the market rate is 10%, the bonds will sell for $187,538. Record the investment in bonds by ALICO on January 1, 2018, and receipt of the first semiannual interest payment on June 30, 2018.

3. If the market rate is 8%, the bonds will sell at $213,590. Record the investment in bonds by ALICO on January 1, 2018, and receipt of the first semiannual interest payment on June 30, 2018.

Solution:

1. Market rate of 9%:

January 1, 2018	Debit	Credit
Investments...	200,000	
Cash		200,000
(Purchase bonds)		
June 30, 2018		
Cash...	9,000	
Interest Revenue		9,000
(Receive semiannual interest revenue)		
($9,000 = $200,000 × 9% × ½)		

2. Market rate of 10%:

January 1, 2018	Debit	Credit
Investments...	187,538	
Cash		187,538
(Purchase bonds)		
June 30, 2018		
Cash (= $200,000 × 9% × ½)	9,000	
Investments (difference)...	377	
Interest Revenue (= $187,538 × 10% × ½)		9,377
(Receive semiannual interest revenue)		

3. Market rate of 8%:

January 1, 2018	Debit	Credit
Investments...	213,590	
Cash		213,590
(Purchase bonds)		
June 30, 2018		
Cash (= $200,000 × 9% × ½)...	9,000	
Investments (difference)...		456
Interest Revenue (= $213,590 × 8% × ½)........................		8,544
(Receive semiannual interest revenue)		

Suggested Homework:
BED–11, BED–12;
ED–10, ED–11;
PD–4A&B

KEY POINTS BY LEARNING OBJECTIVE

LO D-1 Explain why companies invest in other companies.

Companies invest in other companies primarily to receive dividends, earn interest, and gain from the increase in the value of their investment. Companies in seasonal industries often invest excess funds generated during the busy season and draw on these funds in the slow season. Many companies also make investments for strategic purposes to develop closer business ties, increase market share, or expand into new industries.

LO D-2 Account for investments in equity securities when the investor has *insignificant* influence.

We report investments at fair value when a company has an insignificant influence over another company in which it invests, often indicated by an ownership interest of less than 20%. For investments classified as trading securities, unrealized holding gains and losses are included in net income. For investments classified as available-for-sale securities, unrealized holding gains and losses are included as other comprehensive income.

LO D-3 Account for investments in equity securities when the investor has *significant* influence.

We initially record equity investments at cost. Under the equity method, the balance of the Investments account increases for the investor's share of the investee's net income and decreases for the investor's share of the investee's cash dividends. Equity Income reflects the investor's share of the investee's net income.

LO D-4 Account for investments in equity securities when the investor has *controlling* influence.

We account for investments involving the purchase of more than 50% of the voting stock of another company using the consolidation method. Under the consolidation method, the parent company prepares consolidated financial statements, in which the companies are combined as if they were a single company.

LO D-5 Account for investments in debt securities.

Bond investments are the "flip side" of bonds payable. Bond investments are long-term assets that earn interest revenue, while bonds payable are long-term liabilities that incur interest expense.

GLOSSARY

Available-for-sale securities: Securities held for reasons other than attempting to profit from trading in the near future. **p. D-3**

Comprehensive income: A broad measure of income that reports all changes in stockholders' equity other than investment by stockholders and payment of dividends. **p. D-5**

Consolidated financial statements: Combination of the separate financial statements of the parent (purchasing company) and the subsidiary (acquired company) into a single set of financial statements. **p. D-10**

Consolidation method: Method of recording equity investments when one company owns more than 50% of the voting stock of another company. Under this method, the investing company uses *consolidated* financial statements to report operations, as if the two companies were operating as a single combined company. **pp. D-2, D-10**

Debt investments: Investments made in the debt issued by another party. **p. D-11**

Equity investments: Investments made in the equity (or stock) issued by another party. **p. D-2**

Equity method: Method of recording equity investments when an investor has significant influence over, yet does not control, the operations of the investee, often indicated by ownership of between 20% and 50% of the voting shares. Under this method, the investor company records the investment as if the investee is a part of the company. **pp. D-3, D-7**

Fair value: The amount for which the investment could be bought or sold in a current transaction between willing parties. **p. D-3**

Fair value method: Method of recording equity investments when an investor has insignificant influence, often indicated by ownership of less than 20% of the voting shares. Under this method, we classify equity investments as either trading securities or available-for-sale securities and report investments at their fair value. **p. D-3**

Held-to-maturity securities: Debt securities that are expected to be held until they *mature*, which means until they become payable. **p. D-13**

Trading securities: Securities that the investor expects to sell in the near future. **p. D-3**

SELF-STUDY QUESTIONS

1. One of the primary reasons for investing in equity securities includes: **(LO D–1)**
   a. Receiving dividend payments.
   b. Acquiring debt of competing companies.
   c. Earning interest revenue.
   d. Deducting dividend payments for tax purposes.

2. One of the primary reasons for investing in debt securities includes: **(LO D–1)**
   a. Deducting interest payments for tax purposes.
   b. Receiving dividend payments.
   c. Earning interest revenue
   d. Acquiring ownership control in other companies.

3. On November 17, Tasty Foods purchased 1,000 shares (10%) of Eco-Safe Packaging's voting stock for $12 per share. Because Tasty Foods' intent in making the investment is to make a quick profit by trading in the near term, the investment is classified as a trading security. By the end of the year, Eco-Safe Packaging's stock price has dropped to $10 per share. How would the drop in stock price affect Tasty Foods' net income for the year? **(LO D–2)**
   a. Decrease net income by $12,000.
   b. Decrease net income by $10,000.
   c. Decrease net income by $2,000.
   d. No effect.

4. On November 17, Tasty Foods purchased 1,000 shares (10%) of Eco-Safe Packaging's voting stock for $12 per share. Because Tasty Foods has no immediate plans to sell the stock, the investment is classified as an available-for-sale security. By the end of the year, Eco-Safe Packaging's stock price has dropped to $10 per share. How would the drop in stock price affect Tasty Foods' net income for the year? **(LO D–2)**
   a. Decrease net income by $12,000.
   b. Decrease net income by $10,000.
   c. Decrease net income by $2,000.
   d. No effect.

5. On January 1, Tasty Foods purchased 3,000 shares (30%) of Eco-Safe Packaging's voting stock for $12 per share. On December 31, Eco-Safe Packaging reports net income $10,000 and a total dividend payment of $2,000, and the stock price has dropped to $10 per share. For how much would Tasty Foods report its investment in Eco-Safe Packaging at the end of the year? **(LO D–3)**

   a. $30,000.
   b. $38,400.
   c. $36,000.
   d. $39,000.

6. On January 1, Tasty Foods purchased 10,000 shares (100%) of Eco-Safe Packaging's voting stock for $12 per share. Throughout the year, both companies continue to operate as separate legal entities. By December 31, Eco-Safe Packaging's cash balance is $2,000, and Tasty Foods' cash balance is $5,000. In preparing its year-end financial statements, for how much would Tasty Foods report its cash balance? **(LO D–4)**
   a. $7,000.
   b. $5,000.
   c. $3,000.
   d. $2,000.

7. On January 1, Eco-Safe Packaging issues $100,000 of 8%, 5-year bonds with interest payable semiannually on June 30 and December 31. The market interest rate for bonds of similar risk and maturity is 6%. Tasty Foods purchases all of the bonds for $108,530. Which of the following would correctly record Tasty Foods' investment in bonds on January 1? **(LO D–5)**

a. Cash	108,530	
Investments		108,530
b. Investments	108,530	
Cash		108,530
c. Cash	100,000	
Investments		100,000
d. Investments	100,000	
Cash		100,000

8. Refer to Question 7. How much interest revenue would Tasty Foods record at the time it receives the first semiannual payment on June 30? **(LO D–5)**
   a. $4,341.
   b. $8,000.
   c. $6,512.
   d. $3,256.

Note: For answers, see the last page of the appendix.

REVIEW QUESTIONS

1. Explain why a company might invest in another company. ■ LO D-1

2. How can an investor benefit from an equity investment that does not pay dividends? ■ LO D-1

3. How might the investing activity for a company that operates a ski resort vary throughout the year? ■ LO D-1

4. Provide an example of an equity investment in another company undertaken for strategic purposes. ■ LO D-1

5. What is the "flip side" of an investment in equity securities? ■ LO D-1

6. How does a company determine whether to account for an equity investment using the fair value method, equity method, or consolidation method? ■ LO D-1

7. Investments in *equity* securities for which the investor has insignificant influence over the investee are classified for reporting purposes under the fair value method in one of two categories. What are these two categories? ■ LO D-2

8. Explain how we report dividends received from an investment under the fair value method. ■ LO D-2

9. Discuss the difference between an unrealized holding gain and a realized gain. ■ LO D-2

10. When using the fair value method, we adjust the reported amount of the investment for changes in fair value after its acquisition. If the security is classified as trading, how do we report unrealized holding gains and losses? ■ LO D-2

11. When using the fair value method, we adjust the reported amount of the investment for changes in fair value after its acquisition. If the security is classified as available-for-sale, how do we report unrealized holding gains and losses? ■ LO D-2

12. Under what circumstances do we use the equity method to account for an investment in stock? ■ LO D-3

13. Explain how we report dividends received from an investment under the equity method. ■ LO D-3

14. Discuss the meaning of consolidated financial statements.

15. When is it appropriate to consolidate financial statements of two companies? Discuss your answer in terms of the relation between the parent and the subsidiary. ■ LO D-4

16. What is the "flip side" of an investment in debt securities? ■ LO D-5

17. If bonds are purchased at a *discount,* what will happen to the carrying value of the investment in bonds and the amount recorded for interest revenue over time? ■ LO D-5

18. If bonds are purchased at a *premium,* what will happen to the carrying value of the investment in bonds and the amount recorded for interest revenue over time? ■ LO D-5

19. When interest rates go down, what happens to the value of an investment in bonds that pay a fixed interest rate? ■ LO D-5

20. Investments in *debt* securities are classified for reporting purposes in one of three categories. Explain each of these three categories. ■ LO D-5

BRIEF EXERCISES

Mc Graw Hill Education **connect**

Identify reasons why companies invest (LO D–1)

BED–1 Indicate with an "X" any of the following that represent a common reason why companies invest in other companies.

_____ 1. To invest excess cash created by operating in seasonal industries.
_____ 2. To increase employees' morale.
_____ 3. To build strategic alliances.
_____ 4. To reduce government regulation.
_____ 5. To receive interest and dividends.

Record equity investments with insignificant influence (LO D–2)

BED–2 On September 1, Leather Suppliers, Inc., purchases 150 shares of Western Wear Clothing for $13 per share. On November 1, Leather Suppliers sells the investment for $17 per share. Record the transactions made by Leather Suppliers for the purchase and sale of the investment in Western Wear Clothing.

Record trading securities (LO D–2)

BED–3 Summit Financial buys and sells securities, expecting to earn profits on short-term differences in price. On December 28, Summit purchased **Microsoft** common shares for $485,000. On December 31, the shares had a fair value of $483,000. Record the initial investment by Summit and, if appropriate, an adjustment to record the investment at fair value.

Record available-for-sale securities (LO D–2)

BED–4 Summit Financial buys and sells securities that it classifies as available-for-sale. On December 28, Summit purchased **Microsoft** common shares for $485,000. On December 31, the shares had a fair value of $483,000. Record the initial investment by Summit and, if appropriate, an adjustment to record the investment at fair value.

Determine the appropriate classification and reporting for an equity investment (LO D–2)

BED–5 On December 29, Adams Apples purchased 1,000 shares of **General Electric** common stock for $19,000 and placed the investment in an active trading account for immediate resale. On December 31, the market value of the stock is $20 per share. What is the appropriate reporting category for this investment, and at what amount will Adams Apples report it in the year-end balance sheet?

Determine the appropriate classification and reporting for an equity investment (LO D–2)

BED–6 Adams Apples holds 1,000 shares of **General Electric** common stock. The stock was initially purchased in July 2017. On December 31, 2017, and December 31, 2018, the market value of the stock is $18 and $20 per share, respectively. What is the appropriate reporting category for this investment, and at what amount will Adams Apples report it in the 2018 balance sheet?

Explain the effect of net income by the investee in an equity method investment (LO D–3)

BED–7 Wendy Day Kite Company owns 40% of the outstanding stock of Strong String Company. During the current year, Strong String reported net income of $20 million. What effect does Strong String's reported net income have on Wendy Day's financial statements? Explain the reasoning for this effect.

Explain the effect of dividends by the investee in an equity method investment (LO D–3)

BED–8 Wendy Day Kite Company owns 40% of the outstanding stock of Strong String Company. During the current year, Strong String paid a $10 million cash dividend on its common shares. What effect does Strong String's dividend have on Wendy Day's financial statements? Explain the reasoning for this effect.

Calculate consolidated amounts (LO D–4)

BED–9 Wendy Day Kite Company owns 100% of the outstanding stock of Strong String Company. At the end of the year, Wendy Day has total inventory of $14,000 and Strong String has total inventory of $8,000. Determine the amount of inventory that would be reported in Wendy Day's consolidated financial statements (assuming no transactions involving inventory occurred between the two companies).

Record investment in bonds at face value (LO D–5)

BED–10 Salt Foods purchases forty $1,000, 7%, 10-year bonds issued by Pretzelmania, Inc., for $40,000 on January 1. The market interest rate for bonds of similar risk and maturity is 7%. Salt Foods receives interest semiannually on June 30 and December 31.
1. Record the investment in bonds.
2. Record receipt of the first interest payment on June 30.

Record investment in bonds at a discount (LO D–5)

BED–11 Salt Foods purchases forty $1,000, 7%, 10-year bonds issued by Pretzelmania, Inc., for $37,282 on January 1. The market interest rate for bonds of similar risk and maturity is 8%. Salt Foods receives interest semiannually on June 30 and December 31.

1. Record the investment in bonds.
2. Record receipt of the first interest payment on June 30.

BED–12 Salt Foods purchases forty $1,000, 7%, 10-year bonds issued by Pretzelmania, Inc., for $42,975 on January 1. The market interest rate for bonds of similar risk and maturity is 6%. Salt Foods receives interest semiannually on June 30 and December 31.

> *Record investment in bonds at a premium (LO D–5)*

1. Record the investment in bonds.
2. Record receipt of the first interest payment on June 30.

EXERCISES

connect

ED–1 Consider the following statements.

> *Identify reasons why companies invest (LO D–1)*

_____ 1. A reason companies invest in other companies is to build strategic alliances.
_____ 2. All companies are required to pay dividends to their investors.
_____ 3. When market interest rates increase, the market value of a bond increases as well.
_____ 4. One way for a company to expand operations into a new industry is to acquire the majority of common stock in another company that already operates in that industry.
_____ 5. Stocks typically have greater upside potential, providing a higher average return to their investors over the long run than do bonds.
_____ 6. Companies purchase debt securities primarily for the dividend revenue they provide.

Required:
Indicate whether each statement is true (T) or false (F).

ED–2 First National Bank buys and sells securities, expecting to earn profits on short-term differences in price. The company's fiscal year ends on December 31. The following selected transactions relating to First National's trading account occurred during the year.

> *Record trading securities (LO D–2)*

December 20	Purchases 300,000 shares in Classic Computers common stock for $1,500,000.
December 28	Receives cash dividends of $6,000 from the Classic Computers shares.
December 31	The fair value of Classic Computers' stock is $4.80 per share.

Required:
1. Record each of these transactions, including an adjustment on December 31 for the investment's fair value, if appropriate.
2. Calculate the balance of the Investments account on December 31.

ED–3 Mr. T's Fashions, once a direct competitor to Italian Stallion's clothing line, has formed a friendship in recent years leading to a small investment (less than 5%) by Mr. T in the common stock of Italian Stallion. Mr. T's engages in the following transactions relating to its investment.

> *Record available-for-sale investments (LO D–2)*

February	1	Purchases 150 shares of Italian Stallion common stock for $16 per share.
June	15	Sells 50 shares of Italian Stallion stock for $14 per share.
October	31	Receives a cash dividend of $0.50 per share.
December	31	The fair value of Italian Stallion's stock is $12 per share.

Required:
1. Record each of these transactions, including an adjustment on December 31 for the investment's fair value, if appropriate.
2. Calculate the balance of the Investments account on December 31.

ED–4 Gator Shoes, Inc., manufactures a line of stylish waterproof footwear. The following transactions relate to investments in common stock.

> *Record available-for-sale investments (LO D–2)*

March	1	Purchases 3,000 shares of Power Drive Corporation's common stock for $62 per share.
July	1	Receives a cash dividend of $1.25 per share.
October	1	Sells 750 shares of Power Drive Corporation's common stock for $70 per share.
December	31	The fair value of Power Drive Corporation's common stock is $75 per share.

Required:

1. Record each of these transactions, including an adjustment on December 31 for the investment's fair value, if appropriate.
2. Calculate the balance of the Investments account on December 31.

Prepare a statement of comprehensive income (LO D–2)

ED–5 Lefty's Piranha Farm generates sales revenue of $260,000 and incurs operating expenses of $140,000. The company incurs a gain of $13,000 from selling securities classified as available-for-sale and records an unrealized holding loss of $17,000 from adjusting securities available-for-sale to fair value at the end of the year.

Required:

1. What is the meaning of comprehensive income?
2. Prepare a statement of comprehensive income for Lefty's Piranha Farm.

Record transactions under the equity method (LO D–3)

ED–6 On January 1, Lifestyle Pools purchased 25% of Marshall Fence's common stock for $700,000 cash. By the end of the year, Marshall Fence reported net income of $160,000 and paid dividends of $60,000 to all shareholders.

Required:

For Lifestyle Pools, record the initial purchase and its share of Marshall Fence's net income and dividends for the year.

Record transactions under the equity method (LO D–3)

ED–7 On January 1, Marcum's Landscape purchased 10,000 shares (35%) of the common stock of Atlantic Irrigation for $600,000. Below are amounts reported by both companies for the year.

	Marcum's Landscape	Atlantic Irrigation
Stock price on January 1	$85	$60
Net income for the year	$500,000	$130,000
Dividends paid for the year	$60,000	$40,000
Stock price on December 31	$94	$68

Required:

For Marcum's Landscape, record the initial purchase, its share of Atlantic's net income and dividends, and the adjustment for Atlantic's fair value at the end of the year, if appropriate.

Compare available-for-sale securities and equity method investments (LO D–2, LO D–3)

ED–8 As a long-term investment, Fair Company purchased 20% of Midlin Company's 300,000 shares for $360,000 at the beginning of the reporting year of both companies. During the year, Midlin earned net income of $135,000 and distributed cash dividends of $0.25 per share. At year-end, the fair value of the shares is $375,000.

Required:

1. Assume no significant influence was acquired. Record the transactions from the purchase through the end of the year, including any adjustment for the investment's fair value, if appropriate.
2. Assume significant influence was acquired. Record the transactions from the purchase through the end of the year, including any adjustment for the investment's fair value, if appropriate.

Determine which companies to consolidate (LO D–4)

ED–9 Alpha has made the following investments.

_____ 1. 10% of the common stock of Beta.
_____ 2. 40% of the bonds of Gamma.
_____ 3. 75% of the common stock of Delta.
_____ 4. 15% of the bonds of Epsilon.
_____ 5. 25% of the common stock of Zeta.
_____ 6. 60% of the bonds of Eta.
_____ 7. 100% of the common stock of Theta.

Required:

Indicate with an "X" which of the companies above would be accounted for using the consolidation method.

ED–10 On January 1, Dora purchases 175 of the $1,000, 7%, 15-year bonds issued by Splash City, with interest receivable semiannually on June 30 and December 31 each year.

Record investment in bonds at a discount (LO D–5)

Required:

Assuming the market interest rate on the issue date is 8%, Dora will purchase the bonds for $159,869.

1. Complete the first three rows of an amortization table for Dora.
2. Record the purchase of the bonds by Dora on January 1 and the receipt of the first two semiannual interest payments on June 30 and December 31.

ED–11 On January 1, Splash City issues $500,000 of 7% bonds, due in 15 years, with interest payable semiannually on June 30 and December 31 each year. T. Bone Investment Company (TBIC) purchases all of the bonds in a private placement.

Record investment in bonds at a premium (LO D–5)

Required:

Assuming the market interest rate on the issue date is 6%, TBIC will purchase the bonds for $549,001.

1. Complete the first three rows of an amortization table for TBIC.
2. Record the purchase of the bonds by TBIC on January 1 and the receipt of the first two semiannual interest payments on June 30 and December 31.

PROBLEMS: SET A

PD–1A Barry, Hank, and Babe form a company named Long Ball Investments, hoping to find that elusive home run stock. A new clothing company by the name of Major League Apparel has caught their eye. Major League Apparel has two classes of stock authorized: 5%, $10 par preferred and $1 par value common. Long Ball Investments has the following transactions during the year. None of the investments are large enough to exert a significant influence.

Account for investments using the fair value method (LO D–2)

January	2	Purchase 1,500 shares of Major League common stock for $70 per share.
February	14	Purchase 600 shares of Major League preferred stock for $12 per share.
May	15	Sell 300 shares of Major League's common stock for $62 per share.
December	30	Receive a cash dividend on Major League's common stock of $0.50 per share and preferred stock of $0.50 per share.
December	31	The fair values of the common and preferred shares are $73 and $14, respectively.

Required:

1. Record each of these investment transactions. (*Hint:* Preferred stock transactions are recorded like common stock transactions, but preferred stock has no voting rights and therefore ownership provides no influence.)
2. Calculate the balance in the Investments account as of December 31.

PD–2A As a long-term investment at the beginning of the year, Willie Winn Track Shoes purchased 25% of Betty Will Company's 34 million shares outstanding for $178 million. During the year, Betty Will earned net income of $130 million and distributed cash dividends of $1.10 per share.

Account for investments using the equity method (LO D–3)

Required:

Record for Willie Winn Track Shoes the purchase of the investment and its share of Betty Will's net income and dividends using the equity method.

PD–3A On January 1, Twister Enterprises issues $600,000 of 6% bonds, due in 20 years, with interest payable semiannually on June 30 and December 31 each year. The market interest rate on the issue date is 7%. National Hydraulics, a supplier of mechanical parts to Twister Enterprises, purchases 25% of the bond issue ($150,000 face amount) at a discount for $133,984.

Account for investments in debt securities (LO D–5)

Required:
1. Complete the first three rows of an amortization table for National Hydraulics.
2. Record the purchase of the bonds by National Hydraulics and the receipt of the first two semiannual interest payments on June 30 and December 31.
3. Record the sale of the bonds by National Hydraulics on December 31, for $145,000.
4. What happened to market interest rates between the beginning and end of the year?

Account for investments in debt securities (LO D–5)

PD–4A Justin Investor, Inc., purchases $180,000 of 8% bonds from M.R. Bonds Company on January 1. Management intends to hold the debt securities to maturity. For bonds of similar risk and maturity, the market yield is 10%. Justin paid $152,000 for the bonds. It receives interest semiannually on June 30 and December 31. Due to changing market conditions, the fair value of the bonds at December 31 is $160,000.

Required:
1. Record Justin Investor's investment on January 1.
2. Record the interest revenue earned by Justin Investor for the first six months ended June 30.
3. Record the interest revenue earned by Justin Investor for the next six months ended December 31.
4. At what amount will Justin Investor report its investment in the December 31 balance sheet? Why?

PROBLEMS: SET B

Account for investments using the fair value method (LO D–2)

PD–1B Emmitt, Walter, and Barry form a company named Long Run Investments, with the intention of investing in stocks with great long-run potential. A clothing company named National League Gear looks like a great investment prospect. National League Gear has two classes of stock authorized: 6%, $30 par preferred and $5 par value common. Long Run Investments has the following transactions during the year. None of the investments are large enough to exert a significant influence.

February	2	Purchases 1,500 shares of National League Gear's common stock for $35 per share.
February	4	Purchases 600 shares of National League Gear's preferred stock for $32 per share.
July	15	Sells 400 shares of National League Gear's common stock for $40 per share.
November	30	Receives a cash dividend on National League Gear's common stock of $1.10 per share and preferred stock of $1.80 per share.
December	31	The fair value of the common and preferred shares equal $31 and $30, respectively.

Required:
1. Record each of these investment transactions. (*Hint:* Preferred stock transactions are recorded like common stock transactions, but preferred stock has no voting rights and therefore ownership provides no influence.)
2. Calculate the balance in the Investments account as of December 31.

Account for investments using the equity method (LO D–3)

PD–2B As a long-term investment at the beginning of the year, Acquisitions, Inc., purchased 3 million shares (30%) of Takeover Target's 10 million shares outstanding for $52 million. During the year, Takeover Target earned net income of $9 million and distributed cash dividends of $0.50 per share.

Required:
Record for Acquisitions, Inc., the purchase of the investment and its share of Takeover Target's net income and dividends using the equity method.

Account for investments in debt securities (LO D–5)

PD–3B Viking Voyager specializes in the design and production of replica Viking boats. On January 1, the company issues $3,000,000 of 7% bonds, due in 10 years, with interest payable semiannually on June 30 and December 31 each year. The market interest rate on the issue date is 8%. Antique Boat World, one of Viking Voyager's best customers, purchases 15% of the bond issue ($450,000 face amount) at a discount for $419,422.

Required:

1. Complete the first three rows of an amortization table for Antique Boat World.
2. Record the purchase of the bonds by Antique Boat World and the receipt of the first two semiannual interest payments on June 30 and December 31.
3. Record the sale of the bonds by Antique Boat World on December 31 for $415,000.
4. What happened to market interest rates between the beginning and end of the year?

PD–4B Tsunami Sushi purchases $130,000 of 5-year, 7% bonds from Deep Sea Explorers on January 1. Management intends to hold the debt securities to maturity. For bonds of similar risk and maturity, the market rate is 8%. Tsunami paid $124,728 for the bonds. It receives interest semiannually on June 30 and December 31. Due to changing market conditions, the fair value of the bonds at December 31 is $124,000.

Account for investments in debt securities (LO D–5)

Required:

1. Record Tsunami Sushi's investment on January 1.
2. Record the interest revenue earned by Tsunami Sushi for the first six months ended June 30.
3. Record the interest revenue earned by Tsunami Sushi for the next six months ended December 31.
4. At what amount will Tsunami Sushi report its investment in the December 31 balance sheet? Why?

Answers to the Self-Study Questions
1. a   2. c   3. c   4. d   5. b   6. a   7. b   8. d

International Financial Reporting Standards

Learning Objectives

AFTER STUDYING THIS APPENDIX, YOU SHOULD BE ABLE TO:

- **LO E–1** Explain the reasons for differences in accounting practices across countries.
- **LO E–2** Understand the role of the International Accounting Standards Board (IASB) in the development of International Financial Reporting Standards (IFRS).
- **LO E–3** Recognize the major differences between U.S. GAAP and IFRS.

The Globalization of Accounting Standards

On November 15, 2007, the U.S. Securities and Exchange Commission voted unanimously to accept from "foreign private issuers" financial statements that are prepared using International Financial Reporting Standards (IFRS) without reconciliation to U.S. generally accepted accounting principles. There is no doubt that the United States is moving toward converging U.S. GAAP with IFRS. Convergence refers to the process by which U.S. GAAP and IFRS will eventually merge to become a single set of accounting standards.

But convergence of standards hasn't happened yet, and much misunderstanding exists about the status and timing of the convergence process. Why are these changes taking place? Who are the key players? What critical differences between U.S. and international GAAP exist currently? This appendix is designed to answer these questions.

We first explore the reasons for differences in accounting practices across countries. These differences created the need for convergence in the first place. Then, we discuss a brief history and background regarding the development of international financial reporting standards. Finally, we review key differences between U.S. GAAP and IFRS for each chapter.

Differences in Accounting Practices

Most countries have organizations, similar to the FASB in the United States, that are responsible for determining accounting and reporting standards. Financial accounting standards and practices differ from country to country for many reasons, including different legal systems, the influence of tax laws, sources of financing, inflation, culture, political influence of other countries, and the level of economic development. Illustration E–1 (next page) provides a summary and further explanation of the reasons why accounting practices differ across countries.

Note that overlap exists in the reasons described. Accounting research has extensively focused on the legal system (common law vs. code law) as a way to describe overall differences in accounting practices between countries. *Common law* derives from English case law, in which rules are established over time primarily through private-sector professional organizations. *Code law* derives from Roman law, in which rules are an all-embracing set of requirements and procedures. Common-law countries such as the United States, the United Kingdom, Australia, and Canada share many similarities. For instance, these countries have separate rules for financial accounting and tax accounting, rely more on equity

■ LO E–1

Explain the reasons for differences in accounting practices across countries.

ILLUSTRATION E–1

Reasons Why
Accounting Practices
Differ across Countries

Reason	Further Explanation
1. Legal system	Common-law countries (the United States, the United Kingdom, and Canada) place greater emphasis on public information, while code-law countries (Germany, France, and Japan) rely more heavily on private information.
2. Tax laws	For countries whose tax standards are closely tied to financial reporting standards (Central Europe and Japan), accounting earnings tend to be lower so companies can minimize tax payments.
3. Sources of financing	In countries where debt financing is more common (Germany and Japan) than equity financing, there is greater emphasis on reporting the ability of the company to repay debt than on its ability to earn profits for its investors.
4. Inflation	Historically high inflation in some countries (Argentina and Brazil) has created a need to account for the effect of inflation on assets and liabilities.
5. Culture	Some countries (Brazil and Switzerland) are more secretive, leading to fewer financial disclosures.
6. Political and economic ties	Countries that share strong political and/or economic ties (British colonies) often have similar accounting practices.
7. Economic development	More economically developed economies (the United States and the United Kingdom) have a need for more complex accounting standards.

financing, and have political and economic ties with Britain. Code-law countries such as those in Central Europe and Japan also are influenced by the same factors, but in contrasting ways. Code-law countries have similar rules for financial accounting and tax accounting and rely more on debt financing. Many code-law countries have political and economic ties that began with Germany in World War II.

As you might imagine, differences in accounting practices can cause problems for investors trying to compare companies whose financial statements are prepared under different accounting methods. Investors unfamiliar with the accounting practices of a particular country are less likely to invest in firms from that country because of this uncertainty. Many believe that convergence of accounting practices among countries will increase the flow of resources across borders, making it easier for companies to raise international capital.

 **KEY POINT**

Differences in legal systems, tax laws, sources of financing, inflation, culture, political and economic ties, and economic development influence accounting practices across countries.

Divergent accounting rules also can cause problems for multinational corporations. A company doing business in more than one country may find it difficult and costly to comply with more than one set of accounting standards.

International Financial Reporting Standards

INTERNATIONAL ACCOUNTING STANDARDS BOARD

In response to differences in accounting standards and practices across countries, the **International Accounting Standards Committee (IASC)** was formed in 1973 to develop a single set of global accounting standards. The IASC reorganized itself in 2001 and created a new standard-setting body called the International Accounting Standards Board (IASB). The IASB's main objective is to develop a single set of high-quality, understandable, and enforceable global accounting standards to help participants in the world's capital markets and other users make economic decisions.

The IASC issued 41 International Accounting Standards (IAS), which the IASB endorsed at its formation. Since then, the IASB has revised many of the previous standards and has issued standards of its own, called International Financial Reporting Standards (IFRS), sometimes pronounced "eye-furs." More and more countries are basing their national accounting standards on IFRS. Over 140 jurisdictions, including Hong Kong, Australia, and all of the countries in the European Union (EU), either require or permit the use of IFRS or a local variant of IFRS.[1]

■ **LO E–2**
Understand the role of the International Accounting Standards Board (IASB) in the development of International Financial Reporting Standards (IFRS).

PRINCIPLES- VS. RULES-BASED STANDARDS

In comparing IFRS with U.S. GAAP, IFRS is often considered more principles-based while U.S. GAAP is considered more rules-based. *Principles-based accounting standards* emphasize broad principles of accounting with relatively less emphasis on detailed implementation rules. In comparison, *rules-based accounting standards* provide additional detailed guidance to help users implement the standards. An advantage of principles-based standards is that they are more concise, allowing preparers and users of accounting information to exercise judgment in focusing on the key issues. An advantage of rules-based standards is that they are more precise, providing additional guidance to preparers and users on an issue.

In reality, both U.S. GAAP and IFRS have standards that are more principles-based and standards that are more rules-based. However, both standard setters (the FASB and IASB) recognize that in order to achieve convergence and reduce the volume of accounting rules internationally, future international accounting standards will need to be more principles-based.

NORWALK AGREEMENT

The FASB and IASB signed the *Norwalk Agreement* in 2002, formalizing their commitment to the convergence of U.S. GAAP and IFRS. Under this agreement, the two boards pledged to remove existing differences between their standards and to coordinate their future standard-setting agendas so that major issues are worked on together. Robert Herz, as chairman of the FASB, testified before Congress: "We believe now is the appropriate time to develop a plan for moving all U.S. public companies to an improved version of IFRS and to consider any actions needed to strengthen the IASB as the global accounting standard setter." In that testimony he advocated working to develop a blueprint for moving U.S. public companies from U.S. standards to an improved version of IFRS. Herz emphasized that this move would need to be accompanied by consistent, high-quality enforcement, auditing, and education of participants in the capital markets.

Arguments Against Convergence to IFRS.   Not everyone agrees with the idea of convergence set forth in the Norwalk Agreement. Although many argue that a single set of global standards will improve comparability of financial reporting and facilitate access to

---

[1]See *www.ifrs.org/use-around-the-world.*

capital, others argue that U.S. standards should remain customized to fit the stringent legal and regulatory requirements of the U.S. business environment. There also is concern that differences in implementation and enforcement from country to country will make accounting appear more uniform than actually is the case. Another argument for maintaining the two sets of standards is that competition between alternative standard-setting regimes is healthy and can lead to better overall standards.

Where Convergence Currently Stands. The Norwalk Agreement did not specify a timetable for convergence, but active efforts have been ongoing since 2002. At the time this text is being written, it still is unclear whether or how IFRS will be incorporated into U.S. GAAP. The United States, under the authority of the Securities and Exchange Commission (SEC), may require (a) whole-scale adoption of IFRS by U.S. companies or (b) a standard-by-standard endorsement of IFRS standards in the United States, or (c) it may simply continue the process currently in place.

 **KEY POINT**

The IASB's main objective is to develop a single set of high-quality, understandable, and enforceable global accounting standards to help participants in the world's capital markets and other users make economic decisions.

Differences between U.S. GAAP and IFRS

■ **LO E–3**
Recognize the major differences between U.S. GAAP and IFRS.

In this section, we provide chapter-by-chapter descriptions of the important differences between U.S. GAAP and IFRS. Many of these differences are highlighted in IFRS boxes throughout the text.

Chapter 1: Accounting Information and Decision Making. In the United States, the FASB's conceptual framework serves primarily to guide standard setters, while internationally the IASB's conceptual framework also serves to indicate GAAP when more specific standards are not available. The FASB and the IASB are working together to develop a common conceptual framework that would underlie a uniform set of standards internationally.

Chapter 2: The Accounting Information System. U.S. GAAP and IFRS provide similar general guidance concerning the timing and measurement of revenue recognition. However, U.S. GAAP includes many additional rules and other guidance promulgated by the FASB, the SEC, and others.

Chapter 3: The Financial Reporting Process. The FASB and IASB are working on a project to establish a common standard for presenting information in financial statements, including the classification and display of line items and the aggregation of line items into subtotals and totals. This standard will have a major impact on the presentation of financial statements.

An important part of the proposal involves organizing all of the basic financial statements using a common format—operating, investing, and financing activities. These three classifications would be used in the income statement, statement of stockholders' equity, balance sheet, and statement of cash flows.

Chapter 4: Cash and Internal Controls. Accounting for cash under both U.S. GAAP and IFRS is essentially the same. No major convergence efforts are anticipated.

In the United States, *Section 404* of the Sarbanes-Oxley Act (SOX) requires management to document and assess the effectiveness of all internal control processes that could affect financial reporting. In other countries, the burden of documenting effective internal controls is much lower. In fact, the increased burden of compliance with Section 404 has caused many foreign companies to be reluctant to list their shares on U.S. stock exchanges.

Chapter 5: Receivables and Sales. Accounting for receivables, including the allowance for uncollectible accounts, is essentially the same under both U.S. GAAP and IFRS. No major convergence efforts are anticipated.

Chapter 6: Inventory and Cost of Goods Sold

Inventory cost flow assumptions. The LIFO inventory method is not allowed under IFRS, which likely will be a major convergence challenge. The *LIFO conformity rule,* which requires U.S. companies that use LIFO for tax purposes to also use LIFO for financial reporting, means that the elimination of LIFO for financial reporting also would require the elimination of its use for tax purposes. As discussed in Chapter 6, an advantage of using LIFO when inventory costs are rising is that it results in a lower tax burden. Resolving this issue would require agreement not only by the FASB and IASB, but also by the U.S. Congress, as it is responsible for setting tax laws in the United States.

Because of the LIFO restriction, many U.S. multinational companies use LIFO only for their domestic inventories and use FIFO or average cost for their foreign subsidiaries. **General Mills** provides an example (see Illustration E–2) with a disclosure note included in a recent annual report.

CAREER CORNER

Many students believe that if they plan to develop their careers in the United States, they do not need to be familiar with international accounting standards. This most certainly is not true. We are in a global economy. It's likely that the companies you work for during your career will have relationships with companies in other countries and those companies are likely to use international accounting standards. Even if that's not the case, you will likely invest in companies based in other countries using International Financial Reporting Standards.

© BananaStock/Jupiterimages, RF

ILLUSTRATION E–2

Disclosure Note about Inventories

GENERAL MILLS
Notes to the Financial Statements (excerpt)

Inventories

All inventories in the United States other than grain are valued at the lower of cost, using the last-in, first-out (LIFO) method, or market. Inventories outside of the United States are valued at the lower of cost, using the first-in, first-out (FIFO) method, or market.

Lower of cost and net realizable value. Under both U.S. GAAP and IFRS, inventory is reported at the lower of cost and net realizable value. Net realizable value is measured under both standards as the selling price of inventory less any selling costs.

Cadbury Schweppes plc, a U.K. company, prepares its financial statements according to IFRS. The disclosure note in Illustration E–3 shows the designation of market as net realizable value.

ILLUSTRATION E–3

Disclosure Note about Net Realizable Value

CADBURY SCHWEPPES plc
Notes to the Financial Statements (excerpt)

Inventories

Inventories are recorded at the lower of average cost and estimated net realizable value.

When net realizable value falls below cost, companies are required to write down inventory from cost to net realizable value, causing total assets to decrease and total expenses to increase. If in a future period the net realizable value of this inventory increases, reversal of the inventory write-down is *recorded* for most types of inventory under IFRS, but *not allowed* under U.S. GAAP. This means that U.S. GAAP is more conservative by not allowing the asset reduction and expense recognition to be reversed when circumstances indicate that they should.

Chapter 7: Long-Term Assets

Valuation of property, plant, and equipment.   Under U.S. GAAP, companies are not allowed to revalue property, plant, and equipment (PP&E) to fair value for financial reporting purposes. IFRS allows, but does not require, revaluation of PP&E to fair value. *IAS No. 16* allows a company to value PP&E subsequent to initial valuation at (1) cost less accumulated depreciation or (2) fair value (revaluation). If revaluation is chosen, all assets within a class of PP&E must be revalued on a regular basis.

British Airways plc, a U.K. company, prepares its financial statements according to IFRS. The disclosure note in Illustration E–4 describes the company's choice to value PP&E (also referred to as tangible fixed assets) at cost.

ILLUSTRATION E–4

Disclosure Note about Valuation of Property, Plant, and Equipment

> **BRITISH AIRWAYS plc**
> **Notes to the Financial Statements (excerpt)**
>
> **Property, plant, and equipment**
> Property, plant, and equipment is held at cost. The Group has a policy of not revaluing tangible fixed assets.

Valuation of intangible assets.   U.S. GAAP also prohibits revaluation of intangible assets to fair value. *IAS No. 38* allows a company to value an intangible asset subsequent to initial valuation at (1) cost less accumulated amortization or (2) fair value if fair value can be determined by reference to an active market. If revaluation is chosen, all assets within that class of intangibles must be revalued on a regular basis.

 COMMON MISTAKE

Many students have been taught that financial statements are based on historical cost. This is no longer the case. The only historical cost amounts in financial statements are those for cash and land in the domestic currency. All other amounts reflect changes in time, events, or circumstances since the transaction date. For instance, companies record an allowance on accounts receivable, write down inventory to net realizable value, depreciate or amortize long-term assets and write them down to fair value when impaired, recognize most investments at fair value, and amortize the discount or premium on long-term debt.

Research and development expenditures.   U.S. GAAP requires all research and development expenditures to be expensed in the period incurred. IFRS, though, draws a distinction between research activities and development activities. Research expenditures are expensed in the period incurred. However, development expenditures that meet specified criteria are capitalized as an intangible asset.

Heineken, a company based in Amsterdam, prepares its financial statements according to IFRS. The disclosure note in Illustration E–5 describes the criteria used for capitalizing development expenditures.

ILLUSTRATION E–5

Disclosure Note about Capitalization of Development Expenditures

> **HEINEKEN**
> **Notes to the Financial Statements (excerpt)**
>
> **Software, research and development, and other intangible assets**
> Expenditures on research activities, undertaken with the prospect of gaining new technical knowledge and understanding, are recognized in the income statement when incurred. Development activities involve a plan or design for the production of new or substantially improved products and processes. Development expenditures are capitalized only if development costs can be measured reliably, the product or process is technically and commercially feasible, future economic benefits are probable, and Heineken intends to and has sufficient resources to complete development and to use or sell the asset.

Chapter 8: Current Liabilities

Contingencies.   A difference in accounting relates to determining the existence of a contingent liability. Under U.S. GAAP. we accrue a contingent liability if it's both probable and reasonably estimable. IFRS rules are similar, but the threshold for "probable" is defined as "more likely than not" (greater than 50%), representing a lower threshold than "probable" under U.S. GAAP.

Another difference is whether to report a long-term contingency at its face amount or its present value. Under IFRS, the present value of the estimated cash flows is reported when the effect of *time value of money is material.* According to U.S. GAAP, though, discounting of cash flows is allowed when the *timing of cash flows is certain.* Illustration E–6 shows a portion of a disclosure note from the financial statements of **Electrolux,** which reports under IFRS.

ILLUSTRATION E–6

Disclosure Note about Recognition of Contingencies

ELECTROLUX
Notes to the Financial Statements (excerpt)

Note 29: U.S. GAAP information

Discounted provisions
Under IFRS and U.S. GAAP, provisions are recognized when the Group has a present obligation as a result of a past event, and it is probable that an outflow of resources will be required to settle the obligation, and a reliable estimate can be made of the amount of the obligation. Under IFRS, where the effect of time value of money is material, the amount recognized is the present value of the estimated expenditures. *IAS 37* states that long-term provisions shall be discounted if the time value is material. According to U.S. GAAP, discounting of provisions is allowed when the timing of cash flow is certain.

Chapter 9: Long-Term Liabilities

Convertible bonds.   Under IFRS, convertible debt is divided into its liability (bonds) and equity (conversion option) elements. Under U.S. GAAP, the entire issue price is recorded as a liability.

Chapter 10: Stockholders' Equity.   The joint "financial statement presentation" project, referred to earlier under the heading for Chapter 3, will dramatically change the format and display of all financial statements, including the balance sheet—referred to in the project as the *statement of financial position.* The proposed organization of all of the basic financial statements using the same format—operating, investing, and financing activities—will significantly affect the presentation of stockholders' equity items. Current differences between U.S. GAAP and IFRS include the following:

Distinction between debt and equity for preferred stock.   Under IFRS, most preferred stock ("preference shares") is reported as debt, with the dividends reported in the income statement as interest expense. Under U.S. GAAP, most preferred stock is included in stockholders' equity, with the dividends reported as a reduction in retained earnings. Under U.S. GAAP, only "mandatorily redeemable" preferred stock is reported as debt. **Unilever** describes such a difference in a disclosure note, shown in Illustration E–7.

ILLUSTRATION E–7

Disclosure Note about Preferred Stock

UNILEVER
Notes to the Financial Statements (excerpt)

Additional information for U.S. investors

Preference shares
Under *IAS 32,* Unilever recognizes preference shares that provide a fixed preference dividend as borrowings with preference dividends recognized in the income statement. Under U.S. GAAP such preference shares are classified in shareholders' equity with dividends treated as a deduction to shareholders' equity.

Reacquired shares.   IFRS does not permit the "retirement" of shares. All buybacks are treated as treasury stock.

Chapter 11: Statement of Cash Flows.   Like U.S. GAAP, international standards also require a statement of cash flows. Consistent with U.S. GAAP, cash flows are classified as operating, investing, or financing. U.S. GAAP designates cash outflows for interest payments and cash inflows from interest and dividends received as operating cash flows. However, IFRS allows companies to report cash outflows from interest payments as either operating *or* financing cash flows. IFRS also allows companies to report cash inflows from interest and dividends as either operating *or* investing cash flows. U.S. GAAP classifies dividends paid to shareholders as financing cash flows. The international standard allows companies to report dividends paid as either financing *or* operating cash flows.

U.S. GAAP permits *either* the indirect or the direct method in reporting operating cash flows. Most U.S. companies choose the indirect method. IFRS requires the direct method be used in reporting operating cash flows in the statement of cash flows.

U.S. GAAP requires that significant noncash activities be reported either on the face of the statement of cash flows or in a disclosure note. IFRS requires reporting in a disclosure note, disallowing presentation on the face of the statement.

Chapter 12: Financial Statement Analysis

Discontinued operations.   Rather than coming up with separate rules, the IASB reviewed the FASB's extensive work in the area and adopted nearly identical standards for the reporting of discontinued operations. Recently, the FASB simplified its definition of discontinued operations to match the broader definitions already used by international standards.

Extraordinary items.   Under IFRS, the recording or disclosure of items labeled "extraordinary" is not allowed. The FASB required companies to report extraordinary items at the bottom of the income statement in a manner similar to how we report discontinued operations. Now, the FASB has eliminated the reporting of extraordinary items, consistent with international standards.

 **KEY POINT**

U.S. GAAP and IFRS are converging, but many differences still exist.

KEY POINTS BY LEARNING OBJECTIVE

LO E–1   Explain the reasons for differences in accounting practices across countries.

Differences in legal systems, tax laws, sources of financing, inflation, culture, political and economic ties, and economic development influence accounting practices across countries.

LO E–2   Understand the role of the International Accounting Standards Board (IASB) in the development of International Financial Reporting Standards (IFRS).

The IASB's main objective is to develop a single set of high-quality, understandable, and enforceable global accounting standards to help participants in the world's capital markets and other users make economic decisions.

LO E–3   Recognize the major differences between U.S. GAAP and IFRS.

U.S. GAAP and IFRS are converging, but many differences still exist.

GLOSSARY

Convergence: The process by which U.S. GAAP and IFRS will eventually merge to become a single set of accounting standards. **p. E–1**

International Accounting Standards Board (IASB): The body primarily responsible for creating a single set of global accounting standards. **p. E–3**

International Financial Reporting Standards (IFRS): The accounting rules previously set by the International Accounting Standards Committee (IASC) and currently set by the International Accounting Standards Board (IASB). **p. E–3**

SELF-STUDY QUESTIONS

1. Which of the following reason(s) help explain why accounting practices may differ across countries? **(LO E–1)**
   a. Legal system.
   b. Culture.
   c. Political and economic ties.
   d. All of the above.

2. The body primarily responsible for creating a single set of global accounting standards is the: **(LO E–2)**
   a. International Federation of Accountants.
   b. International Accounting Standards Board.
   c. Financial Accounting Standards Board.
   d. International Organization of Securities Commissions.

3. For which of the following topics is accounting under both U.S. GAAP and IFRS essentially the same? **(LO E–3)**
   a. Receivables.
   b. Long-term assets.
   c. Stockholders' equity.
   d. Statement of cash flows.

4. Which inventory cost flow assumption does IFRS not allow? **(LO E–3)**
   a. Specific identification.
   b. FIFO.
   c. LIFO.
   d. Average cost.

5. Which of the following statements is true regarding revaluation of property, plant, and equipment to fair value? **(LO E–3)**
   a. Both U.S. GAAP and IFRS allow revaluation of property, plant, and equipment to fair value.
   b. Neither U.S. GAAP nor IFRS allows revaluation of property, plant, and equipment to fair value.
   c. U.S. GAAP allows, but IFRS does not allow, revaluation of property, plant, and equipment to fair value.
   d. U.S. GAAP does not allow, but IFRS allows, revaluation of property, plant, and equipment to fair value.

Note: Answers appear at the end of the appendix.

REVIEW QUESTIONS

1. What is meant by convergence of U.S. GAAP? ■ **LO E–1**

2. Describe at least five reasons why accounting practices differ across countries. ■ **LO E–1**

3. Which factor explaining why accounting practices differ across countries do you think is most important? Explain why. ■ **LO E–1**

4. What difficulties do differences in accounting standards create for investors? ■ **LO E–1**

5. What difficulties do differences in accounting standards create for multinational corporations in preparing their financial statements? ■ **LO E–1**

6. What is the main objective of the International Accounting Standards Board (the IASB)? ■ **LO E–2**

7. Explain the difference between principles-based accounting standards and rules-based accounting standards. ■ **LO E–2**

8. Describe the Norwalk Agreement. What is the significance of this agreement? ■ **LO E–2**

■ LO E–2

9. Provide at least one argument against the trend toward convergence between U.S. GAAP and IFRS.

■ LO E–3

10. What is meant by a conceptual framework in accounting? Why is it important that the FASB and the IASB develop a common conceptual framework?

■ LO E–3

11. Explain how an income statement might be organized along the same categories currently used in the statement of cash flows—operating, investing, and financing activities.

■ LO E–3

12. Which inventory cost flow assumption is allowed under U.S. GAAP but not under IFRS? Explain why some U.S. companies will lobby strongly to keep this method as an allowable alternative.

■ LO E–3

13. What effect does writing down inventory have on total assets and net income in that reporting period? The reversal of an inventory write-down in a future period, which is recorded under IFRS but not allowed under U.S. GAAP, has what effect on total assets and net income?

■ LO E–3

14. What does it mean to revalue a long-term asset? How do U.S. GAAP and IFRS differ regarding revaluation of long-term assets?

■ LO E–3

15. How do IFRS rules differ in the reporting of research and development costs? Which is more conservative in the reporting of research and development costs, U.S. GAAP or IFRS?

■ LO E–3

16. Would a company be more likely to report a contingent liability under U.S. GAAP or IFRS? Which is more conservative in the reporting of contingent liabilities, U.S. GAAP or IFRS?

■ LO E–3

17. How is preferred stock reported differently under U.S. GAAP and IFRS? Do you think preferred stock is a liability or an equity item? Why?

EXERCISES

Mc Graw Hill Education **connect**

Identify reasons for differences in accounting practices across countries (LO E–1)

EE–1 Match each reason with its description.

Reason	Description
1. Legal system	a. More-developed economies have more-complex business transactions.
2. Tax laws	
3. Sources of financing	b. The extent of public disclosure depends on the secretiveness of society.
4. Inflation	
5. Culture	c. Common-law countries rely more heavily on public information.
6. Political and economic ties	
7. Economic development	d. Countries share business activities and have political connections.
	e. Alignment between financial reporting and tax reporting rules.
	f. In some countries, asset values increase rapidly because of the general price level changes.
	g. Some countries rely more heavily on debt capital than on equity capital to fund operations.

Classify differences in accounting practices across countries (LO E–1)

EE–2 Listed next are seven reasons for differences in accounting practices among countries. For each reason, at least two options are provided.

Reason	Options
1. _____ Legal system	(a) Common-law (b) Code-law
2. _____ Tax laws	(a) Different tax and financial accounting rules (b) Similar tax and financial accounting rules
3. _____ Sources of financing	(a) More equity financing (b) More debt financing
4. _____ Inflation	(a) Low inflation (b) High inflation
5. _____ Culture	(a) Transparent (b) Secretive
6. _____ Political and economic ties	(a) British ties (b) German ties (c) Spanish ties
7. _____ Economic development	(a) Developed economy (b) Developing economy (c) Underdeveloped economy

Required:

For each of the countries listed below, select the seven options that best describe that country. For instance, the United States can be described as common-law, different tax and financial reporting, more equity financing, low inflation, transparent, British ties, and a developed economy. You may wish to search the Internet to learn more about each country.

1. Austria
2. Australia

EE-3 International Financial Reporting Standards are gaining support around the globe. In 2007, the SEC eliminated the requirement for foreign companies that issue stock in the United States to include in their financial statements a reconciliation of IFRS to U.S. GAAP. There also is serious discussion of allowing U.S. companies to choose whether to prepare their financial statements according to U.S. GAAP or IFRS.

Provide arguments for and against allowing U.S. companies to use IFRS (LO E-2)

Required:

Do you think U.S. companies should be allowed the choice of reporting under either U.S. GAAP or IFRS? Provide arguments both for and against this idea.

EE-4 Many outside the United States claim that a problem with U.S. GAAP is that there are too many rules. They argue for principles-based accounting standards in which the broad principles of accounting are emphasized and less emphasis is placed on detailed implementation rules. Americans counter that IFRS may lack quality and rigor. Additional rules are necessary to provide adequate guidance to users.

Discuss principles-based versus rules-based accounting standards (LO E-3)

Required:

1. Explain the difference between principles-based and rules-based accounting standards.
2. What are the advantages of principles-based standards?
3. What are the advantages of rules-based standards?
4. Do you think that future international accounting standards will need to be more principles-based or more rules-based?

EE-5 The format of financial statements varies from country to country. The FASB and IASB propose that financial statements in the future be organized using the same format currently

Format financial statements by operating, investing, and financing activities (LO E-3)

used in the statement of cash flows—operating, investing, and financing activities. This would greatly change the current format used to prepare the income statement and the balance sheet.

Required:

1. Explain the differences among operating, investing, and financing activities. You might want to refer back to the first section in Chapter 11 on the statement of cash flows.
2. Provide at least one example of an account reported in the income statement that would be classified as (a) an operating activity, (b) an investing activity, and (c) a financing activity.
3. Provide at least one example of an account reported in the balance sheet that would be classified as (a) an operating activity, (b) an investing activity, and (c) a financing activity.

Understand the effects of switching from LIFO to FIFO (LO E–3)

EE–6 During 2018, Noval Company sells 270 units of inventory for $100 each. The company has the following inventory purchase transactions for 2018.

Date	Transaction	Number of Units	Unit Cost	Total Cost
Jan. 1	Beginning inventory	70	$83	$ 5,810
Apr. 7	Purchase	190	85	16,150
Oct. 9	Purchase	90	87	7,830
		350		$29,790

Required:

1. Calculate ending inventory, cost of goods sold, and gross profit for 2018, assuming the company uses LIFO with a periodic inventory system.
2. To comply with IFRS, the company decides to instead account for inventory using FIFO. Calculate ending inventory, cost of goods sold, and gross profit for 2018.
3. Explain the effects in the company's income statement and balance sheet of using FIFO instead of LIFO to account for inventory.

Account for research and development (LO E–3)

EE–7 During 2018, Fueltronics spends $200,000 on several different research projects to gain new knowledge about the use of alternative fuels to operate motorized vehicles. Because one of the projects shows very high promise, the company spends an additional $500,000 near the end of the year to develop this product for future use. This project is considered to have a high probability of success, and management intends to continue to develop it for future consumer use.

Required:

1. Explain how the research cost of $200,000 and the development cost of $500,000 would be reported under U.S. GAAP.
2. Explain how the research cost of $200,000 and the development cost of $500,000 would be reported under IFRS.
3. Explain the effects in the company's income statement and balance sheet of using IFRS versus U.S. GAAP to account for these research and development costs.

Report preferred stock (LO E–3)

EE–8 Most preferred stock is reported under IFRS as debt, with the dividends reported in the income statement as interest expense. Under U.S. GAAP, most preferred stock is reported as equity, with the dividends excluded from income and reported as a direct reduction to retained earnings.

Required:

1. What is the definition of a liability? What is the definition of stockholders' equity? You may wish to refer back to Chapter 1.
2. Defend the IFRS position that preferred stock is a liability.
3. Defend the U.S. GAAP position that preferred stock is part of stockholders' equity.
4. Based on the above, where do you recommend preferred stock be reported?

Answers to the Self-Study Questions

1. d   2. b   3. a   4. c   5. d

Subject Index

Note: Page numbers followed by *n* indicate material in footnotes.

Company Index

Future Value and Present Value Tables

This table shows the future value of $1 at various interest rates (i) and time periods (n). It is used to calculate the future value of any single amount.

TABLE 1 Future Value of $1

$$FV = \$1(1 + i)^n$$

n/i	1.0%	1.5%	2.0%	2.5%	3.0%	3.5%	4.0%	4.5%	5.0%	5.5%	6.0%	7.0%	8.0%	9.0%	10.0%	11.0%	12.0%	13.0%
1	1.01000	1.01500	1.02000	1.02500	1.03000	1.03500	1.04000	1.04500	1.05000	1.05500	1.06000	1.07000	1.08000	1.09000	1.10000	1.11000	1.12000	1.13000
2	1.02010	1.03022	1.04040	1.05063	1.06090	1.07123	1.08160	1.09203	1.10250	1.11303	1.12360	1.14490	1.16640	1.18810	1.21000	1.23210	1.25440	1.27690
3	1.03030	1.04568	1.06121	1.07689	1.09273	1.10872	1.12486	1.14117	1.15763	1.17424	1.19102	1.22504	1.25971	1.29503	1.33100	1.36763	1.40493	1.44290
4	1.04060	1.06136	1.08243	1.10381	1.12551	1.14752	1.16986	1.19252	1.21551	1.23882	1.26248	1.31080	1.36049	1.41158	1.46410	1.51807	1.57352	1.63047
5	1.05101	1.07728	1.10408	1.13141	1.15927	1.18769	1.21665	1.24618	1.27628	1.30696	1.33823	1.40255	1.46933	1.53862	1.61051	1.68506	1.76234	1.84244
6	1.06152	1.09344	1.12616	1.15969	1.19405	1.22926	1.26532	1.30226	1.34010	1.37884	1.41852	1.50073	1.58687	1.67710	1.77156	1.87041	1.97382	2.08195
7	1.07214	1.10984	1.14869	1.18869	1.22987	1.27228	1.31593	1.36086	1.40710	1.45468	1.50363	1.60578	1.71382	1.82804	1.94872	2.07616	2.21068	2.35261
8	1.08286	1.12649	1.17166	1.21840	1.26677	1.31681	1.36857	1.42210	1.47746	1.53469	1.59385	1.71819	1.85093	1.99256	2.14359	2.30454	2.47596	2.65844
9	1.09369	1.14339	1.19509	1.24886	1.30477	1.36290	1.42331	1.48610	1.55133	1.61909	1.68948	1.83846	1.99900	2.17189	2.35795	2.55804	2.77308	3.00404
10	1.10462	1.16054	1.21899	1.28008	1.34392	1.41060	1.48024	1.55297	1.62889	1.70814	1.79085	1.96715	2.15892	2.36736	2.59374	2.83942	3.10585	3.39457
11	1.11567	1.17795	1.24337	1.31209	1.38423	1.45997	1.53945	1.62285	1.71034	1.80209	1.89830	2.10485	2.33164	2.58043	2.85312	3.15176	3.47855	3.83586
12	1.12683	1.19562	1.26824	1.34489	1.42576	1.51107	1.60103	1.69588	1.79586	1.90121	2.01220	2.25219	2.51817	2.81266	3.13843	3.49845	3.89598	4.33452
13	1.13809	1.21355	1.29361	1.37851	1.46853	1.56396	1.66507	1.77220	1.88565	2.00577	2.13293	2.40985	2.71962	3.06580	3.45227	3.88328	4.36349	4.89801
14	1.14947	1.23176	1.31948	1.41297	1.51259	1.61869	1.73168	1.85194	1.97993	2.11609	2.26090	2.57853	2.93719	3.34173	3.79750	4.31044	4.88711	5.53475
15	1.16097	1.25023	1.34587	1.44830	1.55797	1.67535	1.80094	1.93528	2.07893	2.23248	2.39656	2.75903	3.17217	3.64248	4.17725	4.78459	5.47357	6.25427
16	1.17258	1.26899	1.37279	1.48451	1.60471	1.73399	1.87298	2.02237	2.18287	2.35526	2.54035	2.95216	3.42594	3.97031	4.59497	5.31089	6.13039	7.06733
17	1.18430	1.28802	1.40024	1.52162	1.65285	1.79468	1.94790	2.11338	2.29202	2.48480	2.69277	3.15882	3.70002	4.32763	5.05447	5.89509	6.86604	7.98608
18	1.19615	1.30734	1.42825	1.55966	1.70243	1.85749	2.02582	2.20848	2.40662	2.62147	2.85434	3.37993	3.99602	4.71712	5.55992	6.54355	7.68997	9.02427
19	1.20811	1.32695	1.45681	1.59865	1.75351	1.92250	2.10685	2.30786	2.52695	2.76565	3.02560	3.61653	4.31570	5.14166	6.11591	7.26334	8.61276	10.19742
20	1.22019	1.34686	1.48595	1.63862	1.80611	1.98979	2.19112	2.41171	2.65330	2.91776	3.20714	3.86968	4.66096	5.60441	6.72750	8.06231	9.64629	11.52309
21	1.23239	1.36706	1.51567	1.67958	1.86029	2.05943	2.27877	2.52024	2.78596	3.07823	3.39956	4.14056	5.03383	6.10881	7.40025	8.94917	10.80385	13.02109
22	1.24472	1.38756	1.54598	1.72157	1.91610	2.13151	2.36992	2.63365	2.92526	3.24754	3.60354	4.43040	5.43654	6.65860	8.14027	9.93357	12.10031	14.71383
23	1.25716	1.40838	1.57690	1.76461	1.97359	2.20611	2.46472	2.75217	3.07152	3.42615	3.81975	4.74053	5.87146	7.25787	8.95430	11.02627	13.55235	16.62663
24	1.26973	1.42950	1.60844	1.80873	2.03279	2.28333	2.56330	2.87601	3.22510	3.61459	4.04893	5.07237	6.34118	7.91108	9.84973	12.23916	15.17863	18.78809
25	1.28243	1.45095	1.64061	1.85394	2.09378	2.36324	2.66584	3.00543	3.38635	3.81339	4.29187	5.42743	6.84848	8.62308	10.83471	13.58546	17.00006	21.23054
30	1.34785	1.56308	1.81136	2.09757	2.42726	2.80679	3.24340	3.74532	4.32194	4.98395	5.74349	7.61226	10.06266	13.26768	17.44940	22.89230	29.95992	39.11590
35	1.41660	1.68388	1.99989	2.37321	2.81386	3.33359	3.94609	4.66735	5.51602	6.51383	7.68609	10.67658	14.78534	20.41397	28.10244	38.57485	52.79962	72.06851
40	1.48886	1.81402	2.20804	2.68506	3.26204	3.95926	4.80102	5.81636	7.03999	8.51331	10.28572	14.97446	21.72452	31.40942	45.25926	65.00087	93.05097	132.78155
45	1.56481	1.95421	2.43785	3.03790	3.78160	4.70236	5.84118	7.24825	8.98501	11.12655	13.76461	21.00245	31.92045	48.32729	72.89048	109.53024	163.98760	244.64140
50	1.64463	2.10524	2.69159	3.43711	4.38391	5.58493	7.10668	9.03264	11.46740	14.54196	18.42015	29.45703	46.90161	74.35752	117.39085	184.56483	289.00219	450.73593

TABLE 2 Present Value of $1

This table shows the present value of $1 at various interest rates (i) and time periods (n). It is used to calculate the present value of any single amount.

$$PV = \frac{\$1}{(1+i)^n}$$

n/i	1.0%	1.5%	2.0%	2.5%	3.0%	3.5%	4.0%	4.5%	5.0%	5.5%	6.0%	7.0%	8.0%	9.0%	10.0%	11.0%	12.0%	13.0%
1	0.99010	0.98522	0.98039	0.97561	0.97087	0.96618	0.96154	0.95694	0.95238	0.94787	0.94340	0.93458	0.92593	0.91743	0.90909	0.90090	0.89286	0.88496
2	0.98030	0.97066	0.96117	0.95181	0.94260	0.93351	0.92456	0.91573	0.90703	0.89845	0.89000	0.87344	0.85734	0.84168	0.82645	0.81162	0.79719	0.78315
3	0.97059	0.95632	0.94232	0.92860	0.91514	0.90194	0.88900	0.87630	0.86384	0.85161	0.83962	0.81630	0.79383	0.77218	0.75131	0.73119	0.71178	0.69305
4	0.96098	0.94218	0.92385	0.90595	0.88849	0.87144	0.85480	0.83856	0.82270	0.80722	0.79209	0.76290	0.73503	0.70843	0.68301	0.65873	0.63552	0.61332
5	0.95147	0.92826	0.90573	0.88385	0.86261	0.84197	0.82193	0.80245	0.78353	0.76513	0.74726	0.71299	0.68058	0.64993	0.62092	0.59345	0.56743	0.54276
6	0.94205	0.91454	0.88797	0.86230	0.83748	0.81350	0.79031	0.76790	0.74622	0.72525	0.70496	0.66634	0.63017	0.59627	0.56447	0.53464	0.50663	0.48032
7	0.93272	0.90103	0.87056	0.84127	0.81309	0.78599	0.75992	0.73483	0.71068	0.68744	0.66506	0.62275	0.58349	0.54703	0.51316	0.48166	0.45235	0.42506
8	0.92348	0.88771	0.85349	0.82075	0.78941	0.75941	0.73069	0.70319	0.67684	0.65160	0.62741	0.58201	0.54027	0.50187	0.46651	0.43393	0.40388	0.37616
9	0.91434	0.87459	0.83676	0.80073	0.76642	0.73373	0.70259	0.67290	0.64461	0.61763	0.59190	0.54393	0.50025	0.46043	0.42410	0.39092	0.36061	0.33288
10	0.90529	0.86167	0.82035	0.78120	0.74409	0.70892	0.67556	0.64393	0.61391	0.58543	0.55839	0.50835	0.46319	0.42241	0.38554	0.35218	0.32197	0.29459
11	0.89632	0.84893	0.80426	0.76214	0.72242	0.68495	0.64958	0.61620	0.58468	0.55491	0.52679	0.47509	0.42888	0.38753	0.35049	0.31728	0.28748	0.26070
12	0.88745	0.83639	0.78849	0.74356	0.70138	0.66178	0.62460	0.58966	0.55684	0.52598	0.49697	0.44401	0.39711	0.35553	0.31863	0.28584	0.25668	0.23071
13	0.87866	0.82403	0.77303	0.72542	0.68095	0.63940	0.60057	0.56427	0.53032	0.49856	0.46884	0.41496	0.36770	0.32618	0.28966	0.25751	0.22917	0.20416
14	0.86996	0.81185	0.75788	0.70773	0.66112	0.61778	0.57748	0.53997	0.50507	0.47257	0.44230	0.38782	0.34046	0.29925	0.26333	0.23199	0.20462	0.18068
15	0.86135	0.79985	0.74301	0.69047	0.64186	0.59689	0.55526	0.51672	0.48102	0.44793	0.41727	0.36245	0.31524	0.27454	0.23939	0.20900	0.18270	0.15989
16	0.85282	0.78803	0.72845	0.67362	0.62317	0.57671	0.53391	0.49447	0.45811	0.42458	0.39365	0.33873	0.29189	0.25187	0.21763	0.18829	0.16312	0.14150
17	0.84438	0.77639	0.71416	0.65720	0.60502	0.55720	0.51337	0.47318	0.43630	0.40245	0.37136	0.31657	0.27027	0.23107	0.19784	0.16963	0.14564	0.12522
18	0.83602	0.76491	0.70016	0.64117	0.58739	0.53836	0.49363	0.45280	0.41552	0.38147	0.35034	0.29586	0.25025	0.21199	0.17986	0.15282	0.13004	0.11081
19	0.82774	0.75361	0.68643	0.62553	0.57029	0.52016	0.47464	0.43330	0.39573	0.36158	0.33051	0.27651	0.23171	0.19449	0.16351	0.13768	0.11611	0.09806
20	0.81954	0.74247	0.67297	0.61027	0.55368	0.50257	0.45639	0.41464	0.37689	0.34273	0.31180	0.25842	0.21455	0.17843	0.14864	0.12403	0.10367	0.08678
21	0.81143	0.73150	0.65978	0.59539	0.53755	0.48557	0.43883	0.39679	0.35894	0.32486	0.29416	0.24151	0.19866	0.16370	0.13513	0.11174	0.09256	0.07680
22	0.80340	0.72069	0.64684	0.58086	0.52189	0.46915	0.42196	0.37970	0.34185	0.30793	0.27751	0.22571	0.18394	0.15018	0.12285	0.10067	0.08264	0.06796
23	0.79544	0.71004	0.63416	0.56670	0.50669	0.45329	0.40573	0.36335	0.32557	0.29187	0.26180	0.21095	0.17032	0.13778	0.11168	0.09069	0.07379	0.06014
24	0.78757	0.69954	0.62172	0.55288	0.49193	0.43796	0.39012	0.34770	0.31007	0.27666	0.24698	0.19715	0.15770	0.12640	0.10153	0.08170	0.06588	0.05323
25	0.77977	0.68921	0.60953	0.53939	0.47761	0.42315	0.37512	0.33273	0.29530	0.26223	0.23300	0.18425	0.14602	0.11597	0.09230	0.07361	0.05882	0.04710
30	0.74192	0.63976	0.55207	0.47674	0.41199	0.35628	0.30832	0.26700	0.23138	0.20064	0.17411	0.13137	0.09938	0.07537	0.05731	0.04368	0.03338	0.02557
35	0.70591	0.59387	0.50003	0.42137	0.35538	0.29998	0.25342	0.21425	0.18129	0.15352	0.13011	0.09366	0.06763	0.04899	0.03558	0.02592	0.01894	0.01388
40	0.67165	0.55126	0.45289	0.37243	0.30656	0.25257	0.20829	0.17193	0.14205	0.11746	0.09722	0.06678	0.04603	0.03184	0.02209	0.01538	0.01075	0.00753
45	0.63905	0.51171	0.41020	0.32917	0.26444	0.21266	0.17120	0.13796	0.11130	0.08988	0.07265	0.04761	0.03133	0.02069	0.01372	0.00913	0.00610	0.00409
50	0.60804	0.47500	0.37153	0.29094	0.22811	0.17905	0.14071	0.11071	0.08720	0.06877	0.05429	0.03395	0.02132	0.01345	0.00852	0.00542	0.00346	0.00222

This table shows the future value of an ordinary annuity of $1 at various interest rates (*i*) and time periods (*n*). It is used to calculate the future value of any series of equal payments made at the *end* of each compounding period.

TABLE 3 Future Value of an Ordinary Annuity of $1

$$FVA = \frac{(1+i)^n - 1}{i}$$

n/i	1.0%	1.5%	2.0%	2.5%	3.0%	3.5%	4.0%	4.5%	5.0%	5.5%	6.0%	7.0%	8.0%	9.0%	10.0%	11.0%	12.0%	13.0%
1	1.0000	1.0000	1.0000	1.0000	1.0000	1.0000	1.0000	1.0000	1.0000	1.0000	1.0000	1.0000	1.0000	1.0000	1.0000	1.0000	1.0000	1.0000
2	2.0100	2.0150	2.0200	2.0250	2.0300	2.0350	2.0400	2.0450	2.0500	2.0550	2.0600	2.0700	2.0800	2.0900	2.1000	2.1100	2.1200	2.1300
3	3.0301	3.0452	3.0604	3.0756	3.0909	3.1062	3.1216	3.1370	3.1525	3.1680	3.1836	3.2149	3.2464	3.2781	3.3100	3.3421	3.3744	3.4069
4	4.0604	4.0909	4.1216	4.1525	4.1836	4.2149	4.2465	4.2782	4.3101	4.3423	4.3746	4.4399	4.5061	4.5731	4.6410	4.7097	4.7793	4.8498
5	5.1010	5.1523	5.2040	5.2563	5.3091	5.3625	5.4163	5.4707	5.5256	5.5811	5.6371	5.7507	5.8666	5.9847	6.1051	6.2278	6.3528	6.4803
6	6.1520	6.2296	6.3081	6.3877	6.4684	6.5502	6.6330	6.7169	6.8019	6.8881	6.9753	7.1533	7.3359	7.5233	7.7156	7.9129	8.1152	8.3227
7	7.2135	7.3230	7.4343	7.5474	7.6625	7.7794	7.8983	8.0192	8.1420	8.2669	8.3938	8.6540	8.9228	9.2004	9.4872	9.7833	10.0890	10.4047
8	8.2857	8.4328	8.5830	8.7361	8.8923	9.0517	9.2142	9.3800	9.5491	9.7216	9.8975	10.2598	10.6366	11.0285	11.4359	11.8594	12.2997	12.7573
9	9.3685	9.5593	9.7546	9.9545	10.1591	10.3685	10.5828	10.8021	11.0266	11.2563	11.4913	11.9780	12.4876	13.0210	13.5795	14.1640	14.7757	15.4157
10	10.4622	10.7027	10.9497	11.2034	11.4639	11.7314	12.0061	12.2882	12.5779	12.8754	13.1808	13.8164	14.4866	15.1929	15.9374	16.7220	17.5487	18.4197
11	11.5668	11.8633	12.1687	12.4835	12.8078	13.1420	13.4864	13.8412	14.2068	14.5835	14.9716	15.7836	16.6455	17.5603	18.5312	19.5614	20.6546	21.8143
12	12.6825	13.0412	13.4121	13.7956	14.1920	14.6020	15.0258	15.4640	15.9171	16.3856	16.8699	17.8885	18.9771	20.1407	21.3843	22.7132	24.1331	25.6502
13	13.8093	14.2368	14.6803	15.1404	15.6178	16.1130	16.6268	17.1599	17.7130	18.2868	18.8821	20.1406	21.4953	22.9534	24.5227	26.2116	28.0291	29.9847
14	14.9474	15.4504	15.9739	16.5190	17.0863	17.6770	18.2919	18.9321	19.5986	20.2926	21.0151	22.5505	24.2149	26.0192	27.9750	30.0949	32.3926	34.8827
15	16.0969	16.6821	17.2934	17.9319	18.5989	19.2957	20.0236	20.7841	21.5786	22.4087	23.2760	25.1290	27.1521	29.3609	31.7725	34.4054	37.2797	40.4175
16	17.2579	17.9324	18.6393	19.3802	20.1569	20.9710	21.8245	22.7193	23.6575	24.6411	25.6725	27.8881	30.3243	33.0034	35.9497	39.1899	42.7533	46.6717
17	18.4304	19.2014	20.0121	20.8647	21.7616	22.7050	23.6975	24.7417	25.8404	26.9964	28.2129	30.8402	33.7502	36.9737	40.5447	44.5008	48.8837	53.7391
18	19.6147	20.4894	21.4123	22.3863	23.4144	24.4997	25.6454	26.8551	28.1324	29.4812	30.9057	33.9990	37.4502	41.3013	45.5992	50.3959	55.7497	61.7251
19	20.8109	21.7967	22.8406	23.9460	25.1169	26.3572	27.6712	29.0636	30.5390	32.1027	33.7600	37.3790	41.4463	46.0185	51.1591	56.9395	63.4397	70.7494
20	22.0190	23.1237	24.2974	25.5447	26.8704	28.2797	29.7781	31.3714	33.0660	34.8683	36.7856	40.9955	45.7620	51.1601	57.2750	64.2028	72.0524	80.9468
21	23.2392	24.4705	25.7833	27.1833	28.6765	30.2695	31.9692	33.7831	35.7193	37.7861	39.9927	44.8652	50.4229	56.7645	64.0025	72.2651	81.6987	92.4699
22	24.4716	25.8376	27.2990	28.8629	30.5368	32.3289	34.2480	36.3034	38.5052	40.8643	43.3923	49.0057	55.4568	62.8733	71.4027	81.2143	92.5026	105.4910
23	25.7163	27.2251	28.8450	30.5844	32.4529	34.4604	36.6179	38.9370	41.4305	44.1118	46.9958	53.4361	60.8933	69.5319	79.5430	91.1479	104.6029	120.2048
24	26.9735	28.6335	30.4219	32.3490	34.4265	36.6665	39.0826	41.6892	44.5020	47.5380	50.8156	58.1767	66.7648	76.7898	88.4973	102.1742	118.1552	136.8315
25	28.2432	30.0630	32.0303	34.1578	36.4593	38.9499	41.6459	44.5652	47.7271	51.1526	54.8645	63.2490	73.1059	84.7009	98.3471	114.4133	133.3339	155.6196
30	34.7849	37.5387	40.5681	43.9027	47.5754	51.6227	56.0849	61.0071	66.4388	72.4355	79.0582	94.4608	113.2832	136.3075	164.4940	199.0209	241.3327	293.1992
35	41.6603	45.5921	49.9945	54.9282	60.4621	66.6740	73.6522	81.4966	90.3203	100.2514	111.4348	138.2369	172.3168	215.7108	271.0244	341.5896	431.6635	546.6808
40	48.8864	54.2679	60.4020	67.4026	75.4013	84.5503	95.0255	107.0303	120.7998	136.6056	154.7620	199.6351	259.0565	337.8824	442.5926	581.8261	767.0914	1013.7042
45	56.4811	63.6142	71.8927	81.5161	92.7199	105.7817	121.0294	138.8500	159.7002	184.1192	212.7435	285.7493	386.5056	525.8587	718.9048	986.6386	1358.2300	1874.1646
50	64.4632	73.6828	84.5794	97.4843	112.7969	130.9979	152.6671	178.5030	209.3480	246.2175	290.3359	406.5289	573.7702	815.0836	1163.9085	1668.7712	2400.0182	3459.5071

This table shows the present value of an ordinary annuity of $1 at various interest rates (*i*) and time periods (*n*). It is used to calculate the present value of any series of equal payments made at the *end* of each compounding period.

TABLE 4 Present Value of an Ordinary Annuity of $1

$$PVA = \dfrac{1 - \dfrac{1}{(1+i)^n}}{i}$$

n/i	1.0%	1.5%	2.0%	2.5%	3.0%	3.5%	4.0%	4.5%	5.0%	5.5%	6.0%	7.0%	8.0%	9.0%	10.0%	11.0%	12.0%	13.0%
1	0.99010	0.98522	0.98039	0.97561	0.97087	0.96618	0.96154	0.95694	0.95238	0.94787	0.94340	0.93458	0.92593	0.91743	0.90909	0.90090	0.89286	0.88496
2	1.97040	1.95588	1.94156	1.92742	1.91347	1.89969	1.88609	1.87267	1.85941	1.84632	1.83339	1.80802	1.78326	1.75911	1.73554	1.71252	1.69005	1.66810
3	2.94099	2.91220	2.88388	2.85602	2.82861	2.80164	2.77509	2.74896	2.72325	2.69793	2.67301	2.62432	2.57710	2.53129	2.48685	2.44371	2.40183	2.36115
4	3.90197	3.85438	3.80773	3.76197	3.71710	3.67308	3.62990	3.58753	3.54595	3.50515	3.46511	3.38721	3.31213	3.23972	3.16987	3.10245	3.03735	2.97447
5	4.85343	4.78264	4.71346	4.64583	4.57971	4.51505	4.45182	4.38998	4.32948	4.27028	4.21236	4.10020	3.99271	3.88965	3.79079	3.69590	3.60478	3.51723
6	5.79548	5.69719	5.60143	5.50813	5.41719	5.32855	5.24214	5.15787	5.07569	4.99553	4.91732	4.76654	4.62288	4.48592	4.35526	4.23054	4.11141	3.99755
7	6.72819	6.59821	6.47199	6.34939	6.23028	6.11454	6.00205	5.89270	5.78637	5.68297	5.58238	5.38929	5.20637	5.03295	4.86842	4.71220	4.56376	4.42261
8	7.65168	7.48593	7.32548	7.17014	7.01969	6.87396	6.73274	6.59589	6.46321	6.33457	6.20979	5.97130	5.74664	5.53482	5.33493	5.14612	4.96764	4.79877
9	8.56602	8.36052	8.16224	7.97087	7.78611	7.60769	7.43533	7.26879	7.10782	6.95220	6.80169	6.51523	6.24689	5.99525	5.75902	5.53705	5.32825	5.13166
10	9.47130	9.22218	8.98259	8.75206	8.53020	8.31661	8.11090	7.91272	7.72173	7.53763	7.36009	7.02358	6.71008	6.41766	6.14457	5.88923	5.65022	5.42624
11	10.36763	10.07112	9.78685	9.51421	9.25262	9.00155	8.76048	8.52892	8.30641	8.09254	7.88687	7.49867	7.13896	6.80519	6.49506	6.20652	5.93770	5.68694
12	11.25508	10.90751	10.57534	10.25776	9.95400	9.66333	9.38507	9.11858	8.86325	8.61852	8.38384	7.94269	7.53608	7.16073	6.81369	6.49236	6.19437	5.91765
13	12.13374	11.73153	11.34837	10.98319	10.63496	10.30274	9.98565	9.68285	9.39357	9.11708	8.85268	8.35765	7.90378	7.48690	7.10336	6.74987	6.42355	6.12181
14	13.00370	12.54338	12.10625	11.69091	11.29607	10.92052	10.56312	10.22283	9.89864	9.58965	9.29498	8.74547	8.24424	7.78615	7.36669	6.98187	6.62817	6.30249
15	13.86505	13.34323	12.84926	12.38138	11.93794	11.51741	11.11839	10.73955	10.37966	10.03758	9.71225	9.10791	8.55948	8.06069	7.60608	7.19087	6.81086	6.46238
16	14.71787	14.13126	13.57771	13.05500	12.56110	12.09412	11.65230	11.23402	10.83777	10.46216	10.10590	9.44665	8.85137	8.31256	7.82371	7.37916	6.97399	6.60388
17	15.56225	14.90765	14.29187	13.71220	13.16612	12.65132	12.16567	11.70719	11.27407	10.86461	10.47726	9.76322	9.12164	8.54363	8.02155	7.54879	7.11963	6.72909
18	16.39827	15.67256	14.99203	14.35336	13.75351	13.18968	12.65930	12.15999	11.68959	11.24607	10.82760	10.05909	9.37189	8.75563	8.20141	7.70162	7.24967	6.83991
19	17.22601	16.42617	15.67846	14.97889	14.32380	13.70984	13.13394	12.59329	12.08532	11.60765	11.15812	10.33560	9.60360	8.95011	8.36492	7.83929	7.36578	6.93797
20	18.04555	17.16864	16.35143	15.58916	14.87747	14.21240	13.59033	13.00794	12.46221	11.95038	11.46992	10.59401	9.81815	9.12855	8.51356	7.96333	7.46944	7.02475
21	18.85698	17.90014	17.01121	16.18455	15.41502	14.69797	14.02916	13.40472	12.82115	12.27524	11.76408	10.83553	10.01680	9.29224	8.64869	8.07507	7.56200	7.10155
22	19.66038	18.62082	17.65805	16.76541	15.93692	15.16712	14.45112	13.78442	13.16300	12.58317	12.04158	11.06124	10.20074	9.44243	8.77154	8.17574	7.64465	7.16951
23	20.45582	19.33086	18.29220	17.33211	16.44361	15.62041	14.85684	14.14777	13.48857	12.87504	12.30338	11.27219	10.37106	9.58021	8.88322	8.26643	7.71843	7.22966
24	21.24339	20.03041	18.91393	17.88499	16.93554	16.05837	15.24696	14.49548	13.79864	13.15170	12.55036	11.46933	10.52876	9.70661	8.98474	8.34814	7.78432	7.28288
25	22.02316	20.71961	19.52346	18.42438	17.41315	16.48151	15.62208	14.82821	14.09394	13.41393	12.78336	11.65358	10.67478	9.82258	9.07704	8.42174	7.84314	7.32998
30	25.80771	24.01584	22.39646	20.93029	19.60044	18.39205	17.29203	16.28889	15.37245	14.53375	13.76483	12.40904	11.25778	10.27365	9.42691	8.69379	8.05518	7.49565
35	29.40858	27.07559	24.99862	23.14516	21.48722	20.00066	18.66461	17.46101	16.37419	15.39055	14.49825	12.94767	11.65457	10.56682	9.64416	8.85524	8.17550	7.58557
40	32.83469	29.91585	27.35548	25.10278	23.11477	21.35507	19.79277	18.40158	17.15909	16.04612	15.04630	13.33171	11.92461	10.75736	9.77905	8.95105	8.24378	7.63438
45	36.09451	32.55234	29.49016	26.83302	24.51871	22.49545	20.72004	19.15635	17.77407	16.54773	15.45583	13.60552	12.10840	10.88120	9.86281	9.00791	8.28252	7.66086
50	39.19612	34.99969	31.42361	28.36231	25.72976	23.45562	21.48218	19.76201	18.25593	16.93152	15.76186	13.80075	12.23348	10.96168	9.91481	9.04165	8.30450	7.67524

Summary of Ratios Used in This Book

	Chapter	Calculations
RISK RATIOS		
Liquidity		
Receivables turnover ratio	5	$\dfrac{\text{Net credit sales}}{\text{Average accounts receivables}}$
Average collection period	5	$\dfrac{365 \text{ days}}{\text{Receivables turnover ratio}}$
Inventory turnover ratio	6	$\dfrac{\text{Cost of goods sold}}{\text{Average inventory}}$
Average days in inventory	6	$\dfrac{365 \text{ days}}{\text{Inventory turnover ratio}}$
Current ratio	8	$\dfrac{\text{Current assets}}{\text{Current liabilities}}$
Acid-test ratio	8	$\dfrac{\text{Cash} + \text{Current investments} + \text{Accounts receivable}}{\text{Current liabilities}}$
Solvency		
Debt to equity ratio	9	$\dfrac{\text{Total liabilities}}{\text{Stockholders' equity}}$
Times interest earned ratio	9	$\dfrac{\text{Net income} + \text{Interest expense} + \text{Tax expense}}{\text{Interest expense}}$
PROFITABILITY RATIOS		
Gross profit ratio	6	$\dfrac{\text{Gross profit}}{\text{Net sales}}$
Return on assets	7	$\dfrac{\text{Net income}}{\text{Average total assets}}$
Profit margin	7	$\dfrac{\text{Net income}}{\text{Net sales}}$
Asset turnover	7	$\dfrac{\text{Net sales}}{\text{Average total assets}}$
Return on equity	10	$\dfrac{\text{Net income}}{\text{Average stockholders' equity}}$
Dividend Yield	10	$\dfrac{\text{Dividends per share}}{\text{Stock price}}$
Earnings per share	10	$\dfrac{\text{Net income} - \text{Preferred stock dividends}}{\text{Average shares of common stock outstanding}}$
Price-earnings ratio	10	$\dfrac{\text{Stock price}}{\text{Earnings per share}}$

Framework for Financial Accounting

Two primary functions of financial accounting are to *measure* activities of a company and *communicate* those measurements to investors and other people for making decisions. The measurement process involves recording transactions into accounts. The balances of these accounts are used to communicate information in the four primary financial statements, which are linked. For more detailed illustrations of financial statements, see the corresponding illustrations in Chapter 1. A comprehensive list of accounts used to measure activities in this textbook is provided on the next page.

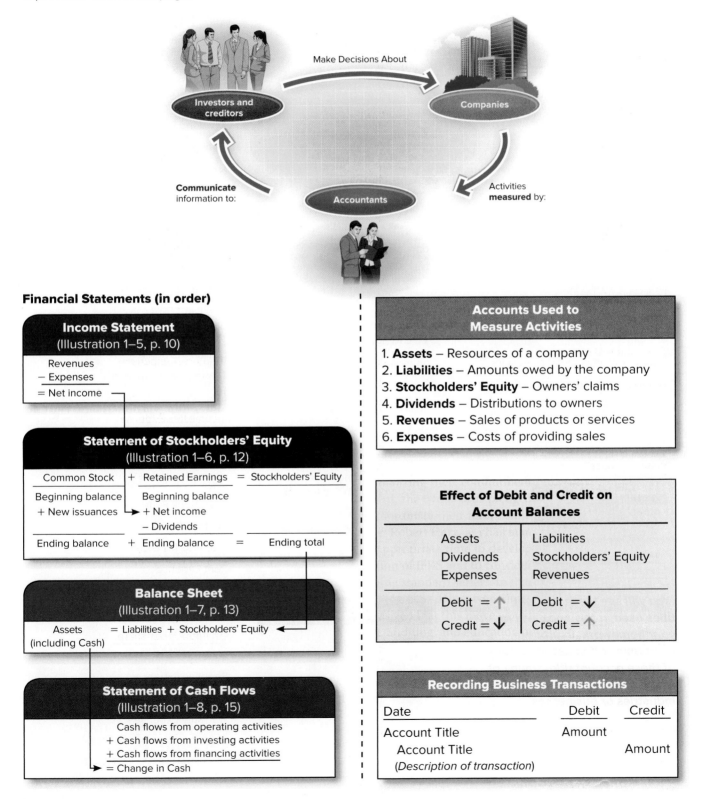

Financial Statements (in order)

Income Statement
(Illustration 1–5, p. 10)

Revenues
− Expenses
= Net income

Statement of Stockholders' Equity
(Illustration 1–6, p. 12)

Common Stock	+ Retained Earnings	= Stockholders' Equity
Beginning balance	Beginning balance	
+ New issuances	+ Net income	
	− Dividends	
Ending balance	+ Ending balance	= Ending total

Balance Sheet
(Illustration 1–7, p. 13)

Assets = Liabilities + Stockholders' Equity
(including Cash)

Statement of Cash Flows
(Illustration 1–8, p. 15)

Cash flows from operating activities
+ Cash flows from investing activities
+ Cash flows from financing activities
= Change in Cash

Accounts Used to Measure Activities

1. **Assets** – Resources of a company
2. **Liabilities** – Amounts owed by the company
3. **Stockholders' Equity** – Owners' claims
4. **Dividends** – Distributions to owners
5. **Revenues** – Sales of products or services
6. **Expenses** – Costs of providing sales

Effect of Debit and Credit on Account Balances

Assets Dividends Expenses	Liabilities Stockholders' Equity Revenues
Debit = ↑	Debit = ↓
Credit = ↓	Credit = ↑

Recording Business Transactions

Date	Debit	Credit
Account Title	Amount	
Account Title		Amount
(Description of transaction)		

Representative Chart of Accounts*

BALANCE SHEET

ASSETS

Cash

Petty Cash

Accounts Receivable

   Less: Allow. for Uncollectible Accts.

Notes Receivable

Interest Receivable

Supplies

Inventory

Prepaid Advertising

Prepaid Insurance

Prepaid Rent

Investments

Land

Land Improvements

Buildings

Equipment

   Less: Accumulated Depreciation

Natural Resources

Patents

Copyrights

Trademarks

Franchises

Goodwill

LIABILITIES

Accounts Payable

Notes Payable

Deferred Revenue

Salaries Payable

Interest Payable

Utilities Payable

Dividends Payable

Income Tax Payable

FICA Tax Payable

Unemployment Tax Payable

Sales Tax Payable

Contingent Liability

Warranty Liability

Bonds Payable

STOCKHOLDERS' EQUITY

Common Stock

Preferred Stock

Additional Paid-in Capital

Retained Earnings

   Less: Treasury Stock

Unrealized Holding Gain—
Other Comprehensive Income

Unrealized Holding Loss—
Other Comprehensive Income

INCOME STATEMENT

REVENUES

Service Revenue

Sales Revenue

   Less: Sales Discounts

   Less: Sales Returns

   Less: Sales Allowances

Interest Revenue

Dividend Revenue

Equity Income

Gain

Unrealized Holding Gain—
Net Income

EXPENSES

Advertising Expense

Amortization Expense

Bad Debt Expense

Cost of Goods Sold

Delivery Expense

Depreciation Expense

Entertainment Expense

Income Tax Expense

Insurance Expense

Interest Expense

Legal Fees Expense

Payroll Tax Expense

Postage Expense

Property Tax Expense

Rent Expense

Repairs and Maintenance Expense

Research and Development Expense

Salaries Expense

Service Fee Expense

Supplies Expense

Utilities Expense

Warranty Expense

Loss

Unrealized Holding Loss—Net Income

You will see these account titles used in this book and in your homework. In practice, companies often use variations of these account titles, many of which are specific to particular industries or businesses.

DIVIDENDS**

Dividends (Cash)

Stock Dividends

**Reported in the statement of stockholders' equity.